Thailand

a Lonely Planet travel survival kit

ประเทศไทย

Joe Cummings
with assistance from Richard Nebesky

Thailand

6th edition

Published by
Lonely Planet Publications
Head Office: PO Box 617, Hawthorn, Vic 3122, Australia
Branches: 155 Filbert St, Suite 251, Oakland, CA 94607, USA
                 10 Barley Mow Passage, Chiswick, London W4 4PH, UK
                 71 bis rue du Cardinal Lemoine, 75005 Paris, France

Printed by
SNP Printing Pte Ltd., Singapore

Photographs by

Glenn Beanland (GB)	Richard I'Anson (RI)	Bill Preston (BP)
Don Campbell (DC)	Chris Lee Ack (CLA)	Tourism Authority of
Joe Cummings (JC)	Peter Morris (PM)	Thailand (TAT)
Mark Downey (MD)	Richard Nebesky (RN)	Dale Wahren (DW)
Meredith Hunnibell (MH)	Joanna O'Brien (JO)	

Front cover: Novice monks, Wat Muay Taw, Mae Hong Son
               The Photo Library–Sydney (Alain Evrard)

First Published
February 1982

This Edition
February 1995
Reprinted with Update supplement June 1996

**Although the authors and publisher have tried to make the information as
accurate as possible, they accept no responsibility for any loss, injury or
inconvenience sustained by any person using this book.**

National Library of Australia Cataloguing-in-Publication Data

Cummings, Joe.
    Thailand.

    6th ed.
    Includes index.
    ISBN 0 86442 252 0.

    1. Thailand – Guidebooks. I. Nebesky, Richard. II. Title.
    (Series: Lonely Planet travel survival kit).

915.930444

text & maps © Lonely Planet 1995
photos © photographers as indicated 1995
climate charts compiled from information supplied by Patrick J Tyson, © Patrick J Tyson, 1995

Joe Cummings

Joe has travelled extensively and frequently in Thailand over the last 18 years. Before travel writing became a full-time job, he was a Peace Corps volunteer in Thailand, a translator/interpreter of Thai, a graduate student of Thai language and Asian art history at the UC Berkeley (MA 1981), a columnist for *The Asia Record*, an East-West Center Scholar in Hawaii, a university lecturer in Malaysia, and a bilingual studies consultant in the USA and Taiwan.

Able to speak, read and write Thai fluently, Joe has travelled through all 76 of the kingdom's provinces by virtually every mode of transport. Joe is also the author of Lonely Planet's *Thai* phrasebook and guides to *Bangkok* and *Laos*, and a contributor to LP guidebooks to South-East Asia, Myanmar, China, Malaysia/Singapore and Indonesia. He occasionally writes for *Geographical, World & I, Outside, Worldview, Earth Journal, BBC Holidays, The Independent* and other periodicals.

Richard Nebesky

Richard was born in Prague but left with his family after the Soviet-led invasion in 1968 and came to Australia. With a BA in politics and history, he took to the road and has travelled, skied and worked in Europe, Asia, North America and Africa.

He joined Lonely Planet in 1987, and since then has been co-author of LP's *Eastern Europe* and *Central Europe* phrasebooks, *Prague* and *Czech & Slovak Republics* guidebooks, has helped to update the guidebooks to *Australia, Indonesia, Thailand* and *Russia*, and has contributed to the *Thailand* travel atlas.

From the Authors

From Joe Thanks to the following people in Thailand and California who assisted along the way: Nancy Chandler, Drs Max & Charles Henn, Guy Gorias, Somdy Mingolo, Roger, Doy & Noi, Karin & Ally, Paul & Bruce Harmon, Jacques Deen, Margot Welk, Mark Pompermayer, Soeren, Gianluigi and Salonge, Gabriel Vallicelli, Chookiet Potito, Prof Poonsak Suvannoparat, Wisoot Buachoom, Chantana Indragarjijta, Nuan Sarnsorn, Manit Boonchim, Saratwadee Asasupakit, Sethaphan Buddhani, Pradthana Pulperm, Adisai Suwanpradhes and Queen Bee Travel Service, Graeme Edgar and Bandhit Ketmala.

The Tourist Authority of Thailand and its employees throughout Thailand, as usual, were of considerable assistance, as were research assistants Davies Stamm and Tom Huhti. Special thanks to Richard Nebesky for his heroic efforts in wading through beach-blanket Babylon.

Thanks also to the hundreds of travellers who have taken time to write, especially letter-writers Roger Holdsworth, Pat Thurgood, Barrie Kerper, Marina Violati, Sai Jantarapat, Bella Intaranan, Tracey & Andrew Mitchell, Jim Enright, Sally Burbage and Bernie Hodges.

I've tried to name everyone who was of direct help but know I've forgotten a few names along the way. Please forgive me if you're not listed and accept my heartfelt thanks.

The 6th edition of this guidebook is dedicated to the memory of Ven Ajaan Buddhadasa (1906-1993).

From Richard Thanks to my partner Loretta for making the trip pleasant, as well as for support during bus journeys and those difficult moments. Also thanks to the following people who helped me along the way; Paulo and his partner, Pissamai Sungkasit, Sayan, Bob Lothian and crew, as well as the Bangkok TAT office and their other branches in south Thailand for valuable assistance. And last but not least to Joe for making the trip possible, for his assistance and for sorting out the Thai script.

Joe's Note to Readers

When using the information contained in this guide to find your way around Thailand, keep in mind the Buddhist concept of *anicca*, or 'impermanence'. All things in the world of travel especially are in a constant state of flux and Thailand is no exception. What you read here are conceptual snapshots of single moments in time, filtered through one person's perceptions. They represent the very best of my research efforts at the time of writing, but were bound to change the second I turned my attention away from research and began writing it all down, a necessary part of the process in getting this book to you. Don't expect to find things to be exactly as described in the text – stay flexible and you'll enjoy yourself more.

This Book

The first five editions of this book were written by Joe Cummings. For the 6th edition Joe was assisted by Richard Nebesky, who contributed to the Central Thailand chapter and updated the Southern Thailand chapter.

From the Publisher

Kim Haglund and Sarah Lewis edited this edition of Thailand in our US office; it was proofed by Katie Purvis, Katie Cody, Sharan Kaur and Tom Smallman in Melbourne; and Katie Purvis took it through production. Alan Marshall, Sandra Smythe and Ann Jeffree were responsible for the maps; the book was designed and laid out by Maliza Kruh; the cover was designed by Jane Hart. Thanks to Joe Cummings for supplying the Thai script, to Dan Levin for the Thai script fonts, and to Sharon Wertheim for indexing. Thanks also to Sue Mitra and Scott Summers in our US office for all their help.

Thanks must also go to the travellers who used the previous editions of this book and wrote to Lonely Planet with information, comments and suggestions. They are listed at the back of the book.

Warning & Request

Things change – prices go up, schedules change, good places go bad and bad places go bankrupt – nothing stays the same. So if you find things better or worse, recently opened or long since closed, please write and tell us and help make the next edition better. Your letters will be used to help update future editions and, where possible, important changes will also be included in an Update section in reprints.

We greatly appreciate all information that is sent to us by travellers. Back at Lonely Planet we employ a hard-working readers' letters team to sort through the many letters we receive. The best ones will be rewarded with a free copy of the next edition or another Lonely Planet guide if you prefer. We give away lots of books, but, unfortunately, not every letter or postcard receives one.

Contents

Map Legend

BOUNDARIES

.... International Boundary

.... Provincial Boundary

ROUTES

.... Freeway

.... Highway

.... Major Road

.... Unsealed Road or Track

.... City Road

.... City Street

.... Railway

.... Underground Railway

.... Tram

.... Walking Track

.... Walking Tour

.... Ferry Route

.... Cable Car or Chairlift

AREA FEATURES

.... Park, Gardens

.... National Park

.... Built-Up Area

.... Pedestrian Mall

.... Market

.... Cemetery

.... Reef

.... Beach or Desert

.... Rocks

HYDROGRAPHIC FEATURES

.... Coastline

.... River, Creek

.... Intermittent River or Creek

.... Lake, Intermittent Lake

.... Canal

.... Swamp

SYMBOLS

✪ CAPITAL		National Capital
◉ Capital		Provincial Capital
🌊 CITY		Major City
● City		City
● Town		Town
● Village		Village
■		Place to Stay
▼		Place to Eat
▮		Pub, Bar
✉	☎	Post Office, Telephone
❶	❸	Tourist Information, Bank
⊖	Ⓟ	Transport, Parking
⛪	✿	Museum, Youth Hostel
🚐	⅄	Caravan Park, Camping Ground
† ☒ †		Church, Cathedral
☪	✡	Mosque, Synagogue
⚊	⚌	Buddhist Temple, Hindu Temple

✚	★	Hospital, Police Station
✈	✝	Airport, Airfield
🏊	✿	Swimming Pool, Gardens
❖	🐘	Shopping Centre, Zoo
☙	⌂	Winery or Vineyard, Picnic Site
←	25	One Way Street, Route Number
	∴	Archaeological Site or Ruins
🏛	▲	Stately Home, Monument
☗	▣	Castle, Tomb
⌒	⌂	Cave, Hut or Chalet
▲	❋	Mountain or Hill, Lookout
⚡	⌇	Lighthouse, Shipwreck
)(	⚬	Pass, Spring
		Ancient or City Wall
		Rapids, Waterfalls
		Cliff or Escarpment, Tunnel
		Railway Station

Note: not all symbols displayed above appear in this book

Introduction

Thailand, or Siam as it was called until 1939, has never been colonised by a foreign power, while all of its South-East Asian neighbours have undergone European imperialism (or more recently, ideological domination by communism – which originated in Europe) at one time or another. True, it has suffered periodic invasions on the part of the Burmese and the Khmers and was briefly occupied by the Japanese in WW II, but the kingdom was never externally controlled long enough to dampen the Thais' serious individualism. Although the Thais are often depicted as fun-loving, happy-go-lucky folk (which they often are), they are also very strong-minded and have struggled for centuries to preserve their independence of spirit.

This is not to say that Thailand has not experienced any Western influence. Like other Asian countries it has both suffered and benefited from contact with foreign cultures. But the ever-changing spirit of Thai culture has remained dominant, even in modern city life.

The end result is that Thailand has much to interest the traveller: historic culture, lively arts, exotic islands, nightlife, a tradition of friendliness and hospitality to strangers, and one of the world's most exciting cuisines.

Travel in this tropical country is fairly comfortable and down-to-earth. The rail, bus and air travel network is extensive and every place worth visiting is easily accessible. There are many places worth visiting, many sights to see, a multifaceted culture to experience and it is all quite affordable by today's international travel standards.

Travellers will, from time to time, notice

that the spelling of place names in this book is at variance with other sources. This is because Thai uses a totally different script from our own 'roman' script. Any Thai name has to be transliterated for those of us who don't read Thai, and transliteration is very often a matter of opinion. For more information on Thai spellings, see the Language section in the Facts about the Country chapter.

Facts about the Country

HISTORY

Prehistory

The history of the geographical area now known as Thailand reaches far back into 'hoary antiquity'. World-renowned scholar Paul Benedict (author of *Austro-Thai Language & Culture*) found that modern linguistic theory, which ties numerous key items in ancient Chinese culture to an early Thai linguistic group, together with recent archaeological finds in Thailand, enable us to establish South-East Asia as a 'focal area in the emergent cultural development of Homo sapiens. It now seems likely that the first true agriculturists anywhere, perhaps also the first true metalworkers, were Austro-Thai speakers'.

The Maekhong River valley and Khorat Plateau areas of what today encompasses significant parts of Laos, Cambodia and Thailand were inhabited as far back as 10,000 years ago. Currently the most reliable sources for archaeological evidence are the Ban Chiang and Ban Prasat areas of northeast Thailand, where rice was cultivated as early as 4000 BC (China by contrast was growing and consuming millet at the time). The Ban Chiang culture had begun bronze metallurgy before 3000 BC; the Middle East's Bronze Age arrived around 2800 BC, China's a thousand years later.

Thai Migration

The ancestors of today's Thais were scattered amidst a vast, nonunified zone of Austro-Thai influence that involved periodic migrations along several different geographic lines. The early Thais proliferated all over South-East Asia, including the islands of Indonesia, and some later settled in south and south-west China, later to 're-migrate' to northern Thailand to establish the first Thai kingdom in the 13th century.

A linguistic map of south China, northeast India and South-East Asia clearly shows that the preferred zones of occupation by the Thai peoples have been river valleys, from the Red River (Hong River) in south China and Vietnam to the Brahmaputra River in Assam. At one time there were two terminals for movement into what is now Thailand – the 'north terminal' in the Yuan Jiang and other river areas in China's Yunnan and Guangxi provinces, and the 'south terminal' along central Thailand's Chao Phraya River. The populations remain quite concentrated in these areas today, while areas between the two were intermediate relay points and as such have always been far less populated.

The Maekhong River valley between Thailand and Laos was one such intermediate migrational zone, as were river valleys along the Nan, Ping, Kok, Yom and Wang rivers in northern Thailand, plus various river areas in Laos and in Myanmar's Shan states. The migrant Thais established local polities along traditional social schemata according to *meuang* (roughly 'principality' or 'district'), under the hereditary rule of chieftains or sovereigns called *jâo meuang* (meuang lord).

Each meuang was based in a river valley or section of a valley. Some meuang were loosely collected under one jâo meuang or an alliance of several. One of the largest collections of meuang – though not necessarily united – was in south China and was known as Nam Chao (Naam Jao) or Lord(s) of the River(s). Yunnan's present-day Xishuangbanna district (Sipsongpanna in Thai), a homeland for Northern Thai and Thai Lü groups, is often cited as the point of origin for all Thais, but in-depth histories place Thai groups everywhere along the Thai diaspora from Dien Bien Phu, Vietnam, to Assam, India.

In the mid-13th century, the rise to power of the Mongols under Kublai Khan in Sung Dynasty China caused a more dramatic southward migration of Thai peoples. Wherever Thais met indigenous populations of Tibeto-Burmans and Mon-Khmers in the move south (into what is now Myanmar (Burma), Thailand, Laos and Cambodia), they were somehow able to displace, assimilate or co-opt them without force. The most probable explanation for this relatively smooth assimilation is that there were already Thai peoples in the area. Such a supposition finds considerable support in current research on the development of Austro-Thai language and culture.

Early Kingdoms

With no written records or chronologies it is difficult to say with certainty what kind of cultures existed among the meuangs of Thailand before the middle of the first millennium. However, by the 6th century AD an important network of agricultural communities was thriving as far south as modern-day Pattani and Yala, and as far north and north-east as Lamphun and Muang Fa Daet (near Khon Kaen). Theravada Buddhism was flourishing and may have entered the region during India's Ashokan period, in the 3rd or 2nd centuries BC, when Indian missionaries were said to have been sent to a land called Suvarnabhumi (Land of Gold). Suvarnabhumi most likely corresponds to a remarkably fertile area stretching from southern Myanmar, across central Thailand, to eastern Cambodia. Two different cities in Thailand's central river basin have long been called Suphanburi (City of Gold) and U Thong (Cradle of Gold).

Dvaravati This loose collection of city-states was given the Sanskrit name Dvaravati (literally, 'place having gates'), the city of Krishna in the Indian epic poem *Mahabharata*. The French art historian George Coedes discovered the name on some coins that were excavated in the Nakhon Pathom area, which seems to have been the centre of Dvaravati culture. The Dvaravati period lasted until the 11th or 12th century AD and produced many fine works of art, including distinctive Buddha images (showing Indian Gupta influence), stucco reliefs on temples and in caves, some architecture (little of which remains intact), some exquisite terracotta heads, votive tablets and other miscellaneous sculpture.

Dvaravati may have been a cultural relay point for the pre-Angkor cultures of ancient Cambodia and Champa to the east. The Chinese, through the travels of the famous pilgrim Xuan Zang, knew the area as Tuoluobodi, located between Sriksetra (north Myanmar) and Tsanapura (Sambor Prei Kuk-Kambuja). The ethnology of the Dvaravati peoples is a controversial subject, though the standard decree is that they were Mons or Mon-Khmers. The Mons themselves seem to have been descended from a group of Indian immigrants from Kalinga, an area overlapping the boundaries of the modern Indian states of Orissa and Andhra Pradesh. The Dvaravati Mons may have been an ethnic mix of these people and people indigenous to the region (the original Thais). In any event, the Dvaravati culture quickly declined in the 11th century under the political domination of the invading Khmers who made their headquarters in Lopburi. The area around Lamphun, then called Hariphunchai, held out until the late 12th or early 13th centuries, as evidenced by the Dvaravati architecture of Wat Kukut in Lamphun.

Khmer Influence The concurrent Khmer conquests of the 7th to 11th centuries brought Khmer cultural influence in the form of art, language and religion. Some of the Sanskrit terms in Mon-Thai vocabulary entered the language during the Khmer or Lopburi period between the 11th and 13th centuries. Monuments from this period located in Kanchanaburi, Lopburi and many locations throughout the north-east were constructed in the Khmer style and compare favourably with architecture in Angkor. Elements of Brahmanism, Theravada Buddhism and Mahayana Buddhism were intermixed as Lopburi became a religious centre, and some of each religious Buddhist school – along with Brahmanism – remain to this day in Thai religious and court ceremonies.

Other Kingdoms While all this was taking place, a distinctly Thai state called Nam Chao (650-1250 AD) was flourishing in what later became Yunnan and Sichuan in China. Nam Chao maintained close relations with imperial China and the two neighbours enjoyed much cultural exchange. The Mongols, under Kublai Khan, conquered Nam Chao in 1253, but long before they came, the Thai peoples began migrating southward, homesteading in and around what is today Laos and northern Thailand.

Some Thais became mercenaries for the Khmer armies in the early 12th century, as depicted on the walls of Angkor Wat. The Thais were called 'Syams' by the Khmers, possibly from the Sanskrit *shyama* meaning 'golden' or 'swarthy', because of their relatively deeper skin colour; another theory claims the word means 'free'. Whatever the meaning, this was how the Thai kingdom eventually came to be called Sayam or Syam. In north-western Thailand and Myanmar the pronunciation of Syam became 'Shan'. English trader James Lancaster penned the first known English transliteration of the name as 'Siam' in 1592.

Meanwhile Southern Thailand – the upper Malay Peninsula – was under the control of the Srivijaya empire, the headquarters of which were in Sumatra, between the 8th and 13th centuries. The regional centre for Srivijaya was Chaiya, near the modern town of Surat Thani. Srivijaya art remains can still be seen in Chaiya and its environs.

Sukhothai & Lan Na Thai

Several Thai principalities in the Maekhong Valley united in the 13th and 14th centuries, when Thai princes wrested the lower north from the Khmers – whose Angkor government was declining fast – to create Sukhothai or 'rising of happiness'. They later took Hariphunchai from the Mons to form Lan Na Thai (literally, 'million Thai rice fields').

The Sukhothai kingdom declared its independence in 1238 under King Si Intharathit and quickly expanded its sphere of influence, taking advantage not only of the declining Khmer power but the weakening Srivijaya domain in the south. Sukhothai is considered by the Thais to be the first true Thai kingdom. It was annexed by Ayuthaya in 1376, by which time a national identity of sorts had been forged. Many Thais today view the Sukhothai period with sentimental vision, seeing it as a golden age of Thai politics, religion and culture – an egalitarian, noble period when everyone had enough to eat and the kingdom was unconquerable. A famous passage from Sukhothai's so-called Ram Khamhaeng Inscription reads:

This land of Sukhothai is thriving. There is fish in the water and rice in the fields...**The King** has hung a bell in the opening of the gate over there; if any commoner has a grievance which sickens his belly and grips his heart, he goes and strikes the bell; **King Ram Khamkhaeng** questions the man, examines the case and decides it justly for him.

Among other accomplishments, the third Sukhothai king, Ram Khamhaeng, sponsored a fledgling Thai writing system which became the basis for modern Thai; he also codified the Thai form of Theravada Buddhism, as borrowed from the Sinhalese. Under Ram Khamhaeng, the Sukhothai kingdom extended as far as Nakhon Si Thammarat in the south, to the upper Maekhong River valley in Laos, and to Bago (Pegu) in southern Myanmar. For a short time (1448-86) the Sukhothai capital was moved to Phitsanulok.

Ram Khamhaeng also supported Chao Mengrai of Chiang Mai and Chao Khun Ngam Muang of Phayao, two northern Thai jâo meuang, in the 1296 AD founding of Lan Na Thai, nowadays often known simply as 'Lanna'. Lanna extended across North Thailand to include the meuang of Wiang Chan along the middle reaches of the Maekhong River. In the 14th century, Wiang Chan was taken from Lanna by Chao Fa Ngum of Luang Prabang, who made it part of his Lan Xang (Million Elephants) kingdom. Wiang Chan later flourished as an independent kingdom for a short time during the mid-16th century and eventually became capital of Laos in its royal, French (where it got its more popular international spelling, 'Vientiane') and now socialist incarnations. After a period of dynastic decline, Lanna fell to the Burmese in 1558.

Ayuthaya Period

The Thai kings of Ayuthaya became very powerful in the 14th and 15th centuries, taking over U Thong and Lopburi, former Khmer strongholds, and moving east in their conquests until Angkor was defeated in 1431. Even though the Khmers were their adversaries in battle, the Ayuthaya kings incorporated Khmer court customs and language. One result of this was that the Thai monarch gained more absolute authority during the Ayuthaya period and assumed the title *devaraja* (god-king; *thewarâat* in Thai) as opposed to the *dhammaraja* (dharma-king; *thammárâat* in Thai) title used in Sukhothai.

Ayuthaya was one of the greatest and wealthiest cities in Asia, a thriving seaport envied not only by the Burmese but by the Europeans who were in great awe of the city. It has been said that London, at the time, was a mere village in comparison. The kingdom sustained an unbroken monarchical succession through 34 reigns, from King U Thong (1350-69) to King Ekathat (1758-67), over a period of 400 years.

In the early 16th century Ayuthaya was receiving European visitors, and a Portuguese embassy was established in 1511. The Portuguese were followed by the Dutch in 1605, the English in 1612, the Danes in 1621 and the French in 1662. In the mid-16th century Ayuthaya and the independent kingdom of Lanna came under the control of the Burmese, but the Thais regained rule of both by the end of the century. In 1690 Londoner Engelbert Campfer proclaimed 'Among the Asian nations, the Kingdom of Siam is the greatest. The magnificence of the Ayuthaya Court is incomparable.'

A rather peculiar episode unfolded in Ayuthaya when a Greek, Constantine Phaulkon, became a very high official in Siam under King Narai from 1675 to 1688. He kept out the Dutch and the English but allowed the French to station 600 soldiers in the kingdom. The Thais, fearing a takeover, forcibly expelled the French and executed Phaulkon. Ironically, the word for a 'foreigner' (of European descent) in modern Thai is *faràng*, an abbreviated form of *faràngsèt*, meaning 'French'. Siam sealed itself from the West for 150 years following this experience with farangs.

The Burmese again invaded Ayuthaya in 1765 and the capital fell after two years of fierce battle. This time the Burmese destroyed everything sacred to the Thais, including manuscripts, temples and religious sculpture. The Burmese, despite their effectiveness in sacking Ayuthaya, could not maintain a foothold in the kingdom, and Phaya Taksin, a Thai general, made himself king in 1769, ruling from the new capital of Thonburi on the banks of the Chao Phraya River, opposite Bangkok. The Thais regained control of their country and further united the disparate provinces to the north with central Siam.

Taksin eventually came to regard himself as the next Buddha; his ministers, who did not approve of his religious fantasies, deposed and then executed him in the custom reserved for royalty – by beating him to death in a velvet sack so that no royal blood touched the ground.

Chakri Dynasty

Another general, Chao Phaya Chakri, came to power and was crowned in 1782 under the title Phraphutthayotfa Chulalok. He moved the royal capital across the river to Bangkok and ruled as the first king of the Chakri dynasty. In 1809, his son Loet La took the throne and reigned until 1824. Both monarchs assumed the task of restoring the culture so severely damaged by the Burmese decades earlier.

The third Chakri king, Phra Nang Klao (1824-51), went beyond reviving tradition and developed trade with China while increasing domestic agricultural production. He also established a new royal title system, posthumously conferring 'Rama I' and 'Rama II' upon his two predecessors and taking the title 'Rama III' for himself. During

Nang Klao's reign, American missionary James Low brought the first printing press to Thailand and produced the country's first printed document in Thai script. Missionary Dan Bradley published the first Thai newspaper, the monthly *Bangkok Recorder*, from 1844 to 1845.

Rama IV, commonly known as King Mongkut (Phra Chom Klao to the Thais), was one of the more colourful and innovative of the early Chakri kings. He originally missed out on the throne in deference to his half-brother Rama III and lived as a Buddhist monk for 27 years. During his long monastic term he became adept in the Sanskrit, Pali, Latin and English languages, studied Western sciences and adopted the strict discipline of local Mon monks. He kept an eye on the outside world and when he took the throne in 1851 immediately courted diplomatic relations with European nations, while avoiding colonialisation.

In addition, he attempted to align Buddhist cosmology with modern science with the aim of demythologising the Thai religion (a process yet to be fully accomplished), and founded the Thammayut monastic sect, based on the strict discipline he had followed as a monk. (Today, the Thammayut remains a minority sect in relation to the Mahanikai, who comprise the largest number of Buddhist monks in Thailand.)

Thai trade restrictions were loosened by King Mongkut and many Western powers signed trade agreements with the monarch. He also established Siam's first printing press and instituted educational reforms, developing a school system along European lines. Mongkut was the first monarch to show Thai commoners his face in public; he died of malaria in 1868.

His son, King Chulalongkorn (known to the Thais as Chulachomklao or Rama V, 1868-1910), continued Mongkut's tradition of reform, especially in the legal and administrative realm. Educated by European tutors, Chula abolished prostration before the king as well as slavery and corvée (state labour). Thailand further benefited from relations with European nations and the

USA: railways were built, a civil service established and the legal code restructured. Though Siam still managed to avoid colonialisation, the king was compelled to concede territory to French Indochina (Laos in 1893, Cambodia in 1907) and British Burma (three Malayan states in 1909) during his reign.

Chula's son King Vajiravudh (also Mongkut Klao or Rama VI, 1910-25) was educated in Britain and during his rather short reign introduced compulsory education and other educational reforms. He further 'Westernised' the nation by making the Thai calendar conform to Western models. His reign was somewhat clouded by a top-down push for Thai nationalism that resulted in strong anti-Chinese sentiment.

Before Rama VI's reign, Thai parents gave each of their children a single, original name, with no surname to identify family origins. In 1909 a royal decree required the adoption of Thai surnames for all Thai citizens – a move designed as much to parallel the European system of family surnames as to weed out Chinese names.

In 1912 a group of Thai military officers unsuccessfully attempted to overthrow the monarchy – the first in a series of 20th-century coup attempts that has continued to the present day. As a show of support for the Allies in WW I, Rama VI sent 1300 Thai troops to France in 1918.

Revolution

While Vajiravudh's brother, King Prajadhipok (Pokklao or Rama VII, 1925-35), ruled, a group of Thai students living in Paris became so enamoured of democratic ideology that they mounted a successful coup d'état against absolute monarchy in Siam. This bloodless revolution led to the development of a constitutional monarchy along British lines, with a mixed military-civilian group in power.

A royalist revolt in 1933 sought to reinstate absolute monarchy, but it failed and left Prajadhipok isolated from both the royalist revolutionaries and the constitution-minded ministers. One of the king's last official acts was to outlaw polygamy in 1934, leaving behind the cultural underpinnings for consorts, concubines and minor wives that now support Thai prostitution.

In 1935 the king abdicated without naming a successor and retired to Britain. The cabinet named his nephew, 10-year-old Ananda Mahidol, to the throne as Rama VIII, though Ananda didn't return to Thailand from school in Switzerland until 1945. Phibun (Phibul) Songkhram, a key military leader in the 1932 coup, maintained an effective position of power from 1938 until the end of WW II. Ananda Mahidol ascended the throne in 1945 but was shot dead in his bedroom under mysterious circumstances in 1946. His brother, Bhumibol Adulyadej, succeeded him as Rama IX.

Under the influence of Phibun's government, the country's name had been officially changed from 'Siam' to 'Thailand' in 1939 – rendered in Thai as 'Prathêt Thai'. ('Prathêt' is derived from the Sanskrit *pradesha* or 'country'; 'thai' is considered to have the connotation of 'free', though in actual usage it simply refers to the Thai, Tai or T'ai peoples, who are found as far east as Tonkin, as far west as Assam, as far north as south China, and as far south as north Malaysia.)

WW II & Postwar Periods

The Japanese outflanked the Allied troops in Malaya and Myanmar in 1941 and the Phibun government complied with the Japanese in this action by allowing them into the Gulf of Thailand; consequently the Japanese troops occupied a portion of Thailand itself. Phibun then declared war on the USA and Great Britain (in 1942) but Seni Pramoj, the Thai ambassador in Washington, refused to deliver the declaration. Phibun resigned in 1944 under pressure from the Thai underground resistance (Thai Seri), and after V-J Day in 1945, Seni became premier.

In 1946, the year King Ananda was shot dead, Seni and his brother Kukrit were unseated in a general election and a democratic civilian group took power under Pridi Phanomyong, a law professor who had been instrumental in the 1932 revolution. Pridi's

civilian government, which changed the country's name back to Siam, ruled for a short time, only to be overthrown by Field Marshal Phibun in 1947. Phibun suspended the constitution and reinstated 'Thailand' as the country's official name in 1949. Under Phibun the government took an extreme anticommunist stance, refused to recognise the People's Republic of China and became a loyal supporter of French and US foreign policy in South-East Asia.

In 1951 power was wrested from Phibun by General Sarit Thanarat, who continued the tradition of military dictatorship. However, Phibun somehow retained the actual position of premier until 1957 when Sarit finally had him exiled. Elections that same year forced Sarit to resign and go abroad for 'medical treatment'; he returned in 1958 to launch another coup. This time he abolished the constitution, dissolved the parliament and banned all political parties, maintaining effective power until his death of cirrhosis in 1963. From 1964 to 1973 the Thai nation was ruled by army officers Thanom Kittikachorn and Praphat Charusathien, during which time Thailand allowed the USA to develop several army bases within its borders in support of the US campaign in Vietnam.

Reacting to political repression, 10,000 Thai students publicly demanded a real constitution in June 1973. In October of the same year the military brutally suppressed a large demonstration at Thammasat University in Bangkok, but General Krit Sivara and King Bhumibol refused to support further bloodshed, forcing Thanom and Praphat to leave Thailand.

Polarisation & Stabilisation

An elected, constitutional government ruled until October 1976 when students demonstrated again, this time protesting Thanom's return to Thailand as a monk. Thammasat University again became a battlefield as border patrol police, along with right-wing, paramilitary civilian groups (Nawaphon, the Red Gaurs and the Village Scouts), assaulted a group of 2000 students holding a sit-in.

Hundreds of students were killed and injured in the fracas; more than a thousand were arrested. Using public disorder as an excuse, the military stepped in and installed a new right-wing government with Thanin Kraivichien as premier.

This bloody incident disillusioned many Thai students and older intellectuals not directly involved with the demonstrations, the result being that numerous idealists 'dropped out' of Thai society and joined the People's Liberation Army of Thailand (PLAT) – armed communist insurgents based in the hills who had been active in Thailand since the 1930s.

In October 1977 Thanin was replaced by the more moderate General Kriangsak Chomanand in an effort to conciliate anti-government factions. When this failed, the military-backed position changed hands again in 1980, leaving Prem Tinsulanonda at the helm. By this time the PLAT had reached a peak force of around 10,000.

Prem served as prime minister through 1988 and is credited with the political and economic stabilisation of Thailand in the post-Indochina War years (only one coup attempt in the 1980s!). The major accomplishment of the Prem years was a complete dismantling of the Communist Party of Thailand and PLAT through an effective combination of amnesty programmes (which brought the students back from the forests) and military action. His administration is also considered responsible for a gradual democratisation of Thailand which culminated in the 1988 election of his successor, Chatichai Choonhavan.

It may be difficult for new arrivals to Thailand to appreciate the political distance Thailand covered in the 1980s. Between 1976 and 1981, freedom of speech and the press were rather curtailed in Thailand and a strict curfew was enforced in Bangkok. Anyone caught in the streets past 1 am risked spending the night in one of Bangkok's mosquito-infested 'detention areas'. Under Prem, the curfew was lifted, and dissenting opinions began to be heard again in public.

Traditionally, every leading political figure in Thailand, including Prem, has had to receive the support of the Thai military, who are generally staunch reactionaries. Considering Thailand's geographic position, it's not difficult to understand, to some extent, the fears of this ultra-conservative group. But as the threat of communist take-over (either from within or from nearby Indochinese states) diminished, the military gradually began loosening its hold on national politics. Under Chatichai, Thailand enjoyed a brief period of unprecedented popular participation in government.

Approximately 60% of Chatichai's cabinet were former business executives rather than ex-military officers, as compared to 38% in the previous cabinet. Thailand seemed to be entering a new era in which the country's double-digit economic boom ran concurrently with democratisation. Critics praised the political maturation of Thailand, even if they grumbled that corruption seemed as rife as ever. By the end of the 1980s, however, certain high-ranking military officers had become increasingly disappointed with this *coup d'argent*, complaining that Thailand was being run by a plutocracy.

February 1991 Coup
On 23 February 1991, in a move that shocked Thailand observers around the world, the military overthrew the Chatichai administration in a bloodless coup (Thai: *pàtìwát)* and handed power to the newly formed National Peace-Keeping Council (NPKC), led by General Suchinda Kraprayoon. It was Thailand's 19th coup attempt and one of 10 successful coups since 1932, however it was only the second coup to overthrow a democratically elected civilian government. Chatichai lasted longer than any other elected prime minister in Thailand's history: two years and seven months. Charging Chatichai's civilian government with corruption and vote-buying, the NPKC abolished the 1978 constitution and dissolved the parliament. Rights of public assembly were curtailed but the press was closed down for only one day.

Whether or not Chatichai's government was guilty of vote-buying, one of his major mistakes was his appointment of General Chaovalit Yongchaiyuth and former army commander Arthit Kamlang-ek as defence and deputy defence minister respectively. Both were adversaries of the generals who engineered the coup, ie army chief Suchinda and his main ally General Sunthorn Kongsompong (both 'Class 5' officers – those who graduated from the Chulachomklao Royal Military Academy in 1958 – a group that forms the backbone of the NPKC's support). Chatichai was also moving into areas of foreign policy traditionally reserved for the military, especially relations with Myanmar, Laos and Cambodia, and the generals may have feared that the prime minister would fire them. It was the same old story: a power struggle between military bureaucrats and capitalist politicians.

Following the coup, the NPKC appointed a hand-picked civilian prime minister, Ananda Panyarachun, former ambassador to the USA, Germany, Canada and the UN, to dispel public fears that the junta was planning a return to 100% military rule. Ananda claimed to be his own man, but like his predecessors – elected or not – he was allowed the freedom to make his own decisions only insofar as they didn't affect the military. In spite of obvious constraints, many observers felt Ananda's temporary premiership and cabinet were the best Thailand had ever had.

In December 1991, Thailand's national assembly passed a new constitution that guaranteed an NPKC-biased parliament – 270 appointed senators in the upper house stacked against 360 elected representatives. Under this constitution, regardless of who is chosen as the next prime minister or which political parties fill the lower house, the government will remain largely in the hands of the military unless the public rises up to demand a more democratic charter. The new charter includes a provisional clause allowing for a 'four-year transitional period' to full democracy – a provision which sounds suspiciously close to the military subterfuge in neighbouring Myanmar.

Elections & Demonstrations

A general election in March 1992 ushered in a five-party coalition government with Narong Wongwan, whose Samakkhitham (Justice Unity) Party received the most votes, as premier. But amid allegations that Narong was involved in Thailand's drug trade, the military exercised its constitutional prerogative and immediately replaced Narong with (surprise, surprise) General Suchinda in April.

The NPKC promised to eradicate corruption and build democracy, a claim that was difficult to accept since they had done little on either score. In many ways, it was like letting the proverbial fox guard the henhouse, as the military is perhaps the most corrupt institution in the country – always claiming to be free of politics and yet forever meddling in them. Thailand's independent political pundits agreed there was more oppression under the NPKC than under any administration since pre-1981 days.

In May 1992, several huge demonstrations demanding Suchinda's resignation – led by charismatic Bangkok governor Chamlong Srimuang – rocked Bangkok and larger provincial capitals. After street confrontations between the protesters and the military near Bangkok's Democracy Monument resulted in nearly 50 deaths and hundreds of injuries, Suchinda resigned after less than six weeks as premier. The military-backed government also agreed to institute a constitutional amendment requiring that Thailand's prime minister come from the ranks of elected MPs. Ananda Panyarachun was reinstated as interim premier for a four-month term, once again winning praise from several circles for his even-handed and efficient administration.

The September 1992 elections squeezed in veteran Democrats Party leader Chuan Leekpai with a five-seat majority. Chuan leads a coalition government consisting of the Democrats, New Aspiration, Palang Dharma and Solidarity parties. A food

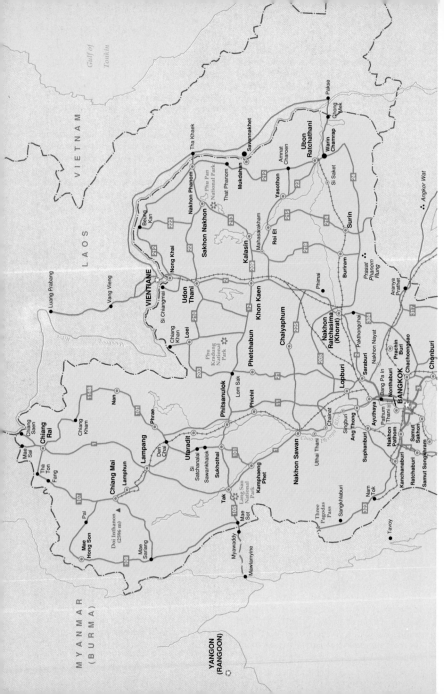

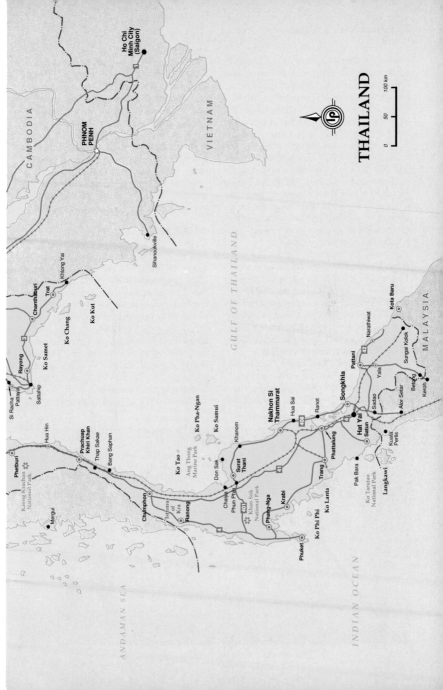

vendor's son and native of Trang Province, the new premier doesn't fit the usual Thai PM mould since he's neither general nor tycoon nor academic. Though well regarded for his honesty and high morals, Chuan has accomplished little in the areas of concern to the majority of Thais – most pointedly Bangkok traffic, national infrastructure and the undemocratic NPKC constitution. By the end of 1993 the opposition was calling for parliamentary dissolution. Meanwhile Bangkok's 'Mr Clean', Chamlong Srimuang (winner of the 1992 Magsaysay Award for his role in galvanising the public to reject General Suchinda), has retired from party politics to an upcountry farm.

In most ways, since the events of 1991 and 1992, Thailand has seen 'business as usual'. Thai cynics will tell you that things *never* change – it depends on how closely you observe politics. The temporary military takeover undoubtedly hurt Thailand's international image, especially among those observers who had seen Thailand moving towards increased democratisation.

Optimists now see Suchinda's hasty resignation as a sign that the coup was only a minor detour on the country's road towards a more responsive national government.

Others say the democratic Chatichai and Chuan governments may merely be short-lived deviations from the norm of military rule. Hardened cynics might hold the view that Thailand's 20th-century coups and counter-coups are a mere extension of the warlordism of early Thai jâo meuangs. Without question, until the constitution is amended to remove objectionable provisions for parliamentary succession, Thailand's claims to democratic status and political stability will remain as shaky as ever.

GEOGRAPHY

Thailand has an area of 517,000 sq km, making it slightly smaller than the state of Texas in the USA, or about the size of France. Its shape on the map has been compared to the head of an elephant, with its trunk extending down the Malay Peninsula, but it looks to me as if someone has squeezed the lower part of the 'boot' of Italy, forcing the volume into the top portion while reducing the bottom. The centre of Thailand, Bangkok, is at about 14° north latitude, putting it on a level with Madras, Manila, Guatemala and Khartoum.

The country's longest north-to-south dis-

Thai woman in rice field, Northern Thailand (MD)

tance is about 1860 km, but its shape makes distances in any other direction a thousand km or less. Because the north-south reach spans roughly 16 latitudinal degrees, Thailand has perhaps the most diverse climate in South-East Asia. The topography varies from high mountains in the north – the southernmost extreme of a series of ranges that extend across northern Myanmar and south-west China to the south-eastern edges of the Tibet Plateau – to limestone-encrusted tropical islands in the south that are part of the Malay Archipelago. The rivers and tributaries of northern and central Thailand drain into the Gulf of Thailand via the Chao Phraya Delta near Bangkok; those of the Mun River and other north-eastern waterways exit into the South China Sea via the Maekhong River.

These broad geographic characteristics divide the country into four main zones: the fertile centre region, dominated by the Chao Phraya River; the north-east plateau, the kingdom's poorest region (thanks to 'thin' soil plus occasional droughts and floods), rising some 300 metres above the central plain; northern Thailand, a region of mountains and fertile valleys; and the southern peninsular region, which extends to the Malaysian frontier and is predominantly rainforest. The southern region receives the most annual rainfall and the north-east the least, although the north is less humid.

Extending from the east coast of peninsular Malaysia to Vietnam, the Sunda Shelf separates the Gulf of Thailand from the South China Sea. On the opposite side of the Thai-Malay Peninsula, the Andaman Sea encompasses that part of the Indian Ocean found east of India's Andaman and Nicobar Islands. Thailand's Andaman Sea and Gulf of Thailand coastlines form 2710 km of beaches, hard shores and wetlands. Hundreds of oceanic and continental islands are found offshore on both sides – those with tourist facilities constitute only a fraction of the total. Offshore depths in the Gulf range from 30 to 80 metres, while offshore Andaman depths reach over 100 metres.

CLIMATE
Rainfall
Thailand's climate is ruled by monsoons. As a result there are three seasons in northern, north-eastern and central Thailand, and two seasons in southern Thailand. The three-season zone, which extends roughly from Thailand's northernmost reaches to the Phetburi Province on the southern peninsula, experiences a 'dry and wet monsoon climate', with the south-west monsoon arriving between May and July and lasting into November. This is followed by a dry period from November to May, a period that begins with lower relative temperatures (because of the influences of the north-east monsoon, which bypasses this part of Thailand but results in cool breezes) till mid-February, followed by much higher relative temperatures from March to May.

It rains more and longer in the south, which is subject to the north-east monsoon from November to January, as well as the south-west monsoon. Hence most of southern Thailand has only two seasons, a wet and a dry, with smaller temperature differences between the two.

Although the rains 'officially' begin in July (according to the Thai agricultural calendar), they actually depend on the monsoons in any given year. As a rule of thumb, the dry season is shorter the farther south you go. From Chiang Mai north the dry season may last six months (mid-November to May); in most of central and north-east Thailand five months (December to May); on the upper peninsula three months (February to May); and below Surat Thani only two months (March and April). Occasional rains in the dry season are known as 'mango showers'.

In central Thailand it rains most during August and September, though there may be floods in October since the ground has reached full saturation by then. If you are in Bangkok in early October don't be surprised if you find yourself in hip-deep water in certain parts of the city. It rains a little less in the north, August being the peak month. The north-east gets less rain and periodically

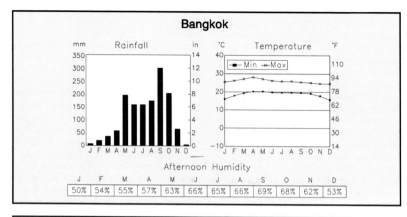

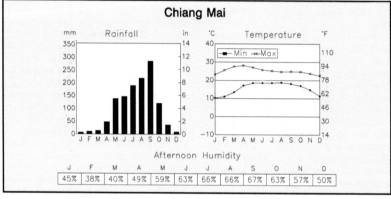

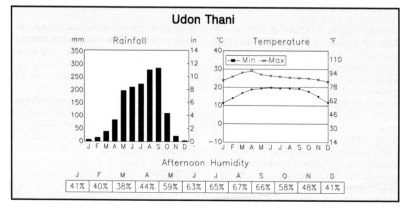

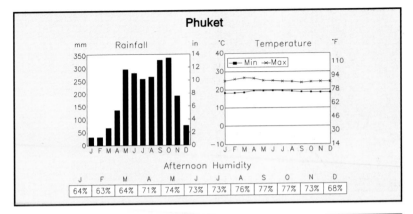

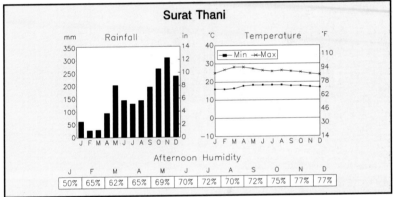

suffers droughts. In Phuket it rains most in May (an average of 21 out of 30 days) and in October (an average of 22 out of 30 days), as this area undergoes both monsoons. Travelling in the rainy season is generally not unpleasant, but unpaved roads may occasionally be impassable.

Temperature
Most of Thailand – with the mountains in the north and the Khorat plateau of the northeast notable exceptions – is very humid, with an overall average humidity of 66% to 82%, depending on the season and time of day. The hot part of the dry season reaches its hottest along the north-east plain, and temperatures easily soar to 39°C in the daytime, dropping only a few degrees at night. The temperature can drop to 13°C at night during the cool season in Chiang Mai and even lower in Mae Hong Son – if you're visiting the north during the cooler months, long-sleeved shirts and pullovers would be in order. Because temperatures are more even year-round in the south, when it is 35°C in Bangkok it may be only 32°C in Phuket.

ECOLOGY
Flora & Fauna
Unique in South-East Asia because its north-

Top: Hat Sai Kaew, Ko Samet (RN)
Middle: Beauty queens, Chiang Mai (JC)
Bottom: Rice harvest, Um Phang (JC)

south axis extends some 1800 km from mainland to peninsular South-East Asia, Thailand thus provides potential habitats for an astounding variety of flora and fauna. As in the rest of tropical Asia, most indigenous vegetation in Thailand is associated with two basic types of tropical forest: monsoon forest (with a distinctive dry season of three months or more) and rainforest (where rain falls more than nine months per year).

Monsoon forests are marked by deciduous tree varieties which shed their leaves during the dry season to conserve water; rainforests are typically evergreen. Central, north, eastern and north-eastern Thailand mainly contain monsoon forests while southern Thailand is predominantly a rainforest zone. There is much overlap of the two – some forest zones support a mix of monsoon forest and rainforest vegetation. The country's most famous flora includes an incredible array of fruit trees (see the Food section in the Facts for the Visitor chapter), bamboo (more species than any country outside China), tropical hardwoods and over 27,000 flowering species, including Thailand's national floral symbol, the orchid.

Wildlife variation is also closely affiliated with geographic and climatic differences. Hence the indigenous fauna of Thailand's northern half is mostly of Indochinese origin while that of the south is generally Sundaic (ie typical of Malaysia, Sumatra, Borneo and Java). The invisible dividing line between the two zoogeographical zones is across the Isthmus of Kra, about halfway down the southern peninsula. The large overlap area between zoogeographical and vegetative zones – extending from around Prachuap Khiri Khan on the southern peninsula to Uthai Thani in the lower north – means that much of Thailand is a potential habitat for plants and animals from both zones.

Thailand is particularly rich in bird life, with over 900 recorded resident and migrating species – approximately 10% of all world bird species. Coastal and inland waterways of the southern peninsula are especially important habitats for South-East Asian waterfowl.

Indigenous mammals – mostly found in dwindling numbers within Thailand's national parks or wildlife sanctuaries – include tigers, leopards, elephants, Asiatic black bears, Malayan sun bears, gaur (Indian bison), banteng (wild cattle), serow (an Asiatic mountain goat), sambar deer, barking deer, mouse deer, tapirs, pangolin, gibbons, macaques, dolphins and dugongs (sea cows). Forty of Thailand's 282 mammal species, including clouded leopard, Malayan tapir, tiger, and pileated gibbon, are on the International Union for Conservation of Nature (IUCN) list of endangered species.

Herpetofauna (298 reptiles, 107 amphibians) include four sea-turtle species along with numerous snake varieties, of which six are venomous: the common cobra (six subspecies), king cobra (hamadryad), banded krait (three species), Malayan viper, green viper and Russell's pit viper. Although the relatively rare king cobra can reach up to six metres in length, the nation's largest snake is the reticulated python, which can reach a whopping 15 metres. The country's many lizard species include two commonly seen in homes and older hotels or guesthouses, the *túk-kae* (a large gecko) and the *jing-jòk* (a smaller house lizard), as well as larger species like the black jungle monitor.

Environmental Policy

Like all countries with high population densities, Thailand has applied enormous pressure on the ecosystems within its borders. Fifty years ago the countryside was around 70% forest; in 1991 an estimated 20 to 30% of the forest cover remained. Logging and agriculture are mainly to blame for the decline, and the loss of forest cover has been accompanied by dwindling wildlife resources. Species notably extinct in Thailand include the kouprey (a type of wild cattle), Schomburgk's deer and the Javan rhino, but innumerable smaller species have also fallen by the wayside.

In response to environmental degradation, the Thai government has created a large number of protected lands (see the National Parks, Marine Parks & Wildlife Sanctuaries

Elephant and mahout, near Mae Sarit (JC)

section in this chapter) since the 1970s, and has enacted legislation to protect specific plant and animal species. The government hopes to raise total forest cover to 40% by the middle of next century. Thailand has also become a signatory to the UN Convention on International Trade in Endangered Species (CITES).

In 1989, logging was banned in Thailand following a 1988 disaster in which hundreds of tonnes of cut timber washed down deforested slopes in Surat Thani Province, killing more than a hundred people and burying a number of villages. It is now illegal to sell timber felled in the country, and all imported timber is theoretically accounted for before going on the market. Illegal timber trade has further diminished with Cambodia's recent ban on all timber exports, along with the termination of all Thai contracts by the Burmese. Laos is now the number one source for imported timber in Thailand, both legal and illegal.

These days builders even need government permission to use timber salvaged from old houses. This has helped curb illegal logging operations in the interior (unfortunately Thai timber brokers are now turning their attention to Laos and Myanmar – neither of which are CITES signatories), but corruption remains a problem.

Corruption also impedes government attempts to shelter 'exotic' species from the illicit global wildlife trade and to preserve Thailand's sensitive coastal areas. The Forestry Department is currently under pressure to take immediate action in those areas where preservation laws have gone unenforced, including coastal zones where illegal tourist accommodation has flourished. There has also been a crackdown on restaurants serving 'jungle food' *(aahāan pàa)*, which consists of exotic and often endangered wildlife species like barking deer, bear, pangolin, civet and gaur.

The tiger is one of the most endangered of

Thailand's large mammals. Although tiger hunting or trapping is illegal, poachers continue to kill the cats for the lucrative overseas Chinese pharmaceutical market; among the Chinese, the ingestion of tiger penis and bone are thought to have curative effects. Taipei, where at least two-thirds of the pharmacies deal in tiger parts (in spite of the fact that such trade is forbidden by Taiwanese law), is the world centre for Thai tiger consumption.

Forestry Department efforts are limited by lack of personnel and funds. The average ranger is paid only 75B a day to face down armed poachers backed by the rich and powerful godfathers who control illicit timber and wildlife businesses.

Marine resources are also threatened by a lack of long-range conservation goals. The upper portion of the Gulf of Thailand between Rayong and Prachuap Khiri Khan, was once one of the most fertile marine areas in the world. Now it is virtually dead due to overfishing and the release of mainland pollutants.

Experts say it's not too late to rehabilitate the upper Gulf by reducing pollution and the number of trawlers, and by restricting commercial fishing to certain zones. An effective ban on the harvest of *plaa tuu* (mackerel) in the spawning stages has brought this fish back from the brink of total depletion. The Bangkok Metropolitan Administration (BMA) is currently developing a system of sewage treatment plants in the Chao Phraya Delta area with the intention of halting all large-scale dumping of sewage into Gulf waters, but similar action needs to be taken along the entire eastern seaboard, which is rapidly becoming Thailand's new industrial centre.

Overdevelopment on Ko Phuket and Ko Phi Phi is starving the surrounding coral reefs by blocking nutrient-rich runoff from the island's interior, as well as smothering the reefs with pollutants. Ko Samui and Ko Samet face a similar fate if action isn't taken soon to control growth and improve waste-disposal standards.

One encouraging move by the government has been the passing of the 1992 Environmental Act, which provides for environmental quality standards and establishes national authority to designate conservation and pollution control areas. Pattaya and Phuket immediately became the first locales to be decreed pollution control areas, thus making them eligible for government

---

Thai Environmentalism

It is obvious that only with strong popular participation can Thailand effect a reasonable enforcement of protective laws - which are already plentiful but often ignored. Current examples of 'people power' include the hundreds of forest monasteries that voluntarily protect chunks of forest throughout Thailand. When one such wat was forcibly removed by the military in Buriram Province, thousands of Thais around the country rallied behind the abbot, Phra Prachak, and the wat's protectorship was re-established. On the other side of the coin, wats with less ecologically minded trustees have sold off virgin lands to developers.

One of the greatest recent victories by Thai environmentalists was the 1986 defeat of government plans to construct a hydroelectric facility across the Khwae Yai River. The dam was to be placed over a river section in the middle of the Thung Yai Naresuan and Huay Kha Khaeng wildlife sanctuaries, one of the largest and best preserved monsoon forest areas in South-East Asia. It took four years of organised protest to halt the dam. Social critics fear that under the new government it will be more difficult to mount this type of extended protest because the NPKC has unchecked power to ban all public assembly.

In 1983 Wildlife Fund Thailand (WFT) was created under Queen Sirikit's patronage as an affiliate of the World-Wide Fund for Nature. The main function of the WFT has been to raise public consciousness with regard to the illegal trade in endangered wildlife. Other Thai groups involved in environmental issues include Santi Pracha Dhamma Institute (SPDI), the brainchild of one of Thailand's leading intellectuals, Sulak Sivaraksa (currently exiled from Thailand to avoid NPKC persecution). ■

cleanup funds. With such assistance, officials in Pattaya now claim they'll be able to restore Pattaya Bay – exposed to improper waste disposal for at least the last 20 years – to its original purity by 1996.

National Parks, Marine Parks & Wildlife Sanctuaries

Despite Thailand's rich diversity of flora and fauna, it has only been in recent years that most of the 66 national parks and 32 wildlife sanctuaries have been established. Together

---

Tourism & the Environment

In some instances tourism has had positive effects on environmental conservation in Thailand. Conscious that the country's natural beauty is a major tourist attraction for both residents and foreigners – and that tourism is one of Thailand's major revenue earners – the government has stepped up efforts to protect wilderness areas and to add more acreage to the park system. In Khao Yai National Park, for example, all hotel and golf-course facilities are being removed in order to reduce human influences on the park environment and upgrade the wilderness. Under government and private sector pressure on the fishing industry, coral dynamiting has been all but eliminated in the Similan and Surin islands, to preserve the area for tourist visitation.

However, tourism has also made negative contributions. Eager to make fistfuls of cash, hotel developers and tour operators have rushed to provide ecologically inappropriate services for visitors in sensitive areas which are unable to sustain high-profile tourism. Concerns about this issue are causing the government to look more closely at Ko Phi Phi and Ko Samet – two national park islands notorious for overdevelopment. Part of the problem is that it's not always clear which lands are protected and which are privately owned.

Common problems in marine areas include the anchoring of tour boats on coral reefs and the dumping of rubbish into the sea. Coral and seashells are also illegally collected and sold in tourist shops. 'Jungle food' restaurants – with endangered species on the menu – flourish near inland national parks. Perhaps the most visible abuses occur in areas without basic garbage and sewage services, where there are piles of rotting garbage, mountains of plastic and open sewage run-off.

One of the saddest sights in Thailand is the piles of discarded plastic water bottles on popular beaches. Worse yet are those seen floating in the sea or in rivers, where they are sometimes ingested by marine or riparian wildlife with fatal results. Many of these bottles started out on a beach only to be washed into the sea during the monsoon season.

What can the average visitor to Thailand do to minimise the impact of tourism on the environment? First off, they can avoid all restaurants serving 'exotic' wildlife species (eg barking deer, pangolin, bear); visitors should also consider taking down the names of any restaurants serving or advertising such fare and filing a letter of complaint with the Tourist Authority of Thailand (TAT), the Wildlife Fund Thailand (WFT) and the Forestry Department (addresses below). The main patrons of this type of cuisine are the Thais themselves, along with visiting Chinese from Hong Kong and Taiwan. Municipal markets selling endangered species, such as Bangkok's Chatuchak Market, should also be duly noted – consider enclosing photographs to support your complaints. For a list of endangered species in Thailand, contact the WFT.

When using hired boats in the vicinity of coral reefs, insist that boat operators not lower anchor onto coral formations. This is becoming less of a problem with established boating outfits – some of whom mark off sensitive areas with blue-flagged buoys – but is common among small-time pilots. Likewise, volunteer to collect (and later dispose of) rubbish if it's obvious that the usual mode is to throw everything overboard.

Obviously, you should refrain from purchasing coral or items made from coral while in Thailand. Thai law forbids the collection of coral or seashells anywhere in the country – report any observed violations in tourist or marine park areas to the TAT and Forestry Department, or in other places to the WFT.

One of the difficulties in dealing with rubbish and sewage problems in tourist areas is that many Thais don't understand why tourists should expect any different methods of disposal than are used elsewhere in the country. In urban areas or populated rural areas throughout Thailand, piles of rotting rubbish and open sewage lines are frequently the norm – after all, Thailand is still a 'developing' country. Thais sensitive to Western paternalism are quick to point out that on a global scale the so-called 'developed' countries contribute far more environmental damage than does

these cover 11.05% of the country's land area, one of the highest ratios of protected to unprotected areas of any nation in the world (compare this figure with India at 4.2%, Malaysia 3.5%, France 8.8% and the USA 10.5%).

A system of wildlife sanctuaries was first provided for in the Wild Animals Reservation and Protection Act of 1960, followed by the National Parks Act of 1961 which established the kingdom's national park programme along with Khao Yai National

---

Thailand (eg per capita greenhouse emissions for Australia, Canada or the USA average over five tons each while ASEAN countries contribute less than 0.5 tonnes per capita).

Hence, in making complaints or suggestions to Thais employed in the tourist industry, it's important to emphasise that you want to work *with* them rather than against them in improving environmental standards.

Whether on land or at sea, refrain from purchasing or accepting drinking water offered in plastic bottles wherever possible. When there's a choice, request glass water bottles, which are recyclable in Thailand. The 4B deposit is refundable when you return the bottle to any vendor who sells drinking water in glass bottles. For those occasions where only plastic-bottled water is available, you might consider transferring the contents from plastic bottles to your own reusable water container – if the vendor/source of the plastic bottle is a more suitable disposal point than your destination. If not, take the bottle with you and dispose of it at a dumpster or other legitimate collection site so that the bottle doesn't end up blowing in the breeze.

A few guesthouses now offer drinking water from large, reusable plastic water containers as an alternative to the disposable individual containers. This service is available in most areas of Thailand (even relatively remote areas like Ko Chang) and is certainly available wherever the disposable plastic bottles are. Encourage hotel and guesthouse staff to switch from disposable plastic to either glass or reusable plastic.

In outdoor areas where rubbish has accumulated, consider organising an impromptu cleanup crew to collect plastic, styrofoam and other nonbiodegradables for delivery to a regular rubbish pick-up point. If there isn't a pick-up somewhere nearby, enquire about the location of the nearest collection point and deliver the refuse yourself.

By expressing your desire to use environmentally friendly materials – and by taking direct action to avoid the use and indiscriminate disposal of plastic – you can provide an example of environmental consciousness not only for the Thais but for other international visitors.

Write to the following organisations to offer your support for stricter environmental policies or to air specific complaints or suggestions:

Tourist Authority of Thailand
372 Bamrung Meuang Rd, Bangkok 10100
Wildlife Fund Thailand
251/88090 Phahonyothin Rd, Bangkhen, Bangkok 10220
or
255 Soi Asoke, Sukhumvit 21, Bangkok 10110
Office of the National Environment Board
60/1 Soi Prachasumphan 4, Rama IV Rd, Bangkok 10400
The Siam Society
131 Soi Asoke, Sukhumvit Rd, Bangkok 10110
Project for Ecological Recovery
77/3 Soi Nomjit, Naret Rd, Bangkok 10500
Royal Forestry Department
Phahonyothin Rd, Bangkhen, Bangkok 10900
Thailand Information Centre of Environmental Foundation
58/1 Sakol Land, Chaeng Wattana Rd, Pakret, Nonthaburi

Magic Eyes
Bangkok Bank Building, 15th Floor, 333 Silom Rd, Bangkok 10400
Community Ecological Development Programme
PO Box 140, Chiang Rai 57000
Asian Society for Environmental Protection
c/o CDG-SEAPO, Asian Institute of Technology, GPO 2754, Bangkok 10501
Raindrop Association
105-107 Ban Pho Rd, Thapthiang, Trang 92000
Siam Environmental Club
Chulalongkorn University, Phayathai Rd, Bangkok 10330

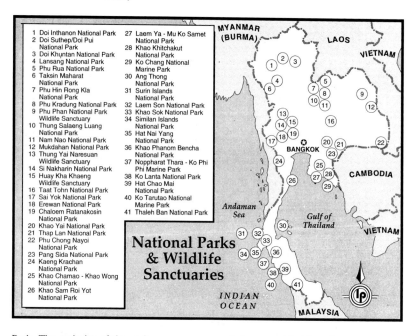

National Parks & Wildlife Sanctuaries

1 Doi Inthanon National Park
2 Doi Suthep/Doi Pui National Park
3 Doi Khuntan National Park
4 Lansang National Park
5 Phu Rua National Park
6 Taksin Maharat National Park
7 Phu Hin Rong Kla National Park
8 Phu Kradung National Park
9 Phu Phan National Park Wildlife Sanctuary
10 Thung Salaeng Luang National Park
11 Nam Nao National Park
12 Mukdahan National Park
13 Thung Yai Naresuan Wildlife Sanctuary
14 Si Nakharin National Park
15 Huay Kha Khaeng Wildlife Sanctuary
16 Taat Tohn National Park
17 Sai Yok National Park
18 Erewan National Park
19 Chaloem Ratanakosin National Park
20 Khao Yai National Park
21 Thap Lan National Park
22 Phu Chong Nayoi National Park
23 Pang Sida National Park
24 Kaeng Krachan National Park
25 Khao Chamao - Khao Wong National Park
26 Khao Sam Roi Yot National Park
27 Laem Ya - Mu Ko Samet National Park
28 Khao Khitchakut National Park
29 Ko Chang National Marine Park
30 Ang Thong National Park
31 Surin Islands National Park
32 Laem Son National Park
33 Khao Sok National Park
34 Similan Islands National Park
35 Hat Nai Yang National Park
36 Khao Phanom Bencha National Park
37 Noppharat Thara - Ko Phi Phi Marine Park
38 Ko Lanta National Park
39 Hat Chao Mai National Park
40 Ko Tarutao National Marine Park
41 Thaleh Ban National Park

Park. The majority of the parks, preserves and sanctuaries are well maintained by the Forestry Department, but a few have allowed rampant tourism to threaten the natural environment, most notably on the islands of Ko Samet and Ko Phi Phi. Poaching, illegal logging and shifting cultivation have also taken their toll on protected lands, but since 1990 the government has been cracking down with some success.

Most of the national parks are easily accessible, yet only 5% of the average annual number of visitors is non-Thai. There is usually somewhere to stay, and sometimes meals are provided, but it's a good idea to take your own sleeping bag or mat; basic camping gear is useful for parks without fixed accommodation. You should also take a torch (flashlight), rain gear, insect repellent, a water container and a small medical kit.

Most parks charge a small fee to visit (typically 3 to 5B for Thais, 15 to 25B for foreigners). Advance bookings for accommodation are advisable at the more popular parks, especially on holidays and weekends. Most national park bungalows cost around 500 to 1500B a night (unless otherwise noted), and usually sleep five to 10 people. During low seasons you can often get a room in one of these park bungalows for 100B per person. A few parks also have *reuan tháew* (long houses) where rooms are around 150 to 200B for two. Some have tents for rent at 50 to 60B a night, but always check the condition of the tents before agreeing to rent one. Finally, if you bring your own tent it's only 5 to 10B per person – almost every park has at least one camping area.

For a true appreciation of Thailand's geography and natural history, a visit to at least one national park is a must. In Bangkok the reservations office is at the national parks division of the Forestry Department (☎ 579-4842/0529), Phahonyothin Rd, Bangkhen (north Bangkok). Bookings from Bangkok must be paid in advance.

GOVERNMENT
The 1991 Constitution

The government of the Kingdom of Thailand is nominally a constitutional monarchy inspired by the bicameral British model but with myriad subtle differences. With the recent change of government and new constitution, government hierarchies have been substantially reshuffled.

Thailand's 15th constitution, enacted on 9 December 1991 by the coup regime's now-defunct National Peace-Keeping Council (NPKC), replaces that promulgated in December 1978 and allows for limited public participation in the choosing of government officials. National polls elect the 360-member lower house and prime minister, but the 270 senators of the upper house are appointed by the prime minister.

Candidates for prime minister need not come from the national assembly, and there is no limit on the number of nonelected cabinet members in the prime minister's council of ministers, which numbers 13 in all. The upper and lower houses vote jointly on no-confidence motions, which means that a majority senate would need only 46 MPs to oust the government and elect a new prime minister. The NPKC claimed that such a system was necessary to guard against the potential for vote-buying, especially in rural areas. However, neither they nor anyone else ever offered conclusive evidence to show that vote-buying was pervasive in previously elected administrations.

A portion of the government's annual budget is provided by over 60 state-owned enterprises – including major manufacturing and transport industries – administered by the PM's office and various government ministries.

Left: Paradise bungalows, Hat Lamai, Ko Samui (RN)
Top Right: Ao Phang-Nga National Park, Phang-Nga (RN)
Bottom Right: Bungalow sight signs, Ao Chalok Ban Kao, Ko Tao (RN)

Thai soldier, Bangkok (MD)

Administrative Divisions

For administrative purposes, Thailand is divided into 76 *jangwàat* or provinces. Each province is subdivided into *amphoe* or districts, which are further subdivided into *kìng-amphoe* (subdistricts), *tambon* (communes or village groups), *mùu-bâan* (villages), *sukhāaphibaan* (sanitation districts) and *thêtsàbaan* (municipalities). Urban areas with more than 50,000 inhabitants and a population density of over 3000 per sq km are designated *nákhon*; those with populations of 10,000 to 50,000 with not less than 3000 per sq km are *meuang* (usually spelt 'muang' on roman-script highway signs). The term 'meuang' is also used loosely to mean metropolitan area (as opposed to an area within strict municipal limits).

A provincial capital is an *amphoe meuang*. An amphoe meuang takes the same name as the province of which it is capital, eg amphoe meuang Chiang Mai (often abbreviated as 'meuang Chiang Mai') means the city of Chiang Mai, capital of Chiang Mai Province.

Except for Krungthep Mahanakhon (Metropolitan Bangkok), provincial governors *(phûu wâa râatchakaan)* are appointed to their four-year terms by the Ministry of the Interior – a system that leaves much potential for corruption. Bangkok's governor and provincial assembly were elected for the first time in November 1985, when Chamlong Srimuang, a strict Buddhist and a former major general, won by a landslide.

District officers *(nai amphoe)* are also appointed by the Interior Ministry but are responsible to their provincial governors. The cities are headed by elected mayors *(naiyók thêtsàmontrii)*, tambons by elected commune heads *(kamnan)* and villages by elected village chiefs *(phûu yài bâan)*.

Armed Forces & Police

Thailand's armed services include the Royal Thai Army (260,000 troops), Royal Thai Air Force (44,000) and Royal Thai Navy (40,000) under the Ministry of Defence, as well as the National Police Department (115,000) under the Ministry of the Interior. The latter department is divided into provincial police, metropolitan police, border patrol police and the central investigation bureau. The central bureau includes railway, marine, highway and forestry police along with special branches concerned with trans-provincial crime and national security issues. Police corruption is common; recruits earn just US$147 a month on salary, so many take 'tea money' whenever they can.

Ever since the 1932 revolution, and particularly following WW II, the Thai military has had a substantial influence on the nation's political affairs. Ananda Panyarachun, interim premier for two short terms in 1991 and 1992, was able to diminish considerably the military's power when he revoked a 14-year-old ministerial order which gave the supreme commander powers as 'internal peace-keeping director'. At the same time he disbanded the Capital Security Command, an organ that was instrumental in the May 1992 bloodbath. This has effectively dissolved all legal and physical structures introduced after the infamous October 1976 coup, including the special command and task forces which had allowed the use of military forces for internal peace-keeping since that time.

Such task forces have not been the military's only source of political ascendancy. High-ranking officers have traditionally held key positions in the telecommunications, shipping and public transport industries as well, thus forming a powerful partnership with big business interests. Another of Ananda's accomplishments was the ousting of military brass from executive posts at the Telephone Organization of Thailand and Thai International Airways.

Following the events of 1991-92, even the generals were admitting that the role of the military had to be reduced. In 1992 General Vimol Wongwanich of the State Railway of Thailand voluntarily resigned his board chairmanship to assume his new position as Commander-in-Chief – a move that would have been unheard-of 20 years ago. Vimol says he intends to depoliticise the army and has declared the coup d'état 'obsolete'. One of his first acts was to reshuffle key postings in the Thai armed forces in order to break up the anti-democratic Class 5 clique.

The Monarchy

His Majesty Bhumibol Adulyadej (pro-nounced 'Phumíphon Adunyádèt') is the ninth king of the Chakri dynasty (founded in 1782) and as of 1988 the longest reigning king in Thai history. Born in the USA in 1927 and schooled in Bangkok and Switzerland, King Bhumibol was a nephew of King Rama VII (King Prajadhipok, 1925-35) as well as the younger brother of King Rama VIII (King Ananda Mahidol). His full name – including royal title – is Phrabaatsomdet Boramintaramahaphumiphonadunyadet.

His Majesty ascended the throne in 1946 following the death of Rama VIII, who had reigned as king for only one year (Ananda served as regent for 10 years after his uncle's abdication in 1935). In June 1946 Ananda was found shot dead in his palace bed, a Colt .45 automatic at his side; no public explana-tion of his mysterious demise has ever been offered. Three palace attendants were arrested in 1948, held in solitary confine-ment for six years, secretly tried and then executed in 1954. Whether their execution was for negligence in protecting the king or for direct involvement in his death is not a matter of public record. The Tourist Author-ity of Thailand (TAT) summarises the circumstances of King Ananda's death as 'untimely.'

A jazz composer and saxophonist, King Bhumibol wrote the royal anthem, *Falling Rain*, which accompanies photos of the royal family shown before every film at cinemas throughout the country. His royal motorcade is occasionally seen passing along Ratcha-damnoen (Royal Promenade) Rd in Bangkok's Banglamphu district; the king is usually seated in a vintage yellow Rolls Royce or a 1950s Cadillac.

Novices on alms-round, Chiang Khan (JC)

Chakri Dynasty

Crown Title	Reign	Common Westernised Name	Thai Pronunciation
Rama I	1782-1809	Yot Fa	Phutthayotfa Chulalok
Rama II	1809-24	Loet La	Phutthaloetla Naphalai
Rama III	1824-51	Nang Klao	same
Rama IV	1851-68	Mongkut	Jawm Klao
Rama V	1868-1910	Chulalongkorn	Chunla Jawm Klao
Rama VI	1910-25	Vajiravudh	Mongkut Klao
Rama VII	1925-35	Prajadhipok	Pok Klao
Rama VIII	1935-46	Ananda Mahidol	Anantha Mahidon
Rama IX	1946-present	Bhumibol Adulyadej	Phumiphon Adunyadet

The king has his own privy council comprised of up to 14 royal appointees who assist with the king's formal duties; the president of the privy council serves as interim regent until an heir is throned.

The king and his wife, Queen Sirikit, have four children: Princess Ubol Ratana (born 1951), Crown Prince Maha Vajiralongkorn (1952), Princess Mahachakri Sirindhorn (1955) and Princess Chulabhorn (1957). A royal decree issued by King Trailok (1448-88) to standardise succession in a polygamous dynasty makes the king's senior son or full brother his *uparaja* (Thai: *ùpàrâat*) or heir apparent. Thus Prince Maha Vajiralongkorn was officially designated as crown prince and heir when he reached 20 years of age in 1972; if he were to decline the crown or be unable to ascend the throne due to incurable illness or death, the senior princess (Ubol Ratana) would be next in line.

Princess Ubol Ratana married American Peter Jensen in 1972 against palace wishes, thus forfeiting her royal rank, but was reinstated as Princess a few years ago. The Crown Prince has married twice, most recently to an ex-actress. His son Prince Juthavachara is the eldest male of the next Chakri generation.

Though Thailand's political system is officially classified as a constitutional monarchy, the Thai constitution stipulates that the king be 'enthroned in a position of revered worship' and not be exposed 'to any sort of accusation or action'. With or without legal writ, the vast majority of Thai citizens regard King Bhumibol as a sort of demigod, partly in deference to tradition but also because of his impressive public works record.

Neither the constitution nor the monarchy's high status prevents Thai people from gossiping about the royal family in private, however. Gathered together, the various whisperings and speculations with regard to royal intrigue would make a fine medieval fable. Many Thais, for example, favour Princess Sirindhorn for succession to the Thai throne, though none would say this publicly, nor would this popular sentiment appear in the Thai print or broadcast media. Among the nation's soothsayers, it has long been prophesied that the Chakri dynasty will end with Rama IX; current political conditions, however, suggest the contrary.

It is often repeated that the Thai king has no political power (by law his position is strictly titular and ceremonial) but in times of national political crisis, Thais have often looked to the king for leadership. Two

Left: Market in Ban Don, Surat Thani (RN)
Top Right: Frangipani (JO)
Middle Right: Bougainvillea (RN)
Bottom Right: Waterlily flower, Ratchaburi (RN)

attempted coups d'état in the 1980s may have failed because they received tacit royal disapproval. By implication, the successful military coup of February 1991 must have had palace approval, whether *post facto* or *a priori*.

The NPKC's 1991 draft constitution was widely condemned until just a few days before its final reading in the national assembly, when the king spoke out during his annual birthday address in favour of leaving the draft unchanged. Not surprisingly, the assembly passed the constitution in spite of a few anti-democratic clauses contained therein, even though it would have taken only a few extra days to revise the draft. This unamended constitution continues to be a major source of friction between Thailand's political parties.

Along with nation and religion, the monarchy is very highly regarded in Thai society – negative comment about the king or any member of the royal family is a social as well as legal taboo. See the Avoiding Offence section in this chapter.

ECONOMY

During the 1980s, Thailand maintained a steady GNP growth rate which in 1988 reached 13% per annum. Now, Thailand has suddenly found itself on the threshold of attaining the exclusive rank of NIC or 'newly industrialised country', which experts forecast will happen within the next six to 10 years. Soon, they say, Thailand will be joining Asia's 'little dragons', also known as the Four Tigers – South Korea, Taiwan, Hong Kong and Singapore – in becoming a leader in the Pacific Rim economic boom.

Sixty per cent of Thailand's exports are agricultural; the country ranks first in the world for rice (a whopping 36% of world exports, followed by 20% from the USA and 9% from Pakistan), second in tapioca (after Brazil) and fifth in coconut (following Indonesia, the Philippines, India and Sri Lanka). Since 1991 Thailand has been the world's largest producer of natural rubber, although it still ranks behind Malaysia in total rubber exports. Other important agricultural exports

include sugar, maize, pineapple, cotton, jute, green bean, soybean and palm oil. Processed food and beverages – especially canned shrimp, tuna and pineapple – also account for significant export earnings. Thailand's top export markets are the USA (21%), Japan (18%) and Singapore (8%).

About 65% of the Thai labour force is currently engaged in agriculture, 10% each in commerce and services, and 10% in manufacturing. By the year 2000, it is expected that close to half of Thailand's labour force will be engaged in the manufacturing and industrial sectors. Manufactured goods have become an increasingly important source of foreign exchange revenue and now account for at least 30% of Thailand's exports. Cement, textiles and electronics lead the way. The country also has substantial natural resources, including tin, petroleum and natural gas.

Since 1987, tourism has become a leading earner of foreign exchange, occasionally outdistancing even Thailand's largest single export, textiles, with receipts as high as US$4 billion per annum. The government's economic strategy remains focused, however, on export-led growth through the development of light industries such as textiles and electronics, backed by rich reserves of natural resources and a large, inexpensive labour force. Observers predict that such a broad-based economy will make Thailand a major economic competitor in Asia in the long term.

Average per capita income by early 1994 was US$1905 per year. Regional inequities, however, mean that local averages range from US$300 in the north-east to US$2600 in Bangkok. The minimum wage in Bangkok and surrounding provinces is 120B (US$4.80) per day; it can be as low as 85B a day in the outer provinces. Although it doesn't reach the world's top 50 list in terms of raw per capita GNP, on a worldwide scale Thailand's economy ranks 21st (between Pakistan at 20th and Iran at 22nd) if figured by the GDP 'purchasing power parity' method. Thais are tied with the Japanese in eighth place for gross savings of GDP

Top: Vendors at Amphoe floating market, Samut Songkhram (RN)
Bottom: Rice farmer, Um Phang (JC)

income at 34% (Singapore ranks first at 45%; Australia and the US are ranked 42nd and 66th, with respective savings rates of 15% and 21%).

The current inflation rate is a low 4% per annum; travellers should keep this in mind when referring to prices in this edition. As in most other countries, prices continue to rise.

Regional Economies

The north-east of Thailand has the lowest inflation rate and cost of living. This region is poorer than the rest of the country and doesn't get as much tourism; it therefore offers excellent value for the traveller and is in dire need of your travel dollar. Hand-woven textiles and farming remain the primary means of livelihood in this area, although Khorat (Nakhon Ratchasima) is an emerging centre for metals and automotive industry. In the south, fishing, tin mining and rubber production keep the local economy fairly stable, with tourism a seasonal runner-up.

Central Thailand grows fruit (especially pineapples), sugar cane and rice for export, and supports most of the ever-growing industry (textiles, food processing and cement). North Thailand produces mountain or dry rice (as opposed to water rice, the bulk of the crop produced in Thailand) for domestic use, maize, tea, various fruits and flowers,

Top: Thai women fishing, Hat Mae Nam, Ko Samui (RN)
Bottom: Boats in harbour, Thong Sala, Ko Pha-Ngan (RN)
Border: Drying fish, Na Thon, Ko Samui (RN)

and is very dependent on tourism. Teak and other lumber were once major products of the north, but since early 1989 all logging has been banned in Thailand in order to prevent further deforestation.

Infrastructure & Growth

Some say that Thailand has been growing faster than its infrastructure can handle. Although adequate for most domestic trade, the transport and telecommunications systems are in dire need of upgrading for purposes of international trade. Incoming ships have to wait a week before they can get a berth at busy Khlong Toey Port. Access to Khlong Toey is limited to ships of less than 10,000 tons or 8.5-metre draft; larger vessels must off-load at the mouth of the Chao Phraya River or offshore near the country's second-largest ports at Si Racha and Sattahip. Thirty smaller ports along the Gulf and Andaman Sea serve fishing fleets and smaller import-export operations.

Engineers are working hard to meet the shipping demands – a new deep-water port has opened at Laem Chabang, near Si Racha, and is linked to an export-processing zone. Another industrial park and port is under development at Mapthaphut, farther east, for petrochemical and fertiliser industries.

One of the biggest dilemmas facing the economic planners is whether to acquire a larger foreign debt in order to finance the development of an infrastructure which is capable of handling continued high growth, or whether to allow growth to slow while the infrastructure catches up. Continued rapid growth will probably result in a disproportionate development of the more industrialised central and southern regions, leaving the agricultural north and north-east behind.

Advocates of a slow-growth approach hope for better distribution of wealth around the country through a combination of agribusiness projects and welfare programmes that would bring a higher standard of living to poor rural areas. This makes good sense when one considers the relative differences between Thailand and the Four Tigers (in the proportion of rural to urban dwellers and the high fertility of the land).

The 1990-92 recession was a blessing in disguise inasmuch as it allowed Thailand's overheated economy to cool down. The current growth rate has slowed to 7.4% and is not expected to increase more than half a per cent or so over the next two years. Even at 8%, Thailand will remain one of the world's fastest growing economies.

Indochina, ASEAN & Pacific Trade

Aside from its own export-oriented growth, Thailand stands to profit from increased international trade in Laos, Cambodia and Vietnam. At the moment Bangkok is the main launching base for foreign investments in Indochina, and the Thai baht is second only to the US dollar as the currency of choice for regional commerce. In Laos and Cambodia the only foreign banks are Thai; Vientiane and Phnom Penh have even started building up portions of their national reserves in baht, thus forming a 'baht bloc'. Thailand continues to profit from the overland transshipment of international goods to Vietnam via Laos, even with the 1994 lifting of the US-Vietnam trade embargo.

In 1994 the ASEAN countries (Thailand, Malaysia, Singapore, Brunei, Philippines and Indonesia) established the ASEAN Free Trade Area (AFTA), which will gradually reduce import tariffs among ASEAN nations until total free trade is reached by 2008. This agreement should prove very advantageous for Thailand's economy since Thailand has a highly educated, inexpensive labour pool and a large manufacturing sector.

Thailand is also a member of the Asia-Pacific Economic Cooperation (APEC) bloc, which comprises the USA, Canada, Japan, Australia, New Zealand, South Korea, Thailand, Malaysia, Singapore, Brunei, Hong Kong, Taiwan, China, Papua New Guinea, Mexico and Chile. APEC meets periodically to discuss trade issues of mutual interest, occasionally agreeing to lower or eliminate trade barriers on specific products.

The kingdom's latest efforts for regional economic influence include plans for a

Opium & the Golden Triangle

The opium poppy, *Papaver somniferum*, has been cultivated and its resins extracted for use as a narcotic at least since the time of the early Greek Empire. The Chinese were introduced to the drug by Arab traders during the time of Kublai Khan (1279-94). It was so highly valued for its medicinal properties that hill-tribe minorities in southern China began cultivating the opium poppy in order to raise money to pay taxes to their Han Chinese rulers. Easy to grow, opium became a way for the nomadic hill tribes to raise what cash they needed in transactions (willing and unwilling) with the lowland world. Many of the hill tribes that migrated to Thailand and Laos in the post WW II era in order to avoid persecution in Myanmar (Burma) and China took with them their one cash crop, the poppy. The poppy is well suited to hillside cultivation as it flourishes on steep slopes and in nutrient-poor soils.

The opium trade became especially lucrative in South-East Asia during the 1960s and early 1970s when US armed forces were embroiled in Vietnam. Alfred McCoy's *The Politics of Heroin in Southeast Asia* recounts how contact with the GI market not only expanded the immediate Asian market, but provided outlets to world markets. Before this time the source of most of the world's heroin was the Middle East. Soon everybody wanted in and various parties alternately quarrelled over and co-operated in illegal opium commerce. Most notable were the Nationalist Chinese Army refugees living in northern Myanmar and northern Thailand, and the anti-Rangoon rebels, in particular the Burmese Communist Party, the Shan States Army and the Shan United Army.

The American CIA eventually became involved in a big way, using profits from heroin runs aboard US aircraft to Vietnam and further afield to finance covert operations throughout Indochina. This of course led to an increase in the availability of heroin throughout the world, which in turn led to increased production in the remote northern areas of Thailand, Myanmar and Laos, where there was little government interference. This area came to be known as the 'Golden Triangle' because of local fortunes amassed by the 'opium warlords' – Burmese and Chinese military-businesspeople who controlled the movement of opium across three international borders.

As more opium was available, more was consumed and the demand increased along with the profits – so the cycle expanded. As a result, opium cultivation became a full-time job for some hill tribes within the Golden Triangle. Hill economies were destabilised to the point where opium production became a necessary means of survival for thousands of people, including the less nomadic Shan people.

One of the Golden Triangle's most colourful figures is Khun Sa (also known as Chang Chi-Fu, or Sao Mong Khawn) a half-Chinese, half-Shan opium warlord. He got his start in the 1950s and 1960s working for the Kuomintang (KMT) – Chiang Kai-shek's Nationalist Chinese troops, some of whom had fled to Myanmar. The KMT were continuing military operations against the Chinese Communists along the Myanmar-China border, financed by the smuggling of opium (with CIA protection). They employed Khun Sa as one of their prime local supporters/advisors. Khun Sa broke with the KMT in the early 1960s after establishing his own opium-smuggling business, with heroin refineries in northern Thailand.

From that time on, the history of heroin smuggling in the Golden Triangle has been intertwined with the exploits of Khun Sa. In 1966, the Burmese government deputised Khun Sa as head of 'village defence forces' against the Burmese Communist Party (BCP), which was at maximum strength at this time and fully involved in opium trade. Khun Sa cleverly used his government backing to consolidate power and build up his own militia by developing the Shan United Army (SUA), an anti-government insurgent group heavily involved in opium throughout the Golden Triangle in competition with the BCP and KMT.

When the KMT attempted an 'embargo' on SUA opium trade by blocking caravan routes into Thailand and Laos, Khun Sa initiated what has come to be known as the Opium War of 1967 and thwarted the embargo. However, the KMT managed to chase Khun Sa, along with a contingent of SUA troops running an opium caravan routed for Thailand, into Laos, where Burmese officials arrested Khun Sa and the Laotian government seized the opium. Khun Sa escaped Burmese custody by means of a carefully planned combination of extortion and bribery in 1975 and returned to take command of the SUA. About the same time, the Burmese government broke KMT control of opium trafficking and Khun Sa stepped in to become the prime opium warlord in the Triangle, working from his headquarters in Ban Hin Taek, Chiang Rai Province, Thailand. Coincidentally, US forces pulled out of Indochina at this time so there was no longer any competition from CIA conduits in Laos. Ironically, since then, the primary law-enforcement conflict has been between US-backed Thai forces and the SUA.

Since the late 1970s, Khun Sa's armies have continued to buy opium from the BCP, Shan and hill-tribe cultivators in Myanmar, Laos and Thailand, transporting and selling the product to Yunnanese-operated heroin refineries in China, Laos and Thailand, who in turn sell to ethnic Chinese (usually Tae Jiu/Chao Zhou) syndicates who control access to world markets via Thailand and Yunnan.

A turning point in Khun Sa's fortunes occurred in 1982 and 1983 when the Thais launched a full-scale attack on his Ban Hin Taek stronghold, forcing him to flee to the mountains of the Kok River valley across the border in Ho Mong, Myanmar, where he directs his independent empire from a fortified network of underground tunnels. This move led to the breaking up of opium and heroin production in the Mae Salong-Ban Hin Taek area.

The SUA has since merged with several other Shan armies to form the Muang Tai Army (MTA), led by the Shan State Restoration Council; in 1992 Khun Sa declared the Shan State an independent nation. Recent MTA strength has been estimated at 25,000 – the largest and best-equipped ethnic army in Myanmar – well beyond that of the Karen National Union, the country's second largest insurgent group (among the 30-odd different groups operating since the 1940s). From time to time Khun Sa announces his 'retirement' but, like his Rangoon nemesis Ne Win, Khun Sa has outwitted many international players before and will probably maintain de facto control until his death or capture. Khun Sa is now a 'marked' man (with a price of 100,000B on his head, roughly the wholesale value of a kilo of pure heroin) who may soon be sacrificed by corrupt Burmese and Thai generals in order to appease the US government.

Since his retreat to Myanmar, Khun Sa's former northern Thailand stronghold has undergone heavy 'pacification' or Thai nationalisation. At great expense to the Thai government, tea, coffee, corn and Chinese herbs are now grown where opium once thrived. Whether this particular project is successful or not is another question, but the government's strategy seems to be one of isolating and then pushing pockets of the opium trade out of Thailand and into Myanmar and Laos, where it continues uninterrupted. Myanmar remains the largest producer of opium in the world, manufacturing an average of 800 tonnes per annum over the last decade. During a bumper year, the entire Triangle output approaches 4000 tonnes; Khun Sa recently boasted that the 1994-95 harvest would reach 6000 tonnes.

During the 1970s, the socialist rulers of Laos took advantage of Thai government action in northern Thailand to encourage an increase in opium production in Lao territory, effectively capturing a large share of the market vacated by the SUA in Thailand. In recent years, however, the Lao government has reversed its official tolerance towards opium production and has invited US participation in a nationwide anti-narcotics drive. In spite of these bilateral efforts, northwestern Laos is dotted with heroin refineries which process Burmese and Laotian opium. Smuggling routes for Laotian opium and heroin continue to intersect the Thai border at several points throughout the north and north-east, including the provinces of Chiang Mai (via Myanmar), Chiang Rai, Nan, Loei, Nong Khai and Nakhon Phanom.

By all estimates there has been a steady increase in Triangle production for the last ten years; only 1.9 to 2.5% of the opium crop is intercepted by national or international authorities each year. Whenever they receive a large financial contribution from the US Drug Enforcement Agency (DEA), Thai army rangers sweep northern Thailand from Tak to Chiang Rai and Mae Hong Son, destroying poppy fields and heroin refineries but rarely making arrests. A typical sweep costs US$1 million and accomplishes the destruction of 25,000 or more *rai* (one rai is equal to 1600 sq metres) of poppy fields in Chiang Mai, Chiang Rai, Mae Hong Son, Tak or Nan. Hill-tribe and Shan cultivators, at the bottom of the profit scale, stand by helplessly while their primary means of livelihood is hacked or burned to the ground. A crop substitution programme, developed by the Thai royal family in 1959 (a year earlier, cultivation of the opium poppy for profit had been made illegal), has had mixed results. Success has only occurred in selected areas where crop substitution is accompanied by a concentrated effort to indoctrinate hill tribes into mainstream Thai culture.

Meanwhile, power shifts from warlord to warlord while the hill-tribe and Shan cultivators continue as unwilling pawns in the opium-heroin cycle. The planting of the poppy and the sale of its collected resins has never been a simple moral issue. Cultivators who have been farming poppies for centuries and heroin addicts who consume the end product have both been exploited by governments and crime syndicates who trade in opium for the advancement of their own interests. Because of the complexities involved, opium production in the Golden Triangle must be dealt with as a political, social, cultural and economic problem and not simply as a conventional law-enforcement matter.

So far, a one-sided approach has resulted only in the unthinking destruction of minority culture and economy in the Golden Triangle area, rather than an end to the opium and heroin problem. Opium cultivation persists in Thailand in hidden valleys not frequented by the Thai armed forces. Although the Thai government outlawed opium trade in 1839, any hill-tribe settlement may legally plant a limited crop of opium poppies for medical consumption. Small plots of land are thus sometimes 'leased' by opium merchants who have allowed production to decentralise in order for poppy resin collection to appear legal. ∎

'southern growth triangle' that would link trade growth in Thailand's five southernmost provinces with Malaysia and Indonesia, and the 'northern growth quadrangle' joining northern Thailand, China's Yunnan Province, northern Laos and north-eastern Myanmar. For the latter plan, the Thai government is offering significant financial assistance for road development between the four countries, beginning with north-south highways connecting Yunnan and northern Thailand via both Myanmar and Laos.

Tourism

According to TAT statistics, the country is currently averaging about five million tourist arrivals per year, a 62-fold increase since 1960 when the government first began keeping statistics. The country's biggest boom occurred during 1986-90, when arrivals grew by 10 to 23% per annum.

In 1993 nearly two-thirds of the visitors came from East Asia and the Pacific, with Malaysians leading the way at 829,700, followed by Japanese (581,800), Taiwanese (524,700) and Singaporeans (364,400). Europeans as a whole made up approximately 1.3 million of the total, with Germans at the top (320,200), followed by Britons (250,000), French (202,000) and Italians (126,400). US visitors accounted for 278,300 of the total, Australians 205,200 and Canadians 59,300. Other major markets include Hong Kong (265,500), China (261,700), India (105,400) and the Netherlands (76,400). Thailand's fastest-growing tourist segments in 1993 were South Africans (up 103%), Chinese (102%) and Turks (57%).

The biggest growth in tourism since 1990 has been among the Thais themselves. Spurred by steady economic growth, an estimated 37 million Thais per year are now taking domestic leisure trips. Ten years ago Western tourists often outnumbered Thais at some of the nation's most famous tourist attractions. Now the opposite is true; except

Poppies in bloom, Chiang Mai Province (JC)

at major international beach destinations like Phuket and Ko Samui, Thai tourists tend to outnumber farangs in most places.

POPULATION & PEOPLE

The population of Thailand is about 59 million and currently growing at a rate of 1.5% per annum (as opposed to 2.5% in 1979), thanks to Khun Mechai's nationwide family-planning campaign.

Bangkok is by far the largest city in the kingdom, with a population of over six million (more than 10% of the total population) – too many for the scope of its public services and what little 'city planning' exists. Ranking the nation's other cities by population depends on whether you look at thetsabaan (municipal district) limits or at meuang (metropolitan district) limits. By the former measure, the four most populated cities in descending order (not counting the densely populated 'suburb' provinces of Samut Prakan and Nonthaburi, which would rank second and third if considered separately from Bangkok) are Khorat, Chiang Mai, Hat Yai and Khon Kaen. Using the rather misleading meuang measure, the ranking runs Udon Thani, Lopburi, Khorat and Khon Kaen. Most of the other towns in

Thailand have populations of well below 100,000.

The literacy rate in Thailand is approximately 93% and increasing, and the average life expectancy is 69 – in both respects Thailand is a leader in mainland South-East Asia. In 1993 the government raised compulsory schooling from six to nine years. Infant mortality figures are 27 per 1000 births (figures for neighbouring countries vary from 117 per 1000 in Cambodia to 14 in Malaysia). Thailand as a whole has a relatively youthful population; only about 12% are older than 50.

The Thai Majority

About 75% of the citizenry are ethnic Thais, who can be divided into the central Thais or Siamese of the Chao Phraya Delta (the most densely populated region of the country); the Thai Lao of north-east Thailand; the Thai Pak Tai of southern Thailand; and the northern Thais. Each of these groups speak their own Thai dialect and to a certain extent practise customs unique to their region. Politically and economically the central Thais are the dominant group, although they barely outnumber the Thai Lao of the northeast.

Thailand's Largest Cities

Population	Thetsabaan (municipal district)	Meuang (metropolitan district)
Bangkok	not applicable	6+ million (1569 sq km)
Chaiyaphum	25,600 (2.8 sq km)	157,700 (1169 sq km)
Chiang Rai	36,542 (10.6 sq km)	167,318 (1622 sq km)
Chiang Mai	154,777 (40 sq km)	164,490 (152 sq km)
Hat Yai	139,400 (21 sq km)	149,800 (1154 sq km)
Khon Kaen	130,300 (46 sq km)	197,400 (953 sq km)
Khorat (Nakhon Ratchasima)	202,403 (37 sq km)	208,800 (571 sq km)
Lampang	43,369 (9 sq km)	184,000 (1156 sq km)
Lopburi	40,000 (6.8 sq km)	211,400 (565 sq km)
Nakhon Pathom	45,000 (5.3 sq km)	181,700 (417 sq km)
Nakhon Si Thammarat	71,500 (11.7 sq km)	216,708 (765 sq km)
Nonthaburi	46,400 (2.5 sq km)	240,000 (77 sq km)
Phetchabun	28,400 (8.6 sq km)	176,000 (2272 sq km)
Sakon Nakhon	24,800 (13 sq km)	178,000 (1815 sq km)
Samut Prakan	71,400 (7.3 sq km)	266,000 (190 sq km)
Surin	40,000 (11.4 sq km)	237,000 (1279 sq km)
Udon Thani	95,000 (3.7 sq km)	277,000 (1094 sq km)

Top Left: Man in field, Ban Chao Doi (RI)
Top Right: Muslim boy (RN)
Middle: Karen family, Um Phang (JC)
Bottom Left: Hill-tribe woman, Ban Huay Phao (RI)
Bottom Right: Hill-tribe woman, Ban Huay Kruy (RI)

Smaller groups with their own Thai dialects include the Shan (Mae Hong Son), the Thai Lü (Nan, Chiang Rai), the Lao Song (Phetchaburi and Ratchaburi), the Phuan (Chaiyaphum, Phetchaburi, Prachinburi), the Thai Khorat or Sawoei (Khorat), the Phu Thai (Mukdahan, Sakon Nakhon), the Yaw (Nakhon Phanom, Sakon Nakhon) and the Thai-Malay (Satun, Trang, Krabi).

The Chinese

People of Chinese ancestry make up 11% of the population, most of whom are second or third-generation Hokkien or Tae Jiu (Chao Zhou/Chiu Chao). Ethnic Chinese probably enjoy better relations with the majority population here than in any other country in South-East Asia, due partly to historical reasons and partly to traditional Thai tolerance of other cultures (although there was a brief spell of anti-Chinese sentiment during the reign of Rama VI). King Rama V used Chinese businesspeople to infiltrate European trading houses, a manoeuvre that helped defeat European colonial designs on Siam. Wealthy Chinese also introduced their daughters to the royal court as consorts, developing royal connections and adding a Chinese bloodline that extends to the current king.

Minorities

The second largest ethnic minority group living in Thailand are the Malays (3.5%), most of whom reside in the provinces of Songkhla, Yala, Pattani and Narathiwat. The remaining 10.5% of the population is divided among smaller non-Thai-speaking groups like the Vietnamese, Khmer, Mon, Semang (Sakai), Moken *(chao leh* or 'sea gypsies'), Htin, Mabri, Khamu and a variety of hill tribes (described more fully in the Northern Thailand chapter).

A small number of Europeans and other non-Asians live in Bangkok and the provinces – their total numbers aren't recorded since very few have immigrant status.

ARTS
Traditional Sculpture & Architecture

The following scheme is the latest one used by Thai art historians to categorise historical styles of Thai art, principally sculpture and architecture (since very little painting prior to the 19th century has survived).

A good way to acquaint yourself with these styles, if you are interested, is to visit the Bangkok National Museum in Bangkok, where works from each of these periods are on display. Then, as you travel upcountry and view old monuments and sculpture, you'll know what you're seeing, as well as what to look for.

Since 1981, the Thai government has made restoration of nine key archaeological sites part of its national economic development plan. As a result, the Fine Arts Department, under the Ministry of Education, has developed nine historical parks *(ùthayaan pràwátìsàat)*: Sukhothai Historical Park and Si Satchanalai Historical Park in Sukhothai Province; Phra Nakhon Si Ayuthaya Historical Park in Ayuthaya Province; Phanom Rung Historical Park in Buriram Province; Si Thep Historical Park in Phetchabun Province; Phra Nakhon Khiri Historical Park in Phetburi Province; Phimai Historical Park in Nakhon Ratchasima Province; Muang Singh Historical Park in Kanchanaburi Province; and Kamphaeng Phet Historical Park in Kamphaeng Phet Province.

These parks are administered by the Fine Arts Department to guard against theft and vandalism, and to protect tourists from bandits at more remote sites. In 1988 the department even managed to get the famous Phra Narai lintel returned to Prasat Phanom Rung from the Art Institute of Chicago Museum. UNESCO has declared the ruins at Ayuthaya, Sukhothai, Si Satchanalai and Kamphaeng Phet as World Heritage Sites, which makes them eligible for UN funds and/or expertise in future restoration projects.

Additional areas of historical interest for art and architecture include Thonburi, Nakhon Pathom, Sawankhalok, Chiang Mai,

Top Left: Gong maker, Ubon Ratchathani Province (JC)
Top Right: Making shadow puppets, Nakhon Si Thammarat (JC)
Bottom Left: Silk weaving, Chonabot (JC)
Bottom Right: Woodcarver, Ancient City (JO)

Thai Art Styles

Style	Duration	Centred in	Characteristics
Mon Art (formerly Dvaravati)	6th to 13th C	Central Thailand, also North and North-East	adaptation of Indian styles, principally Gupta
Khmer Art	7th to 13th C	Central and North-East Thailand	post-classic Khmer styles accompanying spread of Khmer empires
Peninsular Art	(formerly Srivijaya period)	Chaiya and Nakhon Si Thammarat	Indian influence 3rd to 5th C, Mon and local influence 5th to 13th C, Khmer influence 11th to 14th C
Lan Na (formerly Chiang Saen)	13th to 14th C	Chiang Mai, Chiang Rai, Phayao, Lamphun, Lampang	Shan/Burmese and Lao traditions mixed with local styles
Sukhothai	13th to 15th C	Sukhothai, Si Satchanalai, Kamphaeng Phet, Phitsanulok	unique to Thailand
Lopburi	10th to 13th C	Central Thailand	mix of Khmer, Pala and local styles
Suphanburi-Sangkhlaburi (formerly U Thong)	13th to 15th C	Central Thailand	mix of Mon, Khmer, and local styles; prototype for Ayuthaya style
Ayuthaya A	1350-1488	Central Thailand	Khmer influences gradually replaced by revived Sukhothai influences
Ayuthaya B	1488-1630	Central Thailand	ornamentation distinctive of Ayuthaya style, eg crowns and jewels on Buddhas, begins
Ayuthaya C	1630-1767	Central Thailand	baroque stage and decline
Ratanakosin	19th C to present	Bangkok	return to simpler designs, beginning of European influences

Art Styles

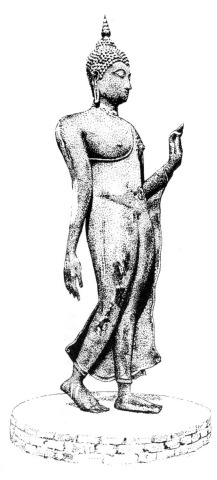

LOPBURI
10th to 13th centuries

SUKHOTHAI
13th to 15th centuries

MON (Dvaravati)
6th to 11th centuries

MON (Hariphunchai)
11th to 13th centuries

SUPHANBURI-SANGKHLABURI
13th to 15th centuries

LAN NA
13th to 14th centuries

Phitsanulok, Chiang Saen, Lamphun, Nan, Lopburi, Khorat, Surin, Buriram, Si Saket, Chaiya and Nakhon Si Thammarat. Some of the monuments at these sites have also been restored by the Fine Arts Department and/or by local interests. For more detail on historical sites, see the relevant regional sections in this book.

Recommended books on Thai art are A B Griswold's classic *Arts of Thailand* (Indiana University Press, 1960), the similarly titled *The Arts of Thailand* (Thames & Hudson, 1991) by Steve Van Beek, and *A Concise History of Buddhist Art in Siam* (Tokyo, 1963) by Reginald Le May. Even the newest of these three books is out of date, since research in Thai art history has evolved quickly in recent years, but they make good introductions. There are several decent English-language books on various aspects of Thai art for sale at the national museums around Thailand (particularly at the Bangkok National Museum) and at the Ancient City (Muang Boran) office on Ratchadamnoen Klang Rd in Bangkok.

For information about the export of antiques or objects of art from Thailand, see the Customs section in the Facts for the Visitor chapter.

Modern Architecture

Modern Thai architects are among the most daring in South-East Asia, as even a short visit to Bangkok will confirm. Thais began mixing traditional Thai with European forms in the late 19th and early 20th centuries, as exemplified by Bangkok's Vimanmek Palace, the Author's Wing of the Oriental Hotel, the Chakri Mahaprasat next to Wat Phra Kaew, the Thai-Chinese Chamber of Commerce on Sathon Tai Rd and any number of older residences and shophouses in Bangkok or provincial capitals throughout Thailand. This style is usually referred to as 'old Bangkok' or 'Ratanakosin'. The recently completed Old Siam Plaza shopping centre, adjacent to Bangkok's Chalermkrung Royal Theatre, is an attempt to revive the old Bangkok school.

In the 1930s a simple Thai Deco style emerged, blending European Art Deco with functionalist restraint; surviving examples include the restored Chalermkrung Royal Theatre, the Royal Hotel and several buildings along Ratchadamnoen Klang Rd. Buildings of mixed heritage in the north and north-east exhibit French and English influences, while those in the south typically show Portuguese influence.

Shophouses throughout the country, whether 100 years or 100 days old, share the basic Chinese shophouse (*hâwng tháew* in Thai) design in which the ground floor is reserved for trading purposes while the upper floors contain offices or residences.

During most of the post-WW II era, the trend in modern Thai architecture – inspired by the European Bauhaus movement – was towards a boring functionalism in which the average building looked like a giant egg carton turned on its side. The Thai aesthetic, so vibrant in prewar eras, almost entirely disappeared in this characterless style of architecture.

When Thai architects finally began experimenting again during the building boom of the mid-1980s, it was to provide high-tech designs like Sumet Jumsai's famous robot-shaped Bank of Asia on Sathon Tai Rd in Bangkok. Few people seemed to find the space-age look endearing, but at least it was different. Another trend affixed gaudy Roman and Greek-style columns to rectangular Art-Deco boxes in what was almost a parody of Western classical architecture. One of the outcomes of this fashion has been the widespread use of curvilinear banisters on the balconies of almost every new shophouse, apartment or condominium throughout Thailand, often with visually disturbing results.

More recently, a handful of rebellious architects have begun reincorporating traditional Thai motifs – mixed with updated Western classics – in new buildings. MIT graduate Rangsan Torsuwan introduced the neoclassic (or neo-Thai) style, the best example of which is the new Grand Hyatt Erawan in Bangkok. Another architect using traditional Thai architecture in modern functions is Pinyo Suwankiri, who has designed a number of government buildings in Bangkok as well as the Cittaphawan Buddhist School in Chonburi.

A good book for those with a general interest in Thai residential design, interior or exterior, is William Warren's *Thai Style* (Asia Books), a coffee-table tome with excellent photography by Luca Invernizzi Tettoni.

Painting

Except for prehistoric and historic cave or rock-wall murals found throughout the country, not much formal painting predating the 18th century exists in Thailand. Presumably there were a great number of temple murals in Ayuthaya that were destroyed by the Burmese invasion of 1767. The earliest surviving temple examples are found at Ayuthaya's Wat Ratburana (1424) and Phetburi's Wat Yai Suwannaram (late 17th century).

Nineteenth-century religious painting has fared better; Ratanakosin-style temple art is in fact more highly esteemed for painting

---

National Museums

Thailand's Fine Arts Department operates an excellent network of national museums in areas of the country known for historic art and archaeology. The museums typically offer a small exhibit of artefacts from around the country as well as more extensive displays featuring works of local provenance. At present visitors have a choice of 35 regional museums to choose from. All are open the same hours, Wednesday to Sunday, 9 am to 5 pm. Those most worth visiting include the following. Museums are in provincial capitals unless otherwise stated.

Provincial Capital	Museum
Ayuthaya	Chan Kasem National Museum
	Chao Sam Phraya National Museum
Bangkok	National Museum
	National Royal Barges Museum
	Wat Benchamabophit National Museum
Chainat	Chainat Muni National Museum
Chiang Mai	Chiang Mai National Museum
Chiang Rai	Chiang Saen National Museum (Chiang Saen)
Kamphaeng Phet	Kamphaeng Phet National Museum
Kanchanaburi	Ban Kao National Museum (Ban Kao)
Khon Kaen	Khon Kaen National Museum
Lamphun	Hariphunchai National Museum
Lopburi	Somdet Phra Narai National Museum
Nakhon Pathom	Phra Pathom Chedi National Museum
Nakhon Ratchasima	Mahawirawong National Museum
	Phimai National Museum (Phimai)
Nakhon Si Thammarat	Nakhon Si Thammarat National Museum
Nan	Nan National Museum
Phetburi	Phra Nakhon Khiri National Museum
Phitsanulok	Phra Phuttha Chinnarat National Museum
Phuket	Thalang National Museum (Thalang)
Prachinburi	Prachinburi National Museum
Ratchaburi	Ratchaburi National Museum
Singburi	In Bun National Museum
Songkhla	Matchimawat National Museum
	Songkhla National Museum
Sukhothai	Ramkhamhaeng National Museum
	Sawanworanayok National Museum (Sawankhalok)
Suphanburi	U Thong National Museum
Surat Thani	Chaiya National Museum (Chaiya)
Surin	Surin National Museum
Ubon Ratchathani	Ubon Ratchathani National Museum
Udon Thani	Ban Chiang National Museum (Ban Chiang)

than for sculpture or architecture. Typical temple murals feature rich colours and lively detail. Some of the finest are found in Wat Phra Kaew's Wihan Phutthaisawan (Buddhaisawan Chapel) in Bangkok and at Wat Suwannaram in Thonburi.

Modern Painting The beginnings of Thailand's modern art movement are usually attributed to Italian artist Corrado Feroci, who was first invited to Thailand by King Rama VI in 1924. Feroci's design of Bangkok's Democracy Monument was inspired by Italy's Fascist art movement of the 1930s – in Italy, he earned his reputation as a designer of war memorials under Mussolini. Feroci founded the country's first fine arts institute in 1933, a school which eventually developed into Silpakorn University, Thailand's premier training ground for artists and art historians. In gratitude for his contributions, the Thai government gave Feroci the Thai name Silpa Bhirasri.

Today contemporary Thai painting is exhibited at a number of Bangkok and Chiang Mai venues. One of the most important modern movements in Thai art was an updating of Buddhist themes, begun in the 1970s by painters Pichai Nirand, Thawan Duchanee and Prateung Emjaroen. The movement has grown stronger since their early efforts combined modern Western schemata with Thai motifs. One Bangkok gallery, the Visual Dhamma Gallery (off Soi Asoke), specialises in the display of modern Thai Buddhist art by a number of different artists.

Another important venue and source of support for modern art is Bangkok's luxury hotels. The largest collection of modern Thai painting anywhere in the world is found in the lobbies and public areas of the Grand Hyatt Erawan; the displays are changed regularly.

Music

Traditional Music From a Western perspective, traditional Thai music is some of the most bizarre on the planet, but to acquire a taste for it is well worth the effort. The clas-

sical, central Thai music is spicy, like Thai food, and features an incredible array of textures and subtleties, hair-raising tempos and pastoral melodies.

The classical orchestra is called the *pìi-phâat* and can include as few as five players or more than 20. Among the more common instruments is the *pìi*, a woodwind instrument which has a reed mouthpiece; it is heard prominently at Thai boxing matches. The pii is a relative of a similar Indian instrument, while the *phin*, a banjo-like stringed instrument whose name comes from the Indian *vina*, is considered native to Thailand. A bowed instrument similar to ones played in China and Japan is aptly called the *saw*. The *ranâat èk* is a bamboo-keyed percussion instrument resembling the Western xylophone, while the *khlui* is a wooden flute.

One of the more amazing Thai instruments is the *khawng wong yài*, tuned gongs arranged in a semicircle. There are also several different kinds of drums, some played with the hands, some with sticks. The most important Thai percussion instrument is the *tà-phon* (or *thon)*, a double-headed hand-drum which sets the tempo for the ensemble. Prior to a performance, the players make offerings of incense and flowers to the taphon, which is considered to be the 'conductor' of the music's spiritual content.

The pii-phaat ensemble was originally developed to accompany classical dance-drama and shadow theatre but can be heard in straightforward performance these days, in temple fairs as well as concerts. One reason classical Thai music may sound strange to the Western ear is that it does not use the tempered scale we have been accustomed to hearing since Bach's time. The standard Thai scale does feature an eight-note octave but it is arranged in seven full-tone intervals, with no semi-tones. Thai scales were first transcribed by Thai-German composer Peter Feit (Phra Chen Duriyanga), who also composed Thailand's national anthem in 1932.

In the north and north-east there are several popular reed instruments with multiple bamboo pipes, which function basically like a mouth-organ. Chief among these is the *khaen*, which originated in Laos; when played by an adept musician it sounds like a rhythmic, churning calliope. The funky *lûuk thûng*, or 'country' (literally 'children of the fields') style, which originated in the north-east, has become a favourite throughout Thailand.

If you're interested in learning how to play traditional Thai instruments, contact the Bangkok YMCA (☎ 286-1542/2580) to enquire about its weekly classes.

Recommended books on the subject are *The Traditional Music of Thailand* by David Morton, and *Thai Music* by Phra Chen Duriyanga (Peter Feit).

Modern Music Popular Thai music has borrowed much from Western music, particularly its instruments, but still retains a distinct flavour of its own. Although Bangkok bar bands can play fair imitations of everything from Hank Williams to Olivia Newton-John, there is a growing preference among Thais for a blend of Thai and international styles.

The best example of this is Thailand's famous rock group Carabao. At the time of writing, Carabao is by far the most popular musical group in Thailand and has even scored hits in Malaysia, Singapore, Indonesia and the Philippines with songs like 'Made in Thailand' (the chorus is in English). This band and others have crafted an exciting fusion of Thai classical and luuk thung forms with heavy metal. These days almost every other Thai pop group sounds like a Carabao clone, and individual members of the original band are putting out their own albums using the now-classic Carabao sound.

Another major influence on Thai pop was a 1970s group called Caravan, which created a modern Thai folk style known as *phleng phêua chii-wít* or 'songs for life'. Songs of this nature have political and environmental topics rather than the usual moonstruck love themes; during the authoritarian dictatorships of the 1970s many of Caravan's songs were officially banned by the government.

Though this band dissolved in the early 1980s, they re-form for the occasional live concert. The group's most gifted songwriter, Surachai, continues to record and release solo efforts.

Yet another inspiring movement in modern Thai music is the fusion of international jazz with Thai classical and folk motifs. The leading exponent of this newer genre is the composer and instrumentalist Tewan Sapsanyakorn (also known as Tong Tewan), whose performances mix Western and Thai instruments. The melodies of his compositions are often Thai-based but the improvisations and rhythms are drawn from such heady sources as Sonny Rollins and Jean-Luc Ponty. Tewan himself plays soprano and alto sax, violin and khlui with equal virtuosity. When Tewan isn't touring internationally you may catch him and his extremely capable band Tewan Noveljazz at the Bangkok clubs Brown Sugar, Fang Dee, Trumpet, or Round Midnight.

Cassette tapes of Thai music are readily available throughout the country in department stores, cassette shops and street vendors. The average price for a Thai music cassette is 50 to 70B. Western tapes are cheaper (about 30B each) if bootlegged, but the days of pirate tapes in Thailand are numbered now that the US music industry is enforcing international copyright laws. Licensed Western music tapes cost 90B, still a good deal by the pricing standards of most Western nations.

Theatre & Dance
Traditional Thai theatre consists of six dramatic forms: *khōn*, formal masked dance-drama depicting scenes from the *Ramakian* (the Thai version of India's *Ramayana)* and originally performed only for the royal court; *lákhon*, a general term covering several types of dance-dramas (usually for non-royal occasions) as well as Western theatre; *lí-khe* (likay), a partly improvised, often bawdy folk play with dancing and music; *mánohra*, the southern Thai equivalent of li-khe, but based on a 2000-year-old Indian story; *năng* or shadow plays, limited to southern Thai-

Thai dancer

land; and *hùn lŭang* or *lákhon lék* – puppet theatre.

Khon In all khon performances, four types of characters are represented – male humans, female humans, monkeys and demons. Monkey and demon figures are always masked with the elaborate head coverings often seen in tourist promo material. Behind the masks and make-up, all actors are male. Traditional khon is a very expensive production – Ravana's retinue alone (Ravana is the story's principal villain) consists of over a hundred demons, each with a distinctive mask. Perhaps because it was once limited to royal venues and hence never gained a popular following, the khon or *Ramakian* dance-drama tradition nearly died out in Thailand. Bangkok's National Theatre was once the only place where khon was regularly performed for the public; the renovated Chalermkrung Royal Theatre now hosts weekly khon performances enhanced by laser graphics and high-tech audio.

Scenes performed in traditional khon (and lakhon performances) come from the *Ramayana*, India's classic 'epic journey' tale with obvious archetypal parallels in the Greek epic the *Odyssey*, and the Greek myth of Jason and the Argonauts. The central story revolves around Prince Rama's search for his beloved Princess Sita, who has been abducted by the evil 10-headed demon Ravana and taken to the island of Lanka. Rama is assisted in his search and in the final battle against Ravana by a host of mythical half-animal, half-human characters including the monkey-god Hanuman. See the following Literature section for some details on the differences between the Indian *Ramayana* and Thai *Ramakian*.

Lakhon The more formal *lákhon nai* (inner lakhon) was originally performed for lower nobility by all-female ensembles; even more than royal khon it's a dying art. In addition to scenes from the *Ramakian*, lakhon nai performances may include traditional Thai folk tales; whatever the story, text is always sung.

Lákhon nâwk (outer lakhon) deals exclusively with folk tales and features a mix of sung and spoken text, sometimes with improvisation. Both male and female performers are permitted. Like khon and lakhon nai, performances are becoming increasingly rare. More common these days is the less refined *lákhon chatrii*, a fast-paced, costumed dance-drama usually performed at upcountry temple festivals or at shrines (commissioned by a shrine devotee whose wish was granted by the shrine deity). Chatrii stories have been influenced by the older manohra theatre of southern Thailand (see Manohra later in this section).

Lákhon phûut (speaking lakhon) is the equivalent of Western theatre based on the Greek model – all dialogue is spoken rather than sung. This is the most modern of Thailand's theatre traditions as well as the most popular in cities and larger towns.

Li-khe In rural and small-town Thailand this is the most popular type of live theatre. Most often performed at festivals by troupes of travelling performers, li-khe presents an intriguing mixture of folk and classical music, outrageous costumes, slapstick comedy, sexual innuendo and up-to-date commentary on Thai politics and society. Farangs – even those who speak fluent Thai – are often left behind by the highly idiomatic, culture-specific language and gestures. Most li-khe performances begin with the *àwk khàek*, a prelude in which an actor dressed in Malay costume takes the stage to pay homage to the troupe's teacher and to narrate a brief summary of the play to the audience. For true li-khe aficionados, the coming of a renowned troupe is a bigger occasion than the release of a new *Terminator* sequel at the local cinema.

Manohra Also known simply as *nora*, this is southern Thailand's equivalent to li-khe and the oldest surviving Thai dance-drama. The basic story line bears some similarities to the *Ramayana*. In this case the protagonist, ◄Prince Suthon (Sudhana in Pali), sets off to rescue the kidnapped Manohra, a *kinnari* or woman-bird princess. As in li-khe, performers add extemporaneous comic rhymed commentary – famed nora masters sometimes compete at local festivals to determine who's the best rapper.

Nang Shadow-puppet theatre – in which two-dimensional figures are manipulated between a cloth screen and light source at night-time performances – has been a South-East Asian tradition for perhaps five centuries. Originally brought to the Malay peninsula by Middle Eastern traders, the technique eventually spread to all parts of mainland and peninsular South-East Asia; in Thailand it is mostly found only in the south. As in Malaysia and Indonesia, shadow puppets in Thailand are carved from dried buffalo or cow hides (*nãng* in Thai).

Two distinct shadow-play traditions survive in Thailand. The most common, *nãng thálung*, is named after Phattalung Province, where it developed based on Malay models. Like their Malay-Indonesian counterparts, the Thai shadow puppets represent an array of characters from classical and folk drama, principally the *Ramakian* and Phra Aphaimani in Thailand. A single puppet master manipulates the cutouts, which are bound to the ends of buffalo-horn handles. Nang thalung is still occasionally seen at temple fairs in the south, mostly in Songkhla and Nakhon Si Thammarat provinces. Performances are also held periodically for tour groups or visiting dignitaries from Bangkok.

The second tradition, *nãng yài* (literally, 'big hide'), uses much larger cutouts, each bound to two wooden poles held by a puppet master; several masters (almost always male) may participate in a single performance. Nang yai is rarely performed nowadays because of the lack of trained nang masters and the expense of the shadow puppets. Most nang yai made today are sold to interior decorators or tourists – a well-crafted hide puppet may cost as much as 5000B.

Lakhon Lek Like khon, lakhon lek or 'little theatre' (also known as hun luang or 'royal puppets') was once reserved for court performances. Metre-high marionettes made of *koi* paper and wire, wearing elaborate costumes modelled on those of the khon, are used to convey similar themes, music and dance movements. Two Thai puppet-masters are required to manipulate each hun luang – including arms, legs, hands, even fingers and eyes – by means of wires attached to long poles. Stories are drawn from Thai folk tales, particularly Phra Aphaimani, and occasionally from the *Ramakian*.

Hun luang is no longer performed, as the performance techniques and puppet-making skills have been lost. The hun luang puppets themselves are highly collectable; the Bangkok National Museum has only one example in its collection. Surviving examples of a smaller, 30-cm court version called *hùn lék* (little puppets) are occasionally used in live performances; only one puppeteer is required for each marionette in hun lek.

Another Thai puppet theatre called *hùn kràbòk* (rod puppets) is based on popular Hainanese puppet shows. It uses 30-cm hand puppets that are carved from wood, and they are viewed from the waist up. Hun krabok marionettes are still being crafted and used in performance.

Literature

Of all classical Thai literature, the *Ramakian* is the most pervasive and influential in Thai culture. The Indian source – the *Ramayana* – came to Thailand with the Khmers 900 years ago, first appearing as stone reliefs on Prasat Hin Phimai and other Angkor-period temples in the north-east. Oral and written versions may also have been available; eventually, though, the Thais developed their own version of the epic, first written down during the reign of Rama I (1782-1809). This version was 60,000 stanzas, about 25% longer than the Sanskrit original.

Although the main theme remains the same, the Thais embroidered the *Ramayana* by providing much more biographic detail on arch-villain Ravana (Dasakantha, called Thótsàkan or '10-necked' in the *Ramakian)* and his wife Montho. Hanuman the monkey-god differs substantially in the Thai version insofar as he is very flirtatious with females (in the Hindu version he follows a strict vow of chastity). One of the classic *Ramakian* reliefs at Bangkok's Wat Pho depicts Hanuman clasping a maiden's bared breast as if it were an apple.

Also passed on from Indian tradition are the many *jatakas* or life stories of the Buddha *(chaa-tòk* in Thai). Of the 547 jataka tales in the Pali *tripitaka* (Buddhist canon) – each one chronicling a different past life – most appear in Thailand almost word-for-word as they were first written down in Sri Lanka. A group of 50 'extra' stories, based on Thai folk tales of the time, were added by Pali scholars in Chiang Mai 300 to 400 years ago. The most popular jataka in Thailand is one of the Pali originals known as the Mahajati or Mahavessandara (Mahaa-Wetsandon in Thai), the story of the Buddha's penultimate life. Interior murals in the *bòt* or ordination

chapel of Thai wats typically depict this jataka and nine others: Temiya, Mahaachan-aka, Suwannasama, Nemiraja, Mahaasotha, Bhuritat, Chantakumara, Nartha and Vithura.

The 30,000-line *Phra Aphaimani*, composed by poet Sunthorn Phu in the late 18th century, is Thailand's most famous classical literary work. Like many of its epic predecessors around the world, it tells the story of an exiled prince who must complete an odyssey of love and war before returning to his kingdom in victory.

Poetry During the Ayuthaya period, Thailand developed a classical poetic tradition based on five types of verse – *chan, kap, khlong, khlon* and *rai.* Each of these forms uses a complex set of strict rules to regulate metre, rhyming patterns and number of syllables. Although all of these poetic systems use Thai language, chan and kap are derived from Sanskrit verse forms from India while khlong, khlon and rai are native forms. The Indian forms have all but disappeared from 20th-century use. During the political upheavals of the 1970s, several Thai newspaper editors, most notably Kukrit Pramoj, composed lightly disguised political commentary in khlon verse. Modern Thai poets seldom use the classical forms, preferring to compose in blank verse or with song-style rhyming.

SPORT
Thai Boxing (Muay Thai)

Almost anything goes in this martial sport, both in the ring and in the stands. If you don't mind the violence (in the ring), a Thai boxing match is worth attending for the pure spectacle – the wild musical accompaniment, the ceremonial beginning of each match and the frenzied betting around the stadium.

Thai boxing is also telecast on Channel 7 every Sunday afternoon; if you're wondering where everyone is, they're probably inside watching the national sport.

History Most of what is known about the early history of Thai boxing comes from Burmese accounts of warfare between

Myanmar and Thailand during the 15th and 16th centuries. The earliest reference (1411 AD) mentions a ferocious style of unarmed combat that decided the fate of Thai kings. A later description tells how Nai Khanom Tom, Thailand's first famous boxer and a prisoner of war in Myanmar, gained his freedom by roundly defeating a dozen Burmese warriors before the Burmese court. To this day, many martial art aficionados consider the Thai style the ultimate in hand-to-hand fighting. Hong Kong, China, Singapore, Taiwan, Korea, Japan, the USA, Netherlands, Germany and France have all sent their best and none of the challengers have been able to defeat top-ranked Thai boxers. On one famous occasion, Hong Kong's top five Kung Fu masters were dispatched in less than 6½ minutes cumulative total, all knockouts.

King Naresuan the Great (1555-1605) was supposed to have been a top-notch boxer himself, and he made muay thai a required part of military training for all Thai soldiers. Later another Thai king, Phra Chao Seua (the Tiger King), further promoted Thai boxing as a national sport by encouraging prize fights and the development of training camps in the early 18th century. There are accounts of massive wagers and bouts to the death during this time. Phra Chao Seua himself is said to have been an incognito participant in many of the matches during the early part of his reign. Combatants' fists were wrapped in thick horsehide for maximum impact with minimum knuckle damage. They also used cotton soaked in glue and ground glass and later hemp. Tree bark and seashells were used to protect the groin from lethal kicks.

Modern Thai Boxing The high incidence of death and physical injury led the Thai government to institute a ban on muay thai in the 1920s, but in the 1930s, the sport was revived under a modern set of regulations based on the international Queensberry rules. Bouts were limited to five three-minute rounds separated with two-minute breaks. Contestants had to wear international-style gloves and trunks (always either in red or blue) and their feet were taped – to this day no shoes are worn.

There are 16 weight divisions in Thai boxing, ranging from mini-flyweight to heavyweight, with the best fighters said to be in the welterweight division (67 kg maximum). As in international-style boxing, matches take place on a 7.3-sq-metre canvas-covered floor with rope retainers supported by four padded posts, rather than the traditional dirt circle.

In spite of these concessions to safety, today all surfaces of the body are still considered fair targets and any part of the body except the head may be used to strike an opponent. Common blows include high kicks to the neck, elbow thrusts to the face and head, knee hooks to the ribs and low crescent kicks to the calf. A contestant may even grasp an opponent's head between his hands and pull it down to meet an upward knee thrust. Punching is considered the weakest of all blows and kicking merely a way to 'soften up' one's opponent; knee and elbow strikes are decisive in most matches.

The training of a Thai boxer and particularly the relationship between boxer and trainer is highly ritualised. When a boxer is considered ready for the ring, he is given a new name by his trainer, usually with the name of the training camp as his surname. For the public, the relationship is perhaps best expressed in the *ram muay* (boxing

Thai boxing

dance) that takes place before every match. The ram muay ceremony usually lasts about five minutes and expresses obeisance to the fighter's guru *(khruu)*, as well as to the guardian spirit of Thai boxing. This is done through a series of gestures and body movements performed in rhythm to the ringside musical accompaniment of Thai oboe (pii) and percussion. Each boxer works out his own dance, in conjunction with his trainer and in accordance with the style of his particular camp.

The woven headbands and armbands worn into the ring by fighters are sacred ornaments which bestow blessings and divine protection; the headband is removed after the ram muay ceremony, but the armband, which actually contains a small Buddha image, is worn throughout the match. After the bout begins, the fighters continue to bob and weave in rhythm until the action begins to heat up. The musicians continue to play throughout the match and the volume and tempo of the music rise and fall along with the events in the ring.

As Thai boxing has become more popular among Westerners (both spectators and participants) there are increasing numbers of bouts staged for tourists in places like Pattaya, Phuket and Ko Samui. In these, the action may be genuine but the judging below par. Nonetheless, dozens of authentic matches are held every day of the year at the major Bangkok stadiums and in the provinces (there are about 60,000 full-time boxers in Thailand), and these are easily sought out.

Several Thai·*nák muay* have gone on to win world championships in international-style boxing. Khaosai Galaxy, the greatest Asian boxer of all time, chalked up 19 WBA bantamweight championships in a row before retiring undefeated in December 1991. As of 1993 Thailand had three concurrent WBA world champions.

In Thailand an English-language periodical called *Muay Thai: Thai Championship Boxing* appears annually at Bangkok, Chiang Mai and Phuket bookshops that sell English-language material. The annual includes features on muay thai events abroad as well as in Thailand.

Krabi-Krabong

Another traditional Thai martial art still practised in Thailand is *kràbìi-kràbong* (literally, 'sword-staff'). As the name implies, this tradition focuses on hand-held weapons techniques, specifically the *kràbìi* (sword), *plông* (quarter-staff), *ngao* (halberd), *dàap sãwng meu* (a pair of swords held in each hand) and *mái sun-sàwk* (a pair of clubs). Although for most Thais krabi-krabong is a ritual artefact to be displayed during festivals or at tourist venues, the art is still solemnly taught according to a 400-year-old tradition handed down from Ayuthaya's Wat Phutthaisawan. The King of Thailand's elite bodyguard are trained in krabi-krabong; many Thai cultural observers perceive it as a 'purer' tradition than muay thai.

Like muay thai of 70 years ago, modern krabi-krabong matches are held within a marked circle, beginning with a *wâi khruu* ceremony and accompanied throughout by a musical ensemble. Thai boxing techniques and judo-like throws are employed in conjunction with weapons techniques. Although sharpened weapons are used, the contestants refrain from striking their opponents – the winner is decided on the basis of stamina and the technical skill displayed. Although an injured fighter may surrender, injuries do not automatically stop a match.

For information on muay thai and krabi-krabong training courses in Thailand, see Martial Arts Training in the Courses section of the Facts for the Visitor chapter.

Takraw

Tàkrâw, sometimes called Siamese football in old English texts, refers to games in which a woven rattan ball about 12 cm in diameter is kicked around. The rattan (or sometimes plastic) ball itself is called a *lûuk tàkrâw*. Takraw is also popular in several neighbouring countries; it was originally introduced to the SEA Games by Thailand but the Malays seem to win most international championships. The traditional way to play takraw in

Thailand is for players to stand in a circle (the size of the circle depends on the number of players) and simply try to keep the ball airborne by kicking it soccer-style. Points are scored for style, difficulty and variety of kicking manoeuvres.

A popular variation on takraw – and the one used in intramural or international competitions – is played with a volleyball net, using all the same rules as in volleyball except that only the feet and head are permitted to touch the ball. It's amazing to see the players perform aerial pirouettes, spiking the ball over the net with their feet. Another variation has players kicking the ball into a hoop 4.5 metres above the ground – basketball with feet, but without a backboard!

AVOIDING OFFENCE

Monarchy and religion are the two sacred cows in Thailand. Thais are tolerant of most kinds of behaviour as long as it doesn't insult one of these.

King & Country

The monarchy is held in considerable respect in Thailand and visitors should be respectful too – avoid disparaging remarks about the king, queen or anyone in the royal family. One of Thailand's leading intellectuals, Sulak Sivaraksa, was arrested in the early 1980s for lese-majesty because of a passing reference to the king's fondness for yachting (Sulak referred to His Majesty as 'the skipper') and again in 1991 when he referred to the royal family as 'ordinary people'. Although on that occasion he received a royal pardon, in 1991 Sulak had to flee the country to avoid prosecution again for alleged remarks delivered at Thammasat University about the ruling military junta, with reference to the king (Sulak has since returned under a suspended sentence). The penalty for lese-majesty is seven years' imprisonment.

While it's OK to criticise the Thai government and even Thai culture openly, it's considered a grave insult to Thai nationhood as well as to the monarchy not to stand when you hear the national or royal anthems.

Radio and TV stations in Thailand broadcast the national anthem daily at 8 am and 6 pm; in towns and villages (even in some Bangkok neighbourhoods) this can be heard over public loudspeakers in the streets. The Thais stop whatever they're doing to stand during the anthem (except in Bangkok where nobody can hear anything above the street noise) and visitors are expected to do likewise. The royal anthem is played just before films are shown in public cinemas; again, the audience always stands until it's over.

Religion

Correct behaviour in temples entails several guidelines, the most important of which is to dress neatly (no shorts or sleeveless shirts) and to take your shoes off when you enter any building that contains a Buddha image. Buddha images are sacred objects, so don't pose in front of them for pictures and definitely do not clamber upon them.

Monks are not supposed to touch or be touched by women. If a woman wants to hand something to a monk, the object should be placed within reach of the monk, not handed directly to him.

When sitting in a religious edifice, keep your feet pointed away from any Buddha images. The usual way to do this is to sit in the 'mermaid' pose in which your legs are folded to the side, with the feet pointing backwards.

Social Gestures

Traditionally Thais greet each other not with a handshake but with a prayer-like palms-together gesture known as a *wâi*. If someone wais you, you should wai back (unless waied by a child).

The feet are the lowest part of the body (spiritually as well as physically) so don't point your feet at people or point at things with your feet. In the same context, the head is regarded as the highest part of the body, so don't touch Thais on the head either.

Terms of Address

Thais are often addressed by their first name with the honorific *khun* or other title preceding it. Other formal terms of address include *nai* (Mr) and *naang* (Miss or Mrs). Friends often use nicknames or kinship terms like *phîi* (elder sibling), *náwng* (younger sibling), *mâe* (mother) or *lung* (uncle) depending on the age differential.

Dress & Attitude
Beach attire is not considered appropriate for trips into town and it is especially counter-productive if worn to government offices (eg when applying for a visa extension). The attitude of 'This is how I dress at home and no-one is going to stop me' gains nothing but contempt/disrespect from the Thais.

As in most parts of Asia, anger and emotions are rarely displayed and generally get you nowhere. In any argument or dispute, remember the paramount rule is to keep your cool.

Nudity
Regardless of what the Thais may (or may not) have been accustomed to centuries ago, they are quite offended by public nudity today. Bathing nude at beaches in Thailand is illegal. If you are at a truly deserted beach and are sure no Thais may come along, there's nothing stopping you – however, at most beaches travellers should wear suitable attire. Likewise, topless bathing for females is frowned upon in most places except on heavily touristed islands like Phuket, Samui, Samet and Pha-Ngan. Many Thais say that nudity on the beaches is what bothers them most about foreign travellers. These Thais take nudity as a sign of disrespect for the locals, rather than as a libertarian symbol or modern custom. Thais are extremely modest in this respect (despite racy billboards in Bangkok) and it should not be the visitor's intention to 'reform' them.

Message from a Reader
As a final comment on avoiding offence, here is a plea from a female reader who wrote to me following an extended visit she had in Thailand:

Please do whatever you can to impress on travellers the importance of treating the Thai people, who are so generous and unassuming, with the respect they deserve. If people sunbathe topless, take snapshots of the people like animals in a zoo, and demand Western standards then they are both offending the Thai people and contributing to the opinion many of them have of us as being rich, demanding and promiscuous.

RELIGION
Buddhism
Approximately 95% of the Thai citizenry are Theravada Buddhists. The Thais themselves frequently call their religion Lankavamsa (Sinhalese lineage) Buddhism because Thailand originally received Buddhism from Sri Lanka during the Sukhothai period. Strictly speaking, Theravada refers only to the earliest forms of Buddhism practised during the Ashokan and immediate post-Ashokan periods in South Asia. The early Dvaravati and pre-Dvaravati forms of Buddhism are not the same as that which has existed in Thai territories since the 13th century.

Since the Sukhothai period, Thailand has maintained an unbroken canonical tradition and 'pure' ordination lineage, the only country among the Theravadin (using Theravada in its doctrinal sense) countries to do so. Ironically, when the ordination lineage in Sri Lanka broke down during the 18th century under Dutch persecution, it was Thailand that restored the Sangha (Buddhist brotherhood) there. To this day the major sect in Sri Lanka is called Siamopalivamsa (Siam-Upali lineage, Upali being the name of the Siamese monk who led the expedition to Ceylon), or simply Siam Nikaya (the Siamese sect).

Basically, the Theravada school of Buddhism is an earlier and, according to its followers, less corrupted form of Buddhism than the Mahayana schools found in East Asia or in the Himalayan lands. The Theravada (literally, 'teaching of the elders') school is also called the 'southern' school since it took the southern route from India, its place of origin, through South-East Asia (Myanmar, Thailand, Laos and Cambodia in this case), while the 'northern' school pro-

Spirit Houses

Every Thai house or building has to have a spirit house to go with it – a place for the spirits of the site, or *phra phum*, to live in. Without this vital structure you're likely to have the spirits living in the house with you, which can cause all sorts of trouble. A spirit house looks rather like a birdhouse-sized Thai temple mounted on a pedestal – at least your average spirit house does. A big hotel may have a shrine covering 100 sq metres or more.

How do you ensure that the spirits take up residence in your spirit house rather than in the main house with you? Mainly by making the spirit house a more auspicious place to live in than the main building, through daily offerings of food, flowers, candles and incense. The spirit house should also have a prominent location and should not be shaded by the main house. Thus its position has to be planned from the very beginning and installed with due ceremony. If your own house is improved or enlarged then the spirit house should be as well. The local *phâw khru* or *mâe khruu* (father or mother teacher) usually presides over the initial installation as well as later improvements.

The interior of a spirit house is usually decorated with ceramic or plastic figurines representing the property's guardian spirits. The most important figurine, the *châo thîi* or 'place lord', embodies a phra phum who reigns over a specific part of the property (see the list of Guardian Spirits below). Larger or more elaborate spirit houses may also contain figurines that serve as family, retainers or servants for these resident spirits. Thai believers purchase these figurines – as well as the bowls, dishes and other accoutrements for making daily offerings – at rural temples or, in larger cities, at supermarkets and department stores.

An abandoned or damaged spirit house can't simply be tossed aside like a broken appliance, left to rot or dismantled for firewood. Instead, it should be deposited against the base of a sacred banyan tree or in the corner of a sympathetic wat where benevolent spirits will watch over it.

Guardian Spirit	Sphere of Influence
Phra Chaimongkhon	houses
Phra Nakhonrat	gates, portals, ladders
Phra Khonthan	honeymoon homes
Phra Khan Thoraphon	corrals, cattle pens
Phra Chai Kassapa	granaries
Phra Thamahora	fields
Phra Than Thirat	gardens, orchards
Phra Chaimongkut	farmyards, compounds
Phra That Tara	temples, shrines, monasteries

ceeded north into Nepal, Tibet, China, Korea, Mongolia, Vietnam and Japan. Because the Theravada school tried to preserve or limit the Buddhist doctrines only to those canons codified in the early Buddhist era, the Mahayana school gave Theravada Buddhism the name Hinayana, or the 'lesser vehicle'. The Mahayana school was the 'great vehicle', because it built upon the earlier teachings, 'expanding' the doctrine in such a way as to respond more to the needs of lay people, or so it is claimed.

Theravada or Hinayana doctrine stresses the three principal aspects of existence: *dukkha* (suffering, unsatisfactoriness, disease), *anicca* (impermanence, transience of all things) and *anatta* (non-substantiality or non-essentiality of reality – no permanent 'soul'). These three concepts, when 'discovered' by Siddhartha Gautama in the 6th century BC, were in direct contrast to the Hindu belief in an eternal, blissful self (*paramatman*), hence Buddhism was originally a 'heresy' against India's Brahmanic religion.

Gautama, an Indian prince-turned-ascetic, subjected himself to many years of severe austerity to arrive at this vision of the world and was given the title Buddha, 'the enlightened' or 'the awakened'. Gautama Buddha spoke of four noble truths which had the power to liberate any human being who could realise them. These four noble truths are:

1. The truth of dukkha: 'All forms of existence are subject to dukkha (dis-ease, unsatisfactoriness, imperfection).'
2. The truth of the cause of dukkha: 'Dukkha is caused by *tanha* (desire).'
3. The truth of the cessation of dukkha: 'Eliminate the cause of dukkha (ie desire) and dukkha will cease to arise.'
4. The truth of the path: 'The Eightfold Path is the way to eliminate desire/extinguish dukkha.'

The Eightfold Path (Atthangika-Magga), which if followed will put an end to dukkha, consists of (1) right understanding, (2) right mindedness (right thought), (3) right speech, (4) right bodily conduct, (5) right livelihood, (6) right effort, (7) right attentiveness and (8) right concentration. These eight limbs belong to three different 'pillars' of practice: morality or *sila* (3 to 5), concentration or *samadhi* (6 to 8), and wisdom or *pañña* (1 and 2). The path is also called the Middle Way, since ideally it avoids both extreme austerity and extreme sensuality. Some Buddhists believe it is to be taken in successive stages, while others say the pillars and/or limbs are interdependent. Another key point is that the word 'right' can also be translated as 'complete' or 'full'.

The ultimate end of Theravada Buddhism is *nibbana* (Sanskrit: *nirvana)*, which literally means the extinction of all desire and thus of all suffering (dukkha). Effectively, it is also an end to the cycle of rebirths (both moment to moment and life to life) that is existence. In reality, most Thai Buddhists aim for rebirth in a 'better' existence rather than the supramundane goal of nibbana, which is highly misunderstood by Asians as well as Westerners.

Many Thais express the feeling that they are somehow unworthy of nibbana. By feeding monks, giving donations to temples and performing regular worship at the local *wat* (temple) they hope to improve their lot, acquiring enough merit (Pali: *puñña*; Thai: *bun)* to prevent or at least lessen the number of rebirths. The making of merit *(tham bun)* is an important social and religious activity in Thailand. The concept of reincarnation is almost universally accepted in Thailand,

even by non-Buddhists, and the Buddhist theory of karma is well expressed in the Thai proverb *tham dii, dâi dii; tham chûa, dâi chûa* – 'do good and receive good; do evil and receive evil'.

The Triratna, or Triple Gems, highly respected by Thai Buddhists, include the Buddha, the Dhamma (the teachings) and the Sangha (the Buddhist brotherhood). Each is quite visible in Thailand. The Buddha, in his myriad and omnipresent sculptural forms, is found on a high shelf in the lowliest roadside restaurants as well as in the lounges of expensive Bangkok hotels. The Dhamma is chanted morning and evening in every wat and taught to every Thai citizen in primary school. The Sangha is seen everywhere in the presence of orange-robed monks, especially in the early morning hours when they perform their alms-rounds, in what has almost become a travel-guide cliché in motion.

Thai Buddhism has no particular 'Sabbath' or day of the week when Thais are supposed to make temple visits. Nor is there anything corresponding to a liturgy or mass over which a priest presides. Instead Thai Buddhists visit the wat whenever they feel like it, most often on *wan phrá* (literally 'excellent days') which occur with every full and new moon, ie every 15 days. On such a visit typical activities include the offering of lotus buds, incense and candles at various altars and bone reliquaries around the wat compound, offering food to the temple Sangha (monks, nuns and lay residents – monks always eat first), meditating (individually or in groups), listening to monks chanting *suttas* or Buddhist discourse, and attending a *thêt* or dhamma talk by the abbot or other respected teacher. Visitors may also seek counsel from individual monks or nuns regarding new or ongoing life problems.

Monks & Nuns Socially, every Thai male is expected to become a monk for a short period in his life, optimally between the time he finishes school and the time he starts a career or marries. Men or boys under 20 years of age may enter the Sangha as novices – this is not unusual since a family earns great merit when one of its sons takes robe and bowl. Traditionally, the length of time spent in the wat is three months, during the Buddhist lent *(phansãa)* which begins in July and coincides with the rainy season. However, nowadays men may spend as little as a week or 15 days to accrue merit as monks. There are about 32,000 monasteries in Thailand and 200,000 monks; many of these monks ordain for a lifetime. Of these a large percentage become scholars and teachers, while some specialise in healing and/or folk magic.

The Sangha is divided into two sects, the Mahanikai and the Thammayut (from the Pali *dhammayutika* or 'dharma-adhering'). The latter is a minority sect (one Thammayut to 35 Mahanikai) begun by King Mongkut and patterned after an early Mon form of monastic discipline which he had practised as a monk *(bhikkhu)*. Members of both sects must adhere to 227 monastic vows or precepts as laid out in the Vinaya Pitaka – Buddhist scriptures dealing with monastic discipline. Overall discipline for Thammayut monks, however, is generally stricter. For example, they eat only once a day – before noon – and must eat only what is in their alms bowl, whereas Mahanikais eat twice before noon and may accept side dishes. Thammayut monks are expected to attain proficiency in meditation as well as Buddhist scholarship or scripture study; the Mahanikai monks typically 'specialise' in one or the other.

At one time the Theravada Buddhist world had a separate Buddhist monastic lineage for females, who called themselves *bhikkhuni* and observed more vows than monks did – 311 precepts as opposed to the 227 followed by monks. Started in Sri Lanka around two centuries after the Buddha's lifetime by the daughter of King Asoka (a Buddhist king in India), the bhikkhuni tradition in Sri Lanka eventually died out and was unfortunately never restored.

In Thailand, the modern equivalent is the *mâe chii* (Thai for 'nun,' literally 'mother priest') – women who live the monastic life as *atthasila* or 'Eight-Precept' nuns. Thai nuns shave their heads, wear white robes, and take vows in an ordination procedure similar to that undergone by monks. Generally speaking, nunhood in Thailand isn't considered as 'prestigious' as monkhood. The average Thai Buddhist makes a great show of offering new robes and household items to the monks at their local wat but pay much less attention to the nuns. This is mainly due to the fact that nuns generally don't perform ceremonies on behalf of laypeople, so there is often less incentive for self-interested laypeople to make offerings to them. Furthermore, many Thais equate the number of precepts observed with the total Buddhist merit achieved, hence nunhood is seen as less 'meritorious' than monkhood since mae chiis keep only eight precepts.

This difference in prestige represents social Buddhism, however, and is not how those with a serious interest in Buddhist practice regard the mae chii. Nuns engage in the same fundamental eremitic activities – meditation and dhamma study – as monks do, activities which are the core of monastic life. The reality is that wats which draw sizeable contingents of mae chiis are highly respected, since women don't choose temples for reasons of clerical status. When more than a few nuns reside at one temple, it's usually a sign that the teachings there are particularly strong.

Recently a small movement to restore the bhikkhuni sangha in Thailand has arisen. Some women now ordain in Taiwan, where the Mahayana tradition has maintained a bhikkhuni lineage, then return to Thailand to practice with full bhikkhuni status.

An increasing number of foreigners come to Thailand to ordain as Buddhist monks or nuns, especially to study with the famed meditation masters of the forest wats in north-east Thailand.

Further Information If you wish to find out more about Buddhism you can contact the World Fellowship of Buddhists (☎ 251-1188), 33 Sukhumvit Rd (between Sois 1 and 3), Bangkok. There's an English meditation class here on the first Sunday of each month; all are welcome.

Sculptural Symbolism

Buddha images throughout Thailand are for the most part sculpted according to strict iconographical rules found in Buddhist art texts dating to the 3rd century AD. The way the monastic robes drape over the body, the direction in which the hair curls, the proportions for each body part are all to some degree canonised by these texts. The tradition does leave room for innovation, however, allowing the various 'schools' of Buddhist art to distinguish themselves over the centuries.

One aspect of the tradition that almost never varies are the postures and hand positions of Buddha images. Four basic postures (Pali: *asana*) are portrayed: standing, sitting, walking and reclining. The first three are associated with daily activities of the Buddha, ie teaching, meditating and offering refuge to his disciples, which can be accomplished in any of these three asanas. The reclining position represents the Buddha's dying moments when he attained *parinibbana* or ultimate nirvana. Another key iconographical element is the figure's *mudra* or hand position.

Bhumisparsa ('touching the earth') In this classic mudra the right hand touches the ground while the left rests in the lap. This hand position symbolises the point in the Buddha's legendary life story when he sat in meditation beneath the banyan tree in Bodh Gaya, India and vowed not to budge from the spot until he gained enlightenment. Mara, the Buddhist equivalent of Satan, tried to interrupt the Buddha's meditation by invoking a series of distractions (including tempests, floods, feasts and nubile young maidens); the Buddha's response was to touch the earth, thus calling on nature to witness his resolve. The bhumisparsa mudra is one of the most common mudras seen in Thai Buddhist sculpture; it's also known as the *maravijaya* ('victory over Mara') mudra.

Dhyana ('meditation') Both hands rest palms up on the Buddha's lap, with the right hand on top, signifying meditation.

Vitarka or Dhammachakka ('exposition' or 'turning of the wheel of dharma') When the thumb and forefinger of one hand (vitarka) or both hands (dhammachakka) form a circle with the other fingers curving outward (similar to the western 'OK' gesture), the mudra evokes the first public discourse on Buddhist doctrine.

Abhaya ('no fear') One or both hands extend forward, palms out, fingers pointing upward, to symbolise the Buddha's offer of protection or freedom from fear to his followers. This mudra is most commonly seen in conjunction with standing or walking Buddhas.

Calling for Rain In Northern Thailand – especially in Chiang Rai, Nan and Phrae provinces (and across the border in Luang Prabang, Laos) – one occasionally sees a non-canonical mudra in which the arms of a standing image extend straight downward on each side with the palms facing the thighs. Among Thai worshippers this pose symbolises a call for rain to nourish the rice fields.

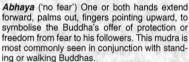

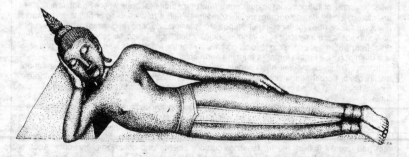

The reclining position represents the Buddha's dying moments when he attained *parinibbana* or the ultimate nirvana.

A Buddhist bookshop across the street from the north entrance to Wat Bovornives (Bowonniwet) in Bangkok sells a variety of English-language books on Buddhism.

For more information on meditation study in Thailand, see the Courses section in the Facts for the Visitor chapter, and also the Meditation Study section in the Bangkok chapter.

Recommended books about Buddhism include:

Buddhism Explained by Phra Khantipalo, Trasvin Publications, 1991 (Chiang Mai)

Buddhism in Thailand: Its Past and Present by K Kusalasaya, Buddhist Publication Society, 1965 (Kandy)

What the Buddha Taught by Walpola Rahula, Motilal Banarsidass, 1971 (Delhi)

Buddhism in Transition by Donald K Swearer, Westminster Press, 1970 (Philadelphia)

Buddhism in the Modern World edited by Heinrich Dumoulin, Macmillan, 1976 (New York)

Buddhism, Imperialism, and War by Trevor Ling, D Reidel Publishing, 1980 (Dordrecht)

World Conqueror and World Renouncer by Stanley Tambiah, Cambridge University Press, 1976 (Cambridge)

Living Buddhist Masters by Jack Kornfield, Buddhist Publication Society, 1989 (Kandy)

The Central Conception of Buddhism by Th Stcherbatsky, Motilal Banarsidass, 1974 (Delhi)

Buddhist Dictionary by Mahathera Nyanatiloka, Island Hermitage Publications, 1950 (Dodanduwa)

Other Religions

A small percentage of Thais and most of the Malays in the south, amounting to about 4% of the total population, are followers of Islam. Half a per cent of the population – primarily missionised hill tribes and Vietnamese immigrants – profess Christianity, while the remaining half per cent are Confucianists, Taoists, Mahayana Buddhists and Hindus. Mosques (in the south) and

---

What's a Wat

Technically speaking, a *wát* (a Thai word, from the Pali-Sanskrit *avasatha* or 'dwelling for pupils and ascetics') is a Buddhist compound where men or women can be ordained as monks or nuns. Virtually every village in Thailand has at least one wat, while in towns and cities they're quite numerous. Without an ordination area (designated by *sěma* or stone ordination markers), a monastic centre where monks or nuns reside is simply a *săm-nák sŏng* (sangha residence). The latter are often established as meditation retreat facilities in forest areas, sometimes in conjunction with larger *wát pàa* or forest monasteries.

The typical wat compound in Thailand will contain: an *uposatha* (*bòt* in Thai), a consecrated chapel where monastic ordinations are held; a *vihara* (*wíhǎan* in Thai), where important Buddha images are housed; a *sala* (*sǎalaa)* or open-sided shelter for community meetings and dhamma talks; a number of *kùti* or monastic quarters; a *hǎw trai* or tripitaka library where Buddhist scriptures are stored; a *hǎw klawng* or drum tower (sometimes with a *hǎw rákhang* or bell tower); various *chedis* or stupas (the smaller squarish stupas are *thâat kràdùk* (bone reliquaries), where the ashes of worshippers are interred; plus various ancillary buildings – such as schools or clinics – that differ from wat to wat according to local community needs. Many wats also have a *hǎw phǐi khun wát* or spirit house for the temple's reigning earth spirit.

In rural Thailand, the wat often serves as a combination religious centre, grammar school, health clinic, herbal sauna house, community centre, astrology house, transient guesthouse, funeral home and geriatric ward, with monks and nuns serving as staff for one or more of these functions.

The typical wat is also a focus for much festival activity and is thus an important social centre for Thais. Especially lively are the *ngaan wát* or temple fairs; these take place regularly on certain auspicious dates (eg the advent and end of the Rains Retreat, the anniversary of the Buddha's birth, enlightenment, and death, the anniversary of the first Dhamma (Buddhist teachings) lecture, etc) and usually feature music, feasting, outdoor cinema and occasional fireworks. Another common type of celebration is the *ngaan sòp* or funeral ceremony. A typical ngaan sop includes a lively procession (with musical accompaniment) from the deceased's home to the wat. ∎

Chinese temples are both common enough that you will probably come across some in your travels in Thailand. Before entering *any* temple, sanctuary or mosque you must remove your shoes, and in a mosque your head must be covered.

LANGUAGE

Learning some Thai is indispensable for travelling in the kingdom; naturally, the more language you pick up, the closer you get to Thailand's culture and people. Foreigners who speak Thai are so rare in Thailand that it doesn't take much to impress most Thais with a few words in their own language.

Your first attempts to speak the language will probably meet with mixed success, but keep trying. When learning new words or phrases, listen closely to the way the Thais themselves use the various tones – you'll catch on quickly. Don't let laughter at your linguistic attempts discourage you; this amusement is an expression of their appreciation.

I would particularly urge travellers, young and old, to make the effort to meet Thai college and university students. Thai students are, by and large, eager to meet their peers from other countries. They will often know some English, so communication is not as difficult as it may be with merchants, civil servants, etc, plus they are generally willing to teach you useful Thai words and phrases.

For a complete selection of phrases, basic vocabulary and grammar for travel in Thailand, see the updated and expanded 2nd edition of Lonely Planet's *Thai Phrasebook*.

Many people have reported modest success with *Robertson's Practical English-Thai Dictionary* (Charles E Tuttle Co, Tokyo), which has a phonetic guide to pronunciation with tones and is compact in size. It may be difficult to find, so write to the publisher, Suido 1-chome, 2-6, Bunkyo-ku, Tokyo, Japan.

More serious learners of the Thai language should get Mary Haas's *Thai-English Student's Dictionary* (Stanford University Press, Stanford, California) and George McFarland's *Thai-English Dictionary* (also Stanford University Press) – the cream of the crop. Both of these require that you know the Thai script before using them. The US State Department's *Thai Reference Grammar* by R B Noss (Foreign Service Institute, Washington, DC, 1964) is good for an in-depth look at Thai syntax.

Other learning texts worth seeking out include:

Foundations of Thai, two volumes, by E M Anthony, University of Michigan Press, 1973
A Programmed Course in Reading Thai Syllables by E M Anthony, University of Hawaii, 1979
AUA Language Center Thai Course, three volumes, AUA Language Center (Bangkok), 1969
AUA Language Center Thai Course: Reading & Writing, two volumes, AUA Language Center (Bangkok), 1979
Thai Basic Reader by Gething & Bilmes, University of Hawaii, 1977
Thai Reader by Mary Haas, American Council of Learned Societies, Program in Oriental Languages, 1954
The Thai System of Writing by Mary Haas, American Council of Learned Societies, Program in Oriental Languages, 1954
Thai Cultural Reader, two volumes, by R B Jones, Cornell University, 1969
A Workbook for Writing Thai by William Kuo, University of California at Berkeley, 1979
Teaching Grammar of Thai by William Kuo, University of California at Berkeley, 1982

For information on language courses, see Thai Language Study under Courses in the Facts for the Visitor chapter.

Dialects

Thailand's official language is Thai as spoken and written in Central Thailand. This dialect has successfully become the lingua franca of all Thai and non-Thai ethnic groups in the kingdom. Of course, native Thai is spoken with differing tonal accents and with slightly differing vocabularies as you move from one part of the country to the next, especially in a north to south direction. But it is the Central Thai dialect that is most widely understood.

All Thai dialects are members of the Thai half of the Thai-Kadai family of languages and are closely related to languages spoken in Laos (Lao, Northern Thai, Thai Lü), northern Myanmar (Shan, Northern Thai), north-western Vietnam (Nung, Tho), Assam (Ahom) and pockets of southern China (Zhuang, Thai Lü).

Modern Thai linguists recognise four basic dialects within Thailand: Central Thai (spoken as a first dialect through Central Thailand and throughout the country as a second dialect); Northern Thai (spoken from Tak Province north to the Burmese border); North-Eastern Thai (north-eastern provinces towards the Lao and Cambodian borders); and Southern Thai (from Chumphon Province south to the Malaysian border). Each of these can be further divided into subdialects; North-Eastern Thai, for example, has nine regional variations easily distinguished by those who know Thai well. There are also a number of Thai minority dialects such as those spoken by the Phu Thai, Thai Dam, Thai Daeng, Phu Noi, Phuan and other tribal Thais, most of whom reside in the north and north-east.

Vocabulary Differences

Like most languages, Thai makes distinctions between 'vulgar' and 'polite' vocabulary, so that *thaan*, for example, is a more polite everyday word for 'eat' than *kin* and *sĭi-sà* for 'head' is more polite than *hŭa*. When given a choice, foreigners are better off learning and using the polite terms since these are less likely to lead to unconscious offence.

A special set of words, collectively called *kham râatchaasàp* (royal vocabulary), is set aside for use with Thai royalty within the semantic fields of kinship, body parts, physical and mental actions, clothing and housing. For example, in everyday language Thais use the word *kin* or *thaan* for 'eat', while with reference to the Royal Family they say *ráppràthaan*. For the most part these terms are used only when speaking to or referring to the King, Queen and their children, hence as a foreigner you will have little need to learn them.

Script

The Thai script, a fairly recent development in comparison with the spoken language, consists of 44 consonants (but only 21 separate sounds) and 48 vowel and diphthong possibilities (32 separate signs). Experts disagree as to the exact origins of the script, but it was apparently developed around 800 years ago using Mon and possibly Khmer models, both of which were in turn inspired by South Indian scripts. Like these languages, written Thai proceeds from left to right, though vowel signs may be written before, above, below, 'around' (before, above *and* after), *or* after consonants, depending on the sign.

Though learning the alphabet is not difficult, the writing system itself is fairly complex, so unless you are planning a lengthy stay in Thailand it should perhaps be foregone in favour of learning to actually speak the language. Where possible, place names occurring in headings in this book are given in Thai script as well as in roman script, so that you can at least 'read' the names of destinations at a pinch, or point to them if necessary.

Tones

In Thai the meaning of a single syllable may be altered by means of five different tones (in standard Central Thai): level or mid tone, low tone, falling tone, high tone and rising tone. Consequently, the syllable *mai*, for example, can mean, depending on the tone, 'new', 'burn', 'wood', 'not?' or 'not', eg *Mái mài mâi mâi mãi*, 'New wood doesn't burn, does it?' This makes it rather tricky to learn at first, especially for those of us who come from non-tonal-language traditions. Even when we 'know' what the correct tone in Thai should be, our tendency to denote emotion, verbal stress, the interrogative, etc, through tone modulation often interferes with speaking the correct tone. Therefore the first rule in learning to speak Thai is to divorce emotions from your speech, at least until you have learned the Thai way to express them without changing essential tone value.

The following is a brief attempt to explain the tones. The only way to really understand the differences is by listening to a native or fluent non-native speaker. The range of all five tones is relative to each speaker's vocal range so there is no fixed 'pitch' intrinsic to the language.

The level or mid tone is pronounced 'flat', at the relative middle of the speaker's vocal range. Example: *dii* means good. (No tone mark used.)

The low tone is 'flat' like the mid tone, but pronounced at the relative *bottom* of one's vocal range. It is low, level and with no inflection. Example: *bàat* means baht (the Thai currency).

The falling tone is pronounced as if you were emphasising a word, or calling someone's name from afar. Example: *mâi* means 'no' or 'not'.

The high tone is usually the most difficult for Westerners. It is pronounced near the relative top of the vocal range, as level as possible. Example: *níi* means 'this'.

The rising tone sounds like the inflection generally given by English speakers to a question – 'Yes?' Example: *săam* means 'three'.

If the tones were to be represented on a visual curve they might look like this:

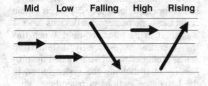

Mid	Low	Falling	High	Rising

Words in Thai that appear to have more than one syllable are usually compounds made up of two or more word units, each with its own tone. They may be words taken directly from Sanskrit, Pali or English, in which case each syllable must still have its own tone. Sometimes the tone of the first syllable is not as important as that of the last, so for these I am omitting the tone mark.

Here is a guide to the phonetic system which has been used in the Language, Food and Drink sections, as well as throughout the book when transcribing directly from Thai. It is based on the Royal Thai General System of transcription (RTGS), except that it distinguishes between vowels of short and long duration (eg 'i' and 'ii'; 'a' and 'aa'; 'e' and 'eh'; 'o' and 'oh'), between 'o' and 'aw' (both would be 'o' in the RTGS), between 'u' and 'eu' (both 'u' in the RTGS); and between 'ch' and 'j' (both 'ch' in the RTGS).

Consonants

th	as the 't' in 'tea'
ph	as the 'p' in 'put' (never as the 'ph' in 'phone')
kh	as the 'k' in 'kite'
k	as the 'k' in 'skin'; similar to 'g' in 'good', but unaspirated (no accompanying puff of air) and unvoiced
t	as the 't' in 'forty', unaspirated; similar to 'd' but unvoiced
p	as the 'p' in 'stopper', unvoiced and unaspirated (not like the 'p' in 'put')
ng	as the 'ng' in 'sing'; used as an initial consonant in Thai (practise by saying 'sing' without the 'si')
r	similar to the 'r' in 'run' but flapped (tongue touches palate); in everyday speech often pronounced like 'l'

All the remaining consonants correspond closely to their English counterparts.

Vowels

i	as the 'i' in 'it'
ii	as the 'ee' in 'feet'
ai	as the 'i' in 'pipe'
aa	as the 'a' in 'father'
a	half as long as *aa*
ae	as the 'a' in 'bat' or 'tab'
e	as the 'e' in 'hen'
eh	as the 'a' in 'hate'
oe	as the 'u' in 'hut' but more closed
u	as the 'u' in 'flute'
uu	as the 'oo' in 'food', longer than *u*
eu	as the 'eu' in French 'deux', or the 'i' in 'sir'
ao	as the 'ow' in 'now'

aw as the 'aw' in 'jaw' or 'prawn'
o as the 'o' in 'bone'
oh as the 'o' in 'toe'
eua diphthong, or combination, of *eu* and *a*
ia as 'ee-ya', or as the 'ie' in French *rien*
ua as the 'ou' in 'tour'
uay as the 'ewy' in 'Dewey'
iu as the 'ew' in 'yew'
iaw as the 'io' in 'Rio' or Italian *mio* or *dio*

Here are a few extra hints to help you with the alphabetic tangle:

1. Remember that 'ph' is not meant to be pronounced like the 'ph' in phone but like the 'p' in 'pound' (the 'h' is added to distinguish this consonant sound from the Thai 'p' which is closer to the English 'b'). This can be seen written as 'p', 'ph', and even 'bh'.
2. There is no 'v' sound in Thai; Sukhumvit is pronounced Sukhumwit and Vieng is really Wieng.
3. 'L' or 'r' at the end of a word is always pronounced like an 'n'; hence, Satul is pronounced Satun, Wihar is really Wihan. The exception to this is when 'er' or 'ur' are used to indicate the sound 'oe', as in 'ampher' *(amphoe)*. In the same way 'or' is sometimes used for the sound 'aw' as in 'Porn' *(phawn)*.
4. 'L' and 'r' are often used interchangeably in speech and this shows up in some transliterations. For example, *naliga* (clock) may appear as 'nariga' and *râat nâa* (a type of noodle dish) might be rendered 'laat naa' or 'lat na'.
5. 'U' is often used to represent the short 'a' sound, as in *tam* or *nam*, which may appear as 'tum' and 'num'. It is also used to represent the 'eu' sound, as when *beung* (swamp) is spelt 'bung'.
6. Phonetically all Thai words end in a vowel (a, e, i, o, u), semi-vowel (y, w), nasal (m, n or ng) or one of three stops: p, t and k. That's it. Words transcribed with 'ch', 'j', 's' or 'd' endings – like Panich, Raj, Chuanpis and Had – should be pronounced as if they end in 't', as in Panit, Rat, Chuanpit and Hat. Likewise 'g' becomes 'k' (Ralug is actually Raluk) and 'b' becomes 'p' (Thab becomes Thap).
7. Finally, the 'r' in 'sri' is *always* silent, so that word should be pronounced 'sii' (extended 'i' sound, too).

Transliteration

Writing Thai in roman script is a perennial problem – no truly satisfactory system has yet been devised to assure both consistency and readability. The Thai government uses the Royal Thai General System of transcription for official government documents in English and for most highway signs. However, local variations crop up on hotel signs, city street signs, menus, and so on in such a way that visitors often become confused. Add to this the fact that even the government system has its flaws. For example, 'o' is used for two very different sounds ('o' and the 'aw' in the Language section above), as is 'u' ('u' and 'eu' above). Likewise for 'ch', which is used to represent two different consonant sounds ('ch' and 'j'). The government transcription system also does not distinguish between short and long vowel sounds, which affect the tonal value of every word.

To top it off, many Thai words (especially people and place names) have Sanskrit and Pali spellings but the actual pronunciation bears little relation to that spelling if romanised strictly according to the original Sanskrit/Pali. Thus Nakhon Si Thammarat, if transliterated literally, becomes 'Nagara Sri Dhammaraja'. If you tried to pronounce it using this Pali transcription, very few Thais would be able to understand you.

Generally, names in this book follow the most common practice or, in the case of hotels for example, simply copy their roman script name, no matter what devious process was used in its transliteration! When this transliteration is especially distant from actual pronunciation, I've included the pronunciation (following the system given in the Language section) in parentheses after the transliteration. Where no roman model was available, names were transliterated phonetically directly from Thai. Of course, this will only be helpful to readers who bother to acquaint themselves with the language – I'm constantly amazed at how many people manage to stay for great lengths of time in Thailand without learning a word of Thai.

Problems often arise when a name is transliterated differently, even at the same place.

Thai Consonants

K	ก	KH	ข	KH	ฃ	KH	ค
KH	ฅ	KH	ฆ	NG	ง	J	จ
CH	ฉ	CH	ช	S	ซ	CH	ฌ
Y	ญ	D	ฎ	T	ฏ	TH	ฐ
TH	ฑ	T	ฒ	N	ณ	D	ด
T	ต	TH	ถ	TH	ท	TH	ธ
N	น	B	บ	P	ป	PH	ผ
F	ฝ	PH	พ	F	ฟ	PH	ภ
M	ม	Y	ย	R	ร	L	ล
W	ว	S	ศ	S	ษ	S	ส
H	ห	L	ฬ	–	อ	H	ฮ

'Thawi', for example, can be Tavi, Thawee, Thavi, Tavee or various other versions. Outside the International Phonetic Alphabet, there is no 'proper' way to transliterate Thai – only wrong ways. The Thais themselves are incredibly inconsistent in this matter, often using English letters that have no equivalent sound in Thai: Faisal for Phaisan, Bhumibol for Phumiphon, Vanich for Wanit, Vibhavadi for Wiphawadi. Sometimes they even mix literal Sanskrit transcription with Thai pronunciation, as in King Bhumibol (which is pronounced Phumiphon and if transliterated according to the Sanskrit would be Bhumibala).

Here are a few words that are commonly spelt in a way that encourages mispronunciation among native English speakers:

Common Spelling	Pronunciation	Meaning
bung	beung	pond or swamp
ko or koh	kàw	island
muang	meuang	city
nakhon or nakorn	nákhawn	large city
raja	usually râatchá if at the beginning of a word, râat at the end of a word	royal

Greetings & Civilities

When being polite, the speaker ends his or her sentence with *khráp* (for men) or *khâ* (for women). It is the gender of the *speaker* that is being expressed here; it is also the common way to answer 'yes' to a question or show agreement.

Greetings/Hello.
sawàt-dii (khráp/khâ)

สวัสดี (ครับ/ค่ะ)

How are you?
pen yangai?

เป็นยังไง?

I'm fine.
sabàay dii

สบายดี

Thank you.
khàwp khun

ขอบคุณ

Small Talk

you
khun (for peers)

คุณ

thâan (for elders, people in authority)

ท่าน

phõm (for men), *diichãn* (for women)

ผม (ผู้ชาย) ดีฉัน (ผู้หญิง)

What is your name?
khun chêu arai?

คุณชื่ออะไร?

My name is...
phõm chêu...(men)

ผมชื่อ...

diichãn chêu...(women)

ดีฉันชื่อ...

Do you have...?
mii...mãi? (or *...mii mãi?*)

มี...ไหม? (...มีไหม?)

Do you have noodles?
mii kũaythĩaw mãi?

มีก๋วยเตี๋ยวไหม?

I/you/he/she/it does not have
mâi mii

ไม่มี

no
mâi châi
ไม่ใช่

no?
mãi? or *châi mãi?*
ไหม?/ใช่ไหม?

when
mêu-arai
เมื่อะไร

It doesn't matter.
mâi pen rai
ไม่เป็นไร

What is this?
níi arai?
นี่อะไร?

What do you call this in Thai?
níi phaasãa thai rîak wâa arai?
นี่ภาษาไทยเรียกว่าอะไร?

(I) understand.
khâo jai
เข้าใจ

Do you understand?
khâo jai mãi?
เข้าใจไหม?

(I) don't understand.
mâi khâo jai.
ไม่เข้าใจ

a little
nít nàwy
นิดหน่อย

Some Verbs
go
pai
ไป

will go
jà pai
จะไป

come
maa
มา

will come
jà maa
จะมา

(I) like...
châwp...
ชอบ...

(I) do not like...
mâi châwp...
ไม่ชอบ...

(I) would like (+ verb)...
yàak jà...
อยากจะ...

(I) would not like...
mâi yàak jà...
ไม่อยากจะ...

(I) would like to eat...
yàak jà thaan...
อยากจะทาน...

(I) would like...(+ noun)
yàak dâi...
อยากได้...

Getting Around
(I) would like a ticket.
yàak dâi tũa
อยากได้ตั๋ว

(I) would like to go...
yàak jà pai...
อยากจะไป...

Where is (the)...?
...yùu thîi nãi?

...อยู่ที่ไหน?

motorcycle
rót maw-toe-sai

รถมอเตอร์ไซ

train
rót fai

รถไฟ

bus
rót meh or *rót bát*

รถเมล์/รถบัส

car
rót yon

รถยนต์

hotel
rohng raem

โรงแรม

station
sathãanii

สถานี

post office
praisanii

ไปรษณีย์

restaurant
ráan aahãan

ร้านอาหาร

hospital
rohng phayaabaan

โรงพยาบาล

airport
sanãam bin

สนามบิน

market
talàat

ตลาด

beach
hàat

หาด

Accommodation

bathroom
hâwng náam

ห้องน้ำ

toilet
hâwng sûam

ห้องส้วม

room
hâwng

ห้อง

hot
ráwn

ร้อน

cold
não

หนาว

bath/shower
àap náam

อาบน้ำ

towel
phâa chét tua

ผ้าเช็ดตัว

Shopping

How much?
thâo raí?

เท่าไร?

How much is this?
níi thâo rai? (or *kìi bàat?*)

นี่เท่าไร (กี่บาท)

too expensive
phaeng pai

แพงไป

cheap, inexpensive
thùuk

ถูก

Emergencies
(I) need a doctor.
tâwng-kaan mǎw

ต้องการหมอ

Time
today
wan níi

วันนี้

tomorrow
phrûng níi

พรุ่งนี้

yesterday
mêua waan

เมื่อวาน

Numbers

0	*sǔun*	ศูนย์
1	*nèung*	หนึ่ง
2	*sǎwng*	สอง
3	*sǎam*	สาม
4	*sìi*	สี่
5	*hâa*	ห้า
6	*hòk*	หก
7	*jèt*	เจ็ด
8	*pàet*	แปด
9	*kâo*	เก้า
10	*sìp*	สิบ
11	*sìp-èt*	สิบเอ็ด
12	*sìp-sǎwng*	สิบสอง
13	*sìp-sǎam*	สิบสาม
14	*sìp-sìi*	สิบสี่
20	*yîi-sìp*	ยี่สิบ
21	*yîi-sìp-èt*	ยี่สิบเอ็ด
22	*yîi-sìp-sǎwng*	ยี่สิบสอง
23	*yîi-sìp-sǎam*	ยี่สิบสาม
30	*sǎam-sìp*	สามสิบ
40	*sìi-sìp*	สี่สิบ

50	*hâa-sìp*	ห้าสิบ	10,0000	*mèun*	หมื่น
100	*ráwy*	ร้อย	100,000	*sāen*	แสน
200	*sǎwng ráwy*	สองร้อย	1,000,000	*láan*	ล้าน
300	*sǎam ráwy*	สามร้อย	billion	*phan láan*	พันล้าน
1000	*phan*	พัน			

Facts for the Visitor

VISAS & EMBASSIES
Visa Requirements
The Thai government allows 35 different nationalities to enter the country without a visa for 15 days at no charge. Shining exceptions are visitors with New Zealand, Swedish or South Korean passports, who may enter Thailand for up to 90 days without a visa!

Certain other nationalities – those from smaller European countries like Andorra or Liechtenstein or from West Africa, South Asia or Latin America – can obtain 15-day Transit Visas on arrival upon payment of a 300B fee. Extensions of the no-visa 15-day Transit Visa aren't allowed unless the visitor comes from a country without a Thai embassy.

A few nationalities – eg Hungarians – must obtain a visa in advance of arrival or they'll be turned back. Check with a Thai embassy or consulate in advance to be sure if you plan to try arriving without a visa.

Without proof of an onward ticket and sufficient funds for one's projected stay any visitor can be denied entry, but in practice your ticket and funds are rarely checked if you're dressed neatly for the immigration check. See Exchange Control in the Money section in this chapter for officially required amounts for each visa type.

There is also a 30-day Transit Visa which can only be purchased in advance from a Thai consulate for US$10. This visa may not be extended.

Next in length of validity is the Tourist Visa, which is good for 60 days and costs US$15. Three passport photos must accompany all applications.

Non-Immigrant Visas are good for 90 days, must be applied for in your home country, cost US$20 and are not difficult to obtain if you can offer a good reason for your visit. Business, study and extended family visits are among the purposes considered valid.

Whichever type of visa you have, be sure to check your passport immediately after stamping. Overworked officials sometimes stamp 15 or 30 days on arrival even when you hold a longer visa; if you point out the error before you've left the immigration area at your port of entry, officials will make the necessary corrections. If you don't notice this until you've left the port of entry, go to Bangkok and plead your case at the central immigration office.

Once a visa is issued, it must be used (ie you must enter Thailand) within 90 days.

Visa Extensions
In the past the 15-day no-visa stay was never extendible but beginning in 1994 most immigration offices would extend a 15-day no-visa entry for another 10 days for 500B.

If you overstay your visa, the usual penalty is a fine of 100B per day of your overstay.

Sixty-day Tourist Visas may be extended at the discretion of Thai immigration authorities. The Bangkok office (☎ 286-9176) is on Soi Suan Phlu, Sathon Tai Rd, but you can apply at any immigration office in the

---

Proposed New Visa Scheme
In early 1994 the Ministry of the Interior proposed a new set of immigration regulations that would allow citizens of 55 countries (including virtually all European countries, the USA, the UK, Australia, and most countries in northern Africa, the Middle East and South-East Asia) to visit Thailand without a visa for 30 days. Under the same plan, visa fees for the two-month Tourist and three-month Non-Immigrant visas would increase to US$20 and US$40 respectively. So far this scheme remains in the proposal stage – check with the nearest Thai embassy or consulate for the latest. ■

country – every provincial capital has one. The usual fee for extension of a Tourist Visa (up to one month) is 500B. Bring along two photos and two copies each of the photo and visa pages of your passport.

Extension of the 15-day, on-arrival Transit Visa is only allowed if you hold a passport from a country that has no Thai embassy. The 30-day Transit Visa cannot usually be extended for any reason.

Re-Entry & Multiple-Entry Visas

If you need a re-entry visa for a return trip to Myanmar or the like, apply at the immigration office on Soi Suan Phlu, Bangkok. The cost is 500B.

Thailand does not issue multiple-entry visas. If you want a visa that enables you to leave the country and then return, the best you can do is to obtain a visa permitting two entries; this will cost double the single-entry visa. For example, a two-entry three-month Non-Immigrant Visa will cost US$40 (or US$80 if the proposed visa regulations go into effect) and will allow you six months in the country, as long as you cross a border with immigration facilities by the end of your first three months. The second half of your visa is validated as soon as you re-cross the Thai border, so there is no need to go to a Thai embassy/consulate abroad. All visas acquired in advance of entry are valid for 90 days from the date of issue.

Working Holidays

If you want to stay longer, a Non-Immigrant Visa is the one to get. Extending it very much depends on how the officials feel about you – if they like you then they will extend it. Money doesn't usually come into it; neat appearance and polite behaviour count for more. Typically, one must collect various signatures and go through various interviews which result in a 'provisional' extension. You may then have to report to a local immigration office every 10 to 14 days for the next three months until the actual extension comes through. Becoming a monk doesn't necessarily mean you'll get a longer visa either – again, it depends on whom you

see and how they feel about you. See the following section for information on tax clearance.

Tax Clearance Anyone who receives income while in Thailand must obtain a tax clearance certificate from the Revenue Department before they'll be permitted to leave the country. The Bangkok office (☎ 281-5777, 282-9899) of the Revenue Department is on Chakkapong Rd not far from the Democracy Monument. There are also Revenue Department offices in every provincial capital.

Old Thai hands note: the tax clearance requirement no longer applies to those who have simply stayed in Thailand beyond a cumulative 90 days within one calendar year – this regulation was abolished in 1991. This makes it much easier for expats or other long-termers who live in Thailand on Non-Immigrant Visas – no more hustling for tax clearance every time you make a visa trip to Penang or Vientiane.

Thai Embassies & Consulates

To apply for a visa, contact one of Thailand's diplomatic missions in any of the following countries. In many cases, if you apply in person you may receive a Tourist or Non-Immigrant Visa on the day of application; by mail it generally takes anywhere from two to six weeks.

Australia
> Royal Thai Embassy, 111 Empire Circuit, Yarralumla, Canberra, ACT 2600 (☎ 273-1149, 273-2937)

Canada
> Royal Thai Embassy, 85 Range Rd, Suite 704, Ottawa, Ontario K1N 8J6 (☎ 237-0476)

China
> Royal Thai Embassy, 40 Guang Hua Lu, Beijing (☎ 521-903, 522-282)

France
> Royal Thai Embassy, 8 Rue Greuze, 75116 Paris (☎ 4704-3222/6892)

Germany
> Royal Thai Embassy, Ubierstrasse 65, 53173 Bonn 2 (☎ 355-065)

Hong Kong
> Royal Thai Embassy, 8th Floor, 8 Cotton Tree Drive, Fairmont House, Central (☎ 216-481)

India
    Royal Thai Embassy, 56-N Nyaya Marg, Chanakyapuri, New Delhi, 110021 (☎ 605-679)
    Royal Thai Consulate, 18-B Mandeville Gardens, Ballygunge, Calcutta 7000019 (☎ 460-836)
Indonesia
    Royal Thai Embassy, Jalan Imam Bonjol 74, Jakarta (☎ 343-762)
Italy
    Royal Thai Embassy, Via Nomentana 132, 00162 Rome (☎ 832-0729)
Japan
    Royal Thai Embassy, 14-6 Kami-Osaki 3-chome, Shinagawa-ku, Tokyo (☎ 441-1386; 442-6750)
Laos
    Royal Thai Embassy, Thanon Phonkheng, Vientiane Poste 128 (☎ 2508, 2543, 2765)
Malaysia
    Royal Thai Embassy, 206 Jalan Ampang, Kuala Lumpur (☎ 488-222/350)
Myanmar (Burma)
    Royal Thai Embassy, 91 Pyi Rd, Yangon (☎ 82471, 76555)
Nepal
    Royal Thai Embassy, Jyoti Kendra Bldg, Thapathali, Kathmandu (☎ 213-910)
Netherlands
    Royal Thai Embassy, Buitenrustweg 1, 2517 KD The Hague (☎ 452-088, 459-703)
New Zealand
    Royal Thai Embassy, 2 Cook St, Karori, Wellington 5 (☎ 735-385/391)
Philippines
    Royal Thai Embassy, 107B Rada St, Legaspi Village Makati, Metro Manila (☎ 815-4219/00)
Singapore
    Royal Thai Embassy, 370 Orchard Rd, 0923 (☎ 737-2158/3372)
Sweden
    Royal Thai Embassy, Sandhamnsgatan 36, 102 51 Stockholm, (☎ 08-6672160, 08-6678090)
Switzerland
    5th Floor, Sandhamnsgatan 36, 3007 Bern (☎ 462-281/2)
UK
    Royal Thai Embassy, 29-30 Queen's Gate, London SW7 5JB (☎ 589-2834/2944)
USA
    Royal Thai Embassy, 2300 Kalorama Rd NW, Washington, DC 20008 (☎ 483-7200)
    Royal Thai Consulate, 801 N LaBrea Ave, Los Angeles, CA 90038 (☎ 937-1894)
Vietnam
    Royal Thai Embassy, So Nha E1, Kho Ngoai Giao Doan, Trung Tu, Hanoi (☎ 56043)

Foreign Embassies & Consulates

Bangkok is a good place to collect visas for westward journeys, and most countries have diplomatic representation in Bangkok. For more information see the Foreign Embassies & Consulates section in the Bangkok chapter.

CUSTOMS

Like most countries, Thailand prohibits the import of illegal drugs, firearms and ammunition (unless registered in advance with the Police Department) and pornographic media. A reasonable amount of clothing for personal use, toiletries and professional instruments are allowed in duty-free, as are one still or one movie/video camera with five rolls of still film or three rolls of movie film or videotape. Up to 200 cigarettes can be brought into the country without paying duty, or for other smoking materials a total of up to 250 grams. One litre of wine or spirits is allowed in duty-free.

Electronic goods like personal stereos, calculators and computers can be a problem if the customs officials have reason to believe you're bringing them in for resale. As long as you don't carry more than one of each, you should be OK. Occasionally, customs will require you to leave a hefty deposit for big-ticket items (eg a lap-top computer or midi-component stereo) which is refunded when you leave the country with the item in question. If you make the mistake of saying you're just passing through and don't plan to use the item while in Thailand, they may ask you to leave it with the Customs Department until you leave the country.

For information on currency import or export, see the Money section.

Antiques & Art ·

Upon leaving Thailand, you must obtain an export licence for any antiques or objects of art you want to take with you. An antique is any 'archaic movable property whether produced by man or by nature, any part of ancient structure, human skeleton or animal carcass, which by its age or characteristic of production or historical evidence is useful in the field of art, history or archaeology'. An object of art is a 'thing produced by craftsmanship and appreciated as being valuable in the field of art'. Obviously these are very sweeping definitions, so if in doubt go to the Department of Fine Arts for inspection and licensing.

Application can be made by submitting two front-view photos of the object(s) (no more than five objects to a photo) and a photocopy of your passport, along with the object(s) in question, to one of three locations in Thailand: the Bangkok National Museum, the Chiang Mai National Museum or the Songkhla National Museum. You need to allow three to five days for the application and inspection process to be completed.

Thailand has special regulations for taking a Buddha or other deity image (or any part thereof) out of the country. These require not only a licence from the Department of Fine Arts but a permit from the Ministry of Commerce as well. The one exception to this are the small Buddha images (*phr phim* or *phr khreûang*) that are meant to be worn on a chain around the neck; these may be exported without a licence as long as the reported purpose is religious.

Temporary Vehicle Importation
Passenger vehicles (car, van, truck or motorcycle) can be brought into Thailand for tourist purposes for up to six months. Documents needed for the crossing are a valid International Driving Licence, passport vehicle registration papers (in the case of a borrowed or hired vehicle, authorisation from the owner) and a cash or bank guarantee equal to the value of the vehicle plus 20%. (For entry through Khlong Toey Port or Bangkok Airport, this means a letter of bank credit; for overland crossings via Malaysia a 'self-guarantee' filled in at the border is sufficient.)

Home Country Customs
Be sure to check the import regulations in your home country before bringing or sending back a large quantity (or high value) of Thailand purchases. The limit varies from country to country; the USA, for example, allows US$400 worth of foreign-purchased goods to enter without duty (with no limit on handicrafts and unset gems), while in Australia the total value is limited to A$400.

MONEY
Currency
The basic unit of Thai currency is the *baht*. There are 100 satang in 1 baht; coins include 25-satang and 50-satang pieces and baht in 1B, 5B and 10B coins. Older coins exhibit Thai numerals only, while newer coins have Thai and roman numerals. At the time of writing, 1B coins come in three sizes: only the middle size works in public pay phones! Likewise, 5B coins also come in three sizes; a large one with a Thai numeral only and two smaller coins that have Thai and roman numerals (one of the smaller 5B coins has nine inset edges along the circumference). The new copper-and-silver 10B coin has Thai and roman-Arabic numerals. Eventually Thailand will phase out the older coins, but in the meantime, counting out change is confusing.

Twenty-five satang equals one *saleng* in colloquial Thai, so if you're quoted a price of six saleng in the market, say, for a very small bunch of bananas or a bag of peanuts, this means 1.50B. The term is becoming increasingly rare as ongoing inflation makes purchases of less than 1B or 2B almost extinct.

Paper currency comes in denominations of 10B (brown), 20B (green), 50B (blue), 100B (red), 500B (purple) and 1000B (beige). Fortunately for newcomers to Thailand, numerals are printed in their Western as well as Thai forms. Notes are also scaled according to the amount; the larger the denomination, the larger the note. Large denominations – 500B and especially 1000B bills – can be hard to change in small towns, but banks will always change them.

Exchange Rates

A$1	=	18B
C$1	=	18.6B
DM1	=	14.86B
FF1	=	4.36B
M$1	=	9.28B
NZ$1	=	14.5B
S$1	=	15.95B
US$1	=	25.25B
UK£1	=	37.60B
¥100	=	23.78B

There is no black-market money exchange for baht, so there's no reason to bring in any Thai currency. Banks or legal money-changers offer the best exchange rate within the country. The baht is firmly attached to the US dollar and is as stable.

Exchange rates are given in the *Bangkok Post* every day. For buying baht, US dollars are the most readily acceptable currency and travellers' cheques get better rates than cash. Since banks charge 10B commission and duty for each travellers' cheque cashed, you will save on commissions if you use larger cheque denominations (eg a US$50 cheque will only cost 10B while five US$10 cheques will cost 50B). Note that you can't exchange Indonesian rupiah, Nepalese rupees or Burmese kyat into Thai currency at banks, though some Bangkok moneychangers carry these currencies. The latter are in fact good places to buy Indian and Nepalese rupees, as well as Burmese kyat, if you're going to any of these countries. Rates are comparable with black-market rates in each of these countries.

Visa credit-card holders can get cash advances of up to US$500 (in baht only) per day through some branches of the Thai Farmers Bank and some Thai Commercial Banks (and also at the night-time exchange windows in well-touristed spots like Banglamphu, Chiang Mai and Ko Samui).

American Express card holders can also get advances, but only in travellers' cheques. The Amex agent is SEA Tours (☎ 251-4862), Suite 414, Siam Center, 965 Rama I Rd, Bangkok.

ATM & Credit/Debit Cards

An alternative to carrying around large amounts of cash or travellers' cheques is to open an account at a Thai bank and request an ATM card. Most major banks in Thailand now have automatic teller machines (ATMs) in provincial capitals and in some smaller towns as well. Once you have a card you'll be able to withdraw cash at machines throughout Thailand. ATM cards issued by Thai Farmers Bank or Bangkok Bank can be used with the ATMs of 14 major banks – there were over 1400 machines nationwide as of the end of 1993.

Debit cards (also known as cash cards or check cards) issued by a bank in your own country can also be used at several Thai banks to withdraw cash (in Thai baht only) directly from your checking or savings account back home, thus avoiding all commissions and finance charges. You can use MasterCard debit cards to buy baht at foreign exchange booths or desks at either Bangkok Bank or Siam Commercial Bank. Visa debit cards can buy cash though Thai Farmers Bank exchange services.

These cards can also be used at many Thai ATMs, though a surcharge of around US$1 is usually subtracted from your account each time you complete a machine transaction. As a general rule, debit cards issued under the MasterCard name work best at Bangkok Bank ATMs, while Visa debit cards work best with Thai Farmers Bank machines. Some travellers now use debit cards in lieu of travellers' cheques because they're quicker and more convenient, although it's a good idea to bring along an emergency travellers' cheque fund in case you lose your card. One disadvantage of debit card accounts – as opposed to credit card accounts – is that you can't arrange a 'chargeback' for unsatisfactory purchases after the transaction is completed – once the money's drawn from your account it's gone.

Plastic money is becoming increasingly popular in Thailand and many shops, hotels and restaurants now accept credit as well as debit cards. The most commonly accepted cards are Visa and MasterCard, followed by

Diner's Club and Japan Card Bureau (JCB). American Express and Carte Blanche are of much more limited use.

Card Problems Occasionally when you try to use a Visa or MasterCard at upcountry hotels or shops, the staff may try to tell you that only cards issued by Thai Farmers Bank or Siam Commercial Bank are acceptable. With a little patience, you should be able to make them understand that the Thai Farmers Bank will pay the merchant and that your bank will pay the Thai Farmers Bank – that any Visa or MasterCard issued anywhere in the world is indeed acceptable.

Another problem concerns illegal surcharges on credit-card purchases. It's against Thai law to pass on to the customer the 3% merchant fee charged by banks, but almost all merchants in Thailand do it anyway. Some even ask 4 or 5%! The only exception seems to be hotels (although even a few hotels will hit you with a credit-card surcharge). If you don't agree to the surcharge they'll simply refuse to accept your card. Begging and pleading or pointing out the law doesn't seem to help. The best way to get around the illegal surcharge is to politely ask that the credit-card receipt be itemised with cost of product or service and the 3% surcharge listed separately. Then when you pay your bill, photocopy all receipts showing the 3% and request a 'charge back'. If a hotel or shop refuses to itemise the surcharge, take down the vendor's name and address and report them to the Tourist Authority of Thailand (TAT) tourist police – they may be able to arrange a refund.

To report a lost or stolen Visa or MasterCard, call either Thai Farmers Bank (☎ 271-0234, daily 7 am to 10 pm) or Siam Commercial Bank (☎ 256-1361, Monday to Friday 8.30 am to 4 pm) in Bangkok.

See the Dangers & Annoyances section in this chapter for important warnings on credit-card theft and fraud.

Safety Deposit Boxes
Travellers can rent safety deposit boxes at Bangkok's Safety Deposit Centre, 3rd Floor, Chan Issara Tower, 942/81 Rama IV Rd (near the Silom Rd intersection) for 150B a month plus 2000B for a refundable key deposit. The centre is open from 10 am to 7 pm, Monday to Friday, and from 10 am to 6 pm Saturday, Sunday and public holidays. A few banks will rent safety deposit boxes as well, but generally you need to open an account with them first.

Exchange Control
Legally, any traveller arriving in Thailand must have at least the following amounts of money in cash, travellers' cheques, bank draft, or letter of credit, according to visa category: Non-Immigrant Visa, US$500 per person or US$1000 per family; Tourist Visa, US$250 per person or US$500 per family; Transit Visa or no visa, US$125 per person or US$250 per family. This may be checked if you arrive on a one-way ticket or if you look as if you're at 'the end of the road'.

According to 1991 regulations, there are no limits to the amounts of Thai or foreign currency you may bring into the country. Upon leaving Thailand, you're permitted to take no more than 50,000B per person without special authorisation; exportation of foreign currencies is unrestricted.

It's legal to open a foreign currency account at any commercial bank in Thailand. As long as the funds originate from abroad, there are no restrictions on their maintenance or withdrawal.

Costs
Food and accommodation outside Bangkok are generally quite inexpensive and even in Bangkok they are fairly cheap, especially considering the value vis-à-vis other countries in South and South-East Asia.

Outside Bangkok, budget-squeezers should be able to get by on 200B per day if they really keep watch on their expenses. This estimate includes basic guesthouse accommodation, food, nonalcoholic beverages and local transport, but not film, souvenirs, tours or vehicle hire. Add another 45 to 70B per day for every large beer (25 to 30B for small bottles) you drink.

Expenses vary, of course, from place to place; where there are high concentrations of budget travellers, for example, accommodation tends to be cheaper and food more expensive. With experience, you can travel in Thailand for even less if you live like a Thai of modest means and learn to speak the language. Average low-to-middle income Thais certainly don't spend 200B a day when travelling in their own country.

Someone with more money to spend will find that for around 350 to 500B per day, life can be quite comfortable: cleaner and quieter accommodation is easier to find once you pass the 200B-a-night zone in room rates. (Of course, a 50B guesthouse room with a mattress on the floor and responsive management is better than a poorly maintained 350B room with air-con that won't turn off and a noisy all-night card game next door.)

In Bangkok there's almost no limit to the amount you *could* spend, but if you live frugally, avoid the tourist ghettos and ride the public bus system you can get by on only slightly more than you would spend upcountry. Where you stay in Bangkok is of primary concern, as since the tourist boom of 1987 accommodation there has generally become a good deal more expensive than upcountry accommodation. Typically, the visitor spends well over 250B per day in Bangkok just for accommodation – this is generally the absolute minimum for air-con (in a twin room). On the other hand, if you can do without air-con, accommodation can be found in Bangkok for as little as 50B per person. But the noise, heat and pollution in Bangkok may drive many budget travellers to seek more comfort than they might otherwise need upcountry.

Food is somewhat more expensive in Bangkok than in the provinces. However, in Thonburi (Bangkok's 'left bank'), where I lived for some time, many dishes are often *cheaper* than they are upcountry, due to the availability of fresh ingredients. This is also true for the working-class districts on the Bangkok side, like Khlong Toey or Makkasan. Bangkok is the typical 'primate city' cited by sociologists, meaning that most goods produced by the country as a whole end up in Bangkok. The glaring exception is Western food, which Bangkok has more of than anywhere else in the kingdom but charges the most for. Eat only Thai and Chinese food if you're trying to spend as little as possible. After all, why go to Thailand to eat steak and potatoes?

Bargaining

Good bargaining, which takes practice, is another way to cut costs. Anything bought in a market should be bargained for; prices in department stores and most non-tourist shops are fixed. Sometimes accommodation rates can be bargained down. One may need to bargain hard in heavily touristed areas since the one-week, all-air-con type of visitor often pays whatever's asked, creating an artificial price zone between the local and tourist market that the budgeteer must deal with.

On the other hand the Thais aren't *always* trying to rip you off, so use some discretion when going for the bone on a price. There's a fine line between bargaining and niggling – getting hot under the collar over 5B makes both seller and buyer lose face. Some more specific suggestions concerning costs can be found in the Accommodation and Things to Buy sections of this chapter.

The cost of transportation between cities and within them is very reasonable; again, bargaining (when hiring a vehicle) can save you a lot of baht. See the Getting Around chapter.

Tipping

Tipping is not normal practice in Thailand, although they're getting used to it in expensive hotels and restaurants. Elsewhere don't bother. In taxis where you have to bargain the fare, it certainly isn't necessary.

Consumer Taxes

In January 1992 Thailand instituted a 7% value-added tax (VAT) for certain goods and services. Unfortunately no-one seems to know what's subject to VAT and what's not, so the whole situation is rather confusing. It doesn't mean that consumers are to be charged 7% over retail – the tax is supposed to be applied to a retailer's cost for the product. For example, if a merchant's wholesale price is 100B for an item that retails at 200B, the maximum adjusted retail including VAT should be 207B, not 214B. In practice the tax is supposed to have caused a net decrease in prices for most goods and services since the VAT replaces a graduated business tax that averaged 9%. But this doesn't always stop Thai merchants from trying to add 'VAT' surcharges to their sales. Like the credit-card surcharge, a direct VAT surcharge is illegal and should be reported to the TAT tourist police.

Tourist hotels add a 7 to 11% hotel tax, and sometimes an 8 to 10% service charge as well, to your room bill.

WHEN TO GO

The best overall time for visiting most of Thailand vis-à-vis climate is between November and February – during these months it rains least and is not so hot. The south is best visited when the rest of Thailand is miserably hot, March to May, while the north is best from mid-November to early December or in February when it begins warming up again. If you're spending time in Bangkok, be prepared to roast in April and do some wading in October – probably the two worst months, weather-wise, for the capital.

The peak months for tourists are December and August – don't go during these months if you want to avoid crowds of farang vacationers. The least crowded months are May, June and September.

WHAT TO BRING

Bring as little as possible – one medium-sized shoulder bag or backpack should do it. Pack light, natural-fibre clothes, unless you're going to be in the north in the cool season, in which case you should have a pullover. Pick up a *phâakhama* (short Thai-style sarong for men) or a *phâasîn* (a longer sarong for women) to wear in your room, on the beach, or when bathing outdoors. These can be bought at any local market (different patterns/colours in different parts of the country) and the vendors will show you how to tie them.

The sarong is a very handy item; it can be used to sleep on or as a light bedspread, as a makeshift 'shopping bag', as a turban/scarf to keep off the sun and absorb perspiration, as a towel, as a small hammock and as a device with which to climb coconut palms – to name just a few of its many functions. It is not considered proper street attire, however.

Sunglasses are a must for most people and can be bought cheaply in Bangkok. Slip-on shoes or sandals are highly recommended – besides being cooler than lace-up shoes, they are easily removed before entering a Thai home or temple. A small torch (flashlight) is a good idea, as it makes it easier to find your way back to your bungalow at night if you are staying at the beach or at a remote guesthouse. A few other handy things are a compass, a plastic lighter for lighting candles and mosquito coils (lighters, candles and mossie coils are available in Thailand) and foam ear plugs for noisy nights.

Toothpaste, soap and most other toiletries can be purchased anywhere in Thailand. Sun block and mosquito repellent (except high-percentage DEET – see the Health section in this chapter) are available, although they're expensive and the quality of both is generally substandard. If you plan to wash your own clothes, bring along a universal sink plug, a few plastic clothespins and three metres of plastic cord or plastic hangers for hanging wet clothes out to dry.

If you plan to spend a great deal of time in one or more of Thailand's beach areas, you might want to bring your own snorkel and mask (see Diving & Snorkelling under Activities in this chapter). This would save you having to rent such gear and would also assure a proper fit. Shoes designed for water sports, eg aquasocks, are great for wearing in the water whether you're diving or not. They protect your feet from coral cuts, which easily become infected.

TOURIST OFFICES

The Tourist Authority of Thailand (TAT) is a government-operated tourist information/promotion service attached to the Prime Minister's office, with several offices within the country and others overseas. In 1991 the TAT was granted regulatory powers for the monitoring of tourism-related businesses throughout Thailand, including hotels, tour operators, travel agencies and transport companies, in an effort to upgrade the quality of these services and prosecute unscrupulous operators. Since 1992 the TAT has opened new provincial offices in Ayuthaya, Lopburi, Khon Kaen, Udon Thai and Sakon Nakhon.

Local Tourist Offices

Ayuthaya
　　Si Sanphet Rd (temporary office), Ayuthaya 13000 (☎ (036) 422768, fax 422769)

Bangkok
　　372 Bamrung Meuang Rd, Bangkok 10100 (☎ (02) 226-0060/72, fax 224-6221)

Cha-am
　　500/51 Phetkasem Highway, Amphoe Cha-am, Phetburi 76000 (☎ (032) 471005, fax 471502)

Chiang Mai
　　105/1 Chiang Mai-Lamphun Rd, Chiang Mai 50000 (☎ (053) 248604/7, fax 248605)

Chiang Rai
　　Singhakai Rd, Chiang Rai 57000 (☎ (053) 717433, fax 717434)

Hat Yai
　　1/1 Soi 2, Niphat Uthit 3 Rd, Hat Yai, Songkhla 90110 (☎ (074) 243747, fax 245986)

Kanchanaburi
　　Saengchuto Rd, Kanchanaburi 71000 (☎ /fax (034) 511200)

Khon Kaen
　　15/5 Prachasamoson Rd, Khon Kaen 40000 (☎ (043) 244498, fax 244487)

Lopburi
　　HM The Queen's Celebration Building (temporary office), Provincial Hall, Narai Maharat Rd, Lopburi 15000 (☎ (036) 422768, fax 422769)

Nakhon Ratchasima (Khorat)
　　2102-2104 Mittaphap Rd, Nakhon Ratchasima 30000 (☎ (044) 213666, fax 213667)

Nakhon Phanom
　　Provincial Offices (temporary office), Abhibanbancha Rd, Nakhon Phanom 4800 (☎ (042) 513490, 513491, fax 513492)

Nakhon Si Thammarat
　　Sanam Na Meuang, Ratchadamnoen Klang Rd, Nakhon Si Thammarat 80000 (☎ (075) 346515, fax 346517)

Pattaya
　　382/1 Chai Hat Rd, Pattaya Beach, South Pattaya 21000 (☎ (038) 428750, fax 429113)

Phitsanulok
　　209/7-8 Surasi Trade Center, Boromtrailokanat Rd, Phitsanulok 85000 (☎ (055) 252743, fax 252742)

Phuket
　　73-75 Phuket Rd, Phuket 83000 (☎ (076) 212213, 211036, fax 213582)

Rayong
　　300/77 Liang Meuang Rd, Rayong 2100 (☎ /fax (038) 611228)

Surat Thani
　　5 Talat Mai Rd, Ban Don, Surat Thani 84000 (☎ /fax (077) 282828)

Ubon Ratchathani
　　264/1 Kheuan Thani Rd, Ubon Ratchathani 34000 (☎ (045) 243770, fax 243771)

Udon Thani
　　Provincial Education Office (temporary office), Phosi Rd, Udon Thani 41000 (☎ /fax (042) 241968)

Representatives Abroad

Australia
　　7th Floor, Royal Exchange Bldg, 56 Pitt St, Sydney NSW 2000 (☎ (02) 247-7549, fax 251-2465)

France
　　Office National de Tourisme de Thailande, 90 Ave des Champs Elysées, 75008 Paris (☎ (01) 4562-8656, fax 4563-7888)

Germany
　　Thailandisches Fremdenverkehrsamt, Bethmannstrasse 58, 60311 Frankfurt/Main (☎ (069) 295704/804, fax 281468)

Hong Kong
　　Rm 401, Fairmont House, 8 Cotton Tree Drive, Central (☎ (05) 868-0732, fax 868-4585)

Italy
　　Ente Nazionale per il Turismo Thailandese, Via Barberini 50, 00187 Rome (☎ (06) 487-3479, fax 487-3500)

Japan
　　Hibiya Mitsui Bldg, 1-2 Yurakucho 1-chome, Chiyoda-ku, Tokyo 100 (☎ (03) 3580-6776, fax 3580-7808)
　　Hiranomachi Yachiyo Bldg, 5F, 1-8-14 Hiranomachi, Chuo-ku, Osaka 541 (☎ (06) 231-4434, 231-4337)

Korea
　　Rm No 2003, 20th fl, Coryo Daeyungek Center Bldg 25-5, 1-ka, Chungmu-Ro, Chung-Ku, Seoul 100-706 (☎ (02) 779-5417, fax 779-5419)

Malaysia
　　c/o Royal Thai Embassy, 206 Jalan Ampang,

504505 Kuala Lumpur (☎ 248-0958, fax 241-3002)

Singapore
c/o Royal Thai Embassy, 370 Orchard Rd 0923 (☎ 235-7694, fax 733-5653)

Taiwan
Thailand Trade & Economic Office, Tourism Division, 2B Central Commercial Bldg, 16-18 Nanking East Rd, Section 4, Taipei 105 (☎ (02) 778-2735, fax 741-9914)

UK
49 Albemarle St, London WIX 3FE (☎ (0171) 499-7679, fax 629-5519)

USA
5 World Trade Center, Suite 2449, New York, NY 10048 (☎ (212) 432-0433, fax 912-0920)
3440 Wilshire Blvd, Suite 1100, Los Angeles, CA 90010 (☎ (213) 382-2353, fax 389-7544)
303 East Wacker Drive, Suite 400, Chicago, IL 60601 (☎ (312) 819-3990, fax 565-0359)

HOLIDAYS & FESTIVALS

The number and frequency of festivals and fairs in Thailand is incredible – there always seems to be something going on, especially during the cool season between November and February.

Exact dates for festivals may vary from year to year, either because of the lunar calendar – which isn't quite in sync with our solar calendar – or because local authorities decide to change festival dates. The TAT publishes an up-to-date *Major Events & Festivals* calendar each year that is useful for anyone planning to attend a particular event.

On dates noted as public holidays, all government offices and banks will be closed.

Major upcoming events not listed below include a *total solar eclipse*, which will occur on 24 October 1995 and will be visible across a wide swath of Thailand from Mae Sot on the Thai-Burmese border to Aranya Prathet on the Thai-Cambodian border. The *13th Asian Games* will be held at the National Stadium in Bangkok in 1998. For information on either event contact a TAT office in Thailand or abroad.

Last week of January
Phra That Phanom Fair – an annual week-long homage to the north-east's most sacred Buddhist stupa in Nakhon Phanom Province. Pilgrims from all over the country attend.

Late January
Don Chedi Memorial Fair – held at the Don Chedi memorial in Suphanburi Province, this event commemorates the victory of King Naresuan of Ayuthaya over Burmese invaders in 1592. The highlight of the fair is dramatised elephant-back duelling.

February
Magha Puja (Makkha Buchaa) – held on the full moon of the third lunar month to commemorate the preaching of the Buddha to 1250 enlightened monks who came to hear him 'without prior summons'. A public holiday throughout the country culminating in a candle-lit walk around the main chapel at every wat.

1st week of February
Chiang Mai Flower Festival – colourful floats and parades exhibit Chiang Mai's cultivated flora.

Phra Nakhon Khiri Diamond Festival, Phetburi – week-long celebration of Phetburi's history and architecture focused on Phra Nakhon Khiri (also known as Khao Wang), a hill topped by a former royal palace overlooking the city. Features a light & sound show on Khao Wang, temples festooned with lights and Thai classical dance-drama.

Young boy at Candle Festival parade

Late February to early March

Chinese New Year – called *trùt jiin* in Thai, Chinese populations all over Thailand celebrate their lunar new year (the date shifts from year to year) with a week of house-cleaning, lion dances and fireworks. The most impressive festivities take place in the Chinese-dominated province capital of Nakhon Sawan.

1st week of March

ASEAN Barred Ground Dove Fair – large dove-singing contest held in Yala that attracts dove-lovers from all over Thailand, Malaysia, Singapore and Indonesia.

1st or 2nd week of March

Phra Phutthabat Fair – annual pilgrimage to the Temple of the Holy Footprint at Saraburi, 236 km north-east of Bangkok. Quite an affair, with music, outdoor drama and many other festivities. If you're in the area, the shrine is worth visiting even in the 'off season'.

3rd week of March

Bangkok International Jewellery Fair – held in several large Bangkok hotels, this is Thailand's most important annual gem and jewellery trade show. Runs concurrently with the Department of Export Promotion's *Bangkok Gems & Jewellery Fair*.

Last week of March

Prasat Phanom Rung Festival – a newly established festival to commemorate the restoration of this impressive Angkor-style temple complex in Buriram Province. Involves a daytime procession to Khao Phanom Rung and spectacular sound & light shows at night. Be prepared for very hot weather.

6 April

Chakri Day – a public holiday commemorating the founder of the Chakri Dynasty, Rama I.

13 to 15 April

Songkran Festival – the New Year's celebration of the lunar year in Thailand. Buddha images are 'bathed', monks and elders receive the respect of younger Thais by the sprinkling of water over their hands, and a lot of water is tossed about for fun. Songkran generally gives everyone a chance to release their frustrations and literally cool off during the peak of the hot season. Hide out in your room or expect to be soaked; the latter is a lot more fun.

May (Full Moon)

Visakha Puja (Wisakha Buchaa) – a public holiday which falls on the 15th day of the waxing moon in the 6th lunar month. This is considered the date of the Buddha's birth, enlightenment and parinibbana, or passing away. Activities are centred around the wat, with candle-lit processions, much chanting and sermonising, etc.

5 May

Coronation Day – public holiday. The King and Queen preside at a ceremony at Wat Phra Kaew in Bangkok, commemorating their 1946 coronation.

2nd week of May

Royal Ploughing Ceremony – to kick off the official rice-planting season, the king participates in this ancient Brahman ritual at Sanam Luang (the large field across from Wat Phra Kaew) in Bangkok. Thousands of Thais gather to watch, and traffic in this part of the city comes to a standstill.

Rocket Festival – all over the north-east, villagers craft large skyrockets of bamboo which they then fire into the sky to bring rain for rice fields. This festival is best celebrated in the town of Yasothon, but is also good in Ubon and Nong Khai. Known in Thai as Bun Bong Fai.

Mid-June

Phii Ta Khon Festival – a unique celebration held in Loei's Dan Sai district (nowadays also in the provincial capital) in which revellers dress in garish 'spirit' costumes and painted masks of coconut wood. The festival commemorates a Buddhist legend in which a host of spirits *(phii)* appeared to greet the Buddha-to-be upon his return to his home town, during his penultimate birth.

Mid-July

Asanha Puja – full moon is a must for this public holiday which commemorates the first sermon preached by the Buddha.

Mid to late July

Khao Phansaa – a public holiday and the beginning of Buddhist 'lent', this is the traditional time of year for young men to enter the monkhood for the rainy season and for all monks to station themselves in a single monastery for the three months. It's a good time to observe a Buddhist ordination.

Candle Festival – Khao Phansaa is celebrated in the north-east by carving huge candles and parading them on floats in the streets. This festival is best celebrated in Ubon.

12 August

Queen's Birthday – public holiday. In Bangkok, Ratchadamnoen Klang Rd and the Grand Palace are festooned with coloured lights.

Mid-September

Thailand International Swan-Boat Races – these take place on the Chao Phraya River in Bangkok near the Rama IX Bridge.

Last week of September

Narathiwat Fair – an annual week-long festival celebrating local culture with boat races, dove-singing contests, handicraft displays, traditional southern Thai music and dance. The King and Queen almost always attend.

Late September to early October

Vegetarian Festival – a nine-day celebration in Trang and Phuket during which devout Chinese Buddhists eat only vegetarian food. There are also various ceremonies at Chinese temples and merit-making processions that bring to mind Hindu Thaipusam in its exhibition of self-mortification. Smaller towns in the south such as Krabi and Phang-Nga also celebrate the veggie fest on a smaller scale.

Mid-October to mid-November

Thawt Kathin – a one-month period at the end of the Buddhist 'lent' *(phansãa)* during which new monastic robes and requisites are offered to the Sangha. In Nan Province longboat races are held on the Nan River.

23 October

Chulalongkorn Day – a public holiday in commemoration of King Chulalongkorn (Rama V).

November

Loi Krathong – on the proper full-moon night, small lotus-shaped baskets or boats made of banana leaves containing flowers, incense, candles and a coin are floated on Thai rivers, lakes and canals. This is a peculiarly Thai festival that probably originated in Sukhothai and is best celebrated in the north. In Chiang Mai, where the festival is called Yi Peng, residents also launch hot-air paper balloons into the sky. At the Sukhothai Historical Park there is an impressive sound & light show.

3rd weekend in November

Surin Annual Elephant Roundup – Thailand's equivalent to the 'running of the bulls' in Pamplona, Spain, is pretty touristy these days. If you ever wanted to see a lot of elephants in one place, though, here's your chance.

Late November to early December

River Khwae Bridge Week – sound & light shows every night at the Death Railway Bridge in Kanchanaburi, plus historical exhibitions and vintage train rides.

5 December

King's Birthday – this is a public holiday which is celebrated with some fervour in Bangkok. As with the Queen's birthday, it features lots of lights along Ratchadamnoen Klang Rd. Some people erect temporary shrines to the King outside their homes or businesses.

10 December

Constitution Day – public holiday.

31 December to 1 January

New Year's Day – a rather recent public holiday in deference to the Western calendar.

BUSINESS HOURS

Most government offices are open from 8.30 am to 4.30 pm, Monday to Friday, but closed from noon to 1 pm for lunch. Banks are open from 8.30 am to 3.30 pm Monday to Friday, but in Bangkok in particular several banks have special foreign-exchange offices which are open longer hours (generally until 8 pm) and every day of the week.

Businesses usually operate between 8.30 am and 5 pm, Monday to Friday and sometimes Saturday morning as well. Larger shops usually open from 10 am to 6.30 or 7 pm but smaller shops may open earlier and close later.

Vegetarian Festival, Phuket

POST & TELECOMMUNICATIONS
Post

Thailand has a very efficient postal service and within the country postage is very cheap.

The poste restante service is also very reliable, though during high tourist months (December and August) you may have to wait in line at the Bangkok GPO. There is a fee of 1B for every piece of mail collected, 2B for each parcel. As with many Asian countries, confusion at poste restante offices is most likely to arise over given names and surnames. Ask people who are writing to you to print your surname clearly and to underline it. If you're certain a letter should be waiting for you and it cannot be found, it's always wise to check it hasn't been filed under your given name. You can take poste restante at almost any post office in Thailand.

The American Express office (☎ 251-4862), Suite 414, Siam Center, Rama I Rd, will also take mail on behalf of Amex card holders. The hours are from 8.30 am to noon and 1 to 4.30 pm, Monday to Friday, and 8.30 to 11.30 am Saturday.

Bangkok's GPO on Charoen Krung (New) Rd is open from 8 am to 8 pm Monday to Friday and from 8 am to 1 pm weekends and holidays. A 24-hour international tele-communications service (including telephone, fax, telex and telegram) is located in a separate building behind and to the right of the main GPO building.

Outside Bangkok the typical provincial GPO is open from 8.30 am to 4.30 pm Monday to Friday, 9 am to noon Saturday. Larger GPOs in provincial capitals may also be open for a half day on Sunday.

Postal Rates Air-mail letters weighing 10 grams or less cost 13B to Europe, Australia and New Zealand, and 16B to the Americas. Aerograms cost 10B regardless of the destination, while postcards are 9B.

Letters sent by registered mail cost 20B in addition to regular air-mail postage. International express mail (EMS) fees vary according to country of destination. Sample rates for items weighing 100 to 250 grams are: Japan 250B; Australia, Germany and the UK 215B; France, Canada and the USA 235B. Within Thailand, this service costs only 20B (100 to 250 grams) in addition to regular postage.

The rates for parcels shipped by post vary according to weight (rising in one-kg increments), country of destination and whether they're shipped by surface (takes up to two

Parcel Postage Rates

Destination		1 kg	5 kg	10 kg	20 kg
Australia	surface	176B	326B	479B	–
	air	280B	872B	1589B	3029B
Canada	surface	152B	278B	400B	717B
	air	339B	1226B	2675B	5229B
France	surface	198B	346B	496B	–
	air	396B	1100B	1919B	3693B
Germany	surface	137B	266B	393B	654B
	air	264B	908B	1687B	3213B
Japan	surface	204B	334B	426B	–
	air	272B	674B	1119B	–
New Zealand	surface	180B	332B	522B	–
	air	315B	1032B	1944B	–
UK	surface	218B	401B	563B	–
	air	337B	1032B	1850B	3519B
USA	surface	135B	454B	824B	1597B
	air	356B	1564B	3035B	6034B

months) or air (one to two weeks). See the Parcel Postage Rates table earlier for sample prices.

Most provincial post offices sell do-it-yourself packing boxes (11 sizes!) costing from 5 to 35B; tape and string are provided at no charge. Some offices even have packing services, which cost from 4 to 10B per parcel depending on size. Private packing services may also be available in the vicinity of large provincial post offices.

You can insure a package's contents for 8.50B for each 1740B of the goods' value.

Telephone

The telephone system in Thailand, operated by the government-subsidised Telephone Organization of Thailand (TOT) under the Communications Authority of Thailand (CAT), is quite efficient and from Bangkok you can usually direct-dial most major centres with little difficulty.

The country code for Thailand is ☎ 66.

International Phone Services A service called Home Direct is available at Bangkok's GPO (Charoen Krung Rd), at airports in Bangkok, Chiang Mai, Phuket, Hat Yai and Surat Thani, and at post office CAT centres in Bangkok, Hat Yai, Phuket, Chiang Mai, Surat Thani, Pattaya, Hua Hin and Kanchanaburi. Home Direct phones offer easy one-button connection with international operators in 20-odd countries around the world. You can also direct-dial Home Direct access numbers from any private phone (most hotel phones won't work) in Thailand.

For Home Direct service, dial ☎ 001-999 followed by:

Australia	61-1000
Canada	15-1000
Denmark	45-1000
Germany	49-1000
Hawaii	14414
Hong Kong	852-1086
Indonesia	62-1000
Italy	39-1000
Japan	81-0051

Korea	82-1000
Netherlands	31-1035
New Zealand	64-1066
Norway	47-1000
Philippines	63-1000
Singapore	351-1000
Taiwan	886-1000
UK	44-1066
USA (AT&T)	1111
USA (MCI)	12001
USA (Sprint)	13877

Hotels generally add surcharges (sometimes as much as 30% over and above the TOT rate) for international long-distance calls; it's always cheaper to call abroad from a CAT telephone office. These offices are almost always attached to a city's GPO, often on the building's 2nd floor, around the side or just behind the GPO. There may also be a separate TOT office down the road, used only for residential or business service (eg billing or installation), not public calls; even when public phone services are offered (as at the TOT office on Ploenchit Rd in Bangkok), TOT offices accept only cash payments – reverse-charge and credit-card calls aren't permitted. Hence the CAT office is generally your best choice.

Once you've found the proper office and window, the procedure for making an international long-distance call *(thorásàp ráwàang pràthêt)* begins with filling out a bilingual form with your name and details pertaining to the call's destination. Except for reverse-charge calls, you must estimate in advance the time you'll be on the phone and pay a deposit equal to the time/distance rate. There is always a minimum three-minute charge, refunded if your call doesn't go through.

Usually, only cash or international phone credit cards are acceptable for payment at CAT offices; some provincial CAT offices also accept American Express and a few take Visa/MasterCard. If the call doesn't go through you must pay a 30B service charge anyway – unless you're calling reverse charges *(kèp plai-thaang)*. For reverse-charge calls it's the opposite, you pay the 30B charge only if the call goes through. Depending on where you're calling, reimbursing someone later for a reverse-charge call to your home country may be less expensive than paying CAT/TOT charges – it pays to compare rates at source and destination. For calls between the USA and Thailand, for example, AT&T collect rates are less than TOT's direct rates.

Private long-distance telephone offices are also available in most towns, but sometimes these are only for calls within Thailand. Often they're just a desk or a couple of booths in the rear of a retail shop. These private offices typically collect a 10B surcharge for long-distance domestic calls, 50B for international calls. The vast majority of such offices accept cash.

Whichever type of phone service you use, the least expensive time of day to make calls is from midnight to 5 am (30% discount from standard rates), followed by 9 pm to midnight and 5 to 7 am (both at 20% discount). You pay full price from 7 am to 9 pm.

Telephone Office Hours GPO phone centres in most provincial capitals are open daily from 7 am to 11 pm; smaller provincial phone offices may be open from 8 am to 8 or 10 pm. Bangkok's international CAT phone office at the Chareon Krung Rd GPO is open 24 hours.

Pay Phones In most places there are two kinds of public pay phones in Thailand, 'red' and 'blue'. The red phones are for local city calls and the blue are for long-distance calls (within Thailand). Local calls from pay phones cost 1B. Although there are three different 1B coins in general circulation, only the middle-sized coin fits the coin slots. Some hotels and guesthouses have private pay phones that cost 5B per call; these take only nine-sided 5B coins.

Card phones are now available at most Thai airports as well as major shopping centres and other public areas throughout urban Thailand. Telephone cards come in 25B, 50B, 100B and 240B denominations, all roughly the same size as a credit card; they can be purchased at any TOT office. In airports you can usually buy them at the airport information counter or at one of the gift shops.

The newest phone booth service in Thailand – found mostly in Bangkok – is called Fonepoint, a system which uses a one-way

---

Area Codes

002	Bangkok, Thonburi, Nonthaburi, PathumThani, Samut Prakan	044	Buriram, Chaiyaphum, Nakhon Ratchasima (Khorat)
032	Phetburi, Cha-am, Prachuap Khiri Khan, Pranburi, Ratchaburi	045	Si Saket, Surin, Ubon Ratchathani, Yasothon
034	Kanchanaburi, Nakhon Pathom, Samut Sakhon, Samut Songkhram	053	Chiang Mai, Chiang Rai, Lamphun, Mae Hong Song
035	Ang Thong, Ayuthaya, Suphanburi	054	Lampang, Nan, Phayao, Phrae
036	Lopburi, Saraburi, Singburi	055	Kamphaeng Phet, Phitsanulok, Sukhothai, Tak, Mae Sot, Uttaradit
037	Nakhon Nayok, Prachinburi, Aranya Prathet	056	Nakhon Sawan, Phetchabun, Phichit, Uthai Thani
038	Chachoengsao, Chonburi, Pattaya, Rayong, Si Racha	073	Narathiwat, Sungai Kolok, Pattani, Yala
039	Chanthaburi, Trat	074	Hat Yai, Phattalung, Satun, Songkhla
042	Loei, Chiang Khan, Mukdahan, Nakhon Phanom, Nong Khai, Sakon Nakhon, Udon Thani	075	Krabi, Nakhon Si Thammarat, Trang
		076	Phang-Nga, Phuket
043	Kalasin, Khon Kaen, Mahasarakham, Roi Et	077	Chumphon, Ranong, Surat Thani, Chaiya, Ko Samui

mobile phone network operated by TOT. Such mobile phones can be used within 100 to 200 metres of a Fonepoint location to communicate with other mobile phones and pagers. For a Fonepoint account the TOT charges a monthly service fee of 350B plus 1B per minute (three-minute minimum) in Bangkok, or normal TOT rates for upcountry and overseas calls, plus registration fees.

Fax, Telex & Telegraph
GPO telephone offices throughout the country offer fax, telegraph and telex services in addition to regular phone service. There's no need to bring your own paper, as the post offices supply their own forms. A few TOT offices also offer fax services. International faxes typically cost a steep 100 to 140B for the first page, and 65 to 110B per page for the remaining pages, depending on size of the paper and destination.

Larger hotels with business centres offer the same telecommunication services but always at higher rates.

TIME
Time Zone
Thailand's time zone is seven hours ahead of GMT/UTC (London). Thus, noon in Bangkok is 3 pm in Sydney, 1 pm in Perth, 5 am in London, 1 am in New York and 10 pm the previous day in Los Angeles.

Thai Calendar
The official year in Thailand is reckoned from 543 BC, the beginning of the Buddhist Era, so that 1995 AD is 2538 BE.

ELECTRICITY
Electric current is 220 V, 50 cycles. Electrical wall outlets are usually of the round, two-pole type; some outlets also accept flat, two-bladed terminals, and some will accept either flat or round terminals. Any electrical supply shop will carry adapters for any international plug shape as well as voltage converters.

LAUNDRY
Virtually every hotel and guesthouse in Thailand offers a laundry service. Rates are generally geared to room rates; the cheaper the accommodation, the cheaper the washing and ironing. Cheapest of all are public laundries, where you pay by the kg.

Many Thai hotels and guesthouses also have laundry areas where you can wash your clothes at no charge; sometimes there's even a hanging area for drying. For accommodation where a laundry area isn't available, do-it-yourselfers can wash their clothes in the sink and hang clothes out to dry in their rooms – see the What to Bring section in this chapter for useful laundry tools. Laundry

---

Thai Time

There are three ways of expressing time in Thailand: the common 12-hour system (eg 11 am is 12 hours distant from 11 pm); 'official' *(râatchakaan)* time, based on the 24-hour clock (eg 11 pm is the same as 2300 hours); and the traditional six-hour system.

From dusk to dawn, most Thais tell time using the traditional six-hour method. In this system, times are expressed the same way as in the 12-hour clock until 6 pm, but from 7 pm to midnight Thais use *thûm* (the sound of a drumstroke), counting from one to six – eg 7 pm is *nèung thûm* or 'one thum', 11 pm is *hâa thûm* or 'five thum'. After midnight *(thîang khêun)*, it's back to one again with the hours referred to as *tii* (the sound of wooden clackers), so that 3 am is *tii sǎam* or 'three tii' (the word order is reversed for tii). After 6 am Thai speakers revert to thum with the addition of the word *cháo* (morning), eg *sǎwng thûm cháo* is 'two thum chao' or 8 am.

At one time drums and wooden clackers were used throughout Thailand to mark the hours during these respective times of day. Today the wooden clackers are often replaced by steel bars, which neighbourhood watchmen clank together on the hour while guarding residential districts. If the neighbourhood's inhabitants don't hear the comforting clanks or clacks throughout the night they become alarmed. ■

detergent is readily available in general mercantile shops and supermarkets.

For dry-cleaning, take clothes to a dry-cleaner. Laundries that advertise dry-cleaning often don't really dry-clean (they just boil everything!) or do it badly. Luxury hotels usually have dependable dry-cleaning services.

Two reliable dry-cleaners in Bangkok are Erawan Dry Cleaners (basement of Landmark Plaza, Sukhumvit Rd) and Spotless Dry Cleaning & Laundry (166 Soi 23 Sukhumvit Rd). Both of these companies can dry-clean large items like sleeping bags as well as clothes.

WEIGHTS & MEASURES

Dimensions and weight are usually expressed using the metric system in Thailand. The exception is land measure, which is often quoted using the traditional Thai system of *waa*, *ngaan* and *râi*. Old-timers in the provinces will occasionally use the traditional Thai system of weights and measures in speech, as will boat-builders, carpenters and other craftspeople when talking about their work. Here are some conversions to use for such occasions:

1 sq *waa*	=	4 sq metres
1 *ngaan* (100 sq waa)	=	400 sq metres
1 *râi* (4 ngaan)	=	1600 sq metres
1 *bàht*	=	15 grams
1 *taleung* or *tamleung* (4 baht)	=	60 grams
1 *châng* (20 taleung)	=	1.2 kg
1 *hàap* (50 chang)	=	60 kg
1 *níu*	=	about 2 cm (or 1 inch)
1 *khêup* (12 niu)	=	25 cm
1 *sàwk* (2 kheup)	=	50 cm
1 *waa* (4 sawk)	=	2 metres
1 *sén* (20 waa)	=	40 metres
1 *yôht* (400 sen)	=	16 km

BOOKS & MAPS
People, Culture & Society

Culture Shock! Thailand & How to Survive It by Robert & Nanthapa Cooper is an interesting outline on getting along with the Thai way of life. *Letters from Thailand* by Botan (translated by Susan Fulop Kepner) and Carol Hollinger's *Mai Pen Rai Means Never Mind* can also be recommended for their insights into traditional Thai culture. *Bangkok Post* reporter Denis Segaller's *Thai Ways* and *More Thai Ways* present yet more expat insights into Thai culture.

Ramakian: The Thai Ramayana by Naga Books (anonymous author) is a thorough exposition of the Thai version of Indian poet Valmiki's timeless epic.

For a look at rural life in Thailand, the books of Pira Sudham are unparalleled. Sudham was born to a poor family in north-east Thailand and has written *Siamese Drama, Monsoon Country* and *People of Esarn (Isaan)*. These books are not translations – Sudham writes in English in order to reach a worldwide audience. These fiction titles are fairly easy to find in Bangkok but can be difficult to find overseas – the publisher is Siam Media International, GPO Box 1534, Bangkok 10501.

Behind the Smile: Voices of Thailand (Post Publishing, 1990) by Sanitsuda Ekachai is a very enlightening collection of interviews with Thai peasants from all over the country. The Siam Society's *Culture & Environment in Thailand* is a collection of scholarly papers by Thai and foreign authors delivered at a 1988 symposium which examined the relationship between Thai culture and the natural world; topics range from the oceanic origins of the Thai race and nature motifs in Thai art to evolving Thai attitudes toward the environment.

Siam in Crisis by Sulak Sivaraksa, one of Thailand's leading intellectuals, analyses modern Thai politics from Sulak's unique Buddhist-nationalist perspective. Sivaraksa has written several other worthwhile titles on Thai culture which have been translated into English.

For books on Buddhism and Buddhism in Thailand, see the Religion section of the Facts about the Country chapter.

Hill Tribes If you are interested in detailed information on hill tribes, seek out the hard-to-find *The Hill Tribes of Northern Thailand* by Gordon Young (Monograph No 1, The

Siam Society). Young was born of third-generation Christian missionaries among the Lahu people, speaks several tribal dialects and is even an honorary Lahu chieftain with the highest Lahu title, the Supreme Hunter. The monograph covers 16 tribes, including descriptions, photographs, tables and maps.

From the Hands of the Hills by Margaret Campbell has lots of beautiful pictures. The recently published *Peoples of the Golden Triangle* by Elaine & Paul Lewis is also very good, very photo-oriented and expensive. Lonely Planet's *Thai Hill Tribes Phrasebook* has descriptions of Thailand's major hill tribes, maps, and phrases in several hill-tribe languages.

For short descriptions of Thai hill tribes in this guidebook, see under Hill Tribes in the Northern Thailand chapter.

History & Politics

George Coedes' classic prewar work on South-East Asian history, *The Indianised States of South-East Asia*, contains groundbreaking historical material on early Thai history, as does W A R Wood's *A History of Siam*, published in the same era. One of the more readable general histories written in the latter half of the 20th century is David Wyatt's *Thailand: A Short History* (Trasvin Publications, Chiang Mai).

Concentrating on post-revolutionary Thailand, *The Balancing Act: A History of Modern Thailand* (Asia Books, 1991), by Joseph Wright Jr, starts with the 1932 revolution and ends with the February 1991 Coup. Wright's semi-academic chronicle concludes that Thai history demonstrates a continuous circulation of elites governed by certain 'natural laws'. Though the book is packed with detail, such deep-structure theorising brings to mind the way Anglo scholars until very recently identified all French political trends as 'Bonapartiste'. Wright's most demonstrable thesis is that, despite the 1932 revolution, democracy has never gained a firm foothold in Thai society.

The best source of information on Thailand's political scene during the turbulent 1960s and 1970s is *Political Conflict in Thailand: Reform, Reaction, Revolution* by David Morrell & Chai-anan Samudavanija.

Although it sheds no new light on the Death Railway's historical significance, WW II buffs may enjoy Clifford Kinvig's *River Kwai Railway: The Story of the Burma-Siam Railroad*, which presents lots of previously hard-to-find details on, for example, the movement of specific military regiments in South-East Asia, types and amounts of explosives used in construction of the railway, and the composition of Japanese forces in Thailand.

Thailand's role in the international narcotics trade is covered thoroughly in Alfred McCoy's *The Politics of Heroin in Southeast Asia* and Francis Belanger's *Drugs, the US, and Khun Sa*.

Natural History

Complete with sketches, photos and maps, *The Mammals of Thailand* (Association for the Conservation of Wildlife, 1988), by Boonsong Lekagul and Jeffrey McNeely, remains the classic on Thai wildlife in spite of a few out-of-date references (it was first published in 1977). Birdlovers should seek out the *Bird Guide of Thailand* (Association for the Conservation of Wildlife, 1972) by Boonsong Lekagul and E W Cronin for comprehensive descriptions of Thailand's avian species.

Detailed summaries of 63 of Thailand's national parks, along with an objective assessment of current park conditions, are available in *National Parks of Thailand* (Communication Resources, Bangkok, 1991) by Gray, Piprell & Graham.

Description & Travel

Charles Nicholls' semi-fictional *Borderlines* (Picador, 1992) takes the reader on a voyage to the Thai-Burmese border in the company of a colourful group of travellers. Along the way the author weaves cultural insights into the storyline, making the book more than just a beach read.

Nicholls, Pico Iyer, Robert Anson Hall and several other well-known and not-so-well-known authors have contributed travel essays of varying style to *Travelers' Tales Thailand* (edited by James O'Reilly & Larry Habegger, 1994). It's the first title in a new series that assembles travel articles and chapters from various sources into a single anthology devoted to a particular country. Savvy travel tips are sprinkled throughout the text.

Temple buffs will find plenty to chew on in *Guide to Thailand* by Achille Clarac, edited and translated by Michael Smithies. Studded with descriptions of obscure temple ruins throughout the kingdom, Clarac's guide originally appeared in English as *Discovering Thailand* in 1971; it hasn't been updated since 1977 but was a pioneering work in its day.

For an insider's view of temple life, read Tim Ward's amusing *What The Buddha Never Taught* (Celestial Arts, Berkeley, 1993), an account of the author's sojourn as a monk at a north-eastern forest wat.

If you can get hold of a copy of *Hudson's Guide to Chiang Mai & the North* you'll learn a lot about this area that is unknown to the average traveller. Much of the information is out of date (since the book is long out of print) but it makes interesting reading and has one of the best Thai phrase sections ever published – 218 phrases *with* tone marks. (Phrase sections without tone marks are next to worthless.) In 1987, Roy Hudson published the minuscule *Hudson's Guide to Mae Hong Son* which you may come across in the north.

If this is your first trip to Asia, you might also want to have a look at *Before You Go to Asia* (Laurel Publications, San Francisco) by John McCarroll. This book weighs the pros and cons of going on your own versus going with a tour group (the author comes out strongly in favour of going on your own) and lists references for further information on Asian travel.

Food & Shopping

Amongst the explosion of Thai cookbooks that have appeared in recent years, one of the best remains *Thai Cooking* (formerly *The Original Thai Cookbook*) by Jennifer Brennan. For those without access to a complete range of Thai herbs and spices, *Cooking Thai Food in American Kitchens* by Malulee Pinsuvana makes reasonable substitutions. Though expensive and unwieldy, the huge, coffee-table-style *Thailand the Beautiful Cookbook* by Panurat Poladitmontri contains excellent photography and very authentic recipes.

Shopping in Exotic Thailand (Impact Publications, USA) by Ronald and Caryl Rae Krannich is packed with general shopping tips as well as lists of speciality shops and markets throughout Thailand. John Hoskins' *Buyer's Guide to Thai Gems & Jewellery* is a must for anyone contemplating a foray into Thailand's gem market.

Bookshops

Bangkok probably has the largest selection of English-language books and bookshops in South-East Asia. The principal chains are Asia Books (headquarters on Sukhumvit Rd near Soi 15) and DK Book House (Siam Square); each has branch shops in half a dozen street locations around Bangkok as well as in well-touristed cities like Chiang Mai, Hat Yai and Phuket. Asia and DK offer a wide variety of fiction and periodicals as well as books on Asia. Some of Thailand's larger tourist hotels also have bookshops with English-language books and periodicals.

In Chiang Mai, the independent Suriwong Book Centre on Si Donchai Rd is especially good for books on Thailand and Asia.

Maps

Lonely Planet is about to publish the 1:1,150,000 scale *Thailand Travel Atlas*, the first in a series of country map booklets designed for maximum accuracy combined with maximum portability. The atlas includes place names in both Thai and roman script, travel information in five languages (English, French, German, Spanish and Japanese), topographic shading and a complete geographic index. It has been spot-checked on the ground for accuracy and currency by this author.

Nelles Maps and Bartholomew Maps each publish decent 1:500,000 scale maps of Thailand with general topographic shading. These are readily available for around US$7 at many Bangkok bookshops as well as overseas. The Bartholomew map is more up-to-date and accurate than the Nelles.

A few years back Bartholomew, in conjunction with DK Book House, came out with the *Handy Map of Thailand*, an ingeniously folded 22 x 13 cm road atlas that can be opened like a book to any section without refolding the map – perfect for the backpacker. Although it's not 100% accurate, the convenience and durable coated paper make it a bargain at 90 to 100B – if you can find it. Other companies have issued similar – but much less readable and accurate – accordion maps.

Even better is the four-map set issued by Thailand's Department of Highways (although also not 100% accurate). For 65B you get a very detailed, full-colour road map of the central, northern, north-eastern and southern regions. The 1:1,000,000 scale maps include information on 'roads not under control by the Highway Department' – many of the roads you may travel on in the north, for example. Bookshops sometimes sell this set for 200B, including a mailing tube, but the Highway Department on Si Ayuthaya Rd in Bangkok offers the set at the lower price. The mailing tube is not worth 135B.

The Roads Association of Thailand publishes a 48-page, bilingual road atlas called *Thailand Highway Map*. The atlas has cut the Highway Department maps to a more manageable size and includes dozens of city maps, driving distances and lots of travel and sightseeing information. It costs 100 to 120B depending on the vendor, but beware of inferior knock-offs.

The maps from the Highway Department or Bartholomew/DK are more than adequate for most people. Thai military maps, which focus on areas no larger than the amphoe (local district), come complete with elevations and contour lines. They are rarely offered for sale (for a while DK Books in Chiang Mai carried a few) but can sometimes be photocopied at university libraries.

City Maps *Bangkok Bus Map*, issued by Bangkok Guide Co, is the most accurate of the general Bangkok maps available. In addition to bus routes, the map shows suggested walking tours. *Latest Tour's Guide to Bangkok & Thailand* has a bus map of Bangkok on one side and a fair map of Thailand on the other. Both maps are usually priced at 35B and are available at most bookshops in Bangkok which carry English-language materials. A bus map is quite necessary if you intend to spend much time in Bangkok and want to use the very economical bus system.

Nancy Chandler's city maps of Bangkok and Chiang Mai are also very useful. Revised annually, these colourful maps serve as up-to-date and informative guides, spotlighting local sights, noting local markets and their wares, outlining local transport and even recommending restaurants. Her maps are available at most bookshops that specialise in English-language material and at some map stores abroad.

MEDIA
Newspapers
Thailand's 1991 constitution guarantees freedom of the press, though the National Police Department reserves power to suspend publishing licences for national security reasons. Editors nevertheless exercise self-censorship in certain realms, particularly with regard to the monarchy. Monarchical issues aside, Thailand is widely considered to have the freest print media in South-East Asia.

Two English-language newspapers are published daily in Thailand and distributed in most provincial capitals throughout the country: the *Bangkok Post* (morning) and the *Nation* (afternoon). The *Nation* is almost entirely staffed by Thais and presents, obviously, a Thai perspective, while the *Post*, which was Thailand's first English daily (established 1946), has a mixed Thai and international staff and represents a more international view. For regional and international news, the *Post* is the better of the two papers and is in fact regarded by many journalists as the best English daily in the region. The *Nation*, on the other hand, is to be commended for taking a harder anti-NPKC stance during the 1991 coup.

A third English-language daily, the less widely available *Thailand Times*, is owned by an investment company with obvious biases regarding growth and development. About the only thing this newspaper has going for it is the page of condensed train and air-con bus timetables which appear near the back of each issue. The bus fares were out of date when last I checked.

The Singapore edition of the *International Herald Tribune* is widely available in Bangkok, Chiang Mai and heavily touristed areas like Pattaya and Phuket.

The most popular Thai-language newspapers are *Thai Rath* and *Daily News*, but they're mostly full of blood-and-guts stories. The best Thai journalism is found in the somewhat less popular *Matichon* and *Siam Rath* dailies. Many Thais read the English-language dailies as they consider them better news sources. The *Bangkok Post* also publishes a Thai-language version of the popular English daily.

Magazines

English-language magazine publishing continues to grow, although the lifespan of individual titles tends to be short. Though mostly devoted to domestic and regional business, the English-language *Manager* occasionally prints very astute, very up-to-date cultural pieces. *Caravan*, a slick lifestyle magazine introduced in 1994, brings a new sophistication to Bangkok publications concerned with art, culture, and music.

Many popular magazines from the UK, USA, Australia and Europe – particularly those concerned with computer technology, autos, fashion, music, and business – are available in bookstores which specialise in English-language publications (see Book-

shops under Books & Maps earlier in this chapter).

Radio

Thailand has more than 400 radio stations, with 41 FM and 35 AM stations in Bangkok alone. Bangkok's national public radio station, Radio Thailand (Sathãanii Wítháyú Hàeng Pràthêt Thai), broadcasts English-language programmes at 97 FM from 6 am to 11 pm. Most of the programmes comprise local, national and international news, sports, business and special news-related features. For up-to-date news reports this is the station to listen to. An official news bulletin (national news sponsored by the government) is broadcast at 7 am, 12.30 pm and 7 pm. The station hosts musical programmes between 9.15 and 11 am, and from 8.30 pm on.

Another public radio station is 107 FM, which is affiliated with Radio Thailand and Channel 9 on Thai public television. It broadcasts Radio Thailand news bulletins at the same hours as Radio Thailand (7 am, 12.30 pm and 7 pm). Between 5 pm and 2 am daily, 107 FM features some surprisingly good music programmes with British, Thai and American DJs. Another station with international pop and English-speaking DJs is Radio Bangkok, 95.5 FM.

Chulalongkorn University broadcasts classical music at 101.5 FM from 9.30 to midnight nightly. A schedule of the evening's programmes can be found in the *Nation* and *Bangkok Post* newspapers.

In the evenings between 6 and 8 pm, several FM stations provide soundtracks in English for local and world satellite news on television Channel 3 (105.5 FM), Channel 7 (103.5 FM), Channel 9 (107 FM) and Channel 11 (8 pm, 88 FM).

The Voice of America, BBC World Service, Radio Canada and Radio Australia all have English and Thai-language broadcasts over short-wave radio from about 6 am to midnight. The radio frequencies and schedules, which change hourly, also appear in the *Post* and the *Nation*. Radio listeners without short-wave receivers can listen to VOA on 95.5 FM, and BBC World Service on 105 FM from midnight to 6 am.

Radio France Internationale and Deutsche Welle carry short-wave programmes in French and German respectively. Deutsche Welle also broadcasts 50 minutes of English programming three times daily.

Television

Thailand has five TV networks based in Bangkok. Following the 1991 coup the Thai government authorised an extension of telecast time to 24 hours and networks are scrambling to fill air time. As a result, there has been a substantial increase in English-language telecasts – mostly in the morning hours when Thais aren't used to watching TV.

Channel 5 is a military network (the only one to operate during coups) and broadcasts from 6 am to midnight; between 6 and 10 am this network presents a mix of ABC, CNN, and English-subtitled Thai news programmes, English-language news at noon and 7 pm, then CNN headlines again at 11.37 pm. Channel 9, the national public television station, broadcasts from 6 am until midnight. An English-language soundtrack is simulcast with Channel 9's evening news program Monday to Friday at 7 pm on radio station FM 107.

Channel 3 is privately owned; broadcast hours vary but there's an English-language news simulcast at 7 pm on FM 105.5. Channel 7 is military-owned but broadcast time is leased to private companies; the channel offers an English-language news simulcast via FM 103.5 at 7 pm. Channel 11 is run by the Ministry of Education and features educational programmes from 5.30 am to 11 pm, including TV correspondence classes from Ramkhamhaeng and Sukhothai Thammathirat open universities. An English-language news simulcast comes over FM 88 at 8 pm.

Upcountry cities will generally receive only two networks – Channel 9 and a local private network with restricted hours.

Satellite & Cable TV As elsewhere in Asia, satellite and cable television services are swiftly arriving in Thailand, and competition for the untapped market is keen. Of the several regional satellite operations aimed at Thailand, the most successful so far is Satellite Television Asian Region (STAR), beamed from Hong Kong via AsiaSat I. STAR offers five free 24-hour channels, including Music TV Asia (a tie-in with America's MTV music-video channel), Prime Sports (international sports coverage), BBC World Service Television (news), and two channels showing movies in Chinese and English. STAR has announced plans to add three to five additional pay channels. CNN and ESPN are available in Thailand via Indonesia's Palapa satellite, a pay-TV service known locally as IBC.

Thailand has recently launched its own ThaiSat as an uplink for AsiaSat. Thai Sky channels 1 to 5 respectively offer the following programmes: news and documentaries, Thai music videos, Thai variety programmes, the BBC World Service, and MTV-Asia.

Tourist-class hotels in Thailand often have one or more satellite TV channels (plus in-house video), including a STAR 'sampler' channel that switches from one STAR offering to another.

Video The predominant video format in Thailand is PAL, a system compatible with that used in most of Europe (France's SECAM format is a notable exception) as well as in Australia. This means if you're bringing videotapes from the USA or Japan, which use the NTSC format, you'll have to bring your own VCR to play them! Some video shops (especially those which carry pirated or unlicensed tapes) sell NTSC as well as PAL and SECAM tapes. A 'multisystem' VCR has the capacity to play both NTSC and PAL, but not SECAM.

FILM & PHOTOGRAPHY

Print film is fairly inexpensive and widely available throughout Thailand. Japanese print film costs 65 to 70B per 36 exposures, US print film 75 to 90B. Fujichrome RDP 100 slide film costs around 150B, Kodak Ektachrome 100HC is 140B and Ektachrome 200 about 200B. Slide film, especially Kodachrome, can be hard to find outside Bangkok and Chiang Mai, so be sure to stock up before heading upcountry. Film processing is generally quite good in the larger cities in Thailand and also quite inexpensive. Kodachrome must be sent out of the country for processing, so it can take up to two weeks to get it back.

Pack some silica gel with your camera to prevent mould growing on the inside of your lenses. A polarising filter could be useful to cut down on tropical glare at certain times of day, particularly around water or highly polished glazed-tile work.

Hill-tribe people in some of the regularly visited areas expect money if you photograph them, while certain Karen and Akha will not allow you to point a camera at them. Use discretion when photographing villagers anywhere in Thailand as a camera can be a very intimidating instrument. You may feel better leaving your camera behind when visiting certain areas.

HEALTH

Travel health depends on your predeparture preparations, your day-to-day health care while travelling and how you handle any medical problem or emergency that does develop. While the list of potential dangers can seem quite frightening, with a little luck, some basic precautions and adequate information few travellers experience more than upset stomachs.

Travel Health Guides

There are a number of books on travel health:

Staying Healthy in Asia, Africa & Latin America, Moon Publications. Probably the best all-round guide to carry, as it's compact but very detailed and well organised

Travellers' Health, Dr Richard Dawood, Oxford University Press. Comprehensive, easy to read, authoritative and also highly recommended, although it's rather large to lug around

Where There is No Doctor, David Werner, Hesperian Foundation. A very detailed guide intended for someone going to work in an undeveloped country (such as a Peace Corps volunteer), rather than for the average traveller

Travel with Children, Maureen Wheeler, Lonely Planet Publications. Includes basic advice on travel health for younger children.

Predeparture Preparations

Health Insurance A travel insurance policy to cover theft, loss and medical problems is a wise idea. There is a wide variety of policies and your travel agent will have recommendations. The international student travel policies handled by STA Travel and other student travel organisations are usually good value. Some policies offer lower and higher medical expenses options but the higher one is chiefly for countries like the USA which have extremely high medical costs. Check the small print:

1. Some policies specifically exclude 'dangerous activities' which can include scuba diving, motorcycling, even trekking. If such activities are on your agenda you don't want that sort of policy. A locally acquired motorcycle licence may not be valid under your policy.
2. You may prefer a policy which pays doctors or hospitals direct rather than one which requires you to pay on the spot and claim later. If you have to claim later, make sure you keep all documentation. Some policies ask you to call back (reverse charges) to a centre in your home country where an immediate assessment of your problem is made.
3. Check if the policy covers ambulances or an emergency flight home. If you have to stretch out you will need two seats and somebody has to pay for them!

Medical Kit A small, straightforward medical kit is a wise thing to carry. A possible kit list includes:

1. Aspirin or Panadol – for pain or fever.
2. Antihistamine (such as Benadryl) – useful as a decongestant for colds, allergies, to ease the itch from insect bites or stings or to help prevent motion sickness. Antihistamines may cause sedation and interact with alcohol so care should be taken when using them.

3. Antibiotics – useful if you're travelling well off the beaten track, but they must be prescribed and you should carry the prescription with you. Some individuals are allergic to commonly prescribed antibiotics such as penicillin or sulfa drugs. It would be sensible always to carry this information when travelling.
4. Kaolin preparation (Pepto-Bismol), Imodium or Lomotil – for stomach upsets.
5. Rehydration mixture – for treatment of severe diarrhoea. This is particularly important if travelling with children, but is recommended for everyone.
6. Antiseptic such as Betadine, which comes as impregnated swabs or ointment, and an antibiotic powder or similar 'dry' spray – for cuts and grazes.
7. Calamine lotion – to ease irritation from bites or stings.
8. Bandages and Band-Aids – for minor injuries.
9. Scissors, tweezers and a thermometer (note that mercury thermometers are prohibited by airlines).
10. Insect repellent, sunscreen, suntan lotion, chap stick and water purification tablets.
11. A couple of syringes, in case you need injections in an area with medical hygiene problems. Ask your doctor for a note explaining why they have been prescribed.
12. Antibiotic eye ointment for all-too-common eye infections.

Ideally, antibiotics should be administered only under medical supervision and should never be taken indiscriminately. Take only the recommended dose at the prescribed intervals and continue using the antibiotic for the prescribed period, even if the illness seems to be cured earlier. Antibiotics are quite specific to the infections they can treat. Stop immediately if there are any serious reactions and don't use the antibiotic at all if you are unsure that you have the correct one.

In Thailand medicine is generally available over the counter and the price will be much cheaper than in the West. However, be careful when buying drugs, particularly where the expiry date may have passed or correct storage conditions may not have been followed. Bogus drugs are not uncommon and it's possible that drugs which are no longer recommended, or have even been banned, in the West are still being dispensed in Thailand.

Health Preparations Make sure you're healthy before you start travelling. If you are embarking on a long trip make sure your teeth are OK; there are lots of places where a visit to the dentist would be the last thing you'd want to do.

If you wear glasses, take a spare pair and your prescription. Losing your glasses can be a real problem, although in many places you can get new spectacles made up quickly, cheaply and competently.

If you require a particular medication take an adequate supply, as it may not be available locally. Take the prescription or, better still, part of the packaging showing the generic rather than the brand name (which may not be locally available), as it will make getting replacements easier. It's a wise idea to have a legible prescription with you to show you legally use the medication – it's surprising how often over-the-counter drugs from one place are illegal without a prescription or even banned in another.

Immunisations Vaccinations provide protection against diseases you might meet along the way. However, there are no health requirements for Thailand in terms of required vaccinations unless you are coming from an infected area (eg Africa).

It is important to understand the distinction between vaccines recommended for travel in certain areas and those required by law. Essentially the number of vaccines subject to international health regulations has been dramatically reduced over the last 10 years. Currently yellow fever is the only vaccine subject to international health regulations. Vaccination as an entry requirement is usually only enforced when coming from an infected area.

All vaccinations should be recorded on an International Health Certificate, which is available from your physician or government health department.

Plan ahead for getting your vaccinations: some of them require an initial shot followed by a booster, while some vaccinations should not be given together. It is recommended you seek medical advice at least six weeks prior to travel.

Most travellers from Western countries will have been immunised against various diseases during childhood but your doctor may still recommend booster shots against measles or polio. The period of protection offered by vaccinations differs widely and some are contraindicated if you are pregnant.

In Thailand immunisations are available from a number of sources, including both public hospitals and private clinics. Bangkok is your best bet in terms of locating less common or more expensive vaccines. The possible list of vaccinations includes:

Smallpox Smallpox has now been wiped out worldwide, so immunisation is no longer necessary.

Cholera Protection is poor and it lasts only six months. It is contraindicated in pregnancy.

Tetanus & Diphtheria Boosters are necessary every 10 years and protection is highly recommended.

Typhoid Available either as an injection or oral capsules. Protection lasts from one to three years and is useful if you are travelling for long in rural, tropical areas. You may get some side effects such as pain at the injection site, fever, headache and a general unwell feeling. A new single-dose injectable vaccine, which appears to have few side effects, is now available but is more expensive. Side effects are unusual with the oral form but occasionally an individual will have stomach cramps.

Infectious Hepatitis The most common travel-acquired illness which can be prevented by vaccination. Protection can be provided in two ways – either with the antibody gammaglobulin or with a new vaccine called Havrix.

Havrix provides long-term immunity (possibly more than 10 years) after an initial course of two injections and a booster at one year. It may be more expensive than gammaglobulin but certainly has many advantages, including length of protection and ease of administration. It is important to know that, being a vaccine, it will take about three weeks to provide satisfactory protection – hence the need for careful planning prior to travel.

Gammaglobulin is not a vaccination but a ready-made antibody which has proven very successful in reducing the chances of hepatitis infection. Because it may interfere with the development of immunity, it should not be given until at least 10 days after administration of the last vaccine needed; it should also be given as close as possible to departure because it is at its most effective in the first few weeks after administration and the effectiveness tapers off gradually between three and six months.

Japanese encephalitis A good idea for those who think they may be at moderate or high risk while in Thailand (see Japanese Encephalitis later in this section for more information).

Basic Rules

Care in what you eat and drink is the most important health rule; stomach upsets are the most likely travel health problem (between 30% and 50% of travellers in a two-week stay experience this) but the majority of these upsets will be relatively minor. Don't become paranoid; trying the local food is part of the experience of travel, after all.

Water The number one rule is *don't drink tap water*. If you don't know for certain that the water is safe always assume the worst. Reputable brands of bottled water or soft drinks are generally fine, although in some places bottles refilled with tap water are not unknown. Only use water from containers with a serrated seal – not tops or corks. Take care with fruit juice, particularly if water may have been added.

Thai soft drinks are safe to drink, as is the weak Chinese tea served in most restaurants. Ice is produced from purified water under hygienic conditions and is therefore theoretically safe. During transit to the local restaurant, however, conditions are not so hygienic (you may see blocks of ice being dragged along the street), but it's very difficult to resist in the hot season. The rule of thumb is that if it's chipped ice, it probably came from an ice block (which may not have been handled well) but if it's ice cubes or 'tubes', it was delivered from the ice factory in sealed plastic. In rural areas, villagers mostly drink collected rainwater. Most travellers can drink this without problems, but some people can't tolerate it.

In Thailand, virtually no-one bothers with filters, tablets or iodine since bottled water is so cheap and readily available.

Food There is an old colonial adage which says: 'If you can cook it, boil it or peel it you can eat it....otherwise forget it'. Salads and fruit should be washed with purified water or peeled where possible. Ice cream is usually OK if it is a reputable brand name, but beware of street vendors and of ice cream that has melted and been refrozen. Thoroughly cooked food is safest but not if it has been left to cool or if it has been reheated. Uncooked shellfish such as mussels, oysters and clams should be avoided as well as undercooked meat, particularly in the form of mince. Steaming does not make shellfish safe for eating.

If a place looks clean and well run and if the vendor also looks clean and healthy, then the food is probably safe. In general, places that are packed with travellers or locals will be fine, while empty restaurants are questionable. Busy restaurants mean the food is being cooked and eaten quite quickly with little standing around and is probably not being reheated.

Nutrition If your food is poor or limited in availability, if you're travelling hard and fast and therefore missing meals, or if you simply lose your appetite, you can soon start to lose weight and place your health at risk.

Make sure your diet is well balanced. Eggs, tofu, beans, lentils and nuts are all safe ways to get protein. Fruit you can peel (eg bananas, oranges or mandarins) is always safe and a good source of vitamins. Try to eat plenty of grains (rice) and bread. Remember that although food is generally safer if it is cooked well, overcooked food loses much of its nutritional value. If your diet isn't well balanced or if your food intake is insufficient, it's a good idea to take vitamin and iron pills.

In hot weather make sure you drink enough – don't rely on feeling thirsty to indicate when you should drink. Not needing to urinate or very dark yellow urine is a danger sign. Always carry a water bottle with you on long trips. Excessive sweating can lead to loss of salt and therefore muscle cramping. Salt tablets are not a good idea as a preventative, but in places where salt is not used much adding salt to food can help.

Everyday Health A normal body temperature is 98.6°F or 37°C; more than 2°C higher is a 'high' fever. A normal adult pulse rate is 60 to 80 per minute (children 80 to 100, babies 100 to 140). You should know how to take a temperature and a pulse rate. As a general rule the pulse increases about 20 beats per minute for each °C rise in fever.

Respiration (breathing) rate is also an indicator of illness. Count the number of breaths per minute: between 12 and 20 is normal for adults and older children (up to 30 for younger children, 40 for babies). People with a high fever or serious respiratory illness (like pneumonia) breathe more quickly than normal. More than 40 shallow breaths a minute usually means pneumonia.

In countries with safe water and excellent human waste disposal systems we often take good health for granted. In years gone by, when public health facilities were not as good as they are today, certain rules attached to eating and drinking were observed, eg washing your hands before a meal. It is important for people travelling in areas of poor sanitation to be aware of this and adjust their own personal hygiene habits.

Clean your teeth with purified water rather than straight from the tap. Avoid climatic extremes: keep out of the sun when it's hot, dress warmly when it's cold. Avoid potential diseases by dressing sensibly. You can get worm infections through walking barefoot or dangerous coral cuts by walking over coral without shoes. You can avoid insect bites by covering bare skin when insects are around, by screening windows or beds or by using insect repellents. Seek local advice: if you're told the water is unsafe due to jellyfish, crocodiles or bilharzia, don't go in. In situations where there is no information, discretion is the better part of valour.

Medical Problems & Treatment

Potential medical problems can be broken down into several areas. First there are the climatic and geographical considerations – problems caused by extremes of temperature, altitude or motion. Then there are diseases and illnesses caused through poor environmental sanitation, insect bites or stings, and animal or human contact. Simple cuts, bites or scratches can also cause problems.

Self-diagnosis and treatment can be risky, so wherever possible seek qualified help. Although we do give treatment dosages in this section, they are for emergency use only. Medical advice should be sought where possible before administering any drugs.

An embassy or consulate can usually recommend a good place to go for such advice. So can five-star hotels, although they often recommend doctors with five-star prices. (This is when that medical insurance really comes in useful!) In some places standards of medical attention are so low that for some ailments the best advice is to get on a plane and go somewhere else.

Climatic & Geographical Considerations

Sunburn In the tropics you can get sunburnt surprisingly quickly, even through cloud. Use a sunscreen and take extra care to cover areas which don't normally see sun – eg, your feet. A hat provides added protection, and you should also use zinc cream or some other barrier cream for your nose and lips. Calamine lotion is good for mild sunburn.

Prickly Heat Prickly heat is an itchy rash caused by excessive perspiration trapped under the skin. It usually strikes people who have just arrived in a hot climate and whose pores have not yet opened sufficiently to cope with greater sweating. Keeping cool but bathing often, using a mild talcum powder or even resorting to air-conditioning may help until you acclimatise.

Heat Exhaustion Dehydration or salt deficiency can cause heat exhaustion. Take time to acclimatise to high temperatures and make sure you get sufficient liquids. Salt deficiency is characterised by fatigue, lethargy, headaches, giddiness and muscle cramps and in this case salt tablets may help. Vomiting or diarrhoea can deplete your liquid and salt levels..

Anhydrotic heat exhaustion, caused by an inability to sweat, is quite rare. Unlike the other forms of heat exhaustion it is likely to strike people who have been in a hot climate for some time, rather than newcomers.

Heat Stroke This serious, sometimes fatal, condition can occur if the body's heat-regulating mechanism breaks down and the body temperature rises to dangerous levels. Long, continuous periods of exposure to high temperatures can leave you vulnerable to heat stroke. You should avoid excessive alcohol or strenuous activity when you first arrive in a hot climate.

The symptoms are feeling unwell, not sweating very much or at all and a high body temperature ($39°C$ to $41°C$). Where sweating has ceased the skin becomes flushed and red. Severe, throbbing headaches and lack of coordination will also occur, and the sufferer may be confused or aggressive. Eventually the victim will become delirious or convulse. Hospitalisation is essential, but meanwhile get victims out of the sun, remove their clothing, cover them with a wet sheet or towel and then fan continually.

Fungal Infections Hot-weather fungal infections are most likely to occur on the scalp, between the toes or fingers (athlete's foot), in the groin (jock itch or crotch rot) and on the body (ringworm). You get ringworm (which is a fungal infection, not a worm) from infected animals or by walking on damp areas, like shower floors.

To prevent fungal infections wear loose, comfortable clothes, avoid artificial fibres, wash frequently and dry carefully. If you do get an infection, wash the infected area daily with a disinfectant or medicated soap and water, and rinse and dry well. Apply an antifungal powder like the widely available Tinaderm. Try to expose the infected area to air or sunlight as much as possible and wash all towels and underwear in hot water as well as changing them often.

Cold Too much cold is just as dangerous as too much heat, particularly if it leads to hypothermia. If you are trekking at high altitudes or simply taking a long bus trip over mountains, particularly at night, be prepared. In Thailand this is usually only a potential problem in the northern and north-eastern areas.

Hypothermia occurs when the body loses heat faster than it can produce it and the core temperature of the body falls. It is surprisingly easy to progress from very cold to dangerously cold due to a combination of wind, wet clothing, fatigue and hunger, even if the air temperature is above freezing. It is best to dress in layers; silk, wool and some of the new artificial fibres are all good insulating materials. A hat is important, as a lot of heat is lost through the head. A strong, waterproof outer layer is essential, as keeping dry is vital. Carry basic supplies, including food containing simple sugars to generate heat quickly and lots of fluid to drink.

Symptoms of hypothermia are exhaustion, numb skin (particularly toes and fingers), shivering, slurred speech, irrational or violent behaviour, lethargy, stumbling, dizzy spells, muscle cramps and violent bursts of energy. Irrationality may take the form of sufferers claiming they are warm and trying to take off their clothes.

To treat hypothermia, first get the person out of the wind and/or rain, remove their clothing if it's wet and replace it with dry, warm clothing. Give them hot liquids – not alcohol – and some high-kilojoule, easily digestible food. This should be enough for the early stages of hypothermia, but if it has gone further it may be necessary to place victims in warm sleeping bags and get in with them. Do not rub victims but place them near a fire or remove their wet clothes in the wind. If possible, place a sufferer in a warm (not hot) bath.

Motion Sickness Eating lightly before and during a trip will reduce the chances of motion sickness. If you are prone to motion sickness try to find a place that minimises disturbance – near the wing on aircraft, close to midships on boats, near the centre on buses. Fresh air usually helps, reading or cigarette smoke doesn't. Commercial anti-motion-sickness preparations, which can cause drowsiness, have to be taken before the trip commences; when you're feeling sick it's too late. Ginger is a natural preventative and is available in capsule form.

Jet Lag Jet lag is experienced when a person travels by air across more than three time zones (each time zone usually represents a one-hour time difference). It occurs because many of the functions of the human body (such as body temperature, pulse rate and emptying of the bladder and bowels) are regulated by internal 24-hour cycles called circadian rhythms. When we travel long distances rapidly, our bodies take time to adjust to the 'new time' of our destination, and we may experience fatigue, disorientation, insomnia, anxiety, impaired concentration and loss of appetite. These effects will usually be gone within three days of arrival, but there are ways of minimising the impact of jet lag:

1. Rest for a couple of days prior to departure; this means you'll have to be organised (ie no last-minute dashes for travellers' cheques, passports etc) and that you should avoid late nights before you commence a long flight.
2. Try to select flight schedules that minimise sleep deprivation; arriving late in the day means you can go to sleep soon after you arrive. For very long flights, try to organise a stopover.
3. Avoid excessive eating (which bloats the stomach) and alcohol (which causes dehydration) during the flight. Instead, drink plenty of non-carbonated non-alcoholic drinks such as fruit juice or water.
4. Avoid smoking, as this reduces the amount of oxygen in the aeroplane cabin even further and causes greater fatigue.
5. Make yourself comfortable by wearing loose-fitting clothes and perhaps bringing an eye mask and ear plugs to help you sleep.

A drug called melatonin, available over the counter in many countries (often at health food shops), has recently been shown to cut the intensity and longevity of jet lag by 50% or more. The recommended dosage is 75 mg starting the night before you fly and every night before you go to bed after arrival until you've adjusted to the new time zone.

Diseases of Poor Sanitation

Diarrhoea A change of water, food or climate can all cause the runs; diarrhoea caused by contaminated food or water is more serious. Despite all your precautions you may still have a bout of mild travellers' diarrhoea but a few rushed toilet trips with no other symptoms is not indicative of a serious problem. Moderate diarrhoea, involving half a dozen loose movements in a day, is more of a nuisance. Dehydration is the main danger with any diarrhoea, particularly for children where dehydration can occur quite quickly. Fluid replacement remains the mainstay of management. Weak black tea with a little sugar, soda water, or soft drinks allowed to go flat and diluted 50% with water are all good. With severe diarrhoea a rehydrating solution is necessary to replace minerals and salts. Commercially available ORS (oral rehydration salts) is very useful; add the contents of one sachet to a litre of boiled or bottled water. In an emergency you can make up a solution of eight teaspoons of sugar to a litre of boiled water and provide salted cracker biscuits at the same time. You should stick to a bland diet as you recover.

Lomotil or Imodium can be used to bring relief from the symptoms, although they do not actually cure the problem. Only use these drugs if absolutely necessary – eg, if you *must* travel. For children Imodium is preferable, but under all circumstances fluid replacement is the main message. Do not use these drugs if the person has a high fever or is severely dehydrated.

In certain situations antibiotics may be indicated:

- Watery diarrhoea with blood and mucus. (Gut-paralysing drugs like Imodium or Lomotil should be avoided in this situation.)
- Watery diarrhoea with fever and lethargy.
- Persistent diarrhoea for more than five days.
- Severe diarrhoea, if it is logistically difficult to stay in one place.

The recommended drugs (adults only) are either norfloxacin 400mg twice daily for three days or ciprofloxacin 500mg twice daily for three days.

The drug bismuth subsalicylate has also been used successfully. It is not available in Australia. The dosage for adults is two tablets or 30 ml; for children it is one tablet or 10 ml. This dose can be repeated every 30 minutes to one hour, with no more than eight doses in a 24-hour period.

The drug of choice for children is co-trimoxazole (Bactrim, Septrin, Resprim) with dosage dependent on weight. A three-day course is also given.

Ampicillin has been recommended in the past and may still be an alternative.

Giardiasis The parasite causing this intestinal disorder is present in contaminated water. The symptoms are stomach cramps, nausea, a bloated stomach, watery, foul-smelling diarrhoea and frequent gas. Giardiasis can appear several weeks after you have been exposed to the parasite. The symptoms may disappear for a few days and then return; this can go on for several weeks. Tinidazole, known as Fasigyn, or metronidazole (Flagyl) are the recommended drugs for treatment. Either can be used in a single treatment dose. Antibiotics are of no use.

Dysentery This serious illness is caused by contaminated food or water and is characterised by severe diarrhoea, often with blood or mucus in the stool. There are two kinds of dysentery. Bacillary dysentery is characterised by a high fever and rapid onset; headache, vomiting and stomach pains are also symptoms. It generally does not last longer than a week, but it is highly contagious.

Amoebic dysentery is often more gradual in the onset of symptoms, with cramping abdominal pain and vomiting less likely; fever may not be present. It is not a self-limiting disease: it will persist until treated and can recur and cause long-term health problems.

A stool test is necessary to diagnose which kind of dysentery you have, so you should seek medical help urgently. In case of an emergency the drugs norfloxacin or ciprofloxacin can be used as presumptive treatment for bacillary dysentery, and metronidazole (Flagyl) for amoebic dysentery.

If you're unable to find either of these drugs then a useful alternative is co-trimoxazole 160/800mg (Bactrim, Septrin, Resprim) twice daily for seven days. This is a sulfa drug and must not be used in people with a known sulfa allergy.

In the case of children, a reasonable first-line treatment is the drug co-trimoxazole.

For amoebic dysentery, the recommended adult dosage of metronidazole (Flagyl) is one 750 mg to 800 mg capsule three times daily for five days. Children aged between eight and 12 years should have half the adult dose; the dosage for younger children is one-third the adult dose.

An alternative to Flagyl is Fasigyn, taken as a two-gram daily dose for three days. Alcohol must be avoided during treatment and for 48 hours afterwards.

Cholera Cholera vaccination is not very effective. The bacteria responsible for this disease are waterborne, so that attention to the rules of eating and drinking should prtect the traveller.

Outbreaks of cholera are generally widely reported, so you can avoid such problem areas. The disease is characterised by a sudden onset of acute diarrhoea with 'rice water' stools, vomiting, muscular cramps, and extreme weakness. You need medical help – but treat for dehydration, which can be extreme, and if there is an appreciable delay in getting to hospital then begin taking tetracycline. The adult dose is 250mg four times daily. It is not recommended in children aged eight years or under nor in pregnant women. An alternative drug would be Ampicillin. Remember that while antibiotics might kill the bacteria, it is a toxin produced by the bacteria which causes the massive fluid loss. Fluid replacement is by far the most important aspect of treatment.

Viral Gastroenteritis This is caused not by bacteria but, as the name suggests, by a virus. It is characterised by stomach cramps, diarrhoea, and sometimes by vomiting and/or a slight fever. All you can do is rest and drink lots of fluids.

Hepatitis Hepatitis A is a very common problem amongst travellers to areas with poor sanitation. With good water and adequate sewage disposal in most industrialised countries since the 1940s, very few young adults now have any natural immunity and must be protected. Protection is through the new vaccine Havrix or the antibody gammaglobulin. The antibody is short-lasting.

The disease is spread by contaminated food or water. The symptoms are fever, chills, headache, fatigue, feelings of weakness and aches and pains, followed by loss of appetite, nausea, vomiting, abdominal pain, dark urine, light coloured faeces, jaundiced skin and the whites of the eyes may turn yellow. In some cases you may feel unwell, tired, have no appetite, experience aches and pains and be jaundiced. You should seek medical advice, but in general there is not much you can do apart from rest, drink lots of fluids, eat lightly and avoid fatty foods. People who have had hepatitis must forgo alcohol for six months after the illness, as hepatitis attacks the liver and it needs that amount of time to recover.

Hepatitis B, which used to be called serum hepatitis, is spread through contact with infected blood, blood products or bodily fluids, eg through sexual contact, unsterilised needles and blood transfusions. Other risk situations include having a shave or tattoo in a local shop, or having your ears pierced. The symptoms of type B are much the same as type A except that they are more severe and may lead to irreparable liver damage or even liver cancer. Although there is no treatment for hepatitis B, an effective prophylactic vaccine is readily available in most countries. The immunisation schedule requires two injections at least a month apart followed by a third dose five months after the second. Persons who should receive a hepatitis B vaccination include anyone who anticipates contact with blood or other bodily secretions, either as a health care worker or through sexual contact with the local population, particularly those who intend to stay in the country for a long period.

Hepatitis Non-A Non-B is a blanket term formerly used for several different strains of hepatitis, which have now been separately identified. Hepatitis C is similar to B but is less common. Hepatitis D (the 'delta particle') is also similar to B and always occurs in concert with it; its occurrence is currently limited to IV drug users. Hepatitis E, however, is similar to A and is spread in the same manner, by water or food contamination.

Tests are available for these strands, but are very expensive. Travellers shouldn't be too paranoid about this apparent proliferation of hepatitis strains; they are fairly rare (so far) and following the same precautions as for A and B should be all that's necessary to avoid them.

Typhoid Typhoid fever is another gut infection that travels the faecal-oral route – ie, contaminated water and food are responsible. Vaccination against typhoid is not totally effective and it is one of the most dangerous infections, so medical help must be sought.

In its early stages typhoid resembles many other illnesses: sufferers may feel like they have a bad cold or flu on the way, as early symptoms are a headache, a sore throat, and a fever which rises a little each day until it is around 40°C or more. The victim's pulse is often slow relative to the degree of fever present and gets slower as the fever rises – unlike a normal fever where the pulse increases. There may also be vomiting, diarrhoea or constipation.

In the second week the high fever and slow pulse continue and a few pink spots may appear on the body; trembling, delirium, weakness, weight loss and dehydration are other symptoms. If there are no further complications, the fever and other symptoms will slowly go during the third week.

However you must get medical help before this because pneumonia (acute infection of the lungs) or peritonitis (perforated bowel) are common complications, and because typhoid is very infectious. The fever should be treated by keeping the victim cool and dehydration should also be watched for.

The drug of choice is ciprofloxacin at a dose of one gram daily for 14 days. It is quite expensive and may not be available. The alternative, chloramphenicol, has been the mainstay of treatment for many years. In many countries it is still the recommended antibiotic but there are fewer side affects with Ampicillin. The adult dosage is two 250 mg capsules, four times a day. Children aged between eight and 12 years should have half the adult dose; younger children should have one-third the adult dose.

People who are allergic to penicillin should not be given Ampicillin.

Worms These parasites are most common in rural, tropical areas and a stool test when you return home is not a bad idea. They can be present on unwashed vegetables or in undercooked meat and you can pick them up through your skin by walking in bare feet. Infestations may not show up for some time, and although they are generally not serious, if left untreated they can cause severe health problems. A stool test is necessary to pinpoint the problem and medication is often available over the counter.

Schistosomiasis Also known as 'blood flukes', this disease is caused by tiny flatworms that burrow their way through the skin and enter the bloodstream. Humans contact the worms when swimming or bathing in contaminated fresh water (the flukes can't survive in salt water). Symptoms include a rash or skin irritation where the worm larvae have penetrated the skin. The rash/irritation disappears after a few days and there are no symptoms for several weeks until the flukes mature in the bloodstream; then fever, chills, weakness and another rash affect the victim, sometimes along with painful or bloody urination. If left untreated, the disease may result in liver, spleen and lymph-node enlargement, and in advanced cases may lead to irreversible damage to organs and the central nervous system.

The overall risk for this disease is quite low, but it's highest in the southern reaches of the Maekhong River and in the lakes of north-east Thailand – avoid swimming or bathing in these waterways. If submersion is for some reasons unavoidable, vigorous towel-drying reduces the risk of penetration. If schistosomiasis symptoms appear, consult a physician; the usual treatment is a regimen of praziquantel (often sold as Biltricide).

Opisthorchiasis Also called 'liver flukes', these are tiny worms that are occasionally present in freshwater fish. The main risk comes from eating raw or undercooked fish. Travellers should in particular avoid eating *plaa r a* (sometimes called *paa daek* in north-east Thailand), an unpasteurised fermented fish used as an accompaniment for rice in the north-east. Plaa r a is not commonly served in restaurants, but is common in rural areas of the north-east, where it's considered a great delicacy. The Thai government is currently trying to discourage north-easterners from eating plaa r a or other uncooked fish products. A common roadside billboard in the region these days reads *isāan mâi kin plaa dìp* or 'north-eastern Thailand doesn't eat raw fish'.

Liver flukes *(wiwâat bai tàp* in Thai) are endemic to villages around Sakon Nakhon Province's Nong Han, the largest natural lake in Thailand. Don't swim in this lake! (As with blood flukes, liver flukes can bore into the skin.) A much less common way to contract liver flukes is through swimming in rivers. The only other known area where the flukes might be contracted by swimming in contaminated waters is in the southern reaches of the Maekhong River.

The intensity of symptoms depends very much on how many of the flukes get into your body. At low levels, there are virtually no symptoms at all; at higher levels, an overall fatigue, low-grade fever and swollen or tender liver (or general abdominal pain) are the usual symptoms, along with worms or worm eggs in the faeces. Persons suspected of having liver flukes should have a stool sample analysed by a competent doctor or clinic. The usual medication is 25 mg per kg of body weight of praziquantel (Biltricide) three times daily after meals for two days.

Diseases Spread by People & Animals

Tetanus This potentially fatal disease is found in undeveloped tropical areas. It is difficult to treat but is preventable with immunisation. Tetanus occurs when a wound becomes infected by a germ which lives in the faeces of animals or people, so clean all cuts, punctures or animal bites. Tetanus is also known as lockjaw, and the first symptom may be discomfort in swallowing, or stiffening of the jaw and neck; this is followed by painful convulsions of the jaw and whole body.

Rabies Rabies is found in many countries and is caused by a bite or scratch by an infected animal. Dogs are noted carriers as are monkeys and cats. Any bite, scratch or even lick from a warm-blooded, furry animal should be cleaned immediately and thoroughly. Scrub with soap and running water, and then clean with an alcohol solution. If there is any possibility that the animal is infected medical help should be sought immediately. Even if the animal is not rabid, all bites should be treated seriously as they can become infected or can result in tetanus. A rabies vaccination is now available and should be considered if you are in a high-risk category – eg, if you intend to explore caves (bat bites could be dangerous) or work with animals.

Tuberculosis (TB) Although this disease is widespread in many developing countries, it is not a serious risk to travellers. Young children are more susceptible than adults and vaccination is a sensible precaution for children under 12 travelling in endemic areas. TB is commonly spread by coughing or by unpasteurised dairy products from infected cows. Milk that has been boiled is safe to drink; the souring of milk to make yoghurt or cheese also kills the bacilli.

Bilharzia Bilharzia is carried in water by minute worms. The larvae infect certain varieties of freshwater snails, found in rivers, streams, lakes and particularly behind dams. The worms multiply and are eventually discharged into the water surrounding the snails.

They attach themselves to your intestines or bladder, where they produce large numbers of eggs. The worm enters through the skin, and the first symptom may be a tingling and sometimes a light rash around the area where it entered. Weeks later, when the worm is busy producing eggs, a high fever may develop. A general feeling of being unwell may be the first symptom; once the disease is established abdominal pain and blood in the urine are other signs.

Avoiding swimming or bathing in fresh water where bilharzia is present is the main method of preventing the disease. Even deep water can be infected. If you do get wet, dry off quickly and dry your clothes as well. Seek medical attention if you have been exposed to the disease and tell the doctor your suspicions, as bilharzia in the early stages can be confused with malaria or typhoid. If you cannot get medical help immediately, praziquantel (Biltricide) is the recommended treatment. The recommended dosage is 40mg/kg in divided doses over one day. Niridazole is an alternative drug.

Diphtheria Diphtheria can be a skin infection or a more dangerous throat infection. It is spread by contaminated dust contacting the skin or by the inhalation of infected cough or sneeze droplets. Frequent washing and keeping the skin dry will help prevent skin infection. A vaccination is available to prevent the throat infection.

Sexually Transmitted Diseases Sexual contact with an infected sexual partner spreads these diseases. While abstinence is the only 100% preventative, using latex condoms is also effective. In Thailand gonorrhoea, non-specific urethritis (NSU) and syphilis are the most common of these diseases; sores, blisters or rashes around the genitals, discharges or pain when urinating are common symptoms. Symptoms may be less marked or not observed at all in women. Syphilis symptoms eventually disappear completely but the disease continues and can cause severe problems in later years. The treatment of gonorrhoea and syphilis is by antibiotics.

There are numerous other sexually transmitted diseases, for most of which effective treatment is available. However, there is no cure for herpes and there is also currently no cure for AIDS.

HIV/AIDS HIV, the Human Immunodeficiency Virus, could develop into AIDS (Acquired Immune Deficiency Syndrome). HIV is a major health problem in Thailand although the overall incidence of infection has slowed over recent years. Any exposure to blood, blood products or bodily fluids may put the individual at risk. In Thailand transmission is predominantly through heterosexual sexual activity; the second most common source of HIV infection is intravenous injection by drug addicts who share needles. Apart from abstinence, the most effective preventative is always to practise safe sex using condoms. It is impossible to detect the HIV-positive status of an otherwise healthy-looking person without a blood test.

The Thai phrase for 'condom' is *thŭng anaamai*. Latex condoms are more effective than animal-membrane condoms in preventing disease transmission; to specify latex condoms ask for *thŭng yaang anaamai*. Good-quality latex condoms are distributed free by offices of the Ministry of Public Health throughout the country – they come in numbered sizes, like shoes! Condoms can also be purchased at any pharmacy, but those issued by the Ministry of Public Health are considered the most effective; a recent ministry survey found that around 11% of

AIDS in Thailand

Because HIV infections are often associated with sexual contact and Thailand has an international reputation for illicit night-time activities, rumours regarding the status of AIDS in the country vary wildly. Some think the threat is greatly exaggerated while others are convinced the Thai government is involved in a massive cover-up of the epidemic. The risks of contracting the disease are very real but should be placed in perspective.

For the record, as of June 1994 the World Health Organisation (WHO) estimated there were approximately 500,000 HIV-positive cases in Thailand (the country's total population is approximately 56 million), a number also supported by the country's Ministry of Health research. To date, 5990 AIDS deaths have been documented in the country but the number will undoubtedly have increased by the time you read this. Eighty per cent of all reported infections are thought to be associated with sexual transmission. Thai women and their children are now the highest risk group, as infection has moved from the homosexual population in the early 1980s to intravenous drug users mid-decade and then from prostitutes in the late 1980s to the general population. In Thailand, homosexual/bisexual males now have the lowest incidence of infection next to blood-transfusion recipients, dispelling the myth that AIDS is a 'gay disease'. In 1991, for example, Phrae Province health authorities recorded four HIV-positive male homosexuals and 414 HIV-positive female prostitutes.

Thus the main risk to the casual male visitor is HIV transmission via sexual contact with prostitutes or any Thai female whose HIV infection status is unknown. According to AIDS researchers, the percentage of HIV-positive prostitutes is much higher in rural areas than in Bangkok, especially in northern Thailand – which, for Thai males, is the 'capital' of Thai prostitution. A 1993 provincial health investigation, for example, found that 70% of prostitutes tested in Chiang Rai Province were HIV-positive; northern Thailand in general accounts for about 75% of all infections reported. The apparent reason for this is that Bangkok sex workers are much more likely to insist on condom use than their provincial counterparts. Thai male customers, on the other hand, are much less likely to use condoms than farang customers, which explains why even Pattaya – the capital for sex service to foreigners – shows a lower rate of infection than anywhere in the north. Of the estimated 210,000 full-time sex workers in the country, the vast majority are patronised by Thai customers, and since Thai males visit prostitutes an average of twice a month the virus is now finding its way to their wives and girlfriends. A recent American study concluded that 12% of military draftees stationed outside Bangkok were HIV-infected.

For female visitors the main risk is having sexual contact with any male – Thai or farang – known to have had intercourse with Thai prostitutes since the mid-1980s. For both genders, the second-highest risk activity would be any use of unsterilised needles, especially in illicit intravenous drug use.

The Thai government is not involved in covering up the epidemic and is in fact very keen to

commercial Thai condoms were damaged, mostly due to improper storage.

HIV/AIDS can also be spread through infected blood transfusions although in Thailand this risk is virtually nil due to vigorous blood-screening procedures. It can also be spread by dirty needles – vaccinations, acupuncture, tattooing and ear or nose piercing can potentially be as dangerous as intravenous drug use if the equipment is not clean. If you do need an injection, ask to see the syringe unwrapped in front of you, or better still, take a needle and syringe pack with you overseas – it is a cheap insurance package against infection with HIV.

Fear of HIV infection should never preclude treatment for serious medical conditions. Although there may be a risk of infection, it is very small indeed.

Insect-Borne Diseases

Malaria This serious disease is spread by mosquito bites. If you are travelling in endemic areas it is extremely important to take malarial prophylactics. Symptoms include headaches, fever, chills and sweating which may subside and recur. Without treatment malaria can develop more serious, potentially fatal effects.

make HIV/AIDS statistics public and to educate the public about the disease and how to prevent transmission. Even the TAT is now addressing the issue in their annual reports. WHO officials report that Thailand has done more than any other country in South-East Asia to combat the AIDS threat, including following a WHO-approved national AIDS-prevention campaign since 1988. Radio and TV ads, public billboards and AIDS-awareness marches became everyday occurrences much sooner in Thailand than in Europe or the USA relative to the occurrence of the country's first known AIDS-related death (1984).

On a local level, Ministry of Public Health offices are undertaking intensive public awareness programmes, conducting regular blood tests in brothels, massage parlours and coffee houses and distributing free condoms at their office locations as well as at sex service locations (including hotels). But health officials don't have the power to close sex service operations; even if they could, officials say this would only force prostitution underground where it would be even more difficult to monitor and educate sex workers.

As with their success in sharply reducing population growth in the 1970s, the ministry's aggressive AIDS campaign in the 1980s and 1990s seems to be having a positive effect. A survey conducted by Thailand's Epidemiology Department during 1993 revealed that the HIV infection rate (the frequency with which new infections develop) among sex workers had dropped 60% over the previous four years. This has been confirmed by long-term Population & Community Development Association (PDA) studies, which note that in the mid to late 1980s HIV figures in Thailand were doubling every six months, a rate which soon slowed to doubling every year, and is now doubling every two years. Between 1991 and 1994 Thailand's overall infection rate dropped 77%, an achievement that earned PDA director Mechai Viravaidya the prestigious Magsaysay Award in 1994. Since the 1970s, when Mechai initiated a vigorous national programme aimed at educating the public about contraception, the most common Thai nickname for 'condom' has been 'Mechai'. At last report an estimated 600 new infections per day were occurring, a rate Thai health officials are confident they can cut in half by the end of the 1990s.

Although the following comparisons shouldn't be taken to mean that precautions aren't absolutely mandatory, WHO officials estimate Thailand has a lower per-capita HIV infection rate than Australia, Switzerland or the USA. Even among Asian countries, WHO reports the infection rate and projected vulnerability for AIDS are now higher in India, Pakistan, Bangladesh and the Philippines. As elsewhere around the globe, however, absolute numbers will only increase with time until/unless a cure is discovered.

In May 1994 the Public Health Ministry – in a somewhat controversial move – authorised a US biomedical company to begin testing a new AIDS vaccine in Thailand, the results of which won't be available for several years to come. In the meantime, behaviour modification is the best strategy available for combating the spread of the disease.

One of Thailand's chief accomplishments in the war against HIV transmission is that the medical blood supply is now considered safe, thanks to vigorous screening procedures. ∎

Antimalarial drugs do not prevent you from being infected but kill the parasites during a stage in their development.

There are a number of different types of malaria. The one of most concern is falciparum malaria, which is responsible for the very serious cerebral malaria. At the moment Thailand's high-risk areas include northern Kanchanaburi Province (especially Thung Yai Naresuan Wildlife Sanctuary) and parts of Trat Province along the Cambodian border (including Ko Chang). According to the CDC and to Thailand's Ministry of Public Health, there is virtually no risk of malaria in urban areas.

The problem in recent years has been the emergence of increasing resistance to commonly used antimalarials like chloroquine, maloprim and proguanil. Newer drugs such as mefloquine (Lariam) and doxycycline (Vibramycin, Doryx) are often recommended for chloroquine and multidrug resistant areas, though in Thailand most strains are also resistant to these. Expert advice should be sought, as there are many factors to consider when deciding on the type of antimalarial medication, including the area to be visited, the risk of exposure to malaria-carrying mosquitoes, your current medical condition, and your age and pregnancy status. It is also important to discuss the side-effect profile of the medication, so you can work out some level of risk-versus-benefit ratio. It is also very important to be sure of the correct dosage of the medication prescribed to you. Some people have inadvertently taken weekly medication (chloroquine) on a daily basis, with disastrous effects. While discussing dosages for prevention of malaria, it is often advisable to include the dosages required for treatment, especially if your trip is through a high-risk area that would isolate you from medical care.

All commonly prescribed malarial suppressants (eg chloroquine) have the potential to cause side effects – chloroquine is in fact now completely banned in Japan. Mefloquine affects motor skills and, although introduced only seven years ago, is now estimated to be 70% ineffective in Thailand due to the quick buildup of drug-resistant strains.

In Thailand, where malaria tends to be resistant to most if not all the previously mentioned prophylactics, the Chinese herb *qinghao* – or its chemical derivative artemether – has proven to be very effective. Its use in Thailand (and other mainland South-East Asian countries) has recently been endorsed by the UN Tropical Disease Programme as well as the WHO director-general.

The main messages are:

1. Primary prevention must always be in the form of mosquito avoidance measures. The mosquitoes (Anopheles) that transmit malaria bite from dusk to dawn and during this period travellers are advised to:
   • wear light coloured clothing
   • wear long pants and long sleeved shirts
   • use mosquito repellents containing the compound DEET on exposed areas – commercial repellents containing no more than 35% DEET can be purchased at well-stocked Thai pharmacies
   • avoid highly scented perfumes or aftershave
   • use a mosquito net – it may be worth taking your own
2. While no antimalarial is 100% effective, taking the most appropriate drug significantly reduces the risk of contracting the disease.

3. No one should ever die from malaria. It can be diagnosed by a simple blood test. Symptoms range from fever, chills and sweating, headache and abdominal pains to a vague feeling of ill-health, so seek examination immediately if there is any suggestion of malaria.

Contrary to popular belief, once a traveller contracts malaria he/she does not have it for life. One of the parasites may lie dormant in the liver but this can also be eradicated using a specific medication. Malaria is curable, as long as the traveller seeks medical help when symptoms occur.

For those with an allergy or aversion to synthetic repellents, citronella makes a good substitute. Mosquito coils *(yaa kan yung bàep jùt)* do an excellent job of repelling mosquitoes in your room and are readily available in Thailand. Day mosquitoes do not carry malaria, so it is only in the night that you have to worry – peak biting hours are a few hours after dusk and a few hours before dawn.

Like many other tropical diseases, malaria is frequently mis-diagnosed in Western countries. If you should develop the symptoms after a return to your home country, be sure to seek medical attention immediately and inform your doctor that you may have been exposed to malaria.

Dengue Fever In some areas of Thailand there is a risk, albeit low, of contracting dengue fever via mosquito transmission. This time it's a day variety (Aedes) you have to worry about. Like malaria, dengue fever seems to be on the increase throughout tropical Asia in recent years. Dengue is found in urban as well as rural areas, especially in areas of human habitation (often indoors) where there is standing water.

Unlike malaria, dengue fever is caused by a virus and there is no chemical prophylactic or vaccination against it. In Thailand there are four strains (serotypes) of dengue and once you've had one you usually develop an immunity specific to that strain. The symptoms come on suddenly and include high fever, severe headache and heavy joint and muscle pain (hence its older name 'break-bone fever'), followed a few days later by a rash that spreads from the torso to the arms, legs and face. Various risk factors such as age, immunity and viral strain may mitigate these symptoms so that they are less severe or last only a few days. Even when the basic symptoms are short-lived, it can take several weeks to recover fully from the resultant weakness.

In rare cases dengue may develop into a more severe condition known as dengue haemorrhagic fever (DHF), or dengue toxic shock syndrome, which is fatal. DHF is most common among Asian children under 15 years who are undergoing a second dengue infection, so the risk of DHF for most international travellers is very low.

Although the latest estimate says you have only a one in 10,000 chance of contracting dengue when bitten by the Aedes mosquito (ie only one in 10,000 Aedes mosquitoes in Thailand is infectious), I have personally known several travellers (including myself) who have come down with the disease over the years. By contrast I've only ever met a couple of farangs who contracted malaria in Thailand. Probably the fact that more people are outdoors in the daytime means exposure is greater. The best way to prevent dengue, as with malaria, is to take care not to be bitten by mosquitoes.

The only treatment for dengue is bed rest, constant rehydration and acetaminophen (Tylenol, Panadol). Avoid aspirin, which increases the risk of haemorrhaging. Hospital supervision is necessary in extreme cases.

Japanese Encephalitis Although long endemic to tropical Asia (as well as China, Korea and Japan), rainy-season epidemics in northern Thailand and Vietnam during the last decade have slightly increased the risk for travellers. A night-biting mosquito (Culex) is the carrier for this disease and the risk is said to be greatest in rural zones near areas where pigs are raised or rice is grown, since pigs and certain wild birds, whose habitat may include rice fields, serve as reservoirs for the virus.

Persons who may be at risk in Thailand are those who will be spending long periods of time in rural areas during the rainy season (July to October). If you belong to this group, you may want to get a Japanese encephalitis vaccination. At the time of writing, the vaccine is only produced in Japan but is available in most European and Asian capitals (but not in the USA). Check with the government health service in your home country before you leave to see if it's available; if not, arrange to be vaccinated in Bangkok, Hong Kong or Singapore, where the vaccine is easy to find.

Timing is important in taking the vaccine; you must receive at least two doses seven to 10 days apart. The Center for Disease Control in Atlanta, USA, recommends a third dose 21 to 30 days after the first for improved immunity. Immunity lasts about a year, at which point it's necessary to get a booster shot; then it's every four years after that.

The symptoms of Japanese encephalitis are sudden fever, chills and headache, followed by vomiting and delirium, a strong aversion to bright light, and sore joints and muscles. Advanced cases may result in convulsions and coma. Most people who contract the virus exhibit no symptoms whatsoever.

As with other mosquito-borne diseases, the best way to prevent JE (outside of the vaccine) is to avoid being bitten.

Cuts, Bites & Stings
Cuts & Scratches Skin punctures can easily become infected in hot climates and may be difficult to heal. Treat any cut with an antiseptic such as Betadine. Where possible avoid bandages and Band-Aids, which can keep wounds wet. Coral cuts are notoriously slow to heal, as the coral injects a weak venom into the wound. Avoid coral cuts by wearing shoes when walking on reefs, and clean any cut thoroughly with sodium peroxide if available.

Bites & Stings Bee and wasp stings are usually painful rather than dangerous. Calamine lotion will give relief and ice packs will reduce the pain and swelling. There are some spiders with dangerous bites but antivenenes are usually available. Scorpion stings are notoriously painful. Scorpions often shelter in shoes or clothing.

There are various fish and other sea creatures which can sting or bite dangerously or which are dangerous to eat. Local advice is the best prevention.

Snakes To minimise your chances of being bitten always wear boots, socks and long trousers when walking through undergrowth where snakes may be present. Don't put your hands into holes and crevices, and be careful when collecting firewood.

Snake bites do not cause instantaneous death and antivenenes are usually available. Keep the victim calm and still, wrap the bitten limb tightly, as you would for a sprained ankle, and then attach a splint to immobilise it. Then seek medical help, if possible with the dead snake for identification. Don't attempt to catch the snake if there is even a remote possibility of being bitten again. Tourniquets and sucking out the poison are now comprehensively discredited.

Snakebite antivenene is available at Chulalongkorn Hospital (☎ 252-8181/9), Rama IV Rd, Bangkok.

Jellyfish Local advice is the best way of avoiding contact with these sea creatures with their stinging tentacles. Dousing in vinegar will de-activate any stingers which have not 'fired'. Calamine lotion, antihistamines and analgesics may reduce the reaction and relieve the pain.

Bedbugs & Lice Bedbugs live in various places, but particularly in dirty mattresses and bedding. Spots of blood on bedclothes or on the wall around the bed can be read as a suggestion to find another hotel. Bedbugs leave itchy bites in neat rows. Calamine lotion may help.

All lice cause itching and discomfort. They make themselves at home in your hair (head lice), your clothing (body lice) or your pubic hair (crabs). You catch lice through direct contact with infected people or by sharing combs, clothing and the like. Powder or shampoo treatment will kill the lice and infected clothing should then be washed in very hot water.

Leeches & Ticks Leeches may be present in damp rainforest conditions; they attach themselves to your skin to suck your blood. Trekkers often get them on their legs or in their boots. Salt or a lighted cigarette end will make them fall off. Do not pull them off, as the bite is then more likely to become infected. An insect repellent may keep them away. Vaseline, alcohol or oil will persuade a tick to let go. You should always check your body if you have been walking through a tick-infested area, as they can spread typhus.

Women's Health
Gynaecological Problems Poor diet, lowered resistance due to the use of antibiotics for stomach upsets and even contraceptive pills can lead to vaginal infections when travelling in hot climates. Keeping the genital area clean, and wearing skirts or loose-fitting trousers and cotton underwear will help to prevent infections.

Yeast infections, characterised by a rash, itch and discharge, can be treated with a vinegar or even lemon-juice douche or with yoghurt. Nystatin suppositories are the usual medical prescription. Trichomonas is a more serious infection; symptoms are a discharge and a burning sensation when urinating. Male sexual partners must also be treated, and if a vinegar-water douche is not effective medical attention should be sought. Metronidazole (Flagyl) is the prescribed drug.

Pregnancy Most miscarriages occur during the first three months of pregnancy, so this is the most risky time to travel as far as your own health is concerned. Miscarriage is not uncommon, and can occasionally lead to severe bleeding. The last three months should also be spent within reasonable distance of good medical care. A baby born as early as 24 weeks stands a chance of survival, but only in a good modern hospital. Pregnant women should avoid all unnecessary medication, but vaccinations and malarial prophylactics should still be taken where possible. Additional care should be taken to prevent illness and particular attention should be paid to diet and nutrition. Alcohol and nicotine, for example, should be avoided.

Women travellers often find that their periods become irregular or even cease while they're on the road. Remember that a missed period in these circumstances doesn't necessarily indicate pregnancy. There are health posts or family planning clinics in many small and large urban centres, where you can seek advice and have a urine test to determine whether you are pregnant or not.

Hospitals & Clinics
Thailand's most technically advanced hospitals are in Bangkok. In the north, Chiang Mai has the best medical care; in the north-east it's Khon Kaen and in the south Hat Yai or Phuket. Elsewhere in the country, every provincial capital has at least one hospital of varying quality as well as several public and private clinics. The best emergency health care, however, can usually be found at military hospitals (*rohng phayaabaan tha-hāan* in Thai); they will usually treat foreigners in an emergency. See the respective destination

chapters for information on specific health-care facilities.

Should you need urgent dental care, suggested contacts in Bangkok include:

Bumrungrad Medical Centre
    33 Soi 3, Sukhumvit Rd (☎ 253-0250)
Dental Polyclinic
    211/3 New Phetburi Rd (☎ 314-5070)
Ploenchit Clinic
    Maneeya Bldg, Ploenchit Rd (☎ 251-1567/8902)
Siam Dental Clinic
    412/11-2 Soi 6, Siam Square (☎ 251-6315)

For urgent eye care, the best choices are in Bangkok – the Rutnin Eye Hospital (80/1 Soi Asoke, ☎ 258-0442) or the Pirompesuy Eye Hospital (117/1 Phayathai Rd, ☎ 252-4141).

Counselling Services
Qualified professionals at Community Services of Bangkok (☎ 258-4998; 15 Soi 33, Sukhumvit Rd) offer a range of counselling services to foreign residents and newcomers to Thailand.

Members of Alcoholics Anonymous who want to contact the Bangkok group or others who are interested in AA services can call 253-6305 from 6 am to 6 pm or 256-6578 from 6 pm to 6 am for information. Weekly meetings are held at Holy Redeemer Catholic Church, 123/19 Soi Ruamrudee.

WOMEN TRAVELLERS
Everyday incidents of sexual harassment are much less common in Thailand than in India, Indonesia or Malaysia and this may lull women who have recently travelled in these countries into thinking that Thailand travel is safer than it is. Over the past seven years, several foreign women have been attacked while travelling alone in remote areas. If you're a woman travelling alone, try to pair up with other travellers when travelling at night or in remote areas. Urban areas seem relatively safe; the exception is Chiang Mai, where there have been several reports of harassment (oddly, we've had no reports from Bangkok). Make sure hotel and guesthouse rooms are secure at night – if they're

Traditional Thai Medicine

Western medical practices are for the most part restricted to modern hospitals and clinics in Thailand's towns and cities. In villages and rural areas a large number of Thais still practise various forms of traditional healing which were codified in Thailand over 500 years ago. Clinics and healers specialising in traditional Thai medicine can also be found in urban areas; many Thai doctors in fact offer a blend of international medicine – a term ethno-medical scholars prefer to 'Western medicine' – and indigenous medical systems.

Traditional Thai medical theory features many parallels with India's Ayurvedic healing tradition as well as Chinese medicine. In practice, however, Thai diagnostic and therapeutic techniques may differ significantly. Obviously influenced to some degree by these traditions, Thai medicine in turn has been the predominant influence on traditional medicine in Cambodia, Laos and Myanmar.

Most Thai medicine as practised today is based on two surviving medical texts from the Ayuthaya era, the *Scripture of Diseases* and the *Pharmacopoeia of King Narai*. Presumably many more texts were available before the Burmese sacked Ayuthaya in 1767 and destroyed the kingdom's national archives. A coexisting oral tradition passed down from healer to healer conforms to the surviving texts; other materia medica developed in the Ratanakosin (Bangkok) era are founded on both these texts and the oral tradition.

Like medical practitioners elsewhere in the world, traditional Thai physicians perform diagnoses by evaluating the pulse, heartbeat, skin colour/texture, body temperature, abnormal physical symptoms and bodily excretions (eg blood, urine, faeces) of their patients. Unlike orthodox Western doctors, Thai healers favour a holistic approach that encompasses internal, external, and psycho-spiritual conditions. Thus, once diagnosed, patients may be prescribed and issued treatments from among three broad therapeutic categories.

Herbal Medicines Traditional pharmacological therapy employs prescribed herbs, either singly or in combination, from among 700 plant varieties (plus a limited number of animal sources) which are infused, boiled, powdered or otherwise rendered into a consumable form. Common household medicines *(yaa klaang bâan* in Thai) include the root and stem of *baw-ráphét (Tinospora rumphii,* a type of woodclimber) for fever reduction, *râak cha-phluu* (Piper roots) for stomach ailments, and various *yaa hǎwm* (fragrant medicines) used as medicinal balms for muscle pain or headaches. Medicines of this type are readily available over the counter at traditional medicine shops and to a lesser extent in modern Thai pharmacies.

More complex remedies called *yaa tamráp luǎng* (royally approved/recorded medicine) are prepared and administered only by herbalists skilled in diagnosis, as the mixture and dosage must be adjusted for each patient. One of the most well-known yaa tamrap luang is *chanthá-liilaa,* a powerful remedy for respiratory infections and influenza-induced fevers.

As in the Chinese tradition, many Thai herbs find their way into regional cuisine with the intent of enhancing health as well as taste. *Phrík thai* (black pepper, *Piper nigrum*), *bai krà-phaw* (stomach leaf) and *bai maeng-lák* (a variety of basil) are common curry ingredients which have proven antacid/carminative properties. Thais eat soups containing *mará* (bitter melon) – a known febrifuge – to bring down a fever.

not, demand another room or move to another hotel/guesthouse.

Jii-Khoh Small upcountry restaurants are sometimes hang-outs for drunken *jii-khōh,* an all-purpose Thai term that refers to the teenage playboy-hoodlum-cowboy who gets his kicks by violating Thai cultural norms. These oafs sometimes bother foreign women (and men) who are trying to have a quiet meal ('Are you married?' and 'I love you' are common conversation openers). It's best to ignore them rather than try to make snappy comebacks – they won't understand them and will most likely take these responses as encouragement. If the jii-khohs persist, find another restaurant. Unfortunately restaurant proprietors will rarely do anything about such disturbances.

Massage The second and most internationally famous type of Thai medical therapy is *ráksǎa thaang nûat* (massage treatment). The extensive and highly refined Thai massage system combines characteristics of massage (stroking and kneading the muscles), chiropractice (manipulating skeletal parts) and acupressure (applying deep, consistent pressure to specific nerves, tendons, or ligaments) in order to balance the functions of the four body elements *(thâat tháng sìi)*. These four elements are: earth *(din* – solid parts of the body, including nerves, skeleton, muscles, blood vessels, tendons and ligaments); water *(náam* – blood and bodily secretions); fire *(fai* – digestion and metabolism); and air *(lom* – respiration and circulation). Borrowing from India's Ayurvedic tradition, some practitioners employ Pali-Sanskrit terms for the four bodily elements: *pathavidhatu, apodhatu, tecodhatu* and *vayodhatu*.

From the Ayuthaya period until early this century, the Thai government's Department of Health included an official massage division *(phanâek mǎw nûat)*. Under the influence of international medicine and modern hospital development, responsibility for the national propagation/maintenance of Thai massage was eventually transferred to Wat Phra Jetuphon (Wat Pho) in Bangkok, where it remains today. Traditional massage therapy has persisted most in the provinces, however, and has recently enjoyed a resurgence of popularity throughout the country.

Within the traditional Thai medical context, a massage therapist *(mǎw nûat*, literally, 'massage doctor') usually applies Thai massage together with pharmacological and/or psycho-spiritual treatments as prescribed for a specific medical problem. Nowadays many Thais also use massage as a tool for relaxation and disease prevention, rather than for specific medical problems. Massage associated with Bangkok's Turkish baths *(àap òp nûat* or 'bathe-steam-massage' in Thai) is for the most part performed for recreational or entertainment purposes only (or as an adjunct to prostitution); the techniques used are loosely based on traditional Thai massage.

For problems affecting the nerves rather than the muscular or skeletal structures, many Thais resort to *nûat jàp sên* (nerve-touch massage), a Chinese-style massage technique that works with the body's nerve meridians, much like acupuncture.

Psycho-Spiritual Healing A third aspect of traditional Thai medicine called *ráksǎa thaang nai* (inner healing) or *kâe kam kaò* (literally, 'old karma repair') includes various types of meditation or visualisation practised by the patient, as well as shamanistic rituals performed by qualified healers. These strategies represent the psycho-spiritual side of Thai medical therapy and, like massage are usually practised in conjunction with other types of treatment. With the increasing acceptance of meditation, hypnosis and biofeedback in Occidental medicine, anthropologists nowadays are less inclined to classify such metaphysical therapy as 'magico-religious', accepting them instead as potentially useful adjunct therapies.

As in the West, psycho-spiritual techniques are most commonly reserved for medical conditions with no apparent physical cause or those for which other therapies have proved unsuccessful. In Thailand they are also occasionally employed as preventive measures, as in the *bai sǐi* ceremony popular in north-eastern Thailand and Laos. This elaborate ceremony, marked by the tying of string loops around a subject's wrists, is intended to bind the 32 *khwǎn* or personal guardian spirits – each associated with a specific organ – to the individual. The ritual is often performed before a person departs on a long or distant journey, based on the reasoning that one is more susceptible to illness when away from home. ■

DANGERS & ANNOYANCES
Precautions

Although Thailand is in no way a dangerous country to visit, it's wise to be a little cautious, particularly if you're travelling alone. Solo women travellers should take special care on arrival at Bangkok International Airport, particularly at night. Don't take one of Bangkok's often very unofficial taxis (black and white licence tags) by yourself – better the THAI bus, or even the public bus. Both men and women should ensure their rooms are securely locked and bolted at night. Inspect cheap rooms with thin walls for strategic peepholes.

Take caution when leaving valuables in hotel safes. Many travellers have reported unpleasant experiences with leaving valuables in Chiang Mai guesthouses while trekking. Make sure you obtain an itemised receipt for property left with hotels or guest-houses – note the exact quantity of travellers' cheques and all other valuables.

On the road, keep zippered luggage secured with small locks, especially while travelling on buses and trains.

Credit Cards

On return to their home countries, some visitors have received huge credit-card bills for purchases (usually jewellery) charged to their cards in Bangkok while the cards had, supposedly, been secure in the hotel or guest-house safe. It's said that over the two peak months that this first began occurring, credit-card companies lost over US$20 million in Thailand – one major company had 40% of their worldwide losses here! You might consider taking your credit cards with you if you go trekking – if they're stolen on the trail at least the bandits won't be able to use them. Organised gangs in Bangkok specialise in arranging stolen credit-card purchases – in some cases they pay 'down and out' foreigners to fake the signatures.

When making credit-card purchases,

Scams

Thais are generally so friendly and laid-back that some visitors are lulled into a false sense of security that makes them particularly vulnerable to scams and con schemes of all kinds. Scammers tend to haunt areas where first-time tourists go, such as Bangkok's Grand Palace area. Though you could meet them anywhere in Thailand, the overwhelming majority of scams take place in Bangkok, with Chiang Mai a very distant second.

Most scams begin the same way: a friendly Thai male approaches a lone visitor – usually newly arrived – and strikes up a seemingly innocuous conversation. Sometimes the con man says he's a university student, other times he may claim to work for the World Bank or a similarly distinguished organisation (some conners even carry cellular phones). If you're on the way to Wat Pho or the Jim Thompson House, for example, he may tell you it's closed for a holiday. Eventually the conversation works its way around to the subject of the scam – the better con men can actually make it seem like *you* initiated the topic. That's one of the most bewildering aspects of the con – afterwards victims remember that the whole thing seemed like their idea, not the con artist's.

The scam itself almost always involves either gems or card playing. With gems, the victims find themselves invited to a gem and jewellery shop – your new-found friend is picking up some merchandise for himself and you're just along for the ride. Somewhere along the way he usually claims to have a connection – often a relative – in your home country (what a coincidence!) with whom he has a regular gem export-import business. One way or another, victims are convinced (usually they convince themselves) that they can turn a profit by arranging a gem purchase and reselling the merchandise at home. After all, the jewellery shop just happens to be offering a generous discount today – it's a government or religious holiday, or perhaps it's the shop's 10th anniversary, or maybe they just take a liking to you!

There is a seemingly infinite number of variations on the gem scam, almost all of which end up with the victim making a purchase of small, low-quality sapphires and posting them to their home countries. (If they let you walk out with them, you might return for a refund after realising you'd been taken.) Once you return home, of course, the cheap sapphires turn out to be worth much less than what you paid for them (perhaps one-tenth to one-half). A jeweller in Perth, Australia says he sees about 12 people a week who have been conned in Thailand.

Many have invested and lost virtually all their savings; some admit they had been scammed even after reading warnings in this guidebook or posted by the TAT around Bangkok. As one letter-writer concluded his story: 'So now I'm US$500 poorer and in possession of potentially worthless sapphires – a very expensive lesson into human nature.'

Even if you were somehow able to return your purchase to the gem shop in question (I knew one fellow who actually intercepted his parcel at the airport before it left Thailand), chances are slim to none they'd give a full refund. The con artist who brings the mark into the shop gets a commission of 10% to 50% per sale – the shop takes the rest.

don't let vendors take your credit card out of your sight to run it through the machine. Unscrupulous merchants have been known to rub off three or four or more receipts with one credit-card purchase; after the customer leaves the shop, they use the one legitimate receipt as a model to forge your signature on the blanks, then fill in astronomical 'purchases'. Sometimes they wait several weeks – even months – between submitting each charge receipt to the bank, so that you can't remember whether you'd been billed at the same vendor more than once.

Druggings

On trains and buses, particularly in the south, beware of friendly strangers offering cigarettes, drinks or sweets (candy). Several travellers have reported waking up with a headache sometime later to find that their valuables have disappeared. One traveller was offered what looked like a machine-wrapped, made-in-England Cadbury's chocolate. His girlfriend spat it out immediately, while he woke up nine hours later in hospital having required emergency resuscitation after his breathing nearly

---

The Thai police are usually of no help whatsoever, believing that merchants are entitled to whatever price they can get. The main victimisers are a handful of shops who get protection from certain high-ranking government officials. These officials put pressure on police not to prosecute or to take as little action as possible. Even the TAT tourist police have never been able to prosecute a Thai jeweller, even in cases of blatant, recurring gem fraud. A Thai police commissioner was recently convicted of fraud in an investigation into a jewellery theft by Thais in Saudi Arabia which resulted in the commissioner's replacing the Saudi gems with fakes!

The card-playing scam starts out much the same – a friendly stranger approaches the lone traveller on the street, strikes up a conversation and then invites you to the house or apartment of his sister (or brother-in-law, etc) for a drink or meal. After a bit of socialising a friend or relative of the con arrives on the scene; it just so happens a little high-stakes card game is planned for later that day. Like the gem scam, the card-game scam has many variations, but eventually the victim is shown some cheating tactics to use with help from the 'dealer', some practice sessions take place and finally the game gets under way with several high rollers at the table. The mark is allowed to win a few hands first, then somehow loses a few, gets bankrolled by one of the friendly Thais, and then loses the Thai's money. Suddenly your new-found buddies aren't so friendly anymore – they want the money you lost. Sometimes the con pretends to be dismayed by it all. Sooner or later you end up cashing in most or all of your travellers' cheques.

Again the police won't take any action – in this case because gambling is illegal in Thailand so you've broken the law by playing cards for money.

The common denominator in all scams of this nature is that the victims' own greed – the desire for an easy score – was their downfall. Other minor scams involve tuk-tuk drivers, hotel employees and bar girls who take new arrivals on city tours; these almost always end up in high-pressure sales situations at silk, jewellery or handicraft shops. In this case greed isn't the ruling motivation – it's simply a matter of weak sales resistance.

Follow TAT's number-one suggestion to tourists: disregard all offers of free shopping or sightseeing help from strangers – they invariably take a commission from your purchases. I would add to this: beware of deals that seem too good to be true – they're usually neither good nor true. You might also try lying whenever a stranger asks how long you've been in Thailand – if it's only been three days, say three weeks! The con artists rarely prey on anyone except new arrivals. Or save your Bangkok sightseeing until after you've been upcountry.

Whether they're able to take any action or not, the TAT now has 'regulatory' powers over shops catering to tourists – you should contact the tourist police if you have any problems with consumer fraud. The tourist police headquarters (☎ 1699, 225-0085) is at the Crime Suppression Division, located at 509 Worachak Rd, Bangkok; you can also contact them through the TAT office on Bamrung Meuang Rd. There is also a police unit that deals specifically with gem swindles (☎ 254-1067, 235-4017). ∎

stopped. This happened on the Surat Thani to Phuket bus.

Travellers have also encountered drugged food or drink from friendly strangers in bars and from prostitutes in their own hotel rooms. Thais are also occasional victims, especially at the Moh Chit bus terminal and Chatuchak Park, where young girls are drugged and sold to brothels. Conclusion – don't accept gifts from strangers.

Assault

Robbery of farangs by force is very rare in Thailand, but it does happen. Statistically Thailand claims only 15 violent crimes – including murder and armed robbery – per 100,000 population per year, some distance behind Malaysia (42), Australia (57.5), Britain (97), Hong Kong (208) and the USA (282) as of 1991. Isolated incidences of armed robbery have tended to occur along the Thai-Burmese and Thai-Cambodian borders and on remote islands. The safest practice in remote areas is not to go out alone at night and, if trekking in north Thailand, always walk in groups. More information on hill trekking is given in the Northern Thailand chapter.

Touts

Touting – grabbing newcomers in the street or in train stations, bus terminals or airports to sell them a service – is a long-time tradition in Asia, and while Thailand doesn't have as many as, say, India, it has its share. In the popular tourist spots it seems like everyone – young boys waving flyers, tuk-tuk drivers, samlor drivers, schoolgirls – is touting something, usually hotels or guesthouses. For the most part they're completely harmless and sometimes they can be very informative. But take anything a tout says with two large grains of salt. Since touts work on commission and get paid just for delivering you to a guesthouse or hotel (whether you check in or not), they'll say anything to get you to the door.

Often the best (most honest and reliable) hotels and guesthouses refuse to pay tout commissions – so the average tout will try to steer you away from such places. Hence don't believe them if they tell you the hotel or guesthouse you're looking for is 'closed', 'full', 'dirty' or 'bad'. Sometimes (rarely) they're right but most times it's just a ruse to get you to a place that pays more commission. Always have a careful look yourself before checking into a place recommended by a tout. Tuk-tuk and samlor drivers often offer free or low-cost rides to the place they're touting; if you have another place you're interested in, you might agree to go with a driver only if he or she promises to deliver you to your first choice after you've had a look at the place being touted. If drivers refuse, chances are it's because they know your first choice is a better one.

This type of commission work isn't limited to low-budget guesthouses. Taxi drivers and even airline employees at Thailand's major airports – including Bangkok and Chiang Mai – reap commissions from the big hotels as well. At either end of the budget spectrum, the customer ends up paying the commission indirectly through raised room rates. Bangkok International Airport employees are notorious for talking newly arrived tourists into staying at badly located, overpriced hotels.

Insurgent Activity

Since the 1920s and 1930s several insurgent groups have operated in Thailand: the Communist Party of Thailand (CPT) with its tactical force the People's Liberation Army of Thailand (PLAT) in rural areas throughout the country; Hmong guerrillas in the north hoping to overthrow the communist regime in Laos; and Malay separatists and Muslim revolutionaries in the extreme south. These groups have been mainly involved in propaganda activity, village infiltration and occasional clashes with Thai government troops. Very rarely have they had any encounters with foreign travellers. Aside from sporadic terrorist bombings – mostly in train stations in the south and sometimes at upcountry festivals – 'innocent' people have not been involved in the insurgent activity.

In 1976, the official government estimate of the number of active communist guerrillas in Thailand was 10,000. By the end of the 1970s, however, many CPT followers had surrendered under the government amnesty programme. In the 1980s new military strategies, as well as political measures, reduced the number to around two to three thousand. Another cause for the CPT's severely curtailed influence stems from the 1979 split between the CPT and the Chinese Communist Party over policy differences regarding Indochinese revolution (eg Chinese support for the Khmer Rouge against Vietnamese communists). Before the split, CPT cadres received training in Kunming, China; afterwards they were isolated.

Only a few dozen CPT guerrillas are still active in Thailand, and these are mainly involved in local extortion rackets under the guise of 'village indoctrination'. New highways in previously remote provinces such as Nan and Loei have contributed to improved communications, stability and central (Bangkok) control. This means that all routes in these provinces that were closed to foreigners in the 1970s are now open for travel, eg Phitsanulok to Loei via Nakhon Thai. Travellers can also travel from Nan to Loei by bus, and from Chiang Rai to Nan via Chiang Muan, routes that formerly ran through hotbeds of rebel activity. A new road between Phattalung and Hat Yai – a route considered 'insecure' until the mid-1980s – has cut travel time between those two cities considerably.

In the north and north-east, the government claims that armed resistance has been virtually eliminated and this appears to be verified by independent sources as well as by my own travel experiences through former CPT strongholds. One area that supposedly remains active is a pocket of eastern Nan Province on the Laos border – the Thai military in fact doesn't allow visitors or even its own citizens into this area. Smaller, militarily inactive pockets reportedly still exist in parts of Sakon Nakhon, Tak and Phetburi provinces.

In the south, traditionally a hot spot, communist forces have been all but limited to Camp 508 in a relatively inaccessible area along the Surat Thani-Nakhon Si Thammarat provincial border. The Betong area of Yala Province on the Thai-Malaysian border was until recently the tactical headquarters for the armed Communist Party of Malaya (CPM). Thai and Malaysian government troops occasionally clashed with the insurgents, who from time to time hijacked trucks along the Yala to Betong road. But in December 1989, in exchange for amnesty, the CPM agreed 'to terminate all armed activities' and to respect the laws of Thailand and Malaysia. It appears that this area is now safe for travel.

Cynics note that it's in the Thai army's best interests to claim that communist insurgency still exists, that this notion is used to justify a larger standing army, higher military budgets and continuing political involvements in Bangkok. Most observers do not expect communist guerrilla activity to flare again any time in the foreseeable future. This seems especially true in light of the great economic strides Thailand has made during the last decade, which have simply made Marxism a less compelling alternative for most of the population. The softening of socialism in adjacent Cambodia and Laos have also greatly reduced the possibility of 'infiltration'.

PULO One continuing thorn in the side of the Thai government is the small but militant Malay-Muslim movement in the south. The Pattani United Liberation Organisation (PULO) formed in 1957, trained in Libya and reached its peak in 1981 with a guerrilla strength of around 1800. The PULO refers to Thailand's three predominantly Muslim, Malay-speaking provinces of Pattani, Yala and Narathiwat collectively as 'Pattani'; their objective is to create a separate, sovereign state or, at the very least, to obtain annexation to Malaysia. Intelligence sources claim the rebels are supported by PAS, Malaysia's main opposition party, which is dedicated to making Malaysia a more Islamic state than it already is.

A group of 111 Muslim separatists belonging to the PULO, Barisan Revolusi Nasional (BRN, or National Revolutionary Front) and Barisan Nasional Pembebasan Pattani (BNPP, or National Front for the Freedom of Pattani) surrendered in late 1991, but PULO remnants persist in southern Thailand's villages and jungles. This was its fourth mass surrender in five years – only a few dozen guerrillas are still active, mainly involved in propaganda and extortion activities plus the occasional attack on Thai government vehicles. PULO members collect regular 'protection' payments, for example, from rubber plantations.

Things may be heating up again, however. In August 1992 a powerful bomb exploded in the Hat Yai train station, killing three and injuring 75; a PULO-signed letter was found in the station. This was the first bombing of this nature since the early 1980s. A second bombing occurred along the Bangkok-Sungai Kolok rail line in Songkhla Province on 30 March; there were no serious injuries this time. In August 1993 a coordinated terrorist effort set fire to 35 schools in Pattani, Yala and Narthiwat. Since the fire incident, law enforcement efforts in the south have been intensified and the area has stayed relatively quiet.

Other Hot Spots Probably the most sensitive areas in Thailand nowadays are the Cambodian and Myanmar border areas. Most dangerous is the Thai-Cambodian border area, where Cambodia's former Vietnamese-backed regime sealed the border against the Khmer Rouge (KR) with heavy armament, land mines and booby traps. Most but not all of the latter are planted inside Cambodian territory, so it is imperative that you stay away from this border – it will be at least 10 years before the mines are cleared. Armed Khmer bandits are occasionally encountered in the vicinity of Aranya Prathet (but not in Aranya Prathet itself), still considered a risky area for casual travel.

The Khao Phra Wihaan ruins just inside Cambodia near Ubon were recently closed to visitors from the Thai side due to heavy skirmishes between KR and Phnom Penh troops. A 1993-94 dry season offensive against KR strongholds has pushed KR troops all along the Thai-Cambodian border; during that period gun and mortar fire could be heard from just about every Thai settlement in the area on a daily basis. Stray bullets and rockets do manage to find their way across national boundaries, so be sure to make security enquiries in the provincial capitals of Surin, Si Saket or Ubon before taking a trip along the border.

The Myanmar border between Mae Sot and Mae Sariang occasionally receives shelling from Burmese troops in pursuit of Karen rebels. The rebels are trying to maintain an independent nation called Kawthoolei along the border with Thailand. If you cross illegally and are captured by the Burmese, you may automatically be suspected of supporting the Karen. If you are captured by the Karen you will probably be released, though they may demand money. The risks of catching a piece of shrapnel are substantially lower if you keep several km between yourself and the Thai-Myanmar border in this area – fighting can break out at any time. Mae Sot itself is quite safe these days, though you can still occasionally hear mortar fire in the distance.

In the Three Pagodas Pass area, there is also occasional fighting between Burmese, Karen and Mon armies, who are competing for control over the smuggling trade between Myanmar and Thailand. Typically, the rebels advance in the rainy season and retreat in the dry; lately this area has been fairly quiet.

Along the Myanmar-Thai border in northern Mae Hong Son and Chiang Rai provinces, the presence of Shan and Kuomintang armies make this area dangerous if you attempt to travel near opium trade border crossings – obviously these are not signposted, so take care anywhere along the border in this area. In late 1992 Thai rangers moved in on the Mae Hong Son border to force opium warlord Khun Sa and his Muang Tai Army (MTA) camp further back from the frontier – his HQ at the time was only a km inside Burmese territory. Although the Thai rangers have delivered an ultimatum that the MTA remain at least two km away from the border, a definite risk of firefights continues.

Although Bangkok has generally been safe from terrorist activity, a couple of large truck bombs bound for the Israeli embassy have been intercepted in the city since 1991. The district known as Little Arabia (Soi Nana Neua, off Sukhumvit Rd) is a known 'hideaway' for Muslim terrorists on the lam from other parts of the world. During the Persian Gulf 'conflict', the US State Department issued a travel advisory suggesting caution in Bangkok because of the perceived potential for acts of terrorism against Westerners (acts which never developed); that advisory has since been rescinded.

Drugs

Opium, heroin and marijuana are widely used in Thailand, but it is illegal to buy, sell or possess these drugs in any quantity (the exception is opium, possession of which is legal for consumption – but not sale – among hill tribes). A lesser known narcotic, *kràtom* (a leaf of the *Mitragyna speciosa* tree), is used by workers and students as a stimulant – similar to Yemen's *qat*. A hundred kratom leaves sell for around 30B, and are sold for

1 to 3B each; the leaf is illegal and said to be addictive.

In the south, especially on the rainy Gulf islands, mushrooms (in Thai *hèt khîi khwai*, 'buffalo-shit mushrooms', or *hèt mao*, 'drunk mushrooms') which contain the hallucinogen psilocybin are sometimes sold to or gathered by foreigners. The legal status of mushroom use or possession is questionable; police have been known to hassle Thais who sell them. Using such mushrooms is a risky proposition as the dosage is always uncertain; I've heard one confirmed story of a farang who swam to his death off Ko Pha-Ngan after a 'special' mushroom omelette.

Although in certain areas of the country drugs seem to be used with some impunity, enforcement is arbitrary – the only way not to risk getting caught is to avoid the scene entirely. Every year perhaps dozens of visiting foreigners are arrested in Thailand for drug use or trafficking and end up doing hard time. A smaller but significant number die of heroin overdoses.

Penalties for drug offences are stiff: if you're caught using marijuana, you face a fine and/or up to one year in prison, while for heroin, the penalty for use can be anywhere from six months' to 10 years' imprisonment. In the table below, 'smuggling' refers to any drug possession at a border or airport customs check.

Drug	Quantity	Penalty
Marijuana		
Smuggling	any amount	2 to 15 years imprisonment
Possession	less than 10 kg	up to 5 years imprisonment
Possession	10 kg +	2 to 15 years imprisonment
Heroin		
Smuggling	any amount	life imprisonment
Smuggling with intent to sell	any amount	execution
Possession	10 grams +	imprisonment or execution

ACTIVITIES
Diving & Snorkelling

Thailand's two coastlines and countless islands are popular among divers for their mild waters and colourful marine life. The biggest diving centre is still Pattaya, simply because it's less than two hours' drive from Bangkok. There are several islands with reefs within a short boat ride from Pattaya and the little town is packed with dive shops.

Phuket is the second biggest jumping-off point and has the advantage of offering the largest variety of places to choose from – small offshore islands less than an hour away, Ao Phang-Nga (a one to two-hour boat ride) with its unusual rock formations and clear green waters, and the world-famous

Similan and Surin islands in the Andaman Sea (about four hours away by fast boat). Reef dives in the Andaman are particularly rewarding – some 210 hard corals and 108 reef fish have so far been catalogued in this under-studied marine zone, where probably thousands more species of reef organisms live.

In recent years a few dive operations have opened on the palmy islands of Ko Samui, Ko Pha-Ngan and Ko Tao in the Gulf of Thailand off Surat Thani. Chumphon Province, just north of Surat Thani, is another up-and-coming area where there are a dozen or so islands with undisturbed reefs. Newer frontiers include the so-called Burma Banks (north-west of the Similans) and islands off the coast of Trang Province.

All of these places with the possible exception of the Burma Banks have areas that are suitable for snorkelling as well as scuba diving, since many reefs are no deeper than two metres. Masks, fins and snorkels are readily available for rent not only at dive centres but also through guesthouses located in beach areas. If you're particular about the quality and condition of the equipment you use, however, you might be better off bringing your own mask and snorkel – some of the stuff for rent is second-rate. And people with large heads may have difficulty finding masks that fit since most of the masks are made or imported for Thai heads.

Dive Centres Most dive shops rent equipment at reasonable rates and some also offer basic instruction and NAUI or PADI qualification for first-timers. See the relevant destination sections of this book for names and locations of established diving centres.

Bangkok
Seat Co, 1175 New Road (near the GPO) (☎ (02) 235-0605, fax 236-3921)

Dolphin Club, 19 Soi 21, Sukhumvit Rd (☎ (02) 259-9170, fax 259-1487)

Thai Diving Centre, 44/1 Soi 21, Sukhumvit Rd (☎ (02) 258-3662)

Sea Fron Thai Co, 397/1 Soi Siri Chulasewok, Silom Rd (☎ (02) 235-9438)

Pattaya
Dave's Divers' Den, 1/1 Pattaya-Naklua Rd, North Pattaya (☎ (038) 221860, fax 221618)

Max's Dive Shop, Nipa Lodge Hotel, North Pattaya Rd (☎ (038) 428321/2)

Mermaid's Dive School, Soi Mermaid, Jomtien Beach (☎ (038) 330272, fax 330516)

The Scuba Professionals, Dusit Resort Hotel (☎ (038) 429901/3)

The Reef Dive Shop, Ocean View Hotel (☎ (038) 428084)

Pattaya International Diving Centre, Siam Bayview Hotel (☎ (038) 423325/1)

Steven's Dive Shop, 579 Soi 4, Beach Rd (☎ (038) 428392)

Phuket
Holiday Diving Club, Patong Beach Hotel, 89/37 Thawiwong Rd, Patong Beach (☎ 321166, fax 340440)

Phuket International Diving Centre, 1/10 Viset Rd, Ao Chalong (☎ /fax (076) 381219)

Loan Island Resort, Ao Chalong (☎ (076) 211253; (02) 314-5332 in Bangkok)

Andaman Divers 83/8 Thawiwong Rd, Patong Beach (☎ (076) 340322)

Fantasea Divers, Patong Beach (☎ /fax (076) 340309)

Marina Divers, Kata-Karon Beach (☎ (076) 381625, fax 213604)

Ocean Divers, 61/12 Muu 3, Thawiwong Rd, Patong Beach (☎ (076) 340166)

Phuket Aquatic Safari, 62/9 Rasada Centre, Rasada Rd, Phuket Town (☎ (076) 216562, fax 214537)

Poseidon Memrod Club, Phuket Island Resort (☎ (076) 215950/5)

Santana, Patong Beach (☎ (076) 292901)

Siam Diving Centre, Kata-Karon Beach (☎ (076) 381608)

Dave's Divers' Den, 9 Chao Fa Rd, Ao Chalong (☎ (076) 3818, fax 381260)

Southeast Asia Divers, Le Meridien, Karon Noi Beach (☎ (076) 340480, fax 340586)

Chumphon

Chumphon Cabana Thung Wua Lan Beach (☎ (077) 511885; 224-1884 in Bangkok)

Pornsawan Home Paknam (☎ (077) 521031; 427-1360 in Bangkok)

Ko Samui

Calypso Diving, 27/5 Chaweng Rd (☎ /fax (077) 422437)

Samui International Diving School, PO Box 40 (☎ (077) 421056, fax 421465)

Several nonprofit diving associations and clubs also exist in Thailand; most of their members are long-term Thai and expat residents. Joining a club trip is an excellent way to meet Thais and farangs with a strong interest in Thailand's dive scene. The country's longest running diving association is the Thailand Sub-Aqua Club (☎ 256-0170, ext 298; ask for Scott Klimo), PO Box 11-1196, Bangkok 10110. The club offers dive trips and certification year-round.

Dive Seasons Generally speaking, the Gulf of Thailand has a year-round dive season, although tropical storms sometimes blow out the visibility temporarily. On the Andaman coast the best diving conditions occur between December and April; from May to November monsoon conditions prevail. Whale sharks and manta rays in the offshore Andaman (eg Similan and Surin island groups) are a major bonus during planktonic blooms in March and April.

Other Water Sports

With countless islands and thousands of km of coastline along the Gulf of Thailand and Andaman Sea, just about any water-related activity imaginable can be enjoyed.

Windsurfing The best combinations of rental facilities and wind conditions are found on Pattaya and Jomtien beaches in Chonburi Province, on Ko Samet, on the west coast of Phuket and on Chaweng Beach on Ko Samui. To a lesser extent you'll also find rental equipment on Ko Pha-Ngan, Ko Tao and Ko Chang.

Rental windsurfing gear generally found at Thai resorts is not the most complete and up-to-date. Original parts may be missing, or may have been replaced by improvised, Thai-made parts. For the novice windsurfer this probably won't matter, but hot-doggers may be disappointed in the selection. Bring your own if you have it. In Thailand's year-round tropical climate, wetsuits aren't necessary.

If you have your own equipment you can set out anywhere you find a coastal breeze. If you're looking for something undiscovered, you might check out the cape running north from Narathiwat's provincial capital in southern Thailand. In general the windier months on the Gulf of Thailand are mid-February to April. On the Andaman Sea side of the Thai-Malay Peninsula winds are strongest September to December.

Surfing This sport has never really taken off in Thailand, not least because there don't seem to be any sizeable, annually dependable breaks (write to me if you find any). Phuket's west coast occasionally kicks up some surfable waves during the south-west monsoon, May to November. I have also seen some fair surf action on the west coast of Ko Chang during the same time of year, and on the east coast of Ko Samet during the dry season, November to February. I'd be willing to bet there's decent surf on Ko Chang's east coast during these latter months.

Low-quality boards can be rented in Pattaya and on Phuket's Patong Beach (but bigger surf is usually found on Laem Singh and Hat Surin). Coastal Trang is historically reputed to receive large waves during the south-west monsoon, but I've never heard of anyone surfing there.

Sea Canoeing Touring the islands and coastal limestone formations around Phuket and Ao Phang-Nga by inflatable canoe has become an increasingly popular activity over the last five years. The typical sea canoe tour seeks out half-submerged caves called 'hongs' (*hâwng*, Thai for 'room'), timing their excursions so that they can paddle into the caverns at low tide. Several outfits on Phuket offer equipment and guides – see the Phuket section for details.

River & Canal Excursions

Numerous opportunities for boat travel along Thailand's major rivers and canals are available through the extensive public boat system and aboard a small number of tourist boat services. So far only the lower Chao Phraya River and a few rivers in northern Thailand have been introduced to regular leisure boating. A variety of watercraft are available, from air-conditioned tourist boats along the Chao Phraya River around

Bangkok to rustic bamboo rafts on the Kok River and sturdy whitewater kayaks on the Pai River.

The Maekhong River, until the late 1980s considered perilous due to regional hostilities, has enormous potential. During the last four years or so short-distance boat trips have been offered in Chiang Rai and Nong Khai provinces, and in early 1994 an experimental tour service between Chiang Saen and China was inaugurated. Central Thailand's vast network of canals, centred around the Chao Phraya River Delta and fanning out for hundreds of km in all directions, offers innumerable boating opportunities. Because of the sometimes imposing motorised boat traffic along these waterways, so far very few foreign visitors have tried canoeing or kayaking this grid; for the adventurous, the potential is tremendous. By public and chartered longtail boat one can piece together canal journeys of several days' duration.

For more information on river and canal travel possibilities, see the introductory Getting Around chapter and the relevant destination sections later in the book.

Trekking

Wilderness walking or trekking is one of northern Thailand's biggest draws. Typical northern Thailand trekking programmes run for four or five days (though it is possible to arrange everything from one to 10-day treks) and feature daily walks through forested mountain areas coupled with overnight stays in hill-tribe villages to satisfy both ethno and eco-touristic urges. See Hill-Tribe Treks in the Northern Thailand chapter for more detail.

Other trekking opportunities are available in Thailand's larger national parks (including Khao Yai, Kaeng Krachan, Khao Sam Roi Yot, Doi Phu Kha, Khao Sok, Thap Lan and Phu Reua) where park rangers may be hired as guides and cooks for a few days at a time. Rates are reasonable. For more information, see the respective park descriptions later in this book.

Courses

Thai Language Study Several language schools in Bangkok and Chiang Mai offer courses for foreigners in Thai language. Tuition fees average around 250B per hour. Some places will let you trade English lessons for Thai lessons; if not, you can usually teach English on the side to offset tuition costs. There are three recommended schools in Bangkok:

Union Language School
  CCT Building, 109 Surawong Rd (☎ 233-4482). Generally recognised as the best and most rigorous course (many missionaries study here). Employs a balance of structure-oriented and communication-oriented methodologies in 80-hour, four-week modules. Private tuition is also available.
AUA Language Center
  179 Rajadamri (Ratchadamri) Rd (☎ 252-8170). American University Alumni (AUA) runs one of the largest English-language teaching institutes in the world, so this is a good place to meet Thai students. On the other hand, farangs who study Thai here complain that there's not enough interaction in class because of an emphasis on the so-called 'natural approach', which focuses on teacher input rather than student practice. AUA also has a branch in Chiang Mai.
Nisa Thai Language School
  YMCA Collins House, 27 Sathon Tai Rd (☎ 286-9323). This school has a fairly good reputation, though teachers may be less qualified than at Union or AUA language schools. In addition to all the usual levels, Nisa offers a course in preparing for the Baw Hok or Grade 6 examination, a must for anyone wishing to work in the public school system.

Chulalongkorn University in Bangkok, the most prestigious university in Thailand, offers an intensive Thai studies course called 'Perspectives on Thailand'.

The eight-week programme includes classes in Thai language, culture, history, politics and economics, plus a 10-day upcountry field trip. Classes meet six hours a day, six days a week (Saturday is usually a field trip) and are offered once a year from the first Monday in July to the last Friday in August. Students who have taken the course say they have found the quality of instruction excellent. Tuition is around US$2400, including meals, transport and accommodation on the 10-day field trip. Room and board on campus are available, though it's much less expensive to live off campus. For further information write to Perspectives on Thailand, Continuing Education Center, 5th floor, Vidhyabhathan Bldg, Soi Chulalongkorn 12 (2), Chulalongkorn University, Bangkok 10330 (☎ (02) 218-3393; fax 214-4515).

The YWCA's Siri Pattana Thai Language School (☎ 286-1936), 13 Sathon Tai Rd, gives Thai language lessons as well as preparation for the Baw Hok exam. Siri Pattana has a second branch at 806 Soi 38, Sukhumvit Rd.

Meditation Study Thailand has long been a popular place for Western students of Buddhism, particularly those interested in a system of meditation known as *vipassana* (Thai: *wí-pàt-sa-nãa*), a Pali word which roughly translated means 'insight'. Foreigners who come to Thailand to study vipassana can choose among dozens of temples and meditation centres (*sãmnák wípàtsanãa*) which specialise in these teachings. Teaching methods vary from place to place but the general emphasis is on learning to observe mind-body processes from moment to moment. Thai language is usually the medium of instruction but several places also provide instruction in English.

Details on some of the more popular meditation-oriented temples and centres are given in the relevant sections. Instruction and accommodation are free of charge at temples, though donations are expected. Short-term students will find that two-month Tourist Visas are ample for most courses of study. Long-term students may want to consider a three or six-month Non-Immigrant Visa. A few Westerners are ordained as monks in order to take full advantage of the monastic environment. Monks are generally (but not always) allowed to stay in Thailand as long as they remain in robes.

Places where English-language instruction is usually available include:

International Buddhist Meditation Centre, Wat Mahathat, Maharat Rd, Tha Phra Chan, Bangkok (☎ (02) 222-6011)

Wat Asokaram, Bang Na-Trat Highway (32 km south of Bangkok), Samut Prakan (☎ (02) 395-0003)

Wiwekasom Vipassana Centre, Ban Suan, Chonburi (☎ 038) 283766)

Sorn-Thawee Vipassana Centre, Bang Kla, Chachoengsao

Boonkanjanaram Meditation Centre, Jomtien Beach, Pattaya, Chonburi (☎ (038) 231865)

Wat Tapotaram (Wat Ram Poeng), Chiang Mai (☎ (053) 278620)

Wat Suanmok, Chaiya, Surat Thani

Wa Khao Tham, Ko Pha-Ngan, Surat Thani

Before visiting one of the above centres, it's a good idea to call or write to make sure space and instruction are available. Some places require that lay persons staying overnight wear white clothes. For even a brief visit, wear clean, polite clothing, ie long trousers or skirt and sleeves which cover the shoulder.

For a detailed look at vipassana study in Thailand, including visa and ordination procedures, read *The Meditation Temples of Thailand: A Guide* (Spirit Rock Center, PO Box 909, Woodacre, CA 94973, USA) or *A Guide to Buddhist Monasteries & Meditation Centres in Thailand* (available from the World Federation of Buddhists in Bangkok).

Martial Arts Training Many Westerners have trained in Thailand (especially since the release of Jean-Claude Van Damme's martial arts flick, *The Kick Boxer*, which was filmed on location in Thailand), but few last more than a week or two in a Thai camp – and fewer still have gone on to compete on Thailand's pro circuit.

Thai Boxing (Muay Thai) One farang who went pro in Thailand was Dale Kvalheim, a Dutch fighter once ranked No 10 at Ratchadamnoen Stadium and champion of North-East Thailand from 1972 to 1975. An Australian, Patrick Cusick, directs muay thai seminars for farangs in Thailand: contact him at Thai Championship Boxing (☎ 234-5360; fax 236-7242), Box 1996, Bangkok. The Pramote Gym (☎ 215-1206) at 210-212

Phetburi Rd, Ratthewi, offers training in Thai boxing as well as other martial arts (judo, karate, tae kwon do, krabi-krabong) to foreigners as well as locals.

Those interested in training at a traditional muay thai camp might try the PB Boxing Gym on Khao San Rd in Bangkok (behind PB Guest House), the Sityodthong-Payakarun Boxing Camp in Naklua (north of Pattaya) or Fairtex Boxing Camp outside Bangkok (c/o Bunjong Busarakamwongs, Fairtex Garments Factory, 734-742 Trok Kai, Anuwong Rd, Bangkok). Be forewarned, though, that the training is gruelling and features full-contact sparring.

For more information about Thai boxing, see the Sport section in the Facts about the Country chapter.

Krabi-Krabong Krabi-krabong (a traditional Thai martial art; see under Sport in the Facts about the Country chapter for more information) is taught at several Thai colleges and universities, but currently the country's best training venue is the Buddhai Sawan Fencing School of Thailand (5/1 Phetkasem Rd, Thonburi), where Ajaan Samai Mesamarna carries on the tradition as passed down from Wat Phutthaisawan. Several farangs have trained here, including one American who recently became the first foreigner to attain *ajaan* (master) status. Pramote Gym (see Thai Boxing earlier) also provides krabi-krabong training.

The *Modern Gladiator Journal* (fax (312) 201-9399, PO Box 5619, Chicago, IL 60680, USA) is a homespun quarterly devoted to Thai martial arts training and competition.

HIGHLIGHTS
Thailand's travel scene has many faces. Exploring all the country has to offer is a lifetime endeavour; time and money constraints will compel most of us to decide – either in advance or as we go along – which parts we're going to see and which parts will have to be left out. In Thailand it usually pays to be a little under-ambitious with one's travel plans; don't try to see too much in too

short an interval or your travels may quickly become a chore.

Most visitors begin their journey in Bangkok. Depending on how much time you have available, you might want to save your Bangkok explorations until after you've seen other parts of the country. That way Bangkok won't seem quite so overwhelming as on first arrival. You'll also understand more about the Thai character after travelling around the country, and in Bangkok it pays to be a good judge of character – in order to separate the touts from the genuinely friendly.

Your recreational and aesthetic inclinations will largely determine which direction you take. The basic threads most visitors are interested in following include beaches/islands, historic temple architecture, trekking, handicrafts, and performing arts. These travel aspects are not necessarily mutually exclusive, though it's hard to find one place that has them all! In Songkhla, for example, you'll find handicrafts and beaches, while many places in the north-east offer temple ruins and handicrafts.

Beaches & Islands

Thailand's coastline boasts some of the finest beaches and islands in Asia. Head to southern Thailand if you have a week or more to spare and will be using ground transportation. Which side of the peninsula you choose – the Gulf of Thailand (for Prachuap Khiri Khan, Ko Samui, Songkhla) or the Andaman Sea (Phuket, Krabi, Trang) – might be determined by the time of year. Both sides are mostly rain-free from March to May, both are somewhat rainy from June to November, while the Gulf side is drier than the Andaman side from November to January.

For shorter beach excursions, check out the beaches and islands along the eastern Gulf coast of central Thailand (Pattaya, Ko Samet, Ko Chang) or upper peninsular Gulf (Cha-am, Hua Hin). Or, if you can afford it, plan to fly to one of the airports in the southern beach resort areas (eg Ko Samui, Phuket).

Historic Temple Architecture

The former Thai capitals of Ayuthaya, Lopburi, Kamphaeng Phet, Sukhothai, Si Satchanalai and Chiang Mai offer a wide range of Buddhist temple architecture, most of it from the 11th to 17th centuries. The Thai government has developed several of these sites into historical parks, complete with on-site museums and impressive temple restorations.

Visits to Ayuthaya and Sukhothai are usually sufficient for those with limited time or a milder interest in Thai temple ruins. The ruins at Kamphaeng Phet and Si Satchanalai are similar to those found at Sukhothai but they offer more of an off-the-beaten-track atmosphere. Because it features a mix of Khmer and Thai monuments, Lopburi is another noteworthy stop. Wat Phra That Lampang Luang in Lampang Province makes an interesting side trip from Chiang Mai and is Thailand's oldest surviving wooden temple.

For Khmer and Lao temple architecture, head to Isaan (north-eastern Thailand). Hundreds of Khmer ruins dating from the 8th to 13th centuries – including many Angkor-period monuments – are dotted around the Isaan countryside. The most impressive sites are those at Prasat Hin Phimai in Nakhon Ratchasima Province and Prasat Hin Khao Phanom Rung in Buriram Province, but don't neglect some of the smaller, out-of-the-way spots if you have the time and inclination. Dozens of famous Lao temples – both ruins and operating wats – can be found along the Maekhong River from Loei Province to Ubon Ratchathani Province.

See the Arts section in the Facts about the Country chapter for more information on art styles and archaeological sites.

Handicrafts

Thailand's ethnic diversity means a wide range of handicrafts is available for study or purchase throughout the country. As the culture and business capital of northern Thailand, Chiang Mai has been the north's main handicrafts centre for over 30 years. Here you'll find virtually every type of craft produced in the region, as well as materials from Myanmar and Laos. Northern specialities include silverwork, woodcarving, painted umbrellas, hill-tribe clothing, ceramics and antique furniture.

North-eastern Thailand is the country's centre for handmade cotton and silk. The best selection of textiles is found in the provincial capitals of Nakhon Ratchasima, Khon Kaen, Roi-Et, Udon Thani, Nakhon Phanom and Nong Khai. The city of Ubon Ratchathani offers a good selection of crafts from nearby Cambodia and Laos, plus locally produced silver and ceramics. For cotton prints, sarongs and batik, visit the provinces of Songkhla, Yala, Pattani and Narathiwat.

Performing Arts

Not surprisingly, Bangkok offers more performing arts – both traditional and modern – than anywhere else in the country. See the Entertainment section in the Bangkok chapter for details on the best venues.

About the only performing arts genre not easily found in Bangkok is traditional Thai shadow play, which is restricted to rare performances in Nakhon Si Thammarat. All over the country, however, you may encounter regional variations on *lí-khe*, or Thai folk opera, such as Trang's famous *lí-khe pàa*.

Li-khe, classical dance-drama and other traditional performing arts are most frequently presented during local or national festivals. Thailand's main festival season arrives after the main rice harvest in September/October and lasts until May.

Culture

One of the main highlights of Thailand travel is just soaking up the general cultural ambience, which can be done just about anywhere in the country. You won't obtain much in terms of Thai culture if you spend most of your time sitting around in guesthouse cafes, hanging out on the beach or trekking with your own kind. At least once during your trip, try going to a small to medium-sized town well off the main tourist circuit, staying at a local hotel, and eating in Thai curry

shops and noodle stands. It's not as easy as going with the crowd but you'll learn a lot more about Thailand.

ACCOMMODATION

Places to stay are abundant, varied and reasonably priced in Thailand.

However, just a word of warning about touts: don't believe them if they say a place is closed, full, dirty or crooked. Sometimes they're right but most times it's just a ruse to get you to a place that pays them more commission. (See the Dangers & Annoyances section earlier for more information about touts.)

Guesthouses, Hostels & YMCA/YWCAs

Guesthouses are generally the cheapest accommodation in Thailand and are found in most areas where travellers go in central, north and south Thailand; they are spreading slowly to the east and north-east as well. Guesthouses vary quite a bit in facilities and are particularly popular in Bangkok and Chiang Mai where stiff competition keeps rates low. Some are especially good value, while others are mere flophouses. Many serve food, although there tends to be a bland sameness to meals in guesthouses wherever you are in Thailand.

There is a Thai branch of Hostelling International (☎ (02) 282-0950, fax 281-6834) at 25/2 Phitsanulok Rd, Sisao Thewet, Dusit, Bangkok 10300, with member hostels in Bangkok (two), Ayuthaya (one), Chiang Mai (two), Chiang Rai (one) and Phitsanulok (one). From time to time there have been others in Kanchanaburi, Ko Phi Phi and Nan but at the time of writing these were closed. Thai youth hostels range in price from 50B for a dorm bed to 250B for an air-con room. Since 1992, only Hostelling International (formerly International Youth Hostel Federation) card-holders are accepted as guests in Thai hostels; memberships cost 300B per year or 50B for a temporary (one-night) membership.

A YMCA or YWCA costs a bit more than a guesthouse or hostel (an average of 250B and above) and sometimes more than a local

> **Bathing in Thailand**
> Upcountry, the typical Thai bathroom consists of a tall earthen water jar fed by a spigot and a plastic or metal bowl. You bathe by scooping water out of the water jar and sluicing it over the body. It's very refreshing during the hot and rainy seasons, but requires a little stamina during the cool season if you're not used to it. If the 'bathroom' has no walls, or if you are bathing at a public well or spring in an area where there are no bathrooms, you should bathe while wearing the *phâakhamáa* (sarong for men) or *phâasîn* (sarong for women); bathing nude would offend the Thais. ■

hotel, but are generally good value. There are Ys in Bangkok, Chiang Mai and Chiang Rai.

Chinese-Thai Hotels

The standard Thai hotels, often run by Chinese-Thai families, are the easiest accommodation to come by and generally have very reasonable rates (average 60 to 100B for rooms without bath or air-con, 100 to 250B with fan and bath, 250 to 500B with air-con). They may be located on the main street of town and/or near bus and train stations.

The most economical hotels to stay in are those without air-con; typical rooms are clean and include a double bed and a ceiling fan. Some have attached Thai-style bathrooms (this will cost a little more). Rates may or may not be posted; if not, they may be increased for the farang, so it is worthwhile bargaining. It is best to have a look around before agreeing to check in, to make sure the room *is* clean, that the fan and lights work and so on. If there is any problem, request another room or a good discount. If possible, always choose a room off the street and away from the front lounge to cut down on ambient noise.

For a room without air-con, ask for a *hâwng thammádaa* (ordinary room) or *hâwng phát lom* (room with fan). A room with air-con is *hâwng ae*. Sometimes farangs asking for air-con are automatically offered a 'VIP' room, which usually comes with air-con, hot water, fridge and TV and is about twice the price of a regular air-con room.

Some Chinese-Thai hotels may double as brothels; the perpetual traffic in and out can be a bit noisy but is generally bearable.

Unaccompanied males are often asked if they want female companionship when checking into inexpensive hotels. Even certain middle-class (by Thai standards) hotels are reserved for the 'salesman' crowd, meaning travelling Thai businessmen who frequently expect extra night-time services.

The cheapest hotels may have their names posted in Thai and Chinese only, but you will learn how to find and identify them with experience. Many of these hotels have restaurants downstairs; if they don't, there are usually restaurants and noodle shops nearby.

National Park Accommodation/Camping

Thailand has 66 national parks and nine historical parks. All but 10 of the national parks have bungalows for rent that sleep as many as 10 people for rates of 500 to 1500B, depending on the park and the size of the bungalow.

Camping is allowed in all but four of the national parks (Nam Tok Phliu in Chanthaburi Province, Doi Suthep-Pui in Chiang Mai Province, Hat Chao Mai in Trang Province and Thap Laan in Prachinburi Province) for only 5B per person per night. A few parks also have *reuan tháew* or long houses, where rooms are around 150 to 200B for two, and/or tents on platforms for 50 to 60B a night.

A few of the historical parks have bungalows with rates comparable to those in the national parks, mostly for use by visiting archaeologists.

Universities/Schools

College and university campuses may be able to provide inexpensive accommodation during the summer vacation (March to June). There are universities in Chiang Mai, Nakhon Pathom, Khon Kaen, Mahasarakham and Songkhla. Outside Bangkok there are also teachers' colleges *(wíthâyálai khruu)* in every provincial capital which may offer accommodation during the summer vacation. The typical teachers' college dorm room lets for 30 to 70B per night during holiday periods.

Tourist-Class & Luxury Hotels

These are found only in the main tourist destinations: Bangkok, Chiang Mai, Chiang Rai, Kanchanaburi, Pattaya, Ko Samui, Songkhla, Phuket and Hat Yai. Prices start at around 600B outside Bangkok and Chiang Mai and proceed to 2000B or more – genuine tourist-class hotels in Bangkok start at 1000B or so and go to 2500B for standard rooms, and up to 5000 or 10,000B for a suite. These will all have air-con, TV, Western-style toilets and restaurants. Added to room charges will be an 11% government tax, and most of these hotels will include an additional service charge of 8 to 10%.

The Oriental in Bangkok, rated as the number-one hotel in the world by several executive travel publications, starts at 3100B for a standard single and tops off at 20,000B for a deluxe suite.

Resorts In most countries 'resort' refers to hotels which offer substantial recreational facilities (eg tennis, golf, swimming, sailing, etc) in addition to accommodation and dining. In Thai hotel lingo, however, the term simply refers to any hotel that isn't located in an urban area. Hence a few thatched beach huts or a cluster of bungalows in a forest may be called a 'resort'. Several places in Thailand fully deserve the name under any definition – but it pays to look into the facilities before making a reservation.

Temple Lodgings

If you are a Buddhist or can behave like one, you may be able to stay overnight in some temples for a small donation. Facilities are very basic, though, and early rising is expected. Temple lodgings are usually for men only, unless the wat has a place for lay women to stay. Neat, clean dress and a basic knowledge of Thai etiquette are mandatory. See the section on Meditation Study in this chapter for information on wats in Thailand which will accommodate long-term lay students.

FOOD

Some people take to the food in Thailand immediately while others don't; Thai dishes can be pungent and spicy – lots of garlic and chillies are used, especially *phrík khîi nũu* (literally, 'mouse-shit peppers' – these are the small torpedo-shaped devils which can be pushed aside if you are timid about red-hot curries). Almost all Thai food is cooked with fresh ingredients, including vegetables, poultry, pork and some beef. Plenty of lime juice, lemon grass and fresh coriander leaf are added to give the food its characteristic tang, and fish sauce *(náam plaa,* generally made from anchovies) or shrimp paste *(kà-pì)* to make it salty.

Other common seasonings include 'laos' or galanga root *(khàa),* black pepper, three kinds of basil, ground peanuts (more often a condiment), tamarind juice *(náam makhãam),*

ginger *(khĭng)* and coconut milk *(kà-tí)*. The Thais eat a lot of what could be called Chinese food, which is generally, but not always, less spicy.

Rice *(khâo)* is eaten with most meals; 'to eat' in Thai is literally 'eat rice' or *kin khâo*. Thais can be very picky about their rice, insisting on the right temperature and cooking times. Ordinary white rice is called *khâo jâo* and there are many varieties and grades. The finest quality Thai rice is known as *khâo hāwm máli* or 'jasmine fragrant rice' for its sweet, inviting smell when cooked. In the north and north-east 'sticky' or glutinous rice *(khâo nĭaw)* is common and is traditionally eaten with the hands.

Where to Eat

Many smaller restaurants and food stalls do not have menus, so it is worthwhile memorising a standard 'repertoire' of dishes. Most provinces have their own local specialities in addition to the standards and you might try asking for 'whatever is good', allowing the proprietors to choose for you. Of course, you might get stuck with a large bill this way, but with a little practice in Thai social relations you may get some very pleasing results.

The most economical places to eat – and the most dependable – are noodle shops *(ráan kŭaytĭaw)*, curry-and-rice shops *(ráan khâo kaeng)* and night markets *(talàat tôh rŭng)*. Most towns and villages have at least one night market and several noodle and/or curry-rice shops. The night markets in Chiang Mai have a slight reputation for overcharging (especially for large parties), but on the other hand I have never been overcharged for food anywhere in Thailand. It helps if you speak Thai as much as possible. Curry shops are generally open for breakfast and lunch only, and are a very cheap source for nutritious food.

Another common food venue in larger cities is the *ráan khâo tôm*, literally 'boiled rice shop', a type of Chinese-Thai restaurant that offers not just boiled rice soups (khâo tôm) but an assortment of *aahāan taam sàng*, 'food according to order'. In the better places

cooks pride themselves in being able to fix any Thai or Chinese dish you name. One attraction of the ráan khâo tôm is that they tend to stay open late – some are even open 24 hours.

If you're interested in learning how to prepare Thai cuisine, see the section on Thai Cooking Schools in the Bangkok chapter.

What to Eat

Thai food is served with a variety of condiments and sauces, including ground red pepper *(phrík bon)*, ground peanuts *(thùa)*, vinegar with sliced chillies *(náam sôm phrík)*, fish sauce with chillies *(náam plaa phrík)*, a spicy orange-red sauce called *náam phrík sĭi raachaa* (from Si Racha, of course) and any number of other dipping sauces *(náam jîm)* for particular dishes. Soy sauce *(náam síi-yú)* can be requested, though this is normally used as a condiment for Chinese food only.

Except for the 'rice plates' and noodle dishes, Thai meals are usually ordered family-style, ie two or more people order together, sharing different dishes. Traditionally, the party orders one of each kind of dish, eg one chicken, one fish, one soup, etc. One dish is generally large enough for two people. One or two extras may be ordered for a large party. If you come to eat at a Thai restaurant alone and order one of these 'entrees', you had better be hungry or know enough Thai to order a small portion. This latter alternative is not really very acceptable socially: Thais generally consider eating alone in a restaurant unusual – but then as a farang you're an exception anyway.

A cheaper alternative is to order dishes 'over rice' or *râat khâo*. Curry *(kaeng)* over rice is called *khâo kaeng*; in a standard curry shop khâo kaeng is only 7 to 12B a plate.

Another category of Thai food is called *kàp klâem* – dishes meant to be eaten while drinking alcoholic beverages. On some menus these are translated as 'snacks' or 'appetisers'. Typical kàp klâem include *thùa thâwt* (fried peanuts), *kài sāam yàang* (literally 'three kinds of chicken', a plate of chopped ginger, peanuts, mouse-shit peppers and bits of lime – to be mixed and eaten by hand) and various kinds of *yam*, Thai-style salads made with lots of chillies and lime juice.

Vegetarian Those visitors who wish to avoid eating animal food while in Thailand can be accommodated with some effort. Vegetarian restaurants are increasing in number throughout the country, thanks largely to Bangkok's ex-Governor Chamlong Srimuang, whose strict vegetarianism has inspired a nonprofit chain of vegetarian restaurants (*ráan aahãan mangsàwírát*) in Bangkok and several provincial capitals. Look for the green sign out the front showing one or two large Thai numerals – each restaurant is numbered according to the order in which it was established. The food at these restaurants is usually served buffet-style and is very inexpensive – typically 5 to 8B per dish.

Other easy though less widespread venues for vegetarian meals include Indian restaurants, which usually feature a vegetarian section on the menu. Currently these are most prevalent in Bangkok, Chiang Mai, Pattaya and Phuket's Patong Beach. Chinese restaurants are also a good bet since many Chinese Buddhists eat vegetarian food during Buddhist festivals, especially in southern Thailand.

More often than not, however, visiting vegetarians are left to their own devices at the average Thai restaurant. In Thai the magic words are *phõm kin jeh* (for men) or *dii-chãn kin jeh* (women). Like other Thai phrases, getting the tones right makes all the difference – the key word, *jeh*, should rhyme with the English 'jay' without the 'y'. Loosely translated this phrase means 'I eat only vegetarian food'. It might also be necessary to follow with the explanation *phõm/dii-chãn kin tàe phàk*, 'I eat only vegetables.' Don't worry – this won't be interpreted to mean no rice, herbs or fruit. For other useful food phrases, see the list later in this section.

In Thai culture, 'brown' (unpolished) rice is said to be reserved for pigs and prisoners! Look for it at the local feed store.

Table Etiquette

Using the correct utensils and eating gestures will garner much respect from the Thais, who are of the general opinion that Western table manners are rather coarse.

Thais eat most dishes with a fork and tablespoon except for noodles, which are eaten with chopsticks (*tà-kìap*); noodle soups are eaten with spoon and chopsticks. Another exception to the fork-and-spoon routine is sticky rice (common in the north and north-east), which is rolled into balls and eaten with the right hand, along with the food accompanying it.

The fork (*sáwm*) is held in the left hand and used as a probe to push food onto the spoon (*cháwn*); you eat from the spoon. To the Thais, pushing a fork into one's mouth is as uncouth as putting a knife into the mouth is in Western countries.

When serving yourself from a common platter, put no more than one or two spoonfuls onto your own plate at a time. It's customary at the start of a shared meal to eat a spoonful of plain rice first – a gesture that recognises rice as the most important part of the meal. If you're being hosted by Thais, they'll undoubtedly encourage you to eat less rice and more curries, seafood, etc as a gesture of their generosity (since rice costs comparatively little). The humble guest, however, takes rice with every spoonful.

Always leave some food on the serving platters as well as on your plate. To clean your plate and leave nothing on the serving platters would be a grave insult to your hosts. This is why Thais tend to 'over-order' at social meal occasions – the more food is left on the table, the more generous the host appears.

The following list gives standard dishes in Thai script with a transliterated pronunciation guide, using the system outlined in the Language section of the Facts about the Country chapter and an English translation and description.

Curries (kaeng) แกง
hot Thai curry with chicken/beef/pork
kaeng phèt kài/néua/mǔu
แกงเผ็ดไก่/เนื้อ/หมู

rich and spicy Muslim-style curry with chicken/beef & potatoes
kaeng mátsàman kài/néua
แกงมัสมั่นไก่/เนื้อ

mild, Indian-style curry with chicken
kaeng kari kài
แกงกะหรี่ไก่

hot & sour fish & vegetable ragout
kaeng sôm
แกงส้ม

'green' curry, made with fish/chicken/beef
kaeng khǐaw-wǎan plaa/kài/néua
แกงเขียวหวานปลา/ไก่/เนื้อ

savoury curry with chicken/beef
kaeng phánaeng kài/néua
แกงพะแนงไก่/เนื้อ

chicken curry with bamboo shoots
kaeng kài nàw mái
แกงไก่หน่อไม้

catfish curry
kaeng plaa dùk
แกงปลาดุก

Soups (súp) ซุป
mild soup with vegetables & pork
kaeng jèut
แกงจืด

mild soup with vegetables, pork & bean curd
kaeng jèut tâo-hûu
แกงจืดเต้าหู้

soup with chicken, galanga root & coconut
tôm khàa kài
ต้มข่าไก่

prawn & lemon grass soup with mushrooms
tôm yam kûng
ต้มยำกุ้ง

fish ball soup
kaeng jèut lûuk chín
แกงจืดลูกชิ้น

rice soup with fish/chicken/shrimp
khâo tôm plaa/kài/kûng
ข้าวต้มปลา/ไก่/กุ้ง

Egg (khài) ไข่
hard-boiled egg
khài tôm
ไข่ต้ม

fried egg
khài dao
ไข่ดาว

plain omelette
khài jiaw
ไข่เจียว

omelette stuffed with vegetables & pork
khài yát sài
ไข่ยัดไส้

scrambled egg
khài kuan
ไข่กวน

Rice Dishes (khâo râat nâa) ข้าวราดหน้า
fried rice with pork/chicken/shrimp
khâo phàt mǔu/kài/kûng
ข้าวผัดหมู/ไก่/กุ้ง

boned, sliced Hainan-style chicken with marinated rice
khâo man kài
ข้าวมันไก่

chicken with sauce over rice
khâo nâa kài
ข้าวหน้าไก่

roast duck over rice
khâo nâa pèt
ข้าวหน้าเป็ด

'red' pork (char siu) with rice
khâo mǔu daeng
ข้าวหมูแดง

curry over rice
khâo kaeng
ข้าวแกง

Noodles *(kǔaytǐaw/bà-mii)*
ก๋วยเตี๋ยว/บะหมี่

wide rice noodle soup with vegetables & meat
kǔaytǐaw náam
ก๋วยเตี๋ยวน้ำ

wide rice noodles with vegetables & meat
kǔaytǐaw hâeng
ก๋วยเตี๋ยวแห้ง

wide rice noodles with gravy
râat nâa
ราดหน้า

thin rice noodles fried with tofu, vegetables, egg & peanuts
phàt thai
ผัดไทย

fried thin noodles with soy sauce
phàt sii-yíw
ผัดซีอิ๊ว

wheat noodles in broth, with vegetables & meat
bà-mii náam
บะหมี่น้ำ

wheat noodles with vegetables & meat
bà-mii hâeng
บะหมี่แห้ง

Seafood *(aahǎan tháleh)* อาหารทะเล
steamed crab
puu nêung
ปูนึ่ง

steamed crab claws
kâam puu nêung
ก้ามปูนึ่ง

shark fin soup
hǔu chalǎam
หูฉลาม

crisp-fried fish
plaa thâwt
ปลาทอด

fried prawns
kûng thâwt
กุ้งทอด

batter-fried prawns
kûng chúp pâeng thâwt
กุ้งชุบแป้งทอด

grilled prawns
kûng phǎo
กุ้งเผา

steamed fish
plaa nêung
ปลานึ่ง

grilled fish
plaa phǎo
ปลาเผา

whole fish cooked in ginger, onions, soy
sauce
  plaa jĭan
  ปลาเจี๋ยน

sweet & sour fish
  plaa prîaw wăan
  ปลาเปรี้ยวหวาน

cellophane noodles baked with crab
  wûn-sên òp puu
  วุ้นเส้นอบปู

spicy fried squid
  plaa mèuk phàt phèt
  ปลาหมึกผัดเผ็ด

roast squid
  plaa mèuk yâang
  ปลาหมึกย่าง

oysters fried in egg batter
  hăwy thâwt
  หอยทอด

squid
  plaa mèuk
  ปลาหมึก

shrimp
  kûng
  กุ้ง

fish
  plaa
  ปลา

catfish
  plaa dùk
  ปลาดุก

freshwater eel
  plaa lăi
  ปลาไหล

saltwater eel
  plaa lòt
  ปลาหลด

tilapia
  plaa nin
  ปลานิล

spiny lobster
  kûng mangkon
  กุ้งมังกร

green mussel
  hăwy malaeng phùu
  หอยแมลงภู่

scallop
  hăwy phát
  หอยพัด

oyster
  hăwy naang rom
  หอยนางรม

Miscellaneous

stir-fried mixed vegetables
  phàt phàk lăi yàang
  ผัดผักหลายอย่าง

spring rolls
  pàw-pía
  เปาะเปี๊ย

beef in oyster sauce
  néua phàt náam-man hăwy
  เนื้อผัดน้ำมันหอย

duck soup
  pèt tŭn
  เป็ดตุ๋น

roast duck
  pèt yâang
  เป็ดย่าง

fried chicken
kài thâwt

ไก่ทอด

chicken fried in holy basil
kài phàt bai kà-phrao

ไก่ผัดใบกะเพรา

grilled chicken
kài yâang

ไก่ย่าง

chicken fried with chillies
kài phàt phrík

ไก่ผัดพริก

chicken fried with cashews
kài phàt mét má-mûang

ไก่ผัดเม็ดมะม่วง

morning-glory vine fried in garlic, chilli &
bean sauce
phàk bûng fai daeng

ผักบุ้งไฟแดง

'satay' or skewers of barbecued meat, sold on
the street
sà-té

สะเต๊ะ

spicy green papaya salad (north-east
speciality)
sôm-tam

ส้มตำ

noodles with fish curry
khănom jiin náam yaa

ขนมจีนน้ำยา

prawns fried with chillies
kûng phàt phrík phão

กุ้งผัดพริกเผา

chicken fried with ginger
kài phàt khĭng

ไก่ผัดขิง

fried wonton
kíaw kràwp

เกี๊ยวกรอบ

cellophane noodle salad
yam wún sên

ยำวุ้นเส้น

spicy chicken or beef salad
lâap kài/néua

ลาบไก่/เนื้อ

hot & sour grilled beef salad
yam néua

ยำเนื้อ

chicken with bean sprouts
kài sàp thùa ngâwk

ไก่สับถั่วงอก

fried fish cakes with cucumber sauce
thâwt man plaa

ทอดมันปลา

Vegetables (*phàk*) ผัก
angle bean
thùa phuu

ถั่วภู

bitter melon
mará-jiin

มะระจีน

brinjal (round eggplant)
mákhĕua pràw

มะเขือเปราะ

cabbage
phàk kà-làm or *kà-làm plii*

ผักกะหล่ำ กะหล่ำปลี

cauliflower
dàwk kà-làm
ดอกกะหล่ำ

Chinese radish (daikon)
phàk kàat hūa
ผักกาดหัว

corn
khâo phôht
ข้าวโพด

cucumber
taeng kwaa
แตงกวา

eggplant
mákhēua mûang
มะเขือม่วง

garlic
kràtiam
กระเทียม

lettuce
phàk kàat
ผักกาด

long bean
thùa fák yao
ถั่วฝักยาว

okra (ladyfingers)
krà-jíap
กระเจี๊ยบ

onion (bulb)
hūa hāwm
หัวหอม

onion (green, 'scallions')
tôn hāwm
ต้นหอม

peanuts (groundnuts)
tùa lísōng
ถั่วลิสง

potato
man faràng
มันฝรั่ง

pumpkin
fák thawng
ฟักทอง

taro
pheùak
เผือก

tomato
mákhēua thêt
มะเขือเทศ

Fruit (*phōn-lá-mái*) ผลไม้
mandarin orange (year-round)
sôm
ส้ม

watermelon (year-round)
taeng moh
แตงโม

guava (year-round)
fa-ràng
ฝรั่ง

lime (year-round)
má-nao
มะนาว

mangosteen – round, purple fruit with juicy
white flesh (April to September)
mang-khút
มังคุด

coconut – grated for cooking when mature, eaten from the shell with a spoon when young; juice is sweetest and most plentiful in young coconuts (year-round)
máphráo

มะพร้าว

rose-apple – small, apple-like texture, very fragrant (April to July)
chom-phûu

ชมพู่

tamarind – comes ·in sweet as well as tart varieties (year-round)
mákhāam

มะขาม

sapodilla – small, brown, oval, sweet but pungent-smelling (July to September)
lámút

ละมุด

pineapple (year-round)
sàp-pàrót

สับปะรด

mango – several varieties & seasons
má-mûang

มะม่วง

custard-apple (July to October)
náwy naa

น้อยหน่า

'rambeh' – small, reddish-brown, sweet, apricot-like (April to May)
máfai

มะไฟ

pomelo – large citrus similar to grapefruit (year-round)
sôm oh

ส้มโอ

papaya (year-round)
málákaw

มะละกอ

durian – held in high esteem by the Thais, but most Westerners dislike this fruit. There are several varieties and seasons, so keep trying
thúrian

ทุเรียน

rambutan – red, hairy-skinned fruit with grape-like interior (July to September)
ngáw

เงาะ

jackfruit – similar in appearance to durian but much easier to take (year-round)
kha-nŭn

ขนุน

banana – over 20 varieties (year-round)
klûay

กล้วย

longan – 'dragon's eyes', small, brown, spherical, similar to rambutan (July to October)
lam yài

ลำไย

Sweets *(khāwng wāan)* ของหวาน
Thai custard
sāngkha-yaa

สังขยา

coconut custard
sāngkha-yaa ma-phráo

สังขยามะพร้าว

sweet shredded egg yolk
fāwy thawng

ฝอยทอง

egg custard
maw kaeng

หม้อแกง

banana in coconut milk
klûay bùat chii

กล้วยบวชชี

'Indian-style' banana, fried
klûay khàek

กล้วยแขก

sweet palm kernels
lûuk taan chêuam

ลูกตาลเชื่อม

Thai jelly with coconut cream
ta-kôh

ตะโก้

sticky rice with coconut cream
khâo nĩaw daeng

ข้าวเหนียวแดง

sticky rice in coconut cream with ripe mango
khâo nĩaw má-mûang

ข้าวเหนียวมะม่วง

Some Useful Food Words

For 'I' men use *phõm*; women use *dii-chãn*

I eat only vegetarian food.
phõm/dii-chãn kin jeh

ผม/ดีฉัน กินเจ

I can't eat pork.
phõm/dii-chãn kin mũu mâi dâi

ผม/ดีฉัน กินหมูไม่ได้

I can't eat beef.
phõm/dii-chãn kin néua mâi dâi

ผม/ดีฉัน กินเนื้อไม่ได้

(I) don't like it hot & spicy.
mâi châwp phèt

ไม่ชอบเผ็ต

(I) like it hot & spicy.
châwp phèt

ชอบเผ็ต

(I) can eat Thai food.
kin aahãan thai pen

กินอาหารไทยเป็น

What do you have that's special?
mii a-rai phí-sèt?

มีอะไรพิเศษ?

I didn't order this.
nîi phõm/dii-chãn mâi dâi sàng

นี้ ผม/ดีฉัน ไม่ได้สั่ง

Do you have...?
mii...mãi?

มี...ไหม?

DRINKS
Nonalcoholic Drinks
Fruit Juices & Shakes The incredible variety of fruits in Thailand means a corresponding availability of nutritious juices and shakes. The all-purpose term for fruit juice is *náam phõn-lá-mái*. Put *náam* (water or juice) together with the name of any fruit and you can get anything from *náam sôm* (orange juice) to *náam taeng moh* (watermelon juice). When a blender or extractor is used, fruit juices may be called *náam khán* or 'squeezed juice' (eg *náam sàppàrót khán*, pineapple juice). When mixed in a blender with ice the result is *náam pon* (literally, 'mixed juice') as in *náam málákaw pon*, a papaya 'smoothie' or 'shake'. Night markets will often have vendors specialising in juices and shakes.

Thais prefer to drink most fruit juices with a little salt mixed in. Unless a vendor is used to serving farangs, your fruit juice or shake will come slightly salted. If you prefer unsalted fruit juices, specify *mâi sài kleua* (without salt).

Sugar cane juice *(náam âwy)* is a Thai favourite and a very refreshing accompaniment to curry-and-rice plates. Many small restaurants or food stalls that don't offer any other juices will have a supply of freshly squeezed náam âwy on hand.

Coffee Over the last 10 years or so, Nescafé and other instant coffees have made deep inroads into the Thai coffee culture at the expense of freshly ground coffee. The typical Thai restaurant – especially those in hotels, guesthouses and other tourist-oriented establishments – serves instant coffee with packets of artificial, non-dairy creamer on the side. Up-market hotels and coffee shops sometimes also offer filtered and espresso coffees at premium prices.

Traditionally, coffee in Thailand is locally grown (mostly in hilly areas of northern and southern Thailand), roasted by wholesalers, ground by vendors and filtered just before serving. Thai-grown coffee may not be as full and rich-tasting as gourmet Sumatran, Jamaican or Kona beans but to my palate it's still considerably tastier than Nescafé or other instant coffees.

Sometimes restaurants or vendors with the proper accoutrements for making traditional filtered coffee will keep a supply of Nescafé just for farangs (or moneyed Thais, since instant always costs a few baht more per cup than filtered). To get real Thai coffee ask for *kafae thǔng* (literally, 'bag coffee'), which refers to the traditional method of preparing a cup of coffee by filtering hot water through a bag-shaped cloth filter. Thailand's best coffee of this sort is served in Hokkien-style cafes in the southern provinces. Elsewhere in Thailand outdoor morning markets are the best place to find kafae thǔng.

The usual kafae thǔng is served mixed with sugar and sweetened condensed milk – if you won't want either be sure to specify *kafae dam* (black coffee) followed with *mâi sài náam-taan* (without sugar). Kafae thǔng is often served in a glass instead of a ceramic

cup – to pick a glass of hot coffee up, grasp it along the top rim.

Tea Both Indian-style (black) and Chinese-style (green or semi-cured) teas are commonly served in Thailand. The latter predominates in Chinese restaurants and is the usual ingredient in *náam chaa*, the weak, often lukewarm tea-water traditionally served in Thai restaurants for free. The aluminium teapots seen on every table in the average restaurant are filled with náam chaa; ask for a plain glass *(kâew plào)* and you can drink as much as you like at no charge. For iced náam chaa ask for a glass of ice (usually 1B) and pour your own; for fresh, undiluted Chinese tea request *chaa jiin*.

Black tea, both imported and Thai-grown, is usually available in the same restaurants or food stalls that serve real coffee. An order of *chaa ráwn* (hot tea) almost always results in a cup (or glass) of black tea with sugar and condensed milk. As with coffee you must specify as you order if you want black tea without milk and/or sugar.

Water Water purified for drinking purposes is simply called *náam dèum* (drinking water), whether boiled or filtered. *All* water offered to customers in restaurants or to guests in an office or home will be purified, so you needn't fret about the safety of taking a sip (for more information on water safety, see the Health section in this chapter). In restaurants you can ask for *náam plào* (plain water), which is always either boiled or taken from a purified source; it's served by the glass at no charge or you can order by the bottle. A bottle of carbonated water (soda) costs about the same as a bottle of plain purified water but the bottles are smaller.

Beverages *(khreûang dèum)*　　เครื่องดื่ม
plain water
　　náam plào
น้ำเปล่า

hot water
náam ráwn
น้ำร้อน

boiled water
náam tôm
น้ำต้ม

cold water
náam yen
น้ำเย็น

ice
náam khāeng
น้ำแข็ง

Chinese tea
chaa jiin
ชาจีน

weak Chinese tea
náam chaa
น้ำชา

iced Thai tea with milk & sugar
chaa yen
ชาเย็น

iced Thai tea with sugar only
chaa dam yen
ชาดำเย็น

no sugar (command)
mâi sài náam-taan
ไม่ใส่น้ำตาล

hot Thai tea with sugar
chaa dam ráwn
ชาดำร้อน

hot Thai tea with milk & sugar
chaa ráwn
ชาร้อน

hot coffee with milk & sugar
kafae ráwn
กาแฟร้อน

traditional filtered coffee with milk & sugar
kafae thūng (ko-píi in southern Thailand)
กาแฟถุง/โกปี๊

iced coffee with sugar, no milk
oh-liang
โอเลี้ยง

Ovaltine
oh-wantin
โอวันติน

orange soda
náam sôm
น้ำส้ม

plain milk
nom jèut
นมจืด

iced lime juice with sugar (usually with salt too)
náam manao
น้ำมะนาว

no salt (command)
mâi sài kleua
ไม่ใส่เกลือ

soda water
náam sōh-daa
น้ำโซดา

bottled drinking water
náam dèum khùat
น้ำดื่มขวด

bottle
khùat
ขวด

glass
kâew

แก้ว

Alcoholic Drinks

Drinking in Thailand can be quite expensive in relation to the cost of other consumer activities. The Thai government has placed increasingly heavy taxes on liquor and beer, so that now about 30B out of the 45 to 55B that you pay for a large beer is tax. Whether this is an effort to raise more tax revenue (the result has been a sharp decrease in the consumption of alcoholic beverages for perhaps a net decrease in revenue) or to discourage consumption, drinking can wreak havoc with your budget. One large bottle (630 ml) of Singha beer costs more than half the minimum daily wage of a Bangkok worker.

Beer Three brands of beer are brewed in Thailand by Thai-owned breweries: Singha, Amarit and Kloster. Singha (pronounced 'Sĭng' by the Thais) is by far the most common beer in Thailand, with some 66% of the domestic market. The original recipe was formulated in 1934 by nobleman Phya Bhirom Bhakdi and his son Prachuap, who was the first Thai to earn a brewmaster's diploma from Munich's Doemens Institute. Singha is a strong, hoppy-tasting brew thought by many to be the best beer produced in Asia. The barley for Singha is grown in Thailand, the hops are imported from Germany and the rated alcohol content is 6%. Singha is sometimes available on tap in pubs and restaurants.

Kloster is quite a bit smoother and lighter than Singha and generally costs 5B more per bottle, but it is a good-tasting brew often favoured by Western visitors, expats and upwardly mobile Thais who view it as somewhat of a status symbol. Amarit NB (the initials stand for 'naturally brewed' though who knows whether it is or not) is similar in taste to Singha but a bit smoother, and is brewed by Thai Amarit, the same company that produces Kloster. Like Kloster it costs a few baht more than the national brew.

Together Amarit and Kloster claim only 7% of Thailand's beer consumption. Alcoholic content for each is 4.7%.

Boon Rawd Breweries, makers of Singha, also produce a lighter beer called Singha Gold which only comes in small bottles; most people seem to prefer either Kloster or regular Singha to Singha Gold, which is a little on the bland side. Better is Singha's new canned 'draft beer' – if you like cans.

Carlsberg, jointly owned by Danish and Thai interests, is a strong newcomer to Thailand. As elsewhere in South-East Asia, Carlsberg has used an aggressive promotion campaign (backed by the makers of Mekong whisky) to grab around 25% of the Thai market in only two years. The company adjusted its recipe to match Singha's 6% alcohol content, which may be one reason they've surpassed Kloster and Amarit so quickly. Singha has retaliated in advertisements suggesting that drinking Carlsberg is unpatriotic. Heineken is about to enter the fray, so look for more sparks to fly.

The Thai word for beer is *bia*. Draught beer is *bia sòt* (literally, 'fresh beer').

Spirits Rice whisky is a big favourite in Thailand and somewhat more affordable than beer for the average Thai. It has a sharp, sweet taste not unlike rum, with an alcoholic content of 35%. The two major liquor manufacturers are Suramaharas Co and the Surathip Group. The first produces the famous Mekong (pronounced 'Mâe-khŏng') and Kwangthong brands, the second the Hong (swan) labels including Hong Thong, Hong Ngoen, Hong Yok and Hong Tho. Mekong and Kwangthong cost around 100 to 120B for a large bottle *(klom)* or 55 to 60B for the flask-sized bottle *(baen)*. An even smaller bottle, the *kòk*, is occasionally available for 30 to 35B. The Hong brands are less expensive.

In the late 1980s, the two liquor giants met and formed a common board of directors to try to end the fierce competition brought about when a 1985 government tax increase led to a 40% drop in Thai whisky sales. The meeting has resulted in an increase in whisky prices but probably also in better distribution – Mekong and Kwangthong have generally not been available in regions where the Hong labels are marketed and vice versa. A third company, Pramuanphon Distillery in Nakhon Pathom, markets a line of cut-rate rice whisky under three labels: Maew Thong (Gold Cat), Sing Chao Phraya (Chao Phraya Lion) and Singharat (Lion-King).

More expensive Thai whiskies appealing to the pre-Johnnie Walker set include Singharaj blended whisky (240B a bottle) and VO Royal Thai whisky (260B), each with 40% alcohol.

One company in Thailand produces a true rum, that is, a distilled liquor made from sugar cane, called Sang Thip (formerly Sang Som). Alcohol content is 40% and the stock is supposedly aged. Sang Thip costs several baht more than the rice whiskies, but for those who find Mekong and the like unpalatable, it is an alternative worth trying.

Other Liquor A cheaper alternative is *lâo khão*, or 'white liquor', of which there are two broad categories: legal and contraband. The legal kind is generally made from sticky rice and is produced for regional consumption. Like Mekong and its competitors, it is 35% alcohol, but sells for 45 to 50B per klom, or roughly half the price. The taste is sweet and raw and much more aromatic than the amber stuff – no amount of mixer will disguise the distinctive taste.

The illegal kinds are made from various agricultural products including sugar palm sap, coconut milk, sugar cane, taro and rice. Alcohol content may vary from as little as 10 or 12% to as much as 95%. Generally this *lâo thèuan* (jungle liquor) is weaker in the south and stronger in the north and northeast. This is the choice of the many Thais who can't afford to pay the heavy government liquor taxes; prices vary but 10 to 15B worth of the stronger concoctions will intoxicate three or four people. These types of home-brew or moonshine are generally taken straight with pure water as a chaser. In smaller towns, almost every garage-type restaurant (except, of course, Muslim restaurants) keeps some under the counter for sale. Sometimes roots and herbs are added to jungle liquor to enhance flavour and colour.

Currently, herbal liquors are fashionable throughout the country and can be found at roadside vendors, small pubs and in a few guesthouses. These liquors are made by soaking various herbs, roots, seeds, fruit and bark in lâo khão to produce a range of concoctions called *yàa dong*. Many of the yàa dong preparations are purported to have specific health-enhancing qualities. Some of them taste fabulous while others are rank.

ENTERTAINMENT
Cinema
Movie theatres are found in towns and cities throughout the country. Typical programmes include US and European shoot-em-ups mixed with Thai comedies and romances. Violent action pictures are always a big draw; as a rule of thumb, the smaller the town, the more violent the film offerings. English-language films are only shown with their original soundtracks in a handful of theatres in Bangkok, Chiang Mai and Hat Yai; elsewhere all foreign films are dubbed in Thai. Ticket prices range from 10 to 50B. Every film in Thailand begins with a playback of the royal anthem, accompanied by projected pictures of the royal family. Viewers are expected to stand during the anthem.

Bars & Member Clubs
Urban Thais are night people and every town of any size has a selection of nightspots. For the most part they are male-dominated, though the situation is changing rapidly in the larger cities, where young couples are increasingly seen in bars.

Of the many types of bars, probably the most popular at the moment is the 'old west' style, patterned after Thai fantasies of the 19th-century American west – lots of wood and cowboy paraphernalia. Another up-and-coming style is the 'Thai classic' pub, which is typically decorated with old black & white photos of Thai kings Rama VI and Rama VII, along with Thai antiques from northern and central Thailand. The old west and Thai-classic nightspots are cosy, friendly and popular with couples as well as singles.

The 'go-go' bars seen in lurid photos published by the Western media are limited to a few areas in Bangkok, Chiang Mai, Pattaya and Phuket's Patong Beach. These are bars in which girls typically wear bathing suits; in some bars they dance to recorded music on a narrow raised stage. To some visitors it's pathetic, to others paradise.

'Member clubs,' similar to old-style Playboy clubs, provide a slinky, James Bond atmosphere of feigned elegance and savoir faire in which women clad in long gowns or tight skirts entertain suited men in softly-lit sofa groups. Private rooms are also available. A couple of drinks and a chat with the hostesses typically costs around US$40, including membership charges. These clubs are thinly scattered across the Soi Lang Suan and Sukhumvit Rd areas in Bangkok.

Coffee Houses

Aside from the Western-style cafe, which is becoming increasingly popular in Bangkok,

---

Prostitution

Thais generally blame 19th-century Chinese immigrants for bringing prostitution to Thailand, but in reality Thailand was fertile ground because of its longstanding concubinary tradition. Until 1934 Siam had no laws forbidding polygamy – or even a word for this Judaeo-Christian concept. Most men of wealth counted among their retinue at least one *sŏhphenii* (from the Sanskrit term for a woman trained in the kama sutra and other amorous arts), a word often translated as 'prostitute' in English today but which might better be translated as 'courtesan'. In addition, the traditional Thai *mia yài mia nói* (major wife, minor wife) system made it socially permissible for a man to keep several mistresses – all Thai kings up to Rama IV had mia noi, as did virtually any Thai male who could afford them until recent times. Even today talk of mia nois hardly raises an eyebrow anywhere in Thailand as the tradition lives on among wealthy businessmen, *jâo phâw* (organised crime 'godfathers') and politicians.

The first brothels in Thailand, however, were indisputably established by Chinese immigrants in Bangkok's Sampeng district in the mid-19th century. In the beginning, only Chinese women worked as prostitutes; when Thai women became involved at the turn of the century, they usually took Chinese names. Prostitution eventually spread from Sampeng to Chinese districts throughout Thailand and is now found in virtually every village, town and city in the kingdom. Ethnic Chinese still control most of the trade, although the prostitutes themselves now come from almost every ethnic background. In the last few years Bangkok has even seen an influx of Russian women – most on Tourist Visas – participating in the sex trade through escort services.

The first true prostitutes – non-cohabiting women who accepted cash for sex services – to appear outside Sampeng came along soon after King Rama VII's 1934 decree banning polygamy. During WW II the Thai government stationed large numbers of Thai troops in the north to prevent Bangkok from becoming a military target. At the beginning of the war Chiang Mai had only two known prostitutes but by 1945 there were hundreds servicing the soldiers. Prostitution wasn't declared illegal until the 1950s when Field Marshal Phibun bullied his way into the PM's seat. In the 1960s and 1970s the Vietnam War brought unprecedented numbers of foreign soldiers to Bangkok and Pattaya on 'rest & recreation' tours, creating a new class of prostitutes who catered to foreigners rather than Thais.

Current estimates of the number of Thai citizens directly involved in offering sex services vary from the Ministry of Public Health's conservative 86,000 to wild bar-stool estimates of 500,000. After an intensive two-year study into the prostitution industry, Chulalongkorn University's Population Institute came up with a reasoned estimate of 200,000 to 210,000, a figure now widely considered the most realistic. This number is thought to include around 10,000 male and child prostitutes. Although often portrayed as Asia's sex capital, Thailand actually ranks third (behind Taiwan and the Philippines) in per-capita number of sex workers, according to international human rights reports.

there are two other kinds of cafes or coffee shops in Thailand. One is the traditional Hokkien-style coffee shop (*ráan kaa-fae*) where thick, black, boiled coffee is served in simple, casual surroundings. These coffee shops are common in the Chinese quarters of southern Thai provincial capitals, less common elsewhere. Frequented mostly by older Thai and Chinese men, they offer a place to read the newspaper, sip coffee and gossip about neighbours and politics.

The other type, called *kaa-feh* (cafe) or 'coffee house', is more akin to a nightclub, where Thai men consort with a variety of Thai female hostesses. This is the Thai counterpart to farang go-go bars, except girls wear dresses instead of bathing suits. A variation on this theme is the 'sing-song' cafe in which a succession of female singers take turns fronting a live band. Small groups of men sit at tables ogling the girls while putting away prodigious amounts of Johnnie Walker, J&B or Mekong whisky. For the price of a few house drinks, the men can invite one of the singers to sit at their table for a while. Some of the singers work double shifts as part-time mistresses, others limit their services to singing and pouring drinks.

Today the highest per-capita concentration of sex workers is found in the north – Chiang Mai, for example, has an estimated 3000 service girls in two brothel districts. Brothels are less common in the southern provinces, except in Chinese-dominated Phuket, Hat Yai and Yala, and in Thai-Malaysian border towns, where the clientele is almost exclusively Malay.

Most of the country's sex industry is invisible to the visiting farang. A typical mid-level coffee house/brothel will offer girls ranked in price according to their beauty or supposed skills; prices are denoted by coloured tags the women wear on their dresses. Back-alley places service low-wage earners for as little as 30 or 40B. At the other end of the spectrum, Thai businessmen and government officials entertain in private brothels and member clubs where services average 1000 to 5000B. Sociologists estimate that 75% of single Thai males engage the services of a prostitute an average of twice a month.

Unlike Western prostitution, there are few 'pimps' (people who manage one or more prostitutes) in Thailand. Instead, a network of procurers/suppliers and brothel owners control the trade, taking a high proportion (or all) of the sex service fees. At its worst, the industry takes girls sold or indentured by their families, sometimes even kidnapped, and forces them to work in conditions of virtual slavery. A few years ago a Phuket brothel of the type rarely patronised by farangs caught fire; several young women who were chained to their beds by the management died in the fire.

In the Patpong-style bar catering to foreigners, most bar girls and go-go dancers are semi-freelance agents; they earn their income from taking a percentage of drinks bought on their behalf and from sex liaisons arranged outside the premises – usually after closing (if they leave during working hours, a customer usually pays a 'bar fine' on their behalf). Fees for services are then negotiated between customer and prostitute.

Most prostitutes – male and female – are young, uneducated and from village areas. Researchers estimate they have a maximum working life of 10 to 12 years – if they haven't saved up enough money to retire by then (few do), they're often unemployable due to mental and physical disabilities acquired during their short working life. Various Thai volunteer groups are engaged in counselling Thailand's sex workers – helping them to escape the industry or to educate them to the dangers of STDs, particularly AIDS.

Officially prostitution is illegal, but the government has been either powerless or unwilling to enforce the laws. In 1992 the Thai cabinet introduced a bill to decriminalise prostitution in the hope that it would make it easier for prostitutes to seek counselling or STD testing without fear of prosecution. So far no such bill has been enacted, but in June 1993 Prime Minister Chuan Leekpai ordered a crackdown on prostitutes under 18, an act which has had quantifiable results but has by no means banished under-18s from the trade. A recent US State Department human rights report of the same year found that the percentage of prostitutes in Thailand under the age of 18 falls well below that found in India, Bangladesh, Sri Lanka or the Philippines. In July 1994 the government strengthened child prostitution laws by making clients of under-age sex workers subject to fines and jail terms. ∎

Discos

Discotheques are popular in larger cities; outside Bangkok they're mostly attached to tourist or luxury hotels. The main disco clientele is Thai, though foreigners are welcome. Some provincial discos retain female staff as professional dance partners for male entertainment, but for the most part discos are considered fairly respectable nightspots for couples.

THINGS TO BUY

Many bargains await you in Thailand if you have the space to carry them back. Always haggle to get the best price, except in department stores. And don't go shopping in the company of touts, tour guides or friendly strangers as they will inevitably – no matter what they say – take a commission on anything you buy, thus driving prices up.

Textiles

Fabric is possibly the best all-round buy in Thailand. Thai silk is considered the best in the world – the coarse weave and soft texture of the silk means it is more easily dyed than harder, smoother silks, resulting in brighter colours and a unique lustre. Silk can be purchased cheaply in the north and north-east where it is made or, more easily, in Bangkok. Excellent and reasonably priced tailor shops can make your choice of fabric into almost any pattern. A silk suit should cost around 3700 to 6300B.

Cottons are also a good deal – common items like the *phâakhamãa* (reputed to have over a hundred uses in Thailand) and the *phâasîn* (the slightly larger female equivalent) make great tablecloths and curtains. Good ready-made cotton shirts are available, such as the *mâw hâwm* (Thai work shirt) and the *kuay haeng* (Chinese-style shirt) – see the sections on Pasang in the north and Ko Yo in the south for where to see cotton-weaving.

In recent years, cotton-weaving has become very popular in the north-east and there are fabulous finds in Nong Khai, Roi-Et, Khon Kaen and Mahasarakham. The *mãwn khwãan*, a hard, triangle-shaped pillow made in the north-east, makes a good souvenir and comes in many sizes. The north-east is also famous for its *mát-mìi* cloth, thick cotton or silk fabric woven from tie-dyed threads – similar to Indonesia's ikat fabrics.

In the north you can find Lanna-style textiles based on intricate Thai Lü patterns from Nan, Laos and China's Sipsongpanna (Xishuangbanna).

Fairly nice batik *(pa-té)* is available in the south in patterns that are more similar to batik found in Malaysia than in Indonesia.

Clothing

Tailor-made and ready-made clothes are relatively inexpensive. If you're not particular about style you could pick up an entire wardrobe of travelling clothes at one of Bangkok's many street markets (eg Pratunam) for what you'd pay for one designer shirt in New York or Paris.

You're more likely to get a good fit if you resort to a tailor but be wary of the quickie 24-hour tailor shops; the clothing is often made of inferior fabric or the poor tailoring means the arms start falling off after three weeks' wear. It's best to ask Thai or longtime foreign residents for a tailor recommendation and then go for two or three fittings.

Yao embroidery made by hill-tribe women

Shoulder Bags

Thai shoulder bags (yâam) are generally quite well made. They come in many varieties, some woven by hill tribes, others by Thai cottage industry. The best are made by the Lahu hill tribes, whom the Thais call 'Musoe'. The weaving is more skilful and the bags tend to last longer than those made by other tribes. For an extra-large yaam, the Karen-made bag is a good choice, and is easy to find in the Mae Hong Son area. These days many hill tribes are copying patterns from tribes other than their own.

Overall, Chiang Mai has the best selection of standard shoulder bags, but Bangkok has the best prices – try the Indian district, Pahurat, for these as well as anything else made of cloth. Roi-Et and Mahasarakham in the north-east are also good hunting grounds for locally made shoulder bags. Prices range from 45B for a cheaply made bag to 200B for something special.

Antiques

Real antiques cannot be taken out of Thailand without a permit from the Department of Fine Arts. No Buddha image, new or old, may be exported without permission – again, refer to the Fine Arts Department, or, in some cases, the Department of Religious Affairs, under the Ministry of Education. Too many private collectors smuggling and hoarding Siamese art (Buddhas in particular) around the world have led to strict controls. See the section on Customs earlier in this chapter for more information on the export of art objects and antiques.

Chinese and Thai antiques are sold in Bangkok's Chinatown in two areas: Wang Burapha (the streets which have Chinese 'gates' over the entrance) and Nakhon Kasem. Some antiques (and many fakes) are sold at the Weekend Market in Chatuchak Park. Objects for sale in the tourist antique shops are fantastically overpriced, as can be expected. In recent years northern Thailand has become a good source of Thai antiques – prices are about half what you'd typically pay in Bangkok.

Jewellery

Thailand is one of the world's largest exporters of gems and ornaments, rivalled only by India and Sri Lanka. The International Colorstones Association (ICA) recently relocated from Los Angeles to Bangkok's Chan Issara Tower, and the World Federation of Diamond Bourses (WFDB) is establishing a bourse in Bangkok – two events that recognise that Thailand has become the world trade and production centre for precious stones. The biggest importers of Thai jewellery are the USA, Japan and Switzerland.

Although rough stone sources in Thailand itself have decreased dramatically, stones are now imported from Australia, Sri Lanka and other countries to be cut, polished and traded here. There are over 30 diamond-cutting houses in Bangkok alone. One of the results of this remarkable growth of the gem industry – in Thailand the gem trade has increased nearly 10% every year for the last 15 years – is that the prices are rising rapidly.

If you know what you are doing you can make some really good buys in both unset gems and finished jewellery. Gold ornaments are sold at a good rate as labour costs are low. The best bargains in gems are jade, rubies and sapphires. Buy from reputable dealers only, unless you're a gemologist.

The biggest gem centres in Thailand are Kanchanaburi, Mae Sot, Mae Sai and Chanthaburi – these areas are where the Bangkok dealers go to buy their stones. The Asian Institute of Gemological Sciences (☎ 513-2112; fax 236-7803), 484 Ratchadaphisek Rd (off Lat Phrao Rd in the Huay Khwang district, north-east Bangkok), offers short-term courses in gemology as well as tours of gem mines for those interested. You can bring gems here for inspection but they don't assess value, only authenticity and grading. John Hoskin's book Buyer's Guide to Thai Gems & Jewellery, available at Bangkok bookshops, is a useful introduction to Thai gems.

Warning Be wary of special 'deals' that are offered for one day only or which set you up as a 'courier' in which you're promised big money. Many travellers end up losing big.

Shop around and *don't be hasty*. Remember: There's no such thing as a 'government sale' or a 'factory price' at a gem or jewellery shop; the Thai government does not own or manage any gem or jewellery shops.

See the Dangers & Annoyances section earlier in this chapter for detailed warnings on gem fraud.

Hill-Tribe Crafts

Interesting embroidery, clothing, bags and jewellery from the north can be bought in Bangkok at Narayan Phand, Lan Luang Rd, at branches of the Queen's Hillcrafts Foundation, and at various tourist shops around town. See Things to Buy in the Bangkok chapter for details.

In Chiang Mai there are shops selling handicrafts all along Thaphae Rd and there is a shop sponsored by missionaries near Prince Royal College. There is a branch of the Queen's Hillcrafts Foundation in Chiang Rai. It's worth shopping around for the best prices and bargaining. The all-round best buys of northern hill-tribe crafts are at the Chiang Mai night bazaar – if you know how to bargain.

Lacquerware

Thailand produces some good Burmese-style lacquerware (a style which actually originated in Thailand) and sells some Burmese-made stuff along the northern Burmese border. Try Mae Sot, Mae Sariang and Mae Sai for the best buys.

Nielloware

This art came from Europe via Nakhon Si Thammarat and has been cultivated in Thailand for over 700 years. Engraved silver is inlaid with niello – an alloy of lead, silver, copper and sulphur – to form striking black-and-silver jewellery designs. Nielloware is one of Thailand's best buys.

Ceramics

Many kinds of hand-thrown pottery, old and new, are available throughout the kingdom. Most well-known are the greenish Sangkhalok or Thai celadon products from the Sukhothai-Si Satchanalai area and Central Thailand's *bencharong* or 'five-colour' style. The latter is based on Chinese patterns while the former is a Thai original that has been imitated throughout China and South-East Asia. Rough, unglazed pottery from the north and north-east can also be very appealing.

Other Crafts

Under Queen Sirikit's Supplementary Occupations & Related Techniques (SUPPORT) foundation, a number of regional crafts from around Thailand have been successfully revived. *Málaeng tháp* collages and sculptures are made by the artful cutting and assembling of the metallic, multicoloured wings and carapaces of female wood-boring beetles *(Sternocera aequisignata)*, harvested after they die at the end of their reproductive cycle between July and September each year. Hailing mostly from the north and north-east, they can nonetheless be found in craft shops all over Thailand.

For 'Damascene ware' (known as *kràm* in Thai), gold and silver wire is hammered into a cross-hatched steel surface to create exquisitely patterned bowls and boxes. Look for them in more upscale Bangkok department stores and craft shops.

Yaan lipao is a type of intricately woven basket made from a hardy grass in southern Thailand. Ever since the Queen and other female members of the royal family began

Lahu belt buckle

carrying delicate yaan lipao purses, they've been a Thai fashion staple. Basketry of this type is most easily found in the southern provincial capitals, or in Bangkok shops that specialise in regional handicrafts.

Furniture

Rattan and hardwood furniture items are often good buys and can be made to order. Bangkok and Chiang Mai have the best selection of styles and quality. Teak furniture has become relatively scarce and expensive; rosewood is a more reasonable buy.

Fake or Pirated Goods

In Bangkok, Chiang Mai and all the tourist centres, there is black-market street trade in fake designer goods; particularly Lacoste (crocodile) and Ralph Lauren polo shirts, Levi's jeans, and Rolex, Dunhill and Cartier watches. Tin-tin T-shirts are also big. No-one pretends they're the real thing, at least not the vendors themselves. The European manufacturers are applying heavy pressure on the Asian governments involved to get this stuff off the street, so it may not be around for much longer.

In some cases foreign name brands are legally produced under licence in Thailand and represent good value. A pair of legally produced Levi's 501s, for example, typically costs US$10 from a Thai street vendor, and US$30 to US$40 in Levi's home town of San Francisco! Careful examination of the product usually reveals telltale characteristics that confirm or deny the item's legality.

Prerecorded cassette tapes are another illegal bargain in Thailand. The tapes are 'pirated', that is, no royalties are paid to the copyright owners. Average prices are from 25 to 35B per cassette for amazingly up-to-date music. Word has it that these will disappear from the streets, too, under pressure from the US music industry.

In 1991 four of the major tape piraters (including market leaders Peacock and Eagle) agreed to stop producing unlicensed tapes, but only on condition that the police prosecute the myriad smaller companies doing business. As of early 1994, it was becoming quite difficult to find pirated tapes anywhere in the country except on Bangkok's Khao San Rd. Licensed tapes, when available, cost 60 to 90B each; Thai music tapes cost the same.

Other Goods

Bangkok is famous the world over for its street markets – Pratunam, Chatuchak Park, Khlong Toey, Sampeng (Chinatown), Banglamphu and many more – where you'll find things you never imagined you wanted but once you see, you feel you can't possibly do without. Even if you don't want to spend any money, they're great places to wander around.

For top-end shopping, the two main centres in Bangkok are the area around the Oriental Hotel off Charoen Krung (New) Rd and the River City shopping complex on the river next to the Royal Orchid Sheraton Hotel. At the other end, Thailand's two big department store chains, Robinson and Central, offer reasonably priced clothing, electronics and housewares at several branches in Bangkok as well as in the larger towns.

Getting There & Away

AIR

The expense of getting to Bangkok per air km varies quite a bit depending on your point of departure. However, you can take heart in the fact that Bangkok is one of the cheapest cities in the world to fly out of, due to the Thai government's loose restrictions on airfares and the close competition between airlines and travel agencies. The result is that with a little shopping around, you can come up with some real bargains. If you can find a cheap one-way ticket to Bangkok, take it, because you are virtually guaranteed to find one of equal or lesser cost for the return trip once you get there.

From most places around the world your best bet will be budget, excursion or promotional fares – when enquiring from airlines ask for the various fares in that order. Each carries its own set of restrictions and it's up to you to decide which set works best in your case. Fares fluctuate, but in general they are cheaper from September to April (northern hemisphere) and from March to November (southern hemisphere).

Fares listed here should serve as a guideline – don't count on them staying this way for long (they may go down!).

Tickets

Although other Asian centres are now competitive with Bangkok for buying discounted airline tickets, this is still a good place for shopping around.

Travellers should note, however, that some Bangkok travel agencies have a shocking reputation. Taking money and then delaying or not coming through with the tickets, as well as providing tickets with limited validity periods or severe use restrictions are all part of the racket. There are a large number of perfectly honest agents, but beware of the rogues.

Some typical discount fares being quoted from Bangkok include:

Around Asia	Fare
Calcutta	3750B
Colombo	5250B
Delhi	5775B
Hong Kong	4150B
Jakarta	5895B
Kathmandu	5025B
Kuala Lumpur	2750B
Penang	2500B
Rangoon	3150B
Singapore	3750B

Australia & New Zealand	Fare
Sydney/Brisbane/Melbourne	11,875B
Darwin/Perth	8750B
Auckland	12,000B

Europe	Fare
Athens, Amsterdam, Frankfurt, London, Paris, Rome or Zurich	11,250B

USA	Fare
San Francisco/Los Angeles	12,500B
via Australia	18,200B
New York	12,500B

Booking Problems During the past couple of years the booking of flights in and out of Bangkok during the high season (December to March) has become increasingly difficult. For air travel during these months you should book as far in advance as possible. THAI is finally loosening its stranglehold on air routes in and out of Thailand, so the situation has improved since the late 1980s when the national carrier refused to allow additional airlines permission to add much-needed services through Bangkok.

Also, be sure to reconfirm return or ongoing tickets when you arrive in Thailand. Failure to reconfirm can mean losing your reservation.

Arriving in Thailand

During the last decade, the airport facilities at Bangkok International Airport have undergone a US$200 million redevelopment, including the construction of an international terminal that is one of the most modern and convenient in Asia. The old terminal is now used for domestic flights only. However, the very slow immigration lines in the upstairs arrival hall are still a big problem. Despite a long row of impressive-looking immigration counters, there never seem to be enough clerks on duty, even at peak arrival times. Even when the booths are fully staffed, waits of 45 minutes to an hour are not unusual. Baggage claim, however, is usually quick and efficient (of course, they have lots of time to get it right while you're inching along through immigration).

The customs area has a green lane for passengers with nothing to declare – just walk through if you're one of these and hand your customs form to one of the clerks by the exit. Baggage trolleys are free for use inside the terminal.

The Thai government has plans to open another international airport about 20 km east of Bangkok at Nong Ngu Hao. This additional airport is expected to be operational by 2000 and will be named Raja Deva (Racha Thewa).

Airport Services In and around the airport various services are available.

Currency Exchange The foreign currency booths (Thai Military Bank, Bangkok Bank, Krung Thai Bank) on the ground floor of the arrival hall and in the departure lounge give a good rate of exchange, so there's no need to wait till you're downtown to change money if you need Thai currency. Each of these banks also operates automatic teller machines in the arrival and departure halls.

Tourist Information On the ground floor of the arrival hall is a tourist information counter and a hotel reservation counter for Thai Hotel Association (THA) members. This doesn't go below the Miami-Malaysia standard of hotel.

Left Luggage & Day Rooms Left-luggage facilities (20B per piece per day, three months maximum) are available in the departure hall (3rd floor). In the Transit Lounge, day rooms with washing and toilet facilities can be rented for 620B per six hours.

Post & Telephone There is a 24-hour post/telephone office with a Home Direct phone service in the departure hall (3rd floor). Another 24-hour post office is located in the departure lounge; a third one in the arrival hall is open Monday to Friday from 9 am to 5 pm.

Food On the 4th floor of the international terminal is the Rajthanee Food Mall, a small 24-hour cafeteria area where you can choose from Thai, Chinese and European dishes at fairly reasonable prices. Next door is the larger THAI restaurant with more expensive fare. On the 2nd level above the arrival area is a coffee shop open from 6 am to 11 pm, and there is also a small snack bar in the waiting area of the ground floor. The departure lounge has two snack bars which serve beer and liquor.

Near the Airport If you leave the airport building area and cross the expressway on the pedestrian bridge (just north of the passenger terminal), you'll find yourself in the Don Meuang town area where there are all sorts of shops, a market, lots of small restaurants and food stalls, even a wat, all within 100 metres or so of the airport. The modern and luxurious Amari Airport Hotel (☎ 566-1020/1) at US$125 up has its own enclosed bridge and 'special mini-stay' daytime rates (8 am to 6 pm) for stays of up to a maximum of three hours for around 400/450B for singles/doubles, including tax and service. Longer daytime rates are available on request. For additional information on overnight accommodation in the Don Meuang area, see Places to Stay in the Bangkok chapter.

Transport to Bangkok For information on transport from the airport to Bangkok, see Local Transport in the Getting Around chapter.

Air Travel Glossary

Apex Apex, or 'advance purchase excursion' is a discounted ticket which must be paid for in advance. There are penalties if you wish to change it.

Baggage Allowance This will be written on your ticket: usually one 20 kg item to go in the hold, plus one item of hand luggage.

Bucket Shop An unbonded travel agency specialising in discounted airline tickets.

Bumped Just because you have a confirmed seat doesn't mean you're going to get on the plane – see Overbooking.

Cancellation Penalties If yo have to cancel or change an Apex ticket there are often heavy penalties involved; insurance can sometimes be taken out against these penalties. Some airlines impose penalties on regular tickets as well, particularly against 'no show' passengers.

Check In Airlines ask you to check in a certain time ahead of the flight departure (usually 1½ hours on international flights). If you fail to check in on time and the flight is overbooked the airline can cancel your booking and give your seat to somebody else.

Confirmation Having a ticket written out with the flight and date you want doesn't mean you have a seat until the agent has checked with the airline that your status is 'OK' or confirmed. Meanwhile you could just be 'on request'.

Discounted Tickets There are two types of discounted fares – officially discounted (see Promotional Fares) and unofficially discounted. The lowest prices often impose drawbacks like flying with unpopular airlines, inconvenient schedules, or unpleasant routes and connections. A discounted ticket can save you other things than money – you may be able to pay Apex prices without the associated Apex advance booking and other requirements. Discounted tickets only exist where there is fierce competition.

Full Fares Airlines traditionally offer first class (coded F), business class (coded J) and economy class (coded Y) tickets. These days there are so many promotional and discounted fares available from the regular economy class that few passengers pay full economy fare.

Lost Tickets If you lose your airline ticket an airline will usually treat it like a travellers' cheque and, after inquiries, issue you with another one. Legally, however, an airline is entitled to treat it like cash and if you lose it then it's gone forever. Take good care of your tickets.

No Shows No shows are passengers who fail to show up for their flight, sometimes due to unexpected delays or disasters, sometimes due to simply forgetting, sometimes because they made more than one booking and didn't bother to cancel the one they didn't want. Full-fare passengers who fail to turn up are sometimes entitled to travel on a later flight. The rest of us are penalised (see Cancellation Penalties).

On Request An unconfirmed booking for a flight; see Confirmation.

Warning Beware of airport touts – this means anyone trying to steer you away from the city taxi counter or asking where you plan to stay while you're in Bangkok. A legion of touts – some in what appear to be airport or airline uniforms – are always waiting for new arrivals in the arrival area, and will begin their badgering as soon as you clear customs. Posing as helpful tourist information agents, their main objective is to get commissions from overpriced taxi rides or hotel rooms. If you're foolish enough to mention the hotel or guesthouse you plan to stay at, chances are they'll tell you it's full and that you must go to another hotel (which will pay them a commission, though they may deny it). Sometimes they'll show you a nice collection of photos; don't get sucked in, as these touted hotels are often substandard and badly located.

Open Jaws A return ticket where you fly out to one place but return from another. If available, this can save you backtracking to your arrival point.

Overbooking Airlines hate to fly empty seats and since every flight has some passengers who fail to show up (see No Shows) airlines often book more passengers than they have seats. Usually the excess passengers balance those who fail to show up, but occasionally somebody gets bumped. If this happens guess who it is most likely to be? The passengers who check in late.

Promotional Fares Officially discounted fares like Apex fares which are available from travel agents or direct from the airline.

Reconfirmation At least 72 hours prior to departure time of an onward or return flight you must contact the airline and 'reconfirm' that you intend to be on the flight. If you don't do this the airline can delete your name from the passenger list and you could lose your seat. You don't have to reconfirm the first flight on your itinerary or if your stopover is less than 72 hours. It doesn't hurt to reconfirm more than once.

Restrictions Discounted tickets often have various restrictions on them – advance purchase is the most usual one (see Apex). Others are restrictions on the minimum and maximum period you must be away, such as a minimum of 14 days or a maximum of one year. See Cancellation Penalties.

Standby A discounted ticket where you only fly if there is a seat free at the last moment. Standby fares are usually only available on domestic routes.

Tickets Out An entry requirement for many countries is that you have an onward or return ticket, in other words, a ticket out of the country. If you're not sure what you intend to do next, the easiest solution is to buy the cheapest onward ticket to a neighbouring country or a ticket from a reliable airline which can later be refunded if you do not use it.

Transferred Tickets Airline tickets cannot be transferred from one person to another. Travellers sometimes try to sell the return half of their ticket, but officials can ask you to prove that you are the person named on the ticket. This is unlikely to happen on domestic flights; on an international flight tickets may be compared with passports.

Travel Agencies Travel agencies vary widely and you should ensure you use one that suits your needs. Some simply handle tours while full-service agencies handle everything from tours and tickets to car rental and hotel bookings. A good one will do all these things and can save you a lot of money but if all you want is a ticket at the lowest possible price, then you really need an agency specialising in discounted tickets. A discounted ticket agency, however, may not be useful for other things, like hotel bookings.

Travel Periods Some officially discounted fares, Apex fares in particular, vary with the time of year. There is often a low (off-peak) season and a high (peak) season. Sometimes there's an intermediate or shoulder season as well. At peak times, when everyone wants to fly, not only will the officially discounted fares be higher but so will unofficially discounted fares or there may simply be no discounted tickets available. Usually the fare depends on your outward flight – if you depart in the high season and return in the low season, you pay the high-season fare. ■

The THA hotel reservation desk at the back of the arrival hall also takes a commission on every booking, but at least they have a wide selection of accommodation. There have been reports that the THA desk occasionally claims a hotel is full when it isn't, just to move you into a hotel that pays higher commissions. If you protest, the staff may ask you to speak to the 'reservations desk' on the phone – usually an accomplice who con-

firms the hotel is full. Dial the hotel yourself if you want to be certain.

Now that the TAT supposedly has regulatory powers, one of its first acts should be to clean the touts out of the airport arrival area, as the present situation gives many visitors a rather negative first impression of Thailand. Then again, some see it as part of the challenge of Asian travel!

To/From Australia

The full economy fare from Australia to Bangkok is around A$4000 from Sydney, Melbourne or Brisbane, A$3330 from Perth. However, tickets discounted either by travel agents or airlines are much cheaper. None of these are advance purchase nowadays, but they tend to sell out early – the airlines only allocate a limited number of these super-cheap seats to each flight. Prices start at about A$550 (one way) and A$770 (return) from Melbourne or Sydney on the cheaper carriers (eg Olympic and Alitalia), and get more expensive the better the airline's 'reputation'.

From Australia to most Asian destinations, including Bangkok, the airlines have recently introduced new seasons: the peak is December to 15 January, mid-year school holiday periods are 'shoulder' season, and the rest of the year is low season. Fares now also vary depending on how long you want to stay away for – a fare valid for 28 days' travel is about A$50 to A$60 cheaper than one valid for 90 days. This rule varies a lot, so check with individual airlines for the best deal.

At the time of writing, fares available through agents specialising in discount fares on the better-known airlines (eg Thai, Qantas and British Airways) are: A$985/$1070/ $1170 (low/shoulder/peak season) from Sydney, Melbourne or Brisbane, A$820/ $900/$1000 from Perth. Garuda Indonesia have cheap fares via Bali or Jakarta to Bangkok, then on to London, for around A$900 one way, A$1550 return.

To/From Europe

London 'bucket shops' will have tickets to Bangkok available for around £250 one way or £490 return. It's also easy to stop over in Bangkok between London and Australia, with return fares for around £650 to the Australian east coast. Good travel agencies to try for these sorts of fares are Trailfinders on Kensington High St (☎ (0171) 938-3939) and Earls Court Rd (☎ (0171) 938-3366), or STA Travel (☎ (0171) 937-9962) on Old Brompton Rd and at the universities of London, Kent, Birmingham and Loughborough. Or you can simply check the travel ads in *Time Out* or the *News & Travel Magazine*. For discounted flights out of Manchester or Gatwick, check with Airbreak Leisure (☎ (0171) 712-0303) at South Quay Plaza 2, 193 Marsh Wall, London, E14 92H.

One of the best deals going is on TAROM (Romanian Air Transport), which has Brussels-Bangkok-Brussels fares valid for a year as low as US$500. Other cheapies are Lauda Air from London (via Vienna) and Czechoslovak Airlines from Prague (via London, Frankfurt and Zurich).

To/From North America

If you fly from the West Coast, you can get some great deals through the many bucket shops (who discount tickets by taking a cut in commissions) and consolidators (agencies that buy airline seats in bulk) operating in Los Angeles and San Francisco. Through agencies such as these a return (round-trip) airfare to Bangkok from any of 10 different West Coast cities starts at around US$750.

One of the most reliable discounters is Avia Travel (☎ (800) 950-AVIA toll-free, (415) 668-0964; fax (415) 386-8519) at 5429 Geary Blvd, San Francisco, CA 94121. Avia specialises in custom-designed around-the-world fares, eg San Francisco-Hong Kong-Calcutta/Bombay-Delhi-Frankfurt/ Rome/Amsterdam/Paris-New York from US$1336. The agency sets aside a portion of its profits for Volunteers in Asia, a non-profit organisation that sends grassroots volunteers to work in South-East Asia.

Another agency that works hard to get the cheapest deals is Air Brokers International (☎ (800) 883-3273 toll-free, (415) 397-1383; fax (415) 397-4767) at 323 Geary St, Suite 411, San Francisco, CA 94102. One of their 'Circle Pacific' fares, for example, offers a Los Angeles-Hong Kong-Bangkok-Jakarta-Yogyakarta-Denpasar-Los Angeles ticket for US$949 plus tax during the low season. East Coast departures generally cost US$100 to US$200 more, although if you're willing to take a 'Circle Europe' fare with several European stops along the way, you can reach Thailand for under US$1000 from New York City.

While the airlines themselves can rarely match the prices of the discounters, they are worth checking if only to get benchmark prices to use for comparison. Tickets bought directly from the airlines may also have fewer restrictions and/or less strict cancellation policies than those bought from discounters (though this is not always true).

Cheapest from the West Coast are: Thai Airways International (THAI), China Airlines, Korean Airlines and CP Air. Each of these has a budget and/or 'super Apex' fare that costs around US$900 to US$1200 return from Los Angeles, San Francisco or Seattle. THAI is the most overbooked of these airlines from December to March and June to August and hence their flights during these months may entail schedule delays (if you're lucky enough to get a seat at all). Several of these airlines also fly out of New York, Dallas, Chicago and Atlanta – add another US$100 to US$200 to their lowest fares.

TAROM, the Romanian carrier, offers one-way excursion fares from New York to Bangkok for US$500.

To/From Asia
Bangkok International Airport There are regular flights to Bangkok from every major city in Asia and it's not so tricky dealing with inter-Asia flights as most airlines offer about the same fares. Here is a sample of current estimated one-way fares:

Route	Fare
Singapore-Bangkok	US$110-$195
Hong Kong-Bangkok	US$140-$200
Kuala Lumpur-Bangkok	US$110-$195
Taipei-Bangkok	US$220-$373
Calcutta-Bangkok	US$170
Kathmandu-Bangkok	US$210-$276
Colombo-Bangkok	US$236
New Delhi-Bangkok	US$236
Manila-Bangkok	US$200-$231
Kunming-Bangkok	US$250

ASEAN promotional fares (return from any city, eg a Bangkok-Manila-Jakarta fare allows you to go between Manila, Jakarta, Bangkok and Manila; or Jakarta, Bangkok, Manila and Jakarta; or Bangkok, Manila, Jakarta and Bangkok):

Route	Fare
Bangkok-Manila-Jakarta	US$545
Bangkok-Singapore-Manila	US$440
Bangkok-Jakarta-Kuala Lumpur	US$410
Bangkok-Manila-Brunei-Jakarta-Singapore-Kuala Lumpur	US$580
Bangkok-Singapore-Jakarta-Yogyakarta-Denpasar	US$580

Other International Airports in Thailand
Air travellers heading for southern or northern Thailand can skip Bangkok altogether by flying directly to these areas. THAI has regular flights to Phuket and Hat Yai from Singapore, to Phuket from Perth and to Chiang Mai from Hong Kong, Beijing and Kunming. During the winter, German carrier LTU offers direct flights to Phuket from Düsseldorf and Munich.

A fourth international airport has recently opened in Chiang Rai. Although this airport only services flights to/from Bangkok so far, THAI hopes to establish international routes to/from other Asian capitals – possibly Luang Prabang (Laos) and Kunming (China) – over the next few years.

Regional Services Thailand's Ministry of Transport now allows several Thailand-based air carriers to provide regional air services to Myanmar, Vietnam, Laos and Cambodia. Bangkok Airways flies five times weekly to Phnom Penh on 56-seat Dash 8 turboprops (2500B one way). SK Air (which was formerly Air Kampuchea, then Air Cambodia) also operates Bangkok-Phnom Penh flights.

Bangkok Airways also fields regular flights to Mandalay from Chiang Mai (5000B return) and Bangkok (8000B return), but these tickets are usually sold only in association with tour packages. Eventually Bangkok Airways also plans to offer services between Bangkok, Danang and Hué (Vietnam).

Newer routes to/from Thailand by foreign carriers include Yunnan Airways and China

Southwest flights from Kunming, to Bangkok; Silk Air between Singapore and Phuket; Dragon Air between Hong Kong and Phuket; MAS between Ipoh, Malaysia, and Hat Yai.

Bangkok Airways is slated to start service to/from Sukhothai to Luang Prabang (Laos) by the end of 1994, when the Sukhothai airport opens. There are also discussions under way for flights from Sukhothai to Jinghong, Dali and Kunming in China's Yunnan Province as well as from Bangkok to Shenzhen and Hainan in southern China. If any of these China services are established, travellers will be able to complete a China route and enter Thailand without having to backtrack to Hong Kong or Beijing (or finish most of Thailand without backtracking to Bangkok, then on to China).

LAND
To/From Malaysia

Hat Yai is the major transport hub in southern Thailand. See that section for more details on land transport to Malaysia.

You can cross the west coast border by taking a bus to one side and another bus from the other side, the most obvious direct route being between Hat Yai and Alor Setar. This is the route used by taxis and buses but there's a long stretch of no-man's-land between the Thai border control at Sadao and the Malaysian one at Changlun. Finding transport across this empty stretch is difficult.

It's much easier to go to Padang Besar, where the train line crosses the border. Here you can get a bus right up to the border, walk across and take another bus or taxi on the other side. On either side you'll most likely be mobbed by taxi and motorcycle drivers wanting to take you to immigration. It's better to walk over the railway by bridge into Thailand, and then ignore the touts until you get to 'official' Thai taxis who will take you all the way to Hat Yai, with a stop at the immigration office (2.5 km from the border), for 30B. A new immigration/customs office and bus/train station complex is currently

under construction on the Thai side, which when completed should make the whole transition smoother.

There's a daily bus running between Alor Setar, Hat Yai and Kota Baru and reverse.

There's also a road crossing at Keroh (Thai side – Betong), right in the middle between the east and west coasts. This may be used more now that the Penang to Kota Baru road is open. For more information on Betong, see the Yala Province section in the Southern Thailand chapter.

See the Sungai Kolok & Ban Taba sections in the Southern Thailand chapter for crossing the border on the east coast.

Riding the rails from Singapore to Bangkok via Butterworth, Malaysia, is a great way to travel to Thailand – as long as you don't count on making a smooth change between the Kereta Api Tanah Melayu (KTM) and State Railway of Thailand (SRT) trains. The Thai train almost always leaves on time; the Malaysian train rarely arrives on time. Unfortunately the Thai train leaves Padang Besar even if the Malaysian railway express from Kuala Lumpur (or the 2nd-class connection from Butterworth) is late. To be on the safe side, purchase the Malaysian and Thai portions of your ticket with departures on consecutive days and plan a Butterworth/Penang stopover.

Bangkok to Butterworth/Penang The daily special express No 11 leaves from Bangkok's Hualamphong station at 3.15 pm, arriving in Hat Yai at 7.04 am the next day and terminating at Padang Besar at 8 am. Everyone disembarks at Padang Besar, proceeds through immigration, then boards 2nd-class KTM train No 99 for a Butterworth arrival around noon Malaysian time (one hour ahead of Thai time). The fare to Padang Besar is 694B for 1st class, 326B for 2nd, plus a 50B special express charge, 100B for air-con. There is no 3rd-class seating on this train.

For a sleeping berth in 2nd class add 100B for an upper berth, 150B for a lower. In 1st class it's 150B per person.

Bangkok to Kuala Lumpur & Singapore

For Kuala Lumpur (KL), make the Thai and Malaysian rail connections to Butterworth as described above, changing to the No 3 Express in Butterworth, which departs for Kuala Lumpur at 1 pm and arrives in Kuala Lumpur at 8.45 pm the same day.

For Singapore, the final leg leaves Kuala Lumpur aboard night express (1st and 2nd class only) No 11 at 11 pm, arriving in Singapore at 7.05 am the next day. Or if the Butterworth connection is on time, try the earlier 2nd and 3rd-class-only night train No 59 at 9 pm, arriving in Singapore at 6.35 am. If you're going straight through from KL, when you get to Butterworth get off quickly and re-book a sleeping berth for the Kuala Lumpur-Singapore leg (M$2 to M$3 booking fee). In Kuala Lumpur you have to get a 2nd-class seat allocation – insist on 2nd or you may be fobbed off with 3rd class on a slower Biasa train. The entire two-day Bangkok to Singapore fare totals around US$80 in 1st class, US$40 in 2nd class, not including express surcharge or berth charges if you get a sleeper.

You can no longer purchase a through-fare to KL or Singapore from Bangkok or vice versa (except on the plush Eastern & Oriental Express). KTM fares from Butterworth to Kuala Lumpur are M$17 3rd class, M$28 2nd class and M$54 1st class. Butterworth to Singapore fares are M$30, M$50 and M$102 respectively.

Eastern & Oriental Express

In 1991 the State Railway of Thailand, the Kereta Api Tanah Melayu (KTM; Malaysia's state railway) and Singapore's Eastern & Oriental Express Co (E&O) purchased the rights from Paris' Venice Simplon to operate the new Eastern & Oriental Express between Singapore and Bangkok. Finally, an Orient Express that actually begins and ends in the Orient! The original Orient Express ran between Paris and Constantinople in the 1880s and was considered the grandest train trip in the world; an updated version along the same route was resurrected around 20 years ago and has been very successful.

The E&O travels at an average speed of 50 km/h, completing the 1943-km Singapore to Bangkok journey in 41 hours, with a two-hour Butterworth stopover and tour of Georgetown, Penang. As in Europe, this new train offers cruise-ship luxury on rails. Passengers dine, sleep and entertain in 22 railway carriages imported from New Zealand and refurbished using lots of brass, teak and old-world tapestry, fitted in 1930s style by the same French designer who remodelled the Venice Simplon Orient Express in Europe. Aside from the locomotive(s), sleeping coaches, staff coach and luggage cars, the train features two restaurant cars, a saloon car and a bar car, with a combination bar car and open-air observation deck bringing up the rear. All accommodation is in deluxe private cabins with shower, toilet and individually controlled air-con; passengers are attended by round-the-clock cabin stewards (38 of 52 front-line staff in 1994 were Thai) in the true pukkah tradition. Tariffs begin at (brace yourself) US$1130 for the full route, US$710 for Bangkok or Singapore to Butterworth or vice versa; spacious Presidential suites are available for a mere US$2950 (US$1860 on the shorter runs). Honeymoon couples comprise a significant part of the clientele.

The train can be booked in Singapore through Eastern & Oriental Express (☎(65) 227-2068; (02) 251-4862 in Bangkok; fax (65) 224-9265), at Carlton Bldg No 14-03, 90 Cecil St, Singapore 0106.

Elsewhere, E&O reservations and information can be obtained by calling the numbers below.

Australia	☎ (02) 232 7499
France	☎ (1) 45 62 0069
Germany	☎ (211) 16 21 06/7
New Zealand	☎ (9) 379 3708
Switzerland	☎ (22) 366 42 22
UK	☎ (71) 928 6000
USA	☎ (800) 524-2420

To/From Laos

By Road Since April 1993 a land crossing from Champasak Province in Laos to Chong Mek in Thailand's Ubon Ratchathani Province has been open to foreign visitors. To use this crossing you'll need a visa valid for entry via Chong Mek and Pakse – this must usually be arranged in advance through a Lao consulate or sponsoring agency. See the Chong Mek Getting There & Away section in the North-East Thailand chapter for more information on this border crossing.

A new 1190-metre Australian-financed bridge across the Mekong near Nong Khai opened in April 1994. Called the Thai-Lao Friendship Bridge (Saphan Mittaphap Thai-Lao), it spans a section of the river between Hat Jommani on the Thai side to Tha Naleng on the Lao side – very near the current vehicle ferry (which presumably will become unnecessary now that the bridge is open).

The next step in the plan is to build a parallel rail bridge in order to extend the Bangkok-Nong Khai railway into Vientiane.

A second Mekong bridge is tentatively planned to span the river at either Tha Khaek (opposite Thailand's Nakhon Phanom) or Savannakhet (opposite Mukdahan).

By River It is now legal for non-Thai foreigners to cross the Maekhong River between Laos and Thailand at the following points: Nong Khai (near Vientiane), Nakhon Phanom (opposite Tha Khaek), Chiang Khong (opposite Ban Huay Sai) and Mukdahan (opposite Savannakhet).

In everyday practice, Nong Khai is the only border crossing that can be used by non-Thai foreigners without special permission attached to their visas. See the Nong Khai Getting There & Away section in the North-East Thailand chapter for more information on this border crossing.

To/From Myanmar & Cambodia

There is currently no legal land passage between Myanmar and Thailand, and the Cambodian border won't be safe for land crossings until mines and booby traps left over from the conflict between the Khmer Rouge and the Vietnamese are removed or detonated.

To/From China

By Road The governments of Thailand, Laos, China and Myanmar recently agreed to the construction of a four-nation ring road through all four countries. The western half of the loop will proceed from Mae Sai, Thailand, to Jinghong, China, via Myanmar's Tachilek (opposite Mae Sai) and Kengtung (near Dalau on the China-Myanmar border), while the eastern half will extend from Chiang Khong, Thailand to Jinghong via Huay Xai, Laos (opposite Chiang Khong) and Boten, Laos (on the Yunnanese border south of Jinghong).

The stretch between Tachilek and Dalau is now under construction but it's possible to arrange one to three-day trips as far as Kengtung in Myanmar's Shan State (see the Mae Sai section in the Northern Thailand chapter for details). A road between Huay Xai and Boten already exists (built by the Chinese in the 1960s and 1970s) but needs upgrading. Once the roads are built and the visa formalities have been worked out, this loop will provide alternative travel connections between China and South-East Asia, in much the same way as the Karakoram Highway has forged new links between China and South Asia. It's difficult to predict when all the logistical variables will be settled, but progress so far points to a cleared path by the end of the decade.

By River A third way to reach China's Yunnan Province from Thailand is by boat along the Maekhong River. Several surveys of the waterway have been completed and a specially constructed express boat made its inaugural run between Sop Ruak, Chiang Rai Province, and China's Yunnan Province in early 1994. For the moment, permission for such travel is restricted to private tour groups, but it's reasonable to assume that in the future – if demand is high enough – some sort of scheduled public service may become available. The boat trip takes six hours –

Monk at festival, Hat Yai (JC)

Top Left: Wat Chao Chan, Chaliang, Sukhothai (JC)
Top Right: Wat Phra That Choeng Chum, Sakon Nakhon (JC)
Bottom: Wat Phra Kaew, Bangkok (RI)

considerably quicker than any now possible road route.

SEA

There are several ways of travelling between Malaysia and the south of Thailand by sea. Simplest is to take a long-tail boat between Satun, right down in the south-west corner of Thailand, and Kuala Perlis. The cost is about M$4, or 40B, and boats cross over fairly regularly. You can also take a ferry to the Malaysian island of Langkawi from Satun.

There are immigration posts at both ports so you can make the crossing quite officially, but they're a bit slack at Satun (since they don't get many foreigners arriving this way) so make sure they stamp your passport. See the Satun section in the Southern Thailand chapter for more information.

From Satun you can take a bus to Hat Yai and then arrange transport to other points in the south or further north. It's possible to bypass Hat Yai altogether, by heading directly for Phuket or Krabi via Trang.

You can also take a ferry to Ban Taba on the east coast of Thailand from near Kota Baru – see the Sungai Kolok and Ban Taba sections in the Southern Thailand chapter.

See the Phuket Getting There & Away section in the Southern Thailand chapter for information on yachts to Penang and other places.

A passenger ferry service also runs between Pulau Langkawi and Phuket, Thailand. It's operated by Syarikat Kuala Perlis-Langkawi Ferry Services.

TOURS

Many tour operators around the world can arrange guided tours of Thailand. Most of them simply serve as brokers for tour companies based in Thailand; they buy their trips from a wholesaler and resell them under various names in travel markets overseas. Hence, one is much like another and you might as well arrange a tour in Thailand at a lower cost. Two of Thailand's largest tour wholesalers are World Travel Service (☎ (02) 233-5900; fax (02) 236-7169) at

1053 Charoen Krung Rd, Bangkok 10500 and Deithelm Travel (☎ (02) 255-9150; fax (02) 256-0248) at Kian Gwan Bldg II, 140/1 Withayu Rd, Bangkok.

The better overseas tour companies build their own Thailand itineraries from scratch and choose their local suppliers based on which ones best serve these itineraries. Of these, several specialise in adventure and/or ecological tours, including those listed below. Bolder Adventures, for example, offers trips across a broad spectrum of Thai destinations and activities, from Northern Thailand trekking to sea canoeing in the Phuket Sea, plus tour options that focus exclusively on north-east Thailand. The average trip runs 14 to 17 days.

Ms Kasma Loha-Unchit (4119 Howe St, Oakland, California 94611 USA (☎ (510) 655-8900), a Thai native living in California, offers highly personalised, 26-day 'cultural immersion' tours of Thailand.

Backroads
  1516 Fifth St, Berkeley, CA 94710, USA (☎ (800) 462-2848, (510) 527-1555; fax (510) 527-1444)
Bolder Adventures
  PO Box 1279, Boulder, CO 80306, USA (☎ (800) 642-2742, (303) 443-6789; fax (303) 443-7078)
Exodus
  9 Weir Rd, London SW12 OLT, UK (☎ (0181) 673-0859)
Intrepid Travel
  801 Nicholson St, North Carlton, Victoria 3054, Australia (☎ (03) 387-3484; fax (03) 387-9460)
Mountain Travel-Sobek
  6420 Fairmount Ave, CA 94530, USA (☎ (800) 227-2384, (510) 527-8100; fax (510) 525-7710)
Odyssey Tours
  20 South Terrace, Clifton Hill, Victoria 3069, Australia (☎ (03) 489-2553)
Venturetreks
  164 Parnell Rd, Parnell, Auckland, NZ (☎ (09) 379-9855; fax (09) 377-0329)
World Expeditions
  3rd floor, 441 Kent St, Sydney, NSW 2000, Australia (☎ (02) 264-3366; fax (02) 261-1974)

LEAVING THAILAND
Departure Tax

Airport departure tax is 200B for international flights and 20B for domestic. Children under two are exempt. See the To/From Bangkok International Airport section in the Getting Around chapter for more details.

WARNING

The information in this chapter is particularly vulnerable to change: prices for international travel are volatile, routes are introduced and cancelled, schedules change, special deals come and go, and rules and visa requirements are amended. Airlines and governments seem to take a perverse pleasure in making price structures and regulations as complicated as possible. You should check directly with the airline or a travel agent to make sure you understand how a fare (and ticket you may buy) works. In addition, the travel industry is highly competitive and there are many lurks and perks.

The upshot of this is that you should get opinions, quotes and advice from as many airlines and travel agents as possible before you part with your hard-earned cash. The details given in this chapter should be regarded as pointers and are not a substitute for your own careful, up-to-date research.

Getting Around

AIR

Most domestic air services in Thailand are operated by Thai Airways International (THAI) and cover 23 airports throughout the kingdom. On certain southern routes, domestic flights through Hat Yai continue on to Malaysia (Penang, Kuala Lumpur), Singapore and Brunei (Bandar Seri Begawan).

THAI operates Boeing 737s or Airbus 300s on all its main domestic routes, but also has Avro 748s on some smaller routes. To the more remote locations, particularly in the north and north-east, there are small Shorts 330s and 360s. Some of the fares to these remote locations are subsidised.

The accompanying chart shows some of the fares on more popular routes. Where routes are operated by 737s and by Avro 748s or Shorts 330s and 360s, the 737 fares will be higher. Note that through fares are generally less than the combination fares – Chiang Rai to Bangkok, for example, is less than the addition of Chiang Rai to Chiang Mai and Chiang Mai to Bangkok fares. This does not always apply to international fares, however. It's much cheaper to fly from Bangkok to Penang via Phuket or Hat Yai than direct, for example.

Air Passes

From time to time THAI offers special four-coupon passes – available only outside Thailand for foreign currency purchases – in which you can book any four domestic flights for one fare of US$240 as long as you don't repeat the same leg. Unless you plan carefully this isn't much of a savings since it's hard to avoid repeating the same leg in and out of Bangkok.

If you were to buy separate tickets from Bangkok to Hat Yai, then Hat Yai to Phuket, Phuket to Bangkok and finally Bangkok to Chiang Mai you'd spend 6230B (US$249), a savings of only US$10. However, if you were to fly from Bangkok to Phuket, Phuket

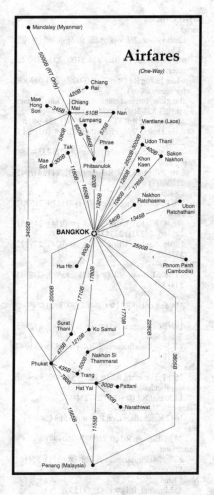

Airfares
(One-Way)

to Bangkok, Bangkok to Chiang Mai – then continue overland to Sakon Nakhon and fly back to Bangkok from there, you'd save approximately US$68 over the total of the individual fares.

For information on the four-coupon deal, enquire at any THAI office outside of Thailand.

THAI Offices

Bangkok
Head Office, 89 Vibhavadi Rangsit Rd (☎ (02) 513-0121)
485 Silom Rd (☎ (02) 234-3100, 233-3810 for reservations)
6 Lan Luang Rd (☎ (02) 280-0090, 280-0070/80 for reservations)
Bangkok International Airport, Don Meuang (☎ (02) 523-2081/3, 523-6121)
45 Anuwong Rd, Yaowarat (☎ (02) 224-9602/8)
Asia Hotel, 296 Phayathai Rd (☎ (02) 215-2020/1)
4th floor, Charn Issara Tower (☎ (02) 235-4588)
Chiang Mai
240 Prapokklao Rd (☎ (053) 211541/042, 211044/7)
Chiang Rai
870 Phahonyothin Rd (☎ (054) 711179, 715207)
Hat Yai
166/4 Niphat Uthit 2 Rd (☎ (074) 245851, 246165, 243711, 233433)
190/6 Niphat Uthit 2 Rd (☎ (074) 231272, 232392),
Khon Kaen
183/6 Maliwan Rd (☎ (043) 236523, 239011, 238835)
Lampang
314 Sanambin Rd (☎ (054) 217078, 218199)
Loei
191/1 Charoenrat Rd (☎ (042) 812344, 812355)
Mae Hong Son
71 Singhanatbamrung Rd (☎ (053) 611297, 611194)
Mae Sot
76/1 Prasatwitthi Rd (☎ (055) 531730, 531440)
Nakhon Ratchasima
14 Manat Rd (☎ (044) 257211/5)
Nakhon Si Thammarat
1612 Ratchadamnoen Rd (☎ (075) 342491)
Nan
34 Mahaprom Rd (☎ 710377, 710498)
Narathiwat
322-324 Phuphaphakdi Rd (☎ (073) 511161, 512178)
Nong Khai
453 Prachak Rd (☎ (042) 411530)
Pattani
9 Preeda Rd (☎ (073) 349149)
Pattaya
Royal Cliff Beach Hotel (☎ (038) 429286/7)
Phitsanulok
209/26-28 Bromtrailokanat Rd (☎ (055) 258020, 251671)

Phrae
42-44 Ratsadamnoen Rd (☎ (054) 511123)
Phuket
78 Ranong Rd (☎ (076) 211195, 212499, 212946)
41/33 Montri Rd (☎ (076) 212400, 212644, 212880)
Sakon Nakhon
1446/73 Yuwapattana Rd (☎ (042) 712259)
Songkhla
2 Soi 4, Saiburi Rd (☎ (074) 311012)
Surat Thani
3/27-28 Karoonrat Rd (☎ 273710, 273355)
Tak
485 Taksin Rd (☎ (055) 512164)
Trang
199/2 Visetkul Rd (☎ (075) 218066)
Ubon
364 Chayanggoon Rd (☎ (045) 254431, 255894)
Udon
60 Makkang Rd (☎ 246697, 243222)

Bangkok Airways

Since January 1989 the Transport Ministry has licensed newcomer Bangkok Airways, owned by Sahakol Air, to fly routes between Bangkok and Loei, Hua Hin, Ko Samui, Phuket and U-Taphao. Planned Bangkok Airways destinations include Sukhothai (by the end of 1994), Chiang Rai, Trang, Krabi, Ubon Ratchathani and Ranong – once airports in these cities are completed. For most of its domestic flights (the company also has daily flights to Phnom Penh), Bangkok Airways uses either 37-seat Dash 8-100s or 56-seat 8-300s – all turboprops.

Bangkok Airways' fares are competitive with THAI's but the company is small and it remains to be seen whether or not it will survive to become a serious contender. At the moment it's like Mekong and Hong Thong whisky, each concentrating on a different share of the market. The airline's head office (☎ 229-3434; fax 229-3450) is at Queen Sirikit National Convention Centre, New Ratchadaphisek Rd, Khlong Toey, Bangkok 10110. There are also offices in Hua Hin, Pattaya, Phuket and Ko Samui.

Domestic Airport Terminal

All domestic flights originate from Bangkok's Don Meuang Airport, a few hundred metres south of Bangkok International Airport. Facilities include a post and telephone office on the ground floor, a snack bar in the departure lounge and a restaurant on the 2nd floor.

THAI operates a free shuttle bus between the international and domestic terminals every 15 minutes between 6 am and 11.20 pm.

BUS
Government Bus
Several different types of buses ply the roads of Thailand. The cheapest and slowest are the ordinary government-run buses (*rót thamádaa*) that stop in every little town and for every waving hand along the highway. For some destinations – smaller towns – these are your only choice, but at least they leave frequently. The government also runs faster, more comfortable, but less frequent air-conditioned buses called *rót ae* or *rót pràp aakàat*. If these are available to your destination, they are your very best choice since they don't cost that much more than the ordinary stop-in-every-town buses. The government bus company is called Baw Khaw Saw, an abbreviation of Borisàt Khõn Sòng (literally, 'the transportation company'). Every city and town in Thailand linked by bus transportation has a Baw Khaw Saw terminal, even if it's just a patch of dirt by the roadside.

The service on the government air-con buses is usually quite good and includes beverage service and video. On longer routes (eg Bangkok to Chiang Mai, Bangkok to Nong Khai), the air-con buses even distribute claim checks (receipt dockets) for your baggage. Longer routes may also offer two classes of air-con buses, regular and 1st class; the latter buses have toilets. A newer innovation are the VIP buses that have fewer seats (30 to 34 instead of 44; some routes have Super VIP, with only 24 seats) so that each seat reclines more. Sometimes these are called *rót nawn* or sleepers. For small-to-medium-sized people they are more comfortable, but if you're big in girth you may find yourself squashed on the 34-seaters when the person in front of you leans back.

Occasionally you'll get a government air bus in which the air-con is broken or the seats are not up to standard, but in general I've found them more reliable than the private tour buses.

Private Bus
Private buses are available between major tourist and business destinations: Chiang Mai, Surat, Ko Samui, Phuket, Hat Yai, Pattaya, Hua Hin and a number of others. To Chiang Mai, for example, several companies run daily buses out of Bangkok. These can be booked through most hotels or any travel agency, although it's best to book directly through a bus office to be assured that you get what you pay for.

Fares may vary from company to company, but usually not by more than a few baht. However, fare differences between the government and private bus companies can be substantial. Using Surat Thani as an example, the state-run buses from the southern bus terminals are 151B for ordinary bus, 222B (1st class) air-con, while the private companies charge up to 385B. On the other hand, to Chiang Mai the private buses often cost less than the government buses, although those that charge less offer inferior service. Departures for some private companies are more frequent than for the equivalent Baw Khaw Saw route.

There are also private buses running between major destinations within the various regions, eg Nakhon Si Thammarat to Hat Yai in the south, and Chiang Mai to Sukhothai in the north. New companies are cropping up all the time. The numbers seemed to reach a peak in the 1980s, but are now somewhat stabilised because of a crackdown on licensing. Minibuses are used on some routes eg Surat to Krabi and Tak to Mae Sot.

The private air-con buses are usually no more comfortable than the government air-con buses and feature similarly narrow seats and a hair-raising ride. The trick the tour companies use to make their buses seem more comfortable is to make you think you're not on a bus by turning up the air-con until your knees knock, handing out pillows and blankets and serving free soft drinks. On overnight journeys the buses usually stop somewhere en route and passengers are awakened to get off the bus for a free meal of fried rice or rice soup. A few companies even treat you to a meal before a long overnight trip.

Like their state-run equivalents, the private companies offer VIP (sleeper) buses on long hauls.

Out of Bangkok, the safest, most reliable private bus services are the ones which operate from the three official Baw Khaw Saw terminals rather than from hotels or guesthouses. Picking up passengers from any points except these official terminals is actually illegal, and services promised are often not delivered. Although it can be a hassle getting out to the Baw Khaw Saw terminals, you're generally rewarded with safer, more reliable, and more punctual service.

Service

Although on average the private companies charge more than the government does on the same routes, the service is not always up to the higher relative cost. In recent years the service on many private lines has in fact declined, especially on the Bangkok to Chiang Mai, Bangkok to Ko Samui, Surat to Phuket and Surat to Krabi routes.

Sometimes the cheaper lines – especially those booked on Khao San Rd in Bangkok – will switch vehicles at the last moment so that instead of the roomy air-con bus advertised, you're stuck with a cramped van with broken air-con. One traveller recounted how his Khao San Rd bus stopped for lunch halfway to Chiang Mai and then zoomed off while the passengers were eating – leaving them to finish the journey on their own! To avoid situations like this, it's always better to book bus tickets directly at a bus office – or at the government Baw Khaw Saw station – rather than through a travel agency.

Another problem with private companies is that they generally spend more time cruising the city for passengers before getting under way, meaning that they rarely leave at the advertised departure time.

Safety

Statistically, private tour buses meet with more accidents than government air-con buses. Turnovers on tight corners and head-on collisions with trucks are probably due to the inexperience of the drivers on a particular route. This in turn is probably a result of the companies opening and folding so frequently and because of the high priority given to making good time – Thais buy tickets on a company's reputation for speed.

As private bus fares are typically higher than government bus fares, the private bus

---

WARNING

While travelling by bus or train, do not accept food, drinks or sweets from strangers no matter how friendly they may seem. You might be drugged or robbed of your belongings.

Tourist Police
509 Vorachak Road
Bangkok
☎ **221-6206/10**

Tourist Assistance Centre
Tourism Authority of Thailand
Ratchadamnoen Nok Avenue, Bangkok
☎ **282-8129, 281-5051**

companies attract a better-heeled clientele among the Thais, as well as among foreign tourists. One result of this is that a tour bus loaded with money or the promise of money is a temptation for upcountry bandits. Hence, private tour buses occasionally get robbed by bands of thieves, but these incidents are diminishing due to increased security under provincial administration.

In an effort to prevent druggings and robbery in southern Thailand, which peaked in the 1980s, Thai police now board tour buses plying the southern roads at unannounced intervals, taking photos and videotapes of the passengers and asking for IDs. Reported incidents are now on the decrease.

Large-scale robberies never occur on the ordinary buses, very rarely on the state-run air-con buses and rarely on the trains. Accidents are not unknown on state-run buses either, so the train still comes out the safest means of transport in Thailand.

Robberies and accidents are relatively infrequent (though more frequent than they should be) considering the number of buses taken daily, and I've never been on a bus that's suffered either mishap – the odds are on your side. Travellers to Thailand should know the risk of tour bus travel against the apparent convenience, especially when there are alternatives. Some travellers really like the tour buses, though, so the private companies will continue to do good business.

Keep an eye on your bags when riding buses – thievery by stealth is still the most popular form of robbery in Thailand (eminently preferable to the forceful variety in my opinion), though again the risks are not that great – just be aware. Most pilfering seems to take place on the private bus runs between Bangkok and Chiang Mai, especially on buses booked on Khao San Rd. Keep zippered bags locked and well secured.

TRAIN

The railway network in Thailand, run by the Thai government, is surprisingly good. After travelling several thousand km by train and bus, I have to say that the train wins hands

down as the best form of public transport in the kingdom. It is not possible to take the train everywhere in Thailand, but if it were that's how I'd go. If you travel 3rd class, it is often the cheapest way to cover a long distance; by 2nd class it's about the same as a 'tour bus' but much safer and more comfortable. Trains take a bit longer than chartered buses on the same journey but, on overnight trips especially, are worth the extra travel time.

The trains offer many advantages; there is more space, more room to breathe and stretch out – even in 3rd class – than there is on the best buses. The windows are big and usually open, so that there is no glass between you and the scenery – good for taking photos – and more to see. The scenery itself is always better along the train routes compared to the scenery along Thai highways – the trains regularly pass small villages, farmland, old temples, etc. The pitch-and-roll of the railway cars is much

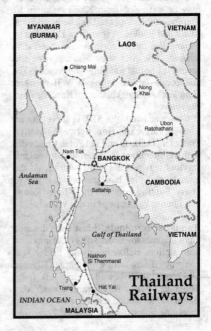

easier on the bones, muscles and nervous system than the quick stops and starts, the harrowing turns and the pothole jolts endured on buses. The train is safer in terms of both accidents and robberies. Last, but certainly not least, you meet a lot more interesting people on the trains, or so it seems to me.

Rail Routes

Four main rail lines cover 4500 km along the northern, southern, north-eastern and eastern routes. There are several side routes, notably between Nakhon Pathom and Nam Tok (stopping in Kanchanaburi) in the west central region, and between Tung Song and Kantang (stopping in Trang) in the south. The southern line splits at Hat Yai, one route going to Sungai Kolok on the Malaysian east coast border, via Yala, and the other route going to Padang Besar in the west, also on the Malaysian border.

A new Bangkok to Pattaya spur, inaugurated in 1991, has met with uneven success. Within the next few years, a southern spur may be extended from Khiriratnikhom to Phuket, establishing a rail link between Surat Thani and Phuket. A spur from Den Chai to Chiang Rai in the north is also under discussion. The SRT may also renovate the Japanese line that was built with forced POW and coolie labour during WW II between Nam Tok and Sangkhlaburi in Kanchanaburi Province.

Closer at hand, the SRT is surveying an unused rail extension between Aranya Prathet in Thailand and Poi Pet in Cambodia with the intention to resume international rail services between the two countries. At the moment this plan has been set aside due to heavy fighting between the Khmer Rouge and Phnom Penh troops in this vicinity.

Bangkok Terminals Most long-distance trains originate from Bangkok's Hualamphong train station. Before a railway bridge was constructed across the Chao Phraya River in 1932, all southbound trains left from Thonburi's Bangkok Noi train station. Today Bangkok Noi station services commuter and short-line trains to Kanchanaburi/Nam Tok,

Suphanburi, Ratchaburi and Nakhon Pathom (Ratchaburi and Nakhon Pathom can also be reached by train from Hualamphong). A slow night train to Chumphon and Lang Suan, both in southern Thailand, leaves nightly from the Bangkok Noi station but it's rarely used by long-distance travellers.

Classes

The SRT operates passenger trains in three classes – 1st, 2nd and 3rd – but each class varies considerably depending on whether you're on an ordinary, rapid, or express train.

Third Class A typical 3rd-class car consists of two rows of bench seats divided into facing pairs. Each bench seat is designed to seat two or three passengers, but on a crowded upcountry line nobody seems to care about design considerations. On a rapid train (which carries 2nd and 3rd-class cars only), 3rd-class seats are padded and reasonably comfortable for shorter trips. On ordinary, 3rd-class-only trains in the east and north-east, seats are sometimes made of hard wooden slats, and are not recommended for more than a couple of hours at a time. Express trains do not carry 3rd-class cars at all. Commuter trains in the Bangkok area are all 3rd class and the cars resemble modern subway or rapid transit trains, with plastic seats and ceiling loops for standing passengers.

Second Class In a 2nd-class car, seating arrangements are similar to those on a bus, with pairs of padded seats all facing towards the front of the train. Usually the seats can be adjusted to a reclining angle, and for some people this is good enough for overnight trips. In a 2nd-class sleeper, you'll find two rows of facing seat pairs; each pair is separated from the next by a dividing wall. A table folds down between each pair and at night the seats convert into two fold-down berths, one over the other. Curtains provide a modicum of privacy and the berths are fairly comfortable, with fresh linen for every trip. A toilet stall is located at one end of the car and washbasins at the other. Second-class cars are found only on rapid and express trains; some routes offer air-con 2nd class as well as ordinary 2nd class.

First Class First-class cars provide private cabins for singles or couples. Each private cabin has individually controlled air-con, an electric fan, a fold-down washbasin and mirror, a small table and a long bench seat (or two in a double cabin) that converts into a bed. Drinking water and towels are provided free of charge. First-class cars are available only on express and special express trains.

Bookings

The disadvantage of travelling by train, in addition to the time factor mentioned earlier, is that it can be difficult to book. This is especially true around holiday time, eg the middle of April approaching Songkran Festival, since many Thais also prefer the train. Trains out of Bangkok should be booked as far in advance as possible – a minimum of a week for popular routes such as the northern line to Chiang Mai and southern line to Hat Yai, especially if you want a sleeper. For the north-eastern and eastern lines a few days will suffice.

Advance bookings may be made one to 90 days before your intended date of departure. If you want to book tickets in advance, go to Hualamphong station in Bangkok, walk through the front of the station house and go straight to the back right-hand corner where a sign says 'Advance Booking' (open 8.30 am to 4 pm Monday to Friday, 8.30 am to noon weekends and holidays). The other ticket windows, on the left-hand side of the station, are for same-day purchases, mostly 3rd class.

Reservations are now computerised in the Advance Booking office. Instead of having to stop at three different desks as in previous years, you simply take a queue number, wait until your number appears on one of the electronic marquees, report to the correct desk (one for the southern line, one for north and north-eastern) and make your ticket

arrangements. Only cash baht is acceptable here.

Note that buying a return ticket does not necessarily guarantee you a seat on the way back, it only means you do not have to buy a ticket for the return. If you want a guaranteed seat reservation it's best to make that reservation for the return immediately upon arrival at your destination.

Booking trains back to Bangkok is generally not as difficult as booking trains out of Bangkok; however, at some stations this can be quite difficult, eg buying a ticket from Surat Thani to Bangkok.

Tickets between any stations in Thailand can be purchased at Hualamphong station (☎ 223-3762, 225-6964, 224-7788; fax 225-6068). You can also make advance bookings at Don Meuang station, across from Bangkok International Airport. SRT ticket offices are open from 8.30 am to 6 pm on weekdays, 8.30 am to noon on weekends and public holidays.

Train tickets can also be purchased at certain travel agencies in Bangkok (see the Travel Agencies section in the Bangkok chapter). It is much simpler to book trains through these agencies than to book them at the station; however, they usually add a surcharge of 50 to 100B to the ticket price.

Rail Passes

For those who plan to travel extensively by train in Thailand, the State Railway of Thailand (SRT) offers a Visit Thailand Rail Pass for international passport holders. The Blue Pass allows 20 days of 2nd and 3rd-class travel at 1100B for adults or 550B for children (aged four to 12), supplementary charges not included; the Red Pass (2000B adults, 1100B children) covers all supplementary charges for 2nd and 3rd class. The rates for both passes have dropped 30% since they were first introduced in 1989 – apparently few visitors were buying them at the higher rates.

Are the passes good value? Suppose you were to take a train from Bangkok to Chiang Mai, spend a week in the north, return to Bangkok and then make a similar excursion to Nong Khai and back; your 2nd-class ticket would cost a total of 1060B by express train, or 1040B by rapid train. In this scenario you'd be paying slightly more per km if you had purchased the Blue Pass. If you were to take even one more lengthy train trip, however, a Blue Pass would more than pay for itself.

If you made the same Chiang Mai and Nong Khai excursions using 'lower berth' sleeper accommodation (ie with a window and a bit more headroom than an 'upper berth' sleeper), you'd pay 1460B by express train, clearly making the 2000B Red Pass less attractive even if you were to take a few shorter side trips. If you had used the 1100B Blue Pass, you'd have had to kick in an extra 400B for the lower berths plus 120B for express surcharges, a total of 1620B and still cheaper than the Red Pass. So for the average visitor who might make four 600 to 700-km train journeys plus a few shorter ones over a 20-day period, it's probably more economical to buy a Blue Pass and pay your own supplementary charges along the way.

On the other hand, if you're a real train freak and were to board trains every other day or so for 20 days, then either pass becomes a bargain. The Red Pass has the advantage of not having to deal with the supplementary charges – all you have to do is flash the pass at the booking office and get a seat. Both passes can be used either for making advance reservations or for taking what's available on the day of departure.

Charges & Surcharges

There is a 30B surcharge for express trains (*rót dùan*) and 20B for rapid trains (*rót raew*). These trains are somewhat faster than the ordinary trains, as they make fewer stops. On the northern line during the day there is a 50B surcharge for 2nd-class seats in air-con cars. For the special express trains (*rót dùan phísèt*) that run between Bangkok and Padang Besar or between Bangkok and Chiang Mai there is a 50B surcharge.

The charge for 2nd-class sleeping berths is 70B for an upper berth and 100B for a lower berth (or 100B and 150B respectively

on a special express). The difference between upper and lower is that there is a window next to the lower berth and a little more headroom. The upper berth is still quite comfortable. For 2nd-class sleepers with air-con add 100B per ticket. No sleepers are available in 3rd class.

All 1st-class cabins are air-con; a two-bed cabin costs 250B per person while a single-bed cabin is 350B.

Train fares in Thailand continue to increase regularly, so train travel is not quite the bargain it once was, especially considering that the charge for 2nd-class berths is as high as the cost of cheaper hotel rooms outside Bangkok. You can figure on 500 km costing around 180B in 2nd class (not counting surcharges for rapid/express service), twice that in 1st class and less than half in 3rd. Note that the fares given in this guidebook are guaranteed to the end of 1994 only. Surprisingly, fares have hardly changed since the 1987 edition, in spite of an overall inflation rate in Thailand of 5% to 7% per annum. Relative to fare trends over the last 12 years, this is unusual and I think they're due for an increase. Although the government continues to subsidise train travel to some extent, I predict that fares will be taking a significant jump in the next two to three years, say around 10% to 15%. (I said the same thing two years ago but it hasn't happened yet!)

Meals

Meal service is available in dining cars and at your seat in 2nd and 1st-class cars. Menus change as frequently as the SRT changes catering services. For a while there were two menus, a 'special food' menu with 'special' prices (generally given to tourists) and a cheaper, more extensive menu. Nowadays all the meals seem a bit overpriced (50 to 150B average) – if you're concerned with saving baht, bring your own.

Train staff sometimes hand out face wipes, then come by later to collect 10B each for them – a racket since there's no indication to passengers that they're not complimentary.

(On government buses they're free, and they're available in the station for 1B.) Drinking water is provided, albeit in plastic bottles; sometimes it's free, sometimes it costs 5 to 10B per bottle.

Several readers have written to complain about being overcharged by meal servers on trains. If you do purchase food on board, be sure to check prices on the menu rather than trusting server quotes. Also check the bill carefully to make sure you haven't been overcharged.

Station Services

Accurate, up-to-date information on train travel is available at the Rail Travel Aids counter in Hualamphong station. There you can pick up timetables or ask questions about fares and scheduling – one person behind the counter usually speaks a little English. There are two types of timetables available: a condensed English timetable with fares, schedules and routes for rapid, express and special express trains on the four trunk lines; and complete, separate Thai timetables for each trunk line, with side lines as well. These latter timetables give fares and schedules for all trains – ordinary, rapid and express.

All train stations in Thailand have baggage storage services (sometimes called the 'cloak room'). The rates and hours of operation vary from station to station. At Hualamphong station the hours are from 4 am to 10.30 pm and left luggage costs 10B per piece per day. Hualamphong station also has a 5B shower service in the rest rooms.

All stations in provincial capitals have restaurants or cafeterias as well as various snack vendors. These stations also offer an advance-booking service for rail travel anywhere in Thailand. Hat Yai station is the only one with a hotel attached, but there are usually hotels within walking distance of other major stations.

Hualamphong station has a travel agency where other kinds of transport can be booked. This station also has a post office that's open from 7.30 am to 5.30 pm Monday to Friday, 9 am to noon Saturdays and holidays, and closed Sundays.

Excursions

The SRT offers a variety of train excursions on Saturdays, Sundays and official holidays. These almost always leave at 6.30 am and return around 7.30 pm.

Sample programmes include Sai Yok National Park (295B per person), Prasat Meuang Singh Historical Park (275B), Erawan National Park (345B), Hua Hin (100B), Damnoen Saduak (360B), Phetburi/Cha-am (380B), Prasat Hin Phimai Historical Park/Ban Prasat/Dan Kwian (1,650B); children's fares are discounted up to 40% depending on the programme. These trips can be booked through the Railway Advance Booking Office (☎ 225-6964, 223-3762).

CAR & MOTORCYCLE
Roadways

Thailand has over 167,000 km of roadways, of which 15,800 km are classified 'national highways' (both two-lane and four-lane), which means they're generally well maintained. Route numberings are fairly consistent; some of the major highways have two numbers, one under the national system and another under the optimistic 'Asia Highway' system which indicates highway links with neighbouring countries. Route 105 to Mae Sot on the Burmese border, for example, is also called 'Asia 1', while Highway 2 from Bangkok to Nong Khai is 'Asia 12'. For the time being, the only border regularly crossed by noncommercial vehicles is the Thai-Malaysian border.

Kilometre stones are placed at regular intervals along most larger roadways, but place names are usually printed on them in Thai script only. Highway signs in both Thai and roman script showing destinations and distances are becoming increasingly common.

New highway bypasses are under construction around Chiang Mai, Ubon, Khorat, Lampang, Khon Kaen, Phitsanulok, Lopburi and Kanchanaburi, which should cut driving time in these areas considerably.

Road Rules

Thais drive on the left-hand side of the road – most of the time. Other than that just about anything goes, in spite of road signs and speed limits – the Thais are notorious scofflaws when it comes to driving. Like many places in Asia, every two-lane road has an invisible third lane in the middle that all drivers feel free to use at any time. Passing on hills and curves is common – as long as you've got the proper Buddhist altar on the dashboard, what could happen?

The main rule to be aware of is that the right of way belongs to the bigger vehicle; this is not what it says in the Thai traffic law, but it's the reality. Maximum speed limits are 60 km/h within city limits, 80 km/h on highways – but on any given stretch of highway you'll see vehicles travelling as slowly as 30 km/h or as fast as 150 km/h. Speed traps are becoming more common; they seem especially common along Highway 4 in the south and Highway 2 in the north-east.

Turn signals are often used to warn passing drivers about oncoming traffic. A left-turn signal means it's okay to pass, while a right-turn signal means someone's approaching from the other direction.

The principal hazard to driving in Thailand besides the general disregard for traffic laws is having to contend with so many different types of vehicles on the same road – bullock carts, 18-wheelers, bicycles, tuktuks and customised racing bikes. In village areas the vehicular traffic is lighter but you have to contend with stray chickens, dogs, water buffaloes, pigs, cats and goats. Once you get used to the challenge, driving in Thailand is very entertaining, but first-time drivers tend to get a bit unnerved.

Checkpoints Military checkpoints are common along highways throughout northern and north-eastern Thailand, especially in border areas. Always slow down for a checkpoint – often the sentries will wave you through without an inspection, but occasionally you'll be stopped and briefly questioned. Use common sense and don't act belligerent or you're likely to be detained longer than you'd like.

Rental

Cars, jeeps and vans can be rented in Bangkok, Chiang Mai, Chiang Rai, Mae Hong Son, Pattaya, Phuket, Ko Samui and Hat Yai. A Japanese sedan (eg Toyota Corolla) typically costs from around 1200 to 1500B per day, minivans (eg Toyota Hi-Ace, Nissan Urvan) go for around 1800B a day. The best deals are usually on 4WD Suzuki Caribians (sic), which can be rented for as low as 700 to 800B per day for long-term rentals or during low seasons. Unless you absolutely need the cheapest vehicle, you might be better off with a larger vehicle (eg the Toyota 4WD Mighty Cab, if you absolutely need 4WD); Caribians are notoriously hard to handle at speeds above 90 km/h and tend to crumple dangerously in crashes. Cars with automatic shift are uncommon. Drivers can usually be hired with a rental for an additional 300B per day.

Check with travel agencies or large hotels for rental locations. It is advisable always to verify that a vehicle is insured for liability before signing a rental contract; you should also ask to see the dated insurance documents. If you have an accident while driving an uninsured vehicle you're in for some major hassles.

Motorcycles can be rented in major towns as well as many smaller tourist centres like Krabi, Ko Samui, Ko Pha-Ngan, Mae Sai, Chiang Saen, Nong Khai, etc (see Motorcycle Touring below). Rental rates vary considerably from one agency to another and from city to city. Since there is a glut of motorcycles for rent in Chiang Mai and Phuket these days, they can be rented in these towns for as little as 80B per day. A substantial deposit is usually required to rent a car; motorcycle rental usually requires that you leave your passport.

Driving Permits

Foreigners who wish to drive motor vehicles

(including motorcycles) in Thailand need a valid International Driving Permit. If you don't have one, you can apply for a Thai driver's licence at the Police Registration Division (PRD) (☎ 513-0051/5) on Phahonyothin Rd in Bangkok. Provincial capitals also have PRDs. If you present a valid foreign driver's licence at the PRD you'll probably only have to take a written test; other requirements include a medical certificate and three passport-sized colour photos. The forms are in Thai only, so you'll also need an interpreter.

Fuel & Oil

Modern petrol (gasoline) stations with electric pumps are in plentiful supply everywhere in Thailand where there are paved roads. In more remote off-road areas petrol (ben-sin or náam-man rót yon) is usually available at small roadside or village stands – typically just a couple of ancient hand-operated pumps fastened to petrol barrels. As this book went to press, regular (thamádaa) petrol cost about 9.30B per litre, super (phísèt) a bit more. Diesel (dii-soen) fuel is available at most pumps for around 8.40B.

The Thai phrase for 'motor oil' is náam-man khrêuang.

Motorcycle Touring

Motorcycle travel is becoming a popular way to get around Thailand, especially in the north. Dozens of places along the guesthouse circuit, including many guesthouses themselves, have set up shop with no more than a couple of motorbikes for rent. It is also possible to buy a new or used motorbike and sell it before you leave the country – a good used 125cc bike costs around 20,000B.

Daily rentals range from 80B a day for an 80cc or 100cc step-through (eg Honda Dream, Suzuki Crystal) to 400B a day for a good 250cc dirt bike. The motorcycle industry in Thailand has stopped assembling dirt bikes, so many of the rental bikes of this nature are getting on in years – when they're well maintained they're fine. When they're

not well maintained, they can leave you stranded if not worse. The latest trend in Thailand is for small, heavy racing bikes that couldn't be less suitable for the typical farang body.

The legal maximum size for motorcycle manufacture in Thailand is 150cc, though in reality few bikes on the road exceed 125cc. Anything over 150cc must be imported, which means an addition of up to 600% in import duties. The odd rental shop specialises in bigger motorbikes (average 200 to 500cc) – some were imported by foreign residents and later sold on the local market but most came into the country as 'parts' and were discreetly assembled, and licensed under the table.

A number of used Japanese dirt bikes have made it to northern Thailand more recently. The 250cc, four-stroke, water-cooled Honda AX-1 combines qualities of both touring and off-road machines, and features economical fuel consumption. If you're looking for a more narrowly defined dirt bike, check out the Honda XL 250. Both of these bikes are hard to find outside Chiang Mai and Pattaya.

While motorcycle touring is undoubtedly one of the best ways to see Thailand, it is also undoubtedly one of the easiest ways to cut your travels short, permanently. You can also run up very large repair and/or hospital bills in the blink of an eye. However, with proper safety precautions and driving conduct adapted to local standards, you can see parts of Thailand inaccessible by other modes of transport and still make it home in one piece. Some guidelines to keep in mind:

1. If you've never driven a motorcycle before, stick to the smaller 80 to 100cc step-through bikes with automatic clutches. If you're an experienced rider but have never done off-the-road driving, take it slow the first few days.

2. Always check a machine over thoroughly before you take it out. Look at the tyres to see if they still have tread, look for oil leaks, test the brakes. You may be held liable for any problems that weren't duly noted before your departure. Newer bikes cost more than clunkers, but are generally safer and more reliable. Street bikes are more comfortable and ride more smoothly on paved roads than dirt bikes; it's silly to rent an expensive dirt bike

if most of your riding is going to be along decent roads. A two-stroke bike suitable for off-roading generally uses twice the fuel of a four-stroke bike with the same engine size, thus lowering your cruising range in areas where roadside pumps are scarce (eg the 125cc Honda Wing gives you about 300 km per tank while a 125cc Honda MTX gets about half that).

3. Wear protective clothing and a helmet (most rental places will provide a helmet with the bike if asked). Without a helmet, a minor slide on gravel can leave you with concussion, cuts or bruises. Long pants, long-sleeved shirts and shoes are highly recommended as protection against sunburn and as a second skin if you fall. If your helmet doesn't have a visor, then wear goggles, glasses or sunglasses to keep bugs, dust and other debris out of your eyes. It is practically suicidal to ride on Thailand's highways without taking these minimum precautions for protecting your body. Gloves are also a good idea, to prevent blisters from holding on to the twist-grips for long periods of time.

4. For distances of over 100 km or so, take along an extra supply of motor oil and, if riding a two-stroke machine, carry two-stroke engine oil. On long trips, oil burns fast.

5. You should never ride alone in remote areas, especially at night. There have been incidents where farang bikers have been shot or harassed while riding alone, mostly in remote rural areas. When riding in pairs or groups, stay spread out so you'll have room to manoeuvre or brake suddenly if necessary.

6. In Thailand the de facto right of way is determined by the size of the vehicle which puts the motorcycle pretty low in the pecking order. Don't fight it and keep clear of trucks and buses.

7. Distribute whatever weight you're carrying on the bike as evenly as possible across the frame. Too much weight at the back of the bike makes the front end less easy to control and prone to rising up suddenly on bumps and inclines.

8. Get insurance with the motorcycle if at all possible. The more reputable motorcycle rental places insure all their bikes; some will do it for an extra charge. Without insurance you're responsible for anything that happens to the bike. If an accident results in a total loss, or if the bike is somehow lost or stolen, you can be out 25,000B plus. To be absolutely clear about your liability, ask for a written estimate of the replacement cost for a similar bike – take photos as a guarantee. Some agencies will only accept the replacement cost of new bike. Health insurance is also a good idea – get it before you leave home and check the conditions in regard to motorcycle riding.

BICYCLE

Bicycles can also be hired in many locations; guesthouses often have a few for rent at only 20 to 30B per day. Just about anywhere outside Bangkok, bikes are the ideal form of local transport because they're cheap, non-polluting and keep you moving slowly enough to see everything. Carefully note the condition of the bike before hiring; if it breaks down you are responsible and parts can be very expensive.

Many visitors are bringing their own touring bikes to Thailand these days. Grades in most parts of the country are moderate; exceptions include the far north, especially Mae Hong Son and Nan provinces, where you'll need iron thighs. There is plenty of opportunity for dirt-road and off-road pedalling, especially in the north, so a sturdy mountain bike would make a good alternative to a touring rig. Favoured touring routes include the two-lane roads along the Maekhong River in the north and the northeast – the terrain is mostly flat and the river scenery is inspiring.

No special permits are needed for bringing a bicycle into the country, although bikes may be registered by customs – which means if you don't leave the country with your bike you'll have to pay a huge customs duty. Most larger cities have bike shops – there are several in Bangkok and Chiang Mai – but they often stock only a few Japanese or locally made parts. All the usual bike trip precautions apply – bring a small repair kit with plenty of spare parts, a helmet, reflective clothing and plenty of insurance.

HITCHING

Hitching is never entirely safe in any country in the world, and we don't recommend it. Travellers who decide to hitch should understand that they are taking a small but serious risk. You may not be able to identify the local rapist/murderer before you get into his vehicle. However, many people do choose to hitch, and the advice that follows should help to make their journeys as fast and safe as possible.

People have mixed success with hitch-hiking in Thailand; sometimes it's great and other times no-one will pick you up. It seems easiest in the more touristed areas of the north and south, most difficult in the central and north-eastern regions where farangs are a relatively rare sight. To stand on a road and try to flag every vehicle that passes by is, to the Thais, something only an uneducated village dweller would do.

If you're prepared to face this perception, the first step is to use the correct gesture used for flagging a ride – the thumb-out gesture isn't recognised by the average Thai. When Thais want a ride they stretch one arm out with the hand open, palm facing down, and move the hand up and down. This is the same gesture used to flag a taxi or bus, which is why some drivers will stop and point to a bus stop if one is nearby.

In general hitching isn't worth the hassle as ordinary buses (no air-con) are frequent and fares are cheap. There's no need to stand at a bus terminal – all you have to do is stand on any road going in your direction and flag down a passing bus or songthaew (described in the Local Transport section of this chapter).

The exception is in areas where there isn't any bus service, though in such places there's not liable to be very much private vehicle traffic either. If you do manage to get a ride it's customary to offer food or cigarettes to the driver if you have any.

BOAT

As any flight over Thailand will reveal, there is plenty of water down there and you'll probably have opportunities to get out on it sometime during your trip. The true Thai river transport is the 'long-tail boat' (reua hang yao), so called because the propeller is mounted at the end of a long drive shaft extending from the engine. The engine, which varies from a small marine engine to a large car engine, is mounted on gimbals and the whole unit is swivelled to steer the boat. Long-tail boats can travel at a phenomenal speed.

Between the mainland and islands in the Gulf of Thailand or Andaman Sea, all sorts of larger ocean-going craft are used. The standard is an all-purpose wooden boat eight to 10 metres long with a large inboard engine, a wheelhouse and a simple roof to shelter passengers and cargo. Faster, more expensive hovercraft or jetfoils are sometimes available in tourist areas.

LOCAL TRANSPORT

The Bangkok Getting Around section has more information on various forms of local transport.

To/From Bangkok International Airport

The main international airport is in Don Meuang district, approximately 25 km north of Bangkok. You have a choice of transport modes from the airport to the city ranging from 3.50 to 300B in cost.

THAI Minibus THAI has a minibus service to major hotels (and minor ones if the driver feels like it) for 100B per person. THAI touts in the arrival hall will try to get you into the 350B limo service first, then the 100B minibus.

To Pattaya THAI operates direct air-con buses to Pattaya from the airport thrice daily at 9 am, 11 am and 7 pm; the fare is 180B one way. Private sedans cost 1500B per trip.

Public Bus Cheapest of all are the public buses to Bangkok which stop on the highway in front of the airport. There are two non-air-con bus routes and four air-con routes that visitors find particularly useful for getting into the city. Ordinary bus No 59 costs only 3.50B and operates 24 hours – it zigzags through the city to Banglamphu (the Democracy Monument area) from the airport, a trip that can take up to an hour and a half or more in traffic.

Ordinary No 29 bus (3.50B, 24 hours) plies one of the most useful, all-purpose routes from the airport into the city. After entering the city limits via Phahonyothin Rd (which turns into Phayathai Rd), the bus passes Phetburi Rd (where you'll want to get off to change buses for Banglamphu if you missed the No 59), then Rama I Rd at the Siam Square/Mahboonkrong intersection (for buses out to Sukhumvit Rd, or to walk to Soi Kasem San 1 for Muangphol Lodging, Reno Hotel, etc) and finally turns right on Rama IV Rd to go to the Hualamphong district (where the main train terminal is located). You'll want to go the opposite way on Rama IV for the Soi Ngam Duphli lodging area.

Air-con bus No 29 costs 16B and follows much the same route as the ordinary No 29 from the airport to the Siam Square and Hualamphong areas. Unless you're really strapped for baht, it's worth the extra 12.50B for the air-con and almost guaranteed seating, especially in the hot season, since the trip downtown by bus usually takes an hour or more. It runs only from 5.45 am to 8 pm, so if you're arriving on a late-night flight you'll miss it.

Air-con bus No 13 (16B, 5.45 am to 8 pm) also goes to Bangkok from the airport, coming down Phahonyothin Rd (like No 29), turning left at the Victory Monument to Ratchaprarop Rd, then south to Ploenchit Rd, where it goes east out Sukhumvit Rd all the way to Bang Na. This is definitely the one to catch if you're heading for the Sukhumvit area.

Air-con bus No 4 (16B, 5.45 am to 8 pm) begins with a route parallel to that of the No 29 bus – down Mitthaphap Rd to Ratchaprarop and Ratchadamri Rds (Pratunam district), crossing Phetburi, Rama I, Ploenchit and Rama IV Rds, then down Silom, left on Charoen Krung, and across the river to Thonburi.

Train You can also get into Bangkok from the airport by train. Just after leaving the passenger terminal, turn right (north), cross the highway via the pedestrian bridge, turn left and walk about 100 metres towards Bangkok. Opposite the big Amari Airport Hotel is the small Don Meuang train station from where trains depart regularly to Bangkok. The 3rd-class fare is only 5B on the ordinary and commuter trains. If you happen to get on a rapid or express train you may have to pay a 20 or 30B surcharge. There are trains every 15 to 30 minutes between 5.52 am and 8 pm and it takes about 45 minutes to reach Hualamphong, the main station in central Bangkok. In the opposite direction trains run frequently between 4.20 am and 8 pm.

You can also ride trains between Hualamphong and Makkasan, which is north of Phetburi Rd near the intersection of Ratchaprarop and Si Ayuthaya Rds, not far from the Indra and Bangkok Palace hotels. There are no direct trains between Don Meuang and Makkasan stations; you have to change in Hualamphong. The trip only takes 15 minutes but there are just 11 trains per day, between 5.30 am and 6 pm.

Two years ago an air-con Airport Express train was established especially for the tourist traffic between Don Meuang and Hualamphong stations. It often leaves the station with few or no passengers, as it's overpriced and a hassle to use. The train ride itself takes about 35 minutes but since you can't purchase the express tickets at the station (only at the THAI limo desk), you're forced to take a shuttle bus, which has to go 12 km south on the highway and make a U-turn to reach the station, a trip of 20 minutes or more.

This train runs only four times between 7.50 am and 7.55 pm. The total journey to reach Hualamphong station, not counting bus and train waits, is hence 55 minutes. The fare has been slashed (from 100B when the service first began) to 20B each way. When you can walk across the open public bridge and take the far more frequent ordinary train – comfortable enough – for 5B, why bother with the tourist express?

Taxi The taxis which wait near the arrival area of the airport are supposed to be airport-regulated. Ignore all the touts waiting like sharks near the customs area and buy a taxi ticket from the public taxi booth at the southern end of the arrival hall (to the far left as you leave customs). Fares are set according to city destination – no haggling should be necessary; most destinations in central Bangkok are 200B (eg Siam Square) or 300B (eg Banglamphu). Taxis using this system are not required to use their meters. Two, three, or even four passengers (if they don't have much luggage) can split the fare. Sometimes unscrupulous drivers will approach you before you reach the desk and try to sell you a ticket for 350B or 400B – ignore them and head straight for the desk. A few touts from the old taxi mafia that used to prowl the arrival area are still around and may approach you with fares of around 150B. Their taxis have white and black plates and are not licensed to carry passengers, hence you have less legal recourse in the event of an incident than if you take a licensed taxi (yellow and black plates).

If you really want to save the 30 to 50B, go upstairs to the departure area and get an incoming city taxi, one that has just dropped passengers off. These will usually take you to Bangkok on the meter for 120 to 150B. The downstairs taxi mafia frowns on this practice, however, and you may be hassled.

Metered taxis flagged down on the highway in front of the airport (turn left from the arrival hall) are even cheaper – 100 to 120B for central Bangkok. When the queue at the public taxi desk is particularly long, it's sometimes faster to go upstairs or walk out to the highway and flag one down.

Going to the airport from the city, a metered taxi costs from 115B (eg from Siam Square) to 150B (from Banglamphu or the Silom Rd area). The occasional driver will refuse to use his meter and quote a flat rate of 150 to 200B.

On a metered taxi trip to/from the airport, passengers are responsible for the 30B or 40B (depending on which entrance the driver chooses) expressway toll. During heavy traffic you can save money by staying on the surface (non-expressway) streets – which are just as speedy as (if not speedier than) the expressway during heavy commuter hours.

THAI Limousine THAI offers an airport limousine, which is really just a glorified air-con taxi service, for 350B downtown, 250B to the northern bus terminal or 400B to the southern bus terminal.

Terminal Shuttle THAI operates a free shuttle bus between the international and domestic terminals every 15 minutes between 6 am and 11.20 pm.

Helicopter The Shangri-La Hotel has its own helicopter service – introduced for the World Bank/IMF meeting in 1991 – from Bangkok Airport to the hotel rooftop for 3500B per person, minimum two passengers. The flight takes only 10 minutes but is reserved for Shangri-La guests only. If you can afford the copter flight you can certainly afford this hotel, which has one of Bangkok's best river locations.

Bus

In most larger provincial capitals, there are extensive local bus services, generally operating with very low fares (2 to 5B).

Taxi

Many regional centres have taxi services, but although there may well be meters, they're never used. Establishing the fare before departure is essential. Try to get an idea from a third party what the fare should be and be prepared to bargain. In general, fares are reasonably low. With the recent success of metered taxis in Bangkok, look for meters to appear in larger upcountry towns like Chiang Mai, Khon Kaen or Hat Yai.

Samlor/Tuk-Tuk

Samlor means 'three' (*sãam*) 'wheels' (*láw*), and that's just what they are – three-wheeled vehicles. There are two types of samlors, motorised and non-motorised. You'll find motorised samlors throughout the country. They're small utility vehicles, powered by a horrendously noisy two-stroke engine – if the noise and vibration doesn't get you, the fumes will. These samlors are more commonly known as *túk-túks* from the noise they make. The non-motorised version, on the other hand, are bicycle rickshaws, just like you find, in various forms, all over Asia. There are no bicycle samlors in Bangkok but you will find them elsewhere in the country. In either form of samlor the fare must be

Samlor

established, by bargaining if necessary, before departure.

Songthaew

A songthaew (sǎwng thǎew, literally 'two rows') is a small pick-up truck with two rows of bench seats down the sides, very similar to an Indonesian bemo and akin to a Filipino jeepney. Songthaews sometimes operate fixed routes, just like buses, but they may also run a share-taxi type of service or even be booked individually just like a regular taxi.

TRAVEL FOR PEOPLE WITH DISABILITIES

Thailand presents one large, ongoing obstacle course for the mobility-impaired. With its high curbs, uneven sidewalks and nonstop traffic, Bangkok can be particularly difficult – many streets must be crossed via pedestrian bridges flanked with steep stairways, while buses and boats don't stop long enough for even the mildly handicapped. Rarely are there any ramps or other access points for wheelchairs.

Hyatt International (Bangkok, Pattaya, Chiang Mai) is the only hotel chain in the country that makes a consistent effort to provide handicapped access for each of its properties. For the rest you're pretty much left to your own resources. For wheelchair travellers, any trip to Thailand will require a good deal of advance planning; fortunately a growing network of information sources can put you in touch with those who have wheeled through Thailand before. There is no better source of information than someone who's done it.

Three international organisations which act as clearing houses for information on world travel for the mobility-impaired are: Mobility International USA (☎ (503) 343-1284), PO Box 10767, Eugene, OR 97440, USA; Access Foundation (☎ (516) 887-5798), PO Box 356, Malverne, NY 11565, USA; and Society for the Advancement of Travel for the Handicapped (SATH) (☎ 718 858-5483), 26 Court St, Brooklyn, NY 11242, USA.

Abilities magazine (☎ (416) 766-9188; fax 762-8716), PO Box 527, Station P, Toronto, ON, Canada M5S 2T1, carries a new column called 'Accessible Planet' which offers tips on foreign travel for people with disabilities. One story described how two French wheelchair travellers trekked around northern Thailand. The book *Exotic Destinations for Wheelchair Travelers* by Ed

Hansen and Bruce Gordon (Full Data Ltd, San Francisco) contains a useful chapter on Thailand.

In Thailand you can also contact Disabled Peoples International, Council of Disabled People of Thailand (☎ (02) 255-1718; fax 252-3676) at 78/2 Tivanond Rd, Pak Kret, Nonthaburi 11120 and Handicapped International at 87/2 Soi 15 Sukhumvit Rd, Bangkok 10110.

Bangkok

The very epitome of the modern, steamy Asian metropolis, Bangkok (560 sq km; population six million) has a surplus of attractions if you can tolerate the traffic, noise, heat (in the hot season), floods (in the rainy season) and somewhat polluted air. The city is incredibly urbanised, but beneath its modern veneer lies an unmistakable Thainess. To say that Bangkok is not Thailand, as has been superciliously claimed by some, is like saying that New York is not the USA, Paris is not France, or London not England.

The capital of Thailand was established at Bangkok in 1782 by the first king of the Chakri dynasty, Rama I. The name Bangkok comes from *bang makok*, meaning 'place of olive plums' and refers to the original site, which is only a very small part of what is today called Bangkok by foreigners. The official Thai name is quite a tongue twister:

Krungthep - mahanakhon - bowon - rattanakosin - mahintara - ayuthaya - mahadilok - popnopparat - ratchathani - burirom - udomratchaniwet - mahasathan - amonpiman - avatansathir - sakkathatitya - visnukamprasit

Fortunately this is shortened to Krung Thep (City of Angels) in everyday usage. Metropolitan Krung Thep includes Thonburi, the older part of the city (and predecessor to Bangkok as the capital), which is across the Chao Phraya River to the west.

Bangkok caters to diverse interests: there are temples, museums and other historic sites for those interested in traditional Thai culture; an endless variety of good restaurants, clubs, international cultural and social events; movies in several different languages; and discos, heavy metal pubs, folk cafes, even modern art galleries for those seeking contemporary Krung Thep. As the dean of expat authors in Thailand, William Warren, has said, 'The gift Bangkok offers me is the assurance I will never be bored'.

Orientation

The east side of the Chao Phraya River, Bangkok proper, can be divided into two by the main north-south train line. The portion between the river and the railway is old Bangkok (often called Ko Ratanakosin), where most of the older temples and the original palace are located, as well as the Chinese and Indian districts. That part of the city east of the railway, which covers many times more area than the old districts, is 'new' Bangkok. It can be divided again into the business/tourist district wedged between Charoen Krung (New) and Rama IV Rds, and the sprawling business/residential/tourist district stretching along Sukhumvit and New Phetburi Rds.

This leaves the hard-to-classify areas below Sathon Tai Rd (which includes Khlong Toey, Bangkok's main port), and the area above Rama IV Rd between the railway and Withayu (Wireless) Rd (which comprises an infinite variety of businesses, several movie theatres, civil service offices, the shopping area of Siam Square, Chulalongkorn University and the National Stadium). The areas along the east bank of the Chao Phraya River are undergoing a surge of redevelopment and many new buildings, particularly condos, are going up.

On the opposite (west) side of the Chao Phraya River is Thonburi, which was Thailand's capital for 15 years before Bangkok was founded. Few tourists ever set foot on the Thonburi side except to visit Wat Arun, the Temple of Dawn. Fang Thon (Thon Bank), as it's often called by Thais,

seems an age away from the glittering high-rises on the river's east bank, although it is an up-and-coming area for condo development.

Finding Addresses Any city as large and unplanned as Bangkok can be tough to get around. Street names often seem unpronounceable to begin with, compounded by the inconsistency of romanised Thai spellings. For example, the street often spelt as Rajadamri is pronounced Ratchadamri (with the appropriate tones), or in abbreviated form Rat'damri. The 'v' in Sukhumvit should be pronounced like a 'w'. The most popular location for foreign embassies is known both as Wireless Rd and Withayu Rd (*wíthávú* is Thai for 'radio').

Many street addresses show a string of numbers divided by slashes and hyphens, for example, 48/3-5 Soi 1, Sukhumvit Rd. This is because undeveloped property in Bangkok was originally bought and sold in lots. The number before the slash refers to the original lot number; the numbers following the slash indicate buildings (or entrances to buildings) constructed within that lot. The pre-slash numbers appear in the order in which they were added to city plans, while the post-slash numbers are arbitrarily assigned by developers. As a result numbers along a given street don't always run consecutively.

The Thai word *thanŏn* means road, street or avenue. Hence Ratchadamnoen Rd (sometimes referred to as 'Ratchadamnoen Ave') is always called Thanon Ratchadamnoen in Thai.

A *soi* is a small street or lane that runs off a larger street. In our example, the address referred to as 48/3-5 Soi 1, Sukhumvit Rd will be located off Sukhumvit Rd on Soi 1. Alternative ways of writing the same address include 48/3-5 Sukhumvit Rd Soi 1, or even just 48/3-5 Sukhumvit 1. Some Bangkok sois have become so large that they can be referred to both as thanon and soi, eg Soi Sarasin/Sarasin Rd and Soi Asoke/Asoke Rd.

Smaller than a soi is a *tràwk* (usually spelt 'trok') or alley. Well-known alleys in Bangkok include Chinatown's Trok Itsanuraphap and Banglamphu's Trok Rong Mai.

Information
Tourist Offices The Tourist Authority of Thailand (TAT) has a desk in the arrivals area at Bangkok International Airport. The TAT's main office (☎ 226-0060, 226-0072) is in a large government compound on the corner of Bamrung Meuang and Worachak Rds. English-speaking staff dispense information from a small round building at the centre of the compound. The TAT produces the usual selection of colourful brochures, but they're also one of the best tourist offices in Asia for putting out useful hard facts – on plain but quite invaluable duplicated sheets.

The TAT also maintains a Tourist Assistance Centre, or TAC (☎ 282-8129, 281-5051) in the same compound for matters relating to theft and other mishaps; it's open from 8 am to midnight. The paramilitary arm of the TAT, the tourist police, can be quite effective in dealing with such matters, particularly 'unethical' business practices – which sometimes turn out to be cultural misunderstandings. Note that if you think you've been overcharged for gems (or any other purchase), there's very little the TAC can do.

Bangkok Primacy
Bangkok has dominated Thailand's urban hierarchy since the late 18th century and is today considered Asia's quintessential 'primate city' by sociologists. A primate city is one that is demographically, politically, economically and culturally dominant over all other cities in the country. Approximately 70% of Thailand's urban population (and 10% of the total population) lives in Bangkok, as compared with 30% in Manila and 27% in Kuala Lumpur (the second and third most primate in the region). More statistics: 79% of the country's university graduates, 78% of its pharmacists and 45% of its physicians live in the capital; 80% of the nation's telephones and 72% of all passenger cars registered in the country (30% of all motor vehicles) are found in Bangkok. ■

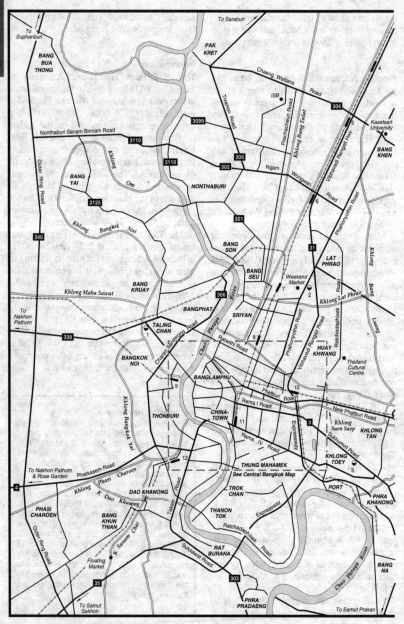

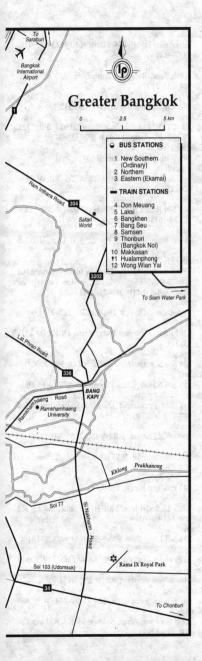

Greater Bangkok

0   2.5   5 km

BUS STATIONS
1 New Southern (Ordinary)
2 Northern
3 Eastern (Ekamai)

TRAIN STATIONS
4 Don Meuang
5 Laksi
6 Bangkhen
7 Bang Seu
8 Samsen
9 Thonburi (Bangkok Noi)
10 Makkasan
11 Hualamphong
12 Wong Wian Yai

To Saraburi

Bangkok International Airport

Ram Inthara Road   304

Safari World

3202

To Siam Water Park

Lat Phrao Road

336

Ramkhamhaeng Road

BANG KAPI

Ramkhamhaeng University

Khlong Prakhanong

Soi 77

Si Nakharin Road

Soi 103 (Udomsuk)

Rama IX Royal Park

34

To Chonburi

Money Major Thai banks have currency exchange offices in many areas of Bangkok which are open from 8.30 am to 8 pm (some even later) every day of the year. You'll find them in several places along Sukhumvit, Nana Neua, Khao San, Patpong, Surawong, Ratchadamri, Rama IV, Rama I, Silom and Charoen Krung Rds. If you're after currency for other countries in Asia, check with the moneychangers along Charoen Krung Rd near the GPO.

Post The GPO is on Charoen Krung (New) Rd. The easiest way to get there is via the Chao Phraya River Express, which stops at Tha Meuang Khae at the river end of Soi Charoen Krung 34, next to Wat Meuang Khae, just south of the GPO. The poste-restante counter is open Monday to Friday from 8 am to 8 pm, and on weekends from 8 am to 1 pm. Each letter you collect costs 1B, parcels 2B, and the staff are very efficient. The bulging boxes of poste-restante mail you must look through are sometimes daunting.

There's also a packaging service at the post office where parcels can be wrapped for 4 to 10B plus the cost of materials (up to 35B). Or you can simply buy the materials at the counter and do it yourself. The packaging counter is open Monday to Friday from 8 am to 4.30 pm, Saturday 9 am to noon. When the parcel counter is closed (weekday evenings and Sunday mornings) an informal packing service (using recycled materials) is open behind the service windows at the centre rear of the building.

Telephone & Fax The CAT international telephone office, around the corner from the main GPO building, is open 24 hours. At last count 16 different countries had Home Direct service, which means you can simply enter a vacant Home Direct booth and get one-button connection to an international operator in any of these countries (see the Telephone section in the Facts for the Visitor chapter for a country list). Other countries (except Laos and Malaysia) can be reached via IDD phones. Faxes can also be sent from the CAT office.

Other Home Direct phones can be found at Queen Sirikit National Convention Centre, World Trade Centre, Sogo Department Store and at the Banglamphu and Hualamphong post offices.

You can also make long-distance calls and faxes at the TOT office on Ploenchit Rd – but this office accepts cash only, no reverse-charge or credit-card calls. Calls to Laos and Malaysia can only be dialled from the TOT office or from private phones.

Foreign Embassies & Consulates

Bangkok is an important place for gathering visas for onward travel. The visa sections of most embassies and consulates are open from around 8.30 to 11.30 am, Monday to Friday only (call first to be sure). If you're heading on to India you'll definitely need a visa, and if you're going to Nepal it's much advisable to have one even though they are granted on entry.

For travel to Myanmar or Laos you'll also need a visa. Both countries are now issuing 14-day tourist visas, although you will probably have to purchase some kind of minimum 'tour' for Laos, even if you plan to travel independently. Check with the individual embassies for a list of agencies authorised to issue visas for each country. Visas are now available on arrival in Cambodia and Vietnam.

Countries with diplomatic representation in Bangkok include:

Argentina
    20/85 Soi 49, Sukhumvit Rd (☎ 259-0401/2)
Australia
    37 Sathon Tai Rd (☎ 287-2680)
Austria
    14 Soi Nantha, Sathon Tai Rd (☎ 254-6970)
Bangladesh
    727 Soi 55, Sukhumvit Rd (☎ 392-9437)
Belgium
    44 Soi Phiphat, Silom Rd (☎ 236-0150, 233-9370)
Brazil
    239 Soi Sarasin, Lumphini (☎ 262-6043/23)
Brunei
    19 Soi 26, Sukhumvit Rd (☎ 260-5884)
Bulgaria
    3/44 Lat Phrao Soi 31 (☎ 513-9781)

Canada
    Boonmitr Bldg, 138 Silom Rd (☎ 234-1561/8, 237-4126)
Chile
    18th floor, Bangkok Bank Bldg, 333 Silom Rd (☎ 233-2177)
China
    57 Ratchadaphisek Rd (☎ 245-7032/49)
Colombia
    c/- TTMC Ltd, 7th floor, Than Settakij Bldg, 222 Vibhavadi Rangsit Rd (☎ 278-4386)
Czechoslovakia
    99 Withayu Rd (☎ 256-6663)
Denmark
    10 Soi Attakanprasit, Sathon Tai Rd (☎ 213-2021)
Egypt
    49 Soi Ruam Rudi, Ploenchit Rd (☎ 252-6139, 253-0161)
Finland
    16th floor, Amarin Tower, 500 Ploenchit Rd (☎ 256-9306/9)
France
    35 Customs House Lane, Charoen Krung Rd (☎ 234-0950/6); consular section (visas): 29 Sathon Tai Rd (☎ 213-2181/4)
Germany
    9 Sathon Tai Rd (☎ 286-4223/7, 213-2331/6)
Greece
    3rd floor, Thanakul Bldg, Rama IX Rd (☎ 251-5111)
Hungary
    28 Soi Sukchai, Sukhumvit Rd (☎ 391-2002/3)
Iceland
    59 Soi Nawin, Chua Ploeng Rd (☎ 249-1300)
India
    46 Soi Prasanmit (Soi 23), Sukhumvit Rd (☎ 258-0300/6)
Indonesia
    600-602 Phetburi Rd (☎ 252-3135/40)
Iran
    602 Sukhumvit Rd (between sois 22 and 24) (☎ 259-0611/3)
Iraq
    47 Pradipat Rd (☎ 278-5335/8)
Ireland
    205 United Flour Mill Bldg, Ratchawong Rd (☎ 223-0876)
Israel
    31 Soi Lang Suan, Ploenchit Rd (☎ 252-3131/4)
Italy
    399 Nang Linchi Rd (☎ 286-4844/6, 287-2054)
Japan
    1674 New Phetburi Rd (☎ 252-6151/9)
Jordan
    47 Soi 63, Sukhumvit Rd (☎ 391-7142)
Kenya
    568 Soi Panit Anan, Sukhumvit Rd, Khlong Tan (☎ 391-8294)

Korea (North)
    81 Soi Ari 7, Phahonyothin Rd (☎ 278-5118)
Korea (South)
    23 Thiam-Ruammit Rd, Huay Khwang, Sam
    Saen Nok (☎ 247-7537)
Laos
    193 Sathon Tai Rd (☎ 254-6963, 213-2573)
Malaysia
    35 Sathon Tai Rd (☎ 286-1390/2)
Mexico
    44/7-8 Convent Rd (☎ 235-6367, 234-0935)
Myanmar (Burma)
    132 Sathon Neua Rd (☎ 233-2237, 234-4698)
Nepal
    189 Soi Phuengsuk (Soi 71), Sukhumvit Rd
    (☎ 391-7240)
Netherlands
    106 Withayu Rd (☎ 254-7701, 252-6103/5)
New Zealand
    93 Withayu Rd (☎ 251-8165)
Norway
    11th floor, Bank of America Bldg, Withayu Rd
    (☎ 253-0390)
Pakistan
    31 Soi Nana Neua (Soi 3), Sukhumvit Rd (☎ 253-
    0288/9)
Panama
    Sarasin Bldg, 14 Surasak Rd, Bangrak (☎ 236-
    0250, ex 239)
Peru
    10 Soi 3, Seri 2 Rd, Soi Ramkhamhaeng 24, Hua
    Mak (☎ 314-1054)
Philippines
    760 Sukhumvit Rd (☎ 259-0139)
Poland
    61 Soi 23, Sukhumvit Rd (☎ 258-4112/3)
Portugal
    26 Captain Bush Lane, Si Phaya Rd (☎ 234-
    0372, 233-7610)
Romania
    105 Soi Charoenpon, Pradipat Rd (☎ 279-7902)
Russia
    108 Sathon Neua Rd (☎ 234-9824, 234-2012,
    235-5599)
Saudi Arabia
    Sathon Thani Bldg, 90 Sathon Neua Rd (☎ 237-
    1938, 235-0875/8)
Singapore
    129 Sathon Tai Rd (☎ 286-2111, 286-1434)
South Africa
    6th floor, Park Place, 231 Soi Sarasin (☎ 253-
    8473)
Spain
    93 Withayu Rd (☎ 252-6112)
Sri Lanka
    48/3 Soi 1, Sukhumvit Rd (☎ 251-2789)
Sweden
    20th floor, Pacific Place, 140 Sukhumvit Rd
    (☎ 254-4954/55)

Switzerland
    35 Withayu Rd (☎ 252-8992/4, 253-0156/60)
Taiwan
    Far East Trade Office, 10/F Kian Gwan Bldg, 140
    Withayu Rd (☎ 251-9274/6, 251-9393)
Turkey
    153/2 Soi Mahatlekluang 1, Ratchadamri Rd
    (☎ 251-2987/8)
UK
    1031 Ploenchit Rd (☎ 253-0191/9)
USA
    95 Withayu Rd (☎ 252-5040/9)
Vietnam
    83/1 Withayu Rd (☎ 251-7201/3, 251-5835/8)
Yugoslavia
    28 Soi 61, Sukhumvit Rd (☎ 391-9090/1)

Cultural Centres Various Thai and foreign
associations organise and support cultural
events of a wide-ranging nature. They can be
good places to meet Thais with an international outlook as well as Bangkok residents.
Some of the more active organisations
include:

Alliance Française
    French language courses; translation services;
    monthly bulletin; French films; small library and
    bookshop; French and Thai cafeteria; music, arts
    and lecture programmes – 29 Sathon Tai Rd
    (☎ 286-3841)
American University Alumni (AUA)
    English and Thai language courses; monthly
    newsletter; American films; TOEFL testing; Thai
    cafeteria; library; music, art and lecture pro-
    grammes – 179 Ratchadamri Rd (☎ 252-7067/9)
British Council
    English language classes; monthly calendar of
    events; British films; music, art and drama pro-
    grammes – 428 Soi 2, Siam Square, Rama I Rd
    (☎ 252-6136/8)
Thailand Cultural Centre (TCC)
    Important centre hosting a variety of local and
    international cultural events, including musical
    and theatrical performances, art exhibits, cultural
    workshops and seminars – Ratchadaphisek Rd,
    Huay Khwang (☎ 247-0028)

The TCC also sponsors the Cultural Information Service Centre, an information
clearing house that issues a bimonthly calendar of notable cultural events throughout the
country. Many of the events listed are held
in Bangkok at foreign culture associations,
universities, art galleries, film societies,

theatres and music centres. This is the best single source for cultural happenings in Thailand; it even keeps track of obscure provincial festivals like Uttaradit's Langsat Fair and Buriram's Sombat Isan Tai Festival. The calendar is available at the TCC as well as at the TAT office on Bamrung Meuang Rd.

Religious Services More than one reader has written to point out that not everyone who comes to Thailand is either an atheist or a Buddhist. For those seeking houses of worship in the Judaeo-Christian-Muslim tradition:

Anglican/Episcopal
    Christ Church, 11 Convent Rd (☎ 234-3634)
Catholic
    Assumption Cathedral, 23 Oriental Lane, Charoen Krung Rd (☎ 234-8556)
    Holy Redeemer Church, 123/19 Soi Ruam Rudi (behind US Embassy) (☎ 253-6305)
Jewish
    Jewish Association of Thailand, 121/3 Soi 22, Sukhumvit Rd (☎ 258-2195)
Muslim
    Haroon Mosque, Charoen Krung Rd (near GPO)
    Darool Aman Mosque, Phetburi Rd (near Ratthewi circle)
Protestant
    Calvary Baptist Church, 88 Soi 2, Sukhumvit Rd (☎ 234-3634)
    International Church, 67 Soi 19, Sukhumvit Rd (☎ 258-5821)
Seventh-Day Adventist
    Bangkok Ekamai Church, 57 Soi Charoenchai, Ekamai Rd (☎ 391-3593)
    Bangkok Chinese Church, 1325 Rama IV Rd (☎ 215-4529)

Travel Agencies Bangkok is packed with travel agencies of every manner and description, but if you're looking for cheap airline tickets it's wise to be cautious. In the past two years, two agencies on Khao San Rd closed up shop and absconded with full airfare payments collected from more than 30 tourists who never received their tickets. The really bad agencies change their names frequently, so ask other travellers for advice. Wherever possible, try to see the tickets before you hand over the money. The STA Travel

agency in Bangkok is at Tour Centre (☎ 281-5314) in the Thai Hotel, 78 Prachatipatai Rd.

Some agencies will book Thai train tickets and pick them up by courier – a service for which there's usually a 100B surcharge. Four agencies permitted to arrange direct train bookings (without surcharge) are:

Airland
    866 Ploenchit Rd (☎ 255-5432)
SEA Tours
    Suite 414, 4th floor, Siam Center, Rama I Rd (☎ 251-4862, 255-2080)
Songserm Travel Center
    121/7 Soi Chalermla, Phayathai Rd (☎ 255-8790)
    172 Khao San Rd (☎ 282-8080)
Viang Travel
    Viengtai Hotel, 42 Rambutri Rd (☎ 280-1708)

The following agencies specialise in arranging tourist travel to Myanmar, Laos, Cambodia and Vietnam:

Diethelm Travel
    Kian Gwan Bldg II, 140/1 Withayu Rd (☎ 255-9150; fax 256-0248)
Exotissimo Travel
    21/17 Soi 4, Sukhumvit Rd (☎ 253-5250; fax 254-7683)
MK Ways
    57/11 Withayu Rd (☎ 254-3390; fax 254-5583)
Skyline Travel Services
    27th floor, Ocean Tower II Bldg, 75/62-63 Sukhumvit Rd, Soi 21 (☎ 260-5525; fax 260-5534)

There are also several brokers on Khao San Rd who arrange visa packages for Thailand's socialist neighbours, but none are authorised for direct sales – they must work through other agencies.

If you are heading onto Europe and need a Eurail Pass, Dits Travel Ltd (☎ 255-9205) at Kian Gwan House, 140 Withayu Rd, is one of the Bangkok agencies authorised to issue them.

Bookshops Bangkok has many good bookshops, possibly the best selection in South-East Asia.

For new books and magazines the two best

bookshop chains are Asia Books and Duang Kamol (DK) Book House. Asia Books lives up to its name by having one of the largest selections of English-language titles on Asia in Bangkok. Asia Books' main branch (☎ 252-7277) is at 221 Sukhumvit Rd at Soi 15; large branch shops are at: Landmark Plaza, sois 3 and 4, Sukhumvit Rd (☎ 253-5839); 2nd floor, Peninsula Plaza, adjacent to the Regent Bangkok on Ratchadamri Rd (☎ 253-9786); 3rd floor, World Trade Centre (☎ 255-6209); and 3rd floor, Thaniya Plaza, Silom Rd (☎ 250-0162). Smaller Asia Books stalls can be found in several of the larger hotels and at Thai airports.

DK Book House (☎ 251-6335) is headquartered at Siam Square, off Rama I Rd, with additional branches on Surawong Rd near Patpong, and on Sukhumvit Rd across from the Ambassador City complex (the latter branches are excellent for fiction titles – the Siam Square branch is better for textbooks). DK also has a branch in the Mahboonkrong shopping centre opposite Siam Square. By the end of 1994, DK Book House Co plans to open what will be South-East Asia's largest book centre, in the new Seacon Square shopping complex on Si Nakharin Rd between Bang Kapi and Bang Na. Inspired by similar book-trade facilities in Frankfurt and Paris, the 5200-sq-metre centre promises to become the book marketing centre for the entire region.

There are two other bookshops with English-language books in the Siam Square complex: the Book Chest (Soi 2) and Odeon Store (Soi 1). In the Silom Rd area, the Bookseller at 81 Patpong 1 has a wide selection. Chom Aksawn, a bookstore on the 2nd floor of the Siam Center shopping complex (opposite Siam Square), carries a good selection of magazines, English-language bestsellers, some German novels, maps and guidebooks.

Suksit Siam, opposite Wat Ratchabophit on Fuang Nakhon Rd, specialises in books on Thai politics, especially those representing the views of Sulak Sivaraksa and the progressive Santi Pracha Dhamma Institute (which has offices next door). The shop also has a number of mainstream titles on Thailand and Asia, both in English and Thai.

Elite Used Books, 593/5 Sukhumvit Rd near Villa supermarket, carries a good selection of used foreign-language titles (English, Chinese, French, German, Swedish). The Weekend Market in Chatuchak Park is also a source of used, often out-of-print books in several languages.

Libraries Besides offering an abundance of reading material, Bangkok's libraries make a peaceful escape from the heat, noise and traffic.

The National Library (☎ 281-5212) on Samsen Rd is an impressive institution with a huge collection of Thai material dating back several centuries as well as smaller numbers of foreign-language books. Membership is free. The Siam Society and National Museum also have collections of English-language materials on the history, art and culture of Thailand.

Both American University Alumni (AUA) and the British Council have lending libraries; the British Council allows only members (residents over 16 years of age only) to borrow books, while AUA has a free public lending service. Both libraries cater primarily to Thai members, hence the emphasis tends to be on English-language teaching rather than, say, the latest fiction. Their main strengths are their up-to-date periodicals sections – the British Council's selection is strictly British of course, while AUA's is all-American.

Although you won't be permitted to borrow books unless you're a Chula student, the library in Chulalongkorn University (south of Siam Square) is a good place to hang out – quiet and air-conditioned.

In a class all its own, the Neilson Hays Library (☎ 233-1731), at 193 Surawong Rd next to the British Club, is a historical monument as well as a good, all-purpose lending library. Built in 1921 by Dr Heyward Hays as a memorial to his wife Jennie Neilson Hays, the classic colonial Asian edifice is operated by the 100-year-old Bangkok Library Association and is the oldest

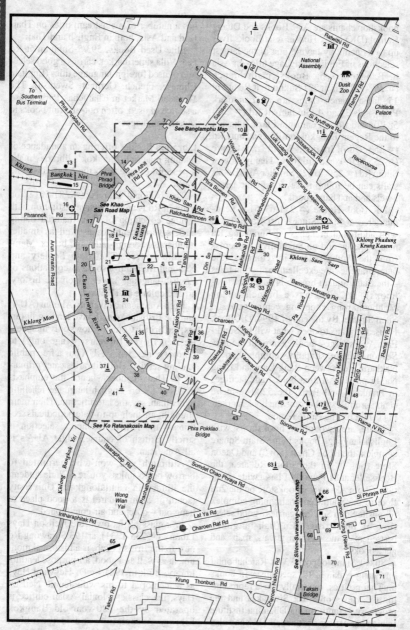

To
Southern Bus Terminal

Phra Pinklao Rd

Khlong

Bangkok
Noi

13

15

16

Phrannok   Rd

17

See Khao
San Road Map

Phra
Phrao
Bridge

14

Phra Athit Rd

See Banglamphu Map

Samsen

Wisut Kasat

Khao San   Rd

Phra Suman Rd

Ratchadamnoen

Ratchadamnoen Nok Ave

Klang Rd

26

National
Assembly

Dusit Zoo

Chitlada
Palace

Ratwithi Rd

2

4   Rd

8

9

Si Ayuthaya

11

Luk Luang Rd

Phitsanulok Rd

Rama V Rd

Racecourse

Krung Kasem Rd

27

28

Lan Luang Rd

Khlong Phadung
Krung Kasem

Khlong   Saen   Saep

10

Maharat

19

20

21

18

Sanam
Luang

22

23

24

29

30

Bamrung Meuang Rd

32

33

Bamrung Meuang Rd

Tanao   Rd

Din So   Rd

Mahachai Rd

Bophit

Waradhat

Luang Rd

Rama VI Rd

Phrannok Rd

Arun Amarin Road

Chao Phraya River

Khlong Mon

34

35

37

38

41

Maharat
Road

25

31

Fuang Nakhon Rd

Triphet Rd

Chakraphet Rd

36

39

40

Charoen

Krung (New) Rd

Chakrawat Rd

Yaowarat Rd

44

45

Sua   Pa   Road

48

47

46

43

Songwat Rd

Rama IV Rd

Muang Rd

42

See Ko Ratanakosin Map

Phra Pokklao
Bridge

Itsaraphap Rd

Prachathipok Rd

Somdet Chao Phraya Rd

63

Khlong Bangkok Yai

Wong
Wian
Yai

Intharaphitak Rd

Lat Ya Rd

Charoen Rat Rd

65

Taksin Rd

Krung Thonburi Rd

Charoen Nakhon Rd

Taksin
Bridge

See Silom-Surawong-Sathon map

66

67

69

68

70

71

Si Phraya Rd

Charoen Krung (New) Rd

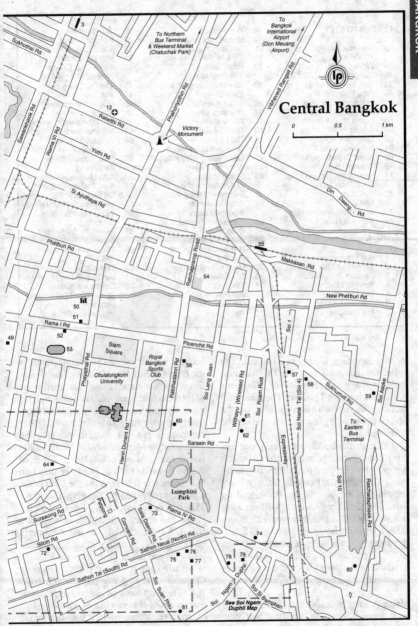

Central Bangkok

Sukhothai Rd

Savankhalock Rd

Rama VI Rd

Ratwithi Rd

Si Ayuthaya Rd

Phetburi Rd

Rama I Rd

Phayathai Rd

To Northern
Bus Terminal
& Weekend Market
(Chatuchak Park)

Phaholyothin Rd

Victory
Monument

Yothi Rd

To
Bangkok
International
Airport
(Don Meuang
Airport)

Vibhavadi Rangsit Rd

Din Daeng Rd

New Phetburi Rd

Ratchaprarop Road

Makkasan Rd

Soi 1

Siam Square

Chulalongkorn University

Royal Bangkok Sports Club

Ploenchit Rd

Ratchadamri Rd

Soi Lang Suan

Soi Ruam Rudi

Withayu (Wireless) Rd

Soi Nana Tai (Soi 4)

Expressway

Sukhumvit Rd

Soi Asoke

To Eastern Bus Terminal

Henri Dunant Rd

Sarasin Rd

Soi 10

Ratchadaphisek Rd

Lumphini Park

Rama IV Rd

Surawong Rd

Patpong

Silom Rd

Convent Rd

Sala Daeng Rd

Sathon Neua (North) Rd

Sathon Tai (South) Rd

Soi Suan Phlu

Soi Ngam Duphli

Soi Si Bamphen

See Soi Ngam
Duphli Map

0   0.5   1 km

PLACES TO STAY

8	Bangkok International Youth Hostel
44	White Orchid
45	Chinatown Hotel
46	New Empire Hotel
49	Tong Poon Hotel
51	Muangphol Building
52	National Scout Hostel
56	Grand Hyatt Erawan
57	Atlanta Hotel
58	Landmark Hotel
64	Mandarin Hotel
67	Royal Orchid Sheraton
70	Oriental Hotel
71	Holiday Inn Crowne Plaza
73	Dusit Thani Hotel
75	YMCA
76	YWCA
77	Beaufort Sukhothai Hotel
79	Malaysia Hotel

OTHER

1	Wat Ratchathiwat
2	Vimanmek Teak Mansion
3	Samsen Train Station
4	National Library
5	Tha Thewet
6	Tha Wisut Kasat
7	Tha Samphey
9	Royal Plaza
10	Wat Intharawihan
11	Wat Benchamabophit
12	Phra Mongkutklao Hospital
13	Royal Barges
14	Tha Phra Athit
15	Thonburi (Bangkok Noi) Train Station
16	Siriraj Hospital
17	Tha Phra Chan
18	Wat Mahathat
19	Tha Maharat
20	Tha Chang
21	Silpakorn University
22	Lak Meuang (City Pillar)
23	Wat Phra Kaew
24	Grand Palace
25	Wat Ratchabophit
26	Democracy Monument
27	Ratchadamnoen BoxingStadium
28	Bangkok Adventist Hospital
29	Wat Ratchanatda
30	Wat Saket
31	Wat Suthat
32	Monk's Bowl Village
33	TAT Office
34	Tha Tien
35	Wat Pho
36	Old Siam Plaza
37	Wat Arun
38	Tha Ratchin
39	Pahurat Market
40	Tha Saphaan Phut
41	Wat Kalayanimit
42	Santa Cruz Church (Wat Kuti Jiin)
43	Tha Ratchawang
47	Wat Traimit
48	Hualamphong Train Station
50	Jim Thompson's House
53	National Stadium
54	Pratunam Market
55	Makkasan Train Station
59	Siam Society (Ban Kamthieng)
60	AUA Language Center
61	New Zealand Embassy
62	US Embassy
63	Wat Thawng Nophakhun
65	Wong Wian Yai Train Station
66	River City Shopping Complex
68	Tha Meuang Khae
69	GPO
72	THAI Office
74	Lumphini Boxing Stadium
78	Goethe Institute
80	Queen Sirikit Convention Centre
81	Immigration Office

English-language library in Thailand. The collection has well over 20,000 volumes, including a good selection of children's books and titles on Thailand. The periodical section offers a few Thai magazines, and the library even has jigsaw puzzles that can be borrowed.

Although the building has only one aircon reading room, the ancient ceiling fans do a good job of keeping the other sitting areas cool. The library's Rotunda Gallery hosts monthly art exhibitions and occasional art sales. Membership rates are 1000B per adult per year, 600B for children or 1250B per family. Opening hours are Monday to Saturday from 9.30 am to 4 pm, Sunday 9.30 am to 12.30 pm. Free parking for members is available at the library's small car park near the corner of Surawong and Naret Rds.

Maps A map is essential for finding your way around Bangkok, and the best one,

because it clearly shows all the bus routes, is the *Bangkok Bus Map (Walking Tours)* published by Bangkok Guide. The map costs 35B (some places ask 40B) and although it's regularly updated, some bus routes will inevitably be wrong, so take care. Other companies put out similar maps called *Tour'n Guide Map to Bangkok Thailand* and *Latest Tour's Map to Bangkok & Thailand* that will also do the job. For more detail on bus routes you'll have to get the *Bus Guide*, a booklet published by Bangkok Guide for 35B. It contains maps and a listing of all the public bus routes in Bangkok as well as a Bangkok train schedule. To use it properly takes some patience since much of the guide is in Thai and the English is horrendous.

Another map to consider is Nancy Chandler's *Map of Bangkok*, which costs 70B. This map has a whole host of information on out-of-the-way places, including lots of stuff on where to buy unusual things around the city. There's a similar companion map to Chiang Mai. The Fine Arts Commission of the Association of Siamese Architects produces a pack of four unusual maps showing temples and important places of cultural interest. The maps are *Bangkok*, *Grand Palace*, *Canals of Thonburi* and *Ayuthaya*. The TAT issues a *Sightseeing & Shopping Map* of Bangkok that has lively three-dimensional drawings of popular tourist spots along Ratchadamri, Rama IV, Rama I and Phayathai Rds.

Medical Services Bangkok is Thailand's leading health care centre, with three university research hospitals, 12 public and private hospitals and hundreds of medical clinics. Australian, US and UK embassies usually keep up-to-date lists of doctors who can speak English; for doctors who speak other languages, contact the relevant embassy or consulate.

Several store-front clinics in the Ploenchit Rd area specialise in lab tests for sexually transmitted diseases. Bangkok's better hospitals include:

Bangkok Adventist Hospital
    430 Phitsanulok Rd (☎ 281-1422)
Bangkok Christian Hospital
    124 Silom Rd (☎ 233-6981/9)
Bangkok Nursing Home
    9 Convent Rd (☎ 233-2610/9)
Phayathai Hospital
    364/1 Si Ayuthaya Rd (☎ 245-2620)
    or 943 Phahonyothin Rd (☎ 270-0780)
Samitivej Hospital
    133 Soi 49, Sukhumvit Rd (☎ 392-0010/9)
Samrong General Hospital
    Soi 78, Sukhumvit Rd (☎ 393-2131/5)
St Louis Hospital
    215 Sathon Tai Rd (☎ 212-0033/48)

Emergency Bangkok does not have an emergency phone system staffed by English-speaking operators. Between the hours of 8 am and midnight, your best bet for English-speaking assistance is the Tourist Assistance Centre (☎ 281-5051, 282-8129). After midnight you'll have to rely on your own resources or on English-speaking hotel staff.

If you can find a Thai to call on your behalf, here are the city's main emergency numbers:

Police   ☎ 191 or 123
Fire   ☎ 199
Ambulance ☎ 252-2171/5

Dangers & Annoyances Bangkok's most heavily touristed areas, especially around Wat Phra Kaew and Khao San Rd, are favourite hunting grounds for Thai con artists of every ilk. Lately I've seen a few hanging out near Soi Kasem San 1 and Soi Kasem San 2, opposite Mahboonkrong Centre and near Jim Thompson's House. The latter typically dress in Thai business suits and carry cell phones.

The clever cons will seemingly meet you on the street or in a cafe by accident. Don't believe anyone on the street who tells you Wat Pho, Jim Thompson's House or some other attraction is closed for a holiday; check for yourself. More obvious are the tuk-tuk drivers who are out to make a commission by dragging you to a local silk or jewellery shop – even though you've requested an entirely different destination. In either case if you accept an invitation for 'free' sightseeing or shopping, you're quite likely to end up wasting an afternoon or – as happens all too often – losing a lot of money.

For full details on common scams, see the Dangers & Annoyances section in the Facts for the Visitor chapter.

Tourist Police Under the Crime Suppression Division of the National Police Department, the tourist police are a separate force established in 1982 to deal with tourist problems. In Bangkok, some 500 English-speaking officers are stationed in tourist areas – their kiosks, cars and uniforms are clearly marked. If you have any problems related to criminal activity, try contacting the tourist police first. When they can't solve the problem, or if it's out of their jurisdiction, they can act as a bilingual liaison with the regular police. The tourist police headquarters is at the TAT compound on Bamrung Meuang Rd; they can be reached by dialling the special four-digit number ☎ 1699. The Crime Suppression Division (☎ 225-0085, at 509 Worachak Rd, near the intersection of Worachak and Charoen Krung Rds) also deals with tourism-related crime, particularly gem fraud.

Highlights

If your visit to Bangkok is a short one, you won't be able to see all the sights the city has to offer. For visits of four or five days, must-dos include Wat Phra Kaew and the Grand Palace along with nearby Wat Pho, the National Museum, either the Lak Meuang or Erawan shrines, Jim Thompson's House, either Vimanmek Teak Mansion or Wang Suan Phakkard, and a river or canal trip.

For a three-day stopover, leave out the National Museum and the shrines. If you have longer – say a week or more – add the Weekend Market, a Thai boxing match and a performance at the National Theatre. Looking for another temple or two? Wat Traimit's Golden Buddha never fails to impress; Wat Arun also makes a pleasant cross-river excursion.

Evenings can be devoted to sampling Bangkok's incredible Thai restaurants – try at least one riverside place to soak up the languid ambience of old Bangkok. You should also seek out at least one Thai musical performance, whether traditional (at a dinner theatre) or modern (at one of the city's many nightclubs).

Wat Phra Kaew & Grand Palace

วัดพระแก้วและพระบรมมหาราชวัง

Also called the Temple of the Emerald Buddha (official name: Wat Phra Si Ratana Satsadaram), this wat adjoins the Grand Palace on common ground which was consecrated in 1782, the first year of Bangkok rule. In aggregate, the 945,000-sq-metre

Statue in the Grand Palace complex

grounds encompass over a hundred buildings that represent 200 years of royal history and architectural experimentation. Most of the architecture, royal or sacred, can be classified Bangkok or Ratanakosin style, with lots of minor variation.

The wat structures are extremely colourful, being comprised of gleaming, gilded chedis, polished orange and green roof tiles, mosaic-encrusted pillars and rich marble pediments. Extensive murals depicting scenes from the *Ramakian* (the Thai version of the Indian epic *Ramayana)* line the inside walls of the compound. Originally painted during Rama I's reign (1782-1809), the murals have undergone several restorations, including a major one finished in time for the 1982 Bangkok/Chakri dynasty bicentennial. Divided into 178 sections, the murals illustrate the epic in its entirety, beginning at the

Top Left: Wat Pho, Bangkok (RI)
Top Right: Wat Phra Kaew, Bangkok (GB)
Bottom Left: Guard, Grand Palace, Bangkok (PM)
Bottom Right: Buddha detail, Wat Si Chum, Sukhothai (BP)

Top Left: Wat Arun, Bangkok (RI)
Top Right: Wat Phra Kaew, Bangkok (RN)
Bottom Left: Lingam (phallus) shrine, Nai Loet Park, Bangkok (JC)
Bottom Right: Wat Doi Kong Mu, Mae Hong Son (RI)

north gate and moving clockwise around the compound.

Except for an anteroom here and there, the interiors of the **Grand Palace** (Phra Borom Maharatchawong in Thai), are today used by the king only for certain ceremonial occasions such as Coronation Day (his current residence is Chitlada Palace in the northern part of the city), and are closed to the public. The exteriors of the four buildings are worth a swift perusal, however, for their royal bombast.

Borobiman Hall (east end), a French-inspired structure that served as a residence for King Rama VI, is occasionally used to house visiting foreign dignitaries. In April 1981 General San Chitpatima used it as headquarters for an attempted coup. Next west is **Amarindra Hall**, originally a hall of justice but used today for coronation ceremonies.

Largest of the palace buildings is the triple-winged **Chakri Mahaprasat**, literally 'Great Holy Hall of Chakri' but usually translated 'Grand Palace Hall'. Built in 1882 by British architects using Thai labour, the exterior shows a peculiar blend of Italian renaissance and traditional Thai architecture, a style often referred to as *faràng sài chá-daa* or 'European wearing a Thai classical dancer's headdress' because each wing is topped by a *mondòp*, a layered, heavily ornamented spire representing a Thai adaptation of the Hindu *mandapa* or shrine. The tallest of the mondops, in the centre, contains the ashes of each Chakri king who has passed away; the flanking mondops enshrine the ashes of Chakri princes who never inherited the throne. Thai kings traditionally housed their huge harems in the mahaprasat's inner palace area, which was guarded by combat-trained female sentries.

Last from east to west is the Ratanakosin-style **Dusit Hall**, which initially served as a venue for royal audiences and later as a royal funerary hall.

Emerald Buddha

The so-called Emerald Buddha or Phra Kaew, 60 to 75 cm high (depending on how it is measured), is actually made of a type of jasper or perhaps nephrite (a type of jade), depending on whom you believe. A definite aura of mystery surrounds the image, enhanced by the fact that it cannot be examined closely – it sits in a glass case, on a pedestal high above the heads of worshippers – and photography within the bot is forbidden. Its mystery further adds to the occult significance of the image, which is considered the 'talisman' of the Thai kingdom, the legitimator of Thai sovereignty.

It is not known for certain where the image originated or who sculpted it, but it first appeared on record in 15th-century Chiang Rai. Legend says it was sculpted in India and brought to Siam by way of Ceylon, but stylistically it seems to belong to the Chiang Saen or Lanna (Lan Na Thai) period (13th to 14th centuries). Sometime in the 15th century, the image is said to have been covered with plaster and gold leaf and placed in Chiang Rai's own Wat Phra Kaew (literally, 'temple of the jewel holy image'). While being transported elsewhere after a storm had damaged the chedi in which the image had been kept, the image supposedly lost its plaster covering in a fall. It next appeared in Lampang where it enjoyed a 32-year stay (again at a Wat Phra Kaew) until it was brought to Wat Chedi Luang in Chiang Mai.

Laotian invaders took the image from Chiang Mai in the mid-16th century and brought it to Luang Prabang in Laos. Later it was moved to Wiang Chan (Vientiane). When Thailand's King Taksin waged war against Laos 200 years later, the image was taken back to the Thai capital of Thonburi by General Chakri, who later succeeded Taksin as Rama I, the founder of the Chakri dynasty. Rama I had the Emerald Buddha moved to the new Thai capital in Bangkok and had two royal robes made for it, one to be worn in the hot season and one for the rainy season. Rama III added another to the wardrobe – to be worn in the cool season. The three robes are still solemnly changed at the beginning of each season by the king himself. The huge bot in which it is displayed was built expressly for the purpose of housing the diminutive image. ■

Admission to the Wat Phra Kaew/Grand Palace compound is 125B, and opening hours are from 8.30 to 11.30 am and 1 to 3.30 pm. The admission fee includes entry to the Royal Thai Decorations & Coins Pavilion (on the same grounds) and to both Vimanmek ('the world's largest golden teak-wood mansion') and Abhisek Dusit Throne Hall, near the Dusit Zoo. (See the later Vimanmek/Abhisek sections for more details.)

Since wats are a sacred place to Thai Buddhists – this one particularly so because of its monarchical associations – visitors should dress and behave decently for their visit. If you wear shorts or sleeveless shirts you may be refused admission; sarongs and baggy pants are sometimes available on loan at the entry area. For walking in the courtyard areas you must wear shoes with closed heels and toes – 'thongs' aren't permitted. As in any temple compound, shoes should be removed before entering the main chapel (bot) or sanctuaries *(wihāan)* of Wat Phra Kaew.

The most economical way of reaching Wat Phra Kaew and the Grand Palace is by aircon bus No 8 or 12. You can also take the Chao Phraya River Express, disembarking at Tha Chang.

Wat Pho (Wat Phra Chetuphon)

A long list of superlatives for this one: the oldest and largest wat in Bangkok, it features the largest reclining Buddha and the largest collection of Buddha images in Thailand and was the earliest centre for public education. As a temple site Wat Pho dates back to the 16th century, but its current history really begins in 1781 with the complete rebuilding of the original monastery.

Narrow Chetuphon Rd divides the grounds in two, with each section surrounded by huge whitewashed walls. The most interesting part is the northern compound, which includes a very large bot enclosed by a gallery of Buddha images and four wihaans, four large chedis commemorating the first three Chakri kings (Rama III

has two chedis), 91 smaller chedis, an old tripitaka (Buddhist scriptures) library, a sermon hall, the large wihaan which houses the reclining Buddha, and a school building for classes in Abhidhamma (Buddhist philosophy), plus several less important structures. The temple is currently undergoing a 53 million baht renovation.

Wat Pho is the national headquarters for the teaching and preservation of traditional Thai medicine, including Thai massage. A massage school convenes in the afternoons at the eastern end of the compound; a massage costs 180B per hour. You can also study massage here in seven to 10-day courses.

The tremendous reclining Buddha, 46 metres long and 15 metres high, illustrates the passing of the Buddha into nirvana. The figure is modelled out of plaster around a brick core and finished in gold leaf. Mother-of-pearl inlay ornaments the eyes and feet of the colossal image, the feet displaying 108 different auspicious *laksanas* or characteristics of a Buddha. The images on display in the four wihaans surrounding the main bot in the eastern part of the compound are interesting. Particularly beautiful are the Phra Jinnarat and Phra Jinachi Buddhas, in the west and south chapels, both from Sukhothai. The galleries extending between the four chapels feature no less than 394 gilded Buddha images. King Rama I's remains are interred in the base of the presiding Buddha image in the bot.

The temple rubbings for sale at Wat Pho and elsewhere in Thailand come from 152 *Ramakian* reliefs, carved in marble and obtained from the ruins of Ayuthaya, which line the base of the large bot. The rubbings are no longer taken directly from the panels but are rubbed from cement casts of the panels made years ago.

You may hire English, French, German or Japanese-speaking guides for 150B for one visitor, 200B for two, 300B for three. Also on the premises are a few astrologers and palm-readers.

The temple is open to the public from 8 am to 5 pm daily; admission is 10B. The ticket booth is closed from noon to 1 pm. Air-con bus Nos 6, 8 and 12 stop near Wat Pho. The nearest Chao Phraya Express pier is Tha Tien.

Wat Mahathat

วัดมหาธาตุ

Founded in the 1700s, Wat Mahathat is a national centre for the Mahanikai monastic sect and houses one of Bangkok's two Buddhist universities, Mahathat Rajavidyalaya. On weekends, a large produce market is held on the grounds. Opposite the main entrance on the other side of Maharat Rd is a large religious amulet market.

The temple is officially open to visitors from 9 am to 5 pm every day and on *wan phrá* – Buddhist holy days (the full and new moons every fortnight). Also in the temple grounds is a daily open-air market which features traditional Thai herbal medicine.

The monastery's International Buddhist Meditation Centre offers meditation instruction in English on the second Saturday of every month from 2 to 6 pm in the Dhamma Vicaya Hall. Those interested in more intensive instruction should contact the monks in Section 5 of the temple compound.

Wat Mahathat is right across the street from Wat Phra Kaew, on the west side of Sanam Luang. Air-con bus Nos 8 and 12 both pass by it, and the nearest Chao Phraya Express pier is Tha Maharat.

Wat Traimit

วัดไตรมิตร

The attraction at the Temple of the Golden Buddha is, of course, the impressive three-metre tall, 5½-tonne, solid-gold Buddha image, which gleams like no other gold artefact I've ever seen.

Sculpted in the graceful Sukhothai style, the image was 'rediscovered' some 40 years ago beneath a stucco or plaster exterior when it fell from a crane while being moved to a new building within the temple compound. It has been theorised that the covering was

added to protect it from 'marauding hordes', either during the late Sukhothai period or later in Ayuthaya when the city was under siege by the Burmese. The temple itself is said to date from the early 13th century.

The golden image can be seen every day from 9 am to 5 pm, and admission is 10B. Wat Traimit is near the intersection of Yaowarat and Charoen Krung Rds, near Hualamphong station.

Wat Arun

วัดอรุณ

The 'Temple of Dawn' is named after the Indian god of dawn, Aruna. It appears in all the tourist brochures and is located on the Thonburi side of the Chao Phraya River. The present wat is built on the site of 17th-century Wat Jang, which was the palace and royal temple of King Taksin when Thonburi was the Thai capital; hence, it was the last home of the Emerald Buddha before Rama I brought it across the river to Bangkok.

The tall, 82-metre *prang* (Khmer-style tower) was constructed during the first half of the 19th century by Rama II and Rama III. The unique design elongates the typical Khmer prang into a distinctly Thai shape. Its brick core has a plaster covering embedded with a mosaic of broken, multi-hued Chinese porcelain; the use of broken porcelain for temple ornamentation was common in the early Ratanakosin period when Chinese ships calling at Bangkok used tons of old porcelain as ballast. Steep stairs reach a lookout point about halfway up the prang from where there are fine views of Thonburi and the river. During certain festivals, hundreds of lights illuminate the outline of the prang at night.

Also worth a look is the interior of the bot. The main Buddha image is said to have been designed by Rama II himself. The murals date to the reign of Rama V; particularly impressive is one that depicts Prince Siddhartha encountering examples of birth, old age, sickness and death outside his palace walls. According to Buddhist legend it was the experience of seeing these phenomena for the first time that led Siddhartha to abandon the worldly life. The ashes of King Rama II are interred in the base of the bot's presiding Buddha image.

The temple looks more impressive from the river than it does from up close, though the peaceful wat grounds make a very nice retreat from the hustle and bustle of Bangkok. Between the prang and the ferry pier is a huge sacred banyan tree.

Wat Arun is open daily from 8.30 am to 5.30 pm; admission is 10B. To reach Wat Arun from the Bangkok side, catch a cross-river ferry from Tha Tien at Thai Wang Rd (see the Ko Ratanakosin map). Crossings are frequent and cost only 1B.

Wat Benchamabophit

วัดเบญจมบพิตร

This wat of white Carrara marble (hence its tourist name, 'Marble Temple') was built at the turn of the century under Chulalongkorn (Rama V). The large cruciform bot is a prime example of modern Thai wat architecture. The base of the central Buddha image, a copy of Phitsanulok's Phra Phuttha Chinnarat, contains the ashes of King Rama V. The courtyard behind the bot exhibits 53 Buddha images (33 originals and 20 copies) representing famous figures and styles from all over Thailand and other Buddhist countries – an education in itself if you're interested in Buddhist iconography.

Wat Ben is on the corner of Si Ayuthaya and Rama V Rds, diagonally opposite the south-west corner of Chitlada Palace; it's open daily and admission is 10B. Bus Nos 2 (air-con) and 72 stop nearby.

Wat Saket

วัดสระเกศ

Wat Saket is an undistinguished temple except for the Golden Mount (Phu Khao Thong) on the western side of the grounds which provides a good view out over Bangkok rooftops. The artificial hill was created when a large chedi under construc-

tion by Rama III collapsed because the soft soil beneath would not support it. The resulting mud-and-brick hill was left to sprout weeds until Rama IV built a small chedi on its crest.

Later his son, Rama V, added to the structure and housed a Buddha relic from India (given to him by the British government) in the chedi. The concrete walls were added during WW II to prevent the hill from eroding. Every November there is a big festival on the grounds of Wat Saket, which includes a candle-lit procession up the Golden Mount.

Admission to Wat Saket is free except for the final approach to the summit of the Golden Mount, which costs 5B. The temple is within walking distance of the Democracy Monument; air-con bus Nos 11 and 12 pass nearby.

Wat Rajanadda (Ratchanatda)

วัดราชนัดดา

Across Mahachai Rd from Wat Saket and behind the old Chalerm Thai movie theatre, this temple dates from the mid-19th century. It was built under Rama III and is an unusual specimen, possibly influenced by Burmese models.

The wat has a well-known market selling Buddhist amulets or magic charms (phrá phim) in all sizes, shapes and styles. The amulets not only feature images of the Buddha, but also famous Thai monks and Indian deities. Full Buddha images are also for sale. Wat Rajanadda is an expensive place to purchase a charm, but a good place to look.

Buddha Images

In the Thai language, Buddhas or phra phim are never 'bought' or 'sold', they are 'rented'. The images are purported to protect the wearer from physical harm, though some act as 'love charms'. Amulets that are considered to be particularly powerful tend to cost thousands of baht and are worn by soldiers, taxi drivers and other Thai believers working in high-risk professions. ∎

Wat Bovornives (Bowonniwet)

วัดบวรนิเวศ

Wat Bowon, on Phra Sumen Rd, is the national headquarters for the Thammayut monastic sect, the minority sect in Mahanikai Buddhism. King Mongkut, founder of the Thammayuts, began a royal tradition by residing here as a monk – in fact he was the abbot of Wat Bowon for several years. King Bhumibol and Crown Prince Vajiralongkorn, as well as several other males in the royal family, have been temporarily ordained as monks here. The temple was originally founded in 1826, when it was known as Wat Mai.

Bangkok's second Buddhist university, Mahamakut University, is housed at Wat Bowon. Across the street from the main entrance to the wat are an English-language Buddhist bookshop and a Thai herbal clinic.

Lak Meuang (City Pillar)

ศาลหลักเมือง

The City Pillar is across the street from the eastern wall of Wat Phra Kaew, at the southern end of Sanam Luang. This shrine encloses a wooden pillar erected by Rama I in 1782 to represent the founding of the new Bangkok capital. Later, during the reign of Rama V, five other idols were added to the shrine. The spirit of the pillar is considered the city's guardian deity and receives the daily supplications of countless Thai worshippers, some of whom commission classical Thai dancers to perform lakhon chatrii at the shrine. Some of the offerings include severed pigs' heads with sticks of incense sprouting from their foreheads.

Maha Uma Devi Temple

วัดมหาอุมาเทวี (วัดแขก)

This small Hindu temple sits alongside busy Silom Rd (near the Pan Rd intersection) in Bangrak, a district with a high concentration of Indian residents. The principal temple structure, built in the 1860s by Tamil immigrants, features a six-metre facade of intertwined, full-colour Hindu deities,

topped by a gold-plated copper dome. The temple's main shrine contains three main deities: Jao Mae Maha Umathewi (Uma Devi, also known as Shakti, Shiva's consort) at the centre; her son Phra Khanthakuman (Khanthakumara or Subramaniam) on the right; and her elephant-headed son Phra Phikhkanesawora (Ganesha) on the left. Along the left interior wall sit rows of Shivas, Vishnus and other Hindu deities, as well as a few Buddhas, so that just about any non-Muslim Asian can worship here – Thai and Chinese devotees come to pray along with Indians. Bright yellow marigold garlands are sold at the entrance for this purpose.

An interesting ritual takes place in the temple at noon on most days, when a priest brings out a tray carrying an oil lamp, coloured powders and holy water. He sprinkles the water on the hands of worshippers who in turn pass their hands through the lamp flame for purification; then they dip their fingers in the coloured powder and daub prayer marks on their foreheads. On Fridays at around 11.30 am, *prasada* (blessed vegetarian food) is offered to devotees.

Thais call this temple Wat Khaek – *khàek* is a Thai colloquial expression for persons of Indian descent. The literal translation is 'guest', an obvious euphemism for a group of people you don't particularly want as permanent residents; hence most Indians living permanently in Thailand don't appreciate the term.

Wat Thammamongkhon

วัดธรรมมงคล

East of Bangkok on Sukhumvit Soi 101, this 95-metre high chedi came about as the result of a monk's vision. While meditating in 1991, Phra Viriyang Sirintharo saw a giant jade boulder; at around the same time a 32-ton block of solid jade was discovered in a Canadian riverbed. Viriyang raised funds to purchase the block (US$560,000) and commissioned a 14-ton Buddha sculpture (carried out by Carrara sculptors) to go in a pavilion at Thammamongkhon; an image of this magnitude deserved a massive chedi. The chedi, which contains a hair of the Buddha presented to Thailand by Bangladesh's Sangharaja (head of a Theravada monastic order), features a lift so you can ride to the top. The chedi's official grand opening ceremony was held in 1993.

A leftover 10-ton chunk of jade is to be carved into a figure of Kuan Yin (the Chinese Buddhist goddess of compassion). Smaller leftovers – a total of nearly eight tons – will be made into amulets and sold to worshippers for US$20 each, raising money to pay for 5000 day-care centres throughout Thailand.

Wat Phailom
วัดไผ่ล้อม

Outside Bangkok, on the eastern bank of the Chao Phraya River in Pathum Thani Province, this old, wooden Mon wat is noted for the tens of thousands of open-billed storks (Anastomus oscitans) that nest in bamboo groves opposite the temple area from December to June. The temple is 51 km from the centre of Bangkok in Pathum Thani's Sam Kok district. Take a Pathum Thani-bound bus (8B) from Bangkok's northern bus terminal and cross the river by ferry to the wat grounds.

Bus No 33 from Sanam Luang goes all the way to Phailom and back. The Chao Phraya River Express tours from Tha Maharat to Bang Pa-In each Sunday also make a stop at Wat Phailom – see River & Canal Trips farther on in this chapter.

Other Temples & Shrines

Marked by its enormous, modern-style 32-metre standing Buddha, **Wat Intharawihan** borders Wisut Kasat Rd, at the northern edge of Banglamphu. Check out the hollowed-out air-con stupa with a lifelike image of Luang Phaw Toh. Entry to Wat In is by donation.

At **Sao Ching-Cha**, the 'Giant Swing', a spectacular Brahman festival in honour of the Hindu god Shiva, used to take place each year until it was stopped during the reign of Rama VII. Participants would swing in ever-

heightening arcs in an effort to reach a bag of gold suspended from a 15-metre bamboo pole – many died trying. The Giant Swing is a block south of the Democracy Monument.

Nearby **Wat Suthat** (see Central Bangkok map), begun by Rama I and completed by Ramas II and III, boasts a wihaan with gilded bronze Buddha images (including Phra Si Sakayamuni, one of the largest surviving Sukhothai bronzes) and colourful jataka murals. Wat Suthat holds a special place in the Thai national religion because of its association with Brahman priests who perform important annual ceremonies, such as the Royal Ploughing Ceremony in May. These priests perform rites at two Hindu shrines near the wat – the Thewa Sathaan (Deva Sthan) across the street to the north-west and the smaller Saan Jao Phitsanu to the east. The former contains images of Shiva and Ganesh while the latter is dedicated to Vishnu. The wat holds the rank of Rachavoramahavihan, the highest royal temple grade; the ashes of King Rama VIII (Ananda Mahidol, the current king's older brother) are contained in the base of the main Buddha image in Suthat's wihaan.

There are also numerous temples on the Thonburi side of the river which are less visited. These include **Wat Kalayanimit** with its towering Buddha statue and, outside, the biggest bronze bell in Thailand; **Wat Pho Bang-O** with its carved gables and Rama III-era murals; **Wat Chaloem Phrakiat**, a temple with tiled gables; and **Wat Thawng Nophakhun** with its Chinese-influenced uposatha (bot). See the Fine Arts Commission Canals of Thonburi map for more information on these wats. **Wat Yannawa**, on the Bangkok bank of the river near Tha Sathon, was built during Rama II's reign (1824-51) and features a building built to resemble a Chinese junk.

Just off Chakraphet Rd in the Pahurat district is a **Sikh Temple** (Sri Gurusingh Sabha) where visitors are welcome to walk around. Basically it's a large hall – somewhat reminiscent of a mosque interior – devoted to the worship of the Guru Granth Sahib, the 16th-century Sikh holy book which is itself considered the last of the religion's 10 great gurus or teachers. *Prasada* (blessed food offerings) is distributed among devotees every morning around 9 am.

On the corner of Ratchaprarop and Ploenchit Rds, next to the Grand Hyatt Erawan Hotel, is a large shrine, Saan Phra Phrom (also known as the **Erawan Shrine**), which was originally built to ward off bad luck during the construction of the first Erawan Hotel (torn down to make way for the Grand Hyatt Erawan some years ago). The four-headed deity at the centre of the shrine is Brahma (Phra Phrom in Thai), the Hindu god of creation. Apparently the developers of the original Erawan – named for

Brahma's three-headed elephant mount – first erected a typical Thai spirit house but decided to replace it with the more impressive Brahman shrine after several serious mishaps delayed the hotel construction. Worshippers who have a wish granted may return to the shrine to commission the musicians and dancers who are always on hand for an impromptu performance.

Since the success of the Erawan Shrine, several other flashy Brahman shrines have been erected around the city next to large hotels and office buildings. Next to the **World Trade Center** on Ploenchit Rd is a large shrine containing a standing Brahma, a rather unusual posture for Thai Brahmas.

Rama V Cult

Since 1991 a new spirit cult has swept the Thai public, involving the veneration of the spirit of King Rama V (1868-1910, also known as King Chulalongkorn or, to the Thais, as Chunla Jawm Klao). The cult is particularly strong in Bangkok and other large urban centres, since its members tend to be middle-class and nouveau riche Thais with careers in commerce or the professions.

In Bangkok the most visible devotional activities are focused on a bronze statue of Rama V standing in Royal Plaza – opposite the south-east corner of the Vimanmek/Abihisek throne hall compound whence the venerated king once ruled the kingdom as absolute monarch. Although originally intended as mere historical commemoration, the statue has quite literally become a religious shrine, where every Tuesday evening thousands of Bangkokians come to offer candles, flowers (predominantly pink roses), incense and bottles of whisky to the newly ordained demigod. Worship of the statue begins at around 9 pm and continues till early in the morning.

All over Thailand Rama V portraits are selling briskly. Some devotees place the portraits at home altars, while others wear tiny, coloured porcelain likenesses of the king on gold chains around their necks in place of the usual Buddhist amulet. In some social circles Rama V amulets are now more common than any other phra phim.

No single event occurred to ignite the Rama V movement; rather, its growth can be traced to a series of events beginning with the 1991 military coup – which caused the intelligentsia to once again lose faith in the constitutional monarchy – on top of the 1990-92 economic recession. Along with worsening traffic and a host of other problems, these events brought about an unfocused, general mistrust of modern politics, technology and affluence among many Thais, who began looking for a new spiritual outlet with some historical relevancy. They seized on Rama V, a king who – without the help of a parliament or the military – brought Thai nationalism to the fore while fending off European colonialisation. He is also considered a champion of the common person for his abolition of slavery and corvée (the requirement that every citizen be available for state labour when called).

Ironically few Rama V cultists realise that the much-revered Rama V conceded substantial Thai territory to French Indochina and British Malaya during his reign – for a total loss of land greater than any Thai king had allowed since before the Sukhothai era. Rama V also deserves more of the blame for 'Westernisation' than any other single monarch. He was the first king to travel to Europe, which he did in 1897 and again in 1907. After seeing Europeans eating with forks, knives and spoons, he discouraged the Thai tradition of taking food with the hands; he also introduced chairs to the kingdom (before his reign Thais sat on the floor or on floor cushions). Following one European visit he asked his number-one concubine to grow her hair long after the European fashion; by custom Thai women had kept their hair cropped short since the Ayuthaya period. ∎

Another hotel shrine worth seeing is the lingam (phallus) shrine behind the Hilton International in tiny Nai Loet Park off Withayu Rd. Clusters of carved stone and wooden lingam surround a spirit house and shrine built by millionaire businessman Nai Loet to honour **Jao Mae Thapthim**, a female deity thought to reside in the old banyan tree on the site. Someone who made an offering shortly thereafter had a baby, and the shrine has received a steady stream of worshippers – mostly young women seeking fertility – ever since. Nai Loet Park is fenced off such that you must now wind your way through the Hilton complex to visit the shrine. Or come via the Khlong Saen Saep canal taxi; ask to get off at Saphaan Withayu (Radio Bridge) – look for the TV 3 building on the north side of the canal.

Churches

Several Catholic churches were founded in Bangkok in the 17th to 19th centuries. Worth seeing is the **Holy Rosary Church** (known in Thai as Wat Kalawan, from the Portuguese 'Calvario') in Talaat Noi near the River City shopping complex. Originally built in 1787 by the Portuguese, the Holy Rosary was rebuilt by Vietnamese and Cambodian Catholics around the turn of the century – hence the French inscriptions beneath the stations of the cross. This old church has a splendid set of Romanesque stained-glass windows, gilded ceilings and a very old Christ statue that is carried through the streets during Easter celebrations. The alley leading to the church is lined with old Bangkok shophouse architecture.

The **Church of the Immaculate Conception** near Krungthon Bridge (north of Phra Pinklao Bridge) was also founded by the Portuguese and later taken over by Cambodians fleeing civil war. The present building is an 1837 reconstruction on the church's 1674 site. One of the original church buildings survives and is now used as a museum housing holy relics. Another Portuguese-built church is 1913-vintage **Santa Cruz** (Wat Kuti Jiin) on the Thonburi side near Phra Phutt Yot Fa Bridge (Saphaan Phut).

The architecture shows Chinese influence, hence the Thai name 'Chinese monastic residence'.

Christ Church, at 11 Convent Rd next to Bangkok Nursing Home, was established as 'English Chapel' in 1864. The current Gothic-style structure, opened in 1904, features thick walls and a tiled roof braced with teak beams; the carved-teak ceiling fans date to 1919.

Temples & River Walking Tour

This walk covers the area of Ko Ratanakosin (Ratanakosin Island), which rests in a bend of the river in the middle of Bangkok and contains some of the city's most historic architecture – Wat Phra Kaew, the Grand Palace, Wat Pho, Wat Mahathat and Wat Suthat (each described in detail earlier) – and prestigious universities. The river bank in this area is busy with piers and markets, worthwhile attractions in themselves. Despite its name, Ko Ratanakosin is not an island at all, though in the days when Bangkok was known as the 'Venice of the East', Khlong Banglamphu and Khlong Ong Ang – two lengthy adjoining canals to the east that run parallel to the river – were probably large enough that the area seemed like an island.

This circular walk (one to three hours depending on your pace) begins at **Lak Meuang** (A), a shrine to Bangkok's city spirit. At the intersection of Ratchadamnoen Nai and Lak Meuang Rds (opposite the southern end of Sanam Luang (Royal Field), the shrine can be reached by taxi, by air-con bus Nos 3, 6, 7 and 39, by ordinary bus Nos 39, 44 and 47 or on foot if you're already in the Royal Hotel area. (If the Chao Phraya River Express is more convenient, you can start this walk from Tha Tien – see (E) below.) By tradition, every city in Thailand must have a foundation stone which embodies the city spirit *(phii meuang)* and from which inter-city distances are measured. This is Bangkok's most important site of animistic worship; believers throng the area day and night, bringing offerings of flowers, incense, whisky, fruit and even cooked food.

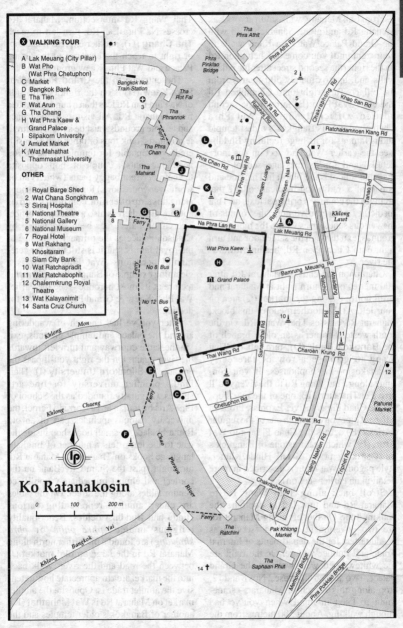

⊗ WALKING TOUR

A Lak Meuang (City Pillar)
B Wat Pho
  (Wat Phra Chetuphon)
C Market
D Bangkok Bank
E Tha Tien
F Wat Arun
G Tha Chang
H Wat Phra Kaew &
  Grand Palace
I Silpakorn University
J Amulet Market
K Wat Mahathat
L Thammasat University

OTHER

1 Royal Barge Shed
2 Wat Chana Songkhram
3 Siriraj Hospital
4 National Theatre
5 National Gallery
6 National Museum
7 Royal Hotel
8 Wat Rakhang
  Khositaram
9 Siam City Bank
10 Wat Ratchapradit
11 Wat Ratchabophit
12 Chalermkrung Royal
  Theatre
13 Wat Kalayanimit
14 Santa Cruz Church

Ko Ratanakosin

0   100   200 m

From Lak Meuang, walk south across Lak Meuang Rd and along Sanamchai Rd with the Grand Palace/Wat Phra Kaew walls to your right until you come to Chetuphon Rd on the right (the second street after the palace walls end, approximately 500 metres from the pillar). Turn right onto Chetuphon Rd and enter **Wat Pho** (B) through the second portico. Officially named Wat Phra Chetuphon, this is Bangkok's oldest temple and is famous for its huge reclining Buddha (see the earlier Wat Pho section for more details) and for its massage school. The massage school is the oldest in Thailand and is part of a traditional medical college that archives the country's principal texts on Thai medicine. After you've done the rounds of the various sanctuaries within the monastery grounds, exit through the same door and turn right onto Chetuphon Rd, heading towards the river.

Chetuphon Rd ends at Maharat Rd after 100 metres or so; turn right at Maharat and stroll north, passing the **market** (C) area on your left. At the northern end of this block, Maharat Rd crosses Thai Wang Rd. On the south-western corner is an older branch of the **Bangkok Bank** (D); turn left on Thai Wang to glimpse a row of rare early Ratanakosin-era shophouses. If you continue along Thai Wang Rd to the river you'll arrive at **Tha Tien** (E), one of the pier stops for the Chao Phraya River Express. From an adjacent pier you can catch one of the regular ferries (1B) across the Chao Phraya to **Wat Arun** (F), which features one of Bangkok's most striking prang, a tall Hindu/Khmer-style pagoda (Wat Arun is described in more detail in an earlier section).

Stroll back along Thai Wang Rd to Maharat Rd and turn left to continue the walking tour. On the left along Maharat Rd are two government buildings serving as headquarters for the departments of Internal Trade and Public Welfare. On the right are the whitewashed west walls of the Grand Palace. Two air-con city buses, Nos 8 and 12, stop along this stretch of Maharat – something to keep in mind when you've had enough walking. About 500 metres from the

Thai Wang Rd intersection, Maharat Rd crosses Na Phra Lan Rd; turn left to reach **Tha Chang** (G), another express boat stop; or right to reach the entrance to the Grand Palace and Wat Phra Kaew grounds.

The entrance to the **Grand Palace/Wat Phra Kaew** (H) is on the right (south) side of Na Phra Lan Rd less than a hundred metres from Maharat Rd. All visitors to the palace and temple grounds must be suitably attired, ie no shorts, tank tops or other dress considered unacceptable for temple visits. If you need long pants, a couple of shops opposite the entrance rent baggy pants (which can be worn over your shorts) for 30B. Other shops along this strip offer film, cold drinks, curries and noodles; there is also a small post office. The Grand Palace has been supplanted by Chitlada Palace as the primary residence of the royal family, but it is still used for ceremonial occasions. Wat Phra Kaew is a gleaming example of Bangkok temple architecture at its most baroque – see the earlier Wat Phra Kaew & Grand Palace section for details.

After you've had enough of wandering around the palace and temple grounds, exit via the same doorway and turn left towards the river again. On the right you'll pass the entrance to **Silpakorn University** (I), Thailand's premier university for fine arts studies. Originally founded as the School of Fine Arts by Italian artist Corrado Feroci, the university campus includes part of an old Rama I palace. A small bookshop inside the gate to the left offers a number of English-language books on Thai art. At Maharat Rd, turn right (past the Siam City Bank on the corner) and almost immediately you'll see vendor tables along the street. On the tables are cheap amulets representing various Hindu and Buddhist deities. Better-quality religious amulets (*phrá phim* or *phrá khrêuang*) are found a bit farther north along Maharat Rd in the large **amulet market** (J) between the road and the river. Walk back into the market area to appreciate how extensive the amulet trade is. Opposite the amulet market on Maharat Rd is **Wat Mahathat** (K), another of Bangkok's older temples and the headquarters for the country's largest monastic sect.

If you're hungry by now, this is an excellent place on the circuit to take time out for a snack or meal. Head back along Maharat Rd from the amulet market just a few metres and turn right at Trok Thawiphon (the sign reads 'Thawephon'). This alley leads to Tha Maharat, yet another express boat stop; on either side of the pier is a riverside restaurant – *Maharat* to the left and *Lan Theh* to the right. Although the food at both of these restaurants is quite adequate, most local residents head past the Lan Theh (no roman-script sign) along the river and into a warren of smaller restaurants and food vendors situated along the river. The food here is very good and extremely inexpensive – to order, all you'll need is a pointing index finger.

Renewed and refuelled, start walking north again along Maharat past the amulet market and Wat Mahathat to Phra Chan Rd, around 80 metres from Trok Thawiphon (perhaps 160 metres from Na Phra Lan Rd). Turn left to reach Tha Phra Chan if you want to catch an express boat north or south along the river, or turn right to reach Sanam Luang, the end of the tour. If you take the latter route, you'll pass **Thammasat University** (L) on the left. Thammasat is known for its law and political science faculties; it was also the site of the bloody October 1976 demonstrations in which hundreds of Thai students were killed or wounded by military troops. Opposite the university entrance are several very good noodle shops.

National Museum
พิพิธภัณฑ์แห่งชาติ

On Na Phra That Rd, the west side of Sanam Luang, the National Museum is the largest museum in South-East Asia and an excellent place to learn something about Thai art before heading upcountry. All periods and styles are represented from Dvaravati to Ratanakosin, and English-language literature is available. Room 23 contains a well-maintained collection of traditional

musical instruments from Thailand, Laos, Cambodia and Indonesia.

The museum buildings themselves were originally built in 1782 as the palace of Rama I's viceroy, Prince Wang Na. Rama V (Chulalongkorn) turned it into a museum in 1884.

In addition to the exhibition halls, the museum grounds contain the restored **Buddhaisawan Chapel**. Inside the chapel (built in 1795) are some well-preserved original murals and one of the country's most revered Buddha images, Phra Phut Sihing. Legend says the image came from Ceylon, but art historians attribute its provenance to 13th-century Sukhothai.

Free English tours of the museum are given by National Museum volunteers on Wednesdays (Buddhism) and Thursdays (Thai art, religion and culture), starting from the ticket pavilion at 9.30 am. These guided tours are excellent and many people have written to recommend them. The tours are also conducted in German (Thursdays), French (Wednesdays) and Japanese (Wednesdays). For more information on the tours, contact the volunteers (☎ 215-8173). The museum is open from 9 am to 4 pm Wednesday to Sunday; admission is 20B.

Royal Barges
เรือพระที่นั่ง

The royal barges are long, fantastically ornamented boats used in ceremonial processions on the river. The largest is 50 metres long and requires a rowing crew of 50 men, plus seven umbrella bearers, two helmsmen, two navigators, and a flagman, rhythm-keeper and chanter. The barges are kept in sheds on the Thonburi side of the river. They're on Khlong Bangkok Noi, near the Phra Pinklao Bridge. *Suphannahong*, the king's personal barge, is the most important of the boats. One of the best times to see the fleet in action on the river is during the royal *kathin* ceremony at the end of phansaa (the Buddhist Rains Retreat, ending with an October or November new moon) when new robes are offered to the monastic contingent.

The barge shed is open daily from 8.30 am to 4.30 pm and admission is 10B. To get there, take a ferry to Tha Rot Fai, then walk down the street parallel to the tracks until you come to a bridge over the khlong (canal). Follow the bridge to a wooden walkway that leads to the barge sheds. You can also get there by taking a khlong taxi (5B) up the canal and getting off near the bridge.

Jim Thompson's House
บ้านจิมทอมสัน

Though it may sound corny when described, this is a great spot to visit for authentic Thai residential architecture and South-East Asian art. Located at the end of an undistinguished soi next to Khlong Saen Saep, the premises once belonged to the American silk entrepreneur Jim Thompson, who deserves most of the credit for the current worldwide popularity of Thai silk.

Born in Delaware in 1906, Thompson was a New York architect who briefly served in the Office of Strategic Services (OSS, forerunner of the CIA) in Thailand during WW II. After the war Thompson found New York too tame and moved to Bangkok. Thai silk caught his connoisseur's eye; he sent samples around to fashion houses in Milan, London and Paris, gradually building a steady worldwide clientele for a craft that had been in danger of dying out.

A tireless promoter of traditional Thai arts and culture, Thompson collected parts of various derelict Thai homes in central Thailand and had them reassembled in the current location in 1959. Although for the most part assembled in typical Thai style, one striking departure from tradition is the way each wall was installed with its exterior side facing the house's interior, thus exposing the wall's bracing system to residents and guests.

While out for an afternoon walk in the Cameron Highlands of west Malaysia in 1967, Thompson disappeared under quite mysterious circumstances; he has never been heard from since. That same year his sister was murdered in the USA, fuelling various conspiracy theories which tried to explain the disappearance. Was it a man-eating tiger? Communist spies? Business rivals? The most recent theory – for which there is apparently some hard evidence – has it that the silk magnate was accidentally run over by a Malaysian truck driver who hid his remains.

The Legendary American – The Remarkable Career & Strange Disappearance of Jim Thompson (Houghton Mifflin, 1970), by William Warren, is an excellent book on Thompson, his career, residence and intriguing disappearance. In Thailand, it has been republished for distribution in Asia as *Jim Thompson: The Legendary American of Thailand* (Jim Thompson Thai Silk Co, Bangkok).

On display in the main house are his small but splendid Asian art collection and his personal belongings. The Jim Thompson Foundation has a table at the front where you can buy prints of old Siam maps and Siamese horoscopes in postcard and poster form.

The house, on Soi Kasem San 2, Rama I Rd, is open Monday to Saturday from 9 am to 5 pm. Admission is 100B (proceeds go to Bangkok's School for the Blind) but you may wander around the grounds for free. Students under 25 years get in for 40B. The rather sleazy khlong at the end of the soi is one of Bangkok's most lively. Beware well-dressed touts in the soi who will tell you Thompson's house is closed – it's just a ruse to take you on a buying spree.

Wang Suan Phakkard (Phakkat)
วังสวนผักกาด

The 'Lettuce Farm Palace', once the residence of Princess Chumbot of Nakhon Sawan, is a collection of five traditional wooden Thai houses containing varied displays of art, antiques and furnishings. The landscaped grounds are a peaceful oasis complete with ducks and swans and a semi-enclosed garden reminiscent of Japanese gardens.

The **Lacquer Pavilion** dates from the Ayuthaya period and features gold-leaf jataka murals. Special exhibitions include seashells and Ban Chiang pottery. In the noise and confusion of Bangkok, the gardens offer a tranquil retreat. The palace is open daily except Sundays from 9 am to 4 pm and admission is 150B (students 30B). It's on Si Ayuthaya Rd, between Phayathai and Ratchaprarop (see Siam Square map); bus No 3 (air-con) passes right in front.

Vimanmek Teak Mansion (Phra Thii Nang Wimanmek)
พระที่นั่งวิมานเมฆ

Originally constructed on Ko Si Chang in 1868 and moved to the present site in 1910, this beautiful L-shaped, three-storey mansion contains 81 rooms, halls and ante-rooms and is said to be the world's largest golden teak building. Teak was once one of Thailand's greatest natural resources (it has since all but disappeared) and makes an especially good wood for building houses because it's so durable. A special oil contained in the wood makes teak resistant to heavy rain and hot sun and also repels insects. A solid piece of teak can easily last 1000 years.

Vimanmek was the first permanent building on the Dusit Palace grounds. It served as King Rama V's residence in the early 1900s, was closed in 1935 and reopened in 1982 for the Ratanakosin bicentennial. The interior of the mansion contains various personal effects of the king, and a treasure trove of early Ratanakosin art objects and antiques.

English-language tours leave every half hour beginning at 9.45 am, with the last one at 3.15 pm. The tours cover around 30 rooms and last an hour. Smaller adjacent buildings display historic photography documenting the Chakri dynasty. Traditional Thai classical and folk dances are performed in the late morning and early afternoon in a pavilion off the canal side of the mansion.

Vimanmek is open from 9.30 am to 4 pm daily; admission is 50B for adults, 20B for children. It's free if you've already been to the Grand Palace/Wat Phra Kaew and kept the entry ticket for Vimanmek/Abhisek. As this is royal property, visitors wearing shorts or sleeveless shirts will be refused entry.

Abhisek Dusit Throne Hall (Phra Thii Nang Aphisek Dusit)
อภิเศกดุสิต

This hall is a smaller wood, brick and stucco structure completed in 1904 for Rama V. Typical of the finer architecture of this era, the Victorian-influenced gingerbread and Moorish porticoes blend to create a striking and distinctly Thai exterior. The hall now houses an excellent display of regional handiwork crafted by members of the Promotion of Supplementary Occupations & Related Techniques (SUPPORT) foundation, an organisation sponsored by the Queen. Among the exhibits are mat-mii cotton and silk, *málaeng tháp* collages (made from metallic, multicoloured beetle wings), Damascene ware, neilloware and *yaan lipao* basketry.

Abhisek is open from 10 am to 4 pm daily and admission is 50B (or free with a Wat Phra Kaew/Grand Palace/Vimanmek ticket). There is souvenir shop on the premises. As at Wat Phra Kaew and Vimanmek, visitors must be properly dressed – no sleeveless shirts or shorts.

Vimanmek and Abhisek lie towards the northern end of the Dusit Palace grounds, off U-Thong Nai Rd (between Si Ayuthaya and Ratwithi Rds), across from the western side of the Dusit Zoo. An air-con No 3 (Si Ayuthaya Rd) or No 10 (Ratwithi Rd) bus will drop you nearby.

Siam Society & Ban Kamthieng
สยามสมาคมบ้านคำเที่ยง

At 131 Soi Asoke, Sukhumvit Rd, the Siam Society is the publisher of the renowned *Journal of the Siam Society* and its members are valiant preservers of traditional Thai culture. The society headquarters are a good place to visit for those with a serious interest in Thailand – a reference library is open to visitors and Siam Society monographs are for sale. Almost anything you'd want to know about Thailand (outside the political sphere, since the society is sponsored by the royal family) can be researched here. An ethnological museum of sorts exhibiting

Thai folk art is located on the Siam Society grounds in the northern-style Kamthieng House. Ban Kamthieng is open Tuesday to Saturday from 9 am to 5 pm. Admission is 25B. For information call ☎ 258-3491.

Other Museums

The **Museum of the Department of Forensic Medicine**, on the ground floor of the Forensic Medicine Building, Siriraj Hospital, in Thonburi (Phrannok Rd, near the Bangkok Noi train station), is the most famous of ten medical museums on the hospital premises. Among the grisly displays are the preserved bodies of famous Thai murderers. Open Monday to Friday, 9 am to 4 pm; free admission.

The **Hall of Railway Heritage** just north of Chatuchak Park displays steam locomotives, model trains and other artefacts related to Thai railroad history. It's open Sundays only from 5 am to noon, and admission is free. Call the Thai Railfan Club (☎ 243-2037) for further information.

The **Bangkok Doll Factory & Museum** (☎ 245-3008) at 85 Soi Ratchataphan (Soi Mo Leng), off Ratchaprarop Rd in the Pratunam district, houses a colourful selection of traditional Thai dolls, both new and antique. Dolls are also available for purchase. It's open Monday to Saturday from 8 am to 5pm; admission is free.

Military aircraft aficionados shouldn't miss the **Royal Thai Air Force Museum**, on Phahonyothin Rd near Wing 6 of the Don Meuang domestic airport terminal. Among the world-class collection of historic aircraft is the only existing Japanese Tachikawa trainer, along with a Spitfire and several Nieuports and Breguets. The museum is open from 8.30 am to 4.30 pm Monday to Friday and on the first weekend of each month; admission is free.

Bangkok also has a **Museum of Science** and a **Planetarium**, both on Sukhumvit Rd between sois 40 and 42.

Art Galleries

Opposite the National Theatre on Chao Fa Rd, the **National Gallery** (☎ 281-2224) displays traditional and contemporary art. Most of the art displayed here is by artists who receive government support; the general consensus is that it's not Thailand's best, but the gallery is worth a visit for die-hard art fans or if you're in the vicinity. The gallery is closed Mondays and Tuesdays, and open from 9 am to 4 pm on other days. Admission is 10B.

At the forefront of the new Buddhist art movement is the **Visual Dhamma Art Gallery** (☎ 258-5879) at 44/28 Soi Asoke (Soi 21, Sukhumvit Rd). Works by some of Thailand's most prominent muralists are sometimes displayed here, along with the occasional foreign exhibition. The gallery is open Monday to Friday from 1 to 6 pm, Saturday from 10 am to 5 pm, or at other times by appointment. Although the address is Soi Asoke, the gallery is actually off Asoke – coming from Sukhumvit Rd, take the second right into a small lane opposite Singha Bier Haus.

Paris New York Bangkok Fine Art, on Soi 31, Sukhumvit Rd, is a new French-owned gallery specialising in modern sculpture. In addition to works on temporary loan from sister galleries in Paris and New York, the gallery displays many bronzes which were cast at Ayuthaya's Fonderie Oceane (under the same ownership as the gallery). It's too soon to say whether this gallery will become a mover and shaker in the Bangkok art world; for the moment it's a small-scale effort to provide a place for Thai and international sculptors to show their work.

Silpakorn University (near Wat Phra Kaew) is Bangkok's fine arts university and has a gallery of student works. The **Thailand Cultural Centre** on Ratchadaphisek Rd (in the Huay Khwang district, between Soi Tiam Ruammit and Din Daeng Rd) has a small gallery with rotating contemporary art exhibits, as does the **River City** shopping complex next to the Royal Orchid Sheraton on the river. Bangkok's foreign cultural centres hold regular exhibits of foreign and local artists – check the monthly bulletins issued by AUA, Alliance Française, the

British Council and the Goethe Institute. For addresses, see Cultural Centres under Information earlier in this chapter.

Several of Bangkok's luxury hotels display top-quality contemporary art in their lobbies and other public areas. The **Grand Hyatt Erawan** (on the corner of Ratchadamri and Ploenchit Rds) and the **Landmark Hotel** (Sukhumvit Rd) have the best collections of contemporary art in the country. The Erawan alone has over 1900 works exhibited on a rotating basis.

The **Neilson Hays Library** at 195 Surawong Rd occasionally hosts small exhibits in its Rotunda Gallery.

Chinatown (Sampeng)

เยาวราช (สำเพ็ง)

Bangkok's Chinatown, off Yaowarat and Ratchawong Rds, comprises a confusing and crowded array of jewellery, hardware, wholesale food, automotive and fabric shops, as well as dozens of other small businesses. It's a good place to shop since goods here are cheaper than almost anywhere else in Bangkok and the Chinese proprietors like to bargain, especially along Soi Wanit 1 (also known as Sampeng Lane). Chinese and Thai antiques in various grades of age and authenticity are available in the so-called Thieves' Market (Nakhon Kasem), but it's better for browsing than buying these days.

During the annual Vegetarian Festival, celebrated fervently by Thai Chinese for the first nine days of the ninth lunar month (September-October), Bangkok's Chinatown becomes a virtual orgy of so-called vegetarian Thai and Chinese food. The festivities are centred around **Wat Mangkon Kamalawat (Neng Noi Yee)**, one of Chinatown's largest temples, on Charoen Krung Rd. All along Charoen Krung Rd in this vicinity, as well as on Yaowarat Rd to the south, restaurants and noodle shops offer hundreds of different vegetarian dishes.

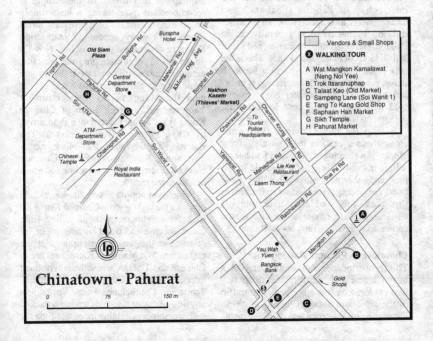

Chinatown - Pahurat

0   75   150 m

Vendors & Small Shops

⊗ WALKING TOUR

A Wat Mangkon Kamalawat (Neng Noi Yee)
B Trok Itsaranuphap
C Talaat Kao (Old Market)
D Sampeng Lane (Soi Wanit 1)
E Tang To Kang Gold Shop
F Saphaan Han Market
G Sikh Temple
H Pahurat Market

A Chinese population has been living in this area ever since the Chinese were moved here from Bang Kok (today's Ko Ratanakosin) by the royal government in 1782 to make room for the new capital. A census in the area taken exactly 100 years later found 245 opium dens, 154 pawnshops, 69 gambling establishments and 26 brothels. Pawnshops, along with myriad gold shops, remain a popular Chinatown business, while the other three vices have gone underground; brothels continue to exist under the guise of 'tea halls' (*róhng chaa*), back-street heroin vendors have replaced the opium dens and illicit card games convene in the private upstairs rooms of certain restaurants. Four Chinese newspapers printed and distributed in the district have a total circulation of over 160,000.

Pahurat

พาหุรัด

At the edge of Chinatown, around the intersection of Pahurat (Phahurat) and Chakraphet (Chakkaphet) Rds, is a small but thriving Indian district, generally called Pahurat. Here dozens of Indian-owned shops sell all kinds of fabric and clothes. This is the best place in the city to bargain for such items, especially silk. The selection is unbelievable, and Thai shoulder bags (yaams) sold here are the cheapest in Bangkok, perhaps in Thailand.

Behind the more obvious storefronts along these streets, in the 'bowels' of the blocks, is a seemingly endless Indian bazaar selling not only fabric but household items, food and other necessities. There are some good, reasonably priced Indian restaurants in this area, too, and a Sikh temple off Chakraphet Rd (for more information see the earlier section Other Temples & Shrines).

Chinatown – Pahurat Walking Tour

This route meanders through Bangkok's busy Chinese and Indian market districts – best explored on foot since vehicular traffic in the area is in almost constant gridlock. Depending on your pace and shopping inten-

tions, this lengthy route could take from 1½ to three hours. You can also do this tour in reverse, beginning from the Pahurat fabric market (H).

Be forewarned that the journey should only be undertaken by those who can withstand extended crowd contact as well as the sometimes unpleasant sights and smells of a traditional fresh market. The reward for tolerating this attack on the senses consists of numerous glimpses into the 'real' day-to-day Bangkok, away from the glittering facade of department stores and office buildings along Bangkok's main avenues – not to mention the opportunity for fabulous bargains. (If you plan to buy anything, you'd better bring along either a phrasebook or an interpreter – very little English is spoken in these areas.)

Start at **Wat Mangkon Kamalawat (Neng Noi Yee)** (A), one of Chinatown's largest and liveliest temples (the name means Dragon Lotus Temple), on Charoen Krung Rd between Mangkon Rd and Trok Itsaranuphap. A taxi direct to the temple is recommended over taking a bus, simply because the district is so congested and street names don't always appear in roman script. If you're determined to go by bus, Nos 35, 48, 53 and 55 pass the temple going west (the temple entrance will be on the right), or you could take an air-con bus No 8 and get off near the Mangkon Rd intersection on Yaowarat Rd, a block south of Charoen Krung. (Yet another alternative is to arrive by Chao Phraya River Express at Tha Ratchawong, then walk four blocks northeast along Ratchawong Rd to Charoen Krung Rd, turn right and walk one and a half blocks to the temple.)

Whichever approach you choose, to help pinpoint the right area on Charoen Krung Rd look for neighbouring shops selling fruit, cakes, incense and ritual burning paper for offering at the temple. Inscriptions at the entrance to Wat Mangkon Kamalawat are in Chinese and Tibetan, while the labyrinthine interior features a succession of Buddhist, Taoist and Confucianist altars. Virtually at any time of day or night this temple is packed with worshippers lighting incense, filling the ever-burning altar lamps with oil and praying to their ancestors.

Leaving the temple, walk left along Charoen Krung Rd about 20 metres to the nearest crosswalk (a policeman is usually directing traffic here), then cross the road and head down the alley on the other side. You're now heading south-west on **Trok Itsaranuphap** (B), one of Chinatown's main market lanes. This section is lined with vendors purveying ready-to-eat or preserved foodstuffs, including cleaned chickens, duck and fish; though not for the squeamish, it's one of the cleanest-looking fresh markets in Bangkok.

One hundred metres or so down Trok Itsaranuphap you'll cross **Yaowarat Rd**, a main Chinatown thoroughfare. This section of Yaowarat is lined with large and small gold shops; for price and selection, this is probably the best place in Thailand to purchase a gold chain (sold by the *bàht*, a unit of weight equal to 15 grams). From the trok entrance, turn right onto Yaowarat Rd, walk 50 metres to the crosswalk and, using a couple of savvy-looking Chinese crones as screens, navigate your way across the avenue.

Trok Itsaranuphap continues southward on the other side. Down the lane almost immediately on your left is the Chinese-ornamented entrance to **Talaat Kao (Old Market)** (C). This market section off Trok Itsaranuphap has been operating continuously for over 200 years. All manner and size of freshwater and saltwater fin and shellfish are displayed here, alive and filleted – or sometimes half alive and half filleted.

About 100 metres farther on down Itsaranuphap, past rows of vendors selling mostly dried fish, you'll come to a major Chinatown market crossroads. Running perpendicular to Itsaranuphap in either direction is famous **Sampeng Lane (Soi Wanit 1)** (D). Turn right onto Sampeng. This is usually the most crowded of Chinatown's market sois, a traffic jam of pedestrians, pushcarts and the occasional annoying motorbike twisting through the crowds. Shops along this section of Sampeng sell dry goods, especially shoes, clothing, fabric, toys and kitchenware.

About 25 metres west, Sampeng Lane crosses Mangkon Rd. On either side of the intersection are two of Bangkok's oldest commercial buildings, a Bangkok Bank and the venerable **Tang To Kang** gold shop (E), both over 100 years old. The exteriors of the buildings are classic early Bangkok, showing lots of European influence; the interiors are heavy with hardwood panelling. Continue walking another 60 metres or so to the Ratchawong Rd crossing (a traffic cop is usually stationed here to part the vehicular Red Sea for pedestrians), cross and re-enter Sampeng Lane on the other side.

At this point, fabric shops – many of them operated by Indian (mostly Sikh) merchants – start dominating the selection as the western edge of Chinatown approaches the Indian district of Pahurat. If you're looking for good deals on Thai textiles you're in the right place. But hold off buying until you've had a chance to look through at least a dozen or more shops – they get better the farther you go. After about 65 metres is the small Mahachak Rd crossing and then, after another 50 metres or so, the larger Chakrawat (Chakkawat) Rd crossing, where yet another traffic cop assists. Along Chakrawat Rd in this vicinity, as well as farther ahead along Sampeng Lane on the other side Chakrawat, there are many gem and jewellery shops.

If you were to follow Chakrawat Rd north from Soi Wanit, you could have a look around the Chinese-Thai antique shops of **Nakhon Kasem** (also known as the Thieves' Market since at one time stolen goods were commonly sold here) between Yaowarat and Charoen Krung Rds. After you re-enter Soi Wanit on the other side of Chakrawat Rd the jewellery shops are mixed with an eclectic array of houseware and clothing shops until you arrive, after another 50 metres, at the **Saphaan Han** (F) market area, named after a short bridge *(saphāan)* over Khlong Ong Ang. Clustered along the khlong on either side of the bridge is a bevy of vendors selling noodles and snacks. On the other side of the bridge, Sampeng Lane ends at Chakraphet Rd, the eastern edge of the Pahurat district.

Chakraphet Rd is well known for its Indian restaurants and shops selling Indian sweets. One of the best eateries in the area is the Royal India Restaurant, which serves north Indian cuisine and is justly famous for its tasty selection of Indian breads. To get there, turn left onto Chakraphet and walk about 70 metres along the east (left) side of the road; look for the Royal India sign pointing down an alley on the left. On the opposite side of Chakraphet Rd from the Royal India is another Chinese temple. North of this temple, in a back alley on the west side of the road, is a large **Sikh temple** (G) – turn left before the ATM department store to find the entrance. Visitors to the temple – reportedly the second-largest Sikh temple outside of India – are welcome but they must remove their shoes. If you arrive on a Sikh festival day you can partake of the *langar* or communal Sikh meal served in the temple.

Several inexpensive Indian food stalls are found in an alley alongside the department store. Behind the store, stretching westward from Chakraphet Rd to Triphet Rd, is the **Pahurat Market** (H), devoted almost exclusively to textiles and clothing. Pahurat Rd itself runs parallel to and just north of the market.

If you're ready to escape the market hustle and bustle, you can catch city buses on Chakraphet Rd (heading north and then east to the Siam Square and Pratunam areas) or along Pahurat Rd (heading west and then north along Tri Thong Rd to the Banglamphu district). Or walk to the river and catch a Chao Phraya River Express boat from Tha Saphaan Phut, which is just to the north-west of Memorial Bridge (Saphaan Phut). If you're doing this route in reverse, you can arrive by Chao Phraya River Express at Tha Saphaan Phut.

Dusit Zoo (Suan Sat Dusit)
สวนสัตว์ดุสิต (เขาดิน)

The collection of animals at Bangkok's 19-hectare zoo comprises over 300 mammals, 200 reptiles and 800 birds, including relatively rare indigenous species such as banteng, gaur, serow and rhinoceros. Originally a private botanical garden for King Rama V, it was converted to a zoo in 1938. The shady grounds feature trees labelled in English, Thai and Latin – plus a lake in the centre with paddle boats for rent. There's also a small children's playground.

If nothing else, the zoo is a nice place to get away from the noise of the city and observe how the Thais amuse themselves – by eating mainly. A couple of lakeside restaurants serve good, inexpensive Thai food. Entry to the zoo is 20B for adults, 5B for children, 10B for those over 60; it's open from 9 am to 6 pm daily. A small circus performs on weekends and holidays between 11 am and 2 pm. Sundays can be a bit crowded – if you want the zoo mostly to yourself, go on a weekday.

The zoo is in the Dusit district between Chitlada Palace and the National Assembly

Great hornbill

Hall; the main entrance is off Ratwithi Rd. Buses that pass the entrance include the ordinary Nos 18 and 28 and the air-con No 10.

Queen Saovabha Memorial Institute (Snake Farm)

สวนเสาวภา

At this research institute (☎ 252-0161), formerly known as the Pasteur Institute, on Rama IV Rd (near Henri Dunant Rd), venomous snakes are milked daily to make snake-bite antidotes which are distributed throughout the country. The milking sessions – at 10.30 am and 2 pm weekdays, 10.30 am only on weekends and holidays – have become a major Bangkok tourist attraction. Unlike other 'snake farms' in Bangkok, this is a serious herpetological research facility; a very informative half-hour slide show on snakes is presented before the milking sessions. This will be boring to some, fascinating to others. Feeding time is 3 pm. Admission is 70B.

A Thai Red Cross pamphlet entitled 'Health Hints for Travellers' is available for 15B; you can also get common vaccinations such as cholera, typhoid and smallpox here.

Monk's Bowl Village

บ้านบาตร

This is the only one remaining of three such villages established in Bangkok by King Rama I for the purpose of handcrafting monk's bowls (bàat). The black bowls, used by Thai monks to receive alms-food from faithful Buddhists every morning, are still made here in the traditional manner. Due to the expense of purchasing a handmade bowl, the 'village' has been reduced to a single alley in a district known as Ban Baht (bâan bàat, Monk's Bowl Village). About half a dozen families still hammer the bowls together from eight separate pieces of steel representing the eight spokes of the wheel of dharma (which in turn symbolise Buddhism's Eightfold Path). The joints are

fused in a wood fire with bits of copper, and the bowl is polished and coated with several layers of black lacquer. A typical bowl-smith's output is one bowl per day.

To find it, walk south on Boriphat Rd south of Bamrung Meuang Rd, then left on Soi Baan Baht. The artisans who fashion the bowls are not always at work, so it's largely a matter of luck whether you'll see them in action. At any of the houses which make them, you can purchase a fine-quality alms bowl for around 400 to 500B. To see monks' robes and bowls on sale, wander down Bamrung Meuang Rd in the vicinity of the Giant Swing.

Lumphini Park

สวนลุมพินี

Named after the Buddha's birthplace in Nepal, this is Bangkok's largest and most popular park. The park is bordered by Rama IV Rd to the south, Sarasin Rd to the north, Withayu Rd to the east and Ratchadamri Rd to the west, with entrance gates on all sides. A large artificial lake in the centre is surrounded by broad, well-tended lawns, wooded areas and walking paths – in other words, it's the best outdoor escape from Bangkok without leaving town.

One of the best times to visit the park is in the early morning before 7 am when the air is fresh (well, relatively so for Bangkok) and legions of Chinese are practising t'ai chi. Also in the morning, vendors set up tables to dispense fresh snake blood and bile, considered health tonics by many Thais and Chinese. Rowboats and paddle boats can be rented at the lake. A weight-lifting area in one section becomes a miniature 'muscle beach' on weekends. Other facilities include a snack bar, an asphalt jogging track, several areas with tables and benches for picnics and a couple of tables where ladies serve Chinese tea. Rest rooms are placed at intervals throughout the park.

During the kite-flying season (mid-February to April), Lumphini becomes a favoured flight zone; kites (wâo) can be purchased in the park in these months.

Rama IX Royal Park

สวนพระรามที่

Opened in 1987 to commemorate King Bhumibol's 60th birthday, Bangkok's newest green area covers 81 hectares and includes a water park and botanical gardens. Since its opening, the latter has developed into a significant horticultural research centre. A museum with an exhibition on the life of the King sits at the centre of the park. Take bus Nos 2 or 23 to Soi Udomsuk (Soi 103), off Sukhumvit Rd in Phrakhanong district, then a green minibus to the park. The park is open from 6am to 6pm daily; admission is 10B.

Sanam Luang

สนามหลวง

Sanam Luang (Royal Field) just north of Wat Phra Kaew is the traditional site for royal cremations, and for the annual Ploughing Ceremony, in which the king officially initiates the rice-growing season. The last ceremonial cremations took place here in 1976, when the king presided over funeral rites for students killed in the demonstrations of that year. A statue of Mae Thorani, the Earth Goddess (borrowed from Hindu mythology's Dharani), stands in a white pavilion at the north end of the field. Erected in the late 19th century by King Chulalongkorn, the statue was originally attached to a well that provided drinking water to the public.

Before 1982, Bangkok's famous Weekend Market was regularly held at Sanam Luang (it's now at Chatuchak Park – see the Things to Buy section in this chapter for details). Nowadays the large field is most popularly used as a picnic and recreational area. A large kite competition is held here during the kite-flying season.

Outskirts of Bangkok

Just outside Bangkok are a host of artificial tourist attractions that provide either the 'see the whole country in an hour' theme or the standard Western-style amusement park. If these attractions appeal to you, it's often worth booking tickets through travel agencies when such a booking includes return transport from your lodgings.

West Thirty-two km west of Bangkok, on the way to Nakhon Pathom, the **Rose Garden Country Resort** (☎ 295-3261), encompasses a canned Thai 'cultural village' (with demos of handicrafts, dancing, traditional ceremonies and martial arts), resort hotel, swimming pools, tennis courts, a three-hectare lake, elephant rides and a golf course. Admission to the 24-hectare garden area – which boasts 20,000 rose bushes – is 10B; it's another 220B for the 2 and 3 pm performances in the cultural village. The resort is open from 8 am to 6 pm daily. Shuttle buses run between the resort and major Bangkok hotels.

Just one km north of the Rose Garden, at the nine-hectare **Samphran Elephant Ground & Zoo** (☎ 284-1873), you can see elephant 'roundups' and crocodile shows; a number of other animals can also be observed in zoo-like conditions. Kids seem to like this place. It's open daily from 8.30 am to 6 pm, with crocodile-wrestling shows at 12.45, 2.20 and 4.30 pm, elephant shows at 1.45 and 3.30 pm weekdays, plus additional shows on weekends and holidays at 11.30 am. Admission is 300B for adults, 150B children.

North-East In Minburi, 10 km north-east of Bangkok, **Siam Water Park** (☎ 517-0075) at 101 Sukhaphiban 2, is a huge recreational park with pools, water slides, a wave pool and the like. It's highly recommended for a splash. Admission is 200B; weekends are best in spite of the crowds, simply because much of the park is inoperative during the week. Saturdays are less crowded than Sundays. Get there on bus Nos 26 or 27 from the Victory Monument.

Also in Minburi is **Safari World** (☎ 518-1000, 99 Ramindra 1), a 69-hectare wildlife park divided into two portions, the drive-through Safari Park and walk-through Marine Park. The five-km drive through Safari Park (aboard air-con coaches or your own vehicle) intersects eight habitats with an assortment of giraffes, lions, zebras, elephants, orang-utans and other African and Asian animals (75 mammal species and 300 bird species in all). A Panda House displays rare white pandas. The Marine Park focuses on trained animal performances by dolphins and the like. Safari World is open daily from 10 am to 6 pm; admission is 400B for adults, 200B for children three to 12, under three free. It's 45 km east of central Bangkok; for public transport catch a No 26 bus from the Victory Monument to Minburi, then a songthaew to the park.

South Billed as the largest open-air museum in the world, **Ancient City (Meuang Boran)** covers more than 80 hectares and presents scaled-down facsimiles of many of the kingdom's most famous monuments. The grounds follow Thailand's general geographical outline, with the monuments placed accordingly. The main entrance places visitors at the country's southern tip, from where you work your way to the 'northernmost' monuments. A sculpture garden focusing on episodes from the *Ramakian* has recently been added. Although the entire facility is in dire need of a facelift, for students of Thai architecture it's worth a day's visit (it takes an entire day to cover the area). It's also a good place for long, undistracted walks, as it's usually quiet and never crowded.

The Ancient City Co (☎ 226-1936/7, 224-1057, 222-8143) also puts out a lavish bilingual periodical devoted to Thai art and architecture called *Meuang Boran*. The journal is edited by some of Thailand's leading art historians. The owner of both journal and park is Bangkok's largest Mercedes Benz dealer, who has an avid interest in Thai art.

Ancient City is in Samut Prakan, 33 km from Bangkok along the Old Sukhumvit Highway. Opening hours are 8 am to 5 pm; admission to the site is 50B. The public bus trip (bus No 25 for 5B or air-con bus No 11 for 16B) to the Samut Prakan terminal can take up to two hours depending on traffic;

from the terminal get a 10-minute songthaew to Meuang Boran for another 5B. Transport can be also arranged through the Bangkok office at 78 Democracy Monument circle, Ratchadamnoen Klang Rd.

In the same area there is a **crocodile farm** (☎ 387-0020), where you can even see crocodile wrestling! There are over 30,000 crocs here, as well as elephants, monkeys and snakes. The farm is open from 7 am to 6 pm daily with trained animal shows every hour between 9 and 11 am and between 2 and 4 pm daily. Croc wrestling takes place at 4 pm and the reptiles usually get their dinner between 4 and 5 pm. Admission is a steep 300B.

For more information on Samut Prakan, see the Samut Prakan section further on.

River & Canal Trips

In 1855 British envoy Sir John Bowring wrote, 'The highways of Bangkok are not streets or roads but the river and the canals. Boats are the universal means of conveyance and communication.' The wheeled motor vehicle has long since become Bangkok's conveyance of choice, but fortunately it hasn't yet become universal. A vast network of canals and river tributaries surrounding Bangkok still carry a motley fleet of watercraft, from paddled canoes to rice barges. In these areas many homes, trading houses and temples remain oriented towards water life and provide a fascinating glimpse into the past, when Thais still considered themselves *jâo nâam* or 'water lords'.

Chao Phraya River Express You can observe urban river life from the water for 1½ hours for only 7B by climbing aboard a Chao Phraya River Express boat at Tha Wat Ratchasingkhon, just north of Krungthep Bridge. If you want to ride the entire length of the express route all the way to Nonthaburi, this is where you must begin. Ordinary bus Nos 1, 17 and 75 and air-con bus No 4 pass Ratchasingkhon pier. Or you could board at any other express boat pier in Bangkok for a shorter ride to Nonthaburi; for example, 20 minutes from Tha Phayap (the

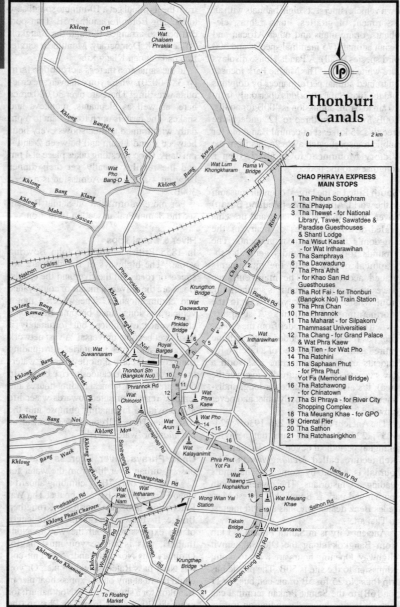

Thonburi Canals

0   1   2 km

CHAO PHRAYA EXPRESS MAIN STOPS

1 Tha Phibun Songkhram
2 Tha Phayap
3 Tha Thewet - for National
   Library, Tavee, Sawatdee &
   Paradise Guesthouses
   & Shanti Lodge
4 Tha Wisut Kasat
   - for Wat Intharawihan
5 Tha Samphraya
6 Tha Daowadung
7 Tha Phra Athit
   - for Khao San Rd
   Guesthouses
8 Tha Rot Fai - for Thonburi
   (Bangkok Noi) Train Station
9 Tha Phra Chan
10 Tha Phrannok
11 Tha Maharat - for Silpakorn/
   Thammasat Universities
12 Tha Chang - for Grand Palace
   & Wat Phra Kaew
13 Tha Tien - for Wat Pho
14 Tha Ratchini
15 Tha Saphaan Phut
   - for Phra Phut
   Yot Fa (Memorial Bridge)
16 Tha Ratchawong
   - for Chinatown
17 Tha Si Phraya - for River City
   Shopping Complex
18 Tha Meuang Khae - for GPO
19 Oriental Pier
20 Tha Sathon
21 Tha Ratchasingkhon

[handwritten annotation: Interesting trips but couldn't find public taxi (hired a longtail boat)]

first stop north of Krungthon Bridge), or 30 minutes from Tha Phra Athit (near the Phra Pinklao Bridge). Express boats run about every 15 minutes from 6 am to 6 pm daily. See the later Getting Around section, under Boat, for more information on the Chao Phraya River Express service.

Khlong Bangkok Noi Taxi Another good boat trip is the Bangkok Noi canal taxi route which leaves from Tha Maharat next to Silpakorn University. The fare is only a few baht and the farther up Khlong Bangkok Noi you go, the better the scenery becomes, with teak houses on stilts, old wats and plenty of greenery.

Stop off at Wat Suwannaram to view 19th-century jataka murals painted by two of early Bangkok's foremost religious muralists. Art historians consider these the best surviving temple paintings in Bangkok.

Other Canal Taxis From Tha Tien pier near Wat Pho, get a canal taxi along **Khlong Mon** (leaving every half hour from 6.30 am to 6 pm, 4B) for more typical canal scenery, including orchid farms. A longer excursion could be made by making a loop along khlongs Bangkok Noi, Chak Phra and Mon, an all-day trip. An outfit called Chao Phraya Charters (☎ 433-5453) runs a tour boat to Khlong Mon from Tha Tien each afternoon from 3 to 5 pm for 300B per person including refreshments.

Boats from Tha Chang pier to **Khlong Bang Yai** (10B) leave every half hour from 6.15 am to 10 pm – this is the same trip that passes the Bang Khu Wiang Floating Market (see Floating Markets later in this chapter). Though the market itself is over by 7 am, this trip is worthwhile later in the day as it passes a number of interesting wats, traditional wooden homes and the Royal Barges.

From the Tha Phibun Songkram pier in Nonthaburi you can board a boat taxi up picturesque **Khlong Om** and see durian plantations. Boats leave every 15 minutes.

Boats to **Khlong Bangkok Yai**, available from either Tha Tien or Tha Ratchini, pass Wat Intharam, where a chedi contains the

ashes of Thonburi's King Taksin Maharaj. Taksin was assassinated by his own ministers in 1782 after they decided he'd gone mad. Fine gold and black lacquerwork adorning the main bot doors depict the mythical *naariiphon* tree, which bears beautiful girls as fruit.

It is possible to go as far from Bangkok as Suphanburi and Ratburi (Ratchaburi) by boat, though this typically involves many boat connections.

For details on boat transport on the Bangkok side of the river, where four lengthy canal routes have been revived, see the Getting Around section at the end of this chapter. Although they provide quick transport, none of the four right-bank canal routes can be recommended for sightseeing.

Boat Charters If you want to see the Thonburi canals at your own pace, the best thing to do is charter a long-tail boat – it needn't be expensive if you can get a small group together to share the costs. The usual price is 300B per hour and you can choose from among eight different canals in Thonburi alone. Beware of 'agents' who will try to put you on the boat and rake off an extra commission. Before travelling by boat, establish the price – you can't bargain when you're in the middle of the river!

The best piers for hiring a boat are **Tha Chang, Tha Saphaan Phut** and **Tha Si Phaya**. Close to the latter, to the rear of the River City complex, the **Boat Tour Centre** charges the same basic hourly price (300B) and there are no hassles with touts. Of these four piers, Tha Chang usually has the largest selection of boats.

Those interested in seeing Bangkok's deep-water port can hire long-tail boats to Khlong Toey or as far downriver as Pak Nam, which means 'river mouth' in Thai. It's about two hours each way by boat, or a bit quicker if you take a bus or taxi one way.

Finally, if you're really a canal freak, look for *50 Trips Through Siam's Canals* (Editions Duang Kamol, 1979) by Geo-Ch Veran (translated from French into English by Sarah Bennett). The book contains 25 detailed maps and clear instructions on how to take the various trips – some of which are very time-consuming. The prolific William Warren has recently written *Bangkok's Waterways*, which may be easier to find but is more photo-oriented and less detailed.

Dinner Cruises A dozen or more companies in Bangkok run regular cruises along the Chao Phraya for rates ranging from 40 to 700B per person, depending on how far they go and whether dinner is included with the fare. Most require advance phone reservations.

The less expensive, more casual boats allow you to order as little or as much as you want from moderately priced menus; a modest charge of 40 to 70B per person is added to the bill for the cruise. It's a fine way to dine outdoors when the weather is hot, away from city traffic and cooled by river breezes. Several of the dinner boats cruise under the illuminated Rama IX Bridge, the longest single-span cable-suspension bridge in the world. This engineering marvel supports the elevated expressway joining Bangkok's Thanon Tok district with Thonburi's Ratburana district. Those dinner cruises offering the à-la-carte menu plus surcharge include:

Ban Khun Luang Restaurant
    Ban Khun Luang Restaurant to Oriental pier,
    Thursday, Friday, Saturday (☎ 243-3235)
Khanap Nam Restaurant
    Krungthon Bridge to Sathon Bridge, twice daily
    (☎ 433-6611)
Riverside Company
    Krungthon Bridge to Rama IX Bridge, daily
    (☎ 434-0090)
River Sight-Seeing Ltd
    Si Phraya pier to Wat Arun or Rama IX Bridge
    (depending on current), daily (☎ 437-4047)
Yok-Yor Restaurant
    Yok-Yor Restaurant (Wisut Kasat pier) to Rama
    IX Bridge, daily (☎ 281-1829, 282-7385)

More swanky dinner cruises charge a set price of 300 to 700B per person for the cruise and dinner; beer and liquor cost extra.

Wanfah Cruise
    River City to Krungthon Bridge, twice daily
    (☎ 433-5453, 424-6218)
Loy Nava Co
    Si Phraya pier to Wasukri pier, twice daily
    (☎ 437-4932/7329)
Oriental Hotel
    Oriental pier to Nonthaburi, Wednesdays only
    (☎ 236-0400/9)

Longer Cruises All-day and overnight cruises on the river are also available. The Chao Phraya River Express Boat Co (☎ 222-5330, 225-3002/3) does a reasonably priced tour starting from Tha Maharat at 8 am and returning at 5.30 pm that includes visits to the Thai Folk Arts & Handicrafts Centre in Bang Sai, Bang Pa-In Palace in Ayuthaya, and the bird sanctuary at Wat Phailom. The price is 180B per person lower deck, 240B upper deck, not including lunch, which you arrange on your own in Bang Pa-In.

Mit Chao Phraya Express Boat Co (☎ 225-6179) operates another moderately priced programme through several Thonburi canals, with stops at Wat Arun, the Royal Barges, an orchid farm and the Snakes & Crocodiles Farm. The tour departs from Tha Maharat at 8.30 am and returns at 6 pm. The cost of the programme is 140B, not including admission fees to the aforementioned attractions.

The Oriental Hotel's luxurious all air-con *Oriental Queen* (☎ 236-0400/9) also does a cruise to Bang Pa-In that leaves at 8 am from the Oriental pier and returns by air-con bus at 5 pm. The *Oriental Queen* cruise costs 1000B including lunch and guided tour. Note that neither of the above cruises really allows enough time to see Ayuthaya properly, so if that's your primary intention, go on your own. On the other hand I've had letters from history-weary readers who thought 15 to 30 minutes was plenty of time to see the ruins! Two other companies running similar Bang Pa-In/Ayuthaya tours for 900B per person are Horizon Cruise (☎ 538-3491) and River Sun Cruise (☎ 237-7608).

Asia Voyages (☎ 235-4100/4, 235-6075) floats the *Mekhala*, a restored teak rice barge that has been transformed into a six-cabin cruiser. The *Mekhala* leaves Bangkok in the afternoon on Saturday, Monday and Thursday (or Ayuthaya on Sunday, Tuesday and Friday) and heads upriver towards Ayuthaya (or downriver towards Bangkok). In the evening it anchors at Wat Praket, where a candle-lit dinner is served. The next morning passengers offer food to the monks from the wat, and then the barge moves on to Bang Pa-In. After a tour of the Summer Palace, a long-tail boat takes passengers on for a tour of the ruins of Ayuthaya. The return to Bangkok is by air-con bus. The cost is 2900B per person double occupancy and includes all meals, accommodation, admission fees in Ayuthaya and hotel transfers.

Floating Markets
ตลาดน้ำ

Among the most heavily published photo images of Thailand are those that depict wooden canoes laden with multicoloured fruits and vegetables, paddled by Thai women wearing indigo-hued clothes and wide-brimmed straw hats. Such floating markets *(talàat náam)* do exist in various locations throughout the huge canal system that surrounds Bangkok – but if you don't know where to go you may end up at a very inauthentic tourist-show scene.

Bang Khu Wiang Floating Market At Khlong Bang Khu Wiang in Thonburi a small floating market operates between 4 and 7 am. Boats to the Khu Wiang Market (Talaat Naam Khuu Wiang) leave from the Tha Chang pier near Wat Phra Kaew every morning between 6.15 and 8 am; take the earliest one to catch the market before it's over, or arrange to charter a long-tail boat at an earlier hour.

Damnoen Saduak Floating Market There is a larger if somewhat more commercial floating market on Khlong Damnoen Saduak in Ratchaburi Province, 104 km south-west of Bangkok, between Nakhon Pathom and Samut Songkhram. You can get buses from the southern bus terminal on Charan Sanit-wong Rd in Thonburi to Damnoen Saduak starting at 5 am. Get there as early in the morning as possible to escape the hordes. See the Ratchaburi section in the Central Thailand chapter for more details.

Wat Sai Floating Market In recent years, visitors to the floating market near Wat Sai on Khlong Sanam Chai (off Khlong Dao Khanong) have outnumbered vendors to the point that opinions are now virtually unanimous – don't waste your time at this so-called market. Go to Bang Khu Wiang or Damnoen Saduak instead – or find your own.

If you're set on doing the Wat Sai trip, take one of the floating-market tours that leave from the Oriental pier (Soi Oriental) or Tha Maharat near Silpakorn University – your only alternative is to charter a whole boat (at the Oriental pier), which can be quite expen-

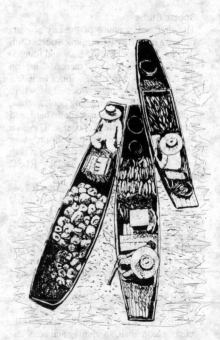

Floating market

The Original Siamese Twins

While walking along Bangkok's Chao Phraya River one afternoon in 1824, English trader Robert Hunter spotted what he thought was a creature with eight limbs and two heads swimming in the river. When it lifted itself onto a canoe, Hunter was surprised to see it was two 13-year-old boys who were fused together at the chest. The Briton was so intrigued that he sponsored a medical exam for the boys (which showed they couldn't be surgically separated) and later introduced them to Bangkok's Western social circuits.

Chang and Eng left Siam five years later to tour Europe and the USA as physiological celebrities. They eventually settled in North Carolina, where they married two sisters and sired 22 children. In 1874 Chang passed away in his sleep; Eng followed him two hours later.

Thais have no known genetic disposition towards joined births (Chang and Eng were actually of Chinese descent), but ever since Hunter's 'discovery', the non-medical world has used the term 'Siamese twins' to describe the phenomena. ∎

sive. Floating-market tours cost from 50B, and give you only 20 minutes or so at the market (probably more than enough for this non-event). Most tours charge 300 to 400B for an hour and a half. Be prepared for a very touristy experience.

Sports Clubs

The first and grandest of the city's sports facilities is the **Royal Bangkok Sports Club** (RBSC) between Henri Dunant and Ratchadamri Rds (the green oval marked 'Turf' on the Bangkok bus maps). Facilities include a horse track, polo grounds (located elsewhere off Withayu Rd), a swimming pool, a sauna, squash and tennis courts (both hard and grass) and an 18-hole golf course. There's a waiting list for membership, so the only way you're likely to frolic at this prestigious club is to be invited there by a lucky RBSC member.

Membership at the **British Club** (☎ 234-0247) is open to citizens of Australia, Canada, New Zealand and the UK or to others by invitation. Among the sports facilities are a pool, squash and tennis courts. The **Mariner Club** (☎ 249-3801) at 27/2 Tha Reua in Khlong Toey has an open membership policy for anyone wanting to use its pool or tennis courts.

Soi Klang Racquet Club (☎ 391-0963, 382-8442), at 8 Soi 49, Sukhumvit Rd, has facilities open to the public for squash, tennis, racquetball, swimming and aerobics. Other sports clubs open to the public include:

Asoke Sports Club – 302/81-81 Asoke-Din Daeng Rd; tennis, swimming (☎ 246-2260)

Bangkhen Tennis Court – 47/2 Viphavadi Rangsit Hwy; tennis (☎ 579-7829)

Central Tennis Court – 13/1 Soi Athakanprasit, Sathon Tai Rd; tennis (☎ 213-1909)

Kanpaibun Tennis Court – 10 Soi 40, Sukhumvit Rd; tennis (☎ 391-8784, 392-1832)

NTT Sports Club – 612/32 Soi Laoladda, Arun Amarin Rd, Thonburi; swimming, weights, aerobics (☎ 433-4623)

Saithip Swimming Pool – 140 Soi 56, Sukhumvit Rd; tennis, badminton, swimming (☎ 331-2037)

Santhikham Court – 217 Soi 109, Sukhumvit Rd; tennis (☎ 393-8480)

Sivalai Club Tennis Court & Swimming Pool – 168 Soi Anantaphum, Itsaraphap Rd, Thonburi; tennis, swimming (☎ 411-2649)

Sukhavadee Swimming Pool – 107/399 Gp 6, Soi 91 Lat Phrao Rd; swimming (☎ 538-6879)

Swim & Slim Family Club – 918 Soi 101/1, Sukhumvit Rd; badminton, swimming, weights (☎ 393-0889)

Meditation Study

Although at times Bangkok may seem like the most un-Buddhist place on earth, there are several places where interested foreigners can learn about Theravada Buddhist meditation. (See the Religion section in the Facts about the Country chapter for background information on Buddhism in Thailand.)

Wat Mahathat This 18th-century wat opposite Sanam Luang provides meditation instruction several times daily at Section 5, a building near the monks' residences. Some of the Thai monks here speak English and there are often Western monks or long-term residents available to translate. There is also a special Saturday session for foreigners at the Dhamma Vicaya Hall. Instruction is based on the Mahasi Sayadaw system of *satipatthana* or mindfulness. Air-con bus Nos 8 and 12 both pass near the wat; the nearest Chao Phraya River Express pier is Tha Maharat.

Wat Pak Nam This very large wat, where hundreds of monks and nuns reside during the Buddhist Rains Retreat, has hosted many foreigners (especially Japanese) over the years. The meditation teacher, Phra Khru Phawana, speaks some English and there are usually people around who can translate. The emphasis is on developing concentration through *nimittas* (acquired mental images), in order to attain trance-absorption states. A small English library is available. Pak Nam is on Thoet Thai Rd, Phasi Charoen, Thonburi. Take bus Nos 4, 9 or 103; the wat can also be reached by chartered long-tail boat from Tha Chang or Tha Saphaan Phut along the river and Thonburi canals.

Wat Rakhang Khositaram Only a few foreigners have studied at this temple, but the meditation teacher, Ajaan Mahathawon from Ubon Province in the north-east, has quite a good reputation. The teaching tradition at Wat Rakhang is strongly Abhidhamma-based, with much emphasis given to Buddhist psychology. Vipassana is considered attainable without strong concentration by means of a dialectic process similar to Krishnamurti's 'choiceless awareness'. To study here, one ought to be able to speak Thai fairly well; otherwise, an interpreter will have to be arranged. Wat Rakhang is on Arun Amarin Rd, Thonburi.

Wat Cholaprathan Rangsarit The teachers here, Ajaan Pañña (the abbot) and Ajaan Khao, employ a modified version of the Mahasi Sayadaw system of *satipatthana* practice. Occasionally there's someone around who can translate; otherwise it will be necessary to arrange in advance for translation. This wat also serves as a Bangkok headquarters for monks from Wat Suanmok (see Chaiya in the Southern Thailand chapter). Wat Cholaprathan is in Pak Kret, Nonthaburi Province; and although not actually part of Bangkok, Nonthaburi is so connected to Bangkok's urban sprawl that you can hardly tell the difference.

World Fellowship of Buddhists The WFB, at 33 Sukhumvit Rd, is a clearing house for information on Theravada Buddhism as well as dialogue between various schools of Buddhism. The centre hosts meditation classes from 2 to 5.30 pm on the first Sunday of every month.

Thai Cooking Schools

More and more travellers are coming to Thailand just to learn how to cook. While passing through Thailand, I often meet foreign chefs seeking out recipe inspirations for the 'East-West' sort of cuisine that seems to be taking the world by storm. You, too, can amaze your friends back home after attending a course in Thai cuisine at one of the following places:

Bussaracum Restaurant – 35 Soi Phiphat 2, Convent Rd (☎ 235-8915)
Modern Housewife Centre – 45/6-7 Sethsiri Rd (☎ 279-2831/4)
Oriental Hotel Cooking School – features a five-day course under the direction of well-known chef Chali (Charlie) Amatyakul – Soi Oriental, Charoen Krung Rd (☎ 236-0400/39)
UFM Food Centre – most classes offered in Thai; need at least four persons to offer an English-language class – 593/29-39 Soi 33/1, Sukhumvit Rd (☎ 259-0620/33)

Other Courses

For more information about language, martial arts and meditation courses in Bangkok, see Courses under Activities in the Facts for the Visitor chapter.

Places to Stay – bottom end

Bangkok has perhaps the best variety and quality of budget places to stay of any Asian capital – which is one of the reasons it's such a popular destination for roving world travellers. Because of the wide distribution of places, your choice actually depends on what part of the city you want to be in – the tourist ghettos of Sukhumvit Rd and Silom-Surawong Rds, the backpackers' ghetto of Banglamphu (north of Ratchadamnoen Klang Rd), the centrally located Siam Square area, Chinatown, or the old travellers' centre around Soi Ngam Duphli, off Rama IV Rd.

Chinatown, Hualamphong station and Banglamphu are the best all-round areas for seeing the real Bangkok, and are the cheapest districts for eating and sleeping. The Siam Square area is also well located, in that it's more or less in the centre of Bangkok – this, coupled with the good selection of city buses that pass through the Rama I and Phayathai Rd intersection, makes even more of the city accessible. In addition, the Siam Square area has good bookshops, several banks, shopping centres, excellent mid-range restaurants,

travel agencies and eight movie theatres within 10 to 15 minutes' walk.

For Bangkok, bottom-end accommodation will be taken to mean places costing from 60 to 500B per night; mid-range from roughly 500 to 1500B per night, and top end from 2000B up.

Banglamphu If you're really on a tight budget head for the Khao San Rd area, near the Democracy Monument, parallel to Ratchadamnoen Klang Rd – ordinary bus Nos 2, 15, 17, 44, 56 or 59 will get you there, also air-con bus Nos 11 and 12. This is the main travellers' centre these days and new guesthouses are continually springing up.

Rates in Banglamphu are generally the lowest in Bangkok and although some of the places are barely adequate (bedbugs are sometimes a problem), a few are excellent value if you can pay just a bit more. At the bottom end, rooms are quite small and the walls dividing them are thin – in fact most are indistinguishable from one another.

PLACES TO STAY

1	Charasri Guest House
3	C & C Guest House
4	Home & Garden GuestHouse
5	Clean & Calm Guest House
6	River House
9	AP Guest House
10	Tatum Guest House
12	Villa Guest House
13	Truly Yours Guest House
14	PS Guest House
16	New World House Apartments & Guest House
17	Canalside Guest House
21	Beer & Peachy Guesthouses
22	New Merry V
23	Apple Guest House
24	Golf Guest House
25	New Siam Guest House
26	Mango Guest House
27	Green Guest House
28	Merry V Guest House
29	P Guest House
30	Super Siam Guest House
31	Chusri Guest House
32	Sawasdee House/Terrace Guest House
37	Rose Garden Guest House
38	Charlie's House & Chai's House
41	59 Guest House
42	Central Guest House
43	PC Guest House
44	Srinthip Guest House
46	Nat II Guest House
47	Sweety Guest House
48	Prasuri Guest House
51	Royal Hotel
52	P Guest House
53	Palace Hotel
54	Hotel 90
55	Bangkok Center Guest House

PLACES TO EAT

36	Wang Ngar Restaurant
49	Vijit Restaurant
56	Arawy Restaurant

OTHER

2	Wat Intharawihan
7	Wat Samphraya
8	Wat Mai Amaratarot
11	Wat Sangwet
15	Siam Commercial Bank
18	New World Shopping Centre
19	Tha Phra Athit (for Chao Phraya Express)
20	UNICEF
33	Banglamphu Department Store
34	Post Office
35	Wat Bovornives (Bowonniwet)
39	Wat Chana Songkhram
40	National Gallery
45	Post Office
50	Democracy Monument
57	City Hall
58	Wat Suthat

Some have small attached cafes with limited menus. Bathrooms are usually down the hall or out the back somewhere; mattresses may be on the floor.

The least expensive rooms are 60/100B (50/80B with haggling in the low season) for singles/doubles, though these are hard to come by due to the hordes of people seeking them out. More common are the 100/120B rooms. Occasionally, triple rooms are available for 160B and dorm beds for 40B. During most of the year, it pays to visit several guesthouses before making a decision, but in the high season (December to February),

you'd better take the first vacant bed you come across. The best time of day to find a vacancy is from around 9 to 10 am. At night during the peak months (December to March), Khao San Rd is bursting with life.

A decade or so ago there were only two Chinese-Thai hotels on Khao San Rd, the Nith Jaroen Suk (now called New Nith Jaroen Hotel) and the Sri Phranakhon (now the Khao San Palace Hotel). Now there are close to a hundred guesthouses in the immediate vicinity, too many to list exhaustively here. If you haven't already arrived with a recommendation in hand, you might

Banglamphu

0   150   300 m

To Grand Palace
(Wat Phra Kaew)
& Wat Pho

Sanam
Luang

best use the Banglamphu and Khao San Rd area maps and simply pick one at random for your first night; if you're not satisfied you can stow your gear and explore the area till something better turns up. A tip: the guesthouses along Khao San Rd tend to be cubicles in modern shophouses, while those in Banglamphu's quieter lanes and alleys are often housed in old homes, some of them with a lot of character.

At the cheaper places it's not worth calling ahead, since the staff usually won't hold a room for you unless you pay in advance. For places that *may* take phone reservations I've included phone numbers.

Central Banglamphu Simple, adequate places with rooms for 60 to 100B single, 80 to 120B double on or just off Khao San Rd – the hub of Bangkok's swirling backpacker universe – include:

Chada Guest House, CH Guest House (dorm available for 40B), *Classic Place, Siri Guest House, Marco Polo Guest House* (also called *160 Guest House*), *Good Luck Guest House, VIP Guest House* (all rooms 80B), *Tong Guest House, Nat Guest House, Bonny Guest House* (dorm beds for 40B), *Top Guest House, Dior Guest House, Grand Guest House, PB Guest House* (dorm beds for 40B, snooker hall & gym), *Khao San Guest House, Buddy Guest House, Lek Guest House, Mam's Guest House, Hello Guest House & Guest House* (many recent complaints on this one for rudeness), *Chart Guest House, NS Guest House, Thai Guest House, Sitdhi Guest House & Restaurant* and, right on the corner of Khao San and Chakraphong Rds, *Ploy Guest House.*

The *Khaosan Palace Hotel* (☎ 282-0578), set off down an alley at 139 Khao San Rd, has seen a facelift; rooms cost 350B with ceiling fan and private bath, 450B with air-con and hot water. Down a parallel alley, the *New Nith Jaroen Hotel* (☎ 281-9872) has similar rates and rooms to the Khaosan Palace, but slightly better service. The new *Nana Plaza Inn* (☎ 281-6402), near the Siri Guest House towards Khao San's east end, is a large, hotel-like enterprise built around a restaurant; air-con/hot-water rooms go for 500B a single/double.

Two narrow alleys between Khao San and Rambutri Rds feature a string of cramped places that nonetheless manage to fill up. The alley furthest west off Khao San sports *Doll, Suneeporn, Leed, Jim's, AT* and *Green House* (☎ 281-0323). Except for Green House, all feature small, luggage-crammed lobbies with staircases leading to rooms layered on several floors and which cost around 60 to 100B. Green House is a bit more expansive, with a pleasant restaurant downstairs and rooms with fan and private bath for 150 to 200B. East down Khao San is a wider alley that's a bit more open, with the small, Indian-run *Best Guest House & Restaurant* (60/100B) and the new, hotel-like *Marco Polo Hostel* (120 to 250B, most rooms with private bath).

Parallel to Khao San Rd but much quieter is Trok Mayom, an alley reserved for mostly pedestrian traffic. *J* and *Joe* (☎ 281-2948) are old teak homes with pleasant rooms for 80 to 150B; not surprisingly, they're almost consistently full. Farther east, towards Tanao Rd, *7-Holder* charges 120/270B for rooms with private bath.

North on Chakraphong Rd you'll find more guesthouses which catch the overflow from Khao San Rd, including an alley with *Siam* and another alley farther north with the Hebrew-speaking *Chuanpis*, both in the 70 to 120B range.

Orchid House (☎ 280-2691), a new guesthouse entry near the Viengtai Hotel on Rambutri Rd (north of Khao San Rd), offers clean apartment-style rooms for 250B single with fan and bath, 350B single/double with air-con or 450B for larger air-con rooms.

West Banglamphu Several long-running guesthouses are on sois between Chakraphong Rd and the Chao Phraya River, putting them within walking distance of the Phra Athit pier where you can catch express boats down or up the river (see Banglamphu map). This area is also close to the Bangkok Noi (Thonburi) train station across the river, the Bangkok National Museum and the National Theatre.

West of Chakraphong on Soi Rambutri, the relatively new *Sawasdee House* (☎ 281-8138) follows the trend towards hotel-style accommodation in the Khao San Rd area, with a large restaurant downstairs and small to medium-sized rooms on several floors upstairs, all with private bath in the 120 to 250B range. Next along Soi Rambutri are the *Chusri* and *Terrace* guesthouses, all of which have adequate rooms for 50 to 60B per person but are nothing special. Right where Soi Rambutri makes a sharp turn to the south-west, the newish *Super Siam* and ordinary *P Guest House* (yes, same name as the one on Trok Sa-Ke) catch the overflow from more preferred houses in the area.

Right around the bend along Soi Rambutri is the popular *Merry V Guest House* (☎ 282-9267) with rooms from 70 to 120B; the cosy, similarly priced *Green* is next door. *Mango*, in a tin-roofed wooden house set back from Soi Rambutri, is another good 70/120B choice in this area. Also in this vicinity, off the southern end of Soi Rambutri, are *Chai's House* and *Charlie's House*. Both feature similar rates and facilities. The dingy, apartment-style *Rose Garden Guest House* offers bare rooms for 60/100B.

Backtracking along Soi Rambutri and turning left into Soi Chana Songkhram, you'll find the *New Siam Guest House*, where OK rooms cost 60 to 100B. Continue on towards the river and you'll reach Phra Athit Rd. On the eastern side of Phra Athit Rd the *Beer Guest House* (☎ 280-0744) and *Peachy Guest House* (☎ 281-6471) are more like small hotels than family-type guesthouses. The Beer is basic but airy, and singles/doubles cost 100B. Peachy has a pleasant garden restaurant and singles/doubles cost 75/120B, 250/320B with air-con. The *New Merry V*, a bit north from Peachy, has comfortable rooms with private hot-water showers for 260B, or with shared bath for 120B.

Parallel to Soi Chana on Trok Rong Mai, off Phra Athit Rd, are a few old-timers, most with only two-bed rooms. The *Apple Guest House*, at 10/1 Trok Rong Mai, may not look like much, but it's popular at 50/80B. There's

also an *Apple Guest House II* out on Trok Kai Chae Rd (off Phra Sumen Rd), for the same price, which one traveller recommended as being better. The *Golf Guest House* next door to Apple I offers similar accommodation at 40B for a dorm bed, 60/100B for singles/doubles.

East Banglamphu There are several guesthouses clustered in the alleys east of Tanao Rd (see Banglamphu map). In general, rooms are bigger and quieter here than at places on or just off Khao San Rd. *Central Guest House* (☎ 282-0667) is just off Tanao Rd on Trok Bowonrangsi (trawk or trok means 'alley') – look for the rather inconspicuous signs. This is a very pleasant guesthouse, with clean, quiet rooms for 60B per person. There are some more spacious doubles for 120B.

Farther south, off Trok Bowonrangsi, are the *59 Guest House*, which has dorm beds at 40B, and singles/doubles from 60/80B, and the similar *Srinthip*. Around the corner on a small road parallel to Ratchadamnoen Klang is *Sweety Guest House* with decent rooms for 50 to 60B per person. Sweety has a roof terrace for lounging and for hanging clothes. Opposite the Sweety and next to the post office are the *Nat II* and *Chart II*, both more like the Khao San Rd standard issue for 80/120B.

If you follow Trok Mayom Rd straight through, away from Tanao Rd, you'll reach Din So Rd. Cross Din So, walk away from the roundabout and you'll see a sign for *Prasuri Guest House* (☎ 280-1428), down Soi Phra Suri on the right; clean singles/doubles/triples cost 190/220/300B with fan, 330/360/390B with air-con – all rooms come with private bath. Also down this soi is the *Democratic*, where rooms are a reasonable 80/100B.

South Banglamphu On the other side of Ratchadamnoen Klang, south of the Khao San Rd area, are a couple of independent hotels and at least one guesthouse worth investigating (see the Banglamphu map). If you walk south along Tanao Rd from

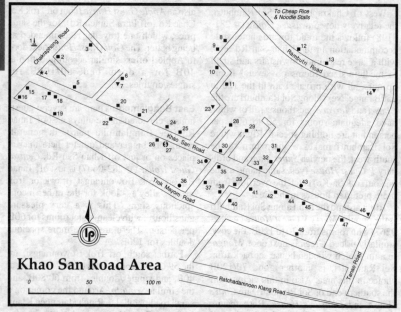

Khao San Road Area

0   50   100 m

To Cheap Rice & Noodle Stalls

Ratchadamnoen Klang, then left at the first soi, you'll come to *Hotel 90* (☎ 224-1843). It's mostly a short-time place but large, clean rooms with fan and private bath are 180/240B, 300B with air-con and TV. A bit farther east along the same soi towards Din So Rd is the quiet, sparsely decorated *Bangkok Center Guest House* (☎ 225-1247; fax 224-9149), an old teak home with 100B rooms that are often full.

Return west on this soi to Tanao Rd, turn left and then take the right at Trok Sa-Ke towards the upper mid-range Royal Hotel, and after 50 metres or so you'll come to the *Palace Hotel* (☎ 224-1876) – an all air-con version of the Hotel 90 with singles/doubles at 250/300B – and the friendly *P Guest House* nearby at 70/120B.

North Banglamphu Up on Phra Sumen Rd, opposite the north entrances to Wat Bowon, is the *Canalside Guest House* which, as its name suggests, overlooks a khlong. Basic

rooms are 80/100B – nothing to get excited about – but at least the guesthouse is away from the Khao San ghetto. Farther north-east on a soi off Prachatipatai Rd, near Wat Makut, is a branch of the Bonny Guest House called *James' Guest House* (☎ 280-0362). Clean singles/doubles here are 100/150B.

At 11/1 Soi Surao, off Chakraphong Rd towards the Banglamphu Department Store and market, the friendly *BK Guest House* (☎ 281-3048) offers clean rooms with shared bath for 100B with fan, 220B with air-con. *PS Guest House* (☎ 282-3932), a Peace Corps favourite, is all the way at the end of Phra Sumen Rd towards the river, off the south side of Khlong Banglamphu; its well-kept rooms go for 70 to 150B. Facing the north side of Khlong Banglamphu off Samsen Rd (the northern extension of Chakraphong Rd), the *New World House Apartment & Guest House* does both short and long-term room rentals starting at 400B per night.

PLACES TO STAY

2 Siam Guest House
3 Chuanpis Guest
   House
5 Sitdhi Guest House
6 Chart Guest House
8 Green House
9 AT, Leed & Jim's
   Guesthouses
10 Suneeporn Guest
   House
11 Doll Guest House &
   Others
12 Viengtai Hotel
13 Orchid House
15 Ploy Guest House
16 J Guest House
17 Thai Guest House
18 NS Guest House
19 Joe Guest House
20 Hello Guest House &
   Restaurant

21 Mam's Guest House
22 Chart Guest House
24 Lek Guest House
25 Buddy Guest House
26 PB Guest House
28 Khao San Palace Hotel
29 New Nith Jaroen Hotel
30 Grand Guest House
31 Marco Polo Hostel
32 Best Guest House
33 Nat Guest House
35 Dior Guest House
37 Bonny & Top
   Guesthouses
38 Marco Polo
   (160 Guest House)
39 Good Luck Guest
   House
40 Tong Guest House
41 VIP Guest House
42 Nana Plaza Inn
44 Siri Guest House
45 CH Guest House

47 Chada Guest House
48 7-Holder Guest House

PLACES TO EAT

7 Royal India
   Restaurant
14 Swensen's & Pizza Hut
23 Buddy Beer & Sonic
   Restaurants
32 Best Restaurant
46 Arawy Det

OTHER

1 Wat Chana
   Songkhram
4 Chana Songkhram
   Police Station
27 Krung Thai Bank
34 Shops
36 School
43 Central Minimart

Also off Samsen Rd, farther north of Khlong Banglamphu, is a small cluster of guesthouses in convenient proximity to the Tha Samphraya river express landing. On Soi 1 Samsen, just off Samsen Rd, the Khao San Rd-style *Truly Yours* (☎ 282-0371) offers 70/140B rooms over a large downstairs restaurant. A bit farther on along Soi 1, *Villa Guest House* offers a quiet, leafy, private home with 10 rooms from 100 to 250B; it's often full. Up on Soi 3 Samsen (also known as Soi Wat Samphraya), are the *River House* (☎ 280-0876), *Home & Garden* (☎ 280-1475) and *Clean & Calm*, each with small but clean rooms with shared bath for 60 to 120B. Note that Soi 3 zigs left, then zags right before reaching these three guesthouses – a good 10-minute walk from Samsen Rd.

Out on noisy Samsen Rd itself, the grungy *Suksawat Hotel* offers basic rooms for 150 to 250B with private bath – plus hot and cold running hookers. Farther north along Samsen, turn east on Soi 6 Samsen, follow the zigzag soi almost all the way to the end and you'll come to the *AP* and *Tatum*, two 70/140B guesthouses near Wat Mai Amaratarot.

The next river express stop north – and the last in the Banglamphu district – is next to Wisut Kasat Rd, where there are a couple of decent choices. The *C & C Guest House* (☎ 280-1974), near Wat Intharawihan at 12 Wisut Kasat Rd (actually on a trok off Wisut Kasat), has very comfortable rooms with fan for 50 to 120B. Farther west along Wisut Kasat Rd, the equally decent *Charasri Guest House* (☎ 282-9305) at 59/3 has a range of rooms with fan from 70 to 250B. The comfortable, mid-range *Trang Hotel* (☎ 282-2141), at 99/8 Wisut Kasat Rd has air-con rooms from 600 to 900B. Each of these is located east of Samsen Rd, so they're a good walk from the river.

Thewet & National Library Area The next district north of Banglamphu near the National Library is another little travellers' enclave. Heading north up Samsen Rd from Wisut Kasat Rd, you'll come to *TV Guest House* (☎ 282-7451) at 7 Soi Phra Sawat, just off Samsen Rd to the east. It's clean, modern and good value at 40B for a dorm bed, 80B a double.

Continue for another half a km or so and cross the canal to the place where Phitsanulok Rd finishes on Samsen Rd and where Si Ayuthaya Rd crosses Samsen Rd. Just beyond this junction is the National Library. On two parallel sois off Si Ayuthaya Rd towards the river (west from Samsen) are five guesthouses run by various members of the same extended family: *Tavee Guest House* (☎ 282-5983), *Sawatdee Guest House* (☎ 282-5349), *Backpacker's Lodge*, *Shanti Lodge* (☎ 281-2497) and *Original Paradise Guest House* (☎ 282-4094/8673). All are clean, well kept, fairly quiet and cost 40 to 50B for a dorm bed, and from 80/110B for singles/doubles.

A fifth, independently run place on the same soi as Paradise is *Little Home Guest House* (☎ 281-3412), which is similar to the others in this area except that it has a busy travel agency in front. There's a good market across the road from both sois, and a few small noodle and rice shops along Krung Kasem Rd, the next parallel street south of Si Ayuthaya (and west of Samsen Rd), which leads to Tha Thewet.

Another way to get to and from the National Library area is by taking advantage of Tha Thewet, a Chao Phraya River Express pier; from the pier you walk east along Krung Kasem Rd to Samsen Rd, turn left, cross the canal and then take another left into Si Ayuthaya Rd. Ordinary bus Nos 16, 30 and 53, and air-con bus Nos 56 and 6 pass Si Ayuthaya Rd while going up and down Samsen Rd; ordinary bus No 72 terminates on the corner of Phitsanulok and Samsen Rds, a short walk from Si Ayuthaya. Air-con bus No 10 from the airport also passes close to the area along Ratwithi Rd to the north, before crossing Krungthon Bridge.

East of Samsen Rd, the *Bangkok International Youth Hostel* (☎ 282-0950, 281-0361) is in the same neighbourhood at 25/2 Phitsanulok Rd. A bed in the air-con dorm is 60B. Rooms with fan and bath are 200B, while air-con singles/doubles with hot water are 250/300B. The rooms with fan are larger than the air-con rooms, and there's a cafeteria downstairs. In 1992 the hostel stopped accepting nonmembers as guests. Annual Hostelling International (formerly IYHF)

membership costs 300B, or you can purchase a temporary membership for 50B. The Bangkok hostel gets mixed reports – the rooms seem nice enough but the staff can be quite rude.

If you want to be close to Ratchadamnoen Boxing Stadium, or simply away from the river guesthouse scene, have a look at *Venice House* (☎ 281-8262) at 548-546/1 Krung Kasem Rd. This friendly, well-maintained guesthouse is next to Wat Somanat, just around the corner from Ratchadamnoen Nok Rd (walk north on Ratchadamnoen Nok from the stadium, turn right on Krung Kasem and walk about 80 metres till you see a sign for Venice House). Rooms are air-con and cost 300/350B. It's about a 15-minute walk from the Tha Thewet landing.

Soi Ngam Duphli This area off Rama IV Rd is where most budget travellers used to come on their first trip to Bangkok. With a couple of notable exceptions, most of the places to stay here are not cheap or even good value any more, and the whole area has taken on a rather seedy atmosphere. Overall, the Banglamphu area has better-value accommodation.

The entrance to Soi Ngam Duphli is on Rama IV Rd, near the Sathon Tai Rd intersection, and within walking distance of the imposing Dusit Thani Hotel and Lumphini Park. Ordinary bus Nos 4, 13, 14, 22, 45, 47, 74, 109 and 115, and air-con bus No 7 all pass by the entrance to Soi Ngam Duphli along Rama IV Rd.

At the northern end of Soi Ngam Duphli near Rama IV Rd is *ETC Guest House* (☎ 286-9424, 287-1478), an efficiently run, multistorey place with a travel agency downstairs. Rooms are small but clean; rates are 120B with shared bath, 160/200B for singles/doubles with private bath. All room rates include a breakfast of cereal, fruit, toast and coffee or tea.

Just south of ETC an alley leads left to the newly constructed Quality Hotel Pinnacle (see Places to Stay – top end). The cheerless *Tokyo Guest House* is farther south down

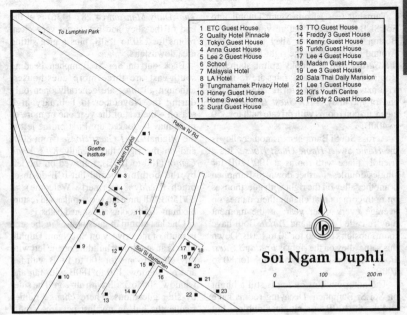

1 ETC Guest House
2 Quality Hotel Pinnacle
3 Tokyo Guest House
4 Anna Guest House
5 Lee 2 Guest House
6 School
7 Malaysia Hotel
8 LA Hotel
9 Tungmahamek Privacy Hotel
10 Honey Guest House
11 Home Sweet Home
12 Surat Guest House
13 TTO Guest House
14 Freddy 3 Guest House
15 Kenny Guest House
16 Turkh Guest House
17 Lee 4 Guest House
18 Madam Guest House
19 Lee 3 Guest House
20 Sala Thai Daily Mansion
21 Lee 1 Guest House
22 Kit's Youth Centre
23 Freddy 2 Guest House

To Lumphini Park

Rama IV Rd

To Goethe Institute

Soi Ngam Duphli

Soi Si Bamphen

Soi Ngam Duphli

0   100   200 m

Ngam Duphli; rooms are 100/140B for singles/doubles with shared bath – not quite up to the Quality's (or even ETC's) standards.

Next south is an alley on the left that leads to the *Anna* and *Lee 2* guesthouses (there are also Lee 1, Lee 3 and Lee 4 guesthouses nearby). Both have rooms with shared bath starting at 80B; Lee is the better value all round.

Back on Soi Ngam Duphli, the *Malaysia Hotel* (☎ 286-3582/7263), at 54 Soi Ngam Duphli, was once Bangkok's most famous travellers' hotel. Its 120 air-con, hot-water rooms cost from 468B for a standard single or double, 546B with a TV and small fridge, and 700B with a TV, larger fridge and carpet. The Malaysia has a swimming pool which may be used by visitors for 50B per day (it's free for guests of course).

Since the 1970s, the Malaysia has made a conscious effort to distance itself from the backpackers' market; for a while it seemed

to be catering directly to the lonely male hired-sex market. The big sign out front advertising 'Day-Off International Club – Paradise for Everyone' has dropped the final phrase 'You'll Never Be Alone Again' and there seem to be fewer hookers around the lobby than in the old days – at least before midnight. After the Patpong bars close, the hotel coffee shop becomes a virtual clearing house for bar girls who didn't pick up an outside customer earlier in the evening.

The *Tungmahamek Privacy Hotel* (☎ 286-2339/8811), across the road to the south of the Malaysia, is also fully air-con and costs 350 to 400B for a double. Many 'short-time' residents here give the place a sleazy feel, though it's less of a 'scene' than the Malaysia. In the other direction from the Malaysia is the *LA Hotel* (the English sign just says 'Hotel'), a bit better value if you don't need air-con but also on the short-time circuit – large rooms with bath and fan are 200B, air-con rooms 500B.

Turn left (east) from Ngam Duphli into Soi Si Bamphen and before you reach the Boston Inn there is an alley to the right. Around the corner on the right-hand side is the *Surat*, with a spooky spiral staircase. Rooms are small but OK; rates are 150B for a room with fan, 200B with air-con. Near the end of the alley, *TTO Guest House* offers clean air-con rooms with private bath for 350 to 400B.

Across Soi Si Bamphen in another alley is the *Home Sweet Home Guest House*. It's a friendly place with rooms at 100/120B for singles/doubles. Farther down Si Bamphen is another alley on the right with guesthouses on both corners that change their names on average every other year; at the moment they're called *Kenny* and *Turkh*. Both have rooms upstairs that go for 80 to 120B. Down this same alley on the right is *Freddy 3 Guest House* with basic accommodation for 80 to 100B.

The notorious *Boston Inn* is still a blight on Soi Si Bamphen. Decaying rooms have slid to 60/120B for singles/doubles, but neither the fan nor the water in the attached bath have been functioning for the last couple of years. A suspicious number of drug overdoses in Boston Inn rooms have been reported to the police; among travellers the hotel has a reputation as a Hell's Fawlty Towers. Rumour has it the owner was planning to renovate (at one time the Boston was one of the better places in the Soi Ngam Duphli area), but for now this one's definitely at the very bottom of the list.

If you turn left at the next soi down Si Bamphen, then take the first right, you'll end up in a cul-de-sac with three very good guesthouses. First up on the right as you enter the soi is the clean, secure and well-managed *Lee 4 Guest House* with rooms for 100/120B with shared bath, and 160/200B with private bath.

Around the corner, *Madam Guest House* also has a legion of loyal followers for its 100 to 120B rooms and friendly service. Next door, the *Lee 3 Guest House*, the best of the four Lee guesthouses, is also quite pleasant and has large rooms from 100B. The *Sala*

Thai Daily Mansion (☎ 287-1436) is at the end of the alley and has large, very clean rooms for 120 to 150B, plus a nice sitting area downstairs.

Back out on Soi Si Bamphen heading south-east are three more guesthouses, although all three are generally open only during the November to February high season – the rest of the year one or more of them may be locked up. First on the left is the original *Lee 1 Guest House* (from 80B) and on the right the friendly *Kit's Youth Centre* (100 to 150B), followed on the left by the nothing-special-but-it'll-do-in-a-pinch *Freddy 2* (formerly Welcome), at 80/150B. All three are very similar and feature medium-sized rooms and shared baths.

One last clump of guesthouses in the area is south of the Privacy on Soi Ngam Duphli. First is an apartment building on the left with tiny, cheap rooms for 100 to 140B with fan and no window, 120 to 180B with fan and window, 300 to 380B with air-con. The side-by-side guesthouses here change names frequently, but on my last pass the whole place was called *Honey*; in high season the building may split into as many as three guesthouses. Hookers rent long-term rooms for short-term use in this row. The original Freddy Guest House, down Soi Ngam Duphli past the Honey on the left, in a building with maze-like passageways, is usually closed these days.

Chinatown & Hualamphong Station This area is central and colourful although rather noisy. There are numerous cheap hotels but it's not a travellers' centre like Soi Ngam Duphli or Banglamphu. Watch your pockets and bag around the Hualamphong area, both on the street and on the bus. The cream of the razor artists operate here as the train passengers make good pickings.

The *New Empire Hotel* (☎ 234-6990/6) is at 572 Yaowarat Rd, near the Charoen Krung Rd intersection, a short walk from Wat Traimit. Air-con singles/doubles with hot water are 400B, with a few more expensive rooms for up to 700B – a bit noisy but a great location if you like Chinatown. The New

Empire is a favourite among Chinese Thais from the southern region.

Other Chinatown hotels of this calibre, most without English signs out the front, can be found along Yaowarat, Chakraphet and Ratchawong Rds. The *Burapha Hotel* (☎ 221-3545/9), situated at the intersection of Mahachai and Charoen Krung Rds, on the edge of Chinatown, is a notch better than the Empire and costs 500B single/double, and up to 1000B for a deluxe room. Likewise for the *Somboon Hotel* (☎ 221-2327), at 415 Yaowarat Rd.

Straddling the bottom and mid-range is the *River View Guest House* (☎ 234-5429, 235-8501) at 768 Soi Phanurangsi, Songwat Rd in the Talaat Noi area – wedged between Bangrak (Silom) and Chinatown. The building is behind the Jao Seu Kong Chinese Shrine, about 400 metres from the Royal Orchid Sheraton, in a neighbourhood filled with small machine shops. To get there, turn right from the corner of Si Phraya Rd (facing the River City shopping complex), take the fourth left, then the first right. Large rooms are 430B with fan and private bath, 645B with air-con and hot water. As the name suggests, many rooms have a Chao Phraya River view; the view from the 8th-floor restaurant is superb, even if you have to wake up the staff to get a meal. If you call from the River City complex, someone from the guesthouse will pick you up.

Along the eastern side of Hualamphong station is Rong Meuang Rd which has several dicey Chinese hotels. The *Sri Hualamphong Hotel*, at No 445, is one of the better ones – all rooms are 100B with fan. The *Sahakit (Shakij) Hotel* is a few doors down from the Sri Hualamphong towards Rama IV Rd and is quite OK too. Rooms are 100B up; if you stay here, try to get a room on the 4th floor which has a terrace with a view and the occasional breeze.

The long-running *Jeep Seng* (☎ 214-2808), at 462-64 Rong Meuang Rd, is not too clean but it's adequate. Rooms are 100/120B for singles/doubles, and they have good khâo man kài downstairs. Just south of the Jeep Seng is the similarly priced *Toonkee Hotel*.

Out towards the front of the station, after Rong Meuang Rd makes a sharp curve, is the *Station Hotel*, a classic Third-World dive. A room with torn curtains, dim sheets and crusty attached bath costs an astounding 140B.

The market area behind the Station Hotel is full of cheap food stalls, and on a small soi parallel to Rong Meuang Rd is the *Hoke Aan Hotel*, yet another 100/120B Chinese hole-in-the-wall (but at least it's away from Rong Meuang traffic). Also off Rong Meuang Rd next to the Chinese market is the noisy but adequate *Nam Ia Hotel* for only 70B.

At least four other cheap Chinese hotels can be found west of the station along Maitrichit Rd, all in the 70 to 100B range.

Also convenient to the Hualamphong station – and more suitable for stays of more than a night or two – are the TT guesthouses. The somewhat easier-to-find *TT 2 Guest House* (☎ 236-2946) is at 516-518 Soi Sawang, Si Phraya Rd near the Mahanakhon Rd intersection. Rooms here are 180B. To find the TT 2 from the train station, turn left onto Rama IV, right on Mahanakhon, left on Soi Kaew Fa and then right on Soi Sawang. Or from Si Phraya Rd (take Microbus 6) turn directly onto Soi Sawang. To find the more hidden *TT 1 Guest House* (☎ 236-3053, 138 Soi Wat Mahaphuttharam, off Mahanakhon Rd) from the station, cross Rama IV Rd, walk left down Rama IV, then right on Mahanakhon, and follow the signs for TT 1. It's only about a 10-minute walk from the station. Dorm beds are just 30B; singles/doubles go for 140B. Baggage storage and laundry service are available; both TTs enforce a strict midnight curfew.

Pahurat There are also several guesthouses in the Indian district of Pahurat, centred around Chakraphet Rd. The *Amarin Guest House*, on Chakraphet has a sign in English, Thai, Hindi and Arabic. Rooms cost from 100B, and are fairly clean. Farther down towards the well-known Royal India Restaurant there is a soi (off to the left if you're walking from the pedestrian bridge) on which you'll find *Moon*, *Kamal*, *Bobby's* and

Tony's Fashion, all offering similar accommodation for around 100B per room. Also in this area are *Rajin*, *Video* and probably a dozen others. The guesthouses in Pahurat cater to mostly South Asian guests, but are happy to take anyone. It's an economical alternative if you need to be in this part of town or if you want to practise speaking Hindi or Punjabi.

Silom & Surawong Rds Several mid-range guesthouses and hotels can be found in and around the Silom and Surawong Rds area.

Another Indian guesthouse is the *Madras Lodge* (☎ 235-6761), on Vaithi Lane off Silom Rd, not far from the Shiva temple. Rooms with fan start at 200B. The proprietor is a friendly Indian man from Madras (a retired gem dealer) and his kitchen serves delicious south Indian food.

Also off Silom Rd is *Bangkok Christian Guest House* (☎ 253-3353) at 123 Sala Daeng Soi 2, Convent Rd. It has very nice air-con rooms from 640B including breakfast. Nearby, at 3 Convent Rd, is the *Swiss Guest House* (☎ 234-1107) where comfortable, clean air-con rooms cost 500 to 700B depending on the size of the room.

Opposite the GPO, on Charoen Krung Rd, are three guesthouses catering mostly to middle-class north Indians, Pakistanis and Bangladeshis – *Mumtaz, Naaz* and *Kabana Inn* – each charging a reasonable 400 to 500B for air-con rooms. Just a bit more expensive but offering better service is the *Woodlands Inn*, on the soi that runs along the northern side of the GPO. Clean, air-con rooms with hot water, TV and fridge are 600B for singles/doubles. Downstairs is an air-con Indian restaurant, the Cholas.

Siam Square Several good places can be found in this centrally located area (see the Siam Square map), which has the additional advantage of being located on the Khlong Saen Saep canal taxi route. There's only one rock-bottom place in the area, the *Scout Hostel* (☎ 215-3533) on Rama I Rd, next to the National Stadium. At the time of writing it was closed for renovation, but when it

opens again beds in gender-segregated dorms will probably cost around 50B per night.

There are several lower mid-range places on or near Soi Kasem San 1, off Rama I Rd near Jim Thompson's house and the National Stadium. The eight-storey *Muangphol (Muangphon) Building* (☎ 215-0033) on the corner of Soi Kasem San 1 and Rama I Rd (931/8 Rama I Rd) has singles/doubles for 450/550B. It's good value – with air-con, hot water, a 24-hour restaurant and good service. Behind the Muangphol, off this soi, is the apartment-style *Pranee Building* (☎ 216-3181), which has one entrance next to the Muangphol and another on Rama I Rd. Fan-cooled rooms with private bath are 300 to 350B; air-con rooms with hot water start at 400B. The Pranee also does long-term rentals at a 10% discount.

Fans of the surreal David Lynch TV series 'Twin Peaks' may feel a twinge when they see the new *White Lodge* (☎ 216-8867, 216-8228), at 36/8 Soi Kasem San 1, past the more expensive Reno Hotel on the left. Clean rooms are 400B for singles/doubles, and there's a pleasant terrace cafe out the front. The next one down on Soi Kasem San 1 is the three-storey *Wendy House* (☎ 216-2436), where small but clean rooms with air-con, hot shower and TV go for 400/450B. If you're carrying unusually heavy bags, note there's no lift. A small restaurant is on the ground floor.

Next up the soi is the ancient *Star Hotel* (☎ 215-3381) at 36/1 Soi Kasem San 1, a classic sort of mid-1960s Thai no-tell motel, with fairly clean, comfortable, air-con rooms with bath and TV for 550 to 650B a double, depending on the room – a bit steep for this area. Perhaps the higher rate is due to the curtained parking slots next to ground floor rooms, which hide cars belonging to guests from casual passers-by.

Opposite the Star is *A-One Inn* (☎ 215-3029; fax 216-4771) at No 25/12-15, a friendly and pleasant place that gets a lot of return business. Fair-sized air-con doubles with bath and hot water are 400B; spacious triples are 500B (rates may drop 100B in low season). The similar *Bed & Breakfast Inn*

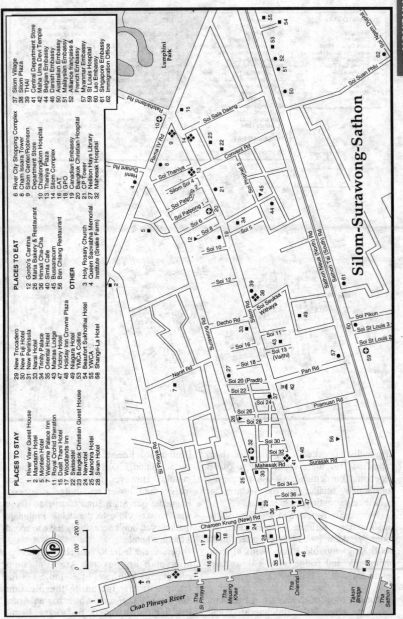

Silom-Surawong-Sathon

PLACES TO STAY

1 River View Guest House
5 Mandarin Hotel
7 Welcome Palace Inn
11 Montien Hotel
15 Royal Orchid Sheraton
17 Dusit Thani Hotel
22 Woodlands Inn
23 Swissotel
24 Bangkok Christian Guest House
25 Manohra Hotel
28 Swan Hotel
29 New Trocadero
30 New Fuji Hotel
31 New Peninsula
33 Narai Hotel
34 Trinity Palace
35 Oriental Hotel
43 Madras Lodge
47 Victory Hotel
48 Holiday Inn Crowne Plaza
49 Niagara Hotel
53 YMCA Collins
55 Beaufort Sukhothai Hotel
55 YWCA
58 Shangri-La Hotel

PLACES TO EAT

12 Gordo's Cantina
26 Maria Bakery & Restaurant
36 Himali Cha-Cha
40 Simla Cafe
45 Bussaracum
56 Ban Chiang Restaurant

OTHER

3 Holy Rosary Church
4 Queen Saovabha Memorial
   Institute (Snake Farm)
6 River City Shopping Complex
9 Cham Issara Tower
8 Silom Center/Robinson
   Department Store
10 Chulalongkorn Hospital
13 Thaniya Plaza
14 Silom Complex
16 CAT
18 GPO
19 Canadian Embassy
20 Bangkok Christian Hospital
21 CP Tower
27 Neilson Hays Library
32 Mahesak Hospital
37 Silom Village
38 Silom Plaza
39 THAI
41 Central Department Store
42 Maha Uma Devi Temple
44 Belgian Embassy
46 Danish Embassy
50 Australian Embassy
51 Malaysian Embassy
52 Alliance française &
   French Embassy
57 Myanmar Embassy
59 St Louis Hospital
60 Lao Embassy
61 Singapore Embassy
62 Immigration Office

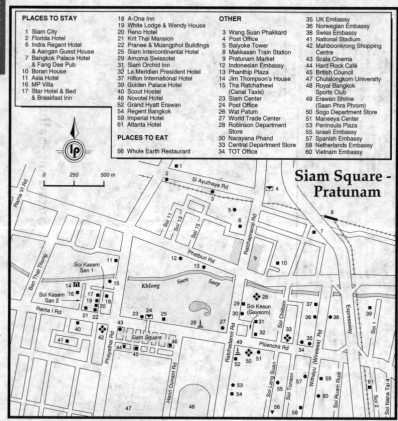

Siam Square - Pratunam

diagonally opposite the A-One has room rates that fluctuate from 350 to 500B depending on demand; air-con rooms are substantially smaller than the A-One's but rates include continental breakfast.

Over on Soi Kasem San 2 – same soi as Jim Thompson's House – the efficient, 54-room *MP Villa* (☎ 214-4495) offers good 500B single/double rooms with air-con, phone, TV and fridge, plus a downstairs restaurant.

Pratunam Most of the hotels in Pratunam (the area around the Ratchaprarop and Phetburi Rds intersection) have rooms starting at around 1200B (see Places to Stay – middle). However, there are a couple of budget and lower mid-range places in Pratunam (see Siam Square map), so if you want to stay close to the dense Pratunam markets you don't necessarily have to spend a lot on a hotel.

Behind the Indra Regent Hotel and shopping mall are several Arab/Pakistani guesthouses with rates of 300 to 500B for air-con rooms, including the pleasant *Aangan Guest House*, which has an Arab/Pakistani/north Indian restaurant downstairs. A walk east along the soi opposite the Indra Hotel (off Ratchaprarop Rd) leads to the mostly short-time *Hotel 38* where the desperate can get a room for 200 to 350B.

Farther north in the district is the *AT Guest House* (☎ 245-2963) at 14/1 Soi Ratchatapan (Maw Leng) off Ratchaprarop Rd. It's operated by Alternative Tour Thailand, a travel agency catering to educational tours for NGOs, and offers accommodation in a big house for 150B per person in air-con, gender-segregated dorms, 350B for an air-con double room (one room has a private bah, two rooms share a bath).

Sukhumvit Rd Staying in this area puts you in the newest part of Bangkok and the furthest from old Bangkok near the river. Taxis take longer to get here because of the one-way street system. The majority of the hotels in this area are in the middle price range.

The oldest hostelry in the Sukhumvit area is the historic *Atlanta Hotel* (☎ 252-1650, 252-6069), at 78 Soi 2 (Soi Phasak), Sukhumvit Rd. Owned since its 1950s construction by Dr Max Henn, a former secretary to the maharajah of Bikaner and sometime DEA-Indochina agent, the Atlanta is a simple but reliable stand-by with clean, comfortable rooms in several price categories. Rooms with shared bath and fan cost 250/350B for singles/doubles, air-con rooms with hot showers go for 400/500/600B single/double/triple, 50B extra for larger rooms with built-in safe boxes. Monthly stays warrant a 10% discount; children under 12 can stay with parents for 50B over the single or double room rate.

The Atlanta's ageing swimming pool, constructed in 1954, was the first hotel pool in Thailand, while the subdued, simply decorated coffee shop is all that remains of the Continental, a restaurant that once served royalty and foreign diplomats. Lingering distinctions include a heavily annotated menu (itself a crash course in Thai cuisine) and the selection of British, German and French newspapers available for perusal in the coffee shop.

The *Golden Palace Hotel*, at 15 Soi 1, Sukhumvit Rd, has a swimming pool, is well situated and costs 400 to 500B for a double with air-con and bath. The clientele here are mostly middle-class tourists 'on a budget', but the Golden Palace has seen better days. On the next soi east, the quiet *Best Inn* (☎ 253-0573) at 75/5-6 Soi 3, Sukhumvit Rd, provides smallish rooms with fan for 350B and air-con rooms for 450B. Another entry in the inner Sukhumvit area is *Thai House Inn* (☎ 255-4698; fax 253-1780), between sois 5 and 7. Rooms with air-con and hot water are 500B a single or double; facilities include a safety-deposit service and a coffee shop. Back on the other side of Sukhumvit Rd, the newish *Uncle Rey* (☎ 252-5565) at 7/10 Soi 4, offers simple air-con lodging for 400B.

Moving farther out on Sukhumvit Rd, the *Miami Hotel* (☎ 252-5140/4759/5036), at Soi 13, Sukhumvit Rd, dates back to 1960s and 1970s R&R peak. The room and service quality seems to seesaw every three years or so but recent reports reckon it's decent value at 500/550B single/double for air-con rooms and a swimming pool. The *Crown Hotel* (☎ 258-0318), at Soi 29, Sukhumvit Rd, is in decline and gets mostly short-time traffic these days.

Disra House (☎ 258-5102), on the access street to Villa Theatre between sois 33 and 33/1, has similar rooms for 80 to 120B.

Places to Stay – middle
Bangkok is saturated with small and medium-sized hotels in this category. The clientele at hotels in this range are a very mixed bunch of Asian business travellers, Western journalists on slim expense accounts, economy-class tour groups, along with a smattering of independent tourists who seem to have chosen their hotels at random. Not quite 'international class', these places often offer guests a better sense of being in Thailand than the luxury hotels.

During the late 1980s, when there was a shortage of tourist accommodation, many mid-range hotels doubled their rates in a grab for short-term profit over long-term good-will. In the off-season (March to November) you may be able to get a low-occupancy discount off the rates listed below.

Banglamphu Before Khao San Rd was 'discovered', the most popular Banglamphu hotel was the *Viengtai Hotel* (☎ 281-5788) at 42 Rambutri Rd. Over the last decade or so the Viengtai has continually raised its prices (not always concomitant with an upgrading of facilities) until it now sits solidly in the middle price range of Bangkok hotels; singles/doubles are 1000 to 1350B.

Besides the Oriental and the Atlanta, the oldest continually operating hotel in the city is the *Royal* (☎ 222-9111/20), still going strong on the corner of Ratchadamnoen Klang and Atsadang Rds near the Democracy Monument. The Royal's 24-hour coffee shop is a favourite local rendezvous; this is one of the few upper mid-range places where there are as many Asian as non-Asian guests. Singles/doubles start at 960B; during low season this can sometimes be negotiated down to around 700B. Incidentally, most of the taxi drivers know this hotel as the 'Ratanakosin' (as the Thai sign on top of the building reads), not as the Royal. During the bloody May 1992 protests against General Suchinda's appointment as prime minister, the Royal served as a makeshift hospital for injured demonstrators.

Other mid-range places in this area include the *Thai Hotel* (☎ 282-2833), at 78 Prachatipatai Rd, which has singles/doubles at 1300/1500B; and the *Welcome Palace* (☎ 234-5402), at 30 Naret Rd, with 450 rooms at 1000B. Welcome Palace occasionally advertises special single room rates of just 400B; the clientele is mostly South Asians and Middle Easterners.

Chinatown Mid-range hotels in the China-town area of Bangkok are tough to find. Best bets are the 80-room *Chinatown* (☎ 226-1267), at 526 Yaowarat Rd, which has rooms starting at 1200B; the *Miramar Hotel* (☎ 222-4191), 777 Mahachai Rd, where standard singles/doubles cost 890 to 1113B; and

the *White Orchid* (☎ 226-0026) at 409-421 Yaowarat Rd.

Silom & Surawong Rds This area is packed with upper mid-range places; discounts are often dispensed from April to October. Bangkok has a YMCA and YWCA, both in the Silom and Surawong Rds area. The *YMCA Collins International House* (☎ 287-1900/2727; fax 287-1996), at 27 Sathon Tai (South) Rd, has air-con rooms with TV, telephone and private bath from 1248B. Guests may use the Y's massage room, gym, track and swimming pool. The *YWCA* (☎ 286-1936) is at 13 Sathon Tai Rd and has cheaper air-con rooms starting at 487B.

On the south side of Silom Rd is Soi Suksavitthaya (Seuksa Withaya), where two good mid-range places are located. First is *Niagara Hotel* (☎ 233-5783/4) at 26 Soi Suksavitthaya, where clean air-con rooms with hot water and telephone are a bargain 560B (rooms with fan are 250B).

Another decent choice in the Silom-Surawong area is the *Newrotel* (☎ 237-1094; fax 237-1102) at 1216/1 Charoen Krung Rd, which is near the GPO and the river. Air-con singles/doubles cost 750B.

The two hotels nearest Patpong Rd – the *Suriwong* and the *Rose* – are in the 700 to 800B range. They can't really be recommended for light sleepers as they suffer from heavy people-traffic from Patpong bars. The Rose has a primarily gay clientele.

Classic mid-range hotels along Surawong Rd include the *New Fuji* (☎ 234-5364) at No 299-310 with rooms from 1124 to 1338B and the *New Trocadero Hotel* (☎ 234-8920/9) at No 34, where singles or doubles cost from 1070 to 1400B. Because they both offer good service and amenities for under 1500B, these two have been favourites among journalists. A fair number of package tours stop here as well. The Thai-style *Manohra Hotel* (☎ 234-5070) at No 412 offers singles/doubles for 1400 to 1600B. A new entry at No 173/8-9, *La Residence* (☎ 235-4795; fax 233-3301), is an intimate 23-room place with rates of 1775 to 1865B.

Siam Square/Hualamphong This area tends to offer either upper-end budget or top-end luxury hotels, with little in the middle. *Krit Thai Mansion* (☎ 215-3042), out on busy Rama I Rd opposite the National Stadium, costs 700 to 800B for rooms with air-con, hot water, private bath, telephone, colour TV/video, fridge and security parking. The coffee shop downstairs is open 24 hours. Reports are mixed on this one – some seem to like it, some don't. An old Siam Square stand-by, the *Reno Hotel* (☎ 215-0026) on Soi Kasem San 1 is a veteran from the Vietnam War days when a spate of hotels opened in Bangkok with names of US cities. Singles/doubles/triples with air-con and hot water cost 600/700/800B; there's a pool on the premises but recent reports say the staff are consistently rude.

The *Siam Orchid Inn* (☎ 255-2119; fax 255-3144), off Soi Gaysorn close to Le Meridien President Hotel, offers well-appointed rooms with all the amenities for around 1500B.

For anyone who wants to be near the Royal Orchid Sheraton, River City complex and river (Tha Si Phraya landing), the *Orchid Inn* (☎ 234-8934; fax 234-4159) at 719/1 Si Phraya Rd provides decent mid-range value at 750/900B (discounts of 100 to 150B often available) for tidy air-con rooms with TV and mini-fridge. Along with its proximity to the river, another advantage here is that the ordinary No 36 bus and Microbus No 6 each terminate almost directly opposite the hotel. The downside is the high number of touts and big-spending tourists in the neighbourhood.

The slightly swanky *Tong Poon Hotel* (☎ 216-0020; fax 215-0450), at 130 Rong Meuang Soi 4, has been recommended as good value. Although rack rates (room rates quoted to walk-ins) for large, nicely done rooms with air-con, colour TV and phones are 1800/2000B single/double, rates of 800 to 1200B were readily dispensed throughout 1993 – better value than anything else in this range in the Siam Square area for the time being. The Tong Poon has a coffee shop and pool, and it's a short tuk-tuk ride from the Hualamphong train station.

Pratunam The *Opera Hotel* (☎ 252-4031; fax 253-5360), at 16 Soi Somprasong 1, Phetburi Rd is very near the heart of Pratunam and features air-con doubles with hot water from 600 to 800B. The Opera also has a swimming pool and coffee shop.

Bangkok Noorie (☎ 252-3340) at 178/7 Soi Wuttiphan, Ratchaprarop Rd near the Indra Hotel, charges 650 to 850B for reasonable air-con rooms. A long walk east along the soi opposite the Indra (off Ratchaprarop Rd) leads eventually to *Borarn House* (☎ 246-4525; fax 253-3639), a Thai-style apartment building at 487/48 Soi Wattanasin, with singles/doubles for 850/950B with air-con and TV. The OK *Siam Hotel* (☎ 252-5081), at 1777 Phetburi Rd, has 120 rooms; singles/doubles cost 833/999B.

Sukhumvit Rd This area is choked with hotels costing 800 to 1500B. Stick to the lower numbered sois to save crosstown travel time.

A long-running farang favourite on Soi 8, *Mermaids Rest* (☎ 253-3648; fax 253-2401), has air-con rooms from 650 to 850B and there is a swimming pool. The reliable *Ruamchit Mansion* (☎ 251-6441), at 1-15 Soi 15, Sukhumvit Rd, has air-con rooms ranging from 450 to 600B and there is hot water, fridge, communal kitchen and a supermarket just below. Monthly rates are available.

The *Federal Hotel* (☎ 253-0175), at 27 Soi 11, Sukhumvit Rd, is a favourite among Vietnam War and Peace Corps vets but I've found the accommodation overpriced at 700 to 1050B, especially for the added-on rooms at ground level; these occasionally flood in the rainy season. The modest pool and coffee shop are the main attractions. The *Golden Gate* at 22/1 Soi 2, Sukhumvit Rd is better value, with large air-con doubles for 750B, including breakfast.

Moving farther east along Sukhumvit Rd, the *Carlton Inn* (☎ 258-0471; fax 258-3717) at 22/2-4 Soi 21, Sukhumvit Rd, has decent rooms from 650B. A bit nicer are the two *City Lodges* on sois 9 (☎ 253-7680) and 19 (☎ 254-4783). Rooms at either location are 950B for a single or double, and include air-con, telephone, TV/video and mini-bar. Other mid-range hotels in the Sukhumvit Rd area include:

Asoke Place, 4/49 Soi 21, Sukhumvit Rd; 20 rooms, singles/doubles 650 to 850B (☎ 258-3742)

Business Inn, 155/4-5 Soi 11, Sukhumvit Rd; 70 rooms, singles/doubles 550 to 950B (☎ 254-7981)

China Inn, 19/27-28 Soi 19, Sukhumvit Rd; 27 rooms, singles/doubles 650 to 850B (☎ 255-7571)

Comfort Inn, 153/11 Soi 11, Sukhumvit Rd; 60 rooms, singles/doubles 900 to 1400B

Dynasty Inn, 5/4-5 Soi 4, Sukhumvit Rd; 55 rooms, singles/doubles 850 to 950B (☎ 250-1397)

Euro Inn, 249 Soi 31, Sukhumvit Rd; 82 rooms, singles/doubles 1444 to 1658B (☎ 259-9480)

Fortuna Hotel, 19 Sukhumvit Rd; 110 rooms, singles/doubles 800/1500B (☎ 251-5121)

Grace Hotel, 12 Nana Neua (Soi 3), Sukhumvit Rd; 550 rooms, singles/doubles 789/1230B (☎ 252-9170/3)

Grand Inn, 2/7-8 Soi 3, Sukhumvit Rd; 24 rooms, 890 to 1390B (☎ 254-9021)

Manhattan, Soi 15, Sukhumvit Rd; 206 rooms, singles/doubles 1350B (☎ 252-7141/9)

Nana Hotel, 4 Nana Tai, Sukhumvit Rd; 224 rooms, singles/doubles from 880B (☎ 250-1210/9, 250-1380/9)

Park Hotel, 6 Soi 7, Sukhumvit Rd; 128 rooms, 1700B (☎ 252-5110/3)

Rajah Hotel, 18 Soi 4, Sukhumvit Rd; 450 rooms, singles/doubles from 1287B (☎ 252-5102/9)

Rex Hotel, 762/1 Soi 32; Sukhumvit Rd; 131 rooms, singles/doubles 1100 to 1310B (☎ 259-0106)

White Inn, 41 Soi 4, Sukhumvit Rd; 24 rooms, singles/doubles 850B

Victory Monument Area Just north of Siam Square, in the Victory Monument area, are several hotels, including the decent *Century Hotel* (☎ 245-3271/3) at 9 Ratchaprarop Rd. This hotel has 96 rooms at 972B for singles or doubles. At the *Continental Hotel* (☎ 278-1596/8), 971/16 Phahonyothin Rd, singles cost from 650 to 695B. The renovated *Florida Hotel* (☎ 245-3221/4, 245-1816/9), at 43 Phayathai Square, Phayathai Rd, has singles/doubles at 800/1300B.

Airport Area Finding decent, moderately priced accommodation in the airport area is difficult. Most of the hotels in this area charge nearly twice as much as comparable hotels in the city. Typical among these price-gougers is *Don Muang Mansion* (☎ 566-3095) at 118/7 Soranakom Rd, Don Meuang, which looks classy on the outside but asks 1200B for a small, stuffy room that in Bangkok would cost at the most 500 to 750B. It's possible to negotiate a lower rate of 800B with some discussion. Even the top-end Amari Airport Hotel (see Places to Stay – top end, following) is guilty of over-charging.

If you can spend a bit more, a better choice is the 150-room *Comfort Inn Airport* (☎ 552-8929; fax 552-8920), about five minutes south of the airport by car at 88/117 Vibhavadi (Wiphaawadi) Rangsit Rd. Large rooms with all the amenities (satellite TV, air-con, hot water bath/shower) cost 1400 to 1600B if you book through a Bangkok travel agent, 2200B for walk-ins. Best of all, the hotel provides a free shuttle to and from the airport every hour. Other facilities include a coffee shop, pool, sauna and health club; about the only drawback is that you can hear planes landing and taking off until around midnight.

For quite a bit less you could stay at the well-run *We-Train Guest House* (☎ 566-1774, 566-2288; fax 566-3481), at 501/1 Mu 3, Dechatung Rd, Sikan, Don Meuang. Simple but very clean air-con rooms with two beds and private bath cost 800B single/double (extra beds cost 150B). You can also get a bed in a fan-cooled dorm for 150B, air-con 200B. To these rates add the usual 10% service charge but no tax since it's operated by a nonprofit women's organisation (male guests are welcome). One major drawback to the We-Train is its distance from the airport – you must get a taxi to cross the highway and railway to Don Meuang, then proceed about three km west along Dechatung Rd to the Thung Sikan school *(rohng rian thûng sĭi-kan)*. There are usually no taxis in this area when you're ready to return to the airport or continue on to

Bangkok, but transportation to and from the airport can be arranged on request.

Other Areas Medium-priced hotels in other areas of the city include:

Baron Hotel, 544 Soi Huay Khwang, Ratchadaphisek Rd, Huay Khwang; 155 rooms, singles/doubles 600B (☎ 246-4525)

Golden Dragon, 20/21 Ngam Wongwan Rd; 114 rooms, singles/doubles 963B (☎ 588-4414/5)

Golden Horse Hotel, 5/1 Damrongrak Rd; 130 rooms, singles/doubles from 1000B (☎ 281-6909)

Liberty Hotel, 215 Pratipat Rd, Saphan Khwai; 209 rooms, singles/doubles 475B to 871B (☎ 271-0880)

Places to Stay – top end

Bangkok has all sorts of international standard tourist hotels, from the straightforward package places to some of Asia's classic hotels. Three of Bangkok's luxury hotels, in fact, made Condé Nasts *Traveler*'s worldwide top 10 list for 1992: the Oriental (No 1), the Regent (No 3) and the Shangri-La (No 10). Although there's no single area for top-end hotels you'll find quite a few of them around the Siam Square area, along the parallel Surawong and Silom Rds, and along the river, while many of the cheaper 'international standard' places are scattered along Sukhumvit Rd.

From 1988 to 1991, luxury-class hotels in Bangkok raised their rates more than any other class of hotel in Thailand, capitalising on the 90%-plus occupancy rates that occurred in the late 1980s. When a hotel construction boom collided with the 1990-91 Gulf War and recession, many of the price-gougers were humbled. With lower occupancy rates, you should be able to negotiate discounts of up to 40% on the rates listed. Booking through a travel agency almost always means lower rates – also try asking for a hotel's 'corporate' discount. Several luxury hotels have even lowered their rack rates since last edition.

A new trend in Bangkok hotels in the past few years has been the appearance of several European-style 'boutique' hotels – small, business-oriented places of around 100 rooms or fewer with rates in the 2000 to 3000B range – like the *Mansion Kempinski* (Soi 11 Sukhumvit Rd), *Princess* (269 Lan Luang Rd), *Somerset* (Soi 15 Sukhumvit Rd), *Swissotel* (Convent Rd) and *Trinity Place* (Soi 5 Silom Rd). Many experienced Bangkok business travellers prefer this type of hotel because they get personal service for about 1000B less than the bigger hotels; also these smaller hotels don't accept tour groups, so regular guests don't have to wade through crowds in the lobby.

New hotel standouts include the 450-room *Monarch Lee Gardens Hotel* (☎ 238-1991; fax 238-1999) at 188 Silom Rd, distinguished by a black marble lobby, Cantonese, Japanese and European restaurants, executive floors, business and health centres and rooms with IDD phones for 4000 to 5000B. The new *Chateau de Bangkok* (☎ 290-0125; fax 290-0167) at 25 Soi Ruam Rudi, Ploenchit Rd, is owned by the French hotel group Accor, and offers 139 'service studios' – one and two-bedroom apartments, each with walk-in closet, IDD phone and fax – for 3500 to 4000B.

The less expensive, tastefully decorated *Hotel Rembrandt* (☎ 261-7100; fax 261-7107) at Soi 18, Sukhumvit Rd, has 406 large rooms that were selling for 2000B in 1993 though rack rates were listed at 3050 to 3550B. Facilities include a swimming pool and the best Mexican restaurant in Bangkok, *Señor Pico's of Los Angeles*. Another advantage is the Rembrandt's proximity to Queen Sirikit National Convention Centre, off Soi 16.

All of the hotels in this category will add a 10% service charge plus 7% tax to hotel bills on departure.

On the River The 118-year-old *Oriental Hotel* (☎ 236-0400/39), on the Chao Phraya River, is one of the most famous hotels in Asia, right up there with the Raffles in Singapore or the Peninsula in Hong Kong. What's more it's also rated as one of the very best hotels in the world, as well as being just about the most expensive in Bangkok. The hotel management prides itself in providing highly personalised service through a staff of 1200 (for 398 rooms) – once you've stayed here they'll remember your name, what you like to eat for breakfast, even what type of flowers you prefer in your room.

Nowadays the Oriental is looking more modern and less classic – the original Author's Wing is dwarfed by the Tower (built in 1958) and River (1976) wings. Authors who have stayed at the Oriental and had suites named for them include Joseph Conrad, Somerset Maugham, Noel Coward, Graham Greene, John Le Carré, James Michener, Gore Vidal and Barbara Cartland. The hotel sits at 48 Oriental Ave; room rates start at 6592B, suites as much as nine times that. It's worth wandering in if only to see the lobby (no shorts, sleeveless shirts or thongs allowed – dress politely or you'll be refused entry).

Two other luxury gems along the river are the *Shangri-La* (☎ 236-7777; fax 236-8570) at 89 Soi Wat Suan Phlu, Charoen Krung Rd; and the *Royal Orchid Sheraton* (☎ 234-5599; fax 236-8320), 2 Captain Bush Lane, Si Phraya Rd. The Shangri-La has 694 rooms starting from 5265B, and its own helicopter transport from the airport, while the Sheraton (776 rooms, from 5649B) is known for crisp, efficient service (the business centre is open 24 hours).

The *Menam* (☎ 289-1148/9; fax 291-9400), towering over the river at 2074 Charoen Krung Rd, Yannawa, has 718 rooms from 4237B up. The *Royal River* (☎ 433-0300; fax 433-5880), at 670/805 Charan Sanitwong Rd, Thonburi, has 403 rooms from 3788B.

Silom & Surawong Rds There are many hotels with similar amenities to the Regent, Hilton and Sheraton, but which are a step down in price because of their location or smaller staff-to-guest ratios. In the Silom and Surawong areas these include the *Montien* (☎ 234-8060; fax 234-8060) at 54 Surawong Rd (600 rooms, 4708B up), a very Thai hotel; the *Dusit Thani* (☎ 233-1130; fax 2366400) at Rama IV Rd (520 rooms, from 6120B), a great hotel in a lousy location; the

Narai (☎ 233-3350; fax 236-7161) at 222 Silom Rd (500 rooms, 3177 to 5885B); and the *Holiday Inn Crowne Plaza* (☎ 238-4300/34; fax 238-5289) at 981 Silom Rd (662 rooms, 3766B up).

Another relatively new entry in the luxury/executive market is the 222-room *Beaufort Sukhothai* (☎ 287-0222; fax 287-4980) at 13/3 Sathon Tai Rd. The Sukhothai features an Asian minimalist decor, including an inner courtyard with lily ponds; the same architect and interior designer created Phuket's landmark Amanpuri. Standard rooms start at 5000B.

Other top-end hotels in this area include:

Mandarin Hotel, 662 Rama IV Rd; 343 rooms, 3178 to 8828B (☎ 233-4980/9; fax 237-1620)
New Peninsula, 295/3 Surawong Rd; 102 rooms, 2250 to 3895B (☎ 234-3910; fax 236-5526)
Silom Plaza, 320 Silom Rd; 209 rooms, 2420B up (☎ 236-8441/84; fax 236-7566)
Swissotel, 3 Convent Rd; 57 rooms, 3885B up (☎ 233-5345; fax 236-9425)
Trinity Palace, 150 Soi 5, Silom Rd; 109 rooms, 2300 up (☎ 238-0052; fax 238-3984)

Siam Square & Ploenchit Rd People accustomed to heady hotels claim the plush *Regent Bangkok* (☎ 251-6127; fax 253-9195), at 155 Ratchadamri Rd, tops the Oriental in overall quality for the money (local calls are free at the Regent – probably the only luxury hotel in the city to offer this courtesy); it's also one of the city's top choices for visiting business travellers because of its efficient business centre and central location. The Regent's 415 rooms start at 5297B.

Another top executive choice is the *Hilton International Bangkok* (☎ 253-0123; fax 253-6509) on Withayu Rd, where you won't find tour groups milling around in the lobby; its 343 rooms start at 3885B.

The 400-room *Siam Intercontinental* (☎ 253-0355; fax 253-0355), ensconced on spacious grounds at 967 Rama I Rd (near Siam Square), takes in a mix of well-heeled pleasure and business travellers. Standard rooms start at 3800B.

The three-year-old *Grand Hyatt Erawan*, at the intersection of Ratchadamri and

Ploenchit Rds, was raised on the site of the original Erawan Hotel (which came up at the same time as the Royal but was torn down some years ago) and has obvious ambitions to become the city's number-one hotel. The neo-Thai architecture has been well executed; inside is the largest collection of contemporary Thai art in the world. Adding to the elite atmosphere, rooms in the rear of the hotel overlook the Bangkok Royal Sports Club racetrack. For most visitors – whether for business or leisure – it probably has the best location of all the city's luxury hotels vis-à-vis transport and proximity to shopping.

During the 1991 opening of the Grand Hyatt, 99 monks ('nine' is considered a lucky number in Thai culture, hence number 99 doubles the good luck) offered Buddhist chants in the lobby and received a sumptuous alms dinner. A Brahman ceremony was performed at the adjacent Erawan Shrine, and at an astrologically auspicious moment, 510 balloons and 99 doves were simultaneously released into the air.

Other top-notch hotels in the Siam Square area include:

Arnoma Swissotel, 99 Ratchadamri Rd; 400 rooms, 4708B up (☎ 255-6888; fax 255-1824)

Asia Hotel, 296 Phayathai Rd; 640 rooms, 3414B up; it's in a good location, but often full of tour groups and conventioneers (☎ 215-0808; fax 215-4360)

Bangkok Palace Hotel, 1091/336 New Phetburi Rd; 650 rooms, 2700B up; contains several lounges, coffee shops, and massage parlours oriented towards the East Asian visitor (☎ 253-0500; fax 253-0556)

Imperial Hotel, Withayu (Wireless) Rd; 370 rooms, 4900B up (☎ 254-0023; fax 253-3190)

Indra Regent, Ratchaprarop Rd; 500 rooms, 3400B up (☎ 251-1111; fax 253-3849)

Le Meridien President, 135/26 Gaysorn Rd; 387 rooms, 3450B up (☎ 253-0444; fax 253-7565)

Sukhumvit Rd Top-end hotels in this area include:

Ambassador Hotel, Soi 11, Sukhumvit Rd; 1050 rooms, 21198B up; an amazing conglomeration of restaurants, food centres, night clubs and cocktail lounges (☎ 254-0444; fax 253-4123)

ANA Grand Pacific Hotel Soi 17-19, Sukhumvit Rd; easy access to Queen Sirikit National Convention Centre; 400 rooms, 4900B up (☎ 233-2922/7; fax 237-5740)

Bel-Aire Princess, 16 Soi 5, Sukhumvit Rd; 160 rooms, 3650B up

Impala Hotel, Soi 24, Sukhumvit Rd; 200 rooms, 2300B up (☎ 258-8612/6; fax 259-2896),

Landmark, 138 Sukhumvit Rd; 415 rooms, 4826 to 9416B; has a Videotex in every room, very good business centre (☎ 254-0404; fax 253-4259)

Mansion Kempinski, 75/23 Soi 11, Sukhumvit Rd; 127 rooms, 6580B; very exclusive (☎ 255-7200; fax 253-2329)

Windsor Hotel, 3 Soi 20, Sukhumvit Rd; 235 rooms, 2589 to 9416B (☎ 258-0160; fax 258-1491)

Airport Area The 300-room *Amari Airport Hotel* (☎ 566-1020; fax 566-1941), directly across from the airport, is quite well appointed but most Bangkok regulars agree it's overpriced at 3800B. A better luxury-class hotel towards the airport is the *Central Plaza Bangkok* (☎ 541-1234; fax 541-1087) at 1695 Phahonyothin Rd. There are 600 rooms, starting at 5297B for a standard room. Or stay five minutes from the airport at the less·expensive *Comfort Inn Airport* (see the earlier entry under Places to Stay – middle).

Other Areas Top-end hotels in other areas include:

Emerald, 99/1 Ratchadaphisek Rd, Huay Khwang; 640 rooms, 3900B up (☎ 281-3088; fax 280-1314)

Quality Hotel Pinnacle, 17 Soi Ngam Duphli, Rama IV Rd; 170 rooms, 2300B up (☎ 287-3411; fax 287-3420)

Rama Gardens, 9/9 Vibhavadi Rangsit Rd; 364 rooms, 3766B up (☎ 561-0011; fax 561-1025)

Royal Lake View, 649/1-76 Asoke-Din Daeng Rd; 176 rooms, 2119 to 4708B

Royal Princess Hotel, 269 Lan Luang Rd; 2900B up (☎ 281-3088; fax 280-1314)

Siam City, 477 Si Ayuthaya Rd; 530 rooms, 4300B up (☎ 247-0120; fax 247-0178)

Places to Eat

No matter where you go in Bangkok, you're almost never more than 50 metres away from a restaurant or sidewalk food vendor. The variety of places to eat is simply astounding and defeats all but the most tireless food samplers in their quests to say they've tried everything. As with seeking a place to stay, you can find something in every price range in most districts – with a few obvious exceptions. Chinatown is naturally a good area for Chinese food, while Bangrak and Pahurat (both districts with high concentrations of Indian residents) are good for Indian and Muslim cuisine. Some parts of the city tend to have higher priced restaurants than others (for example, Siam Square, and Silom, Surawong and Sukhumvit Rds) while other areas are full of cheap eats (eg Banglamphu and the river area around Tha Maharat).

Because transport can be such a hassle in Bangkok, most visitors choose a place to eat according to which district is most convenient to reach (rather than seeking out a specific restaurant); this section has therefore been organised by area, rather than cuisine.

Banglamphu & Thewet This area near the river and old part of the city is one of the best for cheap eating establishments. Many of the guesthouses on Khao San Rd have open-air cafes, which are packed out with travellers from November to February. The typical cafe menu here has a few Thai and Chinese standards plus a variety of traveller favourites like fruit salads, muesli and yoghurt. None of them are particular standouts, though the side-by-side *Orm* and *Wally House* produce fair Thai, farang and vegetarian meals. *Arawy Det*, an old Hokkien-style noodle shop on the corner of Khao San and Tanao Rds, has somehow managed to stay authentic amidst the cosmic swirl.

Pahurat's *Royal India* has a Khao San Rd branch in an alley about 50 metres east of the police station, amidst a cluster of Indian tailor shops. The dining room is air-con and the thalis are filling; though the food is generally not as good as the original on Chakraphet Rd, the Indian bread selection compares favourably. The *Maharajah Restaurant*, above Khao San Rd's Maharajah Boutique, also serves the usual north Indian

dishes. Both are open from 10 am to 11 pm daily.

For more authentic (and cheaper) Thai food check out the next street north of Khao San, Rambutri Rd. At the western end of the street are several open-air restaurants serving excellent Thai food at low prices. A good spot for southern Thai food is a no-name food shop at 8-10 Chakraphong, south of Khao San Rd and two doors south of the Padung Cheep mask shop. In the mornings this one serves khâo mòk kài (Thai chicken biryani) as well as khâo yam, a kind of rice salad which is a traditional breakfast in southern Thailand. Nearby at No 22 is a cheap and efficient Chinese noodle (bàmìi) and wonton (kíaw) shop; No 28 offers tasty Thai curries. A small *Muslim restaurant* on the corner of Phra Athit and Phra Sumen Rds near the river offers good chicken or vegetable mátàbà (a sort of stuffed crepe) for 15B, plus Malay rojak (fruit-vegetable salad) as well as Thai and Indian curries.

Farther north of Khao San Rd, in the heart of Banglamphu's market, are two shopping complexes with food centres, fast-food vendors and supermarkets. At the high-rise *New World shopping centre*, the ground floor features donut shops and meatball vendors, the 5th floor has a supermarket, and on the 8th is a brilliant food centre with city and river views. Centre vendors offer seafood, vegetarian, coffee, noodles, curries and more. The 6th floor of *Banglamphu Department Store* between Krai Si and Rambutri Rds also has a supermarket and small food centre. The department store was recently condemned by the BMA for noncompliance with building codes, so who knows how long it will be before it either closes or collapses.

Many of the Khao San Rd guesthouse cafes offer vegetarian dishes. For an all-veggie menu at low prices, seek out the *Vegetarian Restaurant* at 85/2 Soi Wat Bowon. To find this out-of-the-way spot, turn left on Tanao Rd at the eastern end of Khao San Rd, then cross the street and turn right down the first narrow alley, then left at Soi Wat Bowon – an English sign reads 'Vegetarian'. Another very good vegetarian place is *Arawy* (no English sign), which is south of Khao San Rd, across Ratchadamnoen Klang at 152 Din So Rd (opposite the City Hall). This was one of Bangkok's first Thai vegetarian restaurants, inspired by ex-Bangkok Governor Chamlong Srimuang. The restaurant also serves a few fish and shrimp dishes.

Good curry-and-rice is available for around 10B at the outdoor dining hall at *Thammasat University* near the river; it's open for lunch only. Opposite the southern entrance of the university there are several good noodle and rice shops. For northeastern Thai food, try the restaurants next door to the boxing stadium on Ratchadamnoen Nok Rd, near the TAT office.

At the Tha Wisut Kasat pier in northwestern Banglamphu, there's a very good floating seafood restaurant called *Yok Yor*. Especially good at Yok Yor is the hàw mòk (fish curry). Yok Yor also offers inexpensive evening dining cruises – you order from the regular menu and pay a nominal 50B charge for the boat service. Nearby is the similar *Chawn Ngoen*; it has no English sign, but there is an English menu. *Wang Ngar*, in West Banglamphu next to the Phra Pinklao Bridge, is another decent waterfront place.

At the Democracy Monument circle, Ratchadamnoen Klang Rd, there are a few air-con Thai restaurants, including the *Vijit* and the *Sorn Daeng*, which have reasonable prices considering the food and facilities. At lunchtime on weekdays they're crowded with local government office workers. Both stay open until 11 pm or so.

For authentic, sit-down Thai cuisine, try the long-running *Yod Kum* (Yawt Kham) opposite Wat Bowon on Phra Sumen Rd. Specialities include *phàt phèt plaa dùk* (catfish stir-fried in basil and curry paste), *kaeng khĭaw-wǎan* (green curry) and seafood.

For those in the mood for continental food, *Kanit's* at 68 Tee Thong Rd is just south of the Sao Ching-Cha (Giant Swing) and is another worthwhile semi-splurge. The lasagne and pizza are probably the best you can find in this part of Bangkok.

Silom & Surawong Rds This area has a few restaurants along the main avenues and a greater number tucked away in sois and alleys. The river end of Silom and Surawong Rds towards Charoen Krung Rd (the Bangrak district) is a good hunting ground for Indian food.

Thai & Other Asian The *Soi Pracheun (20) Night Market*, which assembles each evening off Silom Rd in front of the municipal market pavilion, is good for cheap eats. During the day there are also a few food vendors in this soi.

The area to the east of Silom Rd off Convent and Sala Daeng Rds is a Thai gourmets' enclave. Most of the restaurants tucked away here are very good, but a meal for two will cost 600 to 800B. One such up-market spot is *Bussaracum* (pronounced 'boot-sa-ra-kam') at 35 Soi Phipat off Convent Rd. Bussaracum specialises in 'royal Thai' cuisine, that is, recipes that were created for the royal court in days past; these recipes were kept secret from 'commoners' until late this century. Every dish is supposedly prepared only when ordered, from fresh ingredients and freshly ground spices. Live classical Thai music, played at a subdued volume, is also provided. This is a fancy place, recommended for a splurge. Two can eat for around 600 to 800B.

Another great place for traditional Thai – at moderate prices – is *Ban Chiang* (☎ 236-7045), a restored wooden house in a verdant setting at 14 Soi Si Wiang, Pramuan Rd (off Silom Rd west of Wat Khaek).

Moving towards the river, just west of Soi 9 at No 160 Silom Rd, you'll find the open-air *Isn't Classic* (the Thai name is 'Isaan Classic'), a popular restaurant specialising in north-eastern Thai food. Prices are very reasonable for the good-quality sticky rice, kài yâang (spicy grilled chicken), lâap (meat salad), sôm-tam (spicy green papaya salad) and other isǎan delights. Over on Surawong Rd at No 173/8-9, *All Gaengs* is a modern, air-con place specialising in Thai curries and spicy Thai-style salads (yam). *Mandalay* (☎ 237-8812), at 311/5 Surawong Rd opposite the Manohra Hotel, does good Burmese cuisine.

Also on Surawong Rd at No 311/2-4 (on the corner of Soi Pramot), *Maria Bakery & Restaurant* is well known for its fresh Vietnamese and Thai food as well as French pastries, pizza and vegetarian food. A smaller Maria branch can be found next to the GPO on Charoen Krung Rd. Both are clean and air-con, with reasonable prices.

A good one-stop eating place with a lot of variety is the Silom Village Trade Centre, an outdoor shopping complex at Soi 24. Though it's basically a tourist spot with higher than average prices, the restaurants are of high quality and plenty of Thais dine here as well. The centrepiece is *Silom Village*, a place with shaded outdoor tables where the emphasis is on fresh Thai seafood – sold by weight. The menu also has extensive Chinese and Japanese sections. For the quick and casual, *Silom Coffee Bar* makes a good choice. At night *Ruen Thep* offers one of the city's better Thai classical dance-and-dinner venues. During the daytime, vendors dressed in traditional Thai clothing sell a variety of traditional snacks like khanŏm khrók (steamed coconut pastries) and mîang kham (savoury titbits wrapped in wild tea leaves) – more than a little corny, but again the food quality is high.

Towards the eastern end of Surawong, near the Montien Hotel, is the famous *Somboon Seafood* (open from 11 am to midnight), a good, reasonably priced seafood restaurant known for having the best crab curry in town. Somboon has a second branch called *Somboon Chinese* farther north, across Rama IV Rd near Chulalongkorn University at Soi Chulalongkorn 8 (711-717 Chula Soi 8, Ban That Thong Rd).

The Patpong sois themselves are rather bleak when it comes to Thai food, although the long-running *Thai Room* remains a favourite of local Thai farang couples, Peace Corps volunteers and off-duty bar workers. The decor's not much, but prices are reasonable; the menu features several Mexican, Chinese, European and American dishes, as well as Thai food.

The *Sakura Steak House* on Patpong 1 has a loyal Japanese and Thai following for its inexpensive but good Japanese food. Another very good Japanese place – especially for sushi and sashimi – is *Goro* at 399/1 Soi Siri Chulasewok off Silom; prices are reasonable.

Indian & Muslim Farther towards the western end of Silom and Surawong Rds, Indian eateries begin making appearances one by one. For authentic south Indian food (dosa, idli, vada, etc), try the *Madras Cafe* (☎ 235-6761) in the Madras Lodge at 31/10-11 Vaithi Lane (Trok 13), off Silom Rd near the Narai Hotel. Another place serving south Indian (in addition to north Indian) food is the very basic *Simla Cafe* at 382 Soi Tat Mai (opposite Borneo & Co) off Silom Rd, in an alley behind the Victory Hotel. Across from the Narai Hotel, near the Maha Uma Devi temple, street vendors sometimes sell various Indian snacks.

The *Moti Mahal Restaurant* at the old Chartered Bank near the Swan Hotel off Charoen Krung has good Muslim-Indian food, great yoghurt and reasonable prices. *Himali Cha-Cha*, at 1229/11 Charoen Krung Rd, also features good north Indian cuisine, but prices are fairly high.

The *Cholas*, a small air-con place downstairs in the Woodlands Inn on Soi Charoen Krung 32 just north of the GPO, serves decent, no-fuss north Indian food at 40 to 80B a dish. The open-air *Sallim Restaurant* next door to the Woodlands is a cheaper, more working-class place with north Indian, Malay and Thai-Muslim dishes – it's usually packed. Opposite the GPO on Charoen Krung Rd, the *Mumtaz Guest House* has a clean and reasonably priced Muslim restaurant downstairs.

Around the corner on Soi Phutthaosot is the very popular but basic-looking *Naaz* (Naat in Thai), often cited as having the richest khâo mòk kài (chicken biryani) in the city. The milk tea is also very good here, and daily specials include chicken masala and mutton kurma. For dessert, the house speciality is firni, a Middle Eastern pudding spiced with coconut, almonds, cardamom and saffron. Naaz is open from 7.30 am to 10.30 pm daily. There are several other Arab/Indian restaurants in this area.

On Soi Pracheun (Soi 20) off Silom Rd there's a mosque – Masjid Mirasuddeen – so Muslim food vendors are common.

Other Cuisines If you crave German or Japanese food, there are plenty of places serving these cuisines on and around Patpong Rd. *Bobby's Arms*, an Aussie Brit pub, has good fish & chips. The *Brown Derby*, also on Patpong 1, is recommended for American-style deli sandwiches.

Wedged between the go-go bars on Patpong 2 are several fast-food chicken joints, including *Kentucky Fried Chicken, Chicken Divine* and *Magic Grill*. Yet another branch of the *Little Home Bakery & Restaurant* does a booming business serving farang and Filipino food on Soi Thaniya (one soi east of Patpong 2).

Opposite the Silom entrance to Patpong, in the CP Tower building, are a cluster of air-con American and Japanese-style fast-food places: *McDonald's, Pizza Hut, Chester's Grilled Chicken, Suzuki Coffee House* and *Toplight Coffee House*. Several are open late to catch the night-time Patpong traffic.

Mexican food in Thailand is always a big risk – usually the flavours are as distant from cocina mexicana as Bangkok is from Mexico City. One of the city's better Mexican food venues is *El Gordo's Cantina* at 130/8 Soi 8, Silom Rd, opposite the Bangkok Bank headquarters. In addition to a good selection of standard Mexican dishes, the restaurant makes a decent margarita. Live Mexican music starts around 9 pm nightly.

Moving upscale, the trendy *Aztec Bar & Restaurant* (☎ 236-0450), in the Dusit Thani Hotel at Silom and Rama IV Rds, presents an exotic menu of Tex-Mex and Southwestern cuisine amidst banks of TVs playing music videos. The bar section is open from 5 pm to midnight, while the restaurant is only open from 7 to 10 pm. The Narai Hotel on Silom Rd, further capitalising on Bangkok's recent Tex-Mex and Creole food surge, has opened its own Southwest Deco-style *Enigma Party Bistro* (☎ 237-0100, ext 8128), where the creative menu features shrimp ceviche, flautas, blackened red snapper and wine-poached pears. Enigma is open nightly from 5.30pm to 2 am; dinner is served from 6 to 10.30 pm only.

The tiny *Harmonique* on Soi Charoen Krung 34, around the corner from the GPO, is a refreshing oasis in this extremely busy, smog-filled section of Charoen Krung. European-managed and unobtrusive, the little shop serves a variety of teas, fruit shakes and coffee on Hokkien-style marble-topped tables – a pleasant spot to read poste-restante mail while quenching a thirst. The shop also discreetly offers silk and silverwork for sale.

Siam Square This shopping area is interspersed with several low and medium-priced restaurants as well as American fast-food franchises. Chinese food seems to predominate, probably because it's the well-off Chinese Thais that most frequent Siam Square. Soi 1 has three shark-fin places: *Scala, Penang* and *Bangkok*. At the other end of Siam Square, on Henri Dunant Rd, the big noodle restaurant called *Coca Garden* (open from 10.30 am to 10.30 pm) is good for Chinese-style sukiyaki.

Can't decide what kind of Asian or farang food you're in the mood for? Then head for *S&P Restaurant & Bakery* on Soi 12. The extensive menu features Thai, Chinese, Japanese, European and vegetarian specialities, plus a bakery with pies, cakes and pastries – all high-quality fare.

On Soi 11, the Bangkok branch of London's *Hard Rock Cafe* serves good American and Thai food. Look for the tuk-tuk captioned 'God is my co-pilot' coming out of the building's facade. The Hard Rock stays open till 2 am, a bit later than many Siam Square eateries.

Just to the right of the Siam Square's Scala cinema, plunge into the alley that curves behind Phayathai Rd shops to find a row of cheap, good food stalls. A shorter alley with food stalls also leads off the north end of Siam Square's Soi 2.

On the opposite side of Rama I Rd from Siam Square, the green Siam Center has a bounty of coffee shops catering to young Thais, including the recommendable *UCC City Cafe, Takiap, Tea for Two, Dry Fly* and *Highlight Coffeeshop*. Those on the 4th floor feature live Thai pop music in the evenings; the UCC (on the ground floor) has a CD jukebox, also the best coffee in the building (Tea for Two isn't bad either). Menus are mostly Thai, with smaller selections of Chinese, Japanese and European. Prices average around 35 to 75B per dish. *Oldies Goldies* on the 4th floor offers ice cream and fountain drinks, burgers, sandwiches, Thai food, fruit juices, waffles, crepes and salads in a pseudo-1950s American-style ambience.

On both sides of Rama I in Siam Square and Siam Center you'll find a battery of American fast-food franchises, including *Mister Donut, Dunkin Donuts, Pizza Hut, Swensen's Ice Cream, McDonald's, Shakey's Pizza, A&W Root Beer* and *Kentucky Fried Chicken*. Prices are close to what you would pay in the USA.

If you're staying on or nearby Soi Kasem San 1, you don't have to suck motorcycle fumes crossing Rama I and Phayathai Rds to Siam Square, Siam Center or Mahboon-krong to find something to eat. Besides the typical hotel and inn coffee shops found on the soi, there are also two very good, inexpensive curry-and-rice vendors with tables along the east side of the soi. No need to be fluent in Thai, they're used to the 'point-and-serve' system. In front of the White Lodge, *Princesse Terrace* offers an extensive menu of Thai and European food, burgers, pastries, coffees and breakfast – it's good but rather expensive. Right around the corner on Rama I Rd, next to the liquor dealer with the vintage British and US motorcycles out the front, is *Thai Sa Nguan* (no English sign), a fairly clean shop with khâo kaeng (curry and rice) for 12B (two toppings 17B), fried duck with noodles (kŭaytĭaw pèt yâang) and Hainanese-style chicken and rice (khâo man kài).

Mahboonkrong Shopping Centre Another building studded with restaurants, MBK is directly across from Siam Square at the intersection of Phayathai and Rama I Rds. A section on the ground floor called Major Plaza contains two cinemas and a good food centre. An older food centre is on the 7th floor; both places have vendors serving tasty dishes from all over Thailand, including vegetarian, at prices averaging 20 to 25B per plate. Hours are 10 am to 10 pm, but the more popular vendors run out of food as early as 8.30 or 9 pm – come earlier for the best selection. A beer garden on the terrace surrounding two sides of the 7th-floor food centre – with good views of the Bangkok nightscape – is open in the evening.

Scattered around other floors, especially the 3rd and 4th, are a number of popular medium-priced places, including *Little Home Bakery* (an American-style pancake house with a few Filipino dishes), *13 Coins* (steak, pizza and pasta), *Kobune Japanese Restaurant*, *Chester's Grilled Chicken*, *Pizza Hut* and many others.

World Trade Center This relatively new office and shopping complex on the corner of Ploenchit and Ratchadamri Rds contains a few up-market restaurants and the city's trendiest food centre. Located on the ground floor of this huge glossy building are *Kroiss-ant House* (coffees, pastries and gelato) and *La Fontana* (bistro-style Italian). The 6th floor of the centre features *Lai-Lai* and *Chao Sua*, two sumptuous Chinese banquet-style places, plus the elegant traditional Thai *Thanying* and the more casual *Narai Pizzeria*. There are also two food centres on the 7th floor with standard Thai and Chinese dishes, which are only a little more expensive than at the usual Bangkok food centre.

The basement of Zen Department Store contains a Thai deli with many curries, a good Japanese sushi-and-noodle bar (a sizeable plate of sushi costs 60 to 120B), a bakery, sandwich/coffee bar and Western deli. The basement food centre has very few seats, encouraging takeaways.

Soi Lang Suan Farther east from Siam Square, Mahboonkrong and the World Trade Center – off Ploenchit Rd and more or less equidistant from Siam Square, Sukhumvit and Silom Rds – Soi Lang Suan offers a number of medium-priced eating possibilities. Despite its farang name, *Sarah Jane* (☎ 252-6572), on an alley off the west side of Lang Suan about a block and a half south of Ploenchit, serves very good isãan food in a modest air-con dining room. It's open 11 am to 10 pm.

The Italian-owned *Pan Pan* (☎ 252-7501) at 45 Soi Lang Suan is very popular with Western residents for its wood-fired pizza (takeaway orders accepted), pastas, salads, gelato (the best in Thailand) and pastries. A low-kilojoule vegetarian menu is available on request. A second Pan Pan (☎ 258-5071) is located on Soi 33.

The *Whole Earth Restaurant* (☎ 252-5574), at 93/3 Soi Lang Suan, is a good Thai and Indian vegetarian restaurant (non-vegetarian dishes are also served) with service to match, but is a bit pricey if you're on a tight budget. The upstairs room features low tables with floor cushions. A second branch has opened at 71 Soi 26, Sukhumvit Rd (☎ 258-4900).

Nguan Lee Lang Suan, on the corner of Soi Lang Suan and Soi Sarasin, is a semi-outdoor place specialising in Chinese-style seafood and kài lâo daeng (chicken steamed in Chinese herbs).

Sukhumvit Rd This avenue stretching east all the way to the city limits has hundreds of Thai, Chinese and farang restaurants to choose from.

Thai & Other Asian The ground floor of the Ambassador Hotel between sois 11 and 13 has a good food centre. It offers several varieties of Thai, Chinese, Vietnamese, Japanese, Muslim and vegetarian food at 20 to 40B per dish – you must buy coupons first and exchange them for dishes you order.

Cabbages & Condoms at No 10, Soi 12, is run by the Population & Community Development Association (PDA), the brainchild of Mechai Viravaidya who popularised condoms in Thailand – first for birth-control purposes and now as STD prevention. The restaurant offers not only a great selection of condoms, but great Thai food at very reasonable prices as well. The tôm khàa kài (chicken-coconut soup) is particularly tasty here; the restaurant is open from 11 am to 10 pm. The *Mandalay* (☎ 255-2893), at 23/7 Soi Ruam Rudi (along with a second branch on Surawong Rd), is supposedly the only Burmese restaurant in town; it's good but not cheap.

The *Yong Lee Restaurant* at Soi 15, near Asia Books, has excellent Thai and Chinese food at reasonable prices and is a long-time favourite among Thai and farang residents alike. There is a second Yong Lee between sois 35 and 37.

The famous *Djit Pochana* (☎ 258-1578) has a branch on Soi 20 and is one of the best-value restaurants in town for traditional Thai dishes. The all-you-can-eat lunch buffet is 90B. This central section of Sukhumvit Rd is loaded with medium-priced Thai restaurants which feature modern decor but real Thai food. The *Baitarl* (Bai-Taan), at 3 Soi 33, is another very good place for traditional Thai food (though a little more expensive), as is the less expensive *Fuang Fah* across the street.

For nouvelle Thai cuisine, you can try the *Lemongrass* (☎ 258-8637) at 5/21 Soi 24, which has an atmospheric setting in an old Thai house decorated with antiques. The food is exceptional; try the yam pèt (Thai-style duck salad). It is open from 11 am to 2 pm and 6 to 11 pm.

Another restaurant with an inventive kitchen is *L'Orangery* at 48/11 Soi Ruam Rudi (close to where Ploenchit Rd becomes Sukhumvit Rd). Billed as Pacific Rim cuisine, the food shows the dual influences of Californian and Asian cooking; sometimes it works, sometimes it doesn't.

Yet another hidden gem down Sukhumvit Rd is *Laicram* (Laikhram) at Soi 33 (☎ 238-2337) and at Soi 49/4 (☎ 392-5864). The food at Laicram is authentic gourmet Thai, but not outrageously priced. One of the house specialities is hàw mòk hãwy, an exquisite thick fish curry steamed with mussels inside the shell. Sôm-tam (spicy green papaya salad) is also excellent here, usually served with khâo man, rice cooked with coconut milk and bai toei (pandanus leaf). Opening hours are from 10 am to 9 pm Monday to Saturday, 10 am to 3 pm Sunday.

There are many restaurants around the major hotels on Sukhumvit Rd with mixed Thai, Chinese, European and American menus – most of average quality and slightly above-average prices. One of the most authentic – and cheapest – sources of Thai food on Sukhumvit Rd is the regular *Soi 38 Night Market* at the junction of Sukhumvit Rd and Soi 38; in addition to a wide variety of Thai foods, market vendors also serve a few Chinese and Malay dishes.

The upscale *Le Dalat* (☎ 258-0290) at 47/1 Soi 23, Sukhumvit Rd, has the most celebrated Vietnamese cuisine in the city. A house speciality is nãem meuang, grilled meatballs which you place on steamed rice-flour wrappers, then add chunks of garlic, chilli, ginger, starfruit and mango along with a tamarind sauce, and finally wrap the whole thing into a lettuce bundle before popping it in your mouth. There are two other branches at Patpong Business Centre, 2nd floor, Surawong Rd (☎ 234-0290) and Premier Shopping Village, Chaeng Wattana Rd (☎ 573-7017).

Mrs Balbir's (☎ 253-2281) at 155/18 Soi 11 (behind the Siam Commercial Bank) has a good variety of vegetarian and non-vegetarian Indian food (mostly north Indian). Mrs Balbir has been teaching Indian cooking for many years and has her own Indian grocery store as well.

The splurge-worthy *Rang Mahal* (☎ 261-7100), a rooftop restaurant in the Rembrandt Hotel on Soi 18, offers very good north and south Indian 'royal cuisine' with cityscape views. On Sundays the restaurant puts on a sumptuous Indian buffet from 11.30 am to 3 pm. Another decent Indian place is *Bangkok Brindawan* (☎ 258-8793) at 15 Soi 35 near the Fuji supermarket. This one specialises in south Indian food. A few medium to expen-

sive restaurants serving Pakistani and Middle Eastern food can be found in the 'Little Arabia' area of Soi 3 (Soi Nana Neua), including *Akbar's, Al Hamra, Al Helabi, Nana Fondue* and *Shaharazad*.

Other Cuisines Homesick Brits need look no farther than *Jool's Bar & Restaurant* at Soi 4 (Soi Nana Tai), past Nana Plaza on the left walking from Sukhumvit Rd. The British-style bar downstairs is a favourite expat hang-out while the dining room upstairs serves decent English food. Several rather expensive West European restaurants (Swiss, French, German, etc) are also found on touristy Sukhumvit Rd. *Bei Otto*, between sois 12 and 14, is one of the most popular German restaurants in town and has a comfortable bar.

Nostalgic visitors from the USA, especially those from southern USA, will appreciate the well-run *Bourbon St Bar & Restaurant* on Soi 22 (behind the Washington Theatre). The menu here emphasises Cajun and Creole cooking; some nights there is also free live music.

One of the top French restaurants in the city, and probably the best not associated with a luxury hotel – is *Le Banyan* (☎ 253-5556) at 59 Soi 8 in a charming early Bangkok-style house. The kitchen is French-managed and the menu covers the territory from ragout d'escargot to canard maigret avec foie gras. This is definitely a splurge experience – although the prices are moderate when compared with other elegant French restaurants in the city.

If you're looking for Mexican, the city's best can be found at *Señor Pico's of Los Angeles* (☎ 261-7100), on the 2nd floor of the Rembrandt Hotel, Soi 18 Sukhumvit Road. This brightly decorated, festive restaurant offers reasonably authentic Tex-Mex cuisine, including fajitas, carnitas, nachos and combination platters. Expect to spend around 200 to 300B for two.

For American-style pizza, there's a *Pizza Mall* on the corner of Soi 33 and Sukhumvit Rd (the *Uncle Ray's Ice Cream* next door has the best ice cream in Bangkok) and a *Pizza Hut* at Soi 39.

The *Little Home Bakery & Restaurant* (☎ 390-0760), at 413/10-12 Soi 55, has an extensive Western menu along with a few Filipino items – this place has a very loyal Thai following. Unless you're already out this far on Sukhumvit Rd, the Little Home in Mahboonkrong shopping centre would be more convenient to most Bangkok locations.

Chinatown & Pahurat Some of Bangkok's best Chinese and Indian food is found in these adjacent districts but because few tourists stay in this part of town (for good reason – it's simply too congested), they rarely make any eating forays into the area. A few old Chinese restaurants have moved from Chinatown to locations with less traffic, the most famous being Hoi Tien Lao, now called *Hoi Tien Lao Rim Nam* and located adjacent to River House Condominium on the Thonburi bank of the Chao Phraya River, more or less opposite the Portuguese Embassy and River City complex. (The food and decor at Hoi Tien Lao, though far removed from Chinatown, are nonetheless excellent.) But many places are still hanging on to their venerable Chinatown addresses – where the atmosphere is still part of the eating experience.

Most of the city's Chinatown restaurants specialise in southern Chinese cuisine, particularly that of coastal Guangdong and Fujian provinces. This means seafood, rice noodles and dumplings are often the best choices. The large, banquet-style Chinese places are mostly found along Yaowarat and Charoen Krung Rds, and include *Lie Kee* (on the corner of Charoen Krung and Bamrungrat Rds, a block west of Ratchawong Rd), *Laem Thong* (on Soi Bamrungrat just off Charoen Krung Rd) and *Yau Wah Yuen* (near the Yaowarat and Ratchawong Rds intersection). Each of these has an extensive menu, including dim sum before lunch time.

The best noodle and dumpling shops are hidden away on smaller sois and alleys. At No 54 on Soi Bamrungrat is the funky

Chiang Kii, where the 100B khâ tôm plaa (rice soup with fish) belies the casual surroundings – no place does it better. *Kong Lee*, at 137/141 Ratchawong, has a very loyal clientele for its dry-fried wheat noodles (bàmii hâeng in Thai) – again it's reportedly the best in Bangkok. Another great noodle place, *Pet Tun Jao Thaa*, is on the southeastern edge of Chinatown in the direction of the GPO, at 945 Soi Wanit 2 opposite the Harbour Department building. The restaurant's name means 'Harbour Department Stewed Duck' – the speciality is rice noodles (kŭaytĭaw) served with duck or goose, either roasted or stewed.

Over in Pahurat, the Indian fabric district, most Indian places serve north Indian cuisine, which is heavily influenced by Moghul or Persian flavours and spices. For many people, the best north Indian restaurant in town is the *Royal India* at 392/1 Chakraphet Rd in Pahurat. It can be very crowded at lunchtime – almost exclusively with Indian residents – so it might be better to go there after the standard lunch hour or at night. The place has very good curries (both vegetarian and non-vegetarian), dahl, Indian breads (including six kinds of paratha), raita, lassi, etc – all at quite reasonable prices.

The *ATM department store* on Chakraphet Rd near the pedestrian bridge has a food centre on the top floor that features several Indian vendors – the food is cheap and tasty and there's quite a good selection. Running alongside the ATM building on Soi ATM are several small teahouses with very inexpensive Indian and Nepali food, including lots of fresh chapatis and strong milk tea. For a good choice of inexpensive vegetarian food, try the Sikh-operated *Indrathep* on Soi ATM. In the afternoons, a Sikh man sets up a pushcart on the corner of Soi ATM and Chakraphet Rd and sells vegetarian samosas often cited as the best in Bangkok.

Wedged between the western edge of Chinatown and the northern edge of Pahurat, the three-storey *Old Siam Plaza* shopping centre houses a number of Thai, Chinese and Japanese restaurants. The most economical places are on the 3rd floor, where a food centre serves inexpensive Thai and Chinese meals from 10 am to 5 pm. The 3rd floor also has several reasonably priced, Thai-style coffee shops. Attached to the adjacent Chalermkrung Royal Theatre is a branch of the highly efficient, moderately priced *S&P Restaurant & Bakery*, where the extensive menu encompasses everything from authentic Thai to well-prepared Japanese, European and vegetarian dishes, along with a selection of pastries and desserts.

Vegetarian During the annual Vegetarian Festival (centred around Wat Mangkon Kamalawat on Charoen Krung Rd in September-October), Bangkok's Chinatown becomes a virtual orgy of vegetarian Thai and Chinese food. Restaurants and noodle shops in the area offer hundreds of different vegetarian dishes. One of the best spreads is at *Hua Seng Restaurant*, a few doors west of Wat Mangkon on Charoen Krung Rd.

Other Areas *Tum-Nak-Thai (Tamnak Thai)* (☎ 276-7810), 131 Ratchadaphisek Rd, is one of several large outdoor restaurants built over boggy areas of Bangkok's Din Daeng district north of Phetburi. But this one just happens to be billed as the largest outdoor restaurant in the world (verified by the Guinness record book)! It's built on four hectares of land and water and can serve up to 3000 diners at once. The menu exceeds 250 items and includes Thai, Chinese, Japanese and European food. All orders are computer-coordinated and some of the waiters glide by on roller skates. One section of the restaurant offers while-you-dine Thai classical dance performances. Two can eat here for under 300B including beer.

Dinner Cruises There are a number of companies that run cruises during which you eat dinner. Prices range from 40 to 700B per person depending on how far they go and whether dinner is included in the fare. For more information, see Dinner Cruises under River & Canal Trips earlier in this chapter.

Vegetarian The *Bangkok Adventist Hospital cafeteria* (430 Phitsanulok Rd) also serves inexpensive veggie fare. On the southwestern corner of Chatuchak Park (where the Weekend Market is held), near the pedestrian bridge and Chinese shrine, look for a sign reading 'Vegetarian' in green letters and you'll find a small Thai veggie restaurant with great food for only 7 to 12B per dish. All the Indian restaurants in town have vegetarian selections on their menus.

Hotel Restaurants For splurge-level food, many of Bangkok's grand luxury hotels provide memorable – if expensive – eating experiences. With Western cuisine, particularly, the quality usually far exceeds anything found in Bangkok's independent restaurants. Some of the city's best Chinese restaurants are also located in hotels. If you're on a budget, check to see if a lunchtime buffet is available on weekdays; usually these are the best deals, ranging from 150 to 300B per person (up to 490B at the Oriental). Also check the *Bangkok Post* and the *Nation* for weekly specials presented by visiting chefs from far-flung corners of the globe – Morocco, Mexico City, Montreal, no matter how obscure, they've probably done the Bangkok hotel circuit.

The Oriental Hotel has six restaurants, all of them managed by world-class chefs – buffet lunches are offered at several. The hotel's relatively new *China House* (☎ 236-0400, ext 3378), set in a charming wooden house opposite the hotel's main wing, has one of the best Chinese kitchens in Bangkok, with an emphasis on Cantonese cooking. The lunchtime dim sum is superb and is a bargain by luxury hotel standards at 50B or less per plate or all you can eat for 250B. The Oriental's *Lord Jim's* is designed to imitate the interior of a 19th-century Asian steamer, with a view of the river; the menu focuses on seafood (lunch buffet available).

Dusit Thani's *Chinatown* (☎ 236-0450) was probably the inspiration for the Oriental's China House, though here the menu focuses on Chiu Chau (Chao Zhou) cuisine as well as Cantonese. Dim sum lunch is available, but it's a bit more expensive than the Oriental's. As at the Oriental, service is impeccable. Dusit also has the highly reputed *Mayflower*, with pricey Cantonese cuisine, and the Vietnamese *Thien Duong*.

For hotel dim sum almost as good as that at the Dusit or Oriental – but at less than a third the price – try the *Jade Garden* (☎ 233-7060) at the Montien Hotel. Though not quite as fancy in presentation, the food is nonetheless impressive.

For French food, the leading hotel contenders are *Ma Maison* (☎ 253-0123) at the Hilton International, *Normandie* (☎ 236-0400, ext 3380) at the Oriental, and *Regent Grill* (☎ 251-6127) at the Regent Bangkok. All are expensive but the meals and service are virtually guaranteed to be of top quality. The Regent Bangkok also offers the slightly less formal *La Brasserie*, specialising in Parisian cuisine.

The minimalist *Colonnade Restaurant* (☎ 287-0222) at the Beaufort Sukhothai Hotel lays out a huge 500B brunch, including made-to-order lobster bisque, from 11 am to 3 pm on Sundays. A jazz trio supplies background music. Reservations are suggested.

Finally, if eating at one of the above would mean spending your life savings, try this pauper's version of dining amidst the bright hotel lights of Bangkok. Go to the end of the soi in front of the Shangri-La Hotel and take a ferry (1B) across the river to the wooden pier immediately opposite. Next to this pier is the·riverside *Prom*, where you can enjoy an inexpensive Thai seafood meal outdoors with impressive night-time views of the Shangri-La and Oriental hotels opposite. The ferry runs till Prom closes, around 2 am.

High Tea Although Thailand was never a British colony (or anyone's colony for that matter), influences from nearby Kuala Lumpur and Singapore have made afternoon tea (or 'high tea') a custom at the more ritzy hotels. One of the best spreads is afternoon tea in the *Regent Bangkok* lobby from 2 to 5.30 pm on weekdays. The cost is 180B for a selection of herbal, fruit, Japanese, Chinese

and Indian teas plus a variety of hot scones, Devonshire cream, jam, cakes, cookies and sandwiches.

Afternoon tea in the lobby-lounge of the *Shangri-La Hotel* costs 210B weekdays for a variety of teas, sandwiches and cakes; on weekends the Shangri-La does a more lavish 40-item 'high tea buffet' for 235B. The *Hilton International* hosts a 140B Sunday afternoon tea that offers a decent selection of sandwiches; a live classical quartet provides musical atmosphere.

Entertainment
In their round-the-clock search for *khwaam sa-nùk* (fun), Bangkokians have made their metropolis one that literally never sleeps. To get an idea of what's available, check the entertainment listings in the daily *Bangkok Post* and the *Nation*, the tourist-oriented weeklies *This Week* and *Angel City* or the relatively new monthly *Guide of Bangkok: The Trend & Entertainment Newspaper of Bangkok* (the latter three are free at various tourist haunts around town). If you're looking for something more avant-garde, seek out a copy of *Caravan*, a local magazine devoted to trendy lifestyles and events.

Possibilities include classical music performances, rock concerts, videotheque dancing, Asian music/theatre ensembles on tour, art shows, international buffets, etc. Boredom should not be a problem in Bangkok, at least not for a short-term visit; however, save some energy and money for your upcountry trip!

Nightlife Bangkok's naughty nightlife image is linked to the bars, coffee houses, nightclubs and massage parlours left over from the days when the City of Angels was an R&R stop for GIs serving in Vietnam. By and large these throwbacks are seedy, expensive and cater to men only. Then there is the new breed of S&S (sex & sin) bar, some merely refurbished R&R digs, that are more modest, classy and welcome females and couples. Not everybody's cup of tea, but they do a good business. More recently, other places have appeared which are quite chic and suitable for either gender.

All the major hotels have flashy nightclubs too. Many feature live music – rock, country & western, Thai pop music and jazz. Hotels catering to tourists and businesspeople often contain up-to-date discos. You'll find the latest recorded music in the smaller neighbourhood bars as well as the mega-discos.

Go-Go Bars These are concentrated along Sukhumvit Rd (east of Soi 21), off Sukhumvit Rd on Soi Nana (including the infamous Grace Hotel, now an all-Arab nightspot) and in the world-famous Patpong Rd area, between Silom and Surawong Rds. Wherever you go prices are about the same; beers are usually 40 to 50B.

Patpong (named after the Chinese millionaire, Phat Phong, who owns practically everything on Patpong Rds I and II) has calmed down a bit over the years. These days it has more of an open-air market feel as several of the newer bars are literally on the street, and vendors set up shop in the evening hawking everything from roast squid to fake designer watches. The downstairs clubs with names like *King's Castle* and *Pussy Galore* feature go-go dancing while upstairs the real raunch is kept behind closed doors. Don't believe the touts on the street who say the upstairs shows – featuring amazing anatomical feats – are for free: after the show, a huge bill usually arrives. Patpong's *Lipstick* and *Suzie Wong's* are the only 'sexotic' bars that consistently eschew the practice of adding surprise charges to your bill.

Another holdover from the R&R days is *Soi Cowboy* (off Sukhumvit between sois 21 and 23), which still gets pretty wild some nights. *Nana Plaza*, off Soi 4 (Soi Nana Tai) Sukhumvit Rd, is a three-storey complex which has rather recently surged in popularity among resident and visiting oglers. Nana Plaza comes complete with its own guesthouses in the same complex – almost exclusively used by Nana Plaza's female bar workers for illicit assignations.

Soi Tantawan and Thaniya Rd, on either side of and parallel to Patpong Rds I and II, feature expensive Japanese-style hostess bars (which non-Japanese are usually barred from entering) as well as a handful of gay bars with names like *Mandate* and *Golden Cock* that feature male go-go dancers and 'bar boys'.

Transvestite cabarets are big in Bangkok and several are found in the Patpong area. *Calypso Cabaret* has recently moved from its old Soi 24 Sukhumvit Rd location to the Ambassador Hotel at Soi 11. The Calypso (☎ 261-6355) has the largest regularly performing transvestite troupe in town, with nightly shows at 8.30 and 10 pm.

Other Bars Trendy among Bangkok Thais these days are bars which strive for a more sophisticated atmosphere, with good service and choice music played at a volume that doesn't entirely rule out conversation. The Thais call them pubs but they bear little resemblance to any traditional English pub. Some are 'theme' bars, conceived around a particular aesthetic. Soi 33 off Sukhumvit Rd has a string of bars named after European artists: *Vincent Van Gogh, Ea Manet Club, Renoir Club 1841*; you get the idea. Soi Lang Suan off Ploenchit Rd has several live music pubs, including the favourites *Brown Sugar* and *Old West* (see Live Music below).

All the city's major hotels feature Western-style bars as well. Two new trendy, bistro-style places where good food and drink go together are the Dusit Thani's *Aztec Bar & Restaurant* and the Narai Hotel's *Enigma Party Bistro*, both in the Silom Rd area. See the earlier Places to Eat section for more detail.

Bangkok is a little short on plain neighbourhood bars without up-market pretensions or down-market sleaze. One that's close to fitting the bill is the *Front Page*, a one-time journalists' hang-out (before the nearby *Bangkok Post* offices moved to Khlong Toey) on Soi 1, Sala Daeng (off Silom and Rama IV). Two low-key, Brit-style taverns include *Jool's* on Soi 4 near

Nana Plaza and the *Witch's Tavern* at 306/1 Soi 55, Sukhumvit Rd.

The guitar-shaped bar at Bangkok's *Hard Rock Cafe* (☎ 251-0792), Siam Square, Soi 11, features a full line of cocktails and a small assortment of local and imported beers. The crowd is an ever-changing assortment of Thais, expats and tourists. From 10 pm on there's also live music.

TV jocks can keep up with their favourite teams via big-screen satellite TV at *Champs* (☎ 252-7651), a huge American-style sports bar in the Nai Lert Building on Sukhumvit Road, near Soi 5.

Live Music Bangkok's live music scene has expanded rapidly over the past five years or so, with a multiplicity of new, extremely competent bands and new clubs. The three-storey *Saxophone Pub Restaurant* (☎ 246-5472), south-east of the Victory Monument circle at 3/8 Victory Monument, Phayathai Rd, has become a Bangkok institution for musicians of several genres. On the ground floor is a bar/restaurant featuring jazz from 9 pm to 1.30 am; the next floor up has a billiards hall with recorded music; the top floor has live bands playing reggae, R&B or blues from 10.30 pm to 4 am, and on Sundays there's an open jam session. There's never a cover charge at Saxophone and you don't need to dress up.

Along Sarasin Rd, north of Lumphini Park, are a number of live music pubs, including Bangkok's hottest jazz/fusion club, *Brown Sugar* (☎ 250-0103). One of Brown Sugar's top draws has been regular performances by multi-instrumentalist Tewan Sapsanyakorn, probably Thailand's top jazz performer at the moment. Tewan's fusion of international jazz and Thai folk-classical music results in exciting sounds, and his band is always top drawer. The music starts around 10 pm and ends at 1 am. National treasure Tewan also appears regularly at a new cafe-club on the ground floor of the Bangkok Palace Hotel called *Fang Dee* (☎ 253-0510) at 1091/335 New Phetburi Rd.

Other bars with regular live jazz include *The Glass* (☎ 254-3566) at 22/3-5 Soi 11 Sukhumvit Rd, *Round Midnight Pub & Restaurant* (☎ 251-0652) at 106/2 Soi Lang Suan, *Trumpet* on Soi 24 Sukhumvit Rd, and *Blues/Jazz* (☎ 258-7747) at Soi 53 Sukhumvit Rd. The Oriental's famous *Bamboo Bar* has live jazz from 5 to 8.30 pm nightly in an elegant but relaxed atmosphere; other hotel jazz bars include *Entrepreneur* at the Asia Hotel (Saturday night only), the Beaufort Sukhothai Hotel's *Colonnade* (Sunday 11 am to 3 pm) and the Hilton's *Music* bar (Friday night only).

Rock fans should check out the *Co-Bongo Bar* on Din So Rd, about 50 metres north of the Democracy Monument in Banglamphu. Decorated with an eclectic mix of pseudo-African artefacts, Southwest American Indian pottery, and surf gear, this one-of-a-kind club features a high-calibre rock and reggae group nightly from around 9.30 pm. There's a one-drink minimum but no cover.

The imaginatively named *Rock Pub*, opposite the Asia Hotel on Phayathai Rd, offers up Thai heavy metal – with plenty of hair-throwing and lip-jutting – nightly.

Eclectic *The Glass*, mentioned above with regard to jazz, also hosts pop, rock, funk and R&B bands – basically a different style each night of the week. Bangkok's better-than-average *Hard Rock Cafe* (mentioned above under bars) features live rock music most evenings from around 10 pm to 12.30 am, including the occasional big name act (Chris Isaak's incendiary 1994 performance left bootnail dents in the bar top).

Not to be overlooked on Sarasin Rd, the *Old West* (Thailand's original old-west style pub) books good Thai folk and blues groups – look for a rockin' outfit called D-Train here. The *Magic Castle* at 212/33 Sukhumvit Road (next to Soi 12) hires a variety of rock and blues acts nightly, including some of Bangkok's biggest names. The *Front Page* (Soi Sala Daeng, off Rama IV Rd) hosts journeyman folk and blues groups on weekend nights.

Discos & Dance Clubs All the major hotels in the city have international-style discotheques but only a small number of them can really be recommended as attractions in themselves. Cover charges are pretty uniform: around 150 to 200B on weekday nights, including one drink, and around 300 to 350B on weekends, including two drinks. Most places don't begin filling up till after 11 pm. Two consistently good hotel discos are the Dusit Thani's videotheque *Bubbles* (☎ 233-1130), and the Shangri-La's high-tech *Zaza Party House* (☎ 236-7777). The latter attempts to provide a more visceral sound experience through its 'bodysonic' audio system. Well-heeled Thais and Thai celebrities frequent the exclusive, high-tech *Diana's* in the Oriental Plaza off Charoen Krung Rd. The Montien Hotel's new *An-An Fun Theque* (☎ 223-7060) looks promising but it's too soon to tell whether it will take off.

Much more relaxed than the hotel discos is *Rome Club* (☎ 233-8836) at Soi 4 (Soi Jaruwan), Silom Rd, where DJs play the latest US and UK music video hits over a good sound system and huge video screen. Brief, humorous, transvestite/transsexual musical comedy revues are presented twice nightly. Rome's clientele was once predominantly gay but has become more mixed as word got around about the great dance scene.

Bangkok has several huge high-tech discos that hold up to 5000 people each and feature mega-watt sound systems, giant-screen video and the latest in light-show technology. The clientele for these dance palaces is mostly an aggro crowd of young, moneyed Thais experimenting with lifestyles of conspicuous affluence, plus the occasional Bangkok celebrity. The most 'in' discos of this nature are the *Paradise* on Arun Amarin Rd in Thonburi and the *Palace* on Vibhavadi Rangsit Highway towards the airport. Another biggie is *NASA Spaceadrome* at 999 Ramkhamhaeng Rd, which features a sci-fi theme; it's open nightly from 9 pm to 5 am. A mega-disco that gets older as well as younger Thais is the *Galaxy* on Rama IV Rd, from which WBA world boxing champions

Khaosai Galaxy and his brother Khaokor have taken their surname. The Galaxy has also become popular with visiting Japanese.

The relatively new *FM 228* (☎ 231-1228), in the United Center Building, 323 Silom Rd, tries to cover all the bases with separate rooms featuring videotheque dancing, live music, and karaoke, plus an American restaurant and bar.

Temptations, at the Novotel Hotel in Siam Square, provides big band music for *lii-lâat*, the Thai word for ballroom dancing. Every night of the week a dressed-to-the-nines crowd of Bangkok Thais cha-cha, foxtrot, tango and rumba across the glazed dance floor. In addition to serving drinks, waiters and waitresses will lead novices through the steps. The cover charge of 400B includes one drink and all the instruction necessary to turn you into a *nák lii-lâat*.

Karaoke For better or for worse, the worldwide karaoke craze has hit Bangkok with a vengeance. If your idea of fun is singing in front of inebriated strangers, the city's better KTV (video karaoke) haunts include the *Inn Place* in the Holiday Inn Crowne Plaza, 981 Silom Rd; *Cat's Eye Karaoke* at Le Meridien President Hotel on Ploenchit Rd; and the heavily computerised *Carina Club* at 789 Pattanakan Rd, off New Phetburi Rd.

Thai Dance-Drama Thailand's most traditional lakhon and khon performances are held at the National Theatre (☎ 224-1342) on Chao Fa Rd near Phra Pinklao Bridge. The theatre's regular public roster schedules six or seven performances per month, usually on weekends. Admission fees are very reasonable – around 20 to 100B depending on the seating. Attendance at a khon performance (masked dance-drama based on stories from the *Ramakian*) is highly recommended.

Occasionally, classical dance performances are also held at the Thailand Cultural Centre (☎ 245-7711), Ratchadaphisek Rd and at the College of Dramatic Arts (☎ 224-1391), near the National Theatre.

Chalermkrung Royal Theatre The 1993 renovation of this Thai Deco building at the edge of the city's Chinatown-Pahurat district provides a striking new venue for khon performance in Thailand. When originally opened in 1933, the royally funded Chalermkrung was the largest and most modern theatre in Asia, with state-of-the-art motion picture projection technology and the first chilled-water air-con system in the region.

The reborn theatre's 80,000-watt audio system, combined with computer-generated laser graphics, enable the 170-member dance troupe to present a technologically enhanced version of traditional khon. Although the special effects are reasonably impressive, the excellent costuming, set design, dancing and music are reason enough to attend.

The khon performance lasts about two

Classical dancer at the royal court

hours with intermission; when the theatre first reopened in December 1993, performances were held every Tuesday and Thursday at 8 pm, but look for this schedule to alter as the theatre feels its way through the Bangkok cultural market. Other Thai performing arts may also be scheduled at the theatre from time to time.

Khon tickets cost a steep 500, 700, 800, and 1000B. Theatre members can obtain a 200 to 300B discount on these rates; only Bangkok residents are eligible, although for once this includes foreigners as well as Thais. For ticket reservations, call ☎ 222-0434 or visit the box office in person. The theatre requests that patrons dress respectfully, which means no shorts or thongs. Bring a wrap or long-sleeved shirt in case the air-con is running full blast.

The Chalermkrung Royal Theatre stands on the corner of Charoen Krung and Triphet Rds, adjacent to the Old Siam Plaza complex and only a block from the Pahurat fabric market. Air-con bus Nos 8, 48 and 73 pass the theatre (going west on Charoen Krung). You can also comfortably walk to the theatre from the western terminus of the Saen Saep canal ferry. Taxi drivers may know the theatre by its original name, Sala Chalerm Krung, which is spelt out in Thai in the lighted sign surmounting the front of the building.

Dinner Theatres Most tourists view performances put on solely for their benefit at one of the several Thai classical dance/dinner theatres in the city (see list). Admission prices at these evening venues average 200 to 500B per person and include a 'typical' Thai dinner (often toned down for farang palates), a couple of selected dance performances and a martial arts display.

The historic Oriental Hotel has its own dinner theatre on the Thonburi side of the Chao Phraya River opposite the hotel (the Sala Rim Nam). The admission is well above average but so is the food and the performance; the river ferry between the hotel and restaurant is free. The much less expensive dinner performance at Silom Village's Ruen

Thep restaurant on Silom Rd is recommended because of the relaxed, semi-outdoor setting.

Baan Thai Restaurant
  7 Soi 32, Sukhumvit Rd (☎ 258-5403)
Chao Phraya Restaurant
  Phra Pinklao Bridge (☎ 474-2389)
Maneeya's Lotus Room
  Ploenchit Rd (☎ 252-6312)
Phiman Restaurant
  46 Soi 49, Sukhumvit Rd (☎ 258-7866)
Ruen Thep
  Silom Village, Silom Rd (☎ 233-9447)
Sala Norasing
  Soi 4, Sukhumvit Rd (☎ 251-5797)
Sala Rim Nam
  opposite Oriental Hotel, Charoen Nakhon Rd
  (☎ 437-6221/3080)
Suwannahong Restaurant
  Si Ayuthaya Rd (☎ 245-4448/3747)
Tum-Nak-Thai Restaurant
  131 Ratchadaphisek Rd (☎ 277-3828)

Shrine Dancing Free performances of traditional lakhon chatrii dance can be seen daily at the Lak Meuang and Erawan shrines if you happen to arrive when a performance troupe has been commissioned by a worshipper. Although many of the dance movements are the same as those seen in classical lakhon, these relatively crude performances are specially choreographed for ritual purposes and don't represent true classical dance forms. But the dancing is colourful – the dancers wear full costume and are accompanied by live music – so it's worth stopping by to watch a performance if you're in the vicinity. For more information on Thai classical dance see the Arts section in the Facts about the Country chapter.

Thai Boxing *Muay thai* (Thai boxing) can be seen at two boxing stadiums, Lumphini (on Rama IV Rd near Sathon Tai (South) Rd) and Ratchadamnoen (on Ratchadamnoen Nok Rd, next to the TAT office). Admission fees vary according to seating: the cheapest seats in Bangkok are now around 170B and ringside seats cost 500B or more. Monday, Wednesday, Thursday and Sunday, the boxing is at Ratchadamnoen, while Tuesday, Friday and Saturday it's at Lumphini. The Ratchadamnoen matches begin at 6 pm, except for the Sunday shows which start at 5 pm, and the Lumphini matches all begin at 6.20 pm. Aficionados say the best-matched bouts are reserved for Tuesday nights at Lumphini and Thursday nights at Ratchadamnoen. The restaurants on the north side of Ratchadamnoen stadium are well known for their delicious kài yâang and other north-eastern dishes. (For more information on Thai boxing see the Sport section in the Facts about the Country chapter.)

Massage Parlours Massage parlours have been a Bangkok attraction for many years now, though the Tourist Authority of Thailand (TAT) tries to discourage the city's reputation in this respect. Massage as a healing art is a centuries-old tradition in Thailand, and it is possible to get a really legitimate massage in Bangkok – despite the commercialisation of recent years. That many of the modern massage parlours (*àap òp nûat* or 'bathe-steam-massage' in Thai) also deal in prostitution is well known; less well known is the fact that many (but by no means all) of the girls working in the parlours are bonded labour – they are not necessarily there by choice.

All but the most insensitive males will be saddened by the sight of 50 girls/women behind a glass wall with numbers pinned to their dresses. Often the bank of masseuses is divided into sections according to skill and/or appearance. Most expensive is the 'superstar' section, in which the women try to approximate the look of fashion models or actresses. A smaller section is reserved for women who are actually good at giving massages, with no hanky-panky on the side.

Before contemplating anything more than a massage at a modern massage parlour, be sure to read the Health section in the Facts for the Visitor chapter for information on sexually transmitted diseases. There is a definite AIDS presence in Thailand; condom use lowers the risk considerably, but remember that an estimated 11% of commercial Thai condoms are barrier-defective.

Traditional Massage Traditional Thai massage, also called 'ancient' massage, is now widely available in Bangkok as an alternative to the red-light massage parlours. One of the best places to experience a traditional massage is at *Wat Pho*, Bangkok's oldest temple. Massage here costs 180B per hour or 90B for half an hour. There is also a 30-hour course in Thai massage which can be attended three hours per day for 10 days, or two hours per day for 15 days. Tuition for the course is 3000B. You must also pay the regular 10B per day admission fee for Wat Pho whether you are a student or massagee.

Other places to get traditional Thai massage in Bangkok include *Buathip Thai Massage* (☎ 255-1045) at 4/13 Soi 5, Sukhumvit Rd; *Marble House* (☎ 235-3519) at 37/18-19 Soi Surawong Plaza; *SL* (☎ 237-5690) on the 10th floor of Silom-Surawong Condos, 176 Soi Anuman Ratchathon, off Silom Rd Soi 6; and *Winwan* (☎ 251-7467) between sois 1 and 3, Sukhumvit Rd.

Fees for traditional Thai massage should be no more than 150B per hour, though some places have a 1½-hour minimum. Be aware that not every place advertising traditional or ancient massage offers a really good one; sometimes the only thing 'ancient' about the pommelling is the age of the masseuse or masseur. Thai massage aficionados say that the best massages are given by blind masseurs (available at Marble House).

Most hotels also provide legitimate massage service either through their health clubs or as part of room service. The highly praised *Oriental Hotel Spa* offers a 40-minute 'jet lag massage' designed to alleviate body-clock time differences.

Cinema Dozens of movie theatres around town show Thai, Chinese, Indian and occasionally Western movies. The majority of films shown are comedies and shoot-em-ups, with the occasional drama slipping through. These theatres are air-con and quite comfortable, with reasonable rates (20 to 60B). All movies in Thai theatres are preceded by the Thai royal anthem along with projected pictures of King Bhumibol and other members of the royal family. Everyone in the theatre stands quietly and respectfully for the duration of the anthem (written by the king, incidentally).

The main theatres showing commercial English-language films are *Center 1 & 2* at Siam Center; *Scala, Lido* and *Siam* at Siam Square; *Major 1 & 2* at Mahboonkrong; *Century 1 & 2* and *Mackenna* on Phayathai Rd; and the *Washington 1 & 2* at Soi 24 Sukhumvit Rd. Movie ads appear daily in both the *Nation* and the *Bangkok Post*; listings in the *Nation* include addresses and programme times.

Foreign films are often altered before distribution by Thailand's board of censors; usually this involves obscuring nude sequences with Vaseline 'screens'. Some distributors also edit films they consider to be too long; occasionally Thai narration is added to explain the storyline (when *The Omen* was released in Thailand, distributors chopped off the ambiguous ending and added a voice-over, giving the film a 'new' ending).

Film snobs may prefer the weekly or twice-weekly offerings at Bangkok's foreign cultural clubs. French and German films screened at the cultural clubs are almost always subtitled in English. Admission is sometimes free, sometimes 30 to 40B. For addresses and phone numbers see the Cultural Centres section earlier in this chapter.

Video Video rentals are very popular in Bangkok; not only are videos cheaper than regular film admissions, but many films are available on video that aren't approved for theatre distribution by Thailand's board of censors. For those with access to a TV and VCR, the average rental is around 20 to 30B. Sukhumvit Rd has the highest concentration of video shops; the better ones are found in the residential area between sois 39 and 55.

Things to Buy
Regular visitors to Asia know that, in many ways, Bangkok beats Hong Kong and Singapore for deals on handicrafts, textiles, gems, jewellery, art and antiques – nowhere else

will you find the same combination of selection, quality and prices. The trouble is finding the good spots, as the city's intense urban tangle makes orientation sometimes difficult. Nancy Chandler's *Map of Bangkok*, which was originally intended as a guide to the city's markets and shopping venues (but includes much more these days), makes a very good buying companion, with annotations on all sorts of small, out-of-the-way shopping venues.

Be sure to re-read the introductory Things to Buy section in the Facts for the Visitor chapter before setting out on a buying spree. Amidst all the bargains are a number of cleverly disguised rip-off schemes – *caveat emptor*!

The Thai word for 'market' is *tàlàat*.

Weekend Market Also known as Chatuchak Market, this is the Disneyland of Thai markets. Everything is sold here, from live chickens and snakes to opium pipes and herbal remedies. Thai clothing such as the phaakhamaa (sarong for men) and the phaasin (sarong for women), *kaang keng jiin* (Chinese pants) and *sêua mâw hâwm* (blue cotton farmer's shirt) are good buys. You'll also find musical instruments, hill-tribe crafts, religious amulets, antiques, flowers, clothes imported from India and Nepal, camping gear and military surplus. The best bargains of all are household goods like pots and pans, dishes, drinking glasses, etc. If you're moving to Thailand for an extended period, this is the place to pick up stuff for your kitchen. Don't forget to try out your bargaining skills. There is plenty of interesting and tasty food for sale if you're feeling hungry. And if you need some cash, a couple of banks have ATMs and foreign-exchange booths at the Chatuchak Park offices, near the north end of the market's sois 1, 2 and 3.

An unfortunate footnote to add is that Chatuchak Park remains an important hub of Thailand's illegal exotic wildlife trade – in spite of occasional police raids – as well as a conduit for endangered species from surrounding countries. Some species are sold for their exotic food value, eg barking deer, wild boar, crocodiles and pangolins, while some are sold for their supposed medicinal value, eg rare leaf-monkeys. Thai laws protect most of these species, but Thais are notorious scofflaws. Not all wildlife trade here is illicit though; many of the birds sold, including the hill mynah and zebra dove, have been legally raised for sale as pets.

The main part of the Weekend Market is open on Saturday and Sunday from around 8 am to 8 pm. There are a few vendors out on weekday mornings and a daily vegetables/plants/flowers market opposite the market's south side. One section of the latter, known as the Aw Taw Kaw Market, sells organically grown (no chemical sprays or fertilisers) fruits and vegetables.

The Weekend Market lies at the southern end of Chatuchak Park, off Phahonyothin Rd and across from the northern (Maw Chit) bus terminal. Air-con bus Nos 2, 3, 9, 10 and 13, and a dozen other ordinary city buses, all pass the market – just get off before the northern bus terminal. The air-con bus No 12 and ordinary bus No 77 conveniently terminate right next to the market.

Flower Markets & Nurseries A good selection of tropical flowers and plants is available at the Thewet Market near the Tha Thewet pier on Krung Kasem Rd to the north-west of Banglamphu. The city's largest wholesale flower source is Pak Khlong Market on the right bank of the Chao Phraya River at the mouth of Khlong Lawt, between Atsadang Rd and Memorial Bridge. Pak Khlong is also a big market for vegetables. The newest and largest plant market is opposite the south side of Chatuchak Market (the 'Weekend Market'), near the northern bus terminal off Phahonyothin Rd; unlike the Chatuchak market it's open all week long. It's sometimes called 'Talaat Phahonyothin' or Phahonyothin Market.

The best area for nursery plants, including Thailand's world-famous orchid varieties, is Thonburi's Phasi Charoen district, which is accessible via the Phetkasem Highway north of Khlong Phasi Charoen itself. The latter is linked to the Chao Phraya River via Khlong

Bangkok Yai. Two places with good selections are Eima Orchid Co (☎ 454-0366; fax 454-1156) at 999/9 Mu 2, Bang Khae, Phasi Charoen, and Botanical Gardens Bangkok (☎ 467-4955) at 6871 Kuhasawan, Phasi Charoen. Ordinary bus Nos 7 and 80, plus air-con bus No 9, stop in Phasi Charoen district.

Other Markets Under the expressway at the intersection of Rama IV and Narong Rds in the Khlong Toey district is the Khlong Toey Market, possibly the cheapest all-purpose market in Bangkok (best on Wednesday). South of the Khlong Toey Market, closer to the port, is the similar Penang Market, so called because a lot of the goods 'drop off' cargo boats from Penang (and Singapore, Hong Kong, etc).

Pratunam Market, at the intersection of Phetburi and Ratchaprarop Rds, runs every day and is very crowded, but has great deals in new, cheap clothing.

The huge Banglamphu Market spreads several blocks over Chakraphong, Phra Sumen, Tanao and Rambutri Rds – a short walk from the Khao San Rd guesthouse area. The Banglamphu market area is probably the most comprehensive shopping district in the city as it encompasses everything from street vendors to up-market department stores. Also in this part of Bangkok you'll find the Thewet flower market (see Flower Markets & Nurseries above).

The Pahurat and Chinatown districts have interconnected markets selling tons of well-priced fabrics, clothes and household wares, as well as a few places selling gems and jewellery. The Wong Wian Yai Market in Thonburi, next to the large roundabout *(wong wian yài* means 'big circle') directly south-west of Memorial Bridge (Saphaan Phut), is another all-purpose market – but this one rarely gets tourists.

Shopping Centres & Department Stores The growth of large and small shopping centres has accelerated over the last few years into a virtual boom. Central and Robinson department stores, the original

stand-bys, have branches in the Sukhumvit and Silom areas with all the usual stuff – designer clothes, Western cosmetics – plus supermarkets and Thai delis, cassette tapes, fabrics and other local products that might be of interest to some travellers.

Oriental Plaza (Soi Oriental, Charoen Krung Rd) and River City shopping complex (near the Royal Orchid Sheraton, off Charoen Krung and Si Phraya Rds) are centres for high-end consumer goods. They're expensive but do have some unique merchandise; River City has two floors specialising in art and antiques.

The much smaller Silom Village Trade Centre on Silom Rd has a few antique and handicraft shops with merchandise several rungs lower in price. Anchored by Central Department Store, the six-storey Silom Complex nearby remains one of the city's busiest shopping centres. Also on Silom Rd is the posh Thaniya Plaza, a newer arcade housing clothing boutiques, bookshops, jewellery shops and more.

Along Ploenchit and Sukhumvit Rds you'll find many newer department stores and shopping centres, including Sogo, Landmark Plaza and Times Square, but these Tokyo clones tend to be expensive and not that exciting. Peninsula Plaza on Ratchadamri Rd (named after the Bangkok Peninsula Hotel, which has since changed its name to the Regent Bangkok) has a more exclusive selection of shops – many of which have branches at River City and Oriental Plaza – and a good-sized branch of Asia Books.

Another high-end shopping complex is the new World Trade Center near the intersection of Ploenchit and Phayathai Rds; its eight floors seem to go on, wing after wing, with no end in sight. The main focus is the Zen Department Store, which has clothing shops reminiscent of Hong Kong's high-end boutiques. On the 8th floor is Bangkok's premier antidote to the tropics, the World Ice Skating Center. If you're looking for clothing or toys for kids, ABC Babyland on WTC's 2nd floor has just about everything. Asia Books has recently opened a branch in the WTC and more shops are opening as a new wing is being added.

Siam Square, on Rama I Rd near Phayathai Rd, is a network of some 12 sois lined with shops selling mid-priced designer clothes, books, sporting goods and antiques. On the opposite side of Rama I stands Thailand's first shopping centre, the four-storey, 20-year-old Siam Center. It's still going strong, with designer clothing shops – Benetton, Chaps, Esprit, Chanel, Jaspal, Anne Cole, Guy Laroche and Paul Smith to name a few – as well as coffee shops, travel agencies, banks and airline offices.

One of the most varied shopping centres to wander around is the Mahboonkrong (MBK) centre near Siam Square. It's all aircon, but there are many small, inexpensive vendors and shops in addition to the flashy Tokyu department store. Bargains can be found here if you look. The Travel Mart on MBK's 3rd floor stocks a reasonable supply of travel gear and camping equipment – not the highest quality but useful in a pinch.

North of Siam Square on Phetburi Rd, Phanthip Plaza specialises in shops selling computer equipment and software. Until 1992 or so bootleg software was abundant here; some of the shops still knock off a few pirated programmes under the counter.

Old Siam Plaza, bounded by Charoen Krung, Burapha, Pahurat and Triphet Rds, is the first new development of any significance in the Chinatown-Pahurat area in over a decade. Along with the renovation and reopening of the adjacent Chalermkrung Royal Theatre, the old Bangkok-style shopping centre represents a minor renaissance for an otherwise shabby and congested district. Most of the shops purvey Thai-style goods or services; one whole side is devoted to gun dealers, another to gem and jewellery stores, the rest to Thai handicrafts, furniture, restaurants and coffee shops. The only establishments without a Thai theme are McDonald's and Furama, a Japanese restaurant.

Antiques & Decorative Items Real Thai antiques are rare and costly. Most Bangkok antique shops keep a few antiques around for collectors, along with lots of pseudo-antiques or traditionally crafted items that look like antiques. The majority of shop operators are quite candid about what's really old and what isn't. As Thai design becomes more popular abroad, many shops are now specialising in Thai home decorative items.

Reliable antique shops (using the word 'antiques' loosely) include Elephant House (☎ 266-2780) at 67/12 Soi Phra Phinit, Soi Suan Phlu; Peng Seng, on the corner of Rama IV and Surawong Rds; Asian Heritage, at 57 Soi 23, Sukhumvit Rd; Thai House, 720/6 Sukhumvit Rd, near Soi 28; and Artisan's in the Silom Village Trade Centre, Silom Rd. The River City and Oriental Plaza shopping complexes also have several good, if pricey, antique shops.

Gems & Jewellery Recommending specific shops is tricky, since to the average eye one coloured stone looks as good as another, so the risk of a rip-off is much greater than for most other popular shopping items. One shop that's been a long-time favourite with Bangkok expats for service and value in set jewellery is Johnny's Gems (☎ 222-1756) at 199 Fuang Nakhon Rd (off Charoen Krung Rd). Another reputable jewellery place is Merlin et Delauney (☎ 234-3884), with a large showroom and lapidary at 1 Soi Pradit, Surawong Rd and a smaller shop at the Novotel Hotel, Soi 6, Siam Square. Both of the foregoing also have unset stones as well as jewellery; two dependable places that specialise in unset stones are Lambert International (☎ 236-4343) at 807 Silom Rd, and Thai Lapidary (☎ 214-2641), at 277/122 Rama I Rd.

Bronzeware Thailand has the oldest bronze-working tradition in the world and there are several factories in Bangkok producing bronze sculpture and cutlery. Two factories that sell direct to the public (and where you may also be able to observe the bronze-working process) are Siam Bronze Factory (☎ 234-9436), at 1250 Charoen Krung Rd;

and SN Thai Bronze Factory (☎ 215-7743), at 157-33 Phetburi Rd. Make sure any items you buy are silicon-coated, otherwise they'll tarnish. To see the casting process for Buddha images, go to the Buddha-Casting Foundry next to Wat Wiset Khan on Phrannok Rd, Thonburi (take a river ferry from Tha Phra Chan or Tha Maharat on the Bangkok side to reach the foot of Phrannok Rd).

Many vendors at Wat Mahathat's Sunday market sell old and new bronzeware – haggling is imperative.

Handicrafts Bangkok has excellent buys in Thai handicrafts, though for northern hill-tribe materials you might be able to do better in Chiang Mai. Narayana Phand (☎ 252-4670) on Ratchadamri Rd, is a bit on the touristy side but has a large selection and good marked prices – no haggling is necessary. Central Department Store on Ploenchit Rd has a Thai handicrafts section with marked prices.

Two royally sponsored outlets where profits go directly to hill tribes and villages are the Hill Tribe Foundation (☎ 351-9816) at 195 Phayathai Rd, and the Chitlada Shop (☎ 281-4558), Chitlada Palace, Rama V Rd. Lao Song Handicrafts (☎ 311-2277), 2/56 Soi 41, Sukhumvit Rd, is another self-help project selling village handiwork.

Old man's hollow dragon bracelet, Akha hill tribe

International School Bangkok (ISB) (☎ 583-5401/28), at 39/7 Soi Nichadathani Samakhi, puts on a large charity sale of Thai handicrafts every sixth Saturday or so (except during ISB's summer holiday, June to August). Sometimes you can find pieces at the ISB craft sales that are practically unavailable elsewhere. At other times it's not very interesting; it all depends on what the sale managers are able to collect during the year. Call for the latest sale schedule. ISB is north of the city proper, towards the airport, off Route 304 (Chaeng Wattana Rd) on the way to Pak Kret, inside the Nichada Thani condo/townhouse complex.

Perhaps the most interesting places to shop for handicrafts are the smaller, independent handicraft shops – each of which has its own style and character. Quality is high and prices reasonable at Rasi Sayam (☎ 258-4195), 32 Soi 23, Sukhumvit Rd; many of the items they carry – including wall-hangings and pottery – are made specifically for this shop. Another good one for pottery as well as lacquerware and fabrics (especially the latter) is Vilai's (☎ 391-6106) at 731/1 Soi 55 (Thong Lor), Sukhumvit Rd.

Nandakwang (☎ 258-1962), 108/3 Soi 23 (Soi Prasanmit), is a branch of a factory shop of the same name in Pasang, northern Thailand; high-quality woven cotton clothing and household wares (tablecloths, napkins, etc) are their speciality. Prayer Textile Gallery (☎ 251-7549), a small shop on the edge of Siam Square facing Phayathai Rd, stocks a nice selection of new and antique textiles – in both ready-to-wear original fashions or in traditional rectangular lengths – from Thailand, Laos, and Cambodia.

Khon (Thai classical dance-drama) masks of intricately formed wire and papier mâché can be purchased at Padung Chiip (no English sign) on Chakraphong Rd just south of the Khao San Rd intersection. For Thai celadon, check Celadon House at 18/7 Soi 21 (Soi Asoke), Sukhumvit Rd. An inexpensive place to pick up new Thai pottery of all shapes and sizes is the Dutch-managed Waraporn Thai Pottery (☎ 375-7746), at 37/1 Sukhaphiban 2 Rd, Bang Kapi.

Camera Supplies, Film & Processing For a selection of camera supplies across a wide range of models and brand names, two of the best shops are AV Camera (☎ 234-4786) at 301/2 Silom Rd and Sunny Camera (☎ 233-8378 at 1267/1 Charoen Krung Rd, ☎ 237-2054 at 134/5-6 Soi 8 Silom Rd, ☎ 217-9293, 3rd floor, Mahboonkrong Center).

Both slide and print films are widely available in Bangkok, although the highest concentration of photo shops can be found along Silom and Surawong Rds. Quick, professional-quality processing of most film types is available at E6 Processing Centre (☎ 258-4590) at 59/10 Soi 31 Sukhumvit Rd, IQ Lab (☎ 238-4001) at 60 Silom Rd, Berlin Color Lab (☎ 234-4385) at 197/7 Surawong, and Supertouch (☎ 235-4711) at 35/12 Soi Yommarat, Sala Daeng Rd.

Getting There & Away

Air Bangkok is a major centre for international flights throughout Asia, and Bangkok's airport is a busy one. Bangkok is also a major centre for buying discounted airline tickets (see the Getting There & Away chapter for details), but be warned that the Bangkok travel agency business has more than a few crooked operators. Domestic flights operated by THAI and Bangkok Airways also fan out from Bangkok all over the country. Addresses of airline offices in Bangkok are:

Aeroflot
    183 Mezzanine floor, Regent House, Ratchadamri Rd (☎ 251-1223; reservations ☎ 251-0617)
Air France
    Ground floor, Chan Issara Tower, 942/51 Rama IV Rd (☎ 234-1330/9; reservations ☎ 234-9477)
Air India
    16th floor, Amarin Tower, Ploenchit Rd (☎ 256-9620; reservations ☎ 256-9614/8)
Air Lanka
    Chan Issara Tower 942/34-5 Rama IV Rd (☎ 236-4981, 235-4982)
Air New Zealand
    1053 Charoen Krung Rd (☎ 233-5900/9, 237-1560/2)

Alitalia
    8th floor, Boonmitr Bldg, 138 Silom Rd (☎ 233-4000/4)
All Nippon Airways (ANA)
    2nd floor, CP Tower, 313 Silom Rd (☎ 238-5121)
Asiana Airlines
    14th floor, BB Bldg, 54 Soi Asoke (☎ 260-7700/4)
Bangkok Airways
    Queen Sirikit National Convention Centre, New Ratchadaphisek Rd, Khlong Toey (☎ 229-3434)
Biman Bangladesh
    Chongkolnee Building, 56 Surawong Rd (☎ 235-7643/4, 234-0300/9)
British Airways
    Chan Issara Tower, Rama IV Rd (☎ 236-8655/8)
Cambodia International Airlines
    Queen Sirikit National Convention Centre, New Ratchadaphisek Rd, Khlong Toey (☎ 229-3387/9)
Canadian Airlines International
    Maneeya Bldg, 518/5 Ploenchit Rd (251-4521, 254-8376)
Cathay Pacific Airways
    Chan Issara Tower, Rama IV Rd (☎ 235-4330; reservations ☎ 233-6105/9)
China Airlines
    Peninsula Plaza, Ratchadamri Rd (☎ 253-5733; reservations ☎ 253-4438)
China Southern Airlines (formerly CAAC)
    134/1-2 Silom Rd (☎ 235-1880/2, 235-8159)
Czechoslovak Airlines
    2nd floor, Regent House, Ratchadamri Rd (☎ 254-3921/5)
Delta Air Lines
    7th floor, Patpong Bldg, 1 Surawong Rd (☎ 237-6855; reservations ☎ 237-6838)
Druk Air (see Thai Airways International)
EgyptAir
    3rd floor, CP Tower, 313 Silom Rd (☎ 231-0505/8)
Finnair
    Maneeya Bldg, 518/2 Ploenchit Rd (☎ 251-5445; reservations ☎ 251-5012)
Garuda Indonesia
    27th floor, Lumphini Tower, 1168 Rama IV Rd (☎ 285-6470/3)
Gulf Air
    Maneeya Bldg, 518/2 Ploenchit Rd (☎ 254-7931/40)
Japan Airlines
    33/33-4 Wall Street Tower, Surawong Rd (☎ 234-9111; reservations ☎ 233-2440)
KLM Royal Dutch Airlines
    2 Patpong Rd (☎ 235-5150/4, 235-5155/9)
Korean Air
    Kongboonma Bldg, 699 Silom Rd (☎ 234-0957; reservations ☎ 235-9221/6)

Kuwait Airways
159 Ratchadamri Rd (☎ 251-5855)
Lao Aviation
Silom Plaza, Silom Rd (☎ 236-9822)
Lauda Air
33/33-4 Wall Street Tower, Surawong Rd (☎ 233-2565)
LOT Polish Airlines
485/11-12 Silom Rd (☎ 235-2223)
Lufthansa
Bank of America Bldg, 2/2 Wireless Rd (☎ 255-0370)
Malaysian Airlines
98-102 Surawong Rd (☎ 236-5871; reservations ☎ 236-4705/9)
Myanmar Airways
48/5 Pan Rd (☎ 233-3052, 234-9692)
Northwest Airlines
Silom Plaza, 491/39 Silom Rd (☎ 253-4822)
Landmark Plaza, 138 Sukhumvit Rd (☎ 253-4822/4423)
Peninsula Plaza, 153 Ratchadamri Rd (☎ 254-0789, 253-4822)
Pakistan International Airlines
52 Surawong Rd (☎ 234-2961, 233-5215)
Philippine Airlines
Chongkolnee Bldg, 56 Surawong Rd (☎ 233-2350/2)
Silk Air
12th floor, Silom Centre Bldg, Silom Rd (☎ 236-0303)
Qantas
Chan Issara Tower, 942/51 Rama IV Rd (☎ 236-9193/5, 237-6268)
Royal Brunei Airlines
2nd floor, Chan Issara Tower, 942/52 Rama IV Rd (☎ 235-4764)
Royal Jordanian Airlines
Yada Bldg, 56 Silom Rd (☎ 236-0030)
Royal Nepal Airlines
Sivadon Bldg, 1/4 Convent Rd (☎ 233-3921/4)
Sabena Belgian World Airlines
3rd floor, CP Tower, 313 Silom Rd (☎ 238-2201)
Scandinavian Airlines System (SAS)
Soi 25, Sukhumvit Rd (☎ 260-0444)
Saudi Arabian Airlines
Ground floor, CCT Bldg, 109 Surawong Rd (☎ 236-9400/3)
Silk Air
12th floor, Silom Centre Bldg, Silom Rd (☎ 236-0303; reservations ☎ 236-0440)
Singapore Airlines
12th floor, Silom Center Bldg, 2 Silom Rd (☎ 236-0303; reservations ☎ 236-0440)
Swissair
1 Silom Rd (☎ 233-2930/4; reservations ☎ 233-2935/8)

TAROM Romanian Air Transport
89/12 Bangkok Bazaar, Ratchadamri Rd (☎ 253-1681)
Thai Airways International (THAI; also agent for Druk Air)
89 Vibhavadi Rangsit Rd (☎ 513-0121; reservations ☎ 233-3810)
485 Silom Rd (☎ 234-3100/19)
6 Lan Luang Rd (☎ 288-0070/80/90)
Asia Hotel, 296 Phayathai Rd (☎ 215-2020/4)
United Airlines
9th floor, Regent House, 183 Ratchadamri Rd (☎ 253-0558)
Vietnam Airlines (Hang Khong Vietnam)
3rd floor, 572 Ploenchit Rd (☎ 251-4242)
Yunnan Airways
CTC Hainan Aviation & Tourism, Asia Hotel Frontage, Shopping Arcade, 296 Phayathai Rd (☎ 216-3328)

Bus Bangkok is the centre for bus services that fan out all over the kingdom. There are basically three types of long-distance buses. First there are the ordinary public buses, then the air-con public buses. The third choice is the many private air-con services which leave from various offices and hotels all over the city and provide a deluxe service for those people for whom simple air-con isn't enough!

Public Bus There are three main public bus stations. The northern/north-eastern terminal (☎ 279-4484/7) is on Phahonyothin Rd on the way up to the airport. It's also commonly called the Moh Chit station (sathǎanii mǎw chít). Buses depart here for north and north-eastern destinations like Chiang Mai and Khorat, as well as places closer to Bangkok such as Ayuthaya and Lopburi. Buses to Aranyaprathet also go from here, not from the eastern bus terminal as you might expect. Air-con city buses Nos 2, 3, 9, 10, 29 and 39, along with a dozen or more ordinary city buses, all pass the terminal.

The eastern bus terminal (☎ 391-2504 ordinary; ☎ 391-9829 air-con), the departure point for buses to Pattaya, Rayong, Chanthaburi and other points east, is a long way out along Sukhumvit Rd, at Soi 40 (Soi Ekamai) opposite Soi 63. Most folks call it Ekamai station (sathǎanii èk-amai). Air-con bus Nos 1, 8, 11 and 12 all pass this station.

The southern bus terminal (☎ 434-5558 ordinary, 391-9829 air-con) for buses south to Phuket, Surat Thani and closer centres like Nakhon Pathom and Kanchanaburi, now has one Thonburi location for both ordinary and air-con buses at the intersection of Highway 338 (Nakhon Chaisi Rd) and Phra Pinklao Rd. A convenient way to reach the station is by air-con city bus No 7, which terminates here.

When travelling on night buses take care of your belongings. Some of the long-distance buses leaving from Bangkok now issue claim checks for luggage stored under the bus, but valuables are still best kept on your person or within reach.

Private Bus The more reputable private tour buses leave from the public (Baw Khaw Saw) terminals listed above. Some private bus companies arrange pick-ups at Khao San Rd and other guesthouse areas – these pick-ups are illegal since it's against municipal law to carry passengers within the city limits except en route to or from an official terminal. This is why the curtains on these buses are sometimes closed when picking up passengers.

Although fares tend to be lower on private buses, the incidence of reported theft is far greater than on the Baw Khaw Saw buses. They are also generally – but not always – less reliable, promising services (such as air-con or VIP seats) that they don't deliver. For safer, more reliable, and more punctual service, stick to buses which leave from the official Baw Khaw Saw terminals.

See the Getting Around chapter for more information about bus travel in Thailand. Also, for details on bus fares to/from other towns and cities in Thailand, see the Getting There & Away sections under each place.

Train Bangkok is the terminus for rail services to the south, north and north-east. There are two main train stations. The big Hualamphong station on Rama IV Rd handles services to the north, north-east and some of the southern services. The Thonburi (Bangkok Noi) station handles a few ser-

vices to the south. If you're heading south, make sure you know which station your train departs from. See the Train section in the Getting Around chapter for further details on which southern lines correspond to which stations.

Getting Around

Getting around in Bangkok may be difficult at first for the uninitiated but once you're familiar with the bus system the whole city is accessible. The main obstacle is traffic, which moves at a snail's pace during much of the day. This means advance planning is a must when you are attending scheduled events or arranging appointments.

If you can travel by river or canal from one point to another, it's always the best choice. Bangkok was once called the 'Venice of the East', but much of the original canal system has been filled in for road construction; with 10% of Thailand's population living in the capital, water transportation, with a few exceptions, has been relegated to a secondary role. Larger canals, especially on the Thonburi side, remain important commercial arteries but many of the smaller canals are hopelessly polluted and would probably have been filled in by now if it weren't for their important drainage function.

Bus You can save a lot of money in Bangkok by sticking to the public buses, which are 2.50B for any journey under 10 km on the ordinary blue or smaller green buses, 3.50B on the red buses or 6B for the first eight km on the air-con lines. The fare on ordinary buses is 4B for longer trips (eg from Chulalongkorn University to King Mongkut's Institute of Technology in Thonburi on bus No 21) and as high as 16B for air-con buses (eg from Silom Rd to Bangkok Airport on air-con bus No 4). The air-con buses are not only cooler, but are usually less crowded (all bets are off during rush hours).

One air-con bus service that's never overcrowded is the new red Microbus, which stops boarding passengers once every seat is filled. They collect a 15B flat fare – you deposit the money in a box at the front of the bus rather than wait for an attendant to come around and collect it. Newspapers (usually Thai papers only, occasionally a *Thailand Times*) are available on the Microbus. A couple of useful Microbus lines include the No 6, which starts on Si Phraya Rd (near the River City complex) and proceeds to the Mahboonkrong-Siam Square area, then out to Sukhumvit Rd (and vice versa); and the No 1, which runs between the Victory Monument area and Banglamphu district.

Bus Maps To do any serious bus riding you'll need a Bangkok bus map – the easiest to read is the *Bangkok Bus Map (Walking Tours)* published by Bangkok Guide, or Thaveepholcharoen's *Bangkok Thailand Tour'n Guide Map*. If you plan to do a lot of bus riding, the Bangkok Bus Map is the more accurate, but Tour'n Guide Map also has a decent map of the whole country on the flip side. The bus numbers are clearly marked in red, with air-con buses in larger type. Don't expect the routes to be 100% correct, a few will have changed since the maps last came out, but they'll get you where you're going most of the time. These maps usually retail for 35B or sometimes 40B. A more complete 113-page *Bus Guide* is available in some bookshops and newsstands for 35B, but it's not as easy to use as the bus maps.

Bus Safety Be careful with your belongings while riding Bangkok buses. The place you are most likely to be 'touched' is on the crowded ordinary buses. Razor artists abound, particularly on buses in the Hualamphong train station area. These dextrous thieves specialise in slashing your backpack, shoulder bag or even your trouser pockets with a sharp razor and slipping your valuables out unnoticed. Hold your bag in front of you, under your attention, and carry money in a front shirt pocket, preferably (as the Thais do) maintaining a tactile and visual sensitivity to these areas if the bus is packed shoulder to shoulder. Seasoned travellers don't need this advice, as the same precautions are useful all over the world – the trick is to be relaxed but aware (not tense).

Taxi Metered taxis were finally introduced in Bangkok in 1993, and by March 1994 there were 29,000 metered and 13,500 non-metered taxis on city streets. Fares for metered taxis are always lower than for non-metered, the only problem being that they can be a little harder to flag down during peak commuter hours. Demand often outstrips supply from 8 to 9 am and 6 to 7 pm, also late at night when the bars are closing (1 to 2 am). Because metered-taxi drivers use rented vehicles and must return them at the end of their shifts, they sometimes won't take longer fares as quitting time nears.

Metered taxis charge 35B at flagfall for the first two km, then 2B for each half-km increment thereafter when the cab travels at six km/h or more; at speeds under five km/h, a surcharge of 1B per minute kicks in. Freeway tolls – 20 to 40B depending on where you start – must be paid by the passenger. Since the introduction of metered cabs (called 'taxi meter' or *tháeksii miitôe* in Thai), the average passenger fare has dropped considerably. An airport trip from Siam Square, for example, previously cost 150 to 200B (depending on your negotiation skills) in a non-metered cab; the typical meter fare for the same trip is now around 115B. A jaunt to Silom Rd from the same area that previously cost 50 or 60B is now in the neighbourhood of 33B.

A 24-hour 'phone-a-cab' service (☎ 319-9911) is available for an extra 10B over the regular metered fare. This is only really necessary if you're in an area where there aren't a lot of cabs; residents who live down long sois are the main clientele. Previously such residents had to catch a motorcycle taxi or 'baht bus' to the *pàak soi* ('soi mouth', where a soi meets a larger street).

For those times when you're forced to use a non-metered cab, you'll have to negotiate the fare. It's no use telling non-metered cab drivers what a comparable metered trip would cost – they know you wouldn't be wasting your time with them if a metered cab were available. Fares to most places within central Bangkok are 60 to 70B – you should add 10B or so if you're using it during rush

Future Traffic Alternatives

At times, Bangkok's traffic situation seems quite hopeless. An estimated three million vehicles (a figure rising by 1000 per day) crawl through the streets at an average of 13 km/h during commuter hours, and nearly half the municipal traffic police are undergoing treatment for respiratory ailments! It's estimated that the typical Bangkok motorist spends a cumulative 44 days per year in traffic; petrol stations throughout the capital sell the Comfort 100, a portable potty that allows motorists to relieve themselves in their own vehicles during traffic jams. Cellular phones, TVs and food warmers are other commonplace auto accessories among wealthier drivers.

Several mass transit systems (which are either in the planning or very early construction phases) promise much-needed 'decongestion'. The one most likely to be completed first is the Bangkok Metropolitan Authority's (BMA) light rail system, about two-thirds of which will be elevated (Khlong Toey to Lat Phrao via Ratchadaphisek) and a third underground (Hualamphong to Khlong Toey). This project has undergone so many reroutings (initially the north-south leg was to run parallel to Ratchaprarop, Ratchadamri and Sathon Tai Rds) that it's difficult to say with any certainty whether it will ever actually get off the ground. The BMA also plans to add several more elevated expressways; sceptics say building more roadways will simply encourage Bangkokians to buy more cars.

The much ballyhooed Skytrain network, a more extensive elevated rail project that was proposed in 1986, has gone from contractor to contractor and now seems dead in the water. If revived, the plan is to have two Skytrain lines, Phrakhanong-Bang Seu (23 km) and Sathon-Lat Phrao (11 km), with two more lines in each direction to follow. A third contract was awarded to Hong Kong developer Hopewell Holdings to construct 60 km of (mostly elevated) railway, and 48 km of highway; this plan, too, has fallen victim to interdepartmental squabbles but may be taken over by the optimistically named Metropolitan Rapid Transit Authority (MRTA). The main villains in all this appear to be BMA principals, who want inflexible control over every project brought to the table even where there are clear conflicts of interest. In 1993 the BMA shot down a reasonable proposal put before the Interior Ministry to split the 560-sq-km city into five to eight separate townships for ease of traffic administration.

The investments involved in these rail and road projects are enormous, but as current traffic congestion costs the nation over 13 billion baht per year in fuel bills, the potential savings far exceed the outlay. Bangkok recently lost out to Singapore in a bid to be named the site of the new Asia-Pacific Economic Cooperation (APEC) secretariat largely because of the city's appalling traffic congestion.

One cheaper alternative which the government is seriously considering is a toll zone or other area traffic control zone within the central business district. City planners from the Massachusetts Institute of Technology, hired as consultants by BMA, concur that this would be the best approach for quick and lasting traffic congestion relief. This sort of plan has worked very well in nearby Singapore but it remains to be seen whether such a system would work in Bangkok, where even enforcement of traffic lights, parking and one-way streets is shaky.

While you're stuck in a Bangkok traffic jam you can take comfort in knowing that average rush-hour traffic flows are worse in Hong Kong (12.2 km/h), Taipei (11.5 km/h), Bombay (10.4 km/h) and Manila (7.2 km/h). Dirty air? Bangkok didn't even make UNEP/WHO's 1994 list of Asia's five worst cities for air pollution – honours captured by Delhi, Xian, Beijing, Calcutta and Shenyang. Ambient noise ratios are equal to those measured in Seoul, Chongqing and Saigon. ∎

hour or after midnight. For airport trips the non-meter guys still want 150 to 200B. Perhaps sometime in the future there won't be any non-metered cabs left on the street – until that time you'll probably be forced to use them occasionally.

A useful *Taxi Guide* brochure distributed by TAT to both tourists and taxi drivers lists Thai and English addresses of hotels, guest-houses, embassies, airlines, shopping centres, temples and various tourist attractions. The guide can be of considerable help in facilitating communication between non-English-speaking drivers and non-Thai-speaking passengers.

Tuk-Tuk In heavy traffic, tuk-tuks are usually faster than taxis since they're able to weave in and out between cars and trucks. This is the main advantage to taking a tuk-tuk for short hops. On the down side, tuk-tuks are not air-conditioned, so you have to breathe all that lead-soaked air (at its thickest in the middle of Bangkok's wide avenues), and they're also more dangerous since they easily flip when braking into a fast curve. The typical tuk-tuk fare nowadays offers no savings over a metered cab – around 40B for a short hop (eg Siam Square to Soi 2 Sukhumvit).

Tuk-tuk drivers tend to speak less English than taxi drivers, so many new arrivals have a hard time communicating their destinations. Although some travellers have complained about tuk-tuk drivers deliberately taking them to the wrong destination (to collect commissions from certain restaurants or silk shops), others never seem to have a problem with tuk-tuks, and swear by them. Beware tuk-tuk drivers who offer to take you on a sightseeing or factory tour for 10 or 20B – it's a touting scheme designed to pressure you into purchasing overpriced goods.

Motorcycle Taxi As passengers become more desperate in their attempts to beat rush-hour gridlocks, motorcycle taxis have moved from the sois to the main avenues. Fares for a motorcycle taxi are about the same as tuk-tuks except during heavy traffic, when they may cost a bit more.

Riding on the back of a speeding motorcycle taxi is even more of a kamikaze experience than riding in a tuk-tuk. Keep your legs tucked in – the drivers are used to carrying passengers with shorter legs than those of the average farang and they pass perilously close to other vehicles while weaving in and out of traffic.

Boat Although many of Bangkok's canals (khlongs) have been paved over, there is still plenty of transport along and across the Chao Phraya River and up adjoining canals. River transport is one of the nicest ways of getting around Bangkok as well as, quite often, being much faster than any road-based alternatives. For a start you get quite a different view of the city; secondly, it's much less of a hassle than tangling with the polluted, noisy, traffic-crowded streets. (Just try getting from Banglamphu to the GPO as quickly by road.) Over the last couple of years the Bangkok Metropolitan Authority (BMA) has revived four lengthy and very useful canal routes: Khlong Saen Saep (Banglamphu to Bang Kapi), Khlong Phrakhanong (Sukhumvit to Sinakarin campus), Khlong Bang Luang/Khlong Lat Phrao (New Phetburi Rd to Phahonyothin Bridge) and Khlong Phasi Charoen in Thonburi (Kaset Bang Khae port to Rama I Bridge). Although the canal boats can be crowded, the service is generally much faster than either an auto taxi or bus.

Tuk-Tuk Wars

In 18th-century Bangkok, residents got around on foot, by canal, or in human-drawn rickshaws, called *rót chék* or 'Chinese vehicles' by the Thais. During the early 20th century the rickshaw gave way to the three-wheeled pedicab or *samlor*, which then added inexpensive Japanese two-stroke engines after WW II to become the onomatopoeic *túk-túk*.

These small three-wheeled taxicabs sound like power saws gone berserk and commonly leave trails of blue smoke whenever they rev up. Objecting Bangkokians have been trying for years to enact a ban on tuk-tuks. Several years ago the city supposedly forbade the further production of any new three-wheel taxis, but every time I go to Bangkok I see hordes of brand new ones. It's a bit of a moral dilemma actually, since the tuk-tuk drivers are usually poor north-easterners who can't afford to rent the quieter, less polluting Japanese auto-taxis. You can buy one for around US$1200 from Tuk-Tuk Industry Thailand (☎(02) 437-6983), 463-465 Prachathipok Rd, Bangkok. ■

Chao Phraya River Express The first step in using river transport successfully is to know your boats. The main ones you'll want to use are the rapid Chao Phraya Express boats *(reua dùan)*, a sort of river bus service. These cost 5 to 10B (depending on the distance) and follow a regular route up and down the river; a trip from Banglamphu to the GPO, for example, costs 6B. They may not necessarily stop at each pier if there are no people waiting, or no-one wants to get off. You buy your tickets on the boat. Chao Phraya River Express boats are big, long boats with numbers on their roofs; the last boat from either end of the route departs at 6 pm.

Chao Phraya River Express

Cross-River Ferry From the main Chao Phraya stops and also from almost every other jetty, there are slower cross-river ferries *(reua khâam fâak)* which simply shuttle back and forth across the river. The standard fares are 1B and you usually pay this at the entrance to the jetty. Be careful – there will probably be a pay window at the jetty and also a straight-through aisle for people taking other boats.

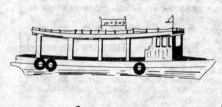

Cross-river ferry

Long-Tail Taxi Finally there are the long-tail boats *(reua haang yao)* which operate a share-taxi system off the main river and up the smaller khlongs. Fares usually start from around 4B – you've really got to know where you're going on these. There are also river charter taxis where you really do take the whole boat – you'll find them at certain jetties (primarily Tha Chang, Tha Si Phraya), and you can charter them for trips around the river-canal system for a standard 300B per hour.

One of the most useful canal services for most visitors runs along Khlong Saen Saep. This one provides a quicker alternative to road transport between the river and eastern Bangkok (ie outer Sukhumvit and Bang Kapi). The boat from Banglamphu to the Ramkhamhaeng University area, for example, costs 10B and takes only 40 minutes. A bus would take at least an hour under normal traffic conditions. The main detraction of this route is the seriously polluted canal – passengers typically hold newspapers over their clothes and faces to prevent being splashed by the stinking black water. Not the best choice of transport if you're dressed for a formal occasion.

Long-tail taxi

A handy little run along this route is by long-tail boat (5B) from the Siam Square area (from Tha Ratchathewi pier by the bridge next to the Asia Hotel) to the Banglamphu pier near Wat Saket and the Democracy Monument. At its western end, this route intersects a north-south boat route along Khlong Banglamphu and Khlong Phadung Krung Kasem. Along this route you can catch a boat from the Khlong Banglamphu pier near the corner of Phra Sumen and Chakraphong Rds (north side of the canal) all the way to Hualamphong station in 15 minutes for 5B.

Walking At first glance Bangkok doesn't seem like a great town for walking – its main avenues are so choked with traffic that the noise and thick air tend to drive one indoors. However, quiet spots where walks are rewarding – Lumphini Park, for example, or neighbourhoods off the main streets – do exist. And certain places are much more conveniently seen on foot, particularly the older sections of town along the Chao Phraya River where the roads are so narrow and twisting that bus lines don't go there.

Car & Motorcycle Cars and motorbikes are easily rented in Bangkok, if you can afford to and have steel nerves. Rates start at around 1200B per day for a small car, much less for a motorcycle, not including insurance. For long-term rentals you can usually arrange a discount of up to 35% off the daily rate. An International Driving Permit and passport are required for all rentals.

For long, cross-country trips, you might consider buying a new or used motorcycle and reselling it when you leave – this can end up being cheaper than renting, especially if you buy a good used bike. See the Getting Around chapter for more details.

Here are the names and addresses of a few car-rental companies:

Avis Rent-a-Car
    2/12 Withayu Rd (☎ 255-5300/4; fax 253-3734); branch offices at the Dusit Thani, Grand Hyatt Erawan, Sukhothai and Royal Princess hotels
Central Car Rent
    24 Soi Tonson, Ploenchit Rd (☎ 251-2778)
Grand Car Rent
    233-5 Asoke-Din Daeng Rd (☎ 248-2991)
Hertz
    420 Soi 71 Sukhumvit Rd (☎ 390-0341)
    1620 New Phetburi Rd (☎ 251-7575)
Highway Car Rent
    1018/5 Rama IV Rd (☎ 233-2991, 235-7746/7)
Inter Car Rent
    45 Sukhumvit Rd, near Soi 3 (☎ 252-9223)
Khlong Toey Car Rent
    1921 Rama IV Rd (☎ 250-1141/1361/1930)
Krung Thai Car Rent
    233-5 Asoke-Din Daeng Rd (☎ 246-0089, 246-1525/7)
Petchburee Car Rent
    23171 New Phetburi Rd (☎ 319-1393)
SMT Rent-a-Car
    931/11 Rama I Rd (☎ 216-8020)
Toyota Rental & Leasing
    U Chuliang Foundation Bldg, 968 Rama IV Rd (☎ 233-4869)
Thongchai Car Rent
    58/117 Si Nakharin Rd (☎ 322-3313)

There are more car-rental agencies along Withayu and New Phetburi Rds. Some also rent motorcycles, but you're better off renting or leasing a bike at a place that specialises in motorcycles. Here are three:

Chusak Yont Shop
    1400 New Phetburi Rd (☎ 251-9225)
SSK Co
    35/33 Lat Phrao Rd (☎ 514-1290)
Visit Laochaiwat
    1 Soi Prommit, Suthisan Rd (☎ 278-1348)

Central Thailand

Officially speaking, central Thailand is made up of 25 provinces, stretching as far north as Nakhon Sawan, south to Prachuap Khiri Khan, west to Kanchanaburi and east to Trat. (For the purposes of this guidebook, the north-south boundaries will be narrowed slightly; Nakhon Sawan will be included in the Northern Thailand chapter, and Prachuap Khiri Khan in the Southern Thailand chapter.) Because of the rain-fed network of rivers and canals in the central region, this is the most fertile part of Thailand, supporting vast fields of rice, sugar cane, pineapples and other fruit, and cassava.

Linguistically, the people of central Thailand share a common dialect which is considered 'standard' Thai simply because Bangkok happens to be in the middle of it. High concentrations of Chinese are found throughout the central provinces since this is where a large number of Chinese immigrants started out as farmers and merchants. Significant numbers of Mon and Burmese live to the west, and Lao and Khmer to the east due to immigration from bordering lands over hundreds of years.

Many places in central Thailand can be visited in day trips from Bangkok, but in most cases they make better stepping stones to places farther afield. You can, for example, pause in Ayuthaya on the way north to Chiang Mai, or in Nakhon Pathom if you're heading south.

Ayuthaya Province

AYUTHAYA

พระนครศรีอยุธยา

Approximately 86 km north of Bangkok, Ayuthaya (population 60,300) was the Thai capital from 1350 to 1767 and by all accounts it was a splendid city. Prior to 1350, when the capital was moved here from U

Thong, it was a Khmer outpost. The city was named after Ayodhya, the home of Rama in the Indian epic *Ramayana*, which is Sanskrit for 'unassailable' or 'undefeatable'. Its full Thai name is Phra Nakhon Si Ayuthaya (Sacred City of Ayodhya).

Thirty-three kings of various Siamese dynasties reigned in Ayuthaya until it was conquered by the Burmese. During its heyday, Thai culture and international commerce flourished in the kingdom – the Ayuthaya period has so far been the apex of Thai history – and Ayuthaya was courted by Dutch, Portuguese, French, English, Chinese and Japanese merchants. By the end of the 17th century Ayuthaya's population had reached one million – virtually all foreign visitors claimed it to be the most illustrious city they had ever seen.

Orientation & Information

The present-day city is located at the confluence of three rivers, the Chao Phraya, the Pa Sak and the smaller Lopburi. A wide canal joins them and makes a complete circle around the town. Long-tail boats can be rented from the boat landing across from Chan Kasem (Chandra Kasem) Palace for a tour around the river/canal; several of the old wat ruins (Wat Phanan Choeng, Wat Phutthaisawan, Wat Kasatthirat and Wat Chai Wattanaram) may be glimpsed from the canal, along with picturesque views of river life. Apart from the historic ruins and museums, Ayuthaya is not particularly interesting, but it is one of three cities in Thailand known for their 'gangster' activity.

Many of the ruins now collect a 10 to 20B admission fee during civil service hours (8 am to 4.30 pm). The ruins are most visited on weekends – visit during the week to avoid the crowds.

Tourist Office TAT recently opened a tourist information office (open from 8.30 am to 4.30 pm daily) next to the Chao Sam Phraya

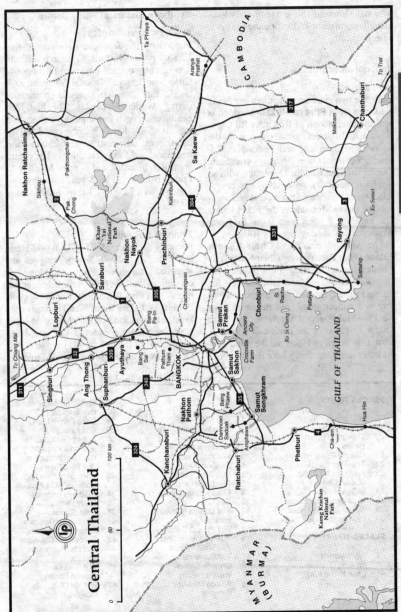

Central Thailand

Ta Phraya

CAMBODIA

To Trat

Aranya
Prathet

Chanthaburi

317

Nakhon Ratchasima

Makham

Pakthongchai

Sikhiew

Sa Kaew

2

Pak
Chong

Kabinburi

304

Ko Samet

3

Rayong

Khao
Yai
National
Park

Nakhon
Nayok

Prachinburi

331

Satahip

Saraburi

305

Chachoengsao

Chonburi

Si
Racha

Pattaya

Lopburi

1

Bang
Pa-in

Samut
Prakan

Ko Si Chang

Ancient
City

To Chiang Mai

32

309

Bang
Sai

Ayuthaya

Pathum
Thani

Crocodile
Farm

GULF OF THAILAND

311

Singburi

Ang Thong

Suphanburi

340

BANGKOK

Samut
Sakhon

Bang
Phaew

Samut
Songkhram

Nakhon
Pathom

35

100 km

324

Kanchanaburi

Damnoen
Saduak

Amphawa

Ratchaburi

Phetburi

Cha-am

4

Hua Hin

50

Kaeng Krachan
National
Park

MYANMAR
(BURMA)

0

National Museum. This is a temporary location; the permanent TAT office site has yet to be announced.

National Museums
พิพิธภัณฑ์แห่งชาติ

There are two museums, the main one being the **Chao Sam Phraya Museum**, which is near the intersection of Rotchana Rd (Ayuthaya's main street, connecting with the highway to Bangkok) and Si Sanphet Rd, near the centre of town. It features your basic roundup of Thai Buddhist sculpture with an emphasis, naturally, on Ayuthaya pieces. A selection of books on Thai art and archaeology are offered for sale at the ticket kiosk. The museum is open from 9 am to 4 pm, Wednesday to Sunday; entry is 10B.

The second museum, **Chan Kasem Palace** (Phra Ratchawong Chan Kasem), is a museum piece in itself, built by the 17th king of Ayuthaya – Maha Thammarat – for his son Prince Naresuan. Among the exhibits here is a collection of gold treasures from Wat Phra Mahathat and Wat Ratburana. Chan Kasem Palace is in the north-east corner of town, near the river. Hours are the same as at the other museum. Entry here is also 10B.

Ayuthaya Historical Study Centre
ศูนย์ศึกษาประวัติศาสตร์อยุธยา

Funded by the Japanese government, this US$6.8 million historical research institute was recently opened on seven rai opposite Chao Sam Phraya National Museum, in a district that housed a Japanese community during Ayuthaya's heyday. The high-tech exhibit area, open to the public, covers five aspects of Ayuthaya's history: city development, port, administration, lifestyles and traditions, and foreign relations. The centre is on Rotchana Rd and is open Monday to Friday from 9 am to 3 pm, Saturday and Sunday from 9 am to 4.30 pm. Admission is 100B.

Temples & Ruins

Recently declared a UNESCO World Heritage Site, Ayuthaya's historic temples are scattered throughout the city and along the encircling rivers. Several of the more central ruins – Wat Phra Si Sanphet, Wat Mongkhon Bophit, Wat Phra Ram, Wat Thammikarat, Wat Ratburana and Wat Phra Mahathat – can easily be visited on foot if you avoid the hottest part of the day from 11 am to 4 pm. Or you could add more temples and ruins to

---

PLACES TO STAY

9	U Thong Hotel
11	Cathay Hotel
20	Thongchai Guest House
21	New BJ Guest House
22	Thai Thai Bungalow
23	Ayuthaya & Old BJ Guesthouses
24	Si Samai Hotel
35	Ayuthaya Youth Hostel
38	Ayuthaya Grand Hotel
39	Pai Thong Guest House

PLACES TO EAT

7	Night Market
36	Floating Restaurants
41	Phae Krung Kao

OTHER

1	Phu Khao Thong Temple (Golden Mount Chedi)
2	Wat Phra Meru
3	Wat Kuti Thong
4	Elephant Kraal
5	Hua Raw Market
6	Pier (Boat Landing)
8	Chan Kasem Palace
10	GPO
12	Wat Lokaya Sutha
13	Palace
14	Wat Phra Si Sanphet
15	Wat Mongkhon Bophit
16	Wat Thammikarat
17	Wat Suwannawat
18	Chinese Shrine
19	Wat Ratburana
25	Air-con Minivans to Bangkok
26	Wat Phra Mahathat
27	Bus Terminal
28	Chao Phrom Market
29	Wat Kasatthirat
30	Queen Suriyothai Memorial Pagoda
31	Wat Chai Wattanaram
32	Wat Phra Ram
33	Chao Sam Phraya Museum/TAT Office
34	Ayuthaya Historical Study Centre
37	Train Station
40	Wat Suwan Dararam
42	Phom Phet Fortress
43	St Joseph's Cathedral
44	Wat Phutthaisawan
45	Mosque
46	Wat Phra Chao Phanan Choeng
47	Wat Yai Chai Mongkhon

CENTRAL THAILAND

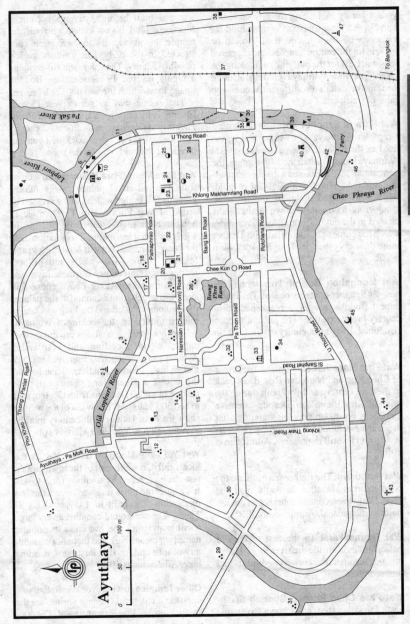

Ayuthaya

0   50   100 m

To Bangkok

Pa Sak River

Lopburi River

Chao Phraya River

Old Lopburi River

Phu Khao Thong – Panjat Road

Ayuthaya – Pa Mok Road

Khlong Thaw Road

Si Sanphet Road

U Thong Road

Pa Thon Road

Rotchana Road

Bang Ian Road

Khlong Makhamriang Road

U Thong Road

Pamaphrao Road

Naresuan (Chao Phrom) Road

Chee Kun Road

Bueng Phra Ram

Ferry

38

47

37

36

35

39

41

40

42

46

11

25   28

24   27

23

22

21

20

18

17

19

26

16

3

2

14

15

13

12

1

30

29

31

45

44

34

32

33

43

9   10

7   8

6

5

4

your itinerary by touring the city on rented bicycle. An ideal transport combination for visitors who want to 'do it all' would be bicycle for the central temples, and chartered long-tail boat for the outlying ruins along the river. See the Ayuthaya Getting Around section for details on different modes and rates of transport.

Wat Phra Si Sanphet This was the largest temple in Ayuthaya in its time, and it was used as the royal temple/palace for several Ayuthaya kings. Built in the 14th century, the compound once contained a 16-metre standing Buddha covered with 250 kg of gold, which was melted down by the Burmese conquerors. It is mainly known for the chedis erected in the quintessential Ayuthaya style, which has come to be identified with Thai art more than any other single style. Admission is 20B.

Wat Mongkhon Bophit This monastery near Si Sanphet contains one of Thailand's largest Buddha images, a blackened 15th-century bronze casting. The present wihaan (Buddhist image sanctuary) was built in 1956.

Wat Phra Mahathat This wat, on the corner of Chee Kun and Naresuan Rds, dates back to the 14th century and was built during the reign of King Ramesuan. Despite extensive damage – not much was left standing after the Burmese hordes – the prang (Khmer-style tower) is still impressive. Admission is 20B.

Wat Ratburana The Ratburana ruins are the counterpart to Mahathat across the road; the chedis, however, contain murals and are not quite as dilapidated. Admission is 20B.

Wat Thammikarat To the east of the old palace grounds, inside the river loop, Thammikarat features overgrown chedi ruins and lion sculptures.

Wat Phra Chao Phanan Choeng Southeast of town on the Chao Phraya River, this wat was built before Ayuthaya became a Siamese capital. It's not known who built the temple, but it appears to have been constructed in the early 14th century so it's possibly Khmer. The main wihaan contains a highly revered 19-metre sitting Buddha image from which the wat derives its name.

The easiest way to get to Wat Phanan Choeng is by ferry from the pier near Phom Phet fortress, inside the south-east corner of the city centre. For a few extra baht you can take a bicycle with you on the boat.

Wat Phra Meru (Phra Mehn/Mane) Across from the old royal palace *(wang lūang)* grounds is a bridge which can be crossed to arrive at Wat Phra Meru. This temple is notable because it escaped destruction in 1767, though it has required restoration over the years. The main bot was built in 1546 and features fortress-like walls and pillars. During the 18th-century Burmese invasion, Myanmar's Chao Along Phaya chose this site from which to fire cannon at the palace; the cannon exploded and the king was fatally injured, thus ending the sacking of Ayuthaya.

The bot interior contains an impressive carved wooden ceiling and a splendid Ayuthaya-era crowned sitting Buddha, six metres high. Inside a smaller wihaan behind the bot is a green-stone, European-pose (sitting in a chair) Buddha from Ceylon, said to be 1300 years old. The walls of the wihaan show traces of 18th or 19th-century murals.

Admission to Wat Phra Meru is 10B.

Wat Yai Chai Mongkhon Wat Yai, as the locals call it, is south-east of the town proper, but can be reached by minibus for 3 to 4B. It's a quiet old place that was once a famous meditation wat, built in 1357 by King U Thong. The compound contains a very large chedi from which the wat takes its popular name *(yài* means big), and there is a community of mae chii, or Buddhist nuns, residing here. Admission is 10B.

Other Temples Just north of Wat Ratburana, opposite a colourful Chinese shrine, are the smaller ruins of **Wat Suwannawat**. The 400-

year-old brick remains of eight chedis, a bot and a wihaan are arranged in a circle – a typical early Ayuthaya layout.

The ruined, typical Ayuthaya-style prang and chedis of **Wat Chai Wattanaram**, on the west bank of the Chao Phraya River southwest of the city island centre, were recently restored. These ruins can be reached by boat, or by bicycle via a nearby bridge. If you go by road, you'll pass **Wat Kasatthirat** on the way.

A short boat ride north along the Lopburi River will bring you to modern **Wat Pa Doh**. In front of the bot, a unique Sukhothai-style walking Buddha image strides over a narrow arch, symbolising the crossing from samsara to nirvana.

Elephant Kraal This is a restored version of the wooden stockade once used for the annual roundup of wild elephants. A huge fence of teak logs planted in the ground at 45-degree angles kept the elephants in; the king had a special raised pavilion from which to observe the thrilling event.

Festivals
Ayuthaya holds one of the country's largest Loi Krathong festivals on the full moon of the 12th lunar month (usually November). Celebrations are held at several spots in the city; the largest spectacle takes place at **Beung Phra Ram**, the large lake in the centre of the city between Wat Phra Ram and Wat Phra Mahathat. Thousands of Thais, many of them from Bangkok, flock to the Beung Phra Ram event to crowd around four or five different outdoor stages offering likhe, Thai pop, cinema and lakhon chatrii – all at the same time (the din can be deafening)! Fireworks are a big part of the show, and there are lots of food vendors on the site.

More low-key and traditional is the celebration at the **Chan Kasem pier**, where families launch their *krathongs* (small lotus-shaped floats topped with incense and candles) onto the Lopburi-Pa Sak river junction. Although kids throw fireworks here, the overall atmosphere is much closer to the heart of Loi Krathong than at Beung Phra

Ram. Krathongs can be purchased at the pier (or you can make your own from materials for sale); for a few baht you can board one of the many waiting canoes at the pier and be paddled out to launch your krathong in the middle of the river. Thai tradition says that any couple who launch a krathong together are destined to be lovers – if not in this lifetime then the next.

Another large Loi Krathong festival takes place at the **Royal Folk Arts & Crafts Centre** in Bang Sai, about 24 km west of Ayuthaya (see the entry on the centre in the Around Ayuthaya section). At this one the emphasis is on traditional costumes and handmade krathongs. If you can put together a small group, any of the hotels or guesthouses in Ayuthaya can arrange a trip to the Bang Sai Loi Krathong for around 200B or less per person.

During the 10 days leading to the Songkran Festival, in mid-April, there is a sound-and-light show with fireworks over the ruins. Every day between 10.30 am and 1.30 pm the local government runs boat tours from the U Thong pier for 50B per person.

Krathong

Places to Stay

Guesthouses & Hostels For budgeteers, there are five guesthouses and one hostel in Ayuthaya to choose from. Four of them are located on or off Naresuan Rd, not far from the bus terminal. As elsewhere in Thailand, tuk-tuk and samlor drivers will tell you anything to steer you towards guesthouses that pay commissions (up to 35B per head in this city).

Near the end of a soi off Naresuan Rd (not far from the Si Samai Hotel), *Ayuthaya Guest House* charges 80/100B for singles/doubles in an old house. Next door, a branch of the same family runs the *Old BJ Guest House* (☎ (035) 251526) at the same rates; the Ayuthaya Guest House is cleaner. Both offer food service and bike rentals (30B a day).

Yet another BJ relative operates the *New BJ Guest House* (☎ (035) 244046) at 19/29 Naresuan Rd. Rooms cost 80 to 100B and there's a nice eating area in front. One drawback is that it's right on Naresuan Rd, a main Ayuthaya thoroughfare, so traffic noise may be distracting. Another newer place is *Thongchai Guest House* (☎ (035) 252083), on a back road parallel to Naresuan Rd and off Chee Kun Rd. A choice of rooms is available in bungalows or in a row house for 120B without bath, 200 to 250B with fan and bath, or 350B for air-con and bath. This might be better value than either of the Ayuthaya hotels in the same price range (ie U Thong or Cathay).

Almost directly across the river from the train station in an old teak house is the *Ayuthaya Youth Hostel* (☎ (035) 241978), also known as Ruendauem (Reuan Doem), at 48/2 U Thong Rd. Plain rooms with ceiling fans and shared bath cost 150B for smaller rooms, 200B for larger ones. A very good floating restaurant extends from the river side of the house; it is open from 10 am till 11 pm. If you can put up with some ambient noise from the restaurant and from the traffic on busy U Thong Rd, it's not a bad choice. No one seems to care whether you show a Hostelling International card or not – if you have one, it wouldn't hurt to ask for a discount.

The *Pai Thong Guest House* (☎ (035) 241830) is also right on the river within walking distance of the train station. Large but very basic rooms are 60B single/double; bike rentals and boat trips are available.

Hotels The *Thai Thai Bungalow* (☎ (035) 244702), at 13/1 Naresuan Rd, set well off the road between the bus terminal and the road to Wat Phra Meru, has large, clean rooms from 120 to 300B with air-con.

Si Samai Hotel (☎ (035) 251104), 12/19 Naresuan Rd, a more up-market place near the Thai Thai, charges 200 to 300B for rooms with fan and bath, 400 to 600B with air-con.

The standard Thai-Chinese style *Cathay Hotel* (☎ (035) 251562), near the U Thong towards Hua Raw Market, costs 150B for a room with fan, 250B with air-con. The *U Thong Hotel* (☎ (035) 251136), on U Thong Rd near Chan Kasem Palace, is similar to the Cathay, with adequate rooms with fan for 150B, air-con for 300B.

Moving towards the top end, the *U-Thong Inn* (☎ (035) 242618) offers recently renovated air-con rooms for 760 to 1500B. It's out on Rotchana Rd past the turn-off for the train station. The newer *Ayuthaya Grand Hotel* (☎ (035) 335483), out towards U-Thong Inn and Wat Yai Chai Mongkhon at 75/5 Rotchana Rd, features rooms with all mod cons for 800 to 1500B. Ayuthaya's flashiest digs can be found at the 202-room *Krung Si River Hotel* (☎ (035) 242996) at 27/2 Rotchana Rd, where decked-out lodgings start at 1400B.

Places to Eat

The most dependable and least expensive places to eat are the Hua Raw market, on the river near Chan Kasem Palace, and the Chao Phrom market, opposite the ferry piers along the east side of the island. The *Chainam* opposite Chan Kasem Palace next to the Cathay Hotel has tables on the river, a bilingual menu and friendly service; it's also open for breakfast. For something a little fancier, try the air-con *Rodeo Saloon* on U Thong Rd. Despite the name and 'old-west' decor, the food is mostly Thai (English menu available); at night a small band plays Thai and international folk music.

Quite a few restaurants can be found on the main road into Ayuthaya, Rotchana Rd, and there are two floating restaurants on the Pa Sak River, one on either side of the Pridi Damrong Bridge on the west bank, and one on the east bank north of the bridge. Of these, the *Phae Krung Kao* – on the south side of the bridge on the west bank – has the better reputation. The floating *Reuan Doem*, in front of the Ayuthaya Youth Hostel, is also quite good.

In the evenings a very choice night market comes to life near the pier opposite Chan Kasem Palace.

Getting There & Away
Bus Ordinary buses leave from the northern bus terminal in Bangkok every 20 minutes between 5 am and 7 pm. The fare is 22B and the trip takes around two hours. Air-con buses leave the same terminal every half hour from 6 am to 6.30 pm and cost 36B; the trip takes 1½ hours when traffic north of Bangkok is light, two hours otherwise.

If you're arriving in Ayuthaya by bus from some place other than Bangkok or other nearby cities, you may be dropped off at the long-distance bus station, five km east of the Pridi Damrong Bridge at the Highway 32 junction.

Train Trains to Ayuthaya leave Bangkok's Hualamphong station every hour or so between 4.20 am and 10 pm. The 3rd-class fare is 15B for the 1½-hour trip; it's hardly worth taking a more expensive seat for this short trip. Train schedules are available from the information booth at Hualamphong station.

After getting off at the Ayuthaya train station, the quickest way to reach the old city is to walk straight west to the river, where you can catch a short ferry ride across to the Chao Phrom pier for 1B.

Upon arrival at Bangkok International Airport, savvy repeat visitors to Thailand sometimes choose to board a northbound train direct to Ayuthaya rather than head south into the Bangkok maelstrom. This only works if you arrive by air during the day, as local trains to Ayuthaya quit running around 7 pm. There are frequent 3rd-class trains throughout the day between Don Muang train station (opposite Bangkok International) and Ayuthaya.

Boat There are no longer any scheduled or chartered boat services between Bangkok and Ayuthaya.

Several companies in Bangkok operate luxury cruises to Bang Pa-In with side trips by bus to Ayuthaya for around 800 to 1000B per person, including a lavish luncheon. (See the Bangkok River & Canal Trips section for more details.)

Getting Around
Songthaews and shared tuk-tuks ply the main city roads for 3B per person. A tuk-tuk from the train station to any point in old Ayuthaya should be around 30B; on the island itself figure no more than 20B per trip. You can hire a samlor, tuk-tuk or songthaew by the hour or by the day to explore the ruins but the prices are quite high by Thai standards (150B per hour for anything with a motor in it, 400B all day when things are slow). It's better to hire a bicycle at one of the guesthouses or walk.

It's also interesting to hire a boat from the palace pier to do a semi-circular tour of the island and see some of the less accessible ruins. A long-tail boat that will take up to eight people can be hired for 300B for a three-hour trip with stops at Wat Phutthaisawan, Wat Phanan Choeng and Wat Chai Wattanaram.

AROUND AYUTHAYA
Bang Pa-In
บางปะอิน
Twenty km south of Ayuthaya is Bang Pa-In, which has a curious collection of palace buildings in a wide variety of architectural styles. It's a nice boat trip from Bangkok if you're taking one of the cruise tours, although in itself it's not particularly note-

worthy. The palace is open from 8.30 am to 3.30 pm daily. Admission is 50B.

Palace Buildings The postcard stereotype here is a pretty little Thai pavilion in the centre of a small lake by the palace entrance. Inside the palace grounds, the Chinese-style **Wehat Chamrun Palace** is the only building open to visitors. The **Withun Thatsana** building looks like a lighthouse with balconies. It was built to give a fine view over gardens and lakes. There are various other buildings, towers and memorials in the grounds plus an interesting example of topiary where the bushes have been trimmed into the shape of a small herd of elephants.

Wat Niwet Thamaprawat Across the river and south from the palace grounds, this unusual wat looks much more like a gothic Christian church than anything from Thailand. It was built by Rama V (Chulalongkorn). You get to the wat by crossing the river in a small trolley-like cable car. The crossing is free.

Getting There & Away Bang Pa-In can be reached by minibus (it's really a large songthaew truck rather than a bus) from Ayuthaya's Chao Phrom Market, Naresuan (Chao Phrom) Rd, for 7B. From Bangkok there are buses every half hour or so from the northern bus terminal and the fare is 17B. You can also reach Bang Pa-In by bus or train from Bangkok.

The Chao Phraya River Express Boat Company does a tour every Sunday from the Maharat pier in Bangkok that goes to Wat Phailom in Pathum Thani (November to June) or Wat Chaloem Phrakiat (July to October) as well as Bang Pa-In and Bang Sai's Royal Folk Arts & Crafts Centre. The trip leaves from Bangkok at 8 am and returns at 5.30 pm. The price is 180B not including lunch, which you arrange on your own in Bang Pa-In. For more expensive, all-inclusive river cruises to Bang Pa-In which include tours of old Ayuthaya, see the Bangkok River & Canal Trips section.

Bang Sai Royal Folk Arts & Crafts Centre

This 115-hectare facility in Beung Yai, Bang Sai District is an important training centre for craftspeople from the central provinces and beyond. Under the auspices of Queen Sirikit's Promotion of Supplementary Occupations & Related Techniques (SUPPORT) foundation, handicraft experts teach craft techniques to novices while at the same time demonstrating them for visitors. The centre is open daily except Wednesday from 8.30 am to 4 pm; admission is 20B. Call ☎ (035) 366-6092 (☎ (035) 225-8265 in Bangkok) for additional information.

The Loi Krathong festival here is considered one of the more traditional versions available in Central Thailand. You can easily book a Loi Krathong trip to Bang Sai from Ayuthaya – see the Ayuthaya section for details.

Lopburi Province

LOPBURI

อ.เมืองลพบุรี

Approximately 154 km north of Bangkok, the town of Lopburi (population 40,000) has been inhabited since at least the Dvaravati period (6th to 11th centuries AD), when it was called Lavo. Nearly all traces of Lavo culture were erased by Khmer and Thai inhabitants following the 10th century, but many Dvaravati artefacts found in Lopburi can be seen in the Lopburi National Museum. Ruins and statuary in Lopburi span a remarkable 12 centuries.

The Khmers extended their Angkor empire to include Lavo in the 10th century. It was during this century that they built the Prang Khaek (Hindu Shrine), San Phra Kan (Kala Shrine) and Prang Sam Yot (Three-Spired Shrine) as well as the impressive prang at Wat Phra Si Ratana Mahathat.

Power over Lopburi was wrested from the Khmers in the 13th century as the Sukhothai Kingdom to the north grew stronger, but the

CENTRAL THAILAND

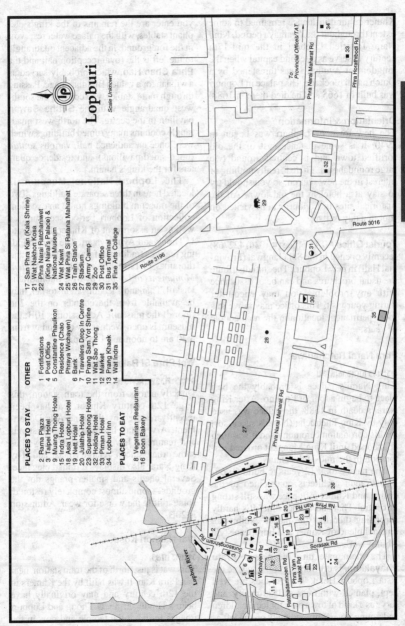

Lopburi

Scale Unknown

PLACES TO STAY

2 Rama Plaza
3 Taipei Hotel
9 Muang Thong Hotel
15 Indra Hotel
18 Asia Lopburi Hotel
19 Nett Hotel
23 Suparaphong Hotel
32 Holiday Hotel
33 Piman Hotel
34 Lopburi Inn

PLACES TO EAT

8 Vegetarian Restaurant
16 Boon Bakery

OTHER

1 Fortifications
4 Post Office
5 Constantine Phaulkon
   Residence (Chao
   Phraya Wichayen)
6 Bank
7 Travellers Drop In Centre
10 Prang Sam Yot Shrine
11 Wat Sao Thong
12 Market
13 Prang Khaek
14 Wat Indra
17 San Phra Kan (Kala Shrine)
21 Wat Nakhon Kosa
22 Phra Narai Ratchaniwet
   (King Narai's Palace) &
   National Museum
24 Wat Kawit
25 Wat Phra Si Ratana Mahathat
26 Train Station
27 Stadium
28 Army Camp
29 Zoo
30 Post Office
31 Bus Terminal
35 Fine Arts College

Khmer cultural influence remained to some extent throughout the Ayuthaya period. King Narai fortified Lopburi in the mid-17th century to serve as a second capital when the kingdom of Ayuthaya was threatened by a Dutch naval blockade. His palace in Lopburi was built in 1665 and he died there in 1688.

Orientation & Information

The new town of Lopburi was begun in 1940. It is some distance east of the old fortified town and is centred around two large roundabouts. There is really nothing of interest in the new section, so you should try to stay at a hotel in the old town. All the historical sites in Lopburi can be visited on foot in a day or two.

Tourist Office A TAT office (☎ (036) 422768) recently opened in the Sala Jangwat (Provincial Hall) in new Lopburi. The staff distribute the usual brochures and can be of assistance with any problems you may encounter during your visit. This office may move to a more permanent location in the next couple of years.

Phra Narai Ratchaniwet

พระนารายณ์ราชนิเวศน์

King Narai's palace is probably the best place to begin a tour of Lopburi. After King Narai's death in 1688, the palace was used only by King Phetracha (Narai's successor) for his coronation ceremony and it was then abandoned until King Mongkut ordered restoration in the mid-19th century.

The palace took 12 years to build (1665-77). French architects contributed to the design and Khmer influence was still strong in central Thailand at that time. It's hardly surprising then that the palace exhibits an unusual blend of Khmer and European style – but it works.

The main gate into the palace, **Pratu Phayakkha**, is off Sorasak Rd, opposite the Asia Lopburi Hotel. The grounds are well kept, planted with trees and shrubbery, and serve as a kind of town park for local children and young lovers. Immediately on the left as

you enter are the remains of the king's elephant stables, with the palace water reservoir in the foreground. In the adjacent quadrangle to the left is the royal reception hall and the **Phra Chao Hao**, which probably served as a wihaan for a valued Buddha image. Passing through more stables, you come to the southwest quadrangle with the **Suttha Sawan** pavilion in the centre. The north-west quadrangle contains many ruined buildings which were once an audience hall, various *saalaa* (open-sided pavilions), and residence quarters for the king's harem.

The **Lopburi National Museum** is located here in three separate buildings. Two of the museum buildings house an excellent collection of Lopburi period sculpture, as well as an assortment of Khmer, Dvaravati, U Thong and Ayuthaya art. The third building features traditional farm implements and dioramas of farm life. *A Guide to Ancient Monuments in Lopburi* by M C Subhadradis Diskul, Thailand's leading art historian, may be available from the counter on the 2nd floor of the museum. Admission is 10B; the museum is open Wednesday to Sunday from 8.30 am to noon and 1 to 4 pm.

Wat Phra Si Ratana Mahathat

วัดพระศรีรัตนมหาธาตุ

Directly across from the train station, this large 12th-century Khmer wat has been recently restored by the Fine Arts Department. A very tall laterite prang still stands and features a few intact lintels, as well as some ornate stucco. A large wihaan added by King Narai also displays a ruined elegance. Several chedis and smaller prangs dot the grounds – some almost completely restored, some a little the worse for wear. Admission is 20B.

Wat Nakhon Kosa

วัดนครโกษา

This wat is just north of the train station, near San Phra Kan. It was built by the Khmers in the 12th century and may originally have been a Hindu shrine. U Thong and Lopburi images found at the temple and now in the

Lopburi National Museum are thought to have been added later. There's not much left of this wat, though the foliage growing on the brick ruins makes an interesting image. However, half-hearted attempts to restore it with modern materials and motifs detract from the overall effect. A recent excavation has uncovered a larger base below the monument.

Wat Indra & Wat Racha
วัดอิทราและวัดราชา

Wat Indra is across the street from Wat Nakhon Kosa. Practically nothing is known of its history and it's now merely a pile of brick rubble. Wat Racha, off Phra Yam Jamkat Rd, is another pile of bricks with little known history.

Wat Sao Thong Thong
วัดเสาธงทอง

This wat is north-west of the palace centre, behind the central market. The buildings here are in pretty poor shape. The wihaan and large seated Buddha are from the Ayuthaya period; King Narai restored the wihaan (changing its windows to an incongruous but intriguing Gothic style) so the wihaan could be used as a Christian chapel. Niches along the inside walls contain Lopburi-style *naga* Buddhas.

Chao Phraya Wichayen (Constantine Phaulkon Residence)
บ้านวิชาเยนทร์

King Narai built this eclectic Thai-European palace as a residence for foreign ambassadors, of whom the Greek Constantine Phaulkon was the most famous. Phaulkon became one of King Narai's principal advisers and was eventually a royal minister. In 1688, as Narai lay dying, Phaulkon was assassinated by Luang Sorasak, who wanted all the power of Narai's throne for himself. The palace is across the street and north-east of Wat Sao Thong Thong; admission is 20B.

San Phra Kan (Kala Shrine)
ศาลพระกาฬ

To the north of Wat Nakhon Kosa, near the train tracks, this unimpressive shrine contains a crude gold-leaf-laden image of Kala, the Hindu god of time and death. A virtual sea of monkeys surrounds the shrine, falling out of the tamarind trees and scurrying along the steps leading to the sanctuary. They are getting fat on hand-outs.

Prang Sam Yot
ปรางค์สามยอด

Opposite the Kala Shrine, near the Muang Thong Hotel, this shrine represents classic Khmer-Lopburi style and is another Hindu-turned-Buddhist temple. Originally, the three prangs symbolised the Hindu *trimurti* of Shiva, Vishnu and Brahma. Now two of them contain ruined Lopburi-style Buddha images. Some Khmer lintels can still be made out, and some appear unfinished.

A rather uninteresting U Thong-Ayuthaya imitation Buddha image sits in the brick sanctuary in front of the linked prangs. At the back, facing the Muang Thong Hotel, are a couple of crudely restored images, probably once Lopburi style. The grounds allotted to Prang Sam Yot by the town are rather small and make the structure difficult to photograph. The grounds are virtually surrounded by modern buildings, as well. The best view of the monument would probably be from one of the upper floors of the Muang Thong. The monument is lit up at night.

Activities

Those interested in Thai classical music and dance should stop by the **Lopburi Fine Arts College** (Withayalai Kalasilpa Lopburi) in the new town – any tuk-tuk driver will know it. Here you can watch young dancers practising the rudiments of classical dance with live musical accompaniment.

A small **zoo** north-east of the first roundabout (coming from the old town) is a quiet place to spend a couple of hours. It's open from 8 am to 6 pm; entry is 10B.

You can also pay a visit to the **Travellers Drop in Centre** at 34 Wichayen Rd, Soi 3 Muang, which is part of the Australian Education Placement Centre, an institute for teaching English. Here travellers can meet Thais at the informal English classes held here three times daily. After the class, the students go with travellers and share a meal in a restaurant.

Places to Stay

Old Lopburi Lopburi can be visited as a day trip en route to the north, but if you want to stay overnight there are a number of hotels in the older part of the city you can try. *Asia Lopburi Hotel* (☎ (036) 411892), on the corner of Sorasak and Phra Yam Jamkat Rds and overlooking King Narai's palace, is clean and comfortable with good service. It has two Chinese restaurants. Rooms are 130/180B for singles/doubles with fan and bath, or up to 250/350B with air-con. Ask for a room off the street if traffic noise is bothersome.

Muang Thong Hotel (☎ (036) 411036), across from Prang Sam Yot, has noisy and not-so-clean rooms for 100 to 120B with fan and bath. Rooms without bath are also available for 80B, or air-con rooms for 200B. Better is the *Taipei Hotel* (☎ (036) 411624), at 24/6-7 Surasongkhram Rd north of the palace area. Clean rooms with private bath cost 120/180B one/two beds; air-con rooms are available for 200/260B one/two beds.

The new *Rama Plaza*, farther north out Surasongkhram Rd, offers clean medium-priced rooms for 180/260B single/double with fan and bath, 260/350B air-con. Popular with business travellers, it's often full.

The *Indra*, on Na Phra Kan Rd across from Wat Nakhon Kosa, is under new – and better – management (though very little English is spoken). It now costs 120B for clean, spacious rooms with fan and bath, 260B air-con. Also on Na Phra Kan Rd, the *Julathip Hotel* is near the Indra but closer to the train station, and has no English sign. This one has also cleaned up a bit (although it still doubles as a brothel) and rooms with fan and bath now

cost 100B; it's a good idea to ask to see a room first.

The similar *Suparaphong Hotel*, also on Na Phra Kan Rd, is not far from Wat Phra Si Ratana Mahathat and the train station. Rooms at the Suparaphong cost 100B and are much the same as at the Julathip and Indra hotels.

The *Nett Hotel* (☎ (036) 411738), at 17/1-2 Ratchadamnoen Rd, is actually on a soi between Ratchadamnoen and Phra Yam Jamkat Rds, parallel to Sorasak Rd. Clean, quiet rooms with fan and bath cost 120/220/250B for one/two/three-bed rooms or 250/350B for air-con one/two-bed rooms.

Finally, the *Travellers Drop in Centre* (☎ (036) 412376, 411439) at 34 Wichayen Rd, Soi 3 Muang (above the Australian Educational Placement Centre), has two double rooms for 60/70B or you can stay at no charge in return for spending an hour talking with Thai students at one of the centre's English classes. Richard (Wichit), the English-speaking Thai man who runs the place, says he may be adding more rooms in the near future. This is not a crash pad – if you plan to trade English conversation for a room, dress politely for his classes.

There are so many hotels along Na Phra Kan Rd that bargaining should be possible. Ask if they have a cheaper room: *Mii hâwng tùuk kwàa mãi?*

New Lopburi If you get stuck in the new part of town for some reason, you can choose from *Piman* (Soi Ekathot, Phra Horathibodi Rd), *Holiday* (Soi Suriyothai 2, Phra Narai Maharat Rd) or *Lopburi Inn* (28/8 Phra Narai Maharat Rd, ☎ 412300; fax 411917). The first two are mostly middle-class short-time places with rates around 250B a night. The Lopburi Inn features very nice rooms with all the amenities from 350B.

Places to Eat

Several Chinese restaurants operate along Na Phra Kan Rd, parallel to the train line, especially near the Julathip and Indra hotels. The food is good but a bit overpriced. Restaurants on the side streets of Ratchadamnöen and Phra Yam Jamkat Rds can be better value. The Chinese-Thai restaurant next to the Asia Lopburi Hotel on Sorasak Rd, across from the main gate to King Narai's palace, is a good standby for most Thai and Chinese dishes. There are also plenty of cheap curry vendors down the alleys and along the smaller streets in old Lopburi.

The market off Ratchadamnoen and Surasongkhram Rds (just north of the palace) is a great place to pick up food to eat in your hotel room – kài thâwt or kài yâang (fried or roast chicken) with sticky rice, hàw mòk (fish and coconut curry steamed in banana leaves), klûay khàek (Indian-style fried bananas), a wide selection of fruits, satay, khâo krìap (crispy rice cakes), thâwt man plaa (fried fish cakes) and other delights.

At 26/47 Soonkangkha Manora, near the Australian Education Placement Centre, is a *Sala Mangsawirat* (Vegetarian Pavilion) with inexpensive Thai veggie food; like most Thai vegetarian restaurants, it's only open from around 10 am to 2 pm.

Boon Bakery, next to the Indra Hotel on Na Phra Kan Rd, serves Western breakfasts, coffee and pastries. In the evenings a night market sets up along Na Phra Kan Rd.

Getting There & Away

Bus Buses leave for Lopburi every 10 minutes from Ayuthaya, or, if you're coming from Bangkok, about every 20 minutes (5.30 am to 8.30 pm) from the northern terminal. It's a three-hour ride which costs 40B (72B air-con) from Bangkok, about half that from Ayuthaya.

Lopburi can also be reached from the west via Kanchanaburi or Suphanburi. If you're coming from Kanchanaburi, you'll have to take a bus (No 411) first to Suphanburi. The trip lasts about 2½ hours, costs 25B, and there's great scenery all the way. In Suphanburi, get off the bus in the town's main street, Malaimaen Rd (it has English signs), at the intersection which has an English sign pointing to Sri Prachan. From here you can catch a direct bus (No 464) to Lopburi for 25B, a trip of around three hours.

If you happen to miss the direct bus, you can also hopscotch to Lopburi by catching a bus first to Singburi or Ang Thong, across the river from Lopburi. The Suphanburi to Singburi leg lasts about 2½ hours for 25B and the scenery gets even better – you'll pass many old, traditional Thai wooden houses (late Ayuthaya style), countless cool rice paddies and small wats of all descriptions. Finally, at the Singburi bus station, catch one of the frequent buses to Lopburi for 10B (45 minutes). The Singburi bus makes a stop in front of Prang Sam Yot in old Lopburi – if you get off here, you won't have to backtrack from the new city. An alternative to the Suphanburi to Singburi route is to take a bus to Ang Thong (10B) and then a share taxi (20B) or bus (15B) to Lopburi. This is a little faster but not quite as scenic.

From the north-east, Lopburi can be reached via Khorat for 50B.

Train Ordinary trains depart Bangkok's Hualamphong station, heading north, every hour or so between 4.20 am and 8 pm, and take only 20 to 30 minutes longer to reach Lopburi than the rapid or express. Only two ordinary trains, the 7.05 am and the 8.30 am, have 2nd-class seats; the rest are 3rd class only. Rapid trains leave at 6.40 am, 3, 6.10, 8 and 10 pm and take about 2½ hours to reach Lopburi. Fares are 57B in 2nd class and 28B in 3rd class, not including surcharges for rapid or express trains.

There are also regular trains from Ayuthaya to Lopburi which take about one hour and cost 13B in 3rd class. It is possible to leave Bangkok or Ayuthaya in the morning, have a look around Lopburi during the day (leaving your bags in the Lopburi train station) and then carry on to Chiang Mai on one of the night trains (departure times are at 5.28 and 8.24 pm, and 12.22 am).

Getting Around

Songthaews run along Wichayen and Phra Narai Maharat Rds between the old and new towns for 3B per passenger. Samlors will go anywhere in the old town for 20B.

Ang Thong & Saraburi Provinces

ANG THONG

อ.เมืองอ่างทอง

There are some places of interest outside small Ang Thong (population 10,000), between Lopburi and Suphanburi, including **Wat Pa Mok** with its 22-metre-long reclining Buddha. The village of **Ban Phae** is famous for the crafting of Thai drums or *klawng*. Ban Phae is behind the Pa Mok Market on the banks of the Chao Phraya River.

Places to Stay

Rooms start at 80B in the *Bua Luang* (☎ (035) 611116) on Ayuthaya Rd. The *Ang Thong Hotel & Bungalows* (☎ (035) 611767/8) at 19 Ang Thong Rd costs 100B for rooms up in the hotel, 120B in the bungalows.

Getting There & Away

A bus from the northern bus terminal in Bangkok costs 31B. See the Lopburi Getting There & Away section for details on transport to Ang Thong from Suphanburi.

SARABURI & AROUND

อ.เมืองสระบุรี

There's nothing of touristic interest in Saraburi (population 64,000), but between Lopburi and here you can turn off to **Wat Phra Buddhabat** (Wat Phra Phutthabaat), one of six royal temples in the country bestowed with the kingdom's highest temple rank, Ratchavoramahavihan. A small and delicately beautiful *mondòp* (square shrine) houses a revered Buddha footprint that was 'discovered' during the reign of King Song Tham (1610-1628). Like all genuine Buddha footprints *(phútthábàat)*, it is massive and identified by its 108 auspicious distinguishing marks. The original Ayuthaya-era mondop perished in a fire; the current one dates to the reign of King Rama I (1782-1809). Twice yearly, in early February and in the middle of March, Phra Buddhabat is the focus of a colourful pilgrimage festival.

Also outside Saraburi is **Krabawk Cave Monastery** (Samnak Song Tham Krabawk), a famous opium and heroin detoxification centre. Originally begun by Mae-chii Mian, a Buddhist nun, the controversial programme has been administered by Luang Phaw Chamrun Panchan since 1959. The programme employs a combination of herbal treatment, counselling and Dhamma to cure addicts and claims a 70% success rate. Thousands of addicts have come to Tham Krabawk to seek treatment, which begins with a rigorous 10-day session involving the ingestion of emetic herbs to purify the body of intoxicants. In 1975, Phra Chamrun was awarded the Magsaysay Prize for his work. Visitors are welcome at the centre.

Recently Tham Krabawk has come under fire from government officials for allegedly harbouring large numbers of Hmong guerrillas – up to 9000 at a time – who hope to overthrow the communist government in Laos.

Places to Stay

Try the *Thanin* (120B) or the *Suk San* (80 to 120B) at Amphoe Phra Buddhabat. In Saraburi there's the *Kiaw An* (☎ (036) 211656) on Phahonyothin Rd where rooms with fan cost from 100B, or from 240B with air-con. Other hotels include the slightly cheaper *Saraburi* (☎ (036) 211646/500) opposite the bus stop, or the *Saen Suk* (☎ (036) 211104) on Phahonyothin Rd.

Getting There & Away

Ordinary buses from Bangkok's northern bus terminal cost 31B to Saraburi, a two to three-hour trip. Songthaews from Saraburi to Phra Buddhabat or Tham Krabawk cost around 5B per person.

Suphanburi Province

SUPHANBURI

อ.เมืองสุพรรณบุรี

Almost 70 km north-east of Kanchanaburi, Suphanburi (population 26,000) is a very old Thai town that may have had some connection with the semi-mythical Suvarnabhumi mentioned in early Buddhist writings. During the Dvaravati period (6th to 10th centuries) it was called Meuang Thawarawadi Si Suphannaphumi. Today the town is a prosperous, typical central Thai town along the Suphanburi River with a high proportion of Chinese among the population. There are some noteworthy Ayuthaya-period chedis and one Khmer-style prang. If you're passing through Suphan on a trip from Kanchanaburi to Lopburi, you might want to stop off for a couple of hours, see the sights, eat and rest.

Temples

Entering Suphan from the direction of Kanchanaburi, you'll see **Wat Paa Lelai** on the right at the town limits. Several of the buildings, originally built during the U Thong period, are old and the bot is very distinctive because of its extremely high whitewashed walls. Looking inside, you'll realise the building was designed that way in order to house the gigantic (24.5 metres) late U Thong or early Ayuthaya-style, 'European-pose' Buddha image inside. Devotees have gilded the figure's feet and ankles with squares of one-baht gold leaf. Exotic-looking goats roam the grounds of this semi-abandoned wat.

Farther in towards the town centre, on the left side of Malaimaen Rd, is **Wat Phra Si Ratana Mahathat** (this must be the most popular name for wats in Thailand). Set back off the road a bit, this quiet wat features a fine Lopburi-style Khmer prang on which much of the stucco is still intact. There is a staircase inside the prang leading to a small chamber in the top.

Two other wats this side of the Suphanburi River, the late U Thong **Wat Phra Rup** and **Wat Chum**, have venerable old Ayuthaya chedis. Wat Phra Rup also contains an impressive reclining Buddha locally known as 'Nen Kaew' and the only wooden Buddha footprint in the country.

Fifteen km north-east, off the road to Ang Thong, is **Wat Sai Ngam**, a famous vipassana monastery under the direction of 80-year-old abbot Ajaan Dhammadharo. Dhammadharo is the originator of an intricate system of developing insight by observing one's own hand and arm movements. As with all meditation wats, only serious meditators or would-be meditators should visit Wat Sai Ngam; an interpreter will be necessary as English isn't spoken at this temple.

Don Chedi

อนุสรณ์ดอนเจดีย์

Seven km west of Suphanburi, off Route 324 on the way to Kanchanaburi, is the road to Don Chedi, a very famous battle site and early war memorial. It was here that King Naresuan, then a prince, defeated the Prince of Myanmar on elephant-back in the late 16th century. In doing so he freed Ayuthaya from domination by the Bago (Pegu) Kingdom.

The chedi itself was built during Naresuan's lifetime but was neglected in the centuries afterwards. By the reign of King Rama V (Chulalongkorn) at the beginning of this century, its location had been forgotten. Rama V began a search for the site but it wasn't until three years after his death in 1913 that Prince Damrong, an accomplished archaeologist, rediscovered the chedi in Suphanburi Province.

The chedi was restored in 1955 and the area developed as a national historic site. Every year during the week of January 25 (Thai Armed Forces Day), there is a week-long Don Chedi Monument Fair which features a full-costume re-enactment of the elephant battle that took place four centuries ago.

During the fair there are regular buses to Don Chedi from Suphanburi, the nearest place to stay. Transport from Bangkok can also be arranged through the bigger travel agencies there.

U Thong National Museum

Seven km west of the amphoe meuang on Route 321 (Malaimaen Rd), this museum houses a collection of art and artefacts collected in Suphanburi Province, from stone and bronze culture tools to Buddhist sculpture of several eras. Dvaravati and U Thong styles are well covered, and there is an exhibit of Lao Song culture and handicrafts. The Lao Song are a local ethnic minority who have all but assimilated with Central Thai culture. The museum is open Wednesday to Sunday from 9 am to 4 pm; admission is 10B.

Places to Stay

The *King Pho Sai* (☎ (035) 522412) at 678 Nen Kaew Rd has rooms from 120B or from 240B with air-con. Other similarly priced hotels are the *K A T* (☎ (035) 521619/639) at 433 Phra Phanwasa, and the *Suk San* (☎ (035) 521668) at 1145 Nang Phim Rd. The *Si Meuang*, 331-6 Phra Phanwasa Rd, is a Chinese hotel with rooms from 90B.

If you're looking for something a little fancier, comfortable air-con rooms are available at the *Kalapreuk Hotel* (☎ (035) 522555), 135/1 Prachathibotai Rd, starting at 600B.

Getting There & Away

See the Getting There & Away information for Lopburi. A bus from the northern bus terminal in Bangkok costs 55B.

Pendant made by Hmong hill tribe

Chachoengsao Province

CHACHOENGSAO

อ.เมืองฉะเชิงเทรา

This provincial town, divided by the wide Bang Pakong River, is hardly visited by foreign tourists, probably because it's not on any of the major road or rail lines out of Bangkok. As a short day trip, however, it's a good way to escape Bangkok and experience provincial Thai life without encountering the tourists and touts of Ayuthaya or Nakhon Pathom.

The main attraction for visitors to Chachoengsao is **Wat Sothon Wararam Worawihaan**, which houses Phra Phuttha Sothon, one of the most sacred Buddha images in the country. The origins of the 198-cm-high image are cloaked in mystery, the only point of agreement being that the image is associated with a famous monk named Luang Phaw Sothon. Sothon was considered a *phrá sàksìt*, a monk with holy powers, and Buddha amulets modelled on the Phuttha Sothon – if blessed by the monk – are thought to be particularly effective protectors. Luang Phaw Sothon supposedly predicted the exact moment of his own death – thousands gathered at the temple to watch him die while sitting in meditation posture.

In the centre of the city, opposite City Hall, is the 90-rai **Somdet Phra Si Nakharin Park** with shade trees and a large pond.

The **Sorn-Thawee Meditation Centre** (Samnak Vipassana Sonthawi), about 17 km north of the city, offers 20 to 50-day meditation courses in the style of Myanmar's late Mahasi Sayadaw. Two German monks can provide instruction in English or German. If you are interested in taking the course, write in advance to Sorn-Thawee Meditation Centre, Bangkla, Chachoengsao 24110.

Places to Stay

Should you want to stay overnight in Chachoengsao, the *River Inn* (☎ (038) 511921) next to the river on Naruphong Rd has good rooms for 150B up.

Getting There & Away

The best way to visit Chachoengsao by public transport is via the eastern railway line. Ten trains a day leave Bangkok's Hualamphong station between 6 am and 5.25 pm; in the reverse direction trains depart between 5.30 am and 5.33 pm. The fare – 3rd class only – is 13B and the trip takes around 1½ hours each way.

Buses to Chachoengsao leave hourly between 6 am and 6 pm from Bangkok's eastern bus terminal (Soi 40, Sukhumvit Rd). The fare is 23B on the ordinary bus (around two hours) or 42B on the air-con bus (1½ hours).

Nakhon Pathom Province

NAKHON PATHOM

อ.เมืองนครปฐม

Only 56 km west of Bangkok, Nakhon Pathom (population 45,000) is regarded as the oldest city in Thailand – the name is derived from the Pali 'Nagara Pathama', meaning 'First City'. It was the centre of the Dvaravati Kingdom, a loose collection of city states that flourished between the 6th and 11th centuries AD in the Chao Phraya River valley. The area may have been inhabited before India's Ashokan period (3rd century BC), as it is theorised that Buddhist missionaries from India visited Nakhon Pathom at that time.

Today's Nakhon Pathom is a typical provincial Thai city whose only visible link to its glorious past is the Phra Pathom Chedi.

Phra Pathom Chedi

พระปฐมเจดีย์

The central attraction in Nakhon Pathom is the famous Phra Pathom Chedi, the tallest Buddhist monument in the world, rising to 127 metres. The original monument, buried within the massive orange-glazed dome, was erected in the early 6th century by Theravada Buddhists of Dvaravati, but in the early 11th century the Khmer King Suryavarman I of Angkor conquered the city and built a Brahman prang over the sanctuary. The Burmese of Pagan, under King Anuruddha, sacked the city in 1057 and the prang lay in ruins until King Mongkut had it restored in 1860. The king had a larger chedi built over the remains according to Buddhist tradition, adding four wihaans, a bot, a replica of the original chedi and assorted salas, prangs and other embellishments. There is even a Chinese temple attached to the outer walls of the Phra Pathom Chedi, next to which

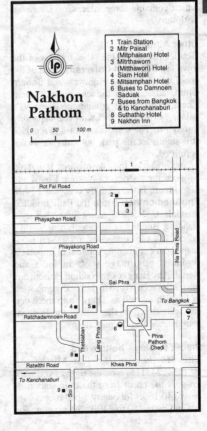

Nakhon Pathom

1 Train Station
2 Mitr Paisal (Mitphaisan) Hotel
3 Mitrthaworn (Mitthawon) Hotel
4 Siam Hotel
5 Mitsamphan Hotel
6 Buses to Damnoen Saduak
7 Buses from Bangkok & to Kanchanaburi
8 Suthathip Hotel
9 Nakhon Inn

0   50   100 m

Rot Fai Road
Phayaphan Road
Phayakong Road
Sai Phra
Ratchadamnoen Road
Ratwithi Road
Khwa Phra
Na Phra Road
Thetsaban
Lang Phra
To Bangkok
To Kanchanaburi
Soi 3
Phra Pathom Chedi

outdoor li-khe (Thai folk dance-drama) is sometimes performed.

On the eastern side of the monument, in the bot, is a Dvaravati-style Buddha seated in 'European pose' similar to the one in Wat Phra Meru in Ayuthaya. It may, in fact, have come from Phra Meru.

The wat surrounding the chedi enjoys the kingdom's highest temple rank, Ratchavoramahavihan, one of only six temples so honoured in Thailand. King Rama VI's ashes are interred in the base of the Sukhothai-era Phra Ruang Rochanarit, a large standing Buddha image in the wat's northern wihaan.

Opposite the bot is a museum, open Wednesday to Sunday from 9 am to 4 pm, which contains some interesting Dvaravati sculpture.

Other Attractions

Besides the chedi, the other focuses of the town are **Silpakorn University**, west of the chedi off Phetkasem Highway, and **Sanam Chan**, adjacent to the university. Sanam Chan, formerly the grounds of Rama VI's palace, is a pleasant park with a canal passing through it. The somewhat run-down palace still stands in the park but entrance is not permitted.

South-east of the city towards Bangkok, between the districts of Nakhon Chaisi and Sam Phran, is the recently completed **Phra Phutthamonthon** (from the Pali 'Buddha-mandala'). This 40.7-metre Sukhothai-style standing Buddha is reportedly the world's tallest; it's surrounded by a 2500-rai landscaped park containing replicas of important Buddhist pilgrimage spots in India and Nepal. Any Bangkok to Nakhon Pathom bus passes the access road to the park (signposted in English as well as Thai); from there you can walk, hitch or flag one of the frequent songthaews into the park itself.

Places to Stay – bottom end

The *Mitrthaworn Hotel* or Mitthawon (☎ (034) 243115) is on the right as you walk towards the chedi from the train station. It costs 140/160B for one/two-bed rooms with fan and bath; 180 to 240B with air-con. The *Mitphaisan Hotel* (☎ (034) 242422) – the English sign reads 'Mitr Paisal' – is farther down the alley to the right from Mitthawon. Rooms here are 150/200B for fan and bath; 270/320B with air-con.

Near the west side of Phra Pathom Chedi, next to a furniture store on Lang Phra Rd, the *Mitsamphan* (☎ (034) 241422) offers clean rooms with fan and bath for 150B. All three of the 'Mit' hotels are owned by the same family. Price differences reflect differences in cleanliness and service. This time around my budget vote stays with Mitphaisan.

West of the chedi a few blocks from Mitsamphan on Thetsaban Rd is the *Siam Hotel* (☎ (034) 241754). The staff here remain curt at best and rooms cost 140/180B for one/two beds with fan and bath or up to 250/280B with air-con. A bit farther south at 24/22 to 44/1 Thetsaban Rd, is the *Suthathip Hotel* (☎ (034) 242242), with a boisterous Chinese restaurant downstairs. Rooms seem like an afterthought here and cost 120/160B for one/two beds with fan and bath.

Places to Stay – top end

The *Nakhon Inn* (☎ (034) 242265, 251152) at 55 Ratwithi Rd is a pleasant 70-room air-con hotel where Thai guests are charged 400B per room, and farangs double that for the same accommodation! Since this is a private establishment (not government-subsidised), this is simple racial discrimination. If you speak Thai well enough, you might be able to get the Thai price.

Places to Eat

Nakhon Pathom has an excellent fruit market along the road between the train station and the Phra Pathom Chedi; the khâo lãam (sticky rice and coconut steamed in a bamboo joint) is reputed to be the best in Thailand. There are many good, inexpensive food vendors and restaurants in this area.

Getting There & Away

Bus Buses for Nakhon Pathom leave the southern bus terminal in Bangkok every 10 minutes from 5.45 am to 9.10 pm; the fare is 16B for the one-hour trip. Air-con buses are

24B and leave about every 20 minutes between 6 am and 10.30 pm.

Buses to Kanchanaburi leave throughout the day from the west side of the Phra Pathom Chedi – get bus No 81.

Train Ordinary trains (3rd class only) leave Bangkok Noi (Thonburi) train station daily at 7.30 and 8 am, 12.30, 1.45, 5.30, 6.15 and 8.20 pm, arriving in Nakhon Pathom in about an hour and 10 minutes. The 3rd-class fare is 14B.

There are also ordinary trains to Nakhon Pathom from Hualamphong station at 9.25 am and 1.40 pm, plus rapid and express trains roughly hourly between 12.25 and 7.45 pm; the 3rd-class fare is 14B, 2nd class 28B, 1st class 54B (add 20B and 30B respectively for rapid and express service); the ordinary and rapid trains from Hualamphong take 1½ hours, the express is only 10 minutes faster. Second and 1st class are available only on rapid and express trains, but it's not worth taking them since travel time is roughly the same; also, the rapid and express surcharges cost more than the ordinary 3rd-class fares alone.

Ratchaburi Province

RATCHABURI
ราชบุรี
Ratchaburi (Ratburi) (population 46,000) is the first major town you reach on the way south from Nakhon Pathom. Like Suphanburi and Nakhon Pathom, its history dates back to the early Dvaravati period.

The city lies on the banks of the Mae Klong River and is connected to the rest of Central Thailand by canal. Chom Bung district, in a north-west section of the province, is the site for a large 'holding centre' (a Thai government euphemism for refugee camp) for Burmese and Karens fleeing political persecution in Myanmar.

Information
Money The First Bangkok City Bank at 250/18 Kraiphet Rd has an exchange facility, open Monday to Friday from 8.30 am to 3.30 pm.

Post Office The post and international telephone office is on the corner of Samutsadarak and Amarin Rds. The phone office upstairs is open daily from 7 am to 10 pm. The telephone area code for Ratchaburi is ☎ 032.

Things to See
In the north-western part of town near the Mae Klong River, the historical **Wat Phra Si Ratana Mahathat** is known for its prang, which is said to be styled after the main prang at Angkor Wat. It is doubtful that it was constructed by the Khmers in the 10th or 11th century as local literature suggests – most likely it was erected during the Ayuthaya period. The wat is a 20-minute walk from the municipal market or a 15B samlor ride (20B by tuk-tuk) from the clock tower near the market.

Two km south-west of the town centre is the abandoned hill monastery **Khao Wang**. Originally built as a palace for Rama V, who only used it once in 1877, it was later converted to Wat Khao Wang by Rama VII. The main wihaan has been restored.

Along the Ratchaburi-Suan Phung Rd, about seven km west of town via Route 3087, is a hermit cave *(tham reusii)* containing a famous Dvaravati-period Buddha stone image. Roughly 20 metres high, the gilded image represents the preaching of the first sermon. Monkeys have taken the figure over and have plenty of fun running along the top of it. To get to **Phra Phutthachai Tham Reusii Khao Ngu**, take one of the numerous minibuses departing from the market near the clock tower. The fare is 4B, and the journey takes about 12 minutes.

Places to Stay
Kuang Hua Hotel (☎ 337119), at 202 Amarin Rd, has reasonable basic rooms for 120B with fan and bath. The *Hong Fa Hotel* (☎ 337484)

at 89/13 Rat Yindi Rd has rooms with fan and bath from 140B. Other hotels include the *Araya* (☎ 337781/2) at 187/1-2 Kraiphet Rd, with not-so-clean rooms for 250B with fan, or 450B with air-con and TV. Almost opposite is the best value in town, the *Numsin Hotel* (☎ 337551) at 2/16 Kraiphet Rd, where good rooms are 220B with fan and 350B with air-con.

Places to Eat

There are plenty of food stalls at the market on the bank of the Mae Klong River. Stalls spread out through the streets all the way to Rotfai Rd, along which runs the train line. This is also a good area for all types of shopping, with a variety of shops lining the streets.

The friendly *Arharnthai* (☎ 337259) at 142 Katathon Rd, in front of the train station, serves a wide variety of Thai dishes in the 40 to 120B range.

Getting There & Away

Bus The ordinary buses to/from Bangkok are stationed on Rotfai Rd, just around the corner from Kraiphet Rd. The fare is 34B and the trip takes 1½ hours. Air-con buses to Bangkok (54B) arrive and depart from in front of the Numsin Hotel on Kraiphet Rd.

Minibuses to Damnoen Saduak depart from Rotfai Rd, near the corner of Kraiphet Rd, and cost 14B. Buses to Phetburi cost 16B and take an hour.

Train Ratchaburi is on the southern line from Bangkok, with seven daily trains passing through. The fare to Bangkok is 25B in 3rd class and 52B in 2nd class (plus rapid or express surcharges for the latter); the trip takes about two hours whether by ordinary, rapid or express train. The ordinary train to Phetburi costs 11B 3rd class and takes about 40 minutes.

Getting Around

Samlors around town cost 10B, or to the outskirts of town 20B. Tuk-tuks are 20B.

AROUND RATCHABURI

Damnoen Saduak Floating Market

If the commercialisation of Bangkok's floating markets puts you off, there is a much more lively floating market *(talaat naam)* on Khlong Damnoen Saduak in Ratchaburi Province, 104 km south-west of Bangkok, between Nakhon Pathom and Samut Songkhram.

Talaat Ton Khem is the main market on Khlong Damnoen Saduak Canal, while **Talaat Hia Kui**, just south on the parallel Khlong Hia Kui, gets the most tourists – one area in fact has been set aside especially for tourists, with a large open shop with souvenirs for bus tours as well as souvenir-laden boats. There is a third, less crowded market on a smaller canal, a bit south of Damnoen Saduak, called **Talaat Khun Phitak**. To get there, take a water taxi going south from the pier on the east side of Thong Lang Canal, which intersects Damnoen Saduak near the larger floating market, and ask for Talaat Khun Phitak. You can rent a boat to tour the canals and all three markets for 100 to 300B per hour – depending on your bargaining skills. Try to arrive by 8 am at the latest – by 9 am the package tours are in full evidence.

One sure way to beat the tour buses from Bangkok is to spend the night in Damnoen Saduak itself and get up before the hordes of tourists arrive. Try the *Noknoi (Little Bird)* (☎ 251382), where rooms cost 100 to 140B with fan, 170 to 250B air-con, or *Ban Sukchoke Guest House*, with comfortable rooms for 120B.

Getting There & Away Bus No 78 goes direct from Bangkok's southern bus terminal to Damnoen Saduak every 20 minutes, beginning at 6 am, but you'll have to get one of the first few buses to arrive in Damnoen Saduak by 8 or 9 am when the market's at its best. The fare is 49B for air-con or 30B for an ordinary bus. From the pier nearest the bus station, take a 20B water taxi to the talaat naam or simply walk west from the station along the canal until you come to the market area.

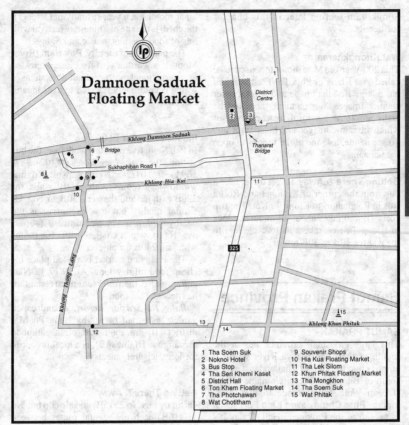

Damnoen Saduak Floating Market

1 Tha Soem Suk
2 Noknoi Hotel
3 Bus Stop
4 Tha Seri Khemi Kaset
5 District Hall
6 Ton Khem Floating Market
7 Tha Photchawan
8 Wat Chotitham
9 Souvenir Shops
10 Hia Kua Floating Market
11 Tha Lek Silom
12 Khun Phitak Floating Market
13 Tha Mongkhon
14 Tha Soem Suk
15 Wat Phitak

Some people spend the night in Nakhon Pathom and catch an early morning bus to Samut Songkhram, asking to be let out at Damnoen Saduak. It is also possible to get to Damnoen Saduak by bus (6B) from Samut Songkhram, a trip of around 25 minutes. A minibus to or from Ratchaburi costs 20B.

One interesting way to get there is by boat from Samut Sakhon. To get to Damnoen Saduak from Samut Sakhon, take a local bus to Kratum Baen and then take a songthaew a few km north to the Tha Angton pier on the right bank of the Tha Chin River. From the pier, catch a ferry boat across the river to the Damnoen Saduak Canal, which runs west off the Tha Chin. From the Bang Yang lock, where ferry passengers disembark, take a 30-km trip by long-tail boat *(reua haang yao)* to the floating market. The fare is 16B and includes a boat change halfway at Ban Phaew – worth it for what is one of Thailand's most beautiful stretches of waterway.

Less touristed floating markets can be reached by boating south from Damnoen Saduak to Amphawa district in Samut Songkhram Province – see the Samut

Songkhram section later in this chapter for details.

Wat Khongkharam

This 200-year-old Mon monastery used to be called Wat Klang or Phia To. The main hall has a large Buddha image and several other smaller images. Surrounding them on the walls are some beautiful frescoes, half of which are rain-damaged and faded with age. To see inside, ask one of the monks to open the wihaan.

Getting There & Away To get there, take a bus from the corner of Kraiphet and Rotfai Rds in Ratchaburi to Klong Ta Kot. The trip costs 7B and takes about 40 minutes. Once in Klong Ta Kot, take a motorcycle taxi to the wat for 10B or 30B return.

Samut Prakan Province

SAMUT PRAKAN

This large city/small province lies at the mouth of the Chao Phraya River where it empties into the Gulf of Thailand just 30 km south of Bangkok. The city's name means 'Ocean Wall', a reference to the 1893-vintage **Phra Chula Jawm Klao Fort** seven km south of the Provincial Hall. Today it's one of Thailand's most densely populated provincial capitals, with 71,500 people packed into 7.3 sq km.

The province's two major attractions, **Ancient City** and the **Crocodile Farm**, are described in the Bangkok Things to See & Do – Outskirts of Bangkok section, since most people visit these as day trips from Bangkok.

The Ayuthaya-era **Phra Samut Chedi**, popularly known as Phra Chedi Klang Nam ('Chedi in the Middle of the River') for its original location on an island in the Chao Phraya River, now sits on the river bank in front of the Provincial Hall. Beginning on the fifth day of the waning moon in the 11th

lunar month each year (usually in October), the chedi is the site of a nine-day festival with lots of food vendors, music and lights.

The port area of the city, **Pak Nam** (River Mouth), is worth a visit for those interested in international ports. Samut Prakan as a whole is commonly referred to as 'Meuang Pak Nam'.

Places to Stay & Eat

In Pak Nam, five minutes' walk from the bus station, the *Pak Num Hotel* (☎ (02) 387-1691) at 101/2-3 Naraiprapsuk Rd has windowless rooms with grotty walls for 220B with fan and shower, 350B air-con. Of similar quality but less expensive is the nearby *Nithra Swan (Nit Sawan)* (☎ (02) 395-1608), which charges 140B for rooms with fan, 240B for air-con.

The Pak Nam market is a good place for cheap food all day long. At 19/17-18 Naraiprapsuk Rd, the *Wall's* ice cream restaurant has decent Thai food.

Bang Pu Seaside Resort, a landscaped garden restaurant in nearby Bang Pu Mai district (10 km south-east of the amphoe meuang via Highway 3), is a local favourite for long, leisurely meals.

Getting There & Away

Ordinary bus No 25 (5B) and air-con bus No 11 (16B) each ply regular routes between central Bangkok and Pak Nam. The journey can take up to two hours depending on traffic.

Getting Around

The bus station is on Srisamut Rd in front of the harbour and market. Songthaews depart from the market area to Ancient City and the Crocodile Farm for 5B each. To get from the Crocodile Farm to Ancient City, turn right from the farm and walk for 10 minutes to Sukhumvit Rd or catch a songthaew or a motorbike taxi. On Sukhumvit Rd, hail a songthaew or a minibus (3B) which will take 10 minutes to get to Ancient City.

Samut Sakhon & Samut Songkhram Provinces

SAMUT SAKHON

Twenty-eight km south-west of Bangkok, Samut Sakhon (Ocean City) is popularly known as Mahachai because it straddles the confluence of the Tha Chin River and Khlong Mahachai. Just a few km from the Gulf of Thailand, this busy port features a lively market area and a pleasant breezy park around the crumbling walls of **Wichian Chodok Fort**. A few rusty cannon pointing towards the river testify to the fort's original purpose in guarding the mouth of the Chao Phraya River from foreign invaders. Before the 17th-century arrival of European traders, the town was known as Tha Jiin (Chinese Pier) because of the large number of Chinese junks that called here.

A few km west of the capital along Highway 35 is the Ayuthaya-period **Wat Yai Chom Prasat**, which is known for the finely carved wooden doors on its bot. You can easily identify the wat from the road by the tall Buddha figure standing in front. To get here from Samut Sakhon, take a west-bound bus (2B) heading towards Samut Song-khram; the wat is only a 10-minute ride from the edge of town.

In Ban Phaew district, around 30 km north-west of the capital via Highway 35 (west) and Route 3079 (north), the **Khlong Pho Hak Floating Market** (talàat náam khlwang phoh hàk) convenes daily except wan phra (full and new moon days) from 6 am to noon. To get there, take a songthaew or bus to Ban Phaew (around 10B) and then catch a long-tail boat taxi along Khlong Pho Hak to the market eight km away – if you share with a group of Thais going to the market the fare should be no more than 10B apiece. It may also be possible to reach this market by chartered long-tail boat from Samut Sakhon through a network of canals. The market is also known as talàat náam làk 5, 'Km 5 Floating Market'.

Places to Stay & Eat

Near the highway at 927/28 Sethakit Rd, only a few minutes' walk from the bus station on the opposite side of the road, is the *Kasem Hotel* (☎ (034) 411078); there is no English sign. It's a standard Thai hotel with fairly clean rooms (but dirty walls) and constant street noise. All rooms feature Western toilets and hot water showers; rates are 180B with fan and 350B with air-con. *Wiang Thai Hotel* (☎ (034) 411151) at 821/5 Sukhon-thawit Rd is similar.

Towards the harbour, Norasing Rd (off Sethakit Rd) fills with food stalls at night, making it a great spot for inexpensive dinners. *Tarua (Thaa Reua) Restaurant* (☎ (034) 411084), on the first floor of the ferry terminal building at the harbour end of Sethakit Rd, is a good seafood place with an English-language menu and seafood dishes ranging from 50 to 100B. *New Sathip* and *Wang Nam Khem* at 927/42 and 927/179 Sethakit Rd serve standard Thai and Chinese dishes at reasonable prices.

Getting There & Away

Ordinary buses to Samut Sakhon (22B) depart from Bangkok's southern terminal all day long. The trip takes about an hour. Buses between Samut Sakhon and Samut Song-khram cost 11B and take about half an hour.

Samut Sakhon is nearly midway along the 3rd-class, short-line train route that runs between Bangkok Noi (Thonburi) station and Samut Songkhram. The fare to/from either Thonburi or Samut Songkhram is 8B; there are only four departures a day.

Getting Around

Samlors and motorbike taxis around town cost 5B to 10B depending on the distance.

SAMUT SONGKHRAM

Wedged between Ratchaburi, Samut Sakhon and Phetburi, 416-sq-km Samut Songkhram is Thailand's smallest province. Commonly known as 'Mae Klong', the capital lies along a sharp bend in the Mae Klong River, 74 km south-west of Bangkok and just a few km from the Gulf of Thailand. Due to flat topography and abundant water sources, the area surrounding the capital is well suited for the steady irrigation needed to grow guava, lychee and grapes. Along the highway from Thonburi, visitors will pass a string of artificial sea lakes used in the production of salt.

Information
The Thai Farmers Bank at 125/5 Prasitphatthana Rd offers foreign-exchange services Monday to Friday from 9 am to 3.30 pm.

Things to See
The capital itself is a fairly modern city with a large market area between the train line and bus terminal. The sizeable **Wat Phet Samut Worawihaan** in the centre of town near the train station and river contains a renowned Buddha image called Luang Phaw Wat Baan Laem – named for the phra saksit (holy monk) who dedicated it, thus transferring mystical powers to the image.

At the mouth of the Mae Klong River, not far from town, is the province's most famous tourist attraction, a bank of fossilised shells known as **Don Hoi Lot**. The type of shells embedded in the bank come from *hǎwy làwt*, clams with a tube-like shell. The shell bank is best seen late in the dry season (typically April and May) when the river surface has receded to its lowest height. To get to Don Hoi Lot you need to charter a boat from the Mae Klong market pier (*thâa talàat mâe klawng*). The trip takes about 45 minutes.

Another local attraction is the **Orchid Farm**, four km north of town on the road to Damnoen Saduak. A bus to the farm costs 3B and takes about 10 minutes.

Floating Markets Samut Songkhram Province is criss-crossed with canals intersecting the lazy bends of the Mae Khlong River, creating the perfect environment for traditional Thai floating markets. Three of the better ones are held in Amphawa district, about seven km north-east of the capital via the Mae Klong River. The **Amphawa Floating Market** (*talàat náam ampháwaa*)

convenes daily in front of Wat Amphawa from 6 to 8 am. The other two meet only six days a month following the traditional lunar calendar; **Bang Noi Floating Market** takes place in nearby Bang Noi from 6 am to 11 am on the 3rd, 8th and 13th days of both the waxing and waning moons, while the **Tha Kha Floating Market** meets on the 2nd, 7th and 12th days of the waxing and waning moons.

Any common Thai calendar, available for a few baht in a housewares market, will show you which days of the solar month coincide with this lunar schedule. These floating markets can be visited by chartered long-tail boat from the Mae Klong market pier – figure on 150 to 300B per hour depending on negotiation.

Places to Stay & Eat
There are four hotels in the centre of the city, none of them very quiet. The cheapest is the *Thai Sawat* (☎ (034) 711205) at 524 Phet Samut Rd, where basic rooms with fan cost 100 to 150B. Also inexpensive is the nearby *Mae Klong Hotel* (☎ (034) 711150) at 546/10-13 Phet Samut Rd, opposite Wat Phet Samut Worawihaan. The owners are pleasant, speak some English and can provide information on the area. The rooms are fairly clean and cost 100B with a fan or 200B with air-con.

The other two places to stay, the *Alongkorn 1 Hotel* (☎ (034) 711017) at 541/15 Kasem Sukhum Rd and *Alongkorn 2 Hotel* (☎ (034) 711709) at 540 Pomkaew Rd are only separated by the cinema on busy Kasem Sukhum Rd. They have very similar rooms and standards at 120B with fan and 170/220B with air-con.

In front of Wat Phet Samut, along Phet Samut Rd, are several food stalls open all day and evening. There is also a lively night market in the square near the bus and taxi stands along Prasitphatthana Rd. *Tang Khai Hong* at 526/4 Phet Samut Rd is a very good Chinese place. *Suan Aahaan Tuk*, on the river off Soi Laem Yai, is a pleasant outdoor spot with an extensive Thai and Chinese menu.

Getting There & Away

Buses and taxis park at the intersection of Ratchayat Raksa and Prasitphatthana Rds. Buses to/from Bangkok depart and arrive here, but some buses from Bangkok may drop you off on the main highway, from where you can either walk or take a samlor or a songthaew. The fare is 22B in an ordinary bus or 40B in an air-con one; either takes about 1½ hours. There are also many daily buses to Samut Sakhon for 11B, taking about half an hour. Samut Songkhram is the southernmost terminus of a 70-km train line that originates at Bangkok Noi (Thonburi) train station, a journey of about an hour. The all 3rd-class train to/from Bangkok costs 16B (8B to/from Samut Sakhon), and there are four departures per day. The train station is a five-minute walk from the bus station, where Kasem Sukhum Rd terminates at Prasitphatthana Rd near the river.

Kanchanaburi Province

The town of Kanchanaburi was originally established by Rama I as a first line of defence against the Burmese, who might use the old invasion route through the Three Pagodas Pass on the Thai-Burmese border. It's still a popular smuggling route into Myanmar today.

During WW II, the Japanese occupation in Thailand used Allied prisoners of war to build the infamous Death Railway along this same invasion route, in reverse, along the Khwae Noi River to the pass. Thousands and thousands of prisoners died as a result of brutal treatment by their captors, a story chronicled by Boulle's book *The Bridge Over the River Kwai* and popularised by a movie based on the same. The bridge is still there (still in use, in fact) and so are the graves of the Allied soldiers. The river is actually spelled and pronounced Khwae (which means 'tributary' in Thai), like 'quack' without the 'ck'.

West and north-west of the capital are several of Thailand's largest waterfalls and most extensive wildlife sanctuaries. Most of the province, in fact, remains sparsely populated and wild.

KANCHANABURI
อ.เมืองกาญจนบุรี

Kanchanaburi (population 37,000) is 130 km west of Bangkok in the slightly elevated valley of the Mae Klong River amidst hills and sugar-cane plantations. The weather here is slightly cooler than in Bangkok and the evenings are especially pleasant. Although Kan (as the locals call it; also Kan'buri) gets enough tourists to warrant its own tourist office, not many Western visitors make it here – most tourists are Thai, Japanese, or Hong Kong and Singapore Chinese, who blaze through on air-con buses, hitting the River Khwae Bridge, the cemetery on Saengchuto Rd, the war museum, and then hurrying off to the nearby sapphire mines or one of the big waterfalls before heading north to Chiang Mai or back to Bangkok.

The Mae Klong River itself is a focus for much weekend and holiday activity among the Thais. Recently the city gave the waterfront area a facelift, planting casuarina trees and moving most of the floating restaurants offshore. A new bridge spanning the river, another bridge on the way and a new highway bypass north-east of town signify that development has arrived in what was previously a provincial backwater.

You may notice the fish-shaped street signs in Meuang Kan – they represent *plaa yisok*, the most common food fish in the Mae Klong River and its tributaries.

Information
Tourist Office The TAT office (☎ 511200) is on Saengchuto Rd, on the right as you enter town before the police station. A free map of the town and province is available, as well as comprehensive information on accommodation and transport. Hours are from 8.30 am to 4.30 pm daily. The office now has a contingent of tourist police – any problems with theft or other criminal occur-

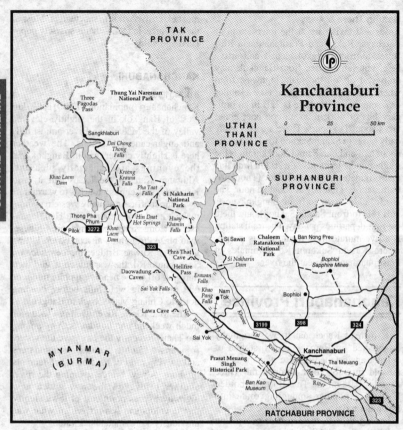

Kanchanaburi Province

rences should be reported to both the tourist police and the regular provincial police.

Post & Telecommunications The GPO on Saengchuto Rd is open weekdays from 8.30 am to 4.30 pm, weekends from 9 am to 2 pm; international telephone service is available daily from 7 am to 11 pm. There is also a small post office on Lak Meuang Rd towards the river, close to the Lak Meuang Shrine. The telephone area code for Kanchanaburi is ☎ 034.

Death Railway Bridge

สะพานข้ามแม่น้ำแคว

The so-called Bridge Over the River Kwai may be of interest to war historians but really looks quite ordinary. It spans the Khwae Yai River, a tributary of the Mae Klong River, a couple of km north of town – Khwae Yai literally translates as 'large tributary'. It is the story behind the bridge that is dramatic. The materials for the bridge were brought from Java by the Imperial Japanese Army during their occupation of Thailand. In 1945 the bridge was bombed several times and was only rebuilt after the war – the curved portions of the bridge are original. The first version of the bridge, completed in February 1943, was all wood. In April of the same year a second bridge of steel was constructed.

It is estimated that 16,000 POWs died while building the Death Railway to Myanmar, of which the bridge was only a small part. The strategic objective of the railway was to secure an alternative supply route for the Japanese conquest of Myanmar and other Asian countries to the west. Construction on the railway began on 16 September 1942 at existing terminals in Thanbyuzayat, Myanmar and Nong Pladuk, Thailand. Japanese engineers at the time estimated that it would take five years to link Thailand and Myanmar by rail, but the Japanese army forced the POWs to complete the 415-km, one-metre-gauge railway, of which roughly two-thirds ran through Thailand, in 16 months. Much of the railway was built in difficult terrain that required high bridges and deep mountain cuttings. The rails were finally joined 37 km south of Three Pagodas Pass; a Japanese brothel train inaugurated the line. The River Khwae Bridge was in use for 20 months before the Allies bombed it in 1945. Only one POW is known to have escaped, a Briton who took refuge among pro-British Karen guerrillas.

Although the statistics of the number of POWs who died during the Japanese occupation are horrifying, the figures for the labourers, many from Thailand, Myanmar, Malaysia and Indonesia, are even worse. It is thought that in total 90,000 to 100,000 coolies died in the area.

Today little remains of the original railway. West of Nam Tok, Karen and Mon carried off most of the track to use in the construction of local buildings and bridges.

Train nuts may enjoy the **railway museum** in front of the bridge, with engines used during WW II on display. Every year during the first week of December there is a nightly sound and light show at the bridge, commemorating the Allied attack on the Death Railway in 1945. It's a pretty big scene, with the sounds of bombers and explosions, fantastic bursts of light, and more. The town gets a lot of Thai tourists during this week, so book early if you want to witness this spectacle.

There are a couple of large outdoor restaurants near the bridge, on the river, but these

River Kwai Bridge

CENTRAL THAILAND

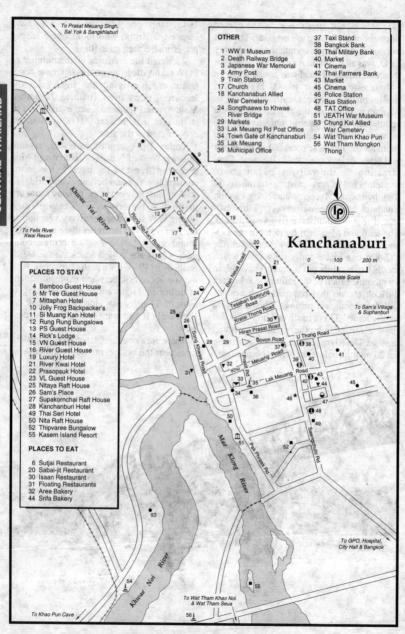

To Prasat Meuang Singh,
Sai Yok & Sangkhlaburi

To Felix River
Kwai Resort

To Sam's Village
& Suphanburi

Kanchanaburi

0   100   200 m

Approximate Scale

To GPO, Hospital,
City Hall & Bangkok

To Wat Tham Khao Noi
& Wat Tham Seua

To Khao Pun Cave

OTHER
1 WW II Museum
2 Death Railway Bridge
3 Japanese War Memorial
8 Army Post
9 Train Station
17 Church
18 Kanchanaburi Allied
    War Cemetery
24 Songthaews to Khwae
    River Bridge
29 Markets
33 Lak Meuang Rd Post Office
34 Town Gate of Kanchanaburi
35 Lak Meuang
36 Municipal Office
37 Taxi Stand
38 Bangkok Bank
39 Thai Military Bank
40 Market
41 Cinema
42 Thai Farmers Bank
43 Market
45 Cinema
46 Police Station
47 Bus Station
48 TAT Office
51 JEATH War Museum
53 Chung Kai Allied
    War Cemetery
54 Wat Tham Khao Pun
56 Wat Tham Mongkon
    Thong

PLACES TO STAY
4 Bamboo Guest House
5 Mr Tee Guest House
7 Mittaphan Hotel
10 Jolly Frog Backpacker's
11 Si Muang Kan Hotel
12 Rung Rung Bungalows
13 PS Guest House
14 Rick's Lodge
15 VN Guest House
16 River Guest House
19 Luxury Hotel
21 River Kwai Hotel
22 Prasopsuk Hotel
23 VL Guest House
25 Nitaya Raft House
26 Sam's Place
27 Supakornchai Raft House
28 Kanchanburi Hotel
49 Thai Seri Hotel
50 Nita Raft House
52 Thipvaree Bungalow
55 Kasem Island Resort

PLACES TO EAT
6 Sutjai Restaurant
20 Sabai-jit Restaurant
30 Isaan Restaurant
31 Floating Restaurants
32 Aree Bakery
44 Srifa Bakery

are for tour groups that arrive en masse throughout the day. If you're hungry, you can save money by eating with the tour bus and songthaew drivers in the little noodle places at the northern end of Pak Phraek Rd.

Getting There & Away The best way to get to the bridge from town is to catch a songthaew along Pak Phraek Rd (parallel to Saengchuto Rd towards the river) heading north. Regular songthaews are 5B and stop at the bridge, which is about four km from the centre of town. You can also take a train from the Kanchanaburi train station to the bridge for 2B.

Allied War Cemeteries

สุสานทหาร

There are two cemeteries containing the remains of Allied POWs who died in captivity during WW II; one is north of town off Saengchuto Rd, just before the train station, and the other is across the Mae Klong River west of town, a few km down the Khwae Noi (Little Tributary) River.

The **Kanchanaburi War Cemetery** is better cared for, with green lawns and healthy flowers. It's usually a cool spot on a hot Kanchanaburi day. It's only a 15-minute walk from the River Kwai Hotel or you can catch a songthaew anywhere along Saengchuto Rd going north – the fare is 5B. Jump off at the English sign in front of the cemetery on the left, or ask to be let off at the *sùsăan* (Thai for cemetery). Just before the cemetery on the same side of the road is a very colourful Chinese cemetery with burial mounds and inscribed tombstones.

To get to the other cemetery, the **Chung Kai Allied War Cemetery**, take a 2B ferry boat from the pier at the west end of Lak Meuang Rd across the Mae Klong, then follow the curving road through picturesque corn and sugar-cane fields until you reach the cemetery on your left. This is a fairly long walk, but the scenery along the way is pleasant. You can also easily take a bicycle along on the ferry. A new bridge may be going in between Sam's Place and Nitaya Raft House

to a large island in the river, with a second bridge to the river's west bank – if this comes to pass the ferry service may be discontinued.

Like the more visited cemetery north of town, the Chung Kai burial plaques carry names, military insignia and short epitaphs for Dutch, British, French and Australian soldiers.

About a km south-west of the Chung Kai Cemetery is a dirt path that leads to **Wat Tham Khao Pun**, one of Kanchanaburi's many cave temples. The path is approximately one km long and passes through thick forest with a few wooden houses along the way.

JEATH War Museum

พิพิธภัณฑ์สงคราม

This odd museum next to Wat Chaichumphon (Wat Tai) is worth visiting just to sit on the cool banks of the Mae Klong. Phra Maha Tomson Tongproh, a Thai monk who devotes much energy to promoting the museum, speaks some English and can answer questions about the exhibits, as well as supply information about what to see around Kanchanaburi and how best to get there. If you show him this book, he'll give you a 5B discount off the usual 20B admission. The museum itself is a replica example of the bamboo-atap huts used to house Allied POWs in the Kanchanaburi area during the Japanese occupation. The long huts contain various photographs taken during the war, drawings and paintings by POWs, maps, weapons and other war memorabilia. The acronym JEATH represents the fated meeting of Japan, England, Australia/America, Thailand and Holland at Kanchanaburi during WW II.

The War Museum is at the end of Wisuttharangsi (Visutrangsi) Rd, near the TAT office, next to the main compound of Wat Chaichumphon. The common Thai name for this museum is *phíphítháphan sŏngkhram wát tâi*. It's open daily from 8.30 am to 4.30 pm.

WW II Museum

พิพิธภัณฑ์สงคราม

Also called 'Art Gallery & War Museum', this new, somewhat garish structure just south of the famous bridge on the river looks like a Chinese temple on the outside. The larger, more lavishly built of the two buildings has nothing to do with WW II and little to do with art unless you can count the garish murals throughout. The bottom floor contains Burmese-style alabaster Buddhas and a *phrá khreûang* (sacred amulets) display. Upper floors exhibit Thai weaponry from the Ayuthaya period and a fair collection of historic and modern ceramics. Brightly painted portraits of all the kings in Thai history fill the 4th floor. Finally, on the 5th and uppermost floor – above the royal portraits (flirting with lese-majesty) – is the history of the Chinese family who built the museum, complete with a huge portrait of the family's original patriarch in China.

A smaller building opposite contains WW II relics, including photos and sketches made during the POW period and a display of Japanese and Allied weapons. Along the front of this building stand life-size sculptures of historical figures associated with the war, including Churchill, MacArthur, Hitler, Einstein, de Gaulle and Hirohito. The English captions are sometimes unintentionally amusing or disturbing – a reference to the atomic bomb dropped on Hiroshima, for example, reads 'Almost the entire city was destroyed in a jiffy'. Inside, a glass case contains 106 skeletons unearthed in a mass grave of Asian labourers. The gossip around town says these remains were stolen from a municipal excavation.

The museum is open from 9 am to 4.30 pm daily. Entry to the museum is 30B.

Lak Meuang Shrine

ศาลหลักเมือง

Like many other older Thai cities, Kanchanaburi has a *làk muang,* or town pillar/phallus, enclosed in a shrine at what was originally the town centre. Kanchanaburi's Lak Meuang Shrine is appropriately located on Lak Meuang Rd, which intersects Saengchuto Rd two blocks north of the TAT office.

The bulbous-tipped pillar is covered with gold leaf and is much worshipped. Unlike Bangkok's Lak Meuang you can get as close to this pillar as you like – no curtain.

Within sight of the pillar, towards the river, stands Kanchanaburi's original **city gate**.

Wat Tham Mongkon Thong

วัดถ้ำมังกรทอง

The 'Cave Temple of the Golden Dragon' is well known because of the 'Floating Nun' – a 70-plus-year-old mae chii who meditates while floating on her back in a pool of water. If you are lucky you might see her, but she seems to be doing this less frequently nowadays (try a Sunday). Thais come from all over Thailand to see her float and to receive her blessings, which she bestows by whistling onto the top of a devotee's head or by stuffing a cluster of burning candles into her mouth, then exhaling the smoke over a devotee's hands or head. A sizeable contingent of young Thai nuns stay here under the old nun's tutelage.

A long and steep series of steps with dragon-sculpted handrails lead up the craggy mountainside behind the main bot to a complex of limestone caves. Follow the string of light bulbs through the front cave and you'll come out above the wat with a view of the valley and mountains below. One section of the cave requires crawling or duck-walking, so wear appropriate clothing. Bats squeak away above your head and the smell of guano permeates the air.

Another cave wat is off this same road about one or two km from Wat Tham Mongkon Thong towards the pier. It can be seen on a limestone outcropping back from the road some 500 metres or so. The name is **Wat Tham Khao Laem**. The cave is less impressive than that at Wat Tham Mongkon Thong, but there are some interesting old temple buildings on the grounds.

Getting There & Away Heading south-east down Saengchuto Rd from the TAT office, turn right on Chukkadon Rd (marked in English – about halfway between the TAT and GPO), or take a songthaew (3B) from the town centre to the end of Chukkadon Rd. A bridge has replaced the river ferry that used to cross here; wait for any songthaew crossing the bridge and you can be dropped off in front of the temple for 5B.

The road to the wat passes sugar-cane fields, karst formations, wooden houses, cattle and rock quarries. Alternatively you could ride a bicycle here from town – the road can be dusty in the dry season but at least it's flat.

Wat Tham Seua & Wat Tham Khao Noi
วัดถ้ำเสือและวัดถ้ำเขาน้อย

These large hilltop monasteries about 15 km south-east of Kanchanaburi are important local pilgrimage spots, especially for Chinese Buddhists. Wat Tham Khao Noi (Little Hill Cave Monastery) is a Chinese temple-monastery similar in size and style to Penang's Kek Lok Si. Adjacent is the half-Thai, half-Chinese-style Wat Tham Seua (Tiger Cave Monastery). Both are built on a ridge over a series of small caves. Wat Tham Khao Noi isn't much of a climb, since it's built onto the side of the slope. Seeing Wat Tham Seua, however, means climbing either a steep set of naga stairs or a meandering set of steps past the cave entrance.

A climb to the top is rewarded with views of the Khwae River on one side, rice fields on the other. Wat Tham Seua features a huge sitting Buddha facing the river, with a conveyor belt that carries money offerings to a huge alms bowl in the image's lap. The easier set of steps to the right of the temple's naga stairs leads to a cave and passes an aviary with peacocks and other exotic birds. The cave itself has the usual assortment of Buddha images.

Getting There & Away By public transport, you can take a bus to Tha Meuang (12 km south-east of Kan), then a motorcycle taxi (30B) from near Tha Meuang Hospital directly to the temples.

If you're travelling by motorcycle or bicycle, take the right fork of the highway when you reach Tha Meuang, turn right past the hospital onto a road along the canal and then across the dam (Meuang Dam). From here to Wat Tham Seua and Khao Noi is another four km. Once you cross the dam, turn right down the other side of the river and follow this unpaved road 1.4 km, then turn left towards the pagodas, which can easily be seen in the distance at this point. The network of roads leading to the base of the hill offers several route possibilities – just keep an eye on the pagodas and you'll be able to make the appropriate turns.

By bicycle, you can avoid taking the highway by using back roads along the river. Follow Pak Phraek Rd in Kan south-east and cross the bridge towards Wat Tham Mongkhon Thong, then turn left on the other side and follow the gravel road parallel to the river. Eventually (after about 14 km) you'll see the Meuang Dam up ahead – at this point you should start looking for the hilltop pagodas on your right. This makes a good day trip by bicycle – the road is flat all the way and avoids the high-speed traffic on the highway. You can break your journey at Ban Tham, a village along the way with its own minor cave wat.

Raft Trips
Several small-time enterprises offer raft trips up and down the Mae Klong River and its various tributaries. The typical raft is a large affair with a two-storey shelter that will carry 15 to 20 people. The average cost for a two-day trip from one of the piers in Kanchanaburi is roughly 500 to 600B per person. Such a trip would include stops at Hat Tha Aw, Wat Tham Mongkon Thong, Khao Pun Cave and the Chung Kai Allied War Cemetery, plus all meals and one night's accommodation on the raft. Alcoholic beverages are usually extra. A one-day trip, no overnight, typically costs 300 to 400B per person including lunch. Add more nights and/or go farther afield and the cost can

escalate quite a bit. It is possible to arrange trips all the way to Sai Yok Falls, for example.

Enquire at any guesthouse, the TAT office, or at the main pier at the end of Lak Meuang Rd about raft trips. Perhaps the best trips are arranged by groups of travellers who get together and plan their own raft excursions with one of the raft operators. One way to see the same river sights at a lower cost is to hire a long-tail boat instead of a raft. Long-tails cost around 100B per hour and can take up to five passengers.

Places to Stay – bottom end

Kanchanaburi has numerous places to stay in every price range but especially in the guest-house category. The ones along the river can be quite noisy on weekends and holidays due to the floating disco traffic (the worst offender is a multi-raft monstrosity called 'Disco Duck'), so choose your accommodation carefully if an all-night beat keeps you awake. Inevitably, there are even karaoke rafts now! A local commission of guesthouse owners is attempting to enact a ban on the floating discos, so perhaps they will soon disappear.

Samlor drivers get a 25B commission for each farang they bring to guesthouses from the bus or train station (on top of what they charge you for the ride), so don't believe everything they say with regard to 'full', 'dirty' or 'closed' – see for yourself.

On the River Down on the riverside, at the junction of the Khwae and Khwae Noi rivers, is the *Nita Raft House* (☎ 514521), where older singles/doubles with mosquito net are 40/60B, doubles with fan are 100B, or with private shower 150B. It's basic but quite well run, though you should heed the warning on floating discos on weekends and holidays. The manager speaks English and has good info on local sights and activities. Don't confuse Nita with the *Nitaya Raft House* farther north along the river near Wat Neua – Nitaya costs from 100B up for substandard accommodation and seems particularly noisy.

Spanning the bottom end to middle range is *Sam's Place* (☎ 513971; fax 511500), near the Nitaya Raft House and the floating restaurants. The owner is a local called Sam who spent 10 years in the USA and speaks excellent English. His raft complex is taste-fully designed and reasonably priced for what you get. A room with fan and private bath is 150B for a single or double, 70/100B with shared bath. For 250 to 300B you can get a room with air-con, plus an extra sitting room. The raft has a small coffee shop. The only drawback to Sam's is that it's within range of the floating discos.

If you want to stay out near the River Khwae Bridge (and away from the floating discos), the *Bamboo House* (☎ 512532) at 3-5 Soi Vietnam, on the river about a km before the Japanese war memorial off Pak Phraek Rd (continuation of Mae Nam Khwae Rd), costs 100B per room with shared bath, 200B with private bath. The owners are very friendly and the setting is peaceful.

Two popular places a little closer to the city centre (but also distant from Disco Duck) are the *River Guest House* (☎ 512491) and the *VN Guest House* (☎ 514082) where small, basic rooms in bamboo raft houses are 40 to 80B, 100 to 150B with bath. Both are in the same vicinity on the river, not far from the train station. They tend to get booked out in the high travel season. A bit farther north on the river is the similar *PS Guest House*, also a good choice.

North of the VN, River and PS is the *Jolly Frog Backpacker's* (☎ 514579), a compara-tively huge, 45-room 'bamboo motel' with a popular restaurant. Singles/doubles with shared bath are 40/70B; doubles with private bath are 100B. For samlor transport to any guesthouse in this vicinity, you shouldn't pay more than 10B from the train station, or 20 to 25B from the bus station.

A bit farther north-west along the river, at the end of Laos Rd on the river, is *Mr Tee*, another two-storey thatched-bamboo place. Rooms upstairs are 100B without bath, while downstairs rooms are 150B with private bath.

In Town The cheapest place in town is the small *Thipvaree Bungalow* (☎ 511063) at 211/1-4 Saengchuto Rd. Basic but clean rooms with fan and private bath are 70B; 120B with air-con. Two rooms are also available without bath for 50B.

On Pak Phraek Rd in the oldest section of town, just a block off the river, stands the ageing *Kanchanaburi Hotel*. With a little fixing up this classic could be turned into a real gem. For now, quite plain rooms cost 60/80B one/two beds with shared bath only.

Places to Stay – middle

Rick's Lodge (☎ 514831) is along the river between the cheaper VN and PS guesthouses. Tastefully decorated bamboo accommodation with fan and private bath cost 250B on the river, 150B back from the river. Very near Sam's Place is *Supakornchai Raft*, which is similar in scope but not quite as nice. Rooms with fan and bath are 200B for a large bed, or 300B for two beds.

One of the better places in this price range is the three-storey *VL Guest House*, across the street from the River Kwai Hotel. A clean, spacious room with fan and hot-water bath is 120B for a single or double. Larger rooms sleeping four to eight people go for 50B per person. A double with air-con and hot water is 250B. The VL has a small dining area downstairs, and you can rent bicycles (20B per day) and motorcycles (200B up). Another plus is the generous 2 pm checkout time.

The family that owns Sam's Place on the river has recently opened a good-value midrange place called *Sam's Village* just east of the city centre, next to a large lotus pond in a quiet housing development. Rooms in sturdy modern houses rent for 150B with two beds, ceiling fan and attached shower, 250B with air-con and hot-water shower, or 350B with air-con, hot-water bath and shower, and fridge. Bicycles and motorcycles are available for rent. To reach Sam's Village, head east on U Thong Rd over the train tracks and turn right just before the power station. Continue alongside the lotus pond till you see Sam's ahead.

The *Prasopsuk Hotel* (☎ 511777) is at 677 Saengchuto Rd, next door to the VL Guest House. Rooms start at 110B with fan, 200 to 240B with air-con, and are off the road a bit. The restaurant and nightclub are a Thai scene at night. *Wang Thong Bungalows* (☎ 511046) at 60/3 Saengchuto Rd, and *Boon Yang Bungalows* (☎ 512598) at 139/9 Saengchuto Rd, offer similar rooms for 140B up. In case you haven't figured this out on your own, 'bungalows' (not the beach kind) are the upcountry equivalent of Bangkok's 'short-time' hotels. They're off the road for the same reason that their Bangkok counterparts have heavy curtains over the carports: so that it will be difficult to spot license plate numbers. Still, they function well as tourist hotels too.

Other hotels in town include the *Si Muang Kan* (☎ 511609), at 313/1-3 Saengchuto Rd (the north end), with clean singles/doubles with fan and bath for 100 to 150B, 170 to 350B with air-con, and the *Thai Seri Hotel* at the southern end of the same road, near the Visutrangsi Rd intersection and the TAT office, with somewhat dilapidated but adequate rooms for 100B up.

The *Luxury Hotel* (☎ 511168) at 284/1-5 Saengchuto Rd is a couple of blocks north of the River Kwai Hotel, and not as centrally located, but good value. Clean one/two-bed rooms with fan and bath start at 100/150B, 200 to 300B with air-con.

River Resorts

The *Kasem Island Resort* (☎ 513359; (02) 255-3604 in Bangkok) sits on an island in the middle of the Mae Klong River just a couple of hundred metres from Tha Chukkadon pier. The tastefully designed thatched cottages and house rafts are cool, clean, quiet and go for 500 to 650B. There are facilities for swimming, fishing and rafting as well as an outdoor bar and restaurant. The resort has an office near Tha Chukkadon pier where you can arrange for a free shuttle boat out to the island.

In the vicinity of the bridge are several river resorts of varying quality. On the river before the bridge is the *River Kwai Resort* (☎ 511313), where rustic bungalows on the

river bank are 350B for two, floating bungalows for two are 450B, and two-bedroom
floating bungalows for four are 650B. Just
above the bridge, two km before the turn-off
for Highway 323, are two more river resorts:
Prasopsuk Garden Resort (☎ 513215) with
air-con town-house doubles for 500B, air-
con bungalows for two at 600B, and large
bungalows for 10 people at 2000B per night;
and *River Kwai Lodge* (☎ 513657; (02) 251-
4377 in Bangkok), where a large room for
two is 600B with fan and bath or 800B with
air-con.

Places to Stay – top end

Kanchanaburi's original 1st-class hotel, the
River Kwai Hotel (☎ 511184/269) at 284/3-
16 Saengchuto Rd offers renovated rooms
with air-con, hot water, telephone and TV for
1200B up. Facilities include a coffee shop,
disco and swimming pool. Next door is the
huge River Paradise massage parlour.

Farther north along Saengchuto Rd, past
the train station, is the new four-storey
Mittaphan Hotel (☎ 514498; (02) 291-9953
in Bangkok). Standard rooms with all the
amenities start at 1000B. A large massage
parlour and snooker club are next door.

The luxurious *Felix River Kwai Resort*
(☎ 515061, fax 515095; (02) 255-3410, fax
255-5769 in Bangkok) sits on the west bank
of the river, about two km north of the new
one-lane bridge. The very nicely landscaped
grounds include two swimming pools. Spacious rooms with IDD phones, cable TV,
minibar and personal safe cost 3000/3200B
for a single/double.

Places to Eat

The greatest proliferation of inexpensive restaurants in Kanchanaburi is along the
northern end of Saengchuto Rd near the
River Kwai Hotel. From here south, to where
U Thong Rd crosses Saengchuto, are many
good Chinese, Thai and Isaan-style restaurants. As elsewhere in Thailand, the best are
generally the most crowded.

For years, one of the most popular has
been the *Isaan*, on Saengchuto Rd between
Hiran Prasat and Kratai Thong Rds. The

Isaan still serves great kài yâang (whole
spicy grilled chicken), khâo niãw (sticky
rice), sôm-tam (spicy green papaya salad),
etc as well as other Thai and local specialities
and inexpensive, ice-cold beer. The kài
yâang is grilled right out front and served
with two sauces – the usual sweet and sour
(náam jîm kài) and a roast red pepper sauce
(náam phrík phão).

Good, inexpensive eating places can also
be found in the markets along Prasit Rd and
between U Thong and Lak Meuang Rds east
of Saengchuto Rd. In the evenings, a sizeable
night market convenes along Saengchuto Rd
near the Lak Meuang Rd intersection.

The *Sabai-jit* restaurant, north of the River
Kwai Hotel on Saengchuto Rd, has an
English menu. Beer and Maekhong whisky
are sold here at quite competitive prices and
the food is consistently good. Other Thai and
Chinese dishes are served apart from those
listed on the English menu. If you see
someone eating something not listed, point.

Punnee Cafe & Bar (☎ 513503) on Ban
Neua Rd serves Thai and European food
according to expat tastes and advertises the
coldest beer in town.

Down on the river there are several large
floating restaurants where the quality of the
food varies but it's hard not to enjoy the
atmosphere. Most of them are pretty good
according to locals, but if you go, don't
expect Western food or large portions – if
you know what to order, you could have a
very nice meal here. Recommended are the
Thongnatee and the *Mae Nam*. Across from
the floating restaurants, along the road, are
several restaurants that are just as good but
less expensive; the best on this row is *Jukkru*
(no English sign – look for blue tables and
chairs). One of the better riverside restaurants in town is *Sutjai*, a garden-style place
on the west bank of the river next to the
one-lane bridge.

There are also food vendors on both sides of
Song Khwae Rd along the river near the new
waterfront park where you can buy inexpensive takeaways and picnic on mats along
the riverbank. This is a festive and prosperous
town and people seem to eat out a lot.

Two bakeries handle most of the pastry and bread business in Kan. *Srifa Bakery* on the north side of the bus terminal is the more modern of the two, with everything from French-style pastries to Singapore-style curry puffs. The *Aree Bakery* on Pak Phraek Rd around the corner from the Lak Meuang post office is less fancy but has coffee, tea, breakfast, ice cream and sandwiches plus tables and chairs for a sit-down break. Aree has great chicken curry puffs and very tasty young coconut pie.

Entertainment

If the floating discos/karaoke bars on the river or the disco at the River Kwai Hotel don't appeal to you, try the Apache Saloon opposite the Sabai-jit Restaurant on Saengchuto Rd. This large, old-west-style bar/restaurant offers live folk-rock music nightly.

Getting There & Away

Bus Buses leave Bangkok from the southern bus terminal on Charan Sanitwong Rd in Thonburi every 20 minutes daily (beginning at 5 am, last bus at 10 pm) for Kanchanaburi. The trip takes about three hours and costs 34B. Buses back to Bangkok leave Kanchanaburi between the same hours.

Air-con buses leave Bangkok's southern air-con terminal every 15 minutes from 5.30 am to 10 pm for 62B. These same buses depart Kanchanaburi for Bangkok from opposite the police station on Saengchuto Rd, not from the bus station. Air-con buses only take about two hours to reach Bangkok. The first bus out is at 5 am; the last one to Bangkok leaves at 7 pm.

There are frequent buses throughout the day from nearby Nakhon Pathom. Bus No 81 leaves from the east side of the Phra Pathom Chedi, costs 20B, and takes about 1½ hours. Other frequent direct bus services are available to/from Ratchaburi (No 461, 26B, 2½ hours) and Suphanburi (No 411, 25B, 2½ to three hours).

Train Ordinary trains leave Bangkok Noi (Thonburi) station at 8 am and 1.45 pm,

arriving at 10.30 am and 4.26 pm. Only 3rd-class seats are available and the fare is 25B. Trains return to Bangkok from Kanchanaburi at 8.03 am and 2.29 pm, arriving at 11 am and 5.15 pm. Ordinary train tickets to Kanchanaburi can be booked on the day of departure.

You can also take the train from the Kanchanaburi station out to the River Khwae Bridge – a three-minute ride for 2B. There are two trains per day at 6 am (No 353) and 10.31 am (No 171).

The same trains go on to the end of the train line at Nam Tok, which is near Sai Yok Falls. You can catch the train in Kanchanaburi at 6 am or 10.31 am or at the bridge at 6.06 or 10.36 am; the fare is the same, 17B. Nam Tok is eight km from Khao Pang Falls and 18 km from Hellfire Pass and the River Khwae Village. A third train (No 197) makes the trip to Nam Tok daily, leaving Kanchanaburi at 4.28 pm. The trip to Nam Tok takes about two hours. Coming back from Nam Tok, there are trains at 6.05 am, 12.35 and 3.15 pm. The early morning trains between Kanchanaburi and Nam Tok (6 am) do not run on weekends and holidays.

Tourist Train The State Railway of Thailand (SRT) has a special tourist train from Hualamphong station on weekends and holidays which departs Bangkok at 6.35 am and returns at 7.30 pm. The return fare is 250B for adults, 120B for children. It includes an hour-long stop in Nakhon Pathom to see the Phra Pathom Chedi, an hour at the River Khwae Bridge, a minibus to Prasat Meuang Singh Historical Park for a short tour, a walk along an elevated 'Death Railway' bridge (no longer in use), a three-hour stop at the river for lunch and a bat-cave visit before returning to Bangkok with a one-hour stopover at the Allied War Cemetery. This ticket should be booked in advance, although it's worth trying on the day even if you're told it's full. The SRT changes the tour itinerary and price from time to time.

Share Taxi & Minivan You can also take a share taxi from Saengchuto Rd to Bangkok for 50B per person. Taxis leave throughout the day whenever five passengers accumulate at the taxi stand. These taxis will make drops at Khao San Rd or in the Pahurat district. Kanchanaburi guesthouses also arrange daily minivans to Bangkok for 80B per person. Passengers are dropped at Khao San Rd.

Getting Around

Prices are very reasonable in Kanchanaburi, especially for food and accommodation, if you are your own tour guide – don't even consider letting a samlor driver show you around, they want big money. The town is not very big, so getting around on foot or bicycle is easy. A samlor to anywhere in Kanchanaburi should be 10 to 15B for one person. Songthaews run up and down Saengchuto Rd for 3B per passenger.

Bicycles and motorcycles can be rented at some guesthouses, at the Suzuki dealer near the bus station and at the Punnee Cafe. Expect to pay about 150B per day for a motorbike (more for a dirt bike), 20 to 30B a day for bicycles. Bikes (motor or push) can be taken across the river by ferry for a few baht.

AROUND KANCHANABURI

Most of the interesting places around Kanchanaburi are to the north and west of the capital, heading towards Three Pagodas Pass. For around 500B per person the PS, River, VN and Rick's Lodge guesthouses can arrange two-day trips to Three Pagodas Pass with stops at Hellfire Pass, various waterfalls and hot springs with an overnight in Sangkhlaburi.

Waterfalls

Kanchanaburi Province has seven major waterfalls, all north-west of the capital. They are Erawan, Pha Lan, Trai Trang, Khao Pang, Sai Yok, Pha That and Huay Khamin. Of these, the three most worth visiting – if you're looking for grandeur and swimming potential – are Erawan, Sai Yok and Huay Khamin. The Erawan Falls are the easiest to get to from Kanchanaburi, while Sai Yok and

Huay Khamin are best visited only if you are able to spend the night in the vicinity of the falls. They're a bit too far for a comfortable day trip from Kanchanaburi.

Any of the waterfalls described here could be visited by motorcycle. Many of the guesthouses in town will rent bikes – offer 150B per day for a 80 to 100cc bike, more for a dirt bike.

Erawan Falls National Park This 550-sq-km park is the most visited national park in Thailand and one of the most beautiful.

Once in the park, you'll have to walk two km from the trail entrance to the end of seven levels of waterfalls (the first step is reached 700 metres from the visitors' centre), which feed into the Khwae Yai River. The trails weave in and out of the numerous pools and falls, sometimes running alongside the water, sometimes leading across footbridges, splitting in different directions. Wear good walking shoes or sneakers. Also, bring a bathing suit as several of the pools beneath the waterfalls are great for swimming. The shape of the topmost fall is said to resemble Erawan, the three-headed elephant of Hindu-Buddhist mythology.

The waterfalls here, as elsewhere in Kanchanaburi, are best visited during the rainy season or in the first two months of the cool season, when the pools are full and the waterfalls most impressive. The peak crowds at Erawan come in mid-April around the time of the Songkran Festival (when there's not much water); weekends can also be crowded. The park is open from 6 am to 6 pm; admission is 25B.

Two limestone caves in the park worth visiting are **Tham Phra That** (12 km north-west of the visitors' centre via a very rough road) and **Tham Wang Badan** (to the west). **Thung Naa Dam** appears 28 km before Erawan.

Places to Stay & Eat Official park bungalows that sleep up to 15 people cost 400 to 1000B per night. The park staff can also make less expensive arrangements in unofficial housing from 50 to 100B per person. You can pitch a tent for 5B. *Erawan Resort Guest House*, off the highway before the park entrance, has small, solid bungalows with attached bath on the river for 200 to 350B.

There are food stalls near the park entrance and at the bus station/market, outside the park. To cut down on rubbish, food is not allowed beyond the second level of the falls.

Getting There & Away The first bus to Erawan leaves the Kanchanaburi bus station at 8 am, takes two hours and costs 19B per person. Ask for *rót thammádaa pai náam tòk eh-raawan* (ordinary bus going to Erawan Falls). Take this first bus, as Erawan takes a full day to appreciate and the last bus back to Kanchanaburi leaves Erawan at 4 pm. During the high tourist season (November to January), minibuses go by all the river guesthouses in Kan around 9 am daily to take visitors to the falls (one hour) for 60B per person. The return trip leaves the park at 4.30 pm.

Huay Khamin Falls Part of little-visited **Si Nakharin National Park**, Huay Khamin (Turmeric Stream) has what are probably Kanchanaburi Province's most powerful waterfalls. The pools under the waterfalls are large and deep and this is an excellent place for swimming. Explorations farther afield in the park can be rewarding for self-contained campers. Elephants and other wildlife are not uncommon.

Getting There & Away Getting to Huay Khamin can be a real problem. The 45-km road from Erawan is in very bad condition and takes at least two hours by motorcycle or rugged 4WD (you must bring your own transport). The falls can also be reached by a similarly rugged – and much longer – dirt road from Route 323 north of Thong Pha Phum.

An alternative is to charter a boat at Tha Reua Khun Phaen, a pier on the south-east shore of Si Nakharin Reservoir in the village of Mongkrathae. The price varies – according to your bargaining skills and the mood of the boat pilots – from 1000 to 3000B; this needn't be as expensive as it sounds if you can bring a group, since the boats can hold up to 20 people. Infrequent Si Sawat buses from Kanchanaburi pass Mongkrathae.

Sai Yok National Park About 100 km north-west of Kanchanaburi, scenic Sai Yok Falls are part of 500-sq-km Sai Yok National Park. In addition to the park's two falls, Sai Yok and Sai Yok Noi, other attractions include the limestone caves of **Tham Sai Yok, Tham Kaew** and **Tham Phra**, the remains of a **Death Railway Bridge** and Japanese cookstoves (actually little more than piles of brick), and a network of clear streams which bubble up from springs in the park. There are established footpaths and trails between the falls, caves, railway bridge and bat cave.

It was at Sai Yok that the famous Russian roulette scenes in the movie *The Deer Hunter* were filmed. The area is well known for overnight raft trips that leave from here along the Khwae Noi River; the waterfalls empty directly into the Khwae Noi. The trips are not cheap, but those who have gone say they're worth the money.

The eight-roomed **Tham Daowadung**, one of Thailand's prettiest limestone caves, is farther north in the park while **Tham Lawa** is in the park's far south-eastern corner; both are best visited by taking boat trips to an access point along the Khwae Noi River, then hiking in. **Hin Daat Hot Springs** is 40 minutes north of Tham Daowadung by boat. The hot springs *(bàw náam ráwn)* are looked after by a Buddhist monastery, so only men are permitted to bathe there.

Notable wildlife in the park includes Kitti's hog-nosed bat (the world's smallest mammal), regal crab, barking deer, blue pittas, wreathed hornbill, gibbons, Malayan porcupines, slow loris and serow. Wild elephants occasionally cross over from Myanmar.

Places to Stay & Eat Forestry Department bungalows are available at Sai Yok for 500 to 1000B per night; they sleep up to six people. On the river near the suspension

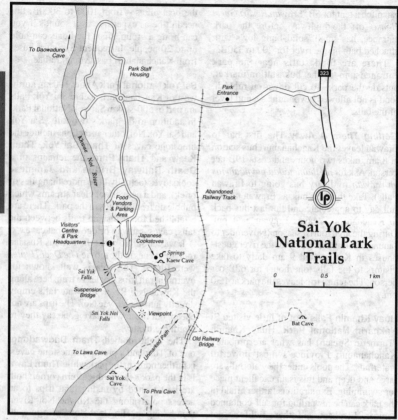

Sai Yok National Park Trails

bridge, *Saiyok View Raft* rents tidy rooms on floating rafts with private bath and air-con for 500B. During the week you may be able to get these raft-house rooms for as low as 300B. There is a row of permanent food stalls next to the parking lot near the visitors' centre. Food vendors here can arrange rooms for 100B per person.

Getting There & Away Sai Yok can be reached by direct bus from Kanchanaburi for 28B and the trip takes a little over an hour. You can also get there by boarding a bus bound for Thong Pha Phum. Tell the driver you're going to Sai Yok Yai and he'll let you off at the road to the falls, on the left side of Route 323. From there you can get local transport to Sai Yok. This method takes about two hours in all and costs about the same as the direct bus. You can also try chartering a boat from Kanchanaburi that can take up to 20 people to Sai Yok for about 600B.

Si Nakharin Reservoir & Si Sawat
เขื่อนศรีนครินทร์และศรีสวัสดิ์

Route 3199 passes Erawan National Park

and continues on to Si Sawat (106 km from Kanchanaburi), a town largely inhabited by north-eastern Thais who came to work on Si Nakharin Dam years ago. On the south-east bank of the huge Si Nakharin Reservoir is a string of rustic lakeside resorts costing from 200 to 700B a night for individual thatched bungalows. Longtail boats can be hired at the village of Mongkrathae for tours around the lake or across to Huay Khamin Falls.

Prasat Meuang Singh Historical Park
อุทยานประวัติศาสตร์ปราสาทเมืองสิงห์

Approximately 43 km from Kanchanaburi are the remains of an important 13th-century Khmer outpost of the Angkor Empire called Meuang Singh (Lion City). Located on a bend in the Khwae Noi River, the recently restored city ruins cover 460 rai (73.6 hectares) and were declared a historical park under the administration of the Fine Arts Department in 1987. Originally this location may have been chosen by the Khmers as a relay point for the trade along the Khwae Noi River.

All the Meuang Singh shrines are constructed of laterite bricks and are situated in a huge grassy compound surrounded by layers of laterite ramparts. Sections of the ramparts show seven additional layers of earthen walls, suggesting cosmological symbolism in the city plan. Evidence of a sophisticated water system has also been discovered amid the ramparts and moats.

The town encompasses four groups of ruins, though only two groups have been excavated and are visible. In the centre of the complex is the principal shrine, Prasat Meuang Singh, which faces east (towards Angkor). Walls surrounding the shrine have gates in each of the cardinal directions. An original sculpture of Avalokitesvara stands on the inside of the northern wall and establishes Meuang Singh as a Mahayana Buddhist centre. The shrine was apparently built during the reign of Jayavarman VII in the 12th century.

To the north-east of the main prasat are the remains of a smaller shrine whose original contents and purpose are unknown. Near the main entrance to the complex at the north gate is a small outdoor museum, which contains various sculptures of Mahayana Buddhist deities and stucco decorations from the shrines.

Clear evidence that this area was inhabited before the arrival of the Khmers can be seen in another small museum to the south of the complex next to the river. The shed-like building contains a couple of prehistoric human skeletons which were found in the area, and that's it. A more complete exhibit of local neolithic remains is at the Ban Kao Museum (see below).

Entry to the historical park is 20B and it's open daily from 8 am to 4 pm.

Ban Kao Neolithic Museum
พิพิธภัณฑ์บ้านเก่า

During the construction of the Death Railway along the Khwae Noi River, a Dutch POW named Van Heekeren uncovered neolithic remains in the village of Ban Kao (Old Town), about seven km south-east of Meuang Singh. After the war, a Thai-Danish team retraced Van Heekeren's discovery and announced that Ban Kao was a major neolithic burial site. Archaeological evidence suggests that this area may have been inhabited as far back as 10,000 years ago.

A small but well-designed museum, displaying 3000 to 4000-year-old artefacts from the excavation of Ban Kao, has been established near the site. Objects are labelled and include a good variety of early pottery and other utensils, as well as human skeletons. Hours are from 8 am to 4.30 pm, Wednesday to Sunday.

Places to Stay & Eat Guest bungalows are available for rent near the south gate of the Prasat Meuang Singh Historical Park for 500B. There are a couple of small restaurants at the north gate.

The *River Khwae Farm* is 3.5 km from the Ban Kao (Tha Kilen) train station. Bungalows and raft houses here start at 500B, including all meals.

Getting There & Away Ban Kao and Meuang Singh are best reached by train from Kanchanaburi via Ban Kao (Tha Kilen) station, which is only one km south of Meuang Singh. Walk west towards the river and follow the signs to Meuang Singh. Trains leave Kanchanaburi daily at 6 and 10.31 am, arriving in Tha Kilen in about an hour. The fare is 10B. To get to Ban Kao, you may have to walk or hitch six km south along the road that follows the Khwae Noi River, though the occasional songthaew passes along this road, too. It's possible to get from Kanchanaburi to Meuang Singh and back in one day by catching the 6 am train there and the 3 pm train back.

If you have your own transport, Ban Kao and/or Meuang Singh would make convenient rest stops on the way to Hellfire Pass or Sangkhlaburi.

Coming from the Erawan National Park area, there's no need to backtrack all the way to Kanchanaburi before heading north on Route 323. A new paved road heads west from Route 3199 at Km 25, then proceeds 16 km to meet Route 323 between Km 37 and 38 – thus cutting half a day's travel from the old loop. This winding, scenic, lightly trafficked short cut is tremendous for cycling.

Chaloem Ratanakosin (Tham Than Lot) National Park

อุทยานแห่งชาติเฉลิมรัตนโกสินทร์

This 59-sq-km park, 97 km north of Kanchanaburi, is of interest to speleologists because of two caves, **Tham Than Lot Yai** and **Tham Than Lot Noi**, and to naturalists for its waterfalls and natural forests. Three waterfalls – **Trai Trang**, **Than Ngun** and **Than Thong** – are within easy hiking distance of the bungalows and campground. Bungalows cost from 500 to 1000B per night and sleep 10 to 12 people. Pitch your own tent for 5B per person.

Getting There & Away To get to Chaloem Ratanakosin, take a bus from Kanchanaburi to Ban Nong Preu for around 35B (a two to three-hour trip) and then try for a songthaew to the park. Most visitors arrive by car, jeep or motorcycle.

Hellfire Pass/Myanmar-Thailand Railway Memorial

The Australian-Thai Chamber of Commerce completed the first phase of the Hellfire Pass memorial project in 1988. The purpose of the project is to honour the Allied prisoners of war and Asian conscripts who died while constructing some of the most difficult stretches of the Myanmar-Thailand Death Railway, 80 km north-west of Kanchanaburi. 'Hellfire Pass' was the name the POWs gave to the largest of a 1000-metre series of mountain cuttings through soil and solid rock, which were accomplished with minimal equipment (3.5-kg hammers, picks, shovels, steel tap drills, cane baskets for removing dirt and rock, and dynamite for blasting).

The original crew of 400 Australian POWs was later augmented with 600 additional Australian and British prisoners, who worked round the clock in 12 to 18-hour shifts for 12 weeks. The prisoners called it Hellfire Pass because of the way the largest cutting at Konyu looked at night by torch light. By the time the cuttings were finished, 70% of the POW crew had died and were buried in the nearby Konyu Cemetery.

The memorial consists of a trail that follows the railway remains through the 110-metre Konyu cutting, then winds up and around the pass for an overhead view. At the far end of the cutting is a memorial plaque fastened to solid stone, commemorating the death of the Allied prisoners. There are actually seven cuttings spread over 3.5 km – four smaller cuttings and three larger ones.

The Australian-Thai Chamber of Commerce also has plans to clear a path to the Hin Tok trestle bridge south-east of the Konyu cutting. This bridge was called the 'Pack of Cards' by the prisoners because it collapsed three times during construction. Eventually

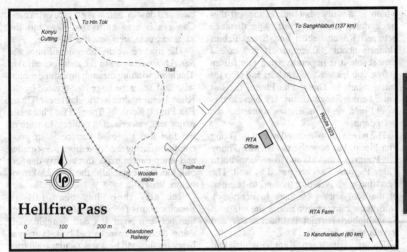

Hellfire Pass

0   100   200 m

To Hin Tok
Konyu Cutting
Trail
Wooden stairs
Trailhead
Abandoned Railway

To Sangkhlaburi (137 km)
Route 323
RTA Office
RTA Farm
To Kanchanaburi (80 km)

some of the track may be restored to exhibit rolling stock from the WW II era.

Getting There & Away Access to Hellfire Pass is via the Royal Thai Army (RTA) farm on Route 323, between Kanchanaburi and Thong Pha Phum. Proceeding north-west along Highway 323, the farm is 80 km from Kanchanaburi, 18 km from the Nam Tok train terminus, and 11 km from the River Kwai Village Hotel. A small roman-script sign near Km 66 marks the turnoff (look for two RST rail coaches on the west side of the highway). Once you arrive at the RTA farm, take one of the dirt roads on either side of the RTA offices about 400 metres around to the posted trailhead. From the trailhead, it's about 340 metres up and down a steep walkway and along the rail bed to reach the pass.

After walking through the pass and viewing the plaque, you can follow another trail/walkway on the right to get a view of the cutting from above. Then you can either double back the way you came or continue on this trail until it wraps around and meets the trailhead.

Any bus from Kanchanaburi to Thong Pha Phum or Sangkhlaburi will pass the RTA farm, but you'll have to let the bus crew know where you want to get off – ask for the *sǔan thahǎan* (army farm). If you're driving, just remember that the farm is about 80 km from Kanchanaburi and look for the English signs announcing Hellfire Pass on Highway 323.

KANCHANABURI TO
THREE PAGODAS PASS

Three Pagodas Pass (Phra Chedi Saam Ong) was one of the terminals of the Death Railway in WW II, and for centuries has been a major relay point for Thai-Burmese trade. Until recently it was a place that the TAT and the Thai government would rather you'd forget about (much like Mae Salong in the north some years ago), but since 1989, when the Burmese government took control of the Burmese side of the border from insurgent armies, it's been promoted as a tourist destination. There's really not much to see at the pass – the attraction lies in the journey itself and the impressive scenery along the way.

It's an all-day journey and will require you to spend at least one night in Sangkhlaburi, which is a somewhat interesting off-the-track destination in itself. The distance between Kanchanaburi and Sangkhlaburi alone is about 200 km, so if you take a motorcycle it is imperative that you fill up before you leave Kanchanaburi and stop for petrol again in Thong Pha Phum, the last town before Sangkhlaburi. By bicycle this would be a very challenging route, but it's been done.

The paved highway used to end in Thong Pha Phum, but now the roads from Thong Pha Phum to Sangkhla and from Sangkhla to Three Pagodas Pass are paved as well. The best time to go is during the mid-to-late part of the cool season (January to February). During the rainy season nearly the whole of Sangkhlaburi District is under water and travel can be difficult.

The road between Kanchanaburi and Thong Pha Phum passes through mostly flat terrain interrupted by the occasional limestone outcropping. This is sugar-cane country, and if you're travelling by bicycle or motorcycle during harvest times you'll have to contend with huge cane trucks, overloaded with cut cane, which strew pieces of cane and dust in their wake – take extra care. Cassava is also cultivated here but the cassava trucks aren't such a nuisance.

The road between Thong Pha Phum and Sangkhlaburi is one of the most beautiful in Thailand, winding through limestone mountains and along the huge lake created by the Khao Laem hydroelectric dam near Thong Pha Phum. North of Thong Pha Phum is a major teak reforestation project. In spite of the fact that the road surface is in good condition during the dry season, steep grades and sharp curves make this a fairly dangerous journey, especially the last 25 km or before Sangkhla.

Recently there has been talk in Kanchanaburi of rebuilding the train connection between Nam Tok and Sangkhlaburi, using the old Japanese rail bed. If it ever happens, this will be a spectacular train trip.

Another pipe dream is the construction of a road between Sangkhlaburi and Um Phang in Tak Province, approximately 120 km to the north. A very bad dirt road exists now, but it crosses the Thai-Burmese border in a couple of places and passes through Karen rebel territory, so it's not really legal. At the

moment it's used mostly by trucks carrying ore from Korean-owned antimony mines near the border on the Thai side. During the rainy season it's often impassable due to deep streams which cross the road.

Thong Pha Phum
ท้องผาภูมิ

Surrounded by scenic karst topography, the area around the small town of Thong Pha Phum is slowly changing from a simple waystation along Route 323 to a destination in itself. Many of the inhabitants – more of whom are Mon or Burman than Thai – originally congregated here to work on Khao Laem Dam.

The Khwae Noi River runs along the east side of town, and it's possible to raft downriver as far as Sai Yok or even all the way to Kanchanaburi. There are some interesting walks and day trips in the area. You can, for example, ford the river over a footbridge close to town to climb a prominent limestone cliff topped by a wat. Farther afield are **Dai Chong Thong Falls** (35 km north via Route 323), **Kroeng Krawia Falls** (33 km north), **Phaa Taat Falls** (30 km south at Km 105) and **Hin Daat Hot Springs** (32 km south at Km 107). All are easily accessed from the highway.

Between Km 32 and Km 33 (some 32 km north of Thong Pha Phum, 42 km before Sangkhlaburi) is the entrance to the **Sunyataram Forest Monastery** (Samnak Paa Sunyataram), a 45-hectare forest meditation retreat centre affiliated with one of Thailand's most famous living monks, Ajaan Yantra. Yantra was accused of sexual improprieties in 1993 (the religious establishment absolved him for lack of evidence) and the monastery is now very touchy about visitors.

Places to Stay & Eat *Somneukjai Hotel*, on the left side of the town's main street off the highway, has basic but clean rooms with fan and attached bath around a shaded courtyard for 120B. A new, all air-con building offers comfortable rooms with hot-water showers

for 600B. *Si Thong Pha Phum Bungalows* farther down the road has large private bungalows for 80 to 100B, but it's located next to a noisy primary school. Better is *Saw Bunyong Bungalows*, which has 120B rooms similar to those at Somneukjai; since it's a bit farther off the street it tends to be quieter.

Green World Hot Spring Resort & Golf Club, 33 km south of town near Km 108, is a huge resort with posh rooms costing 1200 to 2000B. The nearby *Thong Pha Phum River Hills* is similar. Just beyond the dam west of town are nine rustic lakeside resorts, including *Bangkok Flower, Taweechaiphaphum, Wang Phai, Phae VIP, Kho Laem, Phae Rim Kheuan, Bangkok Camping, Weekend Garden* and *Chao Kheuan*. It's mostly a Thai scene, with thatched bungalows in the 200 to 800B range.

In typical Mon style, several shops and vendors along the main street proffer long rows of curry pots; instead of two or three curry choices more typical of Thai vendors, the Mon vendors lay out eight or more – all delicious. The best variety is at a shop called *Rawy Maw* (Hundred Pots); a branch of the same shop can be found in a new shophouse on the highway just south of town.

A small night market convenes near the centre of town each evening with the usual rice and noodle dishes. A riverside restaurant near the highway bridge, *Saep-i-lii*, serves good Isaan food.

Getting There & Away Ordinary buses leave the Kanchanaburi bus terminal for Thong Pha Phum every half hour from 6.45 am until 6 pm; the fare is 39B and the trip takes about three hours. Buses to Sangkhlaburi also stop in Thong Pha Phum – see the Sangkhlaburi Getting There & Away section for details.

SANGKHLABURI
สังขละบุรี

This small but important Kanchanaburi outpost is inhabited by a mixture of Burman, Karen, Mon and Thai, but is mostly Karen and Mon. You'll find very little English spoken out this way – in fact, you may hear as much Burmese, Karen and Mon as Thai.

Hundreds of former residents of Myanmar have moved to the Sangkhla area during the last few years because of the fighting in the Three Pagodas Pass area between the Karen and Mon insurgent armies and between Myanmar government forces and the Karen. These Burmese have fled into Thailand not only to avoid the fighting but to escape being press-ganged as porters for the Burmese army.

The distance between Kanchanaburi and Sangkhlaburi is about 227 km; from Thong Pha Phum it's 74 km.

Money
Sangkhla now has a Siam Commercial Bank where foreigners can change money. It's in the city centre near the market and Sri Daeng Hotel and is open from 8.30 am to 3.30 pm.

Things to See & Do
Sangkhlaburi sits at the edge of the huge lake formed by Khao Laem Dam. The town was in fact created after the dam flooded out an older village near the confluence of the three rivers that now feed the reservoir. There's not much to do in the town itself except explore the small **markets** for Burmese handicrafts such as checked cotton blankets, *longyi* (Burmese sarongs) and cheroots. The town comes alive on Mon National Day, celebrated during the last week of July. Day trips to nearby waterfalls are a possibility – enquire at P Guest House or the Burmese Inn for details.

Thailand's longest wooden bridge leads over a section of the lake near town to a friendly **Mon settlement** of thatched huts and dirt paths. A market in the village purveys goods smuggled from Myanmar, China and India; there are also a few food vendors with pots of rich Mon curry. The village can be reached in five or ten minutes by boat from either of the guesthouses or by walking/biking five km by road and over the bridge.

Wat Wang Wiwekaram Also called Wat Mon since most of the monks here are Mon, this monastery is about three km north of the town on the edge of the reservoir. A tall and much revered stupa, Chedi Luang Phaw Utama, is the centrepiece of the wat. Constructed in the style of the Mahabodhi stupa in Bodhgaya, India, the chedi is topped by 400 baht (about six kg) of gold. An earlier chedi is located some distance behind the tall one and is 300 to 400 years old. From the edge of the monastery grounds is a view of the tremendous lake and three rivers that feed into it.

A new section of the Mon temple built across the road features a flashy, multi-roofed wihaan with stainless steel-plated pillars, heavy carved wooden doors and marble banisters. It's surrounded by a carp-filled moat. Local rumour has it that it was built from profits made selling weapons and other supplies to the Mon and Karen armies; the wildest stories even claim that a huge weapons cache is stashed beneath the wihaan. A more likely source of support for the wat is the black-market tax collected by the Mon rebel soldiers on all goods smuggled through their territory.

Khao Laem Lake & Refugee Camps This huge lake was formed when a dam was erected across the Khwae Noi River near Thong Pha Phum in 1983. The lake submerged an entire village at the confluence of the Khwae Noi, Ranti and Sangkhalia rivers. The spires of the village's **Wat Sam Prasop** (Three-Junction Temple) can be seen protruding from the lake in the dry season.

Canoes can be rented for exploring the lake, or for longer trips you can hire a long-tail boat and pilot. Lake boating is a tranquil pastime, best early in the morning with mist and birdlife – early evening is also good for bird-watching. Two hours across the lake and up the Pikri River by boat from Sangkhla is a huge (population 50,000) **Mon refugee camp**. On the way to the camp you'll pass through a flooded Ayuthaya-period mountain pass marked by a decrepit Buddha image seated under a small tin-roofed sala. This pass was part of the Thai-Burmese border before the border was moved south-east following WW II. During the dry season the camp can only be reached by road.

There are at least four other Mon refugee camps along the border between Three Pagodas Pass and the mining village of Pilok. North-east of Three Pagodas Pass are several Karen refugee settlements but they are very difficult to reach. If you do visit one of the camps, don't go empty-handed; bring blankets, clothes and food supplies for the refugees.

A branch meditation centre of Kanchanaburi's Sunyataram Forest Monastery is found on the lake's **Ko Kaew Sunyataram** (Sunyataram Jewel Isle). Permission to visit must first be obtained from the Sunyataram Forest Monastery, 42 km before Sangkhlaburi.

Places to Stay

Sangkhlaburi has one hotel, the *Sri Daeng Hotel*, which is on the southern edge of town near an army camp and the central market. Rooms are 160/180B for one/two beds with fan and bath or 280B with air-con. The rooms are fairly clean and comfortable.

Down on the lake behind the town, an enterprising Mon-Karen family operates the *P Guest House* (☎ 595061; fax 595139). Bungalows with verandahs are placed along a slope overlooking the lake; singles/doubles with shared bath are a bargain at 40/50B; larger doubles with private bath cost 120B. There's a comfortable dining area with a sunset view of the lake and the chedi at Wat Mon. An information board has maps and suggestions for things to see and do in the area. Canoes can be rented for 10B per hour and there are also bicycles and motorcycles for rent. The staff can arrange jungle treks or long-tail boat tours to Mon refugee camps when enough people are interested. The guesthouse is about 1.2 km from the bus stop in town.

The newer *Burmese Inn* is perched in a stream gorge near the wooden bridge that crosses to the Mon village, about 800 metres from the Sangkhla bus terminal. Run by an Austrian-Thai couple, it offers wooden bungalows with thatched roofs for 60/80B single/double including breakfast. Trips to local waterfalls and to Thung Yai Naresuan Wildlife Sanctuary can be arranged – there is a good, hand-drawn wall map of the area in the dining area.

A motorcycle taxi from the bus stop in Sangkhla to either guesthouse costs 10B; if you come by minivan from Kanchanaburi you can ask the driver to take you to either guesthouse (it's supposed to be door-to-door service).

A couple of km north of Sangkhlaburi on the way to Wat Mon, right on the Sangkhalia River where it meets the lake, is *Songkalia River Huts* (☎ (034) 427-4936). Somewhat run-down floating bungalows that will sleep up to 10 people cost 300 to 600B per night. Above the lake near the bridge, a much better choice is *Samprasop Bungalows*, where rooms with private bath cost 200B, more for air-con.

Out on the lake are several more expensive raft houses, including the *Runtee Palace* (☎ (02) 251-7552 in Bangkok), where bungalows are 800 to 1500B with meals. The Runtee, too, has seen better days, and it's usually open on weekends only.

More places are sprouting up on hillsides along the lake. So far, all are resorts oriented towards Thai tourists in the 300 to 600B range. For now, Sangkhlaburi is very peaceful – one hopes that local entrepreneurs won't turn it into another Kanchanaburi river scene with all-night floating discos.

Places to Eat

The *Sri Daeng Hotel* in Sangkhlaburi has a decent restaurant downstairs. The *Rung Arun* restaurant, opposite the Sri Daeng Hotel, has an extensive menu and is also good, and there are three or four other places to eat down the street. The day market in the centre of town sometimes has a couple of vendor stalls offering Indian nan and curry. The garden restaurant at Samprasop Bungalows is the nicest-looking place in the area and has a good reputation locally.

Getting There & Away

Ordinary bus No 8203 leaves the Kanchanaburi bus terminal for Sangkhlaburi at 6.45, 9, 10.45 am and 1.15 pm and takes four to six hours, depending on how many mishaps occur on the Thong Pha Phum to Sangkhlaburi road. The fare is 70B.

A *rót tûu* (minivan) service to Sangkhla leaves 10 times daily, from 6.30 am to 4.30 pm, from an office on the east side of the Kan bus terminal. The trip takes 3½ hours and costs 100B; if you want to stop off in Thong Pha Phum it's 70B (then from Thong Pha Phum to Sangkhlaburi by van is 50B). Arriving from Kan, the van driver can drop you off at either of the guesthouses or the Sri Daeng Hotel on request. In Sangkhla the vans depart from a spot near the market. From either end it's usually best to reserve your seat a day in advance.

If you go by motorcycle or car, you can count on about five hours to cover the 217 km from Kanchanaburi to Sangkhlaburi, including three or four short rest stops. Alternatively, you can make it an all-day trip and stop off in Ban Kao, Muang Singh, and Hellfire Pass. Be warned, however, that this is not a trip for an inexperienced motorcycle rider. The Thong Pha Phum to Sangkhlaburi section of the journey (74 km) requires sharp reflexes and previous experience on mountain roads. This is also not a motorcycle trip to do alone as stretches of the highway are practically deserted – it's tough to get help if you need it and easy to attract the attention of would-be bandits.

Three Pagodas Pass/Payathonzu

พระเจดีย์สามองค์

The pagodas themselves are rather small, but it is the remote nature of this former black-market outpost that draws a trickle of visitors. Control of the Burmese side of the border once vacillated between the Karen National Union and the Mon Liberation Front, since Three Pagodas was one of several 'toll gates' along the Thai-Burmese border where insurgent armies collected a 5% tax on all merchandise that passed. These ethnic groups used the funds to finance armed resistance against the Burmese government, which has recently increased efforts to regain control of the border area.

The Karen also conduct a huge multi-million dollar business in illegal mining and logging, the products of which are smuggled into Thailand by the truckload under cover of the night – not without the palms-up co-operation of the Thai police, of course. Pressure for control of these border points has increased since the Thai government enacted a ban on all logging in Thailand in 1989, which has of course led to an increase in teak smuggling.

In late 1988, heavy fighting broke out between the Karen and the Mon for control of the 'toll gate' here. Since this is the only place for hundreds of km in either direction where a border crossing is geographically convenient, this is where the Mon army (who have traditionally controlled this area) has customarily collected the 5% tax on smuggling. The Karen insurgents do the same at other points north along the Thai-Burmese border. Burmese government pressure on the Karen farther north led to a conflict between the Karen and the Mon over Three Pagodas trade and the village on the Burmese side was virtually burnt to the ground in the 1988 skirmishes.

In 1989 the Yangon (Rangoon) government wrested control of the town from both the Karen and Mon, and the Burmese seem firmly established at the border for the time being. The Burmese have renamed the town Payathonzu and filled it with shops catering to an odd mix of occupation troops and tourists.

Foreigners are now allowed to cross the border here for day trips for 130B or US$5 cash – this is one of only two such land crossings permitted for non-Thais along Myanmar's entire border perimeters (the other is at Mae Sai in Chiang Rai Province). Payathonzu lies 470 km by road from Yangon but is considered '75% safe' by the

Burmese military. Apparently insurgent Karen forces are still in the area and there are occasional firefights.

A true frontier town, Payathonzu has three Burmese teahouses, one with *nam-bya* – the Burmese equivalent to Indian nan bread – one cinema, several mercantile shops with Burmese longyis, cheroots, jade, clothes, and a few general souvenir shops with Mon-Karen-Burmese handicrafts. Bargaining is necessary (some English is spoken, also Thai) but in general goods are well priced. About 20 Thai merchants operate in town – the Burmese government offers them free rent to open shops. A new temple, **Wat Suwankhiri**, is under construction on a bluff near town.

Kloeng Thaw Falls, 12 km from the border, take a couple of hours by motorcycle to reach from Payathonzu. The road to the falls is only open in the dry season – reportedly the Karen control the waterfall area during the rainy season. Even in good weather, the two-rut track is very rugged, not recommended for motorcycle novices. Lately the falls area has been closed more often than it has been open.

The border is open from 7 am to 6 pm daily. When the border first opened in 1991 cameras had to be left at the border gate but photography is now permitted anywhere in the area.

Places to Stay The only place to stay here is at *Three Pagodas Pass Resort* (☎ (034) 511079; (02) 412-4159 in Bangkok), where large bungalows start at 300B. Most visitors stay in nearby Sangkhla.

Getting There & Away The 19-km paved road to Three Pagodas Pass begins four km before you reach Sangkhla off Route 323. At this intersection is a Thai police checkpoint where you may have to stop for minor interrogation, depending on recent events in the Three Pagodas Pass area. Along the way you'll pass a couple of villages inhabited entirely by Mon or Karen; at one time there was a branch of the All Burma Students Democratic Front here, where self-exiled

Rangoon students had set up an opposition movement with the intention of ousting the Ne Win government from Myanmar. The students have since moved north to Tak Province.

If you don't have your own wheels, songthaews to Three Pagodas Pass leave about every 50 minutes between 6 am and 5 pm from Sangkhlaburi's central market area. The fare is 30B; the last songthaew back to Sangkhlaburi leaves Three Pagodas Pass at around 4.30 pm.

The border is only a short walk from the songthaew stop in Three Pagodas Pass.

Other Attractions around Sangkhlaburi

Along the highway between Thong Pha Phum and Sangkhlaburi are several natural attractions. Those nearest to Thong Pha Phum – south of Km 36 on Route 323 – are described in the earlier Thong Pha Phum section.

Approximately 34 km south of Sangkhlaburi between Km 39 and 40, you'll find a turnoff on the east side of the highway for the 3200-sq-km **Thung Yai Naresuan National Park**, Thailand's largest protected land parcel. This rough dirt road leads to **Takien Thong Falls**, where pools are suitable for swimming nearly all year round. There are at least two other tracks off the highway into the sanctuary, but to find anything of interest you really should go with a guide – check with the Burmese Inn or P Guest House in Sangkhla. Thung Yai Naresuan is one of the last natural habitats in Thailand for the tiger, whose total numbers nationwide are estimated to be less than 500, perhaps no more than 250.

On the opposite side of the highway near the Thung Yai Naresuan turnoff is a paved road into the recently established **Khao Laem National Park**. As yet there are no facilities to speak of, but presumably the park was created to protect the riverine habitats near the reservoir.

Tham Sukho is a large limestone cave shrine just off the highway at Km 42.

Chonburi Province

SI RACHA

ศรีราชา

About 105 km from Bangkok on the east coast of the Gulf of Thailand is the small town of Si Racha (population 23,000), home of the famous spicy sauce *náam phrík sĭi raachaa*. Some of Thailand's best seafood, especially the local oysters, is served here accompanied by this sauce.

The motorised samlors in this fishing town and on Ko Si Chang are unlike those seen anywhere else – huge motorcycles with a side-car at the rear.

On **Ko Loi**, a small rocky island which is connected to the mainland by a long jetty, there is a Thai-Chinese Buddhist temple. Farther off shore is a large island called Ko Si Chang, flanked by two smaller islands – Kham Yai to the north and Khang Kao to the south. As this provides a natural shelter from the wind and sea, it is used as a harbour by large incoming freighters. Smaller boats transport goods to the Chao Phraya delta some 50 km away.

A new deep-water port at nearby **Laem Chabang** may eventually erode the huge barge trade in Ko Si Chang's lee.

Places to Stay

The best places to stay in Si Racha are the hotels built on piers over the waterfront. The *Siriwatana Hotel*, across from Tessaban 1 Rd and the Bangkok Bank, is the cleanest of the lot and has the best service. Their basic fan-cooled rooms start at 120B. The *Siwichai*, next to the Siriwatana, has similar rooms for 200B. The *Samchai*, on Soi 10, across from Surasakdi 1 Rd, has reasonable rooms for 170B and some air-con rooms (350B) as well. All three are open and breezy, with outdoor tables where you can bring food in the evening from nearby markets.

On Soi 18, the *Grand Bungalows* rent bungalows of various sizes, built off the pier, for 500 to 1100B. Each one sleeps several people and they are very popular among holidaying Thais and Chinese.

There are several new top-end hotels in town, including the *Laemthong Residence Hotel* (☎ (038) 322888; fax 312651) in the centre of town, just off Sukhumvit Rd

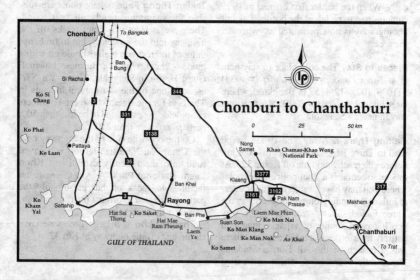

Chonburi to Chanthaburi

(Highway 3). Comfortable rooms with all the amenities cost 749 to 1084B; on the premises are a swimming pool and tennis courts.

Places to Eat

There is plenty of good seafood in Si Racha, but you have to watch the prices. Best known is the Chinese-owned *Chua Lee* on Jermjompol (Choemchomphon) Rd next to Soi 10, across from the Krung Thai Bank. The seafood is great but probably the most expensive in town. Next door and across the street are several seafood places with similar fare at much more reasonable prices, such as the *Fast Food Seafood Restaurant* across the street at 81/26-27. The *Koon Pao* restaurant, near the Chinese temple on Jermjompol Rd across from Sois 16 and 18, is also pretty good.

Jarin, on the Soi 14 pier (the pier with boats to Ko Si Chang), has very good one-plate seafood dishes, especially seafood curry steamed with rice (khâo hàw mòk tha-leh) and Thai-style rice noodles with fresh shrimp (kũaytĩaw phàt thai kûng sòt). It's a great place to kill time while waiting for the next boat to Ko Si Chang.

At the end of the pier at Soi 18 is a new, larger incarnation of the *Seaside Restaurant* – now just about the best all-round seafood place in town for atmosphere, service and value. The full-colour bilingual menu includes a tasty grilled seafood platter stacked with squid, mussels, shrimp and cockles.

The most economical place to eat is in the market near the clock tower at the southern end of town. In the evenings the market offers everything from noodles to fresh seafood, while in the daytime it's mostly an ordinary food and clothing market with some noodle and snack stands.

Outside of town, off Sukhumvit Rd (Highway 3) on the way to Pattaya, there are a couple of cheap, but good, fresh seafood places. Locals favour a place near Laem Chabang, about 10 km south of Si Racha, called *Sut Thang Rak* or 'End of Love Rd'. Closer to town is Ao Udom, a small fishing

bay where there are several open-air seafood places.

Getting There & Away

Buses to Si Racha leave the eastern bus terminal in Bangkok every 25 minutes or so from 5 am to 7 pm. The ordinary bus is 29B, air-con bus is 52B; travel time is around one hour 45 minutes. From Pattaya, buses are 10B and take about 30 minutes. Ordinary direct buses stop near the pier for Ko Si Chang, but through and AC buses stop on Sukhumvit Rd (Highway 3), near the

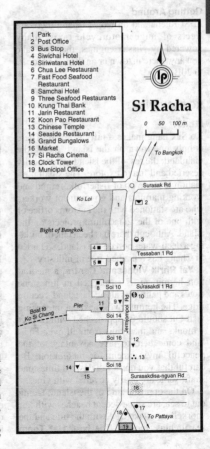

1 Park
2 Post Office
3 Bus Stop
4 Siwichai Hotel
5 Siriwatana Hotel
6 Chua Lee Restaurant
7 Fast Food Seafood Restaurant
8 Samchai Hotel
9 Three Seafood Restaurants
10 Krung Thai Bank
11 Jarin Restaurant
12 Koon Pao Restaurant
13 Chinese Temple
14 Seaside Restaurant
15 Grand Bungalows
16 Market
17 Si Racha Cinema
18 Clock Tower
19 Municipal Office

Si Racha

0   50   100 m

To Bangkok

Surasak Rd
Ko Loi
Bight of Bangkok
Tessaban 1 Rd
Soi 10
Surasakdi 1 Rd
Jermjompol Rd
Boat to Ko Si Chang
Pier
Soi 14
Soi 16
Soi 18
Surasakdisa-nguan Rd
To Pattaya

Laemthong Department Store, from where there are tuk-tuks to the pier.

You can also reach Si Racha by 3rd-class train, though not many people come by this method. Train No 239 leaves Hualamphong station at 6.20 am and arrives at Si Racha at 9.05 am (about an hour slower – but more scenic – than the bus). The fare is 28B. A more realistic train trip would be via the No 195 from Chachoengsao – if you happen to be in Chachoengsao – which leaves daily at 2.40 pm and arrives in Si Racha at 3.54 pm. The Chachoengsao to Si Racha fare is 15B.

Getting Around

In Si Racha and on Ko Si Chang there are fleets of huge motorcycle taxis, many powered by Nissan engines, that will take you anywhere in town or on the island for 10 to 20B.

KO SI CHANG

เกาะสีชัง

Ko Si Chang makes a nifty getaway. There is only one town on the island, facing the mainland; the rest of the island is practically deserted and fun to explore. The small population is made up of fisherfolk, retired and working mariners and government workers who are stationed with the customs office or with one of the aquaculture projects on the island. Although there has been talk of building a deep-water port on the island, so far Ko Si Chang has remained free of industry.

Yai Phrik Vipassana Centre, a meditation hermitage, is ensconced in limestone caves and palm huts along the island's centre ridge. The hermit caves make an interesting visit but should be approached with respect – monks and mae chiis from all over Thailand come here to take advantage of the peaceful environment for meditation. Be careful that you don't fall down a limestone shaft; some are nearly covered with vines.

On the opposite side of the island, facing out to sea, are some decent beaches with fair snorkelling – take care with the tide and the sea urchins, though. The best, **Hat Tham**

(also called Hat Sai), can be reached by following a branch of the ring road on foot to the back of the island. There is also a more public – and less clean – beach at the western end of the island (about two km from the pier) near the old palace grounds, called **Hat Tha Wang**. Thai residents and visitors from the mainland come here for picnics.

The palace was once used by King Chulalongkorn (Rama V) in the summer months, but was abandoned when the French briefly occupied the island in 1893. Little remains of the various palace buildings, but there are a few ruins to see. The main throne hall – a magnificent golden teak structure called Vimanmek – was moved to Bangkok in 1910, but the stairs leading up to it are still there; if you follow these stairs to the crest of the hill overlooking Tha Wang, you'll come to a stone outcropping wrapped in holy cloth. The locals call it 'Bell Rock' because if struck with a rock or heavy stick it rings like a bell. Flanking the rock are what appear to be two ruined chedis. The large chedi on the left actually contains **Wat Atsadangnimit**, a small consecrated chamber where King Chulalongkorn used to meditate. The unique Buddha image inside was fashioned 50 years ago by a local monk who now lives in the cave hermitage. There are attempts to rebuild this palace and some work was going on at the time of writing.

Not far from Wat Atsadangnimit is a large limestone cave called **Tham Saowapha**, which appears to plunge deep into the island. If you have a torch, the cave might be worth exploring.

To the east of town, high on a hill overlooking the sea, is a large **Chinese temple**. During Chinese New Year in February, the island is overrun with Chinese visitors from the mainland. This is one of Thailand's most interesting Chinese temples, with shrine-caves, several different temple levels and a good view of Si Chang and the ocean. It's a long and steep climb from the road below.

Like most islands along Thailand's eastern seaboard, Ko Si Chang is best visited on weekdays; on weekends and holidays the island can get crowded.

CENTRAL THAILAND

Places to Stay

The easiest places to locate are those near the gate to Hat Tha Wang. *Benz Bungalow* (☎ (038) 216091) offers unique stone bungalows for 300 to 400B with fan and bath, 600B with air-con. The rather characterless *Tiewpai Guest House* (☎ (038) 216084), also in this area, has a variety of accommodation ranging from 45B for a dorm bed to 450B for an air-con room.

Near Hat Tham at the back of the island is the friendly *Si Phitsanu Bungalow* (☎ (038) 216024). Rooms in a row house cost 200 to 400B per night, or you can get a one-bedroom bungalow overlooking the small bay for 700B, or a two-bedroom one for 1000B. *Top Bungalow* (☎ (038) 216001), off the road on the way to Si Phitsanu, is similar in price but has no sea view.

The *Green House 84* (☎ (038) 216024) is off the ring road towards the Chinese temple and costs 150/200B for basic, but clean, singles/doubles in a row house. Also in this vicinity is the new *Sichang View Resort* (☎ (038) 216210), where tidy bungalows cost 600B with fan, 1000B air-con.

In town there are a couple of basic hotels, including the *Ban Ari*, that cost 120B a night but are fairly obvious brothel operations.

You can camp anywhere on the island without any hassle, including in Rama V's abandoned palace at Hat Tha Wang.

Places to Eat

The town has several small restaurants, but nothing special, with all the Thai and Chinese standard dishes. Along the road that leads to the public beach are a couple of rustic seafood places.

Getting There & Away

Boats to Ko Si Chang leave regularly from a pier in Si Racha at the end of Soi 14, Jermjompol Rd. The fare is 20B each way; the first boat leaves at about 5 am and the last at 7 pm. The last boat back to Si Racha from Si Chang is at 5 pm. As you approach Ko Si Chang by boat, check out the dozens of barges anchored in the island's lee. Their numbers have multiplied from year to year

as shipping demands by Thailand's booming import and export business have increased.

Getting Around

There are fleets of huge motorcycle taxis that will take you anywhere in town for 10 to 20B. You can also get a complete tour of the island for 100B per hour.

PATTAYA

พัทยา

On the road through Pattaya (population 55,000), before Pattaya Beach, the bus passes a number of prosperous sign-making businesses. Upon arrival at Pattaya Beach, the reason for their prosperity is immediately apparent – the place is lit up like Hollywood Boulevard at night. Many travellers will find Pattaya lacking in culture as well as good taste, since much of the place seems designed to attract the worst kind of Western tourist. Budget travellers, in particular, would do well to scratch it from their itineraries. Pattaya Beach is not such a great beach to begin with and its biggest businesses, water sports and street sex, have driven prices for food and accommodation beyond Bangkok levels. Still, it continues to attract a loyal following of Bangkok oil company expats and package tourists. In a typical November to March season Pattaya receives around a million visitors.

Pattaya got its start as a resort when there was a US base at nearby Sattahip during the Indochina War years – nowadays there are still plenty of sailors about, both Thai and American. Food (especially seafood) is great here, as claimed, but generally way over-priced by national (but not international) standards. That part of South Pattaya known as 'the village' attracts a large number of *ka-toeys* (Thai transvestites), who pose as hookers and ply their trade among the droves of well-heeled European tourists. Germans and Scandinavians lead the pack. Incidentally, the easiest way to tell a ka-toey is by the Adam's apple – a scarf covering the neck is a dead give-away. (Nowadays, though,

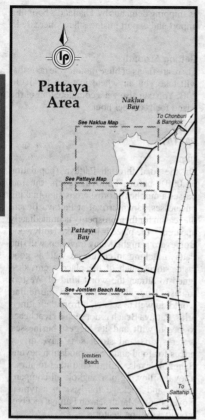

land, the best in the Pattaya area is probably Hat Jomtien (Jawmthian), a couple of km south of Pattaya. Here the water is clean and you're well away from the noisy Pattaya bar scene.

Hat Naklua, north of Pattaya, is also quiet and fairly tastefully developed. Jomtien and Naklua are where visiting families tend to stay, as Pattaya/South Pattaya is pretty much given over to single male tourists or couples on package tours. The glitziest digs are at North Pattaya and Cliff beaches (between South Pattaya and Jomtien).

Changing the Image

After garnering a long streak of bad press in both the domestic and international media, Pattaya has recently begun experiencing a steady decline in tourist visitation. In 1992 Pattaya lost the privilege of hosting the annual Siam World Cup – one of Asia's biggest windsurfing competitions – to Phuket. The two principal complaints have been the sidewalk sex scene and Pattaya Bay's water quality.

Local authorities and travel suppliers are now struggling to upgrade Pattaya's image as well as clean the place up. In many ways Pattaya serves as the prime example of what can happen to a beach resort area if no controls are applied to the quality and quantity of tourism development. I'm actually beginning to feel sorry for Pattaya in spite of the fact that local developers have dug their own graves, so to speak. It's too late to turn Pattaya back into the fishing village it once was, but it's not too late to recreate a clean, safe tourist destination if all concerned cooperate.

Information

Tourist Office The Pattaya TAT office, at the midpoint of Pattaya Beach Rd, keeps an up-to-date list of accommodation in the Pattaya area, and is very helpful. Next door is the Tourist Police (☎ 429371).

Post & Telecommunications The GPO and international telephone office are together in South Pattaya on Soi 15 (Soi Post Office). There are also several private long-distance phone offices in town, but calls from the government office at the GPO are always less expensive. The telephone area code is ☎ 038.

Radio Pattaya has a radio station with English-language broadcasts at FM 107.7

some ka-toeys have their Adam's apples surgically removed.)

The one thing the Pattaya area has going for it is diving centres (see Diving & Snorkelling in the Facts for the Visitor chapter). There are four or five nice islands off Pattaya's shore, although they are expensive to get to. If you're a snorkelling or scuba enthusiast, equipment can be booked at any of the several diving shops/schools at Pattaya Beach. Ko Laan, the most popular of the offshore islands, even has places to stay.

For beach enthusiasts, if you can't get to one of the better beaches in southern Thai-

Top: Ko Phi Phi (TAT)
Bottom: Sunset, Ban Mae Hat, Ko Tao (RN)

Top Left: Waterfall near Sangkhom (JC)
Top Right: Forest on trek from Mae Hong Son (RI)
  Bottom: Ao Phang-Nga (RI)

MHz. American and British announcers offer a mix of local news and music.

Water Sports

Pattaya and Jomtien have some of the best water sports facilities in Thailand. Waterskiing costs 600 to 800B per hour including equipment, boat and driver. Parasailing is 300B a shot (about 10 to 15 minutes) and windsurfing 500B an hour. Game-fishing is also a possibility; rental rates for boats, fishing guides and tackle are quite reasonable.

Jomtien Beach is the best spot for windsurfing, not least because you're a little less likely to run into parasailors or jetskiiers. Surf House on Jomtien Beach Rd rents equipment and offers instruction.

Scuba Diving Pattaya is the most convenient dive location to Bangkok, but it is far from being the best Thailand has to offer. Recent reports say the fish population has dwindled considerably and visibility is often poor due to heavy boat traffic. Shipwrecks off Sattahip and Samae have created artificial reefs which remain the most interesting area dive sites.

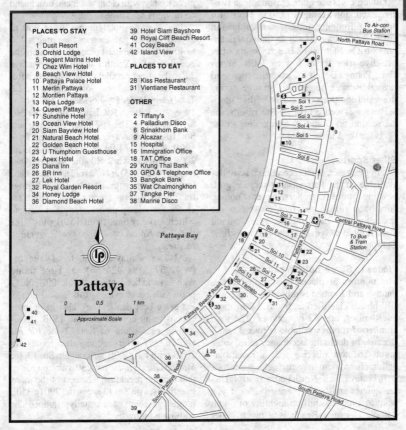

PLACES TO STAY

1 Dusit Resort
3 Orchid Lodge
5 Regent Marina Hotel
7 Chez Wim Hotel
8 Beach View Hotel
10 Pattaya Palace Hotel
11 Merlin Pattaya
12 Montien Pattaya
13 Nipa Lodge
14 Queen Pattaya
17 Sunshine Hotel
19 Ocean View Hotel
20 Siam Bayview Hotel
21 Natural Beach Hotel
22 Golden Beach Hotel
23 U Thumphorn Guesthouse
24 Apex Hotel
25 Diana Inn
26 BR Inn
27 Lek Hotel
32 Royal Garden Resort
34 Honey Lodge
36 Diamond Beach Hotel
39 Hotel Siam Bayshore
40 Royal Cliff Beach Resort
41 Cosy Beach
42 Island View

PLACES TO EAT

28 Kiss Restaurant
31 Vientiane Restaurant

OTHER

2 Tiffany's
4 Palladium Disco
6 Srinakhorn Bank
9 Alcazar
15 Hospital
16 Immigration Office
18 TAT Office
29 Krung Thai Bank
30 GPO & Telephone Office
33 Bangkok Bank
35 Wat Chaimongkhon
37 Tangke Pier
38 Marine Disco

Pattaya Bay

Pattaya

0   0.5   1 km

Approximate Scale

Water Quality

One of Pattaya's main problems during recent years has been the emptying of raw sewage into the bay, a practice that has posed serious health risks for swimmers. Local officials have finally begun to take notice and are now taking regular bacteria counts along the shoreline and fining hotels or other businesses found to be releasing untreated sewage.

The Thai government recently allocated US$60 million to Pattaya for pollution cleanup and prevention. By 1995 water treatment plants in Pattaya, Naklua and Jomtien will be in full operation; authorities claim the coastal waters will be pollution-free by 1997.

In the meantime, according to a TAT pamphlet entitled *Striving to Resolve Pattaya's Problems*, beach areas considered safe for swimming (with a coliform count of less than 1000 MPN per 100 millilitres) include those facing Wong Amat Hotel, Dusit Resort Hotel, Yot Sak shopping centre and the Royal Cliff Hotel. Shoreline areas found to exceed the coliform standard extend from Siam Commercial Bank in South Pattaya to where Khlong Pattaya empties into the sea. Coliform counts here exceeded 1700 MPN per 100 millilitres. ■

Diving costs are quite reasonable: a two-dive excursion averages 1250 to 1750B for boat, equipment, underwater guide and lunch. Some shops, such as the American-run outfit at Mermaid's Beach Resort, offer two-dive trips for as low as 750B. Shops along Pattaya Beach Rd advertise trips, and several Pattaya hotels also arrange excursions and equipment. For a list of dive shops in Pattaya as well as in other Thai resorts, see the section on Diving & Snorkelling in the Facts for the Visitor chapter.

Other Sports

Out of the water, other recreational activities available in the Pattaya area include golf, bowling, snooker, archery, target-shooting, horseback riding and tennis. Among the several gyms and fitness centres around town is Gold's Gym in South Pattaya's Julie Complex.

Places to Stay – bottom end

The number of places to stay in Naklua, Pattaya and Jomtien is mind-boggling: over 140 places classified as hotels, 80 or more guesthouses, and 32 bungalows. The total number of rooms available is over 13,000! Because of declining occupancy rates, some hotels are now offering special rates; bargaining for a room may also net a lower rate.

In Pattaya itself, North Pattaya and Naklua are quieter and better places to stay if you want to avoid the full-on nightlife of South Pattaya. Jomtien Beach is a much better place to stay, with clean water and beach, and no obvious sex scene.

The average hotel ranges from 350 to 2000B, and for guesthouses the range is 150 to 400B. The cheapest places in town are the guesthouses in South Pattaya along Pattaya 2 Rd, the street parallel to Pattaya Beach Rd. Most are clustered near Sois 6, 10, 11 and 12. The *Honey Lodge* (☎ 429133) on 597/8 Moo 10, South Pattaya Rd, has rooms in the 300 to 400B range. The *U-Thumphorn*, opposite Soi 10 on Pattaya 2, has OK rooms from 120B. Nearby is *Wangthong* with rooms for 200B. On Pattaya 2 Rd, the modern *Apex Hotel* (☎ 429233) at No 216/2 near the Diana Inn has rooms with air-con, TV and fridge for 250 to 300B – a great value. There are also a few cheap places along Soi Yamato which have rooms from 150B plus, like the *Nipa House* (☎ 425851) or *Siam Guest House*.

Also on Pattaya 2 Rd, the *Diana Inn* (☎ 429675; fax 424566) has large rooms with fan and hot-water bath for 300B, plus a pool with bar service – this is still one of Pattaya's best deals. They also have more expensive air-con rooms from 450B.

In a lane south of Soi 12 the *BR Inn* (☎ 428229) offers good-value rooms for 200B with fan, 300B air-con. On Soi 13, the *Malibu Guest House* has 250B air-con rooms that include breakfast. The rest of the many guesthouses on Soi 13 are in the 200 to 350B range, but rooms are usually cramped and without windows.

A German reader wrote to say 'Our impression of Pattaya wasn't as bad as yours' and recommended a place called *Garden Villa* on Naklua Rd (North Pattaya). It costs 400 to 550B for an air-con double, is owned by Germans and has 'traditional German food and customs'. Another place that has been recommended is *In de Welkom*, where air-con doubles cost 350B.

In North Pattaya the quiet Soi 1 features the *Chez Wim Hotel* (☎ 429044), where bargain rooms cost 200B with fan or 350B with air-con.

At Jomtien Beach, the bottom end consists of several places around the Surf House at the north end of the beach. The *AA Guest House* (☎ 231183) has 300B air-con rooms. Next to Surf House is *Sunlight* with 400B air-con rooms. One of the cheapest places to stay is *RS Guest House* (☎ 231867/8), which sits at the southern end of the beach, near Chalapruk Rd. Reasonable smallish rooms cost 250B with fan or 350B with air-con. The

similarly priced *DD Inn* (☎ 232995) is at the north end of the beach, where the road turns towards Pattaya.

Places to Stay – middle

Good middle-range places can be found in Naklua, North Pattaya and Jomtien. In Pattaya the *Sunshine Hotel* (☎ 429247; fax 421302) is tucked away at 217/1 Soi 8, and all their fine rooms cost 550B. The hotel also has a pool. On Soi 11 in Pattaya the *Natural Beach Hotel* overlooks the beach with good air-con rooms from 400B. Farther south on the corner of Pattaya 2 Rd and Soi 13 is the high-rise *Lek Hotel* (☎ 425550/2; fax 426629) with decent rooms for 640B.

The *Garden Lodge* (☎ 429109), just off Naklua Rd, has air-con rooms for 450B, a clean pool, good service, and an open-air breakfast buffet. *Pattaya Lodge* (☎ 428014) is farther off Naklua Rd, right on the beach. Air-con rooms here are 2000 to 2800B. The *Riviera Pattaya* (☎ 429230) is between the

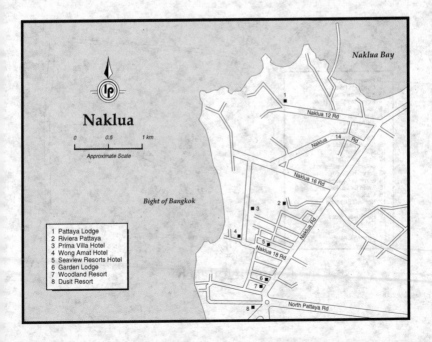

Naklua Bay

Naklua

0   0.5   1 km

Approximate Scale

Bight of Bangkok

Naklua 12 Rd
Naklua 14 Rd
Naklua 16 Rd
Naklua Rd
Naklua 18 Rd
North Pattaya Rd

1 Pattaya Lodge
2 Riviera Pattaya
3 Prima Villa Hotel
4 Wong Amat Hotel
5 Seaview Resorts Hotel
6 Garden Lodge
7 Woodland Resort
8 Dusit Resort

CENTRAL THAILAND

road and the beach and has air-con rooms for 400B.

Peaceful Jomtien Beach has mostly middle-range 'condotel' places ranging in price from 500 to 700B. The *Jomtien Bayview* (☎ 425889) and *Visit House* (☎ 426331) have air-con rooms for 350 to 650B. The *Silver Sand Villa* (☎ 231288/9; fax 231030) has spacious double air-con rooms for 800B, including an American-style breakfast, plus a swimming pool.

The *Surf House* (☎ 231025/6; fax 231029) has air-con rooms from 500B. The *Marine Beach Hotel* (☎ 231129/31) and the well-run *Sea Breeze* (☎ 231057; fax 231059) are just a bit more expensive at 600B per air-con room but the latter is very good value at this rate. Another good-value place is the friendly *Summer Beach Inn* (☎ 231777), near the Marine Beach, where new rooms cost 350 to 650B, including hot water and TV in all rooms. *Seaview Villa* (☎ 422766) has seven bungalows for 300 to 400B, including a fan.

Jomtien also has several more expensive places that rent bungalows in the 1000 to 2000B range (see top end – Jomtien Beach). The high-rise development of Pattaya and Cliff Beach is spreading fast to Jomtien.

At the time of writing there was only one place to stay on Ko Laan. The *Ko Laan Resort* (☎ 428422) was being rebuilt and the mid-range rooms are expected to cost around 600 to 800B.

Places to Stay – top end

Pattaya is really a resort for package tourists so the vast majority of its accommodation is in this bracket. The two reigning monarchs of Pattaya luxury hotels are the *Dusit Resort*, at the northern end of Pattaya Beach, with two pools, tennis courts, a health centre and exceptional dim sum in the rooftop restaurant, and the *Royal Cliff Beach Resort* (at the southern end of Pattaya), which is really three hotels in one: a central section for

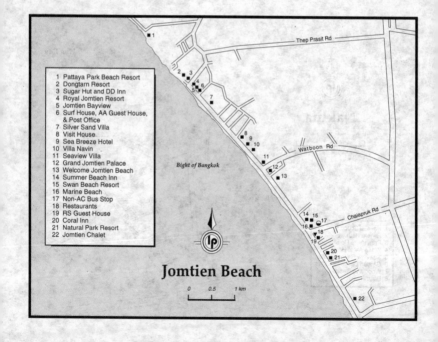

1 Pattaya Park Beach Resort
2 Dongtarn Resort
3 Sugar Hut and DD Inn
4 Royal Jomtien Resort
5 Jomtien Bayview
6 Surf House, AA Guest House, & Post Office
7 Silver Sand Villa
8 Visit House
9 Sea Breeze Hotel
10 Villa Navin
11 Seaview Villa
12 Grand Jomtien Palace
13 Welcome Jomtien Beach
14 Summer Beach Inn
15 Swan Beach Resort
16 Marine Beach
17 Non-AC Bus Stop
18 Restaurants
19 RS Guest House
20 Coral Inn
21 Natural Park Resort
22 Jomtien Chalet

Thep Prasit Rd

Bight of Bangkok

Watboon Rd

Chaiapruk Rd

Jomtien Beach

0   0.5   1 km

package tours and conventions, a family wing and the very up-market Royal Wing.

All of the hotels listed below have air-con rooms and swimming pools (unless otherwise noted). Many of the top-end hotels have lowered rates on standard singles and doubles so it's worth asking if anything cheaper is available when requesting a rate quote. Rooms are also often cheaper when booked through a Bangkok travel agency.

Hat Naklua

Prima Villa Hotel, Naklua Soi 18, 91 rooms, from 1500B (☎ 429398)

Seaview Resorts Hotel, Naklua Rd, 159 rooms, from 1404B (☎ 429317)

Wong Amat Hotel, Naklua Rd, 207 rooms, 1648B up (☎ 426990/9; fax 428599)

Woodland Resort, Naklua Rd, 80 rooms, 1800 and 2000B (☎ 421707; fax 425663)

North Pattaya

Beach View, Soi 2, Beach Rd, 104 rooms, 390 to 590B (discounted from 850B) (☎ 422660; fax 422664)

Dusit Resort, Mu 5, Pattaya-Naklua Rd, 408 rooms, 3000 to 6000B (☎ 428541; (02) 236-0450 jn Bangkok, fax 428239)

Merlin Pattaya, Beach Rd, 360 rooms, singles/doubles 1600/1800B (☎ 428755/9; fax 421673)

Montien Pattaya, Beach Rd, 320 rooms, singles/doubles 2000 to 13,000B (☎ 428155/6; fax 423155)

Orchid Lodge, Beach Rd, 236 rooms, singles/doubles 1500 to 3000B (☎ 428175; fax 428165)

Pattaya Palace Hotel, Beach Rd, 261 rooms, 1600 to 3600B (☎ 428319; fax 428026)

Regent Marina Hotel, North Pattaya Rd, 208 rooms, 1400 to 3504B (☎ 428015, 429298; fax 423296)

Central & South Pattaya

Diamond Beach Hotel, South Pattaya, 120 rooms, 500 to 900B (☎ 428071, 429885/6; fax 424888)

Golden Beach Hotel, 519/29 Pattaya 2 Rd, 1700 and 2000B (☎ 428891; fax 425935)

Nipa Lodge, Beach Rd, 150 rooms, singles/doubles 1000 to 2000B (☎ 428321/2; fax 428097)

Ocean View Hotel, Beach Rd, 111 rooms, 500 to 2600B (☎ 428434; fax 428551)

Royal Garden Resort, Beach Rd, 154 rooms, from 3648B (☎ 428122/6/7)

Hotel Siam Bayshore, South Pattaya Rd, 270 rooms, 1600 (☎ 428678/81; fax 428730)

Siam Bayview Hotel, Beach Rd, 302 rooms, from 2236B up (☎ 423871/7; fax 423879)

Hat Cliff

Asia Pattaya Beach Hotel, Cliff Rd, 314 rooms, 2000 to 7000B (☎ 428602/6; fax 423496)

Cosy Beach, Cliff Rd, no pool, 62 rooms, 900 to 1600B (☎ 428818; fax 422818)

Island View, 150 rooms, 968 to 1452B (☎ 422816)

Royal Cliff Beach Resort, Cliff Rd, 650 rooms, 3679 to 22,000B (☎ 428513, 428613/6; (02) 282-0999 in Bangkok)

Hat Jomtien

Ban Suan, nine bungalows, from 1500 (fan) to 2700B (air-con) (☎ 231072)

Coral Inn, 40 rooms, 700 to 800B (☎ 231283/7)

Dongtarn Resort, 30 bungalows, 1000 to 2000B (☎ 231191)

Grand Jomtien Palace, 356 Jomtien Beach Rd, 252 rooms, 1800 to 2200B (☎ 231405/8; fax 231404)

Jomtien Chalet, 36 bungalows, 1100 to 1600B (☎ 231205)

Marine Beach Hotel, 131/62 Jomtien Beach, 65 rooms, 750 to 1200B (☎ 231129/31)

Natural Park Resort, 412 Jomtien Beach Rd, 87 rooms, from 1050B (☎ 231561; fax 231567)

Pattaya Park Beach Resort, 345 Jomtien Beach, 240 rooms, 1800 to 3600B (☎ 423000/4; fax 423009)

Royal Jomtien Resort, 408 Mou 12 Jomtien Beach Rd 400 rooms, 2400 to 2800B (☎ 231350; fax 231369)

Swan Beach Resort, 126 rooms, from 900B (☎ 231266; fax 231266)

Villa Navin, 74 rooms, from 1000B (☎ 231065/7; fax 231318)

Welcome Jomtien Beach, 400 rooms, from 1900B (☎ 231701/16; fax 232716)

Places to Eat

Most food in Pattaya is expensive, but good Thai food is available in shops along Pattaya's back street (Pattaya 2 Rd), away from the beach. (Also look for cheap rooms to rent here.) The front signs outside the many snack bars reveal that bratwurst mit brot is far more readily available than khâo phàt.

Arabs and South Asians are coming to Pattaya in droves these days, so there is an increasing number of Indian/Pakistani/Middle Eastern restaurants in town, some with fairly moderate prices.

The best seafood restaurants are in South Pattaya, where you pick out the sea creatures yourself and are charged by weight. Prices are sky-high.

CENTRAL THAILAND

One moderately priced yet well-appointed Pattaya restaurant is the *PIC Kitchen* on Soi 5. The Thai-style salas have low wooden tables and cushions for dining and the emphasis is on Thai food with a limited selection of Western dishes. The upstairs bar area occasionally features live jazz. Another interesting place to eat is *Vientiane Restaurant* (☎ 411298) at 485/18 Pattaya 2 Rd, opposite Soi Yamamoto. The restaurant serves Thai and Lao dishes ranging from 50 to 200B, plus lunch specials for 30 to 50B. The 24-hour *Kiss* on Pattaya 2 Rd, near the Diana Inn, has reasonably priced American and European breakfasts, Thai dishes, snacks and drinks.

Opposite the bus station on the corner of Jomtien Beach and Chalapruk Rds are a few basic and cheap restaurants serving the usual Thai/Chinese dishes. Good for a cheap meal in a nice setting is the *Sugar Hut*, next to DD Inn.

San Domenico's (☎ 426871), on Jomtien Rd between South Pattaya and Jomtien Beach, is operated by the same Italian family that started Pan Pan in Bangkok. The Italian menu is superb and though regular meals are pricey there is also an excellent buffet for just under 200B stocked with antipasti, pasta, seafood and Luciano Pantieri's famous desserts.

Entertainment

Eating, drinking and making merry are the big pastimes once the sun goes down. Making merry in Pattaya, aside from the professional sex scene, means everything from hanging out in a video bar to dancing all night at the Marine Bar & Disco in South Pattaya. Three transvestite palaces – Alcazar, Tiffany's and Simon's – offer complete drag-queen shows. Best of the bunch is the Alcazar (78/14 Pattaya 2 Rd, ☎ 428746), which offers three shows nightly at 7, 9 and 10.20 pm.

Among the several discos in town, the very glitzy Palladium has a capacity of 6000 customers, reportedly the largest disco in Thailand. It's close to the Alcazar at 78/33-35 Pattaya 2 Rd.

Actually, one of the best things to do in the evening is just to stroll down Beach Rd and check out the amazing variety of bars – there's one for every proclivity, including a couple of outdoor Thai boxing bars featuring local talent. Truly the Garden of Earthly Delights, in the most Boschean sense.

Getting There & Away

Air At the moment there is no regularly scheduled air service to Pattaya. Two airlines, Tropical Sea Air (formerly Yellowbird) and Bangkok Airways, have each operated flights from Bangkok to Pattaya or nearby U-Taphao at one time or another, but due to a lack of profitability neither lasted.

Bus Ordinary buses from Bangkok's eastern bus terminal cost 37B one way and leave at 30-minute intervals from 5.20 am to 9 pm daily. In Pattaya they leave from the depot on Sukhumvit Rd, where it meets Central Pattaya Rd. Count on around three hours for this trip.

Air-con buses from the same station in Bangkok leave at similar intervals for 66B (or 126B return) between 6.30 am and 8 pm. Buses to Pattaya are also available from Bangkok's northern bus terminal for 67B (air-con). In Pattaya the air-con bus stop is on North Pattaya Rd, near the intersection with Sukhumvit Rd. The air-con route takes around 2½ hours. Several hotels and travel agencies in Bangkok also run thrice-daily air-con tour buses to Pattaya for around 100 to 150B. These buses take around two hours in either direction.

From Si Racha you can grab a public bus on Sukhumvit Rd to Pattaya for 10B.

If you've just flown into Bangkok International Airport and need to get to Pattaya right away, there are airport minibuses that go directly to Pattaya at 9 am, noon and 7 pm daily for 250B one way. In the reverse direction, the THAI minibus leaves from Alcazar Unity (next-door to the Alcazar) in Pattaya at 6.30 am, 1 pm and 7.30 pm. Song Asawin Company also runs an hourly bus to Bangkok International Airport from Pattaya's Regent

Marina Hotel from 7 am to 7 pm for 160B one way.

Train A train goes from Hualamphong station to Pattaya daily at 6.20 am and 1.10 pm. In the opposite direction trains leave at 10.53 am and 5.38 pm daily. The trip takes around three hours and costs 31B one way. Although this is an hour longer than the typical bus ride from Bangkok, it beats biting your nails in traffic jams along the highway from Bang Na to Trat. The Pattaya train station is just north of the T-intersection of Central Pattaya Rd and Sukhumvit Rd.

Getting Around

Songthaew Songthaews cruise up and down Pattaya Beach and Pattaya 2 Rds frequently – just hop on and when you get out pay 5B. If you go to Naklua it's 10B. Don't ask the fare first as the driver may interpret this to mean you want to charter the vehicle. To get to Jomtien you will have to charter a songthaew; the fare should be about 40B.

Many readers have complained about riding the 5B songthaews with local passengers and then being charged a high charter price of 50B or more when they get off. In some instances drivers have threatened to beat farang passengers when they wouldn't pay the exorbitant fare. It's little use complaining to the Tourist Police unless you can give them the licence plate number of the offending driver's vehicle. A refund is highly unlikely but perhaps if the Tourist Police receive enough complaints, they'll take some action to reduce or eliminate the rip-offs.

Boat The ferry to Ko Laan leaves from Tangke Pier, takes 40 minutes and costs a steep 100B. For 250B the ferry service will throw in lunch. Boat charters cost around 1000 to 1200B per day depending on the size of the boat.

Car & Jeep Jeeps can be hired for around 500 to 800B per day, and cars start at 1200B (as low as 800B for a 4WD Suzuki in the low season) depending on size and model; insur-

ance and tax cost up to 160B more. All rentals in Pattaya are on a 24-hour basis. Avis has offices at the Dusit Resort (☎ 429901) and Royal Cliff Beach Resort (☎ 422421); Hertz is at the Royal Garden Resort (☎ 428122). Pattaya Vehicle Rental Service (☎ 425700) and Pop Eye (☎ 429631), both on Pattaya 2 Rd, have lower rates.

Motorbike Motorbikes cost 150 to 200B per day for an 80 or 100cc; a 125cc will cost 250B and you'll even see a few 750cc to 1000cc machines for hire for 500B. There are several motorcycle hire places along Pattaya Beach Rd and a couple on Pattaya 2 Rd. Pattaya is a good place to purchase a used motorcycle – check the rental shops.

AROUND PATTAYA

Farther south and then east from Pattaya are more beaches and more resorts. In fact, the more posh places may, in the future, be restructuring themselves in favour of more middle-class tourists and conventioneers.

Bang Saray Villa (☎ 436070), in Bang Saray, has 24 air-con bungalows for 300B, while the *Bang Saray Bay Resort* and *Ban Saray Fishing Lodge* (☎ 436757) are small hotels with air-con rooms for 450B. *Nong Nooch Village* (☎ 435971/3; fax 435976) has a choice of rooms or bungalows ranging from 300 to 2500B. *Sea Sand Club* (☎ 435163; fax 435166) has 46 air-con bungalows that cost 749B from Sunday to Thursday, and 856B on Friday and Saturday.

There are still some good seafood restaurants for local Thais in Bang Saray – something Pattaya hasn't seen for years.

Still farther south is Sattahip, a vacation spot for the Thai military – some of the best beaches in the area are reserved for their use. There are several Thai navy and air-force bases in the vicinity.

Rayong Province

RAYONG & AROUND

อ.เมืองระยอง

Rayong (population 45,000) is 220 km from Bangkok by the old highway (Highway 3) or 185 km on Highway 36. The province produces fine fruit (especially durian and pineapple) and naam plaa (fish sauce). Rayong itself is not really worth visiting, but nearby beaches are fair and Ko Samet is a favourite island getaway for Bangkokians. Except for Ko Samet, this area has not received many foreign visitors yet, although it has been popular with Thai tourists for several years.

Rayong's beaches are all near **Ban Phe**, a seaside town around 25 km south-east of the provincial capital (this is also the departure point for Ko Samet). If sun and sand are what you've come to Rayong for, head straight for Ban Phe. Then pick out a beach or board a boat bound for Samet.

Another much smaller island nearby is **Ko Saket**, which is a 20-minute boat ride from the beach of Hat Sai Thong (turn south off Highway 3 at Km 208).

The **Suan Son Pine Park**, five km farther down the highway from Ban Phe, is a popular place for Thai picnickers and has white-sand beaches as well.

Suan Wang Kaew is 11 km east of Ban Phe and has more beaches and rather expensive bungalows. **Ko Talu**, across from Wang Kaew, is said to be a good diving area – the proprietors of Suan Wang Kaew, a private park, can arrange boats and gear. Other resort areas along the Rayong coast include **Laem Mae Phim** and **Hat Sai Thong**. **Mae Ramphung Beach**, a 10-km strip of sand between Ban Tapong and Ban Kon Ao (11 km east of amphoe meuang Rayong), is part of Laem Ya-Mu Ko Samet National Park. See the Ko Samet section for more information on the park.

Khao Chamao-Khao Wong National Park is inland about 17 km north of Km 274 off Highway 3. Though less than 85 sq km, the park is famous for limestone mountains, caves, high cliffs, dense forest, waterfalls, and freshwater swimming and fishing. The park service here rents bungalows, long houses and tents. To get here from Ban Phe take a songthaew to Km 274 for 20B, and another songthaew to the park.

Many more resort-type places are popping up along Rayong's coastline. Bangkok developers envisage a string of Thai resorts all the way to Trat along the eastern seaboard, banking on the increasing income and leisure time of Bangkok Thais.

One non-resort development along the coast is the new deep-water port at **Maptaphut** which, along with Chonburi's Laem Chabang Port, is charted to catch the large shipping overflow from Bangkok's Khlong Toey Port.

Information

Money The Bangkok Bank at 56/1 Sukhumvit Rd, between the cinema and Tawan Ok Hotel, has an exchange window open daily from 7 am to 10 pm.

Places to Stay & Eat

Rayong There are three hotels near the bus station off Sukhumvit Rd. The *Rayong*, at 65/3 Sukhumvit Rd, and the *Rayong Otani*, at 69 Sukhumvit, both have rooms from 150B. The latter has some air-con rooms for 350B as well. The *Tawan Ok*, at 52/3 Sukhumvit, has fan-cooled rooms for 90B without bath, 150B with bath.

For cheap food check the market near the Thetsabanteung cinema, or the noodle shop on Taksin Rd next to Wat Lum Mahachaichunphon. There is a very good open-air restaurant along the river belonging to the Fishermen's Association ('Samaakhom Pramong' in Thai).

Ban Phe There are several hotels in Ban Phe near the central market and within walking distance of the pier. *T N Place* (☎ (038) 651078), about 100 metres from the pier, has rooms with fan for 200B or with air-con for 300B. The owners are friendly and provide plenty of information, but the hotel can get a bit noisy. The *Queen* is up the lane from the pier, near the central market, and has rooms for 150B (no bath), 250B with bath, or 300 to 400B with air-con. The most expensive place to stay is the mid-range *Hotel Diamond Phe* (☎ (038) 651826; fax 424888) which is also close to the pier.

The *Thale Thawng* restaurant, where the tour bus from Bangkok stops, has good Thai seafood dishes – especially recommended is the kŭaytĭaw tha-leh, a seafood noodle soup. The shop across the street is a good place to stock up on food, mosquito coils, etc to take to Ko Samet. You'll most likely be spending some time in this spot, waiting either for the boat to leave the nearby pier for Ko Samet or for the bus to arrive from Bangkok.

Nearby Islands Three small islands off the coast of Rayong offer accommodation packages that include boat transport from the nearest pier along with three or four meals a day. These are best arranged by phone in

advance through Bangkok reservation numbers. On **Ko Saket**, opposite Hat Sai Thong (11 km west of amphoe meuang Rayong), the *Ko Saket Phet* (☎ (01) 319042; (02) 319-9929 in Bangkok) has 15 bungalows and 10 'tourist houses' for 1200 to 2500B a night, including boat transport and all meals. *Ko Nok Resort* (☎ (02) 255-0836 in Bangkok) has a similar set-up on **Ko Man Nok**, 15 km off Pak Nam Prasae (53 km east of Ban Phe). Eight km off Laem Mae Phim (27 km east of Ban Phe) on **Ko Man Klang**, the *Raya Island Resort* (☎ (02) 316-6717 in Bangkok) offers bungalows for just 800B with boat transport and meals. Ko Man Klang and Ko Man Nok, along with Ko Man Nai to their immediate west, are part of Laem Ya-Mu Ko Samet National Park. As with Ko Samet, this official designation has not kept away all development, only moderated it. The islands are in fair condition ecologically, the main threat to surrounding corals being the arrival of jet skis.

Public transport to the pier departure points for each of these islands can be arranged in Ban Phe. On weekends and holidays there may be share taxis (or songthaews) out to the piers; otherwise you'll have to charter a vehicle from the market for 50 to 100B one way – be sure to make a pickup appointment for your return.

Getting There & Away

See the Ko Samet Getting There & Away section for details on transport to and from Rayong.

KO SAMET

เกาะเสม็ด

This island earned a permanent place in Thai literature when classical Thai poet Sunthorn Phu set part of his epic *Phra Aphaimani* on the island. The story follows the travails of a prince exiled to an undersea kingdom ruled by a lovesick female giant. A mermaid aids the prince in his escape to Samet where he defeats the giant by playing a magic flute. Formerly Ko Kaew Phitsadan or 'Vast Jewel

Isle' – a reference to the abundant white sand, this island became known as Ko Samet or 'Cajeput Isle' after the cajeput tree which grows in abundance here and which is very highly valued as firewood throughout South-East Asia. Locally, the *samet* tree has also been used in boat-building.

In the early 1980s, the 13.1-sq-km Ko Samet began receiving its first visitors interested in more than cajeput trees and sand – young Thais in search of a retreat from city life. At that time there were only about 40 houses on the island, built by fisherfolk and Ban Phe locals. Rayong and Bangkok spec-ulators saw the sudden interest in Ko Samet as a chance to cash in on an up-and-coming Phuket and began buying up land along the beaches. No-one bothered with the fact that Ko Samet, along with Laem Ya and other nearby islands, was part of a national park (one of seven marine parks now in Thailand) and had been since 1981.

When farangs started coming to Ko Samet in greater and greater numbers, spurred on by rumours that Ko Samet was similar to Ko Samui '10 years ago' (one always seems to miss it by a decade, eh?), the National Parks Division stepped in and built a visitors' office on the island, ordered that all bunga-lows be moved back behind the tree-line and started charging a 5B admission into the park.

This entry fee has since risen to 50B. Other rather recent changes have included the introduction of several vehicles to the island, more frequent boat services from Ban Phe and a much improved water situation. Ko Samet is a very dry island (which makes it an excellent place to visit during the rainy season). Before they started trucking water to the bungalows you had to bathe at often muddy wells. Now most of the bungalow places have proper Thai-style bathrooms and, as a result, Ko Samet is a much more comfortable and convenient place to visit, though it sometimes becomes overcrowded. Because of a ban on the construction of new accommodation (except where they replace old sites), bungalows are spread thinly over most of the island, with the north-east coast being the most crowded area. The beaches really are lovely, with the whitest, squeakiest sand in Thailand. There is even a little surf occasionally (best months are December to January). However, I still think the accom-modation on Samui and Pha-Ngan islands is better value overall, though of course they're much more expensive and time-consuming to reach from Bangkok.

In spite of the fact that the island is sup-posedly under the protection of the National Parks Division, on recent trips to Ko Samet I have been appalled at the runaway growth in the Na Dan and Hat Sai Kaew areas. Piles

To Ban Phe
Laem Noina
Laem Phra
Village
Ao Wiang Wan
Spirit Shrine
Na Dan
Park Office
Temple
Ao Phrao
Hat Sai Kaew
Laem Yai
Ao Hin Khok
Ao Phai
Ao Jampriang
Ao Thap Thim
Ao Phutsa
Laem Kua Taek
Ao Nuan
Ao Cho
Ao Wong Deuan
Ferry Route
Ao Thian
(Candlelight Beach)
GULF OF THAILAND
Ao Wai
Ao Kiu Na Nok
Ao Kiu Na Nai
Laem Khut
Ao Karang
Ko Samet
Ko Chan
0   0.5   1 km

of rubbish and construction materials have really taken away from the island's charm at the northern end. Once you get away from this end of the island, however, things start looking a bit better.

Ko Samet can be very crowded during Thai public holidays: early November (Loi Krathong Festival); 5 December (King's birthday); 31 December to 1 January (New Year); mid-to-late February (Chinese New Year); mid-April (Songkran Festival). During these times there are people sleeping on the floors of beach restaurants, on the beach, everywhere. September gets the lowest number of visitors (average 2500 visitors), March the most (around 40,000 visitors – approximately 36,000 of them Thai). Thais in any month are more prevalent than foreigners but many are day visitors; most stay at White Sand or Wong Deuan in the more up-market accommodation.

In May 1990 the Forestry Department closed the park to all visitors in an effort to halt encroachment on national park lands, but then reopened the island the next month in response to protests by resort operators. Developers reasonably objected that if Ko Samet is to be closed then so must Ko Phi Phi. Court hearings continue monthly; the latest word is that a permanent moratorium on new developments will continue in order to preserve the island's forested interior.

Information

Near Na Dan and on Hat Sai Kaew and Ao Wong Deuan are several small travel agencies that can arrange long-distance phone calls. Citizen Express, between Na Dan and Hat Sai Kaew, can arrange international telephone service, as well as bus and train reservations – they even do air ticketing. A small post office next to Naga Bungalows has poste restante. It's open weekdays from 8.30 am to 12.30 pm and from 2 to 4 pm, Saturday from 8 am to noon. The telephone code for Ko Samet is ☎ 038.

An excellent guide to the history, flora and fauna of Ko Samet is Alan A Alan's 94-page *Samet*, published by Asia Books. Instead of writing a straight-ahead guidebook, Alan has woven the information into an amusing fictional travelogue involving a pair of Swedish twins on their first trip to the island.

Malaria A few years ago, if you entered the park from the northern end of the island near the village, you'd see a large English-language sign warning visitors that Ko Samet was highly malarial. The sign is gone now but the island still has a bit of malaria. If you're taking malarial prophylactics you have little to worry about. If not, take a little extra care to avoid being bitten by mosquitoes at night. Malaria is not that easy to contract, even in malarial areas, unless you allow the mosquitoes open season on your flesh. It's largely a numbers game – you're not likely to get malaria from just a couple of bites (that's what the experts say anyway), so make sure you use repellent and mosquito nets at night.

There is a public health clinic on the island, located halfway between the village harbour and the park entrance. Go there for a blood test if you develop a fever while on Ko Samet, or for any other urgent health problems such as attacks from poisonous sea creatures or snakes.

Activities

Several bungalows on the island can arrange boat trips to nearby reefs and uninhabited islands. Ao Phutsa, Naga Beach (Ao Hin Khok), Hat Sai Kaew and Ao Wong Deuan each have windsurfing equipment rental places that do boat trips as well. Chan's Windsurfing, on Naga Beach, puts together day trips to Ko Thalu, Ko Kuti, etc for 200B per person, including food and beverages (minimum of 10 people). They also rent sailboards at reasonable hourly rates with or without instruction. Other bungalows arrange similar trips from 150 to 210B. Sailboards rent for around 150B per hour or 600B per day. Jaray Windsurfing School on Hat Sai Kaew offers one-hour lessons for 80B.

A Request

The Rayong tourist police request that visitors refrain from hiring jet skis on Samet beaches as they are harmful to coral and dangerous to swimmers. They're hard on the aural environment, too. The local police won't do anything about them even though they're illegal – either because they're afraid of beach developers or are in their pockets. You'll be doing Ko Samet a big favour by avoiding the use of these polluters.

Places to Stay

The two most developed (overdeveloped) beaches are Hat Sai Kaew and Ao Wong Deuan. All of the other spots are still rather peaceful. Every bungalow operation on the island has at least one restaurant and most now have running water and electricity. Some places have electric power from 5 or 6 pm till 2 am only, others till 6 am; only a few have 24-hour power.

On less popular beaches you may come across abandoned bungalow sites, and some of the most expensive places even during the high season offer discounts for accommodation to attract customers. Very basic small huts with a hard mattress on the floor cost in the 50 to 80B range, similar huts with bath start from 80 to 120B, and those including a bed and a fan average 150 to 200B. Bungalows with furniture and air-con start at 600B. Most places offer discounts for stays of four or more days.

Since this is a national park, camping is allowed on any of the beaches. In fact, this is a great island to camp on because it hardly ever rains. There is plenty of room; most of the island is uninhabited and so far, tourism is pretty much restricted to the north-eastern beaches.

Places to Stay – east coast

Hat Sai Kaew Samet's prettiest beach, 'Diamond Sand', is a km or so long and 25 to 30 metres wide. The bungalows here happen to be the most commercial on the island, with video in the restaurants at night and lots of lights. They're all very similar and offer a range of accommodation from 80B (in the low season) for simple huts without fan or bath, 400 to 500B for one with fan,

mosquito net and private bath, or as high as 2500B with air-con. All face the beach and most have outdoor restaurants serving a variety of seafood. Like elsewhere in Thailand, the daily rate for accommodation can soar suddenly with demand. The more scrupulous places don't hike rates by much, though:

Coconut Hut, 300 to 700B with fan
Diamond, 350 to 1200B (☎ (038) 321-0814)
Ploy Talay, 250 to 600B (☎ (038) 321-1109)
Saikaew Villa, 450 to 4500B with air-con, the top-end place of the island on the prettiest part of the beach
Sinsamut, 120 to 250B (☎ (02) 249-0231/3 in Bangkok)
White Sand, 200 to 400B (☎ (038) 321734)

Ao Hin Khok The beach here is about half the size of Sai Kaew but nearly as pretty – the rocks that give the beach its name add a certain character. Hin Khok is separated from Sai Kaew by a rocky point surmounted by a mermaid statue, a representation of the mermaid that carried the mythical Phra Aphaimani to Ko Samet in the Thai epic of the same name. Two of Samet's original bungalow operations still reign here – *Naga* (☎ 321-0732) and *Little Hut* (☎ (01) 323-0264). Naga offers simple bungalows set on a hill overlooking the sea for 80B and decent ones with a good mattress from 120B. The restaurant at Naga sells great bread (which is distributed to several other bungalows on the island), cookies, cakes and other pastries, baked under the supervision of Englishwoman Sue Wild. Water is wisely rationed here.

The bungalows at Little Hut are a little more solid and go for 150B; the restaurant here is also quite good. At the end of the beach is *Jep's*, with standard bungalows for 200B.

Farther down the beach you may see what looks like a Thai 'gathering of the tribes' – a colourful outpost presided over by Chawalee, a free-spirited Thai woman, who has lived on this beach since long before the bungalows came.

Ao Phai Around the next headland is another shallow bay with the friendly *Ao Phai Hut (Nop's Kitchen)* (☎ (01) 211-2967), which has bungalows with bath and fan from 200B and air-con ones for 500B. They organise tours around the island and have an international telephone service, as well as basic postal services. The next place is *Sea Breeze* (☎ (01) 321-1397), with a variety of bungalows from 100 to 500B, followed by *Silver Sand* (☎ (01) 211-0974), with bungalows for 200 and 250B. The *Samed Villa* has good bungalows from 400B.

Ao Phutsa After Ao Phai, the remaining beaches south are separated from one another by steep headlands. To get from one to the next, you have a choice of negotiating rocky paths over the hilly points or walking east to the main road that goes along the centre of the island, then cutting back on side roads to each beach. This is also where the cross-island trail to Ao Phrao starts.

On Ao Phutsa, also known as Ao Thap Thim, you'll find *Phutsa Beach*, where basic huts cost 50 to 100B and newer ones up to 400B, and the larger *Tub Tim*, where nicer huts are 70 to 350B; the more expensive huts come with fans and bath.

Ao Nuan If you blink, you'll miss this one. Lamplit huts at *Ao Nuan* – one of the few to hold off on electricity for the sake of *thammachâat* (natural) ambience – are 100 to 300B. The food is another reported highlight. It's a 10-minute walk over the headland from Ao Phutsa.

Ao Cho (Chaw) A five-minute walk across the next headland from Ao Nuan, this bay has its own pier and can be reached directly from Ban Phe on the boat *White Shark* or aboard the supply boat. *Lung Wang* has small, basic bungalows starting at 80B. The nicely designed *Tantawan* huts range from 150 to 500B. Unfortunately the beach here was full of rubbish at last check.

Ao Wong Deuan This area is now mostly given over to more expensive resort-type

bungalows. The cheaper bungalows that were here a few years ago have nearly all disappeared and those that remain can't be recommended – the whole bay is too crowded with buildings and people. The best of the lot is *Wong Deun Resort* (☎ (038) 651777) with bungalows for 600 to 900B, complete with running water, flush toilet and fan. The air-con ones cost 1000 to 1200B. *Wong Deun Villa* is similar but all air-con, ranging from 600 to 2500B.

The *Malibu Resort (Malibu Garden)* (☎ (038) 651292-3) has cheaper bungalows with no bath from 300B, but it is not a very friendly establishment. More reasonable and more friendly is the *Seahorse* (☎ (01) 323-0049) with bungalows costing 150 to 600B. Three boats go back and forth between Ao Wong Deun and Ban Phe – the *Malibu, Seahorse* and *Wong Deun Villa*.

Ao Thian This is better known by its English name, Candlelight Beach. Far removed from the more active beaches to the north, this is the place to come for a little extra solitude, though the bungalow operations here, *Candle Light Beach* (Sangthian) (☎ (038) 651-1223) and *Lung Dam* (☎ (038) 651810) are no great shakes. Food, I'm told, is a definite minus here too. You can bring your own from the village on the northern tip of the island. Rates are 150 to 350B during high season or on weekends and holidays, 70 to 150B other times.

Other Bays You really have to be determined to get away from it all to go farther south on the east coast of Samet – not a bad idea. Water is only available for an hour or so in the mornings and evenings. Lovely **Ao Wai** is about a km from Ao Thian but can be reached by the boat *Phra Aphai* from Ban Phe. There's only one bungalow operation here, the very private *Sametville Resort* (☎ (01) 321-1284), where two-bed bungalows with attached bath cost 500B inclusive of all meals. Larger bungalows with more beds are available, including a 16-bed one for 3500B. Most bookings are done in Bangkok, but you can try your luck by contacting someone on the *Phra Aphai* at the Ban Phe pier. Finding a vacant bungalow – even in peak season – usually isn't a problem.

Ao Kiu also has only one place to stay at the time of writing, the friendly and clean *Ao Kiu Coral Beach* (☎ (01) 321-1231). Huts are 100 to 600B, or 1200B for a two-room bungalow. The beach here is fairly long and, because so few people use it, quite clean. Just a bit farther is rocky **Ao Karang**, where rustic *Pakarang* charges 100B per wooden hut (no electricity, no running water – just rainwater from ceramic jars). You'll find good coral in this area.

Places to Stay – west coast

Hat Ao Phrao (Coconut Bay Beach) is the only beach on the west side of the island, and has nice sunset views. At the northern end of the beach is *Ao Phrao Resort* where screened huts with fan and attached bath cost 400B. Next down is *Rattana*, with huts for 70 to 150B, possibly more during holidays. In the middle of the beach is *Dome*, with nice huts built on the hillside for 200 to 500B; the more expensive huts feature screened windows and attached bath. At the southern end near the cross-island trail is *SK Hut*, where small bungalows with attached bath are 100B, larger ones up to 500B. There is a daily boat between Ban Phe and Ao Phrao for 50B per person.

Places to Stay – Na Dan area

To the west of Samet's main pier is a long beach called Ao Wiang Wan where several rather characterless bungalows are set up in straight lines facing the mainland. Here you get neither sunrise (maybe a little) nor sunset. The cheapest place is *SK Bungalows* where accommodation is from 80 to 350B. There are several other places with rates in the 200 to 600B range.

Between Na Dan and Hat Sai Kaew, along the north-east corner of the island, are a couple of small beach-bays with bungalow operations. Hardly anyone seems to stay here, and it was only *Pineapple Bungalow* at Laem Yai beach which showed any sign of life. The asking rate of 400B per bungalow was definitely not worth it.

Places to Eat

All bungalows except Pakarang at Ao Karang have restaurants offering mixed menus of Thai and farang travellers' food; prices are typically around 30 to 40B per dish. Fresh seafood is almost always available and costs around 60 to 100B per dish. The pleasant *Bamboo Restaurant* at Ao Cho offers inexpensive but tasty food and good service. It's open for breakfast, lunch and dinner. The 'curry seafood in coconut milk' is very tasty at *Ao Nuan*. *Naga* on Ao Hin Khok has a very good bakery with all kinds of breads and cakes. If you get an urge for some Western food, head for *Pizza Mama* on Ao Wong Deuan where you can have what is almost a real pizza from a Swiss oven for 60 to 110B.

On Hat Sai Kaew, the *White Sands Restaurant* has good seafood in the 100B range. For cheaper fare on this beach, try the popular *Toy Restaurant*.

Getting There & Away

Bus Many Khao San Rd agencies in Bangkok do return transport to Ko Samet, including boat, for around 160B (250B return). This is more expensive than doing it on your own, but for travellers who don't plan to go anywhere else on the east coast it's convenient.

For those who want the flexibility and/or economy of arranging their own travel, the way to go is to take a bus to Ban Phe in Rayong Province, then catch a boat out to Ko Samet. There are regular buses to Rayong throughout the day from the eastern bus terminal, but if your destination is Ban Phe (for Ko Samet) you'd do better to take one of the direct Ban Phe buses, which only cost 5B more; a songthaew to Ban Phe from Rayong is 10B. The Bangkok to Rayong air-con bus is 85B, Bangkok to Ban Phe is 90B. The company that runs the Ban Phe bus, DD Tours, has a reputation for crummy service, often overbooking on the trip back to Bangkok. They also like to put all the farangs in the back of the bus, regardless of reserved seat numbers. Your only alternative is the ordinary bus to Rayong (47B) and then a local bus to Ban Phe. Buses from Bangkok stop in Ban Phe about 300 metres from the pier.

Ordinary buses to Chanthaburi or Pattaya from Rayong cost 30B and take about 1½ hours in either direction. To get one of these, you need to catch a motorcycle taxi to the bus stop on Sukhumvit Rd (Highway 3).

Boat There are various ways to get to and from the island by boat.

To Ko Samet Boats to Ko Samet leave the Ban Phe pier at regular intervals throughout the day starting at around 8 am and finishing at around 7 pm. How frequently they depart mostly depends on whether they have enough passengers and/or cargo to make the trip profitable, so there are more frequent boats in the high season (December to March). Still, there are always at least three or four boats a day going to Na Dan and Ao Wong Deuan.

It can be difficult to find the boat you need, as agents and boat owners want you to go with them rather than with their competitors. In most cases they'll be reluctant to tell you about another boat if they will not be making any money from you. Some travellers have reported being hassled by 'agents' who present photo albums of bungalows on Samet, claiming that they must book a bungalow for several days in order to get onto the island. This is false; ignore such touts and head straight for the boats. Report any problems to the TAT office in Rayong.

For Hat Sai Kaew, Ao Hin Khok, Ao Phai and Ao Phutsa, take one of the regular Na Dan boats (operated by Samet Tour, Suriya Tour and Thepmongkonchai) for 30B. From Na Dan you can either walk to these beaches (10 to 15 minutes) or take one of the trucks that go round the island. See the Getting Around section ahead for standard fares.

The boat *White Shark* also goes directly to Ao Cho from Ban Phe for 30B – have a look around the Ban Phe pier to see if it's available.

The *Seahorse*, *Malibu* and *Wong Deuan Villa* all go to Ao Wong Deuan for 30B. There's no jetty here, so passengers are pulled to shore on a raft or in long-tail boats. You can also get a truck-taxi here from Na Dan, but the fare could be as high as 200B if you're alone. For Ao Thian, you should get either the *White Shark* to Ao Cho or one of the Ao Wong Deuan boats.

The *Phra Aphai* makes direct trips to Ao Wai for 40B. For Ao Kiu or Ao Karang, get the *Thep Chonthaleh* (30B).

For Ao Phrao, you can taxi from Na Dan or possibly get a direct boat from Ban Phe for 30B. The boat generally operates from December to May, but with the increase in passengers this service may soon go all year.

If you arrive in Ban Phe at night and need a boat to Samet, you can usually charter a one-way trip at the Ban Phe pier for 250 to 300B (to Na Dan).

From Ko Samet Samet Tour seems to run a monopoly on return trips from Na Dan and they leave only when they're full – a minimum of 18 people for some boats, 25 for others – unless someone contributes more to the passage. The usual fare is 30B.

These days it is so easy to get boats back from the main beaches to Ban Phe that few tourists go to Na Dan to get a boat. There are four daily boats each from Ao Wong Deuan and Ao Cho, as well as at least one daily boat from Ao Wai, Ao Kiu and Ao Phrao.

While waiting for a boat back to the mainland from Na Dan, you may notice a shrine not far from the pier. This *sǎan jâo phâw* is a spirit shrine to Puu Dam (Grandfather Black), a sage who once lived on the island. Worshippers offer statues of *reusǐi* (hermit sages), flowers, incense and fruit.

Getting Around

If you take the boat from Ban Phe to the village harbour (Na Dan), you can easily walk to Hat Sai Kaew, Ao Phai or Ao Phutsa (Ao Thap Thim). Don't believe the taxi operators who say these beaches are a long distance away. If you're going farther down the island, or have a lot of luggage, you can take the taxi (a truck or a three-wheeled affair with a trailer) as far as Ao Wong Deuan.

Set fares for transport around the island from Na Dan are posted on a tree in the middle of a square in front of the Na Dan harbour: 10B per person to Hat Sai Kaew (or 100B charter); 20B to Ao Phai or Ao Phutsa (150B to charter); 30B to Ao Wong Deuan or Ao Phrao (200B to charter). Exactly how many people it takes to constitute 'public service' rather than a 'charter' is not a hard and fast number. Figure on 20B per person for six to eight people to anywhere between Na Dan and Ao Cho. If they don't have enough people to fill the vehicle, they either won't go, or passengers will have to pay up to 200B to charter the vehicle.

There are trails from Ao Wong Deuan all the way to the southern tip of the island, and a few cross-island trails as well. Taxis will make trips to Ao Phrao when the road isn't too muddy.

Chanthaburi Province

CHANTHABURI

อ.เมืองจันทบุรี

Situated 330 km from Bangkok, the City of the Moon is a busy gem trading centre, particularly noted for sapphires and rubies from all over South-East Asia and farther afield. Chanthaburi (population 39,700) is also renowned for tropical fruit (rambutan, durian, langsat and mangosteen) and rice noodles – Chanthaburi noodles are in fact exported all over the world.

A significant proportion of the local population are Vietnamese Christians who fled religious or political persecution in Vietnam years ago. The first wave arrived in the 19th century as refugees from anti-Catholic persecution in Cochin China (southern Vietnam); the second came between the 1920s and 1940s fleeing French rule; the third wave arrived after the 1975 communist

takeover of South Vietnam. From 1893 to 1905, while negotiating with the Siamese over where to draw the borders for Laos and Cambodia, the French occupied the town.

Chanthaburi's most recent claim to fame arose when 1500 tons of war material was found cached in 12 warehouses throughout the province in 1993. The arms were thought to have been destined for the Khmer Rouge communist rebels who hold parts of western Cambodia. Although the allegations have so far not been proven, it is almost certain the arms were in the control of certain factions within the Thai military.

Things to See & Do

Because of the Vietnamese-French influence, Chanthaburi has some interesting shophouse architecture, particularly along the river. The French-style **cathedral** here is the largest in Thailand. Originally, a small missionary chapel was built on this site in 1711; four reconstructions between 1712 and 1906 (the last carried out by the French) transformed the structure into its current form. The cathedral is 60 metres long and 20 metres wide.

The gem dealers in town are found mostly along Trok Kachang and Thetsaban 4 Rd off Si Chan Rd in the south-east quarter. All day long buyers and sellers haggle over little piles of blue and red stones. During the first week of June every year there is a gems festival and Chanthaburi can get very crowded. Most of the gems bought and sold here come from places other than Chan'buri – chiefly Cambodia, Vietnam, Myanmar and Australia.

King Taksin Park is a large public park with gazebos and an artificial lake near the centre of town – nice for an evening stroll. A few km north of town off Route 3249 is **Khao Phloi Waen**, or 'Sapphire-Ring Mountain', which is only 150 metres high but features a Sri Lankan-style chedi on top, built during the reign of King Mongkut. Tunnels dug into the side of the hill were once gem-mining shafts.

Wat Khao Sukim, a reasonably well-known meditation centre, is 16 km north of

Chanthaburi off Route 3322. Another meditation centre is at **Wat Sapchan**, 27 km west of Chanthaburi in Tha Mai district; Wat Sapchan is a branch of Ajaan Yantra's Sunyataram Forest Monastery in Kanchanaburi.

Places to Stay

The *Kasemsan I Hotel* (☎ (039) 312340), at 98/1 Benchamarachutit Rd, has large, clean rooms with fan for 150 to 180B, or 250B with air-con. As usual, rooms off the street are quieter than those on it. Down by the river at a nice spot on Rim Nam Rd is the

cheaper *Chantha Hotel* (☎ (039) 312310) with rooms without bath for 80B, with bath for 100/120B. Some of the rooms have a view of the river.

In the municipal market area is the *Kasemsan II* on Rong Meuang Rd with the same rates as Kasemsan I but a little noisier due to the location. The nearby *Chai Lee Hotel* on Khwang Rd is similarly priced again, but not as good. In the same area, the *Chanthaburi Hotel* (☎ (039) 311300) on Tha Chalaep Rd is OK if a little pricey for local standards at 250B with fan and bath, 320B with air-con.

CENTRAL THAILAND

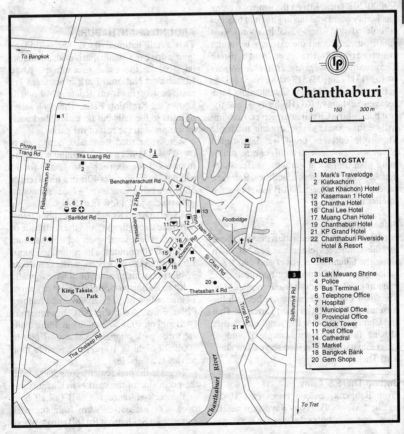

Chanthaburi

0   150   300 m

PLACES TO STAY

1 Mark's Travelodge
2 Kiatkachorn
   (Kiat Khachon) Hotel
12 Kasemsan 1 Hotel
13 Chantha Hotel
16 Chai Lee Hotel
17 Muang Chan Hotel
19 Chanthaburi Hotel
21 KP Grand Hotel
22 Chanthaburi Riverside
   Hotel & Resort

OTHER

3 Lak Meuang Shrine
4 Police
5 Bus Terminal
6 Telephone Office
7 Hospital
8 Municipal Office
9 Provincial Office
10 Clock Tower
11 Post Office
14 Cathedral
15 Market
18 Bangkok Bank
20 Gem Shops

Map labels: To Bangkok, Phraya Trang Rd, Raksakchamun Rd, Tha Luang Rd, Benchamarachutit Rd, Thetsaban 1 & Rds, Saritidet Rd, Rim Nam Rd, Khwang Rd, Si Chan Rd, Footbridge, King Taksin Park, Thetsaban 4 Rd, Tha Chalaep Rd, Trirat Rd, Sukhumvit Rd, Chanthaburi River, To Trat

On Si Chan Rd you'll find *Muang Chan Hotel*, with adequate rooms in the 140 to 250B range. Out on Tha Luang Rd in the north end of town, away from everything, is the *Kiatkachorn (Kiat Khachon) Hotel* (☎ (039) 311212) with rooms from 200 to 450B.

Mark's Travelodge (☎ (039) 311531/ 647), 14 Raksakchamun Rd, is a popular hotel with visiting business travellers. Recently renovated rooms range from 250 to 450B for spacious rooms with air-con, private bath and TV.

The top end in town is the *KP Grand Hotel* (☎ (039) 323201-13; fax 323214-15) at 35/200-201 Trirat Rd. At the time of writing this luxury hotel was having its final touches completed and the available rooms cost 1300B, including all the extras. Also under construction is the even more plush *Chanthaburi Riverside Hotel & Resort* (☎ (039) 311726; (02) 513-8190, fax 512-5726 in Bangkok) at 63 Muu 9, Chanthanimit 5 Rd, between Sukhumvit Rd (Highway 3) and the east bank of the Chanthaburi River. Lodging will be in separate single, double and triple Thai-style cottages on 42-rai landscaped grounds, complete with tennis courts, swimming pool, botanical gardens, coffee shop, nightclub and conference facilities. Rates are expected to be at least 2000B a night for the smaller units.

Places to Eat

For those famous Chanthaburi noodles, head for the Chinese/Vietnamese part of town along the Chanthaburi River and you'll see variations on the basic rice noodle theme, including delicious crab-fried noodles. The *Chanthon Phochana* restaurant beneath the Kasemsan I Hotel has a good variety of Thai and Chinese dishes. At the south-east corner of King Taksin Park are a couple of outdoor ice-cream parlours that also serve a few standard Thai dishes.

Getting There & Away

From Bangkok, air-con buses cost 108B; regular buses 60B. From Rayong it's 32B. There are also buses between Khorat and Chanthaburi via Sa Kaew and Kabinburi to the north. The bus trip takes four to five hours and passes through good mountain scenery. The total fare is about 85B.

If you're on your own set of wheels, take Route 317 north to Sa Kaew, then Highway 33 west to Kabinburi and Route 304 north to Khorat. From Sa Kaew you can also head east and reach Aranya Prathet on the Thai-Cambodian border after just 46 km. Once this border crossing is open you'll be able to take a train straight from Poipet on the Cambodian side of the border to Phnom Penh or stop off at Sisaphon (for buses to Siem Reap/Angkor Wat).

AROUND CHANTHABURI

Two small national parks are within an hour's drive of Chanthaburi. Both are malarial, so take the usual precautions. **Khao Khitchakut National Park** is about 28 km north-east of town off Route 3249 and is known for **Krathing Falls**. There's a series of trails to the falls but no established trails or footpaths in the rest of the park.

Across the road from park headquarters (☎ (039) 431983) are bungalows ranging from 600B for six people to 1200B for 14 people. Camping costs 40B in a hired tent or 5B if you bring your own. A basic restaurant sells snacks and a few rice dishes.

To get to Khao Khitchakut by public transport, take a songthaew from the north side of the market in Chanthaburi for 15B, a jaunt of around 50 minutes. The songthaew stops 1.5 km from the park headquarters on Route 3249, from which point you'll have to walk.

Khao Sabap National Park is only about 14 km south-east off Highway 3 and features **Phliu Falls**. Near the park headquarters (☎ Bangkok (02) 579-4842) at Phliu Falls are three park bungalows that cost 600 to 800B for eight to 10 persons. Simple food service is available.

To get to the park, catch a songthaew from the north side of the market in Chanthaburi to the park entrance for 25B (a half-hour ride) – or get out 2½ km from the park entrance on Sukhumvit Rd (8B), from where you will have to walk (this is how you will have to depart if there are no taxis).

Trat Province

About 400 km from Bangkok, Trat Province borders Cambodia and, as in Chanthaburi, gem mining and gem trading are important occupations. Gem markets (talàat phloi) are open daily at the **Hua Thung Market** in Bo Rai district between 7 and 10 am and at the **Khlong Yaw Market** in the same district between 1 and 3 pm. Bo Rai is about 40 km north of Trat on Route 3389. A smaller market is sometimes open all day in **Khao Saming** district only 20 km north-west of Trat.

Sapphires and rubies are good buys if (and only if) you know what you're buying. Recently, there have been reports of a drop in activity in the gem markets due to the dwindling supply of local gem stock. A sad by-product of the gem mining has been the destruction of vast tracts of land – the topsoil is stripped away, leaving acres of red-orange mud.

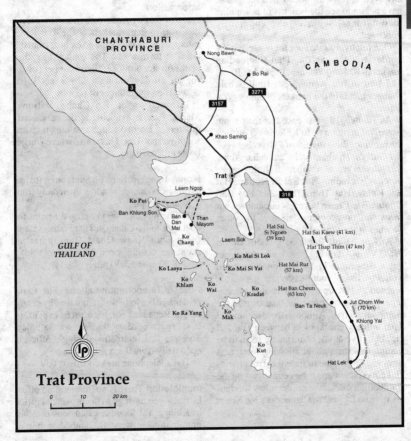

Trat Province

CHANTHABURI PROVINCE

CAMBODIA

Nong Bawn
Bo Rai
3271
3157
Khao Saming
Trat
318
Laem Ngop
Ko Pui
Ban Khlong Son
Ban Dan Mai
Than Mayom
Ko Chang
Laem Sok
Hat Sai Si Ngoen (39 km)
Hat Sai Kaew (41 km)
Hat Thap Thim (47 km)
Ko Mai Si Lek
Ko Laoya
Ko Mai Si Yai
Hat Mai Rut (57 km)
Ko Khlam
Ko Wai
Ko Kradat
Hat Ban Cheun (63 km)
Ban Ta Neuk
Jut Chom Wiw (70 km)
Ko Ra Yang
Ko Mak
Khlong Yai
GULF OF THAILAND
Ko Kut
Hat Lek

0   10   20 km

If the gem business doesn't interest you, another attraction Bo Rai district offers is **Salak Tai Falls** (15 km north-west of Bo Rai). In late 1993 and early 1994 travel in the region was restricted due to Khmer Rouge activity – enquire in amphoe meuang Trat for the latest.

The other big industry in Trat is the smuggling of consumer goods between Cambodia and Trat. For this reason, travelling alone along the border, or in the offshore islands which serve as conduits for sea smuggling, requires caution. More and more people have discovered the beaches and islands of Trat, however, and as the locals and the police have begun to see the benefits of hospitality to outsiders, security has apparently improved.

One relatively safe spot for observing the border trade is at the Thai-Cambodian market in **Khlong Yai**, near the end of Route 318 south of Trat. As much as 10 million baht changes hands in the markets of Khlong Yai daily.

As Route 318 goes east and then south from Trat on the way to Khlong Yai district, the province thins to a narrow sliver between the Gulf of Thailand and Cambodia. Along this sliver are a number of little-known beaches, including **Hat Sai Si Ngoen, Hat Sai Kaew, Hat Thap Thim** and **Hat Ban Cheun**. Ban Cheun has a few bungalows, but there was no accommodation at the other beaches at the time of writing.

At Km 70, off Route 318, is **Jut Chom Wiw** (View-Admiring Point), where you can get a panorama of the surrounding area. Trat Province's south-easternmost point is reached at **Hat Lek**, which is also a semi-legal jumping-off point for boat trips to the Cambodian coast. Although there are several Thai military checkpoints between Trat and Hat Lek (five at last count), they seem to be getting less strict about allowing foreigners through. From time to time the Trat provincial government and their counterpart on the Cambodian side of the border allow foreigners to cross by boat to Cambodia's Ko Kong.

TRAT & AROUND
อ.เมืองตราท

The provincial capital of Trat (population 14,000) has little to offer except as a jumping-off point for the Ko Chang island group or forays into outlying gem and Cambodian markets. The locals are friendly, however, and there are certainly worse places to spend a few days. Market fans will note Trat seems to have more markets for its size than almost any other town in Thailand – probably because it's the closest Thai provincial capital to Cambodian coastal trade.

Information

A few of Trat's guesthouses can arrange local day trips to gem markets or the Trat River estuary. The estuary trips go by boat from the canal in town to the Trat estuary to gather clams (in season) for 100B or less per person for an all-day outing – the exact price depends on the number of people.

Information on Ko Chang National Marine Park is available at the park headquarters in Laem Ngop, a small town 20 km south-west of Trat. This is also where you get boats to Ko Chang.

Money Bangkok Bank on Sukhumvit Rd has a foreign exchange window open daily from 8.30 am to 5 pm.

In Laem Ngop, the jumping-off point for boat trips to Ko Chang, a Thai Farmers Bank (near Chut Kaew Guest House) has an exchange counter open Monday to Friday from 8.30 am to 3.30 pm.

Post & Telecommunications The main post office is a long walk from the city centre on Tha Reua Jang Rd. It's open from 8.30 am to 4.30 pm weekdays, 9 am to noon Saturday. The attached international phone office is open daily from 7 am till 10 pm.

Trat's telephone area code is ☎ 039.

Immigration There is no immigration office in Trat – you must go to the provincial office in Khlong Yai for visa extensions or other immigration matters. If Cambodian border

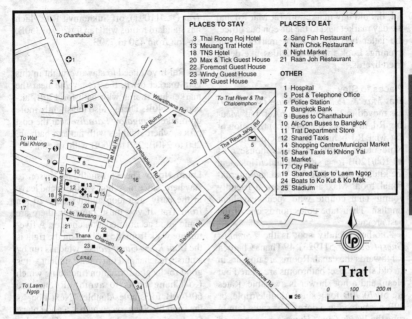

PLACES TO STAY
3 Thai Roong Roj Hotel
13 Meuang Trat Hotel
18 TNS Hotel
20 Max & Tick Guest House
22 Foremost Guest House
23 Windy Guest House
26 NP Guest House

PLACES TO EAT
2 Sang Fah Restaurant
4 Nam Chok Restaurant
8 Night Market
21 Raan Joh Restaurant

OTHER
1 Hospital
5 Post & Telephone Office
6 Police Station
7 Bangkok Bank
9 Buses to Chanthaburi
10 Air-Con Buses to Bangkok
11 Trat Department Store
12 Shared Taxis
14 Shopping Centre/Municipal Market
15 Share Taxis to Khlong Yai
16 Market
17 City Pillar
19 Shared Taxis to Laem Ngop
24 Boats to Ko Kut & Ko Mak
25 Stadium

Trat

0   100   200 m

CENTRAL THAILAND

crossings from Trat by land or sea are permitted in the future, this is where you'll have to come to have your passport stamped upon return from Cambodia.

Malaria Rates of infection for malaria are significantly higher for rural Trat (including Ko Chang) than for much of the rest of Thailand, so take the usual precautions. There is a malaria centre on the main road through Laem Ngop (20 km south-west of Trat), opposite Laem Ngop Inn; here you can get the latest information on the disease. This office can also assist with testing and/or treatment for malaria.

Things to See & Do

Trat town's older homes and shophouses are along the canal – you may be able to rent a canoe from one of the guesthouses for a water-level look. During high tide it's possible to boat from the canal to the Trat estuary on the Gulf. This can also be done from the

Trat River, north of the city; enquire at **Tha Chaloemphon** (also known simply as *thâa reua* or 'boat pier').

Wat Plai Khlong (Wat Bupharam), two km west of the city centre, is over 200 years old and worth a visit if you're looking to kill an hour or so. Several of the wooden buildings date to late Ayuthaya-period, including the wihaan, bell tower and kutis (monk's quarters). The wihaan contains a variety of sacred relics and Buddha images dating from the Ayuthaya period and earlier.

Farther afield, **Ban Nam Chiaw** – about halfway to Laem Ngop (eight km from Trat) – is a mostly Muslim village where one of the main industries is the handweaving of hemispherical straw hats called *ngôp*, the traditional Khmer rice farmer's hat. (*Lāem* means 'cape'.)

Markets Of Trat's several markets, the largest are the new day market beneath the municipal shopping centre off Sukhumvit

Rd, the old day market off Tat Mai Rd and the day market next to the air-con bus office; the latter becomes a night market in the evening. Look for eccentricities like deep-fried lizards.

Places to Stay

Trat *Max & Tick Guest House* (☎ 520799) has moved to 1-3 Soi Luang Aet, Lak Meuang Rd, in a lane which is a continuation of Tat Mai Rd behind the municipal market. Nine clean rooms in a teak house cost 80/100/120B for a single/double/triple, and the kitchen prepares good Thai and international food. Max and Tick are a friendly young Thai couple who speak excellent English. Their tape collection is one of the best around.

Another friendly spot is the *Foremost Guest House* (☎ 511923), 49 Thana Charoen Rd towards the canal. Rooms are upstairs in an old shophouse; bathrooms are shared but clean, and a hot shower is available. Rates are 50/70/90B for a single/double/triple, or 30B per person in a dorm. The same family runs the *Windy Guest House* across the road on the canal; here rooms are 40B dorm, 60/80B single/double. Bicycles and motorcycles are also available for rent for 20B and 180 to 250B per day. Ask about renting canoes for exploring the canal (20B per day) – it depends on who's managing the guesthouse at the time and whether canoes are available.

A fourth place in the southern part of town, *NP Guest House* (☎ 512564), at 952 Nernta-meuw Rd, has rooms with fan and mosquito netting for 120B.

Any of the guesthouses can arrange boat trips along the Trat River or to Ko Chang if enough people are interested.

Most of the hotels in Trat are along or just off Sukhumvit Rd. The *TNS* (☎ 511028) at 66-71 Sukhumvit Rd has rooms from 100 to 180B. The *Thai Roong Roj (Rung Rot)* (☎ 511141) in a lane off Sukhumvit Rd has rooms with fan from 140B or air-con from 250B with air-con. Then at 234 Sukhumvit Rd is *Sukhumvit Inn* (☎ 512151) with 140 to 180B rooms. Top end in town is the *Meuang*

Trat (☎ 511091), off Sukhumvit Rd, which has standard rooms with fan for 200 to 350B, air-con from 450 to 750B.

Bo Rai If you need to stay overnight in this gem-market town, the *Honey Inn* near the market has rooms with bath for 120B, air-con for 240B. There's also the slightly more up-market *Bungalow Paradise* near the post office, where doubles with fan and bath are 200 to 240B, 250 to 360B with air-con.

Laem Ngop There's usually no reason to stay here, since most boats to the island leave in the early afternoon and it's only 20 km from Trat. If you must, however, there are some good accommodation choices. A five-minute walk from the harbour on the right is the *Chut Kaew Guest House*, which is run by a nurse, teacher and university student – it is good for local information (including which Ko Chang boats to avoid). Rooms are 60/100B for singles/doubles. Next door is the friendly *Nong Aye*, which is a good place for breakfast, lunch or dinner. They also provide good information about the islands.

The next place on the right, about 100 metres from the road, is *PI Guest House*, a new, clean place with large rooms in a Thai house. All rooms have one double bed for 60/120B a single/double. The *Laem Ngop Inn Hotel* (☎ 597044) is farther up again, but 300 metres from the road, with rooms with fan for 200B and air-con ones are 300B. The *Paradise Inn* (☎ 512831) has fan-cooled rooms for 150B, air-con for 300B.

At the Laem Ngop pier there are two good seafood restaurants. The *Saengchan Restaurant*, on the right in front of the pier, doesn't have great food but many travellers wait here for minibuses to Trat which connect with air-con buses to Bangkok.

A Bangkok development company is constructing a new pier and commercial site called Koh Chang Centre Point at Laem Ngop. Supposedly the large project will have its own waste-water treatment system to prevent pollution of the strait running between Ko Chang and the mainland.

Khlong Yai The *Suksamran Hotel*, on a street between the market and the highway, offers rooms with fan from 120B, or 250B with air-con. Out of town a bit off Sukhumvit Rd (Highway 3), *Bang In Villa* has similarly priced rooms.

Places to Eat

With all the markets in Trat, you're hardly ever more than 50 metres away from something good to eat. The indoor municipal market beneath the shopping centre has a food section with cheap, good noodle and rice dishes from early morning to early evening. Another good spot for cheap breakfasts is the ancient coffee stand in the old day market on Tat Mai Rd.

In the evenings, there's a good night market next to the air-con bus station. On the Trat River in the northern part of town is a small but atmospheric night market – a good choice for long, leisurely meals.

The *Nam Chok* outdoor restaurant on the corner of Soi Butnoi and Wiwatthana Rd is one of the better local restaurants. Around lunchtime a good find is *Raan Joh* (no English sign) at 90 Lak Meuang Rd. The number is next to impossible to see, just look for the only place making khanõm beûang, a Khmer veggie crepe prepared in a wok. They also do other local specialities – it's very inexpensive but open lunchtime only.

A good mid-range restaurant, the *Sang Fah* (☎ 511222) at 156-7 Sukhumvit Rd, has a large menu with Thai specialities between 50 and 100B. The food is good, and there are plenty of seafood dishes, as well as many mosquitoes buzzing around in the air-con environment. They also serve breakfast, when you might (or might not) want to try the house speciality – 'rice with curdled pig's blood'.

Another good find is *Suan Aahaan Puu* (Crab Garden Restaurant) in Ban Laem Hin, on the way to Laem Sok; the owners originally ran the highly acclaimed but now near-defunct *Jiraporn* restaurant next door to the Trat Hotel in town. Ban Laem Hin is about 15 km south-east of town. The menu is in Thai only, so bring along a Thai friend to translate.

Getting There & Away

To/From Bangkok Buses to/from Bangkok cost 140B air-con or 78B ordinary and leave from the eastern bus terminal. The trip takes five to six hours one-way by air-con bus, or about eight hours by ordinary bus. Three bus companies operate a Trat to Bangkok service; Sahamit, on Sukhumvit Rd near the Trat Hotel and night market, has the best and most frequent (12 trips a day) air-con buses to Bangkok.

To/From Chanthaburi Ordinary buses between Chanthaburi and Trat are 22B and take about 1½ hours for the 66-km trip.

You can also take the quicker share taxis between Trat and Chanthaburi for 40B per person – these take around 45 minutes. During the middle of the day, however, it may take up to an hour to gather the seven passengers necessary for a departure; try to schedule your departure between 7 and 9 am or 4 and 6 pm for the shortest wait.

To/From Laem Ngop Share taxis to Laem Ngop leave Trat from a stand along Sukhumvit Rd next to the municipal market; these cost 10B per person shared or 100B to charter. They depart regularly throughout the day, but after dark you will have to charter.

To/From Khlong Yai, Bo Rai & Hat Lek Share taxis to Khlong Yai cost 25B per person and take about 45 minutes. The share taxi fare from Khlong Yai to Hat Lek is 10B for the 16-km trip; these taxis leave from the back of the municipal market. A door-to-door minibus to Bo Rai is 35B.

Getting Around

Samlors around town should cost 5 to 10B per person.

HAT LEK TO CAMBODIA

At the time of research it was possible to take a boat from Hat Lek to Pak Kong on the Cambodian side of the border for 100B.

From Pak Kong catch another boat to Sihanoukville (100B, 20 hours), and then a three-hour taxi to Phnom Penh for 30B. You may also be able to catch a once-daily bus all the way to Phnom Penh. It is also possible to get to Pak Kong by road – get a motorbike in Hat Lek for 30B. The only problem with this land border crossing is that travellers often get asked for a 600B bribe, which is not the case with the sea crossing.

A Cambodian visa is necessary and obtainable in Bangkok, not at the border. As far as the Thai authorities are concerned this is semi-illegal and while in Cambodia, you are technically in Thailand! You need to do the trip with a valid Thai visa on which you can return to Thailand.

If this option is not available or you feel like getting a taste of Cambodian border life, it is possible to visit Ko Kong, an island on the Cambodian side of the border, by boat (200B). Though not a particularly exciting destination in itself, Ko Kong is an important relay point for goods imported from Singapore into Cambodia, which is now Singapore's largest trade entrepôt in Indochina. You may have to leave your passport and camera behind with the Thai police in Hat Lek. Before setting off to Cambodia, contact the Foremost Guest House in Trat for the latest information about entering the country.

KO CHANG NATIONAL MARINE PARK
อุทยานแห่งชาติทางทะเลหมู่เกาะช้าง

Forty-seven of the islands off Trat's coastline belong to a national park named for Ko Chang, which is the second-largest island (492 sq km) in Thailand after Phuket. Other major islands in the park include Ko Kut and Ko Mak. Ko Chang itself is about 70% virgin forest, with hills and cliffs reaching as high as the 744-metre Khao Jom Prasat. The island has several small bays and beaches including **Ao Khlong Son**, **Hat Sai Khao**, **Hat Khlong Phrao**, **Hat Kaibae**, **Ao Bang Bao** and **Ao Salak Phet**. Near each of these beaches are small villages, eg Ban Khlong Son, Ban Bang Bao and so on.

So far there's not a single paved road on Ko Chang, only red dirt roads between Khlong Son and Hat Kaibae on the west coast of the island, and between Khlong Son and Ban Salak Phet on the east side, plus walking trails passable by motorcycle from Kaibae to Bang Bao and Salak Kok to Salak Phet. Road crews are working to extend the road on the west side, however, and Trat authorities say the island will have a paved ring road – or at least the beginnings of one – within the next two years. The province has plans to 'civilise' the island further by stringing power lines around the island right behind the paved road. In 1993 the island received around 50,000 visitors.

A series of three waterfalls along the stream of Khlong Mayom in the interior of the island, **Than Mayom** (or Thara Mayom) **Falls**, can be reached via Tha Than Mayom or Ban Dan Mai on the east coast. The waterfall closest to the shore can be climbed in about 45 minutes. The view from the top is quite good and there are two inscribed stones bearing the initials of Rama VI and Rama VII nearby. The second waterfall is about 500 metres farther east along Khlong Mayom and the third is about three km from the first. At the third waterfall is another inscribed stone, this one with the initials of Rama V.

A smaller waterfall on the west coast, **Khlong Phu Falls**, can be visited from Ao Phrao (45 minutes) or from Hat Kaibae (one hour) by following Khlong Phrao two km inland. Or pedal a bicycle along the main dirt road until you see the sign on the eastern side of the road. Ride up to the restaurant near the falls, from where it is only a 15-minute walk to the falls themselves. A pool beneath the falls is a good spot for a refreshing swim, and it is possible to stay in the bungalows or camp here.

On **Ko Kut** you'll find beaches mostly along the west side, at Hat Tapho, Hat Khlong Chao and Hat Khlong Yai Kii. A dirt road runs between Ban Khlong Hin Dam, the island's main village on the west coast, and Ao Salat along the north-east shore. Other villages on the island include Ban Ta Poi, Bang Ao Salat, Ban Laem Kluai, Bang

Khlong Phrao and Ban Lak Uan. The nearby small islands of Ko Rang and Ko Rayang have good coral in spots. Ko Kut is best reached from Khlong Yai on the mainland.

Ko Mak, the smallest of the three main islands, has a beach along the north-west bay and possibly others as yet undiscovered. Monsoon forest covers 30% of the island while coconut plantations take up another 60%. A few tractors or jeeps travel along the single paved road which leads from the pier to the main village. It is possible to rent motorbikes and organise diving trips from the resorts on the island.

Ko Wai has some of the best coral and is excellent for snorkelling and diving. The island has one bungalow operation.

Ko Laoya has natural attributes similar to those at Ko Wai, with one rather expensive place to stay.

As with other national marine parks in Thailand, park status versus resort development is a hot issue. On Ko Chang, so far, everyone seems to be in agreement about what is park land and what isn't. Any land that was planted before the conferral of park status in 1982 can be privately deeded, bought, sold and developed – this includes

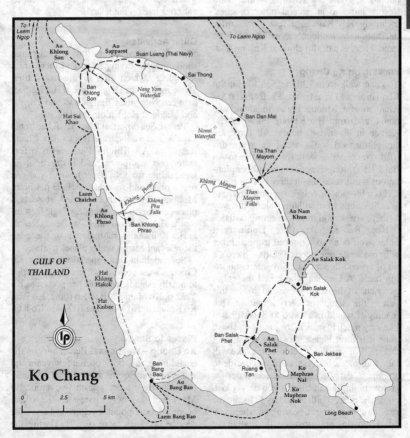

Ko Chang

many beach areas used for coconut plantations, or about 15% of the island. The Forestry Department makes regular flights over the island to check for encroachment on the 85% belonging to the national park – mostly in the interior – and they are said to be very strict with interlopers.

Information
There is no bank on the island, but money-changers will change US dollars at very unfavourable rates. The only post office is near the pier at Ban Khlong Son, where there is a telegram service but no international phones. On Hat Sai Khao at White Sand Resort and also at several other beaches, including Hat Kaibae, a few places offer international telephone service at very high rates. There is a health clinic at Khlong Son.

Walking on Ko Chang
You can walk from Khlong Son to Hat Sai Khao in about 1½ to two hours, from Hat Sai Khao to Hat Khlong Phrao in about two hours, and from Hat Khlong Phrao to Hat Kaibae in about two hours. All three are straightforward walks along the main dirt road. You can also walk from Kaibae to Ao Bang Bao through coconut and rubber plantations – this takes about three to four hours and is a bit more involved (you may have to ask directions from villagers along the way as there are several interconnecting trails).

Bang Bao to Salak Phet? Don't try it unless you're an experienced tropical hiker with moderate orienteering skills – there's a lot of up-and-down and many interconnecting trails. A German who hiked the entire perimeter of the island suggested that for this part of the island you carry a note in Thai reading 'I would like to go to Salak Phet. I like very much to walk in the jungle and have done it before. Please show me the start of this trail'. If you don't get lost, this hike will take four to six hours; should you decide to attempt it, carry enough food and water for an overnight, just in case. If you do get lost, climb the nearest hilltop and try to locate the sea or a stream to get a bearing on where you are. Following any stream will usually take

you either to a village or to the sea. Then you can either follow the coast or ask directions. This advice is also good for hiking anywhere across the island, as it is very easy to get lost on the many intersecting, unmarked trails.

On the east side of the island it's a one-hour walk between Dan Mai and Than Mayom, two hours between Dan Mai and Sai Thong (or Khlong Son and Sai Thong). Salak Kok to Salak Phet is straightforward and takes around three hours.

A hike around the entire island can be done at a comfortable pace in a week to 10 days. Remember to carry plenty of water and watch out for snakes – a few poisonous varieties live on the island.

Other Activities
Most bungalow operations can arrange snorkelling or diving trips, and there are a few places which offer diving instruction. These include the Dive Centre at Hat Kaibae, between Nangnuan Bungalows and Porn's, and Magic at Hat Khlong Makok.

Pethai Sea Sport at Hat Sai Khao rents kayaks and sailboards. Rooks Ko Chang Resort at Ao Khlong Phrao also offers watersport equipment and instruction, eg waterskiing for 1500B per hour or you can rent a mask and snorkel for 100B per hour. Mountain bikes can be rented at several places on the island, including Eagle Restaurant at Hat Sai Khao and Palm Beach Resort at Hat Kaibae. For more details on these see the relevant entries under places to stay.

Several bungalow operations along Ko Chang's west-coast beaches offer boat trips to nearby islands, eg 150B per person to Ko Yuak or Ko Man; 300B to Ko Rang, Ko Wai, Ko Khlam or Ko Mak; and 1000B to Ko Kut.

Places to Stay
Ko Chang – west coast Beach huts on the island have only been open a few years and standards vary quite a bit. Some are only open during the dry season (November to May), but this may change as the island becomes more popular year round and boat service becomes more regular. During the

rainy season, boats usually only go as far as Khlong Son, Dan Mai and Than Mayom – the surf farther south along the west coast can be impassable during heavy rains.

Remember that you can ask the boat pilots to drop you off at almost any bungalow operation on any beach, so if you know where you are going ask the pilot in Laem Ngop. It is also possible to get picked up from any bungalow on any beach – skiffs or long-tail boats take people to the boat if there is no pier. At Hat Sai Khao the boatmen have been known to charge 5B per person to relay passengers from the ferry to the beach.

As the island's better beaches are along the west coast, this is where most of the beach accommodation is. Most huts and bungalows feature one double mattress on the floor or on a raised platform. If you are staying longer than a few days all places will discount their rates, even in peak season. Most of the island has limited electricity or no electricity at all; on the popular beaches most restaurants use generators between 6 pm and midnight, otherwise sites are lit by kerosene or gas lanterns. Only a few places have music and, blessedly, even fewer have videos (Hat Sai Khao is an exception).

At the northern tip of the island is the largest village, Khlong Son, which has a network of piers at the mouth of the khlong, a wat, a school, several noodle shops, a health clinic and one basic friendly bungalow operation on stilts, *Manee Guest House* near the piers for 50/70B a night.

From Khlong Son to Hat Sai Khao (White Sand Beach) is five km. At the lower end of the beach, well off the road and separated from other Hat Sai Khao bungalow developments by a couple of small rocky points, is the nicely landscaped *White Sand Beach Resort* where solid huts go for 100/130B for singles/doubles, and more up-market ones with bath cost 400B; roofs are tarped so that they don't leak in the rain.

Next south are a couple of newer spots beginning with the *Rock Sand*, which has a few rustic wooden huts on a rocky outcrop surrounded by beach on both sides for 100B per hut. The similarly priced grass mat huts

at *KC* are better. There is also a small grocery shop here. Where the short path to the main road ends is *Pethai Sea Sport*, with a handful of bungalows for 120B. They rent out kayaks and sailboards for 100B per hour or 500B per day.

Farther south is a string of cheapies with basic huts for 80 to 200B (70 to 150B in the off season). All are very similar in style and layout; if you get off the boat anywhere along this beach, you can walk from one to the other before deciding. Starting from the north you'll find *Tantawan* and *Bamboo*, which – like several other bungalow operations along this coast – organise trips to other islands. After a small headland are *Apple* and *Honey*. *Sunsai* has the usual basic huts for 100 to 200B, plus some better bungalows with bath for 600B.

A newer place, *Ban Rung Rong* (☎ (039) 597184), offers basic huts for 120 to 200B and nicer ones with bath for 300B. They also have money exchange (5% commission) and rent mountain bikes for 120B per day. Between Ban Rung Rong and Cookie is Eagle Restaurant, where a Dutch guy rents mountain bikes for 100B, with a 1000B deposit. Next is *Cookie* with basic huts for 100B, and a cheaper motorbike rental for 60B per hour or 400B per day. Then there is *Mac* with more basic 100B huts, and nicer bungalows for 300B, including bath. The *Haad Sai Kae* has bungalows from 120B, along with a telephone and a mail service. This is one of the island's more 'social' beaches, where long-termers stoke their bongs with Cambodian herb while watching the sun set.

The German-owned *Phaloma Cliff Resort* is a bit south of Sunsai on the other side of Bubby Bong's bar & restaurant, spread over a rocky cliff. Large tile-and-cement bungalows – shades of Ko Samui – cost 250B, 600B and 1000B per night. The Phaloma also rents motorcycles for 500B a day – the going rate on the island!

About four km south of Hat Sai Khao (nine km from Khlong Son) is Ao Khlong Phrao (Coconut Bay). It stretches south of Laem Chaichet and encompasses the canal

Khlong Phrao as well as its namesake village Ban Khlong Phrao (12 km from Khlong Son). On the north side of the canal is *Chaichet Bungalows* at 80B a single or double. The bungalows are strung out along Laem Chaichet, a gently curving cape, though there's no beach to speak of. Also on the north bank of Khlong Phrao, *Klong Plow Resort* has modern wooden bungalows in a semi-circle around a lagoon for 700B. Near Ban Chaichet south of Ao Khlong Phrao is *Coconut Beach Bungalows*, where typical thatched-roof-style bungalows cost 100B for singles/doubles or you can pay 400B for bamboo or concrete bungalows with bath. The bungalows are well kept and the pleasant beach has its own pier. Chai-chet shares a pier with Coconut Beach Bungalows.

About a 10-minute walk farther south along the beach is the pricey *Rooks Ko Chang Resort* (☎ (01) 329-0434; Bangkok (02) 276-1233). Up-market bungalows here cost 1766 to 2900B and include all the usual comforts with air-con and colour TV.

It is possible to cross the river in a long-tail boat but you need to call for one on the southern bank. If you are staying at PSS Bungalow the service is only 5B but if staying anywhere else it's 10B. The *PSS* huts cost 120B. About a 10-minute walk farther south is *KP*, where basic and small grass mat huts cost 60/100B, larger and nicer ones with bath cost 300B. The food here is good, but the restaurant closes at 8 pm and the lights are out by 9 pm. The service could be a little friendlier; they are closed during the rainy season.

Around another headland to the south are two beach areas separated by a canal, Hat Khlong Makok and Hat Kaibae (15 km south of Khlong Son). These beaches tend to disappear during high tide but they're OK – lots of coconut palms. *Magic* has bungalows for 80B but they're none too clean, while the better bungalows with bath cost from 150 to 300B. There is a pier here, a telephone service, scooter rental for 40B per hour (or 250B per day) and scuba diving. The owner has a boat monopoly from Laem Ngop so is able to funnel many passengers directly to

this beach. Magic's best feature is its restaurant built over the bay. Next door is *Good Luck* (Chokdee), with nicer new thatched huts for 50B or concrete bungalows for 300B – a drawback is that it has no beach.

Next south on Hat Kaibae proper (15 km south of Khlong Son) is an area that has become quite developed, with a new pier and bungalows with generator-powered electricity (yes, this means more videos of Arnold firing large weapons or Van Damme kicking snot from people's faces). Starting in the north, the first place you come to is the German-run *Palm Beach Resort*, where basic huts start at 50B, up to 350B for large bungalows. The food here is reportedly good; mountain bikes rent for 150B per day.

Coral Bungalows is set amidst a bumper crop of coconut palms and costs 50B for basic huts or 450B for larger bungalows with private bath. They also have an international telephone service. *Nangnuan Bungalows* farther along have standard huts for 50B. *Kaibae Hut*, on the south side of the khlong, has a nicely laid out restaurant and fair bungalows, plus a bit of a beach even at high tide; rates are the usual 80B for basic huts and 200 to 250B for nicer bungalows with bath.

There is more of a beach down towards the southern end of Hat Kaibae. *Porn's* has basic 80B huts while the large *Seaview Resort* has similar huts for 100B and nice large bungalows from 800B. Seaview Resort charters boats from 150 to 5000B depending on the destination and trip length. A boat charter to Laem Ngop costs 3000B. The last place on the beach is the secluded and friendly *Siam Bay Resort* with huts for 100B and bungalows with private bath from 200B.

Ko Chang – south coast Down along the south coast at Ao Bang Bao is the *Bang Bao Beach Resort* (☎ (039) 511604) with average bungalows for 100B, and the cheaper *Bang Bao View* and *Sunset Bungalows* for 80 to 100B. Sunset also has tents for 60B. You may also be able to rent rooms cheaply in the village (Ban Bang Bao).

The next bay along the coast, Ao Salak Phet, features the *Ban Salakpetch Bungalow* with the typical thatched huts for 50B. A couple of as yet unnamed bungalow places rent huts for 50B a night near the fishing villages of Ruang Tan and Ban Salak Phet. As at Ao Bang Bao, you may be able to rent a room or house in Ban Salak Phet. Bungalows are under construction farther south-east along the bay at Ban Jekbae.

The very secluded *Long Beach Bungalows*, near the end of the long cape to the south-east of Ao Salak Phet, has well-made huts with electricity for 120B a night. They are closed between July and December. Farther on, right at the tip of the cape, is the friendly *Tantawan House* on a rocky outcrop with only seven huts costing 70/100B. The beach is only a two-minute swim away. To get here take a boat from Ao Salak Phet for 30B.

Ko Chang – east coast Around on the east coast, starting at the northern end, *Sai Thong Bungalows* has the only beachside accommodation on this side of the island. From here it's a two-hour walk north to Khlong Son or south to Dan Mai. The bungalow owner has his own boat that meets the daily minivan from Khao San Rd at Laem Ngop in the late afternoon. It's a bit of a scam actually, as he takes all new arrivals to his bungalows, charging 50B for the boat ride and 100B to stay at his rather average huts.

At the national park headquarters at Than Mayom you can rent Forestry Department bungalows for 400B a night. A couple of private places, *Thanmayom* and *Maeo*, also rent huts for 60 to 100B a night.

Ko Kut At Hat Tapho on the west coast, the aptly named *First* has basic huts for 50B, with outside bath. If this one's closed when you arrive, try village homes in nearby Ban Hin Dam.

Ko Mak On the north-west bay is the Israeli-managed *Lazydays Resort* (☎ (02) 281-3412 in Bangkok), at 100B a night. The generator-powered complex is built over the water. *Au Kao Resort* (☎ (038) 425263) offers comfortable bungalows with fan and private bath

for 500B a night in the low season, 700B high season.

Ko Kradat The *Ko Kradat* has air-con bungalows for 600B. Mr Chumpon in Bangkok (☎ (02) 311-3668) can arrange accommodation at Ko Kradat and transport to the island in advance.

Places to Eat
Menus at all the bungalows on Ko Chang are pretty similar, with highest marks going to Kaibae Hut (Hat Kaibae) for well-prepared meals. Just south of Hat Sai Khao's Sunsai Bungalows, on a rocky hillside overlooking the sea, is Ko Chang's first bar/restaurant, *Bubby Bong's*. Run by two ex-California surfers, the open-sided, torch-lit bamboo eatery serves mostly Thai dishes, including grilled seafood. The menu also includes burgers and their famous garlic-chilli popcorn. You can get here from bungalows at Hat Sai Khao by walking along the beach or along the road – at night just look for the twinkling lights hovering over the sea.

The fairly new *Aloha Bakery* is very popular for items like banana bread and chocolate chip cookies. The food is also quite good at *KP* on Ao Khlong Phrao and at the *Beach Restaurant* at Hat Kaibae.

Getting There & Away
To/From Ko Chang Take a songthaew (10B, 25 minutes) from Trat to Laem Ngop on the coast, then a ferry to Ko Chang. From Laem Ngop you have a choice of several different ferries, depending on the destination and time of day. The chart below lists the kinds of departures available; in many cases the same boat makes two or three stops. All times are approximate and depend on weather, number of passengers and any number of other factors. You should check on fares in advance – sometimes the boat crews overcharge farangs. During the wet season the boat service is erratic and most boats will only go to Ao Khlong Son, where it will be necessary to go to the beaches by pickups or motorbike. Sometimes they'll only go to Khlong Son in spite of good

weather – possibly to rake commissions from the taxi drivers.

Don't take the 250B (400B return) minivan from Khao San Rd in Bangkok to Laem Ngop in hope of getting to Ko Chang on the same day – the only way you can make it is if you board the 4 pm boat to Sai Thong, which meets the van in the late afternoon. If you take that boat you'll end up at Sai Thong Bungalows on the north-east coast, at least two hours' walk from any other bungalow choices. Some people reckon this is OK, others feel cheated.

No matter what time the Khao San Rd people tell you the minivan is leaving Bangkok, they'll most likely stall so that the Sai Thong boat is the only choice – apparently the van people and the Sai Thong people have an agreement. It's better to spend the night in Trat or Laem Ngop and take your time choosing a boat the next day. Or start out earlier in the day by government tour bus to Trat from Bangkok's eastern bus terminal, then in Trat catch a songthaew to Laem Ngop in time for the afternoon boats. You can make the last boat to Ko Chang at 3 pm if you catch the 140B air-con bus to Trat at 8.30 am from Bangkok's eastern bus terminal. This will arrive in Trat around 1.30 pm, leaving plenty of time to get a songthaew to Laem Ngop in time for the boat departure.

If you get enough people together, the Foremost Guest House in Trat can arrange boat trips from the canal in town all the way to Ko Chang (destination of choice, except in high swells when the west coast may be unnavigable) for 100B per person.

To/From Ko Kut Two or three fishing boats a week go to Ko Kut from the pier of Tha Chaloemphon on the Trat River towards the east side of Trat. They'll take passengers for 80B per person. Similar boats leave slightly less frequently (six to eight times a month) from Ban Nam Chiaw, a village about halfway between Trat and Laem Ngop. Departure frequency and times from either pier depend on the weather and the fishing season – it's best to enquire ahead of time.

The boats take around six hours to reach Ko Kut.

Coconut boats go to Ko Kut once or twice a month from a pier next to the slaughterhouse in town – same fare and trip duration as the fishing boats.

If you want to charter a boat to Ko Kut, the best place to do so is from Ban Ta Neuk, near Km 68 south-east of Trat, about six km before Khlong Yai off Highway 318. A long-tail boat, capable of carrying up to 10 people, can be chartered here for 1000B. Travel time is about one hour. During the rainy season these boats may suspend service.

To/From Ko Mak During the November to May dry season boats to Ko Mak leave daily from the Laem Ngop pier at 3 pm (8 am in the reverse direction); the fare is 200B per person and the trip takes around three to $3\frac{1}{2}$ hours. During the rainy season the departure schedule is cut back to every other day – except in high surf when boats may be cancelled altogether for several days.

Coconut boats also go to Ko Mak from the pier near the slaughterhouse in Trat twice a month. The trip takes five hours and costs 100B per person.

To/From Other Islands Daily boats to Ko Khlam also depart at 3 pm (arriving at 6 pm) for 130B. A boat to Ko Wai leaves at 3 pm and arrives at 4.30 pm, costing 70B. Both boats return the next day at around 8 am.

Getting Around
To get from one part of Ko Chang to another you have a choice of motorbike taxi, Japanese pickup, jeep, boat and foot (see the earlier Walking on Ko Chang section).

Motorbike & Truck The motorcycle taxi mafia on the island charge 40B from Khlong Son to Hat Sai Khao, then from Sai Khao south it's 40B to Laem Chaichet and Khlong Phrao (or 70B from Khlong Son) and 60B to Hat Kaibae (100B from Khlong Son). The main motorcycle taxi stand is opposite the north end of Hat Sai Khao; you can also rent one of their motorcycles to drive yourself for

500B a day. Other bungalow operations in Khlong Son and Hat Sai Khao also charge 400 to 600B per day for motorbike hire; elsewhere on the island rental bikes are scarce. The owners claim they have to charge these rates because the island roads are so hard on the bikes.

Between Khlong Son and Sai Khao there are also truck taxis, which charge the same as the motorcycle taxis.

Jeep Between Ao Salak Kok and Ao Salak Phet there's a daily jeep service that costs 10B per person. The jeep leaves Ao Salak Kok at 4.30 pm, returning from Ao Salak Phet the following day at 6 am.

Boat The regular boat to Ao Phrao and Hat Kaibae usually stops first at Hat Sai Khao and Ao Phrao; you can catch a ride from one area to the other along the west coast for 30B. Boat rides up Khlong Phrao to the falls cost 50B per person and can be arranged through most bungalows.

On the east coast, there is a daily boat service between Than Mayom and Ao Salak Kok farther south for 20B per person. On the southern end, you can charter a boat between Salak Phet and Long Beach Bungalows for around 150B.

Charter trips to nearby islands average 500B for a half day. Make sure that the charter includes all user 'fees' for the islands – sometimes the boatmen demand 200B on top of the charter fee for using the beach.

Prachinburi & Sa Kaew Provinces

Lying roughly halfway between Bangkok and the Cambodian border, the largely rural provinces of Prachinburi and Sa Kaew are peppered with many small, unexcavated, unrestored Dvaravati and Khmer ruins. The latter province's name, in fact, means 'Jewel Pool', a reference to various Mon-Khmer reservoirs in the area. Little more than loose collections of laterite blocks, most will be of little interest to the casual visitor. The provincial capitals and larger towns lie next to the banks of the Prachin River – now paralleled by the eastern railway line and Highway 33 – in the midst of a rice-growing region crossed by canals. The eastern districts of Prachinburi centred around amphoe Sa Kaew attained separate provincial status in January 1994.

Ferry Timetable

Destination	Fare	Departure	Arrival	Return
Ban Dan Mai	10B	1 pm	1.30 pm	7 am
Than Mayom	20B	1 pm	1.45 pm	7 am
Khlong Son	20B	1 pm	2 pm	6 & 9 am
Salak Kok	20B	1 pm	2 pm	6.30 to 7 am
Salak Phet	50B	1 pm	3 pm	6 am
Sai Thong	50B	4 pm	4.30 pm	9 am
Hat Sai Khao (White Sand)*	70B	noon & 3 pm	3 & 6 pm	7 to 8 am & 2 pm
Khlong Phrao*	70B	noon & 3 pm	3 & 6 pm	6.30 am & 1.30 pm
Hat Kaibae*	70B	noon & 3 pm	3 & 6 pm	6 am & 1 pm
Ao Bang Bao*	70B	1 & 3 pm	4.30 & 6.30 pm	7 am & 1 pm

* Boats to these beaches may not run in the rainy season.

CENTRAL THAILAND

National Parks

North of Prachinburi, Route 3077 leads to **Khao Yai National Park** (see under Nakhon Ratchasima Province in the North-East Thailand chapter). North and north-east of Kabinburi, along the southern escarpment of the Khorat Plateau, are the contiguous **Thap Lan National Park** and **Pang Sida National Park**. Together these parks encompass 3084 sq km, one of the largest protected natural areas in Thailand.

Thap Lan National Park is well known as a habitat for the abundant *tôn lan*, or talipot palm, the leaves of which were once used for palmleaf Buddhist manuscripts. Wildlife seen in the park includes elephant, gaur, tiger, sambar, barking deer, palm civets, hornbills and gibbons. Lowland bird varieties are particularly well represented here. This area was an important refuge for Thailand's communist guerrillas during the 1960s and 1970s, and remnants of their camps can be seen along the streams Khlong Nam Brang and Khlong Sam Son. Facilities in the park are minimal; anyone who would like to explore the interior should contact the rangers at park headquarters in Thap Lan village, amphoe Na Di. The rangers can arrange for a tour of the park and provide camping permits. There is no public transport to the park entrance, which is around 32 km north of Kabinburi via Route 304 (the road to Khorat).

Pang Sida National Park, centred around 30 km south-east of Thap Lan near Sa Kaew, is smaller but hillier than Thap Lan. Streams that cut through the park form several scenic waterfalls, including **Pang Sida** and **Na Pha Yai Falls** near park headquarters and the more difficult-to-reach **Suan Man Suan Thong** and **Daeng Makha Falls**.

Historical Ruins

South-east of amphoe meuang Prachinburi via Routes 319 and 3070, in the village of Ban Sa Khoi (between Khok Pip and Sa Maha Pho on Route 3070), is the Angkor period **Sa Morakot**. Thai for 'Emerald Pool', this was an important Khmer reservoir during the reign of Angkor's Jayavarman

VII. Original laterite-block sluices next to the dam, along with assorted semas (boundary stones), naga sculptures, pedestals and a sandstone lingam, can still be seen here. Water from this reservoir is still considered sacred and has been used in Thai coronation ceremonies.

Sa Kaew or 'Jewel Pool', another historic reservoir site, is just south of Khok Pip off Route 3070. This one features a Dvaravati-period laterite quarry with some surviving bas-relief on the walls. There are a number of other Dvaravati and Angkor laterite foundations in the area.

ARANYA PRATHET

อรัญประเทศ

This district of 55,000 next to the Thai-Cambodian border has long been an important trade and transport centre. After the Khmer Rouge took over Cambodia in 1975, and again when the Vietnamese invaded Cambodia in 1979, Aranya Prathet became a major recipient of Cambodian refugees. Today, random skirmishes between Khmer Rouge guerrillas and the Phnom Penh government continue to send Cambodian citizens scurrying over the border from time to time.

A large market, where a ragtag crowd of Cambodians sell to the Thais, convenes daily on the Thai side of the border near town.

Incidences of theft and banditry are common in the area, so take care with night travel. Although it's safe to cross the border directly to Poipet, areas to the north and south of the district seat are heavily mined. Audible firefights these days are not uncommon, and Khmer Rouge guerrillas have been known to cross the border into Thailand, especially north of Aranya Prathet towards Buriram Province.

Places to Stay

The *Aran Garden 1* (59/1 Tambon Aranya Prathet) and *Aran Garden 2* (110 Rat Uthit Rd) offer clean, quiet rooms with fan for 100 to 150B a night. The latter also has air-con rooms for 400B. The *Buncharoen Hotel* at

Top Left: Wat Khaek, Nong Khai (JC)
Top Right: Waterlily pads, Ancient City (Meuang Boran) (RN)
Bottom Left: Waterlily flower, Ancient City (Meuang Boran) (RN)
Bottom Right: Wat Phra Kaew, Bangkok (RN)

Top: Water buffalo (DC)
Bottom Left: Monkeys (JC)
Bottom Right: Elephant (CLA)

8-10 Chao Phraya Bodin Rd has OK rooms for 80 to 150B.

Getting There & Away

Ordinary buses from Bangkok's northern/north-eastern bus terminal cost 74B, leave hourly from 5.30 am to 4.30 pm and take around five hours to reach Aranya Prathet. Air-con buses (133B) leave hourly from 5.30 to 10.30 am and from noon to 5 pm. Buses to/from Prachinburi cost 31B and 55B respectively for ordinary and air-con buses.

The 3rd-class-only eastern railway line between Bangkok and Aran leaves Bangkok's Hualamphong station twice daily at 6 am and 1.10 pm, arriving in Aran 5½ hours later. The one-way fare is 48B.

If you have your own wheels you could also reach Aran from Chanthaburi Province to the south via Route 317, or from Buriram Province to the north via Route 3068. Before taking the latter road in either direction,

check the current security situation with a reliable local; Khmer Rouge activity in the area may precipitate the temporary closing of the road.

Crossing to Cambodia The SRT train continues another half hour east of Aran to the border for 5B. From Poipet on the Cambodian side you can catch a Cambodian train all the way to Phnom Penh (420 km) or as far as Sisaphon (49 km), the jumping-off point for buses north to Siem Reap/Angkor Wat.

It's legal to enter Cambodia at Poipet if you are holding a Cambodian visa. Whether or not it's legal to exit Thailand here is another story. Some people have been denied an exit stamp from Thai immigration authorities; others have had no problem. If you're not planning to return to Thailand in the near future, ie you're on your way to Vietnam and then onward from there, it hardly matters.

Northern Thailand

The first true Thai kingdoms (Lanna, Sukhothai, Nan, Chiang Mai and Chiang Saen) arose in what is now northern Thailand, hence this region is endowed with a wide range of traditional architecture, including great temple ruins. It is also the home of most of the Thai hill tribes, whose cultures are dissolving rapidly in the face of Thai modernisation and foreign tourism. Despite this, the scenic beauty of the north has been fairly well preserved, and Chiang Mai is still probably Thailand's most liveable city.

The northern Thai people (who call themselves *khon meuang*) are known for their relaxed, easy-going manner, which shows up in speech – the northern dialect *(kham meuang)* has a rhythm which is slower than that of Thailand's other three main dialects. Northern Thais are very proud of their local customs, considering northern ways to be part of Thailand's 'original' tradition and culture. Symbols expressing cultural solidarity are frequently displayed by northern Thais and include clay water jars placed in front of homes, *kalae* (a carved wooden 'X' motif) which decorate house gables, Shan or hill-tribe style shoulder bags, and the ubiquitous *sêua mâw hâwm* (indigo-dyed rice farmer's shirt) worn on Fridays at many banks, universities and other institutions throughout the north.

Northern Thailand also has its own cuisine, featuring a large variety of vegetables (the region's mountain slopes are well suited to vegetable cultivation). Sticky rice is preferred over the central and southern Thai-style white rice and, as in north-east Thailand and Laos, it is eaten with the hands. Sômtam, a tart and spicy salad usually made with green papaya (the northern Thais also use a variety of other fruits and vegetables), is very popular in the north but, unlike north-eastern Thais, khon meuang tend to eat it as an in-between-meals snack rather than as part of a main meal.

The mountainous north also contains the infamous Golden Triangle, the region where Myanmar, Laos and Thailand meet and where most of the world's illicit opium poppy is grown. Apart from the air of adventure and mystery surrounding the Golden Triangle, it is simply a beautiful area through which to travel.

The Northern Loop
While the straightforward way of travelling north is to head directly from Bangkok to Chiang Mai, there are many interesting alternatives.

Starting north, visit the ancient capitals of Ayuthaya, Lopburi and Sukhothai, or take a longer and less beaten route by heading west to Nakhon Pathom and Kanchanaburi and then travelling north-east by bus to Lopburi via Suphanburi (backtracking to Ayuthaya if desired).

From Lopburi, either head north to Chiang Mai, or stop at Phitsanulok for side trips to Sukhothai, Tak and Mae Sot. It is now possible to travel by road from Mae Sot to Mae Sariang, then on to Mae Hong Son or Chiang Mai.

Once you're in Chiang Mai, the usual route is to continue on to Fang for the Kok River boat ride to Chiang Rai, then on into the Golden Triangle towns of Mae Sai and Chiang Saen. Travellers with more time might add to this the Chiang Mai to Pai to Mae Hong Son to Mae Sariang to Chiang Mai circle. A very rough but traversable road between Tha Ton and Doi Mae Salong is an alternative to the Kok River trip once you get to the Fang area.

From Chiang Mai, proceed to north-eastern Thailand via Phitsanulok and Lom Sak, entering the north-east proper at either Loei or Khon Kaen. From there, Nong Khai, Udon Thani and Khon Kaen are all on the train line back to Bangkok, but there are several other places in the area worth exploring before heading back to the capital.

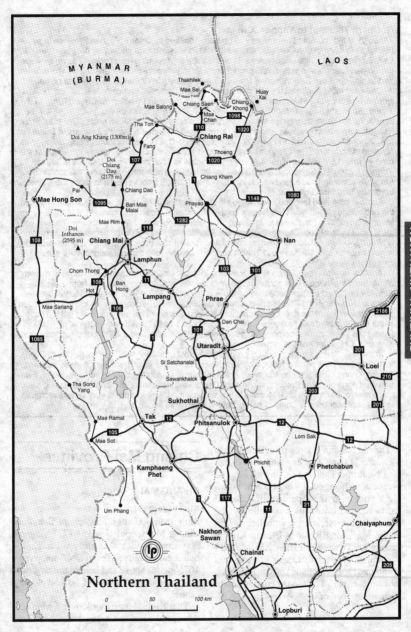

Northern Thailand

0   50   100 km

Northern Thailand to Yunnan, China

Although at the moment the only way to go from Thailand to China's Yunnan Province is by air (Bangkok to Kunming on China Southern Airlines), discussions are under way between the Thai, Lao, Burmese and Chinese governments on the subject of opening road and river travel between the Golden Triangle and Yunnan's Sipsongpanna district in south-western China. The Thais, Shan and Lao all consider Sipsongpanna (called Xishuangbanna in China) to be a cultural homeland.

One land route begins at the Burmese border town Thakhilek (opposite Mae Sai on the Thai side) and proceeds 164 km northward to Myanmar's Kengtung (known as Chiang Tung to the Thais), Shan State. At present this road is a rough track that takes all day to cover when road conditions are good; permission to cross here can be arranged in Mae Sai on the Thai side. From Kengtung the road continues another 100 km north to Myanmar's Mong La (opposite Daluo on the Chinese border); at the moment this latter section isn't approved for tourist travel although its opening is imminent. The Chinese have agreed to finance the Daluo to Kengtung section of the road in return for limited mineral and logging rights in Myanmar. From Daluo it's 300 km to Jinghong, capital of Sipsongpanna. Since Thai immigration authorities hold your passport in Mae Sai while allowing you to travel north into the Shan State, it's not yet legal to cross the Chinese border by land from Myanmar.

Another proposed land route would go via Laos, starting in Nam Tha and proceeding north to the Lao village of Boten on the Chinese border, close to the Sipsongpanna town of Mengla. From Mengla, an existing road leads to Jinghong. To reach Luang Nam Tha from northern Thailand you must cross by ferry from Chiang Khong on the Thai side to Huay Xai on the Lao side. This crossing is already operational; foreigners may enter Laos here with the proper papers. The Boten crossing is now legal for Lao, Chinese and Thai; it shouldn't be very long before foreigners are allowed to cross here as well.

Another way to reach Boten is via Pakbeng in Laos' Udomxai Province. Pakbeng is midway along the Maekhong River route between Huay Xai and Luang Prabang; from Pakbeng a Chinese-built road system continues all the way to Boten. To facilitate trade and travel between China and Thailand, the Chinese have offered to build a new road directly south to the Thai border (Nan Province) from the river bank opposite Pakbeng. For now Thai authorities are not too happy about this proposed road extension, which is seen as a push towards an 'invasion' of Thailand. During the years of Thai communist insurgency, CPT cadres used the Pakbeng road to reach Kunming, China, for training in revolutionary tactics.

In the short term, the river route is probably the most promising. Chinese barges weighing up to 100 tonnes now ply the Maekhong River eight months a year; from the Chinese border to Chiang Khong, Thailand, the trip takes about five days. During the drier months, however, river transport north of Luang Prabang is hampered by rocks and shallows. Blasting and dredging could make way for boats of up to 500 tonnes to travel year-round. A new express ferry service promises to deliver passengers to China from the Chiang Saen area in one day. ∎

The old Laotian Loop – from Bangkok to Vientiane, Luang Prabang and Huay Xai, then back into Thailand to Chiang Rai and eventually Chiang Mai – has become possible again with the opening of Laos to individual tourism. This loop can also be done in the reverse, starting with the crossing of the Maekhong River at Chiang Khong, Chiang Rai Province, to Huay Xai, and then continuing by river to Luang Prabang and Vientiane. From Vientiane you can loop back into north-eastern Thailand or continue on to Vietnam by road or air.

Chiang Mai Province

CHIANG MAI

อ.เมืองเชียงใหม่

More than 700 km north-west of Bangkok, Chiang Mai (population 154,777) has over 300 temples – almost as many as Bangkok – making it visually striking. Doi Suthep rises 1676 metres above and behind the city, providing a nice setting for this fast-developing centre.

Thai King Mengrai took over a Mon settlement to develop Chiang Mai (New City) in 1296. Historically, Chiang Mai succeeded King Mengrai's Chiang Rai kingdom after he conquered the post-Dvaravati kingdom of Hariphunchai (modern Lamphun) in 1281. Mengrai had been a prince of Nam Chao, a Thai kingdom in south-west China.

Later, in the 13th and 14th centuries, Chiang Mai became a part of the larger kingdom of Lan Na Thai (literally, 'million Thai rice fields'), which extended as far south as Kamphaeng Phet and as far north as Luang Prabang in Laos. During this period it became an important religious and cultural centre – the 8th world synod of Theravada Buddhism was held in Chiang Mai in 1477.

The Burmese capture of the city in 1556 was the second time the Burmese had control of Chiang Mai Province: prior to King Mengrai's reign, King Anuruddha of Pagan had ruled the area in the 11th century. As a result, Chiang Mai architecture shows a great deal of Burmese influence.

Chiang Mai was recaptured by the Thais under King Taksin in 1775 and became an important regional trade centre. Many of the later Shan and Burmese-style temples seen around the city were built by wealthy teak merchants who emigrated from Myanmar during the 19th century.

Tourism has replaced commercial trade as Chiang Mai's number-one source of outside revenue. Close behind is the manufacture and sale of handicrafts. Well before tourists started coming to northern Thailand, Chiang Mai was a centre for handcrafted pottery, weaving, umbrellas, silverwork and wood-carving – mainly because it was such a crossroads for travelling artisans from nearby countries. If you visit arts and craft shops anywhere in Thailand today, chances are at least someone working in the shop hails from the Chiang Mai area.

Many visitors stay in Chiang Mai longer than planned because of the high quality of accommodation, food and shopping, the cool nights (in comparison to central Thailand), the international feel of the city and the friendliness of the people. Also, the city is small enough to get around by bicycle.

Not all the foreign faces you see in Chiang Mai are tourists – many live in Chiang Mai part-time or all year round. Chiang Mai residents often comment that living here has all the cultural advantages of being in Bangkok, but fewer of the disadvantages such as traffic jams and air pollution. Lately, however, traffic has increased and the city's main avenues have become noisy and polluted, particularly around the new Tha Phae Gate. This area channels sound and fumes along a 200-metre section of Moon Meuang Rd; in order to restore it in the spirit that motivated the rebuilding of the wall, the city ought to close off all vehicular traffic at the intersection of Moon Meuang and Ratchadamnoen Rds.

To preserve the city's character, it has been proposed that a 'twin city' be built nearby to channel development away from the old city – possibly at San Kamphaeng to the east. Conservation measures include a 1991 ban on the building of any high-rise construction within 93 metres of a temple, thereby protecting about 87% of all lands within municipal limits. This law is designed to halt any future condo developments along the Ping River – the existing condos have already contributed to water pollution and spoiled the city's skyline. As usual, unscrupulous developers have found a loophole – hotels are exempt from the ban, so many condo-type developments are applying for hotel licences. Others are setting their sights on Chiang Rai farther north, where there are no such legal barriers.

Orientation

The old city of Chiang Mai is a neat square bounded by moats. Moon Meuang Rd, along the east moat, is the centre for cheap accommodation and places to eat. Tha Phae Rd runs straight from the middle of this side and crosses the Ping River where it changes to Charoen Meuang Rd.

The train station and the GPO are farther down Charoen Meuang Rd, a fair distance from the centre. There are several bus stations around Chiang Mai, so make sure you're going to the right one.

Several of Chiang Mai's important temples are within the moat area, but there are others to the north and west. Doi Suthep rises up to the west of the city and its temples give you have a fine view over the city.

Information

Tourist Office Chiang Mai has a friendly TAT office (☎ 248604/07) on the Chiang Mai-Lamphun Rd near Nawarat Bridge. It's open daily from 8 am to 5 pm. This is also the headquarters for the city's Tourist Police, who have a good reputation for honesty and efficiency.

Media Several free publications are distributed at tourist spots throughout the city. The monthly *Chiang Mai Newsletter* runs articles on local culture and politics as well as a listing of local events. *Trip Info* is a useful monthly booklet with extensive listings of government agencies, banks, churches, apartments, condos, hotels and resorts.

The amateurish *Siam Chiangmai News* is a one-person show produced by local developer Udom Surin. The tourism-oriented *Chiang Mai Travel Holiday* and *Welcome to Chiangmai & Chiangrai* contain the usual assortment of brief, rather shallow cultural essays embedded among stacks of advertisements for bars, restaurants and antique shops.

Radio Thailand Chiang Mai offers English-language broadcasts – a mix of news and music – from 6 to 8.30 am and 6 to 8.30 pm daily at FM 93.25.

Post & Telecommunications The GPO is near the train station on Charoen Meuang Rd. It's open Monday to Friday from 8.30 am to 4.30 pm, Saturday and Sunday from 9 am to noon. Bus Nos 1 and 3 pass in front of the GPO.

Branch post offices are found at Praisani, Phra Pokklao, Chotana, Mahidon, Chang Pheuak and Chang Klan Rds, and at Chiang Mai University and Chiang Mai International Airport.

Overseas telephone calls, telexes, faxes and telegrams can be arranged 24 hours a day in the telecommunications office around the side and upstairs from the GPO on Charoen Meuang Rd. International calls can also be made from larger hotels for a service charge (up to 30%) and at the international telephone office at 44 Si Donchai Rd from 9 am to 10.30 pm.

Home Direct phones, with easy one-button connection with foreign operators in a number of countries around the world, are available at Chiang Inn Plaza (100/1 Chang Klan Rd, behind the night bazaar), Chiang Mai International Airport, the GPO on Charoen Meuang Rd, THAI (240 Phra Pokklao Rd) and the TAT office.

To phone Bangkok from Chiang Mai, first dial 02. The telephone area code for Chiang Mai is ☎ 053.

Foreign Consulates Chiang Mai has several foreign consular posts where you may be able to arrange visas or extend passports. The Indian consulate here is a familiar stopping-off point for travellers on their way to India because visas can usually be collected on the same day as application.

China
    401 Laddaland Rd, opposite Ladda Land (☎ 511010)
France
    138 Charoen Prathet Rd (☎ 215719)
India
    113 Bamrungrat Rd, opposite British Council (☎ 243066, 242491)
Japan
    Na Watket Rd Soi 1 (☎ 302041)
Sweden
    YMCA Bldg, Mengrairasmi Rd, Santitham (☎ 221820)
UK
    54 Muu 2, Tambon Suthep (☎ 222571)
USA
    387 Wichayanon Rd (☎ 252629/31)

Cultural Centres Several foreign cultural centres in Chiang Mai host film, music, dance, theatre and other events of a socio-cultural nature.

Alliance Française (☎ 275277), 138 Charoen Prathet Rd. French films (subtitled in English) every Tuesday at 4.30 pm, Friday at 8 pm; admission is free to members, 10B students, 20B general public. French language courses are also offered.

USIS/AUA (☎ 278407, 211377), 24 Ratchadamnoen Rd. USIS shows US films every second and fourth Saturday at 2 pm and 7 pm; admission is free. AUA also offers English and Thai language courses (see the Activities section later in this section for details on Thai language study).

British Council (☎ 242103), 198 Bamrungrat Rd. Free British movies every Thursday evening at 7 pm.

Books & Maps Chiang Mai has several bookshops, the best being DK Book House on Tha Phae Rd and Suriwong Book Centre on Si Donchai Rd. DK has a second branch on Chiang Mai University campus.

The USIS/AUA library on Ratchadamnoen Rd inside the east gate has a large selection of English-language newspapers and magazines. The library is open Monday to Friday from noon to 6 pm. The British Council on Bamrungrat Rd also has a small English-language library. The Chiang Mai University library has a collection of foreign-language titles.

The Library Service at 21/1 Ratchamankha Rd Soi 2, not far from Tha Phae Gate, is a small bookshop-cum-cafe with used paperbacks for sale or trade. The staff also have up-to-date information on motorcycle touring, but there is a fee for this service (20B per person) unless you buy breakfast. The shop is open Monday to Saturday from 9 am to 6 pm.

The man who runs the Library Service, David Unkovich, has published a small guidebook entitled *A Pocket Guide for Motorcycle Touring in North Thailand* which is also available at various Chiang Mai bookshops. The book contains accurate odometer distances between various points throughout the north, which is helpful when navigating by motorcycle, bicycle or 4WD. The author has recently produced a second book, *The Mae Hong Son Loop*, devoted to Mae Hong Son Province.

Finding your way around Chiang Mai is fairly simple, although a copy of Nancy Chandler's *Map of Chiang Mai* is a worthwhile investment for 70B. It shows all the main points of interest, bus routes and innumerable oddities which you'd be most unlikely to stumble upon by yourself. Similar in scope are *DK's Chiang Mai Tourist Map* published by DK Book House (this has more emphasis on local transport information but very shaky transliteration) and P&P's *Tourist Map of Chiang Mai*. TAT also puts out a sketchy city map that's free.

Medical Services McCormick Hospital (☎ 241107) on Kaew Nawarat Rd is recommended over Chiang Mai Hospital because they are more geared to foreigners, speak better English and won't keep you waiting for as long. Another good one is the newer, modern Chang Puek Hospital (☎ 220022; fax 218120), at 1/7 Chang Pheuak Rd Soi 2.

Other medical facilities include Ariyawongse Clinic on Changmoi Rd, Chiang Mai Hospital on Suan Dawk Rd, Lanna Hospital on Highway 11 (Super Highway), and the Malaria Centre on 18 Bunreuangrit Rd.

Alcoholics Anonymous (☎ 282627) meets several times weekly at McCormick Hospital, Room 133.

Other The tourist police (☎ 248974) have an office next to the TAT on the Chiang Mai-Lamphun Rd. They are open from 6 am until midnight; there's also an after-hours number (☎ 491420).

The immigration office (☎ 277510) is off Route 1141 near the airport (bus No 6 will take you there).

Outside of Bangkok, Chiang Mai has the best supply of quality photographic film in the country. Broadway Photo (☎ 251253), on Tha Phae Rd about 100 metres east of Tha Phae Gate, has a good selection of slide film, including hard-to-find Fujichrome Pro 400 and Velvia 50.

Wat Chiang Man
วัดเชียงมั่น

The oldest wat in the city, Wat Chiang Man was founded by King Mengrai in 1296 and

NORTHERN THAILAND

features typical northern Thai architecture with massive teak columns inside the bot (main chapel). Two important Buddha images are kept in the smaller wihaan to the right of the bot. The monks once kept it locked, but it's now open daily from 9 am to 5 pm.

The Buddha Sila is a marble bas-relief standing 20 to 30 cm high. It's supposed to have come from Sri Lanka or India about 2500 years ago. The well-known Crystal Buddha, shuttled back and forth between Thailand and Laos like the Emerald Buddha, is kept in the same glass cabinet. It's thought to have come from Lopburi 1800 years ago and stands just 10 cm high.

Wat Chiang Man is off Ratchaphakhinai Rd in the north-east corner of the old city.

Wat Phra Singh
วัดพระสิงห์

Started by King Pa Yo in 1345, the wihaan which houses the Phra Singh image was built between 1385 and 1400 in the classic northern-Thai style found during this period from Chiang Mai to Luang Prabang. The Phra Singh Buddha supposedly comes from Sri Lanka, but it is not particularly Sinhalese in style. As it is identical to two images in Nakhon Si Thammarat and Bangkok, and has quite a travel history (Sukhothai, Ayuthaya, Chiang Rai, Luang Prabang – the usual itinerary for a travelling Buddha image, involving much royal trickery), no-one really knows which image is the real one or can document its provenance. The bot was finished in about 1600.

Wat Phra Singh is at the end of Phra Singh Rd near Suan Dawk Gate.

Wat Chedi Luang
วัดเจดีย์หลวง

This temple complex, on the corner of Phra Pokklao and Phra Singh Rds, contains a very large and venerable chedi dating from 1441. It's now in partial ruins, due to either a 16th-century earthquake or the cannon fire of King Taksin in 1775. It's said that the Emerald Buddha was placed in the eastern

niche here in 1475. The lak meuang (guardian deity post) for the city is within the wat compound in the small building to the left of the main entrance. There are also some very impressive dipterocarp trees on the grounds.

A restoration of the great chedi, financed by UNESCO and the Japanese government, is almost finished. Since no-one knows for sure how the original superstructure looked, Thai artisans are designing a new spire for the chedi. New Buddha images have been placed in the four directional niches, but the new porticoes and naga guardians lack the charm of the originals. Cement elephants in the pediment replace the original brick and stucco ones.

Wat Phan Tao
วัดพันเต้า

Adjacent to Wat Chedi Luang, this wat has a wooden wihaan and some old and interesting monk's quarters. Across Ratchadamnoen Rd from here, at the Phra Pokklao Rd intersection, is an uninteresting monument marking the spot where King Mengrai was struck by lightning!

Wat Jet Yot
วัดเจ็ดยอด

Out of town on the northern highway loop near the Chiang Mai National Museum, this wat was built in the mid-15th century based on the design of the Mahabodhi Temple in Bodhgaya, India. The seven spires represent the seven weeks Buddha spent in Bodhgaya after his enlightenment. The proportions for the Chiang Mai version are quite different from the Indian original, so it was probably modelled from a small votive tablet depicting the Mahabodhi in distorted perspective.

On the outer walls of the old wihaan is some of the original stucco relief. There's an adjacent stupa of undetermined age and a very glossy wihaan. The entire area is surrounded by well-kept lawns. It's a pleasant, relaxing temple to visit, although curiously it's not a very active temple in terms of worship.

Wat Jet Yot is a bit too far from the city centre to reach on foot; by bicycle it's easy or you can take a No 6 city bus (red).

Wat Suan Dok (Dawk)
วัดสวนดอก

Built in 1383, the large open wihaan was rebuilt in 1932. The bot contains a 500-year-old bronze Buddha image and vivid jataka (Buddha life-story) murals. Amulets and Buddhist literature printed in English and Thai can be purchased at quite low prices in the wihaan.

There is an interesting group of white-washed stupas, framed by Doi Suthep. The large central stupa contains a Buddha relic which supposedly self-multiplied. One relic was mounted on the back of a white elephant (commemorated by Chiang Mai's White Elephant Gate) which was allowed to wander until it 'chose' a site on which a wat could be built to shelter the relic. The elephant stopped and died at a spot on Doi Suthep, where Wat Phra That Doi Suthep was built.

Wat Kuu Tao
วัดกู่เต้า

North of the moat, near the Sports Stadium, Wat Kuu Tao dates from 1613 and has a unique chedi which looks like a pile of diminishing spheres. Note the amusing sculptures on the outer wall of the wat.

Wat U Mong
วัดอูโมง

This forest wat was first used during King Mengrai's rule in the 14th century. Brick-lined tunnels here were supposedly built around 1380 for the clairvoyant monk Thera Jan. The monastery was abandoned at a later date and wasn't reinstated until a local Thai prince sponsored a restoration in the late 1940s. The late Ajaan Buddhadasa, a well-known monk and teacher at southern Thailand's Wat Suanmok, sent several monks to re-establish a sangha at U Mong in the 1960s. One building contains modern artwork by various monks who have resided at U Mong, including some foreigners. A marvelously grisly image of the fasting Buddha – ribs, veins and all – can be seen on the grounds.

A small library-museum with English-language books on Buddhism is also on the premises.

To get there, travel west on Suthep Rd for about two km and turn left past Wang Nam Kan, then follow the signs for another couple of km to Wat U Mong. Songthaews to Doi Suthep and city bus No 1 also pass the Wang Nam Kan turn-off.

Wat Ram Poeng
วัดร่ำเปิง

Not far from Wat U Mong, this large monastery supports the well-known Northern Insight Meditation Centre (☎ 211620), where many foreigners have studied vipassana. One-month individual courses are taught by a Thai monk (Ajaan Thong and/or Luang Paw Banyat) with Western students or bilingual Thais acting as interpreters.

A large tripitaka (Buddhist scriptures) library has recently been completed and houses versions of the Theravada Buddhist canon in Pali, Thai, Chinese, English and other languages. The formal name for this wat is Wat Tapotaram.

To get there, take city bus No 1 or a songthaew west on Suthep Rd to Phayom Market (Talaat Pha-yawm). From here, take a songthaew south to the wat entrance (4B).

Wiang Kum Kam
เวียงกุมกำ

These recently excavated ruins are five km south of the city via Route 106 (the Chiang Mai-Lamphun road) near the Ping River. Apparently this was the earliest historical settlement in the Chiang Mai area, established by Mons in the 11th or 12th century (well before King Mengrai's reign, though the city's founding is often mistakenly attributed to Mengrai) as a satellite town for the Hariphunchai kingdom. The walled city was abandoned in the early 18th century due to massive flooding and visible architectural remains are few – only the Mon-style chedi of Wat Chedi Si Liam and the layered brick pediments and stupa of Wat Kan Thom (the Mon name; in Thai the temple was known as Wat Chang Kham).

Altogether over 1300 inscribed stone slabs, bricks, bells and stupas have been excavated at the site – all are currently undergoing translation at Chiang Mai University. So far, the most important archaeological discovery has been a four-piece inscribed stone slab now on display in the Chiang Mai National Museum. These early 11th-century inscriptions indicate that the Thai script actually predates King Ramkhamhaeng's famous Sukhothai inscription (introduced in 1293) by 100 or more years.

The stones – now housed at the Chiang Mai National Museum – display writing in three scripts of varying ages; the earliest is Mon, the latest is classical Sukhothai script, while the middle-period inscription is proto-Thai. Historical linguists studying the slabs now say that the Thai script was developed from Mon models, later to be modified by adding Khmer characteristics. This means Ramkhamhaeng was not the 'inventor' of the script as previously thought, but more of a would-be reformer. His reformations appear on only one slab and weren't accepted by contemporaries – his script in fact died with him.

An ideal way of getting to Wiang Kum Kam is to hire a bicycle; follow the Chiang Mai-Lamphun road south about three km and look for a sign to the ruins on the right. From this junction it's another two km to the ruins. You could also hire a tuk-tuk to take you there for 30 or 40B (one way). Once you're finished looking around you can walk back to the Chiang Mai-Lamphun Rd and catch a No 2 city bus back into the city.

Other Temples

Temple freaks looking for more wat energy can check out **Wat Pheuak Hong**, behind Buak Hat Park off Samlan Rd. The locally revered **Chedi Si Pheuak** is over 100 years old and features the 'stacked spheres' style seen only at Wat Kuu Tao. Another unique local temple is the Burmese-built **Wat Chiang Yuen** on the north side of the moat (across Mani Nopharat Rd) between Chang Pheuak Gate and the north-eastern corner of the old city. Besides the large northern-style chedi here, the main attraction is an old Burmese colonial gate and pavilion on the east side of the school grounds attached to the wat. It looks like it dropped out of the sky from Rangoon or Mandalay.

Three wats along Tha Phae Rd, **Jetawan**, **Maharam** and **Bupharam** feature highly ornate wihaans and chedis designed by Shan or Burmese artisans; most likely they were originally financed by Burmese teak merchants who immigrated to Chiang Mai 100 years ago or more.

Chiang Mai National Museum
พิพิธภัณฑ์แห่งชาติ

The museum has a good selection of Buddha images, in all styles, on display, including a very large bronze Buddha downstairs. Pottery is also displayed downstairs (note the 'failed' jar on the stairs), while upstairs there are household and work items. Look for the amusing wooden 'dog' used for spinning thread.

The museum is open from 9 am to 4 pm, Wednesday to Sunday. Admission is 10B. The museum is close to Wat Jet Yot on Highway 11 which curves around the city; city bus No 6 stops nearby.

Chiang Mai Prison
คุกเชียงใหม่

Near the centre of town, off Ratwithi Rd, this is where dozens of farangs have been incarcerated on drug charges. Chiang Mai is notorious for samlor and tuk-tuk drivers who sell dope and then inform the police about their customers. Fines for even the smallest amounts of ganja are very high – 50,000B for a couple of grams is not unusual. Those who cannot afford to buy out of this dangerous game go to jail.

Night Bazaar

An extensive night market sprawls over the

area between Loi Khraw and Tha Phae Rds, off Chang Klan Rd, just east of the Khlong Mae Kha, near the Chiang Inn. This market is made up of several different concession areas and dozens of street vendors displaying a variety of Thai and northern Thai goods, as well as designer goods (both fake and licensed, look carefully), at very low prices – if you bargain well. Actually, many importers buy here because the prices are so good, especially when buying in quantity.

Good buys include Phrae-style seua maw hawm (blue denim farmers' shirts), northern and north-eastern handwoven fabrics, yaams (shoulder bags), hill-tribe crafts (many tribespeople set up their own concessions here), opium scales, hats, silver jewellery, lacquerware and many other items. Cheap cassette tapes are plentiful too.

If you're in need of new travelling clothes, this is a good place to look. A light cotton dress, trousers or yaams can be bought for between 45 and 60B, and work shirts cost between 50 and 80B, depending on size.

You must bargain patiently but mercilessly. The fact that there are so many different concessions selling the same type of items means that competition effectively keeps prices low, if you haggle. Look over the whole bazaar before you begin buying. If you're not in the mood or don't have the money to buy, it's still worth a stroll, unless you don't like crowds – most nights it's elbow to elbow. Several restaurants and many food trolleys feed the hungry masses.

Tribal Research Institute

ศูนย์ศึกษาชาวเขา

This research institute is on Chiang Mai University campus, five km west of the city. A No 1 bus goes by the university. The institute features a small hill-tribes museum, and literature on hill tribes is available. It's open Monday to Friday from 8.30 am to 4.30 pm.

Other Attractions

The **Old Chiang Mai Cultural Centre** (☎ 275097) on Route 108 south of town is a tourist centre where northern Thai and hill-

tribe dances are performed nightly from 7 to 10 pm. Performances include a *khan tòk* dinner (northern-style food eaten from small round tables) and cost 250B per person. It's a touristy affair but done well.

Buak Hat Park, in the south-western corner of the moat, is Chiang Mai's miniature counterpart to Bangkok's Lumphini Park, with very pleasant grass expanses, fountains and palms. The **Chiang Mai University** campus is another quiet place to wander around. It's also interesting in the evenings, with a busy night bazaar of its own.

Out towards Doi Suthep, six km from the town centre, are the shady, nicely landscaped, hilly **Chiang Mai Zoo** (take city bus No 3) and the nearby **Chiang Mai Arboretum**. Zoo admission is 10B adults, 5B children; you can drive a vehicle through the zoo grounds for 40B per car or truck, 5B for a motorcycle or bicycle. Except for the name of each species, most signs are in Thai only. A few snack vendors scattered around the park offer simple rice and noodle dishes. Along the same road nearby are the **Huay Kaew Fitness Park** and **Huay Kaew Falls**.

Activities

Thai Massage Study Over the years, Chiang Mai has become a centre for Thai massage studies. Not all the places purporting to teach massage are equally good. The oldest and most popular place to study is the Old Medicine Hospital (☎ 275085) on Soi Siwaka Komarat off Wualai Rd, opposite the Old Chiang Mai Cultural Centre. The 11-day course meets daily from 9 am to 4 pm and costs around 2270B, including all teaching materials. There are two courses per month year-round except for the first two weeks of April. The OMH curriculum is very traditional, with a northern Thai slant (the Thai name for the institute is actually Northern Traditional Healing Hospital). Classes tend to be large during the months of December to February. You can also receive a 1½-hour massage here (a requisite for admission to the course) for 150B.

Chaiyuth Priyasith's School of Thai Remedial Massage (no phone), at 52 Soi 3

Tha Phae Rd, offers a course similar to OMH's; Chaiyuth, in fact, taught at OMH for many years and is said to have taught most of the massage instructors working today in Chiang Mai. He charges 200B per hour for both massage and instruction.

The up-and-coming Suan Samoonprai has three locations, one at 105 Wansingkham Rd (☎ 252663), another at 1/11 Chaiyaphum Rd Soi 1 (☎/fax 252706) and a third at 9/3 Moon Meuang Rd Soi 2 (no phone). A seven-day course (six hours per day) costs 2000B; the institute also offers straight massage (100B per hour), herbal massage (400B for two hours), herbal sauna (30B) and herbal facials (50B).

A unique, one-on-one course is available at Baan Nit, Soi 2, Chaiyaphum Rd. The teacher is Nit, a rotund older woman who is a specialist in deep-tissue, nerve and herbal massages. Her methods were handed down to her from a long line of ancestral Chinese healers. Length of study and payment for Nit tutelage is up to the individual – according to what you can afford – but all studies begin with an offering of nine flowers to nine Chinese deities. Nit doesn't speak English so you must know some Thai, though much of the teaching is unspoken. Most students live in and eat meals with Nit and her family while studying. If you want to try Nit's massage talents, you have to pay a minimum of 9B to the same deities; most massagees pay 100B an hour.

Thai Language Study The basic Thai course at AUA (24 Ratchadamnoen Rd, ☎ 278407, 211377) consists of 60 hours of instruction at three levels; there are also 30-hour classes in 'small talk', reading and writing. Costs range from 2000B for the small talk course to 3000B per level for the 60-hour courses. Private tutoring is also available at 180B per hour.

Cooking Classes The Chiang Mai Thai Cookery School (☎ 278033), at 1-3 Moon Meuang Rd opposite Tha Phae Gate, offers a five-hour course in Thai cooking for 500B.

Swimming Landlocked Chiang Mai can get very hot, particularly from March to July. Fortunately, local opportunities for a refreshing swim – providing an alternative to the usual tourist solution (vegetating in refrigerated rooms most of the day) – are many.

Huay Teung Tao Reservoir This sizeable lake about 12 km north-west of the city is a great place for an all-day swim and picnic, especially during the hotter months. By car or motorcycle you can get there by driving 10 km north on Route 107 (follow signs towards Mae Rim), then west two km past an army camp to the reservoir. On public transport, you could take a city bus No 2 until it terminates at the army camp, then walk to the reservoir.

Cyclists would do best to pedal to the reservoir via the canal road (Jon Phra Than). Head west on Huay Kaew Rd, then turn right just before the canal. Follow the canal road until it ends at the unpaved road between the reservoir and the highway; turn left here and you'll reach the lake after another km or so of pedalling. From the north-west corner of the moat, the bike ride takes about an hour.

If you don't bring your own, food is available from vendors at the lake; fishing is permitted if you'd like to try your luck at hooking lunch.

City Pools Chiang Mai has several swimming pools for public use; you can pay on a per-day basis, or buy an annual membership:

Physical Education College
    Chiang Mai Stadium, Sanam Kila Rd (☎ 211422), 5 to 7 pm weekdays, 8 am to 6 pm weekends, 10B members, 20B nonmembers (annual membership 210B)
Pongpat Swimming Pool
    73/2 Chotana Rd (☎ 212812), 9 am to 7 pm, 5B members, 15B nonmembers (annual membership 200B)
Amari Hotel
    Huay Kaew Rd at Nimanhaemin Rd (☎ 221044), 10 am to 6.30 pm, 40B
Chiang Mai University
    Faculty of Education, Huay Kaew Rd (☎ 221699, ext 3050), 10 to 11.45 am and 1 to 5 pm, 15B (annual membership 50B)

Sara Health Club
    109 Bamrungrat Rd (☎ 244371), 8 am to 6 pm, 10 to 40B (annual membership 500B)
Suandok Hospital
    Faculty of Medicine, Suthep Rd (☎ 221699), 9 am to 8 pm (closed Thursday), 8B, plus 15B annual membership
Top North Guest House
    15 Soi 2, Moon Meuang Rd (☎ 213900), 9 am to 8 pm, 50B

Tennis Anantasiri Tennis Courts, off the expressway and opposite the National Museum, is the best public tennis facility in Chiang Mai. The eight courts are illuminated at night, and you can hire a 'knocker' (tennis opponent) for a reasonable hourly fee in addition to the regular court fee.

Other places with public tennis courts include SL Courts (opposite the National Museum) and Suandok Hospital.

Hash House Harriers The Chiang Mai Harriers meet weekly at the Domino Bar, Moon Meuang Rd, and organise a weekly 'hash' (foot race) at various locations in the Chiang Mai area (☎ 278503 for details).

Muay Thai Joe's Gym, off Kotchasan Rd near the Moon Garden Pub, offers muay thai training for foreigners.

Festivals
The week-long Winter Fair in late December and early January is a great occasion, as is the April Songkran Water Festival which is celebrated here with great enthusiasm.

Yet perhaps Chiang Mai's best celebrated festival is the Flower Festival, also called the Flower Carnival, which is held annually in February (actual dates vary from year to year). Events occur over a three-day period and include displays of flower arrangements, a long parade of floats decorated with hundreds and thousands of flowers, folk music, cultural performances and the Queen of the Flower Festival contest. Most activities are centred at Buak Hat Park in the south-west corner of the city moats. People from all over the province and the rest of the country turn out for this occasion, so book early if you want a room in town.

In May the Intakin Festival, held at Wat Chedi Luang and centred around the city lak meuang, propitiates the city's guardian deity to assure that the annual monsoon will arrive on time. Also in May – when the mango crop is ripe – a Mango Fair is celebrated in Buak Hat Park with lots of mango-eating and the coronation of the Mango Queen.

Places to Stay – bottom end
At any one time there are about 300 hotels and guesthouses operating in Chiang Mai. Hotels range from 70B for a dorm room at the YMCA to 3750B for a double room at the new Westin Chiangmai, with an average room costing from 150 to 300B per night. Guesthouses range from 40B per person for a dorm bed to 300B for a room. At the cheaper hotels, 'single' means a room with one large bed (big enough for two) while 'double' means a room with two beds; the number of people staying in the room is irrelevant.

Hotels In Chiang Mai's small Chinatown, the basic *Sri Ratchawongse* (☎ 235864) at 103 Ratchawong Rd, between the east moat and the Ping River, has singles/doubles with fan and bath for 100/160B. Nearby at 94-98 Ratchawong Rd is the nicer *New Mitrapap* (☎ 235436), where rooms are 120 to 200B. Both hotels are close to several good, inexpensive Chinese restaurants, as well as the Warorot Market.

Sri Santitham (☎ 221585) at 15 Soi 4 Chotana Rd, near Chang Pheuak (White Elephant) bus station, has singles with fan and bath from 130B, or from 150B with air-con. A better alternative in this area is *Chiang Mai Phu Viang Hotel* (☎ 221632, 221532) at 5-9 Soi 4, Chotana Rd. Clean, spacious rooms are 200B with fan and bath, up to 500B with air-con.

The funky, old Thai-style *Muang Thong* (☎ 278438) at 5 Ratchamankha Rd, a good location inside the city moats, has singles with fan and bath from just 100B, and two-bed rooms for 150 to 170B. Near the train

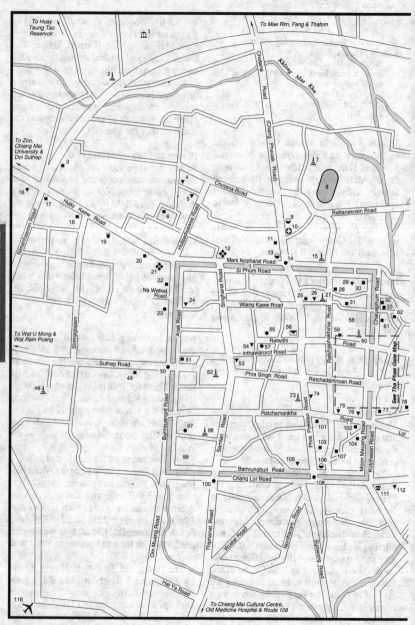

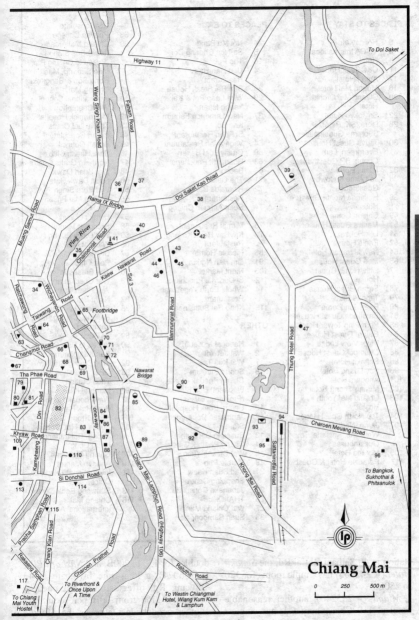

Chiang Mai

0   250   500 m

PLACES TO STAY

3	Holiday Inn
6	YMCA International Hotel
11	C&C Teak House
17	Amari Hotel
18	Muang Mai Hotel
20	Chiang Mai Orchid Hotel
22	Sri Tokyo Hotel
28	Libra, SK, Peter, Supreme Guesthouses
30	Tanya Guest House
31	Evergreen, Lam Chang, SP Guesthouses
32	Miami Hotel
35	Je t'Aime & Cowboy Guesthouses
36	Hollanda Montri Guest House
49	Chiang Come Hotel
51	Manit's Guest House
61	Lek House
62	Eagle House
64	New Mitrapap Hotel
65	Mee Guest House
77	Little Home Guest House
78	Sarah Guest House
79	Taphae Place
80	Baan Jongcome
81	Ratchada Guest House
83	Porn Ping Tower Hotel
84	Galare Guest House
87	River View Lodge
88	Chumpol Guest House
95	Settakit Hotel
96	Poy Luang Hotel
101	Anodard Hotel
102	Muang Thong Hotel
103	Chiang Mai Youth Hostel
104	Top North Guest House
107	Jame, North Star, Welcome, Kritsada, Toy Guesthouses
109	Montha Hotel
117	Paradise Hotel & Guest House

PLACES TO EAT

4	Noi Mu Bang
5	Sa-Nga Choeng Doi
16	The Pub
24	Uan Heh-Haa Restaurant
26	Ban Rai Steak House
29	Wira Laap Pet & Kai Yaang Isaan
37	New Lamduon Faharm Kao Soi
53	Si Phen Restaurant
54	Vegetarian Restaurant
59	Crusty Loaf Bakery
63	Ruam Mit Phochana
68	Bacco
71	The Gallery
72	Riverside Bar & Restaurant
74	Suan Aahaan Chiang Mai
75	Mitmai Restaurant
76	Kaytiaw Reua Koliang Restaurant
86	Piccola Roma
91	Lim Han Nguan
105	Night Market
112	Si Donchai Phochana
114	Whole Earth Vegetarian Restaurant
115	Khao Soi Suthsinee

OTHER

1	National Museum
2	Wat Jet Yot
7	Wat Kuu Tao
8	Sports Stadium
9	Chang Pheuak (White Elephant) Bus Station (Provincial Buses)
10	Chang Puek Hospital
12	Tantrapan Department Store
13	Buses to Doi Suthep
14	Chang Pheuak Gate
15	Wat Chiang Yuen
19	Marble Pub
21	Kad Suan Kaew Shopping Centre
23	Japanese Consulate
25	THAI Office
27	Wat Chiang Man
33	Suan Samoonprai
34	US Consulate
38	Phayap College
39	Chiang Mai Arcade (New) Bus Station (Buses to Chiang Rai, Mae Sariang, Mae Hong Son & Bangkok)
40	Chiang Mai International School
41	Wat Chetuphon
42	McCormick Hospital
43	Thai Tribal Crafts
44	Indian Consulate
45	British Council
46	Sara Health Club
47	Northern Crafts Centre
48	Wat Suan Dawk
50	Suan Dawk Gate
52	Wat Phra Singh
55	Chiang Mai Prison
56	Post Office
57	District Offices
58	Somphet Market
60	Wat Dawk Euang
66	Warorot Market
67	DK Book House
69	Post Office
70	The Brasserie
73	Wat Chedi Luang & Wat Phan Tao
82	Night Bazaar
85	Buses to Lamphun, Pasang, Chiang Rai & Lampang
89	TAT Office
90	Buses to Baw Sang & San Kamphaeng
92	Thai Boxing Stadium
93	GPO
94	Train Station
97	Mengrai Kilns
98	Wat Pheuak Hong
99	Buat Hak Park
100	Suan Prung Gate
106	Buses to Hot, Chom Thong, Doi Inthanon & Hang Dong
108	Chiang Mai Gate
110	Anusan Market
111	International Telephone Offices
113	Suriwong Book Centre
116	Chiang Mai International Airport

station at 46 Sathani Rotfai Rd, the *Settakit Hotel* (☎ 242765) has simple rooms for 120 to 250B.

Miami (☎ 235240), another reasonable hotel at 119 Chaisiphum Rd, has singles/ doubles for 130 to 200B, and *Nakhorn Ping* (☎ 236024), a long-time favourite at 43 Taiwang Rd, offers similar but cheaper accommodation from 90B per room. Yet another good budget hotel is the *Montha*

Rip-Offs
Upon arrival in Chiang Mai – whether by bus, plane or train – you'll quite likely be crowded by touts trying to get you to a particular hotel or guesthouse. As elsewhere in Thailand, the touts get a commission for every prospective guest they bring to a guesthouse/hotel. Commissions run as high as 150B per head; call guesthouses for a ride from the bus or train station and they will be delighted to give you a ride to avoid paying such exorbitant commissions. Even the airport touts get commissions from the large tourist hotels; the commission is often added to your room rate (ie walk-ins get a lower rate than those guests brought by touts).

At the train station, ignore the official-looking table with uniformed attendants who will try to funnel you into hotels and guesthouses paying commissions – they'll say that anything not on their list is either full, dirty, or closed.

Another scam to be aware of is the bus or minivan services from Khao San Rd in Bangkok, which often advertise a free night's accommodation in Chiang Mai if you buy a Bangkok-Chiang Mai ticket. What usually happens on arrival is that the 'free' guesthouse demands you sign up for one of the hill treks immediately; if you don't, the guesthouse is suddenly 'full'. Sometimes they levy a charge for electricity or hot water. Guesthouses involved in this arrangement may also give you the boot if you don't eat at their restaurant. The savings usually don't justify the hassle; the buses are often late and substandard vehicles may be substituted for the shiny ones shown in photos on the travel agency walls. Better guesthouses don't play this game.

The old gem scam has also reached Chiang Mai. The same modus operandi used in Bangkok is employed here: a well-dressed Thai man strikes up a seemingly harmless conversation – often in the vicinity of Wat Chedi Luang and Wat Phra Singh – that ends with your buying worthless sapphires at inflated prices in a local gem shop. ■

Hotel at 20 Loi Khraw Rd, where rooms cost 140 to 240B.

Thaphae Inn (☎ 236640) at 165 Tha Phae Rd, towards the river and between the moat and the TAT office (the Seiko Tour office is in front), has changed its name from Thai Charoen and upgraded its rooms to all air-con for 250 to 400B. This location is convenient to the night bazaar, but be sure to get a room as far away from noisy Tha Phae Rd as possible.

Roong Ruang Hotel (☎ 232017/18), also spelt 'Roong Raeng', is situated in a prime location at 398 Tha Phae Rd, near Tha Phae Gate, on the eastern side of the city moat. The service is good and the rooms, which face an inner courtyard and are therefore quiet, have been renovated with the addition of pleasant sitting areas. Singles/doubles with fan and bath are 270B; with air-con and hot shower they are 370B. The Roong Ruang also has some larger rooms with fan or air-con for a slightly higher cost. This is a good place to stay for the Flower Festival in early February as the Saturday parade passes right by the entrance. Another entrance is on Chang Moi Kao Rd.

YMCA International Hotel (☎ 221819, 222366; fax 215523) is at 2/4 Mengrairasmi Rd, above the north-west corner of the moat. Singles/doubles in the old wing with fan and shared bath are 120/180B, 180B with fan and private bath or 250/300B with air-con. Dorm beds in the old wing are 70B. In the fully air-con new wing, singles/doubles with private bath, telephone and TV are 500/600B. Facilities include a travel agency, handicraft centre and cafeteria. Not far from the Y, the *Patchara Hotel* (☎ 221335) at 404/8 Santitham Rd has decent rooms for 150 to 250B.

The *Montri Hotel* (☎ 211069/70), on the corner of Moon Meuang and Ratchadam-noen Rds, has overpriced singles with fan and bath for 350B, 500B with air-con. The fan rooms are especially poor value, as they're bombarded by noise from Moon Meuang Rd which reflects off Tha Phae wall.

Guesthouses Guesthouses are clustered in several areas: along Charoenrat Rd east of the Ping River, which is far from the centre of the city but near buses to Chiang Rai, Lamphun and the train station; along Moon

Meuang Rd (the inside of the east moat) and on streets off Moon Meuang Rd; along several sois running south off Tha Phae Rd; and along Charoen Prathet Rd, parallel to Charoenrat but west of the Ping River. Several others are scattered elsewhere around the western side of Chiang Mai.

Guesthouses come and go with frequency in Chiang Mai. The best are owned and managed by local families. The worst are those opened by Bangkok Thais who fiddle with your stored belongings while you're off on a trek. There are basically two kinds of budget guesthouse accommodation – old family homes converted into guest rooms (these usually have the best atmosphere though the least privacy) and hotel or apartment-style places with rows of cell-like rooms. In both the furnishings are basic – a bed and few sticks of furniture. Usually you must supply your own towel and soap; the rooms are cleaned only after guests leave. You can assume that rooms under 80B will not have a private bath but will probably have a fan.

The cheaper guesthouses make most of their money from food service and hill-tribe trekking rather than from room charges. Many of the guesthouses can arrange bicycle and motorcycle rental. If you phone a guesthouse, most will collect you from the train or bus station for free if they have a room (this saves them having to pay a commission to a driver).

Guesthouses which belong to the Chiang Mai Guest House Association are probably more secure in terms of theft than those which are not. As members pay government taxes, they are generally more interested in long-term operation. The TAT office on the Chiang Mai-Lamphun Rd can provide an up-to-date list of members. The following list is not exhaustive but hits most of the more reliable, long-running places.

Warning Lonely Planet has received many letters from travellers who have left their valuables in a guesthouse safe while they were trekking. Unfortunately, upon their return, they discovered that their property had been removed from the safe and that items such as travellers' cheques, Swiss army pocket knives and sunglasses were missing. One Australian traveller discovered that A\$2500 had been spent on her MasterCard which had been left in a safe while she had been trekking. An Irish couple had £6000 worth of goods charged to their credit cards in Bangkok while they were on a three-day trek! If you leave your valuables in a safe, make sure you obtain a fully itemised receipt before departing on a trek.

Inner Moat Area *Chiang Mai Youth Hostel* (☎ 272169) at 31 Phra Pokklao Rd has dorm beds for 50B and rooms for 120/160B; both rooms and dorm come with hot showers. A Hostelling International membership is required to stay here; temporary memberships valid for one night cost 50B. Recently the facilities here have really slid downhill.

The *Kent Guest House* (☎ 217578), 5 Soi 1, Ratchamankha Rd, near Tha Phae Gate, has pleasant rooms with fan and bath in a quiet compound for 100B.

Top North Guest House (☎ 213900) at 15 Soi 2, Moon Meuang Rd, is an efficiently run place where rooms cost 200B with fan, 300B with air-con. Facilities include a swimming pool. Also on this soi are the inexpensive *Jame House, Toy House, Welcome House* and *Kritsada*, all in the 100B range.

Nat Guest House (☎ 212878), up from the original youth hostel at 7 Soi 6, Phra Pokklao Rd, is a comfortable place with rooms from 80B.

Manit's Guest House (☎ 213771) is a one-person show at 81/1 Arak near Suan Dawk Gate, in a large off-the-street house inside the city moat. Large rooms with fan and bath cost 100B in the low season, 150B in the high. Manit handles every aspect of this business himself.

The friendly *Chiangmai Garden Guest House* (☎ 210881) at 82-86 Ratchamankha Rd, formerly Racha Guest House, has clean rooms and good food. Singles/doubles cost 100/120B with fan and bath.

Near the Library Service off Soi 2 Moon Meuang Rd, *Saithum* (☎ 211575) offers separate, clean bungalows with balconies in a garden setting for a bargain 60 to 90B.

There are plenty of other guesthouses inside the old city, especially down the little side lanes off Moon Meuang Rd. Soi 9, off Moon Meuang near the north-east corner of the moat, is a particularly good area to look if you're having trouble finding a vacant room during festivals such as Songkran and the Flower Festival. Several tacky, newer buildings here contain cheap guesthouses, including *Libra, SK House, Supreme House, Money, Gamo, SUP Court, PT* and *Peter*, all very similar with 80 to 100B rooms with shared bath, 150 to 180B with private bath (when available). Parallel Soi 7 has the similar apartment-style *Lam Chang, Evergreen House, CM Apartments, Kate House, Chiangmai* and *SP Hotel*.

Bridging the gap between bottom-end and middle-range places are a couple of comfortable guesthouses in the 175 to 400B range. *Gap House* (☎/fax 278140), on Soi 4 Ratchadamnoen (behind the USIS/AUA centre) has northern Thai-style houses built around a quiet garden. All rooms have carpet, air-con and private hot showers; rates are 175/350B for singles/doubles and include a filling breakfast. On the other side of Ratchadamnoen at Soi 5, *Rendezvous Guest House* (☎ 213763) is a newish inn costing 100B for a single with fan, 120 to 150B in a twin room with fan or 280B for an air-con room; add 30B to all rates for hot-water service. Facilities include a video bar.

The hotel-style *Moon Muang Golden Court* (☎ 212779), off Moon Meuang Rd north of Tha Phae Gate, features clean doubles with fan and hot shower for 150B, air-con for 280B.

See under Chang Pheuak Gate Area later in this section for places just inside the moat at the northern end of the old city.

Tha Phae Gate Area *Changmoi House* (☎ 251839) at 29 Chang Moi Kao Rd, behind the New Chiang Mai Hotel, is an old favourite. Clean rooms are only 60, 70 and 80B, depending on the size of the room. Changmoi House also has triples for 120B

and may soon be adding a few new 80B rooms. In mid-1994 Changmoi House suffered a fire and had to close down; hopefully it will be up and running again soon. Down an alley off Chang Moi Kao Rd is the basic but adequate *VK Guest House* with singles/doubles for 50/70B; a three-bed room with bath is available for 35B per person.

Another Chiang Mai original is *Lek House* at 22 Chaiyaphum Rd, near the Chang Moi Kao Rd intersection on the soi to Wat Chompu. It's quiet and has a pleasant garden. Rooms with fan and bath are 80/100B downstairs, 100/120B in the larger, newer rooms upstairs. The French-supervised restaurant is famous for its buffalo steaks (owner Yves started the trend, now imitated throughout the city). Near Lek House is the equally pleasant standby *Pao Come* at 9 Chang Moi Kao Rd. Singles/doubles cost 50/70B.

A bit farther north on Soi 3 Chang Moi Kao Rd is the well-run *Eagle House* (☎ 235387; fax 216368), which offers dorm beds for 30B or clean, quiet rooms with private bath for 80 to 100B a double, 70B a single. The multilingual staff boast French, German, English and Spanish language skills.

In the other direction towards Tha Phae Rd is the hotel-like *Happy House* (☎ 234969) at 11 Chang Moi Kao Rd, towards Tha Phae Gate. Big rooms with hot shower range from 150B with fan, 200 to 250B with air-con.

The Daret Restaurant has moved from its original Moon Meuang Rd location and now operates another restaurant and a rather crowded guesthouse across the moat at 4/5 Chaiyaphum Rd, called *Daret's House*. Rates range from 70 to 100B with a shared bath.

On Soi 6 off Tha Phae Rd, near the gate, is *MEI Guest House* (☎ 282448), which is a bit dingier than Happy House. Rooms range from 80B (with fan) to 250B (with air-con).

Soi 4, farther east (towards the river) along Tha Phae Rd, has several newer, two-storey brick guesthouses with downstairs sitting areas: *Thana, Sarah, Midtown House,*

NORTHERN THAILAND

PLACES TO STAY

2 Changmoi House
3 Daret's House
4 Moon Muang Golden Court
5 VK Guest House
6 Happy House
8 Roong Ruang Hotel
9 Rendezvous Guest House
11 Montri Hotel
15 Gap House
18 Hotel Top North Center
19 MEI Guest House
27 New Saithum Guest House

PLACES TO EAT

1 Thanam Restaurant
7 America Restaurant & Bar
12 JJ Bakery

16 Vegetarian Food Restaurant
21 Suriwong Khao Soi
23 Aroon Rai Restaurant
25 Bierstube
28 Library Service Restaurant

OTHER

10 USIS/AUA
13 Tha Phae Gate
14 USIS/AUA
17 Domino Bar
20 Chiangmai Books
22 Hard Rock Cafe
24 Pinte Blues Pub
26 Black Cat Bar
28 Library Service Bookshop
29 Cozy Corner
30 Pop Motorcycle Rental

Tha Phae Gate Area

0   50   100 m

Thaphae, Flamingo and *Baan Jongcome* (☎ 274823), each with good rooms in the 80 to 350B range. *Fang Guest House* (☎ 282940, 272505) is nearby at 46-48 Soi 1 Kamphaeng Din Rd in a newer building well away from traffic. Clean rooms with fan and bath are 200B a single or double, 250B for triples, and 300B with air-con and carpet. All rooms have hot water; 2nd-floor rooms have windows.

On Tha Phae Rd Soi 3, the *Ratchada Guest House* (☎ 275556) is good value for quiet rooms with fan and shower for 80 to 120B.

Towards the middle range, *Little Home Guest House* (☎ 273662), a newish spot at 1/1 Soi 3, Kotchasan Rd, offers large, comfortable rooms in a modern Thai-style building for 270 to 300B per night or 250B a night for more than three days.

East of the River *Linda Guest House* (☎ 246915), near the train station at 454/67 Banditpattana Rd, has rooms from 60B. German and English are spoken here. *C&C Teak House* (☎ 246966), at 39 Bamrungrat Rd, between the train station and the Ping River, has quiet, comfortable rooms from 60 to 80B. A second branch (☎ 223056) can be found at 27 Chotana Rd.

There are a string of guesthouses along Charoenrat Rd, parallelling the river – a bit far from the centre of town but recommended for those who are seeking a quiet atmosphere. The long-running *Je t'Aime* (☎ 241912), 247-9 Charoenrat Rd, has a variety of bungalow-style accommodation on landscaped grounds for 60 to 150B. *Cowboy Guest House* (☎ 241314), at 233 Charoenrat Rd just before Je t'Aime, is run by a Thai nicknamed Cowboy (with a son named Banjo and daughter named Guitar!) who speaks good English – he once ran a Thai restaurant in the Philippines. Bungalows at Cowboy are 100B with private bath, 60/80B with shared bath. The popular *Gold Riverside* at No 282/3 has rooms from only 60 to 80B. On the same road is *Mee Guest House*, at No 193/1, where doubles with bath cost 60B, and *Pun Pun* (☎ 243362), at No 321, where upgraded air-con rooms now cost 200B.

Farther north along Charoenrat (just about where it turns into Faham Rd) at No 365 is the Dutch-run *Hollanda Montri* (☎ 242450), with clean rooms and hot showers from 160 to 240B. The same family owns the Riverside Bar & Restaurant farther downriver.

Chang Pheuak Gate Area Several guesthouses have sprung up north of the city walls, far from the Tha Phae action but near the Chang Pheuak bus station (for Chiang Dao, Fang and Tha Ton). *Camp of Troppo Guest House* (☎ 279360) at 83/2 Ling Kok Rd, off Chotana Rd, has a relaxed atmosphere and costs from 60 to 80B per room. Farther up Chotana Rd at No 129 is *Chawala Guest House* where rooms range between 120 and 220B with a fan and bath. Just inside the moat at this end, *Mountain View Guest House* (☎ 212866), opposite Chang Pheuak Gate on Si Phum Rd, has large rooms and hot showers. A dorm bed is 50B, rooms with fan and bath are 150 to 250B, and air-con rooms 250 to 350B. Off Si Phum Rd on Soi 1 (around the corner from Wira Laap Pet restaurant) is the newish, Israeli-run *Tanya*

Guest House (☎ 210675) where clean rooms with hot-water bath are 120B, dorm beds 40B.

Chang Klan & Wualai Rds A nicer branch of the *Chiang Mai Youth Hostel* (☎ 236735) at 21/8 Chang Klan Rd has rooms from 100 to 180B.

South of the city at 92 Wualai Rd Soi 2 is the *Srisupan Guest House* (☎ 252811) which has fan-cooled and air-con rooms from 180 to 250B, including private hot shower.

Places to Stay – middle
Some of the places in this price range really blur the line between 'hotel' and 'guesthouse', the difference often being in name only. The well-managed *Galare Guest House* (☎ 273885; fax 279088), for example, at 7/1 Charoen Prathet Rd Soi 2, is fully air-con and has rooms from 300 to 400B. It's popular with repeat visitors for its Ping River location and proximity to both the night bazaar and post office. Another good one on the river is *The Riverfront* (☎ 275125), a large, old teak house at 43/3 Chang Klan Rd with a very good Thai restaurant on the verandah. Rooms with fan and private bath cost 200 to 300B, air-con rooms are 350 to 600B.

One of the best-value places in this range is the new *Paradise Hotel & Guest House* (☎ 270413; fax 273304), at 146/11 Si Chandon Rd (near the intersection of Chang Klan and Rakaeng Rds), with clean, spacious rooms with fan for 300B, air-con for 400B. All rooms come with hot shower and there's a pool on the premises. Also good is the rebuilt *Hotel Top North Center* (☎ 278531; fax 278485), which has replaced the old A&P Hotel at 41 Moon Meuang Rd inside the moat. All rooms come with carpet, air-con, TV and telephone for 500/600B a single/double.

In this range you can expect daily room cleaning, the option of air-con (some places have rooms with fan also) and – in the hotels – TV and telephone. If anything marks a guesthouse, it's the absence of these latter appliances.

Because of a room glut since 1991, room rates for many top-end places have been lowered to the middle range, eg you can sometimes get 1000B rooms for 500B.

Other guesthouses and hotels in this range, with similar facilities, include:

Anodard Hotel, 5 Ratchamankha Rd, 350 to 535B (☎ 270755)

Baan Kaew, 142 Charoen Prathet Rd, 260 to 360B (☎ 271606)

Bua Luang Hotel, 300 to 350B (☎ 221678)

Chang Pheuak Hotel, 133 Chotana Rd, 350 to 500B (☎ 221755)

Chatree Guest House, 11/10 Suriyawong Rd, 280 to 400B (☎ 279085)

Chiang Come Hotel, 7/35 Suthep Rd, 300 to 800B (☎ 222237)

Chiang Mai Phucome Hotel, 21 Huay Kaew, 505 to 750B (☎ 211026)

Chiang Mai Travel Lodge, 18 Kamphaeng Din Rd, 335 to 500B (☎ 271572)

Chomdoi House, 33/3 Huay Kaew Rd, 250 to 400B (☎ 210111, 222749)

Diamond Riverside Hotel, 33/10 Charoen Prathet Rd, 749B (☎ 270080; fax 273947)

Dragon House, 2/1-2 Chang Klan Rd, 350 to 450B (☎ 282305, 279172)

Grand Apartment, 24/1 Ratchaphakhinai Rd, 350 to 600B (☎ 217291)

Iyara Hotel, 126 Chotana Rd, 390 to 690B (☎ 222723)

Lai Thai Guest House, 111/4 Kotchasan Rd, 300 to 400B (☎ 271725/534)

Lanna Thai Guest House, 41/8 Soi 6, Loi Khraw Rd, 280 to 380B (☎ 282421, 275563)

Little Home Guest House, 1/1 Soi 3, Kotchasan Rd, 270 to 300B, 250B for more than three days (☎ 273662)

Living House, 4 Soi 5, Tha Phae Rd, 100 to 350B (☎ 275370)

New Asia Hotel, 55 Ratchawong Rd, 256 to 520B (☎ 235288; fax 252427)

Northern Inn Hotel, 234/12 Mani Nopharat Rd, 554 to 980B (☎ 210002; fax 215828)

Northern Palace, 7/9 Huay Kaew Rd, 250 to 700B (☎ 221549)

Prince Hotel, 3 Taiwang Rd, from 680B (☎ 236396)

The Providence, 99/9 Huay Kaew Rd, 595 to 781B (☎ 221750, 222122)

Sri Tokyo Hotel, 6 Bunreuangrit Rd, from 490B (☎ 213899; fax 211102)

Star Inn, 36 Loi Khraw Rd, 707 to 824B (☎ 270360; fax 273082)

Sumit Hotel, 198 Ratchaphakhinai Rd, 200 to 400B (☎ 211033)

Taphae Place, 2 Soi 3, Tha Phae Rd, 700 to 800B (☎ 270841)

Places to Stay – top end

Chiang Mai has plenty of more expensive hotels, several of which are along Huay Kaew Rd, towards Doi Suthep. In general, hotel rates for luxury hotels are lower in Chiang Mai than in Bangkok. Top properties at the moment are the *Holiday Inn Green Hills, Amari, Chiang Mai Orchid* and *Westin Chiangmai.*

The sparkling new Westin sits on the east bank of the Ping River and is the only five-star, international-class hotel in the city. In addition to large, deluxe guest rooms, facilities include five restaurants (Thai, Chinese, Mediterranean, Japanese, European), a 24-hour business centre, health club, pool and nightclub.

Top-enders, all of which have air-con, TV, IDD telephone and swimming pool, include the following:

Amari Hotel (formerly the Rincome), 301 Huay Kaew Rd, 146 rooms, from 2236B (☎ 221044; fax 221915)

Chiang Inn Hotel, 100 Chang Klan Rd, 170 rooms, from 1600B (☎ 272070; fax 274299)

Chiang Mai Garden Hotel, 330 Super Highway (Highway 11), 990B (☎ 210240; fax 218650)

Chiang Mai Orchid, 100 Huay Kaew Rd, 267 rooms, from 2346B (☎ 222099; fax 221625)

Chiang Mai Plaza, 92 Si Donchai Rd, 444 rooms, from 2000B (☎ 252050; fax 272230)

Chiang Mai President, 226 Wichayanon Rd, 57 rooms, from 900B (☎ 251025; fax 251032)

Empress Hotel, 199 Chang Klan Rd, 1766 to 2783B (☎ 270240; fax 272467)

Felix City Inn, 154 Ratchamankha Rd, 124 rooms, 1200 to 1400B (☎ 270710; fax 270709)

Holiday Inn Green Hills, 24 Chiang Mai-Lampang Rd (Highway 11), 200 rooms, from 1800B (☎ 220100; fax 221602)

Mae Ping, 153 Si Donchai Rd, 374 rooms, 1648 to 1884B (☎ 270160; fax 270181)

Novotel Suriwong Hotel), 110 Chang Klan Rd, 169 rooms, 1900 to 2100B (☎ 236789; fax 271604)

Porn Ping Tower Hotel, 46-48 Charoen Prathet Rd, 325 rooms, from 1500B (☎ 270100; fax 270119)

Poy Luang Hotel, 146 Super Highway (Highway 11), 227 rooms, 1340 to 2340B (☎ 242633; fax 242490)

Quality Chiang Mai Hills, 18 Huay Kaew Rd, 150 rooms, 1600 to 1900B (☎ 211101; fax 210035)

River View Lodge, 25 Charoen Prathet Rd Soi 2, 36 rooms, 1170 to 1400B, with discounts May to August (☎ 271101; fax 279019)

Westin Chiangmai, 324/11 Chiang Mai-Lamphun Rd, 526 rooms, from 3750B (☎ 275300; fax 275299)

Places to Eat

Chiang Mai has the best variety of restaurants of any city in Thailand, apart from Bangkok. Most travellers seem to have better luck here than in Bangkok though, simply because it's so much easier to get around and experiment.

Chiang Mai's guesthouses serve a typical menu of Western food and fruit smoothies along with a few pseudo-Thai dishes.

Thai Food Two good Thai restaurants are the large, open-air *Aroon Rai*, across the moat on Kotchasan Rd, which specialises in northern Thai dishes and has a huge menu, and the smaller but better *Thanam Restaurant* on Chaiyaphum Rd near the New Chiang Mai Hotel and Tha Phae Gate.

Specialities at the super-clean Thanam include phàk náam phrík (fresh vegetables in chilli sauce), plaa dùk phàt phèt (spicy fried catfish), kaeng sôm (hot and sour vegetable ragout with shrimp), as well as local dishes like khâo soi (Burmese chicken curry soup with noodles) and khanŏm jiin náam ngiáw (Chinese noodles with spiced chicken curry). Thanam has a small English sign inside. It closes at about 8 pm, doesn't serve alcohol and won't serve people wearing beach clothes (tank tops, etc).

The highly regarded *Si Phen* (no English sign), on Intharawarorot Rd near Wat Phra Singh, specialises in both northern and north-eastern style dishes. The kitchen prepares some of the best sômtam in the city, including a variation made with pomelo. The kài yâang-khâo nĭaw combo (grilled chicken and sticky rice) is also very good, as is the khâo sòi and khanŏm jiin (with either náam yaa or náam ngíaw) – always incredible. Si Phen is open 9 am to 5 pm only.

A good place for Isaan food is *Wira Laap Pet*, in the north-east corner of the old city on Si Phum Rd, inside the moat. The house speciality here is lâap pèt (duck salad). Just west of Wira Laap Pet is *Kai Yaang Isaan* (no roman script sign), which specialises in tasty Isaan-style grilled chicken.

If you tire of northern and north-eastern Thai cuisines or just want a little coconut in your curry, check out *Khrua Phuket Laikhram* (Classical Phuket Kitchen), a small family-run restaurant at 1/10 Suthep Rd. It's worth hunting down for the delicious, cheap, yet large portions of authentic home-style southern Thai cooking. If there are no seats downstairs, try the upstairs dining room. Specialities include yâwt phráo phàt phèt kûng (spicy stir-fried shrimp with coconut shoots), hèt hŭu nŭu phàt khài (eggs stir-fried with mouse-ear mushrooms) and yam phukèt laikhram (a delicious salad of cashew nuts and squid). The restaurant has daily specials, too. Ask for Khun Manop, who speaks English.

The long-established *Si Donchai Phochana* on Si Donchai Rd near Suriwong Book Centre is famous for the kitchen's ability to prepare virtually any Thai or Chinese dish, going several steps beyond the usual *aahăan taam sàng*. It's usually open late.

If you happen to be in the vicinity of the YMCA, there are two small Santitham district places worth trying. *Sa-Nga Choeng Doi* on Charoensuk Rd, a five-minute walk from the Y, has probably the best khâo mòk kài (Thai chicken biryani) and mátàbà (martabak) in town; it's only open from around 10 am to 2 pm. On the same street, *Noi Muu Bang* has excellent sômtam. Neither restaurant has a roman-script sign – just look for the appropriate dishes on the tables.

Chiang Mai University campus has a very good and inexpensive Thai restaurant called *Busaya*, open from 7 am to 10 pm daily.

Several good splurge places for Thai food are found along the Ping River east of the city centre. *Kala Khrang Neung* (Once Upon A Time) (☎ 274932) is set amidst a traditional teak-wood residence and gardens at 385/2 Charoen Prathet Rd. The menu is excellent and includes several northern Thai dishes. Another elegant eatery along the river on Charoen Prathet Rd is *The Gallery*, a converted Chinese temple that's half art gallery, half restaurant; it's owned by Dutch painter Theo Meier's widow.

Over the years, the most consistent riverside place has been the *Riverside Bar & Restaurant*, on Charoenrat Rd, 200 metres north of Nawarat Bridge. The food is almost always superb (try the kài bai hàw toei – chunks of chicken grilled in pandanus leaves). The atmosphere is convivial and there's good live music nightly. *The Riverfront (Tha Nam) Restaurant* (☎ 275125) on Chang Klan Rd along the west bank of the Ping River follows a similar formula and is also quite good.

Every evening a vendor sets up in the alley just east of the Roong Ruang Hotel, off Tha Phae Rd, and serves exemplary – and cheap – phàt thai.

Chinese Food Chiang Mai has a small Chinatown in an area centred around Ratchawong Rd north of Chang Moi Rd. Here you'll find a whole string of Chinese rice and noodle shops, most of them offering variations on Tae Jiu (Chao Zhou) and Yunnanese cooking. Many of the Chinese living in Chiang Mai are Yunnanese immigrants or direct descendants of Yunnanese immigrants who the Thais call *jiin haw* (literally 'galloping Chinese'). This could be a reference to their migratory ways or to the fact that many brought pack horses from Yunnan.

Two places flanking the New Mitrapap Hotel on Ratchawong Rd are big on roast duck, pork and goose, as well as dim sum: *Hang Yang Hong Kong* (Hong Kong Roast Goose) and *Buatong*. Both are good for what they do. There are several other inexpensive Chinese restaurants along this street.

An old stand-by for Yunnanese food is *Ruam Mit Phochana*, across from the public playground on Sithiwong Rd (one block west of Ratchawong). The food is as good as anything you'll find in Kunming, the capital of China's Yunnan Province; specialities include plaa thâwt náam daeng (whole fried fish in a red sauce, cooked with large, semihot Yunnanese red peppers), mǔu sǎam cham jǐm sǐi-yúu (shredded white pork served with

a chilli, garlic and soy sauce), mǔu tôm khêm (salty, boiled pork or 'Yunnanese ham') and tâo hûu phàt phrík daeng (braised bean curd and red peppers). Apart from a rice accompaniment, you can order mantou, which are plain Chinese steamed buns, similar to the Thai salabao but without stuffing.

Another authentic Yunnanese spot, the clean, simple and spacious *Mitmai Restaurant* (no roman-script sign), specialises in delicious vegetable soups made with pumpkin, taro, Chinese mushrooms, snowpeas or other Chinese vegetables. Especially tasty is the *tôm sôm plaa yâwt máphráo* (hot and sour fish soup with coconut shoots). The very complete bilingual menu also includes *yam* made with Chinese vegetables, Yunnanese steamed ham, Chinese medicine chicken and many vegetarian dishes. Prices are moderate. The Mitmai is on Ratchamankha Rd diagonally opposite the Napoleon Karaoke Club.

For a quick Chinese breakfast, try the food stall opposite JJ Bakery on Ratchadamnoen Rd. It has held out against Tha Phae Gate development for many years and still serves cheap jók (rice congee), paa-thông-kǒ (Chinese 'doughnuts') and náam tâo-hûu (hot soy milk). This is one of the few places in the Tha Phae Gate area that opens early for breakfast – around 6 am. You can also get great jók from the vendor next to the Bangkok Bank on Chang Moi Rd, with a choice of chicken, fish, shrimp or pork.

Lim Han Nguan (no English sign), east of the river on Charoen Meuang Rd near the Bangkok Bank (about midway between the river and the train station) is famous for its 30 kinds of khâo tôm (rice soup), including the traditional khâo tôm kuay – plain boiled rice soup with side dishes of salted egg, salt pork, etc. Other assets include the 1950s Chinese shophouse decor and the fact that it's open until 3 am.

Market Food Stalls Chiang Mai is full of interesting day and night markets stocked with very inexpensive and very tasty foods. The *Somphet Market* on Moon Meuang Rd, north of the Ratwithi Rd intersection, sells cheap takeaway curries, yam, lãap, thâwt man (fish cakes), sweets, seafood, etc. On the opposite side of the moat, along Chaiyaphum Rd north of Lek House, is a small but thriving night market where you can get everything from noodles and seafood to Yunnanese specialities. A lot of farangs eat here, so prices are just a bit higher than average, but the food is usually good.

Another good hunting ground is the very large night market near Chiang Mai Gate along Bamrungburi Rd. People tend to take their time here, making an evening of eating and drinking – there's no hustle to vacate tables for more customers. Over on the east side of the city, a large fruit & vegetable market assembles nightly along Chang Moi Rd near the Charoen Prathet intersection; several rice and noodle vendors are mixed in with the fruit stalls.

In the upstairs section of *Warorot Market* (on the corner of Chang Moi and Wichayanon Rds) are a number of great stalls for khâo tôm, khâo man kài, khâo mũu daeng ('red' pork with rice), jók and khâo sòi (curried chicken and noodle broth), with tables overlooking the market floor. The market is open from 6 am to 5 pm daily.

Anusan Market, near the night bazaar, used to be one of the best places to eat in the city, but many of the stalls have gone downhill during the last few years. If you wander over here, look for the stalls that are crowded – they're usually the best. Several vendors do kũaytĩaw râat nâa thaleh (braised seafood and rice noodles). The large khâo tôm place near the market entrance, *Uan Heh-Haa*, still packs in the customers; the most popular dish is the khâo tôm plaa (fish and rice soup). (Uan Heh-Haa has establshed an additional branch on Arak Rd next to the west moat.) *Sanpakhoi Market*, midway between the river and the train station on Charoen Meuang, has a better selection and lower prices than Anusan.

Noodles Noodles in Chiang Mai are wonderful and the variety astounding. Khâo sòi – a Shan-Burmese concoction of chicken, spicy curried broth and flat, squiggly, wheat noodles which bears a slight resemblance to Malaysian laksa – is one of the most characteristic northern Thai noodle dishes. Most locals say the city's best khâo sòi is found at *New Lamduon Faharm Kao Soi* (formerly Khao Soi Lam Duang) on Charoenrat Rd, just north of Rama IX Bridge opposite Hollanda Montri Guest House. The cook has prepared khâo sòi for no less a personage than King Bhumiphol – and it only costs 8B per bowl. Also on the menu are kâo lao (soup without noodles), mũu saté (grilled spiced pork on bamboo skewers), khâo sòi with beef or pork instead of chicken, khanõm rang pheûng (literally, 'beehive pastry', a coconut-flavoured waffle), Maekhong rice whisky and beer.

Another khâo sòi place on the same road is *White House*, across from the Je t'Aime guesthouse. Inside the old city, *Khao Soi Suthasinee*, on Soi 1 Intharawarorot opposite the district office, also serves exemplary khâo sòi. Suthasinee has another branch at 164/10 Chang Klan Rd near Lanna Commercial College. Other khâo sòi places can be found around the city – just look for the distinctive noodle shape and orange broth. *Khao Soi Islam*, on Soi Charoen Prathet 1 near the Diamond Riverside Hotel and Galare Guest House, is also good and offers a nice selection of sugar-cane, guava and lychee juices. *Suriwong Khao Soi*, on Kotchasan Rd opposite Tha Phae Gate, is a convenient spot for those staying in the Tha Phae Gate vicinity. Most khâo sòi places are open from around 10 am till 2 pm.

If you like khanõm jiin, the thin white noodles served with spicy fish or chicken curry, don't miss the no-name khanõm jiin stall off Moon Meuang Rd on Soi 5, across from Wat Dawk Euang. It's on the left, about 50 metres from Moon Meuang Rd, and serves possibly the best khanõm jiin in town for under 10B a plate, as well as náam âwy (sugar-cane juice) and náam faràng (guava juice).

Kuaytiaw Reua Koliang, on the corner of Ratchamankha and Moon Meuang Rd, has been serving authentic kũaytĩaw reua ('boat noodles', rice noodles served in a dark broth seasoned with ganja leaves) for many years now.

Western Food The amazing *JJ Bakery*, on the corner of Moon Meuang and Ratchadamnoen Rds, offers a very diverse menu of Western, Thai and Chinese dishes. JJ has very good coffee, inexpensive cocktails, and a great selection of pies, cakes, croissants and cookies – a personal fave is the toddy palm pie. JJ Coffeeshop has a new branch at Chiang Inn Plaza, off Chang Klan Rd near the Night Bazaar.

English and American-style breakfasts are also good at the *Library Service* on Soi 2. For something European in the morning, try *Croissant*, next to Wat Jetawan on Tha Phae Rd. Besides its namesake, the cafe has a variety of other breakfast pastries, plus full lunch and dinner menus and free nightly videos.

Yet another hotspot for Western breakfasts is the mellow *Kafé* at 127-129 Moon Meuang (at Soi 5 near Somphet Market); in addition to breakfasts, the menu here features decent Thai, Chinese and European food at very good prices. The slightly more expensive *Crusty Loaf Bakery & Restaurant* offers baked goods, good coffee, yoghurt, muesli, sandwiches, pasta, ice cream, some Thai food, fruit and vegetable juices and a two-for-one paperback swap. The homey indoor section is decorated with Irish kitsch and there's pleasant garden seating out the back.

The *American Restaurant & Bar* on Tha Phae Rd near the Roong Ruang Hotel, specialises in pizza, burgers and Tex-Mex; for the latter the Yank-supervised cooks grind locally grown corn to make the necessary tortillas.

The Pub, 88 Huay Kaew Rd, is one of the oldest restaurants in Chiang Mai serving European food. It is not cheap, but *Newsweek* magazine did name it 'one of the world's best bars' in 1986; beer on tap is served.

The clean and friendly *Dara Steak Shop*, adjacent to Queen Bee Car Rental and the Muang Thong Hotel on the corner of Moon Meuang and Ratchamankha Rds, has an extensive Thai and Western menu. The chef once cooked for farangs on an offshore oil platform in Songkhla.

Two Italian places worth trying include the luxurious *Piccola Roma* (☎ 271256) at 3/2-3 Charoen Prathet Rd and the more casual *Bacco* (☎ 251289) at 158 Tha Phae Rd. Both are operated by Italian expats and serve reasonably authentic Italian food.

Popular among German expats and visitors are the *Bierstube* at 33/6 Moon Meuang Rd (near Tha Phae Gate) and *Haus München* at 115/3 Loi Khraw Rd (opposite the Novotel in the night bazaar area).

The main fast-food district in Chiang Mai runs along Chang Klan Rd, just north of the Night Bazaar area. This strip now features *Swensen's Ice Cream, Pizza Hut, KFC, Seven-Eleven, Mister Donut, Baskin Robbins* and other culinary exotica from the West. Similar franchise-style places can be found in the new Kad Suan Kaew shopping centre on Huay Kaew Rd.

Vegetarian Food Chiang Mai is blessed with several vegetarian restaurants. One of the most popular with travellers is the *Vegetarian Food* (formerly AUM), on Moon Meuang Rd near Tha Phae Gate. The all-veggie menu features a varied list of traditional Thai and Chinese dishes, including northern and north-eastern Thai dishes, prepared without meat or eggs. There is an upstairs eating area with cushions on the floor and low tables. It is open Tuesday to Sunday from 9 am to 2 pm and 5 to 9 pm.

On Soi 1 Intharawarorot Rd near Suthasinee Khao Soi and Wat Phra Singh is another good Thai vegetarian place. The cooks put out 15 to 20 pots of fresh vegetarian dishes daily between 8 am and early afternoon (till everything's sold). The dishes feature lots of bean curd, squash, peas, pineapples, sprouts and potato, etc and the desserts are good.

Out along Si Donchai Rd, past the Chang Klan Rd intersection, is the *Whole Earth Vegetarian Restaurant* in a transcendental meditation centre. The food is Thai and

Indian and the atmosphere is suitably mellow, although the food may be a bit over-priced. *The Cafeteria* at 27-29 Chang Klan also serves Arabic and Indian food in vegetarian variations.

Other veggie spots include the large *Vegetarian Group Restaurant* (no English sign) at 42 Mahidon Rd in amphoe Suthep and *Mama* at 1/9-10 Si Donchai Rd.

Garden Restaurants If you like garden restaurants *(sŭan aahăan)*, Chiang Mai has plenty. Several are along Highway 11 near Wat Jet Yot and the National Museum. The food can be very good, but it is the *banyaakàat* (atmosphere) that is most prized by Thais.

Inside the moat, one of the city's oldest is *Suan Aahaan Chiang Mai*, on Phra Pokklao Rd between Ratchadamnoen and Ratchamankha Rds. *Ta-Krite (Ta-Khrai)*, on the soi that runs along the south side of Wat Phra Singh, is a nice indoor-outdoor place with ironwork chairs in a garden setting. The kitchen focuses on central Thai food for the most part, and prices are very reasonable. Náam phrík is a house speciality, along with *khâo tang nâa tâng* (sticky rice with meat, shrimp and coconut). It's open daily from 11 am to 11 pm; there are at least four other Ta-Krite branches around town.

Food Centres A new food centre on the 3rd floor of the Kad Suan Kaew shopping centre on Huay Kaew Rd gathers together vendors selling all kinds of Thai and Chinese dishes at reasonable prices. *Galare Food Centre*, opposite the main night bazaar building on Chang Klan Rd, is also good; free Thai classical dancing is featured on some evenings.

Entertainment
Live Music Anybody who's anybody makes the scene at the Riverside Rim Ping, a restaurant-cafe on Charoenrat Rd, on the Ping River. It has good food, fruit shakes, cocktails and live music nightly. It's usually packed with both farangs and Thais on weekends, so arrive early to get a table on the outdoor verandah overlooking the river.

A few doors north of the Rim Ping at 37 Charoenrat Rd, The Brasserie has become a favourite late night spot (11.15 pm to 2 am) to listen to a talented Thai guitarist named Took play energetic versions of Pink Floyd, Hendrix, Cream, Dylan and other 1960s gems.

Next to Buak Hat Park on Bamrungburi Rd, the Hill & Bamboo Hut has a large beer garden with live music nightly – a mix of folk and Thai pop. It's worth a visit just to check out this rambling, multilevel wood and thatch complex – it feels like a huge tree house.

Old West, near the north-west corner of the old city on Mani Nopharat Rd (west of Tantrapan department store), is decorated in the typical old-west style found in similar pubs throughout Thailand; most nights a live folk or country band plays after 9 pm. The Smiling Monkey Pub, at 40 Bamrungburi Rd (near Chiang Mai Gate), is popular with Thai students and features good Thai food and live music nightly in a garden setting.

The Arcade, in a former roller rink at the Chiang Mai Arcade bus terminal, is mostly a Thai scene featuring taxi dancing (with paid female dancing partners) to live Thai pop. Couples are welcome – it's not as sleazy as it sounds.

Jazz fans have a choice of several local spots along Huay Kaew Rd. At the new Baritone Pub & Restaurant (☎ 224444, ext 10026) in the Kad Suan Kaew shopping centre on Huay Kaew Rd, the Jazzliners perform nightly, led by a guitarist who graduated from Berklee College of Music in Boston. Other jazz clubs on Huay Kaew Rd include The Level, Marvel and Marble Pub.

Discos All the flashy hotels have discos with high-tech recorded music. Currently the hottest in town are Crystal Cave (Empress Hotel), The Wall (Chiang Inn) and Bubbles (Porn Ping Tower Hotel). The cover charge at each is 90B, which includes one drink. The biggest disco in town is the new Star Wars-style Biosphere Spaceadrome off Charoen Meuang Rd near the train station. Admission is 80B and includes a drink.

All Chiang Mai discos are legally required to close at 2 am, although the Spaceadrome sometimes stays open later.

Bars Along Moon Meuang Rd, between Ratchadamnoen Rd and Soi 3, are a string of small bars with low-volume music that are good for a quiet drink. The Pinte Blues Pub, at 33/6 Moon Meuang Rd, serves espresso and beer, and plays all prerecorded blues. The Bierstube features German grub and beer, while the Cozy Corner and Black Cat Bar are pretty featureless except that an inordinate number of Thai women seem to hang about. Domino has good food, draft beer, videos and is the local Hash House Harriers hang-out. The Blues Pub and Domino are the only bars in Tha Phae Gate vicinity where you generally see couples or farang women.

The Hard Rock Cafe (no legal relation to the worldwide chain), off Kotchasan Rd near Tha Phae Gate, is decorated with old LP covers and contains a pool table. Owned by Roxanna Brown, journalist and author of *Ceramics of Southeast Asia*, the bar features a good selection of rock music tapes – the house mix is even sold on cassette in six volumes.

Chiang Mai has several gay men's bars, including the relaxed Coffee Boy Bar in a 70-year-old teak house at 248 Thung Hotel Rd, not far from the Arcade Bus Terminal. On weekends there's a cabaret show. The Butterfly Room is more centrally located at 126 Loi Khraw Rd near the night bazaar.

Things to Buy

Hundreds of shops all over Chiang Mai sell hill-tribe and northern Thai craftwork, but a lot of it is commercial and touristy junk churned out for the undiscerning. So bargain hard and buy carefully! The nonprofit outlets often have the best quality, and although the prices are sometimes a bit higher than at the night bazaar, a higher percentage of your money goes directly to the hill-tribe artisans. Thai Tribal Crafts (☎ 241043) at 208 Bamrungrat Rd, near the McCormick Hospital, is run by two church groups on a nonprofit basis and has a good selection of quality handicrafts. The YMCA International Hotel also operates a nonprofit handicrafts centre.

The two commercial markets with the widest selections of northern Thai folk crafts are Warorot Market at the eastern end of Chang Moi Kao Rd and the night bazaar off Chang Klan Rd. Warorot (also locally called Kaat Luang) is the oldest market in Chiang Mai. A former royal cremation grounds, it has been a marketplace site since the reign of Chao Inthawararot (1870-97). Although the huge enclosure is quite dilapidated (the escalator and lifts don't work any more), it's an especially good market for fabrics.

In the vicinity of the night bazaar stalls are a couple of dozen permanent shops selling antiques, handicrafts, rattan and hardwood furniture, textiles, jewellery, pottery, basketry, silverwork, woodcarving and other items of local manufacture. One shop that seems to have it all (except jewellery) is the long-running Chiangmai Banyen (☎ 274007) at 201/1 Wualai Rd, south of the Old Chiang Mai Cultural Centre.

As Chiang Mai is Thailand's main handicraft centre, it's ringed by small cottage factories and workshops where you can watch craftspeople at work. In general, though, merchandise you see at factories outside the city will cost more than it would in Chiang Mai unless you're buying in bulk.

Cotton & Silk Very attractive lengths of material can be made into all sorts of things. Thai silk, with its lush colours and pleasantly rough texture, is a particularly good bargain and is usually cheaper here than in Bangkok. Warorot Market is one of the best and least expensive places to look for fabrics, but take care as many items said to be silk are actually polyester.

Several individual shops in town focus on high-quality traditional (sometimes antique) Thai and Lao fabrics, sold by the metre or made up into original-design clothes. A list of the best places in town would have to include royally patronised Duangjit House and Nandakwang, both in a strip of shops opposite the Amari Hotel. Naenna Studio, nearby on Soi 9, off Nimanhaemin Rd, is operated by Patricia Cheeseman, an expert on Thai-Lao textiles who has written extensively on the subject.

The Loom, at 27 Ratchamankha Rd near Soi 3, carries very fine fabrics from north and north-east Thailand, Laos and Cambodia.

If you want to see where and how the cloth is made, go to the nearby town of San Kamphaeng for Thai silk or to Pasang, south of Lamphun, for cotton.

Ceramics Thai Celadon, about six km north of Chiang Mai, turns out ceramics modelled on the Sawankhalok pottery that used to be made hundreds of years ago at Sukhothai and exported all over the region. With their deep, cracked, glazed finish some pieces are very beautiful and prices are often lower than in Bangkok. The factory is closed on Sunday.

The reliable Mengrai Kilns (☎ 241802) has recently moved operations to 31/1 Rat Uthit Rd in the south-west corner of the inner moat area near Buak Hat Park. Other ceramic stores can be found close to the Old Chiang Mai Cultural Centre.

There are also several celadon operations in the nearby town of Hang Dong.

Woodcarving Many types of carvings are available, including countless elephants – but who wants a half-size wooden elephant anyway? Teak salad bowls are good and very cheap. Many shops along Tha Phae Rd and in the vicinity of the night bazaar stock wood crafts.

Antiques You'll see lots of these around, including opium weights (the little animal-shaped weights supposedly used to measure opium in the Golden Triangle). Check prices in Bangkok first, as Chiang Mai's shops are not always cheap. Also remember that worldwide there are a lot more instant antiques than authentic ones. The night bazaar area is probably the best place to look for fake antiques.

For the real thing, visit the many stores along Tha Phae Rd and along Loi Khraw Rd.

Lacquerware Decorated plates, containers, utensils and other items are made by building up layers of lacquer over a wooden or woven bamboo base. Burmese lacquerware, smuggled into the north, can often be seen, especially at Mae Sai. There are several lacquerware factories in San Kamphaeng.

Silverwork There are several silverwork shops on Wualai Rd close to Chiang Mai Gate. Hill-tribe jewellery, which is heavy, chunky stuff, is very nice.

Clothes All sorts of shirts, blouses and dresses, plain and embroidered, are available at very low prices, but check the quality carefully. The night bazaar and stores along Tha Phae and Loi Khraw Rds have good selections. See also the Cotton & Silk section above.

Umbrellas At Baw Sang, the umbrella village, you'll find beautiful hand-painted paper umbrellas. You can also buy very attractive framed leaf paintings from here.

Department Stores Chiang Mai had 15 shopping centres with department stores at last count. Tantrapan, the city's first, now has three branches, one on Tha Phae Rd opposite Huang Men Rd, one near the airport and one on Mani Nopharat Rd outside the north-eastern corner of the old city. Tantrapan stocks a wide selection of ready-made clothing, electrical appliances, toiletries, stationery, and other typical department-store items; each store also has a supermarket on one floor.

The newer Kad Suan Kaew shopping centre on Huay Kaew Rd is centred around a branch of Bangkok's Central department store. There are several other up-market shops in the complex.

Getting There & Away

Air Chiang Mai International Airport lands regularly scheduled flights from eight other cities in Thailand as well as Hong Kong and Taipei. Bangkok Airways has flights to Bagan and Mandalay; in the near future, airlines serving Chiang Mai plan to initiate air connections with Kunming (China) and Vientiane (Laos) as well.

The THAI office (☎ 211541) is within the city moat area at 240 Phra Pokklao Rd, behind Wat Chiang Man. THAI has several daily one-hour flights between Bangkok and Chiang Mai. The fare is 1650B coach or 1950B for business class.

Airfares between Chiang Mai and other Thai cities are:

City	Fare
Chiang Rai	420B
Mae Hong Son	345B
Nan	510B
Mae Sot	590B
Phitsanulok	650B
Tak	765B
Phuket	3455B

Bus From Bangkok's northern bus terminal there are seven ordinary buses daily to Chiang Mai, departing from 5.30 am to 10.30 pm. The 12-hour trip costs 161B via Nakhon Sawan and 164B via Ayuthaya. Seven 1st-class air-con buses leave the adjacent air-con terminal between 8.50 and 10 am and eight buses leave from 8 to 9.45 pm. These buses cost 304B one-way and take from 10 to 11 hours depending on traffic. The public buses from the northern bus terminal are generally more reliable and on schedule than the private ones booked in Banglamphu, etc.

Ten or more private tour companies run air-con buses between Bangkok and Chiang Mai, departing from various points throughout both cities. Return tickets are always somewhat cheaper than one-way tickets. Fares range from 180 to 320B depending on the bus. VIP buses are the most expensive as these have fewer seats per coach to allow for reclining positions; the typical VIP fare is 470B. Similar buses can be booked in the Soi Ngam Duphli area of Bangkok and near the Indra Hotel in Pratunam. The more reliable companies include Setthee (☎ (02) 278-5660), Ambassador (☎ (02) 271-4879), Siam Express (☎ (02) 270-1308), Phumin (☎ (02) 271-2990), Chaiyasit (☎ (02) 279-

1473), Thaworn Farm (☎ (02) 278-4155), Poy Luang (☎ (02) 252-0221) and Sombat (☎ (02) 271-3005).

Several Khao San Rd agencies offer bus tickets to Chiang Mai for as low as 120 to 180B, including a night's free stay at a guesthouse in Chiang Mai. Sometimes this works out well, but the buses can be substandard and the 'free' guesthouse may charge you 40B for electricity or hot water, or apply heavy pressure for you to sign up for one of its treks before you can get a room. Besides, riding in a bus stuffed full of farangs and their bulky backpacks is not the most cultural experience.

The only advantage of the private buses is that they pick you up from where you booked your ticket (supposedly this is legal only for tour operators). If you don't have a lot of baggage it's probably better to leave from the Mo Chit government bus terminal.

Public buses between Chiang Mai and other towns in the north and north-east have frequent departures throughout the day (at least hourly), except for the Mae Sai, Khon Kaen, Udon and Khorat buses which have morning and evening departures only. Here are some fares and trip durations:

City	Fare	Duration
Chiang Khong	91B	6½ hours
Chiang Rai	57B	4 hours
(air-con)	79B	3 hours
(1st class)	102B	3 hours
Chiang Saen	73B	4½ hours
(air-con)	130B	3½ hours
Fang*	40B	3½ hours
Khon Kaen	192B	12 hours
(air-con, Highway 12)	268B	12 hours
(air-con, Highway 11)	307B	11 hours
Khorat	180B	12 hours
(air-con)	262B	11 hours
(1st class air-con)	324B	11 hours
Lampang	29B	2 hours
Lamphun*	7B	½ hour
(air-con)	50B	1 hour
Mae Hong Son		
(Route 108)	105B	8 hours
(Routes 107 & 1095)	90B	7 hours
(air-con)	206B	8 hours
Mae Sai	71B	5 hours
(air-con)	127B	4 hours
Mae Sariang	50B	4-5 hours

Mae Sot	96B	6½ hours
(air-con)	172B *	6 hours
Nan	83B	7 hours
(air-con)	115B	6 hours
(1st class air-con)	148B	6 hours
Pai	45B	4 hours
Pasang*	10B	45 minutes
Phayao	51B	3 hours
Phrae	55B	4 hours
(air-con)	76B	3½ hours
(1st class air-con)	98B	3½ hours
Phetchabun (air-con)	235B	8 hours
Phitsanulok	86B	5-6 hours
(air-con)	128B	5 hours
(1st class air-con)	165B	5 hours
Tak	57B	4 hours
(air-con)	82B	4 hours
Tha Ton*	50B	4 hours

* leaves from White Elephant (Chang Pheuak) bus station, Chotana Rd. All other buses leave from the Chiang Mai Arcade bus station (also called New Station) off Kaew Nawarat Rd.

For buses to destinations within Chiang Mai Province use the Chang Pheuak station, while for buses outside the province use the Chiang Mai Arcade station. City bus No 3 (yellow) goes to the Chiang Mai Arcade station; bus No 2 (yellow) goes to the Chang Pheuak terminal.

Train Chiang Mai-bound express trains leave Bangkok's Hualamphong station daily at 8.10 am (1st and 2nd class), 6 pm (2nd class only) and 7.40 pm (1st and 2nd class), arriving in Chiang Mai at 7 pm, 7.25 am and 8.05 am.

Rapid trains leave at 6.40 am, 3 pm (air-con 2nd class) and 10 pm (no air-con), arriving at 7.45 pm, 5.15 am and 11.55 am respectively. Third-class fares (121B) are available only on the No 189 departure, which leaves Bangkok at 4.20 am, changes to train Nos 95 and 103, and crawls into the Chiang Mai station 16 hours later.

The basic 2nd-class fare is 255B, excluding either the special express (50B), express (30B) or rapid (20B) surcharges. Add 70B for an upper berth and 100B for a lower berth in a 2nd-class sleeping car (100 and 150B respectively on the special express). For air-

con 2nd class, add 50B per ticket for ordinary cars and 100B for sleepers. For example, if you take a 2nd-class upper berth on a rapid train, your total fare will be 345B (255+-70+20B).

The basic 1st-class fare is 537B; berths are 150B per person in a double cabin, 350B in a single and are available only on the special express only.

Trains leave Lopburi for Chiang Mai at 9.03 am (rapid), 5.28 pm (rapid, air-con 2nd class), 8.24 pm (express, air-con 2nd class) and 12.26 am (rapid, no air-con), arriving at the times listed for the same trains from Bangkok. Fares are 245B 2nd class, 130B 3rd class express and 10B less for the rapid.

Berths on sleepers to Chiang Mai are increasingly hard to reserve without booking well in advance. Tour groups sometimes book entire cars. The return trip from Chiang Mai to Bangkok doesn't seem to be as difficult, except during the Songkran (mid-April) and Chinese New Year (February) holiday periods.

The Chiang Mai train station's cloakroom has a left-luggage facility that is open from 6 am to 6 pm daily. The cost is 5B per piece for the first five days and 10B per piece thereafter. The booking office has a computerised reservation system through which you can book train seats for anywhere in Thailand.

City bus Nos 1, 3 and 6 stop in front of the train station.

Getting Around
To/From Chiang Mai International Airport

From the airport to the city you have a choice of standard airport taxi for 70B or the THAI van for 40B. The airport is only two or three km from the city centre. The red bus No 6 goes to the airport but you must catch it somewhere on the Highway 11 loop. You can get a taxi from the centre of Chiang Mai to the airport for less than 50B, although a songthaew would be less again.

The tidy little airport has currency exchange counters, a post office, an international (IDD and Home Direct) phone office

NORTHERN THAILAND

(open from 8.30 am to 8 pm), a tourist information counter, two snack bars (one under the trees by the car park, the other in the arrival area), a bar in an old air force transport aircraft, a THAI-operated restaurant (departure level) and a duty-free shop (departure level).

Bus City buses operate from 6 am to 6 pm and cost 2B in town, up to 6B for the highway loop. Nos 1, 2 and 3 (yellow) cover the whole city, No 5 (red) does a loop around the moat and No 6 (red) goes around the highway loop. Air-con versions of Nos 1, 2 and 3 are less frequent and cost 5B.

Songthaew & Samlor Songthaews go anywhere on their route for 5B. You can also charter a samlor anywhere in the city for 50B or less.

Samlors cost between 10 and 15B for most trips.

Car Rental Cars, jeeps and minivans are readily available at several locations throughout the city. Be sure that the vehicle you rent has insurance (liability) coverage – ask to see the documents and carry a photocopy with you while driving.

Two of the best agencies in town for service and price are Queen Bee (☎ 275525; fax 274349), adjacent to Muang Thong Hotel on Moon Meuang Rd, and North Wheels (☎ 216189, 279554; fax 221709) at 127/2 Moon Meuang Rd near Somphet Market. Both offer hotel pickup and delivery as well as 24-hour emergency road service; North Wheel's rates include insurance, while Queen Bee charges extra for insurance. Sample rentals at North Wheels include Suzuki Caribians for 800B per 24-hour day, 4900B weekly or 18,000B monthly; or a Toyota Mighty-X 4WD for 1800B per day, 11,000B weekly, 30,000B month. At Queen Bee Suzuki Caribians cost 900B per 24-hour day in high season, 700B in low season; other available vehicles include Toyota minivans and Toyota Coronas.

By comparison, Hertz and Avis charge 1200B per day for a Caribian – plus 12%

VAT, plus 150B collision damage waiver and 100B personal accident insurance. This works out to 1594B per day; a three-day minimum rental is required.

Other prominent rental agencies include:

Avis
    14/14 Huay Kaew Rd (☎ 221316)
    Chiang Mai International Airport (☎ 222013)
Erawan PUC
    211/14-15 Chang Klan Rd (☎ 274212; fax 276548)
Hertz
    Diamond Riverside Hotel (☎ 270080)
    Empress Hotel (☎ 270240)
    Chiangmai Plaza Hotel (270040)
North Wheels
    127/2 Moon Meuang Rd (☎ 216189; fax 221709)
PD Express
    138/4 Phra Pokklao Rd (☎ 277876)
Queen Bee
    5 Moon Meuang Rd (☎ 275525; fax 274349)
Chiang Mai MK
    61 Moon Meuang Rd (☎ 270961)

Motorbike These can be rented for 80 to 150B (100cc Honda Dream step-throughs) or 200 to 250B (125 to 150cc Hondas or Yamahas) per day, depending on the size of the motorbike and the length of rental. Prices are very competitive in Chiang Mai because there's a real glut of motorcycles. For two people, it's cheaper to rent a small motorcycle for the day to visit Doi Suthep than to go up and back on a songthaew.

Two of the more reliable places to rent motorcycles for long-distance touring are CS Motorcycle Hire (127/2 Moon Meuang Rd, ☎ 219160) and Hard Rock Bike (6 Kotchasan Rd Soi 1, ☎ 212550). Also popular are Pop (51 Kotchasan Rd on the moat, ☎ 276014) and Queen Bee (5 Moon Meuang Rd, ☎ 274349). These agencies offer motorcycle insurance for 50B per day, not a bad investment considering you could face a 25,000B liability if your bike is stolen. Most policies have a deductible (excess) of 300 to 1000B; so in cases of theft, you're usually responsible for a third to half of the bike's value – even with insurance.

Chiang Mai Motorcycle Touring Club (☎ 210518) at 21/1 Ratchamankha Rd Soi 2

NORTHERN THAILAND

has several well-maintained, larger motor-cycles for rent. The models vary from season to season but at last pass they included a Honda XL600 (550B a day), Honda AX-1 250 (500B), Honda XL 250 (380B), Honda XR 250 (400B) and Honda Wing 175 (bored engine, 175B per day or 1050B per week). The CMMTC also rents helmets, gloves and jackets, leads occasional group bike tours and is the best source of information on northern Thailand bike touring in Chiang Mai.

JK Big Bike on Chaiyaphum Rd next to the Soi 2 entrance rents Honda XL 250s for 350B a day; bigger bikes are available as well. Several car-rental places also rent motorcycles.

Bicycle This is by far the best way to get around Chiang Mai. The city is small enough so that everywhere is accessible by bike, including Chiang Mai University, Wat U Mong, Wat Suan Dawk and the National Museum on the outskirts of town.

Bicycles can be rented for between 20 and 30B per day from several of the guesthouses or from various places along the east moat.

AROUND CHIANG MAI
Doi Suthep

คอยสุเทพ

Sixteen km north-west of Chiang Mai is Doi Suthep, a 1601-metre peak named after the hermit Sudeva, who lived on the mountain's slopes for many years. Near its summit is **Wat Phra That Doi Suthep**, first established in 1383 under King Keu Na. A naga staircase of 300 steps leads to the wat at the end of the winding road up the mountain. If the climb seems too much of a chore, you can take a short tram ride from the parking lot to the wat grounds for 5B. At the top, weather permitting, there are some fine aerial views of Chiang Mai. Inside the cloister is an intriguing copper-plated chedi topped by a five-tier gold umbrella.

About four km beyond Wat Phra That is **Phra Tamnak Phu Phing**, a winter palace for the royal family, the gardens of which are open on weekends and holidays. The road that passes Phu Phing Palace splits off to the left, stopping at the peak of Doi Pui. From there a dirt road proceeds for two or three km to a nearby Hmong hill-tribe village. If you won't have an opportunity to visit more remote villages, it's worth visiting this one, even though it is very well touristed. Some Hmong handiwork can be purchased, and traditional homes and costumes can be seen, although these are mostly posed situations. 'Everyone knows some English,' wrote one visitor, such as 'you buy', 'money' and 'I'll have no profit'.

If you're cycling or driving to the summit, you can stop off along the way at **Monthathon Falls**, which is 2.5 km off the paved road to Doi Suthep. Pools beneath the falls hold water all year round, though swimming is best during or just after the annual monsoon.

Doi Suthep/Doi Pui National Park Most visitors do a quick tour of the temple, the touristy Hmong village and perhaps the winter palace grounds, altogether missing the surrounding park. This 261-sq-km preserve is home to more than 300 bird species and nearly 2000 species of ferns and flowering plants. Because of its proximity to urban Chiang Mai, development of the park has become a very sensitive issue. The west side of the park has been severely disturbed by poachers and land encroachers, including around 500 hill-tribe families. In 1986 a Bangkok company tried to establish a lengthy cable-car system through the park to the temple, but protests, petitions and marches by the newly formed Group for Chiang Mai (Chomrom Pheua Chiang Mai) stopped the plan.

There are extensive hiking trails in the park, including one that climbs 1685-metre Doi Pui; the summit is a favourite picnic spot. Other trails pass Hmong villages that rarely get farang visitors. Bungalow and dormitory accommodation is available near the park headquarters (past the temple car park on the right).

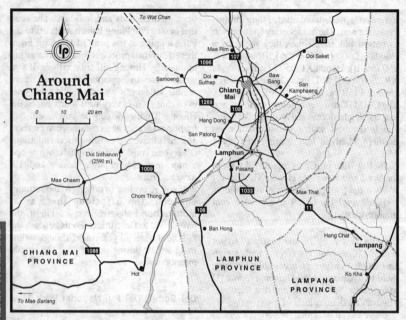

Around Chiang Mai

0   10   20 km

NORTHERN THAILAND

Getting There & Away Songthaews to Doi Suthep leave Chiang Mai throughout the day from the west end of Huay Kaew Rd in front of Chiang Mai University. The fare is 30B up, 20B down. To Phu Phing Palace add 10B and to Doi Pui add 20B in each direction.

Baw Sang

บ่อสร้าง

Baw Sang, nine km east of Chiang Mai on Route 1006, is usually called the umbrella village because of its many umbrella manufacturers. Practically the entire village consists of craft shops selling painted umbrellas, fans, silverware, straw handiwork, bamboo and teak, statuary, china, celadon and lacquerware, along with very tacky Chiang Mai and northern Thai souvenirs, as well as quality items.

The larger shops can arrange overseas shipping at reasonable rates. As in Chiang Mai's night bazaar, discounts are offered for quantity purchases. Some of the places will also pack and post parasols, apparently quite reliably.

San Kamphaeng

สันกำแพง

Four or five km farther down Route 1006 is San Kamphaeng, which flourishes on cotton and silk weaving. Stores offering finished products line the main street, although the actual weaving is done in small factories down side streets. There are some deals to be had here, especially in silk. For cotton, you'd probably do better in Pasang, a lesser known village near Lamphun, although you may see shirt styles here not available in Pasang. A cotton shirt or blouse can cost between 60 and 250B.

Getting There & Away Buses to Baw Sang (sometimes spelled Bo Sang or Bor Sang) and San Kamphaeng leave Chiang Mai frequently during the day from the north side of Charoen Meuang Rd, east of the Ping River. The bus stop is towards the GPO and the train station and across from Sanpakhoi Market. The fare is 5B to Baw Sang and 6B to San Kamphaeng.

Hang Dong

หางดง

Thirteen km south of Chiang Mai on Route 108 is Hang Dong, well known for ceramics, woodcarving and antiques. Many of the shops here deal in wholesale as well as retail, so prices are low. Catch a bus from Chiang Mai Gate to Hang Dong (12B fare). Most of the shops are actually about two km before Hang Dong.

Mae Sa & Samoeng

This forested loop north-west of Chiang Mai via Mae Rim and/or Hang Dong makes a good day or overnight trip. Although dotted with tourist developments – resorts, orchid farms, butterfly parks, elephant camps, snake farms, botanical gardens, antique and handicraft shops – the Route 1096/1269 loop through the Mae Sa Valley is very scenic in spots. **Mae Sa Falls** is only six km from the Mae Rim turnoff from Route 107, which in turn is 12 km north of Chiang Mai. Farther along the loop are several Hmong villages.

There are at least four places along the loop which call themselves elephant 'camp', 'farm' or 'village'. Best of the bunch is the **Mae Sa Elephant Camp** near Mae Sa Falls, where it costs 40B per person for the one-hour elephant show at 9.30 am daily, or 40B per person to ride an elephant any time throughout the day.

Samoeng, at the westernmost extension of the loop (35 km from Mae Rim), is the most peaceful area for an overnight stay, since it's five km north of the main loop junction between the highways to/from Mae Rim and Hang Dong via Route 1269. The *Samoeng Resort*, about 1.5 km outside Samoeng village itself, has quiet, well-designed bungalows from 300B for rooms with fan, more for air-con.

Getting There & Away You can get a songthaew to Samoeng from the Chang Pheuak bus station in Chiang Mai for 14B.

Since it's paved all the way, the winding loop road makes a good ride by bicycle or motorcycle. From Samoeng you can take a north-west detour along Route 1265 to Route 1095 for Pai and Mae Hong Son; the 158-km road (136 km unpaved, 12.2 km paved) breaks north at the Karen village of Wat Chan, where fuel is available. According to motorbike expert David Unkovich, this is the longest unpaved road stretch in northern Thailand and is recommended for experienced off-highway bikers only (and only in the dry season). The road passes a few Hmong and Karen villages.

CHOM THONG AREA

จอมทอง

Chom Thong (pronounced 'jawm thawng') is a necessary stop between Chiang Mai and Doi Inthanon, Thailand's highest peak.

Wat Phra That Si Chom Thong

วัดพระธาตุศรีจอมทอง

If you have time, walk down Chom Thong's main street to Wat Phra That Si Chom Thong. The gilded Burmese chedi in the compound was built in 1451 and the Burmese-style bot, built in 1516, is one of the most beautiful in northern Thailand. Inside and out it is an integrated work of art that deserves admiration; it is well cared for by the local Thais. Fine woodcarving can be seen along the eaves of the roof and inside on the ceiling, which is supported by massive teak columns. The impressive altar is designed like a small prasat (temple) in typical Lanna style and is said to contain a relic of the right side of the Buddha's skull. The abbot is a very serene old man, soft-spoken and radiant.

Behind the prasat-altar is a room containing religious antiques. More interesting is a glass case along one wall of the bot which contains ancient Thai weaponry – a little out of place in a wat, maybe.

Wat Phra Nawn Yai

วัดพระนอนใหญ่

About halfway between Chiang Mai and Chom Thong, off the highway, you may see Wat Phra Nawn Yai (on the right heading towards Chom Thong), with its distinctive Disney-like Buddha figures (standing, sitting and reclining), as well as sculptured scenes from selected Jatakas. The statuary is incredibly garish and cartoonish – good for a giggle.

Doi Inthanon National Park

อุทยานแห่งชาติดอยอินทนนท์

Doi Inthanon, Thailand's highest peak (2595 metres), has three impressive waterfalls cascading down its slopes. Starting from the bottom, these are **Mae Klang Falls**, **Wachiratan Falls** and **Siriphum Falls**. The first two have picnic areas and food vendors nearby. Mae Klang is the largest waterfall and the easiest to get to; you must stop there to get a bus to the top of Doi Inthanon. Mae Klang Falls can be climbed nearly to the top, as there is a footbridge leading to massive rock formations over which the water falls. Wachiratan is also very nice and less crowded.

The views from Inthanon are best in the cool dry season from November to February. You can expect the air to be quite chilly towards the top, so bring a jacket or sweater. For most of the year a mist, formed by the condensation of warm humid air below, hangs around the highest peak. Along the 47-km road to the top are many terraced rice fields, tremendous valleys and a few small hill-tribe villages. Around 4000 Hmong and Karen tribespeople make the mountain slopes their home.

The entire mountain is a national park, despite agriculture and human habitation. One of the top destinations for South-East Asia naturalists and bird-watchers, the mist-shrouded upper slopes produce a bumper crops of orchids, lichens, mosses and epiphytes while supporting nearly 400 bird varieties, more than any other habitat in Thailand. The mountain is also one of the last habitats of the Asiatic black bear, along with Assamese macaque, Phayre's leaf-monkey, and a selection of other rare and not-so-rare monkeys and gibbons, plus the more common Indian civet, barking deer and giant flying squirrel – around 75 mammalian species in all.

Phra Mahathat Naphamethanidon, a chedi built by the Royal Thai Air Force to commemorate the King's 60th birthday in 1989, is off the highway between Km 41 and 42, about four km before reaching the summit. In the base of the octagonal chedi is a hall containing a green stone Buddha image.

A 3B admission is collected for Mae Klang Falls near the foot of mountain. At the park headquarters, 31 km from Chom Thong, you can book park bungalows for 100B per person or tents for 40B. Blankets may be hired for 10B each.

Getting There & Away

Buses to Chom Thong leave regularly from just inside the Chiang Mai Gate at the south moat in Chiang Mai. Some buses go directly to Mae Klang Falls and some terminate in Hot, although the latter will let you off in Chom Thong. The fare to Chom Thong, 58 km away, is 15B.

From Chom Thong there are regular songthaews to Mae Klang, about eight km north, for 10B. Songthaews from Mae Klang to Doi Inthanon leave almost hourly until late afternoon and cost 25 to 30B per person. Most of the passengers are locals who get off at various points along the road up, thus allowing a few stationary views of the valleys below. If you're travelling by private vehicle, you'll have to pay a toll of 20B per car or 5B per motorcycle at the park entrance.

For another 12B you can go from Chom Thong to Hot, where you can get buses on to Mae Sariang or Mae Hong Son. However, if you've gone to Doi Inthanon and the waterfalls, you probably won't have time to make it all the way to Mae Sariang or Mae Hong Son in one day, so you may want to stay overnight in the park or in Chom Thong.

Forestry Service bungalows near the park headquarters (past the Chom Thong park entrance) cost from 300 to 1000B per night. In Chom Thong, enquire at the wat for a place to sleep.

NORTH TO THA TON
Mae Taeng & Chiang Dao

เชียงดาว

The mountainous area around Mae Taeng – especially south-west of the junction of Routes 107 and 1095 – has become a major trekking area because of the variety of Lisu, Lahu, Karen and Hmong villages in the region. Rafting along the Mae Taeng River is now so popular that a permanent rafting centre, Maetaman Rafting, has been established west of Route 107. For the most part, the centre handles groups on trips out of Chiang Mai.

The **Elephant Training Center Taeng-Dao**, off Route 107 between Mae Taeng and Chiang Dao, is one of several in the area that puts on elephant shows for tourists. If you haven't seen the one in Lampang Province (Thung Kwian), this one's a reasonable alternative.

Fang Dao Forest Monastery, off the highway south of Chiang Dao near Km 52, is a meditation wat in the north-eastern forest tradition.

Tham Chiang Dao The main attraction along the way to Fang and Tha Ton is this cave complex five km west of Route 107 and 72 km north of Chiang Mai. The complex is said to extend some 10 to 14 km into 2175-metre Doi Chiang Dao; the interconnected caverns which are open to the public include Tham Maa (7365 metres long), Tham Kaew (477 metres), Tham Phra Nawn (360 metres), Tham Seua Dao (540 metres) and Tham Naam (660 metres). Tham Phra Nawn and Tham Seua Dao contain religious statuary and are electrically illuminated (and thus easily explored on one's own) while Tham Maa, Tham Kaew and Tham Naam have no light fixtures. A lantern and guide can be hired for 20B per cavern or 60B for all three.

Interior cave formations are quite spectacular in places – over 100 of them are named.

Admission to the overall complex is 5B. There is a wat complex outside the cavern and a collection of vendors selling roots, herbs and snacks (mostly noodles). Beyond Tham Chiang Dao along the same rural road is a smaller sacred cave called **Tham Pha Plong**.

Places to Stay *Traveller Inn Hotel*, on the highway in Mae Taeng, is a well-run place with rooms in the 300 to 400B range. An old wooden hotel in Chiang Dao village, the *Pieng Dao*, has rooms for 80B.

Chiang Dao Hill Resort (☎ 236995), off the highway between Km 100 and 101, offers good tourist bungalows for 700B up. The *Royal Ping Garden Resort*, off the highway south of Chiang Dao, has more expensive luxury rooms.

Getting There & Away Buses to Chiang Dao from Chiang Mai's Chang Pheuak station cost 18B.

Doi Ang Khang

ดอยอ่างขาง

About 20 km before Fang is the turn-off for Route 1249 to Doi Ang Khang, Thailand's 'Little Switzerland'. Twenty-five km from the highway, this 1300-metre peak has a cool climate year-round and supports the cultivation of flowers, as well as fruits and vegetables that are usually found only in more temperate climates.

A few hill-tribe villages (Lahu, Lisu and Hmong) can be visited on the slopes. You can pick up a free map of the area at the main military checkpoint on Route 1249.

The Yunnanese village of **Ban Khum** on Doi Ang Khang has some hillside bungalows for rent in the 200B range.

FANG & THA TON

ฝาง/ท่าตอน

The present city of Fang was founded by King Mengrai in the 13th century, although as a human settlement and trading centre the

NORTHERN THAILAND

locale dates back at least 1000 years. North from Chiang Mai along Route 107, Fang doesn't look particularly inviting, but the town's quiet back streets are lined with interesting little shops in wooden buildings. The Burmese-style **Wat Jong Paen** – near the Wiang Kaew Hotel – has an impressive stacked-roof wihaan.

There are also Mien and Karen villages nearby which you can visit on your own, but for most people Fang is just a road marker on the way to Tha Ton, the starting point for Kok River trips to Chiang Rai (and other points along the river in between), and for

guided or solo treks to the many hill-tribe settlements in the region. However, if you're planning to spend the night before catching the boat, Fang is as good a place to stay as Tha Ton. It's only half an hour or so by songthaew to the river from Fang.

Two banks along the main street in Fang offer currency exchange.

About 10 km west of Fang at Ban Meuang Chom, near the agricultural station, is a system of **hot springs**. Just ask for the *bàw náam ráwn* ('baw nâam hâwn' in northern Thai).

Tha Ton

Tha Ton is a collection of riverboats, tourist accommodation, restaurants, souvenir shops and a songthaew stand along a pretty bend in the Kok River. For something to do, climb the hill to **Wat Tha Ton** and attached Chinese shrine for good views of the surrounding area. A large temple bell, which sounds every morning at 4 am (wake-up call for monks) and again at 6 am (meal call), can be heard throughout the valley surrounding Tha Ton.

Trekking & Rafting There are some pleasant walks along the river. Treks and raft trips can be arranged through Thip's Travellers House, Mae Kok River Lodge or the Thaton River View. Thip's arranges economical bamboo house-rafts with pilot and cook for three days for 1200B per person (four-person minimum), including all meals, lodging and rafting. The first day you'll visit several villages near the river and spend the night in a Lisu village; on the second day rafters visit hot springs and more villages, and spend the second night on the raft; and on the third day you dock in Chiang Rai.

The Mae Kok River Lodge uses a sturdy, steel-hulled raft topped with bamboo for one-night, two-day river trips which cost 1500B per person.

You could also pull together a small group of travellers and arrange your own house-raft with a guide and cook for a two or three-day journey downriver, stopping off in villages of your own choosing along the way. A

Fang

1 Ueng Khum Hotel
2 Wiang Kaew Hotel
3 Fang Hotel (Wiang Fang) & Fang Restaurant
4 Bank
5 Police Station
6 District Office
7 Wat Jedi Ngam
8 Market
9 Parichat Restaurant
10 Thai Farmers Bank
11 Bus Station
12 Market
13 Chok Thani & Roza Hotels

To Wat Jong Paen
Tha Phae Road
To Tha Ton (23 km)
To Ban Meuang Chom
Route 107
Rawp Wiang Road
To Chiang Mai
0   50   100 m

house-raft generally costs around 350B per person per day including all meals and takes up to six people – so figure on 1000 to 1200B for a three-day trip with stops at Shan, Lisu and Karen villages along the way. New police regulations require that an experienced boat navigator accompany each raft – the river has lots of tricky spots and there have been some mishaps.

Near the pier you can rent inflatable kayaks to do your own paddling in the area. Upstream a few km the river flows into Myanmar. Khun Sa's Meuang Tai Army occasionally clashes with Rangoon troops in the area; in May 1993 two raftmen sitting next to the bridge in Tha Ton were killed by a stray K-81 rocket that dropped in from a nearby battle.

Places to Stay & Eat

Fang The oldest hotel in town is the *Fang Hotel (Wiang Fang)*, just off the main road in town on the way to Tha Ton, but at last pass it was closed. If and when it reopens, rooms in the old wooden wing should cost around 80B, rooms in the new wing 100B.

A more reliable choice is the friendly *Wiang Kaew Hotel*, behind the Fang Hotel off the main street. Basic but clean rooms with private bath are 100B with hot water, 80B without.

The *Ueng Khum (UK) Hotel* (☎ 451268) around the corner on Tha Phae Rd has large bungalow-style accommodation around a courtyard for 120/180B a single/double; all rooms have hot-water showers. More up-market digs near the market on the highway are available at the *Chok Thani* and *Roza*, both with rooms with fan from 200B, air-con from 320B.

The *Fang Restaurant* (its Thai sign reads 'Khun Pa') next to the Fang Hotel entrance has a bilingual menu and quite decent food. The clean *Parichat Restaurant*, on Rawp Wiang Rd near the highway market, serves an exemplary bowl of khâo sòi with chicken or beef, plus kuãytïaw, khâo phàt and other standards. Farther down this same road is a row of cheap Isaan restaurants and *lâo dong* (herbal liquor) bars.

A few food vendors – not quite enough to make a true 'night market' – set up near the bus terminal at night.

Tha Ton If you want to spend the night near the pier in Tha Ton, there are several options. Old standby *Thip's Travellers House* is a short walk from the pier, quite near the bridge where the road from Fang meets the river. Rates are 40 to 80B for rooms without bath, 80 to 100B with bath. Thip has a new branch location overlooking a stream called Huay Nam Yen about three km past the bridge. Rates are 100B, 200B and 400B depending on the size of the rooms. Enquire at Thip's in town for transport back and forth to Huay Nam Yen.

Chankasem, down near the pier, has a pleasant restaurant on the river and a variety of rooms: 60B with shared bath in the older wooden section; 80B for singles/doubles with fan and bath; 100 to 200B with hot water and 300B for a brick bungalow. Also near the pier is the *Apple Guest House*, with very basic rooms for 40/60B.

On the opposite side of the river there are three more places to choose from. The *Maekok River Lodge* (☎ 222172) has landscaped grounds, a pool and deluxe rooms overlooking the river for 625B, plus a few more basic rooms for 300B. Next door and adjacent to the bridge, the new multi-storey *Parichart Riverside Hotel* was going up until construction was halted by local authorities due to the lack of a proper building permit – probably part of the crackdown that has followed the collapse of Khorat's Royal Plaza Hotel.

On the river another 100 metres or so north from the bridge, the tranquil *Garden Home* offers very clean thatched bungalows spaced well apart on landscaped grounds for 150B with private shower (cold water, but a hot-water shower is available in the restaurant). From the bridge, turn left at the Thaton River View Hotel sign to find it.

Farther on along the river, the well-designed *Thaton River View Hotel* (☎ (01) 510-1781, Bangkok ☎ (02) 287-0123; fax 287-3420) has immaculate, spacious rooms

NORTHERN THAILAND

facing the river for around 1000B. The River View's restaurant is the best in the area, with Shell Chuan Chim honours for four different dishes on the menu.

Two Thai-style resorts near the entrance to Tha Ton from Fang, *Kok Garden Resort* and *Khumphukham Garden*, have rooms with all the amenities from 650B up.

Chao Phae, an indoor-outdoor place opposite Thip's Travellers House, is the best non-hotel restaurant in Tha Ton. There are several rustic foodstalls near the pier and near the bridge. Downriver a bit from the Apple and Chankasem guesthouses, the *Rim Kok Restaurant* has decent Thai and Chinese food. The owners also rent a few rooms for 250B to 500B.

A local specialty is *lûy*, a Northern Thai salad made with pig's blood.

Getting There & Away
Bus & Songthaew Buses to Fang leave from the Chang Pheuak bus station north of the White Elephant (Chang Pheuak) Gate in Chiang Mai. The three-hour trip costs 40B.

From Fang it's 23 km to Tha Ton. A songthaew does the 40-minute trip for 10B; the larger orange buses from Fang leave less frequently and cost only 7B. Buses leave from near the market, or you can wait in front of the Fang Hotel for a bus or songthaew. Both operate from 5.30 am to 5 pm only.

To/From Mae Salong The river isn't the only way to get to points north from Tha Ton. Yellow songthaews leave from the east side of the river in Tha Ton to Mae Salong in Chiang Rai Province several times daily between 7 am and 3 pm. The trip takes about 2½ hours and costs 60B per person. Hold tight – the road is pretty rugged.

To/From Mae Sai & Chiang Rai A new bus service runs several times daily between Tha Ton and Mae Sai via Mae Chan. Look for the green bus – the fare is 33B.

If you'd rather not take the boat downriver, you can hop on an air-con bus to Chiang Rai along Tha Ton's main street for 80B and get there in two hours – half the cost of the boat in half the time.

To/From Pai If you're heading to or coming from Mae Hong Son Province, it's not necessary to dip all the way south to Chiang Mai before continuing westward or eastward. At Ban Mae Malai, the junction of Route 107 (the Chiang Mai-Fang highway), you can pick up a bus to Pai for 38B; if you're coming from Pai, be sure to get off here to catch a bus north to Fang. Buses between Ban Mae Malai and Fang cost 40B.

Motorbike Motorcycle trekkers can also travel between Tha Ton and Doi Mae Salong, 48 km north-east along a sometimes treacherous, partially paved mountain road. There are a couple of Lisu and Akha villages along the way. The 27 km or so between Doi Mae Salong and the KMT village of Hua Muang Ngam are the most difficult, especially in the rainy season. When conditions are good, the trip can be accomplished in 1½ hours. As this road is improved, the adventure factor will decrease.

For an extra charge, you can take a motorcycle on most boats to Chiang Rai.

KOK RIVER TRIP TO CHIANG RAI
From Tha Ton you can make a half-day long-tail boat trip to Chiang Rai down the Kok River. The regular passenger boat leaves at 12.30 pm and costs 160B per person. You can also charter a boat, which between eight or 10 people works out at much the same cost per person but gives you more room to move. The trip is a bit of a tourist trap these days as most of the passengers are farangs and the villages along the way sell Coke and souvenirs, and there are lots of TV aerials – but it's still fun. The best time to do the trip is at the end of the rainy season in November when the river level is high.

To catch a boat on the same day from Chiang Mai you'd have to leave by 7 or 7.30 am at the latest and make no stops on the way. The 6 am bus is the best bet. The travel time downriver depends on river conditions and the skill of the pilot, taking anywhere from three to five hours. You could actually make the boat trip in a day from Chiang Mai, catching a bus back from Chiang Rai as soon as you arrive, but it's far better to stay in Fang or Tha Ton, take the boat trip, then stay in Chiang Rai or Chiang Saen before travelling on. You may sometimes have to get off and walk or push the boat if it gets stuck on sandbars.

Some travellers take the boat to Chiang Rai in two or three stages, stopping first in **Mae Salak**, a large Lahu village which is about a third of the distance, or **Ban Ruammit**, a Karen village about two-thirds of the way down. Both villages are well touristed these days (charter boat tours stop for photos and elephant rides), but from here you can trek to other Shan, Thai and hill-tribe villages, or do longer treks south of Mae Salak to **Wawi**, a large multi-ethnic community of jiin haw (Chinese refugees), Lahu, Lisu, Akha, Shan, Karen, Mien and Thai peoples. The Wawi area has dozens of hill-tribe villages of various ethnicities, including the largest Akha community in Thailand (Saen Charoen) and the oldest Lisu settlement (Doi Chang). A few years ago DK Books in Chiang Mai published helpful Wawi and Kok River trekking maps which marked trails and village locations. These maps are now out of print but if you can manage to get copies they could prove very useful.

Another alternative is to trek south from Mae Salak all the way to the town of **Mae Suai**, where you can catch a bus on to Chiang Rai or back to Chiang Mai. You might also try getting off the boat at one of the smaller villages (see boat fares below) – **Jakheu** looked interesting. Another alternative is to make the trip (much more slowly) upriver from Chiang Rai – this is possible despite the rapids.

Several of the guesthouses in Tha Ton now organise raft trips down the river – see the earlier Tha Ton section.

The following table shows boat fares from Tha Ton:

Destination	Fare
Ban Mai	40B
Mae Salak	50B
Pha Tai	60B
Jakheu	70B
Kok Noi	90B
Pha Khwang	90B
Pha Khiaw	140B
Hat Wua Dam	140B
Ban Ruammit	150B
Chiang Rai	160B

Warning

Whether travelling by raft or long-tail boat, all passengers are required to sign in at police posts three times along the river; once in Tha Ton and once each in Mae Salak and Ban Ruammit. This requirement is part of an overall attempt to improve security along the river following several armed bandit attacks on passing boats during the late 1980s. Since 1988 things have been quiet, so the system seems to be effective. Still, don't travel with any valuables you can't afford to lose.

Bring sun block and a hat (one that you can tie down once the boat reaches warp speed) or scarf, as long-tail boats provide no shelter from the sun.

Hill-Tribe Treks

For years Chiang Mai has been a centre for treks into the mountainous northern areas inhabited by hill tribes. It used to be pretty exciting to knock about the dirt roads of rural Chiang Rai Province, do the boat trip between Fang and Chiang Rai and hike into the various villages of the Karen, Hmong, Akha, Lisu and Mien tribes and the Kuomintang (KMT) settlements. You could spend the night in rustic surroundings and perhaps share some opium with the villagers.

Only a very few Thais living in Chiang Mai had the travel and linguistic knowledge necessary to lead adventurous foreigners through this area. Booking a trip usually meant waiting for optimum conditions and adequate numbers of participants, which sometimes took quite a while.

The trips began to gain popularity in the early 1970s and now virtually every hotel and guesthouse in Chiang Mai books hill-tribe tours for countless tour organisations.

Soon the word was out that the area north of the Kok River in the Golden Triangle was being over-trekked, with treks crisscrossing the area in such a fashion that the hill-tribe villages were starting to become human zoos. With their only contact with the outside world coming through a camera lens and a flow of sweets and cigarettes, many villages faced cultural erosion. So the tours moved south of the Kok River, around Chiang Dao and Wiang Papao, then to Mae Taeng and Mae Hong Son where most of them now operate. It will be only a short time before these areas suffer from the heavy traffic as well.

Meanwhile, thousands of foreign travellers each year continue to take these treks. Most come away with a sense of adventure while a few are disillusioned. The primary ingredient in a good trek is having a good leader/organiser, followed by a good group of trekkers. Some travellers finish a tour complaining more about the other trekkers than about the itinerary, food or trek leader.

Before Trekking

Hill-tribe trekking isn't for everyone. First, you must be physically fit to cope with the demands of sustained up and down walking, exposure to the elements and spotty food. Second, many people feel awkward walking through hill-tribe villages and playing the role of voyeur.

In cities and villages elsewhere in Thailand, Thais and other lowland groups are quite used to foreign faces and foreign ways (from TV if nothing else), but in the hills of northern Thailand the tribes lead largely insular lives. Hence, hill-tribe tourism has pronounced effects, both positive and negative. On the positive side, travellers have a chance to see how traditional subsistence-oriented societies function. Also, since the Thai government is sensitive about the image projected by their minority groups, tourism may actually have forced it to review

and sometimes improve its policies towards hill tribes. On the negative side, trekkers introduce many cultural items and ideas from the outside world that may erode tribal customs to varying degrees.

If you have any qualms about interrupting the traditional patterns of life in hill-tribe areas, you probably should not go trekking. It is undeniable that trekking in northern Thailand is marketed like soap or any other commodity. Anyone who promises you an authentic experience is probably exaggerating at the very least, or at worst contributing to the decline of hill-tribe culture by leading foreigners into unhampered areas.

If you desire to make a trek keep these points in mind: choose your trek operator carefully, try to meet the others in the group (suggest a meeting), and find out exactly what the tour includes and does not include, as usually there are additional expenses beyond the basic rate. In the cool season, make sure sleeping bags are provided, as the thin wool blankets available in most villages are not sufficient for the average visitor. If everything works out, even an organised tour can be worthwhile. A useful check list of questions to ask are:

1. How many people will there be in the group? Six to 10 is a good maximum range.
2. Can the organiser guarantee that no other tourists will visit the same village on the same day, especially overnight?
3. Can the guide speak the language of each village to be visited?
4. Exactly when does the tour begin and end? Some three-day treks turn out to be less than 48 hours in length.
5. Do they provide transport before and after the trek or is it just by public bus (often with long waits)?

Choosing a Company TAT is making efforts to regulate trekking companies operating out of Chiang Mai and recommends that you trek only with members of the Professional Guide Association of Chiang Mai or the Jungle Tour Club of northern Thailand. Still, with more than 100 companies, it's very difficult to guarantee any kind of control.

These days there are plenty of places apart from Chiang Mai where you can arrange treks. Often these places have better and usually less expensive alternatives which originate closer to the more remote and untrekked areas. Also, they are generally smaller, friendlier operations and the trekkers are usually a more determined bunch since they're not looking for a quick in-and-out trek. The treks are often informally arranged, usually involving discussions of duration, destination, cost, etc (it used to be like that in Chiang Mai).

You can easily arrange treks out of the following northern towns: Chiang Rai, Mae Hong Son, Pai, Mae Sai and Tha Ton. With a little time to seek out the right people, you can also go on organised treks from Mae Sariang, Khun Yuam, Soppong (near Pai), Mae Sot, Um Phang and various out-of-the-way guesthouses which are springing up all over northern Thailand.

The down side, of course, is that companies outside of Chiang Mai are generally subject to even less regulation than those in Chiang Mai, and there are fewer guarantees with regard to trekking terms and conditions.

Costs Organised treks out of Chiang Mai average from 1500B for a four-day, three-night trek to 2600B for a deluxe seven-day, six-night trek which includes rafting and/or elephant riding. Rates vary, so it pays to shop around – although these days so many companies are competing for your business that rates have remained pretty stable for the last few years. You can count on an extra 1000B for elephants or other exotic additions to a basic trek. Elephant rides actually become quite boring and even uncomfortable after an hour or two. Some companies now offer quickie day treks or one-night, two-day programmes.

Don't choose a trek by price alone. It's better to talk to other travellers in town who have been on treks. Treks out of other towns in the north are usually less expensive – around 300B per person per day.

The Professional Guide Association in Chiang Mai meets monthly to set trek prices

and to discuss problems, and issues regular, required reports to TAT about individual treks. All trekking guides and companies are supposed to be government-licensed and bonded. As a result, a standard for trekking operators has emerged whereby you can expect the price you pay to include: transport to and from the starting/ending points of a trek (if outside Chiang Mai); food (three meals a day) and accommodation in all villages visited; basic first aid; predeparture valuables storage; and sometimes the loan of specific equipment, such as sleeping bags in cool weather or water bottles.

Not included in the price are beverages other than drinking water or tea, the sometimes available opium-smoking (how many travellers have I heard say '...and then, oh wow, we actually smoked opium with the village headman!'), lunch on the first and last days and personal porters.

Seasons Probably the best time to trek is November to February, when the weather is refreshing with little or no rain and poppies are in bloom everywhere. Between March and May the hills are dry and the weather is quite hot in most northern places. The second-best time to trek is early in the rainy season, between June and July, before the dirt roads become too saturated.

Safety Every year or so there's at least one trekking robbery in northern Thailand. Often the bandits are armed with guns, which they will use without hesitation if they meet resistance. Once they collect a load of cameras, watches, money and jewellery, many bandit gangs hightail it across the border into Myanmar. In spite of this, police have had a good arrest record so far and have created hill-country patrols. Still, gangs can form at any time and anywhere. The problem is that most people living in the rural north believe that all foreigners are very rich (a fair assumption in relation to hill-tribe living standards). Most of these people have never been to Chiang Mai and, from what they have heard about the capital, consider Bangkok to be a virtual paradise of wealth and luxury. So don't take anything with you trekking you can't afford to lose, and don't resist robbery attempts.

Conduct

Once trekking, there are several other guidelines to minimising the negative impact on the local people:

1. Always ask for permission before taking photos of tribal people and/or their dwellings. You can ask through your guide or by using sign language. Because of traditional belief systems, many individuals and even whole tribes may object strongly to being photographed.
2. Show respect for religious symbols and rituals. Don't touch totems at village entrances or any other object of obvious symbolic value without asking permission. Keep your distance from ceremonies being performed unless you're asked to participate.
3. Practise restraint in giving things to tribespeople or bartering with them. Food and medicine are not necessarily appropriate gifts if they result in altering traditional dietary and healing practices. The same goes for clothing. Tribespeople will abandon handwoven tunics for printed T-shirts if they are given a steady supply. If you want to give something to the people you encounter on a trek, the best thing is to make a donation to the village school or other community fund. Your guide can help arrange this.

Opium Smoking Some guides are very strict now about forbidding the smoking of opium on treks. This seems to be a good idea, since one of the problems trekking companies have had in the past is dealing with opium-addicted guides! Volunteers who work in tribal areas also say opium smoking sets a bad example for young people in the villages.

Opium is traditionally a condoned vice of the elderly, yet an increasing number of young people in the villages are now taking opium and heroin. This is possibly due in part to the influence of young trekkers who may smoke once and a few weeks later be hundreds of km away while the villagers continue to face the temptation every day.

Opium overdoses aren't unknown; in 1991 a 23-year-old Brazilian died after smoking 18 pipes of opium while on a trek in northern Thailand.

Independent Trekking

You might consider striking out on your own in a small group of two to five people. Gather as much information as you can about the area you'd like to trek in from the Tribal Research Institute at Chiang Mai University. The institute has an informative pamphlet which is available at its library. Don't bother staff with questions about trekking as they are quite noncommittal, either from fear of liability or fear of retribution from the Chiang Mai trekking companies.

Maps, mostly distributed by guesthouses outside of Chiang Mai, pinpoint various hill-tribe areas in the north.

Be prepared for language difficulties. Few people you meet will know any English. Usually someone in a village will know some Thai, so a Thai phrasebook can be helpful. Lonely Planet now also publishes a *Thai Hill Tribes Phrasebook* with phrase sections for each of the six major hill-tribe languages.

As in Himalayan trekking in Nepal and India, many people now do short treks on their own at the lower elevations, staying in villages along the way. It is not necessary to bring a lot of food or equipment, just money for food which can be bought along the way in small Thai towns and occasionally in the hill-tribe settlements. However, TAT strongly discourages trekking on your own because of the safety risk. Check in with the police when you arrive in a new district so they can tell you if an area is considered safe or not. A lone trekker is an easy target (see the Safety section above).

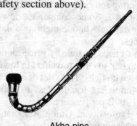

Akha pipe

Trekking Companies

Because of the inherent instability of the trekking business, I can't make any specific recommendations for particular trekking companies in Chiang Mai. Many of the trekking guides are freelance and go from one company to the next, so there's no way to predict which companies are going to give the best service at any time. Many guesthouses that advertise their own trekking companies actually act as brokers for off-site operations; they collect a commission for every guest they book onto a trek.

The TAT office in Chiang Mai maintains and distributes a current list of licensed agencies. Ultimately, the best way to shop for a trek is to talk to travellers who have just returned from treks.

Hill Tribes

The term 'hill tribe' refers to ethnic minorities living in the mountainous regions of northern and western Thailand. The Thais refer to them as *chao khāo*, literally 'mountain people'. Each hill tribe has its own language, customs, mode of dress and spiritual beliefs.

Most are of semi-nomadic origin, having migrated to Thailand from Tibet, Myanmar, China and Laos during the past 200 years or so, although some groups may have been in Thailand much longer. They are 'fourth-world' people in the sense that they belong neither to the main aligned powers nor to the Third-World nations. Rather, they have crossed and continue to cross national borders without regard for recent nationhood. Language and culture constitute the borders of their world – some groups are caught between the 6th and 20th centuries, while others are gradually being assimilated into modern Thai life.

Many tribespeople are moving into lowland areas inhabited by Thais as montane lands become deforested by both traditional swidden (slash-and-burn) cultivation methods and illegal logging.

The Tribal Research Institute in Chiang Mai recognises 10 different hill tribes in Thailand, but there may be up to 20. The Institute estimates the total hill-tribe population to be around 550,000.

The earlier descriptions covered the largest tribes, which are also the groups most likely to be encountered on treks. Linguistically, the tribes can be divided into three main groups: the Tibeto-Burman (Lisu, Lahu, Akha), the Karenic (Karen, Kayah), and the Austro-Thai (Hmong, Mien). Comments on ethnic dress refer mostly to the female members of each group, as hill-tribe men tend to dress like rural Thais. Population figures are 1989 estimates. Within each major group there may also be several subgroups, eg Blue Hmong, White Hmong, Striped Hmong; these names usually refer to predominant elements of clothing.

The Shan (Thai Yai) are not included since they are not a hill-tribe group per se – they live in permanent locations, practise Theravada Buddhism and speak a language very similar to Thai. Thai scholars consider the Shan to have been the original inhabitants (Thai Yai means 'larger' or 'majority Thais') of the area. Nevertheless, Shan villages are common stops on hill-tribe trekking itineraries.

For a more complete description of the dress and customs of each tribe, along with a compendium of useful words and phrases in the language of each, plus maps showing areas of habitation, see Lonely Planet's *Thai Hill Tribes Phrasebook*.

Lamphun Province

LAMPHUN

อ.เมืองลำพูน

Best seen on a day trip from Chiang Mai, along with Pasang, Lamphun (population 14,750) was the centre of the small Hariphunchai principality (750-1281 AD) originally ruled by the Mon princess Chama Thewi. Long after its progenitor, Dvaravati, was vanquished by the Khmers, Hariphunchai succeeded in remaining independent of both the Khmers and the Chiang Mai Thais.

NORTHERN THAILAND

Akha (Thai: *I-kaw*)

Population: 38,000
Origin: Tibet
Present locations: Thailand, Laos, Myanmar, Yunnan
Economy: rice, corn, opium
Belief system: animism, with an emphasis on ancestor worship
Distinctive characteristics: headdresses of beads, feathers and dangling silver ornaments. Villages are along mountain ridges or on steep slopes from 1000 to 1400 metres in altitude. The well known Akha Swing Ceremony takes place mid-August to mid-September – between planting and harvest – and is linked to ancestor worship and spirit offerings. The Akha are amongst the poorest of Thailand's ethnic minorities and tend to resist assimilation into the Thai mainstream. Like the Lahu, they often cultivate opium for their own consumption.

Lisu (Thai: *Lisaw*)

Population: 25,000
Origin: Tibet
Present locations: Thailand, Yunnan
Economy: rice, opium, corn, livestock
Belief system: animism with ancestor worship and spirit possession
Distinctive characteristics: the women wear long multicoloured tunics over trousers and sometimes black turbans with tassels. Men wear baggy green or blue pants pegged in at the ankles. Premarital sex is said to be common, along with freedom in choosing marital partners. Patrilineal clans have pan-tribal jurisdiction, which makes the Lisu unique among hill-tribe groups (most tribes have power centred at the village level with either the shaman or a village headman). Lisu villages are usually in the mountains at about 1000 metres.

Lahu (Thai: *Musoe*)

Population: 58,700
Origin: Tibet
Present locations: south China, Thailand, Myanmar
Economy: rice, corn, opium
Belief system: theistic animism (supreme deity is Geusha) and some groups are Christian
Distinctive characteristics: black and red jackets with narrow skirts for women, bright green or blue-green baggy trousers for men. They live in mountainous areas at about 1000 metres. Their intricately woven shoulder bags (yaam) are prized by collectors. There are five main groups – Red Lahu, Black Lahu, White Lahu, Yellow Lahu and Lahu Sheleh.

Mien (Thai: *Yao*)

Population: 38,000
Origin: central China
Present locations: Thailand, south China, Laos, Myanmar, Vietnam
Economy: rice, corn, opium
Belief system: animism with ancestor worship and Taoism
Distinctive characteristics: women wear black jackets and trousers decorated with intricately embroidered patches and red fur-like collars, along with large dark blue or black turbans. The Mien have been heavily influenced by Chinese traditions and use Chinese characters to write the Mien language. They tend to settle near mountain springs at between 1000 and 1200 metres. Kinship is patrilineal and marriage is polygamous. The Mien are highly skilled at embroidery and silversmithing.

Karen (Thai: *Yang* or *Kariang*)

Population: 285,000
Origin: Myanmar
Present locations: Thailand, Myanmar
Economy: rice, vegetables, livestock
Belief system: animism, Buddhism, Christianity, depending on the group
Distinctive characteristics: thickly woven V-neck tunics of various colours (unmarried women wear white). Kinship is matrilineal and marriage is monogamous. They tend to live in lowland valleys and practise crop rotation rather than swidden (slash-and-burn) agriculture. There are four distinct Karen groups – the White Karen (Skaw Karen), Pwo Karen, Black Karen (Pa-O) and Red Karen (Kayah). These groups combined form the largest hill tribe in Thailand, numbering about half of all hill-tribe people. Many Karen continue to migrate into Thailand from Myanmar, fleeing Burmese government persecution.

Hmong (Thai: *Meo* or *Maew*)

Population: 87,000
Origin: south China
Present locations: south China, Thailand, Laos, Vietnam
Economy: rice, corn, opium
Belief system: animism
Distinctive characteristics: simple black jackets and indigo or black baggy trousers with striped borders or indigo skirts, and silver jewellery. Most women wear their hair in a large bun. They usually live on mountain peaks or plateaus above 1000 metres. Kinship is patrilineal and polygamy is permitted. They are Thailand's second-largest hill-tribe group and are especially numerous in Chiang Mai Province.

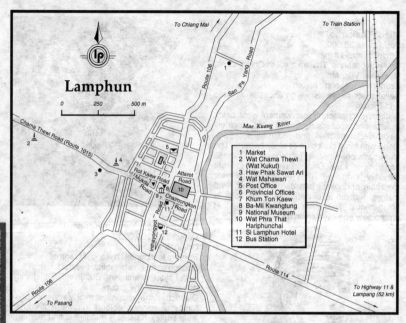

Lamphun

0   250   500 m

To Chiang Mai

Route 106

San Pa Yang Road

To Train Station

Chama Thewi Road (Route 1015)

Mae Kuang River

Rot Kaew Road

Mukda Road

Attarot Road

Chaimongkon Road

Inthayongyot Road

1 Market
2 Wat Chama Thewi
   (Wat Kukut)
3 Haw Phak Sawat Ari
4 Wat Mahawan
5 Post Office
6 Provincial Offices
7 Khum Ton Kaew
8 Ba-Mii Kwangtung
9 National Museum
10 Wat Phra That
   Hariphunchai
11 Si Lamphun Hotel
12 Bus Station

Route 114

Route 106

To Pasang

To Highway 11 &
Lampang (52 km)

This provincial capital is fairly quiet but there are a few places to stay if you want to get away from the hustle and bustle of Chiang Mai or want to study the temples here in depth.

The village just north of Lamphun, Nong Chang Kheun, is known for producing the sweetest lam yai (longan) fruit in the country. During the second week of August, Lamphun hosts the annual Lam Yai Festival, which features floats made of the fruit, and of course a Miss Lam Yai contest.

Wat Phra That Hariphunchai

วัดพระธาตุหริภุญชัย

This wat, which dates to 1157, is on the left on the main road into Lamphun from Chiang Mai. The temple lay derelict for many years until Khrubaa Siwichai, one of Northern Thailand's most famous monks, made renovations in the 1930s. It has some interesting post-Dvaravati architecture, a couple of fine

Buddha images and two old chedis of the original Hariphunchai style. The tallest, Chedi Suwan, dates to 1418; although not built during the Hariphunchai period, it was styled after Hariphunchai models. The chedi's 46-metre height is surmounted by a nine-tier umbrella made of 6.5 kg of pure gold.

Lamphun National Museum

พิพิธภัณฑ์แห่งชาติลำพูน

Across the street from Wat Phra That Hariphunchai, the museum's small collection includes artefacts from the Dvaravati, Hariphunchai and Lanna kingdoms. Opening hours are Wednesday to Sunday from 8.30 am to noon and 1 to 4 pm. Entry is 10B.

Wat Chama Thewi (Wat Kukut)

วัดจามเทวี (วัดกู่กุด)

A larger Hariphunchai chedi can be seen at Wat Chama Thewi (popularly called Wat Kukut), which is said to have been erected in the 8th or 9th century as a Dvaravati monument, then rebuilt by the Hariphunchai Mons in 1218. As it has been restored many times since then it is now a mixture of several schools.

Each of the four sides of the chedi has five rows of three Buddha figures, diminishing in size on each higher level. The stucco standing Buddhas are definitely of the Dvaravati style, though they are of recent creation.

Wat Kukut is on the opposite side of town from Wat Hariphunchai. To get there, walk west down Mukda Rd, perpendicular to the Chiang Mai-Lamphun road (opposite Wat Hari), passing over the town moat, then past the district government offices until you come to the wat on the left.

Places to Stay & Eat

The grotty *Si Lamphun* (☎ (053) 511176) is on the town's main street, Inthayongyot Rd. Singles/twins without bath are 70/90B, or 100/120B with bath.

A better choice is the *Suan Kaew Bungalow* at Km 6 on Lamphun-Lampang Rd (Highway 11), where decent rooms cost 80 to 150B.

Haw Phak Sawat Ari on Chama Thewi Rd near Wat Kukut is where visiting archaeologists stay. For 80B per night or 1200B per month you can have an apartment with a bedroom, bathroom and sitting room.

Ba-Mii Kwangtung (no roman-script sign), on the corner of Rot Kaew and Inthayongyot Rds near the museum, has very good and inexpensive Cantonese-style noodles. Behind the museum, housed in the former teak palace of a local prince, the all air-con *Khum Ton Kaew* offers a Thai and Western menu and is a good place to escape the heat.

Getting There & Away

Buses to Lamphun from Chiang Mai leave at 20-minute intervals throughout the day from the Chiang Mai-Lamphun Rd near the south side of Nawarat Bridge. The 26-km bus ride (7B) goes along a beautiful country road, parts of which are bordered by tall *yang* (dipterocarp) trees.

PASANG

ป่าซาง

Don't confuse this village with Baw Sang, the umbrella village. In Pasang, cotton weaving is the cottage industry. The Nandakwang Laicum shop, one of many that weave and sell their own cotton, is on the right side of the main road going south and is recommended for its wide selection and tasteful designs. A cotton shirt or dress of unique Pasang design can be purchased in town for between 80 and 500B, depending on the quality. Pasang reputedly has the north's most beautiful women.

Wat Phra Phutthabaat Taak Phaa

วัดพระพุทธบาทตากผ้า

About nine km south of Pasang or 20 km south of Lamphun, off Route 106 in the subdistrict (tambon) of Ma-Kawk (follow Route 1133 one km east), is this famous Mahanikai wat. A shrine to one of the north's most famous monks, Luang Puu Phromma, it contains a lifelike wax figure of the deceased monk sitting in meditation.

One of his disciples, Ajaan Thirawattho, teaches meditation to a large contingent of monks who are housed in kutis of laterite brick. Behind the spacious grounds is a type of park and a steep hill mounted by a chedi. The wat is named after an unremarkable Buddha footprint (Phra Phutthabaat) shrine in the middle of the lower temple grounds and another spot where Buddha supposedly dried his robes (Taak Phaa) and left an imprint.

Getting There & Away

A songthaew will take you from Lamphun to Pasang for a few baht. From Chiang Mai it costs 10B by regular bus or 12B by minibus.

If you're heading south to Tak Province

under your own power, traffic is generally much lighter along Route 106 to Thoen than on Highway 11 to Lampang; a winding 10-km section of road north of Thoen is particularly scenic. Both highways intersect Highway 1 south, which leads directly to Tak's capital.

Lampang Province

LAMPANG
อ.เมืองลำปาง

One hundred km from Chiang Mai is Lampang (population 43,369), which was inhabited as far back as the 7th century in the Dvaravati period and played an important part in the history of the Hariphunchai kingdom. Legend says the city was founded by the son of Hariphunchai's Queen Chama Thewi.

Like Chiang Mai, Phrae and other older northern cities, Lampang was built as a walled rectangle alongside a river (in this case the Wang River). At the turn of the century Lampang, along with nearby Phrae, became an important centre for domestic and international teak trade. Because of their familiarity with the teak industry in Myanmar (at the time part of the British Raj along with India), a large British-owned local timber company brought in Burmese supervisors to train Burmese and Thai loggers in the area. These well-paid supervisors, along with independent Burmese teak merchants who plied their trade in Lampang, sponsored the construction of more than a dozen impressive temples in the city. Burmese artisans designed and built the temples out of local materials, especially teak. Their legacy lives on in several of Lampang's most well-maintained wats, now among the city's main visitor attractions.

Many Thais visit Lampang for a taste of urban northern Thailand without the crass commercialism of Chiang Mai. Although the downtown area is quite busy, the shophouses have a more traditional feel.

Horsecarts
Lampang is known throughout Thailand as Meuang Rot Maa (Horsecart City) because it's the only town in Thailand where horsecarts are still used as public transport. These days, Lampang's horsecarts are mainly for tourists. A 15-minute horsecart tour around town costs a standard 20B; for 80B you can get a half-hour tour that goes along the Wang River, and for 100B a one-hour tour which stops at Wat Phra Kaew Don Tao and Wat Si Rong Meuang. If there's not much business you may be able to negotiate to bring the price down to 60B per half-hour or 80B per hour. The main horsecart stands are in front of the City Hall and Thip Chang Hotel.

Wat Phra Kaew Don Tao
วัดพระแก้วดอนเต้า

This wat, on the north side of the Wang River, was built during the reign of King Anantayot and housed the Emerald Buddha (now in Bangkok's Wat Phra Kaew) from 1436 to 1468. The main chedi shows Hariphunchai influence, while the adjacent mondop was built in 1909. The mondop, decorated with glass mosaic in typical Burmese style, contains a Mandalay-style Buddha image. A display of Lanna artefacts – mostly religious paraphernalia and woodwork – can be seen in the wat's **Lanna Museum**.

Other Temples
Two more wats built at the turn of century by Burmese artisans are at **Wat Si Rong Meuang** and **Wat Si Chum.** Both have wihaans and other temple buildings constructed in the Burmese 'layered' style, with tin roofs gabled by intricate woodcarvings.

Besides the wihaan at Wat Phra That Lampang Luang (see the Around Lampang Province section), the mondop at **Wat Pongsanuk Tai** is one of the few remaining local examples of original Lanna-style temple architecture, which emphasised open-sided wooden buildings.

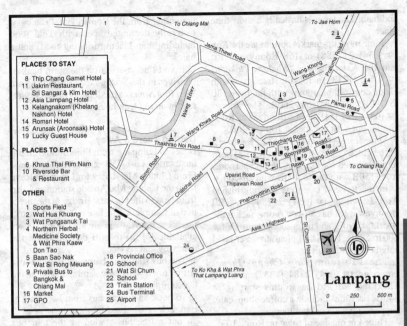

PLACES TO STAY
8 Thip Chang Gamet Hotel
11 Jakrin Restaurant,
   Sri Sangar & Kim Hotel
12 Asia Lampang Hotel
13 Kelangnakorn (Khelang
   Nakhon) Hotel
14 Romsri Hotel
15 Arunsak (Aroonsak) Hotel
19 Lucky Guest House

PLACES TO EAT
6 Khrua Thai Rim Nam
10 Riverside Bar
   & Restaurant

OTHER
1 Sports Field
2 Wat Hua Khuang
3 Wat Pongsanuk Tai
4 Northern Herbal
   Medicine Society
   & Wat Phra Kaew
   Don Tao
5 Baan Sao Nak
7 Wat Si Rong Meuang
9 Private Bus to
   Bangkok &
   Chiang Mai
16 Market
17 GPO

18 Provincial Office
20 School
21 Wat Si Chum
22 School
23 Train Station
24 Bus Terminal
25 Airport

Lampang

0   250   500 m

NORTHERN THAILAND

Baan Sao Nak (Many Pillars House)
บ้านเสานัก

Built in 1896 in the traditional Lanna style, this huge teak house in the old Wiang Neua (North City) section of town is supported by 116 square teak pillars. The local *khun yīng* (a title equivalent to 'lady' in England) who owns the house has opened it to the public as a museum. The entire house is furnished with Burmese and Thai antiques; three rooms display antique silverwork, lacquerware, ceramics and other northern Thai crafts. The area beneath the house is used for khan tok ceremonial dinners.

The house is open daily from 9.30 am to 5.30 pm; admission is 20B.

Traditional Massage
Samakhom Samunphrai Phaak Neua (Northern Herbal Medicine Society) at 149 Pratunam Rd, next to Wat Hua Khuang in the Wiang Neua area, offers traditional northern

Thai massage and herbal saunas. The massage costs 80B per hour; 1½ hours is a recommended minimum for best effect. The outdoor sauna room is pumped with herbal steam created by heating a mixture of 108 medicinal herbs and costs only 30B to use. Once you've paid, you can go in and out of the sauna as many times as you want during one visit.

The massage service and sauna are open from 8 am to 8 pm daily.

Places to Stay
There are several economical choices along Boonyawat Rd, which runs through the centre of town. *Sri Sangar (Si Sa-Nga)* (☎ (054) 217070) at No 213-215 has rooms with fan and bath from 80B and air-con rooms from 250B. *Arunsak (Aroonsak)* (☎ (054) 217344) at No 90/9 is similar but starts at 100B. Cheaper hotels are *Lucky* and *Thap Thim Thong*, both on Kao Mithuna Rd, with basic rooms from 60 to 100B with fan

and bath. The latter is basically a short-time place.

Some more up-market options are the *Kim* (☎ (054) 217588) at 168 Boonyawat Rd and the *Kelangnakorn (Khelang Nakhon)* (☎ (054) 217137) across the street, each with clean, comfortable rooms with fan from 140 to 190B, air-con from 260B. The *Romsri* (☎ (054) 217054) at 142 Boonyawat Rd is similar but a bit cheaper at 100 to 220B.

Siam Hotel (☎ (054) 217472), southwest of the clock circle on Chatchai Rd, has been recommended for its clean, well-kept rooms from 150B with fan to 400B with air-con.

In the top-end category, the refurbished *Asia Lampang* (☎ (054) 217844) at 229 Boonyawat Rd has air-con rooms facing the street for 290B, and nicer rooms with TV for 400 to 500B. The Asia's pleasant street-level cafe is its best feature.

The 130-room *Thip Chang Garnet Lampang* (☎ (054) 218450/337) at 54/22 Thakhrao Noi Rd has rooms starting at 840B. Facilities include a coffee shop, cafe, supper club and cocktail lounge.

Three km outside of town on Route 1035, the road to Chiang Rai, *Bann Fai* (☎ /fax (054) 224602) offers 14 large rooms in a charming teak house decorated with Thai antiques and cotton handwoven on the premises. The landscaped grounds around the house encompass 300 plant species and river frontage, plus views of nearby rice fields and mountains. Rates are 220B per double – four bathrooms are shared.

Places to Eat

In the vicinity of the Kim and Asia hotels there are several good rice and noodle shops. *Jakrin*, beneath the Sri Sangar Hotel opposite the Kim Hotel, is a popular, inexpensive Thai-Chinese place with all the standard dishes.

The outdoor *Riverside Bar & Restaurant* is in an old unrestored teak structure at 328 Thipchang Rd on the river. It's a good choice for a sociable drink or meal, with live folk music nightly and reasonable prices considering the high quality of the food and service. The *Black Horse Pub* on Uparat Rd around

the corner from the Romsri Hotel is a cosy, tastefully decorated spot with Thai food including kàp klâem (drinking food) and a bar.

If you find yourself on the north bank of the river in the Wiang Neua district, *Khrua Thai Rim Nam* is a moderately priced restaurant in an old teak house on the river.

Getting There & Away

Buses to Lampang from Phitsanulok's main bus station cost 75B and take four hours. From Chiang Mai, buses for Lampang leave from the Chiang Mai Arcade station and also from next to the Nawarat Bridge in the direction of Lamphun. The fare is 29B and the trip takes 1½ hours; there are also air-con buses available for 50 to 66B depending on the company and service.

The bus station in Lampang is some way out of town – 10B by samlor if you arrive late at night.

To book an air-con bus from Lampang to Bangkok or Chiang Mai there is no need to go out to the bus station as the tour bus companies have offices in town along Boonyawat Rd near the roundabout. Phaya Yanyon, Thanjit Tour and Thaworn Farm each have 1st-class air-con buses to Bangkok for 262B that leave nightly around 8 pm.

AROUND LAMPANG PROVINCE
Wat Phra That Lampang Luang

วัดพระธาตุลำปางหลวง

Probably the most magnificent temple in all of northern Thailand, Wat Phra That Lampang Luang is also the best compendium of Lanna-style temple architecture. Surrounded by roofed brick cloisters, the centrepiece of the complex is the large, open-sided Wihaan Luang. Thought to have been built in 1476, the impressive building features a triple-tiered wooden roof supported by teak pillars. It's thought to be the oldest existing wooden building in Thailand. A huge gilded mondop in the back of the wihaan contains a Buddha image cast in 1563; the faithful leave small gold-coloured

NORTHERN THAILAND

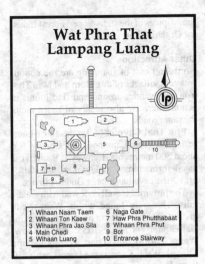

Wat Phra That Lampang Luang

1 Wihaan Naam Taem
2 Wihaan Ton Kaew
3 Wihaan Phra Jao Sila
4 Main Chedi
5 Wihaan Luang
6 Naga Gate
7 Haw Phra Phutthabaat
8 Wihaan Phra Phut
9 Bot
10 Entrance Stairway

Buddha figures close to the mondop and hang Thai Lü weavings behind it.

Early 19th-century jataka murals are painted on wooden panels around the inside upper perimeter of the wihaan. The tall Lanna-style chedi behind the wihaan, raised in 1449 and restored in 1496, measures 24 metres at its base and is 45 metres high. The small, simple Wihaan Ton Kaew to the right of the main wihaan was built in 1476. The oldest structure in the compound is the smaller 13th-century Wihaan Phra Phut to the left (standing with your back to the main gate) of the main chedi; the wihaan to the right of the chedi (Wihaan Naam Taem) was built in the early 16th century and amazingly still contains traces of the original murals.

The Haw Phra Phutthabaat, a small white building behind and to the left of the chedi, has a sign in front that reads 'Women don't step on this place' meaning women are forbidden to climb the steps. You're not missing much – it's just a bare room containing an undistinguished Buddha footprint sculpture. The bot to the left of the Haw Phra dates from 1476 but was reconstructed in 1924.

The lintel over the main entrance to the compound features an impressive inter-twined dragon relief – once common in northern Thai temples but rarely seen these days. Supposedly this gate dates back to the 15th century.

Wat Phra That Lampang Luang is 18 km south-west of Lampang in Ko Kha. To get there by public transport, catch a blue songthaew south on Praisani Rd to the market in Ko Kha (8B), then a Hang Chat-bound songthaew (3B) three km north to the entrance of Wat Phra That Luang. A chartered motorcycle taxi from the Ko Kha songthaew terminal to the temple costs 20 to 30B.

If you're driving or cycling from Lampang, head south on Asia 2 and take the Ko Kha exit, then follow the road over a bridge and bear right. Note the police station on your left and continue for two km over another bridge until you see the temple on the left. If you're coming from Chiang Mai via Highway 11, turn south onto Route 1034 18 km north-west of Lampang at Km 13 – this is a 50-km short cut to Ko Kha that avoids much of Lampang.

Young Elephant Training Centre
ศูนย์ฝึกลูกช้าง

In Hang Chat district north-west of Lampang, outside Thung Kwian at Km 37, is a camp for the training of young elephants. Also called the Thai Elephant Conservation Centre, this camp has moved from its previous location in Ngao, between Lampang and Chiang Rai; the Ngao centre will remain in use as a care facility for elderly tuskers.

In addition to the standard tourist show, the new centre will offer exhibits on the history and culture of Thai elephants as well as elephant rides through the surrounding forest. The animals appreciate a few pieces of fruit – 'feels like feeding a vacuum cleaner with a wet nozzle', reported one visitor. Training takes place daily between 7 and 11 am except on public holidays and during the elephants' summer vacation from March to May.

To reach the camp, you can take a bus or songthaew from Lampang towards Chiang Mai and get off at Km 37.

Thung Kwian Forest Market

ตลาดป่าทุ่งเกวียน

The famous 'forest market' *(talàat pàa)* at Thung Kwian in Hang Chat district (between Lampang and Chiang Mai off Highway 11) sells all manner of wild flora and fauna from the jungle, including medicinal and culinary herbs, wild mushrooms, bamboo shoots, field rats, beetles, snakes, plus a few rare and endangered species like pangolin. Officials are said to be cracking down on the sale of endangered species. The market meets every Wednesday from around 5 am till noon.

The nearby **Thung Kwian Reforestation Centre** protects a new 353-rai forest under the auspices of the state-owned Forest Industry Organisation.

Other Attractions

North and east of Lampang are the cotton-weaving villages of **Jae Hom** and **Mae Tha**. You can wander around and find looms in action; there are also plenty of shops along the main roads.

Pha Thai Cave is 66 km north of Lampang, between Lampang and Chiang Rai about 500 metres off Highway 1. Besides the usual formations – stalagmites and stalactites – the cave has a large Buddha image.

The province is well endowed with waterfalls. Three are found within Wang Neua district, roughly 120 km north of the provincial capital via Route 1053: **Wang Kaew**, **Wang Thong** and **Than Thong** (Jampa Thong). Wang Kaew is the largest, with 110 tiers from summit to bottom. Near the

---

Elephants in Thailand

Current estimates put the number of wild elephants in Thailand at between 3000 and 4000. In 1952 there were 13,397 domestic elephants in Thailand and around 1900 it is estimated that there were at least 100,000 elephants working in Thailand. Until 1917, a white elephant appeared on the Thai national flag.

Elephant mothers carry their calves for 22 months. An adult can run at speeds of up to 23 km per hour and put less weight on the ground per sq cm than a deer. Elephants begin training when they're between three and five years old and the training continues for five years. Tasks they learn under the direction of their mahouts include pushing, carrying and piling logs, as well as bathing and walking in procession.

Working elephants have a career of about 50 years, hence when young they are given two mahouts, one older and one younger (sometimes a father-and-son team) who can see the animal through its lifetime. Thai law requires that elephants be retired and released into the wild at age 61. They often live for 80 years or more.

Now that logging has been banned in Thailand, one wonders if there is going to be less demand for trained elephants. Illegal logging aside, the elephant is still an important mode of jungle transport as it beats any other animal or machine for its ability to move through a forest with minimum environmental damage – its large, soft feet distribute the animal's weight without crushing the ground. ∎

summit is a Mien hill-tribe village. This area became part of the 1172-sq-km **Doi Luang National Park** in 1990; animals protected by the park include serow, barking deer, pangolin and pig-tailed macaque.

In Meuang Pan district, about halfway to Wang Neua from Lampang, is another waterfall, **Jae Sawn**, part of the 593-sq-km **Jae Sawn National Park**. Elevations in the park reach above 2000 metres. Jae Sawn has six drops, each with its own pool; close to the falls are nine hot springs. Camping is permitted in both Jae Sawn and Doi Luang national parks.

Nakhon Sawan Province

NAKHON SAWAN

อ.เมืองนครสวรรค์

A fairly large town on the way north from Bangkok, Nakhon Sawan has an excellent view from the hilltop **Wat Chom Khiri Nak Phrot**. Thais and farangs both agree that Nakhon Sawan is not known for its hospitality, though it's a bustling trade centre. The population (107,000) is largely Chinese and during Chinese New Year celebrations in February every hotel in town is booked. The celebrations here are reportedly the best in Thailand.

Places to Stay

Most of the hotels in the city are located along Phahonyothin Rd (the highway from Bangkok) or along Matuli Rd. The *Si Phitak* (☎ (056) 221076) at 109/5 Matuli Rd has OK rooms with fan and bath for 90 to 120B. Other reasonably priced places include the *Asia* (☎ (056) 213752) at 956 Phahonyothin Rd, where rooms range from 80 to 180B, and the *New Thanchit* (☎ (056) 212027) at 110/1 Sawanwithi Rd, where the cost is from 150 to 250B.

Sala Thai (☎ (056) 222938), at 217-25 Matuli Rd, has air-con rooms from 240 to 380B, and *Airawan (Irawan)* (☎ (056) 221889) at 1-5 Matuli Rd has all air-con rooms from 250 to 450B.

A more expensive hotel is the *Phiman* (☎ (056) 222473), in front of the bus terminal at the Nakhon Sawan shopping centre, where air-con rooms range from 650 to 800B.

Getting There & Away

The ordinary bus fare from Chiang Mai is 98B (180B air-con). From Bangkok, ordinary buses are 57B (107B air-con).

Kamphaeng Phet Province

KAMPHAENG PHET

อ.เมืองกำแพงเพชร

Kamphaeng Phet (population 23,750) was once an important front line of defence for the Sukhothai kingdom but is now mostly known for producing the tastiest *klûay khài* (egg banana) in Thailand.

Old City

เมืองเก่า

Only a couple of km off the Bangkok-Chiang Mai road are some ruins within the old city area of Kamphaeng Phet as well as some very fine remains of the long city wall.

A Kamphaeng Phet Historical Park has been established at the old city site and the area is now cared for by the Department of Fine Arts. There is a 20B entry fee to the ruins within the city wall. Here you'll find **Wat Phra Kaew**, which used to be adjacent to the royal palace. The many weather-corroded Buddha statues here have assumed slender, porous forms which are reminiscent of Giacometti sculpture, as many visitors have commented. About 100 metres southeast of Wat Phra Kaew is **Wat Phra That**, distinguished by a large round-based chedi surrounded by laterite columns.

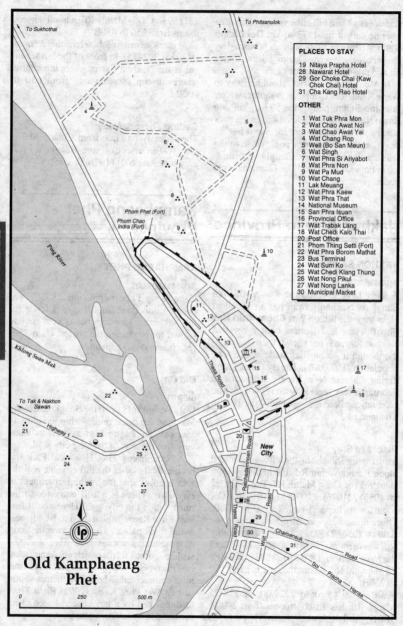

To Sukhothai

To Phitsanulok

PLACES TO STAY

19 Nitaya Prapha Hotel
28 Nawarat Hotel
29 Gor Choke Chai (Kaw Chok Chai) Hotel
31 Cha Kang Rao Hotel

OTHER

1 Wat Tuk Phra Mon
2 Wat Chao Awat Noi
3 Wat Chao Awat Yai
4 Wat Chang Rop
5 Well (Bo San Meun)
6 Wat Singh
7 Wat Phra Si Ariyabot
8 Wat Phra Non
9 Wat Pa Mud
10 Wat Chang
11 Lak Meuang
12 Wat Phra Kaew
13 Wat Phra That
14 National Museum
15 San Phra Isuan
16 Provincial Office
17 Wat Trabak Lang
18 Wat Chedi Kalo Thai
20 Post Office
21 Phom Thing Setti (Fort)
22 Wat Phra Borom Mathat
23 Bus Terminal
24 Wat Sum Ko
25 Wat Chedi Klang Thung
26 Wat Nong Pikul
27 Wat Nong Lanka
30 Municipal Market

Ping River

Khlong Suan Mak

To Tak & Nakhon Sawan

Highway 1

Phom Phet (Fort)
Phom Chao Indra (Fort)

Thesa Road

New City

Ratchadamnoen Road

Charoensuk Road

Wiset Road

Thesa Road

Sol – Pracha – Hansa Road

Old Kamphaeng Phet

0   250   500 m

NORTHERN THAILAND

Kamphaeng Phet National Museum

พิพิธภัณฑ์แห่งชาติกำแพงเพชร

Across the road from these temples is a national museum. Downstairs has the usual survey of Thai art periods while upstairs has a collection of artefacts from the Kamphaeng Phet area, including terracotta ornamentation from ruined temples and Buddha images in the Sukhothai and Ayuthaya styles. The museum is open Wednesday to Sunday from 8.30 am to 4 pm. Admission is 10B.

San Phra Isuan

ศาลพระอิศวร

Near the museum, San Phra Isuan is a shrine with a sandstone base, upon which is a Khmer-style bronze sculpture of Shiva (Isvara). This image is actually a replica, as the original is in the Kamphaeng Phet National Museum.

Wat Phra Borom Mathat

วัดพระบรมธาตุ

Across the Ping River are some more neglected ruins in an area that was settled long before Kamphaeng Phet's heyday, although visible remains are post-classical Sukhothai in design. Wat Phra Borom Mathat features a few small chedis and one large chedi of the late Sukhothai period, which is now crowned with a Burmese-style umbrella added early this century.

Other Wats

North-east of the old city walls, **Wat Phra Si Ariyabot** has the shattered remains of standing, sitting, walking and reclining Buddha images sculpted in the classic Sukhothai style.

North-west of Ariyabot, **Wat Chang Rop** (literally, 'temple surrounded by elephants') is just that – a temple with an elephant-buttressed wall.

Places to Stay

It can be a little difficult finding accommodation since few signs are in roman script.

Nitaya Prapha (☎ (055) 711381) at 118/1 Thesa Rd is an old wooden hotel with rooms from 60 to 80B. It's on the main road leading to the river bridge (near the roundabout) and is the closest hotel to the old city.

Well into the new part of town on the eastern side of Ratchadamnoen Rd is *Ratchadamnoen* (☎ (055) 711029), where fan-cooled rooms range from 100 to 120B (air-con 300B). A bit farther down on the left is the town's top-end hotel, *Cha Kang Rao* (☎ (055) 711315), where all rooms are air-con and rates run from 260 to 1500B. The *Phet Hotel* (☎ (055) 712810) near the municipal market at 99 Wijit Rd is also at the top end, with air-con rooms from 350B.

The next street towards the river is Thesa Rd, and down about 200 metres on the right, set off the road, is the *Navarat (Nawarat)* (☎ (055) 711211), with clean, comfortable air-con rooms starting at 250B, and a coffee shop downstairs. In the centre of the new town, not far from the municipal market, is the bustling but friendly *Gor Choke Chai (Kaw Chok Chai)* (☎ (055) 711247). Rooms with fan and bath cost from 150/180B for one/two beds.

Places to Eat

A small night market sets up every evening in front of the provincial offices near the old city walls and there are also some cheap restaurants near the roundabout.

In the centre of town is a larger day and night market at the intersection of Wijit and Banthoengjit Rds. Several restaurants can be found along Thesa Rd across from Sirijit Park by the river. The *Malai* (no roman-script sign or menu) at 77 Thesa Rd serves good Isaan (north-eastern Thai) food in an outdoor setting. Also on Thesa Rd are a couple of bakeries, *Phayao* and *Tasty*. There are also a few floating restaurants on the river.

Getting There & Away

The bus fare from Bangkok is 84B or 157B air-con. Most visitors arrive from Sukhothai (24B), Phitsanulok (33B) or Tak (17B).

Phitsanulok Province

PHITSANULOK
อ.เมืองพิษณุโลก

Phitsanulok (population 80,000) is often abbreviated as 'Phi-lok'. The town straddles the Nan River about 390 km from Bangkok and makes an excellent base from which to explore the lower north. Besides the venerable temples of Wat Phra Si Ratana Mahathat and Wat Chulamani in town, you can explore the surrounding attractions of historical Sukhothai, Kamphaeng Phet and Si Satchanalai, as well as the national parks of Thung Salaeng Luang and Phu Hin Rong Kla, the former strategic headquarters of the Communist Party of Thailand. All of these places are within a 150-km radius of Phitsanulok.

Check out the markets by the Nan River for bargains on upcountry crafts.

Information
Tourist Office The TAT office (☎ 252742) at 209/7-8 Borom Trailokanat Rd has knowledgeable and helpful staff (some of TAT's best) whose members give out free maps of the town and a sheet that describes a suggested walking tour. The office also distributes info on Sukhothai and Phetchabun provinces.

If you plan to do the trip from Phi-lok to Lom Sak, ask for the sketch map of Highway 12 which marks several waterfalls and resorts along the way.

Post & Telecommunications The GPO on Phuttha Bucha Rd is open Monday to Friday from 8.30 am to 4.30 pm, Saturday and Sunday from 9 am to noon. The attached CAT phone office is open from 7 am to 11 pm daily.

Phitsanulok's area code is ☎ 055.

Money Several banks in town offer foreign-exchange services; only the Bangkok Bank, at 35 Naresuan Rd, has an after-hours exchange window (usually open till 8 pm).

Wat Phra Si Ratana Mahathat
วัดพระศรี

The full name of this temple is Wat Phra Si Ratana Mahathat, but the locals call it Wat Phra Si or Wat Yai. The wat is next to the bridge over the Nan River (on the right as you're heading out of Phi-lok towards Sukhothai). The main wihaan contains the Chinnarat Buddha (Phra Phuttha Chinnarat), one of Thailand's most revered and copied images. This famous bronze image is probably second in importance only to the Emerald Buddha in Bangkok's Wat Phra Kaew. In terms of total annual donations collected (about 12 million baht per year), Wat Yai follows Wat Sothon in Chachoengsao.

The image was cast in the late Sukhothai style, but what makes it strikingly unique is the flame-like halo around the head and torso that turns up at the bottom to become dragon-serpent heads on either side of the image. The head of this Buddha is a little wider than standard Sukhothai, giving the statue a very solid feel.

The story goes that construction of this wat was commissioned under the reign of King Li Thai in 1357. When it was completed, King Li Thai wanted it to contain three high-quality bronze images, so he sent for well-known sculptors from Si Satchanalai, Chiang Saen and Hariphunchai (Lamphun), as well as five Brahman priests. The first two castings worked well, but the third required three attempts before it was decreed the best of all. Legend has it that a white-robed sage appeared from nowhere to assist in the final casting, then disappeared. This last image was named the Chinnarat (Victorious King) Buddha and it became the centrepiece in the wihaan. The other two images, Phra Chinnasi and Phra Si Satsada, were later moved to the royal temple of Wat Bowonniwet in Bangkok. Only the Chinnarat image has the flame-dragon halo.

The walls of the wihaan are low to accommodate the low-swept roof, typical of northern temple architecture, so that the image takes on larger proportions than it might in a central or north-eastern wat. The brilliant interior architecture is such that when you sit on the Italian marble floor in front of the Buddha, the lacquered columns draw your vision towards the image and evoke a strong sense of serenity. The doors of the building are inlaid with mother-of-pearl in a design copied from Bangkok's Wat Phra Kaew.

Another sanctuary to one side has been converted into a museum displaying antique Buddha images, ceramics and other historic artefacts. It's open Wednesday to Sunday from 9 am to 4 pm; admission is free. Dress

appropriately when visiting this most sacred of temples – no shorts or revealing tops.

Near Wat Yai, on the same side of the river, are two other temples of the same period – Wat Ratburan and Wat Nang Phaya.

Wat Chulamani
วัดจุฬามณี

Five km south of the city (a 2B trip on bus No 4 down Borom Trailokanat Rd) is Wat Chulamani, the ruins of which date from the Sukhothai period. The original buildings must have been impressive, judging from

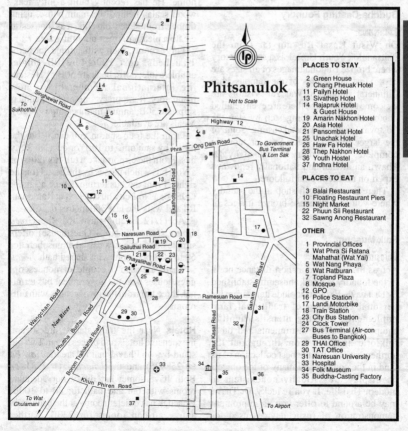

Phitsanulok

Not to Scale

PLACES TO STAY
2 Green House
9 Chang Pheuak Hotel
11 Pailyn Hotel
13 Sivathep Hotel
14 Rajapruk Hotel & Guest House
19 Amarin Nakhon Hotel
20 Asia Hotel
21 Pansombat Hotel
25 Unachak Hotel
26 Haw Fa Hotel
28 Thep Nakhon Hotel
36 Youth Hostel
37 Indhra Hotel

PLACES TO EAT
3 Balai Restaurant
10 Floating Restaurant Piers
15 Night Market
22 Phuun Sii Restaurant
32 Sawng Anong Restaurant

OTHER
1 Provincial Offices
4 Wat Phra Si Ratana Mahathat (Wat Yai)
5 Wat Nang Phaya
6 Wat Ratburan
7 Topland Plaza
8 Mosque
12 GPO
16 Police Station
17 Landi Motorbike
18 Train Station
23 City Bus Station
24 Clock Tower
27 Bus Terminal (Air-con Buses to Bangkok)
29 THAI Office
30 TAT Office
31 Naresuan University
33 Hospital
34 Folk Museum
35 Buddha-Casting Factory

NORTHERN THAILAND

what remains of the ornate Khmer-style tower (prang). King Borom Trailokanat was ordained as a monk here and there is an old Thai inscription to that effect on the ruined wihaan, dating from the reign of King Narai the Great.

The prang itself has little left of its original height, but Khmer-style door lintels remain, including a very nice one with a Sukhothai walking Buddha and a dhammachakka in the background.

Besides the prang and the wihaan, the only original structures left are the remains of the monastery walls. Still, there is a peaceful, neglected atmosphere about the place.

Buddha-Casting Foundry

โรงหล่อพระ

On Wisut Kasat Rd, not far from the Phitsanulok Youth Hostel, is a small factory where bronze Buddha images of all sizes are cast. Most are copies of the famous Phra Chinnarat Buddha at Wat Yai. Visitors are welcome to watch and there are even detailed photo exhibits describing step by step the 'lost wax' method of metal casting. Some of the larger images take a year or more to complete. The foundry is owned by Dr Thawi, an artisan and nationally renowned expert on northern Thai folklore.

There is a small gift shop at the foundry where you can purchase bronze images of various sizes.

Folk Museum

พิพิธภัณฑ์พื้นบ้าน

Across the street and a short distance north of the foundry is a folk museum established by Dr Thawi. Exhibits include items from his personal collection of traditional farm implements, cooking utensils, hunting equipment, musical instruments and other folkloric artefacts from throughout the northern region. It's the best collection of its kind in the country and many of the objects on display are virtually nonexistent in modern Thai life. If you're lucky, Dr Thawi may be around to offer you an impromptu demonstration of rustic devices used for

calling birds and other animals, including elephants! Entrance to the museum is by donation.

Places to Stay – bottom end

Phit has good coverage in the budget accommodation category.

Guesthouses & Hostels The *Phitsanulok Youth Hostel* (☎ 242060) at 38 Sanam Bin Rd is in a 40-year-old house shaded by jasmine vines and is quite comfortable. Sapachai, the owner, worked as a systems analyst in Bangkok for 10 years before giving up the rat race to return to his boyhood home. He has recently built a lofty teakwood saalaa behind the main house, using timber from seven old Tak teak houses to create a pleasant, open-air sitting area.

Large rooms, each with antique northern-Thai beds, cost 100/140/210B single/double/triple; dorm beds are 50B. A Hostelling International membership is now mandatory (temporary one-night memberships are 50B; annual membership is 300B). Meals are available.

From the train station you can get to the hostel by samlor (5 to 10B) or on a No 3 city bus. From the airport take a tuk-tuk (20B) or a No 4 bus which passes by the hostel (on the right). From the bus terminal, take a samlor (20B) or a No 1 city bus (get off at Ramesuan Rd and walk the last 300 metres or so).

At 11/12 Ekathotsarot Rd, the *Green House* (formerly No 4 Guesthouse) offers simple comfort and a casual atmosphere for 60 to 80B per room with shared bath.

There are also a couple of nondescript guesthouses near the government bus terminal, three km from the town centre, with 60B rooms.

Hotels Near the train station are several inexpensive hotels and places to eat. Two old stand-bys on Phayalithai Rd are the *Haw Fa* (☎ 258425) and the *Unachak* (☎ 258387). Both have somewhat dingy but adequate rooms with fan and bath for 80 to 100B; Unachak has quieter rooms at the back, plus a few air-con rooms for 220B. Farther towards the river on Phayalithai Rd is the similar *Chanprasert* for 60 to 120B.

If you turn left out of the station and then take the first right turn on to Sailuthai Rd, you'll come to *Pansombat Hotel* on the left side of the road. Rooms with shared bath and toilet are 70B, or 80 to 150B with toilet. It's noisy and a bit of a brothel, however. The *Sukkit* (☎ 258876) at 20/1-2 Sailuthai Rd is a bit better at 120 to 150B for a room with fan, 300B air-con. Another Sailuthai Rd cheapie, the *Chokeprasit Hotel*, has rock-bottom rooms with shared bath for 40 to 80B.

Not far from the train station on Ekathotsarot Rd is the *Asia Hotel* (☎ 258378), with quite decent rooms for just 100 to 150B.

Places to Stay – middle

Behind the more up-market Rajapruk Hotel on Phra Ong Dam Rd is the *Rajapruk Guest House Hotel* (☎ 258788), where fan-cooled rooms with hot showers go for 214B, air-con 321B. Guests may use the Rajapruk Hotel swimming pool.

Also good is the newish *Indhra Hotel* (☎ 259188, 259638) at 103/8 Sithamatraipidok Rd, south of Phutthachinnarat Provincial Hospital (Phitsanulok Teaching Hospital). Clean air-con singles/doubles with TV are 200 to 800B.

The *Chang Pheuak Hotel* (☎ 252822) at 66/28 Phra Ong Dam Rd and *Sivathep Hotel* (☎ 244933) at 110/21 Prasongprasat were once the top end in Phi-lok. Both offer clean air-con rooms for 220 to 400B.

Places to Stay – top end

Phi-lok's upper-end hotels all start at 1000B or less, making it one of Thailand's bargain provincial capitals. *Rajapruk Hotel* (☎ 258477; fax 251395) at 99/9 Phra Ong Dam Rd offers good upper-range value. All rooms come with air-con, hot showers, carpeting, TV and telephone for 800B for singles/doubles.

Others in this range include *Thep Nakhon Hotel* (☎ 258507) at 43/1 Sithamatraipidok Rd, from 1000B; *Pailyn Hotel* (☎ 252411) at 38 Borom Trailokanat Rd, from 942B; *Nan Chao Hotel* (☎ 252510; fax 244794), from 780B; and *Amarin Nakhon Hotel* (☎ 258588), 3/1 Chao Phraya Phitsanulok Rd, from 640B.

The new 200-room *Topland Plaza Hotel* is under construction next to the Topland Plaza shopping centre at the intersection of Singhawat and Ekathotsarot Rds. Room rates are projected to start at 650B.

Places to Eat

Phitsanulok is a great town for eating – there must be more restaurants per capita here than in just about any other town in Thailand.

Excellent, inexpensive Thai food can be had at the *Phuun Sii* opposite the Haw Fa Hotel on Phayalithai Rd. Recommended dishes here include tôm khàa kài (chicken-coconut soup), lâap (minced meat salad), kaeng mátsàman kài (Muslim chicken curry) and thâwt man plaa (fried fish cakes). *Tui Phochana*, opposite Phuun Sii and operated by a cousin from the same family, makes fabulous yam khanŭn (curried jackfruit) at the beginning of the cool season, plus many other outstanding Thai curries year-round. There are plenty of other cheap Thai restaurants in this area too.

Close to the Phitsanulok Youth Hostel are several small noodle and rice shops. Across from the Naresuan (formerly Sinakharin-wirot) University campus on Sanam Bin Rd is the very popular and very inexpensive *Sawng Anong* outdoor restaurant, open from 9 am to 3 pm daily. It has a great selection of curries, noodles and Thai desserts, all priced at less than 15B. Try the *săo náam*, a mixture of pineapple, coconut, dried shrimp, ginger and garlic served over khanŏm jiin – it's delicious. Also good is the *kaeng yûak*, a curry made from the heart of a banana palm, and kŭaytĭaw sùkhŏthai, thin rice noodles served dry in a bowl with peanuts, barbecued pork, spices, green beans, and bean sprouts.

Early risers should try the small but lively morning market next to Naresuan University. Vendors serve inexpensive khâo man kài (Hainanese chicken and rice), salabao

(Chinese buns), paa-thông-kõ (Chinese doughnuts) and jók (broken-rice soup) from 6 to 10 am daily.

The cheapest meal in town has got to be kũaytĩaw phàt thai (Thai-style fried rice noodles) at the intersection of Phra Ong Dam Rd and Ekathotsarot Rd. The intersection is called Sii-Yaek Baan Khaek (Indian Village Crossroads) and the vendor on the north-west corner has been serving up 5B dishes of phàt thai (10B for two eggs) for many years.

By the mosque on Phra Ong Dam Rd are several Thai-Muslim cafes. One very famous one (no English sign – look for the crowded place near the railroad crossing, with the mosque directly behind it) has thick rotis served with kaeng mátsàman, which is unusual this far north. Ask for roti kaeng to get the set plate. This small cafe also has fresh milk and yoghurt.

A small restaurant next to the Indhra Hotel offers very inexpensive vegetarian food.

Several restaurants along Sanam Bin Rd in the vicinity of the youth hostel serve good medium-priced Thai and Chinese dishes, eg *Feuang Fah* (air-con), *Rak* (air-con) and *Daeng* (outdoors).

If you're out past midnight, your best bet is the very good, 24-hour khâo tôm place next to the train station.

On the River Floating restaurants light up the Nan River at night. Good choices include *Song Khwae, Fa Thai* and *Rim Nam*. South of the main string of floating restaurants is a pier where you can board a restaurant-boat owned by Fa Thai that cruises the Nan River every night. You pay 20B to board the boat and then order from a menu as you please – no minimum charge.

Also along the river is a popular night market area with dozens of food vendors, a couple of whom specialise in *phàk bûng loi fáa* (literally, 'floating-in-the-sky morning glory vine'), which usually translates more simply as 'flying vegetable'. This food fad originated in Chonburi but has somehow taken root in Phi-lok. There are several of these places in town as well as along the river. The dish is basically morning glory vine stir-fried in soy bean sauce and garlic, but with a performance included. The cook fires up a batch in the wok and then flings it through the air to a waiting server who catches it on a plate. The eating places on the river are now so performance-oriented that the server climbs to the top of a van to catch the flying vegetable! Tour companies bring tour groups here and invite tourists to try the catch – it's just as amusing watching the tourists drop phàk bûng all over the place as it is to watch the cook. During the day this area is a sundries market.

The old and established *Balai* – just back from the river and north of Wat Phra Si – is famous for kũaytĩaw hâwy khàa (literally, 'legs-hanging rice noodles'). The name comes from the way customers sit on a bench facing the river, with their legs dangling below. It's only open from 10 am to 4 pm daily.

Entertainment

Along Borom Trailokanat Rd near the Pailyn Hotel is a string of popular Thai pubs. Local favourites include Country Road (old-west style) and Boran Ban Thoeng (classic Thai).

King Kong III, north of the youth hostel on the opposite side of Sanam Bin Rd, is a sing-song club with moderate prices.

Getting There & Away

Air The THAI office (☎ 258020) is at 209/26-28 Borom Trailokanat Rd. THAI has two daily 45-minute flights to Phitsanulok from Bangkok for 920B one way. There are also flights between Phitsanulok and Chiang Mai (daily, 650B), Lampang (daily, 485B), Mae Sot (four times weekly, 495B), Nan (thrice weekly, 575B) and Tak (four times weekly, 325B).

Phitsanulok's airport is just out of town. Songthaews leave the airport every 20 minutes or so and go into town for 5B, otherwise you can catch the No 4 city bus for 2B. The big hotels in town run free buses from the airport, and THAI has a door-to-door van service for 30B per person.

Bus Transport choices out of Phitsanulok are very good, as it's a junction for bus lines running both north and north-east. Bangkok is six hours away by bus and Chiang Mai 5½ hours. Ordinary buses leave Bangkok's northern bus terminal for Phitsanulok several times daily and cost 96B (163B air-con). Be sure to get the *sǎi mài* (new route) bus via Nakhon Sawan (Route 117), as the old route via Tak Fa (Highway 11) takes six hours and costs more. Yan Yon Tour and Win Tour run VIP buses between Bangkok and Phitsanulok for 210B.

Direct buses between Phitsanulok and Loei via Dan Sai cost 58B (104B air-con) and take four hours. Buses to destinations in other north and north-east provinces leave several times a day from the Baw Khaw Saw (government bus terminal), except for the air-con buses which may depart only once or twice a day:

City	Fare	Duration
Chiang Mai (via Den Chai)	86B	5½ hours
(air-con)	155B	5½ hours
Chiang Mai (via Tak)	104B	6 hours
(air-con)	146B	6 hours
Chiang Rai (via Sukhothai)	104B	6½ hours
(air-con)	146B	6 hours
Chiang Rai (via Utaradit)	115B	7½ hours
(air-con)	160B	7 hours
Khon Kaen	92B	5 hours
(air-con)	129 to 156B	5 hours
Khorat (Nakhon Ratchasima)	82B	6 hours
(air-con)	146B	6 hours
Mae Sot	59B	5 hours
(air-con)	83B	5 hours
Udon Thani	91B	7 hours
(air-con)	164B	7 hours

Buses to the following nearby points leave on the hour (*), every two hours (**) or every three hours (***) from early morning until 5 or 6 pm (except for Sukhothai buses, which leave every half-hour):

City	Fare	Duration
Dan Sai**	38B	3 hours
Kamphaeng Phet*	30B	3 hours
Lom Sak*	40B	2 hours
Phetchabun***	47B	3 hours
Sukhothai	16B	1 hour
Tak*	36B	3 hours
Utaradit*	41B	3 hours

Train The 6.40 am and 3 pm rapid trains from Bangkok arrive in Phitsanulok at 12.33 and 9.15 pm. The basic fare is 143B 2nd class or 292B 1st class, plus a 20B surcharge for the rapid service. There is also an all air-con, 1st-class diesel service (No 907) daily at 8.10 am that arrives in Phitsanulok at 1.13 pm, an hour shorter than the rapid service. The 285B fare includes a meal and a snack.

The third-class fare (69B) is only available on ordinary trains; the ordinary train with the most convenient arrival time is No 101, which leaves Bangkok at 7.05 am (or Ayuthaya at 8.40 am) and arrives in Phitsanulok at 2.55 pm.

Trains between Phit and Chiang Mai cost 65B in 3rd class, 136B in 2nd class and 276B in 1st class (not including rapid or express charges for 1st and 2nd-class trains).

If you're going straight on to Sukhothai from Phitsanulok, a tuk-tuk ride from the station to the bus station four km away is 20B. From there you can get a bus to Sukhothai. Or you can catch a Sukhothai-bound bus anywhere along Singhawat Rd on the west side of the river; a tuk-tuk to Singhawat costs 5B from the train station.

Getting Around
Samlor rides within the town centre should cost 10 to 15B per person. City buses are 2B and there are five lines making the rounds, so you should be able to get just about anywhere by bus. A couple of the lines also feature air-con coaches for 5B. The terminal

for city buses is near the train station off Ekathotsarot Rd.

Motorcycles can be rented at Landi Motorbike (☎ 252765) at 57/21-22 Phra Ong Dam Rd (near Rajapruk Hotel). Rates are 150B a day for a 100cc and 200B for a 150cc.

PHU HIN RONG KLA NATIONAL PARK
อุทยานแห่งชาติภูหินร่องกล้า

From 1967 to 1982, Phu Hin Rong Kla was the strategic headquarters for the Communist Party of Thailand (CPT) and its tactical arm, the People's Liberation Army of Thailand (PLAT). The location was perfect for an insurgent army, as it was high in the mountains and there were very few roads into CPT territory. Another benefit was that the headquarters were only 50 km from the Lao border, so lines of retreat were well guarded after 1975 when Laos fell to the Pathet Lao. China's Yunnan Province was only 300 km away and it was in the provincial capital, Kunming, that CPT cadres received their training in revolutionary tactics. Because they were tired of being hassled by the Bangkok government for growing opium, many Hmong from this area became willing recruits for the PLAT and Pathet Lao.

The CPT camp at Phu Hin Rong Kla became especially active after the October 1976 student uprising in Bangkok in which hundreds of students were killed by the Thai military. Many students fled here to join the CPT and they set up a hospital and a school of political and military tactics. For nearly 20 years the area around Phu Hin Rong Kla served as a battlefield for skirmishes between Thailand's 3rd Army Division, garrisoned in Phitsanulok, and the PLAT.

In 1972, the Thai government launched the 1st, 2nd and 3rd armies, plus the navy, air force, and national guard against the PLAT in an attempt to rout them from Phu Hin Rong Kla, but the action was unsuccessful. By 1978 the PLAT here had swelled to 4000. In 1980 and 1981, the Thai armed forces tried again and were able to recapture some parts of CPT territory. But the decisive blow

to the CPT came in 1982 when the government declared an amnesty for all the students who had joined the communists after 1976. The departure of most of the students broke the spine of the movement, which had, by this time, become dependent on their membership. A final military push in 1982 effected the surrender of the PLAT and Phu Hin Rong Kla was declared a national park in 1984.

Orientation & Information

The park covers about 307 sq km of rugged mountains and forest. The elevation at park headquarters is about 1000 metres, so the park is refreshingly cool even in the hot season. The main attractions are the remains of the CPT stronghold, including a rustic courthouse/meeting hall, the school of military tactics and politics and the CPT administration building. Across the road from the school is a waterwheel designed by exiled engineering students.

In another area of the park is a trail that goes to Phaa Chu Thong (Flag Raising Cliff, sometimes called Red Flag Cliff), where the communists would raise the red flag to announce when they had had a military victory. Also in this area is an air-raid shelter, a lookout and the remains of the main CPT headquarters – the most inaccessible point in the territory before a road was constructed by the Thai government. The buildings in the park are bamboo and wood huts with no plumbing or electricity – a testament to how primitive the living conditions were for the insurgents.

At the park headquarters is a small museum which displays relics from CPT days, including medical instruments and weapons. At the end of the road into the park is a small White Hmong village. When the CPT were here, the Hmong were their allies. Now they've switched allegiance to the Thai government and are undergoing 'development'. One wonders what would have happened if the CPT had succeeded in its revolutionary goal. Maybe the 3rd Army headquarters in Phitsanulok would now be a museum instead.

If you're not interested in the history of Phu Hin Rong Kla, there are hiking trails, waterfalls and scenic views, plus some interesting rock formations – an area of jutting boulders called Laan Hin Pum (Million Knotty Rocks) and an area of deep rocky crevices where PLAT troops would hide during air raids, called Laan Hin Taek (Million Broken Rocks).

Places to Stay

The Forestry Department rents out bungalows that sleep five for 600B, eight for 800B, 10 for 1000B and 14 for 1500B. You can pitch your own tent for 10B a night or sleep in park tents for 40B per person (no bedding provided except blankets for 20B per night). If you want to build a fire, you can buy chopped wood for 150B a night.

You can book accommodation in advance through the Forestry Department's Bangkok office (☎ (02) 579-0529/4842), or locally by calling their provincial office (☎ 389002) or Golden House Tour Company (☎ 259973, 389002) in Phitsanulok.

You can also stay at one of several resorts just off Highway 12 west of the Route 2013 junction for Nakhon Thai. Best of the lot is the *Rainforest Resort* (radio ☎ (01) 520-0294; (02) 423-0749 in Bangkok) at Km 44. Spacious, tastefully designed cottages spread over a hillside facing the Khek River cost 800B for two people; there is also one cottage for eight to 10 people for 1500B. All cottages come with air-con and hot water. An indoor-outdoor restaurant serves locally grown coffee and good Thai food. Other resorts in the area, *Wang Nam Yen, Santamas Rimkaeng* and *Thanthong* are similarly priced.

Places to Eat

Near the campground and bungalows are some food vendors. The best is *Duang Jai Cafeteria* – try their famous carrot sômtam.

On the way to or from Phitsanulok, stop at *Blue Mountain Coffee* at Km 42, *Rainfor-*

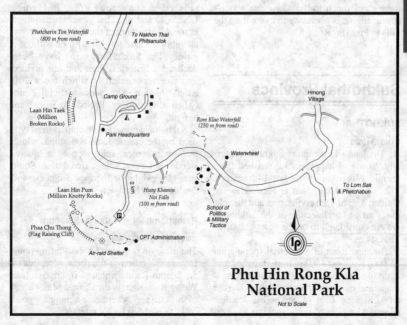

Phu Hin Rong Kla National Park

Not to Scale

Phatcharin Ton Waterfall (800 m from road)

To Nakhon Thai & Phitsanulok

Camp Ground

Hmong Village

Laan Hin Taek (Million Broken Rocks)

Rom Klao Waterfall (250 m from road)

Park Headquarters

Waterwheel

Laan Hin Pum (Million Knotty Rocks)

Huay Khamin Noi Falls (100 m from road)

To Lom Sak & Phetchabun

School of Politics & Military Tactics

Phaa Chu Thong (Flag Raising Cliff)

CPT Administration

Air-raid Shelter

est Resort at Km 44 or *Thawee Fresh Coffee* at Km 45, all on Highway 12 near Ban Kaeng Sawng (close to Kaeng Sawng Waterfall). These restaurants serve some of the best fresh coffee outside of Bangkok; the beans are all locally grown *kafae jàak râi* (literally 'coffee from the fields') but have names like Blue Mountain and Brazil. Freshly brewed coffee costs between 15 and 25B per cup, but it's worth it for 100% Arabica or Robusta beans. Ordinarily, Thai coffee is mixed with ground tamarind seed and other additives.

Getting There & Away
The park headquarters are about 125 km from Phitsanulok. To get there, first take an early bus to Nakhon Thai (32B), where you can catch a songthaew to the park (three times daily between 7.30 am and 4.30 pm for 20B).

A small group could also charter a pick-up and driver in Nakhon Thai to visit all the spots for about 550B for the day. This is a delightful trip if you're on a motorbike as there's not much traffic along the way. A strong engine is necessary to make it up the hills to Phu Hin Rong Kla.

Sukhothai Province

SUKHOTHAI
อ.เมืองสุโขทัย
As Thailand's first capital, Sukhothai (literally, 'rising of happiness') flourished from the mid-13th century to the late-14th century. The Sukhothai kingdom is viewed as the Golden Age of Thai civilisation and the religious art and architecture of the Sukhothai era are considered to be the most classic of Thai styles.

The new town of Sukhothai (population 25,000) is almost 450 km from Bangkok and is undistinguished except for its very good municipal market in the town centre. The old city *(meuang kào)* of Sukhothai features around 45 sq km of ruins, making an over-night stay in New Sukhothai worthwhile, although you could make a day trip to Old Sukhothai from Phitsanulok.

Information
Sky House (☎ 611175), a guesthouse next to the bus terminal, serves as an informal tourist information centre and tourist police headquarters.

The post office on Nikhom Kasem Rd has an attached CAT office with international phone service daily from 7 am to 11 pm. Sukhothai's area code is ☎ 055.

Sukhothai Historical Park
The original capital was surrounded by three concentric ramparts and two moats bridged by four gateways. Today the remains of 21 historical sites and four large ponds can be seen within the old walls, with an additional 70 sites within a five-km radius. The more remote ruins in the hills west of the old city walls, such as Saphaan Hin, used to be considered a dangerous area, but since UNESCO and the Thai government joined in the development of the old city environs, all ruins are safe to visit with or without a guide. The Sukhothai ruins have been declared a historical park and are divided into five zones, each of which has a .20B admission fee. The park's official hours (when admission is collected) are from 6 am to 6 pm.

Sukhothai temple architecture is most typified by the classic lotus-bud stupa, which features a conical spire topping a square-sided structure on a three-tiered base. Some sites also exhibit bell-shaped Sinhalese and double-tiered Srivijaya stupas.

Ramkhamhaeng National Museum
พิพิธภัณฑ์แห่งชาติรามคำแหง
The museum provides a good starting point for an exploration of the ruins. A replica of the famous Ramkhamhaeng inscription (see Wiang Kum Kam in the Chiang Mai section of this chapter) is kept here amongst a good collection of Sukhothai artefacts.

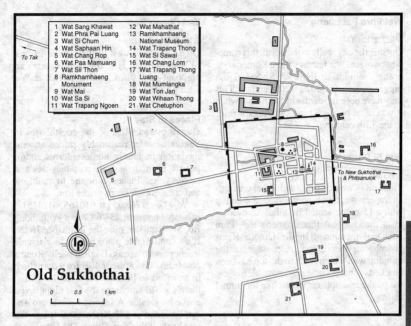

1	Wat Sang Khawat	12	Wat Mahathat
2	Wat Phra Pai Luang	13	Ramkhamhaeng
3	Wat Si Chum		National Museum
4	Wat Saphaan Hin	14	Wat Trapang Thong
5	Wat Chang Rop	15	Wat Si Sawai
6	Wat Paa Mamuang	16	Wat Chang Lom
7	Wat Sil Thon	17	Wat Trapang Thong
8	Ramkhamhaeng		Luang
	Monument	18	Wat Mumlangka
9	Wat Mai	19	Wat Ton Jan
10	Wat Sa Si	20	Wat Wihaan Thong
11	Wat Trapang Ngoen	21	Wat Chetuphon

To Tak

To New Sukhothai
& Phitsanulok

Old Sukhothai

0   0.5   1 km

The museum is open Wednesday to Sunday from 9 am to 4 pm and admission is 20B.

Wat Mahathat

วัดมหาาตุ

The largest in the city and built in the 13th century, Wat Mahathat is surrounded by brick walls (206 metres long and 200 metres wide) and a moat. The stupa spires feature the famous lotus-bud motif and some of the original stately Buddha figures still sit among the ruined columns of the old wihaans. There are 198 chedis within the monastery walls – a lot to explore.

Wat Si Sawai

วัดศรีสวาย

Just south of Wat Mahathat, this shrine (dating from the 12th and 13th centuries) features three corn-cob-like prangs and a

picturesque moat. It was originally built by the Khmers as a Hindu temple.

Wat Sa Si

วัดสระศรี

'Sacred Pond Monastery' sits on an island west of the Ramkhamhaeng Monument. It's a simple, classic Sukhothai-style wat with one large Buddha, one chedi and the columns of the ruined wihaan.

Wat Trapang Thong

วัดตระพังทอง

Next to the museum, this small, still-inhabited wat is reached by a footbridge across the large lotus-filled pond which surrounds it. This reservoir, the original site of the Loy Krathong Festival in Thailand, supplies the Sukhothai community with most of its water.

Wat Phra Pai Luang

วัดพระพายหลวง

Outside the city walls to the north, this somewhat isolated wat features three Khmer-style prangs, similar to those at Si Sawai but bigger, dating from the 12th century. This may have been the centre of Sukhothai when it was ruled by the Khmers of Angkor prior to the 13th century.

Wat Si Chum

วัดศรีชุม

This wat is west of the old city and contains an impressive, much-photographed mondop with a 15-metre seated Buddha. Archaeologists theorise that this image is the 'Phra Atchana' mentioned in the famous Ramkhamhaeng inscription. A passage in the mondop wall which leads to the top has been blocked so that it's no longer possible to view the jataka inscriptions which line the tunnel ceiling.

Wat Chang Lom

วัดช้างลม

Off Highway 12, 'Elephant Circled Monastery' is about a km east of the main park entrance. A large chedi is supported by 36 elephants sculpted into its base.

Wat Saphaan Hin

วัดสะพานหิน

Saphaan Hin is a couple of km to the west of the old city walls, on the crest of a hill that rises about 200 metres above the plain. The name of the wat, which means stone bridge, is a reference to the slate path and staircase leading to the temple, which are still in place. The site affords a good view of the Sukhothai ruins to the south-east and the mountains to the north and south.

All that remains of the original temple are a few chedis and the ruined wihaan, consisting of two rows of laterite columns flanking a 12.5-metre-high standing Buddha image on a brick terrace.

Wat Chang Rop

วัดช้างรอบ

On another hill west of the city, just south of Wat Saphaan Hin, this wat features an elephant-base stupa, similar to that at Wat Chang Lom.

Places to Stay

Guesthouses Most of the guesthouses in Sukhothai offer reasonably priced accommodation in family homes (dorms and/or private rooms), and all rent bicycles and motorcycles. Places continue to multiply, and competition keeps prices low.

No 4 Guest House (☎ 610165, 611315) is in a large house at 234/6 Charot Withithong Rd, Soi Panitsan, near the Rajthanee Hotel. It's a comfortable place run by four female teachers who speak English well. Rooms cost from 60 to 80B, or 40B for a dorm bed; in an effort to beat the local samlor mafia, there's a 20B surcharge the first night if you arrive by samlor. A second branch, No 4B, can be found at 170 Ratchathani Rd on the east bank of the Yom River. The latter is set on spacious grounds, with a garden sitting area, and is quite suitable for long-term stays.

Yupa House (☎ 612578) is near the west bank of the Yom River at 44/10 Prawet Nakhon Rd, Soi Mekhapatthana. The family that runs it is friendly and helpful and often invites guests to share family meals. They have a 30B dorm, plus rooms of various sizes from 60 to 100B. There's a nice view of the city from the roof. *Somprasong Guest House* (☎ 611709) is on the way to Yupa along the same road, at No 32. The rooms are arranged hotel-like on the 2nd floor of a large family house and cost 50/80B for singles/doubles with fan and bath. Also along this road, next door to the Somprasong, is the newer *Ban Thai* (☎ 610163), run by yet another friendly family for 60/80B with shared bath, 80/120B with private bath. Ban Thai is a good place for straight info on things to see and do in the Sukhothai area.

Another new entry to the guesthouse scene is *Friend House* at 52/7 Soi Nissan, off Loet Thai Rd (parallel to Prawet Nakhon

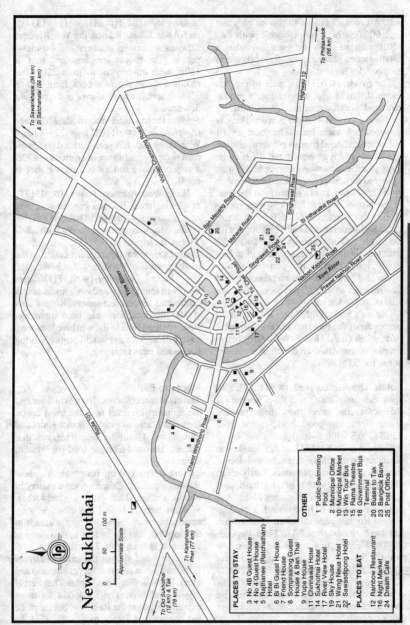

New Sukhothai

To Sawankhalok (36 km)
& Si Satchanalai (56 km)

To Sawankhalok (36 km)

To Phitsanulok (56 km)

Highway 12

Vichian Chamnong Road

Ban Meuang Road

Maharat Road

Singhawat Road

Si Intharathit Road

Singhawat Road

Nikhon Kasem Road

Prawet Nakhon Road

Yom River

Yom River

Charot Withithong Road

Route 101

To Old Sukhothai
(12 km) & Tak

To Kamphaeng
Phet (77 km)

Approximate Scale

0   50   100 m

To Old Sukhothai
(12 km) & Tak (78 km)

PLACES TO STAY

3   No 4B Guest House
4   No 4 Guest House
5   Rajthanee (Ratchathani)
     Hotel
6   Bi Bi Guest House
7   Friend House
8   Somprasong Guest
     House & Ban Thai
9   Yupa House
11 Chinnawat Hotel
14 Sukhothai Hotel
17 River View Hotel
19 Sky House
21 Wang Neua Hotel
22 Sawasdipong Hotel

PLACES TO EAT

12 Rainbow Restaurant
16 Night Market
24 Dream Cafe

OTHER

1   Public Swimming
     Pool
2   Municipal Office
10 Municipal Market
13 Win Tour Bus
15 Rama Theatre
18 Government Bus
     Terminal
20 Buses to Tak
23 Bangkok Bank
25 Post Office

Rd). All rooms come with private bath and cost 60/80B for a single/double with fan, 150B with air-con. The guesthouse has a small garden dining area, free bikes and motorcycles for rent.

Sky House (☎ 611175), next to the bus terminal, has tourist information, a restaurant and singles/doubles for 60/80B, or four-bed rooms at 40B per person. There is a shared hot-water bath. The local tourist police are stationed here so it's very safe, but there's not much ambience and it's become more of an information clearing house than a place to stay. Sky House has a better branch (☎ 612237) two km from town on the road to the historical park. Single/double rooms at this location are 60/80B with bath, 120/150B with fan and bath, 180/200B with fan, bath and mountain views, 260/300B with air-con and hot water. The staff at Sky House 1 will provide free transport to Sky House 2 if you need it. Both branches lend free bicycles to guests, and motorbikes are also available for rent.

Out on Charot Withithong Rd, about 30 metres from the bus stop for the Historical Park, *Bi Bi Guest House* (☎ 610425) offers simple rooms with shared bath in a wooden house for 50 to 80B.

Hotels The *Sawasdipong* (☎ 611567), also spelt *Sawatdiphong*, at 56/2-5 Singhawat Rd, across the street from the expensive Wang Neua, has good, basic rooms from 120B (250B with air-con).

Sukhothai (☎ 611133), at 5/5 Singhawat Rd, is an old travellers' favourite with lots of room to sit around downstairs. Fairly clean singles/doubles with fan and bath cost 120/180B and air-con rooms are 250B.

Chinnawat (☎ 611385), at 1-3 Nikhon Kasem Rd, has gone downhill. Rooms with fan and bath cost from 80 to 140B, depending on whether they are in the old or new wing – the old wing is cheaper and a bit quieter. Air-con rooms cost from 200 to 350B, and there are a couple of large rooms with air-con and hot-water bath for 400B. Be sure to check that the air-con works before booking in.

River View Hotel (☎ 611656; fax 613373), on Nikhon Kasem Rd near the Yom River, is a favourite among truckers and business-people. The rooms are clean and start at 150B, with air-con rooms from 220B and rooms with all the mod-cons from 400 to 650B. There is a large lounge and restaurant downstairs.

Once the top hotel in town, the *Rajthanee (Ratchathani)* (☎ 611031), at 229 Charot Withithong Rd, has seen better days. Standard rooms with fan are overpriced at 470B a single/double and air-con rooms start at 600B.

Wang Neua (Northern Palace) (☎ 611193), at 43 Singhawat Rd, has gone upscale and now charges 475B for Thais, 600B for farangs, for unimpressive rooms with small TVs and refrigerators.

About eight km from the city centre on the road between old and new Sukhothai, the huge *Pailyn Sukhothai* (☎ 613311) caters mostly to tour groups and has a disco, health centre and several restaurants. Rooms start at 1000B; occupancy has been quite low since opening (due to the nowhere location), so a little negotiation would probably bring the quoted rates tumbling.

Places to Eat

The night market across from Win Tour and the municipal market near the town centre are great places to eat. Sukhothai Hotel and Chinnawat Hotel have restaurants that prepare Thai and Chinese food for Western tastes.

Across from Win Tour, the *Rainbow Restaurant & Ice Cream* serves a variety of noodle dishes, Thai curries, sandwiches, Western breakfasts and ice cream at very reasonable prices. The downstairs area is in the open air, and the indoor upstairs area is air-con. It is open from 7 am to 10 pm.

On the same side of the street is *Dream Cafe*, an air-con cafe that serves espresso and other 100% coffee drinks, plus Thai herbal liquors and beer. The food is a bit more expensive than at the Rainbow, but the place has character. A larger, nicer version of the

Dream Cafe is on Singhawat Rd opposite Bangkok Bank. The extensive menu includes a long list of herbal liquors ('stamina drinks'), ice-cream dishes and very well-prepared Thai and Chinese food. The owner is a long-time antique collector and the place is thickly decorated with 19th-century Thai antiques, a look that is very 'in' with young upper-class Thais these days.

Getting There & Away

Air As yet there is no public air service to/from Sukhothai, but Bangkok Airways has plans to open its own airfield by the end of 1994.

Bus Sukhothai can be reached by road from Phitsanulok, Tak or Kamphaeng Phet. If you arrive in Phitsanulok by rail or air, take a city bus No 1 (2B) to the air-con bus terminal in the centre, or to the Baw Khaw Saw (government bus) terminal, for buses out of town. The bus to Sukhothai costs 16B, takes about an hour and leaves regularly throughout the day.

From Tak, get a Sukhothai bus at the Baw Khaw Saw terminal just outside town. The fare is 23B and the trip takes about 1½ hours. Buses from Kamphaeng Phet are 23B and take from one to 1½ hours.

Ordinary Baw Khaw Saw buses to/from Chiang Mai cost 91B via Tak (the shortest, fastest route) and take from 4½ to five hours; air-con is 127B. Buses between Bangkok and Sukhothai are 106B (191B air-con) and take seven hours. Buses to Chiang Rai cost 102B (142B air-con) and take six hours. Buses to Khon Kaen cost 120B (185B air-con) and take from six to seven hours.

Phitsanulok Yan Yon Tour has a daily VIP bus (with reclining seats) to Bangkok for 225B that leaves at 10.45 pm. Ordinary buses to destinations outside Sukhothai Province leave from the government bus terminal; tour buses leave from Win Tour or Phitsanulok Yan Yon Tour near the night market area. Buses to Tak leave from Ban Meuang Rd, two streets east of Singhawat Rd.

Buses to Sawankhalok (10B, 45 minutes) and Si Satchanalai (19B, one hour) leave hourly from the intersection opposite the Sukhothai Hotel, between about 6 am and 6 pm.

Getting Around

Around New Sukhothai, a samlor ride shouldn't cost more than 10 or 15B. Songthaews run frequently between New Sukhothai and the old city (Sukhothai Historical Park), leaving from Charot Withithong Rd near the Yom River; the fare is 5B and it takes 20 to 30 minutes from the river to the park.

The best way to get around Old Sukhothai is by bicycle; these can be rented at shops outside the park entrance for 20B per day or you could borrow or rent one at any guesthouse in the new city.

The park operates a bus tour service through the old city for 20B per person. Local farmers sometimes offer bullock cart rides through the park for about the same rate.

SI SATCHANALAI-CHALIANG HISTORICAL PARK

อุทยานประวัติศาสตร์ศรีสัชนาลัย-ชะเลียง

The Sukhothai-period ruins at the old city sites of Si Satchanalai and Chaliang are in the same basic style as those in Old Sukhothai, but with some slightly larger sites. The 13th to 15th-century ruins cover roughly 720 hectares, surrounded by a 12-metre-wide moat. Chaliang, a km to the south-east, is an older city site (dating to the 11th century) though the two temple remains date to the 14th century.

The ruins at Si Satchanalai are set among hills and are very attractive in the sense that they're not as heavily visited as the Sukhothai ruins. Recent additions to the park include a coffee shop near the ponds in the middle of the complex. Elephant rides through the park are available for 50 to 100B per person.

Admission to the historical park is 20B.

NORTHERN THAILAND

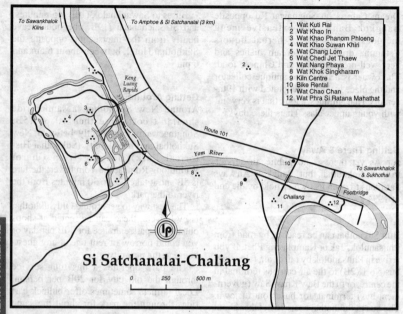

To Sawankhalok Kilns

To Amphoe & Si Satchanalai (3 km)

1 Wat Kuti Rai
2 Wat Khao In
3 Wat Khao Phanom Phloeng
4 Wat Khao Suwan Khiri
5 Wat Chang Lom
6 Wat Chedi Jet Thaew
7 Wat Nang Phaya
8 Wat Khok Singkharam
9 Kiln Centre
10 Bike Rental
11 Wat Chao Chan
12 Wat Phra Si Ratana Mahathat

Keng Luang Rapids

Route 101

Yom River

To Sawankhalok & Sukhothai

Chaliang

Footbridge

Si Satchanalai-Chaliang

0   250   500 m

Wat Chang Lom

วัดช้างล้อม

This temple has the same name and style as the one in Sukhothai – elephants surrounding a stupa – but is somewhat better preserved. A stone inscription says the temple was built by King Ramkhamhaeng between 1285 and 1291.

Wat Khao Phanom Phloeng

วัดเขาพนมเพลิง

On the hill overlooking Wat Chang Lom to the right are the remains of Wat Khao Phanom Phloeng, including a large seated Buddha, a chedi and stone columns which once supported the roof of the wihaan. From this hill you can make out the general design of the once great city. The slightly higher hill west of Phanom Phloeng is capped by a large Sukhothai chedi – all that remains of **Wat Khao Suwan Khiri**.

Wat Chedi Jet Thaew

วัดเจดีย์เจ็ดแถว

Next to Wat Chang Lom, these ruins contain seven rows of lotus-bud chedis, the largest of which is a copy of one at Wat Mahathat in Old Sukhothai. There is also an interesting brick and plaster wihaan designed to look like a wooden structure (an ancient Indian technique used all over South-East Asia). A prasat and chedi are stacked on the roof.

Wat Nang Phaya

วัดนางพญา

South of Wat Chang Lom and Wat Chedi Jet Thaew, this stupa is Sinhalese in style and was built in the 15th or 16th century, a bit later than other monuments at Si Satchanalai. Stucco reliefs on the large laterite wihaan in front of the stupa date to the Ayuthaya period when Si Satchanalai was known as Sawankhalok.

Wat Phra Si Ratana Mahathat
วัดพระศรีรัตนมหาธาตุ

These ruins at Chaliang consist of a large laterite chedi (dating from 1448-88) between two wihaans. One wihaan contains a large seated Sukhothai Buddha image, a smaller standing image and a bas-relief of the famous walking Buddha, so exemplary of the flowing, boneless Sukhothai style. The other wihaan contains less distinguished images.

Wat Chao Chan
วัดเจ้าจันทร์

These wat ruins are about 500 metres west of Wat Phra Si Ratana Mahathat. The central attraction is a large Khmer-style prang similar to later prangs in Lopburi and probably built during the reign of Khmer King Jayavarman VII (1181-1217). The prang has been restored and is in fairly good shape. The roofless wihaan on the right contains a large, ruined, standing Buddha.

Sawankhalok Kilns
เตาไผสวรรคโลก

The Sukhothai-Si Satchanalai area has long been famous for its beautiful pottery, much of which was exported throughout Asia. In China – the biggest importer of Thai pottery during the Sukhothai and Ayuthaya periods – the pieces came to be called 'Sangkalok', a mispronunciation of Sawankhalok (Si Satchanalai's later name). Particularly fine specimens can be seen in the national museums of Jakarta and Pontianak, as the Indonesians of the time were keen collectors.

At one time, more than 200 huge pottery kilns lined the Yom River in this area. Several have been carefully excavated and can be viewed at the **Si Satchanalai Centre for Study & Preservation of Sangkalok Kilns**, which opened in 1987. So far the centre has opened two phases to the public, a small museum in Chaliang with excavated pottery samples and one kiln and a larger outdoor kiln site a couple of km north-west of the Si Satchanalai ruins. The exhibits are very well presented, although there are no English labels. More phases are planned, including one that will feature a working kiln.

Sawankhalok pottery rejects, buried in the fields, are still being found. Shops in Sukhothai and Sawankhalok sell misfired, broken, warped and fused pieces. The **Sawanwaranayok Museum** near Sawankhalok's Wat Sawankhalam on the west bank of the river exhibits pottery and Buddha images unearthed by local villagers and donated to the wat. Thai Celadon near Chiang Mai is a ceramics centre producing a modern interpretation of the old craft.

Ban Hat Siaw

This colourful village south-east of Si Satchanalai is home to the Thai Phuan, a Thai tribal group that immigrated from Xieng Khuang Province in Laos around 100 years ago when the Annamese and Chinese were causing mayhem in north-eastern Laos. The local Thai Phuan are famous for their rich handwoven textiles, known as *phâa hàat sîaw* among the Thais and characterised by patterns of horizontal stripes bordered by brocade.

Traditionally every Thai Phuan woman is taught weaving skills, which are passed from generation to generation. Practically every stilt house in the village has a loom beneath it; cloth can be purchased at the source or from shops in Sawankhalok.

Another Thai Phuan custom is the use of elephant-back processions in local monastic ordinations.

Places to Stay & Eat

Wang Yom Resort, just outside the park, has a number of well-appointed bamboo bungalows and a 'handicraft village' set amid beautifully landscaped grounds. Depending on the location (some are on the river), bungalows here cost from 400B; there are also a few basic huts in the handicraft area that cost 150 to 200B a night. Wang Yom's large restaurant is reportedly very good. Food and drink are also available at a coffee shop in the historical park until 6 pm.

NORTHERN THAILAND

Sawankhalok This charming town on the Yom River about 11 km south of the historical park has a couple of other possibilities for visitors wishing to explore the area in more depth. *Muang In* (☎ (055) 642622) at 21 Kasemrat Rd has rooms with fan for 160B, air-con for 250B. The newer and more centrally located *Sangsin Hotel* (☎ (055) 641859), at 2 Thetsaban Damri Rd (the main street through town) has rooms with fan for 180B, 240 to 320B with air-con. The nearby *Sompasong* has basic but adequate rooms for 60 to 80B.

Ko Heng riverside restaurant has great local food and a view of life along the Yom River. *Van Waw*, a noodle shop opposite Sangsin Hotel, is also recommended; it's open from 8 am to 3 pm only. For khâo kaeng (rice and curry), try the shop opposite Thai Farmers Bank. There is also a night market in town which is bigger than the one in Sukhothai.

Another good eating spot is *Kung Nan*, a Thai and Chinese restaurant on the main road near Muang In Hotel.

Getting There & Away
The Si Satchanalai-Chaliang ruins are off Route 101 between Sawankhalok and New Si Satchanalai. From Sukhothai, take a Si Satchanalai bus (19B) and ask to get off at the old city (meuang kào). There are three places along the left side of the highway where you can get off the bus and reach the ruins; all involve crossing the Yom River. The first leads to a footbridge over the Yom River to Wat Phra Si Ratana Mahathat at Chaliang; the second entrance, about 200 metres past the first, is at a crossroads near the bicycle rental shop and leads over a vehicle bridge to Chaliang's Wat Chao Chan; the third crossing is about two km farther north-west just past two hills and leads directly into the Si Satchanalai ruins.

Getting Around
Bicycle is the best way to see the ruins. These can be rented from a shop at the intersection of Route 101 and the road leading to Wat Chao Chan; rates are a low 20B per day. You can also hire an elephant and mahout to tour Si Satchanalai (but not Chaliang) for 50 to 100B.

Utaradit Province

UTARADIT
อ.เมืองอุตรดิตถ์
Continue north by train from Si Satchanalai and Sawankhalok to Utaradit (population 35,000), the capital of Utaradit Province. Not a big tourist destination, the province is noted for its *langsat* fruit and for the largest earthfilled dam in Thailand, the **Sirikit Dam**, which is 55 km from the town.

Some time in the past, the capital developed a reputation as a city of widows and virgins – perhaps because it served as a battlefront during Burmese invasions. Locals are proud that King Taksin, the Thai monarch who finally reunited the Thai kingdom after the Burmese sacked Ayuthaya in the 18th century, was born here. Another local hero, Phraya Phichai Dap Hak, repelled a Burmese invasion in 1772.

The original city formed around Bang Pho Tha It, an important loading point for trade and transport along the Nan River. Teak was once a major local product; the largest teak tree known in the world was found at **Ton Sak Yai (Big Teak Tree) Park**, in Ban Bang Kleua, 92 km north-east of the provincial capital. The 1500-year-old tree was 47 metres high and 9.8 metres in circumference. The remaining teak stands in the park are protected and should live to a ripe old age.

Temples
Behind the train station towards the river, **Wat Tha Thanon** contains the Luang Phaw Phet, a very sacred, Lanna-style Buddha image considered the focal point of the city's power. More impressive architecturally is **Wat Phra Boromathat**, about five km west of town on the highway to Si Satchanalai. The main wihaan here is built in the Luang

NORTHERN THAILAND

Prabang-Lan Xang style, with carved wooden facades over a deep verandah.

Wat Phra Fang is a Sukhothai-period temple ruin in Ban Phra Fang, 25 km south of town along the Nan River.

Places to Stay

P Vanich (Phaw Wanit) 2 (☎ (055) 411499/749) is by the river in the old section of town at 1 Si Utara Rd, within walking distance of the train station. Rooms with fan cost 100B, or from 200B with air-con. The *Phaw Wanit 3* (☎ (055) 411559) at 47-51 Charoenrat Rd, the *Chai Fah* at 131-33 Borom At Rd and the older *Nam Chai* at No 213/4 on the same street are similarly priced. The *P Vanich 1* at 33-5 Phloen Reudi Rd nearby is cheaper at 90 to 130B per room. Top end is the *Seeharaj Hotel* (☎ (055) 411106) at 163 Borom At Rd; all rooms are air-con and start at 700B. Facilities include a coffee shop, restaurant, nightclub and swimming pool.

Getting There & Away

Although it's roughly midway between Phitsanulok and Lampang, few Westerners stop off in Utaradit (all the more reason to visit!). There is frequent bus transport between the three cities; you can also get there by train. Buses to/from Bangkok cost 113B (ordinary) or 208B (air-con).

Tak Province

Tak, like Loei, Nan, Phetchabun, Krabi and certain other provinces, has traditionally been considered a remote province, that is, one which the central Bangkok government has had little control over. In the 1970s, the mountains of west Tak were a hotbed of communist guerrilla activity. Now the former leader of the local CPT movement is involved in resort hotel development and Tak is open to outsiders, but the area still has an untamed feeling about it. The entire province has a population of only around 350,000.

Western Tak has always presented a distinct contrast with other parts of Thailand because of heavy Karen and Burmese cultural influences. The Thailand-Myanmar border districts of Mae Ramat, Tha Song Yang and Mae Sot are dotted with refugee camps, a result of recent fighting between the Karen National Union (KNU) and the Burmese government which is driving Karen civilians across the border. As of the beginning of 1994 there were an estimated 10,000 Burmese and Karen refugees along the border; repatriation may follow recent ceasefire agreements between the two armies.

The main source of income for people living on both sides of the border is legal and illegal international trade. Black-market dealings are estimated to account for at least 150 million baht per year in local income. The main smuggling gateways on the Thailand side are Tha Song Yang, Mae Sarit, Mae Tan, Wangkha, Mae Sot and Waley. On the Myanmar side, all these gateways except Mae Sot and Waley are controlled by the KNU.

One important contraband product is teak, brought into Thailand from Myanmar on big tractor trailers at night. More than 100,000B in bribes per truckload is distributed among the local Thai authorities responsible for looking the other way. Some of the trade is legal since the Thai and Burmese military leaderships have started cutting deals.

Most of the province is forested and mountainous and is excellent for trekking. Organised trekking occurs, some from out of Chiang Mai farther north. There are Hmong, Musoe (Lahu), Lisu and White and Red Karen settlements throughout the west and north. Many Thais come to Tak to hunt, as the province is known for its abundance of wild animals, especially in the northern section towards Mae Hong Son Province. Much of the hunting is illegal – one even hears rumours of tiger and elephant hunts in national wildlife preserves.

NORTHERN THAILAND

TAK

อ.เมืองตาก

Lying along the east bank of the Ping River, Tak (population 21,000) is not particularly interesting except as a point from which to visit the Lan Sang and Taksin Maharat national parks to the west or Phumiphon Yanhi Dam to the north. Travellers on their way to Mae Sot on the Thai-Burmese border occasionally find themselves here for a few hours or the occasional overnight.

Although most of Tak exhibits nondescript, cement-block architecture, the southern section of the city harbours a few old teak homes. Local residents are proud of the suspension bridge (for motorcycles, pedicabs, bicycles and pedestrians only) over the Ping River, which flows quite broadly here even in the dry season. There's also a larger highway bridge over the river.

Taksin Maharat & Lan Sang National Parks

These small national parks receive a steady trickle of visitors on weekends and holidays but are almost empty during the week. Taksin Maharat (established 1981) covers 149 sq km; the entrance is two km from Km 26 on Route 105/Asia 1, the highway to Mae Sot. The park's most outstanding features are the 30-metre, nine-tiered **Mae Ya Pa Falls** and a record-holding *thábàk*, a dipterocarp that measures 50 metres tall and 16 metres in circumference. Birdwatching is said to be particularly good here; known resident and migrating species include the tiger shrike, forest wagtail and Chinese pond heron.

Lan Sang National Park preserves 104 sq km surrounding an area of rugged, 1000-metre granite peaks, part of the Tenasserim Range. A network of trails leads to several waterfalls, including the park's 40-metre namesake. To reach the park entrance, take Route 1103 three km south off Route 105.

Places to Stay & Eat

Most of Tak's hotels are lined up on Mahat Thai Bamrung Rd in the town centre. The biggest hotel, *Wiang Tak* (☎ (055) 511910), at 25/3 Mahat Thai Bamrung Rd, has air-con rooms from 440 to 650B. A similar *Wiang Tak 2* (☎ (055) 512508) on the Tak River costs the same. In this same price range, the newer *Racha Villa* (☎ (055) 512361) at the intersection of Route 105 and Highway 1, is better value at 350 to 400B for well-appointed rooms.

Back on Mahat Thai Bamrung Rd are the less expensive *Tak* (☎ (055) 511234), which has rooms with fan and bath from 80 to 160B, and the *Mae Ping* (☎ (055) 511807), with similar accommodation for 80 to 140B.

On the next street over is the *Sa-nguan Thai* (☎ (055) 511265) at 619 Taksin Rd. Rooms start from 120B and there is a restaurant downstairs.

Cheap food can be bought in the market across the street from the Mae Ping Hotel.

Getting There & Away

THAI flies to Bangkok (1180B), Chiang Mai (765B), Mae Sot (300B) and Phitsanulok (325B). Tak Airport is 15 km out of town towards Sukhothai on Highway 12.

There are frequent buses to Tak from Sukhothai and fares are 23B for an ordinary Baw Khaw Saw bus or 34B for an air-con bus with Win Tour. The trip takes from one to 1½ hours. The Tak bus station is just outside town, but a motorised samlor will take you to the Tak Hotel (in the town centre) for 10B.

MAE SOT

แม่สอด

Mae Sot is 80 km from Tak on the so-called Pan-Asian Highway (Asia Route 1, which would ostensibly link Istanbul and Singapore if all the intervening countries allowed land crossings), numbered Route 105 under the Thai highway system.

Just a few years ago, several public billboards in town carried the warning (in Thai): 'Have fun, but if you carry a gun, you go to jail', underscoring Mae Sot's reputation as a free-swinging, profiteering wild east town.

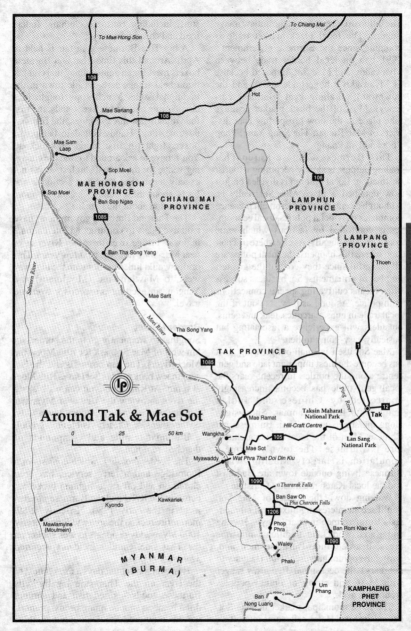

Around Tak & Mae Sot

0   25   50 km

The billboards are gone but the outlaw image lingers. The local black-market trade is booming since the Burmese government's 1991 ban on legal border trade between Myawaddy and Mae Sot, imposed because of Myawaddy's huge trade deficit and the downward spiralling kyat (Burmese currency). Most of the black-market dealings take place in the now-prospering Thai districts of Mae Ramat, Tha Song Yang, Phop Phra and Um Phang.

This Burmese-Chinese-Karen-Thai trading outpost is slowly becoming a tourist destination. Local opinion is divided on just how untamed a place Mae Sot really is. Although a centralised government presence dominates provincial politics, local economics is controlled by factions which settle conflicts extra-legally. As elsewhere in Thailand where this happens, the local police are all-powerful since they control the greatest number of armaments. So, business success often means cultivating special connections with police. As long as they stay out of the local trade in guns, narcotics, teak and gems, outsiders will experience a fascinating but basically easy-going milieu.

Mae Sot itself is small but growing, as it has become the most important jade and gem centre along the border. In recent years the local gem trade has become increasingly controlled by Chinese and Indian immigrants from Myanmar. Shop signs along the streets are in Thai, Burmese and Chinese. Most of the local temple architecture is Burmese. The town's Burmese population is largely Muslim, while Burmese living outside town are Buddhist and the local Karen are mostly Christian.

Walking down the streets of Mae Sot, you'll see an interesting mixture of ethnicities – Burmese men in their longyis, Hmong and Karen women in traditional hill-tribe dress, bearded Indo-Burmese men and, during the opium harvest season (January to February), the occasional Thai army ranger with M-16 and string of opium poppies around his neck.

The large municipal market in Mae Sot, behind the Siam Hotel, sells some interesting stuff, including Burmese clothing, Indian food and cheap takeaways.

A big Thai-Burmese gem fair is held in April. Around this time Thai and Burmese boxers meet for an annual muay thai competition held somewhere outside town in the traditional style. Matches are fought in a circular ring and go for five rounds; the first four rounds last three minutes, the fifth has no time limit. Hands bound in hemp, the boxers fight till first blood or knockout. You'll have to ask around to find the changing venue for the annual slugfest, as it's not exactly legal. (See the Sport section in the Facts about the Country chapter for more information about muay thai.)

The Thai and Burmese governments have tentative plans to construct an international highway bridge over the Moei River at or near Mae Sot within the next few years. This bridge would link Mae Sot with the highway west to Mawlamyine (Moulmein) and Yangon, an exciting prospect for overland travel.

Border Market

Songthaews frequently go to the border, six km west of Mae Sot: ask for Rim Moei (the Moei River). The trip costs 7B and the last songthaew back to Mae Sot leaves Rim Moei at 6 pm. At Rim Moei you can walk along the river and view the Union of Myanmar (Burma) and its eastern outpost, Myawaddy, on the other side. Clearly visible are a school, a Buddhist temple and compounds of thatched-roof houses.

The border crossing, which consists of a footbridge and a ferry service, has been closed on and off since fighting broke out between the KNU and the Burmese government in the early 1980s. In early 1989, mortar fire rocked the area and forced nearly 1000 Myawaddy residents to seek shelter on the Thai side. Similar incidents occurred again in 1993.

However, on calmer days a market next to the river on the Thai side legally sells Burmese goods – dried fish and shrimp, dried bamboo shoots, mung beans, peanuts, woven-straw products, teak carvings, thick

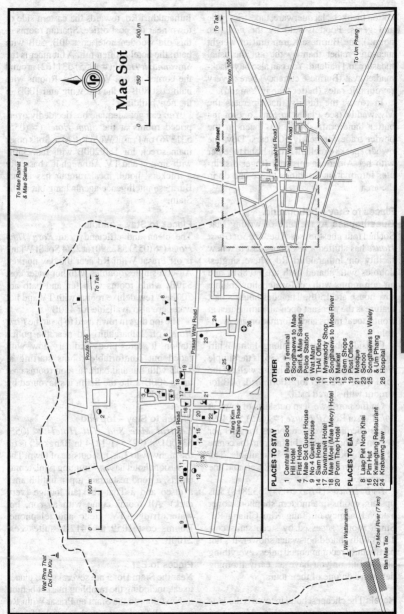

Mae Sot

0   250   500 m

To Tak

To Um Phang

Route 105

Intharakhiri Road

Prasat Withi Road

See Inset

To Mae Ramat
& Mae Sariang

To Tak

Route 105

Prasat Withi Road

Intharakhiri Road

Tang Kim
Chiang Road

0   50   100 m

Wat Phra That
Doi Din Kiu

To Moei River (7 km)

Ban Mae Tao

Wat Wattanaram

PLACES TO STAY

1   Central Mae Sod
    Hill Hotel
4   Hill Hotel
9   Mae Sot Guest House
14 No 4 Guest House
17 Siam Hotel
18 Suwannavit Hotel
    Mae Moei (Mae Meoy) Hotel
20 Porn Thep Hotel

PLACES TO EAT

8   Laap Pet Nong Khai
12 Pim Hut
22 Kwanjing Restaurant
24 Krabawng Jaw

OTHER

2   Bus Terminal
3   Songthaews to Mae
    Sarit & Mae Sariang
5   Mae Sot Police Station
10 THAI Office
11 Myawaddy Shop
13 Songthaews to Moei River
15 Market
16 Gem Shops
19 Post Office
21 Mosque
23 School
    Songthaews to Waley
    & Um Phang
26 Hospital

cotton blankets, lacquerware, tapestries, jade and gems. Food is sold by the *pan* (the pound), the Burmese/Karen unit of weight measure, rather than by the kg, the usual measure in Thailand. You can also buy black-market kyat (Burmese currency) here at very favourable rates (better than in Yangon).

In town, the family that operates the Myawaddy (see Places to Eat), one of the better handicraft shops, has been in the border trade for nearly 50 years. Doy, the owner, speaks excellent English and together with her American husband Roger distributes information on things to see and do in the area.

Places to Stay – bottom end
Guesthouses At the time of writing Mae Sot had four guesthouses. The *Mae Sot Guest House* has shifted a few doors east to a new facility on Intharakhiri Rd where singles/doubles with shared bath are 60/80B, and air-con rooms with cold-water showers in a row house are 150B. The guesthouse's best feature is the pleasant open-air sitting area in front. Local maps and information are available.

Considerably farther along Intharakhiri Rd towards the river, at No 736, is the simple *No 4 Guest House*, a large house well off the road. Rates are 30B for a dorm bed, 60B for a room with shared bath.

On the north-western outskirts of town at 14/21 Asia Rd, *SP House* (☎ (055) 531409) offers adequate wooden rooms for 30B per person. Although it's a bit far from the centre of town, good travel info is available. The staff can arrange various treks around the province.

B+B House (☎/fax (055) 532818) has upstairs rooms in a modern shophouse over a travel agency on Tang Kim Chiang Rd. Small rooms accessed by steep stairs cost 150B with shared hot-water shower. It's not particularly recommended unless everything else is full or you have an early morning departure on one of their tours.

Hotels The cheapest hotel in town is the *Mae Moei Hotel* (a sign reads 'Mae Meoy') on Intharakhiri Rd, towards the eastern side of town near the post office. Spartan rooms in this old wooden hotel cost 40B, 50B with bath; the hotel is often full. A bit nicer is the *Suwannavit Hotel* (☎ (055) 531162) around the corner on Soi Wat Luang. Rooms with bath cost 80B in the old wing and 100B in the new building.

You can get adequate but decidedly over-priced rooms at the *Siam Hotel* (☎ (055) 531376) on Prasat Withi Rd, Mae Sot's other main street, for 180/200B with fan, 350B with air-con and TV. Although it's basically a truckers' hotel, local rumour has it that Burmese intelligence agents hang out at the Siam.

Places to Stay – middle
The clean and efficiently run *Porn Thep Hotel* (☎ (055) 532590) at 25/4 Soi Si Wiang is off Prasat Withi Rd near the day market. Air-con singles/doubles with hot water cost 350B, while rooms with fan and bath are 200B. A few deluxe rooms with TV and hot water are also available for 450B.

The top digs in town used to be at the *First Hotel*, off Intharakhiri Rd near the police station. It seems pretty ordinary now, with faded but comfortable rooms starting at 140B with fan and bath; air-con rooms cost up to 300B. Like the Siam, it's favoured by Thai truckers.

Places to Stay – top end
Central Mae Sod Hill Hotel (☎ (055) 532601/8; (02) 541-1234 in Bangkok) is on the highway to Tak, just outside of town. The 120-room hotel has a swimming pool, tennis courts, a good restaurant (open until 3 am), a disco and a Thai cocktail lounge (very dark). All rooms come with air-con, hot water, fridge, TV, video and telephone. Rooms cost 1059 to 1412B, suites cost 2100B.

Places to Eat
Near the Siam Hotel are several good places to eat, including the rambling market behind it. Next door to the Siam on Prasat Withi Rd is a small food centre with several different

vendors serving noodles and curry. A Burmese-run restaurant opposite the mosque has good roti kaeng (curry and flat bread), fresh milk, curries and khâo sòi (spicy chicken broth with flat noodles). There are other Muslim food stalls in the vicinity.

A favourite local snack is *krabawng jaw* (Burmese for 'fried crispy'), a sort of vegetable tempura. The best place to eat it is at the small vendor stand between Prasat Withi Rd and the hospital, where the same family has been supplying Mae Sot residents with 'fried crispy' for many years. You can sit at a small table near the wok and order fresh chunks of squash, pumpkin or papaya fried in egg batter and dipped in a delicious sauce of peanuts, tamarind, molasses and dried chilli. If you don't want to eat it here they'll wrap for takeaways in two portion sizes, 5B or 10B. The family fires up the wok around 4.30 pm and keeps cooking until 8 pm or until they've run out of ingredients.

Laap Pet Nong Khai, just east of Mae Sot Guest House on Intharakhiri Rd, serves good duck salad and other Isaan specialties.

The best Chinese restaurant in town is the unassuming *Kwangtung Restaurant*, which specialises in Cantonese cooking. It's around the corner from the Porn Thep Hotel, south of Prasat Withi Rd.

The *Myawaddy* handicraft shop on Prasat Withi Rd has a few tables in front where the proprietors serve good meals from a short menu; breakfast is especially good and includes real coffee.

A small, no-name vegetarian restaurant next to the Um Phang songthaew stop offers good, inexpensive Thai vegetarian food from around 7 am to 7 pm or until the food is sold out.

A little farang restaurant enclave has surfaced along Tang Kim Chiang Rd, where you'll find *Pim Hut* with pizza, steak, Thai and Chinese dishes, ice cream and Western breakfasts at moderate prices. Opposite is the brightly lit *Fah Fah 2 Bakery* with a very similar menu which is slightly less expensive. Both cater to tourists, foreign volunteer workers (from nearby Karen-Burmese refugee camps) and upper-middle-class Thais.

Kaphaw Plaa Rim Moei is a popular outdoor restaurant on the road to the Thai-Burmese border, just before it terminates at the river. The house speciality is tangy fish stomach soup but there are plenty of other Thai and Chinese dishes to choose from.

Getting There & Away
Air THAI flies to Mae Sot from Bangkok (1405B) four times a week via Phitsanulok (495B) and Tak (300B).

The THAI office in Mae Sot (☎ (055) 531730) is at 76/1 Prasat Withi Rd.

Bus Buses to Mae Sot leave every half-hour from the Tak bus station, from 6.30 am until 6 pm. An air-con minibus (rot tuu) costs 28B or you can share a taxi for 38B; in Mae Sot, both depart from the First Hotel car park. The trip takes 1½ hours on a beautiful winding road through forested mountains and passes several hill-tribe villages.

Ordinary buses between Bangkok and Mae Sot depart from either end four times daily and cost 125B. VIP buses (24 seats) to Bangkok leave three times daily for 345B; 1st-class air-con buses leave once daily for 224B and there are two 2nd-class air-con buses daily for 174B. The trip takes about 10 hours.

Songthaews to destinations north of Mae Sot (eg Mae Sarit, Mae Sariang) leave from the market north of the police station; those heading south (eg Um Phang) leave from the mosque area.

If you manage to get across the river to Myawaddy, you can take buses to Mawlamyine via Kawkariek. Each leg takes about two hours; the Myawaddy-Kawkariek stretch can be dicey when fighting between Yangon and KNU troops is in progress, while the Kawkariek-Mawlamyine stretch is generally safe. At the moment it's not legal to enter Myanmar this way, but it's very conceivable that this road will open to foreigners within the next three or four years.

Getting Around
Most of Mae Sot can be visited on foot. Jit Alai, a motorcycle dealer on Prasat Withi Rd,

NORTHERN THAILAND

rents motorcycles for 150B (100cc) to 200B (125cc) a day. Make sure you test-ride a bike before renting; some of Jit Alai's machines are in very poor condition.

AROUND MAE SOT
Ban Mae Tao
บ.แม่เต่า
Wat Wattanaram (Phattanaram) is a Burmese temple at Ban Mae Tao, three km west of Mae Sot on the road to the border. A large alabaster sitting Buddha is in a shrine with glass-tile walls, very Burmese in style. In the main wihaan on the 2nd floor is a collection of Burmese musical instruments, including tuned drums and gongs.

Wat Phra That Doi Din Kiu (Ji)
วัดพระธาตุดอยดินกิ่ว(จิ)
This is a forest temple 11 km north-west of Mae Sot on a 300-metre hill overlooking the Moei River and Myanmar. A small chedi mounted on what looks like a boulder balanced on the edge of a cliff is one of the attractions, and is reminiscent of the Kyaiktiyo Pagoda in Myanmar.

The trail that winds up the hill provides good views of thick teak forests across the river in Myanmar. On the Thai side, a scattering of smaller trees is visible. There are a couple of small limestone caves in the side of the hill on the way to the peak. The dirt road that leads to the wat from Mae Tao passes through a couple of Karen villages.

During Myanmar's 1993-94 dry-season offensive against the KNU, this area was considered unsafe and the road to the temple was occasionally blocked by Thai Rangers. Ask in town about the current situation before heading up the road.

Burmese Refugee Camps
ค่ายผู้อพยพพม่า
Several refugee camps have formed along the east bank of the Moei River in either direction from Mae Sot. Most of the refugees in these camps are Karen fleeing battles

between Burmese and KNU troops across the border. The camps have been around for nearly a decade but the Thai government has generally kept their existence quiet, fearing the build-up of a huge refugee volunteer industry such as that which developed around the Indochinese camps in eastern Thailand in the 1970s.

Although many Thai and foreign volunteers have come to the refugees' aid, the camps are very much in need of outside assistance. Visitors are always welcome, as the refugees are starved for recognition by the international community. Donations of clothes, medicines (to be administered by qualified doctors and nurses) and volunteer English teaching are even more welcome.

Most conveniently visited from Mae Sot are those at **Mawker** (7000 refugees), a couple of hours south of Mae Sot on the road to Waley, and **Huaykalok** (3000 refugees), about an hour north of town on the road to Mae Sarit. If you can't travel to any of the camps yourself, you can leave old clothes or other donations at Mae Sot's No 4 Guest House.

For more information on the plight of the Burmese and Karen refugees, contact the Burma Project (☎ (02) 437-9445; fax 222-5788), 124 Soi Watthongnoppakhun, Somdet Chaophraya Rd, Klongsan, Bangkok 10600; or the Santi Pracha Dhamma Institute (☎ (02) 223-4915; fax 222-5188), 117 Fuang Nakhon Rd, Bangkok 10200.

Waley
วะเลย์
Thirty-six km from Mae Sot, Route 1206 splits south-west off Route 1090 at Ban Saw Oh and terminates 25 km south at the border town of Waley, an important smuggling point. The Burmese side was once one of the two main gateways to Kawthoolei, the Karen nation, but in 1989 the Yangon government ousted the KNU. Burmese teak is the main border trade here now; a huge lumberyard just outside Waley is stacked with piles of teak logs which have crossed at Waley. Visitors may be able to arrange a day crossing

by asking nicely at the Thai military post at the Moei River bridge – the guards will radio the Burmese side to see if it's OK.

One can visit hill-tribe villages near **Ban Chedi Kok** as well as the large Mawker (Mawkoe) refugee camp, both off Route 1206 on the way to Waley. Opium is cultivated extensively in this area, much to the chagrin of Thai authorities who send rangers in every year to cut down the production. There is a small hotel in Phop Phra with rooms for 50B.

Getting There & Away Songthaews to Waley depart frequently from a stop south-east of the mosque in Mae Sot for 32B per person. If you go by motorcycle or car, follow Route 1090 south-east towards Um Phang and after 36 km take Route 1206 south-west. From this junction it's 25 km to Waley; the last 10 km of the road are unpaved. Your passport may be checked at a police outpost before Waley.

UM PHANG

อุ้มผาง

Route 1090 goes south from Mae Sot to Um Phang, 150 km away. This road used to be called Death Highway because of the guerrilla activity in the area which hindered highway development. Those days are past, but lives are still lost because of brake failure or treacherous turns on this steep, winding road through incredible mountain scenery. Along the way – short hikes off the highway – are two minor waterfalls, **Thararak Falls** (26 km from Mae Sot) and **Pha Charoen Falls** (41 km). A side road at Km 48 leads to a group of government-sponsored hill-tribe villages (Karen, Lisu, Hmong, Mien, Lahu).

Um Phang itself is an overgrown village populated mostly by Karen at the junction of the Mae Klong and Um Phang rivers. Many Karen villages in this area are very traditional – elephants are used as much as oxen for farm work. Elephant saddles *(yaeng)* and other tack used for elephant wrangling are a common sight on the verandahs of Karen houses outside of town.

An interesting hike can be done following footpaths south-east of the village through rice fields and along a stream called Huay Um Phang to smaller Karen villages.

Near the Burmese border in Um Phang district is the culturally singular village of **Letongkhu** (Leh Tawng Khu). The villagers are for the most part Karen in language and dress, but their spiritual beliefs are unique to this area. They will eat only the meat of wild animals and hence do not raise chickens, ducks, pigs or beef cattle. They do, however, keep buffalo, oxen and elephants as work animals. Some of the men wear their hair in long topknots. The village priests, whom the Thais call reusii (rishi or sage) have long hair and beards and dress in brown or white robes. The priests live apart from the village in a temple and practise traditional medicine based on herbal healing and ritual magic. Antique elephant tusks are kept as talismans. Nobody seems to know where their religion comes from, although there are indications that it may be Hindu-related. Recently an altercation between the Thai Border Police and Letongkhu villagers over hunting rights resulted in the knifing deaths of five policemen.

Thilawsu Falls

น้ำตกทีลอซู

In Um Phang district, you can arrange trips down the Mae Klong River to **Thilawsu Falls** and Karen villages for 500B a day (enquire at Um Phang House or nearby BL Tour). Typical three-day excursions include a raft journey down the river from Um Phang to the falls, then a two-day trek from the falls through the Karen villages of **Khotha** and **Palatha**, where a jeep picks trekkers up and returns them to Um Phang (25 km from Palatha by road). Some people prefer to spend two days on the river, the first night at a cave or hot springs along the river before Thilawsu and a second night at the falls. On the third day you can cross the river by elephant to one of the aforementioned villages to be met by a truck and returned to Um Phang.

The scenery along the river is stunning, especially after the rainy season (November and December) when the cliffs are streaming with water and Thilawsu Falls is at its best. There's a shallow cave behind the falls.

You can also drive to the falls via a rough 47-km road from Um Phang suitable for 4WD or skilled dirt-bike rider only. Or follow the main paved road south of Um Phang to Km 19; the walk to the falls is a stiff four hours from here via **Mo Phado** village. Every two days there's a songthaew for 10 to 15B per person to Km 19; ask for *kii-lôh sìp kâo*.

Places to Stay & Eat

Accommodation in Um Phang is a tad more expensive than elsewhere in northern Thailand, perhaps because it caters to a mostly Thai clientele so far. (The typical Thai tourist won't stay in a place that costs less than 150B a night – too downmarket.) *Um Phang House* (☎ (055) 561073), owned by the local kamnoen, offers a few motel-like rooms with private bath for 150B and nicer wood and brick cottages with hot water and ceiling fans that sleep up to four for 350B (a solo traveller might be able to negotiate the price down a bit). There's a large outdoor restaurant in an open area near the cottages.

West of Um Phang House next to Huay Um Phang are a couple of other new guesthouses (referred to as 'resorts' in typical Thai fashion). *Garden Huts (Garden Resort)* features simple wood and thatch huts for 150 to 200B; it's run by a nice Thai lady who brews good Thai-grown Arabica coffee. Overlooking the stream on the opposite bank is *Umphang Hill Resort*, where large wood and thatch huts cost 100 to 150B per person with two or even three bathrooms. There are also a couple of 300B bungalows for two to three people and some very small huts for 150B.

A further 600 metres west of the checkpoint near the bridge, the atmospheric *Ban Huay Nam Yen* offers Thai-style bungalows furnished with woven mats and axe pillows with terraces overlooking a stream for 200B per person. The larger rooms sleep up to 10 people. It's quiet yet within walking distance of the village.

A newish row house just before the Esso station near the Mae Sot side of town has modern, nondescript rooms with private bath for 150B. Farther out this road towards Mae Sot, about three km before town, *Stray Bird's Hut* and *Gift House* feature simple thatched huts for 60 to 100B a night. *Umphang Country Huts*, off the highway about two km before town, has nicer huts with electricity for 300 to 400B.

You can also rent spartan rooms above BL Tour, on the road to Um Phang House, for just 50B.

Um Phang has three or four simple noodle and rice shops plus one morning market and a small sundries shop. The outdoor restaurant at Um Phang House has the most extensive menu in town.

Getting There & Away

Songthaews to Um Phang cost 100B; there's only one trip a day which leaves Mae Sot at about 8 am and takes five or six hours to complete the 164-km journey. Songthaews usually stop for lunch at windy **Ban Rom Klao 4** (original name Um Piam) along the way. There are a few Hmong villages in the vicinity of Ban Rom Klao 4.

If you decide to try and ride a motorcycle from Mae Sot, be sure it's one with a strong engine as the road has lots of fairly steep grades. Total drive time is around 3½ to four hours. The only petrol pump along the way is in Ban Rom Klao 4, 80 km from Mae Sot, so you may want to carry three or four litres of extra fuel. The road is barely 1½ lanes wide in some spots, and the sealing is rough; the stretch between Ban Rom Klao 4 and Um Phang passes some impressive stands of virgin monsoon forest.

Organised Tours In Um Phang, BL Tour (☎ (055) 561021), on the same street as Um Phang House, charges 800B per person for one day's rafting on the Mae Klong River, plus 50B per person per meal; extra days can be added for just 300B per person. This is significantly less expensive than companies running out of Mae Sot or from Um Phang's guesthouses.

Maesot Conservation Tour (☎ (055) 532818), attached to B+B Guest House in Mae Sot, offers four-day, three-night trips to Um Phang and Thilawsu Falls with camping and rafting for 8000B per person for one or two people, plus 3000B for each additional person. These rates include return transport from Mae Sot, meals and guide service. SP Tour (Mae Sot Travel Centre, ☎ (055) 531409), at SP House in Mae Sot, does Um Phang trips for about the same rates, plus trips north of Mae Sot along the Salawin River.

Um Phang Hills Resort claims to be able to arrange one-week treks from Um Phang south to Sangkhlaburi in Kanchanaburi – this could be quite an interesting trip.

MAE SOT TO MAE SARIANG

Route 1085 runs north from Mae Sot all the way to Mae Sariang in Mae Hong Son Province. The section of the road north of Tha Song Yang has finally been sealed and public transport is now available all the way to Mae Sariang (226 km), passing through Mae Ramat, Mae Sarit, Ban Tha Song Yang and Ban Sop Ngao (Mae Ngao).

Instead of doing the Burmese border run in one go, some people elect to spend the night in Mae Sarit (118 km from Mae Sot), then start fresh in the morning to get to Ban Tha Song Yang in time for a morning songthaew from Ban Tha Song Yang to Mae Sariang. Songthaews to Mae Sarit are 50B and leave frequently from the market north of the police station in Mae Sot and take four hours to reach Mae Sarit. Mae Sarit to Ban Tha Song Yang is 20B and from there to Mae Sariang is 50B; this last leg takes three hours. If you miss the morning songthaew from Mae Sarit to Mae Sariang, you can usually arrange to charter a truck for 100B.

If you decide not to stay overnight in Mae Sarit you can take a direct Mae Sariang songthaew from Mae Sot for 150B. Songthaews leave four times daily between 7 am

and 12.30 pm and the trip takes about six hours. Along the way you'll pass through thick forest, including a few stands of teak, Karen villages, the occasional work elephant and a Thai ranger post called the Black Warrior Kingdom.

Places to Stay

Mae Sarit Mr Narong of *Chai Doi House* (☎ (055) 531782 in Mae Sot) meets the first songthaew of the day from Mae Sot and takes prospective guests to his bungalows on a hill overlooking the border area. Rates are 250B a day including all meals and local trekking guide service. Mr Narong can arrange treks to nearby villages if you'd like to explore the area.

The *Mae Salid Guest House* offers rooms with meals for 120B, but we've had reports that women travellers have been hassled here.

Tha Song Yang There are no guesthouses yet in Tha Song Yang but it would probably be easy to arrange a place to stay by enquiring at the main market (where the songthaews stop) in this prosperous black-market town.

Mae Hong Son Province

Mae Hong Son Province is 368 km from Chiang Mai by the southern route through Mae Sariang (on Route 108), or 270 km by the northern road through Pai (on Route 1095). Thailand's most north-western province is a crossroads for hill tribes (mostly Karen, with some Hmong, Lisu and Lahu), Shan and Burmese immigrants, and opium traders living in and around the forested Pai River valley.

As the province is so far from the influence of sea winds and is thickly forested and mountainous, the temperature seldom rises above 40°C, while in January the temperature can drop to 2°C. The air is often misty with ground fog in the winter and smoke from slash-and-burn agriculture in the hot season.

MYANMAR
(BURMA)

Mae Aw
Pang Tong Palace
Mae La-Na
Tham Lot
Pha Sua Falls
Pangmapha
Fish Cave
Soppong
1095
Pai
Soppong
Ban Huay
Deua
Mae Hong Son
Ban Namrin
Pang Mu
(Pha Pong)
Pai River
To Chiang Mai
Huay Hii
Hot Springs
Wat Chan
Huay Pong
Mae Surin
CHIANG MAI
PROVINCE
Khun Yuam
1253
Doi Inthanon
108
Mae Chaem
Mae La Noi
To Hot &
Chom Thong
Mae Sariang
108
Mae Hong Son
Province
Salaween River
1194
Mae Sam Laep
0   25   50 km
Sop Moei
Sop Moei
Sop Ngao
1085
Ban Tha
Song Yang

To Mae Sot

The province has undergone a tourist mini-boom over the last five years, with many resorts opening in the area around the capital. So far few visitors seem to leave the beaten Mae Hong Son-Soppong-Pai track.

MAE SARIANG & KHUN YUAM

แม่สะเรียง

Many of the hill-tribe settlements in Mae Hong Son Province are concentrated in the districts/towns of Khun Yuam, Mae La Noi and Mae Sariang (population 7600), which are good departure points for treks. Of these three small towns, Mae Sariang is the largest and offers the most facilities for use as a base. Nearby **Mae Sam Laep**, west on the Burmese border, can be reached by songthaew or motorcycle, and from there you can hire boats for trips down the scenic **Salawin River**.

Although there is little to see in Mae Sariang, it's a pleasant enough town and the travel scene is slowly expanding. Two Burmese/Shan temples, **Wat Jong Sung (Uthayarom)** and **Wat Si Bunruang**, just off Mae Sariang's main street not far from the bus station, are worth a visit if you have time.

The Riverside Guest House can arrange day and overnight boat trips on the Salawin River that include stops in Karen villages and Mae Sam Laep. During the dry season, a truck from the Riverside leaves every morning around 6.30 am for Mae Sam Laep, where a boat takes visitors two hours down the Salawin River to a sand beach at Sop Moei. The total cost is 100B per person. There are also songthaews from Mae Sariang to the Karen villages of **Sop Han**, **Mae Han**, and **Ban Huay Pong**.

About 36 km south-east of Mae Sariang at **Ban Mae Waen** is Pan House, where a guide named T Weerapan (Mr Pan) leads local treks. To get to Ban Mae Waen, take a Chiang Mai-bound bus east on Route 108 and get out at the Km 68 marker. Mae Waen is a five-km walk south up a mountain.

On the slopes of **Doi U-Khaw**, 25 km from Khun Yuam via recently upgraded Route

1253, is a Hmong village (Mae U-Khaw) and 250-metre **Mae Surin Falls**, reportedly Thailand's highest cataract. The area blooms with scenic sunflowers in November; this is also the best time to view the waterfall.

Places to Stay

Mae Sariang Mae Sariang's one hotel, *Mitaree Hotel* (☎ (053) 681022), near the bus station on Mae Sariang Rd, has doubles for 120B in the old wooden wing (called the Mitaree Guest House) or for 250B with hot shower in the new wing. Air-con rooms in the new wing cost 300B. The old wing is popular with Thai truckers.

On Wiang Mai Rd near the post office is *New Mitaree Guest House*, run by the same people. Rooms with fan and hot shower cost 120 to 150B in the low-rise building, and similar rooms in the new two-storey building are 200 to 250B, 200 to 350B with air-con.

If you turn left out of the bus terminal and then take the first right you'll come to the small *Mae Sariang Guest House* on Mongkhonchai Rd, opposite the entrance to Wat Jong Sung. Decent rooms are 80/50B with/without bath. Around the corner on Laeng Phanit Rd on the Yuam River is the funky *Riverside Guest House* (☎ (053) 681188) where rooms are 60/80B for singles/doubles, or 120B on the river. The guesthouse has a few quiet, thatched bungalows on the river bank opposite the main building for 150B.

The *See View Guest House* (☎ (053) 681154), on the west side of the Yuam River away from the town centre, offers rooms in a row house for 100B with fan and bath (120B with hot water). The management claim these rates are negotiable in the low season and that they offer free transport to/from the bus terminal.

Out on Route 108 is a combination truck stop and brothel, the *Salawin Inn*, where basic motel-like rooms with attached bath cost 100 to 150B. *Wang Noi Guest House*, at the junction of the main highway and road to Mae Sam Laep, has simple rooms for 100B – sometimes it's open, sometimes not.

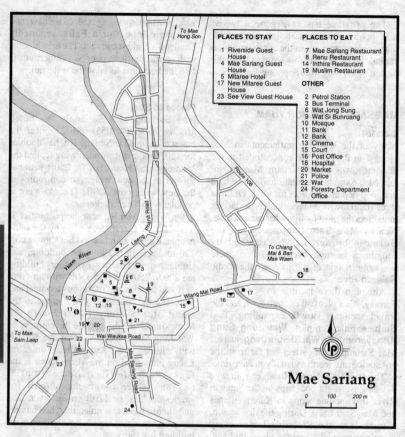

PLACES TO STAY

1 Riverside Guest House
4 Mae Sariang Guest House
5 Mitaree Hotel
17 New Mitaree Guest House
23 See View Guest House

PLACES TO EAT

7 Mae Sariang Restaurant
8 Renu Restaurant
14 Inthira Restaurant
19 Muslim Restaurant

OTHER

2 Petrol Station
3 Bus Terminal
6 Wat Jong Sung
9 Wat Si Bunruang
10 Mosque
11 Bank
12 Bank
13 Cinema
15 Court
16 Post Office
18 Hospital
20 Market
21 Police
22 Wat
24 Forestry Department Office

Mae Sariang

0   100   200 m

Nearby Towns The village headman in Mae Sam Laep lets rooms for 50B per person. In the nearby village of Mae Khong Kha, the *Salween Guest House* also has rooms for 50B per person. There's no public transport to Mae Khong Kha. You can either be dropped off there on a trek or rent a motorcycle.

In Khun Yuam, the *Mit Khun Yuam Hotel* is an old wooden hotel on the main road through the centre of town with rooms from 60B. Off the main road towards the northern end of town (look for the signs) is the super-clean *Ban Farang*, operated by a Frenchman

and his Thai wife. Dorm beds are 50B, rooms 200B a night; they also rent motorcycles.

Rustic accommodation is sometimes available at the Hmong village of Mae U-Khaw, between Khun Yuam and Mae Surin Falls.

Places to Eat

The *Riverside Guest House* on Laeng Phanit Rd has a pleasant restaurant area upstairs overlooking the river.

The *Inthira Restaurant*, on the left side of Wiang Mai Rd as you enter town from Chiang Mai (not far from the Mae Sariang Rd intersection), is well known for its batter-fried frogs, though you won't see them on the English menu. Across the street is the *Renu Restaurant*, decorated with photos of the King playing saxophone and offering such menu delights as nut-hatch curry. Both restaurants have English menus, and both are very good.

Mae Sariang Restaurant, on the corner of Mae Sariang and Wiang Mai Rds, is an indoor-outdoor nightspot with farang and Thai food. It's more popular at night than during the day; the *yam makhēua yao* (roast eggplant salad) is very good, but not listed on the menu.

The food stall next to the bus terminal on Mae Sariang Rd serves excellent khâo sòi and khanŏm jiin for less than 10B – it's only open from morning till early afternoon. A *Muslim restaurant* on Laeng Phanit Rd near the main market in the town centre serves good curries and khâo mòk kài (chicken biryani).

Getting There & Around

Buses to Mae Sariang leave Chiang Mai's Arcade station about every two hours between 6.30 am and 9 pm. The trip takes about four hours and costs 59B. From Mae Sariang to Khun Yuam it's another 32B, or 47B to Mae Hong Son (four to five hours). There's one daily bus between Tak and Mae Sariang for 84B which takes six hours.

A bus for Bangkok leaves from near the Mae Sariang bus terminal daily at 5 pm, arriving in Bangkok at 6 am. The fare is 190B.

Local songthaews go from Mae Sariang to the following Karen villages: Sop Han (5B), Mae Han (10B) and Huay Pong (10B). By motorcycle taxi these destinations are 30, 50 and 35B respectively.

One songthaew goes to Mae Sam Laep on the Salawin River every morning. The fare is 50B except in the rainy season when it rises to 100B – male passengers may have to get out and push the truck on bad sections of the road.

See the Mae Sot to Mae Sariang section earlier for details on songthaew transport between Mae Sot and Mae Sariang.

Motorcycle Rental Next to the service station across from the bus terminal is a small motorcycle rental place.

MAE HONG SON

อ.เมืองแม่ฮ่องสอน

The provincial capital (population 6600) is peaceful (boring to some), despite the intrusion of daily flights from Chiang Mai. Climb the hill west of town, **Doi Kong Mu** (1500 metres), to the Burmese-built **Wat Phra That Doi Kong Mu**, from where there is a nice view of the valley. Much of the capital's prosperity is due to its supply of rice and consumer goods to the drug lords across the border. It's also becoming something of a travellers' scene – there were more than 20 guesthouses at last count. Most of the town's original inhabitants are Shan. Several Karen and Shan villages in the vicinity can be visited as day trips.

Two Hollywood films were shot in the immediate area: *Volunteers*, a comedy-adventure starring Tom Hanks and John Candy about the Peace Corps, and *Air America*, a Mel Gibson vehicle loosely based on events that occurred during the secret US war in Laos during the 1960s.

Mae Hong Son is best visited between November and March when the town is at its most beautiful. During the rainy season (June to October) travel in the province can be difficult because there are few paved roads. During the hot season, the Pai River valley fills with smoke from swidden agriculture. The only problem with going in the cool season is that the nights are downright cold – you'll need at least one thick sweater and a good pair of socks for mornings and evenings and a sleeping bag or several blankets. If you're caught short, you might consider buying a blanket at the market (the Chinese acrylic blankets are cheap) and cutting a hole in the middle for use as a poncho.

The new *Suun Silapaachiip* (Vocational Arts Centre), a km south of the Holiday Inn on Route 108, has a small collection of local handicrafts on display.

NORTHERN THAILAND

Information

Tourist Police Tourist brochures and maps can be picked up at the fledgling Tourist Police office (☎ 611812) on Singhanat Bamrung Rd. Open 24 hrs, this is also the place to come to report mishaps such as theft or to lodge complaints against guesthouses and trek operators.

Money Foreign exchange services are available at Bangkok Bank, Thai Farmers Bank and Bank of Ayudhya, all located along Khunlum Praphat Rd in the centre of town.

Bangkok Bank and Thai Farmers Bank have ATMs.

Post & Telecommunications The Mae Hong Son post office, towards the south end of Khunlum Praphat Rd, is open Monday to Friday from 8.30 am to 4.30 pm, Saturday from 9 am to noon. International telephone service is available at the attached CAT office from 7 am to 11 pm daily.

Mae Hong Son's telephone area code is ☎ 053.

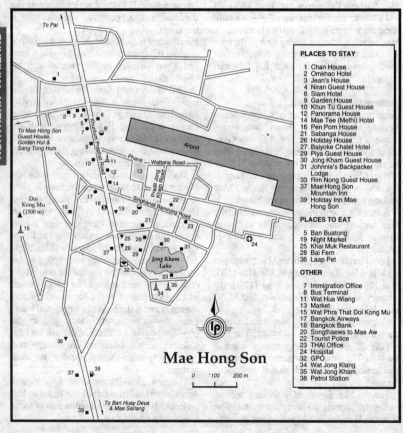

PLACES TO STAY

1 Chan House
2 Omkhao Hotel
3 Jean's House
4 Niran Guest House
6 Siam Hotel
9 Garden House
10 Khun Tu Guest House
12 Panorama House
14 Mae Tee (Methi) Hotel
16 Pen Porn House
26 Sabanga House
27 Holiday House
28 Baiyoke Chalet Hotel
29 Piya Guest House
30 Jong Kham Guest House
31 Johnnie's Backpacker Lodge
33 Rim Nong Guest House
37 Mae Hong Son Mountain Inn
39 Holiday Inn Mae Hong Son

PLACES TO EAT

5 Ban Buatong
19 Night Market
25 Khai Muk Restaurant
28 Bai Fern
36 Laap Pet

OTHER

7 Immigration Office
8 Bus Terminal
11 Wat Hua Wiang
13 Market
15 Wat Phra That Doi Kong Mu
17 Bangkok Airways
18 Bangkok Bank
20 Songthaews to Mae Aw
22 Tourist Police
23 THAI Office
24 Hospital
32 GPO
34 Wat Jong Klang
35 Wat Jong Kham
38 Petrol Station

Mae Hong Son

0   100   200 m

Wat Jong Kham & Wat Jong Klang
วัดจองคำและวัดจองกลาง

Next to a large pond in the southern part of town are a couple of semi-interesting Burmese-style wats – Wat Jong Kham and Wat Jong Klang. Jong Kham was built nearly 200 years ago by Thai Yai (Shan) people, who make up about 50% of the population of Mae Hong Son Province. Jong Klang houses 100-year-old glass paintings and woodcarvings from Myanmar which depict the various lives of the Buddha, but you must ask to see them as they are kept locked away.

Wat Hua Wiang

Although the wooden bot itself is in an advanced state of decay, a famous bronze Buddha in the Mandalay style, called **Chao Phlalakhaeng,** can be seen in this wat on Phanit Wattana Rd, a bit east of Khunlum Praphat Rd.

Trekking

Trekking out of Mae Hong Son can be arranged at several guesthouses and travel agencies; Mae Hong Son Guest House (see Places to Stay – bottom end) has some of the most dependable and experienced guides. Typical rates for two to four nights are from 1500 to 1800B.

Besides the usual routes in the Pai River Valley, Khun Yuam District and north of Soppong, you can also walk from Mae Hong Son to Chiang Mai if you're up to it. A very high, steep mountain path begins in the mountains on the south-east side of town. The trip takes seven days and is supposed to be safe. The trek passes only a few Karen, Hmong and Lisu villages, but the scenery is incredible. Food must be carried part of the way (this is a trek for the hardy and experienced). Ask at the Mae Hong Son Guest House or Don Enterprises (☎ 612236 fax 611682; 77/1 Khunlum Praphat Rd) for details. The latter offers a seven-day walk to Chiang Mai for 500B per person per day (less for five or more trekkers).

Don Enterprises also arranges a special 2200B, three-night trip to Karen, Shan and Burmese refugee camps for those with political or humanitarian interests.

Other trekking agencies are along Khunlum Praphat Rd and Singhanat Bamrung Rd. Nearby Karen villages can be visited without a guide by walking one or two hours outside of town – several guesthouses in town can provide a map.

Festivals

Wat Jong Klang and Wat Jong Kham are the focal point of the Poi Sang Long Festival in March when young Shan boys are ordained as novice monks (bùat lûuk kâew) during the school holidays. Like elsewhere in Thailand, the ordinants are carried on the shoulders of friends or relatives and paraded around the wat under festive parasols, but in the Shan custom the boys are dressed in ornate costumes (rather than simple white robes) and wear flower headdresses and facial make-up. Sometimes they ride on ponies.

Another important local event is the Jong Para Festival held at the end of the Buddhist Rains Retreat in October (actually three days before the full moon of the 11th lunar month – so it varies from year to year). The festival begins with local Shans bringing offerings to monks in the temples in a procession marked by the carrying of castle models on poles. An important part of the festival is the folk theatre and dance performed on the wat grounds, some of which are unique to northwest Thailand.

During Loi Krathong – a national holiday usually celebrated by floating krathongs (small lotus floats) on the nearest pond, lake or river – Mae Hong Son residents launch balloons called krathong sawăn (heaven krathongs) from Doi Kong Mu.

Places to Stay – bottom end

Guesthouses With more than 20 guesthouses in town, the accommodation scene in Mae Hong Son is very competitive – most places are 50 to 80B with shared bath, 80 to 100B with private bath.

The original Mae Hong Son Guest House (☎ 612510) has moved location from near the airport to a more secluded spot on the

NORTHERN THAILAND

north-western outskirts of town (about 700 metres west of Khunlum Praphat Rd). Rooms are 50 to 80B without bath, 100B for a bungalow with private bath. The guesthouse is a good source of information and inexpensive meals.

In the hills nearby are the equally secluded *Sang Tong Huts*, which have panoramic views. The setting is pretty but it's not cheap at 50B for a dorm bed and up to 250B for a hut. In the same area, *Golden Hut* (☎ 611544) has thatched bungalows on a hillside for 200 to 300B with private hot-water bath. Just before the turn-off for Golden Huts, *Paradise* offers thatched huts for 100B a night.

Also at this end of town is the friendly *Jean's House* (☎ 611662) at 6 Pracha Uthit Rd, with rates at 80B for rooms with bath. Next door to Jean's is the guesthouse-style *Omkhao Hotel*, with a very good Thai restaurant and basic bungalow-style rooms for 80B. *Niran Guest House* (☎ 611227) on the nearby corner of Khunlum Praphat Rd has simple rooms behind a large dining area for 100B. A block north, turn left and you'll come to the similar *Chan House*.

Back on Khunlum Praphat Rd, south of the bus terminal on the right and set back off the road a bit, is *Garden House*, where rustic singles/doubles are 50/80B, better rooms as much as 200B. Just a bit farther down is *Khun Tu Guest House (Khun Tu Trading)* where singles/doubles are 70/150B with shared bath. The one four-bed air-con room with hot bath costs 250B. Khun Tu also sells air tickets and rents motorcycles and bicycles.

In the area of Jong Kham Lake are several very pleasant guesthouses. *Jong Kham Guest House* (☎ 611150) overlooks the lake from the north and has very clean rooms in a row house plus some newer thatched huts for 40 to 120B. A shared hot shower is available and towels are provided. East of Jong Kham, also on the northern side of the lake, is *Johnnie's Backpacker Lodge*, a wooden row house with clean rooms and hot showers for 80B.

On the west side of the lake, *Holiday House* has two-bed rooms with shared hot bath for 80B. Just south of Holiday House, *Piya Guest House* (☎ 611260/307) introduced a new sophistication in guesthouse construction to Mae Hong Son when it opened a few years ago. Rooms are built around a garden, with a bar/restaurant in front; rates are 200B with fan, 300B with air-con. All rooms come with private hot showers; it's often full. Around the corner on Udom Chaonithet Rd is the basic *Sabanga House*, a bamboo row house with rooms for 100B.

On the south side of the lake is *Rim Nong Guest House*, a friendly place with a little restaurant on the water's edge. Rates are a low 40B per person in multi-bed rooms, 70 to 100B in private rooms with shared hot-water bath. Across the street, away from the lake, is the very basic *Jo Guest House* with 80B rooms and shared hot-water bath.

On the diagonal street running south-east from Khunlum Praphat Rd to the lake is *Namrin House*, an old wooden building with basic rooms for 60 to 80B. Another inexpensive place in town is *Lanna Lodge* down an alley off Khunlum Praphat Rd, opposite the Thai Farmers Bank. Bungalows here are 80B with shared hot shower. More basic 50B rooms are available in an old Thai house on the premises.

Pen Porn House (☎ 611577), on the road to Wat Phra That Doi Kong Mu, sits in a residential neighbourhood on a slope on the west side of town. Rooms in a newly built row house cost 200B a double, 400B in a four-bed room, all with private hot-water bath.

Hotels Most of the hotels in Mae Hong Son are along the main north-south road, Khunlum Praphat. *Siam Hotel* (☎ 612148), next to the bus station, is overpriced at 180/200B for ordinary rooms with fan, 350B with air-con. Farther down at No 55, *Mae Tee (Methi) Hotel* (☎ 611141) is slightly lower priced but better; rooms with fan cost 160B while air-con rooms start at 300B.

Other less convenient guesthouses can be found around Mae Hong Son – the touts will find you at the bus terminal.

Places to Stay – middle & top end

The new, three-storey *Panorama House* (☎ 611757; fax 611790), at 51 Khunlum Praphat Rd, charges 800B for a simple but clean room with fridge, TV, air-con and hot-water shower. In just about any other Thai town of this size, rooms like this would go for 500B.

Towards the southern end of town, *Baiyoke Chalet Hotel* (☎ 611486) at 90 Khunlum Praphat offers all the typical amenities for 650B in standard rooms, 1200B in VIP ones. The larger and newer *Mae Hong Son Mountain Inn* (☎ 612285), farther south at 112 Khunlum Praphat Rd, charges 800B for similar rooms.

A bit farther south, the 114-room *Holiday Inn Mae Hong Son* (☎ 611390; (02) 254-2614 in Bangkok) at 114/5-7 Khunlum Praphat definitely represents the top end in town. Rooms and bungalows cost 2000 to 3500B. Facilities include a swimming pool, tennis courts, disco, snooker club, coffee shop and restaurant.

Out of Town South-west of town a few km towards Ban Huay Deua are several 'resorts', which in the Thai sense of the term means any hotel located in a rural or semi-rural area. Here you'll find the upscale *Tara Mae Hong Son Hotel* (☎ 611272; fax 611252), with doubles from 2223B. Farther off the highway, three mid-range places are worth considering: *Rim Nam Klang Doi Resort* (☎ 612142; fax 612086), with doubles from 400B; *Mae Hong Son Resort* (☎ 611504, 611406), with doubles from 650B; and *Sam Mok Villa* (☎ 611478), with doubles from 300B.

Places to Eat

Mae Hong Son isn't known for its food, but there are a few decent places to eat besides the guesthouses. *Khai Muk*, an outdoor restaurant just off Khunlum Praphat Rd, is one of the better Thai-Chinese restaurants in town. Another very good spot with an extensive Thai-Chinese menu is *Bai Fern*, around the corner on Khunlum Praphat Rd. Most other restaurants in town pale by comparison with these two.

The jók (broken-rice soup) place near the Mae Tee Hotel is still going strong and sells American breakfasts for 20 to 30B. *Kuaytiaw Chak Thong* (no roman-script sign), next to Garden House, specialises in rice noodles and breakfasts. The morning market behind the Mae Tee Hotel is a good place to buy food for trekking. Get there before 8 am.

Across from the Siam Hotel on Khunlum Praphat Rd is the pleasant *Ban Buatong* cafe/restaurant, which has good, inexpensive Thai and Western food.

Visitors staying at Pen Porn House are close to *Khao Soi Phinnun*, a friendly neighbourhood establishment on the same street which has inexpensive khâo sòi or kūaytĭaw as well as eggs, toast and coffee. A small food centre almost opposite Pen Porn offers pizza, noodles and Shan-style chicken curry.

Laap Pet, just off Khunlum Praphat Rd on the road to Doi Kong Mu, is a nice open-air spot with Isaan food.

Getting There & Away

Air THAI flies to Mae Hong Son from Chiang Mai four times daily. The fare is 345B and the flight takes 40 minutes. It's possible to book a flight to Chiang Mai that links with an onward flight to Mae Hong Son for 1865B. Mae Hong Son's THAI office (☎ 611297, 611194) is at 71 Singhanat Bamrung Rd.

Bangkok Airways operates flights once daily from Bangkok for 1345B; the trip takes an hour and 50 minutes. The Bangkok Airways office (☎ 611784) in Mae Hong Son is on Singhanat Bamrung Rd just west of Khunlum Praphat.

Bus From Chiang Mai there are two bus routes to Mae Hong Son, the northern route through Pai (90B ordinary, 175B air-con, 7 to 8 hours) and the southern route through Mae Sariang (105B ordinary, 206B air-con, 8 to 9 hours).

Although it's longer, the southern route through Mae Sariang is much more comfort-

NORTHERN THAILAND

able because the bus stops every two hours for a 10 to 15-minute break and larger buses – with large seats – are used. The bus to Mae Hong Son via Mae Sariang leaves Chiang Mai's Arcade bus station every two hours between 6.30 am and 9 pm.

The northern route through Pai, originally built by the Japanese in WW II, is very winding and offers spectacular views from time to time. Because the buses used on this road are smaller, they're usually more crowded and there's a lot of motion sickness among the younger passengers. The Pai bus leaves the Chiang Mai Arcade station four times a day at 7, 8.30 and 11 am and 2 pm.

Buses as far as Soppong are 25B or to Pai 42B.

Getting Around

Most of Mae Hong Son is walkable. Motorcycle taxis within town cost 10B, to Doi Kong Mu it's 30B one way or 50B return. Motorcycle drivers will also take passengers farther afield but fares out of town are expensive, eg 500B to Mae Aw.

Several guesthouses in town rent bicycles and motorcycles. Hertz Rent-a-Car (☎ 612108) has an office at the Holiday Inn.

AROUND MAE HONG SON
Rafting

Raft trips on the nearby Pai River are gaining in popularity, as are boat trips into the Karen state (or nation, depending on your political allegiances) of Myanmar. The same guesthouses and trekking agencies that organise treks can arrange the river trips. The most common type of trip sets off from the Pai River pier in **Ban Huay Deua**, eight km south-west of town, for a day-long upriver journey of five km. From the same pier, downriver trips to the 'longneck' village of **Kariang Padawng Kekongdu** on the Thai-Burmese border are also possible. Another popular raft route runs between **Sop Soi** (10 km north-west of town) and the village of **Soppong** to the west (not to be confused with the larger Shan trading village of the same name to the east). These day trips typically cost 400B per person if arranged in

Ban Huay Deua, 700B or more if done through a Mae Hong Son agency.

The Pai River raft trips can be good fun if the raft holds up – it's not uncommon for rafts to fall apart and/or sink. The Myanmar trip, which attracts travellers who want to see the Padaung or long-necked people, is a bit of a rip-off, a four-hour trip through unspectacular scenery to see maybe seven Padaung people who are practically captives of the Karen operators involved.

Mae Aw
แม่ออ

One of the best day trips you can do from the provincial capital is to Mae Aw, 22 km north of Mae Hong Son on a mountain peak at the Burmese border. Since the construction of a better road, songthaew fares to Mae Aw have dropped to 40B per person each way. Vehicles leave from Singhanat Bamrung Rd near the telephone office – it's best to get there at about 9 am to get a seat though the songthaew might not actually depart until around 10. The trip takes two hours and passes Shan, Karen and Hmong villages, the **Pang Tong Summer Palace** and waterfalls.

Mae Aw is a Chinese Kuomintang settlement, one of the last true KMT outposts in Thailand. Occasionally there is fighting along the border between the KMT and the Meuang Tai Army, led by the infamous opium warlord Khun Sa. When this happens, public transport to these areas is usually suspended and you are advised against going without a guide. (See Opium & the Golden Triangle in the Facts about the Country chapter.) The modern Thai name for Mae Aw is 'Ban Rak Thai' (Thai-Loving Village).

Thatched hut accommodation is available for 40B per person in the Hmong village of Na Pa Paek, 7.3 km south of Mae Aw. From Na Pa Paek a rough dirt road leads north-west to the Hmong village of Ma Khua Som (3.5 km) and the KMT village of Pang Ung (6 km) on the Myanmar border.

If you have your own transport, you can stop off at **Pha Sua Falls** on the way to Mae Aw. About 11 km north of Route 108, turn

---

Kuomintang

Following WW II, after eight years of battle against the Japanese, Chiang Kai-shek was forced to release 75% of his Nationalist Army, or Kuomintang (KMT), troops from the Nationalist payroll. Soldiers had to choose between joining the Red Army in China or leaving the country; of the KMT who chose the latter option, those stationed in eastern China fled to Taiwan, while those in the west (mostly from the 8th Battalion) fled to Myanmar and Thailand.

Whole regiments established villages along the Myanmar-Thailand border, including Mae Salong's infamous 93rd Regiment, which eventually acted as enforcers and transporters for the Golden Triangle opium trade. Today most of the KMT remnants in northern Thailand have forsaken opium for legal crops and have settled into a hybrid mountain lifestyle that combines elements from Chinese, Thai and hill-tribe cultures. ∎

NORTHERN THAILAND

onto a marked dirt road. The cataract has water all year round; during the rainy season swimming can be dangerous due to swift water flow.

Mae La-Na
แม่ละนา

Between Mae Hong Son and Pai is an area of forests, mountains, streams and limestone caves dotted with Shan and hill-tribe villages. Some of Mae Hong Son's most beautiful scenery is within a day's walk of the Shan villages of Mae La-Na and Soppong, both of which have accommodation. In the area you can trek to several Red and Black Lahu villages and a couple of large caves (4.5 and eight km away). It's possible to walk a 20-km half loop all the way from Mae La-Na to Tham Lot and Soppong, staying overnight in Red Lahu villages along the way. Ask for a sketch map at the Mae Lana Guest House (see Places to Stay following). Experienced riders can accomplish this route on a sturdy dirt bike – but not alone or during the rainy season.

Twenty-seven km west of Pangmapha is a short turnoff for **Wat Tham Wua Sunyata**, a peaceful forest monastery under the auspices of the famous Phra Ajaan Yantra.

The Mae La-Na junction is 55 km from Mae Hong Son, 10 km from Soppong and 56 km from Pai. The village itself is six km north of the junction. Infrequent songthaews from the highway to the village cost 20B per person – mornings are your best bet.

Soppong
สบปอง

Soppong is a small but relatively prosperous market village a couple of hours north-west of Pai and about 70 km from Mae Hong Son. Since the paving of Route 1095, Soppong and Tham Lot have become popular destinations for minivan tours from Mae Hong Son and Chiang Mai.

Close to Soppong are several Shan, Lisu, Karen and Lahu villages that can easily be visited on foot. Enquire at the Jungle Guest House or Cave Lodge in Soppong for reliable information. It's important to ask about the current situation as the Myanmar border area is somewhat sensitive due to the opium trade.

Tham Lot About eight km north of Soppong is Tham Lot, a large limestone cave with a wide stream running through it. Along with Tham Nam Lang farther west, it's one of the longest known caves in mainland South-East Asia (though some as yet unexplored caves in southern Thailand may be even longer). It is possible to hike all the way through the cave (approximately 400 metres) by following the stream, though it requires some wading back and forth. Apart from the main chamber, there are three side chambers that can be reached by ladders – it takes two or three hours to see the whole thing.

At the park entrance you can hire a gas lantern and guide for 100B to take you through the caverns. If you prefer to go it on your own, you may be able to persuade the guides to rent you a lantern for 50B. The guide fee includes visits to the first and third caverns; to visit the second cavern you must cross the stream. Raftmen waiting inside the cave charge 10B per person per crossing; in the dry season you may be able to wade across. For 100B you can stay on the raft through the third cavern.

The park is open from 8 am to 5 pm every day. A restaurant will soon be built inside the park; for now snacks are available from vendors outside the park entrance. You can camp for free near the park entrance. If you decide to book a Tham Lot day tour from Mae Hong Son, ask if the tour cost includes guide, lamp and raft fees.

Tham Nam Lang Near Ban Nam Khong, 30 km northwest of Soppong, this cave is nine km long and is said to be one of the largest caves in the world in terms of volume. There are many other caves in the area, some of which contain 2000-year-old wooden coffins.

Places to Stay

There is a sprinkling of accommodation in the area, mostly concentrated around Soppong. In town, *Sobpong Guest House* has several simple A-frame huts from 30 to 60B. Also in town you'll find the *Lemon Hill Guest House*, a straightforward teak house with quiet bungalows off the main street for 40 to 60B, and the *Kemarin Garden Lodge*, with nothing-special bungalows for 50/70B a single/double.

The friendly *Jungle Guest House*, one km west on the road to Mae Hong Son, offers well-designed huts for 30 to 40B per person. The restaurant serves better fare than most of the other guesthouses in the area. The nearby *Pangmapa Guest House* is similar.

In the nearby forests and in the vicinity of Tham Lot, several guesthouses have come and gone. Over the last four years, Forestry Department officials have been cracking down on illegal accommodation encroaching on the forest. Accommodation may still be arranged in nearby villages, however.

One place to escape the Forestry Department is the *Cave Lodge* near Tham Lot; it's run by a former trekking guide from Chiang Mai and her Australian husband. They were the first to open regular accommodation in the area, starting the trend. Beds are 40B in a dorm, 80B for bungalows; simple meals cost 20 to 40B. Follow signs in Soppong to get there – it's about a 1½-hour walk to Ban Tham, the village closest to Tham Lot cave. The village headman also rents rooms to travellers, and the Forestry Department has a few bungalows near the cave for 40B per person.

On the banks of the stream that runs through the cave, west of the park entrance, the very shabby *River Lodge* has little to recommend it except for its waterside location.

Just outside Mae La-Na village, the secluded, laid-back *Mae Lana Guest House* rents four large doubles with mosquito nets for 80B per night and a four-bed dorm for 35B per person. *Top Hill*, run by Mae La-Na's village headman, takes the overflow from Mae Lana Guest House at the same basic rates.

At Ban Nam Khong, the *Wilderness Lodge* is run by the same family that owns the Cave Lodge. Huts are 40B per person. The Route 108 turn-off for Wilderness Lodge is located 25 km west of Pangmapha village.

About 12 km north of Mae La-Na in the Black Lahu village of Ban Huay Hea (very close to the Burmese border) is the *Lahu Guest House*, run by a village teacher who speaks English. Simple accommodation is 30B per person and the money goes into a community fund.

Getting There & Away

Pai to Mae Hong Son buses stop in Soppong and there are two or three each day in either direction. From Mae Hong Son, buses take about 2½ hours and cost 25B. The trip between Pai and Soppong costs 22B and takes from 1½ to two hours.

Top Left: Lisu woman (TAT)
Top Right: Red Akha woman (DW)
Bottom: Akha village near Mae Salong (JC)

Top Left: Hmong children (CLA)
Top Right: Hmong family (CLA)
   Bottom: Mien women (TAT)

PAI

ปาย

It first appears that there's not a lot to see in Pai, a peaceful crossroads town about halfway between Chiang Mai and Mae Hong Son on Route 1095. But if you stick around a few days and talk to some of the locals, you may discover some beautiful out-of-town spots in the surrounding hills. Any of the guesthouses in town can provide information on local trekking and a few do guided treks for 200 to 400B per day. Some local trekking guides here specialise in 'hard' treks – one outfit calls itself 'No Mercy Trekking'.

Most of the town's population are Shan and Thai, but there's also a small but visible Muslim population – mostly jiin haw. Northwest of town are several Shan, Lahu, Lisu and KMT villages and a waterfall that can be visited on foot. The waterfall, **Maw Paeng Falls**, is an eight-km walk from town; you can cut the hike in half by taking a Mae Hong Son-bound bus north about five km and getting off at a signpost for the falls; from the highway it's only four km. A pool at the base of the falls is suitable for swimming.

Wat Phra That Mae Yen

วัดพระธาตุแม่เย็น

Simply known as Wat Mae Yen, this is a newish temple built on a hill with a good view overlooking the valley. Walk one km east from the main intersection in town, across a stream and through a village, to get to the stairs (353 steps) which lead to the top. The monks are vegetarian, uncommon in Thai Buddhist temples. Seven km south of the temple via a dirt road are some hot springs.

Traditional Massage

Pai Traditional Massage (☎ 699121), in a house near the river, has very good northern-Thai massage for 120B an hour. The couple

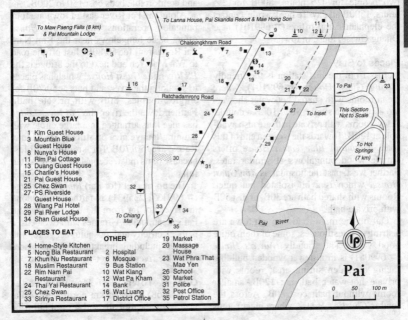

To Maw Paeng Falls (8 km) & Pai Mountain Lodge

To Lanna House, Pai Skandia Resort & Mae Hong Son

Chaisongkhram Road

Ratchadamrong Road

To Pai

This Section Not to Scale

To Hot Springs (7 km)

To Chiang Mai

To Inset

Pai River

PLACES TO STAY
1 Kim Guest House
3 Mountain Blue Guest House
8 Nunya's House
11 Rim Pai Cottage
13 Duang Guest House
15 Charlie's House
21 Pai Guest House
25 Chez Swan
27 PS Riverside Guest House
28 Wiang Pai Hotel
29 Pai River Lodge
34 Shan Guest House

PLACES TO EAT
4 Home-Style Kitchen
5 Nong Bia Restaurant
7 Khun Nu Restaurant
18 Muslim Restaurant
22 Rim Nam Pai Restaurant
24 Thai Yai Restaurant
25 Chez Swan
33 Sirinya Restaurant

OTHER
2 Hospital
6 Mosque
9 Bus Station
10 Wat Klang
12 Wat Pa Kham
14 Bank
16 Wat Luang
17 District Office
19 Market
20 Massage House
23 Wat Phra That Mae Yen
26 School
30 Market
31 Police
32 Post Office
35 Petrol Station

Pai

0   50   100 m

that do the massages are graduates of Chiang Mai's Old Medicine Hospital. They've built their own herbal sauna house where you can steam yourself in *samun phrai* (medicinal herbs) for 50B per visit. The house is open from 4.30 to 8.30 pm Monday to Friday, 8.30 am to 8.30 pm weekends.

Rafting & Elephant Riding

Raft trips on the nearby Pai River operate from July to December, sometimes longer in rainy years; September is usually the best month. Most outfits use flimsy bamboo rafts but it's fun anyway if you don't mind getting wet.

Guy (Khun Kii in Thai), the French proprietor at Chez Swan (☎ /fax 699111), leads excellent two-day trips in sturdy rubber rafts from Pai to Mae Hong Son for 1500B per person including food, rafting equipment, camping gear and dry bags. Guy is fluent in Thai and uses a carefully selected Thai crew.

An elephant camp outside Pai offers jungle rides year-round. The cost is 400B for two people for 1½ hours, 800B for 2½ hours, 1500B all day. To book a ride, contact the elephant camp office (☎ 699101) near Duang Guest House in town.

Places to Stay

Across from the bus station is the friendly *Duang Guest House* (☎ 699101), where clean rooms with shared hot-water showers are 40 to 50B a single, 80 to 100B a double. A few rooms with private bath are also available at 120B. Towards the western end of this road, *Mountain Blue Guest House* offers simple wood bungalows at similar rates. Farther west, past the hospital, is *Kim Guest House*, which is a bit isolated but quiet. Rooms with shared bath are 30B, or just 50B with private bath.

Out on the main road through town are a string of guesthouses, some of them quite good value. The friendly *Nunya's House* (☎ 699051) is in a newer wooden building facing a garden sitting area; rooms with private hot-water bath are 120B, smaller rooms without bath cost 80B. Across the road is *Charlie's House*, where nicer rooms

around a large courtyard cost 60B with shared bath, 120B with hot-water bath, and 160 to 200B in a bungalow. Charlie's is often full during high season.

Behind the Chez Swan restaurant, Guy and his Thai wife have constructed a row of large new rooms with private hot-water showers and thick mattresses for 200B per night.

Farther down the street in the same direction, the *Wiang Pai Hotel* is a traditional wooden hotel with 15 spacious rooms. Single-bed rooms (sleeping one or two) cost 50B; a two-bed room is 100B. Behind the old hotel is a new but characterless wing where a double with a bath is 120B. Hot water is available on request.

On the southern edge of town, off the road a bit, is the *Shan Guest House* (☎ 699162), run by Boonyang, an outgoing Shan who has worked in Bangkok and Saudi Arabia. The atmosphere and food are good and Boonyang tries hard to please. Shan-style bungalows with private hot-water showers and comfortable beds cost 150 to 200B.

Along the Pai River east of town are four bungalow operations. The *Pai Guest House* offers basic bungalows near the Rim Nam Pai Restaurant for 50/80B. Just off the road to Wat Mae Yen and next to the bridge is the *PS Riverside Guest House*, which has places to sit along the river, and huts at 50/70B for singles/doubles, 80B with private bath. Farther down the river, the *Pai River Lodge* has nice huts arranged in a large circle with a dining/lounge area on stilts in the middle. Rates are 50/70B for singles/doubles; because of its quiet, scenic location it's often full.

The up-market (for Pai) *Rim Pai Cottage* (☎ 699133, 235931) is farther north along the river not far from the bus station. Rim Pai's clean, quiet A-frames with two beds, a bath, electricity and mosquito net go for 400 to 600B including breakfast. All four places along the river have hot-water showers.

Out of Town *Pai Mountain Lodge* (☎ 699068) is seven km north-west of Pai near Maw Paeng Falls and several hill-tribe villages. Spacious A-frames with hot-water baths and stone fireplaces sleep four for 400B – good value. In the off season (September to October, April to June) prices drop as low as 150B. In town you can book a room or arrange transport at 89 Chaisongkhram Rd, near the Northern Green bike shop.

Pai Skandia Resort, 4½ km north of town on the highway to Mae Hong Son, features very nice A-frame houses for 400 to 500B a night. Closer in on the same road (2.3 km north of Pai), *Lanna House* rents large wooden bungalows at slightly lower rates.

Places to Eat

Several places to eat along the main north-south and east-west roads in Pai are farang-oriented cafes with the usual not-quite-the-real-thing pizza, felafel, hummus and tacos (the Thai food in these places is equally off). For authentic local food try the *Rim Nam Pai* (no English sign) on the river next to the bridge. This pleasant outdoor spot serves several northern Thai dishes including lâap (Isaan-style meat salad with chillies and lime) and jaew (northern-style noodle hotpot) as well as Thai standards like tôm yam and khâo phàt. A bilingual menu is available.

Young woman, Lahu hill tribe

On Chaisongkhram Rd, the *Khun Nu* has a good variety of Thai and Chinese standards, as does *Nong Bia*. Nong Bia has long been the most popular restaurant in town among local residents. The *Muslim Restaurant* on the main north-south street has khâo sòi and a few rice dishes.

Every evening a row of local food vendors sets up in front of the nearby day market. During the day, takeaway food can also be purchased at the larger Saengthongaram Market on the next street west. Also on this street you'll find a row of noodle shops near the post office.

One traveller-oriented restaurant worth mentioning is *Thai Yai*, which does the best farang breakfast and lunch menu in town – wholemeal bread, real butter, good locally grown coffee, fruit salads, muesli and sandwiches, plus a few Thai dishes. The *Home-Style Kitchen* and *Muang Pai Kitchen*, both a block west of the main drag, attempt similar menus with less success.

Good French food – including several cheeses – is available at the nicely decorated *Chez Swan* on the main north-south strip through town. Especially tasty is the 'Caprice', slices of fresh mozzarella and tomatoes dressed in basil and olive oil.

At the south end of town, the two-storey *Sirinya* caters to Thai tourists with a variety of Thai and Chinese dishes served in a slightly uptown atmosphere.

Getting There & Around

From Chiang Mai's Arcade bus station there are four buses a day at 7, 8.30 and 11 am and 2 pm. The distance is only 134 km but the trip takes about three hours due to the steep and winding road. The fare has dropped to 45B since the road paving was completed. From Mae Hong Son there are three buses a day at 7 and 11 am and 2 pm. This winding, 111-km stretch takes three to four hours; the fare is also 45B.

All of little Pai is accessible on foot. For local excursions you can rent bicycles or motorcycles at Northern Green on Chaisongkhram Rd. Bicycles cost 50B a day, motorcycles (Honda Dreams) are 150B; you get free maps of the area with every rental. Duang Guest House also rents bicycles.

AROUND PAI

Visitors can use Pai as a base for excursions to nearby hill-tribe villages, as described earlier in the Pai section. Farther afield, the area north-east of Pai has so far been little explored. A network of unpaved roads – some little more than footpaths – skirts a mountain ridge and the Taeng River valley all the way to the Burmese border near **Wiang Haeng** and **Ban Piang Haeng**, passing several villages along the way. Near Ban Piang Luang is a Shan temple built by Khun Sa, the infamous Shan-Chinese opium warlord. Printing facilities for *Freedom's Way*, a propaganda journal for the Meuang Tai-Shan United Army, are just across the border.

This area can also be visited by road from Chiang Dao in Chiang Mai Province.

Chiang Rai Province

Chiang Rai (population 167,318), the northernmost province in Thailand, is one of the country's most rural areas. Half of its northern border, separating province and nation from Laos, is formed by the Maekhong (Mekong) River. Mountains form the other half, cleaving Myanmar from Thailand, with the junction of the Sai, Ruak and Maekhong rivers at Thailand's peak. The fertile Maekhong flood plains to the east support most of the agriculture in the province; to the west the land is too mountainous for most crops. One crop that thrives on steep mountain slopes is opium, and until very recently Chiang Rai was the centre for most of the poppy cultivated in Thailand.

Crop substitution and other development projects sponsored by the Princess Mother (the King's mother), along with accelerated law enforcement, have pushed much of the opium trade over the border into Myanmar and Laos. While there are undoubtedly still pockets of the trade here and there, even a few poppy patches, Chiang Rai's Golden Triangle fame is now mostly relegated to history books and museums.

CHIANG RAI

อ.เมืองเชียงราย

A little more than 100 km from Chiang Mai, Chiang Rai (population 36,542; called 'Chiang Hai' in northern Thai dialect) is known as the gateway to the Golden Triangle. Most visitors to the town are interested in hill-tribe trekking or a boat trip on the Kok River.

Chiang Rai was founded by King Mengrai in 1262 as part of the Lanna kingdom. It became a Thai territory in 1786 and a province in 1910. Its most historic monument, Wat Phra Kaew, once hosted the Emerald Buddha during its circuitous travels (the image eventually ended up at the wat of the same name in Bangkok). It now houses a replica of Chiang Mai's Wat Phra Singh Buddha image and a new 'Emerald Buddha' of its own.

Lots of wealthy Thais are moving to Chiang Rai and over the last three years or so the area has seen a development boom as local entrepreneurs speculate on the city's future. Golf courses are going up outside the town, and a new international airport has recently opened 10 km north of the city. From a tourist point of view, Chiang Rai is becoming an alternative to Chiang Mai, especially for Europeans.

Information

Tourist Office The TAT office (☎ 717433) on Singkhlai Rd, north of Wat Phra Singh, distributes maps of the city as well as useful brochures on accommodation and transport. It's open daily from 8.30 am to 5 pm.

Post & Telecommunications The GPO, on Utarakit Rd south of Wat Phra Singh, is open from 8.30 am to 4.30 pm weekdays, 9 am to 1 pm weekends and holidays.

A new CAT office at Damrong and Ngam Meuang Rds offers international telephone, telegram, telex and fax services from 7 am to 11 pm daily.

Chiang Rai's telephone area code is ☎ 053.

Wat Phra Kaew
วัดพระแก้ว

Originally called Wat Paa Yia (Bamboo Forest Monastery) in local dialect, this is the city's most revered Buddhist temple. Legend says that in 1434 lightning struck the temple's octagonal chedi, which fell apart to reveal the Phra Kaew Morakot or Emerald

Buddha (actually made of jade). (See the Bangkok chapter for more information on the Emerald Buddha.)

Around 1990 Chiang Rai commissioned a Chinese artist to sculpt a new image from Canadian jade. Named the Phra Yok Chiang Rai (Chiang Rai Jade Buddha), it was intentionally a very close but not exact replica of the Phra Kaew Morakot in Bangkok, with dimensions of 48.3 cm across the base and 65.9 cm in height (the original is 48.3 and 66 cm respectively). The image was installed at the temple in June 1991. At present, the image sits in a gilded box in front of a larger

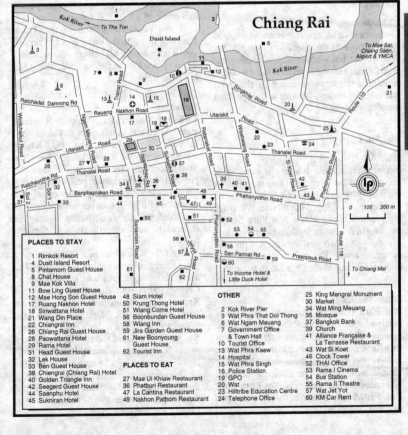

NORTHERN THAILAND

PLACES TO STAY
1 Rimkok Resort
4 Dusit Island Resort
5 Pintamorn Guest House
8 Chat House
9 Mae Kok Villa
11 Bow Ling Guest House
12 Mae Hong Son Guest House
17 Ruang Nakhon Hotel
18 Siriwattana Hotel
21 Wang Din Place
22 Chiangrai Inn
26 Chiang Rai Guest House
28 Paowattana Hotel
29 Rama Hotel
31 Head Guest House
32 Lek House
33 Ben Guest House
38 Chiengrai (Chiang Rai) Hotel
40 Golden Triangle Inn
42 Seegerd Guest House
44 Saenphu Hotel
45 Sukniran Hotel
48 Siam Hotel
50 Krung Thong Hotel
51 Wiang Come Hotel
56 Boonbundan Guest House
58 Wiang Inn
59 Jira Garden Guest House
61 New Boonyoung Guest House
62 Tourist Inn

PLACES TO EAT
27 Mae Ui Khiaw Restaurant
36 Phetburi Restaurant
47 La Cantina Restaurant
49 Nakhon Pathom Restaurant

OTHER
2 Kok River Pier
3 Wat Phra That Doi Thong
6 Wat Ngam Meuang
7 Government Office & Town Hall
10 Tourist Office
13 Wat Phra Kaew
14 Hospital
15 Wat Phra Singh
16 Police Station
19 GPO
20 Wat
23 Hilltribe Education Centre
24 Telephone Office
25 King Mengrai Monument
30 Market
34 Wat Ming Meuang
35 Mosque
37 Bangkok Bank
39 Church
41 Alliance Française & La Terrasse Restaurant
43 Wat Si Koet
46 Clock Tower
52 THAI Office
53 Rama I Cinema
54 Bus Station
55 Rama II Theatre
57 Wat Jet Yot
60 KM Car Rent

seated image in the main wihaan; eventually it will be moved to the new Lanna-style Haw Phra Kaew (Jewel Buddha Hall), soon to be completed. The Princess Mother has honoured the image with the royal title of Phra Phuttha Ratanakon Nawutiwat Sanuson Mongkhon, which roughly translates as 'the ultimate blessed jewel-made Buddha image'.

The main wihaan is a medium-sized, nicely preserved wooden structure with unique carved doors. The chedi behind it dates to the late 14th century and is typical Lanna style.

Wat Jet Yot
วัดเจ็ดยอด

The namesake for this wat is a seven-spired chedi similar to the chedi in Chiang Mai's Wat Jet Yot but without stucco ornamentation. Of more aesthetic interest is the wooden ceiling in the front verandah of the main wihaan; the ceiling features a unique Thai astrological fresco.

Wat Phra Singh
วัดพระสิงห์

Yet another temple housing a copy of a famous Buddha image, this one was built in the late 14th century during the reign of Chiang Rai's King Mahaphrom. A sister temple to Chiang Mai's Wat Phra Singh, the original temple buildings are typical northern-style wooden structures with low, sweeping roofs. The main wihaan houses a copy of Chiang Mai's Phra Singh Buddha.

Other Temples
Wat Phra That Doi Thong is a hilltop wat north-west of Wat Phra Kaew with views of the river and an occasional river breeze. Wat Paa Kaw, near the entrance to the old Chiang Rai Airport south of town, is a Shan-built temple with distinctive Burmese designs. Also near the old airport is Wat Phra That Doi Phrabaat, a northern-style temple perched on a hillside.

Hilltribe Education Centre
ศูนย์การศึกษาชาวเขา

The nonprofit Population & Community Development Association (PDA) operates this combination of museum and handicrafts centre at 620/25 Thanalai Rd (☎ 713410, 711475). Crafts for sale are displayed on the ground floor. The 2nd and 3rd floors of the facility serve as a museum with typical clothing for each tribe, folk implements and other anthropological exhibits. The centre also offers a slide show on Thailand's hill tribes with narration in English, French, German, Japanese and Thai. Admission to the slide show depends on the number of people who want to see it, ranging from 10B per person in a group of 10, to 50B for one person.

If you've already been to the Tribal Research Institute at Chiang Mai University, you'll have seen it all before; otherwise, it's a good place to visit before undertaking any hill-tribe treks.

Activities
Trekking More than 20 travel agencies, guesthouses and hotels offer trekking, typically in the Doi Tung and Chiang Khong areas. Chiang Rai's guesthouses were the first places to offer treks in the area and generally have the most experienced guides. Many of the local travel agencies merely act as brokers for guides associated with one of the local guesthouses; hence it may be cheaper to book directly through a guesthouse.

From the Kok River pier, boats can take you upriver as far as Fang. (See Fang & Tha Ton in this chapter.) An hour's boat ride from Chiang Rai is **Ban Ruammit**, a fair-sized Karen village. From here you can trek on your own to Lahu, Mien, Akha and Lisu villages – all within a day's walk. Inexpensive room and board (20 to 30B per person, meals 10 to 20B) are available in many villages in the river area. Another popular area for do-it-yourself trekkers is Wawi, south of the river town of Mae Salak near the end of the river route. (See the Kok River Trip to Chiang Rai section earlier.)

Places to Stay – bottom end

Guesthouses Near the Kok River pier (for boats from Tha Ton) is *Mae Kok Villa* (☎ 711786) at 445 Singkhlai Rd, which has dorm beds for 40B, bungalows with fan and hot bath for 120B, and large singles/doubles with fan and hot bath for 140/160B. Hostelling International card holders get a 10% discount on these rates; non-members may be required to purchase a membership. Another nice place near the Kok River pier is *Chat House* (☎ 711481), at 1 Trairat Rd. It's an old Thai house with singles/doubles at 40/60B with shared bath, 60/80B with private bath. There are bicycles for rent and guided treks are available.

A bit east of here in a network of sois off Singkhlai Rd are a couple of small family-run guesthouses. First is the clean and friendly *Bow Ling House* (☎ 712704), which has singles/doubles with shared bath for 40/60B and rooms with private bath for 80B. A hot-water shower is available. Next is the very pleasant *Mae Hong Son Guest House of Chiang Rai* (☎ 715367), run by the same family as the original guesthouse in Mae Hong Son. Rooms are 60/80B with shared hot-water showers, 100B with private ones. This guesthouse has a very nice garden cafe, and also rents motorcycles and organises treks.

North of here are a couple of places on a large island separated from the city by a canal. *Chian House* (☎ 713388) at 172 Si Bunruang Rd has simple but nicely done rooms from 60B with cold shower, 80 to 150B for larger rooms with hot shower. Chian House lends free bikes to guests. Also on the island is *Pintamorn Guest House* (☎ 713317, 714161), where comfortable singles/doubles are 80/120B with hot water. There are also doubles with air-con in a separate house for 250B. A 'sports club' on the premises has work-out rooms open to the public for 60B a day, plus a bar/restaurant and sauna.

The original *Chiang Rai Guest House* (☎ 714305) has moved from its old location at Si Koet Rd to larger premises at 77 Pratu Chiang Mai Rd. Room rates are 50B a single, 80B a double with shared bath, and 100 to 120B for doubles with private hot shower. The old house used by the Chiang Rai Guest House at 717/1 Si Koet Rd is now the laid-back *Seegerd Guest House* (☎ 712804), run by knowledgeable trekking guide Adirake. Rooms with shared bath are 50/70B for a single/double.

Lek House (☎ 713337) at 95 Thanalai Rd near the city centre has rooms in an old house for 60/80B single/double with shared bath, or bungalows with private bath for 100B. If you follow Thanalai farther west till it becomes Ratchayotha Rd, you'll find *Head Guest House* at Soi 2. Head's bamboo huts cost from 40 to 60B a single, 70 to 100B a double or triple. Farther down Soi 2, just before it ends at San Khong Noi Rd, is *Chai House* (☎ 716681), a quiet spot away from everything with singles/doubles at 50B.

If you follow Soi 1 Ratchayotha south till it ends, then turn left, you'll come to the ambitious *Ben Guest House* (☎ 714653). Clean rooms in a new building made of salvaged teak cost 80B with fan and hot shower, 60B without bath. The owners speak English very well. About 200 metres past Soi 2 on 21/4 Ratchayotha is *Wisid Guest House* (☎ 713279). Rooms in this old teak and bamboo house are 60B with shared hot bath.

In the southern part of town are *Boon-bundan Guest House* (☎ 712914) and *New Boonyoung Guest House* (☎ 712893), both in walled compounds. The Boonbundan is at 1005/13 Jetyot Rd and offers a choice of accommodation – in small rooms off the garden, in huts or in the new air-con building overlooking the garden – something to suit all budgets. Small rooms with shared bath are 50B, slightly larger singles/doubles with hot bath are 60/80B. Singles/doubles in huts are 100/150B with fan and bath, and large singles/doubles with a fan in the new building are 150/200B, 250/350B with air-con. The Boonbundan loans bicycles, rents out motorcycles and runs treks. New Boonyoung at 1054/5 Sanambin Rd has a similar arrangement minus the new building. Singles/doubles are 50/70B or 100/150B with hot bath.

Also in this vicinity is the friendly and efficient *Tourist Inn* (☎ 714682) at 1004/5-6 Jetyot Rd. Clean, large rooms are 170B with fan and private bath. Due east of Wat Jet Yot, at the end of San Pannat Rd, *Jira Garden Guest House* (☎ 712556) offers a quiet location and spacious grounds. Large doubles with fan and shared hot-water bath are 100 to 120B. Another Jira Garden plus is that it's only a 10-minute walk from the bus station.

Hotels On Suksathit Rd near the clock tower and district government building is the well-run *Chiengrai Hotel* (☎ 311266), a favourite with Thai truck drivers and travelling sales-people. Clean rooms with fan and bath cost 130 to 200B. Also centrally located is the *Sukniran* (☎ 311055) at 424/1 Banphaprakan Rd, between the clock tower and Wat Ming Meuang, around the corner from the Chiang Rai Hotel. Rooms start at 200B for rooms with fan, 350B for air-con.

Similar to the Sukniran but cheaper is *Siam* (☎ 711077) at 531/6-8 Banphaprakan, where rates start at 160B with fan and bath, 200 to 220B with air-con.

Ruang Nakhon (☎ 711566) at 25 Reuang Nakhon Rd, near the hospital, allows four people to share a room with bath for 200B. Bungalows are 160B, doubles 180B, and air-con doubles from 220 to 420B.

If you favour the old Thai-Chinese type of hotel, check out the *Paowattana* (☎ 711722) at 150 Thanalai Rd, which has rooms for 100 to 200B. Another cheap – but noisy – hotel is the *Siriwattana* (☎ 711466) at 485 Utarakit Rd next to the GPO, where singles/doubles cost 100 to 180B and there are a couple of bungalows at 60 to 80B.

The clean and efficient *Krung Thong Hotel* (☎ 711033; fax 711848), at 412 Sanambin Rd, has large one/two-bed rooms with fan and bath for 140/180B; air-con rooms cost 260/300B.

Places to Stay – middle
The centrally located *Rama Hotel* (☎ 311344) at 331/4 Trairat Rd, a couple of blocks from the clock tower, offers rooms with air-con, carpeting and hot-water baths for 420 to 550B. Restaurants, nightclubs and theatres are nearby.

Out of town, at 70 Phahonyothin Rd (the highway to Mae Sai), is the YMCA's *Golden Triangle International House* (☎ 713785). This is a very modern establishment with dorm beds for 80B, singles/doubles with fan and private bath for 240/280B, or 330/440B with air-con. All rooms come with hot water and a telephone. Guests may use the Y's swimming pool.

Places to Stay – top end
The *Golden Triangle Inn* (☎ 711339; fax 713963), at 590 Phahonyothin Rd, has 39 tastefully designed rooms with tile floors, air-con and hot water for 700B including American breakfast. Also on the landscaped grounds are a cafe, a small Japanese-Thai garden and an efficient travel agency. It's a popular place, so book in advance to ensure you get in.

On the same theme, but not quite as successful, is the new *Chiangrai Inn* (☎ 712673; fax 711483) at 661 Utarakit Rd. Large air-con rooms are a bit overpriced at 1100B for singles/doubles.

Ceremonial knife used by priests, Mien hill tribe

Much better value in this range is the centrally located *Saenphu Hotel* (☎ 717300/9; fax 711372). Rooms with all the amenities – air-con, TV, phone, fridge – cost a bargain 545B for a single or double. The hotel's basement nightclub has live music and is a very popular local rendezvous. *Income Hotel* (☎ 717850), on Ratbamrung Rd south of the city centre, offers similar rooms for 600B and has the most popular disco in town.

The *Wiang Inn* (☎ 711543) at 893 Phahonyothin Rd has modestly luxurious rooms from 711B. Facilities include a swimming pool, bar, restaurant, coffee shop and disco. Nearing the top of the Chiang Mai room-rate scale is *Wiang Come* (☎ 711800), at 869/90 Premawiphat Rd in the Chiang Rai Trade Centre. International-class rooms start at 1400B (only 800B for Thais!), complete with TV and fridge. The hotel has a disco, coffee shop, restaurant and nightclub.

A rash of new luxury hotels opened in Chiang Rai just in time for the travel recession of 1990-92. Perched on its own island in the Kok River (you can't miss seeing its stacked white facade if you arrive in Chiang Rai by boat), the 270-room *Dusit Island Resort* (☎ 715777) is an island unto itself, insulating its guests from the rigours of laid-back Chiang Rai. Rooms start at 2800B but since occupancy rates often run below 50%, the Dusit may consider a discount to attract prospective guests.

Opposite the Dusit Island Resort on the other side of river, the Thai-style *Rimkok Resort* (☎ 716445, fax 715859; Bangkok ☎ (02) 278-1154) is probably Chiang Rai's most beautiful hotel. Set on lush grounds, spacious rooms with all the amenities start at 1500B. One drawback is the lack of a nearby bridge, so it's a 15-minute trip back and forth from Chiang Rai via the highway bridge at the east end of town.

Another good choice in this range is *Wang Din Place* (☎ 713363; fax 716790) at 34/1 Khae Wai Rd, in the north-east corner of town near the river. Sturdy, Thai-style bungalows with fridge, TV, air-con and private hot-water bath start at 800B.

The 350-room *Little Duck Hotel* (☎ 715620), south of the city past the old airport, has picked up more of a regular clientele since the last edition in spite of its distance from the new airport and town. Tourist-class rooms start at 1400B. The owner was recently indicted on drug trafficking charges, leading many to believe the hotel may close soon.

North on Phahonyothin Rd just before the road crosses the river on the way to Mae Sai, the *Holiday Park Hotel* (☎ 712243) is also new, but better located. Rooms start at 600B; facilities include an attached shopping plaza, restaurant and a garden sitting area.

Places to Eat

Thai There are plenty of restaurants in Chiang Rai, especially along Banphaprakan and Thanalai Rds. Just east of the once-great (now awful) Haw Naliga Restaurant on Banphaprakan Rd are the inexpensive *Phetburi* and *Ratburi* restaurants. The Phetburi has a particularly good selection of curries and other Thai dishes. One speciality is cha-om thâwt, a type of fried quiche of cha-om greens cut in squares and served with a delicious chilli sauce.

For northern Thai food, the best place in town is *Mae Ui Khiaw* at 106/9 Ngam Meuang Rd, open from 8 am to 5 pm only. Mae Ui Khiaw's simple menu includes such classic northern dishes as kaeng hang leh (vegetable-herb curry) and náam phrík nùm (northern-style chilli sauce). Two other spots specialising in local cuisine as well as standard Thai dishes are *Baan Khun* at 474/6 Singkhlai Rd and *Khrua Mae Korn* at 10/1 Phahonyothin Rd, both of which are open from around 10 am to 10 pm.

Nakhon Pathom, yet another local restaurant named after a central Thailand city, is very popular for inexpensive khâo man kài (Hainanese chicken rice) and kŭaytĭaw pèt yâang (roast duck with rice noodles). The restaurant is on Phahonyothin Rd near the Banphaprakan intersection.

Muang Thong Restaurant, just south of the Wiang Inn, has an extensive Thai and Chinese menu that includes a frog section. The house speciality is kaeng pà pèt, a delicious duck curry made without coconut milk.

Next to the mosque on Itsaraphap Rd is a Thai-Muslim restaurant with delicious khâo mòk kài, a Thai version of chicken biryani. Near the bus station are the usual food stalls; the night market next to the terminal and Rama I cinema is also good. There's a string of inexpensive rice and noodle restaurants along Jetyot Rd between Thanalai Rd and Wat Jet Yot, near the Chiengrai and Wiang Come hotels.

T Hut, on Phahonyothin Rd near the second post office, is a bit pricey for Thai food but is considered one of the best places to eat in the North. The restaurant at the *Little Duck Hotel* puts on a good 80B buffet Monday to Friday from 11 am to 2 pm; come early to beat the crowd.

Western Trapkaset (pronounced 'Sapkaset') Plaza, an L-shaped soi between Banphaprakan and Suksathit Rds, has become something of a farang food and bar centre. *La Cantina* (☎ 716808), operated by an Italian expat, offers an extensive selection of pizza, pasta, Italian regional specialities and wines; Mr Vallicelli even plays Italian opera on the sound system!

Bierstube on Phahonyothin Rd south of the Wiang Inn has been recommended for German food, and there are several other Western-style pubs along here and on Suksathit/Jetyot Rd near the Wiang Come Hotel. *Cafe de Paris* on Jetyot Rd, operated by a Corsican, is good for coffee and European food.

Entertainment
Heuan Kao (Old House), diagonally opposite the Chiengrai Hotel on Suksathit Rd, has live music nightly from 7 pm till midnight. The decor and atmosphere is 'Thai classic' (lots of B&W photos of Rama VII) and there's a reasonable Thai-Chinese menu for munchies, also good ice cream.

The Rama Hotel's Cheers Pub is a lively old-west-style pub with occasional live folk music. Another popular local hang-out is the

basement nightclub of the Saenphu Hotel, which has live Thai pop bands nightly.

Trapkaset Plaza has two go-go bars and the semi-outdoor Easy Bar. The Easy Bar is for video addicts – English-language videos are shown almost nonstop throughout the afternoon and evening.

Homesick Brits may enjoy the Dusit Island Resort's Cellar Pub, which offers pub grub, draught beer and darts; it's open 4 pm till late.

Things to Buy
Prices for antiques and silverwork are sometimes – but not always – lower in Chiang Rai than in Chiang Mai. Several shops worth checking out for handicrafts, silver and antiques are found along Phahonyothin Rd, including Gong Ngoen at No 873/5, Silver Birch at No 891, and Chiangrai Handicrafts Center at No 273. Ego, at 869/81 Premawiphak, carries more up-market items including antique textiles.

Getting There & Away
Air Chiang Rai's new international airport lies 10 km north of the city. THAI flies daily between Chiang Rai and Chiang Mai; the flight takes 30 minutes and costs 420B. Daily flights are also available to/from Bangkok (one hour and 20 minutes, 1855B). There may soon be flights from Hong Kong and Kunming.

Chiang Rai's THAI office (☎ 711179, 715207) is at 870 Phahonyothin Rd, not far from the Wiang Come Hotel.

Bus There are two bus routes to Chiang Rai from Chiang Mai, an old and a new. The old route *(sāi kào)* heads south from Chiang Mai to Lampang before heading north through Ngao, Phayao, Mae Chai and finally to Chiang Rai. If you want to stop at any of these cities, this is the bus to catch, but the trip will take up to seven hours. In Chiang Mai the bus leaves from the Chiang Mai-Lamphun road, near Nawarat Bridge; the fare is 83B (ordinary only).

The new route (sai mai) heads north-east

along Route 1019 to Chiang Rai, stopping in Doi Saket and Wiang Papao, and takes about four hours. The fare is 57B ordinary, 79B 2nd-class air-con or 102B for 1st-class air-con. New-route buses leave from Chiang Mai's Arcade bus station. Chiang Mai to Chiang Rai buses are sometimes stopped for drug searches by police.

Chiang Rai's bus station is on Prasopsuk Rd, several blocks south of Banphaprakan Rd.

Other bus services from Chiang Rai include:

City	Fare	Duration
Bangkok	189B	12 hours
(air-con)	265B	11 hours
(1st class)	364B	
(VIP)	525B	
Chiang Saen	17B	1½ hours
Chiang Khong	31B	3 hours
Khon Kaen	189B	12 hours
(air-con)	264B	11 hours
(1st class)	339B	11 hours
Mae Sai	17B	1¾ hours
Nan	74B	6 hours
Phayao	21B	1¾ hours
Phitsanulok	104B	6 hours
(air-con)	140B	5 hours
Phrae	50B	4 hours

Boat One of the most popular ways of getting to Chiang Rai is the river trip from Tha Ton (see the Kok River Trip to Chiang Rai section earlier in this chapter).

For boats heading upriver on the Mae Kok, go to the pier in the north-western corner of town. Regular long boats from Chiang Rai stop at the following villages along the Kok (times are approximate for ideal river conditions):

Destination	Fare	Duration
Ban Ruammit	25B	1 hour
Pong Nam Rawn	30B	1 hour 20 min
Phaa Muup	35B	1¾ hours
Hat Yao	60B	2¼ hours
Phaa Khwang	70B	2½ hours
Kok Noi	90B	3 hours
Phaa Tai	120B	3½ hours
Mae Salak	130B	4 hours
Tha Ton	160B	4½ to 5 hours

Getting Around

A samlor ride anywhere in central Chiang Rai should cost 10 to 15B. Tuk-tuks cost twice as much. A city songthaew system (2B fare) circulates along the main city streets; there are also route tuk-tuks that charge 5B.

Several small agencies near the Wiang Come Hotel rent cars, vans and jeeps.

Most of the guesthouses in town rent or lend bicycles, which are a good way to get around town. Motorcycles are also easily rented through guesthouses. A reliable motorcycle rental and repair shop is Soon (☎ 714068), on the eastern side of Trairat Rd between Banphaprakan and Thanalai Rds. Another place that rents motorcycles is next to the Sukniran Hotel.

MAE SALONG (SANTIKHIRI)

แม่สลอง (สันติคีรี)

The village of Mae Salong was originally settled by the renegade KMT 93rd Regiment, which fled to Myanmar from China after the 1949 Chinese revolution. The renegades were again forced to flee in 1961 when the Burmese government decided they wouldn't allow the KMT to remain legally in northern Myanmar (some still hide out in the hills).

Ever since the Thai government granted these renegades refugee status in the 1960s, the Thais have been trying to incorporate the Yunnanese KMT and their families into the Thai nation. Before now they weren't having much success, as the KMT persisted in involving themselves in the Golden Triangle opium trade, along with opium warlord Khun Sa and the Shan United Army (SUA).

This area is very mountainous and there are few paved roads, so the outside world has always been somewhat cut off from the goings-on in Mae Salong. Hence, for years the KMT were able to ignore attempts by Thai authorities to suppress opium activity and tame the region. Khun Sa, in fact, made his home in nearby Ban Hin Taek (now Ban Theuat Thai) until the early 1980s when he was finally routed by the Thai military. Khun Sa's retreat to Myanmar seemed to signal a change in local attitudes and the Thai gov-

NORTHERN THAILAND

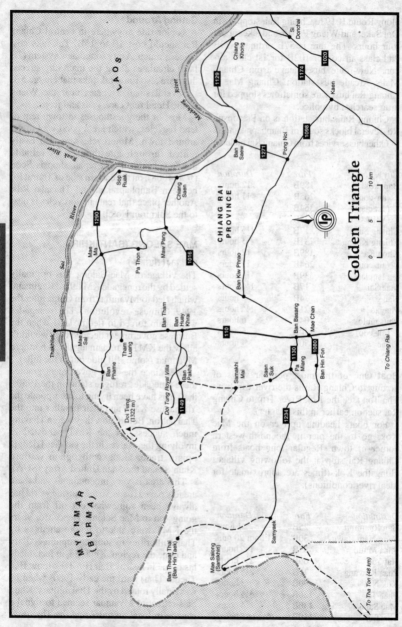

Golden Triangle

ernment finally began making progress in its pacification of Mae Salong and the surrounding area. (See Opium & the Golden Triangle in the Facts about the Country chapter.)

In a further effort to separate the area from its old image as an opium fiefdom, the Thai government officially changed the name of the village from Mae Salong to Santikhiri (Hill of Peace). Until the early 1980s pack horses were used to move goods up the mountain to Mae Salong, but today the 36-km road from Basang (near Mae Chan) to Santikhiri is paved and a Thai-language elementary school has been established. There are also evening adult classes in the Thai language.

Despite government efforts to 'Thai-ise' the area, Mae Salong is unlike any other town in Thailand. The combination of pack horses, hill tribes (Akha, Lisu, Mien, Hmong) and southern Chinese-style houses conjures up images of a small town or village in Yunnan Province in China. Illegal immigrants from Yunnan are still arriving in steady numbers.

Most people in the area speak Yunnanese, except, of course, for members of the local hill tribes, who are mainly Akha and speak hill-tribe dialects. Like other villages throughout rural Thailand undergoing similar pacification programmes, Mae Salong is wired with a loudspeaker system that broadcasts official programming in the streets, starting at 6 am. The locals are reluctant to speak of their KMT past and deny that there are any KMT regulars left in the area. To the Thais, they are simply the jiin haw (galloping Chinese), a reference either to their use of horses or their migratory status.

One of the most important government programmes is the crop-substitution plan to encourage hill tribes to cultivate tea, coffee, corn and fruit trees. This seems to be somewhat successful, as there are plenty of these products for sale in the town markets, and tea and corn are abundant in the surrounding fields. There is a tea factory in town where you can taste the fragrant Mae Salong teas (originally from Taiwan), and there are many fruit wines and liquors for sale at the markets. The local illicit corn whisky is much in demand – perhaps an all too obvious substitution for the poppy.

Another local speciality is Chinese herbs, particularly the kind that are mixed with liquor ('yaa dong' in Thai). Thai and Chinese tourists who come to Mae Salong always take back a bag or two of assorted Chinese herbs.

Minivans full of Thai day-trippers begin arriving in Mae Salong around 10 am and leave by 4 pm. If you can stay overnight you'll pretty much have the place to yourself in the mornings and evenings.

Information
The weather is always a bit cooler on Doi Mae Salong than on the plains below. During the cool and dry months, November to February, nights can actually get cold – be sure to bring sweaters and socks for visits at this time of year.

An interesting morning market convenes from around 5 to 10 am in front of the Mae Salong Guest House and is attended by hill tribespeople from the surrounding districts.

Trekking
Shin Sane Guest House has a wall map showing approximate routes to Akha, Mien, Hmong, Lisu, Lahu and Shan villages in the area. Nearby Mien, Akha and Lisu villages are less than half a day's walk away.

The best hikes are north of Mae Salong between Ban Hin Taek (Ban Theuat Thai) and the Burmese border. Ask about political conditions before heading off in this direction (towards Myanmar), however. In 1989 Khun Sa sent SUA troops to Ban Mae Chan Luang, an Akha village on the northern slopes of Doi Mae Salong. The troops sealed off the village and abducted several villagers including the headman. The conflict had to do with opium-smuggling routes in the area. SUA and Wa National Army forces are competing for control over this section of the Thai-Burmese border and occasionally clash in the area.

It's possible to walk south from Mae Salong to Chiang Rai in three or four days, following trails which pass through fairly remote hill-tribe villages. There are also several easily reached hill-tribe villages along the highway between Ban Basang and Mae Salong, but these days they're full of day tourists from Chiang Rai.

The Mae Salong Guest House arranges six-hour horseback treks to four nearby villages for 500B, including lunch, or a shorter three-hour trek for 300B. Laan Tong Lodge (see Places to Stay below) can also arrange treks.

Places to Stay

The Yunnanese-run *Mae Salong Guest House* is at the high end of town. Clean but spartan rooms with shared hot shower are 60B, 80B with private bath. Yunnanese food, several varieties of local fruit spirits, Mae Salong tea and Chinese herbal medicines are available, and the owners can arrange treks on horseback or advise you on making treks on your own. To reach the guesthouse you must pass through the gateway to Mae Salong Resort or through the Shin Sane Guest House.

Shin Sane (Sin Sae) Guest House, Mae Salong's original hotel, is a wooden Chinese affair with a bit more atmosphere than the Mae Salong Guest House. Basic rooms are 50B per person. Information on trekking is available; there is also a nice little eating area and a place for doing laundry. Next to the Shin Sane, *Akom Guest House* offers cramped, bare rooms for 50/70B with shared bath, 150B with bath – poor value unless everything else is full (not likely).

At the top of the price range is the *Mae Salong Resort* (☎ 714047; (02) 513-9024 in Bangkok), where well-appointed bungalows cost 2000B on weekends, as low as 500B with mid-week discounts. The Yunnanese restaurant here is very good – especially tasty are the fresh mushroom dishes.

Mae Salong Villa (☎ 713444) just below the town centre has bungalow-style accommodation from 500 to 700B. On the opposite side of town near the afternoon market, on the road to Tha Ton, the upscale *Khunnayphol Resort* (☎ 712485) offers modern hotel-style rooms for 800 to 2000B.

Out of Town Three km from Ban Basang on the road to Mae Salong is a turn-off to *Winnipa Lodge* (☎ 712225), on a hillside overlooking the road. Bungalows are 300 to 1000B; there is also tent accommodation available for 100B a night. From here you can see Doi Tung in the distance.

If you're hiking or driving to Chiang Rai from Doi Mae Salong or Tha Ton, you could stop off in Ban Hin Fon and stay at friendly *Laan Tong Lodge* (☎ 771366 in Mae Chan), which is about 13 km west of Mae Chan or 31 km from Mae Salong (17 km east of the Mae Salong-Tha Ton road junction). Otherwise you can reach it by taking a songthaew from Mae Chan to the village (10B) and then hiking the three km to the lodge. Large, well-kept and well-separated huts on impressively landscaped grounds cost 150B without bath, 450B with bath. One of the activities here is tubing along the Mae Chan River.

Places to Eat

Don't miss the many street noodle vendors who sell khanŏm jiin náam ngíaw, a delicious Yunnanese rice-noodle concoction topped with spicy chicken curry – Mae Salong's most famous local dish and a gourmet bargain at 6B per bowl.

Around town you'll find a variety of places serving simple Chinese snacks like fluffy mantou (plain steamed Chinese buns) and salabao (pork-stuffed Chinese buns) with delicious pickled vegetables. Many of the Chinese in Santikhiri are Muslims, so you'll find several Chinese-Muslim restaurants serving khâo sòi (curried chicken and noodles).

Getting There & Away

To get to Mae Salong by public transport, take a bus from Mae Sai or Chiang Rai to Ban Basang, which is about two km north of Mae Chan. From Ban Basang, there are songthaews up the mountain to Mae Salong for 50B per person (down again costs 40B); the trip takes about an hour. The bus fare from Chiang Rai to Ban Basang is 11B.

You can also reach Mae Salong by road from Tha Ton. See the earlier Fang & Tha Ton section for details.

MAE SAI

แม่สาย

The northernmost point in Thailand, Mae Sai is a good place from which to explore the Golden Triangle, Doi Tung and Mae Salong. It's also a spot to observe border life, as Mae Sai is one of only two official land crossings open between Myanmar and Thailand (the other is Three Pagodas Pass).

Burmese authorities have spruced up Thakhilek (the town opposite Mae Sai, also spelt Tachilek) and now foreigners are now allowed across for one to three days as far as Kengtung, 163 km from Thailand and 100 km short of China. Within two years, the road should be open all the way to the Chinese border. (See Around Mae Sai below for current details on this trip.) In spite of the opening, Thai tourists are much more commonly seen in Mae Sai than farangs.

Burmese lacquerware, gems, jade and other goods from Laos and Myanmar are sold in shops along the main street in Mae Sai. Many Burmese come over during the day from Thakhilek to work or do business, hurrying back by sunset. Gem dealers from as far away as Chanthaburi frequent the **gem market** opposite the police station.

Take the steps up the hill near the border to **Wat Phra That Doi Wao**, west of the main street, for superb views over Myanmar and Mae Sai. There are also some interesting trails in the cliffs and hills overlooking the Mae Sai Guest House and the river.

Motorcycle trekking in the area is quite good due to plenty of challenging back roads and trails. Chad House in Mae Sai has good information on motorcycle treks.

Mae Sai is a base for exploring the nearby caves of **Tham Luang** (Great Cave), **Tham Pum**, and **Tham Pla**, as well as the trip to Doi Tung (see Around Mae Sai below).

Places to Stay – bottom end

Guesthouses Near the town entrance and the bus terminal is *Chad House*, off the main street a bit in a residential neighbourhood. The Thai-Shan family that runs it is friendly and helpful, and the food is particularly good. There's a garden with tables for evening repasts. Chad has an extensive knowledge of motorcycle trekking in the area as well as information on trips to Kengtung. Rooms are 80B with shared hot-water bath. There are a couple of 120B bungalows with private bath, and a 10-bed dorm for 40B per person.

Mae Sai Guest House (☎ 732021) is often full due to its scenic location on the river across from Myanmar. It's a walk of about a km from the end of Mae Sai's main road and thus very quiet. Bungalows cost from 40B a single, 100B a double; rooms with private bath are 80 to 150B. A hot shower is available, there's a good restaurant, and treks can be arranged. Recent reports say the staff can be rather unfriendly.

Closer to town and just back from the river is *Mae Sai Plaza Guest House* (☎ 732230). This huge hillside bamboo-and-wood complex has a laid-back atmosphere and a cafe overlooking the river – good for people-watching. Singles/doubles with shared bath cost from 50/80B to 60/100B, doubles with private bath are 120B and there are larger rooms at 200B with hot bath; most rooms have a view of the river. Between Mae Sai Plaza and Mae Sai Guest House, next to the river landing for local Thai-Burmese trade, is the relatively new *Sai Riverside*. Nice, secure rooms are 120B with fan and private bath, 200B with hot water.

Also on the river is *Northern Guest House* (☎ 731537, Bangkok ☎ (02) 468-3266) where a variety of rooms and huts are available from 50/80B for basic singles/doubles with shared bath, or you can pay up to 150B for a double with hot shower. A new air-con building has fancier rooms for 500B. The guesthouse maintains a nicely landscaped sitting area along the river.

Humble *Ya Guest House*, at a quiet location on the river about a km east of the bridge, features singles/doubles with attached shower in a thatch building for 80/100B.

Hotels *Mae Sai Hotel* (☎ 721462), off Phahonyothin Rd in the centre of town, isn't a bad budget choice. Singles/doubles with fan and private bath are 100/150B, air-con rooms with hot bath are 280B.

Sin Wattana (☎ 731950) is on the same side of Phahonyothin Rd across from the market; fairly well-kept rooms cost from 200B with private bath and fan, 350B with air-con.

Places to Stay – middle & top end

Guesthouses Above Mae Sai Guest House on a hill overlooking the river, the new *Rabiengthong House* offers comfortable suites for three or four people at 500B. It gets a mostly Thai clientele and features a fair Thai restaurant.

Petchpradap Guest House (☎ 731820), on a back street east of and parallel to the main strip, rents air-con bungalows with TV and hot water for 600B.

Down on the river strip near Mae Sai Plaza Guest House, the new American-run *King Kobra* features apartment-style rooms with

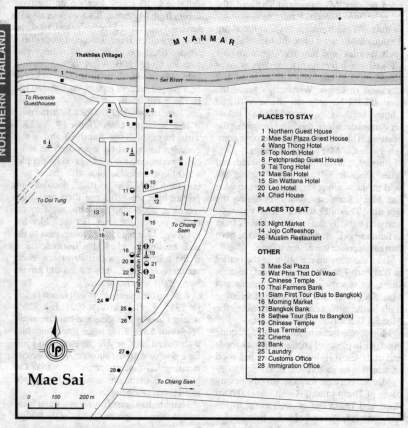

NORTHERN THAILAND

MYANMAR

Thakhilek (Village)

Sai River

To Riverside Guesthouses

To Doi Tung

To Chiang Saen

To Chiang Saen

To Chiang Saen

Phahonyothin Road

Mae Sai

0   100   200 m

PLACES TO STAY

1 Northern Guest House
2 Mae Sai Plaza Guest House
4 Wang Thong Hotel
5 Top North Hotel
8 Petchpradap Guest House
9 Tai Tong Hotel
12 Mae Sai Hotel
15 Sin Wattana Hotel
20 Leo Hotel
24 Chad House

PLACES TO EAT

13 Night Market
14 Jojo Coffeeshop
26 Muslim Restaurant

OTHER

3 Mae Sai Plaza
6 Wat Phra That Doi Wao
7 Chinese Temple
10 Thai Farmers Bank
11 Siam First Tour (Bus to Bangkok)
16 Morning Market
17 Bangkok Bank
18 Sethee Tour (Bus to Bangkok)
19 Chinese Temple
21 Bus Terminal
22 Cinema
23 Bank
25 Laundry
27 Customs Office
28 Immigration Office

private hot-water bath and fans for 200B, or 600B with air-con.

Hotels *Top North Hotel* (☎ 731955), on the west side of Phahonyothin Rd towards the bridge, has comfortable singles/doubles for 300B, 500B with air-con. All rooms have private hot-water showers. The newer *Leo Hotel* (☎ 732064), opposite the bus terminal, has rooms for 500 to 700B including air-con, hot water, TV and fridge – good mid-range value.

Tai Tong (Thai Thong) Hotel (☎ 731975) at 6 Phahonyothin Rd has standard rooms at 600B, and somewhat larger rooms for up to 1000B. All come with air-con and hot water, but considering the rooms, these rates are perhaps a tad high.

The nine-storey, 150-room *Wang Thong Hotel* (☎ 733388, Bangkok ☎ (02) 225-9298) off Phahonyothin Rd in the northern part of town recently opened and is entertaining brisk traffic among business travellers. Spacious, international-class rooms with all the amenities start at 1400/1600B for singles/doubles, not including tax and service. Facilities include a swimming pool, pub, disco and restaurant.

Places to Eat
The night market is rather small but the Chinese vendors do excellent kŭaytǐaw phàt sǐi-yúu (rice noodles stir-fried in soy sauce) and other noodle dishes. You can also get fresh paa-thông-kǒ (Chinese doughnuts) and hot soy milk.

Jojo Coffeeshop on Phahonyothin Rd serves very good Thai curries and Thai vegetarian dishes, plus ice cream and Western snacks. You'll eat well while contemplating the collection of Lanna-style wooden Buddhas along the walls. Down near the bridge on the river is a floating restaurant that's OK.

South of Chad House on the main road is a small Muslim restaurant with good curries and khâo mòk.

Getting There & Away
Buses to Mae Sai leave frequently from

Chiang Rai and cost 17B for the 1½-hour trip. To/from Chiang Saen by bus costs 16B via Mae Chan. (See Getting Around in the Chiang Saen section for details on different routes between Mae Sai and Chiang Saen.)

There are now direct buses to Mae Sai from Fang (33B) and Tha Ton (27B) via the newly paved Tha Ton-Mae Chan road.

To/From Bangkok Sethee Tour and Siam First Tour each have VIP 'sleeper' buses from Mae Sai to Bangkok that leave at about 5.30 or 6 pm daily for 400 to 568B depending on the number of seats; the journey takes around 13 hours. Standard air-con buses to Bangkok cost 364B and depart the main street ten times daily between 7 am and 8 pm. There is no longer a direct non-air-con bus service between Mae Sai and Bangkok; baht-pinchers will have to bus first to Chiang Mai and change to a Bangkok-bound ordinary bus.

Getting Around
Songthaews around town are 10B. Most guesthouses in Mae Sai have stopped renting motorcycles, but they can be rented at Konrakan Motorcycle Shop (☎ 731570) at 415-6 Phahonyothin near the market. In addition to the usual Honda Dreams and MTXs (150 to 160B per day), Konrakan rents a couple of 175cc Yamahas. Pornchai, near the Sethee Tour bus office, also rents motorcycles.

AROUND MAE SAI
Tham Luang (Great Cave)
ถ้ำหลวง
About six km south of Mae Sai off Route 110 is a large cave that extends into the hills for at least a couple of km, possibly more. The first cavern is huge, and a narrow passage at the back leads to a series of other chambers and side tunnels of varying sizes. The first km is fairly easy going but after that you do some climbing over piles of rocks to get further in. At this point the roof formations become more fantastic and tiny crystals make them change colour according to the

angle of the light. For 20B you can borrow a gas lantern from the caretakers in front of the cave or you can take someone along as a guide (for which there's no fixed fee; just give him whatever you want). Guides aren't always available during the week.

Tham Pum/Tham Pla
ถ้ำปุ่มและถ้ำปลา

Only 13 km south of Mae Sai, just off Route 110 at Ban Tham, are a couple of caves with freshwater lakes inside. Bring a torch to explore the caves as there are no lights. Another attraction here is the unique cake-like chedi in front of the cave entrance. It's a very large, multi-tiered structure stylistically different from any other in Thailand.

Doi Tung
ดอยตุง

About halfway between Mae Chan and Mae Sai on Route 110 is the turn-off west for Doi Tung. The name means 'Flag Peak', from the northern Thai word for 'flag' *(tung)*. King Achutarat of Chiang Saen ordered a giant flag to be flown from the peak to mark the spot where two chedis were constructed in 911 AD; the chedis are still there, a pilgrim-age site for Shan Buddhists.

But the main attraction at Doi Tung is getting there. The 'easy' way is via Route 1149, which is mostly paved to the peak of Doi Tung. But it's winding, steep and narrow, so if you're driving or riding a motorcycle, take it slowly.

Along the way are Shan, Akha and Musoe (Lahu) villages. Opium is cultivated in the vicinity of Doi Tung and this can be a dangerous area to explore alone if you go far off the main roads. Travelling after 4 pm – when traffic thins out – is not advised.

Myanmar is a short trek from the peak and many travellers used to climb to the border to view the very large poppy fields guarded by hill tribespeople and KMT soldiers on the other side. Around 1991 the fields were moved three km away from the border to hide them from curious eyes. It is probably not safe to trek in this area without a Thai or

hill-tribe guide simply because you may be mistaken for a USDEA agent (by the opium traders) or drug dealer (by the Thai army rangers who patrol the area). You may hear gunfire from time to time, which might indicate that rangers are in pursuit of MTA, Karen rebels or others caught between two hostile governments.

On the theory that local hill tribes will be so honoured by a royal presence that they will stop cultivating opium, Thailand's royal family maintains the **Doi Tung Royal Villa** on the slopes of Doi Tung near Pa Kluay Reservoir. It's meant to serve as a summer palace for the King's mother.

At the peak, 1800 metres above sea level, **Wat Phra That Doi Tung** is built around twin Lanna-style chedis purportedly erected in 911 AD. The chedis were renovated by famous Chiang Mai monk Khruba Siwichai earlier this century. Pilgrims bang on the usual row of temple bells to gain merit and toss money into the large bellybutton of a fat Chinese Buddha statue. Although the wat isn't that impressive, the high forested setting will make the trip worthwhile. From the walled edge of the temple you can get an aerial view of the snaky road you've just climbed.

A walking path next to the wat leads to a spring, and there are other short walking trails in the vicinity. A bit below the peak is the smaller **Wat Noi Doi Tung**, where food and beverages are available from vendors.

Places to Stay *Kwan Guest House*, on the north side of the road leading to Doi Tung before the palace, offers A-frame bungalows in the 100 to 400B range.

Out on Route 1149, the road to Doi Tung, it's possible to rent a room at the Akha village of Ban Pakha or at *Akha Guest House*, next to the village. The latter no longer officially operates because of a restriction on guest-houses in this area, but sometimes there's someone around to rent out bamboo huts. Neither the village nor the unsigned guest-house has electricity or running water, and the food is not that good, but there are nice views of the valley below. A place to sleep costs 40B per person and guides can be hired for as little as 50B per person for a day trek.

Getting There & Away Buses to the turn-off for Doi Tung are 8B from either Mae Chan or Mae Sai. From Ban Huay Khrai, at the Doi Tung turn-off, a songthaew to Ban Pakha is 10B or 30B all the way to Doi Tung, 18 km away.

The road to Doi Tung has seriously deteriorated above Pakha in the last few years and this section is becoming more of a challenge to climb, whether you're in a truck, jeep or motorcycle.

You can also travel by motorcycle between Doi Tung and Mae Sai along a challenging 15-km half-paved track that starts in the Akha village of Ban Phame, eight km south of Mae Sai (four km south along Route 110, then four km west), and joins the main road about two-thirds of the way up Doi Tung. You can also pick this road up by following the dirt road that starts in front of Mae Sai's Wat Doi Wao. West of Ban Phame this route has lots of tight curves, mud, rocks, precipitous drops, passing lorries and bulldozers – figure on two to 2½ hours by motorbike or jeep from Mae Sai. Eventually this road will be paved all the way but for now it's a road for experienced bikers only. The road also runs high in the mountains along the Burmese border and

Akha village gate

should not be travelled alone or after 4 pm. Ask first in Mae Sai about border conditions.

Cross-Border Trips to Thakhilek & Kengtung, Myanmar

For much of 1993 and 1994, foreigners were permitted to cross the bridge over the Sai River into Thakhilek (a Thai-Shan name which is pronounced Tachilek by the Burmese) upon payment of a US$10 fee and deposit of passport at the Thai immigration post. Besides shopping for Shan and Burmese handicrafts (about the same price as on the Thai side) and eating Shan/Burmese food, there's little to do in Thakhilek. Foreigners were permitted to spend the night in A-frame bungalows strung with coloured lights on the river bank facing Thailand for US$8 to US$14.

In May 1994 Khun Sa's Meuang Tai Army (MTA) bombed the Thakhilek dyke, draining the reservoir that supplied the town with water. Since then the border has been closed to foreigners, but if the security situation improves the crossing may open again soon.

Three-night, four-day excursions 163 km north to the town of Kengtung (called Chiang Tung by the Thais and usually spelt Kyainge Tong by the Burmese) may be arranged through any Mae Sai guesthouse or travel agency or you can do it on your own by paying US$18 for a three-night permit at the border, plus a mandatory exchange of US$100 for Myanmar's Foreign Exchange Certificates. These FECs can be spent on hotel rooms or exchanged on the black market for kyat (the Burmese currency).

Kengtung is a sleepy but historic capital for the Shan State's Khün culture – the Khün speak a Northern Thai language related to Shan and Thai Lü and use a writing script similar to the ancient Lanna script. It's a bit more than halfway between the Thai and Chinese borders – eventually the road will be open all the way to China but for now Kengtung is the limit. Built around a small lake, and dotted with ageing Buddhist temples and crumbling British colonial architecture, it's a much more scenic town than Thakhilek. The road trip allows glimpses of Shan, Akha, Wa and Lahu villages along the way. The *Noi Yee Hotel* costs US$10 per person per night in multi-bed rooms. Myanmar Tours & Travel tries to steer tourists towards the more expensive, government-run *Kyainge Tong Hotel*, where rooms range from US$30 to US$42.

By the time you read this, *Harry's Guest House & Trekking* at 132 Mai Yang Rd, Kanaburoy Village (☎ (101) 21418), should be open somewhere in Kengtung. Harry is an English-speaking Kengtung native who spent many years as a trekking guide in Chiang Mai. His projected room rate is US$5 per person, payable in US, Thai or Burmese currency.

Getting There & Beyond As with the Thakhilek day trips, you must leave your passport at the border. The cheapest form of transport to Kengtung is the 44B songthaew that leaves each morning from Thakhilek. You can rent jeeps on either side of the border, but Thai vehicles with a capacity of five or fewer passengers are charged a flat US$50 entry fee, US$100 for vehicles with a capacity of over five. Burmese vehicle hire is more expensive and requires the use of a driver. Whatever form of transport, count on at least six to ten gruelling hours (depending on road conditions) to cover the 163-km stretch between the border and Kengtung.

The road is currently being improved and will eventually be paved all the way to the Chinese border, 100 km beyond Kengtung. If the Chinese border opens, perhaps Thai immigration authorities in Mae Sai will allow visitors to travel with their passports, which would make an overland trip into China possible.

If current economic and political conditions in Myanmar prevail, the road between Kengtung and Taunggyi should open to foreign travel. At the moment only Myanmar citizens are permitted to use this road. Fighting between Myanmar's Yangon government and the Shan State's Meuang Tai Army (the only ethnic insurgency that hasn't yet signed a ceasefire with Yangon) makes the Kengtung-Taunggyi journey potentially hazardous.

CHIANG SAEN
เชียงแสน

A little more than 60 km from Chiang Rai, Chiang Saen is a small crossroads town on the banks of the Maekhong River. Scattered throughout the town are the ruins of the Chiang Saen kingdom, a Lanna principality founded in 1328 by King Mengrai's nephew Saenphu. Surviving architecture includes chedis, Buddha images, wihaan pillars and earthen city ramparts. A few of the old monuments still standing predate Chiang Saen by a couple of hundred years; legend says this pre-Chiang Saen kingdom was called Yonok. Formerly loosely affiliated with various northern Thai kingdoms, as well as 18th-century Myanmar, Chiang Saen didn't really become a Siamese possession until the 1880s.

The sleepy town hasn't changed much in spite of 'Golden Triangle' commercialisation, which is concentrated in nearby Sop Ruak. Practically everything in Chiang Saen closes down by 9 pm. This may change if passenger boat traffic to/from China along the Maekhong River becomes firmly established.

The Lao side of the mighty Maekhong here looks deserted, but Lao boats occasionally float by. Hill-tribe crafts can be bought in a few shops along the river. Some of the older townspeople, Lao immigrants, speak French.

Information

A new TAT office near the western entrance to town offers town sketch maps and information on the area. Hanging on one of the inside walls is a better area map which extends coverage all the way to Sop Ruak. The office is open daily from 8.30 am to 4.30 pm.

Bicycles can be rented at the guesthouses in town for interesting side trips in the vicinity.

National Museum

พิพิธภัณฑ์แห่งชาติ

Near the town entrance, a small national museum displays artefacts from the Lanna period as well as prehistoric stone tools from the area, and hill-tribe crafts, dress and musical instruments. It's open Wednesday to Sunday from 9 am to 4 pm and admission is 10B.

Wat Chedi Luang

วัดเจดีย์หลวง

Behind the museum to the east, the ruins of this wat feature an 18-metre octagonal chedi in the classic Chiang Saen or Lanna style. Archaeologists argue about its exact construction date but agree it dates to some time between the 12th and 14th centuries.

Wat Paa Sak

วัดป่าสัก

About 200 metres from the Chiang Saen Gate are the remains of Wat Paa Sak, which is undergoing restoration by the Fine Arts Department. The ruins of seven monuments are visible. The main mid-14th century stupa

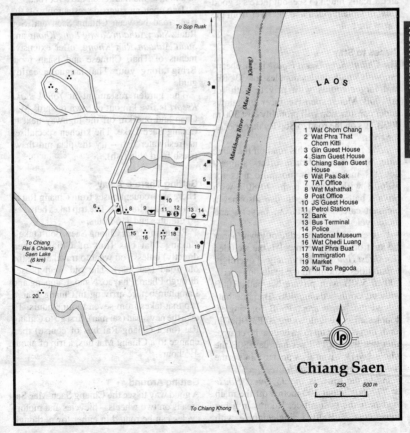

To Sop Ruak

LAOS

Maekhang River (Mae Nam Khong)

1 Wat Chom Chang
2 Wat Phra That Chom Kitti
3 Gin Guest House
4 Siam Guest House
5 Chiang Saen Guest House
6 Wat Paa Sak
7 TAT Office
8 Wat Mahathat
9 Post Office
10 JS Guest House
11 Petrol Station
12 Bank
13 Bus Terminal
14 Police
15 National Museum
16 Wat Chedi Luang
17 Wat Phra Buat
18 Immigration
19 Market
20 Ku Tao Pagoda

To Chiang Rai & Chiang Saen Lake (6 km)

To Chiang Khong

Chiang Saen

0   250   500 m

NORTHERN THAILAND

combines elements of the Hariphunchai and Sukhothai styles with a possible Bagan Burmese influence. Since these ruins are a historical park, there is a 20B admission fee.

Wat Phra That Chom Kitti

วัดพระธาตุจอมกิตติ

About 2.5 km north of Wat Paa Sak on a hilltop are the remains of Wat Phra That Chom Kitti and Wat Chom Chang. The round chedi of Wat Phra That is thought to have been constructed before the founding of the kingdom. The smaller chedi below it belonged to Wat Chom Chang. These chedis aren't really much to see, but there's a good view of Chiang Saen and the river from the top of the hill.

Places to Stay

The *Chiang Saen Guest House* is the cheapest, with small singles/doubles for 30/50B, and larger rooms with private bath for 80/100B. More expensive, nicer bungalows under construction will probably cost 300 to 400B. It's on the road to Sop Ruak, opposite the river.

A bit farther along this road on the same side, *Siam Guest House* offers singles/doubles in huts with mosquito nets for 50/60B with shared bath, 70/80B with private bath. This guesthouse also has a pleasant cafe, and rents out bicycles and motorcycles.

Farther north on the edge of town (about 1.5 km from the bus terminal) is the secluded *Gin Guest House* with a variety of overnight possibilities. Rooms in the main house cost 200 to 500B with private hot bath, 100B without; dorm beds are 40B. Bamboo huts behind the house are 60/80B for singles/doubles; nicer bungalows are 200/300B. Gin lends bicycles for up to an hour at no charge; after that they're 15B per half day, 30B the whole day. Down an alley next to Gin's is the cheaper *Songkler Guest House*.

Inside the town is the *JS Guest House* (☎ 777060), about 100 metres off the main road near the post office. Rooms in a big house cost 80/100B a single/double with shared bath, 200B for singles/doubles with private solar-heated bath. Vegetarian Thai meals are available here.

About five km out of town near Chiang Saen Lake, *Yonok Lake Resort* has a few 500B bungalows with fridge and hot showers, plus a pleasant garden dining area.

Places to Eat

Opposite the bus stop on Chiang Saen's main street, the new bar-restaurant *Dreams* serves Thai and Chinese dishes at moderate prices. The owner speaks English well.

Cheap noodle and rice dishes are available in and near the market on the river road.

Two open-air riverside restaurants off the river road between Chiang Saen and Sop Ruak, *Suan Aahaan Sawng Fang Khong* and *Suan Aahaan Rim Khong*, offer extensive menus of Thai, Chinese and Isaan food. Bring along your Thai-language eating guide.

The garden restaurant at *Yonok Lake Resort* is five km out of town towards Mae Chan and one km off the highway next to Chiang Saen Lake. The kitchen specialises in freshwater fish – try the plaa nin thâwt (fresh fried Nile fish).

Getting There & Away

There are frequent buses from Chiang Rai to Chiang Saen for 17B. The trip takes between 40 minutes and 1½ hours.

Returning from Chiang Saen, don't take a Chiang Mai bus (out of Chiang Saen directly) unless you want to travel along the old road (sai kao). The old road passes through Pham, Phayao, Ngao, Lampang and Lamphun before arriving in Chiang Mai, a trip that takes from seven to nine hours. To take the new road (sai mai), first go to Chiang Rai (on a Chiang Rai bus of course) then change to a Chiang Mai bus, a trip of about 4½ hours.

Getting Around

A good way to see the Chiang Saen-Mae Sai area is on two wheels – bicycles and motorcycles can be rented in either town, though there's usually a better choice of machines in Mae Sai.

From Mae Sai to Chiang Saen there's a choice of two partly paved roads (one from the centre of Mae Sai and one near the town entrance – see the Mae Sai map), or a fully paved road via Route 110 to Mae Chan and then Route 1016 to Chiang Saen.

The roads out of Mae Sai are considerably more direct but there are several forks where you have to make educated guesses on which way to go (there are occasional signs). The two roads join near the village of Mae Ma, where you have a choice of going east through Sop Ruak or south through Pa Thon. The eastern route is more scenic.

AROUND CHIANG SAEN
Sop Ruak
สบรวก

Fourteen km north of Chiang Saen is Sop Ruak, the official centre of the Golden Triangle where the borders of Myanmar, Thailand and Laos meet, at the confluence of the Ruak and Maekhong rivers. In historical terms, 'Golden Triangle' actually refers to a much larger area, stretching thousands of sq km into Myanmar, Laos and Thailand, within which the opium trade is prevalent. Nevertheless hoteliers and tour operators have been quick to cash in on the name by referring to the tiny village of Sop Ruak as 'the Golden Triangle', conjuring up images

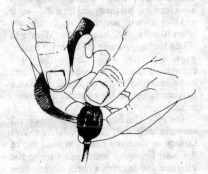

Poppy pod being harvested for opium

of illicit adventure even though the adventure quotient here is close to zero. In Northern Thai this village is pronounced 'Sop Huak'; many out-of-town Thais don't know either Thai name and simply call it 'Saam Liam Thong Kham' (Thai for 'Golden Triangle').

Tourists have replaced opium as the local source of gold. Sop Ruak has in fact become something of a tourist trap, with souvenir stalls, restaurants, a massage place and busloads of package-tour visitors during the day. In the evenings things are quieter. Good yaams can be purchased for 50B without much bargaining.

One place worth a visit is the **House of Opium**, a small museum with historical displays pertaining to opium culture. Exhibits include all the various implements used in the planting, harvest, use and trade of *Papaver somniferum* resin, including pipes, weights, scales and so on, plus photos and maps. Most labels are in Thai only. The museum is at Km 30, at the south-eastern end of Sop Ruak. It's open daily from 7 am to 6 pm; admission is 10B.

On the Burmese side of the river junction you may notice a few temporary buildings and bulldozers. These are the beginnings of the upcoming Golden Triangle Paradise Resort, a huge hotel-and-trade project financed by a wealthy Thai businessman from Suphanburi who has leased nearly 3000 rai from the Myanmar government. The site has become the man's private fiefdom – no-one enters or leaves the area without his permission (visas are superfluous).

In addition to 300 hotel rooms and a trade centre, plans for the complex include an 18-hole golf course, helipad, hospital and hovercraft pier. Rumours persist that the hotel will eventually add a casino, which will not only draw business from Thailand, Laos and Myanmar but will also play host to visiting riverboats from China. Only two currencies – baht and dollars – will be accepted at the hotel. So far development on the project has moved quite slowly, perhaps because the proposed casino is backed by Macau gambling kingpins who are worried about the return of the Portuguese colonial enclave to China in 1999.

Maekhong River Cruises Local boat trips can be arranged through several local agents. The typical trip involves a two-hour circuit around a large island in the river for 100 to

200B per person, with a four-person minimum. Longer trips head downriver as far as Chiang Khong for 450 to 500B return.

Six large express ferries are under construction at a boat camp on the river bank between Chiang Saen and Sop Ruak. Similar in style to the express boats that go to Ko Samui in South Thailand, these boats will be used to ferry passengers back and forth to China's Yunnan Province. A pilot trip was accomplished in January 1994, with regular service to begin sometime in 1995. Most likely these Thailand-China trips will be available only as part of an expensive package that will include meals and some sightseeing.

A regularly scheduled, ordinary passenger service on the Maekhong, if permitted in the future, will most likely use Chiang Khong, farther south, as a terminal. It may be a long time coming; getting the governments of Thailand, Myanmar, Laos and China to agree on regulations is a major obstacle.

Places to Stay & Eat Most budget travellers stay in Chiang Saen these days. Virtually all the former budget places in Sop Ruak have given way to souvenir stalls and larger tourist hotels.

Among the holdouts, *Golden Central Guest House*, opposite the Delta Golden Triangle Resort, has singles/doubles with shared hot bath at 100B. *Phukham Guest House*, next to the House of Opium, has thatched bungalows for about the same rates. *MP World Villa*, at the eastern edge of Sop Ruak, offers new wooden bungalows for 150 to 200B.

In the top-end category, the 73-room *Delta Golden Triangle Resort Hotel* (☎ 777001; (02) 260-6108 in Bangkok) is on a hillside overlooking the river and offers 1st-class accommodation from 2000B.

Also at the top end, *Le Meridien Baan Boran Hotel* (☎ 716678; (02) 254-8147 in Bangkok) is on a secluded hillside spot off the road between Sop Ruak and Mae Sai. Designed by Thai architect M L Tridhosyuth Devakul, the Baan Boran melds classic northern Thai design motifs with modern resort hotel tricks like cathedral ceilings and skylights. To fit the naughty Golden Triangle image, one of the restaurants is called *Suan Fin* (Opium Field) and is decorated with poppy motifs; windows off the dining area serve up a view of Myanmar and Laos in the distance. The hotel bar is called Trafficker Rendezvous. What does it cost to stay amidst this glorification of the regional narcotics trade? Singles are 2000 to 2500B, doubles 2400 to 2800B, and one-bedroom suites 6000B.

Getting There & Away From Chiang Saen to Sop Ruak, a songthaew/share taxi costs 10B; these leave several times a day. It's an easy bike ride from Chiang Saen to Sop Ruak.

Chiang Khong
เชียงของ

At one time Chiang Khong was part of a small riverbank meuang called Juon, founded in 701 AD by King Mahathai. Over the centuries Juon paid tribute to Chiang Rai, then Chiang Saen and finally Nan before being occupied by the Siamese in the 1880s. The territory of Chiang Khong extended all the way to Yunnan province in China until the French turned much of the Maekhong River's left bank into French Indochina in 1893.

More remote yet more lively than Chiang Saen, Chiang Khong is an important market town for local hill tribes and for trade – legal and illegal – with northern Laos. Nearby are several villages inhabited by Mien and White Hmong. Among the latter are contingents who fled Laos during the 1975 communist takeover and who are rumoured to be involved in an organised resistance movement against the current Lao government.

Today's Chiang Khong has several northern-style wats of minor interest. **Wat Luang**, on the main road, was once one of the most important temples in Chiang Rai Province and features a chedi dating to the 13th century (restored in 1881).

On a hill overlooking the town and river is a **Nationalist Chinese Soldiers Cemetery** where over 200 KMT soldiers are interred. The grave mounds are angled on the hill so that they face China. A shrine containing old photos of KMT soldiers-in-arms stands at the top of the hill.

The village of **Ban Hat Khrai**, about a km south of Chiang Khong, is famous as being one of the few places where *plaa bèuk* (giant Maekhong catfish) are still caught.

Huay Xai, the town on the Lao side, was recently designated an official point of entry for Laos. Anyone with a valid Laos visa may cross by ferry (see Crossing to Laos below for details).

The Thai Farmers Bank on the main street is the only place in town with foreign exchange services.

Places to Stay & Eat The friendly *Damrong Phunsuk* (☎ 791036) on the main road in the centre of town has very basic rooms for 70 to 100B with shared bath.

There are two guesthouses at the northern end of town in a neighbourhood called Ban Wiang Kaew. The funky *Ban Tamila Riverside Bungalows* offers simple thatched huts overlooking the river for 100B with shared bath. Next door to the south, the newer and fancier *Reuan Thai Sophapham* (☎ 791234) has rooms in a wooden hotel-like building for 100B with shared bath, 150 to 200B with hot-water shower.

Farther north and towards the river road from Chiang Saen is the *Chiang Khong Hotel* (☎ 791182). Plain but nicely kept singles/doubles with hot shower and fan are 120/150B, 300B with air-con.

On the southern outskirts of town on the river and towards the bus terminal, the *Plabuk Resort* (☎ 791281, Bangkok ☎ (02) 258-0423) features 16 spacious rooms with air-con, hot water and comfortable beds for

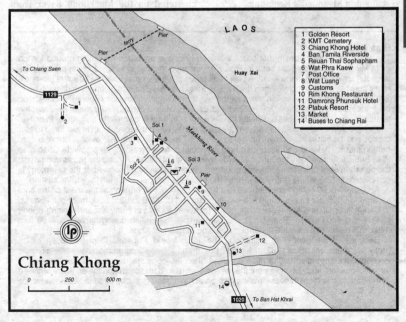

LAOS

Huay Xai

Maekhong River

To Chiang Saen

1129

Soi 1

Soi 2

Soi 3

Pier

ferry

Pier

Pier

1 Golden Resort
2 KMT Cemetery
3 Chiang Khong Hotel
4 Ban Tamila Riverside
5 Reuan Thai Sophapham
6 Wat Phra Kaew
7 Post Office
8 Wat Luang
9 Customs
10 Rim Khong Restaurant
11 Damrong Phunsuk Hotel
12 Plabuk Resort
13 Market
14 Buses to Chiang Rai

Chiang Khong

0   250   500 m

1020   To Ban Hat Khrai

NORTHERN THAILAND

450B a single/double. A restaurant and bar are well separated from the guest rooms.

Next to the KMT cemetery, high on a hill overlooking Chiang Khong, the river, and Huay Xai, is the *Golden Resort* (☎ 791350). Large, well-appointed rooms with air-con and private hot-water bath cost 650B; the resort's entrance is off Route 1129, the road to Chiang Saen. The only drawback is that the resort is so high up that noise from vehicles on the highway and from diesel boats on the Maekhong beams straight into the rooms.

There are a number of rice and noodle shops along the main street, none of them particularly good. The *Rim Khong* on a narrow road down by the river (take the soi opposite the Damrong Phunsuk Hotel) is a simple indoor/outdoor restaurant overlooking the river. The bilingual menu is much shorter than the Thai menu; yam (spicy Thai-style salads) are the house speciality, but the kitchen can make just about anything.

Lawt Tin Lu, off the main street on Soi 2, is a branch of a well-known Shan-Chinese restaurant in Myanmar's Kengtung.

Getting There & Away From Chiang Saen, 52-km Route 1129 – now graded and paved – is the quickest way to come from the west. A second 65-km road curving along the river has just been paved and provides a slower but less trafficked alternative. With mountains in the distance and the Maekhong to one side, this road passes through picturesque villages, tobacco and rice fields before joining Route 1129 just outside Chiang Khong. To travel this road by public transport from Chiang Saen, take a songthaew first to Ban Hap Mae (20B), then another onward to Chiang Khong (20B).

Buses from Chiang Rai and beyond use roads from the south (primarily Route 1020) to reach Chiang Khong. The Chiang Rai bus (No 2127, red) costs 31B and takes about three hours; there are departures approximately every 15 minutes from 4.45 am to 5.45 pm daily.

Air-con buses to/from Bangkok cost 370B and take around 13 hours.

Boats taking up to 10 passengers can be chartered up the Maekhong River from

---

Plaa Beuk

The Maekhong River stretch that passes Chiang Khong is an important fishing ground for the giant Maekhong catfish (plaa beuk in Thai, *Pangasianodon gigas* to ichthyologists) probably the largest freshwater fish in the world. A plaa beuk takes at least six and possibly 12 years (no-one's really sure) to reach full size, when it will measure two to three metres in length and weigh up to 300 kilos. Locals say these fish swim all the way from Qinghai Province (where the Maekhong originates) in northern China. In Thailand and Laos its flesh is considered a major delicacy; the texture is very meaty but has a delicate flavour, similar to tuna or swordfish, only whiter in colour.

These fish are only taken between mid-April and May when the river depth is just three to four metres and the fish are swimming upriver to spawn in Erhai Lake, Yunnan Province, China. Before netting them, Thai and Lao fishermen hold a special annual ceremony to propitiate Chao Mae Plaa Beuk, a female deity thought to preside over the giant catfish. Among the rituals comprising the ceremony are chicken sacrifices performed aboard the fishing boats. After the ceremony is completed, fishing teams draw lots to see who casts the first net, and then take turns casting.

Around 40 to 60 catfish are captured in a typical season. Fishermen sell the meat on the spot for around 500B per kilo (a single fish can bring up to 112,000B in Bangkok); most of it ends up in Bangkok or Chiang Mai restaurants, since local restaurants in Huay Xai and Chiang Khong can't afford such prices. Sometimes you can sample the catfish during harvest season in a makeshift restaurant near the fishermen's landing in Ban Hat Khrai.

Because of the danger of extinction, Thailand's Inland Fisheries Dept has been taking protective measures since 1983, including a breed-and-release programme. Every time a female is caught, it's kept alive until a male is netted, then the eggs are removed (by massaging the female's ovaries) and put into a pan; the male is then milked for sperm and the eggs are fertilised in the pan. In this fashion over a million plaa beuk have been released into the Maekhong since 1983. ∎

Chiang Khong to Chiang Saen for 800B. Boat crews can be contacted near the customs pier behind Wat Luang, or farther north at the pier for ferries to Laos.

Crossing to Laos Ferries to Huay Xai, Laos, leave frequently from a pier at the northern end of Chiang Khong for 20B each way. As long as you hold a visa valid for Laos, there should be no problem crossing. If you don't already have a visa, local agencies can arrange one for 1600B.

Once on the Lao side you can continue on by road to Luang Nam Tha and Udomxai or by boat down the Maekhong to Luang Prabang and Vientiane. Lao Aviation flies from Huay Xai to Vientiane a couple of times a week but seats are difficult to book.

Down from the Maekhong River ferry pier in Huay Xai is the basic *Manirat Hotel* with adequate rooms for 3000/4000 kip (107/142B) single/double. A bigger tourist-oriented hotel is reportedly planned for the near future.

Phrae Province

Phrae Province is probably most famous for the distinctive *seua maw hawm*, the indigo-dyed cotton farmer's shirt seen all over Thailand. 'Made in Phrae' has always been a sign of distinction for these staples of rural Thai life and since the student-worker-farmer political solidarity of the 1970s, even Thai university professors like to wear them. The cloth is made in Ban Thung Hong outside the town of Phrae.

The annual Rocket Festival kicks off the rice-growing season in May. In Phrae the biggest celebrations take place in **Long** and **Sung Men** districts. Look for launching towers in the middle of rice fields for the exact location.

Sung Men district is also known for **Talaat Hua Dong**, a market specialising in carved teak wood. Phrae was, and still is, an important teak centre. Along Route 101 between Phrae and Nan you'll see a steady blur of teak

forests (thickest around Km 25). Since the 1989 national ban on logging, these forests are all protected by law. Most of the provincial teak business now involves recycled timber from old houses. Specially licensed cuts from fallen teak wood may also be used for decorative carving or furniture (but not house construction).

The provinces of Phrae and Nan have been neglected by tourists and travellers alike because of their remoteness from Chiang Mai, but from Den Chai – on a train route – they're easily reached by bus along Route 101.

PHRAE
อ.เมืองแพร่

This provincial capital (population 21,000) is only 23 km from the Den Chai train station on the Chiang Mai line. Like Chiang Mai and Lampang, Phrae has an old city surrounded by a moat alongside a river (here, the Yom River). Unlike Chiang Mai, Phrae's old city still has lots of quiet lanes and old teak houses – if you're a fan of traditional Thai teak architecture, you'll find more of it here than in any other city of similar size anywhere in Thailand. The local temple architecture has successfully resisted central Thai influence over the centuries as well. It's a bit unusual since you'll find a mix of Burmese, northern Thai (Nan and Lanna) and Lao styles.

South-east of the old city, the newer, more modern Phrae looks like any other medium-sized town in Thailand.

If you're in the market for baskets or woven mats, a shop called Kamrai Thong (no roman-script sign) near Kawng Nun restaurant near the Pratuchai gate carries a fine selection of handwoven basketry.

Wat Luang
วัดหลวง

This is the oldest wat in the city, probably dating to the founding of the city in the 12th or 13th century. **Phra That Luang Chang Kham**, the large octagonal Lanna-style chedi, sits on a square base with elephants coming out of all four sides, surrounded by kutis and coconut palms. As is sometimes seen in Phrae and Nan, the chedi is usually swathed in Thai Lü silk.

The verandah of the main wihaan is in the classic Luang Prabang-Lan Xang style but has unfortunately been bricked in with laterite. Opposite the front of the wihaan is **Pratu Khong**, part of the city's original entrance gate. No longer used as a gate, it now contains a statue of Chao Pu, an early Lanna ruler. The image is sacred to local residents, who leave offerings of fruit, flowers, candles and incense.

Also on the wat grounds is a museum displaying temple antiques, ceramics and religious art from the Lanna, Nan, Pegu and Mon periods. A 16th-century, Phrae-made sitting Buddha on the 2nd floor is particularly exquisite. There are also some 19th-century photos with English labels on display, including some gruesome shots of a beheading.

Wat Phra Non

วัดพระนอน

South-west a few hundred metres from Wat

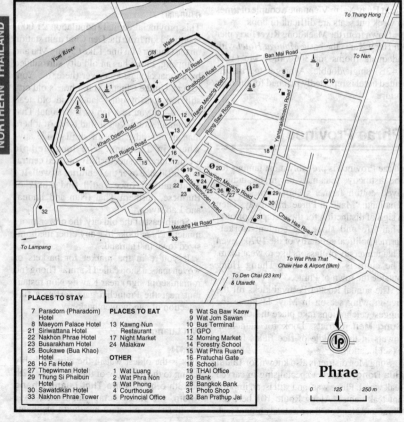

Phrae

PLACES TO STAY
7 Paradorn (Pharadorn) Hotel
8 Maeyom Palace Hotel
21 Siriwattana Hotel
22 Nakhon Phrae Hotel
23 Busarakham Hotel
25 Boukawe (Bua Khao) Hotel
26 Ho Fa Hotel
27 Thepwiman Hotel
29 Thung Si Phaibun Hotel
30 Sawatdikan Hotel
33 Nakhon Phrae Tower

PLACES TO EAT
13 Kawng Nun Restaurant
17 Night Market
24 Malakaw

OTHER
1 Wat Luang
2 Wat Phra Non
3 Wat Phong
4 Courthouse
5 Provincial Office
6 Wat Sa Baw Kaew
9 Wat Jom Sawan
10 Bus Terminal
11 GPO
12 Morning Market
14 Forestry School
15 Wat Phra Ruang
16 Pratuchai Gate
18 School
19 THAI Office
20 Bank
28 Bangkok Bank
31 Photo Shop
32 Ban Prathup Jai

0   125   250 m

NORTHERN THAILAND

Luang is a 300-year-old wat named for its highly revered reclining Buddha image. The bot was built around 200 years ago and has a very impressive three-tiered roof with a separate two-tiered portico and gilded carved wooden facade with *Ramayana* scenes. The wihaan behind the bot contains the Phra Non (a reclining Buddha), swathed in Thai Lü cloth with bead and foil decoration.

Wat Jom Sawan
วัดจอมสวรรค์

Outside the old city on Ban Mai Rd, this temple was built by local Shans early this century, and shows Shan and Burmese influence throughout. The well-preserved wooden wihaans and bot have high, tiered, tower-like roofs like those found in Mandalay. A large copper-crowned chedi has lost most of its stucco to reveal the artful brickwork beneath. A prized temple possession in the main wihaan is a tripitaka (Buddhist scriptures) section consisting of 16 ivory pages engraved in Burmese. As in Lampang, temples like this were originally sponsored by Burmese teak merchants who immigrated to northern Thailand at the turn of the century.

Other Temples

Just outside the north-eastern corner of the moat, **Wat Sa Baw Kaew** is a Shan-Burmese-style temple similar to Wat Jom Sawan. **Wat Phra Ruang**, inside the old city, is typical of Phrae's many old city wats, with a Nan-style, cruciform-plan bot, a Lao-style wihaan and a Lanna chedi.

One day an art historian is going to have to sort out this temple mix – I suspect there's a uniform design of local (Nan-Phrae) provenance that hasn't yet been identified.

Ban Prathup Jai (Prathapjai)
บ้านประทับใจ

You can see lots of good woodcarving in Phrae. On the western outskirts of town is Ban Prathup Jai (Impressive House), also called Ban Sao Roi Tan (Hundred Pillar-Filled House), a large northern-style teak house which was built using more than 130 teak logs, each over 3000 years old. Opened in 1985, the house took four years to build, using timber taken from nine old rural houses. The interior pillars are ornately carved.

Places to Stay – bottom end

Several inexpensive hotels can be found along Charoen Meuang Rd, including *Ho Fa*, *Siriwattana* and *Thepwiman*, all of which have rooms for 80 to 120B; Thepwiman is the best of the bunch, followed closely by Ho Fa.

The friendly *Thung Si Phaibun* (☎ (054) 511011), at 84 Yantarakitkoson Rd, has clean rooms with fan and bath for 90 to 130B, air-con for just 200B. *Sawatdikan* at No 76-8 is similar to the Thung Si Phaibun but not as well kept; rooms start at 80B.

A couple of blocks south-east of the Nakhon Phrae Hotel on the same side of Ratsadamnoen Rd is the *Busarakham Hotel* (☎ (054) 511437), a low-to medium-priced place with decent rooms with fan for 90 to 180B.

Boukawe (Bua Khao) Hotel (☎ (054) 511372), at 8/1 Soi 1 Ratsadamnoen Rd, has rooms with fan for 90B, air-con for 160B – it's mostly a brothel, however, with girls haunting the doorways. The only hotel in the old city, *Neramit* on Wichairacha Rd, is also a brothel, quoting 60B for short-time use, 120B for an all-night stay.

Den Chai If you get stuck in Den Chai waiting for a train, *Saeng Sawang* and *Yaowarat* offer adequate rooms for 80 to 120B.

Places to Stay – medium & top end

Nakhon Phrae Hotel (☎ (054) 511969) at 29 Ratsadamnoen Rd is a short walk from the old city. Large singles/doubles with fan and hot water cost 250B in the old wing; across the street in the new wing standard air-con rooms are 400B or 500B with TV and fridge. Local tourist information is available in the lobbies of both wings.

NORTHERN THAILAND

Paradorn (Pharadon) (☎ (054) 511177), at 177 Yantarakitkoson Rd, has moderately priced singles/doubles with fan and bath for 250B, air-con rooms for up to 550B. Information on local attractions is available in the lobby, but the hotel is looking a bit rundown these days.

Towards the top of the scale in Phrae is the *Maeyom Palace Hotel* (☎ (054) 522906; fax 522904) on Yantarakitkoson Rd 100 metres north-east of the Paradorn. Rooms with air-con, carpet, TV, phone and fridge cost from 1000 to 2000B. Hotel facilities include a pool and two restaurants; the hotel also provides free transport to/from the bus terminal and airport.

A new luxury hotel at 3 Meuang Hit Rd, *Nakhon Phrae Tower* (☎ (054) 521-321; fax 521937), offers quality similar to that found at the Maeyom Palace; rates start at 800B.

Places to Eat

Yantarakitkoson Rd, the main road through Phrae's modern half, is dotted with small restaurants. *Ban Fai*, a large indoor/outdoor restaurant catering to Thai tourists, is at the southern end of Yantarakitkoson. Attached to the restaurant are a folklore museum and craft shop; there's even an auto service so you can have your car worked on while you eat! The menu is Thai-Chinese-farang, with a few northern-Thai dishes, too. Prices are moderately high.

For a slow evening repast, the open-air *Malakaw* on Ratsadamnoen Rd (diagonally opposite the Busarakham Hotel) offers good quality food and drink in a rustic ambience of rough-cut wooden tables and chairs beneath lots of hanging plants. Vegetarians will revel in the *hèt fang pîng* (roasted straw mushrooms served with a chilli dip) and the assortment of yams (Thai-style salads), including a delicious *yam hèt hŭu nŭu* or 'mouse-ear mushroom' salad. Malakaw is open daily from 11.30 am to midnight.

Also on Ratsadamnoen Rd near the Nakhon Phrae Hotel are several other eating spots, including the inexpensive *Phrae Phochana* (opposite the hotel), which specialises in standard Thai fare. Two Chinese coffee shops right next to the Nakhon Phrae Hotel take turns holding court throughout the day – *Sing Ocha* in the morning, *Ah Hui Ocha* in the evening.

Inside the old city near the Pratuchai intersection (Charoen Meuang and Rawp Meuang Rds), the humble but well-known *Kawng Nun* serves excellent and inexpensive curry-and-rice dishes. There's no English sign – it's directly opposite a shop selling maw hawm (indigo cotton) clothes and is run by a friendly, elderly Thai couple. The shop opens early and the food usually runs out by 6 or 7 pm.

A good night market convenes just outside the Pratuchai intersection every evening. Several food vendors also set up nightly in the soi opposite the Sawatdikan Hotel. There's another night market a block or two behind the Paradorn Hotel on weekday evenings only.

Getting There & Away

Air THAI flies to Phrae daily from Bangkok for 1325B; the flight takes an hour and 20 minutes. There are also daily THAI flights between Nan and Phrae (300B, 45 minutes). The THAI office (☎ (054) 511123) is at 42-44 Ratsadamnoen Rd, near the Nakhon Phrae Hotel. The Phrae airport is nine km south-east of town via the same road that goes to Wat Phra That Chaw Hae; THAI operates an airport shuttle for 40B per person.

Bus Ordinary buses from Bangkok's northern bus terminal depart at 11 am and 9 pm for 128B. Air-con buses cost 238B and leave at 8.30, 8.45 and 8.50 pm; VIP (sleeper) buses cost 290 to 395B depending on the number of seats and leave at 8.30, 8.45 and 9 pm.

From Chiang Mai's Arcade bus station, ordinary buses leave several times daily between 8 am and 5 pm (55B, four hours). An air-con bus leaves from the same station at 10 am and 10 pm (78B, 98B 1st class). From Sukhothai, ordinary buses are 48B, air-con 63B.

Train Trains to Den Chai station from Bangkok are 90B for 3rd class, 188B for 2nd class and 389B for 1st class, plus supplementary charges as they apply. The only trains that arrive at a decent hour are the No 101 ordinary (3rd class only, departs Bangkok at 7.05 am and arrives in Den Chai at 5.50 pm) and the No 59 rapid (2nd class only, leaves at 10 pm and arrives at 7.14 am). On the No 59 you can get a 2nd-class sleeper.

Blue songthaews and red buses (No 193) leave the Den Chai station frequently for Phrae and cost 10B. In the opposite direction you can catch them anywhere along the south end of Yantarakitkoson Rd.

Getting Around

A samlor anywhere in the old town costs 10B. Motorcycle taxis are available at the bus terminal; a trip from here to, say, the Pratuchai gate should cost you around 15 to 20B.

AROUND PHRAE PROVINCE
Wat Phra That Chaw Hae

วัดพระธาตุช่อแฮ

On a hill about nine km south-east of town off Route 1022, this wat is famous for its 33-metre-high gilded chedi. Chaw Hae is the name of the cloth that worshippers wrap around the chedi – it's a type of satin said to have originated in Xishuangbanna (Sipsongpanna, literally '12,000 fields' in northern Thai). Like Chiang Mai's Wat Doi Suthep, this is an important pilgrimage site for Thais living in the north. The **Phra Jao Than Jai** Buddha image here – similar in appearance to Phra Jinnarat in Phitsanulok – is reputed to impart fertility to women who make offerings to it.

The bot has a gilded wooden ceiling, rococo pillars and walls with lotus-bud mosaics. Tiered naga stairs lead to the temple compound; the hilltop is surrounded by mature teak trees, protected from cutting since they are on monastic grounds.

Songthaews between the city and Phra That Chaw Hae are frequent and cost 8B.

Phae Meuang Phii

แพะเมืองผี

The name means 'Ghost-Land', a reference to this strange geological phenomenon about 18 km north-east of Phrae off Route 101. Erosion has created bizarre pillars of soil and rock that look like giant fungi. The area has recently been made a provincial park; there are shaded tables and food vendors near the entrance – you may need a drink after wandering around the baked surfaces between the eroded pillars.

Getting there by public transport entails a bus ride nine km towards Nan, getting off at the signposted turn-off for Phae Meuang Phii, and then catching a songthaew another six km to a second right-hand turn-off to the park. From this point you must walk or hitch about 2.5 km to reach the entrance.

Phae Meuang Phii pillars

Mabri Hill Tribe

ชนเผ่ามาบรี

Along the border of Phrae and Nan provinces live the remaining members of the Mabri (sometimes spelt Mrabri or Mlabri) hill tribe, whom the Thais call *phii thong leŭang* (spirits of the yellow leaves). The most nomadic of all the tribes in Thailand, the Mabri customarily move on when the leaves of their temporary huts turn yellow, hence their Thai name. Now, however, their numbers have been greatly reduced (possibly to as few as 150) and experts suspect that few of the Mabri still migrate in the traditional way.

NORTHERN THAILAND

Traditionally, the Mabri are strict hunter-gatherers but many now work as field labourers for Thais, or other hill-tribe groups such as the Hmong, in exchange for pigs and cloth. Little is known about the tribe's belief system, but it is said that the Mabri believe they are not entitled to cultivate the land for themselves. A Mabri woman typically changes mates every five or six years, taking any children from the previous union with her. The Mabris' knowledge of medicinal plants is said to be enormous, encompassing the effective use of herbs for fertility and contraception, and for the treatment of snake or centipede poisoning. When a member of the tribe dies, the body is put in a tree top to be eaten by birds.

In Phrae Province there is a small settlement of around 40 Mabri living in Rong Khwang district (north-east of the capital, near Phae Meuang Phii) under the protection/control of American missionary Eugene Long. Long calls himself 'Boonyuen Suksaneh' and the Mabris' village 'Ban Boonyuen' – a classic scenario right out of Peter Mathiessen's *At Play in the Fields of the Lord*. Ban Boonyuen can only be reached on foot or by elephant; the nearest village linked by road is 12 km away.

Several Mabri families abandoned Ban Boonyuen in early 1992 and are now living in Hmong villages in Phrae and Nan. The remaining 100 or so Mabri live across the provincial border in Nan. The Thai government operates a 'Pre-Agricultural Development of Mabri Society Project' in both provinces to ease the Mabri into modern rural society without an accompanying loss of culture. According to project leaders, the effort is necessary to protect the Mabri from becoming a slave society within northern Thailand's increasingly capitalist rural economy. Because of their anti-materialist beliefs, the Mabri perform menial labour for the Hmong and other hill tribes for little or no compensation.

Nan Province

One of Thailand's remote provinces (an official Thai government designation), Nan was once so choked with bandits and PLAT insurgents that travellers were discouraged from visiting. Before the early 1980s the Thai government couldn't get any roads built in the province because guerrillas would periodically destroy highway building equipment at night.

With the successes of the Thai army and a more stable political machine in Bangkok during the last two decades, Nan has opened up and more roads are being built. The roads

---

Chang

In 1927, just before Nan was made a full-fledged province of Siam, the motion picture team of Ernest Schoedsack and Merian Cooper came here to film the silent motion picture *Chang*. The simple narrative follows a Thai family living in the jungle; recent critiques of the film have praised 'a cast partially made up of villagers with no previous acting experience' – missing the fact that no one who appeared in the film had acting experience! Six years later, following the advent of talkies, the Schoedsack and Cooper produced the classic work *King Kong*.

Cooper, who also made *Mighty Joe Young, The Quiet Man* and *The Searchers*, always held *Chang* to be his best work. The film contains what is considered some of the most authentic wildlife footage in existence, including shots of leopards, buffaloes, snakes, elephants, ant-eaters and monkeys going about their jungle lives, all shot in 'Magnascope', an early wide-screen technique. Of particular historical significance is a sequence showing the herding of wild elephants into a traditional kraal.

A new 35 mm print of the film was released in 1991 with a music soundtrack by Bruce Gaston, an American composer who has lived in Thailand for many years. The original final title card reads 'First there was the jungle. Always there will be the jungle. From the beginning till the end of time it stretches.' If only movie predictions would hold true... ∎

Top: 'Papa Taraporn', Ko Tao (MH)
Middle Left: Villager, Huay Phao (RI)
Middle Right: Sorting mushrooms (JO)
Bottom: Northern village children (TAT)

Top: Drying spring roll wrappers (JC)
Bottom: Hanging out cotton, Ban Huay Khrai (RI)

that link the provincial capital with the nearby provinces of Chiang Rai, Phrae, Utaradit, etc pass through exquisite scenery of rich river valleys and rice fields. Like Loei in the north-east, this is a province to be explored for its natural beauty and its likeable people, who live close to traditional rural rhythms.

Nan remains a largely rural province with not a factory or condo in sight. Most of the inhabitants are agriculturally employed, growing sticky rice, beans, corn, tobacco and vegetables in the fertile river plains. Nan is also famous for two fruits: *fai jiin* (a Chinese version of Thailand's indigenous *má-fai*) and *sôm sĩi thong*, golden-skinned oranges. The latter are Nan's most famous export, commanding high prices in Bangkok and Malaysia. Apparently the cooler winter weather in Nan turns the skin orange (lowland Thai oranges are mostly green) and imparts a unique sweet-tart flavour. **Thung Chang district** supposedly grows the best som sii thong in the province. Nan is also famous for its *phrík yài hâeng*, long hot chillies similar to those grown in China's Sichuan Province. During the hot season, you'll see lots of highly photogenic chillies drying by the roadside.

Geography

Nan shares a 227-km border with Sayaburi (Sainyabuli) Province in Laos. Only 25% of the land is arable (and only half of that actively cultivated), as most of the province is covered by heavily forested mountains; **Doi Phu Kha**, at 2000 metres, is the highest peak. Half the forests in the province are virgin upland monsoon forest. Most of the province's population of 364,000 live in the Nan River valley, a bowl-shaped depression ringed by mountains on all sides.

Major river systems in the province include the Nan, Sam Wa, Samun, Haeng, Lae and Pua. At 627 km, the Nan River is Thailand's third longest after the Maekhong and Mun.

People

Nan is a sparsely populated province, but the ethnic groups found here differ significantly from those in other northern provinces. Outside the Nan River valley, the predominant hill tribes are Mien (around 8000), with smaller numbers of Hmong. During the Indochina War, many Hmong and Mien from Nan (as well as Chiang Rai and Phetchabun) were recruited to fight with the communist Pathet Lao, who promised to create a Hmong-Mien king following a PL victory in Laos. Some of these so-called 'Red Meos' even trained in North Vietnam.

Along the south-western provincial border with Phrae are a few small Mabri settlements as well. What makes Nan unique, however, is the presence of three lesser known groups seldom seen outside this province: the Thai Lü, Htin and Khamu.

Thai Lü This ethnic minority, often called Lua or Lawa by the Thais, began migrating to Nan from China's Xishuangbanna (Sipsongpanna) around 200 years ago and now reside mostly in Pua, Thung Chang, Tha Wang Pha and Mae Jarim districts. Their influence on Nan (and to a lesser extent, Phrae) culture has been very important. The temple architecture at Wat Phra That Chae Haeng, Wat Phumin and Wat Nong Bua – typified by thick walls with small windows, two or three-tiered roofs, curved pediments and naga lintels – is a Thai Lü (who are Theravada Buddhists) inheritance. Thai Lü fabrics are considered among the most

Thai Lü-style temple

NORTHERN THAILAND

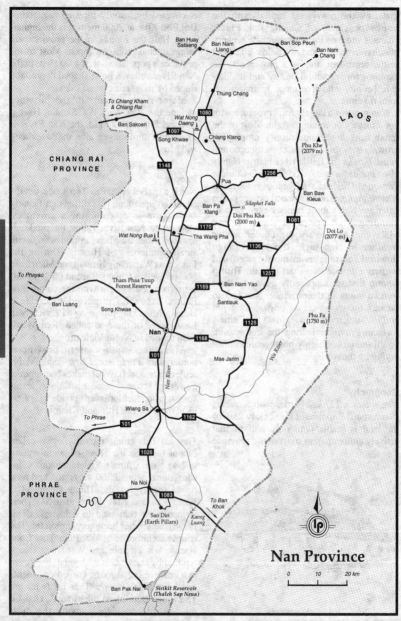

Nan Province

0   10   20 km

prized in northern Thailand and the weaving motifs show up in many Nan handicrafts.

The Thai Lü build traditional wooden or bamboo-thatched houses on thick wooden stilts, beneath which they place their kitchens and weaving looms. Many still make all their own clothes, typically sewn from indigo-dyed cotton fabrics. Many Thai Lü villages support themselves by growing rice and vegetables. In Nan they maintain a strong sense of tradition; most Thai Lü communities still recognise a chao meuang (meuang lord) and maw meuang (meuang astrologer), two older men in the community who serve as political and spiritual consultants.

Htin Pronounced 'Tin', this Mon-Khmer group of about 3000 lives in villages of 50 or so families in remote mountain valleys of Chiang Klang, Pua and Thung Chang districts. A substantial number also live across the border in Sayaburi Province, Laos. They typically subsist by hunting for wild game, breeding domestic animals, farming small plots of land and, in Ban Baw Kleua, by extracting salt from salt wells.

Htin houses are typically made of thatched bamboo and raised on bamboo or wooden stilts. No metal – including nails – is used in house construction because of a Htin taboo. The Htin are particularly skilled at manipulating bamboo to make everything needed around the house; for floor mats and baskets they interweave pared bamboo with a black-coloured grass to create bold geometric patterns. They also use bamboo to fashion a

musical instrument of stepped pipes – similar to the *angklung* of central Thailand and Indonesia – which is shaken to produce musical tones. The Htin don't weave their own fabrics, often buying clothes from neighbouring Miens.

Khamu Like the Thai Lü, the Khamu migrated to Nan around 150 years ago from Sipsongpanna. There are now around 5000 in Nan (more than anywhere else in Thailand), mostly in Wiang Sa, Thung Chang, Chiang Klang and Pua districts. Their villages are established near streams; their houses have dirt floors like those of the Hmong but roofs sport crossed beams similar to the northern Thai kalae (locally called *kapkri-aak*). The Khamu are skilled at metalwork and perform regular rituals to placate Salok, the spirit of the forge. Khamu villages are usually very self-sufficient; villagers hold fast to tradition and are known to value thrift and hard work. Ban Huay Sataeng in Thung Chang district is one of the largest and easiest Khamu villages to visit in the province.

NAN
อ.เมืองน่าน

Just over 668 km from Bangkok, little-known Nan (population 25,000) is steeped in history. For centuries Meuang Nan was an isolated, independent kingdom with few ties to the outside world. Ample evidence of prehistoric habitation exists, but it wasn't until several small meuangs (ancient Thai river-valley states) consolidated to form Nanthaburi on the Nan River in the mid-1300s – concurrent with the founding of Luang Prabang and the Lan Xang (Million Elephants) kingdom in Laos – that the city became a power to contend with. Associated with the powerful Sukhothai kingdom, the city-state took the title Waranakhon (Sanskrit: Varanagara or 'Excellent City') and played a significant role in the development of early Thai nationalism.

Towards the end of the 14th century Nan became one of the nine northern Thai-Lao

Htin house

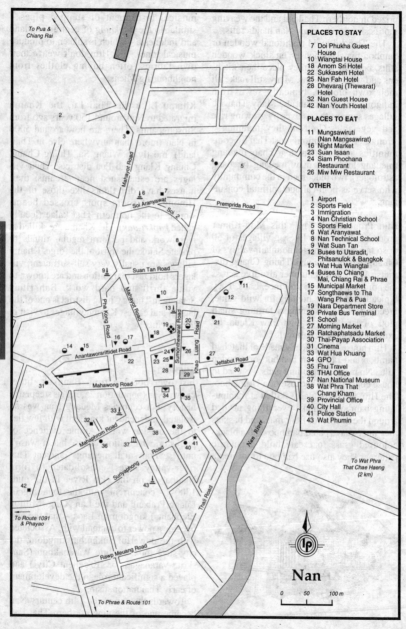

PLACES TO STAY
7 Doi Phukha Guest House
10 Wiangtai House
18 Amorn Sri Hotel
22 Sukkasem Hotel
25 Nan Fah Hotel
28 Dhevaraj (Thewarat) Hotel
32 Nan Guest House
42 Nan Youth Hostel

PLACES TO EAT
11 Mungsawiruti (Nan Mangsawirat)
16 Night Market
23 Suan Isaan
24 Siam Phochana Restaurant
26 Miw Miw Restaurant

OTHER
1 Airport
2 Sports Field
3 Immigration
4 Nan Christian School
5 Sports Field
6 Wat Aranyawat
8 Nan Technical School
9 Wat Suan Tan
12 Buses to Utaradit, Phitsanulok & Bangkok
13 Wat Hua Wiangtai
14 Buses to Chiang Mai, Chiang Rai & Phrae
15 Municipal Market
17 Songthaews to Tha Wang Pha & Pua
19 Nara Department Store
20 Private Bus Terminal
21 School
27 Morning Market
29 Ratchaphatsadu Market
30 Thai-Payap Association
31 Cinema
33 Wat Hua Khuang
34 GPO
35 Fhu Travel
36 THAI Office
37 Nan National Museum
38 Wat Phra That Chang Kham
39 Provincial Office
40 City Hall
41 Police Station
43 Wat Phumin

To Pua & Chiang Rai

Mahayot Road

Soi Aranyawat

Soi 2

Premprida Road

Suan Tan Road

Mahayot Road

Pha Kong Road

Anantaworarittidet Road

Mahawong Road

Mahaphrom Road

Suriyaphong Road

Thai Road

Kha Luang Road

Sumonthewarat Road

Jettabut Road

Nan River

Rawp Meuang Road

To Route 1091 & Phayao

To Phrae & Route 101

To Wat Phra That Chae Haeng (2 km)

Nan

0   50   100 m

NORTHERN THAILAND

principalities that comprised Lan Na Thai (Million Thai Fields, now known as Lanna) and the city-state flourished throughout the 15th century. The Burmese, however, took control of the kingdom in 1558 and transferred many inhabitants to Myanmar as slaves; the city was all but abandoned until western Thailand was wrested from the Burmese in 1786. The local dynasty then regained local sovereignty and remained semi-autonomous until 1931 when Nan finally accepted full Bangkok sponsorship.

Parts of the old city wall and several early wats dating from the Lanna period can be seen in present-day Nan. Meuang Nan's wats are quite distinctive. Some temple structures show Lanna influence, while others belong to the Thai Lü legacy brought from Sipsongpanna, the Thai Lü's historical homeland.

Information

Useful maps of the capital and province – including sketch maps of Nong Bua, Sao Din, Ban Baw Kleua and Phaa Thuup – are available at Doi Phukha Guest House.

Money Bangkok Bank and Thai Farmers Bank on Sumonthewarat Rd, near the Nan Fah and Dhevaraj hotels, operate foreign exchange services. Bangkok Bank has an ATM.

Post & Telecommunications The GPO on Mahawong Rd in the centre of the city is open from 8.30 am to noon and 1 to 3.30 pm, Monday to Friday, and from 8 am to noon on weekends and holidays. The attached CAT office offers international phone service daily from 7 am to 10 pm.

Nan's telephone area code is ☎ 054.

Wat Phumin

วัดภูมินทร์

Nan's most famous temple is celebrated for its cruciform bot which was constructed in 1596 and restored during the reign of Chao Anantavorapitthidet (1867-74). Murals on the walls depicting the Khatta Kumara and

Nimi Jatakas were executed during the restoration by Thai Lü artists; the bot exterior exemplifies the work of Thai Lü architects as well. The murals are considered of historic as well as aesthetic importance since they incorporate scenes of local life from the era in which they were painted.

The ornate altar in the centre of the bot has four sides with four Sukhothai-style sitting Buddhas in *marawichai* pose (victory over Mara, one hand touching the ground) facing in each direction.

Wat Phra That Chae Haeng

วัดพระธาตุแช่แห้ง

Two km past the bridge which spans the Nan River, heading south-east out of town, this very old temple dating from 1355 is the most sacred wat in Nan Province. It is set in a square, walled enclosure on a hill with a view of Nan and the valley. The Lü-influenced bot features a triple-tiered roof with carved wooden eaves, and dragon reliefs over the doors. A gilded Lanna-style chedi sits on a large square base next to the bot with sides measuring 22.5 metres long; the entire chedi is 55.5 metres high.

Wat Phra That Chang Kham

วัดพระธาตุช้างค้ำ

This is the second most important temple in the city after Wat Phumin; the founding date is unknown. The main wihaan, reconstructed in 1458, has a huge seated Buddha image and faint murals in the process of being painstakingly uncovered. (Earlier this century an abbot reportedly ordered the murals to be whitewashed because he thought they were distracting worshippers from concentrating on his sermons.)

Also in the wihaan is a collection of Lanna-period scrolls inscribed (in Lanna script) not only with the usual Buddhist scriptures but with the history, law and astrology of the times. A Nan-style *thammat* – a throne once used by abbots during sermons – sits to one side.

The magnificent chedi behind the wihaan dates to the 14th century, probably around

NORTHERN THAILAND

the same time the temple was founded. It features elephant supports similar to those seen in Sukhothai and Si Satchanalai.

Next to the chedi is a small, undistinguished bot from the same era. Wat Chang Kham's current abbot told me an interesting story involving the bot and a Buddha image that was once kept inside.

According to his holiness, in 1955 art historian A B Griswold offered to purchase the 145-cm-tall Buddha inside the small bot. The image appeared to be a crude Sukhothai-style walking Buddha moulded of plaster. After agreeing to pay the abbot 25,000B for the image, Griswold began removing the image from the bot – but as he did it fell and the plaster around the statue broke away to reveal an original Sukhothai Buddha of pure gold underneath. Needless to say, the abbot made Griswold give it back, much to the latter's chagrin. The image is now kept behind a glass partition, along with other valuable Buddhist images from the area, in the abbot's kuti. Did Griswold suspect what lay beneath the plaster? The abbot refuses to speculate, at least on record.

Wat Chang Kham is also distinguished by having the largest haw trai or tripitaka (Buddhist scripture) library in Thailand. It's as big as or bigger than the average wihaan, but now lies empty.

The wat is opposite the Nan National Museum on Pha Kong Rd.

Wat Hua Khuang
วัดหัวข่วง

Largely ignored by art historians, this small wat diagonally opposite Wat Chang Kham features a distinctive Lanna/Lan Xang-style chedi with four Buddha niches, a wooden tripitaka library (now used as a kuti) and a noteworthy bot with a Luang Prabang-style carved wooden verandah. Inside are a carved wooden ceiling and a huge naga altar. The temple's founding date is unknown, but stylistic cues suggest this may be one of the city's oldest wats.

Wat Suan Tan
วัดสวนตาล

Reportedly established in 1456, Wat Suan Tan (Palm Grove Monastery) features an interesting 15th-century chedi (40 metres high) that combines prang and lotus-bud motifs of obvious Sukhothai influence. The heavily restored wihaan contains an early Sukhothai-style bronze sitting Buddha.

Wat Suan Tan is on Suan Tan Rd, near the north-eastern end of Pha Kong Rd.

Nan National Museum
พิพิธภัณฑ์แห่งชาตินาน

Housed in the 1903-vintage palace of Nan's last two feudal lords (Phra Chao Suriyapongpalidet and Chao Mahaphrom Surathada), this museum first opened its doors in 1973. Recent renovations have made it one of the most up-to-date provincial museums in Thailand. Unlike most provincial museums in the country, this one also has English labels for many items on display.

The ground floor is divided into six exhibition rooms with ethnological exhibits covering the various ethnic groups found in the province, including the northern Thais, Thai Lü, Htin, Khamu, Mabri, Hmong and Mien. Among the items on display are silverwork, textiles, folk utensils and tribal costumes. On the 2nd floor of the museum are exhibits on Nan history, archaeology, local architecture, royal regalia, weapons, ceramics and religious art.

The museum's collection of Buddha images includes rare Lanna styles as well as the floppy-eared local styles, usually wooden standing images in the 'calling for rain' pose (with hands at the sides, pointing down) which show a marked Luang Prabang influence. The astute museum curators posit a Nan style of art in Buddhist sculpture; some examples on display seem very imitative of other Thai styles, while others are quite distinctive – the ears curve outwards. Also on display on the 2nd floor is a rare 'black' (actually reddish-brown) elephant tusk said to have been presented to a Nan lord over 300 years ago. The tusk is held aloft by a wooden Garuda sculpture.

The museum is open Wednesday to Sunday from 9 am to noon and 1 to 4 pm. Admission is 10B. A building adjacent to the museum has a few books on Thai art and archaeology for sale.

Festivals

The Golden Orange Festival (Thetsakaan Som Sii Thong) is held during December-January – the peak harvest time for the oranges. Among the festival events are a parade of floats decorated with Nan oranges and the coronation of an Orange Queen. During the hot season (March to May), in years when there's a bumper crop of phrik yai and the chilli-growers have extra income to spend, Nan occasionally celebrates a Chilli Festival (Ngaan Phrik) with pepper-festooned floats, chilli-eating contests and the coronation of – what else – a Chilli Queen.

Between mid-September and mid-October, Meuang Nan celebrates Thaan Kuay Salaak, a holiday unique to Nan in which special offerings dedicated to one's ancestors are presented to monks in the local temples.

At the end of the Buddhist Rains Retreat (mid-October to mid-November), during the *thâwt kathin* (robes-offering) for Wat Phra That Chang Kham, impressive long-boat races are held on the Nan River. The all-wooden 30-metre-long boats display sculpted naga heads and tails and hold up to 50 rowers.

Although not a festival per se, one local rite unique to Nan that's worth observing (if you have the opportunity) is the Seup Chataa or 'Extend Life' ceremony. Although at one time the ritual was performed annually, it is now most often held when someone is seriously ill or other bad fortune is deemed to have occurred. In the ceremony, the supplicant sits beneath a pyramid-like structure of reeds and flowers while monks and a shaman skilled at Seup Chataa execute a prescribed series of offerings (usually eggs and fruit) and sacred chants.

Places to Stay

Guesthouses *Doi Phukha Guest House* (☎ 771422), 94/5 Soi 1, Sumonthewarat Rd (Soi Aranyawat), offers tidy rooms in a large

wooden house for 80/90B a single/double, 50B for a dorm bed. Meals are available, along with information on exploring Nan.

The *Nan Guest House* (☎ 771849) is in another large house at 57/16 Mahaphrom Rd (actually at the end of a soi off Mahaphrom Rd) near the THAI office. Singles/doubles/triples with shared bath cost 60/80/100B; for rooms with private bath, add 20B per person.

Wiangtai House (☎ 710247), at 21/1 Soi Wat Hua Wiang Tai (off Sumonthewarat Rd near the Nara department store) has upstairs rooms in a large modern house for 100B (one large bed) and 120/150B (two/three beds). Bathrooms are shared but very clean. Mr Tu, the owner, knows the area well and leads treks.

The on-again, off-again *Nan Youth Hostel* (☎ 710322) is in a large, old house near the junction of Mahaphrom and Suriyaphong Rds. For Hostelling International members, dorm accommodation is 30B per person and singles/doubles are 50/70B; non-members pay 40B and 60/80B respectively. Sometimes the name changes (it was 'No Problem Guest House' for a while) and sometimes the place is booked out with Thai students using it as a boarding house for entire school terms.

Hotels *Amorn Si* (☎ 710510) at 97 Mahayot Rd has very basic one/two-bed rooms for 120/170B; it's at a very busy intersection so may not be the quietest choice. *Sukkasem* (☎ 710141) at 29/31 Anantaworarittidet Rd has better rooms costing 150 to 170B with fan and bath, 300B with air-con.

The recently renovated, all-wood *Nan Fah* (☎ 710284) at 438-440 Sumonthewarat (next to the Dhevaraj Hotel) has a bit of atmosphere; one of the teak pillars supporting the hotel extends for three storeys, and there's an antique shop on the ground floor. All rooms come with air-con and cost from 350 to 370B. On the downside, the thin wooden walls are easily penetrated by street noise and by music from the ground floor's Phin Pub (till half past midnight).

The all air-con *Dhevaraj (Thewarat) Hotel* (☎ 710094) at 466 Sumonthewarat Rd is a four-storey place built around a tiled courtyard with a fountain. It's not really fancy but it's a pleasant place and is the best hotel Nan has to offer. Large, clean rooms on the 2nd floor, with fan and private bath, are 300/400B with one/two beds – a bit steep due to the lack of competition, but the rooms are a cut above the usual fan room. Rooms towards the back of the hotel are quieter than those towards the front. Rooms on the 3rd floor are all air-con and cost 500/600B with one/two beds. On the top floor are 'VIP' rooms with double-paned windows; these cost 700/900B with one/two beds.

Out of Town *Nan Resort* (☎ 771034) has 11 well-appointed bungalows at Km 4 on Route 1080 north of town for 700B each. The similar *Kannika Resort* (☎ 772598) has bungalows about six km from town on Route 1168, the road to Mae Jarim.

Places to Eat
A night market assembles on the corner of Pha Kong and Anantaworarittidet Rds every night; it's not that spectacular, but the vendors along the sidewalks nearby have fairly good food. Another group of food vendors sets up along the soi opposite the Dhevaraj Hotel.

The most dependable restaurant in the vicinity of the Nan Fah and Dhevaraj hotels is the old brick and wood *Siam Phochana*. It's a very popular morning spot for jók with a choice of fish, shrimp, chicken or pork; the menu has all the other Thai and Chinese standards as well, and is open late. *Miw Miw*, opposite the Nan Fah Hotel, is a bit cleaner than Siam Phochana and has good jók, noodles and coffee.

If you turn left at the soi next to Siam Phochana and follow it a couple of hundred metres you'll come to the semi-outdoor *Suan Isaan*, the best choice in town for Isaan food – it's clean and the service is good.

The popular *Phin Pub*, behind the craft and antique shop on the ground floor of the Nan Fah Hotel, is decorated with northern Thai antiques; when the weather is dry a few tables are put outdoors. Local Thai ensembles perform folk music on phin (Thai lute)

and saw (Thai violin) in the early evenings, followed by modern Thai folk and pop later. Prices are very reasonable considering the quality of the food and entertainment.

A couple of Chinese-Thai restaurants next to the Sukkasem Hotel prepare the usual aahãan taam sàng at medium prices.

On Khao Luang Rd not far from the bus terminal is *Nan Mangsawirat* (the roman-script sign reads 'Mungsawiruti'), a very simple Thai vegetarian place with just a few tables and chairs under a thatched-roof, open-air sala. It's open from 8 am to 2 pm daily; as usual where meat is absent, prices are quite inexpensive.

Things to Buy
Good buys include local textiles, especially the Thai Lü weaving styles from Sipsong-panna. Typical Thai Lü fabrics feature red and black designs on white cotton in floral, geometric and animal designs; indigo and red on white is also common. A favourite is the 'flowing-water design' *(lai náam lãi)* showing stepped patterns representing streams, rivers and waterfalls.

Local Mien embroidery and Hmong appliqué are of excellent quality – not as mass-produced as that typically found in Chiang Mai. Htin grass-and-bamboo baskets and mats are worth a look, too.

The nonprofit Thai-Payap Association, one of Thailand's most successful village self-help projects, has a shop at 24 Jettabut

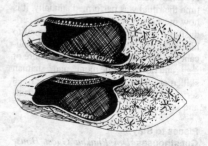

Slippers, Hmong hill tribe

Rd near the morning market and bus terminal. Supported by Britain's Ockenden Venture from 1979 to 1990, the association now involves 21 villages and has become totally self-sufficient. The handiwork offered through Thai-Payap is among the highest quality available, often including more intricate, time-consuming designs. All proceeds go directly to the participating villages – even the administrative staff consists of trained village representatives.

The arts and antique shop on the ground floor of the Nan Fah Hotel has a wide selection of local crafts, including silverwork and jewellery. There are also several small artisan-operated shops in the same vicinity along Sumonthewarat Rd and along Mahawong and Anantaworarittidet Rds.

Getting There & Away

Air You can fly to Nan on THAI from Chiang Mai (510B), Phitsanulok (575B), Phrae (300B) or Bangkok (1530B).

Bus Baw Khaw Saw buses run from Chiang Mai, Chiang Rai and Phrae to Nan. The fare from Chiang Mai's Arcade bus station is 83B (115B air-con, 148B 1st-class air-con) and the trip takes from six to seven hours. From Chiang Rai there's one daily bus at 9.30 am (No 611, 74B) which takes six to seven gruelling hours via treacherous mountain roads – get a window seat as there's usually lots of motion sickness. Buses from Phrae to Nan leave frequently, cost 33B and take from two to 2½ hours.

From Nan, buses to Chiang Mai, Chiang Rai and Phrae leave from a terminal west of the large market on Anantaworarittidet Rd.

Ordinary buses to Utaradit, Phitsanulok, Sukhothai and other points south as far as Bangkok leave from the Baw Khaw Saw terminal off Khao Luang Rd. Regular government-run air-con buses to Bangkok cost 160B (two nightly), 1st-class air-con is 289B (one in the morning, another in the evening) and super-VIP buses are 445B (two nightly).

Private VIP Bangkok buses leave from offices along the eastern end of Anantawo-rarittidet Rd, not far from the Baw Khaw Saw terminal. Sombat Tour runs VIP buses to Bangkok for as low as 320B – check the number of seats before booking, though.

As provincial roads improve, eventually you should be able to bus from Nan to Nakhon Thai and connect with the Phitsanulok to Loei route.

Bus & Train The northern train line makes a stop in Den Chai, which is a 38B, three-hour bus ride from Nan.

A Bangkok-bound train leaves Den Chai at 7 pm (arriving at Bangkok's Hualamphong station at 7.30 am); to be sure of meeting this train, take a 1.15 or 2.30 pm Den Chai-bound bus from Nan's government bus station.

See Getting There & Away in the Phrae section for more Den Chai train information.

Songthaews Pickups to districts in the northern part of the province (Tha Wang Pha, Pua, Phaa Tuup, etc) leave from the petrol station opposite Sukkasem Hotel on Anantaworarittidet Rd. Southbound songthaews (for Mae Jarim, Wiang Sa, Na Noi) depart from the parking lot opposite the new Ratchaphatsadu market on Jettabut Rd.

Getting Around

Fhu Travel Service on Sumonthewarat Rd and Doi Phukha Guest House both rent Honda Dreams for 200B per day, bicycles for 30B. Oversea Shop (☎ 710258) at 488 Sumonthewarat Rd (a few doors down from the Dhevaraj Hotel) rents bicycles and motorbikes at similar rates and can also handle repairs.

Samlors around town cost 10 to 15B.

AROUND NAN PROVINCE
Trekking

Nan has nothing like the organised trekking industry found in Chiang Rai and Chiang Mai, but several local individuals in Nan lead two or three-day excursions into the mountains.

Fhu Travel Service (☎ 710636) at 453/4 Sumonthewarat Rd offers treks to Mabri,

Hmong, Mien, Thai Lü and Htin villages combined with raft trips on the Nan River. A one-day 'soft' trek costs 500B per person (minimum of four to six people); a two-day/one-night trek is 1000 to 1100B, depending on the number of participants; two nights/three days is 1300 to 1400B per person and three nights/four days is 2800B. Fhu tends to concentrate on the northern areas of the province.

Wiangtai House (☎ 710247) at 2/1 Soi Wat Hua Wiang Tai, does two-night/three-day treks for 2500B per person, five-day/four-night trips for 3500B. Wiangtai focuses on the southern areas of the province, including trips to the 'fog sea' on a mountain ridge at the Phrae border.

Doi Phukha Guest House offers one-day tours along the Nong Bua-Doi Phu Kha loop for 500B each with four to six people.

Fees should include guide services, transport and all meals and accommodation.

Doi Phu Kha National Park

อุทยานแห่งชาติดอยภูคา

This very recently established national park is centred around 2000-metre Doi Phu Kha in the Pua and Baw Kleua districts of north-eastern Nan (about 75 km from Nan). There are several Htin, Mien, Hmong and Thai Lü villages in the park and vicinity, as well as a couple of caves and waterfalls and endless opportunities for forest walks. As yet there is no established visitor accommodation in the park; in the meantime rangers will allow visitors to stay in park buildings at no charge. This area gets quite cool in the winter months – evening temperatures of 5 to 10°C are not uncommon – so dress accordingly.

This area was once a hotbed of Thai communist activity; rumour says there are mines on Doi Phu Kha left over from the PLAT days, so stick to obvious footpaths or ask for a ranger guide (the going rate is 100B a day).

To reach the park by public transport you must first take a bus or songthaew north of Nan to Pua (13B), and then pick up one of the infrequent songthaews to the park headquarters (15B). A songthaew to the summit

of Doi Phu Kha costs 35 to 40B. If you come by motorcycle, be forewarned that Route 1256 from Pua deteriorates as you get closer to the summit. Beyond the summit the stretch to Ban Baw Kleua is very rough in spots.

Ban Baw Kleua is a Htin village southeast of the park where the main occupation is the extraction of salt from local salt wells (Baw Kleua means 'salt well'). Route 1256 meets Route 1081 near Baw Kleua; Route 1081 can be followed south back to Nan (107 km) via a network of paved and unpaved roads.

Nong Bua

วัดหนองบัว

This neat and tidy Thai Lü village near the town of Tha Wang Pha, approximately 30 km north of Nan, is famous for Lü-style **Wat Nong Bua**. Featuring a typical two-tiered roof and carved wooden portico, the bot design is simple yet striking - note the carved naga heads at the roof corners. Inside the bot are some noteworthy but faded jataka murals; the building is often locked when religious services aren't in progress, but there's usually someone around to unlock the door. Leave a donation for temple upkeep and restoration at the altar.

You can also see Thai Lü weaving in action in the village. The home of Khun Janthasom Phrompanya, near the wat, serves as a local weaving centre – check there for the locations of looms, or to look at fabrics for purchase. Large yaams are available for just 45B, while nicely woven neck scarves cost more. There are also several weaving houses just behind the wat.

Originally from Sipsongpanna (Xishuangbanna) in China's Yunnan Province, the Thai Lü migrated to Nan in 1836 in the wake of a conflict with a local chao meuang (lord of a Thai river-valley state). Phra Chao Atityawong, ruler of Nan kingdom at the time, allowed the Thai Lü to stay and grow vegetables in what is now Tha Wang Pha district. Nong Bua today is surrounded by picturesque vegetable farms.

Nong Bua Festival
Every three years in early December the Thai Lü at Nong Bua pay homage to their ancestral spirits. On the first day participants don traditional indigo outfits, build a village gate to fend off bad spirits and place offerings at 20 selected spirit houses around the village. The day ends with a feast.

On the second day the villagers form a procession in which they carry trays piled with fruit, incense sticks, betel nut, candles, farm implements and weaponry. The chao meuang, or one of his assistants, carries a basket containing 20 live chickens. When the procession passes one of the 20 selected spirit houses, a feather plucked from one of the chickens is placed in the diminutive house, and then the chicken is tossed into the air. Everyone in the crowd scrambles to catch the chicken for good luck. When the group arrives at the spirit house of Nong Bua's first chao meuang, the participants sacrifice a water buffalo, an ox and two pigs (one white, one black). The meat is cooked and eaten in a feast following the sacrifice. Nowadays Thais from as far away as Bangkok attend the celebration.

The next Nong Bua Festival will be held in December 1996. ■

Getting There & Away Songthaews to Tha Wang Pha (12B) leave from opposite Nan's Sukkasem Hotel. Get off at Samyaek Longbom, a three-way intersection before Tha Wang Pha, and walk west to a bridge over the Nan River, then left at the dead end on the other side of the bridge to Wat Nong Bua. It's a total of 3.1 km from the highway to the wat.

If you're coming from Nan via your own transport on Route 1080, you'll cross a stream called Lam Nam Yang just past the village of Ban Fai Mun but before Tha Wang Pha. Take the first left off Route 1080 and follow it to a dead end; turn right and then left over a bridge across the Nan River and walk until you reach another dead end, then left two km until you can see Wat Nong Bua on the right.

Tham Phaa Tuup Forest Reserve
ถ้ำผาตูบ
This limestone cave complex is about 10 km north of Nan and is part of a new wildlife reserve. Some 17 caves have been counted, of which nine are easily located by means of established (but unmarked) trails.

From Nan, you can catch a songthaew bound for Pua or Thung Chang; it will stop at the turn-off to the caves for 6B. The vehicles leave from the petrol station opposite the Sukkasem Hotel.

Sao Din
เสาดิน
Literally 'Earth Pillars', Sao Din is an erosionary phenomenon similar to that found at Phae Meuang Phii in Phrae Province – tall columns of earth protruding from a barren depression. The area covers nearly 20 rai (3.2 hectares) off Route 1026 in Na Noi district about 30 km south of Nan.

Sao Din is best visited by bicycle or motorcycle since it's time-consuming to reach by public transport. If you don't have your own wheels, take a songthaew to Na Noi from the southbound songthaew terminal opposite the Ratchaphatsadu Market in Nan. From Na Noi you must get yet another songthaew bound for Fak Tha or Ban Khok, getting off at the entrance to Sao Din after five km or so. From here you'll have to walk or hitch four km to Sao Din itself. There are also occasional direct songthaews from Na Noi.

North-west of Sao Din, off Route 1216 West, is a smaller set of earth pillars called Hom Chom.

Other Attractions
There are a couple of interesting destinations in and around the Thai Lü village of **Pua**, roughly 50 km north of Nan. In Pua itself you can check out another famous Thai Lü temple, **Wat Ton Laeng**, which is admired for its classic three-tiered roof. **Silaphet**

Falls is south-east of Pua just off the road between Pua and Ban Nam Yao. The water falls in a wide swath over a cliff and is best seen at the end of the monsoon season in November. On the way to the falls and west of the road is the Mien village of **Ban Pa Klang**, worth a visit to see silversmiths at work. This village supplies many silver shops in Chiang Mai and Bangkok.

Other Mien villages that specialise in silverwork can be found along Route 101 between Nan and Phrae in the vicinity of **Song Khwae** (not to be confused with the village of the same name on Route 1097 farther north).

Off Route 1148, north of the village of Ban Sakoen, is a huge, 200-metre-wide cave called **Tham Luang**. The path to the cave is not signposted, but if you ask at the police checkpoint in Ban Sakoen you should be able to get directions or you might even find a guide.

The **Thaleh Sap Neua** (Northern Lake) formed by the Sirikit Dam is an important freshwater fishery for Nan, as well as a recreational attraction for Nan residents. **Ban Pak Nai** on its north-western shore is the main fishing village. Just before the Nan River feeds into the lake at its extreme northern end, there is a set of river rapids called **Kaeng Luang**.

One area in Nan Province you're not encouraged to visit is the mountainous ridge along the Thai-Lao border. This is a 'restricted area' patrolled by the Thai military, who claim communist insurgents are still holed up here. More likely the real dangers of the area involve undetonated mines left by both insurgency and counter-insurgency forces during the 1960s and 1970s, as well as an ongoing opium trade. The province's two highest peaks, **Phu Khe** (2079 metres) and **Doi Lo** (2077 metres), are found in the restricted area.

North-East Thailand

In many ways, the north-eastern region of Thailand is the kingdom's heartland. Partly due to the area's general non-development, the older Thai customs remain more intact here than elsewhere in the country. The region also hosts fewer tourists – in 1990, for example, only 2% of the country's annual international arrivals ventured into north-east Thailand.

Compared to the rest of Thailand, the pace is slower, the people friendlier and inflation is less effective in the Isaan provinces, and although fewer people speak or understand English, travel in the north-east is easy.

Sites of historical and archaeological significance abound in the north-east; many of them have been restored or excavated. Scattered around the region are 202 known prasats, prangs, kus and chedis, 182 of which are of Khmer origins. Most of them are found in four provinces: Buriram (61), Nakhon Ratchasima (26 sites), Surin (33) and Si Saket (12).

The Khorat Plateau extends across most of north-east Thailand and is divided by the Phu Phan Mountain Range into two wide drainage basins, the Sakon Nakhon Basin in the upper north-east (fed by the Maekhong River and its tributaries) and the Khorat Basin in the lower north-east (fed by the Chi and Mun rivers).

Isaan (the collective term for the region) officially consists of 18 provinces: Buriram, Chaiyaphum, Kalasin, Khon Kaen, Loei, Mahasarakham, Mukdahan, Nakhon Ratchasima (Khorat), Nakhon Phanom, Nong Bualamphu, Nong Khai, Roi Et, Sakon Nakhon, Si Saket, Surin, Ubon Ratchathani, Udon Thani and Yasothon.

History

The region has a long history, beginning with the 2000-year-old bronze culture of Ban Chiang, which predates both Mesopotamia and China as a metallurgical and agricultural site.

Thai use the term *isãan* to classify the region, the people *(khon isãan)* and the food *(aahãan isãan)* of north-east Thailand. The name comes from Isana, the Sanskrit name for the Mon-Khmer kingdom which flourished in what is now north-east Thailand and pre-Angkor Cambodia; Isana was a precursor to the Funan empire (1st to 6th centuries). Funan was in turn absorbed by the Chenla empire during the late 6th to 8th centuries and divided into Upper (Water) and Lower (Land) Chenla, which corresponded with parts of modern-day Isaan, southern Laos and north-western Cambodia. After the 9th century Chenla was superseded by the Angkor empire, which extended well into Isaan and beyond.

Isaan remained more or less autonomous from early Thai kingdoms until the coming of the French in the 1800s created the Indochinese state of Laos, thus forcing Thailand to define its north-eastern boundaries. Rama V divided the region into four *monthon* (from the Pali-Sanskrit 'mandala') or semi-autonomous satellite states, including Lao Phuan (north-eastern Isaan), Roi Et (central Isaan), Lao Klang (south-western Isaan) and Ubon (south-eastern Isaan). The monthon system was abolished in favour of the Bangkok-ruled *jangwàt* (province) system in 1933.

Traditionally Thailand's poorest region due to the infertility of the soil and lack of rain in comparison with the rest of the country, the north-east was nonetheless fertile ground for the communist movement. Ho Chi Minh spent 1928-29 proselytising in Udon Thani, Sakon Nakhon, and Khorat; in the 1940s a number of Indochinese Communist Party leaders fled to Isaan from Laos and helped strengthen the Communist Party of Thailand. From the 1960s until 1982 or so, Isaan was a hotbed of guerrilla activity, especially in the provinces of Buriram, Loei, Ubon, Nakhon Phanom, and Sakon Nakhon. Almost immediately following the amnesty

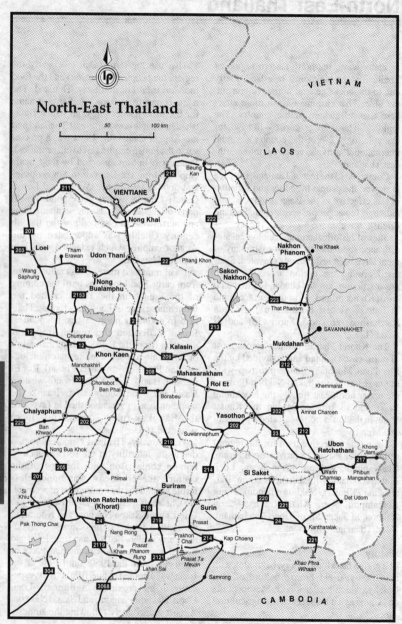

of 1982, the CPT's north-eastern strongholds began a rapid dissolution. The process was hastened by a decade of economic growth which drew large numbers of Isaan peasants from the forests and rice fields to various provincial capitals and to Bangkok.

Opinions today differ on just how far Isaan has been able to ride along on the coat-tails of Thailand's strong economy. The area still has the lowest per capita income of the country's four major regions, but it is definitely more prosperous overall than 15 years ago.

Culture

Isaan culture and language is marked by a mixture of Lao and Khmer influence. The Khmers have left behind Angkor Wat-like monuments near Surin, Khorat, Buriram and other north-eastern towns. Near the Mae-khong River/Lao border in Nakhon Phanom Province are several Lao-style temples, including the famous Wat That Phanom. Many of the people living in this area speak Lao or a Thai dialect which is very close to Lao – in fact there are more people of Lao heritage in north-east Thailand than in all of Laos. In certain areas of the lower north-east, Khmer is the most common language.

Isaan food is famous for its pungency and choice of ingredients. Well-known dishes include *kài yâang* (grilled spiced chicken) and *sômtam* (spicy salad made with grated unripe papaya, lime juice, garlic, fish sauce and fresh chillies). North-easterners eat glutinous rice with their meals, rolling the almost translucent grains into balls with their hands.

The music of the north-east is also highly distinctive in its folk tradition, using instruments such as the khaen, a reed instrument with two long rows of bamboo pipes strung together; the *ponglang*, a xylophone-like instrument made of short wooden logs; and the *phin*, a type of small three-stringed lute played with a large plectrum. The most popular song forms are of the luuk thung (literally, 'children of the fields') type, a very rhythmic style in comparison to the classical music of central Thailand.

The best silk in Thailand is said to come from the north-east, around Khorat (Nakhon Ratchasima), Khon Kaen and Roi Et. A visit to north-eastern silk-weaving towns can uncover bargains, as well as provide an education in Thai weaving techniques. Cotton fabrics from Loei, Nong Khai and Nakhon Phanom are highly regarded, especially those woven using the mat-mii or tie-dye (*ikat*) method.

For real antiquity, Udon Province offers prehistoric cave drawings at Ban Pheu, north of Udon Thani, and a look at the ancient ceramic and bronze culture at Ban Chiang to the east. This latter site, excavated by the late Chester Gorman and his team of anthropologists from the University of Pennsylvania, may prove to be the remains of the world's oldest agricultural society and first bronze metallurgy.

Travellers who want to know more about north-east Thailand should read the works of Pira Sudham, a Thai author born in Buriram. His autobiographical *People of Esarn (Isaan)* is especially recommended.

Getting There & Away

The main train and bus lines in the north-east are between Bangkok and Nong Khai, and between Bangkok and Ubon Ratchathani. The north-east can also be reached from northern Thailand by bus or from Phitsanulok, with Khon Kaen as the 'gateway'.

Nakhon Ratchasima Province

Thailand's largest province (20,500 sq km) is most well known for silk weaving. Some of Thailand's best silk is made in the village of Pak Thong Chai, 30 km south-west of Khorat on Route 304. Many of the Bangkok silk houses have their cloth made there, so don't expect to get any special bargains just because you went all that way. There are also a couple of silk shops in Khorat which are just as good for their selection and price.

Still, Pak Thong Chai is worth a trip if you're interested in observing Thai silk-weaving methods.

Khorat's other big attraction is Angkor-period Khmer ruins scattered about the province. Most are little more than a jumble of stones or a single prang, but the restorations at Prasat Phimai and Wat Phanomwan are very impressive. In addition to Khmer religious shrines, there are some 192 ancient city sites – Mon, Lao and Khmer – scattered around the province. Most are visible only to archaeologists trained to look for the odd earthen rampart, boundary stone or laterite foundation. Little is known about the early history of the province except that, according to a 937 AD inscription, it was part of a kingdom known as Sri Janas (Si Janat), which apparently extended over the entire Khorat Plateau. The inhabitants of Sri Janas – or at least its royal inhabitants – practised a mixture of Mahayana Buddhism and Shiva worship, hence it was probably an Angkor satellite.

NAKHON RATCHASIMA

นครราชสีมา

Exactly 250 km from Bangkok, Nakhon Ratchasima (population 203,000) is also known as Khorat. At one time Khorat was the capital of Lao Klang, a Thai monthon that covered present-day Khorat, Chaiyaphum and Buriram provinces. Up until the mid-Ayuthaya period it was actually two towns, Sema and Khorakpura, which merged under the reign of King Narai. To this day, Khorat has a split personality of sorts, with the older, less commercial half to the west, and the newer downtown half inside the city moats to the east, although neither Sema nor Khorakpura was originally here but in present-day Sung Noen (35 km south-east).

No longer the quaint Isaan town it once was, busy Khorat has become an important transportation hub and burgeoning industrial centre and is Thailand's second largest city. Since 1988 new factory registrations have averaged 1300 per year. Yet only in 1992 did the city get its first international-class hotel.

Often cited only as a train or bus stop from which one reaches the nearby Phimai ruins, Khorat is a fairly interesting place in itself if you don't mind putting up with the generally grubby air, which can be almost as bad as in Bangkok.

One of seven air bases in Thailand used by the US armed forces to launch air strikes on Laos and Vietnam in the 1960s and 1970s was just outside Khorat. A few retired GIs still live in the area with their Thai families, and the Veterans of Foreign Wars Cafeteria is still open on Phoklang Rd. But the heavy US influence that was obvious in the late 1970s after the base was closed has all but faded away. Yes, the big massage parlours are still there, but the clientele is almost exclusively Thai.

Information

Tourist Office The TAT office (☎ 213666; fax 213667) on Mittaphap Rd (western edge of town) is worth a visit, since it has plenty of information on the north-east and a good map of Khorat. To get there, walk straight across from the entrance to the Khorat train station to Mukhamontri Rd, turn left and walk (or catch a No 2 bus) west until you reach the highway to Bangkok – Mittaphap Rd. TAT is just across the road, on the south-west corner. The office is open daily from 8.30 am to 4.30 pm.

A Tourist Police contingent (☎ 213333) is attached to the TAT office.

Post & Telephone The main post office on Mittaphap Rd is open Monday to Friday from 8.30 am to 4.30 pm, Saturday 9 am to 1 pm. There is a convenient branch post office on Jomsurangyat Rd between Klang Plaza 2 shopping centre and the Anachak Hotel and another on Atsadang Rd. International telephone calls are best made from the CAT office attached to the main post office; hours are 7 am to 11 pm daily.

Khorat's telephone area code is ☎ 044.

Money The best area for banks is Chomphon Rd, where you'll find Bangkok Bank, Thai

Farmers Bank and Siam Commercial Bank, all of which offer foreign-exchange services from 8.30 am till 3.30 pm, Monday to Friday.

Mahawirawong National Museum
พิพิธภัณฑ์แห่งชาติมหาวีรวงศ์

In the grounds of Wat Sutchinda, directly across from the government buildings off Ratchadamnoen Rd and just outside the city moat, this museum has a good collection of Khmer art objects, especially door lintels, as well as objects from other periods. It's open from 9 am to noon and 1 to 4 pm, Wednesday to Sunday. Admission is 10B.

Thao Suranari Memorial
อนุสาวรีย์ท้าวสุรนารี

At the Chumphon Gate to downtown Khorat, on the west side, is this much-worshipped memorial shrine to Thao Suranari (also known as Khun Ying Mo), a courageous Thai woman who led the local citizens in a battle against Lao invaders from Vientiane during the rule of Rama III. Hundreds of unique offerings – such as a miniature model of a bus donated by local bus drivers – find their way to the shrine in hopes that Khun Ying Mo's spirit will protect the offerers from danger or ill will.

Khorat Song In the evenings you can see performances of *phleng khorâat*, the traditional Khorat folk song, in an area opposite the shrine near some shops selling preserved pork. It's usually performed by groups of four singers hired by people whose supplications to Thao Suranari have been honoured. To show gratitude to the spirit, they pay for the performance. Over 100 groups are for hire, usually for 300 to 600B per performance.

Wat Phra Narai Maharat
วัดพระนารายณ์

This monastery of indeterminate age is important for two reasons: it contains a Khmer sandstone sculpture of Phra Narai (Vishnu) and, more significantly, Khorat's

lak meuang or city phallus-pillar. It's on Prajak Rd between Atsadang and Chomphon Rds.

Wat Sala Loi
วัดศาลาลอย

This distinctive modern 'Temple of the Floating Pavilion' is 400 metres east of the north-eastern corner of the city moat and has a bot shaped like a Chinese junk.

Wat Paa Salawan
วัดป่าสาละวัน

A Thammayut 'forest monastery' once surrounded by jungle, Salawan has been engulfed by the city, but it's still a fairly quiet escape. The abbot, Luang Phaw Phut, is quite well known as a meditation teacher and has developed a strong lay following in the area. A few relics belonging to the legendary Ajaan Man are on display in the main wihaan, a large but simple wooden affair. A cemetery on the grounds has a couple of markers with photos of US veterans who lived their later years in Khorat. Wat Paa Salawan is in the south-west sector of town behind Nakhon Ratchasima train station.

Swimming & Tennis
Landlocked Khorat is quite warm most of the year – a swim at one of the several local public pools will revive all but the most wilted. Each of the following charges 20B per day per person: Chanya Swimming Pool (☎ 252305) on Seup Siri Rd, Rama Swimming Pool (☎ 242019) on Mittaphap Rd, Puttachart Swimming Pool (☎ 251815) at 29/1 Phetmatukang Rd, and Sripattana Hotel (☎ 242944) on Suranari Rd. The pool at the Sripattana Hotel on Suranari Rd has a good poolside snack bar. Thep Nakhon (off Mittaphap Rd in the north-western section of town) charges 60B a day but is worth it for the newer, more high-tech facilities.

Tennis courts open to the public include Thotsaporn Court (1658 Mittaphap Rd, ☎ 251819, 24B per hour) and the city stadium, north-east of the city centre off Suranari Rd.

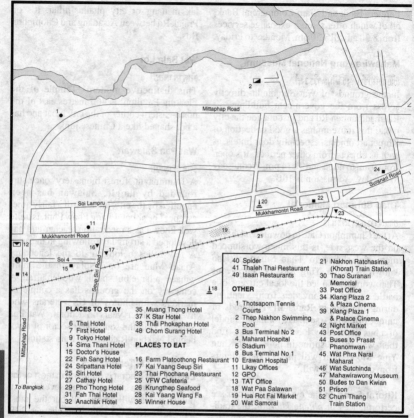

Mittaphap Road

Suranari Road

Soi Lampru

Mukkhamontri Road

Mukkhamontri Road

Soi 4

Seup Siri Road

Mittaphap Road

To Bangkok

NORTH-EAST THAILAND

PLACES TO STAY

6 Thai Hotel
7 First Hotel
9 Tokyo Hotel
14 Sima Thani Hotel
15 Doctor's House
22 Fah Sang Hotel
24 Sripattana Hotel
25 Siri Hotel
27 Cathay Hotel
29 Pho Thong Hotel
31 Fah Thai Hotel
32 Anachak Hotel
35 Muang Thong Hotel
37 K Star Hotel
38 Thai Phokaphan Hotel
48 Chom Surang Hotel

PLACES TO EAT

16 Farm Platoothong Restaurant
17 Kai Yaang Seup Siri
23 Thai Phochana Restaurant
25 VFW Cafeteria
26 Krungthep Seafood
28 Kai Yaang Wang Fa
36 Winner House
40 Spider
41 Thaleh Thai Restaurant
49 Isaan Restaurants

OTHER

1 Thotsaporn Tennis Courts
2 Thep Nakhon Swimming Pool
3 Bus Terminal No 2
4 Maharat Hospital
5 Stadium
8 Bus Terminal No 1
10 Erawan Hospital
11 Likay Offices
12 GPO
13 TAT Office
18 Wat Paa Salawan
19 Hua Rot Fai Market
20 Wat Samorai
21 Nakhon Ratchasima (Khorat) Train Station
30 Thao Suranari Memorial
33 Post Office
34 Klang Plaza 2 & Plaza Cinema
39 Klang Plaza 1 & Palace Cinema
42 Night Market
43 Post Office
44 Buses to Prasat Phanomwan
45 Wat Phra Narai Maharat
46 Wat Sutchinda
47 Mahawirawong Museum
50 Buses to Dan Kwian
51 Prison
52 Chum Thang Train Station

Festival

Khorat's most popular annual event is the Thao Suranari Festival, a celebration of Thao Suranari's victory over the Lao. It's held from late March to early April and features parades, li-khe, phleng khoraat and a beauty contest. Thousands of participants from around Nakhon Ratchasima Province and beyond attend the festivities.

Places to Stay – bottom end

Guesthouses Khorat's only true guesthouse, *Doctor's House* (☎ 255846), is at 78 Soi 4, Seup Siri Rd, in the western area of the city. The house is quiet and comfortable and has four large singles/doubles for 80/160B or 250B with air-con. If you phone from the bus or train station, the guesthouse staff will give you a ride.

Next door to the Tokyo Hotel on Suranari Rd is the *Tokyo Guest House*, actually an extension of the hotel, where large rooms with a bath cost 70 to 80B.

Hotels Visit the TAT office for a map and complete list of Khorat's hotels. *Fah Sang*

Nakhon Ratchasima (Khorat)

0   250   500 m

To Phimai & Khon Kaen

To Dusit Royal Princess & Vegetarian Restaurant

To Wat Sala Loi

To Wat Thung Sawan

To Buriram, Surin, Ubon Ratchathani & Dan Kwian

To Wat Paa Salawan

(☎ 242123), at 68-70 Mukkhamontri Rd not far from Khorat train station, has clean rooms and friendly staff. Rooms with fan and bath are from 110 to 130B for singles, and 140 to 190B for doubles. Air-con singles/doubles with hot water cost 240/280B.

Pho Thong (☎ 242084), 658 Phoklang Rd, has rooms from 100 to 140B with fan and bath. Noisy but liveable, it's on the corner of Ratchadamnoen Rd at the west city gate, right in the centre of things. In the same vicinity is the *Fah Thai Hotel* (☎ 242533) at 3535 Phoklang Rd; this one's a bit better at

150 to 210B for a room with fan and private bath, 300B for air-con.

Siri Hotel (☎ 242831), at 167-8 Phoklang Rd, is well located a couple of blocks west of the city moats. Quiet and friendly, rooms cost 100 to 150B with a fan or 200 to 350B air-con. The VFW Cafeteria is next door.

Muang Thong Hotel (☎ 242090), at 46 Chumphon Rd, is a classic old wooden hotel that's seen better days – look for the green-painted building inside the moat near the Thao Suranari Shrine. Rooms are a rock-bottom 70B a night – be sure to get a room off the street.

Building Failure

Khorat made world headlines in August 1993 when the six-storey Royal Plaza Hotel collapsed, leading to the deaths of 137 people. Over a dozen Thais associated with the hotel construction and operation were arrested for negligence. The hotel started out inauspiciously enough as a massage parlour; the top three floors were later added in violation of construction and safety regulations, then water storage tanks were erected on top, creating a weight load the lower three floors couldn't withstand.

Since this incident, multistorey buildings throughout Thailand have been inspected for similar problems. The owners of those structures found to exhibit building code violations have been required to upgrade the buildings or close them down. Not all have complied; the Banglamphu Department Store in Bangkok, for example, has been condemned yet shoppers and vendors continue to fill the building daily. For what it's worth, the Royal Plaza collapse has been the only such building failure in Thai history. ■

Thai Phokaphan (☎ 242454), 104-6 Atsadang Rd, is inside the city moats, across the street from the more expensive *K Star Hotel* and the KR massage parlour. Good singles/doubles cost 120/180B, 240/280B with air-con.

Cathay (☎ 242889), at 3692/5-6 Ratchadamnoen Rd, has reasonable rates (100 to 130B), and is not far from the bus terminal for Buriram, Surin, Ubon and Chiang Mai. Closer still is the *First Hotel* (☎ 255203) at 132-36 Burin Rd, where ordinary rooms with fan cost 120 to 150B.

Places to Stay – middle

Anachak Hotel (☎ 243925) at 62/1 Jomsurangyat Rd near the Klang Plaza 2 shopping centre, charges a moderate 250 to 500B for its basic but all air-con rooms.

Thai Hotel (☎ 241613), at 640 Mittaphap Rd not far from the main downtown bus terminal, has similar digs for 350 to 450B.

Places to Stay – top end

At the bottom of the top end, *Sripattana* (☎ 242944) on Suranari Rd has air-con rooms from 450B, and a swimming pool. *Chom Surang* (☎ 242940), 2701/2 Mahat Thai Rd, has all air-con rooms from 750B, also with a pool.

The 130-room *Sima Thani Hotel* (☎ 213100; fax 213121; (02) 253-4885 in Bangkok) originally opened in 1992 as a Sheraton but is now owned by a Thai hotel group. Superior singles/doubles start at 1800/2000B, and deluxe rooms cost 2000/2300B. On the premises are a lobby bar, restaurant, pub and swimming pool.

Not to be outdone, Thailand's Dusit Group is about to open its own *Dusit Royal Princess* on Suranari Rd on the north-eastern outskirts of the city. Rates are expected to be in the same league as the Sima Thani's.

Places to Eat

Khorat has many excellent Thai and Chinese restaurants, especially along Ratchadamnoen Rd near the Thao Suranari Shrine and western gate to downtown Khorat. The Hua Rot Fai Market on Mukkhamontri Rd near the train station is a great place to eat in the evening, as is the Manat Rd night bazaar; both are at their best from 6 to 10 pm.

The well-known *Thai Phochana* at 142 Jomsurangyat Rd has a mix of standard Thai and local specialities, including mìi khorâat (Khorat-style noodles) and yam kòp yâang (roast frog salad). Also good here is kaeng phèt pèt (duck curry). The restaurant is now enclosed and air-con, so automotive fumes and street noise from the busy street in front are no longer a problem.

Winner House, at 91 Mahat Thai Rd near the Wacharasarit Rd intersection, has very good Vietnamese food.

Farm Platoothong Restaurant on Seup Siri Rd close to the Doctor's House is a good place for a slow Thai splurge – great service and food. You can also fish for your own food in the farm's ponds for 20B per hour (a rod and reel cost 30B per day).

Thaleh Thai, opposite the Chom Surang Hotel on Mahat Thai Rd, is a very good outdoor seafood restaurant. Also good for fresh seafood – and quite inexpensive – is *Krungthep Seafood* on Phoklang Rd not far from the Siri Hotel. On the same side of Phoklang Rd a little farther east, *Bibi Muslim* does tasty Muslim curries and khâo mòk kài.

The *Vegetarian Restaurant (Sala Mang-sawirat)* has moved once again, this time to an out-of-the-way location on Suranari Rd towards Khorat Teacher's College. If you manage to get out there, you'll find great Thai vegetarian dishes for 5 to 8B. It's open from around 10 am to 3 pm.

Isaan Food A strip of three very unassuming Isaan places along the east side of Wacharasarit Rd between Sanphasit and Kamhaeng Songkhram Rds – *Suan Sin, Samran Laap* and *Si Wiang* – serves such locally popular Isaan fare as plaa chonábòt (freshwater fish steamed with vegetables and served with a tart-spicy sauce), súp haang wua (oxtail soup) and lin yâang (barbecued tongue). They also do lâap and other Isaan standards.

For the best kài yâang and sômtam in town, check out *Kai Yaang Seup Siri*, near Doctor's House on Seup Siri Rd. There are two Isaan places next door to each other here – look for the one with chickens on the grill out the front. They start serving around 10.30 am and are usually sold out by 4 pm.

Also good, and open longer hours, is *Kai Yaang Wang Fa*, on Ratchadamnoen Rd opposite the shrine.

Western *VFW Cafeteria* next to the Siri Hotel on Phoklang Rd has cheap American-style breakfasts, as well as steaks, ice cream, pizza and salads. It gets mixed reviews, however, so let's just say it's a good imitation of an American 'greasy spoon', for all that term implies, both positive and negative. The central tables are often taken by a tight-knit group of American Vietnam War veterans talking in their standard military-issue mid-western accents.

Cleaner and more reliable – if more expensive – are the various American-style restaurants in Klang Plaza 2 shopping centre, including *KFC, Dunkin Donuts, Black Canyon Coffeeshop* and *Royal Home Bakery*. Klang Plaza also has a large supermarket, should you want to shop for groceries.

Many expats swear by *The Spider* on Chomphon Rd, an air-con restaurant/pub with the best farang food in town, plus a list of Thai dishes.

Entertainment

Khorat is a regional headquarters for li-khe (likay) troupes, who maintain several offices along Mukkhamontri Rd near the Seup Siri Rd intersection. Hired performances start at 1000B for a small ensemble – you provide the venue and the troupe will bring their costumes, stage sets, and so on – much like a travelling carnival.

The Phlap-Phla Restaurant in the Sima Thani Hotel hosts a well-executed cultural performance of Thai, Lao and Khmer dancing Monday to Friday from 7 to 9 pm.

Several cinemas in town show motion pictures daily. The better movies – including occasional foreign flicks – seem to turn up at the Plaza, which is behind the Klang Plaza 2 shopping centre off Ratchadamnoen and Jomsurangyat Rds.

The city boasts seven massage parlours, three Thai-style nightclubs and a couple of hotel discos. For a complete list, see the TAT office.

Shopping

A night bazaar along Manat Rd features cheap clothes, fruit, flowers, sunglasses, watches and food vendors – nothing spectacular, but it's a fine place to while away an hour or so.

Klang Plaza 2 shopping centre on Jomsurangyat Rd offers five floors of shops purveying everything from videos to housewares. There's another Klang Plaza on Atsadang Rd near the Thai Phokaphan Hotel.

Khorat has many shops that specialise in Khorat silk. Several are found along Ratchadamnoen Rd near the Thao Suranari Shrine, including Ratri, Thusnee (Thatsani) and Today. Over on Chomphon Rd are a couple of others – Chompol and Jin Chiang.

Getting There & Away

Air THAI flies to Khorat from Bangkok daily; the fare is 540B one way. The THAI office (☎ 257211) is at 14 Manat Rd, off Mahat Thai Rd inside the city moat.

Bus Ordinary buses leave the northern bus terminal in Bangkok every 15 or 20 minutes from 5 am to 10.15 pm. The fare is 64B and the trip takes four hours. Air-con buses cost 115B. In Khorat, air-con buses to Bangkok arrive and depart from the air-con bus terminal on Mittaphap Rd.

For buses to other places in Thailand, there are two main bus terminals. Bus Terminal 1, off Burin Rd downtown near the intersection of the Mittaphap Rd loop and the highway north to Nong Khai, has buses to Phitsanulok, Chiang Mai and Chiang Rai, plus a few buses to Bangkok. This bus station can be extremely congested.

Buses to other points in the north-east (eg Loei, Roi Et, Nakhon Phanom, Ubon, Udon, etc) or in eastern central Thailand (eg Rayong, Pattaya, Chanthaburi) leave from Bus Terminal 2, off the highway to Nong Khai north of downtown. Buses between Khorat and Khon Kaen cost 39B and leave regularly throughout the day. Direct buses between Khorat and Chanthaburi on the south-east coast run hourly between 4.30 am and 4 pm. The fare is 69B and the journey takes about eight hours.

For details on buses to/from other cities in Thailand, see the table following.

Train An express train bound for Ubon Ratchathani departs Bangkok's Hualamphong station at 9 pm, arriving in Khorat at

Buses to/from Nakhon Ratchasima (Khorat)

Buses are air-con unless otherwise noted.

City	Fare	Duration	Departures
Chiang Mai*	262B	8 hours	4.15 and 8 am, 4.15 and 8 pm
Chiang Rai*	279B	9 hours	5 and 7 pm
(ordinary)	155B	10 hours	3.45 am, 2 pm
Loei	150B	3 hours	1 and 2 am
Nakhon Phanom	190B	4.5 hours	12.30 and 11.30 pm
Nong Khai	140B	3.5 hours	11.15 am, 12.30, 2.40 and 11.15 pm
Pattaya	118B	3 hours	11.40 am, 1 and 11.30 pm, 1 am
Phitsanulok*	146B	4 hours	8 am, 8.30 pm
(ordinary)	82B	5 hours	4.30, 6 and 10 am, 3.30 pm
Rayong	142B	4 hours	11.40 am, 1 and 10.40 pm
Roi Et	100B	2.5 hours	11.40 am, 1.30, 2.30 and 11 pm
Sakon Nakhon	190B	4 hours	12.30, 1.30, 2.30 and 11.30 pm
Ubon	150B	4.5 hours	1.30 and 2.40 pm, midnight
Udon	110B	3 hours	every 15 minutes 9 am to 3 am
Yasothon	96B	3 hours	noon, 1 pm, midnight

leaves from Bus Terminal No 1; all others in list leave from Bus Terminal No 2

1.53 am – hardly the best time to look for a hotel.

Rapid trains on the Ubon line depart at 6.50 am and 6.45 pm, arriving in Khorat at 11.31 am and 11.51 pm respectively. These are much more convenient arrival times, especially the morning arrival which leaves plenty of daylight time to explore the town.

There are also ordinary diesel trains on this line at 9.10 am (3rd class only), 11.05 am (2nd and 3rd class), 11.45 am (3rd class only), 3.25 pm (3rd class only), 6.45 pm (2nd and 3rd class), 9.50 pm (2nd and 3rd class), 10.45 pm (3rd class only) and 11.25 pm (3rd class only) which all arrive in Khorat about 5½ to six hours after departure. The 1st-class fare (express train only) is 207B, 2nd class is 104B and 3rd class 50B. Add 20B for the rapid trains and 30B for the express. The train passes through some great scenery on the Khorat Plateau, including a view of the enormous white Buddha figure at Wat Theppitak on a thickly forested hillside.

Getting Around

Samlors around town cost 10 to 15B; tuk-tuks cost 20 to 30B for a short hop, 40 to 50B for longer trips.

The city also has a fairly extensive bus system. From the Khorat train station, bus No 1 heads east along Phoklang Rd; No 2 heads east along Mukkhamontri Rd and No 3 goes east along Jomsurangyat Rd. In the opposite direction, Nos 1, 2 and 3 all end up heading west on Mukkhamontri Rd towards the TAT office. The fare on each line is 3B. Comfortable, air-con versions of bus No 2 are also available for 5B.

AROUND NAKHON RATCHASIMA
Pak Thong Chai

ปักธงชัย

Thirty-two km south of Khorat, on Route 304, is Pak Thong Chai, one of Thailand's most famous silk-weaving villages. Several varieties and prices of silk are available and

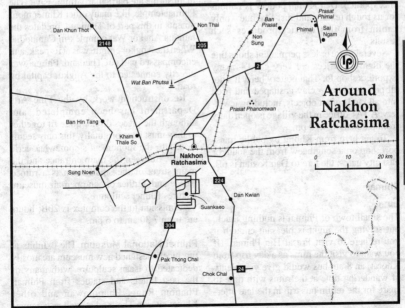

NORTH-EAST THAILAND

most weavers sell directly to the public. However, prices are not necessarily lower than in Khorat or Bangkok. Around 70 silk factories are located in the district. Pak Thong Chai Silk & Cultural Centre opened in 1991 to offer demonstrations of the silk-weaving process as well as the opportunity to purchase silks at reasonable prices.

Bus No 1303 to Pak Thong Chai leaves Bus Terminal No 1 in Khorat every 30 minutes, the last at 4 pm. The fare is 11B.

Achaan Pan and *Pak Thong Chai* hotels are both on the main road through town and have rooms from 60B.

Dan Kwian

ด่านเกวียน

Travellers interested in Thai ceramics might pay a visit to Dan Kwian, a village 15 km south-east of Khorat. This village has been producing pottery for hundreds of years; originally it was a bullock-cart stop for traders on their way to markets in old Khorat (Dan Kwian means 'bullock cart checkpoint'). Dan Kwian pottery is famous for its rough texture and rust-like hue – only kaolin from this district produces such results.

Several more or less permanent shops line the highway. Prices are very good – many exporters shop for Thai pottery here. It's not all pottery either – clay is shaped and fired into all kinds of art objects, including jewellery. A TAT office in the village is open daily from 8.30 am to 4.30 pm.

To get here from Khorat by public transport, hop on a songthaew from the south or east city gates; the fare to Dan Kwian is 6B.

Phimai

พิมาย

The small town of Phimai is nothing much, but staying the night is pleasant enough if you're here to visit Prasat Hin Phimai. (If you want to visit the ruins as a day trip from Khorat, an 8 am bus would give you plenty of wandering time at the ruins with time to spare for the return bus trip in the late afternoon.)

Outside the town entrance, a couple of km down Route 206, is Thailand's largest banyan tree, a mega-florum spread over an island in a large pond (actually a state irrigation reservoir). The locals call it **Sai Ngam**, meaning 'beautiful banyan'; you can walk through the banyan branches via wooden walkways built over the pond. Food vendors and astrologers offer their services to picnickers in the vicinity.

Prasat Hin Phimai National Historical Park This Angkor-period Khmer shrine, 60 km north-east of Khorat, makes Phimai worth a visit. Originally started by Khmer King Jayavarman V in the late 10th century and finished by King Suriyavarman I (1002-49) in the early 11th century, this Hindu-Mahayana Buddhist temple projects a majesty that transcends its size. The 28-metre-tall main shrine, of cruciform design, is made of white sandstone, while the adjunct shrines are of pink sandstone and laterite. The lintel sculpture over the doorways to the main shrine are particularly impressive. The Phimai temple, like many other Khmer monuments in this part of Thailand, predates the famous Angkor Wat complex in Cambodia. When the Angkor empire was at its peak, and encompassed parts of Thailand, Phimai was directly connected to the Angkor capital by road.

Reconstruction work by the Fine Arts Department has been completed, and although the pieces do not quite fit together as they must have originally, this only seems to add to the monument's somewhat eerie quality. Between the main entrance and the main street of the small town is a ruined palace and, farther on, an open-air museum features Khmer sculpture.

Admission to the complex is 20B; hours are from 7.30 am to 6 pm.

Phimai National Museum The exhibits at this nicely designed new museum are mostly dedicated to Isaan sculpture, with many of the best lintels and statues from Phimai, Phanom Rung, Phanomwan and other Khmer sites in Thailand as well as ceramics from nearby Ban Prasat. The museum's most prized possession, a stone sculpture of Angkor King Jayavarman VII, comes from Prasat Hin Phimai – it looks very much like a sitting Buddha. An open-air sculpture garden next to the main hall displays ornate boundary stones and other Khmer figures from Phimai. A small bookshop is attached to the museum.

Opening hours are Wednesday to Sunday from 9 am to 4 pm; admission is 20B.

Festivals Since 1991 the town has hosted a festival during the first week of November to celebrate Prasat Hin Phimai history. Events vary from year to year but typically include a sound-and-light show at the ruins, classical dance-drama performances, historical and cultural exhibits and a lamp-lit procession between temples.

Places to Stay Two guesthouses in Phimai are on opposite sides of an alley off the main street leading to the ruins. *Old Phimai Guest House* (☎ 471725) has dorm beds for 60B, plus singles/doubles/triples for 80/100/140B

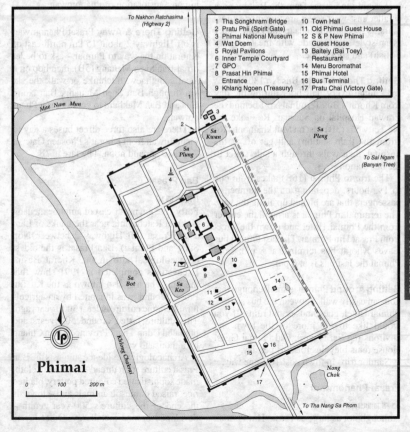

To Nakhon Ratchasima
(Highway 2)

1 Tha Songkhram Bridge	10 Town Hall
2 Pratu Phii (Spirit Gate)	11 Old Phimai Guest House
3 Phimai National Museum	12 S & P New Phimai
4 Wat Doem	Guest House
5 Royal Pavilions	13 Baiteiy (Bai Toey)
6 Inner Temple Courtyard	Restaurant
7 GPO	14 Meru Boromathat
8 Prasat Hin Phimai	15 Phimai Hotel
Entrance	16 Bus Terminal
9 Khlang Ngoen (Treasury)	17 Pratu Chai (Victory Gate)

Mae Nam Mun

Sa Kwan

Sa Plung

Sa Pleng

To Sai Ngam
(Banyan Tree)

Sa Bot

Sa Keo

Nong Chok

Phimai

0   100   200 m

To Tha Nang Sa Phom

with shared bath in a large house. Opposite Old Phimai Guest House is the similar *S&P New Phimai Guest House*.

The town's one hotel, *Phimai Hotel*, is around the corner from the bus terminal and has clean, comfortable rooms from 100 to 120B without bath, 160 to 220B with a bath, and from 350 to 400B with air-con.

Places to Eat Good Thai and Chinese food is available at the *Baiteiy (Bai Toey)* restaurant near the hotel and guesthouses. Daily lunch specials are just 20 to 25B; there are also more expensive à-la-carte items, several vegetarian dishes and ice cream.

Around the corner from the Baiteiy on a smaller east-west street are two modest restaurants specialising in lâap and kâwy (spicy Isaan-style salads made with meat, poultry or fish) and sticky rice.

Getting There & Away Bus No 1305 leaves for Phimai every half hour during the day from Khorat's Bus Terminal No 1 behind the Erawan Hospital on Suranari Rd. Take the No 2 city bus (3B) east on Mukkhamontri Rd (from the train station) and get off at the hospital, then walk through a side street to the bus station.

The trip to Phimai (16B) takes from one to 1½ hours, depending on the number of passengers that are picked up along the way. The terminal in Phimai is around the corner from the Phimai Hotel and down the street from Prasat Hin Phimai. The last Phimai bus leaves Khorat bus terminal at 8 pm; from Phimai the last bus is at 6 pm.

Getting Around Phimai is small enough that you can easily walk between the bus station, Phimai Hotel, guesthouses and ruins. If you would like to see more of the town and environs (eg Sai Ngam), Old Phimai Guest House rents bicycles for 30B per day.

Samlor trips in town cost 10B one way.

Prasat Phanomwan

ปราสาทพนมวัน

Although not as large as Prasat Hin Phimai, the 11th-century ruins at Prasat Phanomwan are nonetheless impressive. Though basically unrestored, the sanctuary is on the grounds of a temple (Wat Phanomwan) that is still used for worship and has resident monks. Inside the sanctuary, surrounded by a moat that fills only in the rainy season, are a number of Buddha images plus a couple of Shivalingams and a Nandi (Shiva's bull-mount), which indicate that the Khmers must have originally built Phanomwan as a Hindu temple. Fifty metres south-west of the main sanctuary is a building that houses other sculpture and artefacts.

A French team has recently begun working on a restoration of Phanomwan.

Getting There & Away Prasat Phanomwan is off Highway 2 about 15 km north-east of Khorat on the way to Phimai – ask to be let off at Ban Saen Meuang (5B), then hop on a local songthaew, hitchhike or walk the six km through Ban Saen Meuang, Ban Nong Bua and Ban Makham to get to Prasat Phanomwan.

There are also three direct buses a day to Phanomwan from Khorat's Phosaen Gate, at 7 am, 10 am and noon. The fare is 7B.

Ban Prasat

บ้านปราสาท

Forty-five km north-east of amphoe meuang Nakhon Ratchasima near the banks of Lam Than Prasat (off Highway 2 between Non Sung and Phimai), Ban Prasat is the oldest archaeological site in the Khorat Basin. Excavations completed in 1991 show that the site, which is also known as the Ku Tan Prasat Mound, was inhabited by an agricultural-ceramic culture at least 3000 years ago. This culture lasted around 500 years and predated Udon Thani Province's Ban Chiang by a thousand years.

Archaeological evidence suggests the Ban Prasat culture spun thread for weaving cloth, made sophisticated coloured pottery, planted rice, raised domestic animals and – towards the end of the culture's 500-year zenith – developed bronze metallurgy. Other layers uncovered indicate the site was later taken over by a pre-Dvaravati Mon city, followed by a 10th-century settlement whose main legacy is a small brick sanctuary known locally as **Ku Than Prasat**. This structure shows both Dvaravati and Khmer characteristics and may have been a cultural transition point between Mon kingdoms to the west and Khmer principalities to the east.

Several preserved excavation pits are on display; the visitors' centre houses pottery and skeletons found in the pits. The visitors' centre is open Wednesday to Sunday from 8.30 am to 4 pm.

KHAO YAI NATIONAL PARK

อุทยานแห่งชาติเขาใหญ่

Established in 1961, this is Thailand's oldest national park; it covers 2172 sq km and includes one of the largest intact monsoon forests in mainland Asia. Considered by many park experts to be among the world's best national parks, Khao Yai was recently designated an ASEAN National Heritage Site and has been nominated for similar international status by the UN. The terrain covers five vegetation zones: evergreen rainforest (100 to 400 metres), semi-evergreen rainforest (400 to 900 metres), mixed deciduous forest (northern slopes at 400 to 600 metres), and hill evergreen forest (over 1000 metres), plus savanna and secondary-growth forest in areas where agriculture and logging occurred before the area was protected.

Some 200 to 300 wild elephants reside within park boundaries; other recorded mammals include sambar deer, barking deer, gaur, wild pig, Malayan sun bear, Asiatic black bear, tiger, leopard, serow, and various gibbons and macaques. In general these animals are most easily spotted during the rainy season from June to October. Khao Yai also has Thailand's largest population of hornbills, including the great hornbill (*nók kòk* or *nók kaahang* in Thai), king of the bird kingdom, as well as wreathed hornbill (*nók ngaa cháang*, literally 'elephant-tusk bird'), Indian pied hornbill (*nók khàek*), and rhinoceros hornbill (*nók râet*). Hornbills breed from January to May, the best time to see them. They also feed on figs, so ficus trees are good places to find them. Caves in the park are home to rare wrinkle-lipped bats and Himalayan ribbed bats.

The park has over 50 km of hiking trails, many of them formed by wildlife movement. Elevations range from 100 to 1400 metres where the western edge of Cambodia's Dongrek mountain range meets the southern edge of the Khorat Plateau. You can get a rather inaccurate trail map from the park headquarters. It's easy to get lost on the longer trails so it's advisable to hire a guide. The charge will be 100B per day no matter how many people go, and the guide is liable to ask for a tip. If you do plan to go walking, it is a good idea to take boots as leeches can be a problem – although apparently mosquito repellent does help to keep leeches away.

In nearby Pak Chong you can also arrange a 1½-day tour from the Jungle Guest House. The tour begins with a half-day jaunt to a bat cave outside park boundaries, followed by an all-day trip through the park, including evening wildlife-spotting. The tour costs 650B per person. Recent evaluations of this tour have been very mixed – some reckon it's OK while others say the guide service has become rather perfunctory. Several other

would-be guides wait at the bus terminals to snare new arrivals.

Places to Stay

In years past, the TAT's *Khao Yai Hotel* offered bungalow, motel and dormitory accommodation at the park, but all permanent visitor accommodation was removed at the end of 1992. Forestry Department bungalows were also slated for removal, but overnight camping is still allowed in camping areas where you can pitch a tent for 5B per person per night. There are also plat-

forms in the park where rangers will allow you to sleep for 10B per night.

In nearby Pak Chong, the *Jungle Guest House* (☎ 312877, 311989), off Soi 3 at 752/11 Kongwaksin Rd, offers basic rooms with mattress on the floor for 70B per night including a substantial breakfast. The guesthouse is a 10 to 15-minute walk from the bus terminals on Friendship Highway; turn right from the Khorat terminal (or left from the Bangkok terminal), then left at the traffic light, left again at Soi 3 and then follow the signs about 200 metres to the guesthouse.

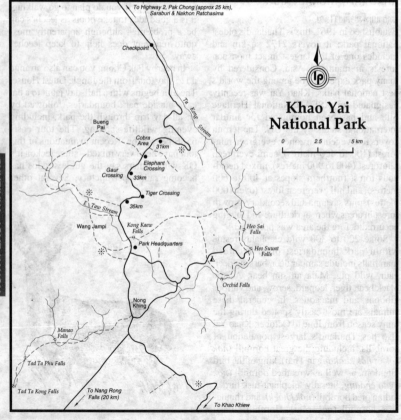

To Highway 2, Pak Chong (approx 25 km), Saraburi & Nakhon Ratchasima

Checkpoint

Ta Kong Stream

Khao Yai National Park

0   2.5   5 km

Bueng Pai

Cobra Area

31km

Elephant Crossing

Gaur Crossing

33km

Tiger Crossing

35km

E Taw Stream

Kong Kaew Falls

Wang Jampi

Park Headquarters

Heo Sai Falls

Heo Suwat Falls

Orchid Falls

Nong Khing

Manao Falls

Tad Ta Phu Falls

Tad Ta Kong Falls

To Nang Rong Falls (20 km)

To Khao Khiew

NORTH-EAST THAILAND

Getting There & Away

From Bangkok take a bus (every 15 minutes from 5 am to 10 pm; 35B ordinary, 65B air-con) from the northern bus station to Pak Chong, from where you can hitch or take a songthaew to the park gates. The fare is 10B from opposite the air-con bus terminal in Pak Chong. You may also be able to take a direct bus from Bangkok at certain times of year – enquire at the northern bus station.

From Khorat take a Bangkok-bound bus and simply get off in Pak Chong (20B ordinary, 47B air-con).

You can also easily get to Pak Chong from Ayuthaya by ordinary train for 23B 3rd class, 47B 2nd class; the trip takes around three hours. From Bangkok the train costs 36B 3rd class, 73B 2nd class, not including the surcharge (20B) for rapid trains. The ordinary train takes around four hours from Bangkok; the rapid is half an hour shorter.

Hitchhiking in the park is usually easy.

Buriram Province

Buriram is a large province (18th-largest out of 76) with a small capital and a long history. During the Angkor period this area was an important part of the Khmer empire. The restored ruins at Prasat Hin Khao Phanom Rung are the most impressive of all Angkor monuments in Thailand; other lesser known ruins in the province include Prasat Meuang Tham, Ku Rasi, Prasat Ban Khok Ngiu, Prasat Nong Hong, Prasat Ban Thai Charoen, Prasat Nong Kong, Prang Ku Samathom, Prang Ku Khao Plaibat, Prang Ku Suwan Taeng, Prang Ku Khao Kadong and many others. If one includes all ancient city sites (including Dvaravati and pre-Dvaravati), the province contains 143, second in number only to Nakhon Ratchasima Province.

Generally speaking, prasat (from the Sanskrit architectural term *prasada*) refers to large temple sanctuaries with a cruciform floor plan, while ku and prang ku are smaller Khmer-style chedis or stupas. However, many Thais use these terms interchangeably. Prasat is sometimes translated in Thai tourist literature as 'castle' or 'palace', but these Khmer monuments were never used as royal residences.

Most of the ruins in Buriram are little more than piles of bricks by the side of a road or out in a field. As the Fine Arts Department and/or the local community continue restoration in the province, more of the Khmer monuments mentioned here may become worth seeing.

Contemporary Buriram Province is famous among Thais for the 320-hectare **Dong Yai Forest** protected by monk Prajak Kuttajitto, who 'ordained' trees with monastic robes and sacred thread so people wouldn't cut them. In 1991 he and his followers were finally run out of the forest by the Thai military, but not without the sustained protests of thousands of sympathetic Thai citizens.

PRASAT HIN KHAO PHANOM RUNG HISTORICAL PARK

ประสาทหินเขาพนมรุ้ง

Phanom Rung is Khmer for 'big hill', but the Thais have added their own word for hill (*khão*) to the name as well as the word for stone (*hĭn*) to describe the prasat.

Orientation & Information

Prasat Phanom Rung is on an extinct volcanic cone, 383 metres above sea level, that dominates the flat countryside for some distance in all directions. To the south-east you can clearly see Cambodia's Dongrek Mountains, and it's in this direction that the capital of the Angkor empire once lay. The prasat's temple complex is the largest and best restored of all the Khmer monuments in Thailand (it took 17 years to complete the restoration) and although it's not the easiest place to reach, it's well worth the effort.

The temple was constructed between the 10th and 13th centuries with the bulk of the work being done during the reign of King Suriyavarman II (1113 to 1150 AD), which by all accounts was the apex of Angkor

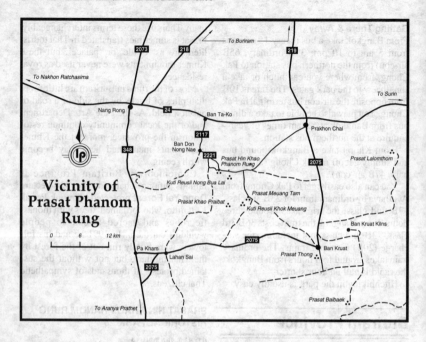

Map: Vicinity of Prasat Phanom Rung

To Buriram
To Nakhon Ratchasima
To Surin
Nang Rong
Ban Ta-Ko
Prakhon Chai
Ban Don Nong Nae
Prasat Hin Khao Phanom Rung
Prasat Lalomthom
Kuti Reusii Nong Bua Lai
Prasat Meuang Tam
Prasat Khao Praibat
Kuti Reusii Khok Meuang
Ban Kruat Kilns

Vicinity of Prasat Phanom Rung

0   6   12 km

Pa Kham
Lahan Sai
Prasat Thong
Ban Kruat
Prasat Baibaek
To Aranya Prathet

architecture. The complex faces east, towards the original Angkor capital. Of the three other great Khmer monuments of South-East Asia, Angkor Wat faces west, Prasat Khao Wihaan faces north and Prasat Hin Phimai faces south-east. Nobody knows for sure whether these orientations have any special significance, especially as most smaller Khmer monuments in Thailand face east (towards the dawn – typical of Hindu temple orientation).

A small museum on the grounds contains some sculpture from the complex and photographs of the 17-year restoration process.

There is a 20B admission fee to the Phanom Rung Historical Park during daylight hours. *The Sanctuary Phanomrung*, by Dr Sorajet Woragamvijya, is an informative booklet put out by the Lower North-East Study Association (LNESA). It may be sold near the entrance to the complex for 20B (vendors may ask 50B, but the LNESA says visitors shouldn't pay more than 20B).

Several English-speaking guides also offer their services at the complex – fee negotiable.

Downhill a bit from the main sanctuary, a number of new structures have been built to house collections of art and artefacts found on the site. When finished, the buildings will become a part of a museum complex that may have a separate admission fee – for now they're free.

The best time to visit Phanom Rung is before 10 am in the morning – this beats most bus tours and it's also cooler then and the light is better for photography.

Design
One of the most remarkable design aspects of Phanom Rung is the promenade leading to the main gate. This is the best surviving example in Thailand. It begins on a slope 400 metres east of the main tower, with three earthen terraces. Next comes a cruciform base for what may have been a wooden

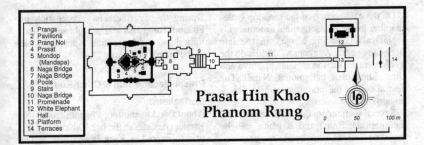

KEY
1 Prangs
2 Pavilions
3 Prang Noi
4 Prasat
5 Mondop (Mandapa)
6 Naga Bridge
7 Naga Bridge
8 Pools
9 Stairs
10 Naga Bridge
11 Promenade
12 White Elephant Hall
13 Platform
14 Terraces

Prasat Hin Khao Phanom Rung

0   50   100 m

pavilion. To the right of this is a stone hall known locally as the White Elephant Hall. On the north side of this hall are two pools that were probably once used for ritual ablutions before entering the temple complex. Flower garlands to be used as offerings in the temple may also have been handed out here.

After you step down from the pavilion area, you'll come to a 160-metre avenue paved with laterite and sandstone blocks and flanked by sandstone pillars with lotus-bud tops, said to be early Angkor style (1100 to 1180 AD). The avenue ends at the first and largest of three naga bridges.

These naga bridges are the only three which have survived in Thailand. The first is flanked by 16 five-headed nagas (cobra deities) in the classic Angkor style – in fact these figures are identical to those found at Angkor Wat. After passing this bridge and climbing the stairway you come to the magnificent east gallery leading into the main sanctuary. The central prasat has a gallery on each of four sides and the entrance to each gallery is itself a smaller version of the main tower. The galleries have curvilinear roofs and false balustraded windows. Once inside the temple walls, have a look at each of the galleries and the *gopura* entrances, paying particular attention to the lintels over the porticoes. The craftwork at Phanom Rung represents the pinnacle of Khmer artistic achievement, on a par with the reliefs at Angkor Wat in Cambodia.

Sculpture

The Phanom Rung complex was originally built as a Hindu monument and exhibits iconography related to the worship of Vishnu and Shiva. Excellent sculptures of both Vaishnava and Shaiva deities can be seen in the lintels or pediments over the doorways to the central monuments and in various other key points on the sanctuary exterior.

Khmer sculpture, Prasat Phanom Rung

NORTH-EAST THAILAND

On the east portico of the mondop (ante-chamber to the prasat or main sanctuary) is a Nataraja (Dancing Shiva), in the late Baphuan or early Angkor style, while on the south entrance are the remains of Shiva and Uma riding their bull mount, Nandi. The central cell of the prasat contains a Shiva-lingam or phallus image.

Several sculpted images of Vishnu and his incarnations, Rama and Krishna, can be found on various other lintels and cornices. Probably the most beautiful is the **Phra Narai Lintel**, a relief depicting Lord Nara-yana, a reclining Vishnu in the midst of the Hindu creation myth. Growing from his navel is a lotus that branches into several blossoms, on one of which sits the creator god Brahma. On either side of Vishnu are heads of Kala, the god of Time and Death. He is asleep on the milky sea of eternity, here represented by a naga snake. This lintel sits above the eastern gate (the main entrance) beneath the Shiva Nataraja relief.

Phanom Rung Festival

During the week of the nationwide Songkran Festival in April, the local people have their own special celebration that commemorates the restoration of Prasat Phanom Rung.

During the day there is a procession up Phanom Rung Hill and at night sound-and-light shows and dance-dramas are performed in the temple complex.

Prasat Meuang Tam & Other Ruins
ประสาทเมืองต่ำ

About five km south of Phanom Rung, this Khmer site dates to the late 10th century and was sponsored by King Jayavarman V. The laterite wall is still in fair condition, but much of the prasat has tumbled down. Restoration is moving steadily along but unless you're attempting an exhaustive tour of Khmer ruins in Thailand, you could skip this one. On the other hand, if you have the time, it gives a good idea of what Prasat Phanom Rung looked like before it was restored. Admission is 20B.

West of Meuang Tam and south of Phanom Rung are the harder-to-find Khmer ruins of **Kuti Reusii Nong Bua Lai**, **Kuti Reusii Khok Meuang** and **Prasat Khao Praibat**. East of these are **Prasat Lalom-thom**, **Prasat Thong** and **Prasat Baibaek**. I haven't explored any of these but they're spotted on the Phanom Rung area map in case anyone out there wants to check them out. To find these it would be best to hire a

---

Phra Narai Lintel

An interesting story goes with the Phra Narai ('Lord Narayana') lintel. In the 1960s local residents noticed the lintel was missing from the sanctuary and an investigation determined that it must have disappeared between 1961 and 1965. A mysterious helicopter was reportedly seen in the vicinity during this period. The Thais later discovered the lintel on display at the Art Institute of Chicago; the lintel had been donated by a James Alsdorf.

The Thai government as well as several private foundations tried unsuccessfully for many years to get the artwork returned to its rightful place. As the complex was reaching the final stages of restoration in preparation for the official opening in May 1988, a public outcry in Thailand demanded the return of the missing lintel. In the USA, Thai residents and American sympathisers demonstrated in front of the Chicago museum. The socially conscious Thai pop group Carabao recorded an album entitled *Thap Lang (Lintel)* that featured an album cover with a picture of the Statue of Liberty cradling the Phra Narai lintel in her left arm! The chorus of the title song went: 'Take back Michael Jackson – Give us back Phra Narai'.

In December 1988 the Alsdorf Foundation returned the Phra Narai lintel to Thailand in exchange for US$250,000 (paid by private sources in the USA) and an arrangement whereby Thailand's Fine Arts Department would make temporary loans of various Thai art objects to the Art Institute of Chicago on a continuing basis. Rumour in Thailand has it that of the seven Thais involved in the original theft and sale of the lintel, only one is still alive. The other six are supposed to have met unnatural deaths. ■

local guide from the Phanom Rung complex or in the village of Prasat Meuang Tam.

From Prasat Meuang Tam you could continue south-east via Ban Kruat and Ban Ta Miang (along routes 2075 and 2121) to **Prasat Ta Meuan**, a secluded Khmer ruins complex on the Thai-Cambodian border (see the Surin section later in this chapter for details). From Ta Miang you could then proceed north to amphoe meuang Surin or continue east along the border to Si Saket and Ubon provinces.

Getting There & Away

Prasat Phanom Rung can be approached from Khorat, Buriram or Surin. From Khorat, take a Surin-bound bus and get out at Ban Ta-Ko, which is a few km past Nang Rong (the turn-off north to Buriram). The fare should be about 20B; Ban Ta-Ko is well marked as the turn-off for Prasat Phanom Rung. Once in Ban Ta-Ko you have several options. At the Ta-Ko intersection you can wait for a songthaew that's going as far as the foot of Khao Phanom Rung (12 km, 15B) or one that's on the way south to Lahan Sai. If you take a Lahan Sai truck, get off at the Ban Don Nong Nae intersection (you'll see signs pointing the way to Phanom Rung to the east). From Ta-Ko to Don Nong Nae will cost 4B. From Don Nong Nae, get another songthaew to the foot of the hill for 10B or charter a pick-up for 40B one way.

If you don't have the patience to wait for a songthaew, take a motorcycle taxi from Ta-Ko to Don Nong Nae (30B) or all the way to Phanom Rung for between 60 and 70B each way. A return trip will cost 120 to 150B; for an extra 50B the drivers will add Meuang Tam. These rates include waiting for you while you tour the ruins.

There are also a couple of morning songthaews from Buriram Market that go directly to Ban Don Nong Nae; these are met by songthaews that go straight to the ruins.

From Surin, take a Khorat-bound bus and get off at the same place on Highway 24, Ban Ta-Ko, then follow the directions as from Khorat.

BURIRAM

อ.เมืองบุรีรัมย์

Buriram is a small provincial capital (population 29,500) where there is not a great deal to do. Nevertheless the town is a good base from which to visit Khmer temple ruins around the province, such as Prasat Phanom Rung.

Places to Stay

Several inexpensive hotels are within walking distance of the Buriram train station. *Chai Jaroen Hotel* (☎ (044) 601559) at 114-6 Niwat Rd in front of the station, has fairly comfortable rooms from 80B with fan and bath.

Cheaper but definitely a step or three down in quality is the *Nivas (Niwat) Hotel*, on a soi just off Niwat Rd. Its barely adequate singles/doubles are 70B (60B a double for less than three hours) – it's not exactly a family place.

The *Grand Hotel* (☎ (044) 611089), up Niwat Rd in the other direction, has fair rooms with fan and bath starting at 120B or with air-con for 250B.

Farther from the train station is the *Prachasamakhi Hotel*, a Chinese hotel with a restaurant downstairs on Sunthonthep Rd. Adequate rooms cost 60/80B with/without bath.

At 38/1 Romburi Rd is the fairly nice *Thai Hotel* (☎ (044) 611112), where clean rooms start at 100B with fan and bath and go as high as 500B for a deluxe room.

The *Buriram Hotel* (☎ (044) 611740) near the town entrance from Route 218 is a renovated, much improved version of the old Krung Rome. Plain, clean air-con rooms go for 400B up.

Buriram's first tourist-class hotel, the 229-room *Buriram Plaza*, is on the southern outskirts of town on the way to Surin. Rooms with all the amenities start at 875B.

You can also stay closer to Prasat Phanom Rung by spending the night at the nondescript hotel in Nang Rong. It's cheap, friendly and noisy, and there's an attached restaurant.

Places to Eat

In front of the train station is a small night market with good, inexpensive food. This area also has a few restaurants that are open during the day for breakfast and lunch. The one on the corner of the clock tower opens early in the morning and sells coffee, tea and paa-thông-kŏ (light Chinese pastries).

At the Samatakan and Thani Rds intersection there is a larger night market that has mostly Chinese as well as a few Isaan vendors.

The *Maitrichit Restaurant* on Sunthonthep Rd near the Prachasamakhi Hotel has a large selection of Thai and Chinese standards which are served from morning until night. Also good is the *Porn Phen (Phawn Phen)* near the Thai Hotel on Romburi Rd.

Just after you turn left (east) from Ban Don Nong Nae on the way to Phanom Rung via Route 2221 there is a nice little family-owned place called *Baan Nit (Nit's House)* where you can get good home-cooked local food. Nit only has a few tables, but out in this area there's not a lot of choice.

Getting There & Away

Air Bangkok Airways has tentative plans to

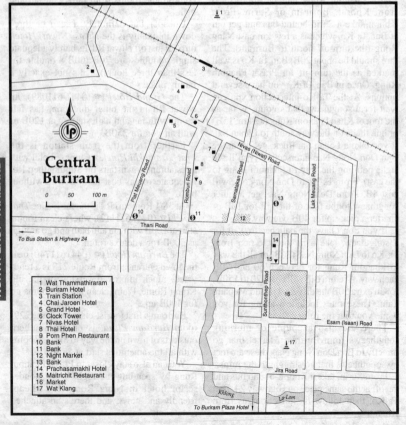

Central Buriram

0   50   100 m

To Bus Station & Highway 24

1 Wat Thammathiraram
2 Buriram Hotel
3 Train Station
4 Chai Jaroen Hotel
5 Grand Hotel
6 Clock Tower
7 Nivas Hotel
8 Thai Hotel
9 Porn Phen Restaurant
10 Bank
11 Bank
12 Night Market
13 Bank
14 Prachasamakhi Hotel
15 Maitrichit Restaurant
16 Market
17 Wat Klang

Pilat Meuang Road
Romburi Road
Samatakan Road
Nivas (Niwat) Road
Lak Meuang Road
Thani Road
Sunthonthep Road
Esarn (Isaan) Road
Jira Road
Khlong La-Lom

To Buriram Plaza Hotel

build an airport near Buriram in 1997, but for now the nearest airport is in Khorat.

Bus Ordinary buses from Khorat to Buriram leave about every 20 minutes between 4.30 am and 7.30 pm. The trip takes about 2½ hours and costs 38B. From Surin ordinary buses head for Buriram at similar frequency for 30B; this trip takes about an hour.

Train Buriram is on the Bangkok-Ubon train line. Fares are 67B 3rd class, 140B 2nd class and 286B 1st class, not including supplementary charges for rapid (20B) or express (30B) service. The fastest 3rd class trains to Buriram from Bangkok are the 11.05 am (No 931) and 9.50 pm (No 933) diesel railcars, which each take around five hours to reach Buriram. Rapid and express trains arrive only a half-hour faster than these – see the Nakhon Ratchasima Getting There & Away section for departure times from Bangkok.

From Khorat there are six daytime trains to Buriram between 11.30 am and 9.51 pm; the 3rd-class fare is 22B, 2nd class 36B for a journey of around one hour 45 minutes. Trains from Surin take only 50 minutes and cost just 6B 3rd class.

Chaiyaphum Province

Bounded by Phetchabun, Lopburi, Nakhon Ratchasima and Khon Kaen provinces, right in the centre of Thailand, Chaiyaphum might as well be in the middle of nowhere considering its low tourist profile. The least visited of any province in the country, it's so remote from national attention that even many Thai citizens can't tell you exactly where it is – or even whether it's in the north or the northeast.

The several Khmer shrine ruins in the province – none of them major sites – indicate that the territory was an Angkor and later Lopburi satellite during the 10th and 11th centuries.

CHAIYAPHUM

During the late 1700s, a Lao court official brought 200 Lao from Vientiane to settle this area, which had been abandoned by the Khmers 500 years earlier. The community paid tribute to Vientiane but were also careful to cultivate relations with Bangkok and Champasak. When Vientiane's Prince Anou declared war on Siam in the early 1800s, the Lao ruler of Chaiyaphum, Jao Phraya Lae, wisely switched allegiance to Bangkok – knowing full well that Anou's armies didn't stand a chance against the more powerful Siamese. Although Jao Phraya Lae lost his life in battle in 1806, the Siamese sacked Vientiane in 1828 and ruled most of western Laos until the coming of the French near the turn of the century. Today a statue of Jao Phraya Lae (renamed Phraya Phakdi Chumphon by the Thais) stands in a prominent spot in downtown Chaiyaphum.

Chaiyaphum's 25,600 residents celebrate a week-long festival in Jao Phraya Lae's honour each year in mid-January. Activities focus on his statue and on a shrine erected on the spot where he was killed by Vientiane troops – at the base of a tamarind tree about three km west of town off the road to Ban Khwao (Route 225).

The town itself is a typical, medium-grade Thai trade centre with little to hold most visitors for more than a day or so. The districts around Chaiyaphum (especially Kut

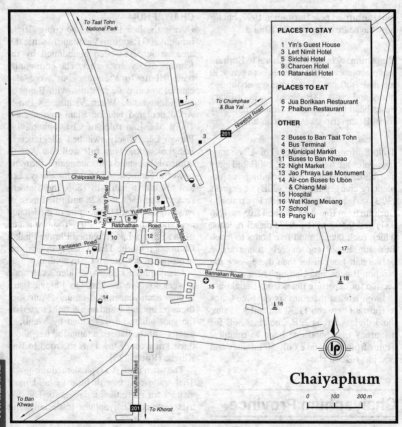

PLACES TO STAY
1 Yin's Guest House
3 Lert Nimit Hotel
5 Sirichai Hotel
9 Charoen Hotel
10 Ratanasiri Hotel

PLACES TO EAT
6 Jua Borikaan Restaurant
7 Phaibun Restaurant

OTHER
2 Buses to Ban Taat Tohn
4 Bus Terminal
8 Municipal Market
11 Buses to Ban Khwao
12 Night Market
13 Jao Phraya Lae Monument
14 Air-con Buses to Ubon
     & Chiang Mai
15 Hospital
16 Wat Klang Meuang
17 School
18 Prang Ku

Chaiyaphum

0   100   200 m

Lalom to the south) are known for trained elephants and elephant trainers, and it's not uncommon to see an elephant or two walking down the capital streets. Since work demand for elephants in Thailand is steadily declining due to the timber ban, many Chaiyaphum elephants are being sold to 'elephant camps' for tourists in the north or to circuses in Europe. The city started an annual elephant roundup a few years back that gained in popularity until the provincial governor had a nightmare in which elephants were injuring people. The roundup has since been cancelled.

The main reason people visit Chaiyaphum nowadays is to tour **Ban Khwao** (15 km west) and other nearby silk villages. Silk can also be purchased at Chaiyaphum shops or in the municipal market in the centre of town. Yin's Guest House (see Places to Stay below) can arrange inexpensive silk village tours. You can also catch a bus to Ban Khwao from the south side of Tantawan Rd just west of Non Muang Rd. If you've never observed the silk process – from the cultivation of mulberry trees and propagation of silkworms to the dyeing and weaving of silk thread – you're in for an interesting day.

Prang Ku
ปรางค์กู่

This hollow Khmer prang was constructed during the reign of the final Angkor king, Jayavarman VII (1121-1220 AD) as a 'healing station' on the Angkor temple route between the Angkor capital in Cambodia and Prasat Singh in Kanchanaburi Province. Chaiyaphum residents consider this a very holy spot; many make daily offerings of flowers, candles and incense. The Buddha figure inside the ku purportedly hails from the Dvāravati period (6th to 10th centuries). Also on the small grounds are a Shivalingam pedestal and a venerable old tamarind tree.

Prang Ku is only about a km east of the Chaiyaphum Provincial Hall.

Taat Tohn National Park
วนอุทยานแห่งชาติตาดโตน

Eighteen km north-west of Chaiyaphum via Route 2051, this seldom-visited, 218-sq-km park at the edge of the Laen Da mountain range is centred around the scenic waterfalls of **Taat Tohn, Taat Klang** and **Phaa Phiang**. Taat Tohn Falls are the largest, reaching 50 metres wide during the May to October monsoon. Most of the vegetation in the park is associated with dry dipterocarp forest. Little wildlife research has been carried out in the park, but since it lies halfway between Nam Nao National Park on the Chaiyaphum-Phetchabun border and Khao Yai National Park on the Nakhon Nayok-Nakhon Ratchasima-Prachinburi border, it's bound to harbour an interesting variety of resident and migrating species.

Park bungalows are available at the usual 400 to 800B rates. It's best to have your own wheels to find the park since there's no regular public transport from Chaiyaphum. Alternatively you can get a songthaew from Chaiyaphum as far as Ban Taat Tohn (around 7B), then hire a pick-up truck on to the park for no more than 50B.

Places to Stay & Eat
Yin's Guest House, about 300 metres from the main bus terminal, is a complex of wooden houses run by a Thai-Norwegian couple who charge 60/80B a single/double. Tours of nearby silk villages can be arranged for 50B per person.

The *Ratanasiri Hotel* on the corner of Non Muang and Ratchathan Rds is an efficiently run place with one floor of rooms with fan for 150B and two floors with air-con and hot water for 280B. All rooms come with TV.

The *Sirichai Hotel* (☎ (044) 811461) on the opposite side of Non Muang Rd farther north has slightly more up-market rooms with air-con for 350B, plus a few rooms with fan in the 150 to 200B range. Less expensive is the standard Thai-Chinese *Phaibun Hotel* at 227/41-4 Yutitham Rd, where basic rooms with fan start at 80B. Farther east off Yutitham Rd at No 196/7 Soi 1, the *Charoën Hotel* (☎ (044) 811184) has rooms for 80 to 200B.

Top end for Chaiyaphum is the *Lert Nimit Hotel* (☎ (044) 811522) on Niwetrat Rd east of the bus terminal on the road to Chumphae (Route 201). Rooms with fan are available for 150 to 200B, or there are nicer air-con bungalows for 400 to 500B.

Phaibun, a large indoor-outdoor restaurant opposite Ratanasiri Hotel on Ratchathan Rd, does the usual Thai and Chinese standards; *Jua Borikaan* on the other corner opposite the hotel is quite similar.

If you're into kài yâang, look no further than the cluster of vendors in front of the hospital on Bannakan Rd – open only during the day.

Chaiyaphum has a splendid night market off Taksin Rd.

Getting There & Away
Chaiyaphum can be reached by bus from Khon Kaen, Khorat and Lom Sak, each of which is about two hours away and costs about 35B.

Buses from Bangkok's northern/north-eastern bus terminal cost 147B air-con (seven hours, nine departures daily) or 65B ordinary (eight hours, every half hour from 6.15 am to 11 pm).

NORTH-EAST THAILAND

Khon Kaen & Roi Et Provinces

Khon Kaen and Roi Et are mostly rural provinces where farming and textiles are the main occupations. At the heart of the Isaan region, these provinces are good places to explore Isaan culture – its language, food and music.

Roi Et Province is also known for the crafting of the quintessential Isaan musical instrument, the khaen, a kind of panpipe made of the *mái kuu* reed and wood. The best khaens are reputedly made in the village of Si Kaew, 15 km north-west of Roi Et. It generally takes about three days to make one khaen, depending on its size. The straight, sturdy reeds, which resemble bamboo, are cut and bound together in pairs of six, eight or nine. The sound box that fits in the middle is made of *tôn pràtuu*, a hardwood that's resistant to moisture.

KHON KAEN

อ.เมืองขอนแก่น

Khon Kaen (population 130,300) is about a 2½-hour bus trip from either Khorat or Udon Thani, and 450 km from Bangkok. It is also the gateway to the north-east if you are coming from Phitsanulok in northern Thailand.

The city is named for **Phra That Kham Kaen**, a revered chedi at Wat Chetiyaphum in the village of Ban Kham in Nam Phawng district, 32 km north-east of the amphoe meuang. Legend says that early in this millennium a *thâat* (reliquary stupa) was built over a tamarind tree stump that miraculously came to life after a contingent of monks carrying Buddha relics to Phra That Phanom (in today's Nakhon Phanom Province) camped here overnight. When it turned out there was no room at That Phanom for more relics, the monks returned to this spot and enshrined the relics in the new That Kham Kaen (Tamarind Heartwood Reliquary). A town developed nearby but was abandoned several times until 1789, when a Suwannaphum ruler founded a city at the current site, which he named Kham Kaen after the chedi. Over the years the name changed to Khon Kaen (Heartwood Log).

The fourth-largest city in Thailand, Khon Kaen is an important commercial, financial, educational and communications centre for Isaan. **Khon Kaen University**, the largest university in the north-east, covers 5000 rai (810 hectares) in the north-west part of town. The city has grown fantastically over the last five years, with lots of added neon and the heaviest automotive traffic in the north-east after Khorat; unlike Khorat the air is fairly clean. A 3.5-km-long airstrip built for American B-52s in nearby Nam Pheung may soon be converted into a maintenance centre for Boeing, McDonnell Douglas and/or Airbus craft – if this comes to pass the centre will be another major boost for the local economy.

For visitors, about the only tourist attraction is the very well curated **Khon Kaen National Museum**, which features Dvaravati objects, *sêma* (ordination marker) stones from Kalasin and Meuang Fa Daet, and bronze and ceramic artefacts from Ban Chiang. It's open Wednesday to Sunday from 9 am to noon and 1 to 5 pm. Admission is 10B.

On the banks of Khon Kaen's 603-rai (in the rainy season) **Beung Kaen Nakhon** (Kaen Nakhon Pond) is the Isaan-style **Wat That**, with elongated spires on the prasat – typical of this area. This lake and **Beung Thung Sang** in the north-east section of town are favourite venues for evening strolls.

With its Western restaurants, air-con hotels and modern banking facilities Khon Kaen makes a good spot to take a rest from small-town and village travel in the north-east. It can also be used as a base for day trips to **Chonabot** (57 km south-west), a centre for good quality mat-mii silk, and the Khmer ruins of **Prasat Peuay Noi** (66 km south-east).

Information

Tourist Office The TAT (☎ 244498; fax 244487) has a new branch office in Khon Kaen at 15/5 Prachasamoson Rd, open daily from 8.30 am to 4 pm. The English-speaking staff distribute good maps of the city and can answer queries on Khon Kaen and surrounding provinces.

Post & Telephone The main post office on the corner of Si Chan and Klang Meuang Rds is open on weekdays from 8.30 am to 4.30 pm, 9 am to noon on Saturday. There is a CAT international phone office attached; you can also make international phone calls at the CAT office on Sun Ratchakan Rd in the northern part of town.

Khon Kaen's telephone area code is ☎ 043.

Money Every major Thai bank has at least one branch in Khon Kaen, most of them clustered along the south side of Si Chan Rd west of Na Meuang Rd, and along Na Meuang Rd between Si Chan and Reun Rom Rds. Bangkok Bank on Si Chan Rd has an ATM and foreign-exchange window.

Festivals
Khon Kaen's biggest annual event is the Silk

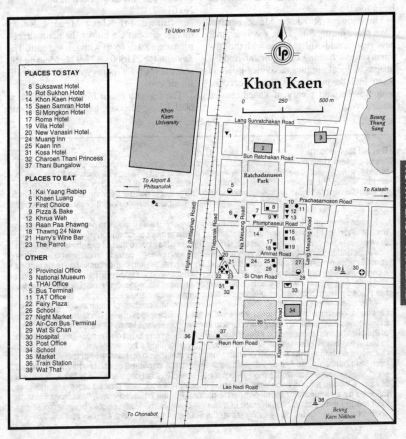

Khon Kaen

0   250   500 m

PLACES TO STAY
8 Suksawat Hotel
10 Rot Sukhon Hotel
14 Khon Kaen Hotel
15 Saen Samran Hotel
16 Si Mongkon Hotel
17 Roma Hotel
19 Villa Hotel
20 New Vanasiri Hotel
24 Muang Inn
25 Kaen Inn
31 Kosa Hotel
32 Charoen Thani Princess
37 Thani Bungalow

PLACES TO EAT
1 Kai Yaang Rabiap
6 Khaen Luang
7 First Choice
9 Pizza & Bake
12 Khrua Weh
13 Raan Paa Phawng
18 Thawng 24 Naw
21 Harry's Wine Bar
23 The Parrot

OTHER
2 Provincial Office
3 National Museum
4 THAI Office
5 Bus Terminal
11 TAT Office
22 Fairy Plaza
26 School
27 Night Market
28 Air-Con Bus Terminal
29 Hospital
30 Wat Si Chan
33 Post Office
34 School
35 Market
36 Train Station
38 Wat That

To Udon Thani
Khon Kaen University
Lang Sunratchakan Road
Sun Ratchakan Road
Ratchadanuson Park
Prachasamoson Road
To Airport & Phitsanulok
Highway 2 (Mittaphap Road)
Theparak Road
Na Meuang Road
Phimphaseut Road
Ammat Road
Si Chan Road
Lang Meuang Road
Reun Rom Road
Lao Nadi Road
To Chonabot
Beung Thung Sang
To Kalasin
Beung Kaen Nakhon

NORTH-EAST THAILAND

& Phuuk Siaw Festival, held for 10 days and nights from late November through early December. Centred at Ratchadanuson Park and in the field in front of the Sala Klang (provincial hall), the festival celebrates the planting of the mulberry tree, a necessary step in the production of silk. Another aspect of the festival is *phùuk sìaw* or 'tying friends', a reference to the *bai sĭi* ceremony in which sacred threads are tied around one's wrists for spiritual protection. The ritual also implies a renewal of the bonds of friendship and reaffirmation of local tradition. Other activities include parades, Isaan music, folk dancing and the preparation and sharing of Isaan food.

The Flowers & Khaen Music Festival takes place during Songkran, the Thai lunar new year in mid-April. Along with the customary ritual bathing of important Buddha images at local temples, activities in Khon Kaen include parades of floats bedecked with flowers and plenty of khaen-centred Isaan music.

Places to Stay – bottom end

As Khon Kaen is a large city and an important transit point, there are many hotels to choose from. *Thani Bungalow* (☎ 221470), on Reun Rom Rd, has shabby singles with shared bath for 60B, better bungalows for 150B, and rooms with air-con and hot water for 300B. It's near the train station and Hua Rot Fai Market.

The part-wooden, part-cement *Saen Samran* (a roman-script sign reads 'Sansumran') at 55/9 Klang Meuang Rd has reasonable rooms that cost 100B with fan or 220B with air-con. Just a bit further down the street is the similarly priced *Si Mongkon* at No 61-67.

Suksawat, off Klang Meuang Rd, is quieter since it's a bit off the main streets; rooms are 80 to 150B with fan and bath. The *Sawatdi* (☎ 221600), 177-9 Na Meuang Rd, starts at 150B for rooms with fan, up to 600B for air-con.

The friendly *Roma Hotel* (☎ 236276), at 50/2 Klang Meuang, has large rooms with

---

Bai Sii Ceremony

North-eastern Thais commonly participate in bai sii ceremonies on auspicious occasions such as birthdays, farewells, times of serious illness, and during certain festivals such as Khon Kaen's annual Ngaan Phuuk Siaw or 'Tying Friends Festival'. In the bai sii (sacred thread) ceremony, the 32 guardian spirits known as *khwǎn* are bound to the guest of honour by white strings tied around the wrists. Each of the 32 khwan are thought to be guardians over different organs in a person's body.

Khwan occasionally wander away from their owner, which isn't thought to be much of a problem except when that person is about to embark on a new project or on a journey away from home, or when they're very ill. Then it's best to perform the bai sii to ensure that all the khwan are present and attached to the person's body. A maw phawn or 'wish priest' – usually an elder who has spent some time as a monk – presides over the ritual. Those participating in the ritual sit on mats around a tiered vase-like centrepiece or *phakhuan* which is decorated with flowers, folded banana leaves and branches with white cotton strings hanging down; pastries, eggs, bananas, liquor and money are placed around the base as offerings to the spirits in attendance.

After a few words of greeting, the maw phawn chants in a mixture of Isaan and Pali to convey blessings on the honoured guest while all in attendance place their hands in a prayer-like, palms-together pose. For part of the chanting segment, everyone leans forward to touch the base of the phakhuan; if there are too many participants for everyone to reach the base, it's permissible to touch the elbow of someone who can reach it, thus forming a human chain.

Once the shaman has finished chanting, each person attending takes two of the white strings from the phakhuan and ties one around each wrist of the honoured guest(s) while whispering a short, well-wishing recitation. When all have performed this action, the guest is left with a stack of strings looped around each wrist and small cups of rice liquor are passed around, sometimes followed by an impromptu *ram wong* (circle dance). For the intended effect, the strings must be kept around the wrists for a minimum of three full days. Some Isaan people believe the strings should be allowed to fall off naturally rather than cut off – this can take weeks. ■

fan for 150 to 200B, plus refurbished air-con rooms for 300 to 500B.

The newish *Coco Guest House*, in a bar area behind the First Choice restaurant between Na Meuang and Klang Meuang Rds has simple, modern singles/doubles for 100/120B behind a noisy beer bar. Similar is the *PS Guest House* at 100B per room, above a beer bar but a bit quieter since it's the only one in the area. The nearby *New Vanasiri Hotel* (☎ 235816), off Si Chan Rd near Soi Yimsiri, has simple but clean rooms with fan and bath for 120 to 180B.

Places to Stay – middle
The new, four-storey *Muang Inn* (☎ 238667), at a convenient location on Na Meuang Rd, offers tidy air-con rooms with phones in the 490 to 650B range.

Phu Inn (☎ 243174), a similar mid-range spot near the market at 26 Satityutitham Rd, has 98 air-con rooms for 400 to 700B.

The *Villa* (☎ 236640, on the corner of Klang Meuang and Ammat Rds, is mostly a short-time place attached to a massage parlour/'entertainment complex', but it has air-con rooms for 300 to 500B.

Places to Stay – top end
More expensive places include the *Khon Kaen Hotel* (☎ 237711) on Phimphaseut Rd, which has air-con singles/doubles for 600/700B, and the similar *Rosesukon (Rot Sukhon) Hotel* (☎ 238576), near the Khon Kaen Hotel on Klang Meuang Rd, where singles/doubles cost 700/800B. Both hotels also have more expensive suites in the 1200 to 2000B range.

The popular *Kosa* (☎ 225014) on Si Chan Rd has rooms with all the amenities for 850/900B. The attached up-market coffee shop-massage parlour attracts a steady flow of Thai businessmen.

Until recently the top hotel in the city was the friendly 200-room *Kaen Inn* (☎ 237744; fax 239457) at 56 Klang Meuang Rd; doubles cost 800 to 1200B with air-con, TV, telephone and fridge. On the premises are Chinese and Japanese restaurants, a karaoke

lounge, coffee shop, barber room and snooker club. This hotel is often full.

The new 320-room *Charoen Thani Princess* (☎ 220400, fax 220438; ☎ (02) 281-3088 in Bangkok) towers over the city at 260 Si Chan Rd. Well-appointed singles/doubles with all mod-cons including cable TV cost a uniform 1444B. Facilities include conference rooms, a banquet-style Chinese restaurant, coffee shop and pool. An attached entertainment complex is under construction.

Places to Stay – Chumphae & Ban Phai
If you're cycling or driving a long distance to Khon Kaen, you could find yourself running out of daylight near the junction towns of Chumphae (81 km west) or Ban Phai (45 km south). Both towns are well-equipped to handle overnight visitors. In Chumphae the easiest place to find is the *Chiwin Palace Hotel* (☎ 311577) right on the highway through town. Modest rooms with fan and private bath cost 100 to 200B. If this one's full, try the *Queen's* (100 to 200B) or the *Suksan* (80 to 200B) along the same road.

In Ban Phai your best bets are either the *Paw Meuang Thong* or the *Thawisuk*, both in the middle of town for 80 to 160B.

Places to Eat
Thai & Isaan Khon Kaen has a lively night market with plenty of good food stalls next to the air-con bus terminal; look for the busy *Khun Aem* jók stall, which serves exemplary broken-rice congee. Opposite the Villa Hotel, the 24-hour *Thawng 24 Naw* is a khâo tôm place with all the usual Thai and Chinese standards.

Raan Paa Phawng (no English sign), on Klang Meuang Rd south of Khrua Weh, has the best kài yâang in town, plus several varieties of sômtam. It's only open from around 9 am to 4 pm. Another good spot for local Isaan food is *Kai Yaang Rabiap*, on Theparak Rd near the corner of Lang Sunratchakan Rd.

Khrua Weh (Tiam An Hue in Vietnamese) is an excellent Vietnamese restaurant in an old house on Klang Meuang Rd near Prachasamoson Rd. Prices are moderate and the bilingual menu features many Thai and Isaan dishes as well. *Yam kài weh*, a spicy chicken and mint salad, is a house speciality, as are *kà-yaw sòt*, fresh spring rolls.

The mid-priced, air-con *First Choice* opposite Khon Kaen Hotel offers an extensive selection of Thai and vegetarian dishes. It opens at 7 am for breakfast.

A food centre on the 4th floor of the Fairy Plaza shopping centre on Si Chan Rd serves decent Thai, Chinese and Muslim food from 10 am to 9 pm. Also on this floor are *Mae Ying*, an elegant Thai restaurant with servers dressed in traditional Thai costumes, and an outdoor seafood restaurant called *Thaleh Kan Eng* – both are open from 5 pm to midnight.

Western *The Parrot*, on Si Chan Rd near Fairy Plaza, offers good Western breakfasts (with wholemeal toast and Dutch coffee) for 40 to 55B. The lengthy menu includes grilled salmon, submarine sandwiches, pizza and good Thai food. Friendly service is a plus, and bread is available for purchase by the loaf. Around the corner on Soi Yimsiri, *Harry's Wine Bar* (☎ 239755) features imported wines by the glass or bottle and a range of fixed-price meals in English and American styles, as well as sandwiches, burgers, ice cream and Thai food; prices are moderate to expensive. Both of these restaurants are popular with the local expat crowd as well as well-to-do Thais; Harry's is open from 10.30 am to 11.30 pm, the Parrot from 8 am to 10 pm.

The family-oriented *Pizza & Bake* has two locations, one near the THAI office on Maliwan Rd west of the train line and another on the corner of Phimphaseut and Klang Meuang Rds. Pizza is the main focus, but the restaurant also prepares a variety of other European and Thai dishes.

In the Fairy Plaza shopping complex on Si Chan Rd, you'll find *Mister Donut* on the ground floor and *Black Canyon Coffee* on the 2nd floor.

Things to Buy
Khon Kaen is a good place to buy handcrafted Isaan goods such as silk and cotton fabrics (you can get mat-mii cotton as well as silk), silver and basketry. A speciality of the north-east is the *māwn khwāan* (axe pillow), a stiff triangle-shaped pillow used as a support while sitting on the floor. These come in many sizes, from small enough to carry in a handbag to large enough to fill your entire backpack. Perhaps the most practical way to acquire axe pillows while on the road is to buy them unstuffed *(mâi sài nûn*, 'no kapok inserted') – the covers are easily carried and you can stuff them when you get home.

If textiles are your main interest, try Prathamakhan at 79/2-3 Reun Rom Rd just west of Na Meuang Rd, Rin Mai Thai at 412 Na Meuang Rd, and the Handicraft Centre for Development of Isaan Women, 90/85 Chetakhon Rd.

Several shops selling local preserved foods and other Isaan products can be found along Klang Meuang Rd between Prachasamoson and Si Chan Rds, including Jerat, Naem Laplae and Heng Nguan Hiang. The emphasis in these shops is *nãem* and other types of sausage or processed meats such as *sâi kràwk, mũu yãw, kun siang mũu* and *kuu siang kài*. Still, behind the stacks of sausage you can often ferret out some good handicraft purchases.

The Fairy Department Store, in the Fairy Plaza shopping complex on Si Chan Rd, has a broad range of everyday goods, clothing, cosmetics and electronics. The centre also contains an ATM Fabric Town, a large supermarket and a number of smaller shops.

Entertainment
Khaen Luang (☎ 241922) on Phimphaseut Rd is a large nightclub that features Isaan music – predominantly maw lam and luuk thung – and folk dancing nightly. You can sit at tables in front or on cushions and mats in the back; Thai and Isaan food is served.

Funan, on Si Chan Rd near the train line, is an old wooden shophouse where local college and university students hang out and listen to live *phleng phêua chii-wít* folk songs.

Thai Classical Massage at the Khon Kaen Hotel offers traditional massage. The Kosa Hotel also has a massage annexe but it's definitely not the traditional kind.

The occasional foreign film makes it to Fairy Cinema 1 & 2 on the 4th floor of Fairy Plaza. Also on the 4th floor is a children's amusement centre with a few simple rides.

Getting There & Away

Air THAI flies daily between Bangkok and Khon Kaen (55 minutes, 1080B one way). There is no longer a THAI flight between Phitsanulok and Khon Kaen, although you should check to see if this has changed.

The Khon Kaen THAI office (☎ 236523, 239011) is at 183/6 Maliwan Rd. The airport is a few km west of the city centre off Highway 12; minivan shuttles between the airport and the city are available through THAI.

Bus Ordinary buses arrive at and depart from a terminal on Prachasamoson Rd, while air-con buses use a depot near the market off Klang Meuang Rd.

An air-con bus from Bangkok's northern bus terminal costs 193B. Departures are every half hour between 8.30 am and 11.30 pm. There are also a couple of VIP bus departures daily that cost 295B. This is a seven to eight-hour bus trip.

The Phitsanulok to Khon Kaen road runs through spectacular scenery, including a couple of national parks. Ordinary buses to Khon Kaen leave Phit hourly between 10 am and 4.30 pm, then again every hour from 6.30 pm to 1 am. The trip takes about five hours and costs 90B. One air-con bus leaves Phitsanulok daily at 2 pm for 126B. Air-con night buses between Khon Kaen and Chiang Mai (11 to 12 hours) are available for 268B (8 pm, old route via Tak) or 307B (8 and 9 pm, new route via Utaradit). An 8 pm VIP bus is also available for 345B.

Other air-con bus destinations include Chiang Rai (339B, 13 hours), Nakhon Phanom (264B, four hours), Ubon (125B, five hours), Nong Khai (79B, five hours) and Loei (95B, four hours).

Ordinary buses leave Khorat for Khon Kaen roughly every half hour from 5.30 am till 5.30 pm, arriving 2½ to three hours later. The cost is 48B. Other destinations include Udon (32B, two hours), Chaiyaphum (34B, two hours) and Surin (69B, 5½ hours).

Train Rapid No 33 and express No 945 depart Bangkok's Hualamphong station at 6.15 and 8.20 am, arriving in Khon Kaen at 2.06 and 3.20 pm respectively. The only overnight sleeper train that arrives at a semi-decent hour is express No 3, which leaves Bangkok at 8.30 pm and arrives in Khon Kaen at 4.47 am. A non-sleeper express railcar, No 947, also leaves at 8.40 pm and arrives at 4.24 am. The basic fare is 333B 1st class, 162B 2nd class, plus appropriate charges for rapid or express service. Direct 3rd-class trains are only available from Saraburi and farther north-east (eg Khorat).

Trains from Khorat leave seven times daily between 6 am and 10.30 pm, arriving in Khon Kaen 4½ to five hours later. The 3rd-class fare is 35B.

AROUND KHON KAEN
Chonabot

This small town south-east of amphoe meuang Khon Kaen is famous throughout Thailand for mat-mii cotton and silk. Mat-mii is a method of tie-dyeing the threads before weaving and is similar to Indonesian ikat. The easiest place to see the fabrics is at the **Suun Silapahattakam Pheun Baan** (Local Handicraft Centre) on Pho Sii Sa-aat Rd opposite Wat Pho Sii Sa-aat – about 10 km from the Highway 2/Ban Phai junction off Route 229 in the north part of town; the centre is really more of a village. It displays and sells silk, cotton, ceramics, fishtraps and other assorted handicrafts (including some weavings from Laos) and is open from 9 am to 6 pm daily.

Better-quality cloth can be found at silk-weaving homes along nearby streets – look

NORTH-EAST THAILAND

for looms beneath the wooden homes. Even if you're not interested in buying it's worth wandering around to see the amazing variety of simple wooden contraptions devised to spin, tie, weave and dry silk.

Some of the more reputable weaving households include those belonging to Khun Songkhram, Khun Suwan, Khun Thongsuk and Khun Chin. Very little English is spoken in Chonabot so it helps considerably if you bring someone along who can speak Thai.

Getting There & Away Songthaews to Chonabot leave the ordinary bus station in Khon Kaen hourly between 5.30 am and 5.30 pm for 12B; the last one back from Chonabot leaves the market around 3.30 or 4 pm. The trip lasts around 45 minutes to an hour.

There is a train station in Ban Phai, around 11 km west of Chonabot. From Khon Kaen to Ban Phai there are nine trains daily between 5 am and 10.16 pm (in the reverse direction six trains depart Ban Phai between 8.47 am and 6.15 pm). The 3rd-class fare is 6B for a journey of around 40 minutes. Songthaews (5B) between the Ban Phai train station and Chonabot leave frequently from around 6 am to 6 pm.

Chonabot can also be reached from the south (eg Khorat) via bus or train to Ban Phai. Ban Phai is 167 km north-east of Khorat.

Prasat Peuay Noi
Also known as Ku Peuay Noi, and locally known as That Ku Thong, this 12th-century Khmer temple ruin is now undergoing restoration at Khon Kaen government expense. About the size of Buriram's Prasat Meuang Tam, the monument consists of a large central sandstone sanctuary surmounted by a Lopburi-style prang and surrounded by stone slab walls with two major gates. The site is very rich in sculpted lintels; during restoration, many of them have been gathered together to one side of the monument in a sort of impromptu sculpture garden.

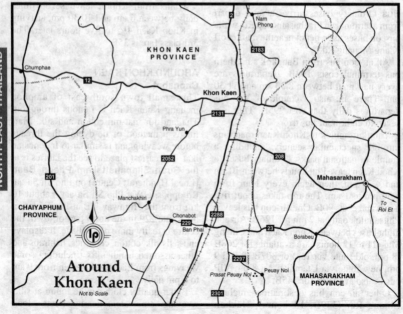

Around Khon Kaen
Not to Scale

Getting There & Away Although Prasat Peuay Noi can be time-consuming to approach if you don't have your own transport, it's a rewarding visit for the quiet scenery along the way even if you're not a Khmer temple buff. On your own from Khon Kaen, proceed 44 km south on Highway 2 to Ban Phai, then east on Highway 23 (signposted to Borabeu) 11 km to Route 2297. Follow Route 2297 24 km south-east through a scenic tableau of rice fields and grazing cattle to the town of Peuay Noi. The ruins are at the western end of town on the south side of the road; you can't miss their grey eminence on your right as you enter the town.

By public transport from Khon Kaen, take a bus or train to Ban Phai, then a songthaew to Peuay Noi. Start early in the morning if you plan to do this in one day; the last songthaew back to Ban Phai from Peuay Noi leaves around 3 pm. Hitching may be possible. See the Around Khon Kaen Getting There & Away section for details on transport to Ban Phai.

ROI ET
อ.เมืองร้อยเอ็ด

Roi Et (population 34,000) is the fairly small but growing capital of a province which, three centuries ago, probably served as a buffer between Thai and Lao political conflict.

Old Roi Et had 11 city gates and was surrounded by its 11 vassal colonies. The name Roi Et means 'one hundred and one'; this could be an exaggeration of the number 11.

The capital is now on an entirely new site, with the large **Beung Phlan Chai** artificial lake in the centre. Paddleboats are available for hire on the lake. An island in the middle, reached by north, west and south causeways, features a fitness park surrounding a tall walking Buddha – demonstrating perhaps that even the Buddha walked for health?

Silk and cotton fabrics from Roi Et are high in quality and generally cheaper than in Khorat and Khon Kaen.

A branch of Bangkok Bank near the Ban Chong Hotel offers foreign-exchange services.

Wat Neua
วัดเหนือ

This wat, in the northern quarter of town, is worth seeing for its 1200-year-old chedi from the Dvaravati period called Phra Satuup Jedi. This chedi exhibits an unusual four-cornered bell-shaped form that is rare in Thailand. Around the bot are a few old Dvaravati sema stones and to one side of the wat is an inscribed pillar, erected by the Khmers when they controlled this area during the 11th and 12th centuries.

Wat Burapha
วัดบูรพา

The tall, standing Buddha that towers above Roi Et's minimal skyline is the Phra Phuttharatana-mongkon-mahamuni (Phra Sung Yai for short) at Wat Burapha. Despite being of little artistic significance, it's hard to ignore. From the ground to the tip of the *ùtsànit* (flame-top head ornament), it's 67.8 metres high, including the base. You can climb a staircase through a building which supports the figure to about as high as the Buddha's knees and get a view of the town.

Places to Stay

The friendly *Ban Chong (Banjong)* (☎ (043) 511235) at 99-101 Suriyadet Bamrung Rd has adequate rooms with fan and bath from 80 to 140B. On the same street at No 133 is the *Saithip*, where fan-cooled rooms start at 90B, air-con from 220B; this one's often full. The *Khaen Kham* (☎ (043) 511508), at 52-62 Rattakit Khlaikhla Rd, has clean rooms with fan and bath for 140B, air-con for 250B. A coffee shop is attached. Also on Rattakit Khlaikhla Rd, at No 46, is the cheaper *Bua Thong* (☎ (043) 511142) at 80B for basic rooms with fan.

The *Phrae Thong Hotel* (☎ (043) 511127), at 45-47 Ploenchit Rd next to a Chinese temple, has comfortable rooms for 120B with fan, 160 to 220B with air-con.

Mai Thai (☎ (043) 511136) at 99 Haisok Rd has all air-con rooms for 400 to 1100B. The *Phetcharat Hotel* (☎ (043) 511741, 514058; fax 511837) opposite the Mai Thai has clean mid-range air-con rooms with hot water for 280 to 480B. Ask for a room off the road.

Places to Eat
Around the edge of Beung Phlan Chai are several medium-priced garden restaurants. The *Neua Yaang Kao-Lii* is on the north-eastern side and has a pleasant atmosphere, an menu in English and good food; the name-sake house speciality is cook-it-yourself Korean beef. Another good lakeside place is the indoors *LA*. You'll find a string of cheaper restaurants along Ratsadan Uthit Rd, which runs east off the lake from the north-eastern corner.

Tako Rai, on Sukkasem Rd around the corner from the Ban Chong Hotel, serves some of the best Isaan food in town. The night market area is a couple of streets east of the Ban Chong and Saithip hotels.

Things to Buy
If you want to buy local handicrafts, the best place to go is the shopping area along Phadung Phanit Rd, where you'll find mawn khwaan (triangular floor pillows), phaa mat-mii (tie-dyed silk and cotton fabric), sticky-rice baskets, khaens and Buddhist paraphernalia. Phaw Kaan Khaa, at 377-9 Phadung Phanit Rd, has a particularly good selection of fabrics, but as always you must bargain well to get good prices. Charin (Jarin), at 383-385 Phadung Phanit Rd, is also good; the owner speaks some English and he also sells gourmet Thai groceries.

Roi Et's street fabric vendors have better prices but less of a selection (and lower quality) than the shops. On the street, four metres of yeoman-quality cotton mat-mii costs as low as 140B. Weavers themselves shop at a weaving supply store at 371 Phadung

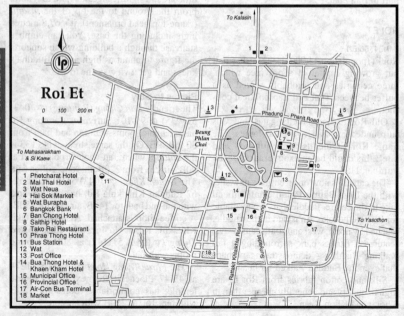

Roi Et

0   100   200 m

To Kalasin
To Mahasarakham & Si Kaew
To Yasothon

Phadung — Phanit Road
Beung Phlan Chai
Rattsakit Khiaikhia Road
Bamrung Road
Sunyadit J.

1 Phetcharat Hotel
2 Mai Thai Hotel
3 Wat Neua
4 Hai Sok Market
5 Wat Burapha
6 Bangkok Bank
7 Ban Chong Hotel
8 Saithip Hotel
9 Tako Rai Restaurant
10 Phrae Thong Hotel
11 Bus Station
12 Wat
13 Post Office
14 Bua Thong Hotel & Khaen Kham Hotel
15 Municipal Office
16 Provincial Office
17 Air-Con Bus Terminal
18 Market

Phanit Rd; here you may see local betel-munchers squatting on the floor checking out dyes, pattern books and pre-knotted skeins.

Getting There & Away
Buses from Udon Thani to Roi Et are 34B (air-con 68B), and from Khon Kaen 30B (air-con 55B). If you're coming straight from Bangkok's northern bus terminal, you can catch an air-con bus for 220B at 8.30 am or 10 am, or every half hour from 8.30 to 11 pm. The trip takes about eight hours. VIP buses cost 420B and leave at 7.30 and 8.10 pm nightly (in the reverse direction at 7.30 pm only).

Ordinary bus destinations include Surin (38B), Ubon (44B) and Khon Kaen (30B).

Getting Around
Samlors around town are 10B; motorised samlors cost 15 to 20B.

AROUND ROI ET
Ku Phra Khona
Around 60 km south-east of amphoe meuang Roi Et, in Suwannaphum district, are the ruins of an 11th-century Khmer shrine. The monument comprises three brick prangs facing east from a sandstone pediment, surrounded by a sandstone slab wall with four gates. The middle prang was replastered in 1928 and Buddha niches were added. A Buddha footprint shrine, added to the front of this prang, is adorned with the Khmer monument's original Bayon-style naga sculptures.

The two remaining prangs have been restored but retain their original forms, which also show Bayon (1017-87) influence. The northern prang features a Narai (Vishnu) lintel over one door and a Ramayana relief on the inside gable.

Getting There & Away Suwannaphum can be reached by frequent buses from the capital via Route 215. From Suwannaphum it's another 17 km south via Route 214 to Ku Phra Khona; any Surin-bound bus can stop on the highway at the town of Ku, which is at the T-intersection with Route 2086 east to

Phon Sai. The ruins are in a wat compound known locally as Wat Ku.

The ruins could also be approached from Surin, 78 km south.

Udon Thani Province

UDON THANI
 อ.เมืองอุดรธานี

Just over 560 km from Bangkok, Udon (often spelt Udorn) is one of several north-eastern cities that boomed virtually overnight when US air bases were established nearby during the Vietnam War (there were seven bases in Thailand until the US pullout in 1976).

Although the bases are long gone, in Udon the US presence lives on, albeit to a much more limited degree. A small number of retired US military personnel and missionaries have settled in the area and a US consulate is still active. Outside the town near the village of Ban Dung a huge Voice of America (VOA) transmitter has recently been constructed at a cost of US$200 million. To reach points throughout South-East Asia, China and Korea, the Ban Dung VOA station will run up an estimated US$3.5 million power bill every year.

In addition to being an American playground, Udon (population 95,000) functions as a transport hub and an agricultural market centre for surrounding provinces. Except as a base for touring for nearby Ban Chiang, Ban Pheu or *khít*-weaving villages, the city has little to offer unless you've spent a long time already in the north-east and seek Western amenities like air-con coffee houses, flashy ice-cream and massage parlours or farang food (though for all of these, Khon Kaen is better).

In the north-east corner of the Thung Si Meuang (city field) is the **Lak Meuang** or city phallus-pillar, where the city's guardian deity is thought to reside. Encrusted with gold leaf and surrounded by offerings of flowers, candles and incense, the pillar

NORTH-EAST THAILAND

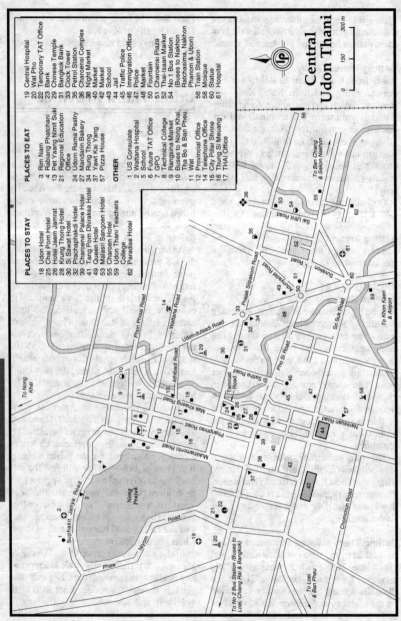

PLACES TO STAY

18 Udon Hotel
25 Chai Porn Hotel
26 Hotel Jaem Jamrat
28 Krung Thong Hotel
30 Si Sawat Hotel
32 Prachapakdi Hotel
39 Charoensi Palace Hotel
41 Tang Porn Dhiraksa Hotel
49 Queen Hotel
53 Malasri Sangoen Hotel
55 Charoen Hotel
59 Udon Thani Teachers
   College
62 Paradise Hotel

PLACES TO EAT

3 Rim Nam
4 Rabiang Phatchani
13 Pet Yaang Nimit Suki
21 Regional Education
   Office
24 Udon Rama Pastry
27 Mandarin Bakery
34 Rung Thong
37 Yawt Kai Yang
57 Pizza House

OTHER

1 US Consulate
5 Wattana Hospital
6 School
7 Future TAT Office
8 GPO
9 Technical College
10 Rangsina Market
10 Buses to Nong Khai,
   Tha Bo & Ban Pheu
11 Wat
12 Provincial Office
14 Telephone Office
15 City Pillar Shrine
16 Thung Si Meuang
17 THAI Office

19 Central Hospital
20 Wat Pho
22 Temporary TAT Office
23 Bank
29 Chinese Temple
33 Clock Tower
35 Petrol Station
36 Charoensi Complex
38 Night Market
40 Market
42 Market
43 School
44 Jail
45 Traffic Police
46 Immigration Office
47 Police
48 Market
50 Fountain
51 Charoensi Plaza
52 Thai-Isaan Market
54 No 1 Bus Station
   (Buses to Nakhon
   Ratchasima, Nakhon
   Phanom & Ubon)
56 Train Station
58 Mosque
60 Statue
61 Hospital

Central
Udon Thani

0   150   300 m

To Nong Khai

To Ban Chiang
& Sakon Nakhon

To Khon Kaen
& Airport

To Loei, Chiang Rai & Bangkok

To Loei
& Ban Pheu

To No 2 Bus Station (Buses to
Loei, Chiang Rai & Bangkok)

shrine sits next to a smaller shrine containing Phra Phuttha Pho Thong, a Buddha stele of undetermined age. Next to this is a sacred banyan tree used as a repository for broken or abandoned spirit houses and Chinese house shrines.

To get away from the busy downtown area, go for a walk around **Nong Prajak**, a reservoir/park in the north-western part of town.

Information

Tourist Office The TAT recently established an office at the Education Division on Pho Si Rd near Nong Prajak. This office carries printed material on Udon, Loei and Nong Khai provinces and is open from 8.30 am to 4.30 pm daily. The staff claim that this office is temporary and that a permanent office will be opened at the northern end of Thesa Rd near the intersection with Athibadi Rd in two to three years.

Post & Telephone The GPO on Wattana Rd is open from 8.30 am to 4.30 pm Monday to Friday and 9 am to noon weekends and holidays. The upstairs telephone office is open from 7 am to 10 pm daily.

Udon's telephone area code is ☎ 042.

Money Several banks along the main avenues provide foreign-exchange services. Only the Bangkok Bank on Prajak Silpakorn Rd has an after-hours exchange window – usually open till 8 pm.

US Consulate There's a small US consulate (☎ 244270) in the north-western section of the city at 35/6 Suphakit Janya Rd, near Nong Prajak park. The staff can assist US citizens with the extension or replacement of their passports and other emergency situations. The consulate also distributes a useful packet of information on Udon for prospective American expat residents. Opening hours are from 7.30 am to 4.30 pm Monday to Friday.

Indochina Visas Kannika Tour (☎ 241378), at 36/9 Si Sattha Rd, and Aranya Tour (☎ 243182), 105 Mak Khaeng Rd, can arrange visas and/or tours of Laos, Cambodia or Vietnam. Most of their clientele are Thai but they're happy to work with farangs as well.

Medical Services Wattana Hospital, on Suphakit Janya Rd near Nong Prajak park and the US consulate, is the best medical facility in the upper north-east.

Places to Stay – bottom end

Udon has a plethora of hotels in all price ranges. The 80 to 100B hotels are generally noisy and more than a little dingy; the better bottom-end places are in the 140 to 250B range. The following are recommended.

Queen Hotel, at 6-8 Udon-dutsadi Rd, has simple rooms with fan and bath from 100 to 140B, air-con for 200B.

Si Sawat, at 123 Prajak Silpakorn Rd, costs 80B for a room with fan and shared bath in the old building, or 120/140B for one/two-bed rooms with fan and private bath in the new building. It's a bit noisy, according to one report, charming according to others. It definitely has more character than most hotels in this range. Another place with character and even cheaper rooms is the old wooden *Hotel Jaem Jarat* on Tamruat Rd near the canal.

The centrally located hotel *Krung Thong* (☎ 221634), at 195-9 Pho Si Rd, offers fair rooms for 140B with fan and bath, 250B with air-con.

There are several other small, inexpensive hotels along the eastern end of Prajak Silpakorn Rd near Charoensi Complex, including the *Mit Sahai* and the *Malasri Sangoen*, which both have rooms for 80B.

Udon Thani Teachers College (☎ 221169) on Thahan Rd lets dorm rooms with shared bath for 30 to 70B during holiday periods (especially March to May). The *Regional Education Office* (☎ 222702), off Pho Si Rd, has 50B rooms most of the year. Accommodation is very simple – one to four beds in a room, a ceiling fan and bathroom facilities down the hall.

NORTH-EAST THAILAND

Places to Stay – middle

Moving up just a bit in quality and price, the friendly *Chai Porn* (☎ 221913, 222144), at 209-211 Mak Khaeng Rd, costs 180 to 230B for rooms with fan and private bath or 240 to 290B with air-con. The *Tang Porn Dhiraksa Hotel* farther south along the same street is very similar.

Another good place in this range is *Prachaphakdi (Prachapakdee) Hotel* (☎ 221804) at 156/8 Prajak Silpakorn Rd. Rooms cost 120 to 160B with fan and bath, 220 to 280B for air-con; it's clean, friendly and relatively quiet for a central hotel.

Paradise Hotel (☎ 221956), 44/29 Pho Si Rd, near the bus station, charges from 250 to 600B for refurbished air-con rooms with bath and hot water.

Places to Stay – top end

The enlarged and upgraded *Udon Hotel* (☎ 248160; fax 242782), at 81-89 Mak Khaeng Rd, is all air-con now, with comfortable rooms from 350 to 800B. A favourite with travelling businesspeople because it has a parking lot, this hotel is often full.

The *Charoen* (☎ 248115), at 549 Pho Si Rd, has air-con rooms in its old wing for 750B, or 1300B in the new wing. Facilities include a pool, cocktail lounge, restaurant and disco.

Charoensi Palace (☎ 222601), at 60 Pho Si Rd, comes a poor third with air-con rooms from 350 to 880B.

The new Charoensi Complex, now undergoing construction at the south-eastern end of Prajak Silpakorn Rd, will supposedly add the 14-floor *Imperial Charoensi Hotel*, with 261 luxury rooms, by the beginning of 1995.

Places to Eat

Thai, Chinese & Isaan There is plenty of good food in Udon, especially Isaan fare. The best kài yâang place is *Yawt Kai Yang*, on the corner of Pho Si and Mukkhamontri Rds. Along with grilled chicken, all the other Isaan specialities are available; prices are very reasonable. Nearby on Mukkhamontri Rd is a good night market.

Rung Thong, on the west side of the clock tower roundabout, sells excellent Thai curries and is also cheap; this is one of the longest-running curry shops in north-east Thailand. *Udorn Rama Pastry*, a small pastry shop, is on Prajak Silpakorn Rd between Tamruat and Mak Khaeng Rds, a few blocks from the clock tower. The cashew-nut brownies are good.

A nicer place for pastries is the *Mandarin Bakery*, next door to the Chai Porn Hotel on Mak Khaeng Rd. In addition to takeaway pastries, this roomy air-con restaurant serves Thai, Chinese and farang food at reasonable prices. Several other small restaurants are scattered along nearly the entire length of Mak Khaeng Rd. Up at the northern end of Mak Khaeng Rd, not far from the Udon Hotel, *Pet Yaang Nimit Suki* specialises in roast duck and Thai-style sukiyaki.

MD Suki, on the ground floor of Charoensi Complex shopping centre, is quite popular with young Thais for noodles and Thai-style sukiyaki. There's also a good food centre on the 3rd floor of this shopping centre.

On the banks of the Nong Prajak reservoir off Suphakit Janya Rd are two decent open-air Thai restaurants, *Rim Nam* and *Rabiang Phatchani*.

Western The 3rd floor of the Charoensi Complex at the south-eastern end of Prajak Silpakorn Rd contains *KFC, Sunmerry Bakery* and a huge supermarket. You'll find coffee shops on both the ground and 2nd floors, including the popular *Black Canyon* with more than 20 kinds of coffee. The *Steak & Pizza House* on the 2nd floor is only passable.

Although it's inconveniently located, the *International Bar Steak House* (☎ 245341), also known as John's International Bar, has the best Western food in town. Outdoor dining is at shaded tables around a pond; there's also an indoor dining area in a small tin-roofed brick hut. The menu is very reasonably priced and the clientele is an equal mix of Thais and expats. The disadvantage is that it's a bit out of town and hard to find – you have to really want farang food to come this far. It's off the highway north of the city (325 Muu 4, Ban Leuam Rawp Meuang). To get there, take a tuk-tuk north to the highway, enter the Thai Samet School grounds and follow the signs for about a km to the restaurant. It's near the No 2 bus station, which is about a 150-metre walk from the school.

Two other places with farang food are the *Pizza House* at 63/1 Naresuan Rd and *TJ's Restaurant*, at 337 Nong Sam Rong Rd.

Entertainment

The Chao Phraya Theatre, at 150 Ratchaphatsadu Rd, has a sound room that plays the original soundtracks for English-language films – probably the only such theatre in north-east Thailand. For somewhere to go at night, the Charoen Hotel has a comfortable bar and also a disco. La Reine at the Udon Hotel is a popular cabaret-style club.

Mak Khaeng Rd, in the vicinity of the Udon Hotel, has a few modern massage parlours left over from the American GI era; nowadays the clientele is mostly Thai.

Things to Buy

Udon's main shopping district is centred around Pho Si Rd between the fountain circle and Mak Khaeng Rd.

Mae Lamun is a good local craft shop on Prajak Silpakorn Rd just east of Mak Khaeng Rd; it's on the 2nd floor of a store selling Buddhist paraphernalia. Mae Lamun has a selection of quality silks and cottons, silver, jewellery, Buddha images and ready-made clothes tailored from local fabrics. Prices start high but are negotiable. Another good craft shop – especially for pillows – is Thi Non Michai at 208 Pho Si Rd.

The new Charoensi Complex, under construction off Prajak Silpakorn Rd, promises to become the largest shopping centre in Isaan, possibly in all of Thailand. If completed as planned it will feature 22,000 sq metres of retail space, a 3000-sq-metre supermarket, swimming pools, an amusement park and a four-star, 14-storey hotel. At the time of writing it was filling up with standard Thai department stores, a flock of

designer clothing boutiques and several restaurants and coffee shops (see Places to Eat above).

Getting There & Away

Air THAI flies to Udon from Bangkok daily. The flight takes an hour and costs 1260B. The Udon office (☎ 246697, 243222) is at 60 Mak Khaeng Rd.

Bus Buses for Udon leave Bangkok's northern bus terminal throughout the day from 5 am to 11 pm. The trip takes 10 to 11 hours and the fare is 134B (241B air-con).

Buses leave the main bus station in Khorat every half hour during the day and arrive five hours later. The cost is 82B (135B air-con).

Getting out of Udon by bus, you must first sort out the tangle of departure points scattered around the city. Ordinary buses to Nong Khai (15 buses a day, 5.30 am to 3.30 pm, 15B) leave from Rangsina Market on the northern outskirts of town; take city bus No 6 or a songthaew north along Udon-dutsadi Rd to get to Talaat Rangsina. You can also get buses to Tha Bo, Si Chiangmai and Ban Pheu from here. The No 2 bus station is on the north-western outskirts of the city next to the highway and has buses to Loei, Nakhon Phanom, Chiang Rai, Si Chiangmai, Nong Khai and Bangkok.

The No 1 bus station is off Sai Uthit Rd near the Charoen Hotel in the south-eastern end of town. Buses from here go mostly to points south and east of Udon, including Khorat, Sakon Nakhon, Nakhon Phanom, Ubon, Khon Kaen, Roi Et and Bangkok, but also go to Beung Kan.

There are also private air-con buses to Bangkok. The company with the best local reputation is 407 Co (☎ 221121) at 125/3 Prajak Silpakorn Rd.

Train The 8.30 pm Nong Khai Express from Bangkok arrives in Udon at 6.33 am the next day. Rapid trains leave Bangkok on the Nong Khai line at 6.15 am and 7 pm, arriving in Udon at 3.56 pm and 5.15 am. The 1st-class fare is 413B, 2nd class is 198B, plus appli-

NORTH-EAST THAILAND

cable charges for sleeper and express service.

A special, all-inclusive 3rd-class fare (110B) applies to faster diesel railcar trains to Udon, which leave Bangkok at 8.20 am and 8.40 am, arriving at 5.05 pm and 6.05 am respectively. Although both the English and Thai train schedules list a 95B 3rd-class fare for ordinary (thammadaa) trains, there are actually no ordinary trains on the Bangkok to Udon run – only diesel railcar, rapid and express.

Getting Around

Samlor drivers in Udon practically doubled their rates overnight when 50 Yanks were brought in to work on the VOA station outside the town in 1990-91; apparently the engineers were throwing their dollars around with abandon. With a permanent contingent of VOA employees in the area, just about any farang who happens through Udon will have to deal with this two-tier price system (which exists to some extent everywhere in Thailand – it's just grossly exaggerated in Udon). Reasonable fares are 10 to 15B on short sprints (eg the No 1 bus station to the Paradise Hotel), 15 to 20B for a medium-length trip (eg No 1 bus station to the Prachaphakdi Hotel) or up to 25B for a longer jaunt (eg Charoensi Plaza to Nong Prajak Park).

A more hassle-free way to get around is by city bus. The most useful city bus for visitors is the yellow No 2, which plies a route from the No 2 bus station, south along Suphakit Janya Rd, and then along Pho Si Rd past the Charoen Hotel. The No 6 bus runs between the No 2 bus station and Rangsina Market, while bus No 23 runs between bus stations Nos 1 and 2. The fare for all city buses is only 3B.

Car Rental

Three car-rental places opposite the Udon Hotel offer sedans, jeeps and vans for hire starting at around 1400B. Should you want to hire a car with driver, a cheaper alternative is to negotiate for one of the old four-door Datsun and Toyota taxis waiting along Phanphrao Rd at the southern end of

the municipal field. Figure on no more than 800B per day for one of these – including the services of a driver. These drivers are happy to go anywhere in the province or as far out of the province as Nong Khai.

AROUND UDON THANI PROVINCE
Ban Chiang

บ้านเชียง

Ban Chiang, 50 km east of Udon Thani, now plays host to a steady trickle of tourists from all over Thailand and a few from beyond. As well as the original excavation at **Wat Pho Si Nai** at the village edge (open to the public), there is a new **National Museum** with extensive Ban Chiang exhibits. This is worth a trip if you're at all interested in the historic Ban Chiang culture, which goes back at least 2000 years. Like all national museums, this one's open Wednesday to Sunday from 9 am to 4 pm. A map of the area is available at the museum.

The Ban Chiang culture, an agricultural society which once thrived in north-east Thailand, is known for its early bronze metallurgy and clay pottery, especially pots and vases with distinctive burnt-ochre swirl designs, most of which were associated with burial sites. The locals attempt to sell Ban Chiang artefacts, real and fake, but neither type will be allowed out of the country, so don't buy them. Some of the local handicrafts, such as thick handwoven cotton fabric, are good buys.

Getting There & Away There is a regular bus between Udon and Ban Chiang for 25B. Buses leave in either direction several times a day, but the last leaves Ban Chiang in the late afternoon.

Ban Pheu

บ้านผือ

Ban Pheu district, 42 km north-west of Udon Thani, has a peculiar mix of prehistoric cave paintings, bizarre geological formations and Buddhist shrines, the bulk of which are at Phra Phutthabat Bua Bok, 12 km outside Ban

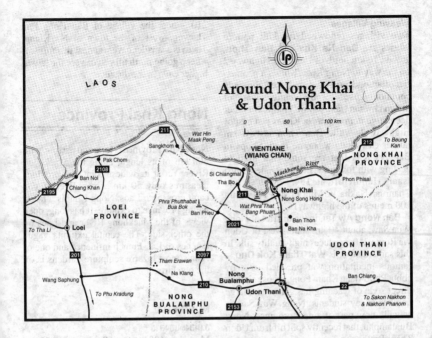

Around Nong Khai & Udon Thani

Pheu on Phra Bat hill. The area has recently been declared **Phu Phra Bat Historical Park**.

The formations are a madhouse of balanced rocks, spires and whale-sized boulders, with several shrines and three wats built in and around the formations. A trail meandering through the park takes around two hours to negotiate at a normal walking pace.

At the entrance to the area is the largest temple in the historical park, **Wat Phra That Phra Phutthabat Bua Bok**. Prehistoric paintings are in several caves and feature wild animals, humans and cryptic symbols. To the south-east of the main wat are the caves of **Tham Lai Meu** and **Tham Non Sao Eh** and to the west are **Tham Khon** and **Tham Wua Daeng**. For Isaan residents, this is an important place of pilgrimage. For visitors, the side-by-side progression from rock art to Buddhist temples represents a localised evolution of thought and aesthetics.

A crude trail map is available at the park entrance, although it doesn't include all the caves nor all the trail branches.

Also in the Ban Pheu district – but outside the park – is **Wat Paa Baan Kaw**, a respected meditation temple under the tutelage of Ajaan Tun (Phikkhu Kippapanyo).

Getting There & Away Ban Pheu has one hotel (70B with shared bath) if you want to spend some time here. Otherwise, it can be visited as a long day trip from either Udon or Nong Khai. From Udon it's an 18B songthaew ride to Ban Pheu; it's 24B from Nong Khai. From Ban Pheu, take a songthaew for 5B to the village nearest the site, Ban Tiu, then walk or hitch the two km to Wat Phra Phutthabat. You could also charter a motorcycle in the Ban Pheu market to take you all the way to Phra Phutthabat.

Easiest of all would be to visit the park by bicycle or motorbike from Nong Khai.

Weaving Villages

Two villages renowned for khit pattern fabrics are **Ban Na Kha** and **Ban Thon**, around 16 km north of Udon via Highway 2 on the way to Nong Khai. Khit is a geometric, diamond-grid minimal weft brocade commonly used for the centre square of mawn khwaan ('axe pillow') fabrics or other decorative items. Ban Na Kha is just east of Highway 2, while Ban Thon is two km farther east along a laterite road. Shops in Ban Na Kha that are somewhat used to dealing with foreign visitors include Songsi Isaan Handicraft at 184/1 Muu 1 and Chanruan Nakha, 92 Muu 1 (Muu 1 is within 100 metres of the highway).

Ban Nong Aw Tai, in the district of Nong Wua Saw, about 40 km south-west of Udon via Route 210, produces high-quality silk. In this same district is **Wat Tham Kok Duu**, a famous meditation wat presided over by abbot Phra Ajaan Kham Fong, whose simple, direct style of teaching has garnered a large number of lay students. Nong Wua Saw is actually now part of a new province, Nong Bualamphu, that recently split off from Udon Thani Province.

Tham Erawan

If you happen to be travelling on your own along Route 210 between Loei Province and Udon, you can stop off and visit Tham Erawan, a large cave shrine high up on the side of a limestone mountain. A huge seated Buddha in the cave can be seen gazing out over the plains from several km away.

The cave is at the back of **Wat Tham Erawan**, which is two km north of a turn-off between Km 31 and 32 markers on Route 210 – near the village of Ban Hong Phu Thawng, west of the town of Na Klang. There is a smaller cave wat near this turn-off – keep going north till you can see the larger, higher cave in the distance.

Nong Khai Province

Nong Khai Province is long and narrow, with 300 km of its length along the Maekhong River. Yet at its widest point, the province measures only 50 km across. Even if you can't cross into Laos, Nong Khai is a fascinating province to explore. It has long, open views of the Maekhong River and Laos on the other side. The capital exhibits vague touches of Lao-French influence and one of Asia's most bizarre sculpture gardens is on the outskirts.

NONG KHAI

อ.เมืองหนองคาย

More than 620 km from Bangkok and 55 km from Udon Thani, Nong Khai (population 25,000) is where Highway 2 – also known as Friendship Highway or Asia 12 – ends, at the Thai-Lao Friendship Bridge over the Maekhong River. Across the river is Laos.

Nong Khai was once part of the Vientiane (Wiang Chan) kingdom, which for much of its history vacillated between independence and tribute to either Lan Xang (1353 to 1694) or Siam (late 1700s to 1893). In 1827 King Rama III gave a Thai lord, Thao Suwothamma, the rights to establish Meuang Nong Khai at the present city site. In 1891,

---

Maekhong

The Thai name for the river is Mae Nam Khong. Mae Nam means river (literally, 'mother water') and Khong is its name, hence the term 'Maekhong River' is a bit redundant. Westerners have called it the 'Mekong River' for decades and the Thais themselves sometimes call it 'Maekhong' for short (on the Laos side they prefer 'Nam Khong'); in this book I'm compromising and calling it the 'Maekhong River'. By agreement between the Thai and Lao governments, all islands in the Maekhong River – including sandbars that appear only in the dry season – belong to Laos. ∎

under Rama V, Nong Khai became the capital of Monthon Lao Phuan, an early Isaan satellite state which included present-day Udon, Loei, Khon Kaen, Sakon Nakhon, Nakhon Phanom and Nong Khai provinces as well as Vientiane. The area came under several attacks by *jiin haw* (Yunnanese) marauders in the late 1800s. The 1886-vintage **Prap Haw Monument** (*pràp haw* means 'putting down the Haw') in front of Nong Khai's city hall commemorates Thai-Lao victories over Haw invasions in 1877 and 1885. When western Laos was partitioned off from Thailand by the French in 1893, the monthon capital was moved to Udon, leaving Nong Khai to fade into a provincial backwater.

Today's Nong Khai has a row of old buildings of French-Chinese architecture along Meechai Rd, east of Soi Si Khun Meuang parallel to the river. Unfortunately, local developers have razed some of the most historic buildings in Nong Khai and have replaced them with the ugly egg-carton architecture common all over urban Asia. Let's hope Nong Khai residents make a plea for historical preservation, or there'll soon be no historic buildings left in Nong Khai. The arrival of the Thai-Lao Bridge largely shifts the focus of international trade from Nong Khai's historic downtown to the bridge area west of the city, so perhaps this will alleviate the pressure to replace older architecture.

The opening of the bridge on 8 April 1994 marks the beginning of a new era of development for Nong Khai as a regional trade and transport centre. New multistorey hotels and office buildings are rising up along the outskirts of town in the vicinity of the new Highway 2 (Mittaphap Hwy) bypass which leads to the Thai-Lao Bridge.

The restaurant next to the immigration office and pier is a good place to sit and watch the ferry boats cross back and forth between Thailand and the Lao People's Democratic Republic. Since pedestrians aren't permitted on the new bridge, this ferry will probably continue to operate until regular bus service is established between Nong Khai and Vientiane. Shops along Meechai Rd near the pier are jammed with Lao, Vietnamese and Chinese goods.

Information

Post & Telephone The GPO on Meechai Rd is open from 8.30 am to 4.30 pm Monday to Friday and 9 am to noon weekends and holidays. The upstairs telephone office is open from 7 am to 10 pm daily.

Nong Khai's telephone area code is ☎ 042.

Money Several banks along Meechai Rd offer ATMs and foreign-exchange services.

Lao Visas Nong Khai is one of six crossings open to non-Thai foreigners along the Thai-Lao border (the other five are Chiang Khong, Nakhon Phanom, That Phanom, Mukdahan and Chong Mek) and citizens of the two countries are allowed to cross at will for day trips. Thais can get visas fairly easily for longer trips.

For foreign visitors, visas to Laos are now readily available through travel agencies in Bangkok. Also try the immigration office in Nong Khai in case they've decided to let foreigners across for day trips too, though this is probably not likely yet.

Several visa brokers in Nong Khai can arrange the necessary paperwork for visits of up to two weeks. Current prices vary from 2000 to 3125B; waiting periods of four to 10 days are typical, depending on the broker. You'll need four passport photos for the visa. One of the more reliable brokers is The Mekong & Laos Co, c/o Nisachol Handicraft Shop (☎ /fax 472457), 115 Mittaphap Hwy in Ban Nong Song Hong (13 km south of the city). A straight Lao visa costs 2500B; add 1500B for each additional provincial travel permit.

If your visit is approved, take a ferry across to Tha Deua in Laos and catch a bus or taxi to Vientiane. You may also be able to catch a direct bus from Nong Khai's bus terminal across the new bridge to Vientiane – once such a service is established. Lonely Planet has a guidebook devoted to Laos

NORTH-EAST THAILAND

which contains extensive visa and travel permit information.

Thai-Lao Friendship Bridge

The US$30 million, Australian-financed Saphaan Mittaphap Thai-Lao spans the Maekhong River from Ban Jommani (three km west of Nong Khai) to Tha Na Laeng (19 km south-east of Vientiane) on the Lao side. The 1174-metre-long bridge opened to vehicular traffic in April 1994; city planners say eventually a rail link will be extended from the Nong Khai railhead across the 12.7-metre-wide bridge. On the Lao side a new train line (the country's first!) will skirt Vientiane to the south-east and terminate in the vicinity of That Luang. The bottom of the bridge features 13.4-metre minimum clearance for boats at the river's highest projected water level. An 8.2-km highway bypass was added to link the bridge with Highway 2/Asia 12 just south of the city.

The bridge is open daily from 8 am to 6 pm. A toll of 20B is collected for cars, 30B for trucks under one ton, 50B for mini or medium buses, 100B for bus coaches and 100 to 300B for larger trucks depending on the number of wheels. Since it's not open to pedestrian traffic, the Tha Sadet ferry in Nong Khai should stay in business. The vehicle ferry to Tha Na Laeng will soon close, however. For further information on vehicle export/import regulations between Thailand and Laos, see Lonely Planet's *Laos* guidebook

Wat Pho Chai

วัดโพธิ์ชัย

This temple off Prajak Rd in the south-eastern part of town is renowned for its large Lan Xang-era sitting Buddha. The head of the image is pure gold, the body is bronze, and the utsanit (flame-top head ornament) is set with rubies.

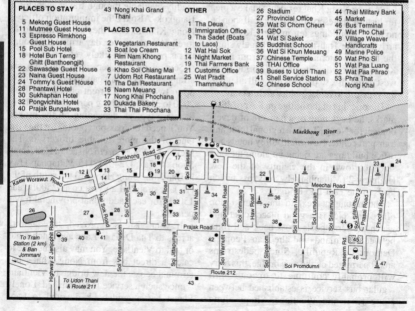

PLACES TO STAY		OTHER	
5 Mekong Guest House	43 Nong Khai Grand Thani	1 Tha Deua	26 Stadium
11 Mutmee Guest House		8 Immigration Office	27 Provincial Office
13 Espresso Rimkhong Guest House	**PLACES TO EAT**	9 Tha Sadet (Boats to Laos)	29 Wat Si Chom Cheun
15 Pool Sub Hotel	2 Vegetarian Restaurant	12 Wat Hai Sok	31 GPO
18 Hotel Bun Terng	3 Boat Ice Cream	14 Night Market	34 Wat Si Saket
Ghitt (Banthoengjit)	4 Rim Nam Khong Restaurant	19 Thai Farmers Bank	35 Buddhist School
22 Sawasdee Guest House	6 Khao Soi Chiang Mai	21 Customs Office	36 Wat Si Khun Meuang
23 Naina Guest House	7 Udom Rot Restaurant	25 Wat Pradit Thammakhun	37 Chinese Temple
24 Tommy's Guest House	10 Tha Dan Restaurant		38 THAI Office
28 Phantawi Hotel	16 Naem Meuang		39 Buses to Udon Thani
30 Sukhaphan Hotel	17 Nong Khai Phochana		41 Shell Service Station
32 Pongvichita Hotel	20 Dukada Bakery		42 Chinese School
40 Prajak Bungalows	33 Thai Thai Phochana		44 Thai Military Bank
			45 Market
			46 Bus Terminal
			47 Wat Pho Chai
			48 Village Weaver Handicrafts
			49 Marine Police
			50 Wat Pho Si
			51 Wat Paa Luang
			52 Wat Paa Phrao
			53 Phra That Nong Khai

Maekhong River

Rimkhong Road

Kaew Worawut Road

Meechai Road

Soi Praisen

Soi Cheunjit

Soi Wat Nak

Sukracha Road

Soi Srimuang

Haw Road

Soi Si Khun Meuang

Soi Lumdjan

Soi Srisumang

Soi Srisulang 2

Prasai Road

Phochai Road

Banthoengjit Road

Soi Sok Yoi

Prajak Road

Soi Jittapunya

Soi Vietnamnusorn

Soi Warnutt

Soi Slipakom

Praesern Rd

Soi Promdumri

To Train Station (2 km) & Ban Jommani

Highway 2 Jenphit Road

To Udon Thani & Route 211

Route 212

Murals in the bot depict the image's travels from the interior of Laos to the banks of the Maekhong, where it was put on a raft. A storm capsized the raft and the image sat at the bottom of the river from 1550 to 1575, when it was salvaged and placed in Wat Haw Kawng (now called Wat Pradit Thammakhun) on the Thai side of the river. The highly revered image was moved to Wat Pho Chai during the reign of King Mongkut (1852-68).

Phra That Nong Khai

Also known as **Phra That Klang Nam** (Holy Reliquary in the Middle of the River) this Lao chedi is submerged in the Maekhong River and can only be seen in the dry season when the Maekhong lowers about 30 metres. The chedi slipped into the river in 1847 and continues to slide – it's near the middle now. For the best view of the chedi, walk east along Meechai Rd past the Marine Police

post, then past two wats on the right, then turn left on Soi Paphraw (Paa Phrao) 3. Follow this soi till it ends at the new riverside promenade and look for the chedi in the river off to your right. Once the top of the chedi has cleared the river surface during the dry season, coloured flags are fastened to the top to make it easier to spot.

Sala Kaew Ku

ศาลาแก้วกู่

Also called **Wat Khaek** (Indian temple) by locals, this strange Hindu-Buddhist shrine, established in 1978, is a tribute to the wild imagination of Luang Puu Bunleua Surirat. Luang Puu (Venerable Grandfather) is a Brahmanic yogi-priest-shaman who merges Hindu and Buddhist philosophy, mythology and iconography into a cryptic whole. He has developed a large following in north-east Thailand and Laos, where he lived for many years before moving to Nong Khai (he still

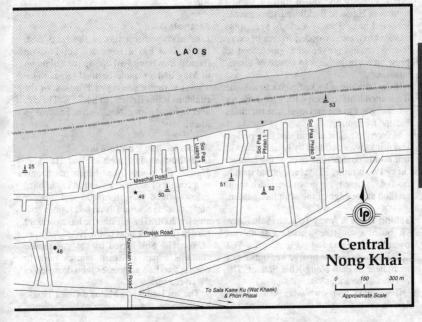

Central Nong Khai

0   150   300 m

Approximate Scale

To Sala Kaew Ku (Wat Khaek) & Phon Phisai

LAOS

Meechai Road

Prajak Road

Kaewkan Uthit Road

Soi Paa Luang 1

Soi Paa Phrao 1

Soi Paa Phrao 3

maintains a temple across the river in Laos). He is supposed to have studied under a Hindu *rishi* in Vietnam; according to legend Luang Puu was walking in the mountains when he fell through a sinkhole and landed in the rishi's lap! He remained in the cave, called Kaew Ku (Jewel Grotto), for several years.

The focus of the temple is the many bizarre cement statues of Shiva, Vishnu, Buddha and every other Hindu or Buddhist deity imaginable, as well as numerous secular figures, all supposedly cast by unskilled artists under Luang Puu's direction. The style of the figures is remarkably uniform, with faces which look like benign Polynesian masks. The tallest, a Buddha seated on a coiled naga with a spectacular multi-headed hood, reaches 25 metres. A sound system wired into the park sometimes plays a bizarre mixture of avant-garde electronic and pop musical selections – Luang Puu's favourite artist is Donna Summer!

In the shrine building there are two large rooms, upstairs and down, full of framed pictures of Hindu or Buddhist deities, temple donors, Luang Puu at various ages, plus smaller bronze and wooden figures of every description and provenance, guaranteed to throw an art historian into a state of disorientation.

If the building is locked, you can ask one of the attendants to open it for you; there are two stairways to the 2nd level, one for males and one for females.

In Nong Khai, it is said that any person who drinks water offered by Luang Puu will turn all his possessions over to the temple. Luang Puu is rather ill these days and spends most of his time lying down beneath a small pavilion at the edge of the sculpture garden.

Getting There & Away To get to Sala Kaew Ku, board a songthaew heading south-east towards Beung Kan and ask to get off at Wat Khaek, which is four or five km outside of town, near St Paul Nong Khai School. The fare should be about 7B.

If you have your own wheels, look for a sign on the right about two turn-offs past St Paul's that reads 'Salakeokoo' referring to the official name, Sala Kaew Ku. It's an easy three-km bike ride from town.

Hat Jommani
This sand 'beach' along the Maekhong River only appears during the dry season. Next to the Thai-Lao Friendship Bridge in Ban Jommani, three km west of Nong Khai, the beach is a favourite picnic spot for local Thais. During the season a rustic thatched shelter with straw mats becomes a restaurant serving delicious kài yâang (grilled chicken), paa yâang (grilled fish), sômtam and cold beer.

Organised Tours
Sunset **boat rides** are available daily at around 5 pm from next to the floating restaurant behind Wat Hai Sok. The city is constructing a new **riverfront promenade** for strolling along the Maekhong. At present the promenade begins at the far eastern end of town and ends two blocks west of Phochai Rd.

Festivals
Like many other cities in the north-east, Nong Khai has a large Rocket Festival (Ngaan Bun Bang Fai) during the full moon of May, and a Candle Festival (Ngaan Hae Thian) at the beginning of Phansaa, or the Buddhist Rains Retreat, in late July. The city also holds its own Nong Khai Festival in March.

Places to Stay – bottom end
Guesthouses Just west of Wat Hai Sok, *Mutmee (Mat-mii) Guest House* has rooms in a couple of old houses and in rustic bungalows which vary from 100 to 150B per night; there is also one three-bed room available for 200B. The guesthouse has a pleasant garden restaurant next to the river. A corner of Wat Hai Sok leased by the guesthouse contains a pair of spirit houses built to honour two Lao princesses who drowned in the river nearby.

The soi leading to Mutmee Guest House has become a miniature travellers' centre, with a well-stocked bookshop, small bakery and rustic studios offering t'ai chi and yoga instruction. Another guesthouse near the mouth of the soi, *Frontier*, offers basic rooms in a house for 80/100B.

In town, the *Mekong Guest House* (☎ 412119) has 16 basic but clean singles/doubles overlooking the river for 70/80B, plus a couple of larger rooms for 130B. Between the Mekong and Mutmee guest-houses, in a quiet spot near the river, the new *Espresso Rimkhong Guest House* has 12 decent rooms with shared bath for 50/100B.

Sawasdee Guest House (☎ 412502) is in one of Nong Khai's old shophouses, restored and refurbished to provide small but very clean rooms for 80 to 120B with fan, 270B air-con (add 30B for hot water). A small inner courtyard is pleasant for sitting. The house is at 402 Meechai Rd, opposite Wat Si Khun Meuang. It would be great if more historic Nong Khai shophouses could be preserved like this one.

Towards the eastern end of town, at the end of the river extension of Phochai Rd, are two guesthouses that catch overflow from the more popular downtown places. *Tommy's*, run by a local Thai musician, is a cluster of basic rooms in an old wooden house; rates are just 50/70B for singles/doubles. On the other side of the soi to the west, *Naina* offers small, side-by-side rooms in a wooden building for 100B per night; a drawback is the collection of noisy fighting cocks on the grounds. The owners are obviously trying to take advantage of people looking for the old Niyana Guest House, which was once located in this area but has since moved to That Phanom.

Hotels The *Phunsap Hotel* (the English sign reads 'Pool Sub'), on Meechai Rd parallel to the river, costs 120B for very basic though large rooms with fan and bath. Hardly anyone ever seems to stay here.

The *Sukhaphan Hotel* (☎ 411894) on Banthoengjit Rd, across the street from the Pongvichita Hotel, is an old wooden Chinese hotel that was great value just after a 1990 renovation but is now in need of another

facelift. The rooms have screened windows and singles/doubles cost 100/150B with fan and shared bath. Two other cheapies on Banthoengjit Rd, which are not as good, are the *Banthoengjit* and the *Kheng Houng (Huang)*, with somewhat dismal rooms for 50 and 60B respectively.

Pongvichita (Phongwichit) (☎ 411583) at 723 Banthoengjit Rd, across the street from the Sukhaphan, is fairly clean and business-like and costs 120/150B for a one/two-bed room with fan and bath, 400/500B with air-con.

Prajak Bungalows (☎ 411116), at 1178 Prajak Rd, has quiet off-street singles/doubles with fan for 150/170B, or 300/400B with air-con and hot water.

Places to Stay – middle & top end

The *Phanthavy (Phantawi)* (☎ 411568), at 1241 Hai Sok Rd, has very tidy air-con rooms with hot water for 350 to 500B. There's a decent coffee shop downstairs. Across the street is *Phantawi Bungalows*, under the same management and at the same rates.

The new 130-room *Nong Khai Grand Thani* (☎ 420033; fax 412026) is out on Route 212 a bit south of the city centre. Modern rooms with all the amenities cost 1000 to 2110B a single, 1200 to 2780B a double. On the premises are a restaurant, coffee shop, swimming pool, conference room and disco.

Built in hopes of reaping a profit from the bridge opening, the 208-room *Holiday Inn Mekong Royal* (☎ 420024; fax 421280) sits on the new highway bypass near Ban Jommani. Plush rooms start at 2119B; hotel facilities include a restaurant, coffee shop, cocktail lounge, pool and conference rooms.

Places to Eat

Udom Rot, which overlooks the Maekhong and Tha Sadet (the ferry pier for boats to and from Laos) has good food and atmosphere, and Isaan-Lao crafts are for sale at the front. Recommended dishes include pàw pía yuan (Vietnamese spring rolls), lâap kài (spicy mint chicken salad) and kài lâo daeng (chicken cooked in red wine). Also on the menu is plaa jòhk, a common Mekong River fish, served either phàt phèt (stir-fried with fresh basil and curry paste) or phanaeng (in a savoury coconut curry). Prices are moderate.

On the other side of the pier is the more expensive *Tha Dan* (Customs Pier) restaurant, which also has a souvenir shop in front. A better riverside choice is the *Rim Nam Khong* next to the Mekong Guest House. On the opposite side of the street is *Nam Tok Rim Khong*, a restaurant specialising in Isaan dishes including neúa náam tòk, or 'waterfall beef' – a spicy/tart salad of barbecued beef served with sticky rice.

The *Dukada Bakery* on Meechai Rd has a variety of pastries, Western breakfasts and Thai food and is one of the few places in Thailand that gives you a choice of Nescafé or Thai coffee (I'll take the real thing over Nescafé any day, even when mixed with tamarind seed). In addition to an extensive selection of Thai and Chinese meals, the menu offers fried chicken, beefsteak or pork chop meals with vegetables and potatoes for just 35B.

For Chinese food, *Nong Khai Phochana* on the corner of Banthoengjit and Rimkhong Rds is good – selections include Chinese roast duck, red pork, kǔaytǐaw and bà-mìi. Very good Isaan and Vietnamese food is available from *Naem Meuang* on the corner opposite Nong Khai Phochana; the house speciality is the namesake *nāem meuang*, spicy Isaan-style pork sausage.

Khao Soi Chiang Mai on Rimkhong Rd, not far from Nong Khai Phochana and Naem Meuang, serves authentic khào soi (Shan-style curry noodles) as well as delicious khanǒm jiin náam ngíaw (spicy Yunnanese-style noodles).

Boat, farther west on Rimkhong Rd, serves ice cream, sundaes, milk shakes and good Thai food; you can choose to sit in the indoor air-con section or in an outdoor riverfront section. A nameless *vegetarian restaurant* a bit farther west on Rimkhong Rd serves tasty and inexpensive Chinese vegetarian food from around 9 am to 6 pm.

Two doors south of Pongvichita Hotel the ráan khâo tôm-style *Thai Thai Phochana* has all the usual Thai and Chinese dishes. Diagonally opposite the Pongvichita is a major jók shop with a choice of chicken or pork jók.

Along a soi inside Wat Hai Sok several coffee and noodle vendors set up each morning. Good *kaa-fae thǔng* (filtered coffee) costs just a few baht.

Things to Buy

A shop called Village Weaver Handicrafts at 786/1 Prajak Rd sells high-quality, moderately priced woven fabrics and ready-made clothes. The staff can also tailor clothing in a day or two from fabric purchased. The shop was established by the Good Shepherd Sisters as part of a project to encourage local girls to stay in the villages and earn money by weaving rather than leaving home to seek work in urban centres. The hand-dyed mat-mii cotton is particularly good here, and visitors are welcome to observe the methods in the weaving workshop behind the shop. It's down Prajak Rd past the bus terminal – 5 to 10B by samlor from the centre of town. The Thai name of the project is Hattakam Sing Thaw.

Wasambe Bookshop, on the soi leading to Mutmee Guest House, sells new and used English-language novels, guidebooks and books on spirituality, plus a small but growing collection of German, French and Dutch titles. The owner is an ex-Peace Corps volunteer who has lived in Morocco and Nepal.

Getting There & Away

Bus Nong Khai's main bus station off Prajak Rd has buses to Si Chiangmai, Beung Kan, Loei, Udon, Ubon, Tha Bo, Bangkok and Rayong.

Buses to Nong Khai (No 221) leave Udon Thani approximately every half hour throughout the day from Udon's Rangsina Market bus terminal. The trip takes about 1¼ hours and costs 15B.

Buses between Loei and Nong Khai (No 506) arrive and depart every half hour in either direction and cost 61B; Nakhon

Phanom buses (No 224) run at a similar frequency and cost 91B.

If you're coming from Loei Province, you can get buses from Chiang Khan or Pak Chom without having to double back to Udon. From Nakhon Phanom you can travel via Beung Kan along the Maekhong River or you can cut through Sakon Nakhon and Udon Thani.

To/From Bangkok Ordinary buses to Nong Khai from Bangkok's northern bus terminal leave 12 times daily between 4.10 am and 10 am. The trip is a long 11 to 12 hours and costs 146B (177B in the reverse direction for some reason). Second-class air-con buses cost 263B and leave three times a day at 8.40 am, 9.15 and 9 pm. First-class air-con and VIP buses leave once nightly at 8 and 9 pm respectively; 1st class costs 319 to 328B, VIP 405B. Most people prefer to take the Bangkok-Nong Khai train – on which they can wander around a bit – rather than sit in a narrow bus seat for 10 or more hours.

Train From Bangkok, the Nong Khai Express leaves Hualamphong station daily at 8.30 pm, arriving in Nong Khai at 7.30 am – about the same speed as the bus but considerably more comfortable. Two rapid trains leave daily at 6.15 am and 7 pm, arriving at 4.50 pm and 6.15 am. Basic one-way fares are 450B 1st class and 215B 2nd class, not including surcharges for express or rapid service (30B and 20B) or sleeping berths.

There are no longer any 3rd-class trains to Nong Khai, but you can take a 3rd-class diesel railcar as far as Udon Thani (110B) and hop on a bus from there for another 15B – see the Udon Thani Getting There & Away section for schedule information.

Boat Ferry boats from Tha Deua on the Laos side of the Maekhong cost 30B each way. At present you must have a visa to board the boat to Laos; in the reverse direction you'll need a visa if you plan to spend more than 15 days in Thailand.

The new Friendship Bridge replaces the Jommani-Tha Na Laeng vehicle ferry between the two countries. Regular bus service between Nong Khai and Vientiane hadn't yet been established at the time of writing but should be available by the time you arrive in Nong Khai. Any travel agency in town can provide car or van transport across the bridge to Vientiane for around 200B.

Getting Around

Samlors around the town centre cost 10B; tuk-tuks are 10 to 20B.

Nana Motor (☎ 411998) at 1160 Meechai Rd rents motorbikes at reasonable rates. Suzuki 4WD Caribians can be rented from Village Weaver Handicrafts at 786/1 Prajak Rd.

AROUND NONG KHAI PROVINCE
Wat Phra That Bang Phuan

วัดพระราธุบังพวน

Twelve km south of Nong Khai, on Highway 2 and then 11 km west on Highway 211, Wat Bang Phuan is one of the most sacred sites in the north-east because of the old Indian-style stupa found here. It's similar to the original chedi beneath the Phra Pathom Chedi in Nakhon Pathom, but no-one knows when either chedi was built. Speculation has it that it must have been in the early centuries AD or possibly even earlier – supposedly the chedi enshrines some chest bones of the Buddha himself.

In 1559 King Jayachettha of Chanthaburi (not the present Chanthaburi in Thailand, but Wiang Chan – known as Vientiane – in Laos) extended his capital across the Maekhong and built a newer, taller, Lao-style chedi over the original as a demonstration of faith (just as King Mongkut did in Nakhon Pathom). Vientiane is the French spelling of the Lao name Wiang Chan, which means City of Sandalwood. Rain caused the chedi to lean precariously and in 1970 it fell over. The Fine Arts Department restored it in 1976-77 with the Sangharaja, Thailand's Supreme Buddhist Patriarch, presiding over the re-dedication in 1978. The current chedi stands 34.25 metres high on a 17.2-sq-metre base.

NORTH-EAST THAILAND

Actually, it is the remaining 16th-century Lao chedis in the compound (two contain semi-intact Buddha images in their niches) that give the wat its charm. There is also a roofless wihaan with a large Buddha image, and a massive round brick base that must have supported another large chedi at one time. Recently, a small museum displaying site relics and a collection of old wooden spirit houses has opened to the public; admission is free, although donations are appreciated.

Getting There & Away To get to Wat Phra That Bang Phuan, get a Si Chiangmai or Sangkhom-bound songthaew or bus in Nong Khai and ask for Ban Bang Phuan (12B). Most Sangkhom-bound buses automatically stop at Phra That Bang Phuan. Otherwise get any bus south on Highway 2 and get off in Ban Nong Song Hong, the junction for Route 211. From there take the next bus (from either Udon or Nong Khai) that's going to Si Chiangmai and get off near the wat. The fare should be about 10B to the road leading off Route 211; it's an easy walk to the wat from that point.

Tha Bo
ท่าบ่อ

Along the Maekhong River and Route 211 between Nong Khai and the Loei Province line are several smaller towns and villages where life revolves around farming and minimal trade between Laos and Thailand.

Surrounded by banana plantations and vegetable fields flourishing in the fertile Maekhong floodplains, Tha Bo (population 16,000) is the most important market centre between Nong Khai and Loei. An open-air market along the main street probably offers more wild plants and herbs than any market along the Maekhong, along with Tha Bo's most famous local product – tomatoes. Tomato exports from Tha Bo reached 86,700 tonnes in 1990. Tobacco is also grown in impressive quantities.

The **Huay Mong Dam**, which crosses the Maekhong at the western edge of town, irri-

gates 10,800 hectares of land around Tha Bo. This relatively small-scale pumping project is one of the most successful hydrology efforts in Thailand, running at a higher efficiency than any of the country's larger dam facilities and with less extreme environmental impact. There is a pleasant public park next to the dam.

Aside from the market and dam, the town's only other claim to fame is **Wat Ong Teu** (also known as Wat Nam Mong), an old Lao-style temple sheltering a 'crying Buddha'. According to local legend, the left hand of the 300-year-old bronze image was once cut off by art thieves; tears streamed from the Buddha's eyes until the hand was returned. The wat is three km west of town off Route 211.

Places to Stay & Eat *Suksan Hotel*, on the main street through town, has basic rooms for 60B. Out on the road from Nong Khai at the town's eastern entrance is *SP Guest House*, a former dive hotel with rooms for 80B. *Tha Bo Bungalow*, on a back street not far from the town centre, has passable rooms with fan and bath for 80B.

Quieter and more unusual accommodation is available at *Isan Orchid Guest Lodge* (☎ (042) 431665) at 87/9 Kaewarawut Rd, a large modern house in the middle of village-like surroundings near the river. Owned by a retired American businessman but managed by Thais, the house has large, comfortable air-con rooms from 500 to 750B including continental breakfast. A smaller bungalow next to the main house is available for 700 to 850B. The manager can arrange Udon airport pick-up as well as trips to Phra Phutthabat Bua Bok; bicycles can be borrowed at no charge.

There are several modest noodle and rice shops on the main street plus a couple of kài yâang places. Near the river at the north-eastern end of town is *Suan Aahaan Taling Naam*, a garden restaurant specialising in 'mountain chicken', which denotes a method of grilling whole chickens standing on end rather than horizontally.

Getting There & Away All songthaews and buses from Nong Khai (25 km to the east) bound for Si Chiangmai will drop passengers in Tha Bo for 10B. If you're cycling from Nong Khai, you have a choice of the scenic but unpaved river road or the paved and fast – but less scenic – Route 211. Eventually the river road will be paved, in which case it will become the fastest and most direct route to Tha Bo and farther west.

Si Chiangmai

ศรีเชียงใหม่

Just across the river from Vientiane, Si Chiangmai has a large number of Lao and Vietnamese who make their living from the manufacture of rice-paper spring-roll wrappers. You can see the translucent disks drying in the sun on bamboo racks all over town. Si Chiangmai is one of the leading exporters of spring-roll wrappers in the world! Many of the Vietnamese and Lao residents are Roman Catholic and there is a small cathedral in town. A local bakery bakes fresh French rolls every morning.

Wat Hin Mak Peng, Ban Pheu, and various local villages can be visited from Si Chiangmai – enquire at Tim Guest House for the latest information.

Ferries now cross regularly to Vientiane; there are immigration and customs offices in town. However, foreigners (non-Thais) are usually referred to Nong Khai for river crossings.

Places to Stay & Eat *Tim Guest House* (☎ (042) 451072), the only guesthouse in town, is run by a friendly young Swiss-French man who speaks English, French, German and Thai. Rooms start at 50B for a small single to 100B for a large double with a river view (but over the street). Simple Thai and farang food is served in a dining area downstairs. Maps of the vicinity, massage and herbal sauna, laundry service and bicycle and motorcycle rental are available. Boat trips along the Maekhong River to Nong Khai, Wat Hin Mak Peng and Sangkhom can also be arranged. The guesthouse is on Rim Khong Rd near the river in the centre of town – walk west from the bus terminal and turn right at Soi 17, then turn left at the end of the road and you'll find it on the left.

Adjacent to Tim is the basic *Hotel Suthisuwan*, with rooms for 50 to 90B.

Getting There & Away Probably because of its importance as a spring-roll wrapper capital, Si Chiangmai has an abundance of public transport in and out. Bus fares to/from Si Chiangmai are:

To/From	Fare
Bangkok	
(air-con)	175 to 205B
Khon Kaen	55B
(air-con)	90B
Khorat	87B
(air-con)	140B
Nong Khai	15B
Pak Chom	35B
Sangkhom	12B
Udon Thani	25B

Wat Hin Maak Peng

วัดหินหมากเป้ง

Sixty-four km north-west of Nong Khai between Si Chiangmai and Sangkhom, Wat Hin is worth a trip just for the scenery along Route 211 from Nong Khai. This monastery is locally known for its *thutong* (Pali: *dhutanga*) monks – men who have taken ascetic vows in addition to the standard 227 precepts. These vows include eating only once a day, wearing only forest robes made from discarded cloth and having a strong emphasis on meditation. There are also several mae chiis (Buddhist nuns) living here.

The place is very quiet and peaceful, set in a cool forest with lots of bamboo groves, overlooking the Maekhong. The monastic kutis are built among giant boulders that form a cliff high above the river; casual visitors aren't allowed into this area however. Below the cliff is a sandy beach and more rock formations. Directly across the river a Lao forest temple can be seen.

NORTH-EAST THAILAND

Fisherfolk occasionally drift by on house rafts.

The abbot at Wat Hin Maak Peng requests that visitors to the wat dress politely – no shorts or sleeveless tops. Those that don't observe the code will be denied entrance.

Getting There & Away To get there, take a songthaew from Nong Khai to Si Chiangmai (15B) and ask for a songthaew directly to Wat Hin (there are a few) or to Sangkhom, which is just past the entrance to Wat Hin – the other passengers will let you know when the truck passes it (the bus usually makes a stop here anyway). The second songthaew is 10B. On the way to Wat Hin you might notice a large topiary at Ban Phran Phrao on the right side of the highway.

Sangkhom
สังคม

The tiny town of Sangkhom could be used as a rest stop on a slow journey along the Maekhong River from Loei to Nong Khai. Wat Hin Maak Peng is nearby and there are some good hikes to caves and waterfalls in the area. The guesthouses hand out maps of the area.

One of the largest local waterfalls is **Than Thip Falls**, three km off Route 211 between Km 97 and 98 a few km west of Sangkhom. The waterfall has two major levels; the upper level is cleaner and has a deep pool (during or just after the rainy season) which is good for a dip. The falls are a long walk from the road – this is a trip best accomplished by motorcycle. **Than Thong Falls**, 11.5 km east of Sangkhom at Km 73 off the north (river) side of Route 211 is more accessible but can be rather crowded on weekends or holidays.

Places to Stay & Eat The town's five guesthouses are off the main road through town near the river.

A flood in 1993 forced two of the guesthouses to shift location to less flood-prone locations. The friendly and efficient *River Huts Guest House* has moved to a more secluded location well off the main road where thatched huts overlooking the river are 60/80B for singles/doubles. The food is good here and the staff offer bicycles for rent. *DD Guest House* also had to move to a new location one km south-east of the village. The setting is lacking in shade but a couple more rainy seasons should take care of that; huts cost 50 to 80B. DD's original restaurant in the middle of town next door to Bouy is still operating.

Out on the main road is the original *Bouy Guest House*, a very pleasant place with huts on the river. Singles/doubles next to the river are 60/80B, or 50/70B nearer the road.

TXK Guest House, off the main road farther west, looked a bit shabby during my last visit but was as welcoming as ever; huts are only 50B. A new thatched-hut place on the river, *Mekong River Guest House*, charges just 40B a single 70B a double.

There are a couple of riverside restaurants. Ask around and you may be able to find a taste of náam yân, the sweetest moonshine from Laos.

Getting There & Away Buses from Nong Khai are 30B and the trip takes about two hours. From Loei it's 50B and three or four hours. Pak Chom is 1½ hours away and the fare is 20B. From nearby Si Chiangmai, it's 12B. Westward beyond Pak Chom, songthaews are less frequent because the road worsens; the fare to Chiang Khan is 15B.

BEUNG KAN
บึงกาฬ

This is a small dusty town on the Maekhong River, 185 km east of Nong Khai by Route 212. You may want to break your journey here if you are working your way around the north-eastern border from Nong Khai to Nakhon Phanom (as opposed to the easier but less interesting Udon-Sakon Nakhon-Nakhon Phanom route). Between Nong Khai and Nakhon Phanom you'll pass many towns with 'Beung' or 'Nong' (Nawng) in their names; both terms refer to shallow bodies of fresh water fed by seasonal streams (a *beung* is usually larger than a *nãwng*).

The closer you get to Nakhon Phanom Province, the more Vietnamese you will see working in the rice fields or herding cows along the road. Nearly all the farmers in this area, whether ethnic Vietnamese or Thai, wear a simple Vietnamese-style straw hat to fend off the sun and rain.

The town of Beung Kan itself isn't much but there are some mildly interesting spots nearby. During the dry season the Maekhong River recedes away from Beung Kan and reaches its narrowest point along the Thai-Lao border. East of town is **Nam Song Sii** (Two-Colour River), where the broad, muddy Huay Songkhram replenishes the Maekhong.

In hopes that it will soon be granted provincial status, amphoe Beung Kan recently constructed a new Sala Jangwat Beung Kan (Beung Kan Provincial Office) next to the highway.

Wat Phu Thawk
(Wat Chedi Khiri Wihaan)
วัดภูทอก (วัดเจดีย์ศรีวิหาร)

Travellers interested in north-eastern forest wats can visit this nearby wat, a massive sandstone outcropping in the middle of a rather arid plain – a real hermit's delight. The entire outcropping, with its amazing network of caves and breathtaking views, belongs to the wat. The wat mountain is climbed by a seven-level series of stairs representing the seven levels of enlightenment in Buddhist psychology. Monastic kutis are scattered around the mountain, in caves and on cliffs. As you make the strenuous climb, each level is cooler than the one before. It is the cool and quiet isolation of this wat that entices monks and mae chiis from all over the north-east to come and meditate here.

This wat used to be the domain of the famous meditation master Ajaan Juan – a disciple of the fierce Ajaan Man who disappeared many years ago. Ajaan Juan died in a plane crash a few years ago, along with several other monks who were flying to

Bangkok for Queen Sirikit's birthday celebration. The plane went down just outside Don Meuang Airport. Many north-easterners have taken this incident as proof that the present queen is a source of misfortune.

To get to Wat Phu Thawk, you'll have to take an early morning songthaew south on Route 222 to Ban Siwilai (25 km, 7B), then another songthaew east (left) on a dirt road, 20 km to the wat (10B). This songthaew carries merit-makers (see Religion in the Facts about the Country chapter). Hitching might be possible if you miss the truck. A reader reported getting a type of local tuk-tuk to the wat in the afternoon from Siwilai for 10B. If solitude is your main objective, it's best to tour Phu Thawk early in the morning before the parade of Thai pilgrims begins.

Ban Ahong
บ้านอาฮง

This village at Km 115 on Route 212 between Beung Kan and Nong Khai (23 km west of Beung Kan) makes an interesting alternative to staying overnight in Beung Kan. The friendly Hideaway Guest House (see Places to Stay & Eat below) next to the Maekhong River is just a 200-metre walk from one of Isaan's smallest and most intriguing wats. Set amongst giant boulders along the river, **Wat Paa Ahong** has only one permanent monastic resident, the highly respected Luang Phaw Praeng. Due to Luang Phaw's skills as a gardener, the wat grounds boast lovely flowers all year round. Luang Phaw also fashions charming sculpture and furniture from bamboo roots, and is locally renowned for the traditional medicines he creates from local herbs. An occasional thutong monk or young novice stops by for a few weeks at a time.

The narrow stretch of Maekhong River opposite the wat has some refreshing pools for swimming during the dry season when the river is fairly clear. This area is also considered a highly auspicious spot to spend the evening of *wan àwk phansãa*, the beginning of the Buddhist Rains Retreat. According to the local legend, supernatural

NORTH-EAST THAILAND

lights, *bawng fai phayaa nàak* (dragon rockets), emerge from beneath the Maekhong River on this evening each year and arc across the sky three times. Several hundred Thai and Lao residents gather along the river for the yearly event. At other times of year there's frequent talk of UFO appearances. Similar stories circulate at Phon Phisai farther south-west towards Nong Khai.

Saksin at Hideaway Guest House can arrange boat trips to nearby river islands for 10B.

Places to Stay & Eat
Beung Kan Hotels in Beung Kan are all in the 50 to 80B price range (forget air-con). The small and funky *Samanmit, Neramit* and *Santisuk* are all on Prasatchai Rd not far from the town clock tower; the Santisuk has the best overall appearance.

In addition to a few nondescript foodstalls in town, the *Mae Nam Restaurant* overlooking the river offers decent Thai and Isaan meals.

Ban Ahong *Hideaway Guest House*, behind the village school next to the river (turn off at Km 115) has a circle of simple, quiet huts on stilts for 50B single, 80B double. Meals are available; there is a pleasant riverside sitting area nearby and one can go for walks in the village.

Getting There & Away
The bus from Nong Khai to Beung Kan is 35B. Nakhon Phanom to Beung Kan buses are 45B.

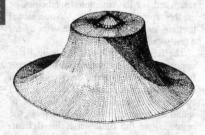

Loei Province

Nearly 520 km from Bangkok, 150 km from Udon, 269 km from Phitsanulok via Lom Sak and 200 km via Nakhon Thai, Loei is one of Thailand's most beautiful and unspoiled provinces. The geography is mountainous and the temperature goes from one extreme to the other, the weather being hotter here than elsewhere in Thailand during the hot season and colder during the cold season. This is the only province in Thailand where temperatures occasionally drop to 0°C.

The culture is an unusual mix of northern and north-eastern influences, which has produced many local dialects. The rural life of Loei outside the provincial capital has retained more of a traditional village flavour than many other places in Thailand, with the possible exceptions of Nan and Phetchabun, also once classified as remote or closed provinces.

Within the province, Phu Kradung, Phu Luang and Phu Reua national parks, as well as the districts of Tha Li and Chiang Khan, are good places to explore for natural attractions.

LOEI
อ.เมืองเลย
In the provincial capital of Loei (population 22,000) there is little to see or do. Cotton is one of Loei's big crops, so it's a pretty good place to buy cotton goods, especially the heavy cotton quilts (quite necessary in the cool months) made in Chiang Khan district – they're priced by the kg. During the first week of February, Loei holds a Cotton Blossom Festival which culminates in a parade of cotton-decorated floats and, naturally, a Cotton Blossom Queen beauty contest.

About three km north of Loei is a water recreation park with a large swimming pool called **Loei Land**. The admission is a reasonable 30B per day.

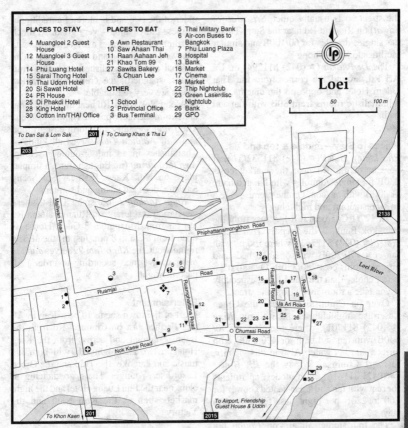

PLACES TO STAY
4 Muangloei 2 Guest House
12 Muangloei 3 Guest House
14 Phu Luang Hotel
15 Sarai Thong Hotel
19 Thai Udom Hotel
20 Si Sawat Hotel
24 PR House
25 Di Phakdi Hotel
28 King Hotel
30 Cotton Inn/THAI Office

PLACES TO EAT
9 Awn Restaurant
10 Saw Ahaan Thai
11 Raan Aahaan Jeh
21 Khao Tom 99
27 Sawita Bakery & Chuan Lee

OTHER
1 School
2 Provincial Office
3 Bus Terminal

5 Thai Military Bank
6 Air-con Buses to Bangkok
7 Phu Luang Plaza
8 Hospital
13 Bank
16 Market
17 Cinema
18 Market
22 Thip Nightclub
23 Green Laserdisc Nightclub
26 Bank
29 GPO

Loei

To Dan Sai & Lom Sak — 201
To Chiang Khan & Tha Li
203

0   50   100 m

Phiphattanamongkhon Road

Maliwan Road

Ruamjai

Ruamphattana Road

Nok Kaew Road

Chumsai Road

Ruamjit Road

Charoenrat Road

Ua Ari Road

Loei River

To Khon Kaen — 201

To Airport, Friendship Guest House & Udon
2015

NORTH-EAST THAILAND

Loei celebrates the annual **Rocket Festival** in May with fervour. The city has even imported the colourful Phi Ta Khon procession from nearby Dan Sai district (see the Dan Sai entry following for details).

Places to Stay – bottom end

Muangloei Guest House has two locations, both within walking distance of the bus terminal. The closest and most amenable is at 103/72 Soi Aw Daw Ruamjai and has basic singles/doubles for 50/80B; this is known as *Muangloei 2 Guest House* (Muangloei 1 has closed) Manager Somdy Mingolo speaks

some English and French and distributes travel information on Loei Province. Luggage may be stored here while you go hiking at Phu Kradung or other national parks in Loei. A Thai brothel sits almost directly across the street from the guesthouse, so soi traffic can be a bit unsavoury at night. Somdy's husband operates a second branch – *Muangloei 3* – with similar rates on a busier street nearby.

Sarai Thong Hotel, off Ruamjit Rd, has 56 none-too-clean rooms in three buildings, costing from 70 to 150B. All rooms have a fan and bath. Service isn't great, but it's off the street so is usually quiet. *Srisawat (Si Sawat)* on Ruamjit Rd near the Sarai Thong has singles/doubles for 60/100B and similar facilities to Sarai Thong.

The *Di Phakdi* (☎ (042) 811294) on Ua Ari Rd, around the corner from the Thai Udom Hotel and opposite the cinema, has minimalistic rooms from 80B with fan and bath.

Places to Stay – middle & top end

Phu Luang Hotel (☎ (042) 811532/570) at 55 Charoenrat Rd near the market costs 230B for singles/doubles with fan and bath, or 300B with air-con. On the premises are a so-so restaurant and nightclub.

At 122/1 Charoenrat Rd, across from the Bangkok Bank, is the friendly *Thai Udom Hotel* (☎ (042) 811763), where rooms with fan cost 170/200B with one/two beds and air-con rooms cost 280/330B. Overall it's a better choice than the Phu Luang, especially if you take a room away from the street.

Over on Chumsai Rd near the Green Laserdisc nightclub is the well-run *King* (☎ (042) 811701), where rooms cost 290/330B with fan and bath, or 420/480B with air-con and hot water. Also in this vicinity, just off Chumsai Rd, is the *PR House* (☎ (042) 811416), with modest apartments for rent with fan and solar-heated shower for 160 to 220B per night, less for long-term stays.

The four-storey, all air-con *Cotton Inn (Meuang Fai)* (☎ (042) 811302; fax 812353), near the THAI office and GPO on Charoenrat Rd, has very pleasant rooms with all the amenities for 400 to 500B.

Places to Eat

The market near the intersection of Ruamjai and Charoenrat Rds has cheap eats and other items of local provenance. Look for the local speciality, khài pîng (eggs-in-the-shell toasted on skewers).

Chuan Lee and *Sawita Bakery* are two pastry/coffee shops on the same side of Charoenrat Rd, not far from the Thai Udom Hotel and Bangkok Bank. Chuan Lee is the older of the two and is more of a traditional Chinese coffee shop – very good. At lunch and dinner it also serves a few curries. Sawita is newer, has air-con and offers a long menu of Thai and farang dishes, including fruit salads, spaghetti, ice cream and cookies. Prices are very reasonable.

Along Nok Kaew Rd near the roundabout are two moderately priced Thai restaurants. The *Isaan* specialises in north-eastern food and *Saw Aahaan Thai* serves all kinds of Thai dishes in an indoor-outdoor setting. *Awn Restaurant* (no English sign), a simpler place on Nok Kaew Rd near Soi Saeng Sawang, does kài yâang and sômtam.

Raan Aahaan Jeh, a small Thai-Chinese vegetarian restaurant on Ruamphattana Rd not far from Muangloei 3 Guest House, is open from 8 am to 8 pm. Just off the nearby roundabout, the *Khao Tom 99* serves aahǎan taam sǎng ('food according to order') till past midnight.

Entertainment

Most of the town seems to be asleep by 10 pm. Farther east on Chumsai Rd from the Isaan restaurant and across from the King Hotel are two Thai nightclubs with both live music and karaoke: the Thip and the Green Laserdisc. Younger Thais go dancing at clubs near the Phu Luang Hotel and the night market, such as the Rim Nam and the Victory.

Getting There & Away

Air THAI flies to Loei from Phitsanulok three times a week for 1490B. This is a fairly new route – typically such experimental north to north-east routes rarely last more than a year or so. At the moment there are no flights from Bangkok. Loei's airport is six km from town on the road to Udon; THAI shuttle vans are available for 30B per person.

Bus Buses to Loei leave Udon regularly until late afternoon for 38B. The 150-km trip takes about four hours. From Nong Khai the fare is 60B and the trip takes five or six hours.

Loei can also be approached from Phit-sanulok by bus via Lom Sak or Nakhon Thai. A direct bus between Phit and Loei is 58B and takes four to five hours; as far as Lom Sak it's about 34B from either end. Buses between Loei and Dan Sai cost about 25B.

To Chiang Mai ordinary buses cost 136B, air-con 300B; the trip takes about eight hours via Utaradit.

Air-con buses from Bangkok's northern terminal leave at 9 am and 12.30, 8.30, 9 and 9.30 pm, arriving in Loei about 10 hours later for a fare of 279B. A VIP bus leaves nightly at 9 pm and costs 340B. Ordinary buses cost 136B and leave at 4.35, 6.30, 7.50 and 10.30 am, and 2, 8.30 and 9.30 pm. In Loei you can get air-con buses to Bangkok from an agency on Ruamjai Rd (188B 2nd-class air-con, 375B VIP) or from the King Hotel.

AROUND LOEI PROVINCE
Phu Kradung National Park

อุทยานแห่งชาติภูกระดึง

At 1360 metres, Phu Kradung is the highest point in Loei. On top of this bell-shaped mountain is a large plateau with 50 km of marked trails to cliffs, meadows, waterfalls and montane forests of pine, beech and oak. The weather is always cool on top (average year-round temperature 20°C), hence the flora is more like that in a temperate zone. Lower down are mixed deciduous and ever-green monsoon forests as well as sections of cloud forest. The 359-sq-km park is a habitat for various forest animals, including ele-phants, Asian jackal, Asiatic black bear, barking deer, sambar, serow, white-handed gibbon and the occasional tiger. A Buddhist shrine near the park headquarters is a favour-ite local pilgrimage site.

The main trail scaling Phu Kradung is six km long and takes about three hours to climb (or rather walk – it's not that challenging since the most difficult parts have bamboo ladders and stairs for support). The climb is quite scenic and there are rest stops with food vendors along the way. It's a further three km to the park headquarters. You can hire porters to carry your gear for 10B per kg.

During the hottest months, from March to June, it's best to start the climb about dawn to avoid the heat. Temperatures in December and January can drop as low as 3 to 4°C; blankets are available for hire then. Bring sweaters and thick socks this time of year.

Phu Kradung is closed to visitors during the rainy season from mid-July to early October because it is considered too hazard-ous, being very slippery and subject to mud slides. The park can get crowded during school holidays (especially March to May when Thai schools are closed).

A visitors' centre at the base of the moun-tain distributes detailed maps and collects a 25B admission fee; this entrance is only open from 7 am to 3 pm.

Places to Stay & Eat Lots of young Thais, mainly friendly college students, camp here. Tents already set up cost 50B a night and boards for the bottom of the tents are avail-able. Check the tents before paying – some are in quite ragged condition. Set up your own tent for 5B per person. Blankets and pillows can be rented for 10B each. Cabins with water and electricity cost from 500 to 1200B depending on size, but even a 600B bungalow will sleep up to 10 people. There are several small restaurants on the plateau.

About two km from the summit, *Phu Kradung Guest House* has small A-frame doubles for 200B and large multi-bed bun-galows with rustic kitchens for 600B.

If you get stuck in Phu Kradung town, *Phu Kradung House* has rooms with fan for 80 to 140B.

Getting There & Away Buses to Phu Kradung town leave the Loei bus station every half hour from 6 am till 5.30 pm (but don't forget the park entrance closes at 3 pm) for the 77-km, 20B trip. From amphoe Phu Kradung, hop a songthaew to the park visitors' centre at the base of the mountain, seven km away, for 7B.

The last bus back to Loei from amphoe Phu Kradung leaves around 6 pm.

NORTH-EAST THAILAND

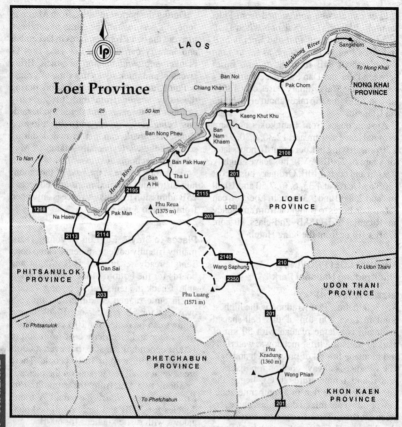

Phu Reua National Park

อุทยานแห่งชาติภูเรือ

This relatively small park of 121 sq km surrounds Phu Reua (Boat Mountain), so named because a cliff jutting from the peak is shaped like a Chinese junk. The easy 2½-hour hike to the summit (1375 metres) passes from tropical to broad-leaf evergreen forest to pine forest. In December, temperatures near the summit approach freezing at night.

The park entrance is about 50 km west of the provincial capital on Route 203. Although there is public transport from Loei to the town of Phu Reua, it is difficult to find songthaews all the way to the park except on weekends and holidays. A well-marked 16-km trail from the park visitors' centre covers a good bit of what the park has to offer, including good views of a mountain range in Sayabuli Province, Laos.

Forestry Department bungalows cost from 250 to 500B a night for up to five people. Tents can be pitched for 5B. On weekends and holidays, food is sometimes available from vendors in the park; at other times you may be able to arrange food through the park rangers.

Phu Luang National Park

อุทยานแห่งชาติภูหลวง

Yet another mountain retreat, Phu Luang (1571 metres) is less visited than either Phu Kradung or Phu Reua. Wildlife is reportedly abundant in the park's higher elevations.

Restrictions Thailand's Forestry Department keeps a tight rein on this national park in order to preserve the wilderness (in contrast to Phu Kradung National Park, which becomes quite trashy on weekends and holidays).

No group larger than 10 people is admitted to the park and visits are restricted to three days and two nights. The park service's control is further enhanced by relatively steep fees totalling 696B for adults, 589B for children aged 12 and under. These fees include permits, two nights' lodging, seven meals, transport from amphoe meuang Loei to the lodging site, guide service and government tax. Guide service usually includes nature walks near the mountain summit and trips to scenic cliffs, springs and waterfalls. Lectures are given in Thai only. The programme ends around 3 pm on the third day.

Permits must be arranged in advance with a 50% deposit – to be sure of obtaining permission allow 15 days' lead time (you can just show up but there's no guarantee of space). Khun Somdy at Muangloei 2 Guest House in Loei can help with the arrangements, or you can write to the District Officer, Amphoe Wang Saphung, Loei 42130 or telephone the park headquarters on ☎ (042) 841141.

To get to the park you'll need your own wheels (hitchhiking is also a possibility); take Route 201 south from Loei for around 20 km to just north of Wang Saphung, then take Route 2250 south-west another 26 km. From there a a nine-km road leads south to the park entrance.

Dan Sai

ด่านซ้าย

About 80 km west of Loei is the small town of Dan Sai, which is famous for its unique Bun Prawet Festival. The three-day festival is part of the larger Rocket Festival that takes place throughout the north-east in May. Nobody seems to know how or when the distinctive festival in Dan Sai first began.

The first day is celebrated in the procession of Phi Ta Khon, a type of masked parade. Participants wear huge masks which are made from carved coconut-tree trunks, topped with a wicker sticky-rice steamer! The procession is marked by a lot of music and dancing. On the second day, Dan Sai residents fire off the usual bamboo rockets and on the third day they retire to **Wat Pon Chai** to listen to Buddhist sermons.

Pak Chom

ปากชม

Pak Chom is the first town of any size you come to in Loei Province if travelling west along the Maekhong River from Nong Khai. It owes much of its erstwhile development to nearby **Ban Winai Refugee Camp**, which was essentially a transplant of Hmong soldiers and families from the secret CIA/USAF base at Long Tieng (Long Chen), Laos, which was evacuated just before the 1975 Pathet Lao takeover. The camp is officially closed and many of the 30,000 Hmong tribespeople at the camp have begun voluntary repatriation to Laos.

There is nothing much to do in Pak Chom except take walks along the river or to nearby villages. The town name means 'Mouth of the Chom', a reference to the confluence of the Chom and Maekhong rivers here. During the dry season, locals pan for gold on Don Chom, a large island at the river junction.

Places to Stay & Eat *Pak Chom Guest House*, on the western edge of town next to the river, has a commanding view of the river and of limestone formations on the opposite banks. The couple who own it have added a few more huts and it's a suitable spot for long-term stays if you're seeking peace and quiet – no dogs or roosters in sight! Huts cost 50/70B single/double; food and boat rentals are available.

To find the guesthouse coming from Chiang Khan on Route 211, get off the bus at the Km 147 stone and walk along a dirt road to the left. Coming from Loei along Route 2108, get off at the T-intersection in town, turn left and look for the Km 147 marker or follow guesthouse signs. Coming from Nong Khai, walk straight across the intersection where the road makes a 90° turn left towards Chiang Khan, and walk about 500 metres till you see the sign pointing right to the Pak Chom Guest House. The huts are another 300 metres towards the river.

Getting There & Away From Chiang Khan, buses to Pak Chom are 15B. Buses from Sangkhom or Loei cost 25B.

CHIANG KHAN

เชียงคาน

Chiang Khan is about 50 km from Loei, on the Maekhong River in a large valley surrounded by mountains. The wooden shophouses along the back streets give the place a bit of a frontier atmosphere and there are some nice views of the river.

Boat trips upriver as far as the Mae Nam Heuang river junction or downriver to Kaeng Khut Khu can be arranged at the Nam and Nong Sam guesthouses for 50 to 150B per person depending on the size of the group and length of the trip.

Visas can be extended at the immigration office, next to the GPO, in Chiang Khan.

Wats

The town's wats feature a style of architecture rarely seen in Thailand – wihaans with colonnaded fronts and painted shutters that seem to indicate a French (via Laos) influence. A good example in the centre of town is **Wat Paa Klang** (Wat Machatimaram), which is about 100 years old and features a new glittery superstructure; in the grounds of this wat is a small Chinese garden with pond, waterfall and Chinese-style sculptures of Buddha and Kuan Yin.

Wat Mahathat in the centre of town is Chiang Khan's oldest temple; the bot, constructed in 1654, has a new roof over old walls, with faded murals on the front.

Temple structures at **Wat Santi** and **Wat Thakhok** are similar to those at Wat Paa Klang (minus the Chinese garden). The walls of the temple buildings are stained red from all the red dust and mud that builds up in the dry and rainy seasons.

Wat Tha Khaek is a 600 to 700-year-old temple, two km outside Chiang Khan, on the way to Ban Noi and Kaeng Khut Khu. The seated Buddha image in the bot is very sacred and it is said that holy water prepared in front of the image has the power to cure any ailing person who drinks it or bathes in it.

Other well-known monastic centres in the area include **Phu Pha Baen**, 10 km east of Chiang Khan, where monks meditate in caves and on tree platforms, and **Wat Si Song Nong**, west of Kaeng Khut Khu (within easy walking distance) on the river. This is a small forest wat where the highly respected Ajaan Maha Bun Nak resides.

Kaeng Khut Khu

แก่งคุดคู้

About four km downstream from Chiang Khan is the Kaeng Khut Khu, a stretch of rapids (best in the dry, hot season) with a park on the Thai side and a village on the Laos side. You can hire a boat to reach the rapids. The park has thatched-roofed picnic areas with reed mats on raised wooden platforms. Vendors sell delicious Isaan food – kài yâang, sômtam and khâo niãw – as well as kûng tên (literally 'dancing shrimp' – fresh river prawns served live in a light sauce of lime juice and chillies), and kûng thâwt (the same fried whole in batter) and drinks. One large restaurant called Khrua Nucha serves sit-down meals. This is a nice place to spend a few hours.

Festivals

Chiang Khan comes alive during awk phansaa, the end of the Buddhist Rains Retreat in October. At that time there's a week-long festival which features displays of large carved wax prasats at each of the

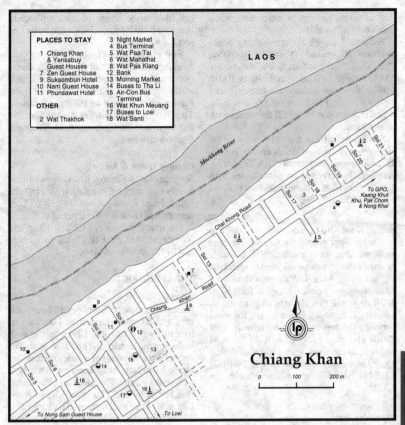

PLACES TO STAY

1   Chiang Khan
    & Yensabuy
    Guest Houses
7   Zen Guest House
9   Suksombun Hotel
10 Nam Guest House
11 Phunsawat Hotel

OTHER

2   Wat Thakhok

3   Night Market
4   Bus Terminal
5   Wat Paa Tai
6   Wat Mahathat
8   Wat Paa Klang
12 Bank
13 Morning Market
14 Buses to Tha Li
15 Air-Con Bus
    Terminal
16 Wat Khun Meuang
17 Buses to Loei
18 Wat Santi

LAOS

Maekhong River

Chai Khong Road

To GPO,
Kaeng Khut
Khu, Pak Chom
& Nong Khai

To Nong Sam Guest House

To Loei

Chiang Khan

0   100   200 m

temples in town as well as boat races on the river. At night there are performances of *măw lam* (Isaan-style musical comedy), in the field facing the GPO.

Places to Stay

Chiang Khan The *Chiang Khan Guest House* (☎ (042) 821029) has fair rooms for 60B, or 80B with two beds and a shared bath. The dining area overlooks the river and inexpensive food is served. At night it's a bit of a Thai hang-out. It's between sois 19 and 20 on Chai Khong Rd, which runs along the Maekhong. *Yensabuy* next door is similar.

Also on Chai Khong Rd, in an old Franco-Chinese building between sois 5 and 6, is the cozy *Nam Guest House* (☎ (042) 821295). Large, nicely furnished upstairs rooms go for 150B with fan, 250B air-con or 300B for a room with three beds (an extra bed in any room costs 50B). In addition to four guest rooms, the house has two outdoor sitting areas – an upstairs verandah with great river views and a downstairs dining area. Meals are available by prior arrangement only.

Turn away from the river altogether on Soi 12 and you'll find *Zen Guest House* (☎ (042) 821119), which is basic but has the largest

NORTH-EAST THAILAND

fleet of rental bicycles in town. Rooms are only 40 to 50B a night.

For hotels, there's the atmospheric *Souksomboon (Suksombun)* (☎ (042) 821064) on Chai Khong Rd just past Soi 9. Rooms are 60 to 80B with fan and shared bath or 100 to 150B with private bath. Around the corner of Soi 9 is the *Phoonsawad (Phunsawat)*, which charges just 50 to 80B for rooms with shared bath.

South-west of town on the river is the easy-going *Nong Sam Guest House*, run by an Englishman and his Thai wife. Large, comfortable, screened singles/doubles with ceiling fans in brick and wood bungalows cost 70/120B.

Kaeng Khut Khu For most people a day trip to Kaeng Khut Khu from Chiang Khan is sufficient, but accommodation is available near the rapids for those inclined to spend the night. *Chiang Khan Hill Resort* offers solid brick bungalows near the rapids for 150 to 800B depending on the size and amenities. *Seeview Huts*, near Ban Noi on the road between the rapids and the highway, cost 200B. The quiet huts are well off the road and next to the river, with a pleasant dining area. The nearby *Cootcoo Resort* (☎ (042) 821248) has similar accommodation for 120B.

Places to Eat
The food situation in Chiang Khan has improved slightly since my last visit. *Chalalai Restaurant* and *Rimkhong Pub* are two new places in old shophouses on the river; they're open evenings and weekends only and serve decent Thai and Isaan meals.

Most of the more modest eating places in town are clustered on Soi 9 and around the intersection of Soi 9 and Chiang Khan Rd. The most popular dish in town seems to be the local version of phàt thai, which here contains thin rice noodles fried with bean sprouts, eggs, and pork (rather than egg, tofu, sprouts, peanuts and dried shrimp). Practically every restaurant in town lists this dish first on its menu! A few places serve khânom

jiin (thin white wheat noodles with chilli sauce), a dish which the locals call by its Lao name, *khào pûn*.

For cheap breakfasts, head for the morning market off Soi 9 near Wat Santi. Between 5 and 7.30 am there are a couple of stalls selling kafae thũng (Thai coffee), curries and paa-thông-kõ (Chinese pastries). The simple riverside restaurant at the Suksombun Hotel serves good Thai and Chinese standards.

Getting There & Away
Songthaews to Chiang Khan leave almost hourly from the Loei bus station for 14B (one hour). From Chiang Khan the bus to Loei departs from near the Shell petrol station.

For transport between Chiang Khan and Nong Khai, see the Pak Chom, Sangkhom and Si Chiangmai sections.

THA LI DISTRICT
อ.ท่าลี่

Perhaps the most beautiful part of Loei is the area which borders Laos from Dan Sai district in the west to Pak Chom in the east, including the district of Tha Li. Much of the district is the Thai half of a valley surrounded by the Khao Noi, Khao Laem and Khao Ngu mountains on the Thai side, and Phu Lane, Phu Hat Sone and Phu Nam Kieng on the Lao side. The small town of Tha Li itself is 50 km from Loei on Route 2115, only about eight km from the Lao border. The border is formed by the Heuang River, a tributary of the Maekhong (which joins the border east of here towards Chiang Khan).

Now that relations between Laos and Thailand have normalised, local commerce back and forth across the Heuang River seems to be growing daily. Ban Nong Pheu, perched on the border, is bustling with a mixture of legal and black-market trade. Handmade products such as cotton fabrics and straw mats, and contraband goods such as ganja and *lâo khão* (white liquor), come across from Laos in exchange for finished goods such as medicine and machine parts. These are 'wild west' villages where travellers go at their own risk – mostly they're easy-going and safe but a lot goes on beneath the apparently calm surface. Sayabuli, the Lao province on the other side of the border, is considered one of the most insecure and lawless in Laos; smuggling is the main source of local income and an armed Hmong guerrilla movement is believed to exist in Sayabuli's mountain ranges.

On the Thai side the village men are prodigious drinkers but rarely touch beer or Maekhong whisky. Instead they drink lao khao, a clear, colourless, fiery liquid with a very high alcohol content, distilled from glutinous rice. In a pun referring to Thailand's famous Maekhong whisky, they call it 'Mae Heuang' after the local tributary. Inside nearly every bottle (30 to 50B per litre) is inserted a thick black medicinal root called *yaa dong*, which is said to dissolve away the aches and pains of the day's work and prevent hangovers. It does seem to mellow the flavour of the lao khao, which has a taste somewhere between high-proof rum and tequila.

In vivid contrast to these villages are several model villages *(mùu bâan tua yàang)* organised by government officials as showcases for counter-insurgency in Loei Province. You'll know if you've stumbled upon one of these by the fenced-in houses with name tags on the doors. They also seem to be mostly empty of people – all hard at work in the fields, say officials. Some model villages even have model families (only one per village) which you are invited to visit – walk right in and see model dad and model mum. Though Thai citizens as near as Loei and Chiang Khan still seem to be ignorant of their existence, I've been able to locate these villages in every visit to Loei since 1983.

Near Ban Pak Huay is one of the best places for swimming in the Heuang River, between January and May when the water is clear. There is now one guesthouse in Ban Pak Huay, or you can usually spend the night at a village temple for a small donation. The wat with the Lao-style chedi off Route 2115 between Tha Li and Pak Huay has hosted several overnight farang visitors.

Ban Nong Pheu & Beyond
บ้านหนองผือ

Fifty km from Chiang Khan along rugged Route 2195, Ban Nong Pheu is a market village for local Thai-Lao trade across the Heuang River, where dozens of ferries flit back and forth all day long. Sit by the border post for an hour or two and you'll be amazed at all the merchandise that comes on and off the narrow boats – cases of Fab detergent, bags of cement, chickens and pigs, lumber, roots, rice. At a wat compound a short walk from the river is an outdoor market where a lot of the goods change hands; there are also a few noodle stalls and cold drink vendors to re-energise visitors who have made it to this little corner of the world. This market doesn't meet every day of the week – enquire in Loei or Chiang Khan for the current schedule. The river traffic is busiest on market days.

About 10 km farther west along Route 2195 is **Ban A Hii**, another market village on the river that's similar to Ban Nong Pheu but usually less lively. The recently paved road continues past Ban A Hii to nondescript Pak Man and ends after about 45 km at Na Haew. This road is not paved to a very high standard; within a year of sealing it was already buckling.

From Na Haew Route 1268 now continues west and north along the Lao border as far as Rom Klao in Phitsanulok Province. A 33-km stretch of Route 1268 north of Rom Klao to Huay Mun in Utaradit Province is unsealed but will probably be reconstructed over the next two or three years; at the moment there's no public transport along this route but it would make an interesting if somewhat rugged bike trip. From Huay Mun you can continue farther north into Nan Province (the provincial border is around 100 km away) along mostly unsealed roads or head west via routes 1239 and 1045 to the amphoe meuang Utaradit.

Places to Stay

Near the junction of routes 2195 and 2115, the low-profile *OTS Guest House* in Ban Pak Huay offers a few simple rooms in a private home for 50B.

NORTH-EAST THAILAND

Getting There & Away
Songthaews from Loei leave almost hourly for Tha Li. The trip takes an hour and costs 15B. Songthaews between Tha Li and Ban A Hi or Ban Pak Huay cost 7B.

NAM NAO NATIONAL PARK
One of Thailand's most beautiful and valuable parks, Nam Nao (Cold Water) covers nearly 1000 sq km, at an average elevation of 800 metres, at the intersection of Chaiyaphum, Phetchabun and Loei provinces. Although the park was first opened in 1972 it remained a PLAT stronghold until the early 1980s. Marked by the sandstone hills of the Phetchabun Mountains, the park features dense mixed evergreen deciduous forest on mountains and hills, open dipterocarp-pine-oak forest on plateaus and hills, dense bamboo mountain forest with wild banana stands in river valleys and savanna in the plains. A fair system of trails branches out from the park headquarters; the scenic and fairly level Phu Khu Khao trail cuts through pine forests and grass meadow for 24 km. The park also features several waterfalls and caves. The park's highest peak, **Phu Phaa Jit**, reaches 1271 metres.

Although it's adjacent to Phu Khiaw Wildlife Sanctuary, a highway bisecting the park has unfortunately made wildlife somewhat more accessible to poachers, so many native species are in decline. There are no villages within park boundaries, however, so incidences of poaching and illegal logging remain fairly minor. Elephant and banteng are occasionally spotted, as well as Malayan sun bear, tigers, leopards, Asian jackals, barking deer, gibbons, langurs and flying squirrels. Rumours of rhinoceros persist (last seen in 1971, but tracks were observed in 1979) and the bizarre fur-coated Sumatran rhino may survive here.

The park headquarters is 55 km east of Lom Sak. A small museum in the visitors' centre contains a collection of confiscated guns and traps used by poachers, an ecological map and bird list. Temperatures are fairly cool all year round, especially nights and mornings; the best time to go is from November to February, when morning frost occasionally occurs.

The Forestry Department operates 10 bungalows (400 to 1200B) and camping areas; tents are available for rent. Vendors next to the visitors' centre offer noodles, Thai and Isaan food. Daily buses run through the park from Lom Sak, Chumphae or Khon Kaen (103 km). Look for the park office sign on Highway 12 at Km 50; the office is two km from here.

LOM SAK
หล่มสัก
It's a scenic trip to/from Phitsanulok via this small town in Phetchabun Province off Highway 12 on the way to/from Loei and Khon Kaen. The ongoing construction of the nearby **Huay Khon Kaen Dam** has brought a small measure of development to Lom Sak.

Places to Stay & Eat
Most convenient to the bus stop is *Sawang Hotel* for 70 to 100B. Near the centre of town, the *PP Guest House* and motel-like *Baan Kaew Guest House* offer better rooms for around 200 to 250B air-con. On the southern outskirts of town towards the highway, opposite a hospital, *Nakhon Inn* has quiet rooms around a courtyard for 120/140B single/double with fan, 240B air-con.

Chawn Ngoen serves very good Thai food in a large saalaa off the main north-south street. Lom Sak's most famous restaurant is the Chinese *Drai-woh*, named for a once-popular detergent called 'Drive-O'! It's the kind of place about which Thais say 'If you haven't eaten at Drive-O you haven't really been to Lom Sak'. *Raan Aahaan Jeh* is a small all-vegetarian restaurant on the east side of the main north-south road through town (just before a bridge).

Nakhon Phanom Province

Nakhon Phanom Province has a large Lao and Vietnamese presence, although the capital is largely ethnic Chinese. If you've come to this province to visit That Phanom, you'll probably have to stop here first to change buses, unless you go directly to That Phanom from Sakon Nakhon via Route 223. The province is dotted with temples with Lao-style thaat – four-sided, curvilinear chedis.

NAKHON PHANOM

อ.เมืองนครพนม

Nakhon Phanom (population 33,400) is 242 km from Udon and 296 km from Nong Khai. It's a rather ordinary town which just happens to have a panoramic view of the Maekhong River and the craggy mountains of Laos beyond – in fact the Sanskrit-Khmer name means 'City of Hills'. A landscaped promenade was recently added along the river at either end of town to take advantage of the views.

Just south of the Grand View Hotel is a river 'beach', where locals and visitors gather to watch the sun set and buy snacks from the evening and weekend vendors. On hot, still days an upside-down mirror image of the river island **Don Don** appears to hang in the air above the real thing.

The interior murals of the bot at **Wat Si Thep**, in town on the street of the same name, show jatakas (life stories of the Buddha) along the upper part, and kings of the Chakri dynasty along the lower part. On the back of the bot is a colourful triptych done in modern style.

The Lao town on the other side of the Maekhong River is **Tha Khaek**. Foreigners are now permitted to cross by ferry provided they hold Lao visas valid for entry at Tha Khaek. Thai and Lao government officials are currently mulling over the possibility of adding a second bridge over the Maekhong

River here (the first, between Thailand's Nong Khai Province and Laos' Vientiane Province, is already open). This would link Nakhon Phanom with the Vietnamese seaport of Vinh on the Gulf of Tonkin via 240-km Route 12 across Laos and Vietnam.

Information

Tourist Office The TAT (☎ 513492) has a temporary office in the Sala Klang Jangwat (Central Provincial Hall) on Aphiban Bancha Rd. The staff distribute information on Nakhon Phanom, Mukdahan and Sakon Nakhon provinces.

By the end of 1995 the TAT office will reportedly be moved to the corner of Sala Klang and Sunthon Wijit Rds.

Post & Telephone The main post office, on the corner of Ratchathan and Sunthon Wijit Rds, is open from 8.30 am to 4.30 pm Monday to Friday, 9 am to noon on weekends and holidays. The attached CAT telephone office is open daily from 7 am to 11 pm.

The telephone area code for Nakhon Phanom is ☎ 042.

Festivals

On the full moon of the 11th lunar month (usually late October), at the end of the Buddhist Rains Retreat, Nakhon Phanom residents celebrate Wan Phra Jao Prot Lok – a holiday in honour of Buddha's ascent to the Devaloka (deity world) to offer the residing devas a Dhamma sermon. Besides the usual wat offering, festival activities include the launching of *reua fai* or 'fire boats' on the Maekhong. Originally these eight to 10-metre boats were made of banana logs or bamboo but modern versions can be fashioned of wood or synthetic materials. The boats carry offerings of cakes, rice and flowers; at night the boats are launched on the river and illuminated in a spectacular display.

During this same festival in the daytime, the city hosts longboat races similar to those seen in many towns along the Maekhong.

Places to Stay – bottom end
Conveniently located on the river, the *River Inn* (☎ 511305) on the Maekhong River used to be one of the nicest places in town but has taken a definite downturn in recent years. Rooms with a fan and bath cost from 120B, with some air-con rooms available for 350B.

The cheapest place in town is the *First Hotel* (☎ 511253) at 370 Si Thep Rd, which has somewhat run-down rooms with fan and bath for 100 to 200B. A bit better is the *Windsor Hotel* (☎ 511946), 692/19 Bamrung Meuang Rd, which has OK singles/doubles for 140/160B with fan and bath, and air-con rooms for 300/350B. Similarly priced yet better than any of the foregoing is the *Grand Hotel* (☎ 511526) on the corner of Si Thep and Ruamjit Rds, which has simple but well-kept rooms for 120/150B or 300B with air-con.

Places to Stay – middle & top end
The *Si Thep Hotel* (☎ 511036), at 708/11 Si Thep Rd, costs 200B for rooms with fan and bath in the old wing, 400B for air-con rooms in the new wing. VIP rooms with fridge and TV are available for 650B.

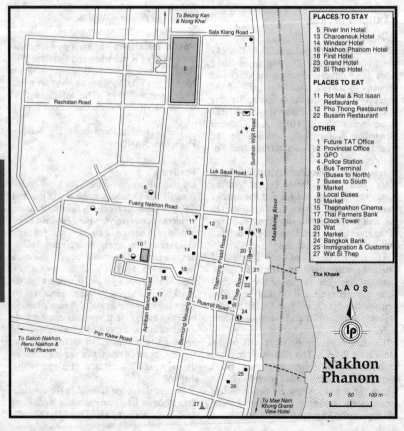

PLACES TO STAY
5 River Inn Hotel
13 Charoensuk Hotel
14 Windsor Hotel
16 Nakhon Phanom Hotel
18 First Hotel
23 Grand Hotel
26 Si Thep Hotel

PLACES TO EAT
11 Rot Mai & Rot Isaan Restaurants
12 Pho Thong Restaurant
22 Busarin Restaurant

OTHER
1 Future TAT Office
2 Provincial Office
3 GPO
4 Police Station
6 Bus Terminal (Buses to North)
7 Buses to South
8 Market
9 Local Buses
10 Market
15 Thepnakhon Cinema
17 Thai Farmers Bank
19 Clock Tower
20 Wat
21 Market
24 Bangkok Bank
25 Immigration & Customs
27 Wat Si Thep

Nakhon Phanom

0   50   100 m

The *Nakhon Phanom Hotel* (☎ 511455) at 403 Aphiban Bancha Rd, has comfortable rooms with fan and bath for 200B, air-con rooms for 300B, air-con with hot water for 450B or VIP rooms (with fridge and TV) for up to 700B.

The new, all air-con *Mae Nam Khong Grand View Hotel* (☎ 513564; fax 511037) overlooking the river at the southern end of town, offers spacious rooms with all the amenities for 850 to 2000B a night.

Places to Eat

Most of the town's better Thai and Chinese restaurants are along the river on Sunthon Wijit Rd; they include *Plaa Beuk Thong (Golden Giant Catfish)*, *New Rapmit*, *Ban Suan*, *Rim Nam* and *New Suan Mai*. I've found New Suan Mai and Plaa Beuk Thong to be the best of the bunch; New Suan Mai has a city map on the wall. At both restaurants, giant Maekhong catfish is served phàt phèt (stir-fried with basil and curry paste), tôm yam (in a spicy lemon-grass broth), phàt kratiam (garlic-fried) or òp mâw din (baked in a clay pot).

There are several good, inexpensive restaurants serving dishes like noodles and curry and rice along Bamrung Meuang Rd north of the Windsor and Charoensuk hotels. Two small rice shops between the Charoensuk Hotel and Honey Massage, *Rot Mai* and *Rot Isaan*, serve local specialities, including jàew háwn, a sukiyaki-style soup with noodles, beef and vegetables. Other popular dishes at these restaurants are lâap pèt (spicy duck salad), ling wua (beef tongue) and yâang sĕua ráwng hâi (literally 'grilled crying tiger' – beef grilled with chillies).

Pho Thong on Bamrung Meuang Rd is a larger place serving Isaan food. Other well-known local Isaan spots include *Somtom Khun Taew* on Sunthon Wijit Rd and *Nawt Laap Pet* at 494 Aphiban Bancha Rd,

If you've had your fill of giant Maekhong catfish and Isaan food but still want Thai fare, try *Khao Kaeng Si Thep*, a standard Thai curry shop in front of the Si Thep Hotel. *Busarin* on Si Thep Rd is a clean, modern Thai restaurant with good food and moderate prices.

Entertainment

The hottest nightspots in town are the Tatiya Club on the corner of Fuang Nakhon and Bamrung Meuang Rds and the nearby Bai Yok, both featuring the usual variety show composed of glittery Thai pop singers. The Nakhon Phanom Hotel's Classic Pub is very popular with moneyed locals. It has the distinction of being the only place in town that serves cocktails. NASA discotheque, next to the Si Thep Hotel, is a pale imitation of its Bangkok namesake.

Getting There & Away

Regular buses run from Nong Khai to Nakhon Phanom via Sakon Nakhon for 50B. There is a direct air-con bus at 9.30 am (it leaves Udon at about 8 am), which costs 120B and takes 7½ hours. If you want to go through Beung Kan, you can get a bus to Beung Kan first (40B), then change to a Nakhon Phanom bus (45B).

Between Nakhon Phanom and Mukdahan there are 13 buses daily for 29B; ordinary buses between Nakhon Phanom and Sakon Nakhon run on a similar schedule for 20B. Buses south to That Phanom run frequently throughout the day and cost 15B.

Air-con buses run between Khorat and Nakhon Phanom thrice daily for 180B.

From Bangkok there are several air-con buses to Nakhon Phanom each evening between 7 and 8 pm for 274B 2nd class or 320 to 375B 1st class, plus one 7 pm VIP departure for 480B.

AROUND NAKHON PHANOM PROVINCE
Renu Nakhon

เรณูนคร

The village of Renu Nakhon is known for the weaving of cotton and silk fabrics, especially mat-mii designs. The local Phu Thai, a Thai tribe separate from mainstream Siamese and Lao, also market their designs here. Each Saturday there's a big handicraft market near

Wat Phra That Renu Nakhon. On other days you can buy from a string of shops and vendors near the temple or directly from weavers in the village. Prices for rough grades of mat-mii are as low as 30B for a 170-cm length.

The thaat at **Wat Phra That Renu Nakhon** exhibits the same basic style characteristics as That Phanom's but in less elongated proportions. The village is definitely worth a visit if you're in the vicinity, even during the week.

During local festivals the Phu Thai sometimes hold folk-dance performances called *fáwn lakhon thai*, which celebrate their unique heritage. They also practise the bai sii custom common in parts of Laos, in which a shaman ties loops of sacred string around a person's wrists during a complicated ceremony involving offerings of blessed water, fruit, flowers, whisky and a variety of other items. On Saturdays at the handicraft market, the Phu Thai put on a music and dance performance for tourists, as well as an abbreviated version of the bai sii ceremony, from 1 to 3 pm.

Getting There & Away The turn-off to Renu Nakhon is south of Nakhon Phanom at the Km 44 marker on Route 212. Since it's only 10 km farther to That Phanom, you could visit Renu on the way, or if you are staying a while in That Phanom, visit here as a day trip. From Route 212, it's seven km west on Route 2031 (5B by songthaew from the junction).

Tha Khaek
ท่าแขก

This Lao town across the river from Nakhon Phanom traces its roots to French colonial construction in 1911-12. Before the war (and during the war until the NVA and Pathet Lao cut the road north to Vientiane), Tha Khaek was a thriving provincial capital and a gambling centre for day-tripping Thais. Today it's a quiet transport and trade outpost with surviving French colonial architecture

similar to that found in Vientiane and Savannakhet.

The *Muanglao* and *Khammouane* hotels offer basic but clean rooms for 2000 kip with shared bath, 4000 kip with private bath.

If you hold a Lao visa valid from entry at Tha Khaek, you can catch a 25B ferry ride across the river; the border is open from 8.30 am to 4 pm daily. Buses from Tha Khaek to Vientiane cost 3000 kip (around 107B) and take 11 hours.

THAT PHANOM
ว ใหญุนม

Fifty-three km from Nakhon Phanom and 70 km from Sakon Nakhon, the centre of activity in this small town is Wat Phra That Phanom.

The short road between Wat Phra That Phanom and the old town on the Maekhong River passes under a large Lao arch of victory which is a miniature version of the arch on Lan Xang Rd in Vientiane (which leads to Vientiane's own Wat That Luang). This section of That Phanom is interesting, with a smattering of French-Chinese architecture reminiscent of old Vientiane or Saigon.

Hundreds of Lao merchants cross the river for the market on Monday and Thursday from around 8.30 am to noon. There are two market locations in town, one on the highway near the wat and one on the river north of the pier. The latter is where the Lao congregate on their twice-weekly visits. Exotic offerings include Lao herbal medicines, forest roots, Vietnamese pigs, and animal skins; the maddest haggling occurs just before the market closes, when Thai buyers try to take advantage of the Lao reluctance to carry unsold merchandise back to Laos.

About 20 km south of town (turn-off for Wan Yai, between Km 187 and 188) is a wooded park next to **Kaeng Kabao**, a set of rapids in the Maekhong River. Nearby hills afford views over the river and Laos on the other side. The usual food vendors make this a good spot for an impromptu picnic – it's an easy bicycle ride from That Phanom.

Information

The Thai Military Bank on Chayangkun Rd offers foreign-exchange services.

Wat Phra That Phanom

The centrepiece of this wat is a huge thaat or Lao-style chedi, more impressive than any chedi in present-day Laos. The monument, which caved in during heavy rains in 1975 and was restored in 1978, is a talismanic symbol of Isaan and is highly revered by Buddhists all over Thailand. The dating of the wat is disputed, but some archaeologists set its age at about 1500 years. The chedi is 57 (or 52, depending on whom you believe) metres high and the spire is decorated with 110 kg of gold. Surrounding the famous chedi is a cloister filled with Buddha images and behind the wat is a shady park.

Festivals

During the That Phanom Festival in mid-February, hordes of visitors descend from all over Isaan, Lao cross over to visit the wat, Thais cross over to Laos, and the town hardly sleeps for seven days.

Places to Stay

That Phanom's first guesthouse, *Niyana Guest House*, on Soi Withi Sawrachon near the That Phanom pier, offers singles with shared bath for 50 to 60B, doubles for 80B, and a few dorm beds for 40B. There's a good information board and a small rooftop garden. In addition to the usual Thai and traveller fare, owner Niyana offers Lao coffee and *khâo jii*, Lao-style French bread. She can also arrange bicycle rentals, short boat trips on the river and excursions to Phu Muu and Mukdahan's Indochina Market.

Relative newcomer *E-San Guest House* at 129/18 Soi Phrempuchani features quiet, tidy rooms in a house on stilts for 60/80B with shared bath.

The old town has three hotels. To reach *Saeng Thong Hotel*, turn right onto Phanom

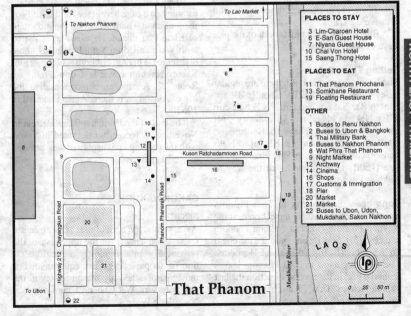

PLACES TO STAY

3 Lim-Charoen Hotel
6 E-San Guest House
7 Niyana Guest House
10 Chai Von Hotel
15 Saeng Thong Hotel

PLACES TO EAT

11 That Phanom Phochana
13 Somkhane Restaurant
19 Floating Restaurant

OTHER

1 Buses to Renu Nakhon
2 Buses to Ubon & Bangkok
4 Thai Military Bank
5 Buses to Nakhon Phanom
8 Wat Phra That Phanom
9 Night Market
12 Archway
14 Cinema
16 Shops
17 Customs & Immigration
18 Pier
20 Market
21 Market
22 Buses to Ubon, Udon, Mukdahan, Sakon Nakhon

To Lao Market

To Nakhon Phanom

Kuson Ratchadamnoen Road

Highway 212

Chayangkun Road

Phanom Phanarak Road

Mae Khong River

To Ubon

LAOS

That Phanom

0   25   50 m

Phanarak Rd as you pass under the arch coming from the wat; it's on the left side of the street 30 metres down. An adequate room with a fan and shared bath costs 60B. It's a funky place (established 1958) with an inner courtyard and lots of character, but pretty basic.

Chai Von (Wan) Hotel, on the opposite side of Phanom Phanarak Rd to the north of the arch (turn left as you pass under the arch), is similar in character but much better kept than the Saeng Thong. Rooms cost 60B with shared bath, 80B with private Thai-style bath.

Lim-Charoen Hotel, on Chayangkun Rd near the bus terminal, has rooms for 80B, but you're better off at the cheaper hotels.

During the February That Phanom Festival, hotel rooms zoom in price and both hotel and guesthouse rooms are booked out well in advance.

Places to Eat
A small night market convenes every evening on Chayangkun Rd. *Somkhane* and *That Phanom Phochana* both serve Thai and Chinese standards.

A floating restaurant just south of the pier has a decent menu.

Getting There & Away
Bus From Chayangkun Rd, there are regular buses to Mukdahan (12B), Ubon (54B, air-con 99B), Sakon Nakhon (20B, air-con 35B), Nakhon Phanom (15B ordinary, 26B air-con) and Udon Thani (62B ordinary, 105B air-con). The air-con Khorat to Nakhon Phanom bus stops at That Phanom. The fare (160B) is the same as all the way to Nakhon Phanom.

Songthaew Songthaews to That Phanom leave regularly from the intersection near the Nakhon Phanom Hotel in Nakhon Phanom and cost 15B. Stay on until you see the chedi on the right. The trip takes about 1½ hours. The last songthaew to That Phanom leaves around 6 pm; in the reverse direction the last vehicle leaves That Phanom for Nakhon Phanom at 8 pm.

Ferry A ferry ride across to Laos costs 10B per person. At the moment only Thai and Lao citizens are permitted to cross the border here.

Sakon Nakhon Province

Sakon Nakhon Province is well known among Thais as the one-time home of two of the most famous Buddhist monks in Thai history, Ajaan Man and Ajaan Fan. Both were ascetic thutong monks who were thought to have attained high levels of proficiency in vipassana meditation. Though born in Ubon, Ajaan Man spent most of his later years at Wat Paa Sutthawat in Sakon Nakhon. Some say he died there, while others say he wandered off into the jungle in 1949 and disappeared. Whatever the story, the wat now has an Ajaan Man museum with a display of some of his monastic possessions.

Ajaan Fan Ajaro, a student of Ajaan Man, established a cave hermitage for the study of meditation at Tham Kham on the mountain of Khao Phu Phaan. He was also affiliated with Wat Paa Udom Somphon in his home district of Phanna Nikhom, 37 km from Sakon Nakhon towards Udon Thani on Route 22. A museum commemorating the life of Ajaan Fan is there. Ajaan Fan died in 1963.

The end of the Buddhist Rains Retreat in November is fervently celebrated in Sakon with the carving and display of wax prasats, as well as parades.

SAKON NAKHON
สกลนคร

As a secondary agricultural market centre (after Udon Thani) for the upper Isaan, the provincial capital is mostly a conglomeration of shops selling farm equipment. For most visitors, the only reason to stay in the city is to visit Wat Choeng Chum and Wat Narai Jeng Weng.

Along the eastern edge of town is **Nong Han**, Thailand's largest natural lake. Don't swim in the lake – it's infested with liver flukes, which can cause a nasty liver infection known as opisthorchiasis. The villages around the lake have recorded among the highest incidences of opisthorchiasis in the world, since many of the villagers eat snails gathered from water plants in the lake. These snails play host to the flukes, which bore through human or animal skin and breed in the internal organs. (See the Health section in the Facts for the Visitor chapter for more information.)

Another of Sakon's claims to fame in Thailand is the relative popularity of dogmeat cuisine. Contrary to common Thai stereotype, not all natives of Sakon are fond of eating dog – in fact it's a custom mostly relegated to the Soh ethnic minority of **Tha Lae district** around 42 km north-west of amphoe meuang Sakon Nakhon. A dog market in Tha Lae sells cooked dog in curries, satay, soups and so on. Since by national law it's illegal to buy and sell live dogs for dining purposes, Sakon residents trade large ceramic water jars with their neighbours for live dogs (usually two to

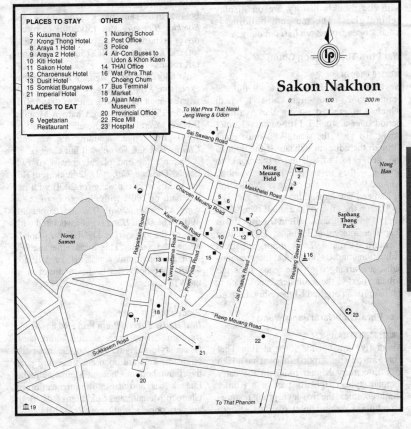

PLACES TO STAY
5 Kusuma Hotel
7 Krong Thong Hotel
8 Araya 1 Hotel
9 Araya 2 Hotel
10 Kiti Hotel
11 Sakon Hotel
12 Charoensuk Hotel
13 Dusit Hotel
15 Somkiat Bungalows
21 Imperial Hotel

PLACES TO EAT
6 Vegetarian Restaurant

OTHER
1 Nursing School
2 Post Office
3 Police
4 Air-Con Buses to Udon & Khon Kaen
14 THAI Office
16 Wat Phra That Choeng Chum
17 Bus Terminal
18 Market
19 Ajaan Man Museum
20 Provincial Office
22 Rice Mill
23 Hospital

Sakon Nakhon

0   100   200 m

To Wat Phra That Narai Jeng Weng & Udon

To Wat Phra That Narai Jeng Weng & Udon

Sai Sawang Road

Ming Meuang Field

Makkhalai Road

Charoen Meuang Road

Kamjat Phai Road

Ratpattana Road

Yuwapattana Road

Prem Prida Road

Jai Phasuk Road

Meuang Sawat Road

Nong Samon

Rawp Meuang Road

Sukkasem Road

Nong Han

Saphang Thong Park

To That Phanom

NORTH-EAST THAILAND

three jars per dog). What does dogmeat taste like? You'll have to take a bite of Rex or Fido to find out for yourself – I've never (knowingly) tasted it.

Ajaan Man Museum

In the grounds of Wat Paa Sutthawat, on the south-west outskirts of town (off the road to Kalasin), this recently completed museum contains an exhibition of the personal effects of Thailand's famous forest monk. The very modern building looks a bit like a modern Christian church, with arches and stained glass windows. A bronze image of Ajaan Man surrounded by flowers sits on a pedestal at one end. Articles and photos associated with the monk's history are on display behind glass. The museum building is usually open from 8 am to 6 pm daily.

Wat Phra That Choeng Chum

วัดพระธาตุเชิงชุม

Next to the Nong Han Lake in town, this wat features a 25-metre-high Lao-style chedi which was erected during the Ayuthaya period over a smaller 11th-century Khmer prang. To view the prang you must enter through the adjacent wihaan. If the door to the chedi is locked, ask one of the monks to open it – they're used to having visitors. Around the base of the prang is a collection of Lao and Khmer Buddha images.

Also on the grounds is a small Lan Xang-era bot and a wihaan built in the cruciform shape reminiscent of Lanna styles found in northern Thailand. Lûuk nímít, spherical ordination markers that look like cannonballs, are arranged on the grass near the wihaan; next to the monastery's east gate is the base for an original Khmer Shivalingam.

Wat Phra That Narai Jeng Weng

วัดพระธาตุนารายณ์เจงเวง

About five km outside town at Ban That (three km past the airport), this wat has a 10th to 11th-century Khmer prang in the early Bapuan style. Originally part of a Khmer Hindu complex, the five-level prang features a reclining Vishnu lintel over its eastern portico and a dancing Shiva over its northern one.

To get to the temple by public transport, catch a songthaew west towards the airport on Sai Sawang Rd and get off at Talaat Ban That Naweng (5B). From here it's a pleasant one-km walk to the wat through a village. The wat is called Phra That Naweng (contraction of Narai Jeng Weng) for short.

Places to Stay

The *Araya 1* on Prem Prida Rd has one/two bed rooms with fan for 150/200B and air-con rooms for 250/300B; diagonally opposite is the wooden *Araya 2* with rooms with fan for only 70/90B and a Thai-Chinese restaurant below. On the same block as the Araya 2 are *Somkiat Bungalows* at 150/200B (a truck-driver favourite because of its inside parking lot) and *Kiti Hotel*, at 100/150B for basic but OK rooms.

At 645/2 Charoen Meuang Rd is the less expensive *Krong Thong* (☎ (042) 711097), where decent rooms with fan are 80 to 150B, air-con 250B. Also along Charoen Meuang Rd are several similar hotels in the 80 to 150B price range, including the *Kusuma, Charoensuk* and *Sakon* – all fair choices.

Sakon's top-end places consist of two hotels. The *Imperial*, at 1892 Sukkasem Rd, has rooms in its old wing for 200B with fan and bath or 290B with air-con; in the new wing VIP rooms with TV and carpet are 490B. The *Dusit Hotel* is not associated with any of the up-market Dusit Group hotels around the country. This one is rather shabby, with air-con rooms for 250B, or VIP for 450B – the hot water is spasmodic even in the VIP rooms.

Places to Eat

Best House Suki on Prem Prida Rd has a nice outdoor eating area, seafood and jàew (Isaan-style sukiyaki – a noodle hot-pot). Night markets are open each evening near the roundabout at Charoen Meuang and Jai Phasuk Rds, and also at the intersection of Charoen Meuang and Sukkasem Rds. Both are very popular nightspots, open till late.

Along Prem Prida Rd are three inexpensive Thai-Chinese restaurants that seem to do half the restaurant business in the city. They're apparent clones of one another; the offerings at all three are similar (buffet-style curries and stir-fries) and all sport names that end in -*rak* (love): *Mitrak* (Friend Love), *Yawt Rak* (Peak of Love) and *Na Rak* (Lovable). All serve passable food at cheap prices.

Laap fans shouldn't miss *Phen Laap Pet*, an inexpensive Sakon institution on Prem Prida Rd with a choice of lâap pèt khão or lâap pèt daeng – white duck salad and red duck salad ('red' means with duck blood). Other house specialities are yam (another kind of Isaan salad, usually with vegetables or seafood), khài yát sâi (ground pork and vegetable omelette), and plaa sãam rót or 'three-flavour fish', a whole fish fried with onions, chillies and garlic.

If duck blood or other animal food isn't your thing, move on over to the *Vegetarian Restaurant* on Charoen Meuang Rd between Sukkasem and Prem Prida Rds. All dishes cost between 5 and 10B, but it's only open from 6 am to 1 pm, Monday to Saturday. Another vegetarian restaurant known simply as *Aahaan Jeh* (Vegetarian Food) has recently opened opposite Phen Laap Pet.

Getting There & Away

Air Should you wish to fly in or out of Sakon Nakhon, THAI has one flight a day from Bangkok (1465B one way). The office in Sakon (☎ (042) 712259) is at 1446 Yuwapattana Rd, near the Dusit Hotel.

Bus Direct buses to Sakon are available from Ubon (69B), Nakhon Phanom (26B), Kalasin (35B), That Phanom (20B) and Udon (42B). Buses from Sakon to Bangkok are 150B (10 departures a day) or 271B air-con (one evening departure a day). Buses between Khorat and Sakon (air-con only) are 138B and leave six times daily.

Private air-con buses to Udon and Khon Kaen leave three times daily from the Udon-Sakon Doen Rot bus office, next to the Esso station on Ratpattana Rd.

AROUND SAKON NAKHON
Phu Phaan National Park
อุทยานแห่งชาติภูพาน

This 645-sq-km nature preserve is in the Phu Phaan Mountains near the Sakon Nakhon-Kalasin border. Deer, monkeys and other smaller forest animals are common to the park and wild elephants and tigers are occasionally seen as well.

The mountain forests are thick and the area is fairly undeveloped. It has been used as a hiding spot by two guerrilla forces – the Thai resistance against the Japanese in WW II and later the PLAT guerrillas in the 1970s.

The park has only a few hiking trails but there are good views along Route 213 between Sakon Nakhon and Kalasin. Three waterfalls – Tat Ton, Hew Sin Chai and Kham Hom – can be visited fairly easily.

The **Tham Seri Thai** cave was used by the Thai Seri during WW II as an arsenal and mess hall.

Yasothon & Mukdahan Provinces

Once encompassed by Ubon Ratchathani and Nakhon Phanom provinces, these adjacent provinces in the lower north-east are two of Thailand's newest and Isaan's smallest. Both are mostly rural in character, with small capital cities serving as market centres for surrounding farms.

YASOTHON

อ.เมืองโสธร

Yasothon (population 29,800) is a bit out of the way, but if you happen to be in the area (say, in Ubon, which is about 100 km away) during May, it might be worth a two-hour bus trip (from Ubon) to catch the annual Rocket Festival which takes place from 8 to 10 May. The festival (Bun Bang Fai in Thai) is prevalent throughout the north-east as a rain and fertility rite, and is celebrated most fervently in Yasothon, where it involves parades and a fantastic fireworks display. The name of the town, which has the largest Muslim population in the north-east, comes from the Sanskrit 'Yasodhara' which means preserver or maintainer of glory, and is also the name of one of Krishna's sons by Rukmini in the *Mahabharata*.

The village of **Si Than** in Pa Tiu district, about 20 km east of Yasothon off Route 202, is renowned for the crafting of firm, triangle-shaped mawn khwaan (axe pillows), which are said to rival those of Roi Et.

Places to Stay

Udomphon, at 80/1-2 Uthairamrit Rd, costs from 80 to 120B for rooms with fan and bath, while the *Surawet Wattana*, at 128/1 Changsanit Rd, costs from 100B. If you can't get into either of these, try the *Yot Nakhon* (☎ (045) 711122), 141-143/1-3 Uthairamrit Rd, where rooms are from 120/220B with/without air-con.

Getting There & Away

A bus to Yasothon from Ubon costs 27B; from Khorat it's 65B ordinary or 134B air-con.

MUKDAHAN

อ.เมืองมุกดาหาร

Fifty-five km south of That Phanom, 170 km north of Ubon Ratchathani and directly opposite the city of Savannakhet in Laos, Mukdahan (population 25,000) is known for its beautiful Maekhong scenery and as a Thai-Lao trade centre. Among Thais it's most known for the **Talaat Indojiin** or Indochina Market, a Thai-Lao-Vietnamese affair that gathers around Wat Si Mongkon Tai near the Mukdahan pier. On weekends the market spills over into nearby streets; you'll see khaens (the Isaan panpipe) and bolts of cloth from around Isaan in addition to the usual Lao, Vietnamese and Chinese imports. The more formal **Danang Market** in the town centre contains actual storefronts selling many of the same goods.

Mukdahan might make a nice stopover between Nakhon Phanom or That Phanom and Ubon. For a view of the town, climb the 500-metre **Phu Narom** hill, three km south of town. **Phu Muu**, a favourite local picnic spot with scenic views, is 34 km south of amphoe meuang Mukdahan off Route 212 – just south of Ban Taw Khet and the Mukdahan Province line between Km 29 and 30.

The Bangkok Bank of Commerce on Samut Sakdarak Rd in town has a currency-exchange service.

Phu Pha Thoep National Park

อุทยานแห่งชาติภูผาเทิบ

Sixteen km south of Mukdahan, off Route 2034, is a hilly area of caves and unusual mushroom-shaped rock formations. Besides the rock formations, the park is a habitat for barking deer, wild boar, monkeys and civets. The main entrance to the park is actually 25 km from town, just south of the Ubon provincial line. About two km south-west into the park, next to a waterfall, is a collection of dozens of small Buddha images.

Places to Stay

None of the hotels in Mukdahan are great deals, but they're adequate. The *Hua Nam Hotel* (☎ (042) 611137), at 20 Samut Sakdarak Rd, quoted 150B for rooms with fan and shared bath – a little high – or 300B with air-con and private bath. On the same road is the cheaper *Banthom Kasem Hotel*, but it's a real dive.

Hong Kong Hotel, over at 161/1-2 Phitak Santirat, is similar in design to the Hua Nam but a bit nicer; rates are 140 to 180B. Better still is *Saensuk Bungalow* at 2 Phitak Santirat Rd, which offers clean, quiet rooms for 100 to 200B fan, 300 to 400B air-con. The *Si Siam* on Wiwit Surakan Rd is another 100B dive.

Mukdahan Hotel (Hotel Muk) is probably the best deal in town – it's a little away from the centre of town on Samut Sakdarak Rd and rooms cost 150B with fan and shared bath, 250 to 600B with air-con.

Places to Eat

The night market along Song Nang Sathit Rd has kài yâang, sôm-tam, khâo jìi (Lao baguette sandwiches), and páw-pía (Vietnamese spring rolls, either fresh (sòt) or fried (thâwt)). *Khao Tom Suanrak*, next to Hua Nam Hotel, is a Chinese rice-soup place that's open all night. Another place that's open in the wee hours is the *Suwa Blend Restaurant/Pub* next to the Hotel Muk. House specialities are American-style breakfast and khâo tôm.

Enjoy Restaurant (no English sign), on the left side of Phitak Santirat Rd on the way to Hotel Muk from the town centre, serves good Vietnamese food.

On the river, about a km south of the pier, the *Riverside* has a shady outdoor area with

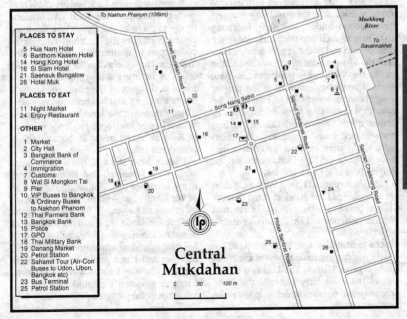

PLACES TO STAY
5 Hua Nam Hotel
6 Banthom Kasem Hotel
14 Hong Kong Hotel
16 Si Siam Hotel
21 Saensuk Bungalow
26 Hotel Muk

PLACES TO EAT
11 Night Market
24 Enjoy Restaurant

OTHER
1 Market
2 City Hall
3 Bangkok Bank of Commerce
4 Immigration
7 Customs
8 Wat Si Mongkon Tai
9 Pier
10 VIP Buses to Bangkok & Ordinary Buses to Nakhon Phanom
12 Thai Farmers Bank
13 Bangkok Bank
15 Police
17 GPO
18 Thai Military Bank
19 Danang Market
20 Petrol Station
22 Sahamit Tour (Air-Con Buses to Udon, Ubon, Bangkok etc)
23 Bus Terminal
25 Petrol Station

To Nakhon Phanom (106km)

Maekhong River

To Savannakhet

Wiwit Surakan Road

Song Nang Sathit

Samut Sakdarak Road

Santran Chaikhrong Road

Phitak Santirat Road

Central Mukdahan

0   50   100 m

a view of Savannakhet. The menu covers mostly Thai and Chinese dishes, but lâap is also served. Prices are moderate and the beer is cold.

Getting There & Away

There are frequent buses from either direction – 29B ordinary (48B air-con) from Nakhon Phanom, half that from That Phanom, or 34B (77B air-con) from Ubon.

VIP (sleeper) buses to Bangkok and ordinary buses to Nakhon Phanom leave from the intersection of Wiwit Surakan and Song Nang Sathit Rds near the government bus office. Sahamit Tour on Samut Sakdarak Rd has air-con buses to Bangkok, Nakhon Phanom, Udon, Ubon and Sakon Nakhon.

Savannakhet

Just across the Maekhong River from Mukdahan, this Lao city of 45,000 is the capital of Savannakhet Province in Southern Laos and a major relay point for trade between Thailand and Vietnam.

Lao and Thai government officials are currently discussing the possibility of erecting a second bridge over the Maekhong River here to facilitate transport among the three countries. On the opposite side of the river, the 570-km Route 9 extends east all the way to the Vietnamese border at Lao Bao, where it continues eastward to the port of Dong Ha on the lower Gulf of Tonkin. At the moment a competing proposal for a bridge farther north (between Nakhon Phanom Province and Laos' Khammuan Province) has a slight edge because the relative distance between the Lao-Thai border and the Gulf of Tonkin is much shorter.

Like Vientiane and Luang Prabang, Savan has a number of French colonial and Franco-Chinese buildings – but with less of a current Western presence and almost no tourists.

Places to Stay For 3000 to 5000 kip (107 to 178B) you can get basic rooms at the *Hotel Santyphab* on Thanon Tha Dan two blocks east of the main ferry pier and the *Hotel Sensabay* on a side street opposite the Santyphab.

Getting There & Away Ferries cross the river between Mukdahan and Savan frequently between 8.30 am and 5 pm weekdays, 8.30 am to 12.30 pm Saturdays, for 30B each way. It's now legal for foreigners to enter and exit the country via Savannakhet – as long as you have a visa endorsed for Savan. From Savan there are daily buses to Vientiane (5000 kip, 12 hours) and Pakse (3000 kip, six hours). A long-distance ferry (5000 kip or 178B) to Vientiane sails twice weekly from June to September.

Ubon Ratchathani Province

Ubon is the north-east's largest province and the provincial capital is one of the larger towns in Thailand. About 300 km of the province borders on Laos and around 60 km borders Cambodia. The local TAT office is trying to promote the area where the three countries meet as the 'Emerald Triangle' in counterpart to northern Thailand's Golden Triangle. The 'emerald' in the title ostensibly refers to the many acres of intact monsoon forest in this part of the province – largely due to the fact that it has been sparsely populated because of war tensions. Now that the Khmer Rouge has stopped military activities in the area, travel in the tri-border zone is considered safe.

Ubon's Mun and Chi river basins were centres for Dvaravati and Khmer cultures many centuries ago. Following the decline of the Khmer empires, the area was settled by groups of Lao in 1773 and 1792. By the early Ratanakosin era it had become part of Monthon Ubon, a south-eastern Isaan satellite state extending across present-day Surin, Si Saket and Ubon provinces – as well as parts of southern Laos – with Champasak, Laos, as monthon capital. Today the Lao influence in the province predominates over the Khmer.

UBON RATCHATHANI
อ.เมืองอุบลราชธานี

Ubon (sometimes spelt Ubol, though the 'l' is pronounced like an 'n') is 557 km from Bangkok, 271 km from Nakhon Phanom and 311 km from Khorat. Situated on the banks of the Mun (pronounced Moon) River – Thailand's second-longest waterway after the Maekhong – Ubon has a population of 90,000 and is a financial, educational, communications and agricultural market centre for eastern Isaan. Like Udon and Khorat, it served as a US air base in the Vietnam War days. The city's main attractions are the October candle festival, a few wats and a national museum.

Information

Tourist Office The TAT (☎ 243770) has a very helpful branch office at 264/1 Kheuan Thani Rd, opposite the Sri Kamol Hotel. The office distributes free maps of Ubon and other information handouts; it's open daily from 8.30 am to 4.30 pm.

Post & Telephone Ubon's GPO is near the intersection of Luang and Si Narong Rds. It's open from 8.30 am to 4.30 pm Monday to Friday, 9 am to noon on weekends. The telephone office is next door and is open daily from 7 am to 11 pm.

Ubon's telephone area code is ☎ 045.

Medical Services The Rom Kao Hospital on Uparat Rd near the bridge is the best medical facility in the lower north-east.

Ubon National Museum
พิพิธภัณฑ์แห่งชาติอุบล

Housed in a former palace of the Rama VI era, west of the TAT office on Kheuan Thani Rd, the National Museum is a good place to learn about Ubon's history and culture before exploring the city or province. Most of the exhibits have bilingual labels.

Flanking the main entrance are a large Dvaravati-period sema (ordination stone)

and some Pallava-inscribed pillars from the Khmer era. The room to the left of the entrance has general information on Ubon history and geography. This is followed by a prehistory room with displays of stone and bronze implements, burial urns and pottery resembling that found in Ban Chiang, plus reproductions of the Phaa Taem rock paintings. The rooms next to it cover the historical era and contain many real treasures of mainland South-East Asian art, including Hindu-Khmer sculpture from the Chenla, Bapuan and Angkor eras, Lao Buddhas, Ubon textiles, local musical instruments, and folk utensils (rice containers, fish traps, betel-nut holders).

Among the museum's most prized possessions are a rare standing Dvaravati Buddha image and a Dong Son bronze drum.

The museum is open from 9 am to noon and 1 to 4 pm, Wednesday to Sunday. Admission is 10B.

Wat Thung Si Meuang
วัดทุ่งศรีเมือง

Off Luang Rd, near the centre of town, this wat was originally built during the reign of Rama III (1824-51) and has a *hǎw trai* (tripitaka library) in good shape. It rests on high-angled stilts in the middle of a small pond. Nearby is an old mondop with a Buddha footprint symbol. The bot's interior is painted with 150-year-old jataka murals.

Wat Phra That Nong Bua
วัดพระธาตุหนองบัว

This wat on the road to Nakhon Phanom on the outskirts of town (catch a white city bus for 2B) is based almost exactly on the Mahabodhi stupa in Bodhgaya, India. It's a much better replica than Wat Jet Yot in Chiang Mai, which is also purported to be a Mahabodhi reproduction, but was designed by people who never saw the real thing. The jataka reliefs on the outside of the chedi are very good. Two groups of four niches on each side of the four-sided chedi contain Buddhas standing in stylised Gupta or Dvaravati closed-robe poses.

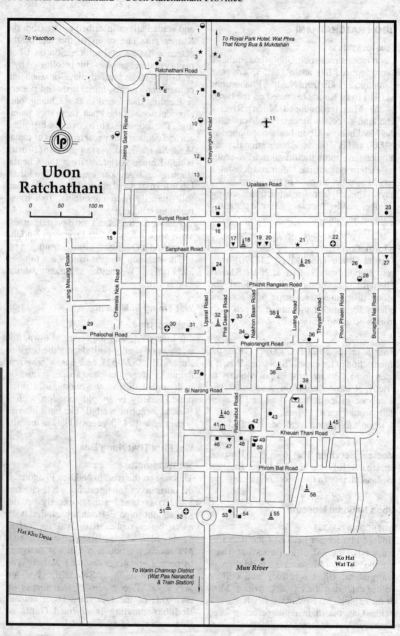

Ubon Ratchathani

To Yasothon

To Royal Park Hotel, Wat Phra
That Nong Bua & Mukdahan

0   50   100 m

Ratchathani Road

Jaeng Sanit Road

Chayanghun Road

Upalisan Road

Suriyat Road

Sanphasit Road

Phichit Rangsan Road

Lang Meuang Road

Chawala Nok Road

Uparat Road

Pha Daeng Road

Nakhon Baan Road

Luang Road

Theyathi Road

Phon Phaen Road

Burapha Nai Road

Phalochai Road

Phalorangrit Road

Si Narong Road

Ratchabut Road

Kheuan Thani Road

Phrom Bat Road

Hat Khu Deua

To Warin Chamrap District
(Wat Paa Nanachat
& Train Station)

Mun River

Ko Hat
Wat Tai

NORTH-EAST THAILAND

Wat Supatanaram

วัดสุปัฏนาราม

Called Wat Supat for short, the unique bot at this temple features a mix of Khmer, European and Thai styles. In contrast to the usual Thai or Lao-style temple structures of the region, the bot is made entirely of stone, like the early Khmer stone prasats; the roof corners display dragons instead of the usual *jâo fáa* or sky spirits.

In front of the bot is the largest wooden bell in Thailand.

Wat Jaeng

วัดแจ้ง

This wat on Sanphasit Rd has a typical Lao-style bot (known locally by the Lao term, *sim*). The carved wooden verandah depicts a *kotchasi*, a mythical cross between an elephant and a horse; above that is Erawan, Indra's three-headed elephant mount.

Warin Chamrap District Temples

Ubon city district is separated from Warin

Chamrap to the south by the Mun River. Two well-known wats in this district are forest monasteries (wat paa) founded by the famous monk and meditation master Ajaan Chaa. The venerable ajaan passed away in January 1992 after a productive and inspirational life, but his teachings live on at these two hermitages.

Wat Nong Paa Phong About 10 km past the train station, in Warin Chamrap district, is Wat Nong Paa Phong. This very famous forest wat was founded by Ajaan Chaa, who also founded many other branch temples in Ubon Province and one in Sussex, England. All of these temples are known for their quiet discipline and daily routine of work and meditation.

Dozens of Westerners have studied here during the past 20 years and many live here or at branch temples as ordained monks.

Ajaan Chaa, a former disciple of the most famous north-eastern teacher of them all, Ajaan Man, was known for his simple and direct teaching method which seemed to

NORTH-EAST THAILAND

cross all international barriers. He passed away in 1992 at age 75; his funeral, which was held here a year later, drew thousands of followers from around the world.

The wat features a small museum and a chedi where Ajaan Chaa's ashes are interred. To get to the wat from Ubon, take a pink city bus No 3 to the Baw Khaw Saw terminal, then catch a songthaew going to the wat.

Wat Paa Nanachat Bung Wai The abbot at Wat Paa Nanachat Bung Wai is Canadian, the vice-abbot is English and most of the monks are European, American or Japanese. As English is the main language spoken here, Wat Paa Nanachat is a better place to visit than Wat Nong Paa Phong if you are interested in more than sightseeing. The wat is very clean, cool and quiet. Generally only those with a serious interest in Buddhism – preferably with previous practice experience – are permitted to stay overnight. Both men and women are welcome, but men are required to shave their heads if they want to stay beyond three days.

From Ubon, take a white city bus No 1 south down Uparat Rd, cross the bridge over the Mun River and get off as the bus turns right in Warin Chamrap for the train station. From there, catch any songthaew heading south (though heading west eventually, on Route 2193 towards Si Saket) and ask to be let off at Wat Nanachat – everybody knows it.

You can also get there by catching a Si Saket bus from Ubon for 4B to Bung Wai, the village across the road from Wat Nanachat. There is a sign in English at the edge of the road – the wat is in the forest behind the rice fields.

You can also hire a tuk-tuk direct to the wat from town for about 70B.

Ko Hat Wat Tai
เกาะหาดวัดใต้
This is a small island in the Mun River on the southern edge of town. During the hot and dry months, from March to May, it is a favourite picnic spot and there are 'beaches'

on the island where you can swim. You can get there by boat from the northern shore of the river.

Hat Khu Deua
หาดคูเดื่อ
Hat Khu Deua is a 'beach' area on the northern bank of the river west of town, off Lang Meuang Rd. Several thatched salas offer shade for picnicking or napping by the river; you can even stay overnight in simple raft houses at no charge.

Festivals
The Candle Festival (Ngaan Hae Thian) is most grandly celebrated in Ubon, with music, parades, floats, beauty contests and enormous carved candles of all shapes – human, animal, divine and abstract. The evening processions are impressive. The festival begins around Khao Phansaa, the first day of the Buddhist Rains Retreat in late July, and lasts five days. Spirits are high and hotels are full. It's worth a trip this time of year just to see the festival.

Places to Stay – bottom end
Suriyat Hotel, at 47/1-4 Suriyat Rd, has divey rooms with fan for 120 to 150B or 200B with air-con. Another cheapie is the *Decha* on Kheuan Thani Rd where rooms are 80 to 100B with fan, 160B with air-con. A better choice in this range is the *Si Isaan (Far East)* (☎ 253204) at 220/6 Ratchabut Rd; singles/doubles are 100/160B with fan and private bath.

The well-kept *Tokyo Hotel* (☎ 241739) is at 178 Uparat Rd where it meets Chayangkun Rd, near the town centre, and is preferable to all of the foregoing if you can afford another 20B or so. Comfortable singles/doubles with fan and bath cost 120/180B or 200/260B with air-con.

Warin *River Moon House* (☎ 322592), at 43-45 Sisaket Soi 2, near the train station in Warin, offers spartan rooms with shared bath in an old teak house for 70 to 100B.

Places to Stay – middle

The friendly *Racha Hotel* at 149/21 Cha-yangkun Rd, north of the town centre, charges 180/220B for clean rooms with fan and bath or 300/320B with air-con. At 24 Si Narong Rd is the *Krung Thong* (☎ 241609) with air-con rooms for a reasonable 380B, fan-cooled rooms for 200/300B.

The *Bodin (Badin)* on Phalo Chai Rd has singles/doubles with fan for 200B and air-con rooms for 320B. It's a bit overpriced for the hotel's shabby condition though it's a favourite with the 'salespeople' crowd.

Ubon Hotel (Kao Chan) at 333 Kheuan Thani Rd used to be the city's number-one lodgings but has gone steadily downhill over the years. Singles/doubles with fan and bath – some quite OK, others rather dank – cost 200/250B or 280/380B with air-con. Similar in price but in better condition is the *Ratcha-thani Hotel* (☎ 254599), at 229 Kheuan Thani Rd, where decent rooms are 220 /300B with fan or 350/500B with air-con.

Places to Stay – top end

The flashy 168-room *Pathumrat Hotel* (☎ 241501; fax 243792) at 173 Chayangkun Rd, once the top hotel in Ubon, has standard air-con rooms for 720 to 920B, 'deluxe' rooms for 1200B and rooms with video for 1850B. Facilities include a coffee shop, res-taurant, travel agency and massage parlour.

Better value in this category is the 116-room *Regent Palace Hotel* (☎ 244031, 245046; fax 241804) at 265-271 Chayang-kun Rd. Clean, quiet, carpeted rooms with TV and phone are 540B single or double, including tax and service. Facilities include a lobby coffee shop, a cocktail lounge and a snooker club.

Another good top-end place is the refur-bished and efficient *Sri Kamol (Si Kamon) Hotel* (☎ 241136; fax 243792) at 22/2 Ubon-sak Rd near the Ratchathani Hotel. Large, comfortable rooms with all the amenities are 750/800B or 1000 to 1200B VIP (with fridge and video); all rates include a Thai or Western complimentary breakfast.

The new 76-room *Tohsang Hotel* (☎ 241925; fax 244814) at 251 Phalo Chai Rd, offers large, pleasant rooms with air-con, TV and minibar for 1200B. Facilities include a coffee shop and Chinese restaurant.

A few km north of town on Route 212, the large *Royal Park Hotel* is under construction. Room rates will probably run in the 1000 to 1500B range.

Ruanrangsi Mansion Park (☎ 244744), in the Ruanrangsi Complex off Ratchathani Rd, offers up-market apartments for rent by the week or month (starting at 12,500B). The landscaped grounds are conveniently adja-cent to the Fern Hut Restaurant, various shops and a branch post office.

Places to Eat

Noodles & Rice On Si Narong Rd, the *Choeng Ubon* (next to the Krung Thong Hotel) and *Song Rot* (opposite the GPO) make good kŭaytĭaw. *Mae Mun 2* and *Thiang Rak* on Kheuan Thani Rd (not far from the Ratchathani Hotel and on the same side of the street) are late-night khâo tôm places that can prepare just about any Thai or Chinese dish you can name.

Maw Khao Maw Kaeng ('Rice Pot – Curry Pot') next to the Sahamit bus office on Kheuan Thani Rd serves good central-Thai curries and hàw mòk (thick, fish-coconut curry steamed in banana leaves).

The cheapest string of rice and noodle places in town runs along Sanphasit Rd just opposite Sanphasit Prasong Hospital.

Regional Ubon is famous for its Isaan food – many Thai gourmets claim it has the best in all of Isaan. Lâap pèt (spicy duck salad) is the local speciality, often eaten with tôm fák (squash soup) and Chinese mushrooms. Good places for lâap pèt include *Jaak Kaan Laap Pet* on Suriyat Rd, *Piak Laap Pet* on Jaeng Sanit Rd (next to a radio relay station) and *Suan Maphrao*, also on Jaeng Sanit Rd (next to Si Mahapho Hospital).

Ubon is also big on kài yâang (grilled Lao-style chicken) and everyone in town agrees that the best is *Kai Yaang Wat Jaeng*, which is just west of Wat Jaeng and is open from around 9 am to 2 pm only. At this rustic, outdoor spot a half chicken costs 35B, sticky rice is 5B, sômtam 5 to 10B. Other specialities include hàw mòk – choice of fish (plaa), or chicken (kài).

A favourite with local families, the simple *Sakhon*, on Pha Daeng Rd near the provincial courthouse, is a long-running Ubon institution with a full array of Isaan dishes. An English menu is available.

Indochine (Indojiin) on Sanphasit Rd near Wat Jaeng specialises in tasty Vietnamese food, including good-value set meals. It's only open from 10 am to 6 pm. A little farther east along the same side of the road, the air-con *Sincere Restaurant* serves an interesting Thai-French cuisine and is open from 9 am to 11 pm; it's closed on Sunday.

Vegetarian Ubon has just one vegetarian restaurant at the moment. It's on Sanphasit Rd east of Sanphasit Prasong Hospital and has Thai vegetarian cuisine at very low prices. Another possible source of vegetarian food is the *Hong Fa Restaurant* opposite the Pathumrat Hotel on Chayangkun Rd. The cooks at Hong Fa will prepare vegetarian Chinese dishes on request; this is where Chinese Buddhists eat when taking vegetarian vows.

Breakfasts & Bakeries The French-Lao influence in Ubon means people are somewhat more accustomed to pastries and Western breakfasts than in many parts of Thailand. *Chiokee (Jiaw Kii)* on Kheuan Thani Rd is very popular among local office workers for both Chinese and Western breakfasts. Prices are good and it has everything from khâo tôm to ham and eggs. One of their specialities is jók (broken-rice soup or congee).

Fern Hut, down a soi opposite the teachers' college (*wítháyalai khruu* in Thai) sells good cakes and other baked items.

In Warin, on Pathumthepphakdi Rd near another Bangkok Bank, *Warin Bakery* offers decent baked goods, coffee and breakfasts.

Night Markets Ubon has two night markets which are open from dusk to dawn, one by the river near the bridge (*talàat yài* or big market), and the other near the bus terminal on Chayangkun Rd – convenient to hotels on Chayangkun and Suriyat Rds.

Entertainment

Nightclubs The top nightspot in town at the moment, the High Class Executive Club at 2/1 Uparat Rd (near the river and bridge), offers live music, karaoke and disco. The Pathumrat Hotel boasts the disco-style Champ and the cabaret-style Pathumma. Rot Isaan, on Si Narong Rd next to the Krung Thong Hotel, is a smoky Thai-style nightclub.

Massage Thai Massage Clinic (☎ 254746) at 369-371 Sanphasit Rd offers traditional massage from 9 am to 9 pm daily. Rates are 100B per hour.

Ubon also has several *àap òp nûat* (bathe-steam-massage) places that probably got their start during the days when a US air base was located outside town. The least seedy is the Pathumrat Hotel's Long Beach.

Things to Buy

One of the major local specialities is silver betel-nut containers moulded using the lost-wax process. The Ubon National Museum on Kheuan Thani Rd has a good exhibit of locally produced betel boxes; to see them being made, visit **Ban Pa-Ao**, a silversmithing village between Ubon and Yasothon off Highway 23.

Phanchat (☎ 243433), at 158 Ratchabut Rd, carries a range of Ubon handicrafts, including fabrics and silverwork, as do several other shops – Ket Kaew, Mit Ying, Dampun – along Ratchabut Rd. Kofak (☎ 254698) at 39 Phalochai Rd, also sells Isaan products. For locally woven fabrics, have a look in Yai Bua (☎ 243287), 182 Sanphasit Rd, and Maybe (☎ 254932), 124 Si Narong Rd.

Getting There & Away

Air THAI has one daily flight from Bangkok to Ubon at 4.45 pm, except on Monday and Saturday when flights leave at 7.10 am. The fare is 1345B and the flight takes an hour.

Bus Two air-con buses a day go to Ubon from Nakhon Phanom, at 7 am and 2 pm, leaving from the intersection of Bamrung Meuang and Ratsadorn Uthit Rds near the Windsor Hotel. The fare is 98B. Ordinary buses from the Baw Khaw Saw station leave regularly from morning until late afternoon for 67B. The trip takes 5½ hours on the tour bus and six to seven hours on the rot thammadaa (ordinary bus).

If you're coming from Northern Thailand, you'll find air-con buses to Ubon from both Phitsanulok (305B) and Chiang Mai (445B).

Ordinary buses to Ubon from Bangkok cost 161B for the 10½-hour route, 159B for the 9½-hour route. Both types leave the northern bus terminal in Bangkok hourly from around 4.30 am through to nearly midnight. First-class air-con buses cost 287 to 290B depending on the bus and leave once in the morning around 9 am and six times in the evening between 8 and 10.30 pm. There is one 400B VIP departure nightly at 8 pm.

Other fares to/from Ubon are listed below. Some fares differ according to alternative routes taken between the same terminals – longer routes are usually cheaper – or class of air-con service.

Destination	Fare
Buriram	50B
(air-con)	120B
Kantharalak	
(for Khao Phra Wihaan)	28B
Khong Jiam	30B
Khon Kaen	70B
(air-con)	125B
Khorat	87 to 102 B
(air-con)	146 to 184B
Mahasarakham	53B
(air-con)	96B
Mukdahan	43B
(air-con)	77B
Phibun Mangsahan	12B
Phimai	74B
(air-con)	133B
Prakhon Chai	
(for Prasat Phanom Rung)	70B
Roi Et	44B
(air-con)	62 to 79B
Sakon Nakhon	69B
(air-con)	125B
Si Saket	18B
(air-con)	32 to 40B
Surin	43B
(air-con)	80B
That Phanom	54B
(air-con)	99B
Udon Thani	97B
(air-con)	125 to 175B
Yasothon	28B
(air-con)	38 to 50B

Train The Ubon Ratchathani express leaves Bangkok daily at 9 pm, arriving in Ubon at 7.05 am the next morning. The basic 1st-class fare is 416B, 2nd class is 200B and 3rd class is 95B, not including surcharges for express service or a sleeping berth. Rapid trains leave at 6.50 am, 6.45 and 10.45 pm, arriving in Ubon about 11 hours later. There is no 1st class on the rapid trains. Ordinary trains take only about an hour longer to reach Ubon; there are five departures daily in either direction between 5.20 am and 11.25 pm.

Rapid trains from Khorat leave at 11.44 am and 12.08 am, arriving in Ubon at 4.45 pm and 5.20 am. The basic fares are 121B 2nd class and 58B 3rd class.

The new all-air-con Sprinter leaves Bangkok at 9.25 am and arrives in Ubon at 5.50 pm; the fare is 345B, including a couple of aeroplane-style meals.

Ubon's train station is in Warin Chamrap; take a white No 2 city bus to reach Chayangkun Rd in the city centre.

Getting Around

A city bus system runs large buses along the main avenues, very convenient for getting from one end of town to the other cheaply (fare is 3B). Samlors around town are 5 to 15B depending on distance.

Motorcycles, vans and cars can be rented at C Wattana (☎ 241906), 269 Suriyat Rd. Other rental places include Chi Chi Tour (☎ 241464), Ubonsak Travel (☎ 311038) and Ubon Tour (☎ 243570), all three on Chayangkun Rd.

Wattana also does day trips to Pakse, Laos, for around 1500B per person (depending on the number of people) as well as more costly overnights to Don Khong, the largest island in the Maekhong River (near the Lao-Cambodian border).

AROUND UBON PROVINCE
Phibun Mangsahan to Khong Jiam
โขงเจียม

The small riverside district of Khong Jiam is 75 km east of Ubon via Route 217 to Phibun Mangsahan and then over the Mun River by bridge at the western end of Route 2222. Visitors often stop in Phibun to see a set of rapids called **Kaeng Sapheu** next to the river crossing.

Ban Khawn Sai, half a km west of Phibun on Route 217 between Km 23 and 24, is a small village whose main livelihood is the forging of bronze gongs for temples and classical Thai music ensembles. You can watch the gongmakers hammering the flat metal discs into beautiful instruments and tempering them in rustic fires – often in temporary shelters just off the road. Should you care to make a purchase or two, small gongs cost 400 to 500B each, larger ones 4000 to 5000B; the huge two-metre gongs run as high as 50,000B.

Farther east along Route 2222 you can stop at **Sae Hua Maew Falls** and **Wat Tham Hehw Sin Chai**. The latter is a cave temple with a waterfall cascading over the front of the cave; it's just a two-km walk south-west of Khong Jiam. Also in the vicinity are two other waterfalls, **Pak Taew Falls** in Nam Yuen district – a tall vertical drop – and the low but wide **Taton Falls**.

Khong Jiam itself sits on a picturesque peninsula formed by the confluence of the Mun and Maekhong rivers. Huge conical fish traps are made here for local use – they look very much like the fish traps that appear in the 3000-year-old prehistoric murals at Pha Taem (see later in this section). Thais visit Khong Jiam to see the so-called **Mae Nam Song Sii** (Two-Colour River), the contrasting coloured currents formed at the junction of the Mun and Maekhong rivers. Along the Maekhong side is a simple but pleasant park with benches and food vendors.

For 150B per hour you can charter longtail boats with 15-person capacities from a rustic landing next to the Pak Mun Restaurant to see Two-Colour River and various small river islands; Thais can cross the Maekhong to Laos. Provincial officials on both sides of the border are trying to arrange permanent permission for day crossings by foreigners. (Foreigners are permitted to cross into Laos 32 km farther south at Chong Mek, however.)

Places to Stay & Eat – Khong Jiam *Apple Guest House* (☎ 351160) on Kaewpradit Rd has rooms in a couple of two-storey buildings off the main road through town. There are two large, clean rooms upstairs and six smaller rooms downstairs, all with shared bath. Rates are a very reasonable 80B per room; windows are screened and soap and towels provided. Good meals can be purchased in a separate dining area; bicycles and motorcycles are available for rent.

Near the river, the friendly, motel-like *Khong Jiam Guest House* (☎ 351160; fax 351074) rooms with fan and bath for 80/170B, 170B for a one-bed room with air-con.

On the Mun River side of town are two restaurants, the floating *Songsat* and the *Hat Mae Mun* on a hillside overlooking the river. The latter has the better food – try the delicious yam mét mámûang sãam sũan, a warm cashew-nut salad made with tomatoes, chillies and fresh green peppercorn.

Along the Maekhong side, *Araya* is very popular on weekends and serves a variety of freshwater fish, Thai-Lao standards, river turtle (ta-phâap náam) and wild pig. *Pak Mun* is a nice wooden restaurant overlooking the junction of the two rivers at the eastern end of town. In town itself, a large Thai-Chinese restaurant called *Jaroen 'cha* is good.

Places to Stay & Eat – Phibun Mangsahan *Sanamchai Guest House* (☎ (045) 441289) has modern bungalows for 100 to 150B with fan, 200 to 250B with air-con. There's a pub and garden restaurant opposite the guesthouse. Near the bridge to Route 2222 is a simple restaurant famous for salabao (Chinese buns) and nãng kòp (frog skin, usually fried). Thais visiting Pha Taem always stop here on the way to stock up on salabao and frog skin.

Getting There & Away From Ubon, direct buses to Khong Jiam (74 km) cost 30B and leave from Market No 5 between 9 am and 1 pm. When direct buses aren't running to Khong Jiam, catch a Phibun bus (12B) from Warin train station between 5 am and 5.30 pm, and change to a Khong Jiam bus (12B) in Phibun.

If you're driving or cycling to Khong Jiam from the Sirinthon Reservoir area via Routes 217 and 2296, you'll have to cross the Mun River by vehicle ferry (30B per vehicle).

Pha Taem
ผาแต้ม

In Khong Jiam district, 94 km north-east of Ubon, near the confluence of the Mun and Maekhong rivers, is a tall stone cliff called Pha Taem. The cliff is about 200 metres long and features prehistoric colour paintings that are at least 3000 years old. Mural subjects include fish traps, *plaa bèuk* (giant Maekhong catfish), turtles, elephants, human hands and a few geometric designs – all very reminiscent of prehistoric rock art found at widely separated sites around the world.

A 500-metre trail descends from the cliff edge to the base past two platforms where visitors can view the rock paintings; from the top of the cliff you get a bird's eye view of Laos. Vendors sell snacks and beverages near the top of the cliff. A cliff-top visitors' centre is planned for future construction and will contain exhibits pertaining to the paintings and local geology.

On the road to Pha Taem is **Sao Chaliang**, an area of unusual stone formations similar to Phu Pha Thoep in Mukdahan.

Getting There & Away Pha Taem is 20 km beyond Khong Jiam via Route 2112, but there's no direct public transport there. The bus from Ubon to Khong Jiam will pass the

final turn-off to Pha Taem on request; then you can walk or hitch five km to the cliff.

By car, bike or motorcycle, go east on Route 217 to Phibun Mangsahan, then turn left (north) across the Mun River on Route 2222 and follow this road to Khong Jiam. From Khong Jiam, take Route 2134 north-west to Ban Huay Phai and then go north-east at the first turn-off to Pha Taem.

Chong Mek & the Emerald Triangle
ช่องเม็ก

South of Khong Jiam via Route 217 is the small trading town of Chong Mek on the Thai-Lao border. Chong Mek has the distinction of being the only town in Thailand where you can cross into Laos by land. At the time of writing you must have a Laos visa valid for Pakse entry to cross here; and you must specify that you want to cross at Chong Mek when applying for the visa. The southern Laos capital of Pakse is three hours by road from Ban Mai Sing Amphon, the village on the Laos side of the border.

Thai visitors come to Chong Mek to drink *oh-líang* (Chinese-style iced coffee) and shop for Lao and Vietnamese souvenirs.

About five km west of Chong Mek is the north-eastern shore of the huge **Sirinthon Reservoir**, an impoundment of a Mun River tributary. On forested hills near the dam at the northern end of the reservoir is a recreation area frequented by local picnickers.

Wat Paa Wanaphothiyaan, a north-eastern forest monastery in the Ajaan Man-Ajaan Chaa tradition, sits on a peninsula jutting from the reservoir's northern shore. Also known locally as Wat Ko (Island Monastery) or Wat Kheuan (Dam Monastery), it's similar in concept to Wat Paa Nanachat Bung Wai in Warin, although there are only about ten monks, most of them Thai. Until recently the abbot was an Australian monk. Serious, experienced meditators may apply to practice here; as at Wat Paa Nanachat, men must shave their heads after three days. To reach here by public transport, take a songthaew bound for Nikhom Neung from Phibun and get off at the wat pier (*thâa* *wát kàw)*, where you can get a boat out to the wat for 20B.

Farther south, near the intersection of the Lao, Thai and Cambodian borders (an area sometimes referred to as the 'Emerald Triangle' for its relatively healthy forest cover), is the little-known **Phu Chong Nayoi National Park**. Established in 1987, the 687-sq-km park's predominant attractions include the **Bak Taew Yai Waterfall** (3½ km from the park headquarters), which plunges 40 metres over a cliff in two separate but parallel streams, a number of interesting rock formations, a couple of fresh springs and some nice views of the surrounding countryside from a cliff called **Phaa Pheung**. The park's highest point reaches 555 metres. Fauna includes the endangered white-winged wood duck.

Surin & Si Saket Provinces

These adjacent provinces between Buriram and Ubon border Cambodia and are dotted with ancient Khmer ruins built during the 11th and 12th-century Angkor empire. Other than the ruins, the only other major attraction in the area is the Surin Annual Elephant Roundup. Few elephants are still used as work animals in Surin; instead they are brought out for ceremonial occasions such as parades and monastic ordinations.

SURIN
สุรินทร์

Surin (population 40,000), 452 km from Bangkok, is a quiet provincial capital except during the Elephant Roundup in late November. At that time a carnival atmosphere reigns, with elephants providing the entertainment. If ever you wanted to see a lot of elephants in one place (there are more elephants now in Thailand than in India), this is your chance.

Culturally, Surin represents an intersection of Lao, Central Thai, Khmer and Suay peoples, resulting in an interesting mix of dialects and customs. A fifth group contributing to the blend consisted of the many volunteers and UN employees working with local refugee camps during the 1970s and 1980s; with the huge refugee industry winding down, their influence is beginning to wane.

To see Surin's elephants during the off season, visit **Ban Tha Klang** in Tha Tum district, about 40 km north of Surin. Many of the performers at the annual festival are trained here.

Silk weaving can be observed at several local villages, including **Khwaosinarin** and **Ban Janrom**.

Prasat Ta Meuan

The most atmospheric – and most difficult to reach – of Surin's temple ruins is a series of three sites known collectively as Prasat Ta Meuan in Ban Ta Miang district on the Cam-

Surin elephant roundup

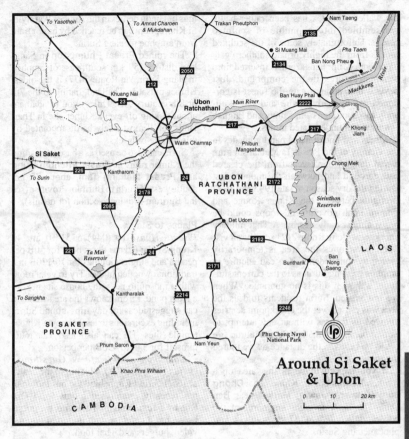

Around Si Saket & Ubon

0   10   20 km

bodian border. Ban Ta Miang is 25 km east of Ban Kruat or 49 km west of Kap Choeng via Route 2121. This trip is best done by hired bicycle, motorcycle or car – Pirom's House can also arrange day trips by van if you can get a small group together.

The first site, **Prasat Ta Meuan** proper, was built in the Jayavarman VII period (1121-1220 AD) as a rest stop for pilgrims. It's a fairly small monument with a two-doored, eight-windowed sanctuary constructed of laterite blocks; only one sculpted sandstone lintel over the rear door remains.

To the south about a half km along a winding road is the more impressive **Prasat Ta Meuan Tot**, which is said to have been a 'healing station' or 'hospital' like Prang Ku outside Chaiyaphum. Large fig trees, cut back to stumps, have attached themselves to the ruins, which consist of a gopura, mondop and main sanctuary surrounded by a laterite wall.

Farther south, right next to the Cambodian border, is the largest site, **Prasat Ta Meuan Thom**. Built mostly of sandstone blocks on a laterite base on a slope that drops off at the southern end to face the Cambodian border, the walled complex has been rather badly reassembled into a jumble of sculpted blocks. Unfortunately some of the sculpted blocks from the highly ornate southern gate have ended up haphazardly inserted into other structures in the compound. Just beyond the southern gate the forest is cordoned off by barbed wire and red skull-and-crossbone signs – in Khmer and English – warning of undetonated mines.

Mines and undetonated hand grenades in the vicinity of the Prasat Ta Meuan sites are a real danger; don't veer from the cleared paths around and between the monuments. During the dry season of late 1993 and 1994 firefights between the Khmer Rouge and Phnom Penh government troops could be heard almost daily nearby. A Thai military checkpoint along Route 2121 screens all visitors; sometimes the area is temporarily closed to nonresidents. You can enquire in amphoe meuang Surin as to the current situation, although this is no guarantee. When we last visited, Surin residents told us the area was closed, yet the checkpoint sentries allowed us to pass without any attempt to turn us back. Automatic rifle and mortar fire could be heard in the distance as we toured the ruins.

If you happen to be in this area on a weekend, check out the Khmer-Thai **Chong Jom (Chawng Jawm) Market** near Ban Dan. The latter is eight km north of the border via Route 214, 57 km south of amphoe meuang Surin.

Other Khmer Temple Ruins

The southern reach of Surin Province along the Cambodian border harbours several minor Angkor-period ruins, including **Prasat Hin Ban Phluang** (30 km south of Surin). The solitary sandstone sanctuary, mounted on a laterite platform, exhibits well-sculpted stone lintels.

A larger Khmer site can be seen 30 km north-east of town at **Prasat Sikhoraphum**. Sikhoraphum (or Si Khonphum) features five Khmer prangs, the tallest of which reaches 32 metres. The doorways to the central prang are decorated with stone carvings of Hindu deities in the Angkor Wat style. Si Khoraphum can be reached by bus or train from amphoe meuang Surin.

The ruined **Prasat Phumphon** in Sangkha district (59 km south-east of amphoe meuang Surin via Route 2077) is the oldest Khmer prasat in Thailand, dating to the 7th or 8th century AD. Unless you're adamant about ticking off every Khmer site in Thailand, you'll most likely be disappointed by this jumble of bricks.

Surin can also be used as a base for visiting the Khmer ruins at **Prasat Phanom Rung** and **Prasat Meuang Tam**, about 75 km south-west of Surin in Buriram Province (see the Buriram Province section for details).

Places to Stay

Pirom's House (☎ (044) 515140) at 242 Krung Si Nai Rd has dorm beds for 50B per person and singles/doubles for 70/120B in a traditional wooden house. Try to get a room with a mosquito net – the house sits next to a lotus pond. Pirom knows the area well and can suggest ideas for day trips around Surin, including excursions to lesser known Khmer temple sites. He can also lead van tours himself for 340 to 450B per person.

Country Roads Cafe & Guesthouse (☎/fax (044) 515721), a bit out of the centre at 165/1 Sirirat Rd, behind the bus terminal, has recently established rooms for 100B. Run by a Texan and his Thai wife, the guesthouse has a cafe/bar with imported liquors, video, burgers and Thai food.

Hotel rates may increase during the Elephant Roundup and hotels may fill up, but otherwise, *Krung Si* (☎ (044) 511037), at 15/11-4 Krung Si Nai Rd, charges from 100 to 120B, and *New Hotel* (☎ (044) 511341/322), next to the train station at 22 Thanasan Rd, charges from 100 to 150B and has some air-con rooms from 200 to 250B. *Thanachai Hotel*, just off the roundabout on Thetsaban 1 Rd near the post office, has somewhat dark and dingy rooms for 100 to 150B, or from 170B with air-con.

Moving up-market just a bit, the very clean and well-run *Saeng Thong* at 155-61 Thanasan Rd offers rooms with fan for 180B with shared bath, 300B with fan and private bath, 400 to 500B with air-con and hot water.

The top-end *Phetkasem Hotel* (☎ (044) 511274, 511576), is at 104 Jit Bamrung Rd. All rooms are air-con, and rates are from 550 to 1200B. *Memorial Hotel* on Lak Meuang Rd just west of Thanasan Rd is similar in price and facilities.

Places to Eat
Along the northern end of Thanasan Rd between the Saeng Thong Hotel and the train station are a number of good, inexpensive Thai and Chinese restaurants. Along this stretch the long-running *Phloen* and *Surin Phochana* serve dependable curries and noodles.

A small night market assembles in front of the train station each evening. There is also a larger night market next to the main municipal market along Krung Si Nai Rd, close to Pirom's House and the Krung Si Hotel.

The popular *Phaw Kin*, near the intersection of Lak Meuang and Krung Si Nai Rds, serves excellent Isaan food at very reasonable prices.

Getting There & Away
Bus Ordinary buses to Surin leave 17 times a day from Bangkok's northern bus terminal between 6 am and 10.50 pm for 108B. Second-class air-con buses cost 152B and leave nightly at 9 and 11 pm, while 1st-class air-con ones depart at 11 am, 9.30, 10 and 10.10 pm for 195B. During the Elephant Roundup, there are many special air-con buses to Surin, organised by major hotels and tour companies.

Surin lies about halfway between Ubon and Khorat; buses from either direction take around four hours and cost 43B ordinary, 80B air-con.

Train Most people travel to Surin by rapid train No 31, which leaves Bangkok at 6.50 am, arriving in Surin at 2.05 pm. The 2nd-class fare is 173B, including the rapid surcharge. Book your seats at least two weeks in advance for travel during November. A faster train is the air-con diesel No 931

to Surin at 11.05 am, arriving at 5.35 pm for 20B less (no surcharges for 3rd class; 50B surcharge in air-con 2nd class). If you prefer night train travel, the rapid No 51 leaves Bangkok at 10.45 pm and arrives in Surin at 6.42 am.

Ordinary 3rd-class trains take around nine hours from Bangkok, cost 73B, and leave daily at 3.25 and 10.25 pm. Surin can also be reached by train from any other station along the Ubon line, including Buriram, Si Saket and Ubon.

Getting Around
Samlors around downtown Surin cost 10 to 20B per trip.

SI SAKET
ศรีสะเกษ
Si Saket's provincial capital (population 34,700) has gained on Surin's; however with nothing like Surin's elephant festival to provide support, the town has less of a tourist infrastructure – a boon for visitors in search of laid-back, authentic Isaan ways. Also, Si Saket Province has more Khmer ruins of significance within its borders than Surin.

With the opening of Khao Phra Wihaan, a major Angkor site just over the provincial border in Cambodia, the town's fortunes may change as it becomes the gateway for visitors to the ruins. The vast majority of visitors to Khao Phra Wihaan so far have been Thais.

Khao Phra Wihaan
เขาพระวิหาร
Lying just across the Cambodian border opposite Si Saket Province's Kantharalak, the Khmer ruins of Khao Phra Wihaan (other common spellings include Kao Prea Vihar and Khao Phra Viharn) are virtually inaccessible from the Cambodian side and until a Khmer Rouge ceasefire was reached in Cambodia they were also off-limits from the Thai side. After a year of negotiations between the Cambodian and Thai governments, the ruins finally opened to the public in 1991, then

closed down again during the Phnom Penh offensive against the Khmer Rouge in 1993-94. Enquire with the TAT in Bangkok or Ubon to find out the latest situation.

Khao Phra Wihaan was built over two centuries under a succession of Khmer kings, beginning with Rajendravarman II in the mid-10th century and ending with Suryavarman II in the early 12th century – it was the latter who also commanded the construction of Angkor Wat. The hill itself was sacred to Khmer Hindus for at least 500 years before the completion of the temple complex, however, and there were smaller brick monuments on the site prior to the reign of Rajendravarman II.

Phra Wihaan sits atop a 600-metre hill at the edge of the Dangrek (Dong Rek) Mountain Range, commanding a view of the Thai plains to the west. Built originally as a Hindu temple in the classic Bapuan and early Angkor styles, the complex extends a linear 850 metres, encompassing four gopuras (entrance pavilions), and a large prasat or sanctuary surrounded by a courtyard and galleries. A stepped naga approach ascends approximately 120 metres from the foot of the hill to the sanctuary.

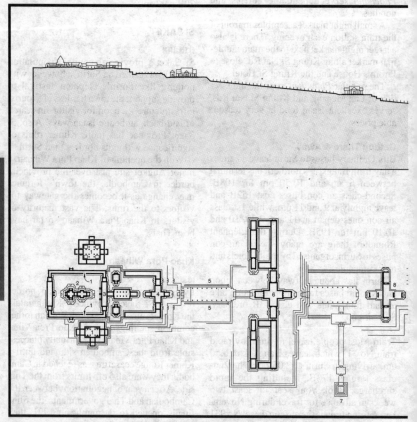

The temple complex is semi-restored – the general condition is somewhere between that of Prasat Phanomwan in Khorat and Prasat Phanom Rung in Buriram. One naga balustrade of around 30 metres is still intact; the first two gopuras have all but fallen down and many of the temple buildings are roofless, but abundant examples of stone carving are intact and visible. The doorways to the third gopura have been nicely preserved and one (the inner door facing south) is surmounted by a well-executed carved stone lintel depicting Shiva and consort Uma sitting on Nandi (Shiva's bull), under the shade of a symmetrised tree. A Vishnu creation lintel is also visible on the second gopura; in contrast to the famous Phanom Rung lintel depicting the same subject, this one shows Vishnu climbing the churning stick rather than reclining on the ocean below.

The main prasat tower in the final court at the summit is in need of major restoration before the viewer can get a true idea of its former magnificence. Many of the stone carvings from the prasat are either missing or lie buried in nearby rubble. The galleries leading to the prasat have fared better and

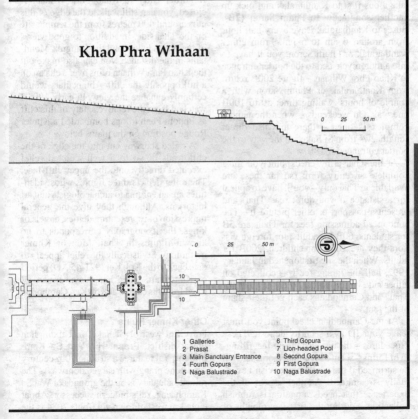

Khao Phra Wihaan

0   25   50 m

0   25   50 m

1 Galleries
2 Prasat
3 Main Sanctuary Entrance
4 Fourth Gopura
5 Naga Balustrade
6 Third Gopura
7 Lion-headed Pool
8 Second Gopura
9 First Gopura
10 Naga Balustrade

have even kept their arched roofs. Eventually the complex may undergo a total restoration but at the moment the money from entrance fees is supposedly going towards the improvement of the road to Phra Wihaan from the Cambodian side (currently Cambodian officials must walk six to eight hours to reach the Thai border).

Getting There & Away Highway 221 leads 95 km south from Si Saket to Phum Saron – 11 km short of the temple – via Kantharalak. Catch a songthaew from near the bus terminal adjacent to the main day market in Si Saket for 15B. If you miss the infrequent direct songthaew service, you may have to take a bus first to Kantharalak and pick up another songthaew to Phum Saron (7B). Buses to Kantharalak leave every half hour from around 6 am to 5 pm. From either Kantharalak or Phum Saron, you'll have to hire a motorcycle taxi to the border entrance to Khao Phra Wihaan – figure 200B return from Kantharalak or Phum Saron with a couple of hours' waiting time; 50 to 100B one way. On weekends – when the temple complex is open – there are also direct songthaews from Si Saket all the way to the border entrance for 18B.

At the Thai army checkpoint you must complete an entry form (so far these are available in Thai only – you'll have to appeal for assistance if you don't read Thai) and present a passport or other picture ID. The announced admission fees for Thais are 5B for students, 60B for adults; for foreign visitors they are 100B for children, 200B for adults. When the site first opened in January 1992, half the farang fee was collected on either side of the border to ensure that the Thais and Cambodians each got their share of the loot.

At the Cambodian checkpoint you must leave your ID as a security deposit. These procedures – the two-instalment fee, filling-in of forms – seem a bit cumbersome and I'll be surprised if the whole process isn't eventually streamlined. Another aspect of the experience that needs attention is rubbish collection – during the first few months of

Khao Phra Wihaan's opening, the accumulation of visitor rubbish at the site was phenomenal.

Only the immediate surroundings to the complex are open. Whether or not Khmer Rouge-Phnom Penh firefights in the area have ceased by the time you arrive, there will still be plenty of land mines and live ordnance in the fields and forests nearby; stick to the designated safety lanes leading to the ruins. Avoid visiting on weekends, when the site is packed with hundreds of local Thai visitors.

Phaa Maw I Daeng

If border entry to Khao Phra Wihaan is closed, you can still walk to the edge of this cliff around 400 metres from the temple site on the Thai side. In addition to good views of the plains below and the Dangrek Mountains in the distance, you can also make out the Khao Phra Wihaan ruins over a chasm on a hill opposite the cliff – binoculars would certainly enhance the view. In early 1994 I watched from the relative safety of this cliff as Phnom Penh troops bombarded a Khmer Rouge position on the plains below.

A railed stairway cut into the edge of the cliff leads down to a well-sculpted relief executed directly onto the upper cliff face. The relief depicts three figures whose identities are an enigma to archaeologists and art historians. Although they give the general impression of representing deities, angels or kings, the iconography corresponds to no known figures in Thai, Mon or Khmer mythology. Stylistically the relief appears to date back to the Koh Ker (921-45 AD) period of Khmer art, when King Jayavarman IV ruled from his capital at Koh Ker, Cambodia.

Other Khmer Ruins

Forty km west of Si Saket in Uthumphon Phisai district, **Prasat Hin Wat Sa Kamphaeng Yai** features a striking 10th-century sandstone prang with carved doorways. The ruined sanctuary is on the grounds of Wat Sa Kamphaeng Yai's modern successor. About eight km west of town via Route 2084 is the similar but smaller **Prasat Hin Wat Sa Kamphaeng Noi**.

Other minor Khmer sites in the province include Prasat Prang Ku, Prasat Ban Prasat and Prasat Phu Fai.

Places to Stay
Si Saket *Phrom Phiman* (☎ (045) 611141), at 849/1 Lak Meuang Rd, has good rooms with fan for 100 to 140B, air-con rooms from 250 to 350B. Everything else in town is in the 80 to 120B range for simple rooms with fan: *Pho Thong* (☎ (045) 611542), 1055/2-5 Ratchakan Rotfai Rd; *Santisuk* (☎ (045) 611496), 573 Soi Wat Phra To; *Si Saket* (☎ (045) 611846), 384-5 Si Saket Rd; and *Thai Soem Thai* (☎ (045) 611458), also on Si Saket Rd.

Kantharalak The *Khwan Yeun Hotel* on the town's main street provides simple, motel-like rooms for 60B. Next door is a good lâap pèt restaurant.

Getting There & Away
From Bangkok's northern bus terminal there are two 1st-class air-con buses daily to Si Saket, one at 9 am and the other at 9.30 pm. The fare is 245B; the trip takes 8½ hours. There is also one 2nd-class air-con bus at 7.30 pm that costs 180B. Ordinary buses leave five times daily and cost 107 to 131B depending on the route taken.

Ordinary buses from Ubon cost 18B (32 to 40B air-con) and take about an hour to reach Si Saket – depending on how many stops the bus makes along the way.

Southern Thailand

History

Although under Thai political domination for several centuries, the south has always remained culturally apart from the other regions of Thailand. Historically, the peninsula has been linked to cultures in ancient Indonesia, particularly the Srivijaya empire, which ruled a string of principalities in what is today Malaysia, southern Thailand and Indonesia. The Srivijaya dynasty was based in Sumatra and lasted nearly 500 years (8th to 13th centuries). The influence of Malay-Indonesian culture is still apparent in the ethnicity, religion, art and language of the *Thai pàk tâi*, the southern Thais.

Geography & Economy

Bounded by water on two sides, the people of southern Thailand are by and large a sea-faring lot. One consequence of this natural affinity with the ocean is the abundance of delectable seafood, prepared southern-style. Brightly painted fishing boats, hanging nets and neat thatched huts add to the pak tai setting; travellers who do a stint in southern Thailand are likely to come face to face with more than a few visions of 'tropical paradise', whatever their expectations might be.

Three of Thailand's most important exports – rubber, tin and coconut – are produced in the south so that the standard of living is a bit higher than in other provincial regions. However, southern Thais claim that most of the wealth is in the hands of ethnic Chinese. In any of the truly southern-Thai provinces (from Chumphon south), it is obvious that the Chinese are concentrated in the urban provincial capitals while the poorer Muslims live in the rural areas. Actually, the urban concentration of Chinese is a fact of life throughout South-East Asia which becomes more noticeable in southern Thailand and the Islamic state of Malaysia because of religious-cultural differences.

In official government terms, southern Thailand is made up of 14 provinces: Chumphon, Krabi, Nakhon Si Thammarat, Narathiwat, Pattani, Phang-Nga, Phattalung, Phuket, Ranong, Satun, Songkhla, Surat Thani, Trang and Yala. For the purposes of this guide, we've included all provinces on the southern peninsula, taking Phetburi and Prachuap Khiri Khan from central Thailand and putting them alongside the others on the official list.

Culture & Language

The Thai pak tai dress differently, build their houses differently and eat differently from Thais in the north. Many are followers of Islam, so there are quite a few mosques in southern cities; men often cover their heads and the long sarong is favoured over the shorter phaakhamaa worn in the northern, central and north-eastern regions. There are also a good many Chinese living in the south – the influence of whom can be seen in the old architecture and in the baggy Chinese pants worn by rural non-Muslims.

All speak a dialect common among southern Thais that confounds even visitors from other Thai regions – diction is short and fast: *pai nāi* (Where are you going?) becomes *p'nái*, and *tham arai* (What are you doing?) becomes *'rái*. The clipped tones fly into the outer regions of intelligibility, giving the aural impression of a tape played at the wrong speed. In the provinces nearest Malaysia – Yala, Pattani, Narathiwat and Satun – many Thai Muslims speak Yawi, an old Malay dialect with some similarities to modern Bahasa Malaysia and Bahasa Indonesia.

You'll notice that 'Ao', 'Hat' and 'Ban' sometimes precede place names; *ao* means bay, *hàat* is beach and *bâan* is village.

Southern Thais are stereotypically regarded as rebellious folk, considering themselves reluctant subjects of Bangkok

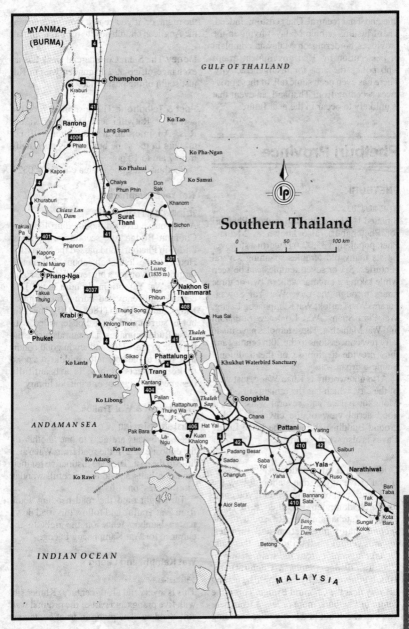

Southern Thailand

MYANMAR (BURMA)

GULF OF THAILAND

Chumphon

Kraburi

Ranong

Lang Suan

Ko Tao

Phato

Kapoe

Ko Phaluai

Ko Pha-Ngan

Khuraburi

Chaiya

Phun Phin

Don Sak

Ko Samui

Chiaw Lan Dam

Surat Thani

Khanom

Sichon

Takua Pa

Phanom

Khao Luang (1835 m)

Kapong

Thai Muang

Phang-Nga

Ron Phibun

Nakhon Si Thammarat

Takua Thung

Krabi

Thung Song

Khlong Thom

Hua Sai

Phuket

Thaleh Luang

Ko Lanta

Sikao

Phattalung

Khukhut Waterbird Sanctuary

Pak Meng

Trang

Kantang

Palian

Ko Libong

Rattaphum

Thung Wa

Thaleh Sap

Songkhla

ANDAMAN SEA

Pak Bara

La-Ngu

Kuan Khalong

Hat Yai

Chana

Pattani

Yaring

Ko Tarutao

Satun

Padang Besar

Sadao

Saba Yoi

Yala

Saiburi

Narathiwat

Ko Adang

Changlun

Yaha

Ruso

Ban Taba

Ko Rawi

Alor Setar

Bannang Sata

Tak Bai

Kota Baru

Bang Lang Dam

Sungai Kolok

INDIAN OCEAN

Betong

MALAYSIA

0   50   100 km

rule and Thai (central Thai) custom. Indeed, Thai Muslims (ethnic Malays) living in the provinces bordering on Malaysia complain of persecution by Thai government troops who police the area for insurgent activity. There has even been some talk of these provinces seceding from Thailand, an event that is unlikely to occur in the near future.

Phetburi Province

PHETBURI

อ.เมืองเพชรบุรี

Situated 160 km south of Bangkok, Phetburi (or Phetchaburi, also known as Meuang Phet; population 35,000) is worth a stopover for its many old temples spanning several centuries. Six or seven temples can be seen while taking a circular walk of two or three hours through the city: Wat Yai Suwannaram, Wat Trailok, Wat Kamphaeng Laeng, Wat Phra Suang, Wat Ko Kaew Sutharam and Wat Mahathat. These temples have made very few concessions to the 20th century and thus provide a glimpse of the traditional Siamese urban wat.

Also noteworthy is Khao Wang, just west of the city, which has the remains of a King Mongkut palace and several wats, plus a good aerial view of the city. The underground Buddhist shrine at the Khao Luang Caves is also worth seeing.

Orientation & Information

If you arrive at the train station, follow the road south-east of the tracks until you come to Ratchadamnoen Rd, then turn right. Follow Ratchadamnoen Rd south to the second major intersection and turn left towards central Phetburi to begin the walk. Or take a samlor from the train station to Chomrut Bridge (Saphaan Chomrut), for 10B. If you've come by bus, you'll be getting off very near the Chomrut Bridge. This is the centre of Phetburi, more or less – from here you can check out hotels if you're spending

the night, or, if you're not, stow your gear at the Anglican church next to the bus terminal.

Money The Siam Commercial Bank has an exchange office at 2 Damnoen Kasem Rd, just south of the post office.

Post & Telephone The post office is on the corner of Ratwithi and Damnoen Kasem Rds. An international telephone office, upstairs in the same building, is open daily from 7 am to 10 pm.

Phetburi's telephone area code is ☎ 032.

Wat Yai Suwannaram

วัดใหญ่สุวรรณาราม

After you've crossed the Phetburi River by Chomrut Bridge (the second-northernmost bridge in Phetburi) and passed the Nam Chai Hotel on the left, walk about 300 metres farther until you see a big temple on the right. This is Wat Yai, originally built in the 17th century and renovated during the reign of King Chulalongkorn (1868-1910). The main bot is surrounded by a cloister filled with sober Buddha images. The murals inside the bot date to the 1730s and are in good condition. Next to the bot, in the middle of a pond to keep insects at bay, is a beautifully designed old haw trai or tripitaka library.

Wat Borom & Wat Trailok

วัดบรมและวัดไตรโลก

These two wats are next to one another on the opposite side of the road from Wat Yai, a little to the east. They are distinctive for their monastic halls and long, graceful, wooden 'dormitories' on stilts.

Turn right onto the road heading south from Wat Trailok and follow this road down past a bamboo fence on the right to the entrance for Wat Kamphaeng Laeng.

Wat Kamphaeng Laeng

วัดกำแพงแลง

This is a very old (13th-century) Khmer site with five prangs and part of the original wall still standing. The prang in front contains a

PLACES TO STAY

4 Khao Wang Hotel
13 Ratanaphakdi Hotel
20 Chom Klao Hotel
21 Phetburi Hotel
22 Nam Chai Hotel

PLACES TO EAT

12 Lamiet Restaurant &
   Other Restaurants
26 Lotuacharaporn
   Food Center
32 Night Market

OTHER

1 Train Station
2 Tram
3 Phra Nakhon Khiri
   Palace
5 Wat Kom Lositaram
6 Wat Sa Bua
7 Wat Phra Phuttaya
   Saiyat
8 Wat Chang
9 Wat Yang
10 Wat Kuti Dao
11 Wat Mahathat
14 Bus Terminal
15 Anglican Church
16 Wat Chi Sa In
17 Siam Commercial Bank
18 GPO & Telephone Office
19 Air-Con Bus Terminal
23 Wat Borom

24 Wat Trailok
25 Wat Yai
   Suwannaram
27 Wat Potaram
28 Day Market
29 Wat Uthai
30 Wat Kamphaeng
   Laeng
31 Wat Phra Suang
33 Digital Clock
   Tower
34 Wat Tho
35 Wat Lat
36 Wat Chi Phra
   Keut
37 Wat Ko Kaew
   Sutharam
38 Clock Tower
39 Wat Chan .
40 Phra Ratchawang
   Ban Beun Palace

Phetburi

0   250   500 m

To Hua Hin

To Khao Luang Caves

To Bangkok, Ratchaburi & Phetkasem Hotel

Phetkasem Road

Rot Fai Road

Khao Phanom Kuat

Khao Wang (Phra Nakhon Khiri)

Ratchadamnoen Road

Ratwithi Road

Te Wiat Road

Chisa-In Road

Chomrut Bridge

Damnoen Kasem Road

Panichacharoen Road

Surinlucha Road

Matayawong Road

Phongsuriya Road

Phrasong Road

Phetburi River

Southern Railway Line

To Hat Chao Samran

Buddha footprint. Of the other four, two contain images dedicated to famous *lŭang phâw* (venerable elderly monks), one was in ruins (but is being restored) and the last has recently been uncovered from a mound of dirt. The Khmers built these as Hindu monuments, so the Buddhist symbols are late additions.

Wat Phra Suang & Wat Lat
วัดพระสวงและวัดลาด

Follow the road beside Wat Kamphaeng Laeng, heading west back towards the river until you pass Wat Phra Suang on the left, undistinguished except for one very nice Ayuthaya-style prasat. Turn left immediately after this wat, heading south again until you come to the clock tower at the southern edge of town. You'll have passed Wat Lat on the left side of the street along the way, but it's not worth breaking your momentum for; this is a long walk.

Wat Ko Kaew Sutharam
วัดแก้วสุทธาราม

Turn right at the clock tower and look for signs leading to the Ayuthaya-period Wat Ko. Two different sois on the left lead to the wat, which is behind the shops along the curving street. The bot features early 18th-century murals that are among the best conceived in Thailand. There is also a large wooden monastic hall on stilts similar to the ones at Wat Borom and Wat Trailok, but in much better condition.

Wat Mahathat
วัดมหาธาตุ

Follow the street in front of Wat Ko north (back towards central Phetburi), and walk over the first bridge you come to on the left, which leads to Wat Mahathat. Alternatively, you can cross the river at Wat Ko, near the clock tower, and take the street on the other side of the river around to Wat Mahathat. The large white prang of this wat can be seen from a distance – a typical late-Ayuthaya, early-Ratanakosin adaptation of the Khmer

prangs of Lopburi and Phimai. This is obviously an important temple in Phetburi, judging from all the activity here.

Khao Wang & Phra Nakhon Khiri Historical Park
เขาวัง/อุทยานประวัติศาสตร์พระนครคีรี

Just west of the city, a 10B samlor ride from the bus station, is Khao Wang. Cobblestone paths lead up and around the hill, which is studded with wats and various components of King Mongkut's palace on Phra Nakhon Khiri (Holy City Hill). The views are great, especially at sunset. The walk up looks easy but is fairly strenuous. Fat monkeys loll about in the trees and on the walls along the main paths. In 1988 Phra Nakhon Khiri was declared a national historical park, so there is now an entry fee of 20B. A tram has been installed to save you walking up to the peak (10B per person one way). The park is open Monday to Friday from 8 am to 5.30 pm and on weekends till 6 pm.

Khao Luang Caves
ถ้ำเขาหลวง

Five km north of Phetburi is the cave sanctuary of Khao Luang (Great Hill). Concrete steps lead down into an anteroom then into the main cavern, which is filled with old Buddha images, many of them put in place by King Mongkut (Rama IV). Sunlight from two holes in the chamber ceiling spray light on the images, which are a favourite subject for photographers. To the rear of the main cavern is an entrance to a third, smaller chamber. On the right of the entrance is Wat Bunthawi, with a sala (open-sided shelter) designed by the abbot himself and a bot with impressively carved wooden door panels.

Admission to the caves is free (donations accepted). A samlor from the city centre to Khao Luang costs 50B.

Festival
The Phra Nakhon Khiri Fair takes place in early February and lasts about eight days. Centred around Khao Wang and the city's historic temples, the festivities include a

sound and light show at the Phra Nakhon Khiri Palace, temples festooned with lights and performances of Thai classical dance-drama, lakhon chatrii, li-khe, and modern-style historical dramas. A twist on the usual beauty contest provides a showcase for Phetburi widows.

Places to Stay

Of the variety of places to stay in Phetburi, the following are recommended. On the eastern side of Chomrut Bridge, on the right bank of Phetburi River, is the *Chom Klao Hotel* (☎ 425398), an ordinary, fairly clean Chinese hotel with friendly staff. It costs 80B for rooms with fan and shared bath, or 120B with private bath.

The *Nam Chai Hotel* is a block farther east from Chomrut Bridge and the Chom Klao Hotel, and has rooms for 90 to 120B, but it is not as good value as the Chom Klao. Another cheapie is the *Ratanaphakdi Hotel*, next to the bus terminal, with rooms for 100 to 200B with private bath, cheaper with shared bath.

Behind the Nam Chai is the *Phetburi Hotel* (☎ 425315), another divey sort of place, with grotty and overpriced rooms for 150B with fan and bath.

The *Khao Wang Hotel* (☎ 425167), opposite Khao Wang (the Hill Palace) used to be my favourite in Phet, but the rooms have gone downhill a bit in recent years. A fairly clean room with fan and bath cost 130/260B for one/two beds. Air-con rooms are 230/500B. Most rooms have TV.

The best hotel in town is the friendly and clean *Phetkasem Hotel* (☎ 425581), 86/1 Phetkasem Rd, which is on the highway north to Bangkok on the edge of town. Rooms are 140 to 170B with fan and bath, 260 to 300B with air-con, and 360 to 450B with hot water.

Places to Eat

There are several good restaurants in the Khao Wang area, with a range of standard Thai and Chinese dishes. A variety of cheap eats is available at the night market at the southern end of Surinleuchai Rd, under the digital clock tower.

Other good eating places can be found in the town centre along the main street to the clock tower. Across from Wat Mahathat, *Lamiet* sells really good khanŏm mâw kaeng (egg custard) and făwy thawng (sweet shredded egg yolk) – which they ship to Bangkok. This shop also has a branch near Khao Wang, where a whole group of egg custard places serve tourists.

Near Wat Yai Suwannaram on Phong-suriya Rd, the *Lotuacharaporn Food Center* is managed by a family who grow their own vegetables and breed their own animals without the use of chemicals. The menu covers a wide variety of Thai and Chinese dishes, none of them prepared with MSG.

Getting There & Away

Bus From Bangkok, buses leave regularly from the southern bus terminal in Thonburi for 36B (ordinary) on the new road, 31B on the old road (via Ratchaburi and Nakhon Pathom), or 65B air-con. The bus takes about 2½ hours.

Buses to Phetburi from Cha-am and Hua Hin are 15 and 20B and take 20 and 40 minutes respectively. Other ordinary bus fares are Ratchaburi 15B (45 minutes), Nakhon Pathom 25B (two hours), Prachuap Khiri Khan 40B (three hours) and Phuket 180B (12 hours).

Train Trains leave Bangkok's Hualamphong station at 9.25 am (ordinary 3rd class), 12.25 pm (rapid 1st and 2nd class), 1.40 pm (ordinary 3rd class), 2 pm (special express, 1st and 2nd class), 3.15 pm (special express 1st and 2nd class), 3.50 pm (rapid 1st and 2nd class), 6.30 pm (rapid 1st and 2nd class), 7.20 pm (express, 1st and 2nd class) and 7.45 pm (rapid 1st and 2nd class). All trains take about 3½ hours to reach Phetburi, so it's not really worth the surcharges for rapid or express service – take an ordinary train. A 3rd-class fare is 34B.

Getting Around

Samlors go anywhere in the town centre for 10B; you can charter one for the whole day for 100B. Share mini-taxis cost 5B around town, including to and from the train station.

KAENG KRACHAN NATIONAL PARK

อุทยานแห่งชาติแก่งกระจาน

This 3000-sq-km park is Thailand's largest, covering nearly half of Phetburi Province along the Burmese border. In spite of its size and proximity to Bangkok, Kaeng Krachan doesn't seem to get many visitors (or perhaps its huge size just swallows them up). Because this part of Phetburi receives some of the heaviest rainfall in Thailand, the rainforest here is particularly thick and abundant in places. There are also areas of savanna-like grasslands, mountains, steep cliffs, caves, waterfalls, long-distance hiking trails and two rivers, the Phetburi and the Pranburi, which are suitable for rafting. Above the **Kaeng Krachan Dam** is a large reservoir stocked with fish. Animals living in Kaeng Krachan include wild elephants, deer, tigers, bears, boars, gaurs and wild cattle. There are small Karen settlements here as well.

Forestry officials at the park headquarters can sometimes be hired as guides for overnight trekking in the park. The standard guide fee is 200B per day. Very little English is spoken so this option is best for those who know some Thai or who don't need any commentary.

You can rent boats on Kaeng Krachan Reservoir lake for 300B per hour or 700B for three hours.

Admission to the park is 25B.

Places to Stay

The six bungalows near the park headquarters cost 100B per person. You can also set up your own tent for 5B per person per night. Near the visitors' centre is a modest restaurant.

Kaeng Krachan Resorts (☎ (02) 513-3238 in Bangkok) offers expensive 'floatel' accommodation at the reservoir.

As malaria is a definite risk in the park, be sure to take precautions against mosquito bites if you're there between dusk and dawn.

Getting There & Around

Kaeng Krachan is about 60 km from Phetburi, off Route 3175. The turn-off for Route 3175 is at Tha Yang on Highway 4, about 18 km south of Phetburi. The park headquarters is eight km past the dam, where the road ends. There is no regular transport all the way to the park, but you can get a songthaew from Phetburi as far as the village of Ban Kaeng Krachan, four km from the park. The songthaews leave from near the clock tower in Phet every half hour between 7 am and 4 pm and cost 20B; there's a half-hour stopover in Tha Yang. From Ban Kaeng Krachan you should be able to hitch or charter a pick-up ride from the locals.

If you have your own wheels, you can explore the park by means of several dirt roads.

CHA-AM

ชะอำ

A tiny town 178 km from Bangkok, 38 km from Phetburi and 25 km from Hua Hin, Cha-am is known for its long, casuarina-lined beach, good seafood and, on weekends and school holidays, its party atmosphere – sort of a Palm Beach or Fort Lauderdale for Thai students. During the week the beach is virtually deserted.

Beach umbrellas and sling chairs are available for hire. The jet skis are a definite minus but not that common yet; if the local tourism promoters want to lure visitors away from fast-developing Hua Hin, the first thing they should do is get rid of the jet skis. There are public bathhouses where you can bathe in fresh water for 5 to 7B.

Near the beach there's not much of a town to speak of – the old centre is on the opposite side of Phetkasem Highway, where you'll find the post office, market, train station and government offices. Inland from the beach (follow the signs) at **Wat Neranchararama** is a fat, white, six-armed Buddha statue; the six hands cover the nine bodily orifices in a symbolic gesture denying the senses.

Information

A new TAT office (☎ 471502) has been established on Phetkasem Highway just 500 metres south of town. The staff are very helpful; they distribute information on Cha-am, Phetburi and Hua Hin. The office is open daily from 6 am to 8 pm.

Cha-am's area telephone code is ☎ 032.

Money A bank window between the corner of Narathip and Ruamjit Rds and the Cha-am Holiday Lodge is open daily from 10 am to 8 pm.

Places to Stay – bottom end & middle

Cha-am Beach has three basic types of accommodation: charming, old-style, spacious wooden beach bungalows on stilts, set back from the road; tacky apartment-style hotels built of cheap materials with faulty plumbing, right on the beach road; and more expensive 'condotel' developments. New places are going up all the time at the northern and southern ends of town. Expect a 20% to 50% discount on posted rates for weekday stays.

One main road leads to the beach area from the highway; if you turn right you'll find the places listed under 'South' below; turn left and you'll see those listed under 'North'.

South Near the air-con bus terminal, *Jack* and *Donut* guesthouses are in a row of modern shophouses similar to the scourge of Pattaya, Hua Hin and Phuket's Patong Beach – they all look the same. Rooms are 200B with fan and shared bath; Donut also has 500B rooms.

South of the air-con bus terminal, the *Anantachai Guest House* has nice rooms with a beach view, air-con, TV, shower and toilet for 500B. They also provide information about the area and have a cheap Thai restaurant.

Santisuk Bungalows & Beach Resort (☎ 471212) is a long-time favourite, with both the early Cha-am style wooden cottages and a newer, equally tasteful section. A room in a hotel-style section with bath is 300B with fan, 400B air-con. Larger two-bedroom cottages with bath and sitting area are 1000B, and it's 2000B for a three-bedroom, two-bath place. The *Nirandorn Resort* (☎ 471893) has similar cottages for 300B with fan, 500 to 600B air-con.

Saeng Thong Condominiums (☎ 471466) costs 800B per night, less in the rainy season. The *White Hotel*, an air-con apartment-style place, costs 400 to 800B. *Arunthip* has tacky but cheap two-bedroom bungalows for 300 to 400B on weekdays.

North *JJ Hotel* and *Somkheat Villa* (☎ 471229; fax 471229) are adjacent apartment-style hotels with rooms in the 300 to 500B and 600 to 800B range respectively.

Thiptari Place (☎ /fax 471879) is a fairly reasonable place, with air-con rooms from 500 to 800B. Farther up, *Rua Makam Villa* (☎ 471073) has old-style wooden cottages, spacious and off the road, for 500 to 800B. *Happy Home* has older-style wooden cottages from 350 to 1500B.

The *Kaen-Chan Hotel* (☎ 471314) has a variety of accommodation – bungalows are 150 to 250B with fan, 200 to 350B with air-con; air-con rooms in the hotel are 1200 to 1500B, with a 20% discount on weekdays. There is a pool on the grounds.

The next cheapest places are the *Jitravee Resort* (☎ 471382) and *Cha-am Villa* (☎ 471010/241), which will let you have rooms for 200B mid-week (300B on weekends); air-con rooms cost 500B.

Cha-am Holiday Lodge has ordinary bungalows for 300B with fan and 500B with air-con.

At the northern end of the beach are the closely clustered bungalows of *Paradise Bungalow* which cost from 350 to 600B, including air-con and TV.

Inthira Plaza This complex off the main road (Narathip Rd) running to the beach from the highway is striving to become a Pattaya-style bar centre ('entertainment centre' in the jargon of the moment). A couple of the bars have apartment-style rooms upstairs for 250B with fan and bath, 350B with air-con. They could be noisy at night.

Places to Stay – top end

Many places in Cha-am call themselves 'resorts' but the only place in the central area that comes close to the term is *Cha-am Methavalai Hotel* (☎ 471480; fax 471590); it has well-kept, modern rooms with flowers spilling from every balcony, plus a pool and a small beach area of its own in front. Walk-in rates are 2100B but during the week an automatic 40% discount is subtracted.

North of town a bit, the *Regent Cha-am Beach Resort* (☎ 47180/91; fax 471491) has rooms starting at 1800B; they advertise a 30% to 40% discount for weekdays. Facilities include a swimming pool, squash and tennis courts and a fitness centre.

Also on the beach north of town is the posh *Dusit Resort & Polo Club* (☎ 520009; fax 520296), where rates start at 3872B. The Dusit offers a fitness centre, mini-golf, horseback riding, pool, tennis and squash courts and, of course, polo.

Places to Eat

Vendors on the beach sell fair chow. Opposite the beach are several good seafood restaurants which, unlike the bungalows, are reasonably priced.

Cha-am Coffee House, at 274/5 Ruamjit Rd, is good and fairly inexpensive. They are open early for breakfast and serve plenty of seafood dishes. Only a few doors away, the similarly priced *Khan Had Restaurant* has a more extensive menu but is also more expensive. Anantachai Guest House is another good place for inexpensive to moderately priced Thai and seafood dishes.

The luxury hotels have generally fine Thai, seafood and western cuisine at the standard high prices. Seafood and Thai cuisine are especially good at the Methavalai Hotel's *Sorndaeng Restaurant*, a branch of the famous Bangkok restaurant of the same name.

Getting There & Away

Buses from Phetburi and Hua Hin cost 15B. From Hua Hin, take a Phetburi-bound bus and ask to be let off at Hat Cha-am (Cha-am Beach); the fare is 10B.

Ordinary buses from Bangkok's southern bus terminal (Thonburi) to Cha-am cost 50B (92B air-con). In Cha-am ordinary buses stop on Phetkasem Highway, from where you can take a motorbike-taxi (10B) or a share-taxi (5B) out to the beach. A few hundred metres south of the corner of Narathip and Ruamjit Rds, a private bus company operates six daily air-con buses to Bangkok for 83B.

The train station is on Narathip Rd, west of Phetkasem Highway and a 10B motorcycle ride to/from the beach. Trains depart Hualamphong station at 9.25 am and 1.40 pm, and return at 6.25 am, 12.12 and 2.49 pm. The train is slower than the bus by one hour, takes about four hours and costs 36B.

Getting Around

Standard prices for motorbike taxi and public songthaew are 10B and 5B (30B to charter) respectively.

AROUND CHA-AM
Hat Peuktian

หาดปึกเตียน

This sandy beach between Cha-am and Phetburi has the usual casuarina trees and food vendors favoured by Thai beach-goers, and hardly a farang in sight. Three rocky islets are within wading distance of shore, one with a sala for shade. Also standing knee-deep just offshore is a six-metre statue of Phi Seua Samut, the undersea female deity that terrorised the protagonist of the Thai classical epic *Phra Aphaimani*. A statue of the prince himself sits on a nearby rock playing a flute.

A tasteless two-storey townhouse-style development has recently been built off the beach. Designed in the pseudo-classical style prevalent in modern city blocks all over Thailand, it looks rather incongruous with the natural beach surroundings.

Prachuap Khiri Khan Province

Pineapples and fishing are the main livelihoods of the Thais living in this narrow province along the upper part of the peninsula. Along the Gulf coast are a variety of small seaside resorts, most of them very low-key.

HUA HIN

หัวหิน

The beaches of Hua Hin first came to the country's attention when King Rama VII built Klai Kangwon, a seafront summer palace just north of what was then a small fishing village, in the early 1900s. Rama VII learned of Thailand's first coup d'état in 1932 while playing golf at the Royal Hua Hin Golf Course. Once endorsed by the royal family, Hua Hin remained a traditional favourite among the Thais long after the beaches of Pattaya and Phuket had been taken over by foreign tourists.

During the last five years, the secret has got out: Hua Hin (population 34,500) is a fairly quiet and fairly economical place to get away from it all, yet it's less than four hours by train from Bangkok. The private sector in Hua Hin have been promoting Hua Hin tourism, and developers have moved in. The resort now attracts a mix of Thais and older farang tourists who are seeking a comfortable beach holiday near Bangkok but don't want the sleaziness of Pattaya.

Unfortunately Hua Hin may go the way of Pattaya unless the local community and the interlopers start planning now, before the sleaze and environmental destruction sets in. Already appearing are a lot of the same kind of cheap, unsightly shophouse-apartment buildings with plumbing problems seen in Pattaya and Phuket's Patong Beach, as well as a recent invasion of girlie bars. Hua Hin has almost entirely lost its fishing-village atmosphere – the fishing fleet is being

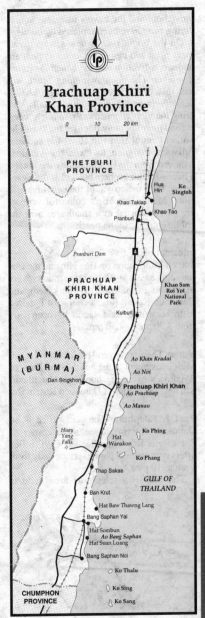

Prachuap Khiri Khan Province

0   10   20 km

PHETBURI PROVINCE

Hua Hin
Ko Singtoh
Khao Takiap
Khao Tao
Pranburi

Pranburi Dam

PRACHUAP KHIRI KHAN PROVINCE

Khao Sam Roi Yot National Park

Kuiburi

MYANMAR (BURMA)

Ao Khan Kradai
Ao Noi
Dan Singkhon

Prachuap Khiri Khan
Ao Prachuap
Ao Manao

Ko Phing

Huay Yang Falls

Hat Wanakon

Ko Phang

Thap Sakae

GULF OF THAILAND

Ban Krut
Hat Baw Thawng Lang
Bang Saphan Yai
Hat Sombun
Ao Bang Saphan
Hat Suan Luang
Bang Saphan Noi

Ko Thalu

Ko Sing

CHUMPHON PROVINCE

Ko Sang

moved out and the town's infamous squid-drying piers have been replaced by hotels.

On the bright side, a new sewage treatment plant and municipal sewer system are under construction and the beach is cleaner than ever. The main swimming beach still has thatched umbrellas and long chairs; vendors from the nearby food stalls will bring loungers steamed crab, mussels, beer, etc and there are pony rides for the kids. The Sofitel Central Hua Hin Hotel has successfully campaigned to have the vendors removed from the beach fronting the hotel – a minus for atmosphere but a plus for cleanliness. With the arrival of the new high-rise Hotel Meliá, Hua Hin's colourful vendors are now restricted to a small area near the public entrance to the beach.

Information

Tourist information on Hua Hin and the surrounding area is available at the municipality office on the corner of Phetkasem and Damnoen Kasem Rds, a couple of hundred metres east of the train station. It's open daily from 8.30 am to 4.30 pm.

Money There are several banks around town. Most convenient to the beach is the Bank of Ayudhya's exchange booth on Naretdamri Rd, near the corner of Damnoen Kasem Rd.

Post & Telephone The post office is on Damnoen Kasem Rd near the corner of Phetkasem Rd. The attached CAT office offers international phone service daily from 6 am to 10 pm.

The Hua Hin telephone area code is ☎ 032.

Ao Takiap
อ่าวตะเกียบ

Eight to 13 km south of Hua Hin along Ao Takiap (Chopsticks Bay) are the beaches of **Hat Khao Takiap**, **Suan Son** and **Khao Tao**, all of which are undergoing resort development. Two hilltop temples can be visited here. **Wat Khao Thairalat** is well off the beach on a rocky hill and is nothing special. At the end of the bay is the more well-endowed **Wat Khao Takiap**; climb the steps for a good bay view.

The southern end of the bay is now one big construction site as one high-rise after another goes up, blocking the sea view from all points inland. North along the bay, however, are several quiet, wooded spots with cabins and beach houses.

If you're driving, the turn-off for Ao Takiap is four km south of Hua Hin. There are regular songthaews back and forth from town.

Places to Stay – bottom end

Prices are moving up quickly for places near the beach. Hotels in town are still reasonable and it's only a five or 10-minute walk to the beach from most of them.

Guesthouses Near – but not on – the beach, the cheapest places are found along or just off Naretdamri Rd. Several small hotels and guesthouses in this area have rooms for 100 to 300B a night. Rooms at *Dang's House (Khun Daeng House)* on Naretdamri Rd cost 100 to 150B with private bath. On the next block north, the Pakistani-run *Moti Mahal* (☎ 513769) at 152/1 Naretdamri costs 150B for a small room with bath and fan, 200B for larger rooms. Also on this block, the *Europa* (☎ 513235) at No 158 has rooms for 150B with bath, and a European restaurant downstairs. *Sunee Guest House*, next door, is an old wooden building with rooms for 150B with shared bath.

Along a soi off Naretdamri Rd just north of Damnoen Kasem Rd is the comfortable-looking *Forum Guest House*. Rooms cost 150 to 180B, some rooms with bath, some

PLACES TO STAY

2 Thanachai Hotel
4 Phananchai Hotel
6 Damrong Hotel
7 Chaat Chai Hotel
10 Thancote Guest House
14 All Nations
15 Siripetchkasem
(Siri Phetkasem) Hotel
17 Subhamitra (Suphamit)
Hotel
20 Seabreeze & Mod
(Mot) Guesthouses
21 Meliá Hua Hin
22 Sukvilay Guest House
23 Phuen Guest House
24 Fresh Inn
26 Joy Guest House
& Ban Pak Hua Hin
27 Sriosraupsin, Europa
& Sunee Guest Houses
28 Forum Guest House
29 Parichart Guest House
& Dang's House
30 City Beach Hotel
31 Ban Boosarin Hotel
32 Sirin Hotel
33 Thai Tae Guest House
36 Golf Inn

40 Jed Pee Nong Hotel
41 Ban Somboon
42 Patchara House
43 Baan Soontree
44 Hotel Sofitel Central

PLACES TO EAT

5 Kiwi Corner
9 Seafood Restaurants
13 Maria Ice Cream
18 Chinese-Thai Restaurants
39 Angus Steak House

OTHER

1 Klai Kangwon Palace
3 Bank
8 Fishing Pier (Tha Thiap
Reua Pramong)
11 Bus Terminal
12 Chatchai Market
16 Pran Tour
19 Rock Walk Pub
25 Wat Hua Hin
29 Bank of Ayudhya
34 Royal Hua Hin Golf Course
35 Train Station
37 Tourist Information
38 GPO & CAT Office

Hua Hin

0   50   100 m

Damrongrat Road

To Bangkok

2

Phetkasem Road

Naep Khehat Road

3

4

5

Chomsin Road

Sasong Road

6

7

8

9

10

11

13

14

Dechanuchit Road

12

18

19

20

15

16

17

Amnuaysin Road

Phunsuk (Poonsuk) Road

Naretdamri Road

22 23

24

21

25

26 27

28

29

30

31 32

33

Damnoen Kasem Road

34

35

36

37

38

39 40

41

42

43

44

Soi Kasem
Samphan

To Prachuap Khiri Khan,
Ao Takiab Beaches & Royal
Garden Resort (200m)

without. On the same soi are the similar *MP* and *SM* guesthouses.

Parichart Guest House (☎ 513863), next to Dang's House, is a more up-market place with rooms for 350B with fan and private bath, 450 to 550B with air-con.

Along the next soi north off Naretdamri Rd are a couple of charming old wooden guesthouses. *Phuen Guest House* is a fairly quiet place with a nice atmosphere and rates in the 200B range. Farther along is the pleasant looking *Sukvilay Guest House*, which is similar in quality and price to the neighbouring places. *Joy Guest House*, on the opposite side of the soi, has similar charm and room rates are 200 and 250B. Also on this soi is the modern, apartment-style *Ban Pak Hua Hin*; it's quiet, exceptionally clean, and costs 200B with fan and bath, 300B with air-con.

Farther up Naretdamri Rd, where the old squid piers used to be, are two wooden motel-like places built on piers over the edge of the sea. *Mod (Mot) Guest House* has rather small rooms for 150 to 250B with fan, 400B with air-con, while the *Seabreeze (Sirima)* costs 250B for rooms with fan and bath overlooking the water, or 160B for rooms closer to the road without bath. One problem here: during low tide the exposed beach beneath the piers emits a terrible smell, probably arising from inadequate waste disposal.

Towards the fishing pier on the right, the friendly *Thancote Guest House* has rooms with fan for 200B and air-con for 400B. They also have a cheap seafood restaurant.

Sukwilai Guest House is a modern house next to Wat Hua Hin with fan-cooled rooms in the 100 to 200B range and air-con for 300B. Around the corner on Phunsuk Rd is *Nature Guest House*, a row of older, two-storey Thai-style bungalows that cost only 80B downstairs, 100B upstairs. Rooms are very basic, furnished with only a mattress on the floor; the upstairs rooms have a small sitting terrace.

Farther north on Dechanuchit Rd (east of Phunsuk Rd), over a New Zealander-managed pub, is the friendly and clean *All Nations*, where rooms cost 150 to 250B depending on

the size. Each room in the tall, narrow building comes with its own balcony and fan; each floor has a bathroom shared by two or three rooms.

Baan Soontree, on Soi Kasem Samphan near the corner of Damnoen Kasem Rd, is a large private home with rooms for 200B with fan and private bath.

Back across the street again next to the more top-end Sirin Hotel, the *Thai Tae (Thae) Guest House* offers rooms with fan and bath for 200B.

Hotels To find hotels under 300B, you'll have to go up to Phetkasem Rd, the main north-south road through town. *Chaat Chai* at 59/1 Phetkasem Rd has rooms with fan and bath for 140 to 220B. Just off Phetkasem, behind the bank, is *Subhamitra (Suphamit)* (☎ 511208/487) with very clean rooms with fan and bath for 250B, air-con for 350 to 800B. Just past the market at 46 Phetkasem Rd is *Damrong* (☎ 511574), where rooms with fan and bath are 120 to 150B, 350B with air-con.

Behind the Chatchai Market area on Sasong Rd, *Siripetchkasem (Siri Phetkasem)* (☎ 511394) is similar to the hotels along Phetkasem Rd. Rooms with fan are 200B and air-con rooms are 400B.

Finally, a bit farther north at 11 Damrongrat Rd, is *Thanachai* (☎ 511755), a good upper bottom-end place for 250B with fan and bath, 500B for air-con. The Thanachai accepts credit cards.

Places to Stay – middle

Hua Hin's middle-range places are typically small, sedate, modern hotels with air-con rooms and such luxuries as telephones. The forerunner of this trend, *Ban Boosarin* (☎ 512076), calls itself a 'mini-deluxe hotel' and although it's 696B a night, all rooms come with air-con, hot water, telephone, colour TV, fridge and private terrace. It's super-clean and rates don't rise on weekends. There's a 10% discount for stays of a week or more.

Along Soi Kasem Samphan next to the Jed Pee Nong Hotel are a couple of Ban Boosarin clones. *Patchara House* (☎ 511787) costs 300B for rooms with fan or 550/610B for singles/doubles with air-con, TV/video, telephone, hot water and fridge. Also on this soi is the similar *Ban Somboon*, where nicely decorated rooms are 300B with fan and hot showers, 550B with air-con; all rates include breakfast and there is a pleasant sitting garden on the premises. Also in this area is *PP Villa*, which has a garden and clean, air-con rooms for 450B (no hot water, however). These hotels, as well as the Jed Pee Nong and City Beach described below, are only a couple of hundred metres from the beach.

The popular *Jed Pee Nong* (☎ 512381) is on Damnoen Kasem Rd. Modern, clean but otherwise unimpressive rooms cost 400B with fan and bath, 500B with air-con or 600B for air-con rooms by the new swimming pool behind the hotel.

On Naretdamri Rd, the modern *Fresh Inn* (☎ 511389) has all air-con rooms for 700 to 875B; this pleasant tourist-class hotel would have had a sea view if not for the construction of the high-rise Meliá Hua Hin between it and the sea.

Running north-east from Chomsin Rd (the road leading to the main pier) is Naep Khehat Rd. At No 73/5-7, the *Phananchai Hotel* (☎ 511707) has air-con rooms for 350 to 600B. It's a bit of a walk from the swimming beaches but all rooms come with air-con, hot water, TV and telephone.

Places to Stay – top end

The air-con *Sirin Hotel* (☎ 511150; fax 513571) is on Damnoen Kasem Rd towards the beach, down from the City Beach Hotel. The rooms here are well kept and come with hot water and a fridge. The semi-outdoor restaurant area is pleasant. Double rooms are 890B during the week and 1290B on weekends and holidays.

Nearby, the old Hua Hin Raluk Hotel has been rebuilt and resurrected as the *City Beach Hotel* (☎ 512870/75; fax 512448) at 16 Damnoen Kasem Rd. Luxurious rooms with the usual service and extras cost from 1600B.

Near the train station, off Damnoen Kasem Rd near the Hua Hin golf course, is the *Golf Inn* (☎ 512473), where air-con rooms are 700 to 1290B.

Hua Hin has two other top-end hotels. *Hotel Sofitel Central Hua Hin* (☎ 512021/40; (02) 233-0974/0980 in Bangkok), formerly the Hua Hin Railway Hotel, is a magnificent two-storey colonial-style place on the beach at the end of Damnoen Kasem Rd. Rooms in the original L-shaped colonial wing cost 3100B; rooms in the new wing are more expensive but there is also a Villa Wing across the road with original one and two-bedroom beach bungalows for 3100 to 5000B. From 20 December to 20 February there's a 700B peak-season supplement on all room charges.

The all-new *Meliá Hua Hin* (☎ 511053; fax 511135), off Naretdamri Rd, is part of the Spanish-owned Meliá hotel chain and is Hua Hin's first high-rise hotel (also the first to mar the skyline, unfortunately). Rooms with all the amenities cost from 3000 to 7200B depending on the time of year.

There are also a few top-end places on beaches just north and south of town. Some add peak-season (November to April) supplements, others offer 40% discounts in the off season:

Hua Hin Highland Resort, from 4600B; it's on a hill north of town, and is a favourite of golfers who frequent the nearby Royal Hua Hin Golf Course (☎ 512487)

Hua Hin Palace Hotel, 700 to 900B (☎ 511151; fax 512117)

Royal Garden Resort 107/1 Phetkasem Rd, from 3000B; discounts of 40% available even in peak season (☎ 511881, fax 512422; (02) 251-8659 in Bangkok)

Royal Garden Village, 45 Phetkasem Rd, from 3884B, plus 700B peak-season supplement November to April (☎ 512412/5, fax 520259; (02) 251-8659 in Bangkok)

Sailom Hotel, 1450 to 3900B (☎ 511890/1, fax 512047; (02) 258-0652 in Bangkok)

Places to Stay – Out of Town

In Hat Takiap, the *Fangkhlun Guest House* (☎ 512402) has five fan-cooled rooms from

---

Hua Hin Railway Hotel

In 1922 the State Railway of Thailand (then the Royal Thai Railway) extended the national rail network to Hua Hin to allow easier access to the Hua Hin summer palace. The area proved to be a popular vacation spot among non-royals too, so in the following year they built the Hua Hin Railway Hotel, a graceful colonial-style inn on the sea, with sweeping teak stairways and high-ceilinged rooms. When I researched the first edition of this guide in 1981, a double room was still only 90B and the service was just as unhurried as it had been when I first stayed here in 1977. It probably hadn't changed much since 1923, except for the addition of electric lighting and screened doors and windows. Big-bladed ceiling fans stirred the humid sea air and in the dining room one ate using State Railway silverware and thick china from the 1920s. Unfortunately, when Bangkok's Central Department Store took over the management of the hotel they floundered in their attempt to upgrade the facilities, failing to take advantage of the hotel's original ambience.

In 1986 the French hotel chain Sofitel became part of a joint venture with Central and together they restored the hotel to most of its former glory. It now bears the awkward name *Hotel Sofitel Central Hua Hin*, but if you've been looking for a historic South-East Asian hotel to spend some money on, this might be it. All of the wood panelling and brass fixtures throughout the rooms and open hallways have been restored. While the old railway silverware and china have been resigned to antique cabinet displays, the spacious, lazy ambience of a previous age remains. Even if you don't want to spend the money to stay here, it's worth a stroll through the grounds and open sitting areas for a little history. It's more interesting in terms of atmosphere than either the Raffles in Singapore or the Oriental in Bangkok (neither of which have eight-hectare grounds), and somewhere in between in terms of luxury. Latest reports, however, say standards have slipped since the lay-off of all European management.

Incidentally, in 1983 this hotel was used as Hotel Le Phnom for the filming of *The Killing Fields*. Also, the State Railway of Thailand still owns the hotel; Sofitel/Central are just leasing it. ∎

---

400 to 500B. The *Takiap Beach Resort* (☎/fax 512639) is south of Khao Takiap, and has air-con rooms from 1500B a night. The *Sri Pathum Guest House* (☎ 512339) is cheaper and has 11 rooms from 250B with fan, 350B air-con; and the *Vegas Guest House* (☎ 512290) has 32 rooms priced from 390B for a small room, 890B for something larger.

In a forested area called Nong Khae at the north end of Ao Takiap are the quiet *Rung Arun Guest House* (☎ 511291), with cabins ranging from 150 to 700B, and *Chaihat Noen Chale* (☎ 511288), with 14 air-con rooms for 1500B each.

In Hat Khao Tao, the *Nanthasuda Guesthouse (Nanthasuda Restaurant)* has rooms from 300B, while Hat Suan Son has the modern *Suan Son Padiphat* (☎ 511239) with fan-cooled rooms for 250B (600B on the sea) or air-con rooms for 500 to 1000B.

In Pranburi, the *Pranburi Beach Resort* has rooms priced from 1400B; the *Pransiri Hotel* (☎ 621061), at 283 Phetkasem Rd, has rooms starting from 140B.

Places to Eat

The best seafood in Hua Hin is found in three main areas. Firstly, along Damnoen Kasem Rd near the Jed Pee Nong and City Beach hotels, and off Damnoen Kasem, on Phunsuk and Naretdamri Rds, there are some medium-priced restaurants. Secondly, there's excellent and inexpensive food in the Chatchai night market, off Phetkasem Rd on Dechanuchit Rd, and in nearby Chinese-Thai restaurants. The third area is next to Tha Thiap Reua Pramong, the big fishing pier at the end of Chomsin Rd. The fish is, of course, fresh off the boats but not necessarily the cheapest in town. One of the places near the pier, *Saeng Thai*, is the oldest seafood restaurant in Hua Hin and quite reliable if you know how to order. The best value for the money can be found in the smaller eating places on and off Chomsin Rd and in the Chatchai night market. There is also a night market on Chomsin Rd.

The best seafood to order in Hua Hin is plaa sǎmlii (cotton fish or kingfish), plaa kapõng (perch), plaa mèuk (squid), hǎwy malaeng phùu (mussels) and puu (crab). The various forms of preparation include:

dìp	raw
nêung	steamed
phão	grilled
phàt	sliced, filleted and fried
râat phrík	smothered in garlic and chillies
thâwt	fried whole
tôm yam	in a hot and tangy broth
yâang	roast (squid only)

Chatchai Market is excellent for Thai breakfast – they sell very good jók and khâo tôm (rice soups). Fresh-fried paa-thông-kŏ Hua Hin-style (small and crispy, not oily), are 1B for three. A few vendors also serve hot soy milk in bowls (4B) – break a few paa-thông-kŏ into the soy milk and drink free náam chaa – a very tasty and filling breakfast for 7B if you can eat nine paa-thông-kŏ.

Gee Cuisine, next to the Jed Pee Nong, caters mostly to farangs but the Thai food is generally good. The nonstop video in the evenings, however, is a curse one hopes won't spread to other restaurants in town.

Phunsuk and Naretdamri Rds are becoming centres for farang-oriented eateries. The *Tan Thong* does good seafood and also has a bar. The *Beergarden* is just what it sounds like – an outdoor pub with Western food. The *Headrock Cafe* (not a misspelling but a pun on the name Hua Hin – 'head rock') is more of a drinking place, but also has Thai and Western food. On the next street up, Phunsuk Rd, is the Italian *La Villa*, with pizza, spaghetti, lasagne and so on. The new *Le Paris Bangkok* restaurant at 54/2 Dechanuchit Rd specialises in French cuisine, with dishes starting from 100B. Europa Guest House also has a continental restaurant. *Kiwi Corner* at 21 Chomsin serves Western breakfasts.

The lavish breakfast buffet at the *Hotel Sofitel Central* is a fair deal at 200 to 250B (depending on the season).

Maria Ice Cream, at 54/2 Dechanuchit Rd, offers fabulous home-made ice cream, including flavours like papaya, watermelon and coconut. Steak-lovers can get their fill at *Angus Steak House* on Damnoen Kasem Rd, just down from the post office.

Entertainment

Several farang bars under German, Swiss, Italian, French and New Zealand management can be found in and around Naretdamri and Phunsuk Rds. Most offer the familiar Thai hostess atmosphere. One that dares to be different is the All Nations Bar at 10-10/1 Dechanuchit Rd, which successfully recreates a pub atmosphere and has quite a collection of flags and other memorabilia from around the world.

Stone Town, an old-west style pub next to Jed Pee Nong Hotel on Damnoen Kasem Rd, features live folk and country music nightly. For Thai rock'n'roll, check out the Rock Walk Pub off Dechanuchit Rd, where live Thai bands – many from Bangkok – appear nightly. The room and sound system are well designed for listening; there's no cover charge and drinks are no more expensive than at any of the town's farang bars.

Getting There & Away

Air Bangkok Airways (☎ 512083; (02) 253-8942 in Bangkok) flies to Hua Hin daily for 900B one way; the flight takes 35 minutes. The airport is five km north of the city.

Bus Buses from Bangkok's southern bus terminal are 92B air-con, 51B ordinary. The trip takes 3½ to four hours. Pran Tour on Sasong Rd near the Siripetchkasem Hotel in Hua Hin runs air-con buses to Bangkok every half hour from 3 am to 9 pm, for 63B 2nd-class air-con or 92B 1st-class air-con. Pran Tour air-con buses to Phetburi are 60B.

MP Travel, at Nana Plaza Inn (☎ (02) 281-5954) on Khao San Rd in Bangkok, operates minivans to Hua Hin for 150B per person.

Ordinary buses for Hua Hin leave Phetburi regularly for 20B. The same bus can be picked up in Cha-am for 15B. From Nakhon Pathom an ordinary bus is 39B.

For local buses from Hua Hin to the beaches of Khao Takiap (5B), Khao Tam (4B) and Suan Son (4B), go to the ordinary bus terminal on Sasong Rd. These buses run from around 6 am until 5 pm. Buses to Pranburi are 7B. Other ordinary buses are to Prachuap Khiri Khan (35B), Chumphon (66B), Surat Thani (112B), Phuket (163B, seven a day), Krabi (158B, two a day) and Hat Yai (178B, three per day).

Train The same trains south apply here as those described under Phetburi's Getting There & Away section. The train trip takes three hours and 45 minutes from Bangkok; 1st-class fare is 182B (express only), 2nd class 92B (rapid and express only), 3rd class is 44B.

You can also come by train from any other station on the southern railway line, including Phetburi (3rd class, 13B), Nakhon Pathom (2nd/3rd class 52/33B), Prachuap (3rd class, 19B), Surat Thani (2nd/3rd class, 116/74B) and Hat Yai (2nd/3rd class, 183/116B). The 1st and 2nd-class fares do not include rapid or express surcharges.

Getting Around

Samlor fares in Hua Hin have been set by the municipal authorities so there shouldn't be any haggling. Here are some sample fares: the train station to the beach, 10B; the bus terminal to the Hotel Sofitel Central, 15B; Chatchai Market to the fishing pier, 10B; the train station to the Royal Garden Resort, 20B.

Motorcycles and bicycles can be rented from a couple of places on Damnoen Kasem Rd near the Jed Pee Nong Hotel. Motorcycle rates are reasonable: 150 to 200B per day for 100cc to 300B for 125cc. Occasionally larger bikes – 400 to 750cc – are available for 500 to 600B a day. Bicycles are 30 to 70B per day.

At the fishing pier in Hua Hin you can hire boats out to Ko Singtoh for 800B a day. On Hat Takiap you can get boats for 700B.

KHAO SAM ROI YOT NATIONAL PARK

อุทยานแห่งชาติเขาสามร้อยยอด

This 98-sq-km park (established 1955) has magnificent views of the Prachuap coastline if you can stand a little climbing. Khao Daeng is only about half an hour's walk from the park headquarters, and from here you can see the ocean as well as some freshwater lagoons. If you have the time and energy, climb the 605-metre **Khao Krachom** for even better views. If you're lucky, you may come across a serow (Asian goat-antelope) while hiking. The lagoons and coastal marshes are great places for bird-watching. Along the coast you may see the occasional pod of Irrawaddy dolphins passing by.

Fauna

Notable wildlife around Khao Sam Roi Yot (Three Hundred Peaks) includes crab-eating macaque, dusky langur, slow loris (the park is considered one of the best spots in the world for viewing dusky langurs and slow loris), barking deer, Malayan pangolin, fishing cat, palm civet, otter, serow, Javan mongoose and monitor lizard.

Because the park lies at the intersection of the East Asian and Australian flyways, as many as 300 migratory and resident bird species have been recorded, including yellow bittern, cinnamon bittern, purple swamp hen, water rail, ruddy-breasted crake, bronze-winged jacana, grey heron, painted stork, whistling duck, spotted eagle and black-headed ibis. The park protects Thailand's largest freshwater marsh (along with considerable mangroves and mudflats), and is one of only two places in the country where the purple heron breeds.

Waterfowl are most commonly seen in the cool season. Encroachment by shrimp farmers in the vicinity has sadly destroyed substantial portions of mangroves, thus depriving the birds of an important habitat.

Beaches, Canals & Marshes

A sandy beach flanked on three sides by dry limestone hills and casuarinas, **Hat Laem Sala** is the location for the main visitors' centre, restaurant, bungalows and camping area. Boats with a capacity of up to 10 people can be hired from Bang Pu to the beach for

150B return. You can also reach the beach from Bang Pu via a steep trail, about a 20-minute walk. The visitors' centre features well-curated exhibits; there are nature trails nearby.

Hat Sam Phraya, five km south of Hat Laem Sala, is a km-long beach with a restaurant and washrooms. The park headquarters is located just past the village of Khao Daeng, about four km south-east of Hat Sam Phraya.

A four-km canal trip in a 10-person boat along **Khlong Khao Daeng** can be arranged in the nearby village of Khao Daeng for 150B. The trip lasts 1½ to two hours and passes mangrove remnants and waterfowl habitats. The birds are most active in early morning or late afternoon.

Caves

The other big attraction at Sam Roi Yot are the three caves of Tham Kaew, Tham Sai and Tham Phraya Nakhon. **Tham Phraya Nakhon** is the most visited and can be reached by boat or on foot. The boat trip only takes about half an hour there and back, while it's half an hour each way on foot along a steep, rocky trail. There are actually two large caverns, both with sinkholes that allow light in. In one cave is a royal sala built for King Chulalongkorn, who would stop off here when travelling back and forth between Bangkok and Nakhon Si Thammarat.

Tham Kaew, two km from the Bang Pu turn-off, features a series of chambers connected by narrow passageways; you enter the first cavern by means of a permanent ladder. Lamps can be rented for 100B, but Tham Kaew is best visited in the company of a park guide because of the dangerous footing.

Tham Sai is ensconced in a hill near Ban Khrun Tanot, about 2½ km from the main road between Lae Sala and Sam Phraya beaches. Villagers rent lamps for around 30B at a shelter near the cave mouth. A 280-metre trail leads up the hillside to the cave, which features a large single cavern. Be careful of steep drop-offs in the cave.

English-speaking guides can be hired at the park office for 100B per hike.

Places to Stay

The Forestry Department hires out large bungalows near the visitors' centre as well as at Hat Laem Sala for 500 to 1000B per night or 100B per person; they sleep 10 to 20 people. You can also pitch your own tent for 10B per person at campsites at the park headquarters, Hat Laem Sala or Hat Sam Phraya. There are restaurants at all three places. Bring insect repellent along as the park is rife with mosquitoes.

Getting There & Away

The park is 37 km south of Pranburi. Catch a bus to Pranburi (8B from Hua Hin) and then a songthaew to Bang Pu for 20B – these run between 6 am and 4 pm. From Bang Pu you must charter a vehicle, hitch or walk.

You can save the hassle of finding a ride in Bang Pu by chartering a songthaew for 300B or a motorcycle taxi for 150B from Pranburi all the way to the park. Most convenient of all would be to rent a car or motorbike in Hua Hin. If you're coming by car or motorcycle from Hua Hin, it's about 25 km to the park turn-off, then another 38 km to park headquarters.

PRACHUAP KHIRI KHAN

อ.เมืองประจวบคีรีขันธ์

Roughly 80 km south of Hua Hin, Prachuap Khiri Khan (population 14,500) is the provincial capital, though it is somewhat smaller than Hua Hin. There are no real swimming beaches in town, but the eight-km-long bay of Ao Prachuap is pretty enough. The seafood here is fantastic, however, and cheaper than in Hua Hin. Fishing is still the mainstay of the local economy.

Orientation & Information

South of Ao Prachuap, around a small headland, is the scenic **Ao Manao**, a bay ringed by a clean white-sand beach with small islands offshore. Because a Thai air-force base is near the bay, the beach was closed to the public until 1990, when the local authorities decided to open the area to day visitors. The beach is two or three km from the base

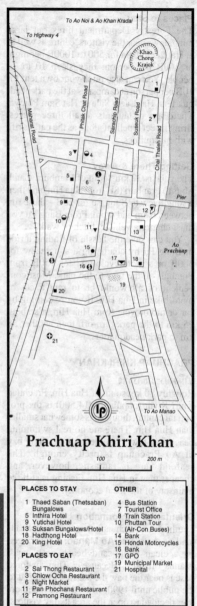

Prachuap Khiri Khan

```
0          100         200 m
```

PLACES TO STAY		OTHER	
1	Thaed Saban (Thetsaban) Bungalows	4	Bus Station
5	Inthira Hotel	7	Tourist Office
9	Yutichai Hotel	8	Train Station
13	Suksan Bungalows/Hotel	10	Phuttan Tour
18	Hadthong Hotel		(Air-Con Buses)
20	King Hotel	14	Bank
		15	Honda Motorcycles
PLACES TO EAT		16	Bank
2	Sai Thong Restaurant	17	GPO
3	Chiow Ocha Restaurant	19	Municipal Market
6	Night Market	21	Hospital
11	Pan Phochana Restaurant		
12	Pramong Restaurant		

entrance; you must leave your passport at the gate and sign in. There are several salas along the beach, one restaurant, toilets and a shower.

At the northern end of Ao Prachuap is **Khao Chong Krajok** (Mirror Tunnel Mountain – named after the hole through the side of the mountain which appears to reflect the sky). At the top is **Wat Thammikaram**, established by King Rama VI. You can climb the hill for a view of the town and bay – and entertain the hordes of monkeys who live here. A metal ladder leads into the tunnel from the wat grounds.

If you continue north from Prachuap Khiri Khan around Ao Prachuap to the headland you'll come to a small boat-building village on **Ao Bang Nang Lom** where they still make wooden fishing vessels using traditional Thai methods. It takes about two months to finish a 12-metre boat, which will sell for around 400,000B without an engine. West of the beach at Ao Bang Nang Lom is a canal, **Khlong Bang Nang Lom**, lined with picturesque mangroves.

A few km north of Ao Prachuap is another bay, **Ao Noi**, the site of a small fishing village with a few rooms to let.

Prachuap has its own city-run tourist office in the centre of town. The staff are very friendly and they have maps and photos of all the attractions in the area.

Local resident Pinit Ounope has been recommended for his inexpensive day tours to Khao Sam Roi Yot, Dan Singkhon and to nearby beaches, national parks and waterfalls. He lives at 144 Chai Thaleh Rd near the beach in town and invites travellers to visit him. His house is rather difficult to find, so take a tuk-tuk or a motorcycle taxi. The typical day tour is 200B for two people, plus 50B for each extra person.

Places to Stay

Prachuap Khiri Khan The *Yutichai Hotel* (☎ 611055) at 35 Kong Kiat Rd has fair rooms with fan and bath for 100 to 120B. Around the corner on Phitak Chat Rd is the *Inthira Hotel* with similar rooms in the 90 to 130B range, but it's noisier and has peepholes. Both of these are quite near the night market and tourist office. The *King Hotel* (☎ 611170), farther south on the same street, has fan-cooled rooms at 150 to 200B. Facing Ao Prachuap is the *Suksan*, with fan-cooled rooms for 160 to 200B and air-con bungalows from 240 to 280B, but it's very much one big brothel in the evenings.

Also facing the bay are the plain but well-kept *Thaed Saban Bungalows* (Thetsaban Bungalows, meaning Municipal Bungalows but also known as Mirror Mountain Bungalows), which are owned by the city. A one-room bungalow (sleeps two) is 200B with fan and bath or 300B for air-con; a two-room (sleeps four) is 500B; a three-room (sleeps six) is 700B; a four-room (sleeps eight) is 1700B. There are also a couple of newer three-room bungalows for 1000B.

The newish *Hadthong Hotel* (☎ 611960; fax 611003) next to the bay in town has modern air-con rooms with balconies for 600 (mountain view) and 728B (sea view), plus a 200B surcharge from 20 December to 31 January. A pool is on the premises.

North of the city, on the road to Ao Noi, *Rimhad Bungalow* offers tiny fan-cooled rooms for 200B, larger rooms with air-con for 400B. The bungalows face Khlong Bang Nang Lom and mangroves. *Happy Inn* nearby has the same prices and similar accommodation.

Ao Noi In Ao Noi there are several rooms and small 'weekend inns', most catering to Thais. *Aow Noi Beach Bungalows* (☎ (02) 510-9790 in Bangkok) offers well-kept cottages for 300 to 600B a night with breakfast. Run by a former German volunteer worker and his Thai wife, facilities include a small bar and restaurant with Thai and Western food, plus a clean, secluded beach.

Places to Eat

Because of its well-deserved reputation for fine seafood, Prachuap has many restaurants for its size. Best place for the money is the night market that convenes near the government offices in the middle of town. On Chai

Thaleh Rd near the Hadthong Hotel is a smaller night market that's also quite good; tables set up along the sea wall sometimes get a good breeze.

Of the many seafood restaurants, the best are the *Pan Phochana* on Sarachip Rd and the *Sai Thong* on Chai Thaleh Rd near the municipal bungalows. Both serve great-tasting seafood at reasonable prices. The Pan Phochana is famous for its hàw mòk hãwy, ground fish curry steamed in mussels on the half-shell. One of the seafood specialities of Prachuap that you shouldn't miss is plaa sãmlii tàet dìaw, whole cottonfish that's sliced lengthways and left to dry in the sun for half a day, then fried quickly in a wok. It's often served with mango salad on the side. It may sound awful, but the taste is sublime.

Just south of the Pan Phochana is a good night market with many seafood stalls.

Other good restaurants include the *Chiow Ocha* (a bit higher priced – this is where the Thai tour buses stop), the *Pramong* and the *Chao Reua*. The *Phloen Samut Restaurant*, adjacent to Hadthong Hotel, is a good outdoor seafood place though it doesn't have everything listed on the menu.

Several good seafood restaurants can also be found along the road north of Ao Prachuap on the way to Ao Noi. *Rap Lom* (literally, 'breeze-receiving') is the most popular – look for the Green Spot sign.

The Hadthong Hotel's dining room offers a bargain Thai buffet lunch on weekdays for just 59B.

Across from the Inthira Hotel is a small morning market with tea stalls that serve cheap curries and noodles.

Getting There & Away

Bus From Bangkok, ordinary buses are 72B; they leave the southern bus terminal frequently between 3 and 9.20 pm. Air-con buses cost 130B from the southern air-con terminal. In the opposite direction, air-con buses to Bangkok cost 135B and leave from Phuttan Tour (☎ 611411) on Phitak Chat Rd at 8.30 am, noon, 3.30 pm and 1 am. In either direction the trip takes four to five hours.

From Hua Hin buses are 30B and leave from the bus station on Sasong Rd every 20 minutes from 7 am to 3 pm, taking 1½ to two hours.

From Prachuap you can catch ordinary buses to Chumphon (50B), Surat Thani (100B), Nakhon Si Thammarat (125B), Krabi (140B) and Phuket (145B).

The air-con bus from Bangkok to Samui stops on the highway in Prachuap at 12.30 am – if seats are available you can buy a through ticket to Samui for 190B. It's a five-minute, 10B motorcycle taxi ride from the town centre to the highway bus stop.

Train For departure details from Bangkok, see the earlier Phetburi Getting There & Away section: the same services apply. Fares from Bangkok are 122B for 2nd class and 58B for 3rd class. Ordinary trains between Hua Hin and Prachuap are 19B; from Hua Hin they leave at 10.30 and 11.47 am, and 6.25 pm, arriving in Prachuap 1½ hours later. There are also a couple of rapid trains between the two towns, but the time saved is only about 20 minutes.

A 3rd-class ticket on to Chumphon is 34B.

Getting Around

Prachuap is small enough to get around on foot, or you can hop on a tuk-tuk for 5B anywhere on the main roads.

A tuk-tuk to Ao Noi costs 20B. The Honda dealer on Sarachip Rd rents motorcycles, as does the Suzuki dealer on Phitak Chat Rd.

A motorbike taxi to Ao Manao costs 20B. They aren't permitted past the gate, from where it is necessary to walk the three km to the beach.

AROUND PRACHUAP KHIRI KHAN TOWN
Wat Khao Tham Khan Kradai
วัดเขาถ้ำคั่นกระไ่ด

About eight km north of town, following the same road beyond Ao Noi, is this small cave wat at one end of lengthy **Ao Khan Kradai**. A trail at the base of the limestone hill leads up and around the side to a small cavern and

then to a larger one which contains a reclining Buddha. If you have a torch you can proceed to a larger second chamber also containing Buddha images. From this trail you get a good view of Ao Khan Kradai (also known as Ao Khan Bandai), a long, beautiful bay that stretches out below. The beach here is suitable for swimming and is virtually deserted. It's not far from Ao Noi, so you could stay in Ao Noi and walk to this beach. Or you could stay in town, rent a motorcycle and make a day trip to Ao Khan Kradai.

Dan Singkhon
ด่านสิงขร

Just south of Prachuap is a road leading west to Dan Singkhon on the Myanmar border. This is the narrowest point in Thailand between the Gulf of Thailand and Myanmar – only 12 km across. The Burmese side changed from Karen to Yangon control following skirmishes in 1988-89. The border is closed; on the Thai side is a small frontier village and a Thai police camp with wooden semi-underground bunkers built in a circle.

Off the road on the way to Dan Singkhon are a couple of small cave hermitages. The more famous one at **Khao Hin Thoen**, surrounded by a park of the same name, has some interesting rock formations and sculptures – but watch out for the dogs. The road to Khao Hin Thoen starts where the paved road to Dan Singkhon breaks left. **Khao Khan Hawk** (also known as Phutthakan Bang Kao) is a less well-known cave nearby where elderly monk Luang Phaw Buaphan Chatimetho lives. Devotees from a local village bring him food each morning.

THAP SAKAE & BANG SAPHAN
ทับสะแกและบางสะพาน

These two districts lie south of Prachuap Khiri Khan and together they offer a string of fairly good beaches that get hardly any tourists.

The town of Thap Sakae is set back from the coast and isn't much, but along the seashore there are a few places to stay (see below). The beach opposite Thap Sakae isn't anything special either, but north and south of town are the beaches of **Hat Wanakon** and **Hat Laem Kum**. There is no private accommodation at these beaches at the moment, but you could ask permission to camp at Wat Laem Kum, which is on a prime spot right in the middle of Hat Laem Kum. Laem Kum is only 3.5 km from Thap Sakae and at the northern end is the fishing village of Ban Don Sai, where you can buy food.

Bang Saphan (Bang Saphan Yai) is no great shakes as a town either, but the long beaches here are beginning to attract some speculative development. In the vicinity of Bang Saphan you'll find the beaches of **Hat Sai Kaew**, **Hat Ban Krut**, **Hat Khiriwong**, **Hat Ban Nong Mongkon**, **Hat (Ao) Baw Thawng Lang**, **Hat Pha Daeng** and **Hat Bang Boet**, all of which are worth looking up. Getting around can be a problem since there isn't much public transport between these beaches.

There are also islands off the coast, including **Ko Thalu** and **Ko Sing**, where there is good snorkelling and diving from the end of January to mid-May.

Places to Stay & Eat

Thap Sakae In Thap Sakae, there are two hotels to choose from: the *Chawalit*, right off the highway, with rooms for 150 to 200B with fan and bath, and the very basic *Sukkasem*, near the centre of town, with rooms for 60 to 90B. On the coast opposite Thap Sakae are a couple of concrete block-style bungalows for 200 to 400B, eg *Chan Reua*. Much more congenial and economical – if it's open – is the *Talay Inn* (☎ 671417), a cluster of neglected bamboo huts on a lake fed by the Huay Yang waterfall, but back from the beach a bit in the fishing village. Accommodation is 60B per person. The place was recently sold, so it may close or take new directions. It's about one km east of the Thap Sakae train station, which is about 1.5 km from Thap Sakae. Talay Inn is within easy walking distance of the sea.

Hat Sai Kaew Between Thap Sakae and Bang Saphan on the beach of Hat Kaew (Km

372, Highway 4) is *Haad Kaeo Beach Resort* (☎ 601035). It's actually just 200 metres from the Ban Koktahom train station, which can only be reached by ordinary train from the Hua Hin, Prachuap, Thap Sakae, Bang Saphan Yai or Chumphon terminals. Pretty, white, air-con bungalows with green roofs are 900 to 1200B per day.

Hat Khiriwong *Tawee Beach Resort* (also *Tawees*, *Tawee Sea*) has bungalows with private bath for 70 to 150B, or you can pitch a tent for 10B. Take a train or bus to the nearby town of Ban Krut, then a motorcycle taxi (30B) to Hat Khiriwong.

Bang Saphan Along the bay of Ao Bang Saphan are several beach hotels and bungalows. At Hat Somboon, the *Hat Somboon Sea View* is 400 or 500B per room with private hot-water bath and air-con. The cheaper *Boonsom Guest House* (☎ 691273) has rooms with fan for 250 and 350B. The *Wanwina Bungalows* (☎ 691251), also in this area, offers rooms with fan for 200B or air-con for 550B, including TV and video. Bungalows are also available for 200B and 400B. The same management handles *Bangsaphan Resort* (☎ 691152-3), which has similarly priced rooms.

Karol L's (☎ 691058), operated by an American and his Thai wife, has 80B and 100B bungalows in the old Samui style six km south of Bang Saphan Yai. If you call from the train or bus terminal, they'll provide free transport. Recently they've had problems with their telephone, so if they don't answer you may need to find your own way there.

The new *Suan Luang Resort* (☎ (01) 212-5687; fax 691054), at 97 Muu 1, is 600 metres from the beach, just up from Karol's. They will also pick up customers from the train station if you give them a call. The resort is run by a friendly and helpful Thai-French couple, a combination also reflected in their dining-room menu. New and spacious bungalows with mosquito proofing cost 150B for wooden ones, 300B for concrete. There are discounts for longer stays. If you have your own tent, camping is free, and they have four motorbikes for rent. They can organise boat trips to nearby islands, or motorbike trips to surrounding areas, including Myanmar if the border is open.

The *Krua Klang Ao* restaurant, right near the centre of Ao Bang Saphan, is a good place for seafood. Because of an Italian-staffed development project nearby, many of the local hotel and restaurant staff speak a smattering of Italian.

Getting There & Away

Buses from Prachuap to Thap Sakae are 12B and from Thap Sakae to Bang Saphan Yai 8B. If you're coming from farther south, buses from Chumphon to Bang Saphan Yai are 25B.

You can also get 3rd-class trains between Hua Hin, Prachuap, Thap Sakae, Ban Koktahom, Ban Krut and Bang Saphan Yai for a few baht each leg, as all of them have train stations (the rapid and express lines do not stop in Thap Sakae, Ban Krut or Bang Saphan). Each of these train stations is around four km from the beach, with motor-cycle taxis the only form of public transport available. It's possible to rent 100cc motor-bikes in Bang Saphan for 150B per day.

Chumphon Province

CHUMPHON

ອ.ເมืองชุมพร

About 500 km south of Bangkok and 184 km from Prachuap Khiri Khan, Chumphon (population 15,000) is the junction town where you turn west to Ranong and Phuket or continue south on the newer road to Surat Thani, Nakhon Si Thammarat and Songkhla. The name is derived from the Thai *chumnumphon*, which means 'meeting place'. The provincial capital is a busy place but of no particular interest except that this is where southern Thailand really begins in terms of ethnic markers like dialect and religion. Pak Nam, Chumphon's port, is 10 km

from Chumphon, and in this area there are a few beaches and a handful of islands with good reefs for diving.

Pak Nam is a major departure point for boats to Ko Tao, a popular island north of Ko Samui and Ko Pha-Ngan. Hence many travellers bound for Ko Tao stop over for a night or two in Chumphon.

Nearer islands include Ko Samet, Ko Mattara, Ko Rang Kachiu, Ko Ngam Yai and Ko Raet. Landing on Ko Rang Kachiu is restricted as this is where the precious swallow's nest is collected for the gourmet market. If you want to visit, you can request permission from the Laem Thong Bird Nest Company in Chumphon. For several years now, rumour has said the bird's nest island may open to tourism, but so far this hasn't happened. The other islands in the vicinity are uninhabited; the reefs around Ko Raet and Ko Mattara are the most colourful.

There are many other islands a bit farther out that are also suitable for diving – get information from the diving centre at Chumphon Cabana Resort on Thung Wua Laen beach or from Chumphon Travel Service on Tha Taphao Rd in town. You can hire boats and diving equipment here as well during the diving season, June to October. Fishing is also popular around the islands.

Information

Money Thai Farmers Bank on Sala Daeng Rd offers foreign exchange services Monday to Friday from 8.30 am to 3.30 pm. There are several other banks along the city's main central streets.

Post & Telephone The GPO on Pobaminthra Manka Rd is open Monday to Friday from 8.30 am to 4.30 pm, weekends 9 am to noon. The CAT office on the 2nd floor of the same building is open for inter-national telephone service daily from 8.30 am to 9 pm.

Chumphon's telephone area code is ☎ 077.

Organised Tours

Several travel agents and guesthouses orga-nise outdoor tours to the surrounding areas.

Top: Damnoen Saduak Floating Market (RN)
Bottom: Fruit vendor, Bangkok (JC)

Top Left: Erawan Shrine, Bangkok (JC)
Top Right: Festival shrine float (JC)
  Bottom: Vegetarian Festival, Phuket (JC)

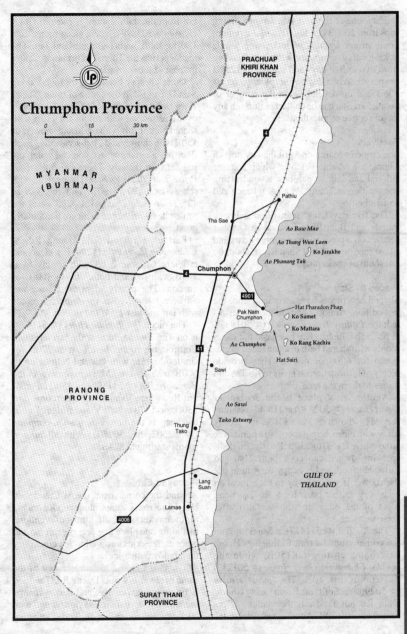

Chumphon Province

0   15   30 km

MYANMAR
(BURMA)

PRACHUAP
KHIRI KHAN
PROVINCE

4

Pathiu

Tha Sae

Ao Baw Mao

Ao Thung Wua Laen

Ko Jarakhe

Ao Phanang Tak

Chumphon

4

4901

Hat Pharadon Phap

Pak Nam
Chumphon

Ko Samet

Ko Mattara

Ko Rang Kachiu

Ao Chumphon

41

Hat Sairi

Sawi

RANONG
PROVINCE

Ao Sawi

Tako Estuary

Thung
Tako

Lang Suan

*GULF OF
THAILAND*

Lamae

4006

SURAT THANI
PROVINCE

Infinity, one of the best, can arrange diving trips from 2000B per day. Tri Star Adventure Tours offers a series of interesting jungle treks, local cave trips and island tours lasting from two to five days and starting at 1250B per person. A one-day cave exploration costs 500B and up depending on the number of people. Tri Star can be contacted through any travel service or guesthouse.

Festivals

Sometime in March or April the city hosts a Chumphon Marine Festival, which features cultural and folk art exhibits, a windsurfing competition at Thung Wua Laen beach and a marathon.

The five-day Lang Suan Buddha Image Parade and Boat Race Festival in October focuses on a procession of temple boats and a boat race on the Lang Suan River, about 60 km south of the capital.

Places to Stay

Several new places have sprung up since the last edition. Almost opposite the bus terminal, the *Infinity Travel Service* (☎ 501937), at 68/2 Tha Taphao Rd, has basic but clean rooms with shared bath in an attached guesthouse for 60B per person. They provide plenty of information on boats to Ko Tao and things to do in the area.

Another new place is the *Sooksamer Guest House* (☎ 502430) at 118/4 Suksamoe Rd. Also known as Pat's Place, it's a cosy place with clean, bright rooms in a home-like atmosphere for 80 to 150B. Pat, the English-speaking owner, can cook both Thai and European food, and is happy for you to use the shower if you drop by to eat a meal on your way to Pak Nam for a Ko Tao boat. Most of the other guesthouses also offer these services.

The *Ko Tao* (☎ 511417) at Soi 3, around the corner from Jansom Chumphon Hotel, has rooms costing 60/150B, while the popular *Chumphon Guest House* (☎ 501242) has rooms for 70B. *Tiw Guest House* (☎ 502900) at Soi 1, off Krom Luang Chumphon Rd not far from the station, offers rooms for 70/120B. Another new place, 1.2

km from the train station, is *Puenjai Guest House* (☎ 503898), where clean rooms cost 150 to 250B with bathroom and fan. The manager runs the Tourist Information Center in front of the train station.

Other cheaper hotels can be found along Sala Daeng Rd in the centre of town. The *Si Taifa Hotel* is a clean, old Chinese hotel built over a restaurant with rooms for 110B with shared bath, 130B with basin and shower, or 150B with shower and Thai-style toilet. Each floor has a terrace where you can watch the sun set over the city. There's also the *Thai Prasert* at 202-204 Sala Daeng Rd, with rooms from 70 to 90B; and the *Suriya*, 125/24-26 Sala Daeng Rd, which has the same rates – neither of them are particularly good.

Farther north on Sala Daeng Rd, *Si Chumphon Hotel* (☎ 511280) is a clean and efficient Chinese hotel with rooms from 180B with fan and bath, 300 to 400B for air-con. The nearly identical *Chumphon Suriwong Hotel* costs the same for rooms with fan and just 280B for air-con.

The nicer *Tha Taphao Hotel* (☎ 511479) is on Tha Taphao Rd near the bus terminal. Comfortable rooms here start at 270B for singles/doubles with fan and bath or up to 600B with air-con. More expensive is the *Paradorn Inn* (☎ 511598), at 180/12 Paradorn Rd, where standard air-con rooms cost 330B, or 530B with TV and fridge. Top of the heap is the newer *Jansom Chumphon* (☎ 502502; fax 502503) with all air-con rooms starting at 824B.

Places to Eat

Around the corner from the Si Chumphon Hotel on Krom Luang Chumphon Rd is a big night market with all kinds of vendors, including one place that serves espresso and other coffee drinks as well as ice cream (try the brandy coffee-ice).

Tiw Guest House has a restaurant of the same name at 174 Sala Daeng Rd. The food is fine and inexpensive, and during mango season they serve delicious ripe mango with sticky rice in coconut milk. Travel informa-

PLACES TO STAY

2 Tiw Guest House
5 Si Chumphon Hotel
6 Thai Prasert Hotel
8 Ko Tao Guest House
9 Sooksamer Guest House
12 Chumphon Suriwong Hotel
13 Paradorn Inn
14 Jansom Chumphon Hotel
18 Infinity & Chumphon Guest House
19 Tha Taphao Hotel
27 Si Taifa Hotel

PLACES TO EAT

3 Night Market
7 Curry Shops
11 Esan
15 Tiw Restaurant
23 Phloen Phochana
24 Day & Night Market
26 Night Market
29 Tang Soon Kee

OTHER

1 Train Station
4 Shopping Centre
10 Hospital
16 Cinema
17 Mini-Buses to Ranong
18 Infinity & Chumphon Travel Service
20 Bank
21 Buses to Ao Thung Wua Laen
22 Air-Con Bus Terminal
25 Bus Terminal
28 Cinema
30 Market
31 Songthaews to Ko Tao Boat Pier
32 GPO & Telephone Office
33 Buses (Local)
34 Wat Suphannimit

Chumphon

0   100   200 m

tion is available on bulletin boards and from the owner.

The several curry shops along Sala Daeng Rd are proof that you are now in southern Thailand. Over on Tha Taphao Rd is a smaller night market and a very popular Chinese place called *Tang Soon Kee*. Farther north on this street just past the bus terminal on the left is another Chinese place, *Phloen Phochana*, which opens early in the morning with 1B paa-thông-kõ, soy milk and coffee or tea. Up on Tawee Sinka Rd near the Chumphon Suriwong Hotel is the *Esan* with good north-eastern Thai food in the eve-

nings. Several more Isaan-style places can be found along Krom Luang Chumphon Rd.

Chumphon Province is famous for klûay lép meu naang, 'princess fingernail bananas'. They're very tasty and cheap – 25B would buy around a hundred of the small, slender bananas.

Getting There & Away

Bus From Bangkok's southern bus terminal ordinary buses cost 112B and depart at 3.30, 4, 6.05 and 6.50 am only. First-class air-con buses are 202B and leave at 2, 9.40 and 10 pm; 2nd-class costs 157B and leaves nightly at 9 pm. There is also a 9.40 pm VIP departure for 280B.

Buses run regularly between Surat Thani and Chumphon for 60B (80B air-con, 3½ hours), and to/from Ranong for 35B, Bang Saphan 30B, Prachuap 45B and Phuket 102B. Air-con minibuses run to/from Ranong daily between 8 am and 5.30 pm for 140B. There is also one to Bangkok which meets the Ko Tao boat at the Pak Nam pier, and leaves from Chumphon Travel Service at noon and 5 pm, costing 290B. Others go to Surat Thani (110B, 2½ hours, several departures per day), Hat Yai and Phattalung (150B, four to five hours).

Train Rapid and express trains from Bangkok take about 7½ hours to reach Chumphon and cost 82B (3rd class), 172B (2nd class), or 356B (1st class, express only). See the Phetburi Getting There & Away section for departure times.

There are several ordinary 3rd-class trains daily to Prachuap Khiri Khan (34B), Surat Thani (34B) and Hat Yai (99B). Southbound rapid and express trains – the only trains with 1st and 2nd-class service – are much less frequent and can be difficult to book out of Chumphon.

Boat to Ko Tao This small island north of Ko Samui and Ko Pha-Ngan (covered in a later section) can be reached by boat from Tha Reua Ko Tao (Ko Tao boat pier), 10 km south-east of town. The regular daily boat leaves at midnight, costs 200B and takes about six hours to reach Ko Tao. From Ko Tao the boat usually leaves at 10 am and arrives at Tha Reua Ko Tao around 3.30 pm.

More expensive but faster is the speed boat from the Tha Yang pier, which takes only one hour and 45 minutes and costs 400B. Depending on the weather, it usually departs at 8 am daily.

Songthaews run to both piers frequently between 6 am and 6 pm for 10B. After 6 pm, Infinity and most other travel services and guesthouses can send a van to the pier around 9.30 pm for 50B per person. Going by van means you won't have to wait at the pier for

six hours before the boat departs. The only other alternative is a 150B motorcycle taxi ride to the pier.

Regular air-con minibuses to/from Bangkok's Khao San Rd guesthouses and travel agencies also connect with the slow boat for 290B. MP Travel at Nana Plaza Inn (☎ (02) 281-5954) on Khao San Rd operates an all-inclusive minivan and boat trip from Bangkok to Ko Tao for 650B per person, a saving of 40B over separate minivan and speed boat fares (but keep in mind you can buy separate 3rd-class train and slow boat tickets for just 282B).

You can also charter a boat to Ko Tao from Pak Nam for maybe 2500B.

Getting Around

Motorcycle taxis around town cost a flat 10B per trip.

Songthaews to the port of Chumphon (Pak Nam Chumphon) are 13B per person. To Hat Sairi they cost 15B and to Thung Wua Laen 13B. Buses to Tako Estuary (for Hat Arunothai) are 15B. A motorcycle taxi out to Thung Wua Laen should be no more than 50B.

The Chumphon Travel Service can arrange motorcycle and car rental.

AROUND CHUMPHON PROVINCE

The best beaches in Chumphon Province are north of Chumphon at **Ao Phanang Tak**, **Ao Thung Wua Laen** and **Ao Baw Mao**. Nearer to town, in the vicinity of Pak Nam Chumphon, are the lesser beaches of **Hat Pharadon Phap** and **Hat Sairi**. Then about 40 km south of Chumphon, past the town of Sawi, is the Tako Estuary and the fair beach of Hat Arunothai. Most of these beaches have at least one set of resort bungalows.

Places to Stay

The air-con *Porn Sawan Home Beach Resort* (☎ 521031) is at Pak Nam Chumphon on Pharadon Phap beach and has rooms starting at 700B. *Sai Ree Lodge* (☎ 502023; fax 502479) at nearby Hat Sairi has concrete bungalows with thatched roofs for 600 to 800B with fan, 1000B with air-con.

Chumphon Cabana Resort (☎ 501990; (02) 224-1994 in Bangkok) on Hat Thung Wua Laen (12 km north of Chumphon) has 26 well-appointed bungalows and 20 sets of diving equipment. The nightly tariff is 500B with fan, or from 800B for air-con.

Chumphon Sunny Beach (☎ 541895) is at the Tako Estuary on Hat Arunothai, about 50 km south of Chumphon. Bungalows are 300 to 450B with fan or 550B with air-con.

At Pak Nam the *Siriphet Hotel* (☎ 521304) has basic rooms from 70B.

Ranong Province

This is Thailand's least populous province; 67% of it is mountains, over 80% forests. Like much of southern Thailand, it undergoes two monsoons, but its mountains tend to hold the rains over the area longer, so it gets the highest average annual rainfall in the country. Hence, it's incredibly green overall, with lots of waterfalls, although it's swampy near the coastline so there isn't much in the way of beaches. A recent letter-writer who stopped over during the height of the rainy season decided that Ranong must be a corruption of the English 'Rained On'!

The provincial economy is supported mainly by mineral extraction and fishing, along with rubber, coconut and cashew-nut production. In Ranong they call cashews *ka-yuu* (in other southern provinces the word is *ka-yii* and in the rest of Thailand it's *mét má-mûang*).

RANONG

อ.เมืองระนอง

The small capital and port of Ranong (population 18,000) is only separated from Myanmar by the Chan River. Burmese residents from nearby Victoria Point (called Kaw/Ko Sawng by the Thais, meaning 'second island', or Kaw Thaung in the Burmese pronunciation) hop across to trade in Thailand or to work on fishing boats. Although there is nothing of great cultural interest in the town, the buildings are architecturally interesting since this area was originally settled by Hokkien Chinese.

Information

Ranong is about 600 km south of Bangkok, 300 km north of Phuket. Most of Ranong's banks are on Tha Meuang Rd, the road to the fishing pier. There is a post office with an attached international telephone office on Ruangrat Rd in the old town district.

Ranong's telephone area code is ☎ 077.

Nai Khai Ranong

ไนค่ายระนอง

During the reign of King Rama V, a Hokkien named Koh Su Chiang became governor of Ranong (thus gaining the new name Phraya Damrong Na Ranong) and his former residence, Nai Khai Ranong, has become a combination clan house and shrine. It's on the northern edge of town and is worth a visit while you're in Ranong.

Of the three original buildings, one still stands and is filled with mementos of the Koh family glory days. The main gate and part of the original wall also remain. Koh Su Chiang's great-grandson Koh Sim Kong is the caretaker and he speaks some English. Several shophouses on Ruangrat Rd preserve the old Hokkien style, too. Koh Su Chiang's mausoleum is set into the side of a hill a bit farther north on the road to Hat Chandamri.

Hot Springs & Wat Hat Som Paen

บ่อน้ำร้อน/วัดหาดส้มแป้น

About one km east of the Jansom Thara Hotel is the Ranong Mineral Hot Springs at Wat Tapotaram. Water temperature hovers around 65°C, hot enough to boil eggs. The Jansom Thara pipes water from the springs into the hotel, where you can take a 42°C mineral bath in their large public jacuzzi for 50B.

If you continue on the same road past the hot springs for about seven km, you'll come to the village of Hat Som Paen, a former tin-mining community. At Wat Hat Som

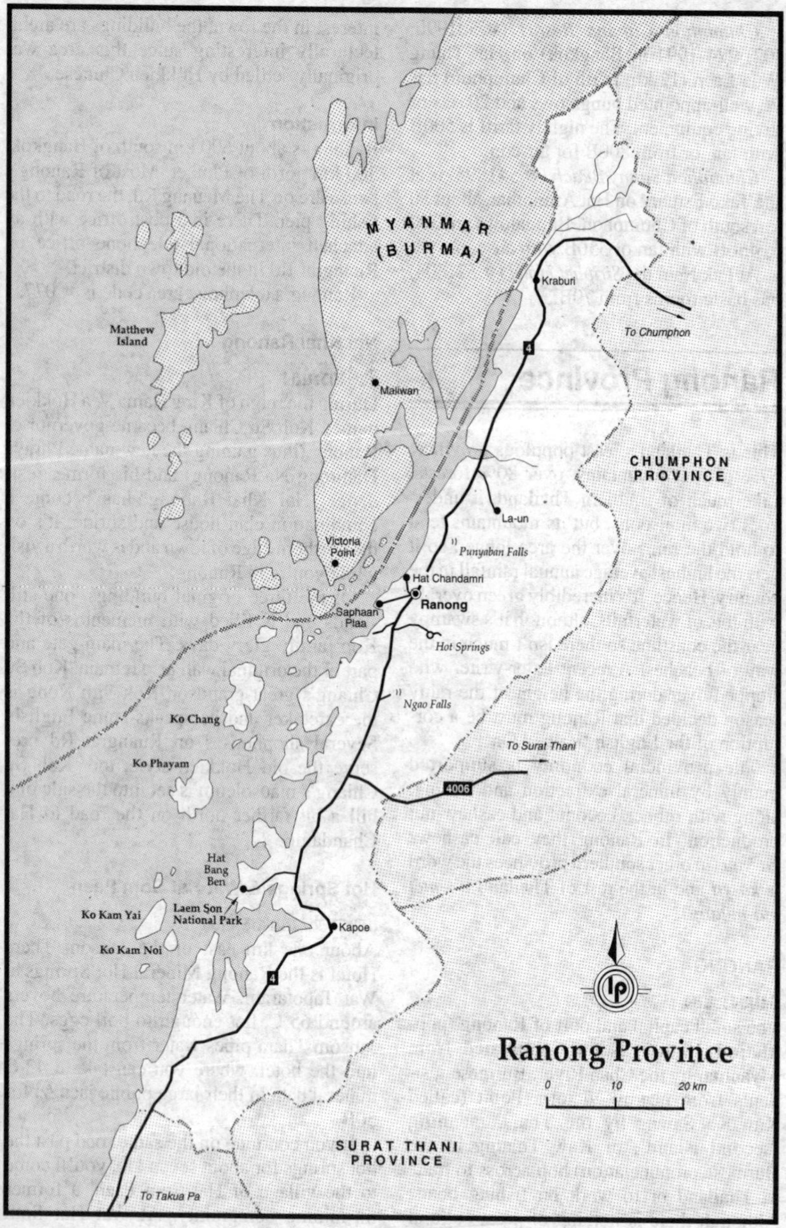

MYANMAR
(BURMA)

Kraburi

To Chumphon

Matthew Island

Maliwan

CHUMPHON PROVINCE

La-un

Punyaban Falls

Victoria Point

Hat Chandamri

Ranong

Saphaan Plaa

Hot Springs

Ngao Falls

Ko Chang

To Surat Thani

Ko Phayam

4006

Hat Bang Ben

Ko Kam Yai

Laem Son National Park

Ko Kam Noi

Kapoe

4

Ranong Province

0   10   20 km

SURAT THANI PROVINCE

To Takua Pa

SOUTHERN THAILAND

Paen, visitors feed fruit to the huge black carp (plaa phluang) in the temple stream. The faithful believe these carp are actually thewada, a type of angel, and it's forbidden to catch and eat them. Legend has it that those who do will contract leprosy.

Another three km down a bumpy dirt road is **Marakot Thara**, an emerald-green reservoir that fills an old tin quarry. Although tin production in Ranong has slackened off due to the depressed global market, the mining of calcium compounds, used to make porcelain, is still profitable.

Boat Trips & Victoria Point Visits

Jansom Thara does boat trips to nearby islands, including Ko Phayam, which has a fairly good beach for swimming. The average cost for a day trip is 400B per person, including lunch. The boat, the JS Queen, can also be chartered for trips to further islands like the Ko Surin group. It holds up to 40 people.

At the time of writing the most popular tour was to Victoria Point in Myanmar. The 600B per person fee (minimum of eight people) includes a 9 am to 1 pm tour, immigration and 'entry' fees, boat transportation, guide and lunch. No passport is necessary as the hotel organises a Border Pass. This is a cheaper and easier way of getting there than doing it by yourself. Independently, you will have to bargain for a boat and bribe your way past customs, all of which will cost at least 50% more than the tour. There is also no guarantee that you will make it across, as the Thai border guards can be fickle.

Places to Stay

The Asia Hotel (☎ 811113), at 39/9 Ruangrat Rd near the day market, has fair rooms with fan and bath for 180 to 240B and air-con rooms for 450B. Across from the market is the Sin Ranong Hotel with adequate rooms with fan for 150B, air-con for 350B. North a bit, at No 81/1 Ruangrat Rd, is the Sin Tavee (Thawi) Hotel (☎ 811213) with similar rooms for 120B, plus air-con rooms for 240B.

Farther up Ruangrat Rd are the Rattanasin Hotel on the right and the Suriyanon Hotel on the left across from the post office. The Rattanasin was being rebuilt at the time of writing, but will probably be in the 150B range when it reopens. The Suriyanon is dark and decaying, but the staff are friendly and claim they don't allow any hookers in the hotel. A basic room is 60B, 80B with a fan, and 100B with fan and bath.

Across the highway on the road to the hot springs is Jansom Thara Hotel (☎ 811511, fax 821821; (02) 448-6096 in Bangkok), which has just about everything you could possibly want in a hotel. Standard rooms come with air-con and colour TV and there's in-house video, hot-water bath with jacuzzi (piped in from the hot springs), and a refrigerator stocked with booze. There are also two restaurants, one of which specialises in Chinese dim sum and noodles, two large mineral jacuzzis, a fitness centre, a disco, a coffee house/cocktail lounge, a swimming pool and a travel agency. Rates start at 1200B, but sometimes they offer discounted rooms for as little as 321B.

Places to Eat

For inexpensive Thai and Burmese breakfasts, try the morning market on Ruangrat Rd. Also along Ruangrat Rd are several traditional Hokkien coffee shops with marble-topped tables and enamelled metal teapots. Between the Rattanasin and Sin Tavee Hotels (same side of Ruangrat Rd as the Rattanasin) is a small Burmese Muslim place where you can get curry, rice, roti, pickled cucumbers and tea for 16B.

Kakok, at 14-19 Ruangrat Rd, is an inexpensive place for basic Chinese and Thai dishes – average plates cost 15 to 20B. The nicer Jansom Thara Restaurant at 259 Ruangrat Rd offers a large variety of Thai and Chinese dishes starting at around 35B. They even serve whole piglets for 700B. The top restaurant in town is the Jansom Thara Hotel's Palm Court.

Getting There & Away

You can get to Ranong via Chumphon (27B),

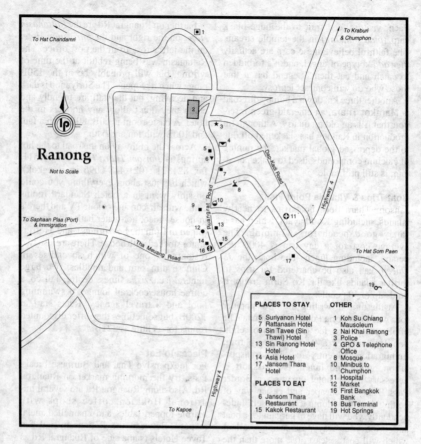

Ranong

Not to Scale

To Hat Chandamri

To Kraburi & Chumphon

To Saphaan Plaa (Port) & Immigration

Tha Meuang Road

Ruangrat Road

Dap-Kadi Road

Highway 4

Highway 4

To Hat Som Paen

To Kapoe

PLACES TO STAY	OTHER
5 Suriyanon Hotel	1 Koh Su Chiang Mausoleum
7 Rattanasin Hotel	2 Nai Khai Ranong
9 Sin Tavee (Sin Thawi) Hotel	3 Police
13 Sin Ranong Hotel Hotel	4 GPO & Telephone Office
14 Asia Hotel	8 Mosque
17 Jansom Thara Hotel	10 Minibus to Chumphon
	11 Hospital
PLACES TO EAT	12 Market
6 Jansom Thara Restaurant	16 First Bangkok Bank
15 Kakok Restaurant	18 Bus Terminal
	19 Hot Springs

Surat Thani (60B, 80B air-con), Takua Pa (32B) and Phuket (60B). The bus terminal in Ranong is out of town near the Jansom Thara Hotel, but buses stop in town on Ruangrat Rd before proceeding on to the terminal.

To/from Bangkok, ordinary buses cost 140B, air-con 250B, VIP 350 to 385B.

Air-con minivans run between Phuket (opposite the Imperial Hotel) and the Jansom Thara Hotel in Ranong for 140B. The van leaves Ranong at around 3.30 pm and arrives in Phuket four or five hours later; in the opposite direction it leaves Phuket at 2 pm and arrives in Ranong at 6.30 pm. In either

direction the van stops in Takua Pa for a meal (not included in the fare). The Jansom Thara Hotel also has a minivan that runs between Surat Thani (Muang Tai Hotel) and Ranong for 170B. Departure from Ranong is at 8 am, arriving in Surat at 11.30 am. From Surat the van leaves at 12.10 pm and arrives in Ranong at 3.40 pm.

A daily air-con minibus to Chumphon costs 140B and departs between 7 am and 5.30 pm from the front of Sin Tavee Hotel, where you can book a seat in advance. Buses to Khuraburi cost 35B and take an hour and 20 minutes.

SOUTHERN THAILAND

Getting Around

Songthaews ply the roads around Ranong and out to the hot springs and Hat Som Paen (No 2), Hat Chandamri (No 3) and Saphaan Plaa (No 2). The fare is 5B to any of these places. See the Around Ranong section for details. Motorcycle taxis (look for the orange vests) will take you anywhere in town for 10B, or to the area around the Jansom Thara for 15 to 20B.

AROUND RANONG
Hat Chandamri
หาดชาญคำรี

Touted as the nearest beach to Ranong, Hat Chandamri is really more of a mud flat. A sister hotel to the Jansom Thara in Ranong, the *Jansom Thara Resort* has similarly equipped bungalows (but no jacuzzis) for 1200B. From the dining terrace overlooking the bay, you can eat seafood and watch the sun set over Myanmar's Victoria Point.

Hat Chandamri is 10 km north-west of Ranong, about 20B by motorcycle taxi or 5B by songthaew.

Fishermen's Pier
สะพานปลา

The provincial fishing port, Tha Thiap Reua Pramong, is eight km south-west of Ranong. It's called **Saphaan Plaa** (Fish Bridge) for short and is always bustling with activity as fishing boats are loaded and unloaded with great cargoes of flapping fish. About half the boats are Burmese, as the fish traders buy from anyone who lands fish here. Boats can be chartered here for day trips to nearby islands. Unless you want to see heaps of fish or charter a fishing boat, there's really no reason to go out to the port.

Isthmus of Kra
คอคอดกระ

About 60 km north of Ranong, in Kraburi district, is the Isthmus of Kra, the narrowest point in Thailand. Barely 50 km separates the Gulf of Thailand from the Indian Ocean at this point. Just off Highway 4 is a monument commemorating this geographical wonder. At one time the Thai government had plans to construct the so-called Kra Canal here, but the latest word is that the canal – if it's built – will run east from Satun Province through Songkhla, about 500 km farther south.

Waterfalls
น้ำตก

Of the several well-known waterfalls in Ranong Province, **Ngao Falls** and **Punyaban Falls** are within walking distance of Highway 4. Ngao is 13 km south of Ranong while Punyaban is 15 km north. Just ride a songthaew in either direction and ask to be let off at the *náam tòk* (waterfall).

LAEM SON NATIONAL PARK
อุทยานแห่งชาติแหลมสน

The Laem Son (Pine Cape) Wildlife & Forest Preserve stretches 315 sq km over the Kapoe district of Ranong and Khuraburi district in Phang-Nga. This area includes about 100 km of Andaman Sea coastline as well as over 20 islands. Much of the coast here is covered with mangrove swamps, home to various

species of birds, fish, deer and monkeys, including the crab-eating macaques which are easily seen while driving along the road to the park headquarters.

The best known and most accessible beach is **Hat Bang Ben**, where the main park offices, restaurant and bungalows are. This is a long, sandy beach backed by shady casuarina trees and it is said to be safe for swimming year-round. From Hat Bang Ben you can see several islands, including the nearby Ko Kam Yai, Ko Kam Noi, Mu Ko Yipun, Ko Kang Kao and, to the north, Ko Phayam. The park staff can arrange boat trips out to any of these islands. During low tide you can walk to a nearby island just a couple of hundred metres away from Hat Bang Ben.

Ko Phayam is inhabited by around 100 Thais, who mostly make their living by fishing or growing cashews. There are good swimming beaches on Phayam and on the western side of some of the Kam islands, as well as some live coral. The beach on **Ko Kam Noi** has particularly clear water for swimming and snorkelling plus the added bonus of fresh water year-round and plenty of grassy areas for camping. One island on the other side of Ko Kam Yai which can't be seen from the beach is **Ko Kam Tok** (also called Ko Ao Khao Khwai). It's only about 200 metres from Ko Kam Yai, and, like Ko Kam Noi, has a good beach, coral, fresh water and a camping area. **Ko Kam Yai** is 14 km south-west of Hat Bang Ben.

About three km north of Hat Bang Ben, across the canal, is another beach, **Hat Laem Son**, which is almost always deserted and is 'undeveloped' according to park authorities (which means they won't guarantee your safety). The only way to get there is to hike from Bang Ben. In the opposite direction, about 50 km south of Hat Bang Ben, is **Hat Praphat**, very similar to Bang Ben with casuarina trees and a long beach. A second park office is located here and this one can be reached by road via the Phetkasem Highway.

In the canals you ford coming into the park, you may notice large wooden racks which are used for raising oysters.

Places to Stay & Eat

According to park authorities at Laem Son, the cost for accommodation in any of the park bungalows is 'by donation', which means you should be able to stay there for about 100B per person. Camping is allowed anywhere amongst the casuarina trees for 5B per person. Just outside the park entrance is the private *Komain Villa* where small bungalows are 100B per night. The food at the park cafe is rather pricey, but considering it has to be brought over 10 km of rough road, the prices are understandable. Slightly cheaper places can be found near Komain Villa.

On Ko Phayam there are several places to stay. The *Payam Island Resort* (☎ 812297; (02) 390-2681 in Bangkok) has bungalows from 300 to 2500B. There is also the *Thawon Resort* (☎ 811186) with bungalows for 100B and 120B.

On neighbouring Ko Chang there are also several places to stay, among them the inexpensive *Cashew Resort* with bungalows for 100B. For more information and booking contact Jansom Thara Restaurant in Ranong. This island also has the similarly priced *Ko Chang Resort*.

Getting There & Away

The turn-off for Laem Son is about 58 km down the Phetkasem Highway (Highway 4) from Ranong, between Km 657 and 658. Any bus heading south from Ranong can drop you off here or you could hitch fairly easily – there is plenty of traffic along Highway 4. Once you're off the highway, however, you'll have to wait a bit to flag down pick-up trucks going to the village near Laem Son. If you can't get a ride all the way, it's a two-km walk from the village to the park. If you have your own vehicle, don't attempt this road when it's wet unless you have 4WD or a good off-road bike.

To Ko Chang there is a daily 9 am boat from Saphaan Plaa in Ranong which takes 4½ hours and costs just 30B. It returns the same afternoon. To Ko Phayam boats are irregular, unless you are willing to charter one for 2000B. Sometimes the Ko Chang boat continues to Ko Phayam – enquire at

Ranong's Jansom Thara Hotel or at Saphaan Plaa.

Phang-Nga Province

KHURABURI, TAKUA PA & THAI MUANG

คุระบุรี,ตะกั่วป่าและท้ายเมือง

These districts of Phang-Nga Province are of minor interest in themselves but are departure points for other destinations. From Khuraburi you can reach the remote Surin and Similan islands, or from Takua Pa you can head east to Khao Sok National Park and Surat Thani.

Takua Pa is also about halfway between Ranong and Phuket so buses often make rest stops here. Just off the highway is the *Extra Hotel* with rooms from 120B if you want to stop for the night.

In the district of Thai Muang is **Thai Muang Beach National Park**, where sea turtles come to lay eggs between November and February. **Thap Lamu**, about 23 km north of Thai Muang, has a pier with boats to the Similan Islands.

HAT BANG SAK & HAT KHAO LAK

หาดบางสัก/หาดเขาหลัก

South of Takua Pa, 13 and 25 km respectively, are the beaches of Bang Sak and Khao Lak. The beach at Khao Lak is pretty, but somewhat stony. An offshore coral reef suitable for snorkelling is 45 minutes away by long-tail boat, and some of the bungalow resorts here offer dive excursions to this reef as well as to the Similan and Surin island groups.

The adjacent Hat Bang Sak is a long sandy beach backed by casuarina trees. Thais claim the roasted fish sold by vendors in Bang Sak is the best in Thailand. Both beaches are just a couple of km off Highway 4.

Places to Stay *Poseidon Bungalows* (☎ (01) 723-1418), in a sheltered bay south of Hat Khao Lak, rents basic double huts for 100B

with shared bath, larger huts with private bath for 280B or 350B for three people. The owners dispense information on the area and organise boat excursions and dive trips to the local reef and to the Similan Islands. A restaurant built on stilts over the sea serves Thai and European food.

Also at the south end, the *Khao Lak Resort* has bungalows for 100B with shared bath, 200 to 350B with private bath.

The slightly more up-market *Nang Thong Bay Resort* (☎ (01) 723-1181) has a variety of bungalows, all with private bath, for 150 to 350B. This is the only place in Khao Lak where you can change money (cash or travellers' cheques). Motorbikes are available for 200B per day, Suzuki jeeps 800B. The nearby *Garden Beach Resort* (☎ (01) 723-1179) has similar rates and also offers motorcycle and jeep hire.

At the northern end of Hat Khao Lak, *Khao Lak Bungalows* (☎ (01) 723-1197) offers small rooms with shared bath for 150B or larger Thai-style bungalows with private bath for 800B. Beneath the attached beachfront restaurant, the Gypsy Bar is the only place on the beach that's open late.

Getting There & Away

To reach Khao Lak, take a motorcycle taxi from the Thap Lamu highway junction for 30B.

SURIN ISLANDS NATIONAL PARK

อุทยานแห่งชาติหมู่เกาะสุรินทร์

A national park since 1981, the Surin Islands are famous for excellent diving and sport-fishing. The two main islands (there are five in all) of Ko Surin Neua and Ko Surin Tai (North Surin Island and South Surin Island) are about 60 km from Khuraburi. The park office and visitors' centre are on the south-west side of the north island at Ao Mae Yai, where boats anchor. Admission to the park is 20B.

On the southern island is a village of sea gypsies (*chao le* or *chao náam*) and this is also where the official camping ground is located. The best diving is said to be in the

SOUTHERN THAILAND

channel between these two islands. The chao naam hold a large ceremony, involving ancestral worship, on Ko Surin Tai during the full moon in March. The island may be off limits during that time, so ask at the park office.

Places to Stay & Eat

Accommodation at the park bungalows is 100B per person. At the camping ground, two-person tents are 80B a night or you can use you own (or camp without a tent) for 40B per night per person. The park also offers a daily package of three meals (mostly seafood) for 250B.

Getting There & Away

The mainland office of Surin Islands National Park is in Ban Hin Lat, from where boats to the islands depart. The road to Ban Hin Lat turns off Highway 4 at Km 110, seven km north of the Khuraburi turn-off, about 70 km south of Ranong. Buses between Khuraburi and Ranong cost 35B and take about an hour and 20 minutes; ask to be let off at the turn-off for Ban Hin Lat. To/from Phuket, buses cost 50B and take about three hours.

You can charter a boat out to the Surin Islands from Ban Hin Lat either through the park officers (who will merely serve as brokers/interpreters) or from the Phae Plaa Chumphon pier at Ban Hin Lat. A 15-metre boat that takes up to eight people can be chartered for 5000 to 6000B return – it takes four to five hours each way. Ordinarily boat travel is only considered safe between December and early May, between the two monsoons.

You can also get boats to the Surin Islands from Hat Patong in Phuket. A regular charter boat from Phuket takes 10 hours, or you can get a Songserm express boat during the diving season (December to April) that takes only three hours 15 minutes. However, the fare for the express boat is 1600B per person – if you have more than a couple of people it's cheaper to go from Khuraburi. Group tours sometimes go from Khuraburi for 800B per person.

SIMILAN ISLANDS NATIONAL PARK
อุทยานแห่งชาติหมู่เกาะสิมิลัน

The Similan Islands are world-renowned among diving enthusiasts for incredible underwater sightseeing at depths ranging from two to 30 metres. As elsewhere in the Andaman Sea, the best diving months are December to May when the weather is good and the sea is at its clearest (and boat trips are much safer). West of the islands is a reef zone known among divers as 'Burmese Banks', a favourite among shark enthusiasts because of the swirling schools of sharks (mostly harmless leopard sharks) that frequent the area.

The Similans are also sometimes called Ko Kao, or Nine Islands, because there are nine of them – each has a number as well as a name. The word 'Similan' in fact comes from the Malay word 'sembilan' for 'nine'. Counting in order from the north, they are Ko Bon, Ko Ba Ngu, Ko Similan, Ko Payu, Ko Miang (which is actually two islands close together), Ko Payan, Ko Payang and Ko Hu Yong. Sometimes you see these listed in the reverse order. They're relatively small islands and uninhabited except for park officials and occasional tourist groups from Phuket. The park office is now on Ko Miang, and admission is 20B.

Places to Stay

Bungalows and camping cost the same in the Similans as in the Surin Islands. Officially camping is permitted on Ko Miang only.

Getting There & Away

The Similans can be reached from Ban Hin Lat (near Khuraburi, same pier as for the Surin Islands), Thap Lamu (about 40 km south of Takua Pa off Highway 4, or 20 km north of Thai Muang), Hat Khao Lak or Phuket.

From Ban Hin Lat the Similans are about 80 km away, about five hours by boat, and from Thap Lamu they are only 40 km away, about three hours by boat. Figure on roughly 3000 to 4000B return to charter a boat for eight people from Ban Hin Lat, less from

Thap Lamu. From November to March the Parks Division in Thap Lamu runs boats daily that cost 600B each way; they stop only at Island No 4 (Ko Miang), however.

Boat Excursions from Phuket Overnight diving excursions from Phuket's Patong Beach are fairly reasonable in cost – about 3500B a day including food, accommodation, diving equipment and underwater guides. Equipment is extra. Non-divers can join these trips for around half the cost – snorkellers are welcome.

Seatran Travel (☎ 211809; fax 213510), 65 Phang-Nga Rd, Phuket, runs their Jet Cat – a high-speed, Norwegian-built, catamaran jetfoil – from Phuket to the Similans between November and April. The Jet Cat leaves Phuket at 8.30 am, takes 2½ hours to reach the islands, and returns to Phuket at 6 pm. Rates are 2200B per adult and 1600B for children aged two to 12, and include hotel-pier-hotel transport, snorkelling equipment, lunch, soft drinks and snacks. A companion surface submarine, the *Pakarang*, offers reef-viewing excursions for non-divers.

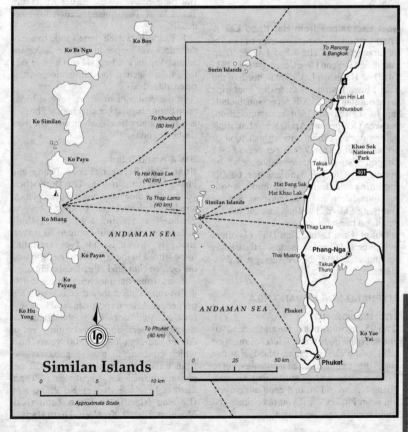

You can also spend the night offshore aboard the company's *Seatran Queen*, which remains at sea from Wednesday to Friday for most of the season (the boat keeps all waste on board until it is collected and disposed of in Phuket). Overnight rates are 1500B for a two-berth cabin, 2100B for a three-berth, 2700B four-berth or 3900B six-berth. Breakfast is complimentary.

Phuket's Songserm Travel (☎ 214272), 64/2 Rasada Center, offers a less luxurious package at slightly lower rates.

From Phuket's Hat Rawai you're supposed to be able to charter your own boat for about 8000B – one that will take up to 30 people.

Boat Excursions from Hat Khao Lak & Thap Lamu Less expensive trips can easily be arranged from Hat Khao Lak or Thap Lamu. Sea Dragon Dive Centre (☎ (01) 723-1418), at Hat Khao Lak (30 km north of the Thai Muang), arranges three-day boat trips to the Similans for 2500B per person, including food, transport and accommodation, between October and April. Khao Lak Bungalows does a similar trip without food or accommodation for 2000B per person. Sea Dragon also runs more elaborate scuba diving trips to the Similans for 6800B including all diving equipment, food, accommodation and boat transport. See the Hat Bang Sak & Hat Khao Lak section for details on transport.

Out of Thap Lamu, *Thai Dive Co* offers two, three and five-day charters to the islands starting at 6900B. Non-divers get a 25% discount.

AO PHANG-NGA & PHANG-NGA
อ่าวพังงา/อ.เมืองพังงา

Over 95 km from Phuket, the area around Ao Phang-Nga is quite scenic – lots of limestone cliffs, odd rock formations, islands that rise out of the sea like inverted mountains, not to mention caves and quaint fishing villages. Phang-Nga would make a good motorcycle trip from Phuket, or, if you have time, you could spend a few days there.

On the way to Phang-Nga (population 9000), turn left off Highway 4 just five km past the small town of Takua Thung, to get to **Tham Suwan Khuha** (Heaven Grotto), a cave temple full of Buddha images. Other nearby caves in the province include **Tham Reusisawan** (Hermit Heaven; three km south of Phang-Nga) and **Tham Phung Chang** (Elephant Belly Cave; also three km south). **Manohra Falls** is nine km north of Phang-Nga.

Phang-Nga's best beach areas are on the west coast facing the Andaman Sea. Between Thai Muang in the south and Takua Pa in the north are the beaches of Hat Thai Muang and Hat Bang Sak – see the earlier Khuraburi, Takua Pa & Thai Muang section for more details.

In Phang-Nga itself there's little to see or do unless you happen to be there during the annual Vegetarian Festival in October (see the Phuket section for information on this unusual festival).

In the centre of town are several banks open during regular banking hours. The post and telephone office is about two km from the bus station.

Bay & Island Tours
Boat Trips Between Takua Thung and Phang-Nga is the road to **Tha Don**, where you can find the Phang-Nga customs pier. At an adjacent pier boats can be hired to tour Ao Phang-Nga, visiting a Muslim fishing village on stilts, half-submerged caves, strangely shaped islands (yes, including those filmed in the 007 flick, *The Man with the Golden Gun*) and other local oddities.

Tours from the pier vary from 150 to 400B; from Phuket they cost at least 300B per person. A former postman from Ko Panyi (one of Ao Phang-Nga's islands) named Sayan has been doing overnight tours of Ao Phang-Nga for several years now which continue to receive good reviews from travellers. The tour costs 300B per person and includes a boat tour of **Tham Lawt** (a large water cave), **Ko Phing Kan** (Leaning Island), **Ko Khao Tapu** (Nail Mountain Island), **Ko Maju**, **Tham Naga**, a former mangrove charcoal factory and **Ko Panyi**, a mangrove swamp, plus dinner, breakfast and accommodation in a Muslim fishing village on Ko Panyi. Sayan also leads morning (rainy season) and afternoon (dry season) trips for 150B that include a seafood lunch and return in the afternoon. The overnight trip is recommended over the day trip; the latter tends to be a bit rushed. Sayan can be contacted at the Thawisuk Hotel in Phang-Nga or at his office (☎ (076) 411521) at the Phang-Nga bus terminal (look for a sign reading 'Tourist Information'). Beware of touts posing as Sayan at Tha Don.

You can also take a ferry to Ko Panyi on your own for 25B.

Whatever you do, try to avoid touring the bay in the middle of the day (10 am to 4 pm) when hundreds of package tourists crowd the islands. The Ko Panyi Muslim village is very commercialised during the day when hordes of tourist boats invade to eat lunch at the village's many overpriced seafood restaurants, and to buy tacky souvenirs at the many stalls. The village returns to its normal self after the boats depart. On Ko Panyi, always ask the price before eating as the restaurants often overcharge.

Canoe Tours A Phuket company called Phuket Sea Canoeing (☎ /fax (076) 212172), at 367/3 Yaowarat Rd, offers inflatable canoe excursions on the bay. The canoes are able to enter semi-submerged caves inaccessible by the long-tail boats. A day paddle costs 2675B per person and includes meals, beverages and equipment, while an all-inclusive three-day camping trip is 7500B per person. Other companies, including Santana Diving on Phuket's Patong Beach, offer similar inflatable canoe trips for about half these prices.

Places to Stay
Phang-Nga Phang-Nga has several small hotels. The *Thawisuk* is right in the middle of town, a bright blue building with the English sign 'Hotel'. Fairly clean, quiet rooms upstairs go for 80B with fan and bath, plus towel and soap on request. You can sit

and have a beer on the roof of Thawisuk while watching the sun set over Phang-Nga's rooftops and the limestone cliffs surrounding the town.

The *Lak Meuang* (☎ (076) 411125/1288), on Phetkasem Rd, just outside town towards Krabi, has rooms from 80 to 200B and a restaurant. The *Rak Phang-Nga*, across the street from Thawisuk towards Phuket, is 80B but somewhat dirty and noisy. Opposite the Rak Phang-Nga is the noisy *Ratanapong Hotel*, overpriced at 120 to 380B. Farther down the road towards Phuket is the *Muang Thong*, with clean, quiet singles/doubles for 120/180B with fan, 250 to 320B with aircon. Outside town, even farther towards Phuket, is *New Lak Meuang II*, with all aircon rooms from 350B.

Tha Don About 100 metres before the tour pier are the *National Park Bungalows*, which cost 350 to 750B a night. Farther on towards town, before the customs pier, the *Phang-Nga Bay Resort Hotel* (☎ (076) 411067/70) costs 906 to 1177B. Facilities include a swimming pool and a decent restaurant. All rooms come with TV, telephone and fridge.

Places to Eat
Duang Restaurant, next to Bangkok Bank on the main road, has a bilingual menu and a good selection of Thai and Chinese dishes, including southern-Thai specialities.

Several food stalls on the main street of Phang-Nga sell cheap and delicious khanõm jiin with chicken curry, náam yaa (spicy ground-fish curry) or náam phrík (sweet and spicy peanut sauce). One vendor in front of the market (opposite Bangkok Bank) serves khanõm jiin with an amazing 12 varieties of free vegetable accompaniments. Roti kaeng (flatbread and curry) is available in the morning market from around 5 am to 10 am. There are also the usual Chinese khâo man kài places around town.

On the edge of town towards Tha Don, just before the New Lak Meuang II Hotel, *Krua Thai Restaurant* offers affordable seafood dishes starting at around 50B. Menu items are listed in English and French as well as

Thai – the 'prawns in coconut sauce' is worth a try.

Getting There & Away

Buses for Phang-Nga leave from the Phuket bus terminal on Phang-Nga Rd, near the Thepkasatri Rd intersection, hourly between 6.20 am and 6 pm. The trip to Phang-Nga takes 1¾ hours and the one-way fare is 25B (air-con 50B). Alternatively you can rent a motorcycle from Phuket.

Buses to/from Krabi cost 28B and take 1½ hours; to/from Surat Thani they cost 50B and take 3½ hours.

Ordinary buses to/from Bangkok cost 207B and take 14 hours, while air-con is 346B and VIP is 515B, both taking 13 hours.

Getting Around

Most of the town is easily accessible on foot. The Fuji photo shop on the main road rents motorcycles.

Songthaews between Phang-Nga and Tha Don (the Phang-Nga customs pier) are 10B.

Phuket Province

Dubbed 'Pearl of the South', by the tourist industry, Phuket (pronounced 'Poo-get') is Thailand's largest island (810 sq km) and a province in itself. While tourism and tin are Phuket's major moneymakers, the island is still big enough to accommodate escapists of nearly all budget levels. Formerly called Ko Thalang ('Phuket' and 'Thalang' are both Malay names), Phuket has a culture all of its own, combining Chinese and Portuguese influences (like Songkhla) with that of the chao naam, the indigenous ocean-going people. About 35% of the island's population are Thai Muslims.

Lying in the Andaman Sea off southern Thailand's west coast, the island's terrain is incredibly varied, with rocky beaches, long, broad, sandy beaches, limestone cliffs, forested hills and tropical vegetation of all kinds. Great seafood is available all over the island and several offshore islands are known for good snorkelling and scuba-diving.

Comparisons with Ko Samui, off the east coast, as well as with other Thai islands, are inevitable, of course. All in all, there is more to do in Phuket, but that means more to spend your money on, too. There are more tourists in Phuket but they are concentrated at certain beaches – eg Patong, Karon and Kata. Beaches like Nai Han and Kamala are relatively quiet, in spite of major tourist development at both. Ko Samui is gradually starting to develop along Phuket lines but the feel of the two islands is different – Samui is much farther out in the sea and as such gives one more of a feeling of adventure than Phuket, which is connected to the mainland by a bridge.

Development on Phuket has been influenced by the fact that Phuket is Thailand's richest province (on a per capita basis), with plenty of money available for investment. The turning point was probably reached when a Club Méditerranée was established at Hat Kata, followed by the construction of the more lavish Phuket Yacht Club on Nai Han and Le Meridien on Karon Noi (Relax Bay). This marked an end to the era of cheap bungalows which started in the early 1970s and lasted a decade. Now the cheapies have just about all been bought out. However, Phuket still has a few secluded and undeveloped beaches, at least for the time being.

The geography of Phuket is more varied than any other island in Thailand, and its large size has allowed microclimates to develop in different areas of the island. Check out the whole island if you have time. Don't ignore the interior of the island, which offers rice paddies, plantations of rubber, cashew nut, cacao, pineapple and coconut, as well as Phuket's last bit of island rainforest.

PHUKET

อ.เมืองภูเก็ต

At the south-eastern end of the island is Phuket (population 50,000).

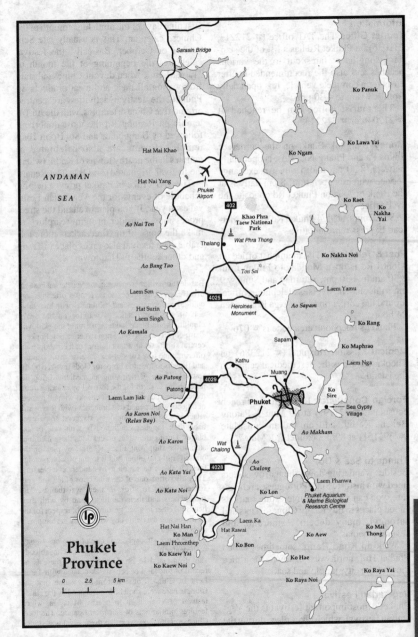

ANDAMAN

SEA

Sarasin Bridge

Ko Panuk

Ko Lawa Yai

Hat Mai Khao

Ko Ngam

Hat Nai Yang

Phuket
Airport

402

Ko Raet

Ko
Nakha
Yai

Ao Nai Ton

Khao Phra
Taew National
Park

Thalang ● Wat Phra Thong

Ko Nakha Noi

Ao Bang Tao

Ton Sai

Laem Yamu

Laem Son

4025

Heroines
Monument

Ao Sapam

Hat Surin
Laem Singh

Ko Rang

Ao Kamala

Sapam ●

Ko Maphrao

Kathu ●

Laem Nga

Ao Patong

4029

Muang ●

Patong ●

Ko Sire

Laem Lam Jiak

Phuket

Sea Gypsy
Village

Ao Karon Noi
(Relax Bay)

Ao Makham

Ao Karon

Wat
Chalong

Ao Kata Yai

4028

Ao Chalong

Ao Kata Noi

Laem Phanwa

Phuket Aquarium
& Marine Biological
Research Centre

Ko Lon

Hat Nai Han
Ko Man

Laem Ka

Hat Rawai

Ko Mai
Thong

Laem Phromthep

Ko Aew

Ko Kaew Yai

Ko Bon

**Phuket
Province**

Ko Hae

Ko Kaew Noi

0   2.5   5 km

Ko Raya Yai

Ko Raya Noi

Information

Tourist Office The TAT office (☎ 212213, 211036) on Phuket Rd has a list of the standard songthaew fares out to the various beaches and also the recommended charter costs for a complete vehicle. It is open daily from 8.30 am to 4.30 pm.

The tourist police can be reached at ☎ 212046 or ☎ 212213.

Money Bangkok Bank, on the corner of Takua Pa and Phang-Nga Rds, is open daily between 8.30 am and 5 pm. An exchange service which is open until 8 pm daily is at the Bank of Asia on Phuket Rd opposite the TAT office.

SEA Tours, at 95/4 Phuket Rd, is an American Express representative.

Post & Telephone The main post office on Montri Rd is open Monday to Friday from 8.30 am to 4.30 pm, Saturday and Sunday 9 am to noon. The overseas telephone office, around the corner on Phang-Nga Rd, is open 24 hours.

Phuket's telephone area code is ☎ 076.

Medical Mission Hospital (☎ 212386) on Thepkasatri Rd is the best medical centre on the island.

Foreign Consulates Phuket has a French consulate (☎ 321199) at 89 Muu 3, Patong Beach, Kathu, and an Italian consulate (☎ 391151) at 89/2 Sakdidet Rd, Muu 7.

Things to See & Do

Besides wandering down the narrow streets lined with historic Sino-Portuguese architecture, you can visit some interesting markets (good places to buy baggy Chinese pants and sarongs), many decent restaurants and several cinemas.

Walk up **Khao Rang**, sometimes called Phuket Hill, north-west of town, for a nice view of the city, jungle and sea.

Vegetarian Festival

Phuket's most important festival is the Vegetarian Festival, which takes place during the first nine days of the ninth lunar month of the Chinese calendar. This is usually late September or October. Basically, the festival celebrates the beginning of the month of 'Taoist Lent', when devout Chinese abstain from eating all meat and meat products. In Phuket, the festival activities are centred around five Chinese temples, with the Jui Tui temple on Ranong Rd the most important, followed by Bang Niaw and Sui Boon Tong temples. Events are also celebrated at temples in the nearby towns of Kathu (where the festival originated) and Ban Tha Reua.

The TAT office in Phuket prints a helpful schedule of events for the Vegetarian Festival each year. If you plan to attend the street processions, consider bringing earplugs to make the noise of the firecrackers more tolerable. The festival also takes place in Trang and other southern-Thai towns.

Besides abstention from meat, the Vegetarian Festival involves various processions, temple offerings and cultural performances and culminates with incredible acts of self-mortification – walking on hot coals, climbing knife-blade ladders, piercing the skin with sharp objects and so on. Shopowners along Phuket's central streets set up altars in front of their shopfronts offering nine tiny cups of tea, incense, fruit, candles and flowers to the nine Emperor Gods invoked by the festival. Those participating as mediums bring the nine deities to earth for the festival by entering into a trance state – and piercing their cheeks with all manner of objects – sharpened tree branches (with leaves still attached!), spears, trombones, daggers; some even hack their tongues continuously with saw or axe blades. During the street processions these mediums stop at the shopfront altars, where they pick up the offered fruit and either add it to the objects piercing their cheeks or pass it on to bystanders as a blessing. They also drink one of the nine cups of tea and grab some flowers to stick in their waistbands. The shopowners and their families stand by with their hands together in a wai gesture, out of respect for the mediums and the deities by whom they are temporarily possessed.

The entire atmosphere is one of religious frenzy, with deafening firecrackers, ritual dancing, bloody shirt fronts and so on. Oddly enough, there is no record of this kind of activity associated with Taoist Lent in China. Some historians assume that the Chinese here were somehow influenced by the Hindu festival of Thaipusam in nearby Malaysia, which features similar acts of self-mortification. The local Chinese claim, however, that the festival was started

To Mission Hospital, Airport & Phang-Nga

Komarapat Road

Nakhon Road

Khao Rang (Phuket Hill)

Chumphon Road

Damrong Road

Thungkha Road

Narison Road

Soi Rommani

Maeluan Road

Deebuk Road

Vichitsongkram Road

To Ao Patong

Krabi   Road

Thalang Road

Sattol Road

Patipat Road

Phang-Nga   Road

Fountain Circle

Ranong Road

Rasada Road

Soi Prathom

Bangkok Road

Takua Pra Road

Soi 9

Poonpol Road

Kra   Road

Phuket Road

Soi Sutin

Soi Talingchan

Chao Fa Road

To Ao Chalong, Ao Rawai, Ao Kata & Ao Karon

To Laem Phanwa & Phuket Aquarium

Ao Makham

Phuket

0   50   100 m

PLACES TO STAY

1 Sukchai Hotel
2 Phuket Merlin Hotel
3 Thara Hotel
5 Suksabai Hotel
7 Laem Thong Hotel
9 Montri Hotel
12 On On Hotel
13 Sinthavee Hotel
14 Siam Hotel
18 Wasana Guest House
21 Phuket Garden Hotel
25 Thawon Hotel
26 Pearl Hotel
27 Imperial Hotel 1
31 Metropole Phuket
34 Ko Sawan Hotel

PLACES TO EAT

6 Raan Jee Nguat Restaurant

8 Muslim Restaurant
15 Kaew Jai Restaurant
23 Mae Porn Restaurant
29 Night Market

OTHER

4 Timber Hut
10 Bus Terminal
11 THAI Office
16 GPO
17 Jui Tui Temple
19 Day Market
20 Songthaews
22 Bangkok Bank
24 Rasda Center
28 TAT Office
30 SEA Tours
32 Bank of Asia
33 Ocean Department Store
35 Immigration Office

SOUTHERN THAILAND

by a theatre troupe from China who stopped off in nearby Kathu around 150 years ago. The story goes that the troupe was struck seriously ill and that they decided the illness had befallen them because they had failed to propitiate the nine 'Emperor Gods' of Taoism. The nine-day penance they performed included self-piercing, meditation and a strict vegetarian diet.

Places to Stay – bottom end

Near the centre of town, and close to the songthaew terminal for most outlying beaches, is the *On On Hotel* (☎ 211154) at 19 Phang-Nga Rd. This hotel's old Sino-Portuguese architecture (established 1929) gives it real character, though the rooms are in dire need of a revamp – rates range from 150 to 220B with fan, 360B with air-con. The *Pengman* (☎ 211486, ext 169) nearby at 69 Phang-Nga Rd, above a Chinese restaurant, costs 100 to 120B with fan and bath, but is not too special. Another rock-bottom place is the Chinese *Laem Thong* (☎ 212310) on funky Soi Rommani, where rooms are 60 to 80B.

The *Ko Sawan Hotel*, 19/8 Poonpol Rd, out towards the waterfront in a red-light district, is 70B and over but deals mostly in short-time trade. The *Thara Hotel* (☎ 216208) on Thepkasatri Rd is 120B with fan and bath; the nearby *Suksabai Hotel* (☎ 212287) is a bit better at 120B for similar but cleaner rooms. The *Siam Hotel*, 13-15 Phuket Rd, has clean rooms with fan and bath for 150B.

A notch higher are *Sukchai* (☎ 223313), 17/1 Komarapat Rd, at 120B with fan and bath, 200B with air-con, and *Taweekit* at 7/3 Chao Fa Rd which costs about the same. The *Thawon Hotel* (☎ 211333) at 74 Rasada Rd has also been recommended – it has good air-con rooms for 250B, or 380 to 550B with hot water, and a swimming pool. Similar is the *Montri* (☎ 212936), 12/6 Montri Rd, without a swimming pool; rooms are 180B with fan, 320B with air-con.

Wasana Guest House (☎ 211754, 213385), at 159 Ranong Rd (next to the fresh market) has clean rooms for 161B with fan and bath or 268B with air-con.

Places to Stay – middle

The clean and friendly *Imperial Hotel 1* (☎ 212311), at 51 Phuket Rd, has good rooms for 300B with fan, 400B with air-con.

In the centre of town, at 81 Phang-Nga Rd, is the renovated *Sinthavee Hotel* (☎ 212153) with comfortable air-con rooms for 471/589B a single/double or 850/950B for deluxe rooms. All rooms come with carpeting, hot-water bath and refrigerators (add TV/video for deluxe); other facilities include a 24-hour coffee shop, business centre, spa and disco.

Places to Stay – top end

The *Pearl Hotel* (☎ 211044) at 42 Montri Rd has 221 rooms from 800B, a rooftop restaurant, swimming pool and so on. The *Phuket Merlin* (☎ 211618) at 158/1 Yaowarat Rd has 185 rooms for 1150/1250B; again there's a swimming pool.

The *Phuket Garden Hotel* (☎ 216900/8) on Bangkok Rd costs from 600B with a pool and all the usual facilities.

Topping off all the top-enders is the plush *Metropole Phuket* (☎ 215050; fax 215990) on Montri Rd. 'Superior' singles/doubles cost 2400/2600B; 2800/3000B for deluxe. Facilities include two Chinese restaurants, a coffee shop, three bars, swimming pool, fitness centre, business centre and airport shuttle service.

Places to Eat

If there's one thing the town of Phuket is known for, it's good food. One long-running local institution is *Raan Jee Nguat*, a Phuket-style restaurant run by Hokkien Chinese, across the street from the now defunct Siam Cinema on the corner of historic Yaowarat and Deebuk Rds. Jee Nguat serves Phuket's most famous dish – delicious khanŏm jiin náam yaa phukèt – Chinese noodles in a pureed fish and curry sauce, Phuket-style, with fresh cucumbers, long green beans and other fresh vegetables on the side – for under 10B. Also good are khài plaa mòk, a Phuket version of hàw mòk (eggs, fish and curry paste steamed in banana leaves), and the kari mai fan, similar to Malaysian laksa, but using rice noodles. The curries are highly esteemed as well. Don't leave it too late, though; they open early in the morning but close around 2 pm.

Very popular with Thais and farangs alike, and deservedly so, is the *Mae Porn*, a restaurant on the corner of Phang-Nga Rd and Soi Pradit, close to the On On and Sinthavee hotels. There's an air-con room as well as outdoor tables. They sell curries, seafood, fruit shakes – you name it and Mae Porn has it – all at very reasonable prices. Another popular spot in town is *Kanda Bakery* on Rasada Rd. It's open early in the morning with fresh-baked whole-wheat bread, baguettes, croissants, cakes and real brewed coffee.

Kaw Yam (Khao Yam), on Thungkha Rd in front of the Phuket Merlin, has a middle-class, indoor-outdoor atmosphere enjoyed by local office workers for breakfast and lunch. The kitchen serves very well-prepared khâo yam, the southern-Thai rice salad, as well as khanŏm jiin and many other Phuket specialities. Just as good for khanŏm jiin but cheaper is *Khwan Khanom Jiin* (no English sign) next door.

Another good local discovery is the simple Muslim restaurant on the corner of Thepkasatri and Thalang Rds – look for the star and crescent. This friendly family-run place serves delicious and inexpensive mátsaman kài (chicken-potato curry), roti kaeng (flatbread and curry – in the morning only) and khâo mòk kài (chicken biryani – usually gone by 1 pm).

Fried rice and pastry fans shouldn't miss *Kaew Jai* (no English sign), at 151 Phang-Nga Rd between Phuket and Montri Rds. More basic than Kanda Bakery, this is the Thai idea of pastry heaven – especially the custard cake, cashew cake and crème caramel – even if the service is a bit surly. Among the fried rice dishes on hand are khâo phàt náam phrík phão (fried rice with roasted chilli paste), khâo phàt khreûang kaeng (rice fried in curry paste) and khâo phàt bai kà-phrao (with holy basil), each with a choice of chicken, pork, crab, shrimp or squid.

The 24-hour coffee shop at the *Sinthavee Hotel* has cheap lunch specials and late-night khâo tôm service. For a splurge, the dim sum service (11 am to 2 pm) at the Hotel Metropole's *Fortuna Pavilion* is an excellent choice. Or their popular Thai buffet lunch is good for 119B, but come early.

The newish, tourist-oriented Rasda Center, a shopping complex around the 24-hour Phuket Department Store off Rasada Rd, has several small, up-market eating places like *Le Glacier* (ice cream), *Krua Thai* (fancy Thai cuisine), *Rasada Cafe* and *Le Café* (good coffees).

Finally, there's the ever-dependable and ever-tasty night market on Phuket Rd, which is fast and cheap. *Nai Yao*, two doors south of the night market and open only at night, has an excellent, inexpensive seafood menu (bilingual), cold beer and tables on the sidewalk. The house speciality is the unique and highly recommended tôm yam hâeng (dry tôm yam), which can be ordered with chicken, shrimp or squid.

Khao Rang (Phuket Hill) *Thungkha Kafae* is an outdoor restaurant at the top of the hill with a very pleasant atmosphere and good food. Try the tôm khàa kài (chicken coconut soup) or khài jiaw hãwy naang rom (oyster omelette). It's open from 11 am to 11 pm daily.

Ao Chalong Just past Wat Chalong (on the left past the five-road intersection, *hâa yâek* Wat Chalong) is *Kan Aeng*, a good fresh seafood place that used to sit on a pier over the bay itself. Now housed in an enclosed air-con restaurant, it still sets a standard for Phuket seafood though prices have risen considerably. You order by weight, choosing from squid, oysters, cockles, crab, mussels and several kinds of fish, and then specify the method of cooking, whether grilled (phão), steamed (nêung), fried (thâwt), parboiled (lûak – for squid), or in soup (tôm yam).

Entertainment
The Pearl Cinema, on the corner of Phang-

Nga and Montri Rds near the Pearl Hotel, has a sound room where the original soundtracks for English-language films are played, though the sound system is not that good. The Alliance Française (☎ 222988), at 3 Soi 1, Pattana Rd, shows French films (subtitled in English) weekly. They also have a TV with up-to-date news broadcasts and a library.

The major hotels have discos and/or karaoke clubs. The Timber Hut, on the eastern side of Yaowarat Rd just south of Thungkha Rd, is a well-run pub with an attractive woodsy decor, lots of Phuket and Thai food and live music after 9 pm. This is perhaps the only non-hotel bar in town with cocktails (80B).

Municipal law allows only one modern massage parlour to operate – in the Pearl Hotel.

Phuket once had four traditional *ram wong* (circle dance) clubs along Montri and Thalang Rds, but there now seems to be only one lone survivor, opposite the Metropole Hotel. Ram wong is a standard Thai couples' dance, and like most couples dancing around the world, it's really a sort of courtship ritual. At these clubs, however, it's more like Chinese tea-dancing, where men pay hostesses to dance with them. The clientele is mostly older Thais.

Getting There & Away

Air THAI has several daily flights from Bangkok for 2000B each way. The flight takes just over an hour, except for departures which have a half-hour stopover in Surat Thani.

There are also regular flights to and from Hat Yai (780B), Trang (435B), Nakhon Si Thammarat (340B) and Surat Thani (475B).

THAI flies to Penang (Malaysia) daily; the trip takes an hour and costs 1565B. Other international destinations from Phuket include Langkawi (2075B), Kuala Lumpur, Singapore, Hong Kong, Taipei and Sydney.

THAI has two offices: one at 78 Ranong Rd (☎ 211195) and the other at 41/33 Montri Rd (☎ 212880).

Southern Helicopter Service (☎ 327111; fax 327113) at the airport charters a Kawa-saki BK117 helicopter, which carries up to seven passengers, for 48,000B per hour. The service covers all of Phuket and Ao Phang-Nga, including Ko Phi Phi.

Bus From Bangkok, one 1st-class air-con and one VIP bus leave the southern bus terminal at 6.50 pm for 368B and 450B respectively. The trip takes 13 to 14 hours. Ordinary buses leave seven times a day from 7.30 am until 10.30 pm for 210B.

Several private tour buses run from Bangkok to Phuket regularly with fares of 378B one way or 700B return. Most have one bus a day which leaves at 6 or 7 pm. In Bangkok try Thai Transport on Rat-chadamnoen Klang Rd near the Benz showroom, not far from Khao San Rd. The ride along the west coast between Ranong and Phuket can be hair-raising if you are awake, so it is fortunate that this part of the trip takes place during the wee hours of the morning.

From Phuket, most tour buses to Bangkok leave at 3 pm. Several agencies have their offices on Rasada and Phang-Nga Rds downtown.

Fares and trip durations for bus trips to and from Phuket include:

Destination	Fare	Hours
Hat Yai	112B	8
(air-con)	240B	6
Krabi	47B	4½
(air-con)	85B	4
Nakhon Si Thammarat	93B	8
Phang-Nga	22B	2½
(air-con)	50B	1½
Surat Thani	77B	6
Takua Pa	38B	3
Trang	78B	6

Taxi & Minivan There are also share taxis between Phuket and other provincial capitals in the south; taxi fares are generally double the fare of an ordinary bus (Krabi 80B, Surat 150B, Trang 120B). The taxi stand for Nakhon Si Thammarat, Surat Thani, Krabi, Trang and Hat Yai is on Phang-Nga Rd, near the Pearl Cinema.

Some companies run air-con minivans (rot tuu) with through tickets to Ko Samui from Phuket – part of a minivan circuit that covers Phuket, Surat, Krabi and Ranong. As in share taxis, fares are about double the public bus fares. You can also get vans to Hat Yai (220B), Krabi (150B), Penang (550B), Kuala Lumpur (650B) and Singapore (700B). Vans can be booked at the same intersection as the share taxis.

Boat A ferry service between Phuket and Malaysia's Langkawi Island has come and gone several times. When running it usually costs around 800B.

You can often travel by yacht between Phuket and Penang. Ask around at Patong Beach to see what's available. The *Szygie* usually sails from Phuket to Penang periodically between 1 December and 30 April. Contact the operators at Restaurant Number Four, Hat Patong, Phuket or J Travel, Chulia St, Georgetown, Penang. They sail Phuket, Ko Phi Phi, Langkawi and Penang.

You can also find yachts going further afield, particularly to Sri Lanka. December and early January are the best months to look for them. The crossing takes about 10 to 15 days.

Getting Around

To/From the Airport THAI operates a shuttle bus between the town and airport (29 km from town) for 70B per person. There's a similar service to Patong, Kata or Karon beaches for 100B.

You can also take one of the rather infrequent songthaews for 15B. Taxis ask 250B for the trip from the airport to the city; in the reverse direction you should be able to negotiate a fare of 150B or so.

Songthaew Songthaews run regularly from Phuket to the various Phuket beaches for 10 to 20B – see the following Phuket Beaches section for details. Beware of tales about the tourist office being five km away, or that the only way to reach the beaches is by taxi, or even that you'll need a taxi to get from the bus station to the town centre.

Songthaews or tuk-tuks around town cost a standard 7B, but some travellers have reported that at times some drivers have insisted on 10B. Songthaews to the beaches depart from close to the town centre and the tourist office. Officially songthaews stop running at 5 pm, so after that time you must charter your own songthaew to the beaches.

Motorcycle Motorcycle taxis around town are 10B. You can hire motorcycles (usually 80 to 125cc Japanese bikes) from various places at the beaches or in Phuket. Costs are in the 150 to 250B per day range. Take care when riding a bike – if you have an accident you're unlikely to find that medical attention is up to Western standards. People who ride around in shorts and T-shirt and a pair of thongs are asking for trouble. A minor spill whilst wearing reasonable clothes would leave you bruised and shaken, but for somebody clad in shorts it could result in enough skin loss to end your travels right there.

Bigger bikes (over 150cc) can be rented at a couple of shops at Patong and Karon.

Car Rental Several agencies in town rent Suzuki jeeps for 900B per day, including insurance. If you rent for a week or more you can get the price down to 800B per day. Avis charges a bit more (around 1100B a day) but has outlets around the island at Le Meridien, Holiday Inn, Phuket Acadia, Dusit Laguna, Phuket Cabana, Club Med, Phuket Island Resort and the airport.

AROUND THE ISLAND

Ko Sire This island, four km east of the capital and separated from the main island by a canal, is known for its chao naam (sea-gypsy) village and a hill-top reclining Buddha. How much longer the chao naam can hold out here in the face of Thai land encroachment is uncertain. Thai fishing trawlers continue to infringe on the chao naam's traditional fishing grounds – even though these are supposedly protected by a three-km limit. On top of this, local housing developers are wreaking havoc on local mangroves, an important source of food and wood for the chao naam.

Laem Phanwa A classic Sino-Portuguese mansion called **Phanwa House**, on the grounds of the Cape Panwa Sheraton Resort on Laem Phanwa, is open to the public. The mansion has a library and a collection of antique furniture and art; high tea is served daily on the verandah.

At the tip of the cape, **Phuket Aquarium & Marine Biological Research Center** displays a varied collection of tropical fish. Admission is 20B.

Khao Phra Taew National Park There are some nice jungle hikes in this park, which features the last of the island's virgin rainforest, and a couple of waterfalls, Ton Sai and Bang Pae. The falls are best seen in the rainy season between June and November. Near Bang Pae Falls is a gibbon rehabilitation centre open to the public.

To get to the park from the provincial capital, take Thepkasatri Rd about 20 km to the district of Thalang, and turn right at the intersection for Ton Sai Waterfall three km down the road.

Also in Thalang district, just north of the crossroads near Thalang village, is **Wat Phra Thong**, Phuket's 'Temple of the Gold Buddha'. The image is half buried – those who have tried to excavate it have met with unfortunate consequences. Parts of the movie *Good Morning Vietnam* were filmed in Thalang.

Diving Phuket is ringed by good dive sites. Among the more popular are the small islands to the south-east for coral, and Shark Point (a habitat for harmless leopard sharks) at the southern tip of the island.

The centre for most Phuket diving operations is Patong Beach. In amphoe meuang Phuket, four dive shops rent equipment and lead dives: Andaman Sea Sports (☎ 211752), Phuket Aquatic Safaris (☎ 216562), PFC Diving Centre (☎ 215527) and Phuket Divers (☎ 215738).

A one-day trip including two dives starts at around 800B per person. A three-day trip to the Similan Islands costs around 10,000B. Rates include all transfers, food and equipment rental. Songserm Travel (☎ 222570/4), at 51-53 Satun Rd, has overnight diving trips to the Similans from 3500B.

Shooting & Riding Phuket's Shooting Range (☎ 381667), on the road between Ao Chalong and Hat Kata, is open to the public for target practice. If blasting away at human-shaped paper targets doesn't excite you, the same owners offer horseback riding at the nearby Phuket Riding Club.

PHUKET BEACHES

Phuket beach accommodation has come a long way since 1977 when I first stayed at Kata and Nai Han in simple thatched-roof huts for 10B a night. Nowadays 80 or 100B is rock-bottom. Any remaining accommodation costing under 300B will probably be upgraded within the next couple of years to a minimum of 500B as Phuket completes the final stages of moving from rustic beach hideaway to full-fledged international resort.

Patong

ป่าตอง

Directly west of Phuket, Patong is a large curved beach around Ao Patong. In the last few years, Hat Patong has been rapidly turning into another Pattaya in all respects. It is now a strip of hotels, up-market bungalows, German restaurants, expensive seafood places, beer bars, nightclubs and coffee houses. Ironically, though this began as Phuket's most expensive beach, the prices are stabilising as the local accommodation market has become saturated with over 70 places to stay. Eventually this will probably become one of the cheapest beaches on the island to stay at, as it becomes funkier and rowdier.

The local authorities are struggling with waste problems; on our most recent visit we saw top-range hotels dumping raw sewage into the sea.

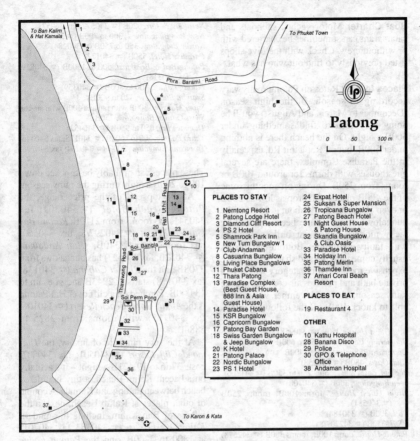

Patong

0   50   100 m

PLACES TO STAY

1 Nerntong Resort
2 Patong Lodge Hotel
3 Diamond Cliff Resort
4 PS 2 Hotel
5 Shamrock Park Inn
6 New Tum Bungalow 1
7 Club Andaman
8 Casuarina Bungalow
9 Living Place Bungalows
11 Phuket Cabana
12 Thara Patong
13 Paradise Complex
   (Best Guest House,
   888 Inn & Asia
   Guest House)
14 Paradise Hotel
15 KSR Bungalow
16 Capricorn Bungalow
17 Patong Bay Garden
18 Swiss Garden Bungalow
   & Jeep Bungalow
20 K Hotel
21 Patong Palace
22 Nordic Bungalow
23 PS 1 Hotel

24 Expat Hotel
25 Suksan & Super Mansion
26 Tropicana Bungalow
27 Patong Beach Hotel
31 Night Guest House
   & Patong House
32 Skandia Bungalow
   & Club Oasis
33 Paradise Hotel
34 Holiday Inn
35 Patong Merlin
36 Thamdee Inn
37 Amari Coral Beach
   Resort

PLACES TO EAT

19 Restaurant 4

OTHER

10 Kathu Hospital
28 Banana Disco
29 Police
30 GPO & Telephone
   Office
38 Andaman Hospital

Information Patong has many foreign-exchange booths, plus its own post and telephone office on the corner of Soi Perm Pong and Thawiwong Rd.

Dive Shops Patong is the diving centre of the island and the following shops rent equipment and lead dive tours: Holiday Diving Club at the Patong Beach Hotel (☎ 321166), Santana International Diving (☎/fax 340360), South-East Asia Yacht Charter (☎ 340406; fax 340586) and Fantasea Divers (☎ 340309).

Boat Trips Several different companies on Patong do one-day cruises to nearby islands. For excursions to the Similan and Surin islands off the Andaman coast of Phang-Nga Province, see the sections on those islands in the Ranong Province section.

Hash House Harriers Phuket's chapter of the running-and-drinking HHH meets regularly at the Expat Bar on Soi Bangla. Hashes (foot races) are held on Saturday afternoons; all interested people are welcome to participate.

SOUTHERN THAILAND

Boat Charter Motor yachts, sailboats and catamarans can sometimes be chartered with or without crew. Check with the dive shops listed previously to find out who has what.

Places to Stay Rates on Patong really vary according to season. In the high season (December to March, and August) you'll be doing very well to find something under 300B a night. On the beach there is nothing under 500B, but on Rat Uthit Rd, especially in the Paradise Complex, there are several guesthouses with dorms for around 100B or rooms from 250B. During off-months some of the 400B places will drop as low as 200B or even 100B, but that's about it. Most of the bungalows of yore have been replaced by tacky modern apartment buildings, often with faulty plumbing. Bottom-end places usually come with fan and shared bath; more expensive rooms in this category will have a private bath and perhaps air-con. During the rainy season, May to November, you may be able to knock 100B off the following rates:

Best Guest House, 250B (☎ 340958)
Boomerang Cafe & Inn, 250 to 600B
Capricorn Bungalow, 300 to 400B
Club Oasis, 480B (☎ 340258)
888 Inn, dorm 80B, rooms 250 to 350B (☎ 341306)
Jeep Bungalow, 300B (☎ 340100)
Night Guest House, dorm 100B, rooms 250B (☎ 340581)
PS I, 300B (☎ 340184)
PS II, 350B (☎ 342207/8)
Patong House, dorm 100B, rooms 300B (☎ 342678)
Sea Dragon Guest House 250B
Shamrock Park Inn, 450B (☎ 340991)
Suksan Mansion, 350B

The middle range at Patong Beach is 400 to 900B, which usually includes air-con and private bath. In this range are:

Asia Guest House, dorm 80B, rooms 350 to 600B (☎ 340962/3)
Casuarina Bungalow, 1200 to 1600B (☎ 340123; fax 342123)
Coconut Villa, 350 to 800B (☎ 340161; fax 340144)
Expat Hotel, 490 to 690B (☎/fax 340300)
K Hotel, 700 to 1100B (☎ 340833; fax 340124)
KSR Bungalow, 350 to 600B (☎ 340938; fax 340322)
The Living Place, 650 to 800B (☎/fax 340121)

Nerntong Resort, 620B (☎ 340572; fax 340571
New Tum Bungalow 1, 300 to 700B (☎ 340159)
Nordic Bungalow, 350 to 750B (☎ 340284)
Paradise Hotel, 550B (☎ 340172)
Patong Bed & Breakfast, 500 to 1500B (☎ 340819; fax 340818)
Patong Palace, 400 to 800B (☎ 340359)
Skandia Bungalow, 420 to 900B
Super Mansion, 300B with fan and 400B with air-con
Swiss Garden Bungalow, 750B
Thamdee Inn, 650 to 950B (☎ 340452)
Thara Patong, 500 to 1600B (☎ 340135; fax 340446)
Tropicana Bungalow, 900B (☎ 340204; fax 340206)

These places can probably be knocked down 100 to 200B a night during the rainy season.

At the top end of the price range, the *Patong Beach Hotel* (☎ 340301; fax 340541) has rooms from 2119B. *Patong Bay Garden Resort* (☎ 340297/8; fax 340560) has rooms from 2340B, *Club Andaman* (☎ 340530; fax 340527) has bungalows from 3708B and the *Phuket Cabana* (☎ 340138; fax 340178) starts at 2943B and goes up to 13,000B. Perched on a cliff over Hat Patong is the *Amari Coral Beach Resort* (☎ 340106; fax 340115) with rooms from 2825 to 5886B.

At the very pinnacle of luxury, the *Diamond Cliff Resort* (☎ 340501; fax 340507) costs 3766 to 19,421B a night – it's actually on adjacent Kalim Beach, a tiny bouldered beach between Patong and Kamala. A couple of other places at Kalim Beach, next to the village of Ban Kalim, include the modern *Kalim Guest House* (☎ 340353; fax 340701) at 1800 to 2200B, and the *Patong Lodge Hotel* (☎ 340286; fax 340287) at 1600 to 1800B. At the northern end of Patong, not quite as far north as Ban Kalim, is the *Thavorn Palm Beach Hotel* (☎ 340034), with 250 rooms for 2400B and up; the Thavorn has its own beach area. A newer entry, *The Residence* (☎ 340456; fax 342213), has rooms for 2100B.

The new *Holiday Inn Phuket* (☎ 340608/9; fax 340435) offers their usual international standards starting at 3414B.

Places to Eat Patong has stacks of restaurants, some of them quite good. The seafood restaurants are concentrated along Soi

Bangla; *Restaurant 4* is the best priced and is popular with Thais.

Another popular place is the *Chilli Restaurant* on Soi Perm Pong, where a range of Thai dishes cost 45 to 60B and breakfast is also available. Around the intersection of Rat Uthit Rd and Soi Bangla are a few inexpensive places worth trying. *Sam's Place*, on a soi just off this intersection, offers inexpensive Thai and Chinese dishes and owner Sam dispenses good local information. For inexpensive noodle and rice vendors, check the soi near the Living Place.

Every Wednesday and Friday evening from 7 to 10 pm the Merlin Hotel serves a buffet of French, Italian, German, Thai and Chinese food – accompanied by a traditional Thai dance performance – for 360B per person.

Entertainment & Shopping There are many bars around town, as well as a few cabarets and discos. *Banana Discotheque* at 96 Thawiwong Rd is one of the more popular dance clubs. If you like transvestite shows, check out the *Simon Cabaret* at 100/6-8 Muu 4.

A string of shops and stalls along the central part of Thawiwong Rd sell clothing, silk, jewellery and souvenirs from all over Thailand. Prices are higher than average.

Getting There & Away Songthaews to Patong from Phuket leave from Ranong Rd, near the day market and fountain circle; the fare is 10B. The after-hours charter fare is 130B.

Getting Around Tuk-tuks circulate Patong for 5B per ride. Patong Big Bike on Rat Uthit Rd rents 250cc to 750cc bikes.

Karon

กะรน

Karon is a long, gently curving beach with small sand dunes and a few evergreen trees. Some insist on calling this two beaches: Karon Yai and Karon Noi. Karon Noi, also known as Relax Bay, can only be reached from Hat Patong. It's completely monopolised by the relatively new Le Meridien Hotel.

Karon used to be quite a spot for budget travellers, but now it's lined with multistorey inns and deluxe bungalows, of which only three offer any rooms or huts for under 200B. It is still a fairly peaceful beach where fisherfolk cast nets, and where you can buy fresh seafood from their boats, though the rice fields between the beach and the surrounding hills have been abandoned. A few bars are moving in, too – signs of a Patong-like growth. See the Kata Getting There & Away section for details on transport to Karon.

Places to Stay On the north of the headland straddling Karon and Kata is the *Kata Tropicana* (☎/fax 330408), with new bungalows for 350 to 900B. *Happy Hut* next door has 150B bungalows; both of these are well off the beach, though. At the northern end of the beach is *Dream Hut* with rooms for 100 to 200B; the nearby *Coco Cabana* and *Lume & Yai* (☎/fax 396096) cost 300 to 500B.

In the commercial centre of Karon, near the roundabout, *Karon Seaview Bungalow* (☎ 396912) offers reasonable bungalows for 200B. On the main road away from the beach is the *Crystal Beach Hotel* (☎ 396580/5), it's good value at 300 to 400B for air-con rooms.

In the mid-range (averaging 500B and up) are the *Karon Village* (☎ 381431), 600 to 800B; *Kampong Karon* (☎ 212901 ext 103), 700B; *Karon Guest House* (☎ 396860; fax 396117), 400 to 700B; *Thepsomboon Inn* (☎ 214630), 500 to 1175B; *Phuket Ocean Resort* (☎ 396599; fax 396470), 1150 to 1250B; and *Ruam Thep Inn* (☎ (01) 723-0231), 350 to 800B.

The remaining places on Karon are new resort-type hotels – which have more than doubled in number over the last two years – with rooms starting at 1000B or above, with air-con, swimming pools, etc.

The top end is:

SOUTHERN THAILAND

Felix (Karon) View Point, 2590 to 7062B (☎ 396666; fax 396853)

The Islandia Park Resort, 128 rooms, 2589 to 7886B (☎ 396492; fax 396491)

Karon Inn, 100 rooms, 1184 to 2966B (☎ 396519; fax 330529)

Karon Villa & Karon Royal Wing, 324 rooms, from 2943B (☎ 396139; fax 396122)

Le Meridien Hotel, 470 rooms, from 3767B (☎ 340480; fax 340479)

Phuket Arcadia Hotel, 225 rooms, from 3296B (☎ 396038)

Phuket Golden Sand Inn, 95 rooms, 500 to 1200B (☎ 396493; fax 396117)

Phuket Green Valley Resort, 42 rooms, 1200B (☎ /fax 396468)

Phuket Island View, 81 rooms, 1500B (☎ 396919; fax 396632)

Sand Resort, 32 rooms, 1500B (☎ 212901, ext 036; fax 216961)

South Sea Resort, 100 rooms, from 3472B (☎ 396611; fax 396618)

Thavorn Palm Beach Hotel, 210 rooms, 4237 to 17,655B (☎ 396090; fax 396555)

Places to Eat As usual, almost every place to stay provides some food. The cheapest Thai places to eat are off the roundabout near the commercial centre. Supposedly one of the best restaurants for Thai food is *Old Siam*, which has dishes from 105 to 220B and good desserts for 55B. Another cosy inexpensive place with excellent food is *Sunset Restaurant*.

Kata

กะตะ

Just around a headland, south from Karon, Kata is more interesting as a beach than Karon, and is divided into two – Ao Kata Yai (Big Kata Bay) and Ao Kata Noi (Little Kata Bay). The small island of Ko Pu is within swimming distance of the shore and on the way are some pretty nice coral reefs. The water here is usually very clear and snorkelling gear can be rented from several of the bungalow groups. With a dozen sets of bungalows and a Club Med it can get a bit crowded, and the video bars are starting to take over. Concrete walls, protecting upmarket resorts from the riff-raff, seem to be sprouting everywhere. The centre for this kind of development seems to be the Kata-

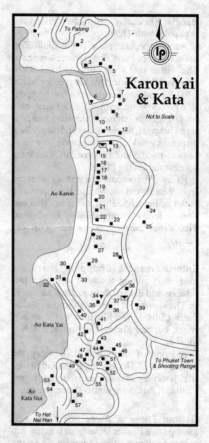

Karon area, the hills at the northern end that lead to either Karon or Kata Yai.

Contrary to rumour, the beach in front of Club Med is open to the public.

Along the main road through the area, near the Rose Inn, are a Thai Farmers Bank (with exchange services) and a post office.

Places to Stay Bungalow rates have really gone up in Kata in recent years but are still less expensive than at Karon. Now the crowd of 34 places to stay ranges from 150B at the *Cool Breeze* in Kata Noi (certain huts only;

PLACES TO STAY

1   Le Meridien
2   Thepsomboon Inn
3   Felix (Karon) View Point
4   Kampong Karon
5   Lume & Yai Bungalows
7   Phuket Ocean Resort
8   Coco Cabana
9   Dream Hut
10 Phuket Golden Sand Inn
11 The Islandia Park Resort
12 Karon Guest House
13 Crystal Beach Hotel
15 Karon Bungalows
16 South Sea Resort
17 Karon Villa
18 Karon Royal Wing
19 Sand Resort
20 Karon Seaview Bungalow
21 Phuket Arcadia
22 Thavorn Palm Beach

23 Karon Inn
24 Kata Village
25 Phuket Green Valley Resort
27 Phuket Island View
28 Happy Hut
29 Kata Tropicana
30 Ruam Thep Inn
31 Marina Cottages
32 Laem Sai Village
33 Kata Villa
35 Hallo
36 Kokchang Village
38 Rose Inn
39 Bougainville Terrace House
40 Peach Hill Hotel
41 Dome Bungalow
42 Club Med
43 Kata Sanuk Village
45 Sea Bees
46 Bell Guest House
47 Kata Beach Resort

48 Boathouse Inn
49 Kata Delight
50 Friendship Bungalow
51 Sea Wind Hotel
52 Cool Breeze
53 Kata Thani Amari Resort
54 Island Lodge Bungalow
55 Pop Cottage
56 Kata Noi Riviera
57 Mountain Beach Resort

PLACES TO EAT

6   Seafood Restaurants
34 Kampong-Kata Hill

OTHER

14 Post Office
26 Maxim Supermarket
37 Post Office
44 Kata Plaza

others with toilet and shower are more expensive) to over 4000B at the new *Boathouse Inn*, just a step above the Club Méditerranée on Kata Yai. The less expensive places tend to be off the beach between Kata Yai (north) and Kata Noi (south) or well off the beach on the road to the island interior.

Friendship Bungalow (☎ 330499), off the beach at the headland between Kata Yai and Kata Noi, is now 350 to 600B. A sprinkling of others under 500B include *Kata Villa* (☎ 330602, 200 to 300B), *Kata Noi Riviera* (☎ 330726, 300 to 600B), *Kata Sanuk Village* (☎ 330476, 300 to 450B), *Kullapang-ha* (150 to 200B), *Kokchang Village* (☎ 330575, 300B), *Dome Bungalow* (☎ 330620, 350B), *Sea Bees* (☎ (01) 723-1070, 200B), *Bell Guest House* (250B), *Island Lodge Bungalow* (150B) and *Rose Inn* (☎ 330135; fax 381735, 300 to 500B). All of the bungalows will give discounts during the low season, from May to October.

Medium-range places (all air-con) in Kata include *Pop Cottage* (☎ 330794) from 300 to 700B; *Peach Hill Hotel* (☎ 330603; fax 330895), in a nice setting with a pool from 400 to 600B; and *Hallo Guest House* (☎ 330631), from 500 to 700B.

The *Kata Thani Amari Resort* (☎ 330417; fax 330426) on the beach at Kata Noi has up-market rooms and bungalows for 2589 to 12,000B. Other top-end places include:

Boathouse Inn, 36 rooms, 3531 to 7062B (☎ 330557)
Bougainville Terrace House, 21 rooms, 1404 to 2806B (☎ 330087; fax 330463)
Club Méditerranée, 300 rooms, 2650 to 3750B (☎ 381455; fax 330461)
Kata Beach Resort, 280 rooms, from 1276B (☎ 330530; fax 330128)
Kata Delight, six rooms, 1400 to 1600B (☎ 330481)
Laem Sai Village, 34 rooms, 1600 to 2500B (☎ 212901)
Marina Cottage, 104 rooms, 1498 to 2354B (☎ 330625)
Mountain Beach Resort, 33 rooms, 650 to 1250B (☎ 330565; fax 330567)
Sea Wind Hotel, 22 rooms, 1936 to 2178B (☎ 330564)

Places to Eat Most of the restaurants in Kata offer standard tourist food and service. One that stands out is the *Kampong-Kata Hill Restaurant*, a Thai-style place decorated with antiques and overlooking the bay. It's open only for dinner, from 5 pm till midnight.

The *Dive Café* serves a multi-course Thai dinner for two for 100B per person.

SOUTHERN THAILAND

Getting There & Away Songthaews to both Kata and Karon leave frequently from the Ranong Rd market in Phuket for 10B per person. After-hour charters cost 130B.

Nai Han

ในทาน

A few km south of Kata, this beach around a picturesque bay is similar to Kata and Karon but, in spite of the 1986 construction of the Phuket Yacht Club, not as developed – thanks to the presence of Samnak Song Nai Han, a monastic centre in the middle of the beach that claims most of the beachfront land. To make up for the loss of saleable beachfront, developers started cutting away the forests on the hillsides overlooking the beach. Recently, however, the development seems to have reached a halt. This means that Nai Han is usually one of the least crowded beaches on the southern part of the island.

The TAT says Nai Han beach is a dangerous place to swim during the monsoon season (May to October), but it really varies according to daily or weekly weather changes – look for the red flag, which means dangerous swimming conditions.

Places to Stay Except for the Yacht Club, there's really not much accommodation available on or even near the beach. *Coconut Huts* is still surviving on the slope behind the Coconut Cafe, near the Phuket Yacht Club entrance. Simple huts are 100B a night. Well back from the beach, in a rubber plantation opposite rice fields, is the quiet *Nockayang Bungalows* for 140B with bath. You should be able to talk them down to 100B, since the huts really aren't very well maintained. On the way to Nockayang is the motel-like *Nai Han Resort* (☎ 381810), with decent rooms for 600 with fan, up to 800B for air-con.

The *Phuket Yacht Club* (☎ 381156; fax 381164) sits on the northern end of Nai Han. Originally built at the astronomical cost of 145 million baht, the hotel has given up on the idea of becoming a true yacht club (apparently the bay currents aren't right for such an endeavour) with a mobile pier. The pier has been removed but luxurious 'state rooms' are still available for 7768B a night and up.

If you follow the road through the Yacht Club and beyond to the next cape, you'll come to the simple *Ao Sane Bungalows*, which cost 100 to 300B depending on the season and condition of the huts. Farther on at the end of this road is the secluded *Jungle Beach Resort* (☎/fax 381108). The nicely done cottages are well-spaced along a naturally wooded slope with a small beach below. Low-season rates start at 300B for a sturdy hut without bath; high-season rates peak at 4000B for a large terraced cottage with private bath.

Getting There & Away Nai Han is 18 km from Phuket and a songthaew (leaving from the intersection of Bangkok Rd and the fountain circle) costs 20B per person. Tuk-tuk charters are 130B one way.

Rawai

ราไวย์

Rawai was one of the first coastal areas on Phuket to be developed, simply because it was near Phuket and there was already a rather large fishing community there. Once other, nicer beach areas like Patong and Karon were 'discovered', Rawai gradually began to lose popularity and today it is a rather spiritless place – but at least it's not crowded.

The beach is not so great, but there is a lot happening in or near Rawai: a local sea-gypsy village; Hat Laem Kha (better than Rawai) to the north; boats to the nearby islands of Ko Lon, Ko Hae, Ko Aew, Ko Phi and others; and good snorkelling off **Laem Phromthep** at the southern tip of Phuket island, easy to approach from Rawai. In fact, most of the visitors who stay at Rawai these days are divers who want to be near Phromthep and/or boat facilities for offshore diving trips.

Laem Phromthep is also a popular viewing point at sunset, when lots of shutterbugs gather to take the cliched Phromthep photo. On a hill next to the viewpoint is a shrine to Phra Phrom (Brahma).

The diving around the offshore islands is not bad, especially at Kaew Yai/Kaew Noi, off Phromthep and at Ko Hae. It's a good idea to shop around for boat trips to these islands to find the least expensive passage – the larger the group, the cheaper the cost per person.

Places to Stay *Pornmae Bungalows*, at 58/1 Wiset Rd, has bungalows for 250B with fan, up to 800B with air-con. Their restaurant is one of the better – and more moderately

priced – ones in the area. Long-runner *Salaloi Resort* is in the 500 to 800B range.

The *Rawai Garden Resort* (☎ 381292) has eight rooms for 250B, while *Rawai Plaza & Bungalow* (☎ 381346; fax 381647) has 50 rooms and bungalows ranging from 450 to 900B.

Round at Laem Kha, the well-managed *Phuket Island Resort* (☎ 381010/7; fax 381018) has air-con rooms from 2943B, a swimming pool and other mod-cons. The *Laem Kha Beach Inn* (☎ 381305) has 15 rooms for 550B.

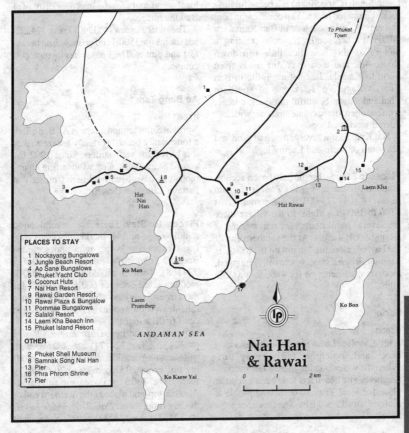

PLACES TO STAY
1 Nockayang Bungalows
3 Jungle Beach Resort
4 Ao Sane Bungalows
5 Phuket Yacht Club
6 Coconut Huts
7 Nai Han Resort
9 Rawai Garden Resort
10 Rawai Plaza & Bungalow
11 Pornmae Bungalows
12 Salaloi Resort
14 Laem Kha Beach Inn
15 Phuket Island Resort

OTHER
2 Phuket Shell Museum
8 Samnak Song Nai Han
13 Pier
16 Phra Phrom Shrine
17 Pier

Nai Han
& Rawai

0   1   2 km

SOUTHERN THAILAND

Places to Eat An attraction in itself is the *Jambalaya Cafe* near Rawai on the road to Phuket. The food is Thai – sorry, no jambalaya – but the Restless Cowboys band play Hank Williams nightly except Sunday.

Getting There & Away Rawai is about 16 km from Phuket and getting there costs 10B by songthaew from the circle at Bangkok Rd. Tuk-tuk charters cost 90B from Phuket.

Laem Singh & Kamala

แหลมสิงห์/กะหลามลา

North of Ao Patong, 24 km from Phuket, Laem Singh (Cape Singh) is a beautiful little rock-dominated beach. You could camp here and eat on Surin beach or in Ban Kamala, a village farther south. If you're renting a motorbike, this is a nice little trip down Route 402 and then over dirt roads from Surin to Kamala. Just before Surin, in Ban Thao village No 2, is one of southern Thailand's most beautiful mosques, a large, whitewashed, immaculate structure with lacquered wooden doors.

Hat Kamala is a lovely stretch of sand and sea south of Surin and Laem Singh.

Places to Stay So far the only beach accommodation is the up-market *Phuket Kamala Resort* (☎ (01) 723-0010), where rooms cost 1700 to 1900B a night. In the village there are several small houses for rent starting at around 500B a night. At the southern end of the bay, overlooking but not on the beach, is *Kamala Beach Estate*, where fully equipped, modern apartments go for 4800 to 8000B a night.

Surin

สุรินทร์

A little north of Laem Singh, Surin has a long beach and sometimes fairly heavy surf. When the water is calm, there's fair snorkelling here. The beach has long been a popular place for local Thais to come and nibble at seafood snacks sold by vendors along the beach.

Places to Stay So far the southern stretches of Surin have been spared hotel development. The northern end has been dubbed 'Pansea Beach' by developers and is claimed by the exclusive Amanpuri and Pansea resorts. *Amanpuri Resort* (☎ 324333; fax 324100) plays host to Thailand's celebrity traffic, each of whom gets a 133-sq-metre pavilion and a personal attendant; the staff to guest ratio is 3½ to one. It's owned by Indonesian Adrian Zecha and designed by the architect who designed the former Shah of Iran's Winter Palace. You can expect to pay 8500B and up per day for a room here. The Amanpuri was recently censured by the local community for the improper display of Buddha images.

The older *Pansea* (☎ 324017; fax 324252) has rooms for 3500B and up including breakfast and dinner. The Pansea has its own golf course.

Ao Bang Tao

บางเทา

North of Surin around a cape is Ao Bang Tao, a long sandy beach. A steady breeze makes it a haven for sailboarders; since 1992 the annual Siam World Cup windsurfing championships have been held here (formerly at Pattaya's Jomtien Beach).

Places to Stay There are several good middle-range and up-market places to stay. Least expensive is the quiet and secluded *Bangtao Lagoon Bungalow* (☎ 324260; fax 324168), with small cottages for 200B, medium-sized ones for 600B, or 1000B for the largest. *Bangtao Cottage* is built on a hillside over the southern end of the bay and costs 650B a night.

Rooms at the new *Dusit Laguna Resort* (☎ 324320; fax 324174) are 4826B, with suites costing considerably more, not including tax. From 20 December to 20 February there is a 400B peak-season surcharge. Another top-end place at the northern end of the bay is the *Royal Park Travelodge Resort* (☎ 324021; fax 324243), where rooms start

Top Left: Ceramic detail, Wat Arun, Bangkok (GB)
Top Right: Shrine wall detail, Wat Phra Kaew, Bangkok (RN)
Bottom Left: Design detail, reua kaw-lae boat, Kao Saen, Songkhla (RN)
Bottom Right: Mosaic, Wat Chiang Man, Chiang Mai (JC)

Top: Traditional masked dance-drama (khon) (TAT)
Bottom: Practising traditional dancing (TAT)

at 2825B. The Grand Sheraton Hotel is on its way to Bang Tao.

Getting There & Away A songthaew from Phuket's Ranong Rd to Surin, Kamala or Bang Tao costs 15B. Tuk-tuk charters are 200B to Surin and Kamala, 170B to Bang Tao.

Nai Yang & Mai Khao
ไนยาง/ไม้ขาว
Both of these beaches are near Phuket Airport, about 30 km from Phuket. Nai Yang, a fairly secluded beach favoured by Thais, is actually a national park, with one set of government-run bungalows. It's about five km farther north along Route 402 (Thepkasatri Rd) to Phuket's longest beach, Hat Mai Khao, where sea turtles lay their eggs between November and February each year. About a km off Nai Yang is a decent reef at a depth of 10 to 20 metres.

Places to Stay Camping is allowed on both Nai Yang and Mai Khao beaches. The park accommodation on Nai Yang costs 200B in a dorm-like long house, 300B in a four-bed bungalow, 600B in a 12-bed one. Two-person tents can be rented for 60B a night.

Although this is a national park, somehow the fancy *Pearl Village Beach Hotel* (☎ 327006; fax 327338) managed to slip in on 8.1 hectares at the southern end of the beach. Air-con rooms and cottages start at 3884B. Another apparent encroacher is the 2943B-per-night *Crown Nai Yang Condotel*.

Getting There & Away A songthaew from Phuket to Nai Yang costs 20B. A tuk-tuk charter costs 250B.

Other Beaches
Out on Laem Phanwa by itself is the *Cape Phanwa Sheraton* (☎ 391123; fax 391177), where luxury digs start at 3237B.

There are a couple of places to stay on Ko Sire, including *Madam Puye Bungalow* for 200B and *Siray Seaview Bungalow* for 300 to 500B.

On Ko Hae, the *Coral Island Resort* (☎ 216381; fax 216263) has up-market bungalows from 2000B with air-con.

Warning
All of the western Phuket beaches, including Surin, Laem Singh and Kamala, have strong riptides during the monsoons. Take care when swimming, or don't go in the water at all if you're not a strong swimmer.

Surat Thani Province

CHAIYA
ไชยา
About 640 km from Bangkok, Chaiya is just north of Surat Thani and best visited as a day trip from there. Chaiya is one of the oldest cities in Thailand, dating back to the Srivijaya empire. In fact, the name may be a contraction of Siwichaiya, the Thai pronunciation of the city that was a regional capital between the 8th and 10th centuries. Previous to this time the area was on the Indian trade route in South-East Asia. Many Srivijaya artefacts in the National Museum in Bangkok were found in Chaiya, including the Avalokitesvara Bodhisattva bronze, considered to be a masterpiece of Buddhist art.

Wat Phra Boromathat, Wat Kaew & Chaiya National Museum
The restored **Borom That Chaiya** stupa at Wat Phra Boromathat, just outside of town, is a fine example of Srivijaya architecture and strongly resembles the *candis* of central Java. A ruined stupa at nearby Wat Kaew, also from the Srivijaya period, again shows central Javanese influence (or perhaps vice versa) as well as Cham (9th-century South Vietnam) characteristics.

The national museum at Wat Phra Boromathat displays prehistoric and historic artefacts of local provenance, as well as local handicrafts and a shadow puppet exhibit. Admission to the museum is 10B; it's open Wednesday to Sunday from 9 am to 4 pm.

SOUTHERN THAILAND

Wat Suan Mokkhaphalaram

วัดสวนโมกขพลาราม

Wat Suanmok (short for Wat Suan Mokkhaphalaram – literally, 'garden of liberation'), west of Wat Kaew, is a modern forest wat founded by Ajaan Buddhadasa Bhikkhu (Thai: Phutthathat), Thailand's most famous monk. Born in Chaiya in 1906, Buddhadasa ordained as a monk when he was 21 years old, spent many years studying the Pali scriptures and then retired to the forest for six years of solitary meditation. Returning to ecclesiastical society, he was made abbot of Wat Phra Boromathat, a high distinction, but conceived of Suanmok as an alternative to orthodox Thai temples. During Thailand's turbulent 1970s, he was branded a communist because of his critiques of capitalism, which he saw as a catalyst for greed. Buddhadasa died in July 1993 after a long illness.

Buddhadasa's philosophy was ecumenical in nature, comprising Zen, Taoist and Christian elements as well as the traditional Theravada schemata. Today the hermitage is spread over 120 hectares of wooded hillside and features huts for up to 70 monks, a museum/library, and a 'spiritual theatre'. This latter building has bas-reliefs on the outer walls which are facsimiles of sculpture at Sanchi, Bharhut and Amaravati in India. The interior walls feature modern Buddhist painting – eclectic to say the least – executed by the resident monks.

At the affiliated International Dhamma Heritage, across the highway 1.5 km from Wat Suanmok, resident farang monks hold meditation retreats during the first 10 days of every month. Anyone is welcome to participate; a 50B donation per day is requested to cover food costs.

Places to Stay

Travellers could stay in Surat Thani for visits to Chaiya or request permission from the monks to stay in the guest quarters at Wat Suanmok. *Udomlap Hotel*, an old Chinese-Thai hotel in Chaiya, has rooms for 80 to 100B.

Getting There & Away

If you're going to Surat Thani by train from Bangkok, you can get off at the small Chaiya train station, then later catch another train to Phun Phin, Surat's train station.

From Surat you can either take a songthaew from Talaat Kaset II in Ban Don (18B to Wat Suanmok or 20B to Chaiya) or get a train going north from Phun Phin. The trains between Phun Phin and Chaiya may be full but you can always stand or squat in a 3rd-class car for the short trip. The ordinary train costs 8B in 3rd class to Chaiya and takes about an hour to get there. The songthaew takes around 45 minutes.

Suanmok is about seven km outside town on the highway to Surat and Chumphon. Until late afternoon there are songthaews from the Chaiya train station to Wat Suanmok for 8B per passenger. From Chaiya you can also catch a Surat-bound bus from the front of the movie theatre on Chaiya's main street and ask to be let off at Wat Suanmok. (Turn right on the road in front of the train station.) The fare to Wat Suanmok is 5B. If buses aren't running you can hire a motorcycle (and driver) for 15 to 20B anywhere along Chaiya's main street.

SURAT THANI/BAN DON

อ.เมืองสุราษฎร์ธานี/บ้านดอน

There is little of particular historical interest at Surat Thani (population 41,800), a busy commercial centre and port dealing in rubber and coconut, but the town has character nonetheless. It's 651 km from Bangkok and the first point in a southbound journey towards Malaysia that really feels and looks like southern Thailand. For most people Surat Thani (often known as Surat) is only a stop on the way to Ko Samui or Ko Pha-Ngan, luscious islands 32 km off the coast – so the Talaat Kaset bus station in Ban Don and the ferry piers to the east become the centres of attention.

Information

Tourist Office The friendly TAT office

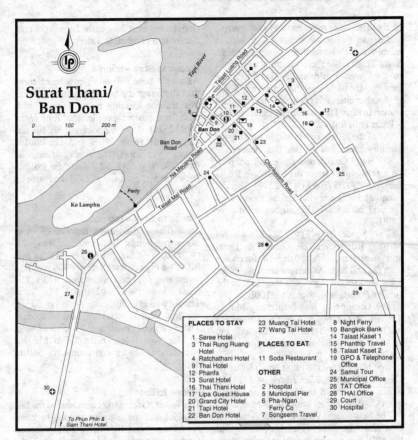

Surat Thani/ Ban Don

0   100   200 m

Tapi River

Talaat Luang Road

Ban Don

Ban Don Road

Na Meuang Road

Chonkasem Road

Talaat Mai Road

Ko Lamphu

Ferry

To Phun Phin & Siam Thani Hotel

PLACES TO STAY	23 Muang Tai Hotel	8 Night Ferry
	27 Wang Tai Hotel	10 Bangkok Bank
1 Seree Hotel		14 Talaat Kaset 1
3 Thai Rung Ruang	**PLACES TO EAT**	15 Phanthip Travel
Hotel		18 Talaat Kaset 2
4 Ratchathani Hotel	11 Soda Restaurant	19 GPO & Telephone
9 Thai Hotel		Office
12 Phanfa	**OTHER**	24 Samui Tour
13 Surat Hotel		25 Municipal Office
16 Thai Thani Hotel	2 Hospital	26 TAT Office
17 Lipa Guest House	5 Municipal Pier	28 THAI Office
20 Grand City Hotel	6 Pha-Ngan	29 Court
21 Tapi Hotel	Ferry Co	30 Hospital
22 Ban Don Hotel	7 Songserm Travel	

(☎ 282828), at 5 Talaat Mai Rd near the south-western end of town, distributes plenty of useful brochures and maps. It's open daily from 8.30 am to 4.30 pm.

Several travel agents in town handle travel to the islands or elsewhere in southern Thailand, including: Songserm Travel (☎ 285124; fax 285127) at 30/2 Mu 3 Bangkoong Rd, with another office opposite the pier; Pha-Ngan Ferry Co (☎ 286461; fax 282713) on the corner of 2-6 Chonkasem and Ban Don Rds; Phanthip Travel (☎ 272230) at 442/24-5 Talaat Mai Rd; and Island Jet (☎ 272230, 272906) at Talaat Mai Rd.

Money Bangkok Bank at 193 Na Meuang Rd has an exchange booth open daily from 8.30 am to 5 pm.

Post & Telephone The GPO and telephone office are on Na Meuang Rd.

Surat's telephone area code is ☎ 077.

Places to Stay – bottom end

For many of Surat Thani's cheaper hotels, business consists largely of 'short-time' trade. This doesn't make them any less suitable as regular hotels – it's just that there's

SOUTHERN THAILAND

likely to be rather more noise as guests arrive and depart with some frequency. In fact, in many ways it's better to zip straight through Surat Thani since there's nothing of interest to hold you. You're quite likely to sleep better on the night boat than in a noisy hotel.

Another alternative is to stay near the train station in Phun Phin (see under Places to Stay – Phun Phin following).

All of the following are within walking (or samlor) distance of the Ban Don boat pier.

Off Ban Don Rd, near the municipal pier, on a fairly quiet street off Si Chaiya Rd, is the *Seree (Seri) Hotel* (☎ 272279). You get adequate but somewhat airless rooms with fan and bath for 290B, air-con rooms for 290B.

The *Surat Hotel* (☎ 272243) on Na Meuang Rd, between the Grand City Hotel and bus station, costs 150 to 300B for rooms with fan and bath. At the rear are some quiet, renovated rooms. Opposite the Surat is the similar *Phanfa* with rooms for 100B.

The *Grand City Hotel* (formerly Muang Thong) (☎ 272560) at 428 Na Meuang Rd has been renovated and has rooms with fan and bath for 160B, and clean air-con rooms for 300B.

One block from the night boat pier on Si Chaiya Rd is the *Thai Hotel* (☎ 272932), which is 150/180B for adequate and fairly quiet singles/doubles with fan and bath.

The best budget value in Surat is the *Ban Don Hotel* (☎ 272167) on Na Meuang Rd towards the morning market, with clean singles/doubles with fan and bath for 110/150B. Enter the hotel through a Chinese restaurant. The *Thai Rung Ruang Hotel* (☎ 273249), 191/199 Mitkasem Rd, is also good with rooms from 260B (fan), and 430B (air-con).

On the corner of Si Chaiya Rd and the road between the river and bus station is the adequate *Ratchathani Hotel* (☎ 272972/143), which starts at 260B for rooms with fan and bath and from 280B for air-con. The *Lipa Guest House* (☎ 282136), a relatively new place at the Talaat Kaset 2 bus station, has rooms for 100B. We've had one report complaining that the noise from chickens being slaughtered next door to the Lipa is not conducive to a good night's sleep.

Places to Stay – middle

Although these two don't cost much more than the foregoing budget places, the facilities are considerably better. Popular with travelling businesspeople, the *Tapi Hotel* (☎ 272575), at 100 Chonkasem Rd, has air-con rooms from 350B and fan-cooled rooms from 250B. The similar *Muang Tai* (☎ 272367), at 390-392 Talaat Mai Rd, has fan-cooled rooms from 200B and air-con rooms from 300B.

Places to Stay – top end

Surat Thani also has a number of more expensive hotels, including the *Wang Tai* (☎ 283020/39; fax 281007) at 1 Talaat Mai Rd. It's a big hotel with nearly 300 rooms, a swimming pool and prices from 970B. The *Siam Thani* (☎ 391-0280), at 180 Surat Thani-Phun Phin Rd, costs 840B but during the low season offers a 50% discount. There's a good restaurant. The *Siam Thara*, on Don Nok Rd near the Talaat Mai Rd intersection, has air-con rooms for 560 to 640B.

Places to Eat

The Talaat Kaset market area next to the bus terminal and the morning market between Na Meuang and Si Chaiya Rds are good food-hunting places. Many stalls near the bus station specialise in khâo kài òp, a marinated baked chicken on rice which is very tasty. During mango season, a lot of street vendors in Surat sell incredible khâo niâw má-mûang, coconut-sweetened sticky rice with sliced ripe mango.

J Home Bakery, around the corner from the Grand City Hotel, is a dark, poorly ventilated air-con place, but it has inexpensive Western breakfasts, a few baked goods, plus Thai and Chinese dishes on a bilingual menu. Better bakery choices are the *Valaisak Bakery* next to the Tapi Hotel or the *Home Bakery* next to the Phanfa Hotel. Next door to J Home is the inexpensive and popular

Yong Hua Long, a decent Chinese restaurant with roast duck and a large buffet table.

Soda Restaurant at 15 Na Meuang Rd features some vegetarian dishes (20 to 30B) on its Thai/Chinese menu and is open for breakfast, lunch and dinner.

Places to Stay & Eat – Phun Phin

You may find yourself needing accommodation in Phun Phin, either because you've become stranded there due to booked-out trains or because you've come in from Samui in the evening and plan to get an early morning train out of Surat before the Surat to Phun Phin bus service starts. If so, there are several cheap but adequate hotels just across from the train station. The *Tai Fah* has rooms for 100B with shared bath, 120B with attached bath. Slightly better at the same location is the *Sri Thani*, also with rooms at 100B.

Around the corner on the road to Surat, but still quite close to the train station, is the decent *Queen* (☎ 311003) where rooms cost 160 to 200B with fan and 250 to 300B with air-con.

Across from the Queen is a good night market with cheap eats. The Tai Fah and Sri Thani do Thai, Chinese and farang food at reasonable prices.

Getting There & Away

Air THAI flies to Surat Thani from Bangkok (daily, 1710B), Chiang Mai (twice a week, 2970B), Nakhon Si Thammarat (three times a week, 340B), Hat Yai (via Phuket, 1200B), Phuket (daily, 475B) and Trang (three times a week, 495B).

The THAI office (☎ 272610) is at 3/27-28 Karunarat Rd (☎ 272610, 273/355). A THAI shuttle van between Surat Thani and the airport costs 40B per person. THAI also runs a more expensive limo service for 150B.

Bus, Share Taxi & Minivan First-class air-con buses leave Bangkok's southern air-con bus terminal in Thonburi daily at 8, 8.20 and 8.30 pm, arriving in Surat 11 hours later; the fare is 285B. There is also one 2nd-class

air-con departure at 10 pm that costs 222B and one VIP departure at 8 pm for 350B. Private companies also run 'Super VIP' buses with only 30 seats for 440B.

Ordinary buses leave the ordinary southern bus terminal at 9.20 and 11 pm for 158B.

Take care when booking private air-con and VIP buses out of Surat. A company called Harmony Tours has been known to sell tickets for VIP buses to Bangkok, then pile hapless travellers onto an ordinary air-con bus and refuse to refund the fare difference. If possible get a recommendation from another traveller or enquire at the TAT office.

Public buses and share taxis run from the Talaat Kaset 1 or 2 markets. Muang Tai bus company books air-con bus tickets to several destinations in southern Thailand from its desk in the lobby of the Surat Hotel, including VIP buses to Bangkok. Phanthip (Phuntip) Travel handles minivan bookings.

Several private tour companies run buses to Surat from Bangkok for around 260B. Other fares to/from Surat are:

Destination	Fare	Hours
Hat Yai	85B	5
(air-con)	120B	4
(share taxi or van)	150B	3½
Krabi	51B	4
(air-con)	91B	3
(share taxi or van)	150B	2
Nakhon Si Thammarat	36B	2½
(air-con)	55B	2
(share taxi)	60B	2
Narathiwat	127B	6
Phang-Nga	50B	4
(air-con)	70B	3
(share taxi)	80B	2½
Phuket	77B	6
(air-con)	139B	5
(share taxi or van)	150B	4
Ranong	70B	4
(air-con)	80B	4
(share taxi or van)	150B	3½
Satun	76B	4
Trang	50B	3
(share taxi)	100B	3
Yala	100B	6

Train Trains for Surat, which don't really stop in Surat but in Phun Phin, 14 km west of town, leave Bangkok's Hualamphong terminal at 12.25 pm (rapid), 2 pm (special express), 3.15 pm (special express), 3.50 pm (rapid), 5.05 pm (rapid), 6.30 pm (rapid), 7.20 pm (express) and 7.45 pm (rapid), arriving 10½ to 11 hours later.

The 6.30 pm train (rapid No 41) is the most convenient, arriving at 6.03 am and giving you plenty of time to catch a boat to Samui, if that's your destination. Fares are 470B in 1st class (available only on the 2 and 3.15 pm special express) and 224B in 2nd class, not including the rapid/express/special express surcharges or berths.

There are no direct 3rd-class trains to Surat from Bangkok, but you can travel from Chumphon to Surat on the ordinary No 119 or No 149 for 25B.

The all 1st-class special express No 981 (formerly called the Sprinter) leaves Bangkok daily at 10.35 pm and arrives in Phun Phin at 7.30 am for 370B. No sleeping berths are available on this train.

The Phun Phin train station has a 24-hour left-luggage room that costs 5B for the first five days, 10B thereafter. The advance ticket office is open daily from 6 to 11 am and noon to 6 pm.

It can be difficult to book long-distance trains out of Phun Phin – for long-distance travel, it may be easier to take a bus, especially if heading south. The trains are very often full and it's a drag to take the bus 14 km from town to the Phun Phin train station and be turned away. You could buy a 'standing room only' 3rd-class ticket and stand for an hour or two until someone vacates a seat down the line.

Advance train reservations can be made, without going all the way out to Phun Phin station, at Phanthip travel agency on Talaat Mai Rd in Ban Don, near the market/bus station. You might try making an onward reservation *before* boarding a boat for Samui. The Songserm Travel Service on Samui can also assist travellers with reservations.

Here is a list of other train fares out of Surat (not including surcharges on rapid, express or air-con coaches):

Destination	1st Class	2nd Class	3rd Class
Bangkok	470B	224B	107B
Chaiya	–	–	8B
Chumphon	71B	34B	25B
Hat Yai	228B	114B	55B
Nakhon Si Thammarat (Thung Song)	103B	54B	26B
Prachuap Khiri Khan	255B	127B	61B

Train/Bus/Boat Combinations These days many travellers are buying tickets from the State Railway that go straight through to Ko Samui or Ko Pha-Ngan from Bangkok on a train, bus and boat combination. For example, a 2nd-class air-con sleeper that includes bus to boat transfers through to Samui costs 549B. See the Getting There & Away sections under each island for more details.

Getting Around

Buses to Ban Don from Phun Phin train station leave every 10 minutes or so from 6 am to 8 pm for 7B per person. Some of the buses drive straight to the pier (if they have enough tourists on the bus), while others will terminate at the Ban Don bus station, from where you must get another bus to Tha Thong (or to Ban Don if you're taking the night ferry).

If you arrive in Phun Phin on one of the night trains, you can get a free bus from the train station to the pier, courtesy of the boat service, for the morning boat departures. If your train arrives in Phun Phin when the buses aren't running (which includes all trains except No 41), then you're out of luck and will have to hire a taxi to Ban Don for about 60 to 70B, or hang out in one of the Phun Phin street cafes until buses start running.

Orange buses run from Ban Don bus station to Phun Phin train station every five minutes from 5 am to 7.30 pm for 7B per person. Empty buses also wait at the Tha Thong pier for passengers arriving from Ko Samui on the express boat, ready to drive them directly to the train station or destinations further afield.

Around town, share tuk-tuks cost 5B and samlors are 10B.

KHAO SOK NATIONAL PARK
อุทยานแห่งชาติเขาสก

This 646-sq-km park is in the western part of Surat Thani Province, off Route 401 about a third of the way from Takua Pa to Surat Thani. The park features 65,000 hectares of thick native rainforest with waterfalls, limestone cliffs, numerous streams, an island-studded lake formed by the Chiaw Lan Dam and many trails, mostly along rivers. Connected to the Khlong Saen Wildlife Sanctuary and three smaller preserves (thus forming the largest contiguous nature preserve on the Thai peninsula), Khao Sok shelters a plathora of wildlife, including wild elephant, leopard, serow, banteng, gaur, dusky langur, tiger and Malayan sun bear as well as over 175 bird species. In 1986 Slorm's stork – a new species for Thailand – was confirmed.

The park is 1.5 km off Route 401 between Takua Pa and Surat Thani at Km 109. Besides the camping area at the park headquarters, there are several private bungalow operations featuring 'tree-house' style accommodation.

Entrance to the park is 30B; the rangers also take jungle tours and/or rafting trips for 150B per day.

Places to Stay

Khao Sok has a camping area and several places to stay. The national park has a house with rooms for 350B. Tents can be rented for 50B per person. A small restaurant near the entrance serves inexpensive meals.

Accommodation is also available just outside the park at *Tree Tops River Huts* (radio ☎ 421155/613, both ext 107), which offers six rooms with bath for 200/300B a single/double, or a tree house with bath for 400B, and meals for 40 to 70B. *Bamboo House*, off the main road to the park, has seven rooms for 100/120B with shared bath, 170/230B with private bath, plus 120B extra for three meals a day.

Art's Jungle House, off the same road beyond the Bamboo House, about a km from the park, has seven rooms for 200 to 300B, plus tree houses for 400B and two large houses with rooms with private bath and deck for 600B; meals cost 250B a day or you order à la carte at breakfast and lunch, 80B for a set Thai dinner. Contact Lost Horizon Travel (☎ (02) 279-4967) in Bangkok, or the Jungle House itself (radio ☎ 076-421155, ext 205). All places have guides for jungle trips. Meals are available for 40 to 60B.

Tree Tops Guest House started the Khao Sok experience several years ago but these days the guesthouse accepts only package tours booked through Vieng Travel (☎ (02) 280-3537) in Bangkok. A typical package for four nights (two nights at Tree Tops, two nights at their raft house) with meals is 4900B.

Getting There & Away

From Phun Phin or Surat there are frequent buses to Km 109 (the park's entrance) for 75B air-con, 28B ordinary. You can also come from the Phuket side of the peninsula by bus.

KO SAMUI
เกาะสมุย

Ko Samui (population 32,000) is part of an island group that used to be called Muu Ko Samui, though you rarely hear that term these days. It's Thailand's third-largest island, at 247 sq km, and is surrounded by 80 smaller islands. Six of these, Pha-Ngan, Ta Loy, Tao, Taen, Ma Ko and Ta Pao, are inhabited as well.

The island long ago attained a somewhat legendary status among Asian travellers, yet until relatively recently it never really escalated to the touristic proportions of other similar getaways found between Goa and Bali. With the advent of the Don Sak auto/bus ferry and the opening of the airport, things have been changing fast. During the high seasons, late December to February and July to August, it can be difficult to find a place to stay, even though most beaches are crowded with bungalows. The port town teems with farangs getting on and off the ferry boats, booking tickets onward, and collecting mail at the post office. With daily flights to Samui from Bangkok, the island is rushing headlong into top-end development.

Airport or no airport, Samui is still an enjoyable place to spend some time. It still has some of the best accommodation values in Thailand and a laid-back atmosphere that makes it quite relaxing. Even with an airport, it still has the advantage of being off the mainland and far away from Bangkok. Coconuts are still the mainstay of the local economy – up to two million are shipped to Bangkok each month. But there's no going back to 1971, when the first two tourists arrived on a coconut boat from Bangkok (much to the surprise of a friend who had been living on the island for four years as a Peace Corps volunteer).

Samui is different from other islands in southern Thailand and its inhabitants refer to themselves as *chao samŭi* (Samui folk) rather than Thais. They are even friendlier than the average upcountry Thai, in my opinion, and have a great sense of humour, although those who are in constant contact with tourists can be a bit jaded.

The island has a distinctive cuisine, influenced by the omnipresent coconut, the main source of income for chao samui. Coconut palms blanket the island, from the hillocks right up to the beaches. The durian, rambutan and langsat fruits are also cultivated.

The population of Ko Samui is for the most part concentrated in the port town of Na Thon, on the western side of the island facing the mainland, and in 10 or 11 small villages scattered around the island. One road encircles the island with several side roads poking into the interior; this main road is now paved all the way around.

One of my main complaints about Samui today is that the Reggae Pub (a large, commercial dance club at Chaweng Beach) has nailed too many signs to palms around the island – not only does it get quite monotonous, it spoils the natural scenery. Truer to

the reggae message, someone should start a campaign to get these removed.

Information

When to Go The best time to visit the Samui group of islands is during the hot and dry season, February to late June. From July to October it can be raining on and off, and from October to January there are sometimes heavy winds. However, many travellers have reported fine weather (and fewer crowds) in September and October. November tends to get some of the rain which also affects the east coast of Malaysia at this time. Prices tend to soar from December to July, whatever the weather.

Tourist Information A new TAT office at the northern end of Na Thon, past the post office on the west side of the road, dispenses the usual handy brochures and maps.

Surat Thani travel agents Songserm (☎ 421288), Island Jet (☎ 421222) and Phanthip have offices in Na Thon.

The nearest decent medical care is at the Taksin Hospital in Ban Don on the mainland.

Money Changing money isn't a problem in Na Thon, Chaweng or Lamai, where several banks or exchange booths offer daily exchange services.

Post & Telephone The island's main post office is in Na Thon, but in other parts of the island there are privately run branches. Many bungalow operations also sell stamps and mail letters, but most charge a commission.

International telephone service is available on the 1st floor of the post office. Many private phone offices around the island will make a connection for a surcharge over the usual TOT fees.

Immigration Travellers have been able to extend their tourist visas at the Ko Samui immigration office in Na Thon for 500B.

Maps In Surat or on Ko Samui, you can pick up TAT's helpful Surat Thani map, which has maps of Surat Thani, the province, Ang

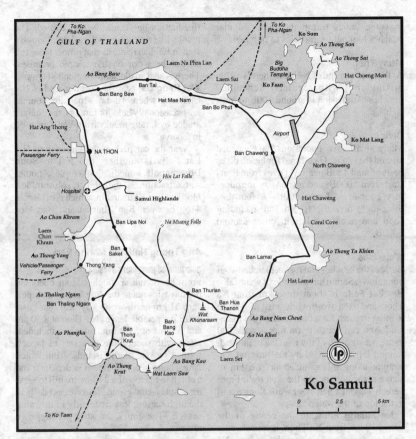

Ko Samui

0   2.5   5 km

Thong National Marine Park and Ko Samui, along with travel info. A couple of private companies now do good maps of Ko Samui, Pha-Ngan and Tao, which are available in tourist areas of Surat and on the islands for 35 to 40B. The most accurate and up-to-date is V Hongsombud's *Guide Map of Koh Samui, Koh Pha-Ngan & Koh Tao*.

Warning Several travellers have written to say take care with local agents for train and bus bookings. Bookings sometimes don't get made at all, the bus turns out to be far inferior to what was expected or other hassles develop. Take care with local boat trips to nearby islands reported another visitor. His boat was nearly swamped on a windy day and he eventually had to spend the night stranded on an uninhabited island.

Massage

Massages by male masseurs are often available for 50B at the sala opposite the post office in Na Thon, but women travellers should think about having massages only with women masseurs elsewhere. Several traditional massage houses are opening around the island as well, and the usual massage ladies tramp the more popular beaches looking for muscles to pummel.

Muay Thai
At the northern end of Na Thon there's a Thai boxing ring with regularly scheduled matches. Admission is around 100B to most fights.

Diving
Many small dive operations have opened around the island. Gear hired for beach dives costs around 450B per day. Dives from boats start from 1000B, and a four-day introductory course is about 5000B. A four-day, three-night dive trip to Ko Tao, including food and accommodation, costs around 5000B.

Waterfalls
Besides the beaches and rustic, thatched-roof bungalows, Samui has a couple of waterfalls. **Hin Lat Falls** is about three km from Na Thon and is a worthwhile visit if you're waiting in town for a boat back to the mainland. You can get there on foot – walk 100 metres or so south of town on the main road, turning left at the road by the hospital. Go straight along this road about two km to arrive at the entrance to the waterfall. From here, it's about a half-hour walk along a trail to the top of the waterfall.

Na Muang Falls, in the centre of the island 10 km from Na Thon, is more scenic and less frequented. A songthaew from Na Thon should be about 20B. Songthaews can also be hired at Chaweng and Lamai beaches.

Temples
For temple enthusiasts, at the southern end of the island, near the village of Bang Kao, **Wat Laem Saw** features an interesting old Srivijaya-style chedi. At the northern end, on a small rocky island joined to Samui by a causeway, is the so-called **Temple of the Big Buddha**, or Phra Yai. The modern image, about 12 metres in height, makes a nice silhouette against the tropical sky and sea behind it. The image is surrounded by kutis

(meditation huts), mostly unoccupied. The monks like receiving visitors there, though a sign in English requests that proper attire (no shorts) be worn on the temple premises. There is also an old semi-abandoned temple, **Wat Pang Ba**, near the northern end of Hat Chaweng where 10-day vipassana courses are occasionally held for farangs; the courses are led by farang monks from Wat Suanmok in Chaiya.

Near the car park at the entrance to Hin Lat Falls is another trail left to **Suan Dharmapala**, a meditation temple. Another wat attraction is the ghostly **Mummified Monk** at Wat Khunaraam, which is off Route 4169 between Ban Thurian and Ban Hua Thanon.

Ang Thong National Marine Park
อุทยานแห่งชาติทางทะเลอ่างทอง
From Ko Samui, a couple of tour operators run day trips out to the Ang Thong archipelago, 31 km north-west. A typical tour costs 300B per person, leaves Na Thon at 8.30 am and returns at 5.30 pm. Lunch is included, along with snorkelling in a sort of lagoon formed by one of the islands, from which Ang Thong gets its name (Golden Jar), and a climb to the top of a 240-metre hill to view the whole island group. Tours depart daily in the high season, less frequently in the rainy season. The tours are still getting rave reviews.

At least once a month there's also an overnight tour, as there are bungalows on Ko Wua Ta Lap. These cost 400B per person and include three meals and accommodation at the bungalows. You may be able to book a passage alone to the Ang Thong islands; enquire at Songserm Travel Service or Ko Samui Travel Centre in Na Thon.

Na Thon
หน้าทอน
On the upper west side of the island, Na Thon (pronounced *nâa thâwn*) is where express and night passenger ferries from the piers in Surat disembark. Car ferries from Don Sak

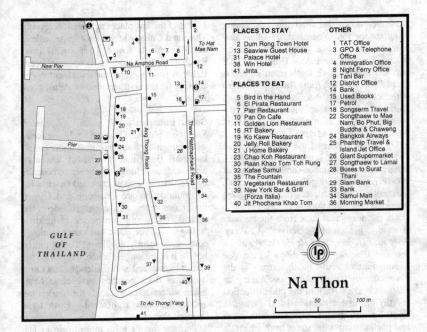

PLACES TO STAY
2 Dum Rong Town Hotel
13 Seaview Guest House
31 Palace Hotel
38 Win Hotel
41 Jinta

PLACES TO EAT
5 Bird in the Hand
6 El Pirata Restaurant
7 Pier Restaurant
10 Pan On Cafe
11 Golden Lion Restaurant
16 RT Bakery
19 Ko Kaew Restaurant
20 Jelly Roll Bakery
21 J Home Bakery
23 Chao Koh Restaurant
30 Raan Kham Tom Toh Rung
32 Kafae Samui
35 The Fountain
37 Vegetarian Restaurant
39 New York Bar & Grill (Forza Italia)
40 Jit Phochana Khao Tom

OTHER
1 TAT Office
3 GPO & Telephone Office
4 Immigration Office
8 Night Ferry Office
9 Tani Bar
12 District Office
14 Bank
15 Used Books
17 Petrol
18 Songserm Travel
22 Songthaew to Mae Nam, Bo Phut, Big Buddha & Chaweng
24 Bangkok Airways
25 Phanthip Travel & Island Jet Office
26 Giant Supermarket
27 Songthaew to Lamai
28 Buses to Surat Thani
29 Siam Bank
33 Bank
34 Samui Mart
36 Morning Market

Na Thon

and Khanom land at Ao Thong Yang, about 10 km south of Na Thon (see the Samui Beaches section later). If you're not travelling on a combination ticket you'll probably end up spending some time in Na Thon on your way in and/or out, waiting for the next ferry. Or if you're a long-term beachcomber, it makes a nice change to come into Na Thon once in a while for a little town life.

Although it's basically a tourist town now, Na Thon still sports a few old teak Chinese shophouses and cafes.

Places to Stay If you want or need to stay in Ko Samui's largest settlement there are six places to choose from at the time of writing.

If you're looking for something inexpensive, take a look at the *Seaview Guest House* on Wattana Rd, which has Khao San-style rooms with fan and shared bath for 150B, fan and private bath for 180 to 200B, and air-con for 300B – none of the rooms actually have sea views.

The *Palace Hotel* (Thai name: *Chai Thaleh*) has clean, spacious rooms starting at 280B with fan or 400B with air-con.

The *Win Hotel* farther down the road has all air-con rooms with TV and telephone for 420B, plus a nice coffee shop downstairs.

On the main road north out of town is the *Dum Rong Town Hotel*, which charges from 500B for rooms with fan and bath. *Chao Koh Bungalow*, just north of town nearer to the sea, is 300 to 800B. On the southern edge of town, the *Jinta* has pretty basic rooms for 150B.

Places to Eat There are several good restaurants and watering holes in Na Thon. On the road facing the harbour, the *Chao Koh Restaurant* is still serving good seafood and Thai standards at reasonable prices. *Ko Kaew* is a similar standby. A good place for breakfast is the *Jelly Roll*, a bakery with home-made pastries and coffee; other meals include burgers, sandwiches and pizza.

SOUTHERN THAILAND

Farther down the road towards Thong Yang are the *Pha-Ngan* and *Sri Samui* restaurants, both quite good Thai seafood places. Towards the Palace Hotel is a Thai rice and noodle place that's open all night, *Raan Khao Tom Toh Rung* (no English sign) – the cheapest place to eat on this strip. During the high season, many of these restaurants fill up at night with travellers waiting for the night ferry.

Up on the corner of the waterfront road and Na Amphoe Rd is the *Bird in the Hand*, a bar with a few tables and a variety of Western breakfasts (listed 'American', 'Australian', 'English', etc), plus sandwiches, imported beers and liquors.

On the next street back from the harbour is another branch of the Jelly Roll bakery, *Jelly Roll II*, then the *J Home Bakery* and a few old Chinese coffee shops like *Kafae Samui*. Farther south on this street is the *Fountain*, an Italian place specialising in pasta and pizza. Back in the other direction (north) on an intersection is *El Pirata*, a small Spanish garden restaurant with pizza and paella. Across the street from El Pirata is the *Golden Lion*, a medium-priced seafood place. Down the street a bit from El Pirata is the *Pier Restaurant*, a popular bar/restaurant with video to keep everyone seated and glassy-eyed. Other bars in the vicinity include the *Tani Bar* and the *Golden Lion Pub*, open only at night from around 6 pm to midnight. After midnight the only places open are the Khao Tom Toh Rung and the flashy Thai nightclub *Pan On Cafe*, which is rather expensive, dark and well chilled.

The third street back from the harbour is mostly travel agencies, photo shops and other small businesses. Two small supermarkets, Samui Mart and Giant Supermarket are also back here. The Charoen Laap morning market is still in operation on this street as well. Down at the southern end is the *New York Bar & Grill (Forza Italia)* with Italian and American-style deli food. The nearby *Tang's Restaurant & Bakery* is yet another place catering to farang tastes. The *RT Bakery* farther north on the same street is similar.

One of the few places in town still serving Thai (and Chinese) food on a large scale is *Jit Phochana Khao Tom* on Thawi Ratchaphakdi Rd, diagonally opposite Forza Italia. A small *vegetarian restaurant* opens at night on the southern end of Ang Thong Rd.

Samui Beaches

Samui has plenty of beaches to choose from, with bungalows appearing at more small bays all the time. Transport has also improved, so getting from beach to beach is no problem. The most crowded beaches for accommodation are Chaweng and Lamai, both more or less on the eastern side of the island. Chaweng has more bungalow 'villages' – over 80 at last count – plus a couple of recently developed flashy tourist hotels. It is the longest beach, over twice the size of Lamai, and has the island of **Mat Lang** opposite. Both beaches have clear blue-green waters and coral reefs for snorkelling and underwater sightseeing. Both have open-air discos.

Perhaps there's a bit more to do in Hat Lamai because of its proximity to two villages – Ban Lamai and Ban Hua Thanon. At the wat in Ban Lamai is the **Ban Lamai Cultural Hall**, a sort of folk museum displaying local ceramics, household utensils, hunting weapons and musical instruments.

Chaweng is definitely the target of current up-market development because of its long beach. Another factor is that only Chaweng Beach (and the northern part of Lamai) has water deep enough for swimming from October to April; most other beaches on the island become very shallow during these months.

For more peace and quiet, try the beaches along the north, south and west coasts. Mae Nam, Bo Phut and Big Buddha are along the northern end; Bo Phut and Big Buddha are part of a bay that holds **Ko Faan** (the island with the 'big Buddha'), separated by a small headland. The water here is not quite as clear as at Chaweng or Lamai, but the feeling of seclusion is greater, and accommodation is cheaper.

Hat Thong Yang is on the western side of the island and is even more secluded (only a few sets of bungalows there), but the beach isn't that great by Samui standards. There is also Hat Ang Thong, just north of Na Thon, very rocky but with more local colour (eg fishing boats) than the others. The southern end of the island now has many bungalows as well, set in little out-of-the-way coves – worth seeking out. And then there's everywhere in-between – every bay, cove or cape with a strip of sand gets a bungalow nowadays, right around the island.

Accommodation & Food Prices vary considerably according to the time of year and occupancy rates. Some of the bungalow operators on Samui have a nasty habit of tripling room rates when rooms are scarce, so a hut that's 80B in June could be 250B in August. Rates given in this section can only serve as a guideline – they could go lower if you bargain or higher if space is tight.

Everyone has his or her own idea of what the perfect beach bungalow is. At Ko Samui, the search could take a month or two, with over 200 operations to choose from. Most offer roughly the same services and accommodation for 80 to 400B, though some cost quite a bit more. The best thing to do is to go to the beach you think you want to stay at and pick one you like – look inside the huts,

check out the restaurant, the menu, the guests. You can always move if you're not satisfied.

Beach accommodation around Samui now falls into four basic categories chronicling the evolution of places to stay on the island. The first phase included simple bungalows with thatched roofs and walls of local, easily replaceable materials; the next phase brought concrete bathrooms attached to the old-style huts, a transition to the third phase of cement walls and tile roofs – the predominant style now, with more advanced facilities like fans and sometimes air-con. The latest wave is luxury rooms and bungalows indistinguishable from mainland inns and hotels.

Generally anything that costs less than 100B a night will mean a shared bath, which may be preferable when you remember that mosquitoes breed in standing water. For a pretty basic bungalow with private bath, 100 to 150B is the minimum on Ko Samui.

Theft isn't unknown on the island. If you're staying in a beach bungalow, consider depositing your valuables with the management while off on excursions around the island or while you're swimming at the beach. Most of the theft reports have come from Lamai and Mae Nam beaches.

Food is touch and go at all the beaches – one meal can be great, the next at the very

same place not so great. Fresh seafood is usually what they do best and the cheapest way to eat it is to catch it yourself and have the bungalow cooks prepare it for you, or buy it in one of the many fishing villages around the island, direct from the fisherfolk themselves, or in the village markets. Good places to buy are in the relatively large Muslim fishing villages of Mae Nam, Bo Phut and Hua Thanon.

The island has changed so much in the years between editions of this book (not to mention the way it has changed since 1971, when the first tourists arrived), that I hesitate to name favourites. Cooks come and go, bungalows flourish and go bankrupt, owners are assassinated by competitors – you never can tell from season to season. Prices have remained fairly stable here in recent years, unlike at Phuket, but they are creeping up. It's easy to get from one beach to another, so you can always change bungalows. The jet-set seems to be discovering Samui but, thank goodness, Club Med and Amanpuri decided to build on Phuket rather than here. Finally, if Samui isn't to your liking, move islands! Think about Ko Pha-Ngan or Ko Tao.

What follows are some general comments on staying at Samui's various beaches, moving clockwise around the island from Na Thon.

Ban Tai (Ao Bang Baw)
บ้านใต้ (อ่าวบางบ่อ)

Ban Tai is the first beach area north of Na Thon; so far there are six places to stay here. The beach has fair snorkelling and swimming. The *Axolotl Village*, run by an Italian-German partnership, caters to Europeans (the staff speaks English, Italian, German and French) with tastefully designed, mid-range rooms for 300B or bungalows for 400 to 600B. Meditation and massage rooms are available – a massage costs 150B per hour. A very pleasant restaurant area overlooking the beach has an inventive international menu.

Next door to the Axolotl is the similar-looking and similarly-priced *Blue River*,

under Thai management. Also at Ban Tai is *Sunbeam*, a set of bungalows in a very nice setting. Huts are 250 to 300B, all with private bath.

Hat Mae Nam
หาดแม่น้ำ

Hat Mae Nam is 14 km from Na Thon and expanding rapidly in terms of budget bungalow development – definitely the cheapest area on the island at the time of writing.

At the headland (Laem Na Phra Lan) where Ao Bang Baw ends and Mae Nam begins is the *Home Bay Bungalows* with basic huts for 80B and bungalows with bath for 200 to 400B. Next is *Coco Palm Village*, followed by *Plant Inn*, also spelt *Phalarn*, with bungalows from 50 to 200B.

Also in this area are *Naplarn Villa*, *Harry's* and *OK Village* – all in the 100 to 400B range. The beach in front of Wat Na Phalaan is undeveloped and the locals hope it will stay that way – topless bathing is strongly discouraged here.

The next group of places east includes *Shangrilah Bungalows*, *Anong Villa*, *Maenam Resort*, *Palm Point Village* and *Shady Shack Bungalows*, where prices start at 100 to 150B at Anong Villa. Maenam Resort (☎ 425116) is a good mid-range place with spacious bungalows for 250 to 700B.

Ban Mae Nam's huge *Santiburi Resort Hotel* (☎ 425338) – complete with tennis courts, waterways, ponds, bakery and sports facilities – costs from 7651B.

Right in Ban Mae Nam are *Lolita Bungalows* (200 to 400B) and the new *Maenam Inn*, a hotel on the circuit road with air-con rooms for 430B in the low season, 650B in the high, or 780B with TV.

Down on Hat Mae Nam proper is *Friendly*, which has clean, well-kept huts for 80B, or 100 to 200B with private bath. Also good are *New La Paz Villa* (60 to 200B, or up to 400 with air-con) and *Silent* (70 to 150B).

Moving towards Bo Phut you'll find *Moon Hut Bungalows*, *Rose Bungalows*, *Laem Sai Bungalows*, *Maenam Villa* and *Rainbow Bungalows*.

There are at least 10 or 15 other bungalow operations between Laem Na Phra Lan and Laem Sai, where Ao Mae Nam ends. The *Ubon Villa* (100 to 150B) is one of the better ones.

Hat Bo Phut

หาดบ่อผุด

This beach has a reputation for peace and quiet; there are about 20 places to stay here in total.

Near Bo Phut village there's a string of bungalows in all price ranges, including *Bo Phut Guesthouse* (80 to 200B), *Sandy Resort* (400 to 800B), *World Resort* (150 to 1000B), *New Sala Thai* (80 to 200B), *Samui Palm Beach* (1404 to 2340B), *Palm Garden* (100 to 250B), *Calm Beach Resort* (100 to 400B), *Peace* (150 to 350B), plus the *Allson Resort Samui Euphoria* (☎ 425100; fax 425107), a semi-luxury place in the 3400 to 4000B range.

Proceeding east, a road off the main round-island road runs to the left and along the bay towards the village. Here you'll find the original *Boon Bungalows*, a small operation with simple 50B huts, as well as large, comfortable bungalows with two beds, fan and hot water for 600 to 800B. The restaurant at Boon is good. West of Boon's is *Ziggy Stardust*, a clean and popular place with huts for 500B. Next to Ziggy's is the *Siam Sea Lodge*, a small hotel with rooms for 250B with fan, hot water and fridge, or 400B with ocean view. You'll find several more cheapies along this strip, including *Miami*, in the 120 to 200B range, and *Oasis*, with huts in the 50 to 150B range. In the same vicinity, *Smile House* now starts at 350B.

If you continue through the village along the water, you'll find the isolated *Sand Blue* with huts for 200 to 400B, and *Sky Blue* in the 40 to 80B range. This area is sometimes called Hat Bang Rak.

The village has a couple of cheap local-style restaurants as well as French, German, Spanish and Italian restaurants. The Australian-managed *Boathouse* has good Western and Thai food in a nice setting, and great cocktails. They are also an agent for a PADI diving school.

Big Buddha Beach (Hat Phra Yai)

หาดพระใหญ่

This now has nearly 20 bungalow operations, including the moderately expensive air-con *Comfort Resort Nara Garden* (☎ 421364), with rooms for 1590 to 2080B and a swimming pool. *Family Village* gets good reviews and costs 200 to 700B. *Big Buddha Bungalows* (250 to 500B) is still OK. *Sun Set* is about the cheapest places here now, with simple huts at 70 to 120B. *Como's*, *Champ Resort*, *Beach House*, *Kinnaree* and *Number One* are in the 150 to 300B range. The Beach House also has huts for 100B. *Niphon* has been rebuilt and the new bungalows now cost from 350 to 800B.

Ao Thong Son & Ao Thong Sai

อ่าวท้องสน/อ่าวท้องไทร

The big cape between Big Buddha and Chaweng is actually a series of four capes and coves, the first of which is Ao Thong Son. The road to Thong Son is a bit on the hellish side, but that keeps this area quiet and secluded. *Samui Thongson Resort* has its own cove and bungalows for 200B with fan, 850 to 1200B with air-con. *Thongson Bay Bungalows* next door has old-style bungalows for 100 to 150B; farther on is the similar *Golden Pine* with 300B bungalows.

The next cove over is as yet undeveloped and there isn't even a dirt road there yet. The third, Ao Thong Sai, has *Tongsai Bay Hotel & Cottages* (☎ 421451), a heavily guarded resort with a private beach, swimming pool and tennis courts. Rates start at 4700B.

Hat Choeng Mon

หาดเชิงมน

The largest cove following Ao Thong Sai has been called by several names, but the beach is generally known as Hat Choeng Mon. Here you'll find *PS Villa* (250 to 600B), *Choeng Mon Palace* (80 to 650B), *Chat Kaew Resort* (500 to 1000B), *Island View*

(200 to 300B) and the well laid-out *Sun Sand Resort* (1250B), which has sturdy thatched-roof bungalows connected by wooden walkways on a breezy hillside. Across from the beach is **Ko Faan Yai**, an island that can be reached on foot in low tide.

Next is a smaller bay called Ao Yai Noi, just before north Chaweng. This little bay is quite picturesque, with large boulders framing the beach. The secluded *IKK* bungalows are 300 to 500B and the *Coral Bay Resort* has larger bungalows with air-con for 1800B.

Hat Chaweng

หาดเฉวง

Hat Chaweng, Samui's longest beach, also has the island's highest concentration of bungalows and is even getting a few tourist hotels. Prices are moving up-market fast; accommodation is now perhaps 50B at the lowest in the off season, and up to 2500B at the Imperial Samui. There is a little commercial 'strip' behind the central beach with restaurants, souvenir shops and discos. If there are a lot of vacant huts (there usually are during the low season) you can sometimes talk prices down to 50B for a basic hut. The beach is beautiful here, and local developers are finally cleaning up some of the trashy areas behind the bungalows that were becoming a problem in the early 1980s.

Chaweng has km after km of beach and bungalows – perhaps 70 or more in all – so have a look around before deciding on a place. There are basically three sections: North Chaweng, Hat Chaweng proper and Chaweng Noi.

North Chaweng places are mostly in the 100 to 800B range, with simple bungalows with private bath at the northernmost end. These include the *Matlang Resort* (400 to 800B), *Samui Island Resort* (400 to 700B), *Marine* (150 to 300B), *Moon* (100 to 300B), *Family* (150 to 300) and *K John Resort* (150 to 350B). The most inexpensive place, *Blue Lagoon Bungalow*, charges 80 to 400B. At the end nearest to central Chaweng are a group of up-market places starting at 2000B:

Samui Villa Flora, *Amari Palm Reef Hotel* and *Blue Lagoon Hotel* (☎ 422037; fax 422401). There are also two mid-range places in the area, the *J P Palace* (350B to 1200B) and *The Island* (200 to 1500B).

The central area, Hat Chaweng proper, is the longest and has the most bungalows and hotels. This is also where the strip behind the hotels and huts is centred, with restaurants (most with videos), bars (yes, the girlie bar scene is sneaking in), discos, video parlours, pool halls, tourist police, TAT office, post office, mini-marts, one-hour photo-developing labs, tailors, souvenir shops and currency exchange booths. The *Manohra* restaurant here features classical southern-Thai dance performances with dinner.

Water sports are big here, too, so you can rent sailboards, go diving, sail a catamaran, charter a junk and so on. Parasailing costs around 400B and water-skiing is about 300B per hour. This area also has the highest average prices on the island, not only because accommodation is more up-market but simply because this is/was the prettiest beach on the island. In general, the places get more expensive as you move from north to south; many of these are owned by the same families who owned them under different names 10 or 15 years ago, some have just added the word 'Resort' to the name. The *Reggae Pub* has built a huge new zoo-like complex off the beach with many bars, a huge dance floor with high-tech equipment and trendy DJs who play music customers can bop to most of the night. Another popular dance place is the *Green Mango*, which closes earlier – this is where people usually start the night. Rather than list all the places on Chaweng Central, I'll just give examples across the spectrum, starting at the north:

Chaweng Villa, 600 to 1200B (air-con)
Lucky Mother, 100 to 250B
Coconut Grove, 200 to 300B
Chaweng Garden, 400 to 800B
Malibu Resort, 400 (fan) to 1300B (air-con)
Long Beach, 1200B
Thai House, 150 to 200B
Charlie's Hut, 100 to 350B
The Village, 1100 to 1400B

Joy Resort, 150 to 700B
Munchies Resort, 200 to 700B

If you're getting the idea that this isn't the beach for backpackers, you're right, but surprisingly a string of popular cheapies has survived between the Beachcomber and Central Bay Resort. From the northern end is *Silver Sand* (150 to 300B), followed by the least expensive, *Cheap Charlie*, with rustic huts in the 60 to 80B range. Better but more expensive huts can be found at *Charlie's Hut III* for 150 to 250B, while next door *Viking* starts at 100B, followed by the similarly priced *Thai House* and *Charlie's Hut*. In peak season these places fill early, so to save money it may be easier to go to another beach entirely – or try North Chaweng.

Chaweng Noi is off by itself around a headland at the southern end of central Hat Chaweng. One place that straddles the headland on both bays is the aptly named *First Bungalows* (they were the first to build on this beach 14 years ago), with wooden bungalows for 550B and concrete-and-tile types for 700B up. The *New Star* starts at 350B. Nearby *Fair House* has fan-cooled rooms for 450B, air-con up to 1200B.

Samui's top property at the moment, the *Imperial Samui*, is built on a slope in the middle of Chaweng Noi proper and costs 3500 to 5100B for air-con accommodation with telephone and colour TV – up to 40% less in the off-season. The Imperial's 56 cottages and 24-room hotel are built in a pseudo-Mediterranean style with a 700-sq-metre salt-water swimming pool and a terrace restaurant with a view. Not very far from the Imperial is the upgraded *Sunshine*, which at the time of writing was being rebuilt yet again. The *Chaweng Noi*, at the southern end of the beach, is the only cheap place left – huts cost 100 to 140B. Finally there's the *Tropicana Beach Resort* with all air-con rooms at 800 to 1200B.

Coral Cove (Ao Thong Yang)
อ่าวท้องยาง
Another series of capes and coves starts at

the end of Chaweng Noi, beginning with scenic Coral Cove. Somehow the Thais have managed to squeeze three places around the cove, plus one across the road. The only one with immediate beach access is *Coral Cove Resort*, where basic huts start at 150B and go up to 500B for a decent bungalow with fan, 850B with air-con. The *Hi Coral Cove* above is 180 to 250B. The *Coral Mountain Chalets*, on the hill opposite the road, costs 350 to 500B.

Ao Thong Ta Khian
อ่าวท้องตะเคียน
This is another small, steep-sided cove, similar to Coral Cove and banked by huge boulders. The *Samui Silver Beach Resort* has bungalows overlooking the bay for 400B with fan or 850B with air-con. On the other side of the road is the *Little Mermaid* with bungalows for 200 and 325B. This is a good spot for fishing, and there are a couple of good seafood restaurants down on the bay.

Hat Lamai
หาดละไม
After Chaweng, this is Samui's most popular beach for farangs. Hat Lamai rates are just a bit lower than at Chaweng overall, without the larger places like the Pansea or Imperial (yet) and fewer of the 500B-plus places. As at Chaweng, the bay has developed in sections, with a long central beach flanked by hilly areas. Recently there have been reports of burglaries and muggings at Lamai. Take care with valuables – have them locked away in a guesthouse or hotel office if possible. Muggings mostly occur in dark lanes and along unlit parts of the beach at night.

Accommodation prices at the northeastern end of the beach are moderate. At the top of the beach is the friendly and peaceful *New Hut*, with 60B huts which can accommodate two people. Others farther south are *Thong Gaid Garden* (120 to 200B), *Royal Blue Lagoon Beach Resort* (250B), *Comfort* (200 to 400B) and, back from the beach, *My Friend* (60 to 120B). More expensive are the newer places, including *Island Resort* (300

SOUTHERN THAILAND

to 500B), *Rose Garden* (250 to 400B) and *Suksamer* (150 to 300B). There are a sprinkling of others here that seem to come and go with the seasons.

Down into the main section of Lamai is a string of places for 100 to 600B including *Mui*, *Utopia*, *Magic*, *Coconut Villa* and the *Weekender*. The Weekender has a wide variety of bungalows and activities to choose from, including a bit of a nightlife. Moving into the centre of Ao Lamai, you'll come across *Coconut Beach* (80 to 200B), *Animal House* (skip this one, it's received several complaints), *Lamai Inn* (300 to 800B) and the *Best Resort* (350 to 700B).

This is the part of the bay closest to Ban Lamai village and the beginning of the Lamai 'scene'. Just about every kind of service is available here, including exchange offices, medical service units, supermarkets, one-hour photo labs, clothing shops, bike and jeep-rental places, travel agencies with postal and international telephone services, restaurants (many with videos), discos, bars, bungee-jumping and food stalls. The girlie bar scene has invaded this part of the island, with several lanes lined with Pattaya-style outdoor bars. The difference here is that unlike in Pattaya and other similar mainland places, where Western males tend to be seen in the company of Thai females, you'll see many Western women spending their holiday with Thai boys.

Next comes a string of slightly up-market 100 to 600B places: *Thai House Inn*, *Marina Villa*, *Sawatdi*, *Mira Mare*, *Sea Breeze*, and *Varinda Resort*. The *Aloha* (☎ 421418) has been rebuilt into a two-storey luxury hotel where bungalows start from 1400B, rooms from 2200B. All of these have fairly elaborate dining areas; the Aloha has a good restaurant with seafood, Thai and European food. Also in this area are the *Galaxy Resort* (250 to 600B) and *Golden Sand* (450 to 950B).

Finishing up central Hat Lamai is a mixture of 50 to 80B and 100 to 200B places. *Paradise* has been here for 19 years and is the second-longest-running place on the beach, with thatched huts from 80B and con-

crete bungalows for 500B. The *White Sand* is another Lamai original and huts are still 50B and up. A farang flea market is held here on Sundays – many travellers sell handmade jewellery. The long-standing *Palm* is still here as well, but they've upgraded the bungalows to the 150 to 250B price range. The *Nice Resort* has huts for 150B up but they're really too close together. Finally, there's the *Sun Rise*, where acceptable huts go for 100 and 200B, new bungalows for 400B with fan or 1000B with air-con.

A place with good French bread, croissants and cakes is *Will Wait* in the centre of the village. They open very early for breakfast, close after 10 pm and are popular for inexpensive travellers' food. Bauhaus Pub is Lamai's most popular disco.

At this point a headland interrupts Ao Lamai and the bay beyond is known as **Ao Bang Nam Cheut**, named after the freshwater stream that runs into the bay here. During the dry months the sea is too shallow for swimming here, but in the late rainy season when the surf is too high elsewhere on the island's beaches, south Lamai is one of the best for swimming. Look for the well-known, phallus-like 'Grandmother' and 'Grandfather' rock formations.

Closer to the road than the coast is the *Samui Park*, with bungalows from 1800B. Down further, *Noi* offers huts starting at 80B and bungalows from 150B. Next is *Chinda House*, with air-con bungalows for 1200 to 2000B. The *Swiss Chalet* has large bungalows overlooking the sea for 200B and the restaurant does Swiss as well as Thai food. Then comes the old-timer *Rocky*, with thatched huts from 80B and sturdier bungalows for up to 400B.

Ao Na Khai & Laem Set
อ่าวหน้าค่าย/แหลมเส็ด

Just beyond the village of Ban Hua Thanon at the southern end of Ao Na Khai is an area sometimes called Hat Na Thian. As at Lanai, the places along the southern end of the island are pretty rocky, which means good snorkelling (there's a long reef here), but perhaps not such good swimming. Prices in this area seem fairly reasonable – 100B here gets you what 200B might in Chaweng. The hard part is finding these places, since they're off the round-island road, down dirt tracks, and most don't have phones. You might try exploring this area on a motorcycle first. The *Cosy Resort* has 11 well-spaced huts for 100 to 200B. Next is the *Royal Resort* with bungalows for 400B with fan and up to 1000B with air-con. The cheaper *Wanna Samui Resort* has bungalows with fan for 250 and air-con for 950B.

Down a different road in the same area is the *Samui Orchid Resort* (☎ 424017), which, with huts for 650 to 1200B and a swimming pool, is slightly up-market.

Turn right here, follow the coast and you'll come to the basic *Sonny View* (60B) and the nicely designed *Na Thian* (100 to 150B). At the end of the road is the secluded *Laem Set Inn* (☎ (01) 212-2762). Rates vary from 2500B for a standard bungalow to 4500B for a larger one – priced at least 1000B above market.

Ao Bang Kao
อ่าวบางเก่า

This bay is at the very south end of the island between Laem Set and Laem So (Saw). Again, you have to go off the round-island road a couple of km to find these places: *River Garden* (60 to 150B), *Diamond Villa* (60 to 300B), *Samui Coral Beach* (120 to 400B) and *Waikiki* (300 to 400B).

Ao Thong Krut & Ko Taen
อ่าวท้องกรูดและเกาะแตน

Next to the village of Ban Thong Krut on Ao Thong Krut is, what else, *Thong Krut*, where huts with private bath are only 100B.

Ban Thong Krut is also the jumping-off point for boat trips to four offshore islands: **Ko Taen, Ko Raap, Ko Mat Daeng** (best coral) and **Ko Mat Sum**. Ko Taen has three bungalow villages along the east-coast beach at Ao Awk: *Tan Village*, *Ko Tan Resort* and *Coral Beach*, all in the range of 80 to 250B

a night. Ko Mat Sum has g... some travellers have camped...

Boats to Ko Taen cost 40B... you want to have a good look..., you can charter a boat at the *Sunset Restaurant* in Thong Krut from 9 am to 4 pm for 900 to 1100B; the boats carry up to 10 people. The Sunset Restaurant has good seafood (best to arrange in advance) and delicious coconut shakes.

West Coast

Several bays along Samui's western side have places to stay, including Thong Yang, where the Don Sak ferry docks. The beaches here turn to mud flats during low tide, however, so they're more or less for people seeking to get away from the east coast scene, not for beach fanatics.

Ao Phangka Around Laem Hin Khom on the bottom of Samui's western side is this little bay, sometimes called Emerald Cove. The secluded *Emerald Cove* and *Sea Gull* have huts with rates from 80 to 300B – it's a nice setting and perfectly quiet. Between them are the newer and slightly cheaper *Gem House* and *Pearl Bay*.

Ao Thong Yang The car ferry jetty is here in Ao Thong Yang. Near the pier are *In Foo Palace* (60 to 400B), *Coco Cabana Beach Club* (400B) and the motel-like *Samui Ferry Inn* (500 to 900B). The Coco Cabana is the best of the lot.

Ao Chon Khram On the way to Na Thon is sweeping Ao Chon Khram, with the *Lipa Lodge* and *International*. The Lipa Lodge is especially nice, with a good site on the bay. Rates start at 80B; most huts are about 100 to 120B, with a few as high as 650B. There is a good restaurant and bar here, not bad for the money. On the other hand, the International is nothing special at 200 to 500B. Between them is the up-market *Rajapruek Samui Resort* (1500 to 3500B), and farther north the isolated and slightly more expensive *The Siam Residence Resort*.

...tting There & Away

Air Bangkok Airways flies daily to Ko Samui using 56-seat Dash 80-300 planes. There is an office in Na Thon opposite the pier and another at the airport (☎ 425012). The fare is 2080B one way – no discount for a return ticket. The flight duration is one hour and 10 minutes, with flights departing Bangkok five times daily.

Bangkok Airways also offers two flights a week between Samui and Phuket for 1120B one way. This flight takes 40 minutes.

During high season flights may be completely booked out as much as six weeks in advance, so be sure to plan accordingly. An alternative is to fly out of Surat Thani on THAI (see the Surat Thani Getting There & Away section for details).

The Samui Airport departure tax is 100B. Bangkok Airways has a limo for 60B per person to/from its Na Thon office; the limo also departs from JR Bungalow on Chaweng Beach and Best Resort in Lamai. Chartered taxis from the airport cost 150B to anywhere on the island.

Bus The government bus/ferry combo fare from Bangkok's northern air-con bus terminal is 327B. Most private buses from Bangkok charge around 350B for the same journey. From Khao San Rd in Bangkok it's possible to get bus/ferry combination tickets for as low as 220B, but service is substandard and theft is more frequent than on the more expensive buses.

Train The SRT also does train/bus/ferry tickets straight through to Samui from Bangkok. The fares are 419B for a 2nd-class upper berth, 449B for a 2nd-class lower berth, 344B for a 2nd-class seat and 244B for a 3rd-class seat. This includes rapid service and berth charges; add 100B for air-con. This only comes out cheaper than doing the connections yourself if you buy the 2nd-class seat. For all other tickets it's 30 to 50B more expensive – which may be worth it to avoid the hassles of separate bookings.

Boat To sort out the ferry situation you have to understand first that there are two ferry companies, one jetboat company and three ferry piers on the Surat Thani coast (actually four but only three are in use at one time) and two on Ko Samui. Neither ferry company is going to tell you about the other. Songserm Travel runs express ferry boats from the Tha Thong pier, six km north-east of central Surat, and slow night boats from the Ban Don pier in town. These take passengers only. The express boats used to leave from the same pier in Ban Don as the night ferry – when the river is unusually high they may use this pier again.

Samui Ferry Co runs vehicle ferries from Don Sak (or Khanom when the sea is high). This is the company that gets most of the bus/boat and some of the train/bus/boat combination business.

Which boat you take will depend on what's next available when you arrive at the bus terminal in Surat or train station in Phun Phin – touts working for the two ferry companies will lead you to one or the other.

During the low season (ie any time except November to February or August), Thai girls may throng the piers around departure time for the Ko Samui boats, inviting farangs to stay at this or that bungalow. This same tactic is employed at the Na Thon and Thong Yang piers upon arrival at Ko Samui. During the high tourist season, however, this isn't necessary as every place is just about booked out. Some of the more out-of-the-way places to stay put touts on the boats to pass around photo albums advertising their establishments.

Express Boat to/from Tha Thong From November to May three express boats go to Samui (Na Thon) daily from Tha Thong and each takes two to 2½ hours to reach the island. From November to May the departure times are usually 7.15 am, 11.30 am and 2.45 pm, though these change from time to time. From June to October there are only two express boats a day, at 7.15 am and 12.30 pm – the seas are usually too high in the late afternoon for a third sailing in this direction during the rainy season. Passage is 105B one way, 170B return. The express ferry boats have two decks, one with seats below and an upper deck that is really just a big luggage rack – good for sunbathing.

From Na Thon back to Surat, there are departures at 7.15 am, noon and 2.30 pm from November to May, or 7.30 am and 2.30 pm from June to October. The 7.15 am boat includes a bus ride to the train station in Phun Phin; the afternoon boats include a bus to the train station and to the Talaat Kaset bus station in Ban Don.

Night Ferry to/from Ban Don There is also a slow boat for Samui that leaves the Ban Don pier each night at 11 pm, reaching Na Thon around 5 am. This one costs 70B for the upper deck (includes pillows and mattresses), or 50B down below (straw mats only). This trip is not particularly recommended unless you arrive in Surat Thani too late for the fast boat and don't want to stay in Ban Don. Some travellers have reported, however, that a night on the boat is preferable to a night in a noisy Surat Thani short-time hotel. And it does give you more sun time on Samui, after all. The night ferry back to Samui leaves Na Thon at 9 pm, arriving at 3 am.

Don't leave your bags unattended on the night ferry, as thefts can be a problem. The thefts usually occur after you drop your bags on the ferry well before departure and then go for a walk around the pier area. Most victims don't notice anything's missing until they unpack after arrival on Samui.

Jet Boat to/from Tha Thong The new Island Jet service takes 1½ hours from Tha Thong to Na Thon and costs 130B each way. Island Jet or Phanthip Travel can book the jet boat in Surat or in Na Thon. For some people a saving of an hour's time (over the regular express boat) is worth 25B; for others maybe not.

The Island Jet departs for Samui from Surat Thani at 8 am and continues to Ko Pha-Ngan at 10.20 am. On the return journey it leaves Pha-Ngan at 12.30 pm, stopping at

Na Thon at 2 pm for the final return to Tha Thong.

Vehicle Ferry to/from Don Sak Tour buses run directly from Bangkok to Ko Samui, via the car ferry from Don Sak in Surat Thani Province, for around 327B. Check with the big tour bus companies or any travel agency.

From Talaat Mai Rd in Surat Thani you can also get bus/ferry combination tickets straight through to Na Thon. These cost 70B for an ordinary bus, 90B for an air-con bus. Pedestrians or people in private vehicles can also take the ferry directly from Don Sak, which leaves at 6.50, 8, 10 am, noon, 2 and 5 pm, and takes one hour to reach the Thong Yang pier on Samui. In the opposite direction, ferries leave Thong Yang at 7.30 and 10 am, noon, 2 and 4 pm.

The fare for pedestrians is 40B, for a motorcycle and driver 70B, and for a car and driver 180B. Passengers on private vehicles pay the pedestrian fare. The ferry trip takes about 1½ hours to reach Don Sak, which is 60 km from Surat Thani.

Buses between the Surat Thani bus station and Don Sak cost 14B and take 45 minutes to an hour to arrive at the ferry terminal. If you're coming north from Nakhon Si Thammarat, this might be the ferry to take, though from Surat Thani the Tha Thong ferry is definitely more convenient.

From Ko Samui, air-con buses to Bangkok leave from near the old pier in Na Thon at 1.30 and 3.30 pm daily, both arriving in Bangkok around 5 am due to a stopover in Surat. Other through bus services from Na Thon include Hat Yai (200B), Krabi (191B) and Phuket (193B); all of these buses leave Na Thon around 7 am, arriving at their respective destinations around six hours later. Check with the several travel agencies in Na Thon for the latest routes.

Getting Around

It is quite possible to hitch around the island, despite the fact that anyone on the island with a car is likely to want to boost their income by charging for rides.

Local Transport The official songthaew fares are 15B from Na Thon to Lamai, 10B to Mae Nam or Bo Phut, 15B to Big Buddha, 20B to Chaweng or Choeng Mon. From the car-ferry landing in Thong Yang, rates are 20B for Lamai, Mae Nam and Bo Phut/Big Buddha, 25B for Chaweng, 30B for Choeng Mon. These minibuses run regularly during daylight hours only. A bus between Thong Yang and Na Thon is 10B. Songthaew drivers like to overcharge newcomers, so take care. Note that if you're arriving in Thong Yang on a bus (via the vehicle ferry), your bus/boat fare includes a ride into Na Thon.

Car & Motorbike Rental Several places rent motorcycles in Na Thon and at various bungalows around the island. The going rate is 150B per day for a 100cc bike, but for longer periods you can get the price down (say 280B for two days, 400B for three days, etc). Rates are generally lower in Na Thon and it makes more sense to rent them there if you're going back that way. Take it easy on the bikes; several farangs die or are seriously injured in motorcycle accidents every year on Samui, and, besides, the locals really don't like seeing their roads become race tracks.

Suzuki Caribian jeeps can be hired for around 700 to 800B per day from various Na Thon agencies as well as at Chaweng and Lamai.

KO PHA-NGAN
เกาะพะงัน

Ko Pha-Ngan, about a half-hour boat ride north of Ko Samui, has become the island of choice for those who find Samui too crowded. It started out as sort of 'back-door escape' from Samui but is well established now, with a regular boat service and over 180 places to stay around the 190-sq-km island. It's definitely worth a visit for its remaining deserted beaches (they haven't all been built upon) and, if you like snorkelling, for its live-coral formations.

In the interior of this somewhat smaller island are the **Than Sadet** and **Phaeng** waterfalls.

Although hordes of backpackers have discovered Ko Pha-Ngan, a lack of roads has so far spared it from tourist-hotel and package-tour development. Compared to Samui, Ko Pha-Ngan has a lower concentration of bungalows, less crowded beaches and coves, and an overall less 'spoiled' atmosphere. Pha-Ngan aficionados say the seafood is fresher and cheaper than on Samui's beaches, but it really varies from place to place. As Samui becomes more expensive for both travellers and investors, more and more people will be drawn to Pha-Ngan. But for the time being, overall living costs are about half what you'd pay on Samui.

Except at the island's party capital, Hat Rin, the island hasn't yet been cursed with video and blaring stereos; unlike on Samui, travellers actually interact instead of staring over one another's shoulders at a video screen.

Wat Khao Tham
วัดเขาถ้ำ

This cave temple is beautifully situated on top of a hill near the little village of Ban Tai. An American monk lived here for over a decade and his ashes are interred on a cliff overlooking a field of palms below the wat. It's not a true wat since there are only two monks and a nun in residence (a quorum of five monks is necessary for wat status).

Ten-day meditation retreats taught by an American-Australian couple are held here during the latter half of most months. The cost is 900B; write in advance for information or pre-register in person. A bulletin board at the temple also has information.

Thong Sala
ท้องศาลา

Ko Pha-Ngan has a total population of roughly 7500 and about half of them live in and around the small port town of Thong Sala. This is where the ferry boats from Surat and Samui (Na Thon) dock, although there

Ko Pha-Ngan

0   2.5   5 km

are also smaller boats from Mae Nam and Bo Phut on Samui.

Information Thong Sala is the only place on the island where you can post or receive mail, and is one of only two places (the other is Hat Rin) where you can change money at regular bank rates. The post office is at the southern end of town, in the direction of Hat Rin. Opposite is a shop with a parcel/packaging service; they also sell stamps. Next door is the Siam City Bank, with an exchange facility open daily from 8.30 am to 6 pm.

The town sports several restaurants, travel agents, clothing shops and general stores. You can also rent motorcycles here for 150 to 250B per day.

Places to Stay Although it is possible to rent rooms in Thong Sala, most people of course choose to stay at one of Pha-Ngan's beaches.

In town the *Shady Nook Guest House* offers basic rooms for 100B a night. *Blackhouse Guest House* has fine rooms for 150B. The new *Buakao Inn* is also good, with clean singles/doubles for 150/250B with fan or 350B with air-con, while the similarly priced

...is not as nice. There is also a ...me hotel that's mostly used as the ...el for 80 to 100B a night.

The new luxury *Pha-Nga Central Hotel* (☎ 377068; fax 377032) is about 150 metres south of the pier. Fan-cooled rooms cost 400B, while air-con rooms with an ocean view and TV cost 900B.

Ao Nai Wok

There are a few beach bungalows within a couple of km north of the pier. Although the beach here isn't spectacular, it's a fairly nice area to while away a few days – especially if you need to be near Thong Sala for some reason. People waiting for an early boat back to Surat or on to Ko Tao may choose to stay here (or south of Thong Sala at Ao Bang Charu) since transport times from other parts of the island can be unpredictable.

Turn left at the first crossing from the pier, then walk straight till the road becomes a sandy trail, cross a concrete footbridge, and then turn left again at a larger dirt road. Soon you'll come to *Phangan* (40 to 300B), *Chan* (80B), *Siriphun* (100 to 400B) and *Tranquil Resort* (60 to 200B) – a distance of about two km in all. Siriphun seems particularly good value and has a good kitchen.

Ko Pha-Ngan Beaches

A few years ago the only beaches with accommodation were just north and south of Thong Sala and on the southern end of the island at Hat Rin. The bungalow operations are still mostly concentrated in these areas, but now there are many other places to stay around the island as well. Because there are almost no paved roads on Pha-Ngan, transport can be a bit of a problem, though the situation is constantly improving as enterprising Thais set up taxi and boat services between the various beaches.

Many of the huts on Pha-Ngan have been established by entrepreneurs from Ko Samui with several years' experience in the bungalow business. Huts go for 60 to 100B a night on average; many do not have electricity or running water. Some have generators which are only on for limited hours in the evening

– the lights dim when they make a fruit shake. For many people, of course, this adds to Pha-Ngan's appeal. Other places are moving into the 100 to 300B range, which almost always includes a private bath. As travel to Pha-Ngan seems particularly seasonal, you should be able to talk bungalow rates down 30% to 40% when occupancy is low. During the peak months (December to February and July and August), there can be an acute shortage of rooms at the most popular beaches and even the boats coming to the island can be dangerously over-crowded.

Since many of the cheaper bungalows make the bulk of their profits from their restaurants rather than from renting huts, bungalow owners have been known to eject guests who don't take meals where they're staying after a few days. The only way to avoid this, besides foregoing your own choice of restaurants, is to get a clear agreement beforehand on how many days you can stay. This seems to be a problem only at the cheaper (40 to 60B) places.

There are a number of beaches with accommodation on Pha-Ngan; the following are listed moving in an anti-clockwise direction away from Thong Sala.

Ao Bang Charu South of Thong Sala, the shallow beach here is not one of the island's best, but it's close to town and so is popular with people waiting for boats or bank business.

Petchr Cottage, Phangan Villa, Nawin House, Moonlight, Sun Dance, Weang Thai, Bamboo Huts, Charm Beach Resort and *Chokkhana Resort* are all in the 60 to 300B range. The Charm Beach Resort is recommended for its well-maintained bungalows, which cost up to 500B, and its restaurant. Farther south-east towards Ban Tai are a few other places strung along the coast, including the *First Villa, First Bay Resort, Laem Tanote Resort* and *P Park*, all for 40B up.

Ban Tai & Ban Khai Between the villages of Ban Tai and Ban Khai is a series of sandy beaches with well-spaced bungalow operations, mostly in the 40 to 100B range (a few also have 200B bungalows). Here you'll find *Birdville, Pink, Wave House, Jup, Sabai, Lee's Garden, Free Lover, Copa, Pan Beach, Pha-Ngan Rainbow, Green Peace, Golden Beach, Sun Sea, Banja Beach, Thong Yang, Pha-Ngan Island Resort* (350 to 450B), *Booms Cafe* and *Silvery Moon.*

In Ban Khai the locals also rent rooms to travellers, especially from December to February when just about everything is filled up. You can get a hut for a month at very low rates here.

Long-tail boats to/from Hat Rin cost 50B per person for one or two passengers, 30B if there are more than two passengers.

Laem Hat Rin This long cape juts south-east and has beaches along both its westward and eastward sides. The eastward side has the best beach, Hat Rin Nok, a long sandy strip lined with coconut palms. The snorkelling here is pretty good, but between October and March the surf can be a little hairy. The western side more or less acts as an overflow for people who can't find a place to stay on the eastern side, as the beach is often too shallow for swimming. Together these beaches have become the most popular on the island.

Along the central western beach, sometimes called Hat Rin Nai (Inner Rin Beach), you'll find long-runners *Palm Beach* (50 to 150B) and *Sunset Bay Resort* (80 to 200B), plus a string of places in the 70 to 250B range: *Neptune's Villa, Dolphin, Charung, Black & White, Friendly, Family House* and, down near the tip of the cape, *Lighthouse* (80B up). The *Rin Beach Resort* has a few larger huts with private bath and fan from 300B as well as concrete air-con bungalows for 1500B.

At the northern end of Hat Rin Nai, around a small headland, are the newer *Bang Son Villa, Blue Hill, Sun Beach, Sandy, Sea Side, Rainbow, Coral, Grammy* and *Sooksom*, all in the 50 to 100B range. For 80B, the nicest thatched bungalows are those at Blue Hill, situated on a hill above the beach.

Across the ridge on the east side is Hat Rin Nok (Outer Rin Beach), famous for its monthly 'full moon parties' featuring all-night beach dancing and the ingestion of various illicit substances – forget about sleeping on these nights. There are plenty of drugs available from the local drug mafia and drug-dependent visitors, and the police occasionally conduct raids. Travellers should be watchful of their personal safety at these parties, especially female travellers; assaults have occasionally been reported. Even when the moon isn't full, several establishments blast dance music all night long – head for the western side if you prefer a quieter atmosphere.

The bungalows here are stacked rather closely together and are among the most expensive on the island. They include *Seaview* (100 to 250B), *Tommy's Resort* (100 to 200B), *Phangan Bayshore Resort* (120 to 500B), *Sunrise* (150 to 350B), *Hat Rin Resort* (250 to 650B), *Pearl Resort* (150 to 250B), *Haad Rin* (100 to 150B), *Sea Garden* (80 to 150B) and *Paradise* on the hill side (150 to 250B). The *Palita Lodge* at the northern end of the beach has huts with private bath for 180 to 250B, plus cheaper 100B huts. The northern end of the beach (Seaview, Palita Lodge, Tommy's Resort) tends to be a little less congested than the central beach area.

Hat Rin Nok beach huts generally have electricity from 6 pm till midnight, though on full-moon nights the generators keep pumping out trance and hip-hop till 1 pm the next day! On both sides of Hat Rin, hammers and saws are busy putting together new huts, so there may be quite a few more places by now. Not only are the cliffs on each side of the bay filling up, but many one-storey hotels are now under construction back from the beach due to the popularity of the area. The dirt track behind the beach is lined with restaurants (most of which show videos nightly), bars, travel agents and mini-mart shops.

Restaurants here are getting almost as expensive as on Samui, but the seafood is good and fresh. One of the better restaurants (no video) is *Sand*; another is *Crab*. The *Haadrin Bakery & Restaurant* offers a wide variety of cakes, rolls and other baked goods.

East Coast Beaches Above Hat Rin Nok around a headland, at the north-eastern end of the bay, are the secluded *Mountain Sea* and *Serenity* with bungalows from 80 to 200B. Farther north along the coast there is accommodation at Hat Thian's *Sanctuary* (40 to 250B), but there was nothing else at the time of writing until **Hat Sadet**. A dirt track (traversable on foot but only partially by motorcycle) runs along the coast from Hat Rin before heading inland to Ban Nam Tok and Than Sadet Falls.

Between Hat Rin and the village of Ban Nam Tok are several little coves with the white-sand beaches of **Hat Yuan** (2.5 km north of Hat Rin), **Hat Yai Nam** (3.5 km), **Hat Yao** (five km) and **Hat Yang** (six km), all virtually deserted. Then, 2.5 km north of Ban Nam Tok by dirt track, is the pretty double bay of **Ao Thong Reng**, where *No Name* bungalows are 40B. Above the beach on the headland, *Than Wung Thong Resort* offers huts for 60 to 150B. North of the headland, a pretty cove ringed by Hat Sadet features *Nid's*, *J S Hut*, *Joke Bar* and *Mai Pen Rai*, all in the 50 to 80B range. The rough dirt track from Thong Sala is subject to weather; the 'Reggae boat' to/from Hat Rin (50B) and Thong Sala (70B) makes the trip by water every morning between September and April.

Ao Thong Nai Pan This bay is really made up of two bays, **Ao Thong Nai Pan Yai** and **Ao Thong Nai Pan Noi**. On the beach at Thong Nai Pan Yai, near Ban Thong Nai Pan village, are the *White Sand*, *A D V* and *Nice Beach*, all with huts from 60B with shared bath up to 300B for nicer ones with attached bath. The other end of the beach features the similarly priced *Pen's* and *Pingjun Resort*, along with the more basic *Chanchit Dreamland* at 70B per hut.

Up on Thong Nai Pan Noi are the very nicely situated *Panviman Resort* (☎ /fax 377048) and *Thong Ta Pan Resort*. Panvi-

man's wooden bungalows cost 300B with fan or up to 1500B with air-con, all with private bath. The more basic Thong Ta Pan Resort costs 80 to 150B. Between them is the similarly priced *Star Hut*, and the rock-bottom *Bio Guest House* with basic huts for 50B.

Hat Khuat & Chalok Lam These are two pretty bays with beaches on the northern end of Pha-Ngan, still largely undeveloped because of the distances involved from major transport points to Samui and the mainland. Some of the island's least expensive accommodation is found here – hence it's popular with long-termers – but that means more likelihood of being evicted from your hut if you don't buy meals from the bungalow kitchens. Be sure to establish whether you'll be required to buy meals before taking a hut.

Hat Khuat (Bottle Beach) is the smaller of the two and currently has three sets of bungalows, all in the 60 to 250B range – *Bottle Beach*, *Bottle Beach II* and *Rock Beach*. West of Hat Khuat, 2.5 km across Laem Kung Yai, is **Hat Khom**, where the *Coral Bay* rents standard huts for 40 and 50B. *Buddy*, on the Chalok Lam side, has huts for just 30B. You can walk to Hat Khuat from Ban Chalok Lam but until they build a better bridge over Khlong Ok, no jeeps or motorcycles can access it – all the better for quiet days and nights.

East of the fishing village of Ban Chalok Lam, where the drying of squid seems to be the main activity, are *Mr Phol's*, *Fanta*, *Try Tong Resort* and *Thai Life*, all with simple huts for 40B, and better bungalows with facilities for up to 200B. At the other end of long Chalok Lam beach, west of the village, is the slightly nicer *Wattana* with huts for 60 to 80B and bungalows with fan for 150 to 250B. The beach is better here, too.

In friendly Ban Chalok Lam you can rent bikes and diving equipment. There are also several restaurants – none of them very good.

Ao Hat Thong Lang & Ao Mae Hat As you move west on Pha-Ngan, as on Samui, the sand gets browner and coarser. The secluded beach and cove at Ao Hat Thong Lang has no accommodation at the moment, though there was once a small bungalow operation here with huts at the usual 30 to 40B rate.

The beach at Ao Mae Hat is no great shakes, but there is a bit of coral offshore. The village of Ban Mae Hat is nearby. The *Mae Hat*, *Mae Hat Bay Resort* and *Island View Cabana* have simple huts for 50B plus huts with private bath for up to 150B. The Island View also has a good restaurant. Opposite the beach on the islet of Ko Mae are five huts that go for just 30B.

Hat Salat & Hat Yao These coral-fringed beaches are fairly difficult to reach – the road from Ban Si Thanu to the south is very bad in spots, even for experienced dirt-bikers – come by boat if possible.

Hat Salat has *My Way* with huts for 60B. Down at Hat Yao are the basic *Benjawan*, *Dream Hill*, *Blue Coral Beach*, *Silver Beach*, *Sandy Bay*, *Ibiza* and *Hat Thian* (isolated on a beach north of Hat Yao around the headland) – all with basic 30 to 120B huts. Also on this beach is *Hat Yao*, which sensibly charges extra for basic accommodation if you don't eat here and also has 200 to 500B bungalows. The *Bay View*, above the northern end of the beach apart from the others, offers 50B huts as well as bungalows with fan and attached bath for up to 600B.

Ao Chaophao & Si Thanu Ao Chaophao is a bay two headlands south of Hat Yao; then around a larger headland at the south end of Ao Chaophao is Ao Si Thanu. In these areas you begin to see the occasional mangrove along the coast.

There are four places to stay along the beach at Ao Chaophao, perhaps too many for the attractions this part of the island holds. The popular *Sea Flower*, *Seetanu* and *Great Bay* all have bungalows with private bath for 80 to 180B, and some without for 50 to 80B. *Hat Chaophao*, sandwiched between the others, has only 300B bungalows. At the south end of the bay, past curving Laem Niat, *Bovy Resort* has standard huts for 70B.

Just around the good-sized cape of Laem Son, at the north end of Ao Si Thanu proper, is the 40 to 70B *Laem Son*. South over a creek comes *Seaview Rainbow* with similar rates. Down towards the south end of the bay, *Lada* offers 200B bungalows with fan and bath. *Loy Fah*, at the southern end of the bay on the cape, has good 100 to 300B huts with bath and mosquito net, plus simpler huts for 50 and 80B. In the same area is the similarly priced *Nantakarn* – clean and friendly. A handful of others here seem to come and go with the seasons.

Ao Hin Kong/Ao Wok Tum This long bay – sometimes divided in two by a stream which feeds into the sea – is just a few km north of Thong Sala but so far has hardly any development. At the centre of Hin Kong, not far from the village of Ban Hin Kong, is the basic *Lipstick Cabana* for the usual 40 to 150B. On the southern end of the village is the similarly priced *Hin Kong*. Down at the southern end of Ao Wok Tum on the cape between this bay and Ao Nai Wok are *Tuk* and *Kiat*, both in the 40 to 60B range. A little farther down around the cape that separates Ao Wok Tum from Ao Nai Wok are *OK*, *Chuenjitt*, *Darin*, *Sea Scene*, *Porn Sawan*, *Cookies* and *Beach*, most with simple 30 to 80B huts – Darin, Sea Scene and Porn Sawan also have bungalows with private bath in the 120 to 300B range.

See the earlier Thong Sala section for accommodation just north of Thong Sala at Ao Nai Wok.

Getting There & Away
To/From Ko Samui – Express Boat
Songserm Co express boats to Ko Pha-Ngan leave from the Na Thon pier on Ko Samui every day at 10.30 am and 4.30 pm. The trip takes 50 minutes and costs 50B one way. Boats back to Samui leave Pha-Ngan's Thong Sala pier at 6.15 and 12.30 pm daily.

There is also an express-boat route to Pha-Ngan that is an extension of the Surat to Ko Samui routes, so you can go straight to Pha-Ngan from Surat with a stopover in Na Thon (see the Ko Samui Getting There & Away section for express boat times from Surat) for 100B one way.

To/From Ko Samui – Other Boats A small boat goes direct from Samui's Bang Rak (near Bo Phut village) to Hat Rin on Ko Pha-Ngan for 60B (depending on who's got the concession, the boat sometimes leaves from Bo Phut instead). This boat departs Bang Rak/Bo Phut just about every day at 10.30 am and 3.30 pm, depending on the weather and number of prospective passengers, and takes 40 to 45 minutes to reach the bay at Hat Rin. As more and more people choose this route to Ko Pha-Ngan, services will probably become more regular. In the reverse direction it usually leaves at 9.30 am and 2.30 pm.

From January to September there is also one boat a day from Hat Mae Nam on Samui to Ao Thong Nai Pan on Pha-Ngan, with a stop at Hat Rin. The fares are 120B and 60B respectively and the boat usually leaves Mae Nam around noon. In the reverse direction the boat starts from Ao Thong Nai Pan around 8 am.

To/From Surat Thani – Jet Boat The Island Jet departs daily at 8 am from Surat Thani (Tha Thong pier) to Ko Samui's Na Thon, then continues to the Thong Sala pier on Ko Pha-Ngan at 10.20 am. From Na Thon the trip lasts just 30 minutes and the fare is 60B. In the reverse direction the Island Jet leaves Thong Sala at noon. The fare all the way to/from Surat is 150B.

To/From Surat Thani – Speed Ferry Ferry Pha-Ngan Co has one direct boat daily to Ko Pha-Ngan. The company's bus meets the night train from Bangkok at Phun Phin station at 7 am, then there's another pick-up at the ferry office in Ban Don at 8 am. The ferry leaves from Don Sak pier at 9.15 am and arrives in Ko Pha-Ngan at 11.45 am. On the return trip the ferry leaves Ko Pha-Ngan at 12.30 pm; connecting buses arrive at the train station at 5.15 pm in time for the

evening rapid and express trains north or south. The ferry fare is 105B each way.

To/From Surat Thani – Night Ferry You can also take the slow night ferry direct to Pha-Ngan from the Ban Don pier in Surat. It leaves nightly at 11 pm, takes 6½ hours to arrive at Thong Sala, and costs 90B on the upper deck, 60B on the lower.

As with the night ferry to Samui, don't leave your bags unattended on the boat – there have been several reports of theft.

To/From Ko Tao Subject to weather conditions, there are daily boats between Thong Sala and Ko Tao, 47 km north. The trip takes 2½ hours and costs 150B one way.

Train/Bus/Boat Combinations At Bangkok's Hualamphong train station you can purchase train tickets that include a bus from the Surat Thani train station (Phun Phin) to the Ban Don pier and then a ferry to Ko Pha-Ngan. A 2nd-class seat costs 309B inclusive, while a 3rd-class seat is 235B. Second-class sleeper combinations cost 459B for an upper berth, 489B for a lower. Add 50 (rapid, express) to 100B (special express) for an air-con coach.

Getting Around

A couple of roads branch out from Thong Sala, primarily to the north and the south. One road goes north-west from Thong Sala a few km along the shoreline to the villages of Ban Hin Kong and Ban Si Thanu. From Ban Si Thanu the road travels north-east across the island to Ban Chalok Lam. Another road goes straight north from Thong Sala to Chalok Lam. There is also a very poor dirt road along the west coast from Ban Si Thanu to Ao Hat Yao and Ao Hat Salat.

Hat Khuat (Bottle Beach) can be reached on foot from Ban Fai Mai (two km) or Ban Chalok Lam (four km) or there are boats.

The road south from Thong Sala to Ban Khai passes an intersection where another road goes north to Ban Thong Nang and Ban

Thong Nai Pan. The dirt road to Hat Rin becomes almost impassable during heavy rains, but during the dry season there is regular transport between Thong Sala and Hat Rin. Until the road to Hat Rin is improved, only experienced motorbike riders should attempt it on their own.

Songthaews and motorcycle taxis handle all the public transport along island roads. Some places can only be reached by motorcycle; some places only by boat or foot.

You can rent motorcycles in Thong Sala for 150 to 250B a day.

Songthaew & Motorcycle Taxi From Thong Sala, songthaews to Hat Chaophao and Hat Yao are 30B and 50B per person respectively, while motorcycle taxis cost 40B and 70B. To Ban Khai, it's 30B by songthaew or motorcycle; if you're only going as far as Wat Khao Tham or Ban Tai the fare remains the same for motorcycles but drops to 20B for a songthaew.

A songthaew from Thong Sala to Ban Chalok Lam is 30B, a motorcycle taxi 40B.

To get to Hat Rin from Thong Sala, a songthaew costs 50B one way while a motorbike is 70B. You can also get there by boat, which is the only option in wet conditions; see the following Boat section.

Thong Nai Pan can be reached from Thong Sala by motorcycle (120B) or songthaew (60B). See the following Boat section for water transport to Thong Nai Pan.

Boat There are daily boats from Ao Chalok Lam to Hat Khuat at 1 and 4 pm (returning at 9.30 am and 3 pm) for 30B. The service operates from January to September, depending on the weather.

Thong Nai Pan can be reached by boat from Hat Rin on south Pha-Ngan at 12.30 pm for 60B, but these boats generally run only between January and September, depending on the weather. When the speed ferry arrives at the Thong Sala pier from Surat or Samui, there are usually boats waiting to take passengers on to Hat Rin for 50B – it takes about 45 minutes. Passengers already on Pha-Ngan

can take these boats, too – they go in each direction two or three times daily.

KO TAO
เกาะเต่า

Ko Tao translates as 'Turtle Island', named for its shape. It's only about 21 sq km in area and the population of 750 are mostly involved in fishing and growing coconuts. Snorkelling and diving are particularly good here due to the relative abundance of coral, though most of the beaches are too shallow for swimming. Until 1994 the only electricity on the island was provided by small gas or diesel generators, but as we went to press a power plant and power lines were reportedly on their way.

Since it takes at least five hours to get there from the mainland (from either Chumphon or Surat Thani via Ko Pha-Ngan), Ko Tao doesn't get people coming over for day trips or for quick overnighters. Still, the island can become quite crowded during high season, when Mae Hat, Hat Sai Ri and Ao Chalok Ban Kao have people sleeping on the beach waiting for huts to vacate.

Ban Mae Hat on the western side of the island is where inter-island boats land. The only other villages on the island are **Ban Hat Sai Ri** in the centre of the northern part and **Ban Chalok Ban Kao** to the south. Just a km off the north-west shore of the island is **Ko Nang Yuan**, which is really three islands joined by a sand bar.

The granite promontory of **Laem Tato** at the southern tip of Ko Tao makes a nice hike from Ban Chalok Ban Kao.

Information
Ban Mae Hat, a one-street town with a busy pier, is the main – the only! – commercial centre on the island. Here you'll find a police station, post and telephone office (open daily from 8.30 am to 4 pm), travel agents, dive shops, restaurants and general stores. There is no bank on the island, but several moneychangers offer exchange services below the usual bank rates. Mr J, past Paew Bungalows, south of Ban Mae, usually has

the best rate. He also has a telephone service and a book exchange.

Boat tickets can be purchased at a booking office by the harbour as well as from travel agents.

Diving & Snorkelling

Ko Tao has an incredible number of diving shops, with some of Thailand's lowest prices for training and/or excursions. Underwater visibility is high and the water is cleaner than around most other inhabited islands in the Gulf. Because of the farang presence, the best diving spots have English names, eg White Rock, Shark Island, South-West Pinnacles.

At the time of writing there were nine shops (Master Divers, Big Blue, Ko Tao Divers, Nangyuan, Bans, Caribou, Samui, Gecko and Dolphin) on the island, most charging basically the same dive rates. Master Divers has a friendly staff and offers good dive site information. Rates typically run 500 to 600B per dive (including gear, boat, guide, food and beverages) or 350B if you bring your own gear. An all-inclusive introductory dive lesson costs 1500B while a four-day, open-water PADI certificate course goes for around 6500B – these rates include gear, boat, instructor, food and beverages. A snorkel mask and fins typically rent for 100B (or 50B separately) per day.

Places to Stay

Most huts on Ko Tao are very simple, inexpensive and made with local materials, although concrete is becoming increasingly common. At last count there were about 600 huts in 46 locations around the island. At most places electricity is provided by generators from 6 pm to midnight. Simple thatched or wooden huts typically cost 50 to 100B per night, while larger wood, brick or concrete bungalows with private bath range from 150 to 600B.

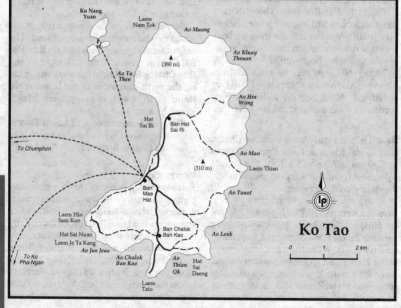

Ko Tao

During the 1994 peak season, it was difficult to find accommodation anywhere on the island – no matter what the time of the day – and people were sleeping on the beach or in restaurants for one or two nights until a hut became available. On arrival at Ban Mae it may be best to follow a tout who can find vacant huts, otherwise your chances of finding a place on your own might be very slim. In the off season it can be a problem finding a bungalow operation that hasn't closed down till next high season.

Ao Mae At Hat Ao Mae, just north of Ban Mae Hat, the shallow bay has plenty of coral. *Crystal* offers basic plywood huts for 100B and concrete and wood bungalows with bath for 400 to 600B – the most expensive on the island. *Dam* has nice thatched huts for 100B. On the headland overlooking the bay are *Queen Resort* (100 to 200B) and *Tommy Resort* (80 to 500B).

Hat Sai Ri Around the headland to the north is long Hat Sai Ri, with a string of bungalow operations starting with *AC Resort*, *Haad Sai Resort* and *Ko Tao Cabana* in the 250 to 350B range. *Bing*, on the other side of the road, has cheaper huts for 100B. Farther north along Hat Sai Ri are four places in the 80 to 250B range: *Sai Ri Cottage*, *New Way*, *Haad Sai Ree Villa* and *O-Chai*.

North of the beach in an area sometimes called Ao Ta Then are several bungalow operations built on the rocks, including *Golden Cape*, *Silver Cliff*, *Sun Sea*, *Sun Lord*, *Eden Resort* and *Mahana Bay* in the 60 to 100B range. Farther north, the lone *C F T* has basic huts for 80B and bungalows with attached bath for up to 300B.

Ao Muang & Ao Kluay Theuan On the northern and north-eastern tip of the island, accessible only by boat, are two coral-fringed coves without bungalow accommodation. As the pressure for places to stay increases, new operations should start appearing at both.

Ao Hin Wong South of Ao Kluay Theuan by sea, or two km north-east of Ban Hat Sai Ri by trail, Ao Hin Wong has a handful of huts called *Hin Wong* for 80 to 100B.

Ao Mao, Laem Thian & Ao Tanot Continuing clockwise around the island, Ao Mao, connected by a two-km dirt trail with Ban Hat Sai Ri, is another cove with no beach accommodation so far. On the cape which juts out over the north end of Ao Tanot, *Laem Thian* has huts from 60B. Ao Tanot proper, to the south, has *Tanote Bay Resort* (60 to 200B) and *Sunrise* (60B).

Ao Leuk & Hat Sai Daeng Ao Leuk, connected by a 2.2-km dirt road with Ban Mae Hat, has the lone *Ao Leuk Resort*, with huts from 60B. Another km or so south is Hat Sai Daeng, where *Kiet* offers simple huts from 60B or nicer ones with private bath for up to 300B. The latter has received complaints regarding rudeness and lack of food service.

Ao Thian Ok & Laem Tato Farther west on the side of the impressive Laem Tato is pretty Ao Thian Ok with *Rocky* at 80 to 300B. We have had several complaints from people who have been violently ejected from the place for not buying enough meals there.

Ao Chalok Ban Kao This nicely situated coral beach, about 1.7 km south of Ban Mae Hat by road, has become quite crowded. In peak season it can be very difficult to find a free hut here and travellers end up sleeping on the floor of a restaurant for a night or two until something becomes available.

Taraporn (50 to 80B) sits on the hill overlooking the western part of the bay, where you'll find *Laem Khlong* (100 to 500B, no beach) and *Nang Nuan* (250 to 300B). Next is the friendly *Sunshine* with spacious bungalows for 250 to 300B. Sunshine's restaurant is one of the best on the island. *Buddha View* next door has similar bungalows for 200B and an equally good restaurant, famous for its garlic bread and the beach's only video. Next are two cheaper places, the *Carabao* (50 to 80B) and *K See*

(130B – with bath). Towards the eastern end of the bay, *Ko Tao Cottages* has the island's most luxurious bungalows for 500 to 600B.

Around a couple of small points to the south along Laem Tato is a beach which can only be reached on foot and at low tide. Here *Tatoo Lagoon* offers basic huts for 60B, plus more elaborate ones with attached bath for up to 300B.

South-West of Mae Hat A few hundred metres south-west of Mae Hat, across a stream and down a footpath, *Paew* has sturdy bungalows for 250 to 350B, while *Coral Beach* offers standard huts for 80B, bungalows from 150B.

A couple of km farther south of Ban Mae Hat is a series of small beaches collectively known as **Hat Sai Nuan**, where you'll find *Sai Thong* (40 to 250B), then *Siam Cookie* (80 to 250B) and *Cha* (50 to 250B).

Around at **Laem Je Ta Kang** (about 1.2 km west of Ao Chalok Ban Kao) is another tiny beach with *Tao Thong Villa* (50 to 80B). South of Laem Je Ta Kang, by itself on **Ao Jun Jeua**, is *Sunset* (40 to 80B). The only way to get to these is to walk along the dirt track from Mae Hat or take long-tail boats.

Ko Nang Yuan Finally, on Ko Nang Yuan are the *Nang Yuan* bungalows for 170 to 600B. One problem with staying on Ko Nang Yuan might be putting up with diving groups that occasionally take over the island. Another is the Nang Yuan's tendency to kick out impecunious guests who don't order enough food at the restaurant. On the positive side, the management does not allow any plastic bottles on the island – these will be confiscated on arrival. Regular twice-daily boats to Nang Yuan from the Ban Mae Hat pier are 20B per person. You can easily charter a ride there for 50B.

Getting There & Away
To/From Bangkok Bus/boat combination tickets from Bangkok cost 450 to 650B and are available from travel agents on Khao San Rd. One of the most reliable services on Khao San Rd, MP Travel (☎ (02) 281-5954)

at Nana Plaza Inn, operates minivans to Ko Tao for 650B per person.

To/From Chumphon Two boats from the mainland – a slow boat and a 'speed boat' leave daily from Chumphon to Ko Tao – some weeks departures may be fewer if the swells are high. The slow boat leaves Chumphon at midnight, takes five hours or so to reach Ko Tao and costs 200B one way. In the opposite direction it departs from Ko Tao at 10 am. See the Chumphon section for more details.

The speed boat departs Chumphon at 8 am (from Ban Mae Hat at 11 am) and takes about one hour and 40 minutes. The speed boat fare is 400B. See the Chumphon section for more details.

To/From Surat Thani Every third day, depending on the weather, a boat runs between Surat Thani (Tha Thong) and Ko Tao, a seven to eight-hour trip for 250B one way. From Surat, boats depart Surat at 11 pm and Ban Mae at 9 am.

To/From Ko Pha-Ngan Depending on weather conditions, boats run daily between the Thong Sala pier on Ko Pha-Ngan and Ban Mae Hat on Ko Tao. The trip takes anywhere from 2½ to three hours and costs 150B per person. Boats leave Thong Sala around noon and return from Ko Tao at 9 am.

Getting Around
The various pick-ups cost 20B per person to anywhere on the island during the day, but to charter one after hours costs 100B. Long-tail boats are also available to any beach on the island, and generally cost 20B to western parts of the island from Ban Mae and up to 50B to anywhere else on the island, or to go right around it.

Walking is an easy way to get around the island, but some trails aren't clearly marked and can be difficult to follow. You can walk around the whole island in a day. The *Guide Map of Koh Samui, Koh Pha-Ngan & Koh Tao* by V Hongsombud offers a rough outline of the trails.

Nakhon Si Thammarat Province

Much of this large southern province is covered with rugged mountains and forests, which were, until very recently, the last refuge of Thailand's communist insurgents. The province's eastern border is formed by the Gulf of Thailand and much of the provincial economy is dependent on fishing and shrimp farming. Along the north coast are several nice beaches: **Khanom, Nai Phlao, Tong Yi, Sichon** and **Hin Ngam**.

In the interior are several caves and waterfalls, including **Phrom Lok Falls, Thong Phannara Cave** and **Yong Falls**. Besides fishing, Nakhon residents earn a living by growing coffee, rice, rubber and fruit (especially *mongkhút*, or mangosteen).

KHAO LUANG NATIONAL PARK

อุทยานแห่งชาติเขาหลวง

This 570-sq-km park in the centre of the province surrounds **Khao Luang**, at 1835 metres the highest peak in peninsular Thailand. The park is known for beautiful mountain and forest walks, cool streams, waterfalls (Karom and Krung Ching are the largest) and fruit orchards. Wildlife includes clouded leopard, tiger, elephant, banteng, gaur and Javan mongoose, plus over 200 bird species.

To get to the park, take a songthaew (15B) from Nakhon Si Thammarat to the village of Khiriwong at the base of Khao Luang. Twice a year the villagers lead groups on a special climb up the mountain – ask at the TAT office in Nakhon Si Thammarat for details.

NAKHON SI THAMMARAT

อ.เมืองนครศรีธรรมราช

Nakhon Si Thammarat (population 71,500) is 780 km from Bangkok. Centuries before the 8th-century Srivijaya empire subjugated the peninsula, there was a city-state here called Ligor or Lagor, capital of the Tambralinga kingdom, which was well known throughout Oceania. Later, when Sri Lankan-ordained Buddhist monks established a cloister at the city, the name was changed to the Pali-Sanskrit *Nagara Sri Dhammaraja* (City of the Sacred Dharma-King), rendered in Thai phonetics as Nakhon Si Thammarat. During the early development of the various Thai kingdoms, Nakhon Si Thammarat was a very important centre of religion and culture. Thai shadow play (nang thalung) and classical dance-drama (lakhon – Thai pronunciation of Lagor) are supposed to have been developed in Nakhon Si Thammarat; buffalo-hide shadow puppets and dance masks are still made here.

Today Nakhon Si Thammarat is also known for its nielloware *(khrêuang tom)*, a silver and black alloy/enamel jewellery technique borrowed from China many centuries ago. Another indigenous handicraft is *yaan lipao*, basketry woven from a hardy local grass into intricate contrasting designs. Yaan lipao handbags are a fashion staple among Thai women, so you should see lots for sale around town.

Until recently the city was also known for its higher-than-average crime rate, but lately the city has been trying to change its image by cracking down on gangster activity.

A new civic pride has developed in recent years and the natives are now quite fond of being called *khon khawn* (Nakhon people). Bovorn (Bowon) Bazaar, a cluster of restaurants and handicraft shops off Ratchadamnoen Rd, serves as a commercial centre for the city's attempted revitalisation process.

Orientation & Information

Nakhon Si Thammarat can be divided into two sections, the historic half south of the clock tower and the new city centre north of the clock tower and Khlong Na Meuang. The new city has all the hotels and most of the restaurants, as well as more movie theatres per sq km than any other city in Thailand.

A new TAT office (☎ 346516) stands opposite the Sanaam Naa Meuang (City Park) off Ratchadamnoen Rd, near the police station. They distribute the usual helpful information printed in English, and can also assist with any tourism-related problems.

The main post office is also on Ratchadamnoen Rd, along with the attached international telephone office upstairs (open from 8 am to 11 pm).

Nakhon's telephone area code is ☎ 075.

Suan Nang Seu Nakhon Bowonrat

The Suan Nang Seu or 'Book Garden', at 116 Ratchadamnoen Rd next to Bovorn Bazaar and Siam Commercial Bank, is Nakhon's intellectual centre (look for the traditional water jar on a platform in front). Housed in an 80-year-old building that once served variously as a *sinsae* (Chinese doctor) clinic, opium den and hotel, this nonprofit bookshop specialises in books (mostly in Thai) on local history as well as national politics and religion. It also co-ordinates Dhamma lectures and sponsors local arts and craft exhibits.

Wat Phra Mahathat

วัดพระมหาธาตุ

This is the city's oldest site, reputed to be over 1000 years old. Reconstructed in the mid-13th century, it features a 78-metre chedi, crowned by a solid gold spire weighing several hundred kg. The temple's bot contains one of Thailand's three identical Phra Singh Buddhas, one of which is supposed to have been originally cast in Sri Lanka before being brought to Sukhothai (through Nakhon Si Thammarat), Chiang Mai and later, Ayuthaya. The other images are at Wat Phra Singh in Chiang Mai and the National Museum in Bangkok – each is claimed to be the original.

Besides the distinctive bot and chedi there are many intricately designed wihaans surrounding the chedi, several of which contain crowned Nakhon Si Thammarat/Ayuthaya-style Buddhas in glass cabinets. One wihaan houses a funky museum (admission 10B) with carved wooden kruts (garudas, Vishnu's mythical bird-mount), old Siwichai votive tablets, Buddha figures of every description including a standing Dvaravati

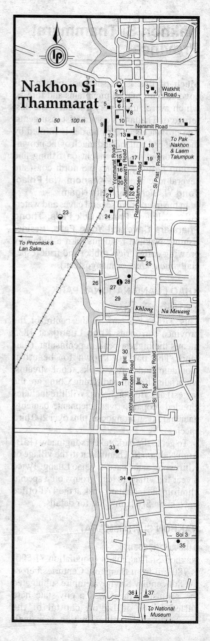

Nakhon Si Thammarat

0   50   100 m

Watkhit Road
Neramit Road
To Pak Nakhon & Laem Talumpuk
Yommarat Road
Jamroenwithi Road
Ratchadamnoen Road
Si Pratt
To Phromlok & Lan Saka
Khlong   Na Meuang
Ratchadamnoen Road
Si Thammasok Road
Soi 3
To National Museum

PLACES TO STAY		PLACES TO EAT		23	Bus Station
				25	GPO & Telephone Office
4	Taksin Hotel	2	Ruam Rot	26	Handicraft Shops
5	Phetphailin Hotel	3	Dam Kan Aeng	27	TAT Office
7	Thai Fa Hotel	8	Yong Seng Restaurant	28	Lak Meuang (City Pillar)
10	Si Thong Hotel			29	Sanaam Naa Meuang (City Park)
11	Nakhon Garden Inn		OTHER	30	Wat Sema Muang
12	Montien Hotel			31	Shiva Shrine
13	Siam Hotel	1	Taxis to Surat,	32	Brahma Shrine
14	Thai Hotel		Chumphon &	33	Provincial Offices
15	Yaowarat Hotel		Ranong	34	Clock Tower
16	Bue Loung (Bua Luang) Hotel	6	Minivans to Sichon & Khanom	35	Suchart's Workshop
17	Muang Thong Hotel	9	Train Station	36	Wat Phra Mahathat
19	Thai Lee Hotel	18	Bovorn Bazaar	37	Wat Na Phra Boromathat
20	Nakhon Hotel	21	Shared Taxi Stand		
24	Laem Thong Hotel	22	Songthaews to Khao Luang		

figure and a Siwichai naga Buddha, pearl-inlaid alms bowls and other oddities. It would be better if the artefacts were labelled – at present many are not identified in either Thai or English. This is the biggest wat in the south, comparable to Wat Pho and other large Bangkok wats. If you like wats, this one is well worth a trip.

Wat Phra Mahathat's full name, Wat Phra Mahathat Woramahawihaan, is sometimes abbreviated to Wat Phra Boromathat. It's about two km from the new town centre – hop on any bus or songthaew going down Ratchadamnoen Rd.

Wat Na Phra Boromathat

วัดหน้าพระบรมธาตุ

Across the road from Wat Mahathat, this is the residence for monks serving at Mahathat. There is a nice Gandhara-style fasting Buddha in front of the bot here.

Nakhon Si Thammarat National Museum

พิพิธภัณฑ์แห่งชาตินครศรีธรรมราช

This is past the principal wats on Ratchadamnoen Rd heading south, across from Wat Thao Khot and Wat Phet Jarik, on the left – 2B by city bus or 3B by songthaew. Since the Tampaling (or Tambralinga) kingdom traded with Indian, Arabic, Dvaravati and Champa states, much art from these places found its way to the Nakhon Si Thammarat area, and some is now on display in the national museum here. Notable are Dong-Son bronze drums, Dvaravati Buddha images and Pallava (south Indian) Hindu sculpture. Locally produced art is also on display.

If you've already had your fill of the usual Thai art history surveys from Ban Chiang to Ayuthaya, go straight to the Art of Southern Thailand exhibit in a room on the left of the foyer. Here you'll find many fine images of Nakhon Si Thammarat provenance, including Phutthasihing, U Thong and late Ayuthaya styles. The Nakhon Si Thammarat-produced Ayuthaya style seems to be the most common, with distinctive, almost comical, crowned faces. The so-called Phutthasihing-style Buddha looks a little like the Palla-influenced Chiang Saen Buddha, but is shorter and more 'pneumatic'.

Admission to the museum is 10B and hours are Wednesday to Sunday from 9 am to 4 pm.

Hindu Temples

There are also three Hindu temples in Nakhon Si Thammarat, along Ratchadamnoen Rd inside the city walls. Brahman priests from these temples take part each year

SOUTHERN THAILAND

in the Royal Ploughing Ceremony in Bangkok. One temple houses a locally famous Shivalingam (phallic shrine) which is worshipped by women hoping to bear children.

Shadow Puppet Workshop

Traditionally, there are two styles of shadow puppets, nang thalung and nang yai; the former are similar in size to the typical Malay-Indonesian style puppets while the latter are nearly life-size and unique to Thailand. Both are intricately carved from buffalo-hide. Performances of Thai shadow theatre are rare nowadays (usually only during festivals) but there are two places in town where you can see the puppets being made.

The acknowledged master of shadow puppet craft – both manufacture and performance – is Suchart Subsin (Suchaat Sapsin), a Nakhon resident with a workshop at 110/18 Si Thammasok Soi 3, not far from Wat Phra Mahathat. Khun Suchart has received several awards for his mastery and preservation of the craft and has performed for the king. His workshop is open to the public; if enough people are assembled he may even be talked into providing a performance at his small outdoor studio. Puppets can be purchased here at reasonable prices – and here only, as he refuses to sell them through distributors. On some puppets the fur is left on the hide for additional effect – these cost a bit more as special care must be taken in tanning them.

Another craftsperson, Mesa Chotiphan, welcomes visitors to her workshop in the northern part of town. Mesa sells to distributors but will also sell direct at lower prices. Her house is at 558/4 Soi Rong Jeh, Ratchadamnoen Rd (☎ 343979). If you call she will pick you up from anywhere in the city. To get there on your own, go north from the city centre on Ratchadamnoen Rd and after about half a km north of the sports field, take the soi opposite the Chinese cemetery (before reaching the golf course and military base).

Festivals

Every year in mid-October there is a southern-Thai festival called Chak Phra Pak Tai held in Songkhla, Surat Thani and Nakhon Si Thammarat. In Nakhon Si Thammarat the festival is centred around Wat Mahathat and includes performances of nang thalung and lakhon as well as the parading of Buddha images around the city to collection donations for local temples.

In the third lunar month (February to March) the city holds the colourful Hae Phaa Khun That, in which a lengthy cloth jataka painting is wrapped around the main chedi at Wat Phra Mahathat.

Places to Stay – bottom end

Most of Nakhon Si Thammarat's hotels are near the train and bus stations.

On Yommarat (spelt 'Yammaraj' on some signs) Rd, almost across from the train station, is the *Si Thong Hotel* (☎ 356357), with adequate rooms for 120B with fan and bath. Also on Yommarat Rd are the *Nakhon Hotel* (☎ 356318) and *Yaowarat* (☎ 356089), with similar rates and facilities as the Si Thong.

On Jamroenwithi Rd (walk straight down Neramit Rd opposite the train station two blocks and turn right into Jamroenwithi Rd) is the large *Siam Hotel* (☎ 356090); rooms with fan and bath cost from 120 and 160B. Farther south on this street is the *Muang Thong Hotel*, where 100B will get you a clean room with fan and bath. A block north of the Siam, on the same side of the street, is the *Thai Fa Hotel*, which, at 90 to 140B, has better rooms than either the Nakhon or the Si Thong.

Others are the newer *Thai Lee* (☎ 356948), at 1130 Ratchadamnoen Rd, where rooms with fan and bath cost 100 to 150B, and the similarly priced *Laem Thong* (☎ 356478) at 1213/5-6 Yommarat Rd.

Places to Stay – middle & top end

Nakhon Si Thammarat's flashiest hotels are the *Thai Hotel* (☎ 356505/451) on Ratchadamnoen Rd, two blocks from the train station, and the *Taksin* (☎ 356788/90) on Si

Prat Rd. The Thai Hotel has fan-cooled singles/doubles for 280/300B, and air-con rooms ranging for 600B. At the Taksin air-con rooms start at 350B.

The newer *Bue Loung (Bua Luang) Hotel* (☎ 341518), on Soi Luang Meuang off Jamroenwithi Rd, has large, clean singles/doubles with fan and bath for 150/220B, and air-con doubles for 320B.

On Yommarat Rd near the train station, the *Montien* (☎ 341908) has decent rooms with fan and attached bath from 200B and air-con for 420B. The nearby *Phetpailin* (☎ 341896; fax 343943) has rooms starting at 150B (air-con from 350B).

The best top-end choice is the quiet *Nakhon Garden Inn* (☎ 344831) at 1/4 Pak Nakhon Rd east of the centre. All 50 rooms with air-con and TV cost 500 to 600B.

Places to Eat

There are lots of funky old Chinese restaurants along Yommarat and Jamroenwithi Rds. The latter street is the city's main culinary centre – at night it's lined with cheap food vendors and by day there are plenty of rice and noodle shops. *Yong Seng* (no English sign) is a very good, inexpensive Chinese restaurant on Jamroenwithi Rd.

To try some of Nakhon's excellent Thai coffee, stop by *Hao Coffee* at Bovorn Bazaar. Basically an update of an original Hokkien-style coffee shop once run by the owner's family in Nakhon, Hao Coffee serves international coffees as well as southern-Thai Hokkien-style coffee (listed as 'Hao coffee' on the menu) served with a tea chaser. Ask for fresh milk (nom sòt) if you abhor powdered non-dairy creamer.

Adjacent to Hao Coffee is *Khrua Nakhon*, a large open-air restaurant serving real Nakhon cuisine, including khâo yam (southern-style rice salad), kaeng tai plaa (spicy fish curry) khanõm jiin (curry noodles served with a huge tray of veggies) and seafood. The restaurant also has egg-and-toast breakfasts; you can order Hao coffee from next door if you'd like. With a banyan tree in front and a modest display of southern-Thai folk art, the atmosphere is hard to beat.

Get there early as it's only open from 7 am to 3 pm. Next to Khrua Nakhon is *Ban Lakhon*, in an old house, which is also very good for Thai food and is open for dinner.

On the corner of the alley leading into Bovorn Bazaar, Nakhon's most famous roti vendors set up nightly. In Nakhon, roti klûay (banana roti) is a tradition – the vendors here use only fresh mashed bananas, no banana preserves or the like. Other offerings here include roti with curry (roti kaeng), with egg (roti khài) or as mataba (stuffed with meat and vegetables). They also do great khanõm jiip, dumplings stuffed with a chicken-shrimp mixture, along with Nakhon coffee and better-than-average milk tea.

Among a cluster of restaurants near the intersection of Jamroenwithi and Watkhit Rds is *Ruam Rot*, which serves very good curries and khanõm jiin. They claim they use no preservatives or artificial flavours; the emphasis is on southern-Thai curries like kaeng mátsàman and kaeng tai plaa. East of this intersection, on the corner of Ratchadamnoen and Watkhit Rds, is the very popular Thai-Chinese *Dam Kan Aeng*, which is packed with hungry customers every night.

Entertainment

Beyond the cinemas in town, there's not a lot of nightlife. The Dallas Cowboy, a pub in Bovorn Bazaar, is a small, convincingly decorated old-west bar with a long list of cocktails from Tom Collins to Señor Playboy.

Getting There & Away

Air THAI has four flights a week to/from Bangkok (1770B), three flights a week to/from Phuket (690B) via Hat Yai and three flights weekly to/from Surat Thani (340B). The THAI office (☎ 342491) in Nakhon is at 1612 Ratchadamnoen Rd.

Bus Air-con buses bound for Nakhon Si Thammarat leave Bangkok's southern air-con bus terminal daily every 30 minutes from 6 to 8.30 pm, arriving 12 hours later, for 342B. Air-con buses in the reverse direction leave at about the same times. There are also two 2nd-class air-con departures (266B) and one VIP departure (420B) nightly. Ordinary buses leave Bangkok at 6.40 am and 5, 6, 7 and 9.30 pm for 192B.

From Surat Thani there are daily buses to Nakhon; check with the tour-bus companies on Na Meuang Rd. A tour bus from Surat to Nakhon should cost 70 to 75B one way. Direct buses run from Songkhla via a bridge over the entrance to Thaleh Noi (the inland sea). Check with one of the tour-bus companies on Niphat Uthit 2 Rd in Hat Yai. Muang Tai Tours, on Jamroenwithi Rd in Nakhon Si Thammarat, does a 70B trip to Surat that includes a good meal and a video movie.

Hourly buses to Nakhon Si Thammarat leave Krabi's Talaat Kao for 50B per person and take about four hours. Less frequent air-con buses cost 70B. Other routes include Trang (37B ordinary, 60B air-con), Phattalung (31B ordinary, 50B air-con) and Hat Yai (53B ordinary, 60B air-con).

Train Most southbound trains stop at the junction of Thung Song, about 40 km west of Nakhon Si Thammarat, from where you must take a bus or taxi to the coast. However, two trains actually go all the way to Nakhon Si Thammarat (there is a branch line from Khao Chum Thong to Nakhon Si Thammarat): the rapid No 47, which leaves Bangkok's Hualamphong station at 7.45 pm, arriving in Nakhon Si Thammarat at 11.10 am, and the express No 15, which leaves Bangkok at 7.20 pm and arrives in Nakhon Si Thammarat at 10.05 am. Most travellers will not be booking a train directly to Nakhon Si Thammarat, but if you want to, 1st class costs 590B, 2nd class 279B, not including surcharges for rapid/express service or sleeping berths. There are no direct 3rd-class trains to Nakhon Si Thammarat.

Share Taxis This seems to be the most popular form of inter-city travel out of Nakhon. The huge share-taxi terminal on Yommarat Rd has taxis to Thung Song (25B), Khanom (40B), Sichon (30B), Krabi

(80B), Trang (60B), Phuket (150B) and Phattalung (50B). A second, smaller stand on Thewarat Rd has taxis to Surat (60B), Chumphon (130B) and Ranong (180B).

Getting Around

City buses run north-south along Ratchadamnoen and Si Thammasok Rds for 3B. Songthaews do similar routes for 3B during the day, 4B at night. Motorbike taxis cost 5 to 10B.

AROUND NAKHON SI THAMMARAT PROVINCE
Laem Talumpuk

แหลมตะลุมพุก

This is a small scenic cape not far from Nakhon Si Thammarat. Take a bus from Neramit Rd going east to Pak Nakhon for 10B, then cross the inlet by ferry to Laem Talumpuk.

Hat Sa Bua

หาดสระบัว

Sixteen km north of Nakhon Si Thammarat in the Tha Sala district, about 11B by songthaew, off Route 401 to Surat, are some semi-deserted white-sand beaches with few tourists. As yet accommodation isn't available, but there are some very reasonably priced restaurants here.

Hat Sichon & Hat Hin Ngam

หาดสิชล/หาดหินงาม

Hat Sichon and Hat Hin Ngam are stunning beaches 37 km north of Nakhon Si Thammarat in Sichon district. Another good beach, **Hat Tong Yi**, is accessible only by boat and is hence almost always deserted – it's between Sichon and Hin Ngam (a chartered boat to Tong Yi from either beach costs 150 to 250B).

Get the bus for Hat Hin Ngam or Sichon from the Nakhon Si Thammarat bus station for 18B or take a share taxi for 30B. Hat Sichon comes first; Hin Ngam is another 1.5 km. *Prasansuk Villa* has 30 bungalows for rent at 320 to 440B.

Ao Khanom

อ่าวขนอม

About 25 km from Sichon, 70 km from Surat and 80 km from Nakhon Si Thammarat is the bay of Ao Khanom. Not far from the vehicle-ferry landing for Ko Samui in Khanom is a string of four white-sand beaches – Hat Nai Praet, Hat Nai Phlao, Hat Na Dan and Hat Pak Nam. *Khanom Hills Resort* (☎ 529403) at Nai Phlao has six rooms for 500 to 800B. Also at Nai Phlao are *Fern Bay Resort*, 400B, the *Nai Phlao Bay Resort* (☎ 529039), 650 to 750B, *Supa Villa* (☎ 529237), 400 to 600B and the *Khanab Nam Diamond Cliff Resort* (☎ 529000/111) with 25 rooms for 600 to 1100B.

Hat Na Dan has the *Watanyoo Villa* (☎ 529224) for 120B up.

Phattalung Province

Over 840 km from Bangkok and 95 km from Hat Yai, Phattalung is one of the south's only rice-growing provinces and it has prospered as a result.

PHATTALUNG & AROUND

อ.เมืองพัทลุง

The provincial capital (population 34,000) is fairly small (you can walk around the perimeter of central Phattalung in an hour, even stopping for rice). Judging from the number of *hang thong* (gold dealers) on Poh Saat Rd, there's a large Chinese population.

Phattalung is famous for the original nang thalung (shadow play) which was probably named after Phattalung – *nãng* means hide (untanned leather), and *thalung* is taken from Phattalung. The Thai shadow-play tradition remains only in Nakhon Si Thammarat and Phattalung, though the best performances are seen in the former. A typical performance begins at midnight and lasts four to five hours. Usually they take place during ngaan wat (temple fairs).

The town is situated between two picturesque, foliage-trimmed limestone peaks, Khao Ok Thalu (literally, 'punctured-chest mountain') and Khao Hua Taek (or 'broken-head mountain'). Local myth has it that these two mountains were the wife and mistress of a third mountain to the north, Khao Meuang, who fought a fierce battle over the adulterous husband, leaving them with their 'wounds'. The names refer to their geographic peculiarities – Ok Thalu has a tunnel through its upper peak, while Hua Taek is sort of split at the top.

Like most Thai towns, Phattalung's street plan is laid out in a grid pattern. Most of the local sights are nearby.

Information

The new tourist centre (☎ 611201), on the corner of Ramesuan and Kanasan Rds near the town hall, is actually a trade handicraft information office also acting as tourist office for the area. They also sell some handicrafts.

To change moneyyour best option is to go to the Thai Farmers Bank on Ramet Rd, near the intersection of Nivas (Niwat) Rd. The post office on Rot Fai Rd offers international telephone service upstairs daily from 8 am to 8 pm.

Phattalung's telephone area code is ☎ 074.

Wat Khuhasawan

วัดคูหาสวรรค์

On the western side of town – straight down Khuhasawan Rd from the train station – Wat Khuhasawan comprises one large cave with rather ugly statues, but the cave is high and cool. A tall passageway leads deeper into the cave – lights can be switched on by the monks. Steps lead around the cave to the top of the mountain for a nice view of rice fields and mountains farther west.

To the right of the main cave is an old hermit's cave – the monk died in 1973 and his form is commemorated by a statue at the second level of stairs. Good views of Khao Ok Thalu and most of Phattalung City can be had from certain points around this cave.

SOUTHERN THAILAND

Wat Wang
วัดวัง

Over 100 years old, this is the oldest wat in Phattalung. The palace of a Thai prince was originally located just east of the wat (*wang* means palace), but only the wall remains. The original chedi is in front of the wat. A closed bot has a decaying set of murals with Buddhist and *Ramayana* themes. You have to open the doors and windows to see them. Wat Wang is about four km east of Phattalung on the road to Lam Pam. Take a songthaew from next to the post office (3B).

Lam Pam
ลำปำ

If you follow Phattalung's main street, Ramet Rd, east over the train tracks past Wat Wang, you'll come to Lam Pam on the banks of the Thaleh Luang, the upper part of the south's inland sea (Thaleh Noi). For 5B you can ride a songthaew from next to the post office out to Lam Pam in 15 minutes, or hire a motorcycle for 10B.

Under shady trees next to the freshwater 'sea' are beach chairs and tables where you can relax, enjoy the breeze and order food – crab, mussels, other shellfish, squid, plus beer, soda, etc. Although the inland sea itself is not at all spectacular, this is a nice spot to while away a few hours drinking beer and eating the fabulous speciality plaa mèuk klûay yâang (literally, 'banana squid' – an egg-carrying squid, roasted over charcoal), along with miang kham, the unique do-it-yourself concoction of dried shrimp, peanuts, lime, garlic, ginger, chilli, toasted coconut and salty-sweet sauce wrapped in wild tea leaves.

Tham Malai
ถ้ำมาลัย

Three km north of Phattalung, near the train line, is a hill with a large cave, Tham Malai, at its base. On top of the hill are some Chinese shrines, though a Thai mae chii resides there. There are excellent views of Phattalung and surrounding mountains from the top.

The cave itself is only slightly more interesting than the shrines. Bring a torch (flashlight) and you can explore the various rooms within the cavern. The cave is more or less in its natural state, with its stalagmites and stalactites still intact. Even without a light, it's worth exploring a bit – when the cave reaches its darkest point, you'll come upon an opening leading back around to daylight.

If the canal running parallel to the train line has enough water, you can get a boat for 5B as far as Tham Malai – easiest in December and January. If the water is too low, walk along the tracks until you come to a foot-bridge which will take you over the canal onto a path leading to the cave.

Bullfighting

A rustic stadium four to five km south of town on Highway 4 (3B by songthaew) holds southern Thai-style bullfights – in which two Brahma bulls butt each other till one retreats – on occasional Sundays. Matches start around 10 am and last at least six hours. Entry is 10B; most of the spectators are men, who bet furiously before and during the matches.

Thaleh Noi Waterbird Sanctuary
อุทยานนกน้ำทะเลน้อย

Thaleh Noi is a small inland sea or lake, 32 km north-east of Phattalung, which is a waterbird sanctuary protected by the Forestry Department. Among the 182 species of waterbird here, the most prominent is the *nók i kong*, with its long, funny feet which quiver like malfunctioning landing gear as the bird takes flight, and the *nók pèt daeng*, a small, red-headed 'duck bird', related to the whistling teal, that skitters along the water. The best time for bird sightings is November and December; the least number of birds is seen from May to August.

The sea itself is sort of a large swamp similar to the Everglades in the southern USA. The major forms of vegetation are

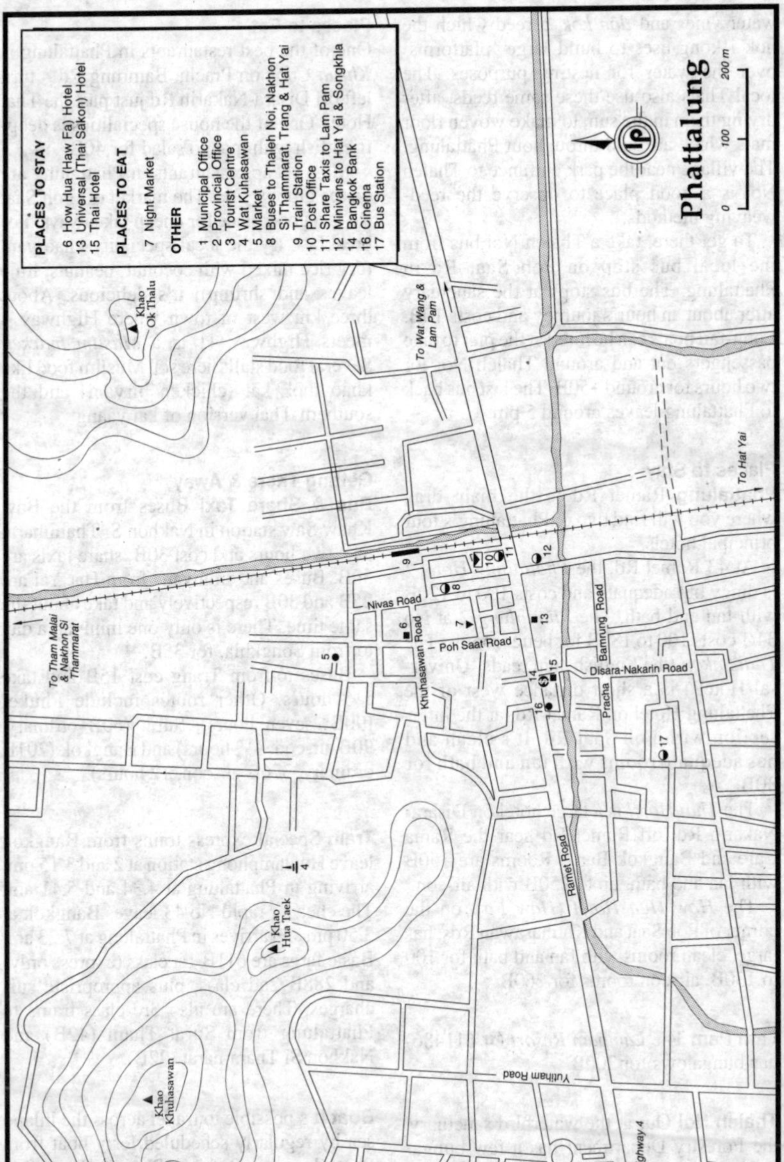

Phattalung
0
100
200 m
PLACES TO STAY
6 How Hua (Haw Fa) Hotel
13 Universal (Thai Sakon) Hotel
15 Thai Hotel
PLACES TO EAT
7 Night Market
OTHER
1 Municipal Office
2 Provincial Office
3 Tourist Centre
4 Wat Kuhasawan
5 Market
8 Buses to Thaleh Noi, Nakhon Si Thammarat, Trang & Hat Yai
9 Train Station
10 Post Office
11 Share Taxis to Lam Pam
12 Minivans to Hat Yai & Songkhla
14 Bangkok Bank
16 Cinema
17 Bus Station
Khao Ok Thalu
Khao Hua Taek
Khao Khuhasawan
To Tham Malai & Nakhon Si Thammarat
To Wat Wang & Lam Pam
To Hat Yai
To Highway 4
Nivas Road
Poh Saat Road
Khuhasawan Road
Pracha Bamrung Road
Disara-Nakarin Road
Ramet Road
Yuthitham Road

water vines and *dôn kòk*, a reed which the nok i kong uses to build large 'platforms' over the water for nesting purposes. The local Thais also use these same reeds, after drying them in the sun, to make woven floor mats which are sold throughout Phattalung. The village near the park entrance to Thaleh Noi is a good place to observe the reed-weaving methods.

To get there, take a Thaleh Noi bus from the local bus stop on Poh Saat Rd in Phattalung. The bus stops at the sanctuary after about an hour's journey and costs 10B. Long-tail boats can be hired at the pier to take passengers out and around Thaleh Noi for two hours for around 150B. The last bus back to Phattalung leaves around 5 pm.

Places to Stay
Phattalung Ramet Rd is the main drag where you will find two of Phattalung's four principal hotels.

At 43 Ramet Rd, the *Phattalung Hotel 1* is dingy but adequate and costs 100 to 120B with fan and bath. The *Phattalung 2* at No 34/1 costs 100 to 180B for better rooms. The *Thai Sakon* (the English sign reads 'Universal Hotel') is a short distance west of the Phattalung Hotel on Ramet Rd, at the intersection with Poh Saat Rd. It's clean and has adequate rooms with fan and bath for 80B.

The *Thai Hotel* is a large hotel on Disara-Nakarin Rd, off Ramet Rd near the Rama Cafe and Bangkok Bank. Rooms are 150B with fan and bath, up to 250B with air-con.

The *How Hua Hotel (Haw Fa)*, on the corner of Poh Saat and Khuhasawan Rds, has large, clean rooms with fan and bath for 100 to 130B, air-con rooms for 260B.

Lam Pam The *Lampam Resort* (☎ 611486) has bungalows for 200B.

Thaleh Noi Out at the waterbird sanctuary, the Forestry Department has a few bungalows for rent for 300B.

Places to Eat
One of the best restaurants in Phattalung is *Khrua Cook* on Pracha Bamrung Rd – turn left off Disara-Nakarin Rd just past the Thai Hotel. One of the house specialities is deep-fried fish with mango salad for 40B.

Most cheap restaurants in Phattalung are on the grubby side. The market off Poh Saat Rd is a good place for cheap takeaways. For breakfast, try the local speciality khâo yam (dry rice mixed with coconut, peanuts, lime leaves and shrimp); it's delicious. About three km west of town where Highway 4 meets Highway 41 is a *Muslim market*. Several food stalls here sell Muslim food like khâo mòk kài (chicken biryani) and the southern-Thai version of kài yâang.

Getting There & Away
Bus & Share Taxi Buses from the Baw Khaw Saw station in Nakhon Si Thammarat take two hours and cost 30B; share taxis are 50B. Buses and minivans from Hat Yai are 25B and 30B respectively and take about the same time. There is only one minivan a day to/from Songkhla, for 35B.

Buses to/from Trang cost 15B and take 1½ hours. Other routes include Phuket (90B, seven hours), Surat (60B ordinary, 90B air-con, 4½ hours) and Bangkok (201B ordinary, 376B air-con, 12 hours).

Train Special express trains from Bangkok leave Hualamphong station at 2 and 3.15 pm, arriving in Phattalung at 4.34 and 5.41 am. The cheaper rapid No 43 leaves Bangkok at 3.50 pm and arrives in Phattalung at 7.23 am. Basic fares are 611B 1st class (express only) and 288B 2nd class, plus appropriate surcharges. There are also 3rd-class trains to Phattalung from Surat Thani (42B) and Nakhon Si Thammarat (22B).

Boat It's possible to travel across the inland sea by regularly scheduled ferry boat from Phattalung to Sathing Phra in Songkhla Province – see the Khukhut Waterbird Sanctuary section following for details.

Songkhla Province

SONGKHLA

อ.เมืองสงขลา

Songkhla (population 84,000), 950 km from Bangkok, is another former Srivijaya satellite on the east coast. Not much is known about the pre-8th century history of Songkhla, a name derived from the Yawi 'Singora' – a reference to a lion-shaped mountain (today called Khao Daeng) opposite the harbour. Originally the settlement lay at the foot of Khao Daeng, where two cemeteries and the ruins of a fort are among the oldest structural remains.

About three km north of Khao Daeng village off the road to Nakhon Si Thammarat is the tomb of Suleiman (1592-1668), a Muslim trader who was largely responsible for Songkhla's commercial eminence during the 17th century. Just south of Suleiman's tomb, a Dutch graveyard testifies to a 17th-century Dutch presence as well (look for large granite slabs in an overgrown area next to a Total warehouse). Suleiman's son Mustapha subsequently fell out of grace with Ayuthaya's King Narai, who burned the settlement to the ground in the next century.

Songkhla later moved across the harbour to its present site on a peninsula between the Thaleh Sap Songkhla (an inland sea) and the South China Sea (or Gulf of Thailand, depending on how you look at it). Today's inhabitants are a colourful mixture of Thais, Chinese and Muslims (ethnic Malays), and the local architecture and cuisine reflect the combination. Older southern Thais still refer to the city as Singora or Singkhon.

The seafood served along the white Hat Samila is excellent, though the beach itself is not that great for swimming, especially if you've just come from Ko Samui. However, beaches are not Songkhla's main attraction, even if the TAT promotes them as such – the town has plenty of other curiosities to offer, though the evergreen trees along Hat Samila give it a rather nice visual effect.

In recent years Songkhla has become increasingly Westernised due to the influx of multinational oil company employees – particularly British and Americans. A short string of farang bars has opened up along Sadao Rd to serve oil workers.

Orientation & Information

The town has a split personality, with the charming older town west of Ramwithi Rd towards the waterfront, and the new town east of Ramwithi Rd – a modern mix of business and suburbia.

Post & Telephone The post office is on Vichianchom Rd; international calls can be made upstairs daily from 8 am to 8 pm.

Songkhla's telephone area code is ☎ 074.

Consulates The Malaysian Consulate (☎ 311062, 311104) is next to Khao Noi at 4 Sukhum Rd, near Hat Samila. Songkhla's US Consulate recently closed.

Around Songkhla

0   2   4 km

To Sathing
Phra & Nakhon
Si Thammarat   4063

Port

See Songkhla Map

Gulf of Thailand

4146

Khao
Daeng

Songkhla

Kao
Seng

Insitute
of Southern
Thai Studies

Thaleh Sap Songkhla

Ko Yo

407

4146

To Hat Yai

Hash House Harriers With all the expats living in Songkhla, there would have to be an HHH chapter. Songkhla's HHH, founded in 1981, usually holds hashes on Saturday at 4.30 pm at different locations around the city. Information is available in the lobbies of the Pavilion and Royal Crown hotels.

Thaleh Sap Songkhla

ทะเลสาบสงขลา

Stretching north-west of the city is the huge brackish lake or 'inland sea' of Thaleh Sap Songkhla. Parts of the Thaleh Sap are heavily fished, the most sought-after catch being the famous black tiger prawn. Illegal gill-net trawling for the prawn is now threatening the overall fish population; legal fishermen have begun organising against gill-net use.

The city's waterfront on the inland sea is buzzing with activity: ice is loaded onto fishing boats on their way out to sea, baskets and baskets of fish are unloaded onto the pier from boats just arrived, fish markets are setting up and disassembling, long-tail boats doing taxi business between islands and mainland are tooling about. The fish smell along the piers is pretty powerful though, so be warned.

National Museum

พิพิธภัณฑ์แห่งชาติ

This is in a 100-year-old building of southern Sino-Portuguese architecture, between Rong Meuang and Jana Rds (off Vichianchom Rd). The museum contains exhibits from all national art-style periods, particularly the Srivijaya. Unfortunately the museum has become rather neglected. Hours are the usual 9 am to noon and 1 to 4 pm, Wednesday to Sunday; admission is 10B.

Temples & Chedis

On Saiburi Rd towards Hat Yai, **Wat Matchimawat** has an old marble Buddha image and a small museum. There is also a Sinhalese-style chedi and royal pavilion at the top of **Khao Tang Kuan**, a hill rising up at the northern end of the peninsula.

Beaches

Besides the strip of white sand along **Hat Samila**, there's the less frequented **Hat Son Awn** on a slender cape jutting out between the Gulf of Thailand and Thaleh Sap, north of Samila.

Other Attractions

Songkhla is southern Thailand's educational centre; there is one university, several colleges, technical schools and research institutes, a nursing college and a military training camp, all situated in or near the town.

Suan Tun, a topiary park across from the Samila Hotel, has yew hedges trimmed into animal shapes.

If you are interested in seeing some traditional Songkhla architecture, walk along the back streets parallel to the inland sea waterfront – Nang Ngam, Nakhon Nai and Nakhon Nawk Rds all have some older Songkhla architecture showing Chinese, Portuguese and Malay influence, but it's disappearing fast.

A few km south of Hat Samila is **Kao Seng**, a quaint Muslim fishing village – this is where the tourist photos of gaily painted fishing vessels are taken. Songthaews run regularly between Songkhla and Kao Seng for 7B per person.

Places to Stay – bottom end

The popular and clean *Amsterdam Guest House* at 15/3 Rong Meuang Rd has nice rooms with shared bath for 150 and 180B. It is run by a friendly Dutch woman. On the same street, near the corner of Vichianchom Rd, the rather unsavoury *Holland House* has rooms for 150/175B and an apartment for 350B.

One of the best deals in Songkhla is the *Narai Hotel* (☎ 311078), at 14 Chai Khao Rd, near the foot of Khao Tang Kuan. It's an older wooden hotel with clean, quiet singles/doubles with fan and shared bath for 100B. A huge double room with bath is 150B.

Another place with character is the *Nang Ngam Hotel*, a small Chinese Hotel on Nang

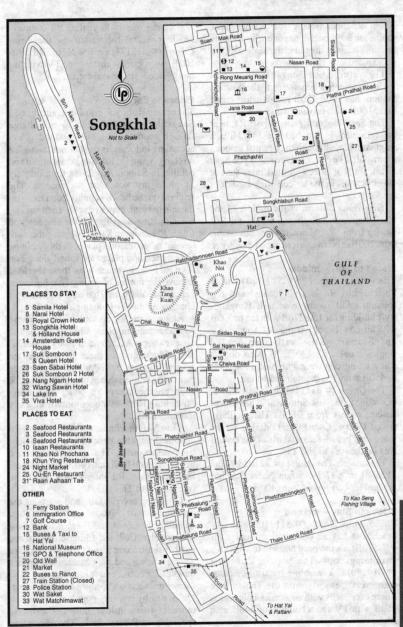

Songkhla

Not to Scale

GULF OF THAILAND

PLACES TO STAY

5 Samila Hotel
8 Narai Hotel
9 Royal Crown Hotel
13 Songkhla Hotel & Holland House
14 Amsterdam Guest House
17 Suk Somboon 1 & Queen Hotel
23 Saen Sabai Hotel
26 Suk Somboon 2 Hotel
29 Nang Ngam Hotel
32 Wiang Sawan Hotel
34 Lake Inn
35 Viva Hotel

PLACES TO EAT

2 Seafood Restaurants
3 Seafood Restaurants
4 Seafood Restaurants
10 Isaan Restaurants
11 Khao Noi Phochana
12 Khun Ying Restaurant
24 Night Market
25 Ou-En Restaurant
31 Raan Aahaan Tae

OTHER

1 Ferry Station
6 Immigration Office
7 Golf Course
12 Bank
15 Buses & Taxi to Hat Yai
16 National Museum
19 GPO & Telephone Office
20 Old Wall
21 Market
22 Buses to Ranot
27 Train Station (Closed)
28 Police Station
30 Wat Saket
33 Wat Matchimawat

To Kao Seng Fishing Village

To Hat Yai & Pattani

Ngam Rd near Yaring Rd. Rather basic rooms are 80B, but for anyone who wants to be in the heart of the old Chinese district this is the place.

The refurbished *Songkhla Hotel*, on Vichianchom Rd across from the Fishing Station, has good 120B rooms with shared bath, 160B with private bath.

The *Suk Somboon 1* on Saiburi Rd, near the museum, is not bad for 140/240B a single/double, although they're just wooden rooms, off a large central area, and you have to ask for that price – posted rates start at 180B. Rooms in the air-con wing next door are 380B.

The *Wiang Sawan*, in the middle of the block between Saiburi and Ramwithi Rds not far from Wat Matchimawat, has rooms from 200B, a bit overpriced for what you get.

Places to Stay – middle

The *Saen Sabai* (☎ 311090) at 1 Phetchakhiri Rd is well located and has clean, if small, rooms in an early Bangkok-style building for 150/270B with fan or 300B with air-con. Nearby is the *Suk Somboon 2* on Saiburi Rd, with fan-cooled singles/doubles for 140/220B. Next door is a new all-air-con wing with rooms for 300B or 450B with TV, bathtub and fridge.

The *Queen* (☎ 311138) at 20 Saiburi Rd, next door to the Suk Somboon 2, has decent air-con rooms from 280B. The similarly priced *Charn (Chan)* (☎ 311903) is on the same road but on the outskirts of the central area on the way to Hat Yai.

The newish *Viva Hotel* (☎ 321033/7; fax 312608), at 547/2 Nakhon Nawk Rd, has modern air-con rooms from 400B.

Places to Stay – top end

The *Samila Hotel* (☎ 311310/4) on the beachfront has air-con singles/doubles for 495/570B; it's the only hotel in town with a swimming pool. The popular *Lake Inn* (☎ 314240) is a rambling multistorey place with great views right on the Thaleh Sap. Rooms are 360B with air-con and hot water, 450B with TV and a bathtub, or 540B with a lake view.

Catering mostly to visiting oil company employees and their families, the *Royal Crown* (☎ 312174) on Sai Ngam Rd costs 605B for rooms with air-con, TV with in-house video, fridge and carpet.

Places to Eat

There are lots of good restaurants in Songkhla but a few tend to overcharge foreign tourists. The best seafood place, according to locals, is the *Raan Aahaan Tae* on Nang Ngam Rd (off Songkhlaburi Rd and parallel to Saiburi Rd). Look for a brightly lit place just south of the cinema. The seafood on the beach is pretty good too – try the curried crab claws or spicy fried squid.

Competing with Tae for the best seafood title is *Buakaew* on Samila Beach – there are several other seafood places in this vicinity. Fancier seafood places are found along Son Awn Rd near the beach – but these also tend to have the hordes of young Thai hostesses kept on to satisfy the Thai male penchant for chatting up *áw-áw* (young girls).

Along Nang Ngam Rd in the Chinese section are several cheap Chinese noodle and congee shops. At the end of Nang Ngam Rd along Phattalung Rd (near the mosque) are several modest Thai-Muslim restaurants; roti kaeng is available at an old worn coffee shop on the corner of Nang Ngam and Phattalung Rds – it's open only from early morning till lunchtime.

Khao Noi Phochana, on Vichianchom Rd near the Songkhla Hotel, has a good lunchtime selection of Thai and Chinese rice dishes. Several food stalls on Sisuda Rd, near the Sai Ngam Rd intersection, do Isaan (north-eastern Thai) food.

There are several fast-food spots at the intersection of Sisuda and Platha Rds, including *Jam Quik* and *Fresh Baker*, plus a few popular Thai and Chinese restaurants. Farther south along Sisuda near the Chalerm Thong cinema and the old train station is a hawkers' centre and night market. The former train station is now a casual cafe-bar. *Ou-en* nearby is a very popular Chinese restaurant with outdoor tables; the house speciality is Peking duck. The very clean

Khun Ying, next door to the Jazzy Blue Pub on Sisuda near the Platha intersection, has inexpensive curries and khanõm jiin.

Entertainment

The Lipstick Bar and Cheeky Pub on Saket Rd next to Wat Saket cater to oil workers and other expats in town with imported liquors, air-con and cable TV. The Offshore and Anytime on Sadao are similar.

Thais tend to congregate at bars with live music in the vicinity of the Sisuda-Platha Rds intersection.

Getting There & Away

Bus Air-con public buses leave Bangkok's southern bus terminal daily at 5, 6.45 and 7.30 pm, arriving in Songkhla 13 hours later for 425B. Ordinary buses are 224B from Bangkok. The privately owned tour buses out of Bangkok (and there are several available) are quicker but cost around 350B. VIP buses are available for 500 to 630B depending on the number of seats.

Air-con buses from Surat to Songkhla and Hat Yai cost 120B one way. From Songkhla to Hat Yai, big green buses leave every 15 minutes (7B) from Rong Meuang Rd, across from the Songkhla National Museum, around the corner from the Songkhla Hotel, or they can be flagged down anywhere along Vichianchom or Saiburi Rds, towards Hat Yai.

Air-con minivans to Hat Yai are 15B. Share taxis are 12B to Hat Yai, 50B to Pattani and 50B to Yala.

Train The old railway spur to Songkhla no longer has a passenger service. See Hat Yai's Getting There & Away section for trains to nearby Hat Yai.

Getting Around

For getting around in town, songthaews circulate Songkhla and take passengers, for 5B, to any point on their route. Motorcycle taxis anywhere in town cost 5 to 10B.

KO YO

เกาะยอ

An island on the inland sea, Ko Yo (pronounced Kaw Yaw) is worth visiting just to see the cotton-weaving cottage industry there. The good-quality, distinctive *phâa kàw yaw* is hand-woven on rustic looms and available on the spot at 'wholesale' prices – meaning you still have to bargain but have a chance of undercutting the usual city price.

Many different households around this thickly forested, sultry island are engaged in cotton-weaving, and there is a central market off the highway so you don't have to go from place to place comparing prices and fabric quality. At the market, prices for cloth and ready-made clothes are excellent if you bargain, and especially if you speak Thai. If you're more interested in observing the weaving process, take a walk down the road behind the market where virtually every other house has a loom or two – listen for the clacking sound made by the hand-operated wooden looms.

There are also a couple of semi-interesting wats, Khao Bo and Thai Yaw, to visit. Along the main road through Ko Yo are several large seafood restaurants overlooking Thaleh Sap. *Pornthip* (about half a km before the market) is reportedly the best.

Folklore Museum

At the northern end of the island at Ban Ao Sai, about two km past the Ko Yo cloth market, is a large folklore museum run by the Institute of Southern Thai Studies, a division of Si Nakharinwirot University. Opened in 1991, the complex of Thai-style pavilions overlooking the Thaleh Sap Songkhla contain well-curated collections (but unfortunately no English labels) of folk art as well as a library and souvenir shop. Displays include pottery, beads, shadow puppets, basketry, textiles, musical instruments, boats, religious art, weapons and various household, agricultural and fishing implements. Among these is a superb collection of coconut-grater seats carved into various animal and human shapes.

On the institute grounds are a series of small gardens, including one occasionally used for traditional shadow theatre performances, a medicinal herb garden and a bamboo culture garden.

Admission to the museum is 10B.

Getting There & Away

From Hat Yai, direct Ko Yo buses – actually large wooden songthaews – leave from near the clock tower on Phetkasem Rd frequently throughout the day. The fare to Ko Yo is 8B; although the bus terminates on Ko Yai further on, it will stop in front of the cloth market on Ko Yo (ask for *nâa talàat*, 'in front of the market'). To get off at the museum, about two km past the market, ask for *phíphítaphan*. From Songkhla, buses to Ranot pass through Ko Yo for the same fare.

Nakhon Si Thammarat or Ranot-bound buses from Hat Yai also pass through Ko Yo via the new bridge system (part of Route 4146) and will stop at the market or museum. Another way to get there is to take a Hat Yai-Songkhla bus to the junction for Ko Yo (5B), then catch the Songkhla-Ranot bus for 3B to the market or museum.

KHUKHUT WATERBIRD SANCTUARY

อุทยานนกน้ำคูขุด

On the eastern shore of the Songkhla inland sea, near Sathing Phra, about 30 km north of Songkhla, is a 520-sq-km sanctuary for waterbirds. Together with the similar Thaleh Noi Waterbird Sanctuary in Phattalung, the wetlands are a habitat for over 200 resident and migrant bird species over the entire Thaleh Sap, including bitterns, egrets and herons (these three are called *nók yang* in Thai), rare Javanese pond heron, fishing eagles (*nók yiaw*), cormorants (*nók kaa*), storks, kites, hawks, falcons, plovers, sandpipers, terns (*nók nang*) and kingfishers.

A book available at the park office has very detailed information on the waterbirds and maps showing habitats. The best birdwatching months are November and December, the worst are May to August.

You can arrange boat trips through the park service – it's 150B for a one-hour birdwatching excursion, or 300B for a three-hour trip to see birds and stop at two islands.

Places to Stay & Eat

At the time of writing there were no guesthouses or hotels in the village (the former *Khukhon Guest House* is now a restaurant only), but it's easy to find rooms in the village for 100B a night.

About five km from the turn-off to the park towards Songkhla (opposite the Km 129 marker), the friendly *Sathing Phra Resort* rents bungalows near the Gulf side of the peninsula for 150 to 270B; you can also pitch a tent here for 50B. A motorcycle taxi from Sathing Phra to the resort costs 10B.

A rustic eating area over the lake next to the park office serves good Thai food. The Sathing Phra Resort offers reasonably priced seafood.

Getting There & Away

Buses to Sathing Phra are 13B from Songkhla – take a red Ranot-bound bus. From the bus stop in front of the Sathing Phra district office you can walk the three km to the park or get a motorcycle taxi for 7 to 10B.

You can also get boats to Khukhut from Phattalung. A long-tail boat (40B) usually leaves Lam Pam daily at 12.30 pm and takes about two hours.

HAT YAI

หาดใหญ่

Hat Yai (population 139,400), 933 km from Bangkok, is southern Thailand's commercial centre and one of the kingdom's largest cities, though it is only a district of Songkhla Province. A steady stream of customers from Malaysia keeps Hat Yai's central business district booming. Everything from dried fruit to stereos are sold in the shops along Niphat Uthit Rds Nos 1, 2 and 3, not far from the train station. Many travellers stay in Hat Yai on their way to and from Malaysia.

Culturally, Hat Yai is very much a Chinese town at its centre, with loads of gold shops and Chinese restaurants. A substantial Muslim minority is concentrated in certain sections of the city, eg near the mosque off Niphat Songkhrao Rd.

Information

Tourist Office The TAT Office (☎ 243747) is at 1/1 Soi 2 Niphat Uthit 3 Rd and is open daily from 8.30 am to 4.30 pm. The tourist police (☎ 246733) can also be found here.

Post & Telephone Hat Yai's GPO is on Niphat Songkhrao 1 Rd just south of the stadium and is open from 8.30 am to 4.30 pm weekdays, 9 am to noon weekends. The adjacent telephone office is open from 7 am to 11 pm daily. There is also a more convenient branch post office on Rattakan Rd, just north of the train station. A private packing service is available next door to the Rattakan post office.

Immigration The immigration office is on Rattakan Rd near the railway bridge. The nearest Malaysian Consulate is in Songkhla.

Money Hat Yai is loaded with banks. Several after-hours exchange windows are along Niphat Uthit 2 and 3 Rds near the Thamnoonvithi Rd (pronounced Thammanun Withi) intersection.

Photography The Chia Colour Lab at 58-60 Suphasan Rangsan Rd, next to the Singapore Hotel, offers a good selection of films and quality processing.

Wat Hat Yai Nai

วัดหาดใหญ่ใน

A few km west of town, off Phetkasem Rd towards the airport, is Wat Hat Yai Nai. A very large (35-metre) reclining Buddha is on the premises (Phra Phut Mahatamongkon). Inside the image's gigantic base is a curious little museum/souvenir shop/mausoleum. To get there, hop on a songthaew near the inter-section of Niphat Uthit 1 and Phetkasem Rds and get off after crossing the U Taphao Bridge.

Bullfighting

Bullfighting, involving two bulls in opposition rather than person and bull, takes place as a spectator sport twice monthly in Hat Yai. On the first Saturday of each month it's at an arena next to the Nora Hotel off Thamnoonvithi Rd, and on the second Saturday it's at the Hat Yai Arena on Highway 4, near the airport. Matches take place continuously all day from 10.30 am until 6 pm and admission is 50B – although many hundred times that amount changes hands during the nonstop betting by Thai spectators.

Because the times and venues for these bullfights tend to change every other year or so, check with the TAT office for the latest.

Places to Stay – bottom end

Hat Yai has dozens of hotels within walking distance of the train station.

Cheaper places nearby include the *Cathay Guest House* (☎ 243815), on the corner of Thamnoonvithi and Niphat Uthit 2 Rds three blocks from the station, with rooms ranging from 120 to 180B; there is also a 60B dorm. The Cathay has become a travellers' centre in Hat Yai because of its good location, helpful staff and plentiful travel info for trips onward, including tips on travel in Malaysia. They have a laundry service and serve inexpensive breakfasts as well as other meals (and also don't mind if you bring takeaways in and eat in the lounge). There is a reliable bus ticket agency downstairs with irregular hours.

Cheaper still are some of the older Chinese hotels in the central area. Rooms are very basic but they're usually secure and service is quite OK – you can get towels and soap on request. The *Tong Nam Hotel* at 118-120 Niphat Uthit 3 Rd is a basic Chinese hotel with rooms for 100B with shared bath, 120B with private bath. *Kim Hua*, opposite and farther south on the same road is 150 to 270B for fan and bath.

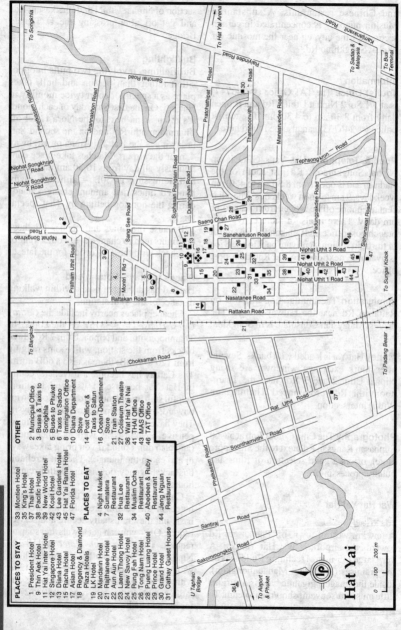

Hat Yai

0   100   200 m

PLACES TO STAY

1   President Hotel
9   Thin Aek Hotel
11 Hat Yai Inter Hotel
12 Singapore Hotel
13 Diana Hotel
15 Racha Hotel
17 Asian Hotel
18 Regency & Diamond
    Plaza Hotels
19 LK Hotel
20 Mandarin Hotel
21 Rajthanee Hotel
22 Aun Aun Hotel
23 Laem Thong Hotel
24 New Savoy Hotel
25 Rung Fah Hotel
26 Pong Nam Hotel
28 Pueng Luang Hotel
29 Prince Hotel
30 Grand Hotel
31 Cathay Guest House
33 Montien Hotel
35 King's Hotel
37 Thai Hotel
38 Pacific Hotel
39 New World Hotel
42 Kosit Hotel
43 Lee Gardens Hotel
45 Hat Yai Rama Hotel
47 Florida Hotel

PLACES TO EAT

4   Night Market
7   Sumatera
    Restaurant
32 Hua Lee
    Restaurant
34 Muslim Ocha
    Restaurant
40 Abedeen & Ruby
    Restaurant
44 Jeng Nguan
    Restaurant

OTHER

2   Municipal Office
3   Buses & Taxis to
    Songkhla
5   Buses to Phuket
6   Taxis to Sadao
8   Immigration Office
10 Diana Department
    Store
14 Post Office &
    Taxis to Satun
16 Ocean Department
    Store
21 Train Station
27 Coliseum Theatre
36 Wat Hat Yai Nai
41 THAI Office
43 MAS Office
46 TAT Office

The *New Savoy Hotel* (☎ 243546), 3½ blocks from the station on Niphat Uthit 2 Rd, has rooms for 120B up. The name might have been changed to New Savoy, but it's as rundown as ever.

On Niphat Uthit 1 Rd is the *Mandarin Hotel*, with rather overpriced rooms for 150B a double with fan and bath, 250B triple. The *Grand Hotel*, at 257-9 Thamnoonvithi Rd, is better, with fairly clean rooms with fan and bath from 130B.

The *Weng Aun* is an old Chinese Hotel across from King's Hotel on Niphat Uthit 1 Rd, four doors down from the Muslim Ocha restaurant. Very basic singles start at 70B.

The friendly *Thin Aek Hotel* at 16 Duangchan Rd (behind Diana Department Store on Niphat Uthit 3 Rd) is another old Chinese relic; it's mostly a holding place for Bangladeshis trying to immigrate to Malaysia, but the owner caters to farang travellers as well. Rooms are 80B with shared bath, 100B with shower, 120B with shower and two large beds (four can sleep for 150B). The toilet is outside for all rooms. Hat Yai used to have more hotels like this, but they're closing down one by one.

Places to Stay – middle

For some reason hotels in Hat Yai take a disproportionate leap upward in quality once you go from 100B a night to 150B and above.

Very popular with Malaysian visitors as well as travellers is the *King's Hotel* on Niphat Uthit 1 Rd. Rooms start at 220B with fan and bath, 310B with air-con. Not far from the train station on Thamnoonvithi Rd is the *Laem Thong Hotel* (☎ 244433) with fairly comfortable singles/doubles for 200B with fan and bath, or 350 to 600B with air-con.

The *OH Hotel (Oriental)* (☎ 245977), at 137-9 Niphat Uthit 3 Rd, has very good fan-cooled singles/doubles in the old wing for 150/200B. In the new wing rooms with air-con, TV, phone and hot water cost 380B.

Rung Fah (☎ 246643), at 117/5-6 Niphat Uthit 3 Rd, has been remodelled and upgraded. Clean rooms are 170 to 200B with fan and bath or a bargain 250 to 280B with air-con.

The *Thai Hotel* on Rat Uthit Rd southwest of the train station has fan-cooled rooms from 130B and air-con rooms up to 300B. There are also cheaper rooms on the top floor for 100B.

The *Pueng Luang (Pheung Luang) Hotel* (☎ 244548), at 241-5 Saeng Chan Rd, has air-con rooms for just 150 to 250B. Nearby, the *Wang Noi* (☎ 245729), 114/1 Saeng Chan Rd, has clean rooms for 150 to 200B with fan or 280 to 300B with air-con.

At 138/2-3 Thamnoonvithi Rd is a place similar to King's called the *Prince Hotel* (☎ 243160). A small room with one bed is 120B; a large room with two beds is 240B. Also good is the *Pacific Hotel* (☎ 244062) at 149/1 Niphat Uthit 2 Rd, with clean fan-cooled rooms for 200B, or 380B for air-con.

The upgraded *Singapore Hotel* (☎ 237478), at 62-66 Suphasan Rangsan Rd, has clean rooms with fan and bath for 170 to 200B, air-con 270 to 300B, and air-con rooms with two beds, TV and hot water for 370B.

There's a rash of places in town calling themselves 'guesthouses' that are really small mid-range hotels. *Louise Guest House* (☎ 220966) at 21-23 Thamnoonvithi Rd costs 220B for air-con, or 330B with hot water – not such a great bargain compared to some of the previously described places. *Lada Guest House* next to the Haad Yai City shopping complex near the train station is similar with rooms with fan from 160B and air-con from 250B. Near the Songkhla bus stand off Phetkasem Rd is *Sorasilp Guest House*, where clean rooms with fan and bath are 150 to 200B.

Places to Stay – top end

The top end in Hat Yai is mainly geared towards Malaysian weekenders, which keeps rates considerably lower than in Bangkok or Chiang Mai. All of the following are fully air-con:

Asian Hotel, 55 Niphat Uthit 3 Rd, 104 rooms, from 530B (☎ 245455; fax 234890)

Diamond Plaza, 62 Niphat Uthit 3 Rd, 280 rooms, from 852B (☎ 230130; fax 230924)

Dusit JB Hotel, 99 Chuti Anuson Rd, 209 rooms, from 1400B (☎ 234300/8; fax 243499)

Emperor, 1 Ranrattankhon Rd, 108 rooms, 420 to 756B (☎ 245166, 235457)

The Florida, 8 Siphunawat Rd, 119 rooms, from 945B (☎ 234555/9; fax 234553)

Grand Plaza, 24/1 Sanehanuson Rd, 145 rooms, from 640B (☎ 234340; fax 234428)

Hat Yai Central, 180 Niphat Uthit 3 Rd, 250 rooms, from 675B (☎ 230000/11; fax 230990)

Hat Yai Inter Hotel, 42-44 Niphat Uthit 3 Rd, 210 rooms, doubles from 400B (☎ 244744; fax 232539)

Kosit, 199 Niphat Uthit 2 Rd, 182 rooms, doubles from 576B in low season, 1006B high (☎ 244711; fax 232365)

Lee Gardens Hotel, 1 Lee Pattana Rd, doubles from 559B (☎ 245888; fax 231888)

LK Hotel, 150 Saeng Chan Rd, 196 rooms, doubles from 692B (☎ 235034; fax 238112)

Manhattan Palace, 29 Chaiyakun Uthit 4 Rd, 180 rooms, 1331 to 1694B (☎ 230724; fax 231315)

Montien, Niphat Uthit 1 Rd, 180 rooms, doubles from 506B (☎ 245593; fax 230043)

New World, 144-158 Niphat Uthit 2 Rd, 133 rooms, 605 to 1212B (☎ 246993)

President, 420 Phetkasem Rd, 110 rooms, doubles from 620B (☎ 244477; fax 235355)

Rajthanee, train station, closed at the time of writing (☎ 232288)

Racha Hotel, 40-42 Niphat Uthit 1 Rd, from 453B (☎ 230951-5; fax 234668)

The Regency, 23 Prachathipat Rd, 189 rooms, doubles from 750B (☎ 245454, 231021)

The Royal Hotel, 106 Prachathipat Rd, 136 rooms, 470 to 1000B (☎ 232162)

Scala Hotel, 43/42-43 Tanrattanakhon Rd, 84 rooms, 400 to 710B (☎ 246983)

Places to Eat

Hat Yai is southern Thailand's gourmet mecca, offering fresh seafood from both the Gulf of Thailand and the Andaman Sea, bird's nests, shark fins, Muslim roti and curries, Chinese noodles and dim sum. Lots of good, cheap restaurants can be found along the three Niphat Uthit Rds, in the markets off side streets between them, and also near the train station.

Chinese Start the day with inexpensive dim sum at *Shangrila* on Thamnoonvithi Rd near the Cathay Guest House. Specialities include khanŏm jìip (dumplings), salabao (Chinese buns) and khâo nâa pèt (roast duck on rice).

In the evenings the Chinese-food action moves to *Hua Lee* on the corner of Niphat Uthit 3 and Thamnoonvithi Rds; it's open till the wee hours.

Jeng Nguan is an old feasting stand-by near the end of Niphat Uthit 1 Rd (turn right from the station; it's on a corner on the left-hand side). Try the tâo hûu thâwt kràwp (fried bean curd), hũu chalãam (shark-fin soup), bàmìi plaa phàt (fried noodles with fish), or kíaw plaa (fish wonton). It's open from 9 am until late at night.

Noodle Garden, opposite the Ocean shopping mall on Sanehanuson Rd, is a more up-market noodle restaurant; there's a second branch on the ground floor of Diana Department Store (Niphat Uthit 3 Rd). Several hotels in town also have good splurge-style Chinese restaurants, including *China Town* (Scala Hotel), *Hong Kong* (Lee Gardens Hotel) and *Dynasty* (Dusit JB Hotel).

Malay & Indian The *Muslim-O-Cha* (Muslim Ocha), across from the King's Hotel, is still going strong, with roti kaeng (roti chanai in Malay) in the mornings and curries all day. This is one of the few Muslim cafes in town where women – even non-Muslim – seem welcome. There are a couple of other Muslim restaurants near this one.

On Niyomrat Rd between Niphat Uthit 1 and 2 are *Ruby*, *Abedeen* and *Mustafa* restaurants, all specialising in Muslim food. Ruby has the best selection of dishes, including Indian paratha, dal, chapati, biryani, and various mutton, chicken, fish and veggie dishes. Abedeen is good for tôm yam kûng (spicy shrimp lemon-grass soup).

Sumatera Restaurant, next to the Pakistan Mosque near the Holiday Plaza Hotel, does Malay dishes like rojak (peanut-sauce salad) and nasi biryani (spiced rice plate).

Thai Although Chinese and Malay food rules in Hat Yai, there are a few Thai places as well. *Noppakao*, a Chinese-owned place on Thamnoonvithi Rd, has an inexpensive and tasty Thai food buffet in the middle of the day and an à-la-carte menu at other times. Another good Thai restaurant is *Niyom Rot* (the English sign says 'Niyom Rosh'), in front of the Nora Hotel on Thamnoonvithi Rd. The plaa krabàwk thâwt, whole sea mullet fried with eggs intact, is particularly prized here.

Although the name is Lao, the *Viang Chan* at 12 Niphat Uthit 2 Rd serves Thai and north-eastern Thai dishes along with Chinese. The food centre below the Tong Nam Hotel has both Thai and Chinese dishes.

Night Markets The extensive night market along Montri 1 Rd specialises in fresh seafood; you can dine on three seafood dishes and one vegetable dish for less than 150B here if you speak Thai. There are smaller night markets along Suphasan Rangsan Rd and Siphuwanat Rd.

Other Food The *Satellite Restaurant*, on Thamnoonvithi Rd next door to Noppakao Restaurant, has a great selection of ice creams, sundaes, shakes, banana splits and Western breakfasts. The menu features colour photos of all the ice cream dishes; prices are reasonable. *Royal Bakery*, at 41 Thamnoonvithi Rd (between Niphat Uthit 1 & 2), has assorted Chinese and Western pastries.

For something very different, cruise down Thanon Nguu (Snake Street – Soi 2, Channiwet Rd), Hat Yai's most popular spot for snake fetishists. After a live snake is slit lengthwise with a scalpel, the blood is drained and drunk with honey, Chinese rice wine or herbal liquor. Besides the blood, the heart, gall bladder and penis are also highly regarded. Skins are sold to manufacturers of wallets, belts and other accessories, while the meat is given away to customers for soup. Rates range from 100B for the evisceration of a small-to-medium cobra to 2000B for a king cobra three or four metres in length.

Entertainment

Most of the many clubs and coffee shops in town cater to Malaysian clientele. The bigger hotels have discos; among the most popular discos are the Disco Palace (Emperor Hotel), the Metro (JB Hotel) and the Inter (Hat Yai Inter Hotel). Cover-charges are only 100 to 120B.

The Post Laserdisc on Thamnoonvithi Rd, a block east of the Cathay Guest House, is a music video/laserdisc bar with an excellent sound system and well-placed monitors. It has mostly Western movies, and programmes change nightly – the fairly up-to-date music videos are a filler between the films. The daily schedule starts at 10 am and goes until 1 am – mostly Thais and farangs come here. There's no admission charge and drink prices are only a little higher than at the average bar.

Opposite the Post Laserdisc, Sugar Rock is one of the more durable Hat Yai pubs, with good food, good prices and a low-key atmosphere.

Four of Hat Yai's six cinemas have sound rooms where the original English soundtrack of English-language films can be heard while watching films that have been dubbed in Thai for the rest of the theatre: Siam (Phetkasem Rd), Coliseum (Prachathipat Rd), Chalerm Thai (Suphasan Rangsan Rd) and the Hat Yai Rama (Phetkasem Rd).

Things to Buy

Shopping is Hat Yai's number-one draw, with most of the market action taking place along Niphat Uthit 2 and 3 Rds. Here you'll find Thai and Malaysian batik, cheap electronics and inexpensive clothing.

SMS Muslim Store, 17 Niphat Uthit 1, has an excellent selection of south Indian sarongs, plus Thai, Malay and Indonesian batiks; although the markets are cheaper they can't compare with SMS in terms of quality and selection.

DK Book House, about 50 metres from the train station on Thamnoonvithi Rd, carries English-language books and maps.

Hat Yai has three major department stores on Niphat Uthit 3 Rd (Diana, Ocean and Yongdee) and two on Thamnoonvithi Rd (World and Haad Yai City).

Getting There & Away – Within Thailand
Air THAI operates flights between Hat Yai and Bangkok every day. Flights take one hour and 20 minutes; the fare is 2280B one way.

There are also THAI flights to Hat Yai from Narathiwat (three times weekly, 420B), Pattani (twice weekly, 300B) and Phuket (daily, 780B).

Bus To Songkhla the green buses leave from outside the small clock tower on Phetkasem Rd. Share taxis leave from around the corner near the President Hotel.

Air-con buses from Bangkok are 428B (VIP 500 to 625B) and leave the southern air-con bus terminal at 7 am and 4, 5.30, 6, 6.15, 6.30, 7, 8 and 8.20 pm. The trip takes 14 hours. Private companies sometimes have fares as low as 300B. Ordinary government buses cost 227B and leave Bangkok at 9.45 and 10.50 pm.

There are lots of buses running between Phuket and Hat Yai; ordinary buses are 122B (eight hours) and air-con 197B (six hours). Air-con minivans to Nakhon Si Thammarat are available for 100B from the Rado Hotel on Sanehanuson Rd. Three daily buses go to Pak Bara (for Ko Tarutao) for 35B (three hours).

Magic Tour (☎ 234535), a travel agency downstairs from the Cathay Guest House, does express air-con buses and minivans to Phuket (220B), Krabi (150B), Ko Samui (250B) and Bangkok. Other buses from Hat Yai include:

Destination	Fare	Hours
Ko Samui	200B	6
Narathiwat	50B	3
(air-con)	65B	3
Pattani	26B	2½
(air-con)	43B	1½
Phattalung	24B	2
Satun	27B	1½
(air-con)	40B	1
Surat Thani	84B	5
(air-con)	150B	4
Trang	35B	2
Yala	35B	2½

Private tour-bus companies include:

Golden Way Travel, 132 Niphat Uthit 3 Rd (☎ 233917; fax 235083)
Magic Tour, ground floor, Cathay Guest House (☎ 234535)
Hat Yai Swanthai Tours, 108 Thamnoonvithi Rd (☎ 246706)
Sunny Tour, Niphat Uthit 2 Rd (☎ 244156)
Pan Siam, 99 Niphat Uthit 2 Rd (☎ 237440)

Share Taxi Share taxis are an important way of getting from one province to another quickly in the south. There are seven share-taxi stands in Hat Yai, each specialising in certain destinations.

In general, share-taxi fares cost about the same as an air-con bus, but the taxis are about 30% faster. Share taxis also offer door-to-door drop-offs at the destination. The downside is that the drivers wait around for enough passengers (usually five minimum) for a departure. If you hit it right the taxi may leave immediately; otherwise you may have to wait for half an hour or more. The drivers also drive at hair-raising speeds – not a pleasant experience for highly-strung passengers.

According to the TAT, the city may soon be establishing a single share-taxi stand on Siphuwanat Rd. Whether or not it will work (each of the current share-taxi stands takes advantage of the quickest route out of the city towards its respective destination) remains to be seen.

Train Trains from Bangkok to Hat Yai leave Hualamphong station daily at 2 pm (special express No 19), 3.15 pm (special express No 11) and 3.50 pm (rapid No 43), arriving in Hat Yai at 5.57 am, 7.05 am and 8.58 am. The basic fare is 664B 1st class (express only), 313B 2nd class. In the reverse direction to Bangkok you can take the 3.20 pm (rapid No 46), 4.55 pm (rapid No 44), 6.10 pm (special express No 12) and 6.40 pm (special express No 20), arriving in Bangkok at 8.35 am, 10.05 am, 9.50 am and 10.35 am.

Third-class trains to Hat Yai start only as far north as Chumphon (99B) and Surat Thani (55B).

The Advance Booking office at Hat Yai station is open from 7 am to 5 pm daily. The station's Rajthanee Restaurant in the Rajthanee Hotel was closed at the time of writing; there's a cheaper eating area on the platform. A left-luggage office (the sign reads 'Cloak Room') is open daily from 5.30 to 11 am and 1 to 7 pm. The cost is 5B per piece for the first five days, 10B thereafter.

Getting There & Away – International

Hat Yai is a very important travel junction – almost any Thailand-Malaysia overland trip involves a stop here.

Air Both THAI and MAS fly from Penang; there are also Silk Air flights from Singapore.

THAI (☎ 243711) has offices in the centre of town at 166/4 Niphat Uthit 2 Rd (☎ 245851) and 190/6 Niphat Uthit 2 Rd (☎ 231272). Malaysia Airlines (MAS, ☎ 245443) has its office in the Lee Gardens Hotel, with a separate entrance on Niphat Uthit 1 Rd.

Hat Yai International Airport has a post office with an IDD telephone in the arrival area; it's open from 8.30 am to 4.30 pm weekdays, 9 am to noon Saturday, closed Sunday. Other airport facilities include the Sky Lounge Cafe & Restaurant on the ground floor near the domestic check-in, a less expensive coffee shop on the 2nd-floor departure level and foreign-exchange kiosks.

Bus From Padang Besar at the Malaysian border, buses are 18B and take an hour to reach Hat Yai. Bus services operate between 6 am and 8 pm.

Magic Tour (☎ 234535), a travel agency downstairs from the Cathay Guest House, does express air-con buses and minivans to Penang (200B and five hours by bus), Kuala Lumpur, Singapore, and destinations within Thailand. Golden Way Travel (☎ 233917; fax 235083), 132 Niphat Uthit 3 Rd, runs VIP (30 reclining seats) buses to Singapore for 380B including all meals; super VIP (24 seats) costs 500B.

Other bus information out of Hat Yai is:

Destination	Fare	Hours
Butterworth (for Penang)	200B	6
Kuala Lumpur*	250 to 300B	12
Singapore*	300 to 400B	15

* denotes private tour-bus companies; see the earlier list for contact details

Warning Care should be taken in selecting travel agencies for bus trips into Malaysia. Recently there have been reports of bus companies demanding 'visa fees' before crossing the border – since visas aren't required for most nationalities, this is a blatant rip-off. The offending company collects your passport on the bus and then asks for the fee – holding your passport hostage. Refuse all requests for visa or border-crossing fees – all services are supposed to be included in the ticket price. One Hat Yai company that has repeatedly perpetrated this scam is Chaw Weng Tours.

Share Taxis Share taxis are a popular way of travelling between Hat Yai and Penang in Malaysia. They're faster than the tour buses, although less comfortable and more expensive. Big old Thai-registered Chevys or Mercedes depart from Hat Yai around 9 am every morning. You'll find them at the train station or along Niphat Uthit 2. In Penang you can find them around the cheap travellers' hotels in Georgetown. The cost is about M$22 – this is probably the fastest way of travelling between the two countries, and you cross the border with a minimum of fuss.

From Hat Yai the fare to Padang Besar is 35B for the one-hour trip; taxis are on Duangchan Rd. For Penang the stand is on Niphat Uthit 1 Rd and the three-hour trip costs 220B.

Getting Around

To/From the Airport The THAI van costs 40B per person for transport to the city; there's also a private 150B THAI limo service. A regular taxi costs 150B from the airport, about half that from the city.

Share Taxi Fares

Destination	Fare	Hours	Taxi Stand
Songkhla	15B	½	near the President Hotel off Phetkasem Rd
Phattalung	50B	1¼	Suphasan Rangsan Rd near Wat Cheu Chang
Trang	60B	2½	Suphasan Rangsan Rd near Wat Cheu Chang
Sungai Kolok	120B	3½	Suphasan Rangsan Rd near Wat Cheu Chang
Betong	100B	3½	Suphasan Rangsan Rd near Wat Cheu Chang
Nakhon Si Thammarat	70B	2½	Suphasan Rangsan Rd near Wat Cheu Chang
Phuket	220B	6	Duangchan Rd
Surat Thani	150B	5	Duangchan Rd
Krabi	150B	5	Duangchan Rd
Narathiwat	80B	3	Niphat Uthit 1 Rd
Sadao	25B	1	Siam Nakarin Department Store, Phetkasem Rd
Khukhut	25B	1	Siam Nakarin Department Store, Phetkasem Rd
Ranot	30B	2	Siam Nakarin Department Store, Phetkasem Rd
Yala	60B	2	Niphat Uthit 2 Rd, near Cathay Guest House
Satun	35B	1½	Rattakan Rd, near the post office
La-Ngu	50B	1½	Rattakan Rd, near the post office

Local Transport The innumerable song-thaews around Hat Yai cost 5B per person. Watch out when you cross the street or they'll mow you down.

AROUND HAT YAI
Ton Nga Chang Falls

น้ำตกโตนงาช้าง

'Elephant Tusk' Falls, 24 km west of Hat Yai via Highway 4 in Rattaphum district, is a seven-tier cascade that falls in two streams (thus resembling two tusks). If you're staying over in Hat Yai, the falls make a nice break from the hustle and bustle of the city. The waterfall looks its best at the end of the rainy season, October to December.

To get to the falls take a Rattaphum-bound songthaew (10B) and ask to get off at the *náam tòk* (waterfall).

Krabi Province

Krabi Province has scenic karst formations near the coast, similar to those in Phang-Nga Province, even in the middle of the Krabi River. Krabi itself sits on the banks of the river right before it empties into the Andaman. Near town you can see Bird, Cat and Mouse Islands, named for their shapes.

Offshore, over 150 islands offer excellent recreational opportunities; many of the islands belong to the **Hat Noppharat Thara - Ko Phi Phi National Marine Park**. Hundreds of years ago, Krabi's waters were a favourite hide-out for Asian pirates because of all the islands and water caves. Latter-day pirates now steal islands or parts of islands for development – land encroachment is reportedly taking place on Phi Phi Don, Poda, Bubu, Jam (Pu), Po, Bilek (Hong), Kamyai and Kluang.

The interior of the province, noted for its tropical forests and the Phanom Bencha mountain range, has barely been explored. Birdwatchers come from far and wide to view Gurney's pitta (formerly thought to be extinct) and Nordmann's greenshank.

Krabi has a nearly new, but hardly used, deep-sea port financed by local speculators

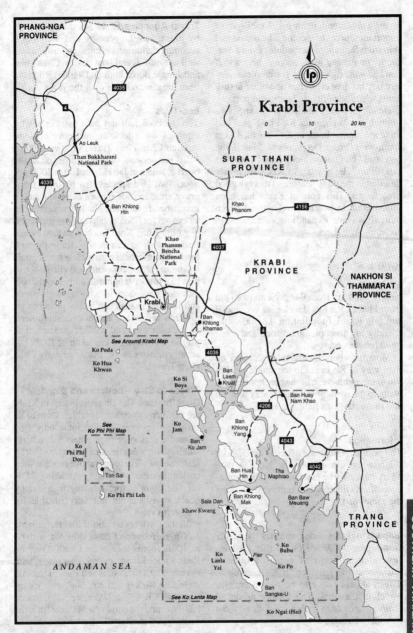

PHANG-NGA PROVINCE

4035

4

Ao Leuk

Than Bokkharani National Park

4039

Ban Khlong Hin

Khao Phanom Bencha National Park

Krabi Province

0   10   20 km

SURAT THANI PROVINCE

Khao Phanom

4156

4037

KRABI PROVINCE

NAKHON SI THAMMARAT PROVINCE

Krabi

Ban Khlong Khamao

See Around Krabi Map

Ko Poda

Ko Hua Khwan

Ko Si Boya

4036

Ban Laem Kruat

Ban Huay Nam Khao

4206

Ban Khlong Yang

4043

See Ko Phi Phi Map

Ko Jam

Ko Phi Phi Don

Ban Ko Jam

Ton Sai

Ko Phi Phi Leh

Ban Hua Hin

Tha Maphrao

4042

Ban Baw Meuang

Sala Dan

Khaw Kwang

Ban Khlong Mak

TRANG PROVINCE

Ko Bubu

Ko Lanta Yai

Pier

Ko Po

ANDAMAN SEA

Ban Sangka-U

See Ko Lanta Map

Ko Ngai (Hai)

in tin, rubber and palm oil, Krabi's most important sources of income. The occasional ship from Singapore (sometimes even a Singapore or Penang junk) anchors here and if you know the right people you can occasionally buy tax-free cigarettes and other luxury items while one of these boats is in port.

Beach accommodation is inexpensive (though not as cheap as Ko Pha-Ngan) and there are regular boats to Ko Phi Phi, 42 km south-west. From December to March, the hotels and bungalows along Krabi's beaches can fill up. The beaches of Krabi are nearly deserted in the rainy season, so this is a good time to go. This part of Krabi has been 'discovered' by world travellers and beach bungalows are expanding operations to accommodate them.

KRABI

อ.เมืองกระบี่

Nearly 1000 km from Bangkok and 180 km from Phuket, the fast-developing provincial capital, Krabi (population 18,000), has friendly townspeople, good food and some good beaches nearby.

Most travellers breeze through town on their way to Ko Lanta to the south, Ko Phi Phi to the south-west, or the beaches near Ao Nang to the west. Some elect to stay in town and make day trips to the latter.

Information

The post and telephone office is on Utarakit Rd past the turn-off for the Jao Fah pier. Visas can easily be extended at the immigration office, which is a bit farther south along the same road.

Maps Bangkok Guide publishes the handy *Guide Map of Krabi* (40B) that contains several mini-maps of areas of interest throughout the province. If it's kept up to date it should prove to be very useful for travel in the area. The locally produced *Krabi Tourist Map* is also good, though not as widely circulated.

Travel Agencies Krabi has dozens of fly-by-night travel agencies that will book accommodation at beaches and islands as well as tour-bus and boat tickets. Chan Phen and Jungle Book, both on Utarakit Rd, have been the most reliable over the years.

Eco-Trips

You can book half-day boat tours to nearby estuaries for a look at mangrove ecology through Chan Phen Travel in town (200 to 350B per person), or simply hire one of the boats at Saphaan Jao Fah for 100 to 200B per hour. Two bird species that frequent mangrove areas include the sea eagle and ruddy kingfisher. In mud and shallow waters, keep an eye out for fiddler crabs and mudskippers.

At the Khao Nor Chuchi Lowland Forest Project, visitors can follow trails through lowland rainforest, swim in clear forest pools and observe/participate in local village activities like rubber-tapping. A daily fee of 250B includes these activities along with meals and lodging in thatched huts – proceeds go towards reforestation, rural development, nature education and wildlife research. The project is located 56 km south of Krabi but arrangements can be made through Chan Phen Travel.

Places to Stay – bottom end & middle

Guesthouses The cheapest places in Krabi are the many guesthouses which seem to be springing up everywhere. Some only stay around a season or two, others seem fairly stable. The ones in the business district feature closet-like rooms above modern shop buildings, often with faulty plumbing – OK for one night before heading to a nearby beach or island but not very suitable for long-term stays.

In the town centre you'll find the reliable *Su Guest House* on Preusa Uthit Rd, with 60 to 100B rooms with shared bath. Over on Ruen Rudee Rd are several other places with the usual upstairs rooms and slow plumbing, including *Walker* and *KL*, both with rooms for 80/100B a single/double with shared bath. Around the corner on Maharat Rd is the *Seaside*, of similar ilk. Better than any of

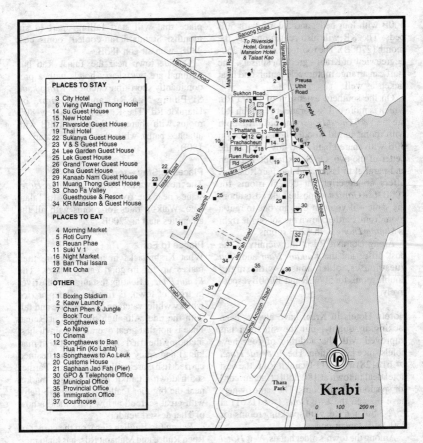

PLACES TO STAY
3 City Hotel
6 Vieng (Wiang) Thong Hotel
14 Su Guest House
15 New Hotel
17 Riverside Guest House
19 Thai Hotel
22 Sukanya Guest House
23 V & S Guest House
24 Lee Garden Guest House
25 Lek Guest House
26 Grand Tower Guest House
28 Cha Guest House
29 Kanaab Nam Guest House
31 Muang Thong Guest House
33 Chao Fa Valley
    Guesthouse & Resort
34 KR Mansion & Guest House

PLACES TO EAT
4 Morning Market
5 Roti Curry
8 Reuan Phae
11 Suki V 1
16 Night Market
18 Ban Thai Issara
27 Mit Ocha

OTHER
1 Boxing Stadium
2 Kaew Laundry
7 Chan Phen & Jungle
    Book Tour
9 Songthaews to
    Ao Nang
10 Cinema
12 Songthaews to Ban
    Hua Hin (Ko Lanta)
13 Songthaews to Ao Leuk
20 Customs House
21 Saphaan Jao Fah (Pier)
30 GPO & Telephone Office
32 Municipal Office
35 Provincial Office
36 Immigration Office
37 Courthouse

Krabi

0   100   200 m

these are the large, fairly clean rooms with private bath at *Grand Tower Guest House* (☎ 612948), over Grand Travel Center on Utarakit Rd. Rates here are 180/220B for singles/doubles. There are also a few rooms with shared bath for 80/120B.

The new *Riverside Guest House*, on Kongkha Rd near the Customs House, has decent 80B rooms and a restaurant with good vegetarian food.

On Prachacheun Rd *Swallow Guest House* is a new place with shipshape rooms for 80/100B a single/double with private bath. Farther north off Maharat Rd, the unsavoury *Anu Guest House* charges 150 to 180B for rooms with fan, 250B for air-con, with hot and cold females of questionable professional status.

Quieter and more comfortable are the guesthouses just south-west of town near the courthouse. On Jao Fah Rd the *Chao Fa Valley Guesthouse & Resort* has good-sized bungalows for 150B with fan, 300B with air-con. Next, on the same side of Jao Fah Rd, *KR Mansion & Guest House* (☎ 612761; fax 612545) offers hotel-style rooms for 120 to 150B with fan and shared bath, 200B a single or double with fan and private bath,

400B with four beds, and a dorm with 50B beds. The KR will also rent rooms by the month (2700B). The rooftop provides a 360-degree view of Krabi – great for sunsets. The staff can arrange motorcycle rentals and boat tickets as well.

On the southern extension of Issara Rd, which is more or less parallel to Jao Fah Rd, are the *V&S Guest House* and *Sukanya*, both with rooms in old wooden houses for 50 to 80B with shared bath. The tidy V&S is the better of the two. On Soi Ruamjit, between and parallel to Issara and Jao Fah Rds, *Lek* offers nondescript but decent rooms for 100B. *Lee Garden*, opposite Lek, costs about the same – if you can find anyone to rent a room from. Farther down the soi on the right is *Muang Thong* with 120B rooms.

Along Utarakit Rd in the vicinity of the post office are the *Kanaab Nam* and *Cha* guesthouses, older houses with single/double rooms for 50/60B and 30/60B respectively.

Hotels Hotels in Krabi have always been lacking in quality, but the situation has improved with the addition of four new hotels since last edition. The *Riverside Hotel* (☎ 612128) at 287/11 Utarakit Rd is the best hotel deal in town at 180/350B (fan/air-con) for spacious, clean rooms. The same owners have opened the *City Hotel* (☎ 611961) at 15/2-3 Sukhon Rd, with sparkling rooms for 250/480B fan/air-con.

Among the town's older hotels, *New Hotel* (☎ 611541) on Phattana Rd has adequate rooms for 120/150B with fan and bath, 300B with air-con. The *Thai Hotel* (☎ 611122) on Issara Rd used to be good value, but they continue to raise the rates and lower the standards. Overpriced rooms with fan start at 300B, air-con from 550B.

Vieng (Wiang) Thong (☎ 611188/288), at 155 Utarakit Rd, is somewhat better. Large doubles with fan and bath are 250B or 400B with air-con; add hot water and TV for 500B and a fridge for 800B.

Standing next to a noisy machine shop, the new *Grand Mansion Hotel* (☎ 611371) at 289/1 Utarakit Rd looks like the kind of place that will start falling apart in six months. Standard fan-cooled rooms cost 280B, with air-con 480B.

Outside town near the Talaat Kao bus terminal are two sleazy hotels with a predominantly short-time clientele: *Kittisuk*, on Si Phang-Nga Rd, and *Naowarat*, on Utarakit Rd. The Kittisuk has a few 80B rooms with shared bath (80 to 140B with attached bath), while the Naowarat starts at 180B.

Places to Stay – top end
The new, swanky *Krabi Meritime Hotel* stands near the river on the way to Talaat Kao. Walk-in rates for rooms with all the amenities start at 2200B.

Places to Eat
What Krabi lacks in hotels it more than makes up for in good eating places. The *Reuan Phae*, a floating restaurant on the river in front of town, is fine for a beer or rice whisky while watching the river rise and fall with the tide. Although the food at Reuan Phae is not that great overall, certain dishes, including the fried shrimp cakes (thâwt man kûng) and spicy hàw mók tháleh (steamed curried fish), are well worth trying. Farther south down Utarakit Rd is a night market near the big pier (called Saphaan Jao Fah), with great seafood at low prices and a host of Thai dessert vendors.

Panan (no English sign), on the corner of Ruen Rudee and Maharat Rds, has khâo mòk kài (chicken biryani) in the mornings, inexpensive curries and kũaytĩaw the rest of day. The roman-script sign reads 'Makanan Islam' (Malay for 'Muslim Food').

Two places on Ruen Rudee Rd specialising in Western breakfasts and a mixed menu of decent Thai and farang food are the nicely decorated *Ban Thai Issara* and *May & Mark* next door.

One of the better restaurants in town for standard Thai dishes and local cuisine is the *Kotung* near Saphaan Jao Fah pier. The tôm yam kûng is especially good, as is anything else made with fresh seafood. Prices are reasonable. Also good, and quite popular with the local Thais, is the air-con *Suki V 1* on Prachacheun Rd. The menu ranges far and wide over Thai and Chinese territory, though the house speciality is of course Thai-style sukiyaki.

For cheap Thai breakfasts, the morning market off Si Sawat Rd in the middle of town is good. Not far from the morning market, on Preusa Uthit Rd, is a Muslim place that serves roti chanai, the Malaysian-style breakfast of flat bread and curry. Look for a sign that says 'Hot Roti Curry Service'. Another cheap and tasty breakfast spot is *Mit Ocha*, a funky coffee shop on the corner of Khongkha and Jao Fah Rds, opposite the customs house. Besides Thai-style coffee and tea, the old Chinese couple here serves khanŏm jiin (served with chunks of pineapple as well as the usual assorted veggies), and custard and sticky rice wrapped in banana leaves (khâo nĭaw săngkha-yaa) – help yourself from the plates on the tables. A good place to hang out if waiting for the morning boat to Phi Phi.

Entertainment

Krabi is pretty quiet at night. About the only thing going is the cinema on Maharat Rd, which has been converted into a dance and sing-song club. The 70B cover charge includes drink, show and dancing – it's good fun.

Getting There & Away

Air When the renovation of the airport is complete (estimated 1997 opening), Bangkok Airways will operate regular flights to Krabi from Bangkok.

Bus, Share Taxi & Minivan Government buses to/from Bangkok cost 161B ordinary, 368 to 377B air-con or 440B VIP (540B for super VIP – 24 seats). Air-con buses leave Bangkok's southern bus terminal between 6.30 and 8 pm; in the reverse direction they leave Krabi between 4 and 5 pm.

Buses to/from Phuket leave hourly during daylight hours, cost 46B (85B with air-con) and take three to four hours. Share taxis to/from Phuket cost 70B; air-con minivans cost 180B.

Buses for Krabi leave Phang-Nga several times a day for 30B.

Ordinary buses between Surat Thani and Krabi make the four-hour trip 13 times daily between 5 am and 2.30 pm for 60B. Air-con buses depart three times a day between 7 am and 3.30 pm for 90B and take around 3½ hours. Through various agencies in town you can pay 90B for a private air-con bus or 150B for air-con minivan.

From Hat Yai buses cost 78B (132B air-con) and take five hours; from Trang, 36B (66B air-con) and 2½ hours. There are also share taxis to/from Trang, Hat Yai and Satun; fares are roughly twice the ordinary bus fare.

Out-of-province buses to/from Krabi arrive at and depart from Talaat Kao, a junction about four km north of Krabi on the highway between Phang-Nga and Trang. To get to the centre of Krabi, catch a songthaew for 5B or motorcycle taxi for 10B. Private air-con buses leaves from Songserm Travel Centre on Utarakit Rd.

Songthaews to Ban Hua Hin (for Ko Lanta) leave from Phattana Rd in town, with a second stop in Talaat Kao, for 30B. They leave about every half hour from 10 am to 2 pm. There are also more expensive air-con minivans available from Krabi travel agencies.

Boat Krabi can be reached by sea from Ko Phi Phi and Ko Lanta. See the respective Phi Phi and Lanta sections for details.

Getting Around

Any place in town can easily be reached on foot, but if you plan to do a lot of exploring out of town, renting a motorcycle might be a good idea. The Suzuki dealer on Preusa Uthit Rd rents bikes for 150 to 200B a day. A couple of other places do motorcycle rental as well, including the Grand Travel Centre on the corner of Jao Fah and Utarakit Rds.

Songthaews to Ao Leuk (for Than Bokkharani Park) leave from the intersection of Phattana and Preusa Uthit Rds for 20B. To Ao Nang (15B) they leave from Utarakit Rd near the New Hotel. Boats to the islands and beaches mostly leave from Jao Fah pier. See the Ao Nang Area Getting There & Away section for boat details.

AROUND KRABI TOWN
Su-Saan Hawy (Shell Cemetery)

สุสานหอย

Nineteen km west of Krabi, on Laem Pho, is the so-called Shell Fossil Cemetery, a shell 'graveyard', where 75-million-year-old shell fossils have formed giant slabs jutting into the sea.

To get there, take a songthaew from the Krabi waterfront for 20B – ask for 'Su-Saan Hawy'.

Wat Tham Seua

วัดถ้ำเสือ

In the other direction, about five km north and then two km east of town, is Wat Tham Seua (Tiger Cave Temple), one of southern Thailand's most famous forest wats. The main wihaan is built into a long, shallow limestone cave, on either side of which dozens of kutis (monastic cells) are built into various cliffs and caves.

The abbot is Ajaan Jamnien, a Thai monk in his forties who has allowed a rather obvious personality cult to develop around him. The usual pictures of split cadavers and decaying corpses on the walls (useful meditation objects for countering lust) are interspersed with large portraits of Ajaan Jamnien, who is well known as a teacher of vipassana and *metta* (loving-kindness). It is said that he was apprenticed at an early age to a blind lay priest and astrologer who practised folk medicine and that he has been celibate his entire life. Many young women come here to practise as eight-precept nuns.

The best part of the temple grounds can be found in a little valley behind the ridge where the bot is located. Follow the path past the main wat buildings, through a little village with nuns' quarters, until you come to some steep stairways on the left. The first leads to an arduous climb to the top of a karst hill with a good view of the area.

The second stairway, next to a large statue of Kuan Yin, leads over a gap in the ridge and into a valley of tall trees and limestone caves. Enter the caves on your left and look for light switches on the walls – the network of caves is wired so that you can light your way chamber by chamber through the labyrinth until you rejoin the path on the other side. There are several kutis in and around the caves, and it's interesting to see the differences in interior decorating – some are very spartan and others are outfitted like oriental bachelor pads.

A path winds through a grove of trees surrounded by tall limestone cliffs covered with a patchwork of foliage. If you continue to follow the path you'll eventually end up where you started, at the bottom of the staircase.

Getting There & Away To get to Wat Tham Seua, take a songthaew from Utarakit Rd to the Talaat Kao junction for 4B, then change to any bus or songthaew east on Highway 4 towards Trang and Hat Yai and get off at the road on the left just after Km 108 – if you tell the bus operators 'Wat Tham Seua' they'll let you off in the right place. It's a two-km walk straight up this road to the wat.

In the mornings there are a few songthaews from Phattana Rd in town that pass the turn-off for Wat Tham Seua (10B) on their way to Ban Hua Hin. Also in the morning there is usually a songthaew or two going direct to Wat Tham Seua from Talaat Kao for around 6B.

Hat Noppharat Thara

หาดนพรัตน์ธารา

Eighteen km north-west of Krabi, this beach used to be called Hat Khlong Haeng (Dry Canal Beach) because the canal that flows into the Andaman Sea here is dry except during, and just after, the monsoon season. Field Marshal Sarit gave the beach its current Pali-Sanskrit name, which means 'Beach of the Nine-Gemmed Stream', as a tribute to its beauty. Recently the Thai navy has cleared

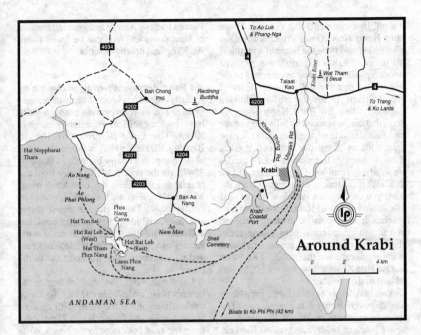

Around Krabi

0   2   4 km

ANDAMAN SEA

Boats to Ko Phi Phi (42 km)

the forest backing the beach to make way for a new royal residence.

The two-km-long beach, part of Hat Noppharat Thara – Ko Phi Phi National Marine Park, is a favourite spot for Thai picnickers. There are some government bungalows for rent and a visitors' centre of sorts, with wall maps of the marine park.

Places to Stay The park pier at the eastern end of Noppharat Thara has boats across the canal to Hat Khlong Muang, where the *Andaman Inn* (50B shared bath, 100/200B attached bath), *Emerald Bungalows* (80B shared bath, 150 to 350B attached bath), *Bamboo Bungalows* (100B with attached bath) and *Sara Cove* (300B with attached bath) offer secluded beach accommodation.

Ao Nang Area

อ่าวนาง

South of Noppharat Thara is a series of bays

where limestone cliffs and caves drop right into the sea. The water is quite clear and there are some coral reefs in the shallows. The longest beach is along Ao Nang, a lovely spot easily reached by road from Krabi.

Over the headlands to the south are the beaches of **Phai Phlong, Ton Sai, Rai Leh**, and then the cape of Laem Phra Nang, which encompasses **Hat Tham Phra Nang** (Princess Cave Beach) on the western side, a beach facing east usually called **East Rai Leh**, and another beach called **Hat Nam Mao**.

All these beaches are accessible either by hiking over the headland cliffs, or by taking a boat from Ao Nang or Krabi – although for several years now rumours have said that a tunnel road will be built to Hat Phai Phlong to provide access to a new resort hotel that is being constructed there.

Hat Tham Phra Nang This is perhaps the most beautiful beach in the area. At one end

SOUTHERN THAILAND

is a tall limestone cliff that contains **Tham Phra Nang Nok** (Outer Princess Cave), a cave that is said to be the home of a mythical sea princess. Local fisherfolk place carved wooden phalli in the cave as offerings to the princess so that she will provide plenty of fish for them. Inside the cliff is a hidden 'lagoon' called **Sa Phra Nang** (Princess Pool) that can be reached by following a cave trail into the side of the mountain. A rope guides hikers along the way and it takes about 45 minutes to reach the pool – guides are available from local guesthouses. If you turn left off the trail after 50 metres from the start, you can reach a 'window' in the cliff that affords a view of Rai Leh West and East beaches. It's also possible to climb to the top of the mountain from here (some rock-climbing is involved) and get an aerial view of the entire cape and the islands of **Ko Poda** and **Ko Hua Khwan** (also known as Chicken Island) in the distance.

A second, larger cave on Laem Phra Nang was discovered only a few years ago. The entrance is in the middle of the peninsula near a batch of beach huts on East Rai Leh. This one is called **Tham Phra Nang Nai** (Inner Princess Cave) and consists of three caverns. All three contain some of the most beautiful limestone formations in the country, including a golden 'stone waterfall' of sparkling quartz. Local mythology now says that this cave is the 'grand palace' of the sea princess while Tham Phra Nang on the beach is her 'summer palace'.

The islands off Laem Phra Nang are good areas for snorkelling. Besides Ko Poda and Ko Hua Khwan there is the nearer island of **Ko Rang Nok** (Bird Nest Island) and, next to that, a larger, unnamed island (possibly part of the same island at low tide) with an undersea cave. One fairly interesting dive site is the sunken boat just south of Ko Rang Nok, a favoured fish habitat. Some of the bungalows do reasonably priced day trips to these as well as other islands in the area. Fun three-day snorkelling/camping trips – sometimes led by chao naam – can be arranged for around 1000B per person.

Places to Stay A large and growing number of bungalows and inns can be found along Ao Nang and nearby beaches.

Ao Nang Because it's easily accessible by road, this beach has become fairly developed of late. The more expensive places usually have booking offices in amphoe meuang Krabi. The *Krabi Resort* (☎ 612160; in Bangkok (02) 208-9165), at the northern end of Ao Nang, has luxury bungalows that cost 2367B on the beach, 1415B away from the beach, and 2047B in the new hotel wing. Most of the guests are with package tours or conferences. There are the usual resort amenities, including a swimming pool, bar and restaurant. Bookings can be made at the Krabi Resort office on Phattana Rd in Krabi and guests receive free transport out to the resort.

Off Route 4203, the road leading to the beach's north end, *Timber House* has tacky modern bungalows for 880B with air-con, hot water, TV and fridge. *Beach Terrace*, on the same road but closer to the beach, costs 1340B for similar accommodation, while the *Ao Nang Ban Lae* next door has simple but well-maintained bungalows for 150 to 250B. On the opposite side of the road, *Ban Ao Nang* is a modern hotel with rooms for 500 to 950B.

Down on the water, *PS Cottage* doesn't seem to have huts any more – at last pass just the restaurant was open. Going south along the beach you'll come to *Ao Nang Beach, Wanna's Place* and *Sea Breeze*, all 100 to 150B for fairly simple huts, and *Gift's*, a nicer spot with larger huts with bath for 250 to 350B. Next along the beach is a strip of gift shops and food stalls – at one time a hotel called *Ao Nang Plaza* was supposed to be constructed here but the project is apparently on hold.

The beach road intersects Route 4203 to Krabi just before you arrive at *Phra-Nang Inn* (☎ 612173/4), a tastefully designed 'tropical hotel' with sweeping views of the bay and a small pool. Large air-con rooms are 1749B a night in the high season (usually

December to February), 1300B the remainder of the year. They have a good restaurant.

Next door is the *Ao Nang Villa* (☎ 612431), with recently upgraded roomy cottages with all the amenities for 1400 to 2200B. Right around the corner on Route 423, the new *Ao Nang Royal* (☎ 611606) has decent bungalows for 400/500B with fan and private bath, up to 1000B with air-con.

Up Route 4203, 100 or so metres from the beach, is the small *BB Ao Nang Bungalow* with relatively modern but simple accommodation for 250 to 350B. Farther up the road the *Green Park* is one of the better cheapies with well-maintained huts for 80B with shared bath, 100/150B with attached bath. Moving further away from the beach, along Route 4203, is *Krabi Seaview Resort* (☎ 611648) with modern A-frames for 500/980B fan/air-con, followed by *Jungle Hut* with adequate bungalows for 70B with shared bath, 120B with private bath. On the opposite side of Route 4203, well back from the road, the *Peace Laguna Resort* (☎ 611972) has gone more up-market with new bungalows for 450B with fan and private bath, 1000B with air-con.

Farther east along Route 4203 is the newer *Mountain View Bungalows* with small fan-cooled bungalows for 150 to 250B and larger ones for 350B, followed by the simple 100B *Ao Nang Village*. Farther on yet, *Flamingo House*, *Hillock* and *Backpacker* offer motel-like rooms for around 100B – take Hillock if you must choose one of these.

Ao Phai Phlong This peaceful, palm-studded cove is worth boating to for the day. At the moment there is no accommodation here. A few years back a hotel conglomerate was rumoured to have purchased the land but so far there are no signs of construction.

Hat Ton Sai This beach can only be reached by boat from Ao Nang, Ao Nam Mao or Krabi. New management has taken over *Andaman Bungalows* here, providing accommodation for 80 to 350B per night. The old setup was highly praised, and recent reports say the tradition continues.

Hat Rai Leh (West) Towards the north-west end of this pretty bay, *Railay Village* (☎ 611944, ext 27) offers huts with bath for 200B up, possibly lower in the off season. The *Sand Sea* and *Railey Bay* have similar accommodation starting at 150B. All three have pleasant dining areas. At the northern end of the beach is a private beach condominium development. It's possible to rent vacant bungalows from the caretakers for 500 to 2000B a night.

West Rai Leh can be reached by boat from Ao Nang, Ao Nam Mao or Krabi, or on foot from Hat Phra Nang and Hat Rai Leh (east) (but these must be approached by boat as well).

Hat Tham Phra Nang The only place to stay at this beautiful beach is the *Dusit Rayavadee* (☎ (02) 238-0032), a tastefully designed and fairly unobtrusive resort with 179 luxurious rooms starting at 8000B.

The beach is not Dusit's exclusive domain – a wooden walkway has been left around the perimeter of the limestone bluff so that you can walk to Hat Tham Phra Nang from East Rai Leh. From West Rai Leh a footpath leads through the forest around to the beach. Phra Nang is accessible by boat or foot only.

Hat Rai Leh (East) The beach along here tends towards mud flats during low tide; most people who stay here walk over to Hat Tham Phra Nang for beach activities.

Railey Beach 2 (formerly Queen), *Sunrise Bay*, *Ya-Ya* and *Coco Bungalows* all offer fair bungalows for 100 to 150B in December and January, half that the rest of the year. Ya-Ya is still the best maintained – they also offer guide service for Phra Nang caving excursions. Ya-Ya and Coco have the best food.

At the northern end of the beach *Viewpoint Bungalows* has bungalows with attached bath for 300 to 450B, negotiable in the off season. Phra Nang Diving School, headquartered at Viewpoint, offers reasonable dive courses and excursions.

A bit farther, near the Phra Nang Nai caves, the *Diamond Cave Bungalows* rents poorly maintained huts in a rubber grove for 80B up. An outdoor bar set against a rock cliff next to the cave and bungalows is atmospheric, but the night-time din carries for some distance – light sleepers beware.

Ao Nam Mao This large bay, around a headland to the north-east of East Rai Leh, about 1½ km from the Shell Cemetery, has a coastal environment similar to that of East Rai Leh – mangroves and shallow, muddy beaches.

Here you'll find the environmentally friendly *Dawn of Happiness Beach Resort* (☎ 612730; fax 612251), where natural, locally available building materials are used wherever possible and no sewage or rubbish ends up in the bay. Thatched bungalows with private baths and mosquito nets cost 200 to 400B per night depending on the season. The staff can arrange trips to nearby natural attractions.

Ao Nam Mao is accessible by road via Route 4204. If you phone from Krabi, the Dawn of Happiness will arrange free transport.

Getting There & Away Hat Noppharat Thara and Ao Nang can be reached by songthaews that leave about every 15 minutes from 7 am to 5 pm from Utarakit Rd in Krabi, near the New Hotel. The fare is 15B and the trip takes 30 to 40 minutes.

You can get boats to Ton Sai, West Rai Leh and Laem Phra Nang at several places. For Ton Sai, the best thing to do is get a songthaew out to Ao Nang, then a boat from Ao Nang to Ton Sai. It's 15B per person for two people or more, 30B if you don't want to wait for a second passenger to show up. You may have to bargain to get this fare.

For West Rai Leh or anywhere on Laem Phra Nang, you can get a boat direct from Krabi's Jao Fah pier for 40B. It takes about 45 minutes to reach Phra Nang. However, boats will only go all the way round the cape to West Rai Leh and Hat Phra Nang from October to April when the sea is tame enough. During the other half of the year they only go as far as East Rai Leh, but you

can easily walk from here to West Rai Leh or Hat Phra Nang. You can also get boats from Ao Nang for 20B all year round, but in this case they only go as far as West Rai Leh and Hat Phra Nang (again, you can walk to East Rai Leh from here). From Ao Nang you'll have to pay 20B per person for two or more passengers, 40B for just one.

Another alternative is to take a songthaew as far as Ao Nam Mao, to the small fishing bay near the Shell Cemetery, for 15B and then a boat to Laem Phra Nang for 20B (three or more people required).

Some of the beach bungalows have agents in Krabi who can help arrange boats – but there's still a charge.

AROUND KRABI PROVINCE
Than Bokkharani National Park

อุทยานแห่งชาติธารโบกขรณี

Than Bokkharani National Park was established in 1991 and encompasses nine caves throughout the Ao Leuk area in northern Krabi Province as well as the former botanical gardens for which the park was named.

The park is best visited just after the monsoons – when it has been dry a long time the water levels go down and in the midst of the rains it can be a bit murky. In December Than Bokkharani looks like something cooked up by Disney, but it's real and entirely natural. Emerald-green waters flow out of a narrow cave in a tall cliff and into a large lotus pool, which overflows steadily into a wide stream, itself dividing into many smaller streams in several stages. At each stage there's a pool and a little waterfall. Tall trees spread over 40 rai (6.4 sq km) provide plenty of cool shade. Thais from Ao Leuk come to bathe here on weekends and then it's full of laughing people playing in the streams and pools. During the week there are only a few people about, mostly kids doing a little fishing. Vendors sell noodles, roast chicken, delicious batter-fried squid and sôm-tam under a roofed area to one side.

Caves Among the park-protected caves scattered around the Ao Leuk district, one of the most interesting is **Tham Hua Kalok**, set in a limestone hill in a seldom-visited bend of mangrove-lined Khlong Baw Thaw. Besides impressive stalactite formations, the high-ceilinged cave features 2000 to 3000-year-old cave paintings of human and animal figures and geometric designs.

Nearby **Tham Lawt** (literally, 'tube cave') is distinguished by a navigable stream flowing through it – it's longer than Phang-Nga's Tham Lawt but shorter than Mae Hong Son's.

Places to Stay *Ao Leuk Bungalow*, on the highway half a km before Than Bok, offers decent if overpriced cottages for 200B with private bath; you may be able to bargain for a lower rate if there are empty rooms.

In nearby Ao Leuk Tai, the wooden *Thai Wiwat Hotel* next to the district office has plain rooms for 70B.

Getting There & Away Than Bok, as the locals call it, is off Highway 4 between Krabi and Phang-Nga, near the town of Ao Leuk, one km south-west towards Laem Sak. To get there, take a songthaew from the intersection of Phattana and Preusa Uthit Rds in Krabi to Ao Leuk for 17B; get off just before town and it's an easy walk to the park entrance on the left.

To visit Tham Lawt and Tham Hua Kalok you must charter a boat from Tha Baw Thaw, around 6.5 km south-west of Than Bok. The tours are run exclusively by Ao Leuk native Uma Kumat and his son Bunma. They'll take one or two people for 100B; up to 10 can charter a boat for 250B. The boats run along secluded Khlong Baw Thaw and through Tham Lawt before stopping at Tham Hua Kalok. The pier at Tha Baw Thaw is 4.3 km from Than Bok via Route 4039, then two km by dirt road through an oil palm plantation. You must provide your own transport to Tha Baw Thaw.

Khao Phanom Bencha National Park

อุทยานแห่งชาติเขาพนมเบญจา

This 50-sq-km park is in the middle of virgin rainforest along the Phanom Bencha mountain range. The main scenic attractions are the three-level **Huay To Falls, Khao Pheung Cave** and **Huay Sadeh Falls**, all within three km of the park office. Other less well-known streams and waterfalls can be discovered as well. Clouded leopards, black panthers, Asiatic black bears, deer, leaf monkeys, gibbons and various tropical birds make their home here. The park has a camping ground where you are welcome to pitch your own tent for 5B per person per night.

Getting There & Away Public transport direct to Khao Phanom Bencha National Park from Krabi or Talaat Kao is rare. Two roads run to the park off Highway 4. One is only about half a km from Talaat Kao – you could walk to this junction and hitch, or hire a truck in Talaat Kao all the way for 100B or so. The other road is about 10 km north of Krabi off Highway 4. You could get to this junction via a songthaew or a bus heading north to Ao Leuk.

It would be cheaper to rent a motorcycle in Krabi for a day trip to Phanom Bencha than to charter a pick-up. Try to have someone at the park watch your bike while hiking to nearby falls – motorcycle theft at Phanom Bencha has been a real problem lately.

KO PHI PHI

เกาะพีพี

Ko Phi Phi actually consists of two islands about 40 km from Krabi, Phi Phi Leh and Phi Phi Don. Both are part of Hat Noppharat Thara – Ko Phi Phi National Marine Park, though this means little in the face of the blatant land encroachment now taking place on Phi Phi Don.

Only parts of Phi Phi Don are actually under the administration of the Park Division of the Royal Thai Forestry Department. Phi Phi Leh and the western cliffs of Phi Phi Don are left to the nest collectors and the part of Phi Phi Don where the chao naam live is also not included in the park.

Phi Phi Don
พีพีดอน

Phi Phi Don is the larger of the two islands, a sort of dumbbell-shaped island with scenic hills, awesome cliffs, long beaches, emerald waters and remarkable bird and sea life. The 'handle' in the middle has long, white-sand beaches on either side, only a few hundred metres apart. The beach on the southern side curves around **Ao Ton Sai**, where boats from Phuket and Krabi dock. There is also a Thai-Muslim village here. On the northern side of the handle is **Ao Lo Dalam**.

The uninhabited (except for beach huts) western section of the island is called Ko Nawk (Outer Island), and the eastern section, which is much larger, is Ko Nai (Inner Island). At the north of the eastern end is Laem Tong, where the island's chao naam (sea gypsy) population lives. The number of chao naam here varies from time to time, as they are still a somewhat nomadic people, sailing from island to island, stopping off to repair their boats or fishing nets, but there are generally about 100. With stones tied to their waists as ballast, chao naam divers can reportedly descend up to 60 metres while

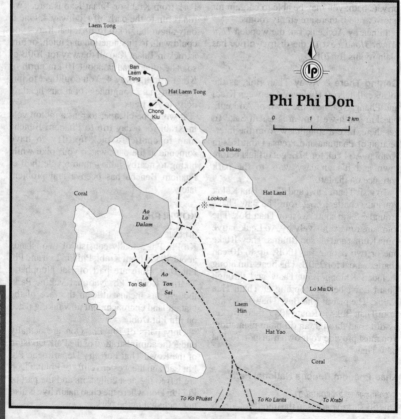

Phi Phi Don

breathing through an air hose held above the water surface. Like Pacific islanders of perhaps 100 years ago, they tend to be very warm and friendly horizon-gazers. Of late, resort developers have been buying up their land.

Hat Yao (Long Beach) faces south and has some of Phi Phi Don's best coral reefs. Ton Sai, Lo Dalam and Hat Yao all have beach bungalows. Over a ridge north-west from Hat Yao is another very beautiful beach, **Hat Lanti**, with good surf. For several years the locals wouldn't allow any bungalows here out of respect for the large village mosque situated in a coconut grove above the beach – but money talked, and the chao naam walked. Farther north is the sizeable bay of **Lo Bakao**, where there is a small resort, and near the tip of Laem Tong are three luxury resorts.

Unfortunately, the park administrators have allowed development on Phi Phi Don to continue unchecked. Rumour has it that park officials won't dare even set foot on Ko Phi Phi for fear of being attacked by village chiefs and bungalow developers profiting from tourism. Beautiful Ao Ton Sai is becoming littered, and more and more bungalows have been crowded onto this section of the island. The noise of the generators is only drowned out by the sounds of Arnold firing large weapons at his enemies during the latest Schwarzenegger epic showing at every other bungalow restaurant.

A friend who recently visited Ton Sai had this report:

Bay packed with boats, small and large, grimy and grand luxe. New hotels building by the pier; scaffolding, dust and din, tin shacks for construction workers all about. Plenty of illegally obtained shell art, hamburgers, pizza, beer bars – Pattaya without the prostitutes. Huge piles of garbage and endless rows of dreary, crowded bungalow developments. Where's the nature? Everywhere the horrid smell of rotting cashew fruit. No-one harvests the nuts any more and no one fishes. Why bother when you can ferry farangs around the coral reefs?

Other parts of Phi Phi Don aren't this bad, though the once-brilliant coral reefs around the island are suffering from anchor drag and runoff from large beach developments. The least disturbed parts of the island so far are those still belonging to those few chao naam who haven't cashed in.

Phi Phi Leh

พีพีเล

Phi Phi Leh is almost all sheer cliffs, with a few caves and a sea lake formed by a cleft between two cliffs that allows water to enter into a bowl-shaped canyon. The so-called **Viking Cave** contains prehistoric paintings of stylised human and animal figures alongside later paintings of ships (Asian junks) no more than 100 years old.

The cave is also a collection point for sea swallow nests. The sea swallows (*Collocalia esculenta*, also known as edible-nest swiftlets) like to build their nests high up in the caves in rocky hollows which can be very difficult to reach. Agile collectors build vine-and-bamboo scaffolding to get at the nests but are occasionally injured or killed in falls. Before ascending the scaffolds, the collectors pray and make offerings of tobacco, incense and liquor to the cavern spirits.

Those who want to collect sea swallow nests must bid for a licence which gives them a franchise to harvest the nests for four years. In one year there are only three harvests, as the birds build seasonally, and the first harvest fetches the highest prices. The collectors sell the nests to intermediaries who then sell them to Chinese restaurants in Thailand and abroad. Known as 'white gold', premium teacup-sized nests sell for US$2000 per kilo – Hong Kong alone imports US$25 million worth every year. The nests are made of saliva which the birds secrete – the saliva hardens when exposed to the air. When cooked in chicken broth, the nests soften and separate and look like bean thread noodles. The Chinese value the expensive bird secretions highly, believing them to be a medicinal food that imparts vigour.

No-one is allowed to stay on Phi Phi Leh because of the bird-nest business, but boats can be hired from Phi Phi Don for the short jaunt over to see the caves and to do a little snorkelling at the coral reefs in Ao Ma-Ya.

Places to Stay

I'm all for boycotting travel to Ko Phi Phi until the national park comes to terms with greedy developers. On the other hand, if people don't see what's happening to Phi Phi they won't protest and the island will fall further into the iron grip of those who would turn this rare island into one big, polluted resort. What follows is a brief summary of places to stay for those who choose to go in the spirit of investigation (or for those who can ignore the obvious impact of unchecked development). If you go with the former intention, please contact one of the organisations listed under Ecology (Tourism & the Environment) in the Facts about the Country chapter with your assessments, whether good or bad.

During the high tourist months of December to February, July and August, nearly all the accommodation on the island gets booked out. As elsewhere during these months, it's best to arrive early in the morning to stake out a room or bungalow. During the off season, rates are negotiable.

Ao Ton Sai

Chao Koh Phi Phi Lodge, 400 to 500B
Gypsy Village, 25 rooms, 300B
Pee Pee Island Cabana, 116 rooms, from 760B
Pee Pee Princess, 60 rooms, 300 to 1200B
Phi Phi Andaman Bungalow, 80 rooms, 100 to 300B
Rim Na Villa, 14 rooms, 300 to 500B
Tonsai Village, 50 rooms, 90 to 1500B

Lo Dalam

Chong Khao, 37 rooms, 100 to 300B
Pee Pee Pavilion Resort, 52 rooms, 900 to 1800B
PP Charlie Beach, 79 rooms, 200 to 600B
PP Viewpoint, 50 rooms, 500 to 800B

Ao Maphrao

Maphrao Resort, 100 to 320B

Hat Yao

Coral Bay Resort, closed for repairs
Long Beach, 60 rooms, 100 to 300B
PP Paradise Pearl, 90 rooms, 180 to 700B

Laem Tong

Phi Phi Palm Beach, 78 rooms, 1000 to 3500B
PP Coral Resort, 51 rooms, 1000 to 1500B
PP International Resort, 70 rooms, 2200 to 3200B

Lo Bakao

Pee Pee Island Village, 60 rooms, 100 to 1500B

Getting There & Away

Ko Phi Phi is equidistant from Phuket and Krabi, but Krabi is your most economical point of departure. Until recently, boats travelled only during the dry season, from late October to May, as the seas are often too rough during the monsoons for safe navigation.

Nowadays the boat operators risk sending boats out all year round – we've received several reports of boats losing power and drifting in heavy swells during the monsoons. It all depends on the weather – some rainy season departures are quite safe, others are risky. If the weather looks chancy, keep in mind that there usually aren't enough life jackets to go around on these boats.

Another cautionary note regards the purchase of return-trip boat tickets. From Krabi there are currently two boat services and if you buy a return ticket from one company you must use that service in both directions. Neither service will recognise tickets from its competitor; not only that, they will refuse to sell you a new ticket back to Krabi if you hold a return ticket from the competitor. The advisable thing, then, is to buy one-way tickets only.

To/From Krabi From Krabi's Jao Fah pier, there are usually three boats a day leaving at 9 am, 1 and 3 pm. The official fare is 125B per person, but this is sometimes discounted by agents in town to as low as 90 or 100B. The trip takes about 1¾ hours on the faster boats or 2½ hours on the slower ones, to reach the public pier at Ao Ton Sai. In the reverse direction the boats leave at the same times.

The second service, operated by Pee Pee Island Cabana, leaves from a pier adjacent to the Jao Fah pier at 10 am and 1 pm for the same fare. This boat is air-con and takes 80 to 90 minutes to reach the Pee Pee Island Cabana pier. The fare is 200B.

There is talk of a new concrete pier being built at Laem Tong, the northern tip of Ko Phi Phi Don. If the pier comes about, it will probably mean the introduction of a third boat service from Krabi.

To/From Ao Nang You can also get boats from Ao Nang on the Krabi Province coast for 100B per person from October to April; there's usually only one departure a day at around 2 pm.

To/From Phuket A variety of boats leave Patong throughout the day for 150 to 200B per person. This trip takes 1½ hours on the fast boat, and up to three hours on the slow boat. There is also a new jet-boat service from Phuket at 2.30 pm that takes 40 minutes and costs 350B.

To/From Other Islands As Ko Lanta is becoming more touristed, there are now fairly regular boats between that island and Ko Phi Phi from October to April. Boats generally leave from the pier on Lanta Yai around 1 pm, arriving at Phi Phi Don around 3 pm. In the reverse direction the departure is usually at 11.30 am. Passage is 150B per person. It's also possible to get boats to/from Ko Jam; the same approximate departure time, fare and trip duration applies.

Organised Tours Various tour companies in Phuket offer day trips to Phi Phi for 350 to 500B per person, including return transport, lunch and a tour. If you want to stay overnight and catch another tour boat back, you have to pay another 100B. Of course it's cheaper to book one-way passage on the regular ferry service.

Pee Pee Island Cabana also does package deals from Krabi or Phuket that include accommodation and a tour of Phi Phi Leh.

Getting Around
Transport on the island is mostly on foot,

although fishing boats can be chartered at Ao Ton Sai for short hops around Phi Phi Don and Phi Phi Leh. There is an irregular boat service between Ton Sai and Hat Yao (Long Beach) for 10B per person.

KO JAM (KO PU) & KO SI BOYA
เกาะจำ(ปู)/เกาะสีบอยา
These large islands are inhabited by a small number of fishing families. At this writing there is one set of bungalows on the western side of Ko Si Boya called *Islander Hut* for 80 to 200B per night. Ko Jam's southern tip is occupied by a private residential development. *Joy Resort* on the south-western coast of Ko Jam has bungalows for 150 to 250B.

Getting There & Away
Boats to both islands leave two or three times a day from Ban Laem Kruat, a village about 30 km from Krabi, at the end of Route 4036, off Highway 4. Passage is 15B to Si Boya, 20B to Ban Ko Jam.

You can also take boats bound for Ko Lanta from Krabi's Jao Fah pier and ask to be let off at Ko Jam. There are generally two boats daily which leave at 8 am and 1 pm; the fare is 130B.

KO LANTA
เกาะลันตา
Ko Lanta (population 18,000) is a district of Krabi Province that consists of 52 islands. The island geography here is typified by stretches of mangrove interrupted by coral-rimmed beaches, rugged hills and huge umbrella trees. Twelve of the islands are inhabited and, of these, three are large enough to be worth exploring: **Ko Klang, Ko Lanta Noi** and **Ko Lanta Yai**. At present you have to get there by ferry from either Ban Hua Hin, on the mainland across from Ko Lanta Noi, or from Baw Meuang, farther south.

Ko Lanta Yai is the largest of the three islands – district offices and piers are found in **Ban Sala Dan**, at the northern tip of the island, and **Ban Ko Lanta**, on the lower east

SOUTHERN THAILAND

coast. The western sides of all the islands have beaches. The best are along the southwest end of Lanta Yai, but practically the whole west coast of Lanta Yai is one long beach interrupted by the occasional stream or shell bed. There are coral reefs along parts of the western side of Lanta Yai and along the Khaw Kwang (Deer Neck) cape at its north-western tip. A hill on the cape gives a good aerial view of the island.

The people in this district are a mixture of Muslim Thais and chao naam who settled here long ago. There is now a long string of

inexpensive bungalow operations on Lanta Yai and you can camp on any of the islands – all have sources of fresh water. The village of **Ban Sangka-U** on Lanta Yai's southern tip is a traditional Muslim fishing village and the people are friendly. Ban Sala Dan at the northern end is the largest village on the island and even has a few TVs.

The little island between Ko Lanta Noi and Ko Klang has a nice beach called **Hat Thung Thaleh** – hire a boat from Ko Klang. Also worth exploring is Ko Ngai (Hai) – see the Trang Province section for more details,

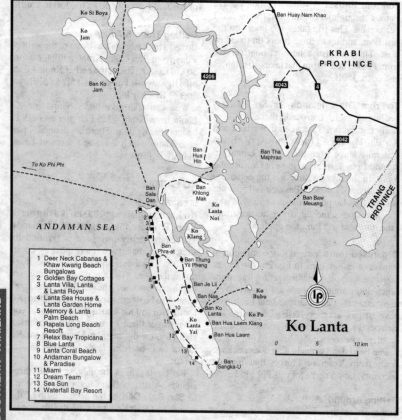

1 Deer Neck Cabanas & Khaw Kwang Beach Bungalows
2 Golden Bay Cottages
3 Lanta Villa, Lanta & Lanta Royal
4 Lanta Sea House & Lanta Garden Home
5 Memory & Lanta Palm Beach
6 Rapala Long Beach Resort
7 Relax Bay Tropicana
8 Blue Lanta
9 Lanta Coral Beach
10 Andaman Bungalow & Paradise
11 Miami
12 Dream Team
13 Sea Sun
14 Waterfall Bay Resort

Ko Lanta

as Ko Ngai is more accessible from that province.

Ko Lanta National Marine Park
อุทยานแห่งชาติทางทะเลหมู่เกาะลันตา

In 1990, 15 islands in the Lanta group (covering an area of 134 sq km) were declared part of the new Ko Lanta National Marine Park in an effort to protect the fragile coastal environment. **Ko Rok Nok** is especially beautiful, with a crescent-shaped bay featuring cliffs and a white-sand beach and a stand of banyan trees in the interior. The intact coral at **Ko Rok Nai** and limestone caves of **Ko Talang** are also worth seeing.

Ko Lanta Yai itself is only partially protected since most of the island belongs to chao naam. So far many bungalows have been built on lands protected by the Forestry Department – if the rangers or the villagers don't crack down soon it will become another Ko Phi Phi.

The park headquarters is situated at the southern tip of Ko Lanta Yai.

Places to Stay
Ko Lanta Outside of Ban Sala Dan, Ko Lanta doesn't have regular electric service yet. Quiet nights are still the rule at the less expensive places, while generators are buzzing at new up-market bungalows. Two Krabi hotels have bought tracts of land here in anticipation of the arrival of a power grid – rumours say Prime Minister Chuan Leekpai also has land on the island.

Ko Lanta has the opportunity of becoming a model for environmentally conscious island tourism if the beach developers here will cooperate to keep the island clean and noise-free. Deforestation is becoming a problem as unscrupulous developers cut down trees to build up-market bungalows with hectares of decks. The simple places catering to backpackers still use renewable bamboo. As seems obvious elsewhere in Thailand, the national park system cannot be relied upon to protect the lands.

At the northern end of Lanta Yai near Ban Sala Dan is the *Deer Neck Cabanas*. It's actually on the south-east side of the small peninsula of the same name that juts west from the island. Nicely separated huts with private bath on a long curving beach cost 200 to 300B. The adjacent *Khaw Kwang Beach Bungalows* is similar.

Starting about 2½ km south of Ban Sala Dan along the western side of the island are a cluster of places in the 200 to 300B range – *Golden Bay Cottages, Lanta Villa, Lanta* and *Lanta Royal*, followed by the more modern *Lanta Sea House* with bungalows for 400 to 600B. *Lanta Garden Home* next door has more basic huts with shared bath for 80B.

Just around a headland famous for a triple-trunked coconut palm are *Memory* at 50 to 100B and the friendly *Lanta Palm Beach*, where good huts rent for 80 to 120B. The beach here is good, and the affiliated Impossible Bar is a nice spot for a sunset drink.

A couple of km farther south along the beach is the new, up-market, poorly designed *Rapala Long Beach Resort* where prices hadn't been set at the time of writing. The nearby *Relax Bay Tropicana* features spacious bungalows with large decks for 200 to 600B – though one wonders whether the copious hardwoods came from the island's officially protected interior. The beach along this stretch – and for the next two km – is nothing special.

Another km south are the *Blue Lanta* and *Lanta Coral Beach* with bungalows for 50 to 80B with shared bath, 100 to 250B with private bath.

Farther south another km or so the beach begins improving. On the left-hand side of the road opposite the beach, *Andaman Bungalow* (formerly Lanta Had Beach) has basic huts for 80 to 100B. This one closes during the off season. The nearby *Paradise* has a family atmosphere, decent food and simple huts for 60B; huts with private bath are 300B. *Miami*, to the immediate south, offers OK bungalows with good beach frontage for 100 to 250B.

Sitting by itself on a rather uninspiring stretch of beach is the beautifully landscaped

Dream Team with new bungalows in the 100 to 400B range.

Just before the road ends is the secluded *Sea Sun* with 50/100B cement bungalows. Right at the end of the road, *Waterfall Bay Resort* costs from 250 to 350B for huts with fan and bath. A dirt track continues to the park headquarters and Ban Sangka-U. This is a good spot to stay if you're interested in hiking into the park interior.

Ban Ko Lanta On the island's lower east coast, near the pier for boats to/from Baw Meuang on the mainland, *No Name* provides very basic accommodation for 50B a night. Just north of here in the village of Ban Si Fa Ya, *Kedah Hut* offers slightly better lodging.

Ko Bubu This tiny island has one bungalow village with 13 huts. Rates are 100B per person in a dormitory, 200B in a bungalow with shared bath or 500B in a two-bed bungalow with private bath.

To get to Bubu from Lanta you can charter a boat from Samsan pier (Ban Ko Lanta) for 150 to 200B. From Krabi the boat to Ban Sala Dan on Ko Lanta Yai continues on to Baw Meuang with a stop at Bubu. You can also get boats from Baw Meuang. More information is available at the Samsan pier on Ko Lanta or from Thammachat (☎ (075) 612536), on Kongkha Rd near the Jao Fah pier in Krabi.

Places to Eat
If you get tired of bungalow food there are a couple of basic places to eat in Ban Sala Dan at the northern end of Lanta Yai. *Pier 1 Restaurant* next to the pier has good coffee and pastries. A more traditional place near the pier has great khâo yam and paa-thông-kŏ in the mornings. *Danny's*, on the beach near Lanta Garden Home, does decent pizza, home-made bread and Mexican food.

Getting There & Away
To/From Ban Hua Hin The slow way to get to Ko Lanta is to take a songthaew (30B) from Phattana Rd in Krabi all the way to Ban Hua Hin, and then a boat (10B) across the

narrow channel to Ban Khlong Mak on Ko Lanta Noi. From there, get a motorcycle taxi (20B) across to another pier on the other side, then a long-tail ferry (5B) to Ban Sala Dan on Ko Lanta Yai. Ban Hua Hin is 26 km down Route 4206 from Ban Huay Nam Khao, which is about 44 km from Krabi along Highway 4.

Songthaews from Krabi (Talaat Kao junction) to Ban Hua Hin run regularly until about 3 pm. Count on two hours to complete the trip, including ferry crossing. If you're travelling by private car or motorcycle, the turn-off for Route 4206 is near Km 63 on Highway 4. Cars have to be parked near the pier in Ban Hua Hin. Motorcycles can be taken on both ferries all the way to Ko Lanta Yai.

To/From Krabi by Boat The quickest way to reach Ko Lanta from Krabi is to take a boat from Krabi's Jao Fah pier. Boats usually depart at 10.30 am and 1.30 pm and take one to 1½ hours to reach Ban Sala Dan; the fare is 150B. In the reverse direction boats leave at 8 am and 3 pm.

To/From Ban Baw Meuang You can also take a boat from Ban Baw Meuang, which is about 35 km from Ban Huay Nam Khao at the end of Route 4042 (about 80 km in total from Krabi). The turn-off for Route 4042 is at Km 46 near the village of Sai Khao. It's 13 km from Ban Sai Khao to Ban Baw Meuang on this dirt road. The boats from Ban Baw Meuang are fairly large, holding up to 80 people, and they take an hour to reach Samsan pier on Lanta Yai's eastern shore. The fare is 30B.

To/From Ko Phi Phi During the dry season, October to April, there are fairly regular boats from Ko Phi Phi for 150B per person. They take about an hour and 20 minutes to reach Ban Sala Dan. There are also occasional boats to Lanta from the pier on Ko Jam.

Getting Around
Most of the bungalows on Ko Lanta will

provide free transport to and from Ban Sala Dan. Motorcycle taxis are available from Ban Sala Dan to almost anywhere along the beaches for 10 to 40B depending on the distance. From Ban Ko Lanta, motorcycle taxi fares fall in the same range.

Motorcycles can be rented in Ban Sala Dan for a steep 250B a day.

Trang Province

The province of Trang has a geography similar to that of Krabi and Phang-Nga, with islands and beaches along the coast and limestone-buttressed mountains inland, but is much less frequented by tourists. Caves and waterfalls are the major attractions in the interior of the province – Trang seems to have more than its share.

Twenty km north of the capital is a 3500-rai (5.6-sq-km) provincial park, which preserves a tropical forest in its original state. In the park there are three waterfalls and government rest houses. Between Trang and Huay Yot to the north is Thaleh Song Hong (Sea of Two Rooms), a large lake surrounded by limestone hills. Hills in the middle of the lake nearly divide it in half, hence the name.

Music & Dance

As in other southern provinces, public holidays and temple fairs feature performances of *Manohra*, the classical southern Thai dance-drama, and nang thalung (shadow play). But because of its early role as a trade centre, Trang has a unique Indian-influenced music and dance tradition as well. *Li-khe pàa* (also called *li-khe bòk* and *li-khe ram manaa*) is a local folk opera with a story line that depicts Indian merchants taking their Thai wives back to India for a visit. It's part farce, part drama, with Thais costumed as Indians with long beards and turbans.

Traditional funerals and Buddhist ordinations often feature a musical ensemble called *kaa-law*, which consists of four or five players sitting on a small stage under a temporary coconut-leaf roof or awning. The instruments include two long Indian drums, a *pii haw* (a large oboe similar to the Indian *shahnai*) and two gongs.

TRANG

 อ.เมืองตรัง

Historically, Trang (population 49,400) has played an important role as a centre of trade since at least the 1st century AD and was especially important between the 7th and 12th centuries, when it was a sea port for ocean-going sampans sailing between Trang and the Straits of Malacca. Nakhon Si Thammarat and Surat Thani were major commercial and cultural centres for the Srivijaya empire at this time, and Trang served as a relay point for communications between the east coast of the Thai peninsula and Palembang, Sumatra. Trang was then known as Krung Thani and later as Trangkhapura (City of Waves) until the name was shortened during the early years of the Ratanakosin period.

During the Ayuthaya period, Trang was a common port of entry for seafaring Western visitors, who continued by land to Nakhon Si Thammarat or Ayuthaya. The town was then located at the mouth of the Trang River, but King Mongkut later gave orders to move the city to its present location inland because of frequent flooding. Today Trang is still an important point of exit for rubber from the province's many plantations.

One of Trang's claims to fame is that it often wins awards for 'Cleanest City in Thailand' – its main rival in this regard is Yala. One odd aspect of the city is the seeming lack of Thai Buddhist temples. Most of those living in the central business district are Chinese, so you do see a few joss houses but that's about it. Meun Ram, a Chinese temple between sois 1 and 2, Visetkul Rd, sometimes sponsors performances of southern-Thai shadow theatre.

Trang's main attractions are the nearby beaches and islands, plus the fact that it can be reached by train. The Vegetarian Festival

SOUTHERN THAILAND

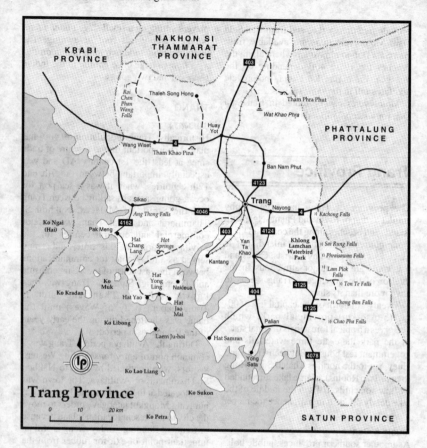

Trang Province

0   10   20 km

is celebrated fervently in Trang in September or October (see the Phuket section for details).

The post & telephone office is on the corner of Phra Ram VI and Yermpanya Rds.

Trang's telephone area code is ☎ 075.

Places to Stay

A number of hotels are found along the city's two main thoroughfares, Phra Ram VI Rd and Visetkul (Wisetkun) Rd, which run from the clock tower. The *Ko Teng* (☎ 218622) on Phra Ram VI Rd has large singles/doubles for a reasonable 140/200B, and a good res-

taurant downstairs. The management can be very helpful with enquiries on what to see and do around Trang, and they also have an information board of sorts with details on local attractions.

The *Wattana Hotel* (☎ 218184), on the same street, offers upgraded rooms for 200B with fan and bath or 430B for air-con.

Over on Ratchadamnoen Rd is the inexpensive *Petch (Phet) Hotel* (☎ 218002), with fair rooms with fan and shared bath for 70B, or with attached bath for 90 to 140B. They also have a restaurant downstairs. Another inexpensive place is the *Mai Tri Hotel* on

SOUTHERN THAILAND

Phra Ram VI near the train station. Basic but clean rooms are 80B. As we went to press we received an unconfirmed report that this hotel had closed.

On Visetkul Rd are the *Queen Hotel* (☎ 218522), with large clean rooms with fan for 200B, or 300B with air-con, and the business-like *Trang Hotel* (☎ 218944), near the clock tower, with upgraded fan-cooled rooms for 420B or air-con from 480B.

The 10-storey *Thamrin* (☎ 211011; fax 218057) is an up-market place on Kantang Rd near the train and bus stations. Modern air-con rooms cost 600B standard, 900B deluxe.

Places to Eat

Plenty of good restaurants can be found in the vicinity of the hotels. Next door to the Queen Hotel is the *Phailin Restaurant*, which has a very broad selection of rice and noodle dishes. The menu has several vegetarian dishes including wûn-sên phàt jeh sài phõng kari (bean-thread noodles stir-fried with curry powder), kũaytĩaw phàt hâeng tâo-hûu (rice noodles fried with tofu) and khâo nâa kà-phrao tâo-hûu (tofu stir-fried with holy basil over rice). Or make it simple and get khâo phàt jeh, vegetarian fried rice. Another house speciality is kafae phailin, a spiced coffee made with local Khao Chong coffee.

The restaurant below the Ko Teng Hotel has good one-plate rice dishes and reputable kaeng kari kài (chicken curry), as well as ko-píi, Trang's famous Hokkien-style coffee.

Two khâo tôm places on Phra Ram VI Rd, *Khao Tom Phui* and *Khao Tom Je Uan*, serve all manner of Thai and Chinese standards in the evenings till 2 am. Phui has been honoured with the Shell Chuan Chim designation for its tôm yam (available with shrimp, fish or squid), sea bass in red sauce (plaa kraphõng náam daeng) and stir-fried greens in bean sauce (pûm pûy kha-náa fai daeng).

Khanõm Jiin

Trang is famous for khanõm jiin (Chinese noodles with curry). One of the best places to try it is at the tables set up on the corner of Visetkul and Phra Ram VI Rds. You have a choice of dousing your noodles in náam yaa (a spicy ground fish curry), náam phrík (a sweet and slightly spicy peanut sauce), or kaeng tai plaa (a very spicy mixture of green beans, fish, bamboo shoots and potato). To this you can add your choice of fresh grated papaya, pickled veggies, cucumber and bean sprouts – all for just 5B per bowl.

Across the street from this vendor, in front of the municipal offices, is a small night market that usually includes a couple of khanõm jiin vendors.

Ko-píi Shops

Trang is even more famous for its coffee and ráan kafae or ráan ko-píi (coffee shops), which are easily identified by the charcoal-fired aluminium boilers with stubby smokestacks seen somewhere in the middle or back of the open-sided shops. Usually run by Hokkien Chinese, these shops serve real filtered coffee (called kafae thũng in the rest of the country) along with a variety of snacks, typically paa-thông-kõ, salabao (Chinese buns), khanõm jiip (dumplings), Trang-style sweets, mũu yâang (barbecued pork) and jók (thick rice soup).

When you order coffee in these places, be sure to use the Hokkien word ko-píi rather than the Thai kafae, otherwise you may end up with Nescafé or instant Khao Chong coffee – the proprietors often think this is what farangs want. Coffee is usually served with milk and sugar – ask for ko-píi dam for sweetened black coffee or ko-píi dam, mâi sài náam-taan for black coffee without sugar.

The best ráan ko-píi in town are the *Sin Jiew* (open 24 hours) on Kantang Rd near Phra Ram VI Rd; *Bo Daeng* (open from 6 am till midnight), next to a Chinese clan house and Bangkok Bank on Phra Ram VI Rd near Kantang Rd; *Huat Ocha* (open from 5 am to 5 pm) on Visetkul Rd next to Wattana School; and *Khao Ocha* (open from 6 am to 8 pm) on Visetkul Rd Soi 5.

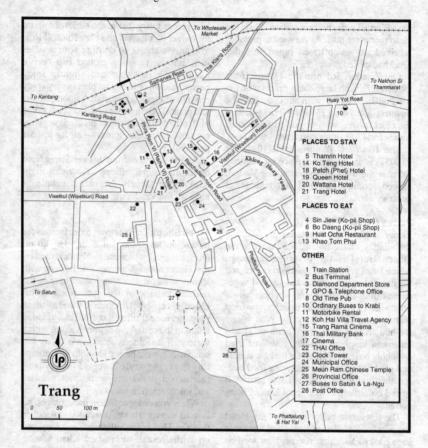

PLACES TO STAY

5 Thamrin Hotel
14 Ko Teng Hotel
18 Petch (Phet) Hotel
19 Queen Hotel
20 Wattana Hotel
21 Trang Hotel

PLACES TO EAT

4 Sin Jiew (Ko-pii Shop)
6 Bo Daeng (Ko-pii Shop)
9 Huat Ocha Restaurant
13 Khao Tom Phui

OTHER

1 Train Station
2 Bus Terminal
3 Diamond Department Store
7 GPO & Telephone Office
8 Old Time Pub
10 Ordinary Buses to Krabi
11 Motorbike Rental
12 Koh Hai Villa Travel Agency
15 Trang Rama Cinema
16 Thai Military Bank
17 Cinema
22 THAI Office
23 Clock Tower
24 Municipal Office
25 Meun Ram Chinese Temple
26 Provincial Office
27 Buses to Satun & La-Ngu
28 Post Office

Trang

0   50   100 m

To Kantang
To Wholesale Market
To Nakhon Si Thammarat
Huay Yot Road
Sathanee Road
Tha Klang Road
Kantang Road
Phra Ram VI (Rama VI) Road
Ratchadamnoen Road
Visetkul (Wisetkun) Road
Khlong Huay Yang
Phattalung Road
Visetkul (Wisetkun) Road
To Satun
To Phattalung & Hat Yai

Entertainment

Old Time Pub, on Kao Rd a bit east of the town centre, is a cosy, air-con place with good service and no jii-khoh hassles. The Relax Pub at 25/50 Huay Yot Rd is a dark, expensive place with the usual parade of Thai female singers. Underneath the Trang Rama cinema is the Boss Club, with a mix of sing-song and disco action.

Things to Buy

Trang is known for its wickerwork and, especially, mats woven of *bai toei* (pandanus leaves), which are called *sèua paa-nan*, or Panan mats. Panan mats are important bridal gifts in rural Trang, and are a common feature of rural households. The process of softening and drying the pandanus leaves before weaving takes many days. They can be purchased in Trang for about 100 to 200B.

The province also has its own distinctive cotton-weaving styles. The villages of Na Paw and Na Meun Si are the most highly regarded sources for these fabrics, especially the intricate diamond-shaped *lai lûuk kâew* pattern, once reserved for nobility.

The best place in town for good buys is the

Tha Klang wholesale market along Tha Klang Rd.

Getting There & Away
Air THAI operates three flights weekly from Bangkok (2005B), four from Phuket (435B), and three from Surat Thani (495B). The Trang THAI office (☎ 218066) is at 199/2 Visetkul Rd.

Bus & Share Taxi A bus from Satun or Krabi to Trang is 35B; from Hat Yai it's 30B. A share taxi from the same cities is around 60B. Air-con buses from Krabi cost 66B and take three to four hours. From Phattalung it's 15B by bus, 30B by share taxi.

From Ban Huay Nam Khao, the junction for Highway 4 and the road to Ko Lanta, a bus to Trang is 20B.

Air-con buses to/from Bangkok are 375B (203B for an ordinary bus) or 565B for a VIP bus. The air-con buses take about 12 hours.

Train Only two trains go all the way from Bangkok to Trang, the rapid No 41, which leaves Hualamphong station at 6.30 pm, arriving in Trang at 10.10 am the next day and the express No 13, which leaves Bangkok at 5.05 pm and arrives in Trang at 8 am. The fare is 597B 1st class, 282B 2nd class, not including rapid or express surcharges. There are no direct 3rd-class trains to Trang; you must change in Thung Song, a rail junction town in Nakhon Si Thammarat Province. From Thung Song there are two trains daily to Trang, leaving at 9.30 am and 3.20 pm, arriving an hour and 45 minutes later.

If you want to continue on to Kantang on the coast, there is one daily ordinary train out of Trang at 5.02 pm which arrives in Kantang at 5.20 pm; the rapid No 41 also terminates in Kantang, arriving at 10.45 am. The fare from Trang to Kantang is 5B in 3rd class (5.02 pm train only) or 28B in 2nd class on the rapid No 41.

Getting Around
Samlors around town cost 10B per trip. Honda 100cc motorbikes can be rented from a shophouse (☎ 218473) at 44A Phra Ram VI Rd for 180B per day.

BEACHES
Trang Province has several sandy beaches and coves along the coast, especially in the Sikao and Kantang districts. On Route 403 between Trang and Kantang is a turn-off west onto an unpaved road that leads down to the coast through some interesting Thai-Muslim villages. At the end, it splits north and south. The road south leads to Hat Yao, Hat Yong Ling and Hat Jao Mai. The road north leads to Hat Chang Lang and Hat Pak Meng.

Hat Jao Mai & Ko Libong
หาดเจ้าไหมและเกาะลิบง
Both Hat Jao Mai and Ko Libong can be found in Kantang district, about 35 km from Trang. The wide white-sand beach is five km long and gets some of Thailand's biggest surf (probably the source of the Trang's original unshortened name, City of Waves). Hat Jao Mai is backed by casuarina trees and lime-stone hills with caves, some of which contain prehistoric human skeletal remains. **Tham Jao Mai** is the most interesting of the caves, a large cavern with lots of stalactites and stalagmites. In their only known appearance on the Thai-Malay peninsula, rare black-necked storks frequent Jao Mai to feed on molluscs and crustaceans.

This beach is part of 231-sq-km **Hat Jao Mai National Park**, which includes Hat Chang Lang farther north and the islands of Ko Muk, Ko Kradan, Ko Jao Mai, Ko Waen, Ko Cheuak, Ko Pling and Ko Meng. Camping is permitted on Jao Mai and there are a few bungalows for rent as well.

Off the coast here is **Ko Libong**, Trang's largest island. There are three fishing villages on the island, so boats from Kantang Port are easy to get for the one-hour trip. The Botanical Department maintains free shelters on Laem Ju-Hoi, a cape on the western tip of Ko Libong. On the south-western side of the island is a beach where camping is permitted. The *Libong Beach Resort*

(☎ 210013) has A-frame thatched bunga-lows for 300 to 400B. About one km from the pier on Libong is the *Tongrop Bungalow* with basic huts for 40B.

Hat Yong Ling & Hat Yao

หาดหยงหลิง/หาดยาว

A few km north of Hat Jao Mai are these two white-sand beaches separated by limestone cliffs. There is no accommodation here as yet.

Hat Chang Lang

หาดช้างหลาง

Hat Chang Lang is part of the Hat Jao Mai National Park, and this is where the park office is located. The beach is about two km long and very flat and shallow. At the north-ern end is Khlong Chang Lang, a stream that empties into the sea.

Ko Muk & Ko Kradan

เกาะมุก/เกาะกระดาน

Ko Muk is nearly opposite Hat Chang Lang and can be reached by boat from Kantang or Pak Meng. The coral around Ko Muk is lively, and there are several small beaches on the island suitable for camping and swim-ming. The best beach, Hat Sai Yao, is on the opposite side of the island from the mainland and is nicknamed Hat Farang because it's 'owned' by a farang from Phuket.

Near the northern end is **Tham Morakot** (Emerald Cave), a beautiful limestone tunnel that can be entered by boat during low tide. At the southern end of the island is pretty Phangka Cove and the fishing village of Hua Laem.

Ko Kradan is the largest and most beauti-ful of the islands that belong to Hat Jao Mai National Park. Actually, only five of six pre-cincts on the island belong to the park: one is devoted to coconut and rubber plantation. There are fewer white-sand beaches on Ko Kradan than on Ko Muk, but the coral reef on the side facing Ko Muk is quite good for diving.

Places to Stay & Eat *Ko Muk Resort* (Trang office: 25/36 Sathanee Rd, next to the train station; ☎ 211367, 211381), on Muk facing the mainland next to the Muslim fishing village of Hua Laem, has simple but nicely designed bungalows for 125B with shared bath, 200B with bath. The beach in front tends towards mud flats during low tide; the beach in front of the nearby village is slightly better but modest dress is called for. The resort organises boats to nearby islands like Ko Ngai, Waen, Kradan and Lanta. The only telephone on the island is a radio phone in the village.

Ko Kradan Resort (☎ 211391 in Trang; (02) 392-0635 in Bangkok) has OK bunga-lows and ugly cement shophouse-style rooms for 400B a night and up. The beach isn't bad, but this resort gets low marks for serving lousy, expensive food and for litter-ing the area – a perfect example of the worst kind of beach resort development.

Getting There & Away The easiest place to get a boat to either Ko Muk or Ko Kradan is Kantang. Songthaews or vans from Trang to Kantang leave regularly and cost 10B. Once in Kantang you must charter another songthaew to the ferry pier for 20B, where you can get a regular long-tail boat to Ko Muk for 50B (or charter for 300B), to Ko Kradan for 100B or to Ko Libong for 25B (noon daily).

You can also get to the islands from Hat Pak Meng. There are two piers, one at the northern end of the beach and one at the southern end. Boats are more frequent from the southern pier, especially during the rainy season. Boats costs 30 to 60B per person to Ko Muk (depending on the number of pas-sengers), 120B to Ko Kradan.

Hat Pak Meng

หาดปากเมง

Thirty-nine km from Trang in Sikao district, north of Hat Jao Mai, Yao and Yong Ling, is another long, broad, sand beach near the village of Ban Pak Meng. The waters are usually shallow and calm, even in the rainy season. A couple of hundred metres offshore are several limestone rock formations, including a very large one with caves. Several vendors and a couple of restaurants offer fresh seafood. There are newish brick bungalows for rent at 200 to 300B a night, plus the new *Relax Bay Parkmeng Resort* (☎ 218940) with thatched bungalows in the 100 to 300B range.

Around the beginning of November, locals flock to Hat Pak Meng to collect *hǎwy taphao*, a delicious type of clam. The tide reaches its lowest this time of year, so it's relatively easy to pick up the shells.

About halfway between Pak Meng and Trang, off Route 4046, is the 20-metre-high **Ang Thong Falls**.

Getting There & Away Take a van (20B) or songthaew (15B) to Sikao from Trang, and then a songthaew (10B) to Hat Pak Meng. There are also one or two direct vans daily to Pak Meng from Trang for 30B. A paved road now connects Pak Meng with the other beaches south, so if you have your own wheels there's no need to backtrack through Sikao.

Hat Samran & Ko Sukon

หาดสำราญและเกาะสุกร

Hat Samran is a beautiful and shady white-sand beach in Palian district, about 40 km south-west of Trang city. From the customs pier at nearby Yong Sata you should be able to get a boat to **Ko Sukon** (also called Ko Muu), an island populated by Thai Muslims, where there are more beaches.

Sukon Island Resort (☎ 219679 in Trang; 211460 on the island) has bungalow accommodation for 600B a night.

Ko Ngai (Hai)

เกาะไหง(ไห)

This island is actually part of Krabi Province to the north, but is most accessible from Trang. It's a fairly small island, covering about 3000 rai (4.8 sq km), but the beaches are fine white sand and the water is clear. The resorts on the island operate half-day boat tours of nearby islands, including Morakot Cave on Ko Muk, for around 200B per person.

Places to Stay Along the east shore of Ko Ngai are two 'resorts'. Towards the middle of the island is *Koh Hai Villa* (☎ 218029 in Trang; (02) 318-3107 in Bangkok), with fan-cooled bungalows for 300B a day and tents for 150B. The vapid food here is overpriced, and the staff are surly.

At the southern end is *Ko Ngai Resort* (☎ 210317 in Trang; (02) 316-7916 in Bangkok), where one-bed seaside huts cost 250B, two-bed rooms in large bungalows are 600 to 950B and a six-bed bungalow is 1300B. Tents are also available for 150B.

You can book any of these through the Koh Hai Villa Travel Agency in Trang (☎ 210496; in Bangkok (02) 246-4399), at 112 Phra Ram VI Rd. Each resort has its own office in the city, but this one is the most conveniently located if you're staying in the central business district. The Ko Teng Hotel in Trang also has contact information.

Getting There & Away Two boats a day leave the southern pier at Pak Meng for Ko Ngai at 10.30 am and 2 pm. The fare is 100B and the trip takes about 40 minutes. You can also charter a boat at the pier for 300B. Songthaews to Pak Meng from Trang cost 30B.

Ban Tung Laem Sai

At Ban Tung Laem Sai in Sikao district is an alternative homestay for visitors interested in ecotourism. Operated by Yat Fon, a local nonprofit organisation that promotes community development and environmental conservation, the staff can educate visitors about local mangroves, coral reefs, coastal resources and the Thai-Muslim way of life. No sunbathing or drinking is allowed in the vicinity. Contact Khun Suwit at Yat Fon, 105-107 Ban Pho Rd in Trang, for reservations and transport.

WATERFALLS

A lightly trafficked, paved road runs south

from Highway 4 near the Trang-Phattalung border past a number of scenic waterfalls where the Trang and Palian rivers (and/or their tributaries) meet the Khao Banthat Mountains. **Ton Te Falls**, 46 km from Trang, is the loftiest. It's best seen during or just after the rainy season, say from September to November, when the 320-metre vertical waterfall reaches its fullest.

Chao Pha Falls in the Palian district near Laem Som has about 25 stepped falls of five to 10 metres each, with pools at every level. The semi-nomadic Sakai tribe are sometimes seen in this area.

Perhaps the most unusual waterfall in the province is **Roi Chan Phan Wang** (literally, 'hundred levels – thousand palaces'), about 70 km north-west of Trang in Wang Wiset district, a little-explored corner of the province. Surrounded by rubber groves, dozens of thin cascades of water tumble down limestone rock formations into pools below. The entire area is well shaded and a good spot for picnics. There is no public transport to the falls, however, and the road is none too good – motorcycle or jeep would be the best choice of transport.

CAVES

A limestone cave in the north-eastern district of Huay Yot, **Tham Phra Phut**, contains a large Ayuthaya-period reclining Buddha. When the cave was re-discovered earlier this century, a cache of royal-class silverwork, nielloware, pottery and lacquerware was found hidden behind the image – probably stashed there during the mid-18th century Burmese invasion.

Also in this district, near the village of Ban Huay Nang, is **Tham Tra** (Seal Cave), with mysterious red seals carved into the cave walls which have yet to be explained by archaeologists. Similar symbols have been found in the nearby cave temple of **Wat Khao Phra**.

More easily visited is **Tham Khao Pina**, off Highway 4 between Krabi and Trang at Km 43, which contains a large, multilevel Buddhist shrine popular with Thai tourists.

Another famous cave, **Tham Khao Chang Hai** near Na Meun Si village, Nayong district, contains large caverns with impressive interior formations.

KHLONG LAMCHAN WATERBIRD PARK
อุทยานนกน้ำคลองลำชาน

This large swampy area in the Nayong district, east of Trang, is an important habitat for several waterbird species – similar to Thaleh Noi or Khukhut in Songkhla province. Accommodation is available.

Satun Province

Bordering Malaysia, Satun (or Satul) is the west coast's southernmost province. Besides crossing the Malaysian border by land or sea, the principal visitor attractions are Ko Tarutao Marine Park and Thaleh Ban National Park.

Eighty per cent of Satun's population – Thai, Malay and chao naam – profess Islam (some of the chao naam also practise animism). In fact throughout the entire province there are only 11 or 12 Buddhist temples, versus 117 mosques.

SATUN
อ.เมืองสตูล

Satun itself is not that interesting, but you may enter or leave Thailand here by boat via Kuala Perlis in Malaysia. Sixty km north-west of Satun is the small port of Pak Bara, the departure point for boats to Ko Tarutao.

As in Thailand's other three predominantly Muslim provinces (Yala, Pattani and Narathiwat), the Thai government has installed a loudspeaker system in the streets which broadcasts government programmes at 6 am and 6 pm (beginning with a wake-up call to work and ending with the Thai national anthem, for which everyone must stop and stand in the streets), either to instil a sense of nationalism in the typically rebel-

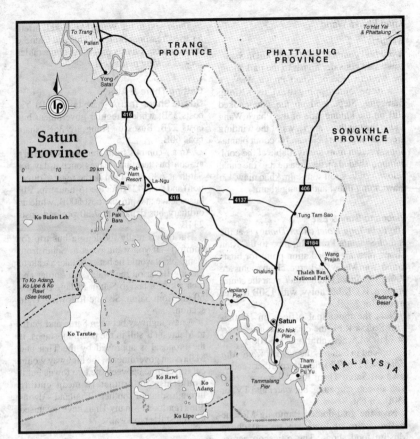

lious southern Thais, or perhaps to try and drown out the prayer calls and amplified sermons from local mosques. As in Pattani and Narathiwat, one hears a lot of Yawi spoken in the streets.

Information

Tourist Office The Satun Tourist Information Centre at 4/5 Samanta Prasit Rd is a temporary office that will be relocated within twelve months. It's open from 9 am to 9 pm daily. The staff are very helpful and provide much information about the town and surrounding area.

Money If you are going to Kuala Perlis in Malaysia, remember that banks on the east coast of Malaysia are not open on Thursday afternoon or Friday, due to the observance of Islam. If you're heading south at either of these times, be sure to buy Malaysian ringgit on the Thai side first so you won't be caught short on the Muslim sabbath.

Post & Telephone The main post and telephone office is on the corner of Samanta Prasit and Satun Thani Rds.

Satun's telephone area code is ☎ 074.

Khao Phaya Wang

เขาพญาวัง

If you find yourself with time to kill in Satun, you might consider a visit to the park along the western side of Khao Phaya Wang, a limestone outcropping next to Khlong Bambang. Steps lead up the vine-choked cliff on the khlong side of the Phaya Wang and at the top there are views of the winding green khlong, rice fields and coconut plantations. Pandan mats are available at the cool, bamboo-shaded picnic area next to the canal below. Vendors sell sôm-tam, khâo niãw, kài thâwt, kûng thâwt and miang kham.

Places to Stay & Eat

The *Rain Tong Hotel (Rian Thong)* is at the end of Samanta Prasit Rd, next to the Rian Thong pier, an embarkation point for boats to and from Malaysia. Large, clean rooms are 100B. The *Satun Thani Hotel*, near the centre of town, is OK but noisy, with 150B rooms, air-con for 230B.

Near the municipal offices on Hatthakam Seuksa Rd is the clean *Udomsuk Hotel* (☎ 711006), where all rooms are 100B.

Top-end in Satun is the newish *Wang Mai Hotel* (☎ 711607/8), near the northern end of town off Satun Thani Rd. All rooms come with air-con, carpeting, hot water and TV for 530B a night.

Near the gold-domed Bambang Mosque in the centre of town are several cheap Muslim food shops. The roti shop across from the Shell service station on Satun Thani Rd serves great roti kaeng all day and into the night. It's 3B per roti or 5B with egg – the curry dip is free. Two roti khài (egg roti) make a filling breakfast. Roti kaeng and Malay-style curries are also available at the clean Muslim shop opposite the Bangkok Bank on Buriwanit Rd.

The *Ajjara (Atjara)* garden restaurant near the municipal office and the Udomsuk Hotel has good Isaan food and is not too expensive.

For Chinese food, wander about the little Chinese district near the Rain Tong Hotel. There's nothing fancy, just a few noodle shops and small seafood places.

Time, next to the Wang Mai Hotel, offers a varied, reasonably priced Thai and Chinese menu in a curious decor – some of the tables are old sewing machines!

Getting There & Away

Bus & Share Taxi A share taxi to Hat Yai costs 35B, while a regular government bus costs 27B. Buses to Trang are 35B, share taxis 60B.

An air-con bus from Bangkok's southern air-con bus terminal leaves once a day for Satun at 7.30 pm (4 pm in the reverse direction) and costs 427B for the 15-hour trip. VIP buses leave at 6 pm and cost 500B, while an ordinary bus departs at 7.30 pm and costs 234B.

But this is really too long a bus trip for comfort – if you want to get to Satun from Bangkok, it would be better to take a train to Padang Besar on the Malaysian border and then a bus or taxi to Satun. Padang Besar is 60 km from Satun. See the following Train section.

A new highway between Satun and Perlis in Malaysia is still in the planning stages. If the proposal is approved by the Thai and Malaysian governments, the highway would cut travel time between the two towns but it would also unfortunately mean cutting through some of southern Thailand's dwindling rainforest – many Thais have organised to protest the proposal.

Train The only train that goes all the way to Padang Besar is the special express No 11, which leaves Hualamphong station at 3.15 pm and arrives in Padang Besar around 8 am the next day. The basic fare is 744B for 1st class, 376B for 2nd class, including the special express surcharge.

Boat From Kuala Perlis in Malaysia, boats are M$4. Depending on the time of year and the tides, boats from Malaysia will either dock at Tammalang pier in the estuary south of Satun, or right in Satun, on Khlong Bambang near the Rain Tong Hotel. To/from either pier, boats to Perlis cost 30B.

PLACES TO STAY

2 Wang Mai Hotel
6 Satun Thani Hotel
15 Udomsuk Hotel
19 Rain Tong (Rian Thong) Hotel

PLACES TO EAT

14 Ajjara (Atjara) Restaurant

OTHER

1 Provincial Office
3 Provincial Office
4 Satun Travel
5 Buses to Trang & Hat Yai
7 Immigration Office
8 Library
9 Bambang Mosque
10 School
11 Bangkok Bank
12 Share Taxis
13 Municipal Office & Buses to Bangkok
16 Forestry Office
17 Pier for boats to Malaysia (High Water Only)
18 Market
20 Cinema
21 Chinese Temple
22 GPO & Telephone Office
23 Provincial Court
24 Church
25 Thai Farmers Bank
26 Wat Chanathip

Satun

0   250   500 m

There's a Thai immigration post at the Tammalang pier but not at the Rian Thong pier. If you arrive at the latter by boat from Malaysia, you must go to the immigration office in town to get your passport stamped. Be sure to get an exit stamp in Perlis on the Malaysian side. In the reverse direction it's best to leave from the Tammalang pier to be sure of getting a Thai exit stamp.

From Langkawi Island in Malaysia boats for Tammalang leave daily at 7.30 am, 11 am and 2 pm. The crossing takes 1½ to two hours and costs M$15 one way. Bring Thai money from Langkawi, as there are no money-changing facilities at Tammalang pier. In the reverse direction boats leave Tammalang for Langkawi at 9 am, 1 and 4 pm and cost 150B.

Getting Around

An orange songthaew to Tammalang pier (for boats to Malaysia) costs 10B from Satun. The songthaews run every 20 minutes between 8 am and 5 pm; catch one from opposite Wat Chanathip on Buriwanit Rd. A motorcycle taxi from the same area costs 20B.

KO TARUTAO NATIONAL MARINE PARK

อุทยานแห่งชาติตามทะเลหมู่เกาะตะรุเตา

This park is actually a large archipelago of 51 islands, approximately 30 km from Pak Bara in La-Ngu district, which is 60 km north-west of Satun. Ko Tarutao, the biggest of the group, is only five km from Langkawi Island in Malaysia. Only five of the islands (Tarutao, Adang, Rawi, Lipe and Klang) have any kind of regular boat service to them, and of these, only the first three are generally visited by tourists.

The Forestry Department has been considering requests from private firms to build hotels and bungalows in Tarutao National Park. This would be a very unfortunate event if it means Ko Tarutao is going to become like Ko Phi Phi or Ko Samet, both of which are national parks that have permitted private development, with disastrous results. So far nothing has transpired.

Ko Tarutao

เกาะตะรุเตา

The park's namesake is about 151 sq km in size and features waterfalls, inland streams, beaches, caves and protected wildlife that includes dolphins, sea turtles and lobster. Nobody lives on this island except for employees of the Forestry Department. The island was a place of exile for political prisoners between 1939 and 1947, and remains of the prisons can be seen near Ao Talo Udang, on the southern tip of the island, and at Ao Talo Wao, on the middle of the east coast. There is also a graveyard, charcoal furnaces and fermentation tanks for making fish sauce.

Tarutao's largest stream, Khlong Phante Malaka, enters the sea at the north-west tip of the island at Ao Phante; the brackish waters flow out of **Tham Jara-Khe** (Crocodile Cave – the stream was once inhabited by ferocious crocodiles, which seem to have disappeared). The cave extends for at least a km under a limestone mountain – no-one has yet followed the stream to the cave's end.

The mangrove-lined watercourse should not be navigated at high tide, when the mouth of the cave fills.

The park pier, headquarters and bungalows are also here at Ao Phante Malaka. A 50B park fee is payable on arrival. The best camping is at the beaches of **Ao Jak** and **Ao San**, two bays south of park headquarters. For a view of the bays, climb Topu Hill, 500 metres north of the park office. There is also camping at Ao Makham (Tamarind Bay), at the south-west end of the island, about 2.5 km from another park office at Ao Talo Udang.

There is a road between Ao Phante Malaka, in the north, and Ao Talo Udang, in the south, of which 11 km were constructed by political prisoners in the 1940s, and 12 km were more recently constructed by the park division. The road is, for the most part, overgrown, but park personnel have kept a path open to make it easier to get from north to south without having to climb over rocky headlands along the shore.

Ko Rang Nok (Bird Nest Island), in Ao Talo Udang, is another trove of the expensive swallow nests craved by Chinese throughout the world. Good coral reefs are at the north-west part of Ko Tarutao at **Pha Papinyong** (Papillon Cliffs), at Ao San and in the channel between Ko Tarutao and Ko Takiang (Ko Lela) off the north-east shore.

Ko Adang

เกาะอาดัง

Ko Adang is 43 km west of Tarutao, and about 80 km from Pak Bara. Ko Adang's 30 sq km are covered with forests and freshwater streams, which fortunately supply water year-round. At **Laem Son** (Pine Cape), on the southern tip of the island where the pier and park office are located, visitors can stay in a thatched longhouse. Camping is also allowed. The restaurant is a little expensive considering the low quality of the food served – but then considering the transport problems, perhaps not. As on Tarutao, it's a good idea to bring some food of your own from the mainland.

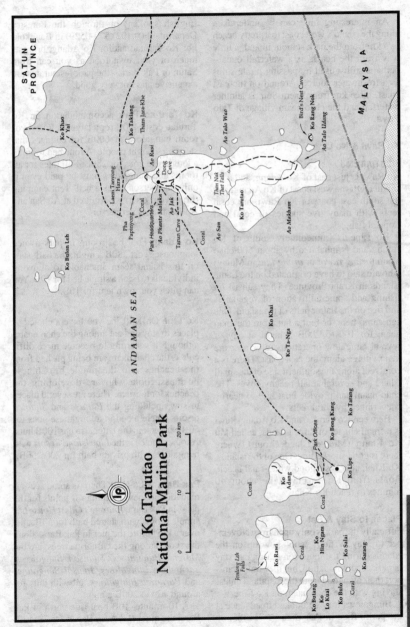

SOUTHERN THAILAND

Ko Tarutao
National Marine Park

ANDAMAN SEA

SATUN PROVINCE

MALAYSIA

Ko Bulon Leh

Ko Khao Yai

Laem Tanyong Hara
Pha Papiyong
Coral
Park Headquarters
Ao Phante Malaka
Ao Jak
Tarun Cave
Coral

Ko Takiang
Tham Jara-Khe
Ao Rasi
Dong Cave
Ao San
Coral

Ao Talo War
Tham Nak
That Falls
Ko Tarutao
Ao Makham

Bird's Nest Cave
Ko Kang Nok
Ao Talo Udang

Ko Khai
Ko Ta-Nga

Ko Turang
Ko Bong Kang
Park Offices
Ko Lipe
Ko Adang
Coral

Ko Rawi
Tanjong Leh
Falls
Ko Hin Ngam
Coral
Ko Salai
Ko Sarang

Ko Butang
Ko Lo Kuai
Ko Bulo
Coral

0   10   20 km

An interesting hike can be undertaken along the island's west coast to a pretty beach two km from the park station. Inland, a little way from the beach, is a waterfall once – perhaps still – used by passing pirate ships as a freshwater source. Around on the east coast, three km from Laem Son, is another waterfall and the chao naam village of **Talo Puya**.

Ko Rawi & Ko Lipe

เกาะราวี/เกาะลิเป

Ko Rawi is just east of Ko Adang, and a bit smaller. Off the west coast of Ko Adang, and the south-east coast of Ko Rawi, are coral reefs with many live species of coral and tropical fish.

Ko Lipe is immediately south of Ko Adang and is inhabited by about 500 chao naam (*orang rawot* or *orang laut* in Malay) who are said to have originated on the Lanta islands in Krabi Province. They subsist on fishing and some cultivation of vegetables and rice on the flatter parts of the island. One can camp here, or rent a hut from the chao naam for 100 to 200B a night at any of several bungalow operations in or near the main village along the east coast. There is a coral reef along the southern side of the small island and several small beachy coves. The chao naam can provide boat hire to nearby islets ringed by coral reefs.

Between Ko Tarutao and Ko Adang-Rawi is a small cluster of three islands, called **Mu Ko Klang** (Middle Island Group), where there is good snorkelling. One of the islands, Ko Khai, also has a good white-sand beach. Boats from Ko Tarutao take about 40 minutes to reach Ko Khai.

Places to Stay & Eat

Officially the park is only open from November to May. Visitors who show up on the islands during the monsoon season can stay in park accommodation, but they must transport their own food from the mainland unless staying with the chao naam on Ko Lipe.

Bungalows may be booked in advance at the park office in Pak Bara (☎ 711383, no English spoken) or through the Forestry Department (☎ (02) 579-0529) in Bangkok. For Ko Tarutao and/or Ko Adang, bring as much of your own food as you can from Satun or Pak Bara – the park restaurants are expensive and not very good.

Ko Tarutao Park accommodation on Ko Tarutao costs 400B for a large 'deluxe' two-room bungalow, or 600B for cottages that sleep up to eight people. A four-bed room in a longhouse goes for 280B. Full rates for all rooms and bungalows must be paid even if only one person takes a bed. Tent camping (bring your own) is permitted at Ao San and Ao Jak for 5B per person.

Ko Adang Four-bed rooms in park-owned longhouses cost 280B a night; the park staff on this island seem amenable to allowing individuals to book a single bed for 70B. You can pitch your own tent for 10B.

Ko Lipe On Ko Lipe you have a choice of places to stay and eat among the chao naam, although it's starting to become more difficult as the chao naam are being pushed from the beaches into the jungle by Chinese businesspeople who are developing the beaches for tourism. There are several places to stay, including the *Pattaya* and *Shaolea* resorts where a bed in a longhouse goes for 50B per person; the latter also has 100B huts. Another choice is the *Lipe Island Resort* with bungalows with private bath for 200/250B.

Pak Bara & La-Ngu There is some accommodation in these jumping-off points for the park. In Pak Bara, *Andrew's Guest House* has simple rooms with shared bath for 50B. Just over a km before the pier in Pak Bara, along the shore among the casuarina trees, are the *Marena Bungalows, Suanson Bungalows, Saengthien Bungalows, Jomsai Bungalows* and *Pornarea Bungalows*, all with huts for around 120 to 200B a night.

A 10-minute, 10B boat ride north of Pak Bara, the quiet *Pak Nam Resort* (☎ 781129) offers beds in a longhouse for 100B per person and thatched bungalows for 150 to 250B.

Marena Bungalows has reputable seafood. There are several food stalls near the Pak Bara pier that do fruit shakes and seafood.

La-Ngu has a couple of cheap hotels on its main street, but Pak Bara has a much better atmosphere.

Getting There & Away – Ko Tarutao
To/From Pak Bara Boats to Tarutao leave regularly between November and April from the pier in Pak Bara, 60 km north-west of Satun and 22 km from Ko Tarutao. During the rest of the year boat service is irregular, since the park is supposedly closed. Satun Province officials are planning to construct a new pier in Tan Yong Po district, nearer Satun, that will serve tourist boats to Tarutao and other islands, possibly on a year-round basis.

For now, boats leave Pak Bara for Tarutao in season daily at 10.30 am and 3 pm. The return fare is 200B, and it takes one to two hours, depending on the boat. Food and beverages are available on the boat. Departures back to Pak Bara are at 10 am and 3 pm.

There are also occasional tour boats out to Tarutao, but these are usually several hundred baht per person, as they include a guided tour, meals, etc. Your final alternative is to charter a boat with a group of people. The cheapest are the hang yao (long-tail boats), which can take eight to 10 people out from Pak Bara's commercial pier for 800B. On holidays, boats may travel back and forth to Tarutao every hour or so to accommodate the increased traffic.

To get to Pak Bara from Satun, you must take a share taxi or bus to La-Ngu, then a songthaew on to Pak Bara. Taxis to La-Ngu leave from in front of the defunct Thai Niyom Hotel when there are enough people to fill a taxi for 20B per person. Buses leave frequently from in front of the public library along the same road and they cost 13B. From La-Ngu, songthaew rides to Pak Bara are 7B and terminate right at the harbour.

From Hat Yai, there are daily buses to La-Ngu and Pak Bara at 7.05 am, 11.05 am and 2.55 pm which cost 34B and take 2½ hours. If you miss one of the direct La-Ngu buses, you can also hop on any Satun-bound bus to the junction town of Chalung (20B, 1½ hours), which is about 15 km short of Satun, then get a songthaew north on Route 4078 for the 10B, 45-minute trip to La-Ngu.

You can also travel to La-Ngu from Trang by songthaew for 30B, or by share taxi for 40B.

To/From Other Piers It is also possible to hire boats to Ko Tarutao from three different piers *(thâa reua)* on the coast near Satun. The nearest is the Ko Nok pier, four km south of Satun (40 km from Tarutao). Then there is the Tammalang pier, nine km from Satun, on the opposite side of the estuary from Ko Nok pier. Tammalang is 35 km from Tarutao. Finally there's the Jepilang pier, 13 km east of Satun (30 km from Tarutao).

Getting There & Away – Ko Adang & Ko Lipe
On Tuesday, Thursday and Saturday (November to May), a boat leaves Pak Bara at 10.30 am for Ko Adang and Ko Lipe, with a stop at Ko Tarutao along the way. The boat continues on from Ko Tarutao to Adang and Lipe at 12.30 pm, arriving at the Ko Adang pier around 3 pm. The following day (Wednesday, Friday and Sunday), the boat starts out from Ko Lipe at 9 am. A return ticket costs 360B.

KO BULON LEH
เกาะบุโหลนเล
Approximately 20 km west of Pak Bara is the small island group of Ko Bulon, of which the largest is Ko Bulon Leh. Though considerably smaller than the major islands of Mu Ko Tarutao, Bulon Leh shares many of the geographical characteristics, including sandy beaches and coral reefs. Aside from the beach in front of Pansand Resort, one of the best coral sites can be found along the north-east side of the island.

Pansand Resort has A-frame bungalows on Bulon Leh's best beach from 100B a night for huts with shared bath to 200/220B with bath. Two-person tents can be hired for 60B or you can pitch your own for 10B. Facilities include badminton, volleyball, table tennis and boats for hire. More information is available from First Andaman Travel (π (072) 218035; fax 219513), 82-84 Visetkul Rd in Trang (opposite the Queen Hotel).

Other places to stay include *Rawi House*, *Adang House* and *Panka House*, each with huts in the 100 to 200B range. Panka House reputedly has the best food on the island.

Getting There & Away

Boats to Ko Bulon Leh depart from the Pak Bara pier at 2 pm and cost 80B per person. The trip takes 45 minutes each way. On the return, boats usually leave Bulon Leh at 9 am.

THALEH BAN NATIONAL PARK

อุทยานแห่งชาติทะเลบัน

This 101-sq-km park on the Thai-Malaysian border in Satun Province encompasses the best preserved section of white meranti rainforest (named for the dominant species of dipterocarp trees) on either side of the border. Although the forest straddles the border, the Malaysian side is becoming steadily deforested by agricultural development. The terrain is hilly, with a maximum elevation of 740 metres at Khao Chin.

The park headquarters, situated on a 100-rai lake in a valley formed by limestone outcroppings, is only two km from the border. Five km north of the office is **Yaroi Falls**, a nine-tiered waterfall with pools suitable for swimming. Climb the limestone cliffs next to the park buildings for a view of the lake and surrounding area. A network of trails leads to a number of other waterfalls and caves in the park, including **Rani Falls, Ton Pliw Falls, Chingrit Falls, Ton Din Cave** and **Pu Yu Tunnel Cave (Tham Lawt Pu Yu)**.

Wildlife found within park boundaries tends to be of the Sundaic variety, which includes species generally found in Peninsular Malaysia, Sumatra, Borneo and Java. Common mammals include mouse deer, serow, various gibbons and macaques. Some of the rare bird species found here are the great argus hornbill, rhinoceros hornbill, helmeted hornbill, masked finfoot, dusky crag martin and black Baza hawk.

The park entrance is about 37 km east of Satun's provincial capital or 90 km south of Hat Yai via Route 406 and Route 4184; coming from Malaysia it's about 75 km from Alor Setar. The best time to visit is from December to March, between seasonal monsoons.

Places to Stay

Near the park office (π 797073) beside the lake are longhouses sleeping eight to 20 people for 500 to 800B per night. It costs 10B per person to set up your own tent.

Getting There & Away

The park is about 40 km from Satun in *tambon* Khuan Sataw. Take a songthaew or share taxi from near the Rain Tong Hotel in Satun to Wang Prajan on Route 4184 for 20B. Wang Prajan is just a few km from the park entrance. Sometimes these vehicles might take you to the park gate, otherwise you can hitch or hop on one of the infrequent songthaews from Wang Prajan into the park.

Yala Province

Yala is the most prosperous of the four predominantly Muslim provinces in southern Thailand, mainly due to income from rubber production. It is also the number-one business and education centre for the region.

YALA

อ.เมืองยะลา

The fast-developing capital (population 68,500) is known as 'the cleanest city in Thailand' and has won awards to that effect three times in the last 25 years (its main competitor is Trang). It's a city of parks, wide boulevards and orderly traffic.

During the dry season there are nightly musical performances in Chang Pheuak Park, in the south-east part of the city just before the big Lak Meuang roundabout, off Pipitpakdee Rd. **Phrupakoi Park**, just west of the lak meuang (city pillar), has a big artificial lake where people can fish, go boating and eat in floating restaurants. Yala residents seem obsessed with water recreation, possibly as a consequence of living in the only land-locked province in the entire south. There is a public swimming pool in town at the Grand Palace restaurant and disco.

One of the biggest regional festivals in Thailand is held in Yala during the last six days of June to pay respect to the city guardian spirit, Jao Phaw Lak Meuang. Chinese New Year is also celebrated here with some zest, as there are many Chinese living in the capital. The Muslim population is settled in the rural areas of the province, for the most part, though there is a sizeable Muslim quarter near the train station in town – you'll know it by the sheep and goats wandering in the streets and by the modern mosque – Yala's tallest building and the largest mosque in Thailand.

Information

The post & telephone office on Siriros Rd offers international telephone service daily from 8 am to 10 pm.

Yala's telphone area code is ☎ 073.

Wat Naa Tham

วัดหน้าถ้ำ

Outside town, about eight km west off the Yala-Hat Yai highway, is Wat Khuhaphimuk (also called Wat Naa Tham – the Cave-Front Temple), a Srivijaya-period cave temple established around 750 AD. Inside the cave is Phra Phutthasaiyat, a long reclining Buddha image sculpted in the Srivijaya style. For Thais, this is one of the three most venerated Buddhist pilgrimage points in southern Thailand (the other two are Wat

Boromathat in Nakhon Si Thammarat and Wat Phra Boromathat Chaiya in Surat Thani). There is a small museum in front of the cave, with artefacts of local provenance.

To get there, take a songthaew going west towards the town of Yaha via Route 4065, and ask to get off at the road to Wat Naa Tham – the fare is 3B. It's about a one-km walk to the wat from the highway.

Two km past Wat Naa Tham is **Tham Silpa**, a well-known cave with Buddhist polychrome murals from the Srivijaya era as well as prehistoric, monochromatic paintings of primitive hunters. A monk from Wat Naa Tham may be able to guide you there. There are several other caves in the vicinity worth exploring for their impressive stalactite and stalagmite formations.

Places to Stay

Yala has quite a few hotels at low to moderate price levels. Starting from the bottom, the *Shanghai Hotel* at 36-34 Ratakit Rd and *Saen Suk* are nearly identical Chinese hotels with Chinese restaurants on the ground floor. Both are on the same block on Ratakit Rd, in the business district, not far from the train station. They have somewhat dreary rooms from 70B and 60B respectively; the Saen Suk is a bit cleaner, and its restaurant is also better, specialising in generous plates of chicken rice (khâo man kài) for 15B. Nearby, on the other side of Ratakit Rd, the *Metro Hotel* at No 7/1-2 has better rooms for 80 to 150B.

The *Hawaii* and *Aun Aun* hotels, on Pipitpakdee Rd, are the first hotels you see as you walk into town from the train station. The Hawaii is OK at 150B, but the Aun Aun is more economical at 90B without bath, 100B with. The manager at Aun Aun also speaks good English.

The *Thepwiman Hotel* (☎ 212400), a left turn from the station on Sribumrung (Si Bamrung) Rd, across from the Yala Rama, is the best value in this range. It's a friendly place, with clean, large rooms with fan and bath for 130B, or 370B with air-con.

The *Yala Merry* (☎ 212693), on the corner of Phutthaphumwithi and Kotchaseni 3 Rds,

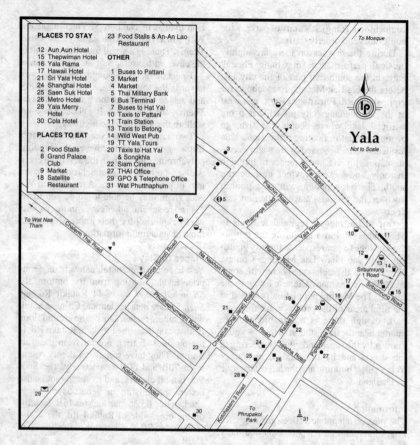

PLACES TO STAY
12 Aun Aun Hotel
15 Thepwiman Hotel
16 Yala Rama
17 Hawaii Hotel
21 Sri Yala Hotel
24 Shanghai Hotel
25 Saen Suk Hotel
26 Metro Hotel
28 Yala Merry Hotel
30 Cola Hotel

PLACES TO EAT
2 Food Stalls
8 Grand Palace Club
9 Market
18 Satellite Restaurant
23 Food Stalls & An-An Lao Restaurant

OTHER
1 Buses to Pattani
3 Market
4 Market
5 Thai Military Bank
6 Bus Terminal
7 Buses to Hat Yai
10 Taxis to Pattani
11 Train Station
13 Taxis to Betong
14 Wild West Pub
19 TT Yala Tours
20 Taxis to Hat Yai & Songkhla
22 Siam Cinema
27 THAI Office
29 GPO & Telephone Office
31 Wat Phutthaphum

Yala
Not to Scale

has seen better days and is not very good value at 130/180B for a one/two-bed room with fan and bath, or 300B for air-con. At the southern end of this block, around the corner on Kotchaseni 1 Rd, is the *Cola Hotel* with 160B rooms (240B air-con) similar to those at the Thepwiman – a bit overpriced.

At the next level is the *Sri Yala Hotel* (☎ 212815) at 18-22 Chai Jarat Rd (the street sign says 'Chaijarus'), with clean rooms for 150B with fan, 200B air-con, a restaurant and a popular coffee shop.

Top end is the *Yala Rama* (☎ 212563; fax 214532) at 21 Sribumrung Rd near the

station. Here, a room with fan and bath goes for 276B, while air-con rooms are 475B. All rooms have two beds. The coffee shop and nightclub here are quite popular.

Places to Eat

There are plenty of inexpensive places to eat in central Yala near all the hotels, especially Chinese restaurants along Ratakit and Ranong Rds. The *Saen Suk* hotel restaurant has good khâo man kài.

The *Suay Suay* indoor/outdoor restaurant, on Sribumrung Rd near the Yala Rama Hotel, and the big *Satellite* restaurant, on the corner of Pipitpakdee and Ranong Rds, specialise in steamed cockles. Near the Satellite, at 39 Pipitpakdee Rd, the *Ta Ra Restaurant* also has good seafood.

Off Chai Jarat Rd, a couple of blocks down the street from Sri Yala Hotel, is the *An An Lao Restaurant*, a large garden restaurant specialising in kài betong – quite good and inexpensive. The *Grand Palace Club*, on Chalerm Thai Rd, in the opposite direction from Wat Phutthaphum, serves fancy Thai and Chinese food at fancy prices to go along with the floor show.

The day market on Siroros (Sirorot) Rd has a good selection of fresh fruit. The Muslim food stalls nearby serve roti kaeng in the early morning – a cheap and filling breakfast.

Entertainment

In addition to the popular hotel coffee shop/nightclubs, you could look in at Wild West, an old-west theme pub near the corner of Rot Fai and Pipitpakdee Rd near the train station. The Wild West has live music in the evenings.

Getting There & Away

Air The nearest commercial airport is in Pattani, 40 km north of Yala.

Bus & Share Taxi Air-con buses between Bangkok and Yala are 460B, VIPs are 530 to 715B and ordinary buses cost 255B for the 16-hour haul.

Buses to/from Pattani cost 11B for the one-hour trip, while share taxis are 20B and take about 40 minutes. Buses south to Sungai Kolok or Pattani leave from Siroros Rd near the train tracks. A share taxi to Sungai Kolok is 70B and takes about two hours. An ordinary bus along the same route is only 14B but takes three to 3½ hours.

Buses north (to Hat Yai, etc) leave from Siroros Rd, opposite the main bus terminal. Buses to/from Hat Yai cost 41B and take 2½ hours; by share taxi or air-con minivan the trip is 50B and takes two hours.

Train The rapid No 45 leaves Bangkok daily at 12.35 pm and arrives in Yala at 6.48 am the next day. The special express No 19 leaves at 2 pm and arrives at 7.49 am. Fares are 346B 2nd class, 738B 1st class, not including air-con (mandatory on the special express) and rapid or special express surcharges.

From Hat Yai, ordinary trains are 23B for 3rd class, and take 2½ hours. From Sungai Kolok, at the Malaysian border, trains are 22B for a 2½-hour trip. To/from Surat Thani the 3rd-class fare is 91B.

BAN SAKAI

บ.ซาไก

The well-known village of Ban Sakai is in Tharato district, about 80 km south of Yala on the way to Betong. Ban Sakai is the home of some of Thailand's last remaining Sakai tribes, called 'Ngaw' by Thais because their frizzy heads and dark complexions remind Thais of the outer skin of the rambutan fruit (*ngáw* in Thai).

Anthropologists speculate that the Sakai are the direct descendants of a Proto-Malay race that once inhabited the entire Thai-Malay peninsula and beyond (also called Negritos, described by George McFarland as 'an aboriginal jungle race allied to negroid pygmies found in the Philippines, New Guinea and parts of Africa').

Speculation says the Sakai's numbers decreased as they were pushed farther back into the jungle upon the expansion of the technologically more advanced Austro-Thai cultures from the north. At any rate, the peaceful, short-statured Sakai continue to lead a traditional village life of hunting and gathering, practising very little agriculture and expressing themselves through their own unique language, music and dance. Recently a development project has got the Sakai involved in tending rubber plantations.

Also in Tharato district is **Tharato Falls**, which is now a national park.

BETONG

เบตง

Betong is 140 km south-west of Yala on the Malaysian border and is Thailand's southern-most point. The area surrounding Betong is mountainous and jungle-foliated; morning fog is not uncommon in the district. Three km north of town is a pleasant hot springs.

Until recently the Communist Party of Malaysia had its hidden headquarters in the Betong vicinity. In December 1989 the CPM finally laid down arms; many guerrillas were given minor land grants in the area by the Thai government in return for their capitula-tion. Others – mainly Chinese – have blended into the Betong woodwork and now make their way as peddlers, Chinese-language tutors, odd-job labourers, rubber tappers and tailors. A number of former CPM members live in nearby 'Peace Village' and regale visiting journalists with tales of jungle life and how they once lived on elephant, tiger and bear meat.

The Pattani United Liberation Organisa-tion (PULO), Thai-Muslim separatists who want Yala and other Muslim provinces to secede from Thailand, still have minor forces in this area but the word is that they, too, will soon give up the fight.

Malaysians are allowed to cross the border at Betong, so the little town is often crowded on weekends as they come across to shop for cheaper Thai merchandise including, for the Malay men, Thai women. Many townspeople speak English and Chinese as well as Thai and Malay.

Places to Stay & Eat

Most hotels in Betong are in the 150 to 200B range for basic rooms – Malaysian price levels – eg the *Cathay*, *Fortuna*, *Khong Kha*, *Thai*, *King's*, *Venus* and *My House*. Payment in Malaysian ringgit is as acceptable as baht at most hotels. One of the hassles for single male visitors is constantly being approached by pimps at many of the hotels.

The *Betong Hotel*, 13/6 Sarit Det Rd, is OK for 100 to 150B. *Si Betong* has two branches, one on Chaiya Chaowalit Rd

which is primarily a brothel, and a better one on Sukayang Rd. Both cost 150B for fan-cooled rooms; *Si Betong 1* (Sukayang Rd) also has some air-con rooms for 280B.

The best budget bet is *Fa Un Rong Hotel* on Jantharothai Rd for 90B. Another decent place to stay is the *Si Charoen (Sea World Long) Hotel* at 17 Soi Praphan Phesat, where good rooms with a bit of a view cost 150B with fan and bath, 220 to 280B with air-con. The hotel's business card is written in Chinese and prices are quoted in Malaysian currency.

Betong has more Muslim and Chinese restaurants than Thai. The town is famous for kài betong, the tasty local chicken, and also roasted or fried mountain frogs, which are said to be even more delicious than the mountain frogs of Mae Hong Son.

Getting There & Away

A share taxi to Betong from Yala is 60B; bus is 38B.

RAMAN

รามัน

Twenty-five km south-east of Yala by road or train, Raman is well known as a centre for the Malay-Indonesian martial art of *silat*. Two very famous teachers of silat reside here, Hajisa Haji Sama-ae and Je Wae. If you're interested in pure Thai-Muslim culture, this is the place.

Pattani Province

PATTANI

อ.เมืองปัตตานี

The provincial capital of Pattani (population 41,000) provides a heavy contrast with Yala. In spite of its basic function as a trading post operated by the Chinese for the benefit (or exploitation, depending on your perspective) of the surrounding Muslim villages, the town has a more Muslim character than Yala. In the streets, you are more likely to hear Yawi, the traditional language of Java, Sumatra and

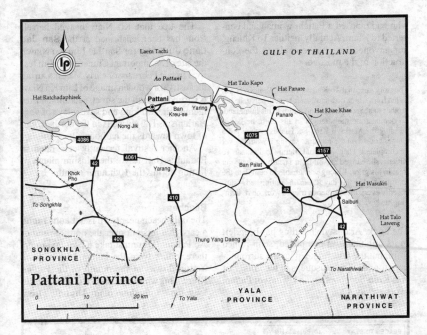

Pattani Province

the Malay peninsula (which when written uses the classic Arabic script plus five more letters), than any Thai dialect. The markets are visually quite similar to markets in Kota Baru in Malaysia. The town as a whole is a bit dirtier than Yala, but the riverfront area is interesting.

Pattani was until rather recently the centre of an independent principality that included Yala and Narathiwat. It was also one of the earliest kingdoms in Thailand to host international trade; the Portuguese established a trading post here in 1516, the Japanese in 1605, the Dutch in 1609 and the British in 1612. During WW II, Japanese troops landed in Pattani to launch attacks on Malaya and Singapore.

Orientation & Information

The centre of this mostly concrete town is at the intersection of Naklua/Yarang Rd, the north-south road between Yala and Pattani harbour, and Ramkomud Rd, which runs east-west between Songkhla and Narathiwat. Intercity buses and taxis stop at this intersection. Ramkomud Rd becomes Rudee Rd after crossing Yarang Rd, and it is along Rudee Rd that you can see what is left of old Pattani architecture – the Sino-Portuguese style that was once so prevalent in southern Thailand.

Pattani's main post office is on Pipit Rd, near the bridge. The attached CAT office provides overseas telephone service daily between 7 am and 10 pm.

Pattani's telephone area code is ☎ 073.

Mosques

Thailand's second-largest mosque is the **Matsayit Klang**, a traditional structure of green hue, probably still the south's most important mosque. It was built in the early 1960s.

The oldest mosque in Pattani is the **Matsayit Kreu-Se**, built in 1578 by an immigrant Chinese named Lim To Khieng who had married a Pattani woman and converted to Islam. Actually, neither To Khieng, nor anyone else, ever completed the construction of the mosque.

The story goes that To Khieng's sister, Lim Ko Niaw, sailed from China on a sampan to try and persuade her brother to abandon Islam and return to his homeland. To demonstrate the strength of his faith, he began building the Matsayit Kreu-Se. His sister then put a Chinese curse on the mosque, saying it would never be completed. Then, in a final attempt to dissuade To Khieng, she hanged herself from a nearby cashew-nut tree. In his grief, Khieng was unable to complete the mosque, and to this day it remains unfinished – supposedly every time someone tries to work on it, lightning strikes.

The brick, Arab-style building has been left in its original semi-completed, semi-ruined form, but the faithful keep up the surrounding grounds. The mosque is in the village of Ban Kreu-Se, about seven km east of Pattani off Highway 42.

The tree that Ko Niaw hanged herself from has been enshrined at the **San Jao Leng Ju Kieng** (or San Jao Lim Ko Niaw), the site of an important Chinese-Muslim festival in late February or early March. During the festival a wooden image of Lim Ko Niaw is carried through the streets; additional rites include fire-walking and seven days of vegetarianism. The shrine is in the northern end of town towards the harbour.

Another festival fervently celebrated in Pattani is Hari Rayo, the Muslim month of fasting during the 10th lunar month.

Beaches

The only beach near town is at **Laem Tachi**, a cape that juts out over the northern end of Ao Pattani. You must take a boat taxi to get there, either from the Pattani pier or from Yaring district at the mouth of the Pattani River. This white-sand beach is about 11 km long, but is sometimes marred by refuse from

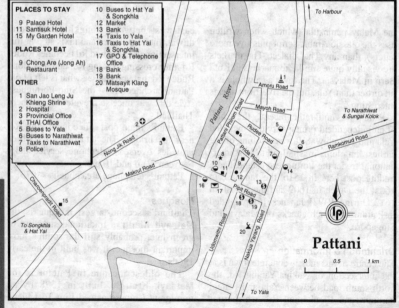

PLACES TO STAY
9 Palace Hotel
11 Santisuk Hotel
15 My Garden Hotel

PLACES TO EAT
9 Chong Are (Jong Ah) Restaurant

OTHER
1 San Jao Leng Ju Kieng Shrine
2 Hospital
3 Provincial Office
4 THAI Office
5 Buses to Yala
6 Buses to Narathiwat
7 Taxis to Narathiwat
8 Police
10 Buses to Hat Yai & Songkhla
12 Market
13 Bank
14 Taxis to Yala
16 Taxis to Hat Yai & Songkhla
17 GPO & Telephone Office
18 Bank
19 Bank
20 Matsayit Klang Mosque

To Harbour
Amoru Road
Mayoh Road
To Narathiwat & Sungai Kolok
Pattani River
Pattani Phirom Road
Rudee Road
Pride Road
Ramkomud Road
Nong Jik Road
Makrut Road
Charoenpradit Road
To Songkhla & Hat Yai
Pipit Road
Naklua Yarang Road
Udomwith Road
To Yala

Pattani

0   0.5   1 km

Ao Pattani, depending on the time of year and the tides.

Batik

Thai Muslims in southern Thailand have their own traditional batik methods that are similar but not identical to the batik of north-east Malaysia. The best place to shop for local batik is at the Palat Market (talàat nát paalát), which is off Highway 42 between Pattani and Saiburi in Ban Palat. The market is held all day Wednesday and Sunday only. If you can't make it to this market, the shops of Muslim Phanit and Nadi Brothers on Rudee Rd in Pattani sell local and Malaysian batik at perhaps slightly higher prices.

Places to Stay & Eat

The Palace Hotel (☎ 349171) at 38 Soi Talaat Tetiwat, off Prida Rd, is a decent place with rooms for 140B with fan and bath, 200B with two beds or air-con, plus another 50B if you want TV.

The Santisuk (☎ 349122), at 1/16 Pipit Rd, has OK rooms for 80B without a bath, 130 with private bath and 200B with air-con. As in Yala, Narathiwat, Satun and Trang, all street signs are in tortured English transliterations of Thai (better than no transliterations at all, for those who can't read Thai).

My Garden (☎ 331055; fax 348200) at 8/28 Chareonpradit Rd, about a km outside town, is a good-value middle-range hotel – 275B for a large two-bed room with fan and bath, 440 to 495B for air-con, 660B with TV. The disco is very popular on weekends. Samlor or songthaew drivers may know it by its former name, the Dina.

The Chong Are (Jong Ah) restaurant, next to the Palace Hotel on Prida Rd, serves decent Thai and Chinese food.

Getting There & Away

Air Pattani has an airport and until mid-1994 THAI operated twice weekly flights to/from Narathiwat and Hat Yai. These flights have since been discontinued – check at Pattani's THAI office (☎ 349149) on 9 Prida Rd to see if these or other flights out of Pattani have been reinstated.

Bus & Share Taxi Pattani is only 40 km from Yala. Share taxis are 20B and take about half an hour; buses cost only 11B but take around an hour. From Narathiwat, a taxi is 40B, bus 28B. From Hat Yai ordinary buses cost 30B and air-con 50B.

From Bangkok there is only one ordinary bus departure at 6.30 pm; the fare for the 15 to 16-hour trip is 258B. A 1st-class air-con bus departs at 10 am for 464B. In the reverse direction these buses depart Pattani at 6.30 pm and 2 pm respectively.

Boat Reportedly certain boats between Songkhla and Pattani will take paying passengers – the fare depends on the size of the boat.

Getting Around

Songthaews go anywhere in town for 5B per person.

AROUND PATTANI PROVINCE
Beaches

About 15 km west of Pattani, **Hat Ratcha-daphisek** (or Hat Sai Maw) is a relaxing spot, with lots of sea pines for shade, but the water is a bit on the murky side. Then there's **Hat Talo Kapo**, 14 km east of Pattani, near Yaring district, a pretty beach that's also a harbour for kaw-lae, the traditional fishing boats of southern Thailand. A string of vendors at Talo Kapo sell fresh seafood; during the week it's practically deserted.

Other beaches can be found south-east of Pattani, on the way to Narathiwat, especially in the Panare and Saiburi districts where there are km of virtually deserted beach. **Hat Chala Lai** is a broad white-sand beach 43 km south-east of Pattani, near Panare. Eight km farther on towards Narathiwat is **Hat Khae Khae**, a pretty beach studded with boulders. Three km north of Panare is **Hat Panare**, which is another colourful kaw-lae harbour.

Near Saiburi is **Hat Wasukri**, also called Chaihat Ban Patatimaw, a beautiful white-sand beach with shade. It's 53 km from Pattani. Some private bungalows here rent for 200B, but this may be negotiable when occupancy is low. Farther south still, a few km before you reach the Narathiwat provincial border, is **Hat Talo Laweng**, possibly Pattani Province's prettiest beach.

A good place to watch the building of kaw-lae is in the village of Pase Yawo (Ya-Waw), near the mouth of the Saiburi River. It's a tradition that is slowly dying out as the kaw-lae is replaced by long-tail boats with auto engines.

Narathiwat Province

NARATHIWAT

อ.เมืองนราธิวาส

Narathiwat (population 40,500) is a pleasant, even-tempered little town, one of Thailand's smallest provincial capitals, with a character all of its own. Many of the buildings are old wooden structures, a hundred or more years old. The local businesses seem to be owned by both the Muslims and the Chinese, and nights are particularly peaceful because of the relative absence of male drinking sessions typical of most upcountry towns in Thailand. The town is right on the sea, and some of the prettiest beaches on southern Thailand's east coast are just outside town.

Information

The post office is at the southern end of Pichitbamrung Rd. An attached international phone office is open daily from 7 am to 10 pm.

Narathiwat's telephone area code is ☎ 073.

Hat Narathat

หาดนราทัศน์

Just north of town is a small Thai-Muslim fishing village at the mouth of the Bang Nara River, lined with the large painted fishing boats called *reua kaw-lae* which are peculiar to Narathiwat and Pattani. Near the fishing village is Hat Narathat, a sandy beach, four to five km long, which serves as a kind of public park for locals, with outdoor seafood restaurants, tables and umbrellas, etc. The

constant breeze here is excellent for windsurfing, a favourite sport of Narathiwat citizens as well as visiting Malaysians. The beach is only two km north of the town centre – you can easily walk there or take a samlor.

Almost the entire coast between Narathiwat and Malaysia, 40 km south, is sandy beach.

Taksin Palace

พระตำหนักทักษิณ

About seven km south of town is Tanyongmat Hill, where Taksin Palace (Phra Taksin Ratchaniwet) is located. The royal couple stay here for about two months between August and October every year. When they're not in residence, the palace is open to the public daily from 8.30 am to noon and 1 to 4.30 pm. The buildings themselves are not that special, but there are gardens with the Bangsuriya palm, a rare fan-like palm named after the embroidered sunshades used by monks and royalty as a sign of rank. A small zoo and a ceramics workshop are also on the grounds, and in front is Ao Manao, a pretty, curved bay lined with sea pines. A songthaew from the town to the palace area is 7B.

Wat Khao Kong

วัดเขากง

The tallest seated-Buddha image in Thailand is at Wat Khao Kong, six km south-west on the way to the train station in Tanyongmat. Called Phra Phuttha Taksin Mingmongkon, the image is 25 metres high and made of bronze. The wat itself isn't much to see. A songthaew to Wat Khao Kong is 5B from the Narathiwat Hotel.

Narathiwat Fair

งานนราธิวาส

Every year during the third week of September, the Narathiwat Fair features kaw-lae boat racing, a singing dove contest judged by the Queen, handicraft displays and silat martial arts exhibitions. Other highlights

GULF OF
THAILAND

Hat
Narathat

To Airport &
Ban Thon

Fishing
Village

Ko Pula
Yama

Punyapridee (Phupha Phakdi) Road

Sophapisai Road

Chamroonnara Road

Pichitbamrung Road

Wichit – Chaibun Road

Bang Nara River

Narathiwat

0   100   200 m

PLACES TO STAY
8 Tan Yong Hotel
9 Yaowaraj Hotel
10 Rex Hotel
11 Cathay Hotel
13 Bang Nara Hotel
17 Narathiwat Hotel
21 Pacific Hotel

PLACES TO EAT
15 Night Market
26 Rim Nam Restaurant

OTHER
1 Mosque
2 Buses to Pattani
3 Market
4 Evening Fish Market
5 Customs
6 Chinese Shrine
7 Songthaews to Ban Thon
12 Siam Commercial Bank
14 Cinema
16 THAI Office
18 Bus Terminal
19 Clock Tower
20 Central Mosque
22 Provincial Office
23 GPO & Telephone Office
24 Police
25 Police

Padungaram Road

Jaturong Ratsami Road

To Pattani

To Wat Khao Kong
& Tanyongmat

To Taksin Palace,
Ao Manao,
& Tak Bai

include performances of the local dance forms, *ram sam pen* and *ram ngeng*.

Places to Stay

The cheapest places to stay are all on Puphapugdee (Phupha Phakdi) Rd along the Bang Nara River. The best deal is the *Narathiwat Hotel* (☎ 511063), a funky wooden building that's quiet, breezy, clean and comfortable. Rooms on the waterfront cost 100B with shared bath; the downstairs rooms can sometimes get a bit noisy from the night trade – try to get an upstairs room. Mosquitoes could be a problem – don't forget your repellent or mossie coils.

Another OK place, across the street and next to the Si Ayuthaya Bank, is the *Bang Nara Hotel* (☎ 511036) – friendly staff and large, clean rooms for 100B with shared bathroom. A last resort is the *Cathay Hotel*, with rooms with hard beds for 100B and 150B; the owner speaks English.

The *Rex Hotel* (☎ 511134), at 6/1-3 Chamroonnara Rd, is a fair place with 150B for rooms with fan, 220B for air-con. Similar rooms with fan for 120 to 180B, 200 to 280B air-con, are available at the *Yaowaraj Hotel* on the corner of Chamroonnara and Pichitbamrung Rds. Because of its busy location, it's not as quiet as the previously mentioned places.

The newer *Pacific Hotel* costs 300B for large, clean rooms with fan and bath – this price may be negotiable – plus air-con for 410B. The top end is the *Tan Yong Hotel* (☎ 511148), on Sophapisai Rd, with air-con rooms from 550B. Most of the guests are Malaysians and Thai government officials.

Places to Eat

For eating, the night market off Chamroonnara Rd behind the Bang Nara Hotel is good. There are also several inexpensive places along Chamroonnara Rd, especially the khâo kaeng place next to the Yaowaraj Hotel, for curries.

Along Wichit Chaibun Rd west of Puphapugdee Rd are several inexpensive Muslim food shops. The *Rim Nam* restaurant, on Jaturong Ratsami Rd a couple of km south of town, has good seafood and curries.

Getting There & Away

Air THAI has three flights weekly between Narathiwat and Hat Yai, connecting with flights to Bangkok. The fare to Hat Yai is 420B, through to Bangkok it's 2620B. Their office (☎ 511161) is at 322-5 Puphapugdee (Phupha Phakdi) Rd; a THAI van between Nara Airport and the THAI office costs 30B per person.

Bus & Taxi Share taxis between Yala and Narathiwat are 40B, buses 35B (with a change in Pattani). Buses cost 28B from Pattani. From Sungai Kolok, buses are 18B, share taxis 40B. To/from Tak Bai, the other border crossing, it is 10B by songthaew (catch one in front of the Narathiwat Hotel), 20B by taxi. Other share-taxi destinations include Hat Yai (80B) and Songkhla (80B).

Air-con minivans to Hat Yai leave several times a day from opposite the Rex Hotel for 100B per person.

It's best not to travel around Narathiwat Province at night, because that's when the Muslim separatist guerrillas go around shooting up trucks and buses.

Train The train costs 13B for 3rd-class seats to Tanyongmat, 20 km west of Narathiwat, then it's either a 15B taxi to Narathiwat, or 10B by songthaew.

AROUND NARATHIWAT
Wadin Husen Mosque

มัสยิดวาดินฮูเซ็น

One of the most interesting mosques in Thailand, the Wadin Husen was built in 1769 and mixes Thai, Chinese and Malay architectural styles to good effect. It's in the village of Lubosawo in Bajo (Ba-Jaw) district, about 15 km north-west of Narathiwat off Highway 42, about 8B by songthaew.

Wat Chonthara Sing-He

วัดชลธาราสิงเห

During the British colonisation of Malaysia (then called Malaya), the Brits tried to claim Narathiwat as part of their Malayan empire. The Thais constructed Wat Chonthara Sing-He (also known as Wat Phitak Phaendin Thai) in Tak Bai district near the Malayan border to prove that Narathiwat was indeed part of Siam, and as a result the British relinquished their claim.

Today it's most notable because of the genuine southern-Thai architecture, rarely seen in a Buddhist temple – sort of the Thai-Buddhist equivalent of the Wadin Husen Mosque. A wooden wihaan here very much resembles a Sumatran-style mosque. An 1873 wihaan on the grounds contains a reclining Buddha decorated with Chinese ceramics from the Song dynasty. Another wihaan on the spacious grounds contains murals painted by a famous Songkhla monk during the reign of King Mongkut. The murals are religious in message but also depict traditional southern-Thai life. There is also a larger, typical Thai wihaan.

Wat Chon is 34 km south-east of Narathiwat in Tak Bai. It's probably not worth a trip from Narathiwat just to see this 100-year old temple unless you're a real temple freak, but if you're killing time in Tak Bai or Sungai Kolok this is one of the prime local sights. It's next to the river and the quiet, expansive grounds provide a retreat from the busy border atmosphere.

To get there from Narathiwat, take a bus or songthaew bound for Ban Taba and get off in Tak Bai. The wat is on the river about 500 metres from the main Tak Bai intersection.

SUNGAI KOLOK & BAN TABA

These small towns in the south-east of Narathiwat Province are departure points for the east coast of Malaysia. There is a fair batik (Thai: paa-té) cottage industry in this district.

Be prepared for culture shock coming from Malaysia, warned one traveller. Not only are most signs in Thai script, but fewer people speak English in Thailand than in Malaysia.

Sungai Kolok

สุไหงโก-ลก

The Thai government once planned to move the border crossing from Sungai Kolok to Ban Taba in Tak Bai district, which is on the coast 32 km east. The Taba crossing is now open and is a shorter and quicker route to Kota Baru, the first Malaysian town of any size, but it looks like Sungai Kolok will remain open as well for a long time. They're even building new hotels in Sungai Kolok and have established a TAT office next to the immigration post.

The border is open from 5 am to 5 pm (6 am to 6 pm Malaysian time). On slow days they may close the border as early as 4.30 pm.

Information The TAT office (☎ 612126), next to the immigration post, is open daily from 8.30 am to 5 pm. The post and telephone office is on Thetpathom Rd.

Ban Taba

บ้านตาบา

Ban Taba, five km south of bustling Tak Bai, is just a blip of a town with only one bank and a couple of hotels. You can change money at street vendors by the ferry on the Thai side.

A ferry across the river into Malaysia is 5B. The border crossing here is open the same hours as in Sungai Kolok. From the Malaysian side you can get buses direct to Kota Baru for M$1.50.

Places to Stay & Eat – Sungai Kolok

The Tourist Business Association brochure says there are 60 hotels in Sungai Kolok, but only 39 of these are in the town itself. The main reason Sungai Kolok has so many hotels is to accommodate the weekend trips of Malaysian males. Of the cheaper hotels, only a handful are under 120B and they're mainly for those only crossing for a couple of hours. So if you have to spend the night here it's best to pay a little more and get away from the short-time trade.

Most places in Sungai Kolok will take Malaysian ringgit as well as Thai baht for food or accommodation.

The most reasonably priced places are along Charoenkhet Rd. Here you can find the fairly clean *Thailiang Hotel* (☎ 611132) at No 12 for 150B, the *Savoy Hotel* (☎ 611093) at No 8/2 for 100 to 150B, and the *Asia Hotel* (☎ 611101) at No 4-4/1 for 160B (fan and bath), or 200 to 250B with air-con. The *Pimarn Hotel* (☎ 611464) at No 76-4 is also quite good at 150B with fan and bath.

On the corner of Thetpathom and Waman Amnoey Rds is the pleasant *Valentine Hotel* (☎ 611229), with rooms for 180B with fan, 330B with air-con. There's a coffee shop downstairs.

Other reasonably decent hotels in the 100 to 200B range include the *Star Hotel* (☎ 611508) at 20 Saritwong Rd, the *An An Hotel* (☎ 611058) at 183/1-2 Prachawiwat Rd, the *Taksin 2* (☎ 611088) at 4 Prachasamran Rd, the *San Sabai 2* (☎ 611313) at 38 Waman Amnoey Rd, the cheaper *San Sabai 1* (☎ 612157) at 32/34 Bussayapan Rd and the *Nam Thai 2* (☎ 611163) at Soi

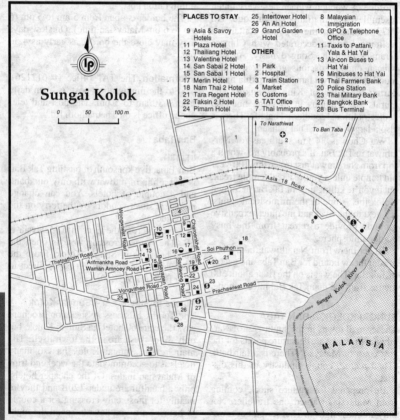

Sungai Kolok

0   50   100 m

PLACES TO STAY	25 Intertower Hotel	8 Malaysian
	26 An An Hotel	Immigration
9 Asia & Savoy	29 Grand Garden	10 GPO & Telephone
Hotels	Hotel	Office
11 Plaza Hotel		11 Taxis to Pattani,
12 Thailiang Hotel	**OTHER**	Yala & Hat Yai
13 Valentine Hotel		13 Air-con Buses to
14 San Sabai 2 Hotel	1 Park	Hat Yai
15 San Sabai 1 Hotel	2 Hospital	16 Minibuses to Hat Yai
17 Merlin Hotel	3 Train Station	19 Thai Farmers Bank
18 Nam Thai 2 Hotel	4 Market	20 Police Station
21 Tara Regent Hotel	5 Customs	23 Thai Military Bank
22 Taksin 2 Hotel	6 TAT Office	27 Bangkok Bank
24 Pimarn Hotel	7 Thai Immigration	28 Bus Terminal

To Narathiwat
To Ban Taba

Asia 18 Road

Soi Phuthon

Thetpathom Road
Arifmankha Road
Waman Amnoey Road
Vongvithee Road
Mongvivat Road
Charoenkhet Road
Bussayapan Road
Saritwong Road
Prachawiwat Road

Sungai Kolok River

MALAYSIA

Phuthon, Charoenkhet Rd. Some of these hotels also offer air-con rooms for 200 to 360B.

Top-end hotels in Sungai Kolok include:

Genting, Asia 18 Rd, from 650B (☎ 613231; fax 611259)
Grand Garden, 104 Arifmankha Rd, from 480B (☎ 611868; fax 613500)
Intertower Hotel, Prachawiwat Rd, from 399B (☎ 611586; fax 613400)
Merlin Hotel, 40 Charoenkhet Rd, from 350B (☎ 611003; fax 613325)
Plaza Hotel, off Bussayapan Rd, from 274B (☎ 611875; fax 613402)
Tara Regent Hotel, Soi Phuthon, Charoenkhet Rd, from 390B (☎ 611401; fax 613385)

The town has plenty of food stalls selling Thai, Chinese and Malaysian food. The *Siam* restaurant next to the Merlin is good for Thai food, and the *Bak Mui* near the Tara Regent for Chinese. For an economical and delicious breakfast very early in the morning, try coffee and doughnuts at the station buffet. Some of the Malay shops also do roti kaeng (Malay: roti chanai – flat bread with curry dip), in the mornings.

Places to Stay – Ban Taba

Masya (☎ 581125) has good rooms for 270B with fan and bath, 300B with air-con or 350B with air-con and TV. It's set back off the road leading from the Malaysian border and a bit difficult to find; take a motorcycle taxi there for 5B. The *Phan Phet* next door is more expensive but not as good. Further from the border is a no-name motel for 180B – look for *Ta Wan Seafood*.

Getting There & Around

Bus & Share Taxi Air-con buses to/from Bangkok cost 533B, take 18 hours and depart from Bangkok at 6.30 pm (from Sungai Kolok at noon). Standard bus fares are 296B, departing from each end at 9 pm. To Surat Thani standard buses are 143B (taking 10 hours), air-con 200B.

Share taxis from Yala to Sungai Kolok costs 60B, from Narathiwat 40B. There are also buses from Narathiwat for 18B (25B air-con). From Sungai Kolok taxis to Narathiwat leave from in front of the An An Hotel.

Air-con buses to Hat Yai cost 80B and leave from the Valentine Hotel at 7 am, and 12.30, 1 and 3 pm. From Hat Yai, departure times are the same. The trip takes about four hours.

The border is about a km from the centre of Sungai Kolok or the train station. Transport around town is by motorcycle taxi – it's 10B for a ride to the border. Coming from Malaysia, just follow the old train tracks to your right, or, for the town, turn left at the first junction and head for the high-rises.

From Rantau Panjang (Malaysian side), a share taxi to Kota Baru costs M$3.50 per person (M$14 to charter the whole car) and takes about an hour. The regular yellow-and-orange bus to KB costs M$2.20.

Train The daily special express No 19 to Sungai Kolok departs Bangkok at 2 pm and arrives at 9.50 am the next day. This train has 1st (808B) and 2nd-class fares (378B), not including the special-express surcharge of 50B (and 1st or 2nd-class sleeping berths if you so choose).

You can also get trains to Sungai Kolok from Yala and Tanyongmat (for Narathiwat), but buses are really faster and more convenient along these routes.

From Sungai Kolok to points farther north (via Yala), however, the train is a reasonable alternative. A train to Hat Yai takes about 4½ hours and costs 31B for a 3rd-class seat, 65B 2nd class. Train Nos 124 and 132 leave Sungai Kolok at 6.05 and 8.40 am, arriving in Hat Yai at 10.49 am and 1.08 pm.

From Sungai Kolok special express No 20 leaves at 3 pm and arrives in Bangkok at 10.35 am the next day, with stops in Hat Yai (6.24 pm), Surat Thani (11.47 pm) and Hua Hin (6.47 am) among other towns along the way.

Glossary

aahãan – food

aahãan pàa – jungle food

ajaan – respectful title for teacher, from the Sanskrit term *acharya*

amphoe – district; next subdivision down from province; sometimes spelt *amphur*

amphoe meuang – provincial capital

ao – bay or gulf

bâan – house or village; often spelt *ban*

bai toey – pandanus leaf

bàw náam ráwn – hot springs

bhikku – Buddhist monk in Pali; Thai pronunciation *phík-khù*

bòt – central sanctuary or chapel in a Thai temple; from Pali *uposatha*

chaa – tea

chaihàat – beach; also spelt *hat*

chao le (chao náam) – sea gypsies

chedi – stupa; monument erected to house a Buddha relic; called *pagoda* in Burma, *dagoba* in Sri Lanka, *cetiya* in India

dhammachakka – Buddhist wheel of law

doi – peak, as in mountain

farang – foreigner of European descent

hàat – beach; short for *chaihaat*; also *hat*

hang yao – long-tailed boat

hãw trai – a tripitaka (Buddhist scripture) library

hĭn – stone

isãan – general term for north-east Thailand, from the Sanskrit name for the medieval kingdom *Isana*, which encompassed parts of Cambodia and north-east Thailand

jangwàat – province

Jataka – life-stories of the Buddha

jii-khõh – Thai hoodlum

jiin – Chinese

kâew – crystal, jewel, glass, or gem; also spelt *keo*

kafae thũng – filtered coffee; sometimes called *ko-píi* in southern Thailand

kàp klâem – drinking food

ka-toey – Thai transvestite

kaw lae – traditional fishing boats of southern Thailand

khaen – reed instrument common in north-east Thailand

khão – hill or mountain

khlong – canal

khon – masked dance-drama based on stories from the *Ramakian*

khon isãan – the people of north-east Thailand

klawng – Thai drums

ko – island; also spelt *koh*; pronounced *kàw*

kuay haeng – Chinese-style work shirt

kuti – meditation hut

lâap – spicy mint salad with mint leaves

lãem – cape (in the geographical sense)

lakhon – classical Thai dance-drama

làk meuang – city pillar/phallus

lâo khão – white liquor

lâo thèuan – jungle liquor

lí-khe – Thai folk dance-drama

longyi – Burmese sarong

mâe chii – Thai Buddhist nun

mâe náam – river; literally 'mother water'

Maha That – literally 'great element', from the Sanskrit-Pali *mahadhatu*; common name for temples which contain Buddha relics

mát-mii – tie-dye silk method

mâw hâwm – Thai work shirt

mãwn khwan – triangular pillow popular in northern and north-east Thailand

metta – Buddhist practice of loving kindness

meuang – city; pronounced *meu-ang*

mondòp – small square building in a *wat* complex generally used by laypeople, as opposed to monks; from the Sanskrit *mandapa*

muay thai – Thai boxing

náam – water
náam phrík – chilli sauce
náam plaa – fish sauce
náam tòk – waterfall
naga – dragon-headed serpent
nakhon – city; from Sanskrit-Pali *nagara*; also spelt *nakhorn*
nãng – Thai shadow play
ngaan wát – temple fair
ngôp – traditional Khmer rice farmer's hat
noeng khão – hill

pàak náam – estuary
paa-té – batik
paa-thông-kõ – Chinese 'doughnut', a common breakfast food
pàk tâi – southern Thai
phâakhamãa – piece of cotton cloth worn as a wraparound by men
phâasîn – same as above for women
phrá – monk or Buddha image; an honorific term from the Pali *vara*, 'excellent'
phrá phum – earth spirits
phuu khão – 'mountain' in Central Thai
pìi-phâat – classical Thai orchestra
ponglang – north-east Thai marimba made of short logs
prang – Khmer-style tower on temples
prasat – small ornate building with a cruciform ground plan and needle-like spire, used for religious purposes, located on wat grounds; from the Sanskrit term *prasada*

rai – one *rai* is equal to 1600 sq metres
reua hang yao – long-tail taxi boat
reuan thãew – long-house
reu-sĩi – a Hindu *rishi* or 'sage'
rót thammada – ordinary bus (non air-con) or ordinary train (not rapid or express)
roti – round flatbread, common street food; also found in Muslim restaurants

sãalaa (sala) – an open-sided, covered meeting hall or resting place; from the Portuguese *sala* or 'room'
sala klang – provincial office

samlor – three-wheeled pedicab
sẽma – boundary stones used to consecrate ground used for monastic ordinations; from the Sanskrit-Pali *sima*
serow – Asian mountain goat
sêua mâw hâwm – blue cotton farmer's shirt
soi – lane or small street
sôm-tam – green papaya salad
sõngkhran – Thai new year, held in mid-April
sõngthãew – literally 'two rows'; common name for small pick-up trucks with two benches in the back, used as buses/taxis
susãan – cemetery

talàat nàam – floating market
tambon – 'precinct', next subdivision below *amphoe*; also spelled *tambol*
thâat – four-sided, curvilinear Buddhist reliquary, common in north-east Thailand; also spelt *that*
thale sàap – inland sea or large lake
thêp – angel or divine being; from Sanskrit *deva*
thewada – a kind of angel
thudong – monks who have taken ascetic vows
tripitaka – Theravada Buddhist scriptures
tuk-tuk – motorised *samlor*

vipassana – Buddhist insight meditation

wai – palms-together Thai greeting
wang – palace
wát – temple-monastery; from Pali *avasa*, monk's dwelling
wíhãan – counterpart to *bot* in Thai temple, containing Buddha images but not circumscribed by *sema* stones. Also spelt *wihan* or *viharn*; from Sanskrit *vihara*

yaa dong – herbal liquor; also the herbs inserted in *lao khao*
yam – Thai-style salad; usually made with meat or seafood

Index

TEXT

Map references are in **bold** type.

accommodation 130-132
  building failure 500
AIDS 109-111
air travel
  departure tax 161
  glossary 154-155
  to/from Thailand 152-158
  within Thailand 163-165
airports
  Bangkok International
  157-158, 175
Akien Thong Falls 315
Amphawa Floating Market 292
Ancient City (Meuang Boran)
  213, 290
Ang Thong 282
Ang Thong NMP 650
Ang Thong Province 282
Ao Bang Bao 344
Ao Bang Charu 664
Ao Bang Kao 659
Ao Bang Nang Lom 604
Ao Bang Tao 640-641
Ao Chaophao 667
Ao Cho 333, 334
Ao Chon Khram 659
Ao Hat Thong Lang 666-667
Ao Hin Khok 332, 334
Ao Hin Kong 667
Ao Karang 334
Ao Khanom 679
Ao Khlong Phrao 346
Ao Khlong Son 344
Ao Kiu 334
Ao Mae Hat 666-667
Ao Manao 603
Ao Na Khai 658-659
Ao Nai Wok 664
Ao Nam Mao 706
Ao Nang 703-706
Ao Noi 604
Ao Nuan 333
Ao Phai 333
Ao Phang-Nga 622-624

Ao Phangka 659
Ao Phutsa 333
Ao Salak Phet 344
Ao Takiap 596
Ao Thian 333
Ao Thong Krut 659
Ao Thong Nai Pan 666
Ao Thong Reng 666
Ao Thong Sai 655
Ao Thong Son 655
Ao Thong Ta Khian 657
Ao Thong Yang 659
Ao Ton Sai 705
Ao Wai 333
Ao Wiang Wan 334
Ao Wok Tum 667
Ao Wong Deuan 332, 333, 334
Aran 353
Aranya Prathet 352-353
architecture 45-51, 129
Ayuthaya 268-275, **271**
Ayuthaya Province 268-276

Bai Sii Ceremony 520
Ban A Hii 555
Ban Ahong 545-546
Ban Chalok Ban Kao 669
Ban Chiang 532
Ban Don 642-647, **643**
Ban Hat Sai Ri 669
Ban Hin Lat 620
Ban Hong Phu Thawng 534
Ban Hua Thanon 652
Ban Janrom 578
Ban Khai 664
Ban Khawn Sai 576
Ban Lamai 652
Ban Mae Hat 669
Ban Na Kha 534
Ban Nam Chiaw 341
Ban Nong Aw Tai 534
Ban Nong Pheu 555
Ban Pak 555
Ban Phae 282
Ban Phai 521
Ban Phe 328-329

Ban Pheu 532-533
Ban Prasat 506-507
Ban Sakai 733
Ban Salak Phet 344
Ban Sangka-U 712
Ban Ta Miang 579
Ban Taba 741-743
Ban Tai 654, 664
Ban Tha Klang 578
Ban Thon 534
Ban Tung Laem Sai 721
Bang Noi Floating Market 292
Bang Pa In 275-276
Bang Pu 602
Bang Sai Royal Folk Arts &
  Crafts Centre 276
Bang Saphan 606-608
Bang Saray 327
Bangkok 180-267, **182-183, 188,
  189, 201, 214, 221, 224, 227,
  231, 232**
  Ancient City (Meuang Boran)
  213
  Chinatown (Sampeng)
  207-210, **207**
  churches 200
  cultural centres 185-186
  department stores 257, 258
  Dusit Zoo 210-211
  embassies & consulates
  184-185
  Emerald Buddha 192
  entertainment 249-255
  floating markets 217-218
  future traffic alternatives 264
  galleries 206-207
  getting around 262-267
  getting there & away 260-262
  Grand Palace 192-194
  Jim Thompson's House 204
  Lak Meuang (City Pillar) 197
  Lumphini Park 211
  markets 256-257
  medical services 191
  Monk's Bowl Village 211
  National Museum 203

THANKS

Thanks to all the following travellers and others (apologies if we've misspelt your name) who took the time and trouble to write to us about their experiences of Thailand.

Dr M Abernethy (UK), Ceely Ackerman (USA), Russell Adams (NZ), Jessica Adolfsson (S), Irene Aebi (CH), M Affonso (Dk), Paulo Affonso, Thomas Agoston (USA), Mrs Edna Ahrens (UK), Patsy Alexander (Aus), R Alker (UK), A Anamnart, Bodo Andrae (D), Niyana Angkawut (Thai), Katherine Anning, A J Aplin (UK), David Ashford (UK), David Aus (USA), Eddi Aver (D), Kenneth Baar (USA), Stephen Backes (UK), Helen Backhouse (UK), Wendy Onche Bakketun Bakketun (Nl), Joy Bannett (USA), Sandra Bao, Ron & Chamnong Barber, Jane Barnacle (Aus), Marg Barr-Brown (NZ), R Barrett (UK), Bonnie Baskin (USA), Chris Battle (Aus), K B Bayley (Aus), John Beales (UK), Shane Beary, Louis R Bechtel (USA), Richard Bell (UK), Daphne Bell (NZ), Peter Bennett (Aus), Steen Bergerud (Dk), Lena Berglow (S), June & Eddy Berkhout (C), Annika Beskow (S), John J Bevan (UK), John Biale (USA), Lucy Bingham (UK), Ross Bishop (USA), David Blake, Fritz Blatter (USA), Richard Blitstein, Arjan Blok (Nl), Jan Blok (Nl), Anders Blomqvist (S), Andris Blums (Aus), Luen de Boer (Nl), Michael Bohm (D), Martin Bohnstedt (A), V Bolton (UK), Luis Bonsembiante (Arg), Ken Boom (USA), Paolo Borsoni (I), Karen Bowles (Aus), DC Boyall (Aus), David Boyall (Aus), David Bradley (Aus), Catherine Brahams (UK), Darren Brasher (UK), France Brassard (C), Gwen Brice-Pickering (C), Susanne Brischle (CH), Israel Broner (USA), T Scott Bryan (USA), Jamie Buckner (USA), Corey Buffo (USA), Suzanne Bunker (Aus), Sally Burbage (UK), Glen Burns (Aus), Dean Burrow, Robb Cadwell (USA), Frank Caglioti (Aus), Peter Callaghan (Aus), Angela Callis, Margaretha Carlsson (S), Eugene Casey, Rudd & Ida Cazemier (Nl), Anker Cedvic (CH), Assunta Cha (USA), Anthony Chambers (USA), John Chanthaisay (USA), Robert Cherubin (USA), Alan Cheung (C), Jason Teo Chin Soon (Sin), Kristina & Colin Cho (USA), Chusack Chongsmack (Thai), Lisa Choy Zafra (USA), Margaret Clarke (NZ), Darran Clarke (UK), Michael A Clarke, Jeff Clarke (USA), Michelle Clifford (UK), Cecil Clifton (USA), Hilary Colcord (USA), Bernie Colditz (Aus), Nicholas Collis (Aus), George Conder (USA), Cynthia C Cook (USA), A G Cooke, A Cooper, Gerda Coppens (B), Brett Corlett (NZ), Joop & Rose Cornelissen (Nl), Nicholas Couis (Aus), J R Coupe (Aus), Nick Crivich (UK), Hans & Miriam Damen (Nl), Gindraux Daniel (CH), Richard Dankin (Aus), Mike Darley (UK), Jay Davidson (USA), Lynne Davis (C), Marjan de Bruijn (Nl), Shirley Deakin (UK), Klaus Derwanz, Gavthier Didier (F), G Donovan (UK), Nancy Drilling (USA),

Paul Drymalski (F), Beth Dudley (NZ), Thomas Duggan, Pieter Dujardin (Nl), Steve Dumire (UK), Lynne & Mark Duncan (C), Linda Dupont (C), Guy Dusselier (B), Anne Dykstra, David Thomas Eaton (USA), Roger Edwards (USA), Dr John Eggleton (UK), Tony van Eijden (Nl), Roger Eitel (Aus), Andrew Elliot (UK), Mark Elliott, Jodie Ellis, Jim Enright, Marcus Farmer (UK), Claire & Duncan Fisher (UK), Robert Fleming, Andrew Florides (UK), Lisa Foresee (USA), Daivd Francis, Denis Freney (Aus), David & Mandy Galbraith (Aus), Marios Gavalas (UK), Bas Geerts (Nl), Michael Geist, Danilatou Gelly, Toni Gerber (CH), Ruth Gerson, Margot Gerster (CH), Brian J Gilbert-Denham (UK), Heng Golf, Carol Goodman (USA), Trevor Graham (Aus), Susan Grant (Aus), Mark Gray (Aus), Martin Gray (UK), David Green (UK), Paul Greenhaf (UK), Linda Greenwood (C), Bill Grier (USA), Julie Grimshaw, Ian Grundy (UK), Diane Guest (USA), Stephen Guignon (Aus), Stephen Guise, C Gwenlan (UK), Clemens Hageraats (Nl), Soeren Halkier (Dk), Tony Hallett (UK), Gary Hammack (USA), Stefan Hammond (USA), Susan Hansell (USA), Amanda Harlow (UK), Lewis Harper (USA), Candy Harrington (USA), Jen Harrison (USA), Wayne Harrison (USA), Sarah Harvey (Aus), Joni Hatashita (C), Chris Hayward, Michiel Heijstek (Nl), Fionna Heiton (UK), Alison Henderson (Aus), Alice Henderson (UK), Rob Hendriks (Nl), Armin Hermann (A), Michael Hess (USA), Anette Hildebrand (D), M Hilditch (UK), Vicki Hinchcliffe (Aus), Kathryn Hinkles (UK), Neil Hipkiss (UK), Matthew Hird (UK), Bernie Hodges, M Hodgkinson (USA), Dr Wolfgang Hoeffer (D), Gunter Hoffman (S), Richard Holbrook (J), Roger Holdsworth (Aus), Hollie Hollander (NZ), Guy & Toi Hopkins, Ronald Hoppen (UK), Kristina Horlin (I), John Howes (J), Zack Huchulak (C), Shirley Hudson (USA), Wendy & Brian Hughes (UK), D Hughes (USA), Harry Hunter (USA), Jimmy Huppe (USA), Roel Hurkens (C), Charlotte Hurley (NZ), Valby Langgade Aicksine (Dk), Bella Intaranan, Kim Ivy (USA), Doni Jacklin (C), Karen Jackson (UK), Kathleen Jalhiert (USA), Sai Jantarapat, Richard Jenkins (USA), S E Jenkins (UK), Gregory Jensen (USA), Henning Jensen (Dk), L & H Jesse (Aus), Robert Johnson (USA), Astrid Joosten (Nl), Dr Iris Kalka (Isr), A Karp, Tim Kasser (USA), Eviatar Katkati (Isr), John & Eliz Kauffman (USA), Peter Kauffner (USA), Jack Kay (USA), Roy Kellett (UK), Brett Kellett (UK), Caitlin Kelly (USA), Phillip Kendon (UK), Kalervo Kiianmaa (Fin), Glen King (UK), Patrick King (Ire), Ralf Kirschenmann (D), Cathy Kitson (UK), Lud Klaauw (Nl), Jiri Klaska (Nl), Alan Klein (USA), Frits Klija (Nl), Peter Kok (Nl), M Krijnen & G Konig (Nl), Henry Koster (Nl), B Kowalczyk (D), Monika Kralik, B Krane (UK), Mascha Kranse (Nl), Ittipol Krisanasuwan, Anne Kronsell (Dk), Kathryn Kulis (USA), P La Bong (USA), Victor Lam (Sin), David Lambert (USA),

Brian Paul Landles (C), Ed & Lois Langerak (USA), Richard Laprise (C), Michael Larsen (USA), Alena Lasure (B), David Latchford (UK), Wayne Lauchlan (Aus), Robert Lavicka (Nl), Todd Lawrence (USA), John Le Long, Adrain Leaver (UK), Robyn Lee (Aus), Andy Lewin (USA), Roger Lewis (UK), Dr C M Leyland (UK), Hermes Liberty (C), Steve Lidgey (UK), Susanne Liljkefors (S), Ulli Link (D), Marcel Lisi (USA), G K Little (UK), David Lollar (USA), Alette Los (Nl), Lorraine Luciano (USA), Elisa & Pietro Luka (I), Dr Niclas Lundin (S), Susan Lupton (UK), Sean Luxton (C), Peter Lysy (D), Michael MacCrystall (USA), Jim Mackie (UK), Brian MacMahon (Ire), Sean Maguire (UK), Frances Mantak, Mario Maric (S), Harvey Marshall (USA), Glenn & Fran Marshall (D), Marg Marshall (Aus), Michael Martensen (USA), Steve Martin, Lisa Martin, Michelle Martin (USA), Samantha Maton (UK), Marlon Maus (USA), Peter May (UK), Roland Mayer (D), Thomas Mayes (USA), Christopher McDermott (USA), Max McGowan, Noel McGuire (Aus), Shawn McGuyer (USA), Kate McMahon (Aus), Bob McMeechan (USA), Joe Meline, Steven Mendoza (Aus), Jean & Mel Merzon (USA), Maria Meylan (CH), Michael Michiel (C), Rhona Millar, Rob Miller, Tracey & Andrew Mitchell, Jakob Modeer (S), Stephen Morey (Aus), Peter Morony (Aus), Damian Mottram (UK), Marianne Mouild (Nl), Tony Moulsdale (UK), Peter Mui (USA), Lynda Murphy (UK), B J Murphy-Bridge (USA), Adrian Murrell (UK), Peter Nang, Bob Nash (USA), Fam Nauta (Nl), Shane Neely (USA), Ann Neilsen (Dk), Andrew Nemiciolo (USA), Caroline Newhouse (UK), Prehn Nichols (Aus), Shelley Nieder (C), Wolfgang Niegl (D), Andrea Nitsche (D), Jonathan Nolan (C), Hazel Norbury (J), Mary Nosek (USA), Hugo Nothdog (UK), Tom Nowak (USA), Garan O'Dowda (UK), Michael O'Reilly (UK), Olov & Tukkata (Thai), Linwi Ongsakun (Thai), Andrew Osborne (UK), Nicola Otterspoor (Nl), Pinat Ounope, Alex Ovenden (Aus), R S J Paauwe (Nl), Nick Pacey (NZ), Julian Page (UK), Rachael Parker (UK), David Parry, Vincent Patrick, Gerry Patterson (C), Jenny Peacock, Sue Pearce (UK), Les Pearton (UK), Nina Pees (D), Patrick Percy (USA), Lidija Perenic, Clem Perry (Aus), Liana Piccoli (Aus), Simonetta Pietrasanta (I), Mike Pihea (USA), Miriam Pinchok (USA), John Plampin (UK), Cecilia Pleshakov, Dan Pool, Ramu Popuri (UK), A J Power (NZ), Matthew Price (UK), Marion Price (Aus), Miss K Pryor (UK), Robert Putnam (Nl), Nicole Puts (Nl), Timothy Quan (C), Agnes Radvanyi, Leilae & Sergio Ramirez, Eric Rayner (USA), Clive Reader (UK), Lucie Redwood, Sharon Regev (Isr), Debbie Reiskind (C), Lisa Renkin (Aus), Heather Renton (Aus), Edith Ressenaar (UK), Mike Rhea (USA), David Richards (USA), Audrey Richter (C), Anita Riemersma (Nl), Jess River (USA), David Roberts (Aus), Richard Robinson (C), Andy Roedlach (A), Ann Rooney (Aus), Andy Roscoe (UK), Dr Rouset (USA), Jean Michel Rousina (F), Paul Rousseau (USA), Karin Ruscher (D), Polly Russel-Stracey (UK), Robyn Russell (USA), Moti Sabag (Isr), Wolfgang Sackenheim, Douglas Samuel (C), Merrilee Sandcastles (USA), Ross Sanford (UK), Justin Sare (Sp), Stewart Saunders (Aus), Brian Savage (UK), Carmelia Saxon, Dean Schluter (NZ), Thomas Schmidt (USA), David Schmidt (USA), Norbert Schmiedeberg (Aus), Matthras Schnrter (D), Anna Scholey (UK), Michael Schumacher (Nl), Anne K Scott (Ire), Phillip Seely (UK), Kaine Seeoophaehar, Dr Olarn Seriniyom, Guy Shapiro (Isr), John Shardlow (UK), Sandee Sharpe (USA), Gerard Sheehy (UK), Jill Sheldon, Lucile Shelton (Aus), Wayne Sheridan (Aus), Kate Shew (Aus), Sonia Short (Aus), Susie Siedentop (USA), Tom Simmons (USA), Tara Singh (USA), Ernst-Otto Smith, Mrs Pat Smith (Aus), Roger Smith (Aus), Anthony Smith (Nl), Brad Smith (Aus), Goulias Sotiris, S Clay Sparkman (USA), Lord Sparrow (UK), Orly & Moshe Spiegler (Isr), Ronald Spiers (Aus), Richard Stajnings, Tony Stanbridge, Pete & Helen Stanger (UK), Marvin & Jasmin Stanley (USA), Jon. Stefansson (Dk), Lenhardt Stevens (USA), John Stevenson (Aus), Annette Stieber, J E Stitfall (NZ), Susanne Strackbein (D), Eileen Stuart (UK), Lisa Studdart (Aus), Caroline Sturm (Aus), Frank Swartjes (Nl), Kate Swinburn (UK), Mark Talleytire, Victoria Tanner (Aus), Kenneth-David Tavalin, Dale & Diane Tayln (Aus), Jim Taylor (UK), Gary Taylor (UK), Andrea Thalemann, Alison Thomas (UK), Henrik Thomsen (Dk), Adriana Tomassetti (I), Peter Tse (UK), Richard & Marijke Tucker (UK), Maggie S Tucker (USA), Martin Tuckey (UK), Rob Tulleken (Nl), Shirley Thei Tun, Jan Valkenburg (Nl), Gabriel Vallicelli, N C van Beek (Nl), Henk van Cann (Nl), J A van der Louw (Nl), Dr Hajonides van der Meulen (Nl), Marcel van der Roest, Hans van der Stock (B), Monique van Erp (Nl), Bas van Gemeren (Nl), Mark van Landingham (USA), A van Soest (Nl), Inge Veen (Nl), S A Op het Veld (Nl), Caroline Verhage (Nl), Frits Verwijnen (Nl), John Vloet, Michael Wadman (USA), Peter Wainwright (Dk), Bernadette Walter, James Ward (Aus), Andrew Warren, David Washington (Aus), Rob Wassink (Nl), David Watkins (Aus), Arnold Weisz (Nl), G J Westenbunk (Nl), Paul Wheaton (UK), Esther White (USA), Pete & Sandy Whitehead (UK), Tanja Wiegloss (D), Bob Williams (USA), Eldrid Williamson (USA), Mark Wilson (USA), Paul Windrig (UK), Joel Winston, Alexander Winter, Brian Winthrop (NZ), Michael Wolfe (USA), Eva Wolmefelt (S), Leslie Gabriel Wong, Peter Woodard, Robert Wyburn (UK), Rubrecht Zaat (Nl), Adam Zanetti (Aus), Stuart Zang, Doris Zingg (S)

A – Austria, Arg – Argentina, Aus – Australia, B – Belgium, C – Canada, CH – Switzerland, D – Germany, Dk – Denmark, F – France, Fin – Finland, I – Italy, Ire – Ireland, Isr – Israel, J – Japan, Nl – Netherlands, NZ – New Zealand, S – Sweden, Sin – Singapore, Sp – Spain, Thai – Thailand, UK – United Kingdom, USA – United States of America

Update – April 1996

Thailand remains one of the most popular destinations in South-East Asia, ranking second behind Singapore.

Visas & Embassies

Transit visas for 56 nationalities, including Australians, New Zealanders, Americans, British, Germans and French, have been extended from 15 to 30 days. It is now also possible to extend a transit visa in Thailand for up to 10 days for 500B. If you want to stay longer you need a tourist visa. Note that some consulates require colour photos for visa applications.

Only people arriving by air are now theoretically required to show onward tickets.

The Embassy of the Lao People's Democratic Republic in Bangkok has moved to 520, 5-2/1-2 Soi Ramkhamhaeng 39, Bang Kapi, Bangkok (☎ 539 6667).

The phone numbers for the Royal Thai Embassy in Japan are ☎ (03) 3441-1386 for visas and ☎ 3441-7352 and ☎ 3442-6750 for information.

Money & Costs

The Thai economy is in reasonable shape and growing at a rapid rate, although inflation is around 7%. Prices have not increased greatly, apart for accommodation, which in some places has increased by as much as 15 to 20% since this edition was researched.

Some banks in the UK have warned that they do not refund commissions (generally from 3 to 5%) charged on Visa transactions by some merchants in Thailand.

In April 1996, US$1 = 25B.

Dangers & Annoyances

The government has launched a programme to eradicate rabies within five years. Meanwhile, stay well away from those stray dogs!

Car & Motorbike Rental The Australian Embassy warns of problems with the hire of motor vehicles, particularly motorcycles. Tourists are being told that they do not need

a driver's licence to ride motorcycles. This is not so; they must have a valid local or international driver's licence for the class of vehicle being hired, or they run the risk of being charged by the police.

A second problem is that quite often neither the vehicle nor any third party is covered by insurance. The person hiring the vehicle must therefore take full responsibility for costs and injuries incurred in an accident. They are also not covered for injury and should ensure that their travel insurance covers any injury sustained. Some travel insurance companies don't pay if the injured party was unlicensed.

Most rental operators insist that you hand over your passport as security. If you do, you might be slapped with ludicrously high claims for damage to the machine when you return it. If they have your passport, there's not much you can do about this, so be sure to inspect the vehicle carefully before renting, and notify the owner of existing damage. It's best to rent only from companies that provide full insurance.

Gem Scams Travellers are still falling for the gem scam by unscrupulous gemshop owners, who now use dishonest foreigners to help them lure naive travellers. Remember there are no government gemshops in Thailand. People are still losing hundreds and sometimes thousands of dollars.

Thai-Myanmar Border In 1995 there was fighting along parts of the Thai western border with Myanmar, which spilled over into Thailand. These might have been isolated incidents, but the border crossings around Mae Sot and Mai Sai were closed temporarily. In early 1996 Khun Sa, the infamous leader of the Myanmar Shan insurgency, surrendered along with most of his troops. The border crossings at Mae Sai, Three Pagodas Pass and Ranong are scheduled to reopen. There is a slight risk that fighting will resume, especially along the border between Mae Sarit and Mae Sariang.

Ko Pha-Ngan Hat Rin beach is well known for its 'full moon parties'. Over the last few years we have been receiving reports of robberies and assaults during the parties, and also at other times. Many of the reports allege that the vicinity of the Cactus Club is the most dangerous place, but problems are by no means restricted to this area. Be warned that the police carry out drug busts at the parties, with the help of Interpol, if rumours are to be believed.

Since early 1996, local tourism authorities have been hosting 'official' full moon parties which incorporate Thai cultural activities and sports events. The general atmosphere at Hat Rin is becoming tamer, while full moon/techno/rave parties (as well as 'dark moon' parties celebrating moonless nights) are being held elsewhere on the island.

Activities

At beautiful Laem Phra Nang, on Hat Rai

Leh east, Ya-Ya Bungalows and Railay Bay Bungalows offer guided rock-climbing as well as instruction and equipment rental.

Sysygie, a 14-m ketch now based at Hat Rai Leh, has five-day trips to/from Penang, with some instruction. There are four sailings per year, between January and March.

Getting There & Away

The Chiang Khong river crossing into Laos is open to travellers with Lao visas. Two-week tourist visas are available at travel agencies in Chiang Khong for about 1700B.

Here is a traveller's report on travelling from Yunnan (China) to northern Thailand:

Sleeper buses run from Kunming to Jinghong, capital of Xishuangbanna (25 hours, Y200). From Jinghong there are seven daily buses to Mengla (5 to 6 hours). If you are in hurry, it's possible to get off the bus from Kunming just before Ming-Luan (I think that's the name), which is a bit before Jinghong, and catch a bus or a ride from there to Mengla. Beware – all accommodation in Mengla is very expensive, Y80 for single.

Then take a short bus ride from Mengla to Mohan on the Lao border (1.5 hours, Y8). From Botan, on the Lao side of the border, take a pickup truck through the jungle to Luang Namtha (3.5 hours, K1500), a small, cute town, capital of the province, complete with a small bank for exchange and two small hotels.

From there the best, fastest and nicest way to get to Thailand is by river: take a small tuk-tuk-like car to the Nam Tha river landing (7 km) and catch a boat going downstream to Pak Tha, a town where Nam Tha River meets the Mekong. Travel for 30 minutes upstream on the Mekong and you're in Huay Xai. Across the river is Chiang Khong, Thailand.

Noam Urbach

From Joe Cummings *In order to cross from China into Laos, you'll need to hold a valid visa for Laos. These are available at the Lao Consulate in Kunming. Boats along the Nam Tha run only during the rainy season and for a short time thereafter, roughly June to October. Buses, however, run year-round along the road between Luang Nam Tha and Huay Xai. A new bridge is under construction across the Mekong River between Huay Xai and Chiang Khong.*

We've had reports that officials at the Chong Mek border crossing from Thailand to Laos refuse to give departure stamps and tell travellers to return to Ubon Ratchathani and get them there.

Ayuthaya

Ayuthaya Historical Study Centre is closed on Monday and Tuesday.

Bangkok

The Tourist Police (☎ 255 2964/8) at 29/1 Soi Lang Suan, Ploenchit Rd, Lumpini, is the only office in Bangkok to report theft if you want a written document for insurance purposes. The process can take as little as half an hour, but there are often long queues. The report is written in Thai but your insurance company will want an English translation as well. You can get a translation at various translation offices around Bangkok. Alternatively, ask the police for a photocopy of your original report in English, which they normally keep.

A traveller highly recommends Bangkok General Hospital on Phetburi Rd, Soi Sunwichai 7. She says that you'll find at least one doctor who is a specialist in tropical diseases and speaks excellent English.

Free guided tours of Wat Phra Kaew and the Grand Palace run approximately half-hourly – you don't need to pay one of the freelance guides who approach you at the main gates.

STA Travel (☎ 233 25882/2626) has moved to Room 1405, 14th Floor, Wall St Tower Building, 33 Surawong Rd, Bangkok 10500.

The authorities are evicting vendors in the Wat Mahathat/Thammasat University area, and at Pak Khlong Market, as part of a plan to renovate the entire Ko Ratanakosin area.

A good way to cool off is to visit the World Ice Skating Centre, on the 8th floor of the World Trade Centre, 4 Rajdamri Rd.

Getting There & Away Bangkok International Airport's new Terminal 2 (connected to Terminal 1 by interior walkways) opened in late 1995. Facilities are similar to those in Terminal 1, including an exchange counter and a taxi desk. On the 4th floor is a new food centre.

Getting Around Apparently you can take the Air Force bus which runs between the airport, the railway station and Laksi Shopping Mall. If you are taking the train from the airport, note that the pedestrian bridge mentioned on page 176 is the enclosed concrete bridge which connects to international Terminal 1.

Ongoing construction of new freeways and elevated railway lines has meant even more disruption to Bangkok's traffic. On the positive side, the staggering of business hours for banks (initially 10 am to 4 pm, but this could change), along with the installation of over 200 computer-controlled traffic lights and the addition of several hundred traffic police has increased the average traffic flow by an estimated 20%. Most tuk-tuks are now powered by LP gas, rather than petrol, and a small fleet of electric-powered tuk-tuks has been introduced. Three major mass-transit projects are under construction, with the first (60 km of elevated light rail and expressways) due to be completed in 1998. However, because of problems in coordinating the three projects, it's doubtful whether any will stay on schedule.

Microbuses now cost a flat rate of 25B.

The Khlong Bangkok Noi taxi now departs at Tha Chan due to renovation works at Tha Maharat. When you take a boat, try to pay on the boat, rather than beforehand, or you might be overcharged. The best seats for seeing the Khlong are in front. The other seats offer lesser views because of the water spraying up along the sides of the boat – which can also mean that you get wet.

Ubon Ratchathani

If you plan to stay at the Wat Paa Nanachat Bung Wai, the monks recommend that you notify them in advance. During the hot season months of March to May, the monks are on retreat and don't take guests.

Chiang Mai

The Arcade bus station can be reached by tuk-tuks and red 'rot sii daeng' from all over the city, merely by saying 'Arcade'. Be aware that you can only buy bus tickets on the day of departure, and there are long queues.

Laem Son National Park

The road in from the highway has been upgraded and there is now no problem with wet season access.

Phuket

Thai Airways no longer runs a shuttle to/from the airport. The service has been taken over by Holiday Charter (☎ 246 088), which has buses running approximately hourly.

A doctor has written to say that the best medical centre on the island is now the Phuket International Hospital (☎ 249 400; 210 935 for emergencies), on the airport bypass road.

Travellers' Tips & Comments

At 80 cm in diameter, *bua phuut* is Thailand's largest and most spectacular flower. It is also one of the world's rarest plant species, occurring only at Khao Sok National Park and the adjoining Khlong Saen Wildlife Sanctuary. Bua phuut is a parasite and has not roots or leaves of its own. For most of the year it exists as microscopic threads, growing inside the roots of lianas (woody climbing plants), absorbing nutrients. Once a year small flower buds develop beneath the bark of the host's roots. As they grow, the buds burst through the root bark and swell to the size of a football. When the flower opens it emits a powerful smell to attract insects which are thought to be responsible for pollination. Within three to four days the flowers shrivel and turn black. Pollinated female flowers develop thousands of small seeds. It is not known how the seeds are dispersed to infect a new host liana.

Wim Klasen

When in Krabi, a somewhat pricey 'must do' activity is a trip with Sea Canoe, based on Ao Phra Nang. They also have offices in Phuket and Samui. The day trip from Krabi may not be as well publicised as the one in Phuket, but is definitely worth the time and money and is much less touristy. A guide leads small groups through the maze of canyons and caves that are the highlight of Krabi province. The solitude and beauty of the trip will be enjoyed by even the most jaded travellers.

Diving in Krabi is also very good, while not as well known as Phi Phi or Phuket. During the high season, day trips leave from Krabi to both Phi Phi and Shark Point which is a popular Phuket day trip. The prices are cheaper and because diving is not a primary attraction in Krabi yet, the groups tend to be smaller.

Because accommodation is still limited in Krabi, travellers would be smart to make advance bookings during the high season. When arranging one of the longtails that travel between Ao Nang and Ralie or Ko Poda, do not pay extra if the captain says he will wait for you. The captains state higher prices for trips if he waits while you spend the day on the beach. Soon as you are out of sight he is off to get another passenger to ferry about. Also, agree on a price for the boat and not per person

Carol Leligdon

We booked an all day sightseeing/snorkelling trip [on Ko Phi-Phi] and were assured that the calm waters would be fine for my friend, a weak swimmer. They ended up depositing us at the mouth of a large bay during an outgoing tide and then proceeded to go to sleep in the boat. We were rapidly swept into the open ocean and some pretty rough waters. Fortunately we were rescued by another snorkeller.

Often the tour companies are too busy scooping up tourist dollars to take what we think of as adequate precautions. There are still some risks in doing everyday things, in spite of all the tourist hordes doing just the same thing.

Peter Ridgway

Songserm Travel Company Ltd has the sole licence to run ferries for tourists from Surat Thani to the islands. They operate from a pier called Tha Thong, which seemed to be their headquarters. They have no competition and now run almost all the tourist buses in Southern Thailand between the ports.

When I got off the train at Surat Thani I was hustled on to a bus which was meant to go to Krabi and the boat to Phi Phi. It took me to the Songserm depot in the middle of nowhere, 20 km from Surat Thani. The bus to Krabi didn't appear for 2.5 hours. I complained about this deception but was simply told where the main road was and that I could get a songthaew back to Surat Thani if I did not like it. Because they run the boats, their own buses, often free, take you to this Songserm depot where you wait for the next bus. They have the route so sewn up that it is difficult to get to the government bus stations.

Nicholas Redfearn

I worked as a volunteer with the Gibbon Rehabilitation Project. Goals of the project include rehabilitating captive gibbons and returning them to the forest. The project received the sanction of the Thai Royal Forestry Department, which allocated some land in Khao Phra Thaew Forest Reserve and later the complete island Ko Boi in Phang-Nga Bay.

The project started in 1992 with three gibbons; now there are almost 30 in the centre. All released gibbons seem to adapt well to their new situation. The Gibbon Centre is a touristy attraction which creates financial support for the project. Europe Conservation has started an eco-volunteer programme.

Elly Bloem

On my first visit to Thailand I bought sleeveless dresses, only to discover that Thai women almost universally cover their arms to the elbow and that I was not acceptably dressed. More women's fashion notes: Pants are more popular in Bangkok, with about 50% of women wearing them on weekends. Most days they are even letting them in Wat Phra Kaew, but not always.

For business-women suits and straight skirts are most common – tough if you're not used to the climate. It depends on how much of your day is air-conditioned and how badly you need a professional image. It's important to realise that Thai people are by and large so polite that even in the Moslem south they will not offer obvious negative feedback on even offensive outfits and behaviour.

Anon

Internet Info
For the latest travel information, check out the Lonely Planet web site:

http://www.lonelyplanet.com

This award-winning site contains updates, recent travellers' letters and a useful travellers' bulletin board.

Acknowledgments
The information in this Stop Press was compiled from various sources, including author Joe Cummings, and reports by the following travellers: Dr B Abtmaier, Donna Acord, Liisa & Polly Arrowsmith, Anny Bussieres, S Cue, Andreas M Faul, David Francis, Margarita Ginty, Peter Hansen & Susanne Lisby, Wim Klasen, Rosalind Knowlson, David Kulka, Phil Miller, Colin Pendry, Nicholas Redfearn, Leni V Reeves, Steve Rogowski, Felix Roth, Ed & Marie Scarpari, Maria Svensson, Dr John Tigue, Noam Urbach, Andris Vizbaras, and Michael Wolff.

LONELY PLANET JOURNEYS

JOURNEYS is a unique collection of travellers' tales – published by the company that understands travel better than anyone else. It is a series for anyone who has ever experienced – or dreamed of – the magical moment when they encountered a strange culture or saw a place for the first time. They are tales to read while you're planning a trip, while you're on the road or while you're in an armchair, in front of a fire.

JOURNEYS books will catch the spirit of a place, illuminate a culture, recount a crazy adventure, or introduce a fascinating way of life. They will always entertain, and always enrich the experience of travel.

ISLANDS IN THE CLOUDS
Travels in the Highlands of New Guinea
Isabella Tree

This is the fascinating account of a journey to the remote and beautiful Highlands of Papua New Guinea and Irian Jaya. The author travels with a PNG Highlander who introduces her to his intriguing and complex world. *Islands in the Clouds* is a thoughtful, moving book, full of insights into a region that is rarely noticed by the rest of the world.

'One of the most accomplished travel writers to appear on the horizon for many years ... the dialogue is brilliant' – Eric Newby

LOST JAPAN
Alex Kerr

Lost Japan draws on the author's personal experiences of Japan over a period of 30 years. Alex Kerr takes his readers on a backstage tour: friendships with Kabuki actors, buying and selling art, studying calligraphy, exploring rarely visited temples and shrines ... The Japanese edition of this book was awarded the 1994 Shincho Gakugei Literature Prize for the best work of non-fiction.

'This deeply personal witness to Japan's wilful loss of its traditional culture is at the same time an immensely valuable evaluation of just what that culture was' – Donald Richie of the Japan Times

THE GATES OF DAMASCUS
Lieve Joris
Translated by Sam Garrett

This best-selling book is a beautifully drawn portrait of day-to-day life in modern Syria. Through her intimate contact with local people, Lieve Joris draws us into the fascinating world that lies behind the gates of Damascus.

'A brilliant book ... Not since Naguib Mahfouz has the everyday life of the modern Arab world been so intimately described' – William Dalrymple

SEAN & DAVID'S LONG DRIVE
Sean Condon

Sean and David are young townies who have rarely strayed beyond city limits. One day, for no good reason, they set out to discover their homeland, and what follows is a wildly entertaining adventure that covers half of Australia. Sean Condon has written a hilarious, offbeat road book that mixes sharp insights with deadpan humour and outright lies.

'Funny, pithy, kitsch and surreal ... This book will do for Australia what Chernobyl did for Kiev, but hey you'll laugh as the stereotypes go boom' – Andrew Tuck, Time Out

LONELY PLANET TRAVEL ATLASES

Lonely Planet has long been famous for the number and quality of its guidebook maps. Now we've gone one step further and in conjunction with Steinhart Katzir Publishers produced a handy companion series: Lonely Planet travel atlases – maps of a country produced in book form.

Unlike other maps, which look good but lead travellers astray, our travel atlases have been researched on the road by Lonely Planet's experienced team of writers. All details are carefully checked to ensure the atlas corresponds with the equivalent Lonely Planet guidebook.

The handy atlas format means no holes, wrinkles, torn sections or constant folding and unfolding. These atlases can survive long periods on the road, unlike cumbersome fold-out maps. The comprehensive index ensures easy reference.

- full-colour throughout
- maps researched and checked by Lonely Planet authors
- place names correspond with Lonely Planet guidebooks
  – no confusing spelling differences
- legend and travelling information in English, French, German, Japanese and Spanish
- size: 230 x 160 mm

Available now:
Thailand; India & Bangladesh; Vietnam;
Zimbabwe, Botswana & Namibia

Coming soon:
Chile; Egypt; Israel; Laos; Turkey

LONELY PLANET TV SERIES & VIDEOS

Lonely Planet travel guides have been brought to life on television screens around the world. Like our guides, the programmes are based on the joy of independent travel, and look honestly at some of the most exciting, picturesque and frustrating places in the world. Each show is presented by one of three travellers from Australia, England or the USA and combines an innovative mixture of video, Super-8 film, atmospheric soundscapes and original music.

Videos of each episode – containing additional footage not shown on television – are available from good book and video shops, but the availability of individual videos varies with regional screening schedules.

Video destinations include: Alaska; Australia (Southeast); Brazil; Ecuador & the Galápagos Islands; Indonesia; Israel & the Sinai Desert; Japan; La Ruta Maya (Yucatán, Guatemala & Belize); Morocco; North India (Varanasi to the Himalaya); Pacific Islands; Vietnam; Zimbabwe, Botswana & Namibia.

Coming soon: The Arctic (Norway & Finland); Baja California; Chile & Easter Island; China (Southeast); Costa Rica; East Africa (Tanzania & Zanzibar); Great Barrier Reef (Australia); Jamaica; Papua New Guinea; the Rockies (USA); Syria & Jordan; Turkey.

The Lonely Planet TV series is produced by:
Pilot Productions
Duke of Sussex Studios
44 Uxbridge St
London W8 7TG UK

Lonely Planet videos are distributed by:
IVN Communications Inc
2246 Camino Ramon
California 94583, USA

107 Power Road, Chiswick
London W4 5PL UK

Music from the TV series is available on CD & cassette.
For ordering information contact your nearest Lonely Planet office.

PLANET TALK

Lonely Planet's FREE quarterly newsletter

We love hearing from you and think you'd like to hear from us.

*When...*is the right time to see reindeer in Finland?
*Where...*can you hear the best palm-wine music in Ghana?
*How...*do you get from Asunción to Areguá by steam train?
*What...*is the best way to see India?

For the answer to these and many other questions read PLANET TALK.

Every issue is packed with up-to-date travel news and advice including:

- a letter from Lonely Planet co-founders Tony and Maureen Wheeler
- go behind the scenes on the road with a Lonely Planet author
- feature article on an important and topical travel issue
- a selection of recent letters from travellers
- details on forthcoming Lonely Planet promotions
- complete list of Lonely Planet products

To join our mailing list contact any Lonely Planet office.

Also available: Lonely Planet T-shirts. 100% heavyweight cotton..

LONELY PLANET ONLINE

Get the latest travel information before you leave or while you're on the road

Whether you've just begun planning your next trip, or you're chasing down specific info on currency regulations or visa requirements, check out the Lonely Planet World Wide Web site for up-to-the-minute travel information.

As well as travel profiles of your favourite destinations (including interactive maps and full-colour photos), you'll find current reports from our army of researchers and other travellers, updates on health and visas, travel advisories, and the ecological and political issues you need to be aware of as you travel.

There's an online travellers' forum (the Thorn Tree) where you can share your experiences of life on the road, meet travel companions and ask other travellers for their recommendations and advice. We also have plenty of links to other Web sites useful to independent travellers.

With tens of thousands of visitors a month, the Lonely Planet Web site is one of the most popular on the Internet and has won a number of awards including GNN's Best of the Net travel award.

http://www.lonelyplanet.com

LONELY PLANET PRODUCTS

Lonely Planet is known worldwide for publishing practical, reliable and no-nonsense travel information in our guides and on our web site. The Lonely Planet list covers just about every accessible part of the world. Currently there are eight series: *travel guides, shoestring guides, walking guides, city guides, phrasebooks, audio packs, travel atlases* and *Journeys* – a unique collection of travellers' tales.

EUROPE

Austria • Baltic States & Kaliningrad • Baltic States phrasebook • Britain • Central Europe on a shoestring • Central Europe phrasebook • Czech & Slovak Republics • Denmark • Dublin city guide • Eastern Europe on a shoestring • Eastern Europe phrasebook • Finland • France • Greece • Greek phrasebook • Hungary • Iceland, Greenland & the Faroe Islands • Ireland • Italy • Mediterranean Europe on a shoestring • Mediterranean Europe phrasebook • Poland • Prague city guide • Russia, Ukraine & Belarus • Russian phrasebook • Scandinavian & Baltic Europe on a shoestring • Scandinavian Europe phrasebook • Slovenia • St Petersburg city guide • Switzerland • Trekking in Greece • Trekking in Spain • Ukranian phrasebook • Vienna city guide • Walking in Switzerland • Western Europe on a shoestring • Western Europe phrasebook

NORTH AMERICA

Alaska • Backpacking in Alaska • Baja California • California & Nevada • Canada • Hawaii • Honolulu city guide • Los Angeles city guide • Mexico • Pacific Northwest USA • Rocky Mountain States • San Francisco city guide • Southwest USA • USA phrasebook

CENTRAL AMERICA & THE CARIBBEAN

Central America on a shoestring • Costa Rica • Eastern Caribbean • Guatemala, Belize & Yucatán: La Ruta Maya • Jamaica

SOUTH AMERICA

Argentina, Uruguay & Paraguay • Bolivia • Brazil • Brazilian phrasebook • Buenos Aires city guide • Chile & Easter Island • Colombia • Ecuador & the Galápagos Islands • Latin American Spanish phrasebook • Peru • Quechua phrasebook • Rio de Janeiro city guide • South America on a shoestring • Trekking in the Patagonian Andes • Venezuela

AFRICA

Arabic (Moroccan) phrasebook • Africa on a shoestring • Cape Town city guide • Central Africa • East Africa • Egypt & the Sudan • Ethiopian (Amharic) phrasebook • Kenya • Morocco • North Africa • South Africa, Lesotho & Swaziland • Swahili phrasebook • Trekking in East Africa • West Africa • Zimbabwe, Botswana & Namibia • Zimbabwe, Botswana & Namibia travel atlas

ALSO AVAILABLE:

Travel with Children • Traveller's Tales

MAIL ORDER

Lonely Planet products are distributed worldwide. They are also available by mail order from Lonely Planet, so if you have difficulty finding a title please write to us. North American and South American residents should write to Embarcadero West, 155 Filbert St, Suite 251, Oakland CA 94607, USA; European and African residents should write to 10 Barley Mow Passage, Chiswick, London W4 4PH; and residents of other countries to PO Box 617, Hawthorn, Victoria 3122, Australia.

NORTH-EAST ASIA

Beijing city guide • Cantonese phrasebook • China • Hong Kong, Macau & Canton • Hong Kong city guide • Japan • Japanese phrasebook • Japanese audio pack • Korea • Korean phrasebook • Mandarin phrasebook • Mongolia • Mongolian phrasebook • North-East Asia on a shoestring • Seoul city guide • Taiwan • Tibet • Tibet phrasebook • Tokyo city guide

INDIAN SUBCONTINENT

Bengali phrasebook • Bangladesh • Delhi city guide • Hindi/Urdu phrasebook • India • India & Bangladesh travel atlas • Karakoram Highway • Kashmir, Ladakh & Zanskar • Nepal • Nepali phrasebook • Pakistan • Sri Lanka • Sri Lanka phrasebook • Trekking in the Indian Himalaya • Trekking in the Nepal Himalaya

SOUTH-EAST ASIA

Bali & Lombok • Bangkok city guide • Burmese phrasebook • Cambodia • Ho Chi Minh city guide • Indonesia • Indonesian phrasebook • Indonesian audio pack • Jakarta city guide • Java • Laos • Lao phrasebook • Malaysia, Singapore & Brunei • Myanmar (Burma) • Philippines • Pilipino phrasebook • Singapore city guide • South-East Asia on a shoestring • Thailand • Thailand travel atlas • Thai phrasebook • Thai audio pack • Thai Hill Tribes phrasebook • Vietnam • Vietnamese phrasebook • Vietnam travel atlas

MIDDLE EAST & CENTRAL ASIA

Arab Gulf States • Arabic (Egyptian) phrasebook • Central Asia • Iran • Israel • Jordan & Syria • Middle East • Turkey • Turkish phrasebook • Trekking in Turkey • Yemen

Travel Literature: The Gates of Damascus

ISLANDS OF THE INDIAN OCEAN

Madagascar & Comoros • Maldives & Islands of the East Indian Ocean • Mauritius, Réunion & Seychelles

AUSTRALIA & THE PACIFIC

Australia • Australian phrasebook • Bushwalking in Australia • Bushwalking in Papua New Guinea • Fiji • Fijian phrasebook • Islands of Australia's Great Barrier Reef • Melbourne city guide • Micronesia • New Caledonia • New South Wales & the ACT • New Zealand • Outback Australia • Papua New Guinea • Papua New Guinea phrasebook • Queensland • Rarotonga & the Cook Islands • Samoa • Solomon Islands • South Australia • Sydney city guide • Tahiti & French Polynesia • Tonga • Tramping in New Zealand • Vanuatu • Victoria • Western Australia

Travel Literature: Islands in the Clouds • Sean & David's Long Drive

THE LONELY PLANET STORY

Lonely Planet published its first book in 1973 in response to the numerous 'How did you do it?' questions Maureen and Tony Wheeler were asked after driving, bussing, hitching, sailing and railing their way from England to Australia.

Written at a kitchen table and hand collated, trimmed and stapled, *Across Asia on the Cheap* became an instant local bestseller, inspiring thoughts of another book.

Eighteen months in South-East Asia resulted in their second guide, *South-East Asia on a shoestring*, which they put together in a backstreet Chinese hotel in Singapore in 1975. The 'yellow bible', as it quickly became known to backpackers around the world, soon became *the* guide to the region. It has sold well over half a million copies and is now in its 8th edition, still retaining its familiar yellow cover.

Today there are over 180 titles, including travel guides, walking guides, language kits & phrasebooks, travel atlases and travel literature. The company is one of the largest travel publishers in the world. Although Lonely Planet initially specialised in guides to Asia, we now cover most regions of the world, including the Pacific, North America, South America, Africa, the Middle East and Europe.

The emphasis continues to be on travel for independent travellers. Tony and Maureen still travel for several months of each year and play an active part in the writing, updating and quality control of Lonely Planet's guides.

They have been joined by over 70 authors and 170 staff at our offices in Melbourne (Australia), Oakland (USA), London (UK) and Paris (France). Travellers themselves also make a valuable contribution to the guides through the feedback we receive in thousands of letters each year.

The people at Lonely Planet strongly believe that travellers can make a positive contribution to the countries they visit, both through their appreciation of the countries' culture, wildlife and natural features, and through the money they spend. In addition, the company makes a direct contribution to the countries and regions it covers. Since 1986 a percentage of the income from each book has been donated to ventures such as famine relief in Africa; aid projects in India; agricultural projects in Central America; Greenpeace's efforts to halt French nuclear testing in the Pacific; and Amnesty International.

'I hope we send the people out with the right attitude about travel. You realise when you travel that there are so many different perspectives about the world, so we hope these books will make people more interested in what they see. These are guidebooks, but you can't really guide people. All you can do is point them in the right direction.'
– Tony Wheeler

LONELY PLANET PUBLICATIONS

Australia
PO Box 617, Hawthorn 3122, Victoria
tel: (03) 9819 1877 fax: (03) 9819 6459
e-mail: talk2us@lonelyplanet.com.au

USA
Embarcadero West, 155 Filbert St, Suite 251,
Oakland, CA 94607
tel: (510) 893 8555 TOLL FREE: 800 275-8555
fax: (510) 893 8563
e-mail: info@lonelyplanet.com

UK
10 Barley Mow Passage, Chiswick,
London W4 4PH
tel: (0181) 742 3161 fax: (0181) 742 2772
e-mail: 100413.3551@compuserve.com

France:
71 bis rue du Cardinal Lemoine, 75005 Paris
tel: 1 44 32 06 20 fax: 1 46 34 72 55
e-mail: 100560.415@compuserve.com

World Wide Web: http://www.lonelyplanet.com